Y0-BQU-660

People on the Move

A United States History

Published as a complete one-volume text and *in two volumes:*

Complete (hardbound):
PEOPLE ON THE MOVE—A UNITED STATES HISTORY

Two-volume (softbound):
PEOPLE ON THE MOVE—A UNITED STATES HISTORY (TO 1877)
PEOPLE ON THE MOVE—A UNITED STATES HISTORY (SINCE 1860)

PEOPLE ON THE MOVE

A United States History

RAY GINGER
The University of Calgary

with the aid of
VICTORIA GINGER

Allyn and Bacon, Inc.   Boston

"Huswifery" by Edward Taylor, from *The Poetical Works
of Edward Taylor,* edited by Thomas H. Johnson (Princeton Paperback, 1966), copyright Rockland, 1939, and
Princeton University Press, 1943.

"After Apple Picking" by Robert Frost, from *The Poetry of
Robert Frost* edited by Edward Connery Lathem. Copy-
right 1930, 1939, © 1969 by Holt, Rinehart, and Winston,
Inc. Copyright © 1958 by Robert Frost. Copyright © 1967
by Lesley Frost Ballantine. Reprinted by permission of
Holt, Rinehart, and Winston, Inc.

From "The Love Song of J. Alfred Prufrock" by T. S. Eliot,
from *Collected Poems 1909–1962,* by permission of Har-
court Brace Jovanovich, Inc.

LIBRARY OF CONGRESS CATALOGING IN PUBLICATION DATA

Ginger, Ray.
  People on the move.

  Bibliography: p.
  Includes indexes.
  1. United States—History. I. Title.
E178.1.G54   1975   973   74-22242

ISB#   0-205-04284-8

Contents

CHAPTER 30
The Decline (and Fall?) of the American Empire

Preface

Often in the middle of the night I reach for some printed words that do not require much attention. This kind of junk reading, whether Westerns or mysteries or science fiction, helps to cross the abyss between alertness and full sleep. It serves a need. But the present book is intended to meet quite different needs. What is said here is not, so far as I am aware, written down in any sense of those words. It is aimed by two adults at other adults. Frequently it uses analogies from our own lives in an attempt to illuminate what happened at earlier times and in separate places; this mode of comparison is a type of thinking that we all use whether we observe our actions or not. Here it is made explicit. Readers are entitled to some advance warning about other features of this volume that might seem unusual.

1. THE NARRATIVE. These pages try to tell a story. They assume that a portrait, however brief, of John Fitch or Benjamin Franklin or the Kennedy brothers, can help you to understand some salient traits of human nature as exposed in the American experience. But this work tries to reach farther yet. It tries to make sense of the lives that people have struggled through in the United States. Facts, like persons, do not carry their meanings on their sleeves. Out of the mists of the past, a historian must select certain events because he cannot tell it all, even if he knew it all, which he does not. But his standards of selection he should try to state clearly. Here are some of mine.

The main theme of this study is put down in the title. Americans more than any other nation known to me have been *People on the Move.* Whatever criterion be chosen—whether geographical or socioeconomic or ethical—we have hustled. Perhaps the most unAmerican of all traits is contentment. Beneath this broadest rubric, however, subcategories can be discerned. Recognizing that the most pervasive American symbol is the moving van, let us list other topics that will recur repeatedly below:

a) *Technology and its applications.* Almost everybody would believe that development of the automobile has been a socially desirable innovation even though it results in air pollution and so many traffic deaths. But can an affirmative verdict be given on the space program that first put men on the moon?

b) *Economic institutions and their evolution.* Using a lackadaisical vocabulary, some historians have characterized Americans as a "materialistic" people. The same writers, in their hope of wiping out the enemy with a questionable epithet, do not heed the types of organization that have helped to make a specific country—so far—the most productive in the history of the earth. To give three examples, they have vaguely opined that money and banking has been important in American history, but they have not tried to explain clearly just what these devices do and have done. They have written about labor relations chiefly in terms of trade unions, which are only a marginal piece of the tale. They have not even tried to look closely at the psychology of leaders who fabricated industrial empires. The following pages try to remedy these ailments.

c) *The phrase "think ethnic"* is unquestionably a great one in its application to American history. But it has been applied chiefly to political events, with some attention to social ones. Here an effort is made to roam into the significance of immigration for economic growth. Obviously if each individual invader from Europe had been forced to make it on his own, he would never have made it at all. But considering the population as a whole, and ignoring the influx of people including the importation of slaves prior to 1860, would the United States now have a Gross National Product of $100,000,000,000 had it not been for the influx of peoples in the last hundred years?

d) The last question opens the realm of *social changes.* The inquiry starts with alterations in birth rates, in death rates, in distributions of the population by age and by sex. But the problems do not end with demography narrowly construed. The structure of American families has altered enormously from Puritan times to the present; indeed, the child-centered entity has emerged in the last hundred years. As infant mortality has fallen, the care lavished on individual offspring has risen rapidly. One of the most searching essays of recent years explores the meaning for character formation of a society that is so affluent that each member of the family can have a private room. The rise of cities has meant manifold revision of male-female relations.

e) *Life of the mind.* The shifting attitudes of the common man have found some of their most intense expressions in the work of intellectuals. Writers and painters and musicians have tried to evoke the hidden meanings of their contemporary ambience. Speaking of the most profound artists, it seems too trite to say that they tried to touch the pulse of their own times: they reached through the skin to reach the heart that drove the pulse. These pages try to give a fair sampling of American achievements in belles lettres and other exalted crafts. Attention will be paid to the ways in which architects, by their design of dwellings as well as of public buildings, have reflected the values of their age. Although knowledge is widespread about the emergence in the twentieth century of native American music, remarks will be made about lesser known aspects of this achievement. Finally, it will be argued that photography and its derivatives are the most significant new departure in the arts since 1800.

f) *Constitutional and political conflicts.* The social and economic tensions of a country also are exposed by the struggles for control of its governments. From the Kansas-Nebraska Act to black power, from the National Association of Manufacturers to trade unions with their Political Action Committee, the clashes have gone on. For twenty-five years after World War II, the fashionable school of historians chose to depict the United States as a nation of consensus, where we all agreed that free-enterprise and republican government were the be-all and end-all. Stated in this form, the view should not be brushed aside. But it must be strictly qualified. American politicians are not pantywaists or paper tigers; they play a body-contact sport. The United States has not been noted for its Christian brotherhood—at least not when power is at stake. The American attitude in the strife for control and use of government has been: I can take you, Buster, so I will.

g) *Foreign policy.* Official attitudes toward the rest of the world have been shaped above all by the stresses within the United States. To cite one example, Washington's Farewell Address cannot be understood without knowing the domestic problems that prompted it. The Monroe Doctrine was a brilliant exploitation of the home difficulties, not of the United States, but of England. In 1914–18 the English found a means to reverse the exploitation: whereas earlier John Quincy Adams had used British power to accomplish American goals, now Sir Edward Grey used American power to carry out British intentions.

h) *Military affairs.* Warfare has been a central element in the history of the United States. From the days of the English colonies in North America to the present, the musket, the Gatling gun, or the hydrogen bomb have been kept close to hand. This brute fact has been pervasive: on the economy, on constitutional relations, on psychology, even in some respects on religion. To speak thus is not to assert that Americans have been "militaristic"—a charge that is about as senseless as to say that they have been "materialistic." Quite the contrary. The United States from earliest days until World War II put its reliance on a civilian militia. The country never bothered to mobilize a fighting force until a war had started, but its advantage was that it held in reserve a devastating capacity that had not been frittered away on the maintenance of a standing army.

i) *The total man.* These pages insist that history is about human beings, and that man is a highly complicated animism. They urge that the diverse facets of man's activities cannot be segmented cleanly from each other. At the same time, however, the making of historical categories can be carried beyond the point of usefulness as requisite tools for our thinking; artificial categories can also betray some connections that existed in other times. In any case, historians do not know enough to reveal all of the linkages that occurred in the past, and I cheerfully although regretfully concede that I have only a part of the knowledge that is owned by the totality of the historical guild. Thus nobody will find this book compartmented by a system of self-contained topics in which one chapter talks about railroads and the next talks about money and banking, while the foresaid topics never touch on one another. The connections I have asserted often fluctuate—a complexity that seems to be dictated by reality. Chapter 3 ties international commerce to the transplantation of culture, suggesting that the movement of goods meant also the movement of ideas from the same parts of the Old World. But two centuries later, in Chapter 14, intellectual tides are joined not to economic ones but to social ones.

This ebb and flow of complications can be avoided only by tactics that are simplistic in the extreme. To quote a great French historian:

> Only a divine mind could make a whole of the infinite variety of aspects of history. . . . Whoever pursues religious history must not neglect economic history, because it is the same man who believes in some religion and is also part of an economic system, or a legal, or a political one. I think that this idea of the concrete historic man is what joins together all the special fields, and gives historical research its full richness.

j) *Mobility.* While these subthemes keep emerging through the book, it should be emphasized that the main motif is mobility. Some three generations of American scholars have gone to the skeet ranges to shoot down Frederick Jackson Turner. But he remains, together with that nonesuch visitor Alexis de Tocqueville, one of the two greatest commentators on the American story. To say that Turner did not know everything is hardly a devastating rebuttal. Fine research has shown that he neglected the stimuli provided by towns and cities in the settlement of the frontier. No analyst of the westward movement would today leave out the pioneers who came westward across the ocean from Europe. The fringes of settlement were not the seedbed of egalitarianism that Turner thought them to be. But few philosophers—Plato, Machiavelli, Marx-Engels, Lincoln—have provided a platform from which we can soar higher. For those interested in American history, Turner's writings, slender though they are, remain the springboard.

k) *What we don't know.* It may seem dogged and even bullheaded, but large parts of this volume are a confession of ignorance. Large and vital parts of American history are still uncharted ground. The maps of our coast lines and rivers that were done in the eighteenth century evoke more confidence than we can feel in charts of portions of the national life which were made two centuries later. One instance is the dubious picture of the origins of political parties in the United States. Several books have appeared recently that purport to deal with the administrations of Washington and Adams. But when they try to explain how the nation arrived at a mode of managing its government that was not approved by any powerful man of the age, no existing work offers a picture that is convincing.

Some portions of history need not remain as befogged forever as they are today. Where a hiatus appears, I have tried to identify it. Where I had an idea of methods that might fill the gap, I have stated them.

2. SOME NOTABLE EVENTS. A common complaint against academic historians is that they ask readers to "memorize . . . kings . . . dates . . . battles." Much can be said for the scholars' attitude: frequently we cannot dissect event B unless we know that event A preceded. But this outlook can result in some mighty dreary tomes. Every book should be fun to read, and an outlook of crude empiricism can butcher the most lively period. You will encounter below an experiment, which is nothing more than a variation on precedents. Most chapters are followed by chronological charts of major or notable episodes, in the hope of freeing the text of many items that might be regarded as "clutter." As to the question of why we list occurrences on these pages that are not discussed in the narrative, the reply is: That was the whole idea in the first place.

3. DOCUMENTS. The chapters are also followed by extracts from the words of contemporaries. In addition to knowing the conclusions that were reached by our predecessors, it is enlightening to know the exact phrases in which they posed their problems, and the lines of reasoning that satisfied them in reaching solutions. Here is the Puritan poet Edward Taylor seeking words to express his gratitude to God; here too is the Mormon banker Marriner Eccles explaining why deficit financing was the best implement to use against the Great Depression. I have sought to enliven the game a bit by talking about the gains that can be won by deliberately inventing false sources and putting them onto the pens of our ancestors.

4. WAYS TO STUDY HISTORY. Practitioners in the natural sciences and also in the humanities have been far ahead of the historians in explaining their craft to outsiders. No respectable teacher would begin an introductory course in the biological sciences without talking about the history of genetics, how DNA was discovered, how two English scientists formulated a hypothesis about its structure and used simple but highly ingenious reasoning to prove that they were right. Similarly in presenting literature the New Critics were not content merely to proclaim that a certain poem was

great; they presented a word-by-word analysis of those qualities that made it so. But by and large, historians have been satisfied to tell what (they thought) the truth was, without condescending to explain why they thought so. In this abstention they have grievously damaged their credibility. How does a historian fix on a particular problem for study? How does he set about gathering evidence? Evaluating its reliability? What other disciplines does he draw on in telling his tale? Each chapter in this book is followed by a brief account of the ways in which an individual historian went about his profession.

5. COLOR PLATES AND BLACK-AND-WHITE HALFTONE ILLUSTRA-TIONS. Choosing the pictures for this volume has involved balancing several considerations. Foremost has been an evaluation of merit as a work of art. No known product of the years before 1770 can be assigned to the first rank; however, it seemed important to offer a glimpse into the painting of the colonial period, and the four-color Figure A retains its charms after the passage of 300 years. Especially with the four-color (lettered) figures, attention had to be paid to the question of whether it would reproduce well on a page of a given size. He who dares to select a wall-size mural for use in a smallish book is a brash man. Some styles reproduce well; others become, if not a blur of mud, a grotesquely distorted and diminished version of the original, as copies of Van Gogh and Gauguin will testify. Then we come to matters of cost. It was possible to use only eight four-color figures. Some artists, Audubon for example, cannot sing out their song if they are deprived of hues and tints, whereas the portrait by Thomas Eakins does not lose by being offered in black and white. Also it seemed desirable to show many different modes of expression. In addition to paintings these pages hold buildings, a cartoon, civil engineering, photography. The buildings range from domestic dwellings to a courthouse to an office building. Regard to a proper distribution in time and space was also an influence. In the earliest years, architecture was far ahead of the "finer" arts, so it is stressed. The late nineteenth century was one of America's finest periods in painting, so you will find a bunching up of oils and watercolors. Also I have tried to suggest that no region has had a monopoly of long standing on talent. If Winslow Homer was a New Englander, Charles Marion Russell tried to set down the evolution of the Northern plains, Frederic Remington that of the Southern ones. As with artists, so with repositories. I started from the dogma that I would not take more than one black-and-white illustration from any museum. This was done in the hope that readers might be encouraged to visit previously unknown resources in their own areas.

Finally, each picture had to point at one or more significant strands in American history. After all the balances had been cast, I ended up with a group of pictures that I liked.

6. HOW DID IT WORK? The tendency of historians, with notable exceptions, to talk about the Homestead Act or the National Banking Act without clearly expounding its operation has been distressing. This defect has been equally glaring in expositions of technological innovations. "The cotton gin revolutionized American history." But look, man, what did the cotton gin do? What happens during the vulcanization of rubber? What were some of the main changes that led to the creation of an economical automobile? My effort was to break longstanding convention by offering diagrams of the workings of these mechanical devices, so that a layman like myself could follow the operation step by step. The accompanying captions are meant to read almost like the recipes on boxes of cake mix.

7. MAPS. Visual aids can be an enormous aid to understanding. If you want to follow the shifting centers of wheat production, for instance, a couple of good maps are more helpful than a thousand words of text. But a map that requires thirty minutes of concentration before its point begins to come across is useless or worse in that it diverts attention from the flow of the narrative. For the same reason, the topics for maps must be highly selective and the subject to be conveyed should be defined narrowly. The graphic impression should be one that the reader can carry with fair accuracy in his head for the rest of his life. This book does not contain any page that shows the location of a certain regiment at the opening of firing on the second day of the Battle of Gettysburg because nobody in the audience would remember the facts for a half hour; certainly I would not. Just as there are no maps of battles, so are there no maps of military campaigns.

Some themes, however, are eminently appropriate for maps. Two series are contained here. One shows the outlines at least of population shifts. We talk of "the westward movement" and it has happened, but the relevant maps show that it has become a drift to the southwest. The other series, because of the immense importance of water transportation in American history, shows the major river basins and the topography that hewed them out. A few political events seemed to lend themselves to cartographic presentation: ratification of the Constitution, abolition of slavery in the North, Presidential election of 1860, secession from the Union in 1861, adoption of woman suffrage. And loose ends but striking ones had to be handled, such as the location of the iron and steel regions.

8. CHARTS AND GRAPHS. Other points can best be made in a variety of visual schemes. These line drawings fall into two categories. Some are historically as precise as present information enables us to make them; they are based on real data drawn from the past. If you master the material in Figure 15-1 showing the percentage of slaveholding families, by state, in 1860, you will know in summation what the best historian knows. But some charts are conceived in another way. Being what an economist or a sociologist would call a model, these graphics use imagined or hypothetical facts in trying to reveal the realities of past relationships.

9. BIBLIOGRAPHIES. Readers are entitled to know in advance the limitations of these tools as used below. Only seven lists of suggested readings are given, one for each Part and a general list. The titles proffered tend to be a middle level of abstraction. On the one hand, you will not find other one- or two-volume histories of the United States. On the other, neither will you find many scholarly monographs. If you want to know as much as possible about cotton cultivation in South Carolina from 1815 to 1860, three steps will be required: from the bibliographies in this book, to the bibliographies given by those volumes, to the books annotated in said lists.

Since my own text relies heavily on articles in scholarly journals, I had originally hoped to cite articles as well as books. But I also reminded myself that the aim of any catalog of suggested readings is to steer the reader to the best work that has been done on a given subject, and the worst guide is an endless maze. So a limit, admittedly arbitrary, of fifty books for each Part was set. All articles, however meritorious, went out. So did quite a few worthy books. I apologize now to all of the authors whose creations are slighted.

The fiction, poetry, and expository texts cited in bibliographies are in my judgment the finest writing that was done in the respective periods. Obviously they are not exhaustive; inevitably the choices are subjective. The general bibliography, which immediately follows the one for Part VI, exists because several outstanding volumes could not be cramped into one of the designated time slots. Most of the works listed there contrast with the chronological ones by using the other mode of organization favored by historians: the topical approach—history of taxation, history of cities, history of the frontier.

10. THREE INDEXES. Ordinarily a tome will give only one (not very helpful) index. This volume has three. First, an *Index of Defined Terms* is provided. A major goal of these pages is to be brief and clear, in which cause technical terms are often used, in ways that I hope will seem reasonable. Whenever such a term crops up for the first time, the narrative should define it or give examples that will make clear its meaning. A catalog of the relevant phrases and page numbers is the first of the indexes. Besides this, there is a *Subject Index* and an *Index of Proper Names.* Of course the first two of these lists overlap, but the Subject Index gives a wider range of references. The Index of Proper Names is meant to be exhaustive within that pigeonhole. For each president of the United States, the dates of his incumbency are given. You will not find below any pages wasted on Appendices to reprint the Constitution and the Declaration of Independence. Such documents are found in *The World Almanac* and other available sources.

People on the Move

A United States History

PART I

Leap into the Wilderness
1492–1763

Origins of Colonization

      Good Christians hated Moslems. Repeatedly in the twelfth and thirteenth centuries, the Pope at Rome urged Catholic Christianity to squander its resources in trying to eject the apostles of Mohammed out of the Holy Land. The Holy Shrine of Jerusalem must be redeemed. The realization of this desire was encouraged by the fact that venturers could get rich through the expansion of shipping through Italian ports to the eastern Mediterranean. For a time the Christian forays had some success; in the twelfth century Islam was evicted from parts of Palestine and Syria. Then the tide ebbed. Later land crusades were failures.

      But despite skimpy results, the dream of reclaiming the Holy Land remained. Some men sought new approaches to the task, not by land but by water. Foremost among them was a prince of Portugal, usually called Henry the Navigator, who was bemused by rumors of a legendary Christian king in east central Africa. By linking up with him, thought Henry, he might win back the citadel of his faith and earn an eternal site in Heaven. Since it was impossible for an expedition to cross solidly Moslem North Africa, Prince Henry started sending ships farther and farther down the west coast, seeking the passage around the Cape of Good Hope and then to sail northward. Such voyages through the fifteenth century were discovering new lands and new opportunities for trade as a by-product of religious zeal. While the commerce of Portugal burgeoned, that of the Mediterranean was waning, and once proud cities were wasting: Venice, Naples, Genoa.

Thus it made sense for the venturesome young Christopher Columbus to abandon his native Genoa and repair to bustling Lisbon in Portugal. Already by 1477 he had sailed to Chios in the Aegean, and to Iceland; by 1485 he had made several voyages to Guinea in western Africa. Journeys of discovery call for sailors who are more than seamen; they must be explorers, seafarers. Columbus was among the foremost. His saga makes a fine beginning for the story of European impact on the Western Hemisphere. It features many themes destined to remain eminent in American history, and includes, for instance, two human traits in astounding measure—boundless Courage, and boundless Greed.

Fortunately, there is today more available evidence about Columbus than about any other explorer before 1600. Not only are there several primary sources of book length, but they have been woven into majestic literary cloth by Samuel Eliot Morison in *Admiral of the Ocean Sea.* As shown in this biography, Columbus is bifocal, with part of his vision in medieval mysticism and another portion in modern science. He lusted to know about nature. His observations of the New World were many and precise. His descriptions were vivid. But his thinking tended to be deductive; he started with an authority and went ahead as if all life could be reduced to geometry. On his first voyage he expected to find kinky-haired black people. Why? Because he had seen such people in Guinea; and Aristotle had declaimed that any given latitude must contain similar peoples. Here was no science, no observation, only dogma. Columbus was a pious man. A prayer stands at the top of his surviving letters:

Jesus cum Maria
Sit nobis in via   ("Jesus with Mary / Be with us on our way")

Henry the Navigator stated the aim of his voyages as both "the exaltation of the faith" and "the honor of the kingdom." The same duality will serve for Columbus; again, with both discoverers, the inspiration of gold and silver soon entered the mixture.

Columbus was encumbered by some wrong notions about the nature of the earth. Not that he thought it was flat; no informed man believed it so in the fifteenth century. But he did make it out to be too small, taking 45 nautical miles as one degree at the equator instead of the true 59.5 miles. And his conception had Asia extending thousands of miles farther eastward than it does. He persisted in these beliefs to the end of his life, and died convinced that he had discovered, not an unknown continent, but a group of outlying Asian islands. Inspired by religion, ambition, and curiosity, and encumbered by misinformation and a didactic habit of mind, Columbus tried to find financial support for an expedition to tap the riches of the Orient by sailing west. In 1484 he tried to interest the king of Portugal in his plan. Rebuffed in Lisbon, he sought support in Spain. For years he endured ridicule; his scheme was a standing joke. Mention of it drew sneers. And the times were wrong, since Ferdinand and Isabella were hurling men and money into their effort to drive Islam from adjacent Granada. After all, Christians (almost all Roman Catholics at that time) hated Moslems. Then, early in 1492, Granada surrendered, and the times came right for new adventures. The monarchs agreed to finance a modest fleet for Columbus, probably fewer than 100 men and boys, and three ships.

But the needs of exploration still had to yield to religious bigotry. With the Moors cast out, Christian Spain could turn its hatred upon its Jews. For centuries they had lived in peace in Spain, where some had played important roles in society. Now it was decreed that all infidels must become Catholic Christians in four months or leave the country. In the summer of 1492 the main port of Cadiz was clogged with forlorn refugees, and Columbus sailed from a lesser harbor. Dropping southward to the Canary Islands off Africa, he headed due west on September 9.

Having gained one miracle by winning royal backing, he now faced problems that only a dauntless captain could bear to look at. First, he had to control his sailors. To them, Spaniards, he was a foreigner, Italian. And this in an age when aliens were everywhere mistrusted and feared. Second, he had to control his ships by finding a course. His tools were few. He could not sail by the stars; his few celestial observations were grossly wrong. He could not use an astrolabe (no evidence exists that he had one on any of his later voyages). The method of measuring distances by "casting the log" was not devised until the next century, and he merely estimated his speed by eye. He knew that the difference of magnetic from true north distorted a compass, but he did not know how to make adjustments. In truth, Columbus sailed by dead reckoning; he simply guessed the number of miles that he sailed each day and estimated his new location. By this technique he got results that verge on fantasy. His third great hazard stemmed from the length of his voyage. Even Columbus himself, one of the most widely travelled men in Europe, had not envisaged a journey of such duration, and his crew, mostly ignorant sailors accustomed to hug the shores of the Mediterranean, were understandably terrified at being out of sight of land for what seemed like eternity.

For ten days the fleet made fine time, riding the trade winds westward. Then it hit a calm as it was entering a vast meadow of gulfweed. Anxieties rose high; men feared that they would be locked into the yellow and green weeds (just as a ship might be frozen into the arctic ice.) The captain pushed on, and discontent grew. The unknown always seems risky, and probably no man in the fleet, perhaps no man in the world, had ever before been out of sight of land for so long as three weeks. Thirty days out, they were far beyond all earlier records for ocean navigation. More to the point, they had long since passed the time when Columbus had predicted they would find land. Twice the cry "Land" had gone up, and both times it had proved false. On October 10 the wind freshened and drove the ships flying forward. Far from allaying the sense of doom, this development brought new fears that they would never be able to double back and sail eastward to home. Open mutiny broke out on the flagship. Nobody knows just how Columbus managed to bring it under control—presumably by pledging that if land was not sighted soon he would turn back.

Ruthlessness is common among great men, and now the shark in Columbus surfaced. His sovereigns had promised a sizable prize to the man who first sighted land. About 10 P.M. on October 11 a seaman said he saw a light. Columbus replied that he already had seen it himself. Future events would show that the captain was eager for riches, but evidently in this episode his chief aim was glory.

The next morning the Spaniards landed on San Salvador in the Bahama Islands. On the flat beach they were met by Taino Indians. Thus at once the question was posed: What should be the relations between white invaders and dark-skinned peoples? Entries in his Journal for that very day show that Columbus had his mind made up from the beginning. He thought the Tainoes handsome, and he piously recorded that they "could better be freed and converted to our Holy Faith by love than by force. . . ." But some of his other observations more accurately predicted their fate. The Indians carried darts, some tipped with a fish-tooth. They knew nothing of metal weapons. So ignorant were they that a man, when handed a sword, might grasp it by the blade and cut himself. "They ought to be good servants and of good skill, for I see that they repeat very quickly all that is said to them; and I believe that they would easily be made Christians, because it seemed to me that they belonged to no religion. I, please Our Lord, will carry off six of them at my departure to Your Highnesses, so that they may learn to speak." Two days later he declared: "These people are very unskilled in arms, . . . with fifty men they could all be subjected and made to do all that one wished."

Everywhere his reaction was the same. Two months later he landed on Hispaniola, the large island that now holds the Dominican Republic and Haiti. Of the Tainoes there he noted: "They bear no arms, and are all unprotected and so very cowardly that a thousand would not face three, so they are fit to be ordered about, made to work, made to sow and do aught else that may be needed, and you may build towns and teach them to go clothed and to adopt our customs." In brief, they should be converted, civilized, and enslaved. This

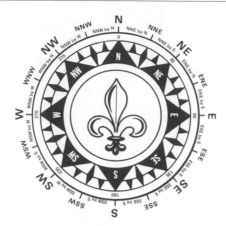

The first definite mention of the magnetic compass occurred in the 12th century. At that time it was probably not a permanent part of a ship's equipment, but was used only when clouds hid the north star. A needle would be magnetized (by rubbing it with a piece of lodestone, which is a naturally occurring magnet), placed on a bit of straw, and floated in a dish of water. It would swing around and point north.

Later mariners began to use the compass to hold a constant course, for which a more permanent arrangement was needed. A metal bowl would be suspended near the helmsman, and a card showing 32 possible points of direction fixed to its bottom. A pin projected up from the center of the bowl, and the compass needle was hung on the pin. Since the needle must be suspended at its precise center, and the pitch of the ship caused it to constantly waver, the instrument was fragile. Another difficulty arose from the fact that the magnetic poles are not located precisely at the geographic poles; compass needles point to the magnetic poles, causing a variation between their readings and true north which becomes more significant the farther north you travel. Although this variation was noticed late in the 15th century (Columbus carried a compass which attempted to compensate for it) charts showing its effect worldwide were not published until 1701.

With a reliable compass, it would seem that the problems of the navigator were solved; knowing where he had started from, he need only hold a given course for a given distance, and he would know where he would end up. This method, known as dead reckoning, was inac-curate for several reasons. First, it is impossible to tell with precision how fast a sailing vessel is traveling, or how far it has gone in a given period of time. Second, a sailing ship can only rarely hold a constant course, but must often move in zig-zags (a maneuver known as tacking) depending on wind direction. Since the navigator can't be sure how far the ship has travelled in any one direction, he would soon be lost if he did not have some independent means of checking his position.

From the time of the ancient Greeks, it had been known that the relationship between the sun and the horizon at noon varied with the latitude and the time of year. They devised a mechanism by which they could measure the angle formed by the sun, the horizon, and the eye of the observer; if you knew the day of the year, that angle would tell you the line of north or south latitude you were on. Similarly, the angles formed between certain stars and the horizon varied with the latitude, and could tell you how far south or north you were. Devices to determine latitude have always worked on this principle, although they have become increasingly precise.

The sun and stars are of no practical help in determining longitude. No matter how far west you go, they look the same. But you can tell the time of day from the stars, if you know your latitude and the day of the year. If you can determine, by some independent means, the simultaneous time at another place of known location, you can find out where you are. This development had to wait until the manufacture of accurate chronometers, in the mid-18th century.

last feature might embrace a wide range of services, as is reflected in an occurrence on the Second Voyage. At St. Croix in the Virgin Islands the Spaniards had their first skirmish against Indians. A Spaniard who had been a chum of the captain since boyhood captured a native girl. Columbus let the man keep her as a slave. Wrote the new master: "Having taken her into my cabin, she being naked according to their custom, I conceived a desire to take pleasure. I wanted to put my desire into execution but she did not want it and treated me with her finger nails in such a manner that I wished I had never begun. But seeing that (to tell you the end of it all), I took a rope and thrashed her well, for which she raised such unheard of screams that you would not have believed your ears. Finally we came to an agreement in such manner that I can tell you that she seemed to have been brought up in a school of harlots."

By early 1494 Columbus was advancing a plan for a regular trade in Carib slaves. In February 1495, back in Hispaniola, he sent off four ships to take 500 Indians to slave markets in Spain; some 200 died on the voyage. Decimation of the natives on Hispaniola was rapid. They were enslaved—or killed—or they fled into the hills to die of starvation and disease. Thousands committed suicide with cassava poison. Here are estimates of the number of aborigines on the island:

1494	300,000
1496	200,000
1508	60,000
1512	20,000
1548	500

Having wiped out most of the Indians in the Caribbean, the Spaniards belatedly realized that they could not extract its wealth without other nonwhite workers. As one of them explained: "Although the soil is very black and good they have not yet found the way or the time to sow: *the reason is that nobody wants to live in these countries.*" So European gentlemen came to a clear objective: to live as absentee landlords in their home countries while using involuntary labor to wrest riches from foreign lands that only labor could make productive. This goal brought with it the use of African slaves throughout the Caribbean.

The congeries of ideas which motivated the Spanish adventurers seem strange to a modern mind. They combined genuine piety and courage with a desire to win glory for themselves and their nation, and to acquire riches and power. Slavery, rape, genocide, and renewed slavery were acceptable means to the end of living like gentlemen of leisure. And yet pious platitudes were not just hypocritically mouthed; most people meant them, and considered that they were living in accordance with their credo. Another theme which casts a hypocritical shadow in the twentieth century, yet was fervently believed in the fifteenth and succeeding centuries, was the doctrine of "special providences." That is, men believed that God intervened directly in human affairs. If a community thrived, it did so because God had chosen to reward its virtuousness. If a calamity hit, the Almighty had chosen to strike at its derelictions. This belief, which was to be crucial in American history, can be illustrated by an event on Columbus' first voyage. On Christmas Eve, 1492, the *Santa Maria*, the fleet's largest vessel, ran aground on a coral reef off Hispaniola. Columbus thought he knew how to get her free, and gave orders. But he ran into the rebellion of inertia; his subordinate failed to act promptly. By Christmas morning the ship was clearly lost, so the day was spent salvaging her cargo onto the beach. There Columbus was approached by an Indian chief who showed him some gold. Now the great navigator had the conceptual tools to chart the situation. What had seemed an undeserved disaster now became for Columbus a special providence, a sign of God's blessing, since without the wreck no landing would have been made at that spot at all. Had no gold been found, the First Voyage might have been seen by Ferdinand and Isabella as a costly misadventure.

Although Columbus made four voyages to the Caribbean, and although by landing in Venezuela and sailing its coast he discovered South America, the zenith of his star came on his return from the First Voyage. His sovereigns received him personally. They fitted out for him a great fleet, 17 ships, more than 1,000 men. Thereafter his luck fluctuated. As governor of Hispaniola he learned—and he was far from the last European governor in the New World to learn the same lesson—that it was not easy to control unruly men who sought only to win riches in a hurry and get back home. On his Third Voyage he barely missed finding the pearl beds off Venezuela, with the result that he was later charged with having held back the news for his own gain. Complaints against him caused a royal commissioner to be sent across the Atlantic to investigate. Columbus was shipped back to Spain in chains. He won his freedom and made another voyage. Although he never got anything like the rewards he thought he deserved, at the end of his life he was quite well-to-do.

Columbus' life brought to him glorious adventures, splendid achievements, and moderate wealth. It brought to mankind one of the greatest of all revolutions. Prior to the First Voyage, the mood of Christendom had been grim. Its future looked bleak. The Great Schism in the Church had been mended, but the stitches seemed untidy and frail. All the resources poured into the Crusades had failed to win back the Holy Sepulchre. The infidel Turks had swarmed over most of Albania, Greece, and Serbia. In 1492 a corrupt Borgia was crowned Pope Alexander VI. Then came the discoveries. Suddenly the potential realm of the Roman Church knew no limits. The number of converts to be made, the amount of wealth to be won, the hosts of subjects to be enrolled under the true flag—each of these quantities was undetermined, but each seemed vast. The degree to which Europe could expand was unknown, but the new lands offered opportunities that were enormous. They also held new threats. The notion of the balance of power among the states of Europe acquired an added range of meanings. Any European state that failed to seize its share of New World resources would find its status subverted.

The effect in Europe was an accelerating spasm. Every one of the main maritime countries eventually made at least a foray into the struggle for the Americas: England, France, Portugal, Spain, Sweden, and the Netherlands. Portugal seized control of Brazil in the sixteenth century, but never amounted to anything in North America. A tiny colony called New Sweden was set up on the Delaware River in the seventeenth century, but the Dutch and then the English finally seized that area. New Netherlands was founded by the Dutch West Indies Company (See Chapter 2), but it lasted only about six decades before the English grabbed it and renamed it New York. In spite of their eventual defeat in the New World, the Low Countries in the seventeenth century were at least as powerful a nation as England. A somewhat similar statement can be made about Spain. Although English weather (not the English Navy) destroyed her Armada in 1588, she was widely regarded until well into the eighteenth century as the most powerful country in Europe. France had the largest population of the maritime nations, and under the reigns of Louis XIII and XIV she constructed a centralized administration that enabled her to mobilize her resources much more efficiently than England could. Nonetheless, it was the English colonizers—scantily financed, often so disorganized as to seem haphazard—who were to have the most lasting impact on North America.

In considering the efforts of Englishmen to gain a foothold in the New World, it is convenient to ask three distinct questions:

1. Where did the liquid capital for the ventures come from? Amusingly, even though most of the persons who put up the money remained safely at home by their firesides and never got to the wilderness across the Atlantic at all, they were termed in the language of the day "the adventurers." Why did investors turn to foreign lands?

2. Who were the settlers, and why did they come? What made a few thousands of men willing to leave their native land and take a leap into the wilderness? These were "the planters"—they "planted" a new colony in America.

3. What devices were used to organize a project? How were adventurers and planters brought together so as to constitute a feasible undertaking? Three forms must be distinguished: joint-stock companies, rather like modern publicly owned corporations; proprietorships, held under charter from the crown by a powerful man or a small group; and royal colonies, ruled directly by the king and his agents.

Several factors that influenced the supply of capital are still obscure, and will probably remain so. From about 1540 to 1640 the general level of

·GRANDIBVS EXIGVI SVNT PISCES PISCIBVS ESCA·
Siet sone dit geb't sik zeer langhe ghisecten dat die groote visschen de cleyne

Victoria and Albert Museum, Vienna

FIGURE 1-1. *Pieter Breughel,* Big Fish Eat Little Fish
　　It's a dog-eat-dog world. The import of this engraving is as sharp and short as that. But the meanings proliferate. So far as we know, the original pen drawing by Pieter Breughel (1502?–1569) was meant to portray the interpersonal relations of the sixteenth century. But since Breughel was one of the foremost artists in an age of great painters, we can also read into this picture a prophecy of the fate of the nation-states then emerging in Europe. The title of the painting can be deciphered with no hesitation, since it is given in both Latin and Flemish: "Grandibus Exigui Sunt Pisces Piscibus Esca" (little fish are food for big fish).
　　Apart from its general import, some facts about the illustration are clear. The drawing is dated 1556, and it was engraved the following year by van der Heyden. A copy is now in the Albertina Museum in Vienna. But what is the meaning of the inscription in the lower left corner?—"Hieronymus Bos. inventor" (—referring to a lost work of Hieronymus Bosch, 1450–1516?). A common practice in the period was to revise or reinterpret a work by an earlier artist, much as a composer might issue "Variations on a Theme by Paganini." The derivative piece might even strive to be an exact copy, the sort of rendition for which the visual arts would later turn to photography. As to this engraving, the publisher may simply have added the name of Bosch in the belief that he was better known and that his name would boost sales.

11

prices in England rose, sometimes rapidly, sometimes slowly. Why did this inflation occur? Nobody knows for certain, but it seems worthwhile to indulge in a bit of speculation. What was probably the chief element can be summarized thus: Population rose more rapidly than did the output of goods and services, especially of agricultural products. The price of foodstuffs rose more rapidly than the price of industrial outputs, and, since food was the largest single factor in the standard of living, the consequence was to carry the general level of prices upward. Seemingly the level of rents also rose—which brings up another murky point. It is a fair guess that while rents were rising, many of them did not rise as rapidly as did the costs of the landowners. So these men, and they were unquestionably the ruling group in England at the time and for centuries to come, were caught in a profit squeeze between rapidly rising costs and relatively fixed rents. Their incomes fell. To make bad matters worse, England suffered severe plagues in 1591–1592 and 1621–1622, and the resultant fluctuations in population created labor shortages in some regions. It grew difficult for landowners to hike rents as they might otherwise have done. Some landowners, then, were desperately seeking new outlets that might yield a higher rate of return, a greater margin of profit.

The preceding paragraph pokes at what was apparently the chief cause of the inflation in England during the century after 1540. It points at the pressure of a fluctuating but rising population against more stable production (we do not know exactly what the population was at any given time, or when it began to increase, or what the rate of increase was, but the fact of growth seems clear). As distinguished from this "real" or "physical" element in the process, the possibility of a "monetary" element should be considered. Whereas Columbus had not found a substantial amount of gold or silver in the New World, some of his successors did. The mining of precious metals in Europe had been rising for some time before the Americas became a significant source of supply, but the dribble of ores from the Old World became a torrent from the New.

What has this to do with expanding English venture capital? In order to answer this question, a definition and an explanation are needed. First, the word *money* must be given a fairly precise meaning, and a basically sound response is to say that money is whatever you can use to pay your bills. In this sense, gold and silver were the main forms of money in 1600. According to a theory of the time (one that held popularity for centuries and is still not dead today), any increase in the amount of money in an economy would be reflected by a proportionate rise in prices. This notion cannot be sustained. To use technical language, a growth in the stock of money can be counterbalanced by a decline in the velocity of circulation; that is, a fall in the number of times that a "typical" dollar is spent per year. (One example of this phenomenon is the hoarding of money that occurred in the later months of 1933.) Further, prices will not rise if the expansion of the stock of money is counterbalanced by a rise in the output of goods and services. These complexities make the problem of finding the causes of the inflation in England four centuries ago even more perplexing than it would be otherwise. The needed facts simply are not available.

Some scholars even maintain that precious metals from the New World were not flowing into England. They hold, on the contrary, that the country was suffering a net outflow of gold. This helps to account, so they say, for the strident demands by Renaissance economists that England export more goods than she imported so as to build up her monetary stocks. The assertion seems most unlikely. Clearly gold was moving out of the Americas—and also out of Spain. It had to go somewhere. One mechanism by which it went to England can be illustrated by a single event. In 1577 Queen Elizabeth helped to finance an expedition to the Caribbean by Sir Francis Drake in the *Golden Hind.* When Drake arrived back in England three years later, his trip showed a net yield of some £1,500,000. Perhaps £600,000 of this sum was in specie. By the standards of 1580, so much wealth is astounding. According to an estimate made soon after World War II, the fruits of this one voyage, if invested at 6 per cent compound interest, would have brought a bigger harvest in the succeeding 350 years than had been garnered in that same period from the entire British Empire.

Notice also must be taken of certain elements that partially offset the imbalance of a population surge against relatively steady production outputs. Plagues and the generally poor sanitation wiped out many people at early ages. At the same time, referring to the other term in the equation, production of many commodities rose dramatically. The output of coal soared tenfold in the hundred years prior to 1640; of iron, lead, glass, ships, and salt, from five to ten times. Several trades that had been known little if at all were started up: copper and brass, paper, tobacco. What portents for the New World they proved to be. The survival of Virginia and Maryland can scarcely be imagined without the English and European demand for tobacco. Nor can we readily imagine how New England could have endured without the English fleet's steady demand for ships, timber, and naval stores. In a sense, however, these figures on the rising yields of minerals and metals might be misleading, since even in 1640 the total output of these commodities was not large. If the aim is to understand the operations of the economy as a whole, the key terms are foodstuffs and the rents of land.

After the many complications have been taken into account, it seems likely that the main source of funds for overseas ventures can be explained by a few remarks. The distribution of income was highly skewed; a few very wealthy families owned an appalling portion of the riches of the country (although probably not as great a share in 1600 as they would own in 1750). As a yardstick, the income per year of the typical parish priest in the Church of England was £8 to £10. Agricultural workers and tradesmen got less. At the other extreme stood the peers of the realm. By one guess their average annual income "may" have been £10,000. This figure seems considerably too high.

But recent estimates by Lawrence Stone put the average for the 63 peers in 1559 at £2,200, more than 200 times as great as for a parish clergyman. Incomes of this group seem to have fallen over the balance of the century, which inclined a few men to embrace foreign opportunities. Other adventurers emerged from the gentry, substantial landowners who were being caught in the profit squeeze. Still others belonged to the professional and commercial classes. Few if any fell into the category popularly denominated as "the common people," some 75 per cent of the inhabitants of England. It was this last group that contributed most of the planters.

Several pressures combined to persuade some men to leave England for the New World. Before we turn to those strains in English society, a preliminary warning is in order, namely, that the people who emigrated were few. In Virginia, founded in 1607, the peak period was 1618 to 1623 when about 4,500 entered the colony. For Massachusetts Bay the Great Migration occurred from 1630 to 1641, a span in which about a thousand people a year arrived from across the Atlantic.

It seems clear that the typical migrant was induced to leave England by economic stresses; he came to America in search of material improvement, just as others would do in the future. For a dozen generations before 1600 English landlords had been both enclosing what had been common land and also evicting tenants in order to fence in their acres and raise flocks of sheep. The result was a growing horde of erstwhile farm laborers. Under the best of circumstances the enclosures in agriculture would have created sizable pools of unemployed workers, and the situation was worsened by the growth of population. England and Wales, which together had about 4 million people in 1600, reached 5.25 million a hundred years later. People swarmed into towns and cities; the population of London doubled in the century to reach 400,000 by 1700. Quite a few men wanted a fresh start—especially if they could get somebody else to finance it. If they could not get a toehold in some expanding urban cluster in England, they might be persuaded to join an exodus to a promising spot overseas.

By the late sixteenth century there were two principal requirements for colonizing the New World: money, and men. A handful of well-to-do merchants and landowners were seeking promising investments in whatever part of the earth. Another group of a few thousand men might be induced to risk their lives and families in an unknown wilderness. But the techniques had to be invented that would combine these two elements to take initiative in a common enterprise. The invention of colonizing organizations was made mainly by private promoters.

The earliest, the most tireless, and perhaps the greatest of the propagandists for settlement in the Western Hemisphere was Richard Hakluyt. From a prominent if untitled family, he had friends at court and in London.

Englishmen had already made efforts—all disastrous—to plant transatlantic colonies before 1589 when Hakluyt brought out his *Principall Navigations, Voiages and Discoveries of the English Nation.* The true agitation may be said to begin with this series, which remains today invaluable as a source of information. Trying to stir up the old crusading spirit, Hakluyt talked a bit about the need to make converts and spread Christianity. But his chief bait was the abundance of land. Here already, in the sixteenth century and in the Old Country, can be found a theme that would be central to American history until the twentieth century: Greed for Land. To put the matter another way, we might discover a rewarding road into the past by asking this question: At a given time and place, what words would prompt the most fervor in the most people? In 1600 the most effective trigger was "God." Next on the list was "Land." In 1776 the brightest spark was "Liberty." Next on the list still was "Land." We may safely guess that at the time of the American Revolution most citizens of the country spent more time, if less spleen, thinking about land than about liberty. But land-hungry citizens alone would not bring rapid change; they merely stood as a historical constant.

During the sixteenth century in England, several elements worked to stimulate land hunger. One was simply the growth of population. Confronting this pressure was a supply restricted by the so-called Fixed Settlement, which tied up about half the land in the kingdom. By these legislative provisions an owner could not alienate his estate. The law of entail forbade him to sell it. The law of primogeniture said that he could not divide it among his heirs, but must leave it intact to his oldest son. Added to these long-term considerations was the sharp spur to speculation that developed when Henry VIII confiscated the lands owned by the monasteries of Roman Catholic orders. Some he gave to his favorites; some he sold. To use a technical term, the new owner might "reach for liquidity" by selling it in his turn. Land, unencumbered land, came onto the market, and many merchants grasped for it eagerly.

The tactics of real-estate boomers have not changed much since 1600. Some of the lies they told then were like the ones told now on matchbook covers that are trying to sell you a piece of desert in New Mexico. And of course they tried to get the government to help in various ways. Richard Hakluyt, at the request of Sir Walter Raleigh, presented Queen Elizabeth with his "Discourse on the Western Planting." An effort to get royal funds, it urged colonization as a means of bolstering England's claim to America and as an offset to the power that had accrued to Spain by virtue of her New World colonies. Elizabeth would not buy it. She would give moral support, no more. She was fighting Spain, and the soaring costs of warfare were flattening the crown's treasury. Only after peace came in 1604 did colonizing prove success-ful. Even then it was not money from the monarch but money from merchants in London that paid for it.

The form taken by their overseas ventures was the joint stock company. This device was already common in foreign trade. A group of promoters would

FIGURE 1-2. *Bartolome Murillo*, San Diego de Alcala

Bartolome Esteban Murillo (1617–1682) may well be the first of the great Spanish painters, unless one chooses also to assign that nationality to El Greco. His depiction of *San Diego de Alcala* is a reminder that poverty was everywhere in the sixteenth and seventeenth centuries. Although succor to the poor was often given by personal charity, in Latin countries it often came from the Church. It may be popular—in Protestant countries—to depict the Roman Papacy of three hundred years ago as the sponsor of Inquisitorial tortures against heretics, but it also spawned many humanitarian works.

The elderly man holding the bowl at the far right of this picture is a *picaro*. Such people were a segment of the Spanish nobility often referred to in English as "rogues," but the label is too simple. Their code of honor denied them the option of practicing a menial trade, but they could see nothing wrong in working as beggars; they became wanderers, outcasts, and as such, models for a great tradition of social mavericks (see Chapter 19 on *Huckleberry Finn*). "Picaresque novel" derives from the Spanish word *picaro*, and the prototype example is the title-role hero of the sixteenth-century novel *Don Quixote*, by Cervantes.

unite to secure a charter from the crown which gave members of their organization the exclusive right to trade with a given area abroad. But the joint stock companies were not so monopolistic as has often been argued. Except for the East India Company and the Levant Company, they were so-called regulated companies. That is, their doors were open to any merchant who would pay their dues and abide by their rules. It was joint stock companies that planted the first successful English colonies in North America, Virginia and Massachusetts.

Other colonies began as proprietorships. In them the charter from the king was held not by a company but by a wealthy man or small group. The proprietor originally held title to all the land in the colony. He could name its governor, and he had the right, always hard to enforce, of making rules. Examples are the planting of Maryland by Lord Baltimore, of Pennsylvania by William Penn, or of the Carolinas by a group of eight proprietors.

Several colonies that were begun by joint stock companies or by proprietors were later converted into a third form of organization: the royal colony, which was governed directly by the king and his agents. After the Virginia Company went bankrupt in 1623 its holdings became a royal colony. The same fate befell Massachusetts in 1691 after its original charter was voided in 1684. Connecticut and Rhode Island—both spinoffs formed by migration from Massachusetts—held charters from the monarch and ostensibly were royal colonies; in point of fact they were well-nigh independent, even having the right to elect their own governors. New York had a peculiar history in this regard. When New Amsterdam was taken from the Dutch in 1664, Charles II gave the colony to his brother James, the Duke of York, to hold as proprietor. When James acceded to the throne in 1685 New York became a royal colony. Thus by the eighteenth century most of the provinces had passed legally under the control of the monarch. But note that the government of England had not founded a single one of them.

The various colonies used different techniques to attract planters. The Virginia Company at first hoped to rent land to tenants, a scheme that soon proved unworkable. Tenancy did not satisfy land hunger, and the vast tracts of unoccupied land drew off renters. Empty land made cash sale difficult as well. All colonies were forced to assume a system of free grants. The "headright" became a commonly used device. If a man "planted" himself—paid his own passage—he would receive title to a specified acreage, commonly 50 acres. For every other person that he planted he would receive as much more. Indentured servants often received wilderness land at the close of their period of service. In New England land was normally distributed not in plots to individuals, but in large tracts to groups, which would organize as towns. The original members of a town would then parcel out a small portion of their holdings among themselves and to others who came among them, usually according to a complicated formula which took both family size and stature in the community into account.

Although the typical migrant journeyed across the Atlantic in search of land, it was not he who guided the new American ventures. To understand the attitudes and purposes of the men who would govern the new colonies, we must start from the religious situation in England. For more than a millenium the Roman Church had struggled to unite Christendom. Its gains were fitful. However, until the reign of Henry VIII (1509–1547) it had maintained the allegiance of the king of England and his subjects. Henry, on the occasion of one of his marital difficulties but undoubtedly for reasons of state also, repudiated the Pope, severed all ties with the Vatican, and won a law proclaiming himself to be the "Protector and Only Supreme Head of the Church and Clergy of England." As legislated early in the reign of Queen Elizabeth, the religion of the entire kingdom stood on the principles of Supremacy and Uniformity. By the mere act of being born, all subjects of the king became also members of the Church of England. Any other form of worship was illegal. There were to be no foolish efforts at religious diversity or toleration. The policy was stated curtly by James I: "I will have one Doctrine and one discipline, one religion in substance, and in ceremonie." This was easier to decree than to accomplish.

As to "substance," nearly everybody agreed to certain maxims. Throughout western Europe it was believed that a state could not allow more than one church to exist. This church must be "established," meaning that all residents would be taxed to support it. Church and state should work together to retrain and to restrain the evil impulses of human beings, for since the Fall of Adam all men had been born into a state of original sin. The main task of each person while alive was to seek eternal salvation for himself and for others. Life on this earth inevitably contains much misery. Religious men had a dismal opinion of human existence; the founder of Rhode Island would call men just "poor grasshoppers, hopping and skipping from branch to twig in this vale of tears." Or, to quote a funeral sermon for the richest man in Boston: ". . . his living above the World, and keeping his heart disentangled, and his mind in Heaven, in the midst of all the outward occasions and urgency of Business, bespake him not to be of this World, but a Pilgrim on the Earth, a citizen of Heaven. . . ." This attitude the New Englanders had carried with them across the Atlantic from their homeland.

While men held all of these attitudes in common, they could quarrel furiously about matters of "ceremonie." It was not theological doctrine but ecclesiastical issues, questions of church organization, that set off most of the bitter disputes. Perhaps every church must acknowledge some absolute authority. For Catholics the final arbiter took an institutional form; wrangles were submitted to a hierarchy that culminated in the Pope and Curia. The crown in England had tried to uphold a similar form, but replaced the Pope with itself at the apex. Many Protestants dissented. To them the ultimate word was invested not in an institution but in a book: the Holy Writ. The Bible was literally the word of God. It had been written down long ago. It was infallible.

It was unchanging. It told mankind all that God wanted us to know about the means to our salvation. Any Scriptural text, declared John Calvin, "obtains the same complete credit and authority with believers . . . as if they heard the very words pronounced by God himself."

From its origins this doctrine of Protestantism was subversive. If everything to be learned about the commands of the Almighty were told us by the Bible, it might logically follow that anybody who could read the Bible could determine for himself what God's injunctions were. The notion that one man or a small group had the exclusive right to proclaim theological truths would be undercut. The central thrust of this attitude was toward individualism; its force was centrifugal, tending increasingly over the years to propel each man outward in some unprecedented direction along a path of his own. Any practices of a church that could not be justified by an explicit passage in the Bible must be abandoned. To the other shattering trends of the sixteenth century was now added a disintegration of religious unity. Moreover, this development could threaten the existence of the civil government as well. It could lead beyond individualism to anarchy. Already by 1581 a young Englishman was saying: "Therefore the Magistrates commaundment must not be a rule unto me . . . but as I see it agree with the worde of God." On those terms, no government could exist.

These considerations help to explain how dissenting creeds could exist even though the Church of England was the established religion with the full backing of the government. The early Christian martyrs in Rome were better equipped to face lions in the Colosseum than to face an outraged Jehovah on the Day of Judgment. Similarly with British sectaries. By the time Charles I and Archbishop Laud tried to enforce "one Doctrine and one discipline," opposing views had spread throughout society, even reaching men who were sworn to uphold the official monopoly of worship. When people fear for their immortal souls, they are armed against earthly persecutions.

All Protestants were agreed that the overriding public issue of the time was the battle against the Roman Catholic Church. Their animosity was ferocious; they talked repeatedly about "the common enemy, the Romish wolf," about "the bloody whore of Rome," about "the reign of the beast and Antichrist of Rome." But even the existence of a common enemy could not bind Englishmen together on religious topics. Protestants hated other Protestants.

In order to understand the trends in British religion, four significant groups must be discerned. The most conservative organization was the Church of England (subsequently to be called the Anglican Church)—the only legal church in the nation. Its government by a hierarchy of bishops, archbishops, and monarch did not satisfy the Presbyterians, who set up a polity ruled by presbyters, or elders, over whom there was no higher rank. This ecclesiastical system was especially strong in Scotland. At the radical end of the Protestant spectrum were several fragmented sects such as the Diggers and Levellers, who often urged a drastic sort of equality in both religion and social relations. Finally, somewhere between the radical groups and Presbyterians, there was the influential faction called the Independents in Great Britain and known as the Puritans in the New World. Their aim, as their name implies, was to restore the primitive church "pure and unspotted." Although in the eyes of the law they could not depart from the Church of England, at the same time they could find no scriptural sanction for many of its practices. They resented ceremonial trappings in religious services. They put no stock in Anglican forms of set prayer. They rejected robes and vestments. These devices violated the word of God. On many aspects of ecclesiastical organization the Puritans were in conflict with the established church.

They were also in conflict with themselves. They got into a bind because their creed could not be reconciled with their intense longing for salvation. At the Creation, so they thought, the final fate of each individual had already been determined by God; this was the doctrine of predestination. Nothing a man did could lever him into heaven; no man could ever earn salvation. It could come only from the free grace of God. This dilemma imposed an incredible tension upon believers. The primary calling of everyone was to win Divine rescue from sin and death—and he could never be sure that he had succeeded. The strain could be unbearable. To resolve this clash between theological doctrine and emotional cravings, some Puritan thinkers hit upon an ingenious construction of the Bible.

They seized upon the 17th chapter of Genesis, which reads:

> And when Abram was ninety years old and nine, the Lord appeared to Abram, and said unto him, I am the Almighty God; walk before me, and be thou perfect.
> And I will make my covenant between me and thee, and will multiply thee exceedingly.
> And Abram fell on his face: and God talked with him, saying,
> As for me, behold, my covenant is with thee, and thou shalt be a father of many nations.

God then changed Abram's name to Abraham, from whom many nations were to descend. We, said the Puritans, are one of those nations. We are a chosen people. The claim may seem presumptuous, but they made it nonetheless.

The result was what is called the federal theology. While we note the incurably authoritarian nature of Puritan thought, we must also notice that it was incurably legalistic. It was fascinated by the idea of laws and contracts. A compact was a compact; a bargain was a bargain. Once a contract had been entered into, all parties were obliged to observe its terms. God had made a compact with Abraham and his descendents. If the human partners in the contract lived up to their commitments and abided by the precepts of the Almighty, then surely God would look on them with special favor. Here was a technique that enabled a man to be more or less sure that he belonged to the elect, that he would pass inspection on the Day of Judgment. Conversely, of course, if the descendents of Abraham should falter and fall, they would be smitten by Divine retribution more severe than that imposed on an ordinary community. This is the doctrine of special providences with a vengeance.

The Puritans used the idea of contract or covenant in dealing with many other problems. They used it to set up civil governments. More pertinent for present purposes is its use to found a novel kind of ecclesiastical structure. They went beyond rejection of the episcopal forms of the Church of England Anglicans; they also rejected Presbyterianism with its rule by councils of elders. They believed that the only church prescribed by the Bible was the individual parish or congregation: hence their name, Congregationalists. They thought further that only the elect were eligible for membership in a congregation. Right at this point, in the conversion experience, was the essence of Puritanism. A sinner might be led step by step toward redemption by learned preachers and elders. But he could not be admitted to the church until he had experienced a magic instant when God touched his heart and he knew himself to be saved. He would feel that he was utterly helpless, a creature of no worth, stained with sin, and simultaneously knew that God of his own grace had granted him salvation. Every candidate for admission to a church had to stand before a congregation or its elders and describe in a satisfactory fashion his instant of illumination. Only after demonstrating that he had entered into a contract with God was he thought fit to join in covenant with the congregation.

For generations the Congregationalists tried, and ultimately failed, to give each parish full power over its own affairs. The more extreme of them raced headlong for untarnished virtue. They were convinced that they could never be regenerated so long as they met in unclean modes of worship with unclean men. Since all Englishmen were by birth members of the Church of England or Anglican Church, and since everyone knew that more than one inhabitant of the nation was a sinner, the only course for one of the elect was to turn his back and walk away. These Separatists wished to leave the Church of England altogether, a course of action that at least had the merits of internal consistency. Few Congregationalists were willing to go so far. No less anxious than their irreligious (by the Puritan code) brethren to preserve uniformity of religion in the nation, they were also hesitant to subject themselves to imprisonment or other persecutions. So, while worshipping by their own creed in secret enclaves, they overtly remained within the Church of England, and justified their two-faced behavior by some fantastic rationalizations. They held that an unregenerate parishioner was not really a "member" and therefore they did not worship with him. By their rules a minister could only be chosen by a congregation, whereas a Church of England priest was installed by a bishop. The Puritans argued that it sufficed for the minister to be chosen later by his congregation, after the bishop had tapped his shoulder. Besides, bishops were not "really" part of the church, so their actions would have no significance.

21

As so often in history, the group with the greater intellectual rigor had the least influence on events. The ideas of the Separatists, usually called the Pilgrims, carried across the Atlantic on the *Mayflower,* went to found the plantation at Plymouth Rock. The Pilgrims and their Thanksgiving Day may be known to every school child, but they are marginal to American history. Coming to the New World a decade later than the Pilgrims, the non-Separating Puritans set up the colony of Massachusetts Bay, centering on Boston. They may have been in some ways a hopelessly illogical bunch, but their colony prospered from the beginning, and their technique of compromise, however shabby, became integral to the American way of life.

To understand the early years in America we must also examine political events in England, where compromise was a seldom-used device. The frustrations and hopes of the sixteenth century bore bloody fruit in the long seventeenth-century struggle for control of her government. From the coronation of James I in 1603 until the Glorious Revolution of 1688–1689, the conflict of king against Parliament was unrelenting on both sides. At the end of Elizabeth's reign the power of the monarch was enormous. All expenses of the armed forces, both army and navy, were met by her moneys. The expenditures of the entire diplomatic corps were paid from her purse. The crown lands were so extensive and yielded such a high income that they could support the government even if Parliament refused to vote appropriations. As for Parliament, the crucial house in the fray would prove to be Commons rather than Lords. Commons had something under 440 members. There were about 50 counties in England plus 12 in Wales, each with two members of Parliament ("MPs"). More than 300 MPs sat for boroughs. What was a borough? Presumably, an incorporated town. But Parliament had determined the representation of the boroughs centuries before; by 1600 some had almost no population, yet still sent two men to Commons. Some rapidly growing cities had no representatives at all. (When Americans in 1765 demanded direct representation and raised the banner, "No taxation without representation," more than one Englishman could not understand what they were talking about.) Although many boroughs were densely populated urban areas, they tended to pick as MPs not local citizens but country gentlemen. Such was the prestige of owning land and being one of the gentry.

The Century of Revolution was a stirring but terrifying age. To kill a king was to oppose the deepest pieties of the time, but the English beheaded Charles I in 1649. To try to govern a country without a king was truly to take a leap into the dark, but the English made the effort for more than a decade. They slaughtered each other until bloody bodies were stacked like cordwood, all for the glory of Christ; small wonder that the great philosopher Thomas Hobbes would advocate an all-powerful state on the grounds that any kind of government was better than anarchy and civil war; small wonder that he would capsulate his life in the sentence, "My mother bore twins: me and fear." No conflict is more brutal than when Cain turns on Abel, when brother turns on brother.

The recent quarrel among historians as to what set off the English civil war has not resulted in any deaths to date, but it may come to that. Certainly it has been heated enough to satisfy all except the sanguinary. Was the key factor the rising cost of warfare, which prompted monarchs to extract ever heavier taxes from a groaning populace? Did the increase in taxation lead to a "crisis of the aristocracy"? Was an indispensable element "the rise of the gentry," an attempt by country landowners to achieve in politics and government a status equivalent to that they had won economically and socially? Was the revolution a thrust by gentlemen in the outlying counties against domination by the court at Westminster? What part was played by prospering merchants in London and Bristol? Does it make sense in this period to distinguish between landowners and merchants? (Very little. A successful person in either field soon diversified into the other.) Disputes about the relative weights to be given to these various "causes" seem likely to go on forever.

But at least two statements can be made with some certitude. The place where existing grievances came to a focus and found expression was Parliament, at least until Oliver Cromwell took command at mid-century. Second, a sound approach by government and Church to the question of religion could have averted the outbreak of armed conflict. By the time Elizabeth died, most Puritans had become fairly moderate in their expectations; they wanted only to be left alone. There were exceptions. The Separatists of course were irreconcilable. Other Puritans were nasty and intolerable. Consider the story of an Exeter merchant who was journeying home from a session of Parliament with another MP: The companion invites the Puritan to lodge at his home for the night; the Puritan agrees only on condition that neither the MP nor his wife nor his servants will curse while he is under their roof; the next day, Sunday, he demands that the usual morning mass be supplemented by an afternoon mass. When this same Puritan became mayor of Exeter, he stopped the sale of fruit or the operation of grist mills on the Sabbath. But he was not the norm. The average Puritan would have settled for half a loaf. That was just what was denied him by four Stuart kings: James I, Charles I (who lost both crown and head), Charles II, and James II.

The clash came to center on two disputes: the king and his top archbishop tried to suppress all dissenting sects, and the king battled with Parliament for the power of the purse. Already by 1610 James I was at loggerheads with Commons; no laws at all were enacted during the following fourteen years. Several were passed in 1624. Parliament met again in 1625, 1626, and 1628–1629. Then it was not convened for more than a decade. When it came together in 1640 the radicals among its members had both organization and a program—part of which, as it evolved, came to be the drastic expedient of imprisoning Charles I. His followers took to the field, and after August of 1642 the nation was at war with itself.

The greatest of the Independent generals proved to be Oliver Cromwell; he proved also to be a towering statesman. Brilliant, absolutely determined, unscrupulous in pursuit of his goals, he smashed even his closest lieutenants if they presumed to disagree with him on matters that he deemed vital. Having previously purged the opposition in Commons, he induced the Rump Parliament to order the execution of Charles I in 1649. Four years later he dissolved the Rump Parliament too. From then until his death in 1658 he ruled alone as Lord Protector. This period of the Commonwealth suggests a fascinating speculation, the answer to which might cast a beacon on the nature of seventeenth-century England. Namely, could the nation be governed without a king? Probably not. One historian has plausibly hypothesized that, if Oliver Cromwell had lived a few years longer, the turbulence in the country would have compelled him to declare himself the monarch and to re-establish a hereditary succession.

But Cromwell did not live, and his son was unable to hold power. The monarchy was restored in 1660 when the son of the dead Charles I ascended to the throne. But the Restoration did not wipe out all of the results of the Commonwealth. Apart from laws affecting the relations of England to her colonies overseas, the chief consequences had to do with religion. Military necessity forced the Protectorate to grant a considerable measure of religious freedom. On one occasion when Cromwell was about to promote in his New Model Army a man known to be an Anabaptist, another general protested that the man was nothing but a heretic. Cromwell, asking caustically whether that trait was likely to alter the man's skill as a soldier, made the promotion.

During the twenty-five years that Charles II reigned, the country was reasonably quiet. But he died without issue, and the accession in 1685 of his brother James meant a renewal of chaos, for James was a professing Roman Catholic. The situation was insane: in an age when religion to most Englishmen was a living throbbing faith, no Catholic, not even one with immense abilities, could have ruled an overwhelmingly Protestant nation. And James was not an able man. He promptly set about removing Protestant judges and replacing them with Catholics. He stuffed the army and navy with Catholic officers. The sequel was a palace revolt. A civil war was averted only because James, fortunately for all, fled to Catholic France. This was the Glorious Revolution—a bloodless one.

The Revolution Settlement brought two new principles. In a sense the question in dispute had been this: Is the king above the law, or is the law above the king? If the second, then Parliament would be the supreme power in the state, since nobody doubted that it could change the law. But legislation would be meaningless if the king could remove and replace by his own whim the judges who would have to interpret and apply the laws. So the Settlement provided that a judge could only be removed for cause. The other new principle was of equal importance: that all Protestants would enjoy toleration of their religious worship.

Every schoolboy knows that expansion of Europe began with Columbus. But there are fascinating and less well-known aspects of his career that reveal some basic and persistent habits of mind of the Explorer Age and later. His discoveries, following a century of European exploratory voyages and based on some recent advances in seafaring, were nevertheless made with only a very few navigational aids. The motives of Columbus, combining dynastic drives with religious ones, fused a need for adventure with lust for wealth. This syndrome demanded from the beginning that his attitude toward Indians in the Caribbean should be that he would dominate them, enslave and Christianize them. More than a century passed before Columbus' achievements had an impact in America north of the Rio Grande. That Englishmen after 1600 should have ventured so successfully into colonization was the product of the emergence of three cooperating factors: surplus capital, surplus manpower, and growing mastery of new forms of organization that could control both money and men. Each of these three essential elements has its own causes, and each is worth careful discussion to illuminate these backgrounds. While this complex of developments was weaving an intricate web that served to carry a few thousand "planters" (really a slight trickle) to the New World, the homeland was torn by decades of struggle. Civil war broke out. A king was beheaded. A commonwealth was tried. The monarch was restored to the throne. When his successor avowed Roman Catholicism in a violently Protestant land, he was deposed in a palace revolution and replaced by a Protestant monarch imported from the Netherlands. Fundamental changes were made in the English constitution, and these would have momentous significance in the American colonies.

SOME NOTABLE EVENTS

1492 Moors expelled from Granada.

Columbus lands at San Salvador (Guanahani, Watling's Island) in Bahamas.

1497 John Cabot makes his first voyage to America.

1498 Vasco da Gama reaches India.

1519 Martin Luther publicly launches what became the Protestant Reformation.

1526 William Tyndale's English translation of Bible.

1534 Act of Supremacy names Henry VIII head of Church of England.

1536 Henry VIII begins to seize lands of Catholic monasteries.

John Calvin, *Institutes of the Christian Religion*, in Latin.

1543 Vesalius, *The Structure of the Human Body*.

Nicholas Copernicus, *On the Revolutions of the Heavenly Orbs*.

1558 Coronation of Elizabeth I of England.

1559 Acts of Supremacy and Uniformity in England.

1577–
1580 Francis Drake's memorable voyage in the *Golden Hind*.

1587 Founding of Sir Walter Raleigh's "Lost Colony" at Roanoke, Virginia.

1587–
1604 England at war against Spain.

1589 Richard Hakluyt, *Principall Navigations, Voiages and Discoveries . . .*

1598 Edict of Nantes grants substantial freedoms to French Protestants.

1603 James VI of Scotland becomes also James I of England

1607 Virginia Company plants colony at Jamestown.

1608 Quebec founded by Samuel de Champlain.

1611 Publication of the King James Authorized Version of the Bible.

1618–
1648 Thirty Years' War on the Continent, largely over religious disputes.

1620 Francis Bacon, *Novum Organum*.

Planting of Pilgrim (Separatist) colony at Plymouth, Massachusetts.

1624 Beginnings of Dutch settlement of Manhattan and the Hudson valley.

1625 Hugo Grotius, *On the Law of War and Peace*.

1628 William Harvey, *On the Movement of the Heart and Blood*.

1629–
1640 Charles I governs England without summoning Parliament.

1630 Massachusetts Bay Company plants colony at Boston.

1630–
1640 The Great Migration to Massachusetts Bay (Boston and environs).

1637 René Descartes, *Discourse on Method*.

1640 What became the Long Parliament convenes.

1642–
1646 Civil war in England.

1648–
1649 Second and last period of civil war in England.

1649 Charles I beheaded on January 30.

1649–
1653 The Commonwealth period, governed by Parliament.

1651 Thomas Hobbes, *Leviathan*.

1652–
1654 First Anglo-Dutch War.

1653–
1658 Protectorate of Oliver Cromwell.

1660 English monarchy restored in the person of Charles II, son of Charles I.

1664 New Netherlands captured by English and renamed New York.

1665–
1667 Second Anglo-Dutch War.

1670–
1674 Third Anglo-Dutch War.

1685 Edict of Nantes revoked by Louis XIV of France; Protestants suppressed.

1685–
  1688 Reign of James II, brother of
        Charles II.
1687 Isaac Newton, *Mathematical Principles of Natural Philosophy.*
1688–
  1689 The Glorious Revolution; William
        and Mary come to throne.
1689 The Act of Toleration in England.
1690 John Locke, *Two Treatises of Government.*

Ways to Study History I

Buy your own ship. Most of us cannot afford to take this advice literally, but Samuel Eliot Morison managed to do it. In his efforts to sail the courses that Columbus had sailed he used not only a ketch and a yawl but also a schooner that was 147 feet long. Morison has done more than his share of working through manuscripts in fusty archives, but he did not quit there. Nobody could ever write of him, as he wrote of some predecessors, "Most biographies of the Admiral might well be entitled, 'Columbus to the Water's Edge.'"

Born in Boston, Morison spent much of his boyhood scudding around the harbor. This left him enchanted for life by the briny deeps. While a professor of history at Harvard he wrote a staggering number of books, and the major part of them concern the sea and seamen. During World War II he became a Rear Admiral charged with writing a history of the naval aspects of the conflict; happily he synopsized his fourteen large volumes on the subject into one book, *The Two-Ocean War.*

His love for the sea was an immense aid to Morison as he tried to think as Columbus thought and to feel as Columbus felt, and this identification was intensified by his tracing of the great explorer's voyages. The yield from this re-living of another's experiences is sometimes hilarious, as in Morison's analysis of the claim made by Columbus that he had seen a light at 10 p.m. on 11 October, 1492. The fleet at that hour was at least 35 miles from land: "The 400,000 candlepower light now on San Salvador, 170 feet above sea level, is not visible nearly so far. One writer has advanced the theory that the light was made by Indians torching for fish —why not lighting a cigar?—but Indians do not go fishing in 3000 fathoms of water 35 miles offshore at night in a gale of wind."

Document 1-1

The pamphlet "Nova Britannia," the source of these excerpts, was propaganda for the new Virginia. Issued in 1609, it was probably written by a London alderman whose father-in-law, Sir Thomas Smith, was a leader of the Virginia Company, the East India Company, and numerous other ventures.

. . . *So I wish and entreat all well affected subjects, some in their persons, others in their purses, cheerfully to adventure, and jointly take in hand this high and acceptable work, tending to advance and spread the kingdom of God and the knowledge of the truth among so many millions of men and women, Savage and blind, that never yet saw the true light shine before their eyes, to enlighten their minds and comfort their souls, as also for the honor of our King and enlarging of his kingdom, . . . The country itself is large and great assuredly, though as yet no exact discovery can be made of all. It is also commendable and hopeful every way, the air and climate most sweet and wholesome, much warmer than England, and very agreeable to our natures. . . .*

There are valleys and plains streaming with sweet springs, like veins in a natural body. There are hills and mountains making sensible proffer of hidden treasure, never yet searched. The land is full of minerals, plenty of woods (the wants of England). There are growing goodly oaks and elms, beech and birch, spruce, walnut, cedar, and fir trees, in great abundance. The soil is strong and lusty of its own nature, and sendeth out naturally fruitful vines running upon trees, and shrubs. . . . But of this that I have said, if bare nature be so amiable in its naked kind, what may we hope when art and nature both shall join, and strive together to give best content to man and beast? . . .

Securing the Beachheads

The first permanent colony to be planted by Englishmen amid the forests of the New World was Virginia. The date was 1607. Several attempts had been made earlier, at scattered locations ranging from Virginia all the way to Newfoundland. All had failed. The survivors of some plantations had retreated back to England in despair. Other ventures, such as the Lost Colony that Walter Raleigh had started at Roanoke, simply were swallowed up by the woods and left no trace. By 1530 at the latest, fishermen from England, the Netherlands, Brittany, and the Basque provinces of France and Spain were pitching their summer quarters in Newfoundland or coastal Maine, but their custom was to return to their homelands every autumn. No stabilized English settlement existed anywhere in North America.

This degree of desolation could not persist; the same energies that led to creation of the East India Company in 1600 were bound to find an outlet to the westward also. An attempt to set up a post in Maine in 1606 proved as futile as

FIGURE 2-1. *River Systems of Virginia*

all of its predecessors, but the next year a colony was founded farther south at Jamestown. It contrived to hold out and, ultimately, to grow. In retrospect the survival seems miraculous. Not only was the project highly hazardous in itself as shown by the destruction of all prior ventures, but the Virginia Company and its planters went about their work in hopelessly wrongheaded fashion. They hoped to turn a handsome profit by concentrating on a narrow range of economic pursuits: mining, preferably of precious metals, finding a water route to the Far East, monopolizing commerce. Jamestown was to be not a permanent farming settlement but a trading post. By July of 1609 some 320 men had been sent over from England. Considering their new environment and the nature of their tasks in it, their occupations were ludicrous. Perhaps as many as a quarter of these early immigrants were "gentlemen." Predictably, more than two thirds of the settlers perished in the first two years. Nor was that the worst of it. Another 600 men arrived in 1609, and they did not bring adequate provisions. The winter of 1609–1610 was "the starving time" in Virginia history; only sixty men managed to make it through the cold months.

The investors in England were understandably eager to recoup their funds quickly, and they had especially charged the planters with finding goods that could be marketed in Great Britain or Europe. But to date the only exports had been a little timber and its derivatives: pitch, tar, ashes for making soap. Then two momentous events took place, both featuring John Rolfe. First, in 1612, he planted the first tobacco grown by a white man; this crop was to dominate the economy of the province for the next two centuries. Although King James wrote a pamphlet condemning the filthy weed, many did not heed him. The market in Great Britain and on the Continent seemed insatiable. American exports of tobacco, a mere 2,000 pounds in 1616, would hit 35,000,000 pounds a year by 1697. It is amusing today to learn that in the 17th century tobacco was widely thought to be a medical remedy; there are reports that schoolboys at Eton were flogged by their masters if they refused to smoke.

Then in 1613 Rolfe took Pocahontas to wife. The marriage has meaning beyond its efficacy in bringing a measure of temporary peace in Indian-white relations. It also yields insight into the rationalizations that appealed to English settlers. In view of God's order to the Israelites not to enter into wedlock with strangers, how could Rolfe justify marrying a heathen? Well, he finally concluded, he could convert her to Christianity, marry her, and thus become the means of saving her soul. In his letter to the governor asking permission for the rites he declared that he made the request not "with the unbridled desire of carnall affection: but for the good of this plantation, for the honour of our countrie, for the glory of God, for my owne salvation, and converting to the true knowledge of God and Jesus Christ, an unbeleeving creature."

Some of Rolfe's contemporaries must have listened askance to his claims about the religious character of his impulses. Captain John Smith, for instance, was no stranger to the baser motives; of Virginia he wrote, "For, I am not so simple to thinke, that ever any other motive than wealth will ever erect there a Commonweale." He sneered at the directors of the Virginia Company for "making Religion their colour, when all their aime was nothing but present profit." But even a skeptic like Smith could not hold to the distinction between religious and material advancement. Men simply did not think in terms of that dichotomy. To quote Smith about his colony at Jamestown, "So then here is a place a nurse for souldiers, a practice for marriners, a trade for marchants, a reward for the good, and that which is most of all, a businesse (most acceptable to God) to bring such poore infidels to the true knowledge of God and his holy Gospell."

Of course a man's behavior in his secondary calling (his secular occupation) could not change his predestined fate at his primary calling, but still common sense suggested that if he kept his covenant with Jehovah, the Lord would grant him worldly goods. Thus in a sermon in 1610 to the Virginia Company in London, a minister of the Church of England could argue that the best way to get monetary gains was manifest: "Now the high way to obtain that, is to forget your own affectiones, & to neglect your own private profit in respect of Gods glorie, . . . and he that seekes only or principally *spirituall* things, God will reward him both with those *spirituall and temporal* things." Doubtless there was dissent from such unction; as one man put it: "Conscience is a pretty thing to carry to church but he that useth it in a fair market or shop may die a beggar." Despite cynical remarks, many men swallowed the soothing syrup. Moreover it was spread through all faiths, so that Jesuit fathers in Maryland could declaim, "Yet we trust in the goodness of God and the piety of the Catholics that, while we sow spiritual seed, we shall reap carnal things in abundance, and that to those who seek the kingdom of God the other things shall be added."

An extreme version of this exultant optimism (have your heaven and eat it too) was published in 1625 as *Purchas His Pilgrims*. It told how, after the Fall, God to avoid mutual slaughter among the different races had sent each to its own segregated part of the globe. Thereafter mankind had to re-achieve its own unity, and God in His helpful way had given some hints. At the Creation every product had grown everywhere, but since the Almighty had instituted regional specialization after the Fall, it had become impossible for any man to meet his needs except by foreign trade. Thus international commerce would lead to eternal salvation. And foremost among the regenerate, so Americans held, would be Americans. To cite John Rolfe again, the migration of Englishmen to the New World had been undertaken by "a peculiar people, marked and chosen by the finger of God, to possess it, for undoubtedly he is with us."

Certainly within fifteen years or so after the starving time it began to seem that indeed the inhabitants of Virginia may have been favored by Divine Agency. The standard of living in the new colony was already higher—perhaps half again as high—as in England, and the typical Englishman lived a good bit better than the average man on the Continent. By 1622 the colony could claim what may be America's first rags-to-riches boast, that "any honest laborious man" could quickly grow rich in the new country.

Success did not come without many trials and many errors. Assuming that the Virginia Company had raised the capital needed to transport immigrants to the Western Hemisphere and to sustain them until they became self-sufficient, the vital question seems obvious: How could potential immigrants be induced to go to Virginia and to work hard after they got there? The Company in London appointed the governor; everybody else in Jamestown was made subordinate to him in a rigid hierarchy. An effort was made to reduce each man to a cipher, so that none of his traits were recognized except his duties to the Company and his rank in the table of organization. Understandably this scheme attracted few men and those were of dubious virtues. The next resort was to involuntary migration, such as the deportation from England of orphans, indigent children, and convicts. These measures seemed ill-suited to supply efficient and disciplined labor, so they were used reluctant-ly and rarely. Hindsight suggests that another possibility had opened up as early as 1619 when the first group of blacks was reportedly brought to Jamestown by a Dutch ship. Clearly the white colonists had no moral antagonism to slavery, but in fact—probably because of a lack of resources with which to buy blacks—the institution did not become significant in Virginia for more than fifty years. Only in 1670 did the colony enact that "all servants not being Christians" who arrived by sea should be slaves for life. Apparently all whites including servants were assumed to be "Christians," and investigators have concluded that perpetual slavery for whites did not exist in any colony.

The behavior of early inhabitants was far from Christian. To maintain control of the motley and mottled population, governors tried several tactics. Their chief reliance was on the cooperation of church with state to enforce discipline. Theological tests were employed to weed out applicants for immigration. In the colony at one point all residents were marched to prayers every day. Not only gambling and drunkenness, but idleness and fancy clothes were illegal. Ministers were to suppress "all ungodly disorders . . . as suspi-cions of whoredoms, dishonest company keeping with woemen and such like." Strict Sabbatarian rules were enforced against such activities as carrying a gun and shucking corn. Everybody was taxed to sustain the church. If a man objected, he had to pay double.

Repression might obtain a modicum of peace, but it was not calculated to draw in more labor or to induce the inhabitants to work hard. Originally the Company owned all the land itself, and it planned to go on that way. But private ownership of real estate was one of the few carrots that it had. By 1614 some better settlers were being given a qualified right to private property. It was not enough. Five years later a further concession was made; the popula-tion was divided into eight categories, which were to get varying amounts of land on varying terms. In 1620 the government's attempt to preserve an all-male society (except for nearby Indians) finally ended and Englishwomen were imported to become wives. Soon a tide of people started. Immigration in the next five years was 4,800—nearly twice as much as in the period from 1607 to 1619.

Economic changes had a grave impress on the structure of society. The seventeenth century had inherited from the Middle Ages the notion that every community must be ordered into a hierarchy of superior and inferior ranks. An early governor of Virginia affirmed his intention of having a society "like our native country"; each person was to stay at his "proper station," the station that he held at birth, and to show a fitting deference to his betters. The class composition that quickly emerged is revealing. Early in 1625 there were 48 families in the colony whose heads bore titles of distinction. These privileged families employed more than half of the 500 servants in the colony.

Until slaves became more numerous, these menials were the bottom of the social scale. Many, perhaps most, of them had crossed the ocean as indentured servants. That is, a ship captain or a future employer already in Virginia would pay for their oceanic crossing. In turn the servant would sign indentures by which he agreed to labor faithfully at the master's command for a fixed period. The term was often seven years or, for a minor, until he was twenty-one years old. But the provisions of indentures varied greatly; a great deal of individual bargaining took place. The servant lived on the master's property and was furnished with the necessities of life. He might even get some education or be trained in a skilled craft. When he completed his term he normally received some sort of stake to give him a start in a life of independence. That was the crux. An indentured servant with a cruel or grasping master might be battered and beaten and abused and underfed and overworked. But he was always aware that his subjection would end, that he was not a slave forever, that if he worked hard his children could begin at a higher rank in the society.

The step upward was likely to be tenancy on a small farm, hopefully followed by ownership. A new owner would then turn to expanding his farm with hope of becoming fully his own master. Several circumstances worked toward this culmination. The English had grown up in a country that fed ambition to a greater extent than did any society on the Continent except perhaps for the Low Countries. For all its stratification and for all the efforts to stabilize the hierarchy, England did hold openings for personal mobility. A young man might desert his yeoman father, go to London, become apprenticed to a draper, grab the chance at his master's death to marry the widow, build up the business, and at last become an alderman. When men migrated to America they did not abandon their traditions or ambitions. Their aim was to transplant their conventional culture to a new location.* They still thought that a hierarchical society was the best—indeed the only—kind to have, but each immigrant wanted a higher rung on the ladder for himself.

In two respects they found room to move ahead. The first elite in Jamestown had been English gentry; it included, for instance, four West brothers who were the sons of Lord de la Warr, the wife being a second cousin of the late Queen Elizabeth. These men died or returned home in less than a generation. Filling the vacuum were a coarser cruder band, men who had torn from the wilderness first a living and then a surplus. Their power was not a legacy but an achievement. Their way of life was far from genteel. Many were wholly taken up by their private business, which consisted in grabbing every acre possible and developing it quickly. The social gulf left by the gentry's emigration back to England was matched by a gulf of economic opportunity

---

*American history holds many incidents to suggest that migrants, whether from abroad or within the nation, are deeply conservative. Where so much is new, they try to save what they can of the old. (See the middle of Chapter 15 on frontier democracy.)

on the receding frontier. As with their predecessors, however, these self-made men did not long remain at the pinnacle of the Virginia pyramid. Many of them did keep their wealth and considerable influence, but soon a group of newcomers moved in over their heads. This wave of migrants was set moving during the Civil Wars in England, lasting from about 1645 to 1665. Several who came were well connected in London, younger sons of substantial families. (The best way to get wealth is to inherit it; next best is to marry it.) These men founded the clans that would be prominent in Virginia for centuries; the first William Byrd arrived in 1670, and 300 years later another Byrd succeeded his own father in the United States Senate. (Did they regard Tudors, Stuarts, and Hanovers as merely other and perhaps lesser dynasties?) Certain it is that the Byrds came to think of political power as being theirs by right—a hereditary matter.

The relation should be stated precisely. A deferential society produced a politics based on deference. Not every man of "good family" could gain public office; some made themselves obnoxious to their neighbors. But very few climbed high in the government who did not have the right parents.

Insistence upon reverence for the high-born saturated Virginia. In 1609 the company gave the governor a body guard to insure "the more regard and respect of your place. . . ." After 1624 members of the governor's Council were consistently called "esquire." Even in noting exceptions to the system, colonists implied an acceptance of the system itself. When the Virginia Company wanted to name a man without social standing as governor, it carefully got him knighted first; when a malcontent said the officials of York County were "Hogg trough Makers" and other craftsmen, he made clear that he scorned them because they were "not fitting to sit where they doe sit." Law required that an orphan be given "the benefit of the estate and station to which he was born." One complaint against Quakers was that they would not take off their hats in court and that they otherwise defied authority. At a time when much of the land was being farmed by tenants and when nearly all horses and cattle were owned by wealthier planters,* it was enacted that men should "fence in the crop and turn out the stock." A farmer had to build a "sufficient" fence to protect his crops. What was "sufficient"? It came to mean "pig-tight, horse-high, and bull-strong." When a Virginian was expecting his sister to come from England, he wrote that she must be "handsomely and gentelely and well cloathed, with a maid to wait on her."

Men with this cast of mind manipulated a government well suited to their aims. By 1624 the Virginia Company was impoverished, and unable even to protect its colonists from Indian attacks; the king vacated its charter and made the settlement into a royal colony. Thereafter he appointed the governor, and the governor named his council. But an earlier governor had in 1619

---

*Tradition distinguished between the men who rode to battle and those who walked to it.

FIGURE 2-2 *King William Courthouse, Virginia*

King William Courthouse in Virginia was built before 1675 to serve the needs of New Kent County. It manifests cardinal features of the transport of European civilization to the New World. As to architecture, it has the rounded arches of English Gothic rather than the pointed ones traditional to French Gothic; these settlers were born British to their marrow. The matter goes further: early colonists remained true to the conventions of their particular areas at home. Immigrants to New England came in large numbers from the southeastern counties of the mother country where wood was abundant; they built in wood. Inhabitants of the Southern provinces had learned to build in brick, and continued to do so.

Note too that Virginia provided a court for each new county, and organized counties as fast as each was settled. South Carolina, in contrast, dispensed justice only in the capital, Charles Town granted to the citizens the right of electing what became a popular assembly. The evolution was gradual, but already in 1624 the assembly was asserting that only it and not the governor had the power to levy taxes or to make appropriations. A republican institution grew by royal neglect; only in 1639 did Charles I recognize that an assembly existed at all. Having reached out to seize the power of the purse, the assembly in 1652 went further in shackling the appointed officials; those worthies, the House of Burgesses decreed, can be members of our body only after taking the oath of a burgess. The colony had now in effect set itself up as a self-governing commonwealth, with its assembly claiming powers analogous to those of the House of Commons. Rules general to the entire colony were to be made by burgesses, council, and governor. That left open the question of local jurisdiction, and here too the precedent was from England: the county court with its justices of the peace and its sheriff.

After the perilous beginnings, population grew rather quickly, being 8,000 in 1640 and 40,000 in 1666. The process of pushing the area of settlement outward carried men beyond convenient reach of the nearest county court. Such access was vital: a man couldn't even move to another county without permission from his court. New counties were formed; there were ten in 1643 and nineteen in 1673. And county by county the justices of the peace were the wealthy landowners. They were also the burgesses for the county. Power had been fragmented, and the future would see renewed clashes of the governor versus county magnates lording it over their own turf.

A major rival against England for a share of North America was the Netherlands. This tiny land had only one asset—its access to the ocean. But the citizens of Holland improved their opportunities. From fishing they moved into shipbuilding and overseas trade, and thence into manufacturing and money-lending. By 1650 the carrying trade of the world was in Dutch hands and she had more than 35,000 vessels on the oceans. Amsterdam was a great city with 260,000 residents. Dutch fishing boats scoured the North Sea to the doorsteps of England; rivalry between the two nations led to three distinct wars from 1652 to 1674. The Dutch colonial empire began in 1602 with the formation of the Dutch East India Company, which was empowered to govern possessions, sign treaties, operate its own army and navy.

Holland's maritime activity led to the foundation in 1621 of the Dutch West India Company with the same expansive powers as its predecessor. It had sole right to trade not only with the Americas but also with West Africa. Its nineteen directors, managing from Amsterdam and with total control of all activities, turned their eyes almost exclusively to two objectives. One was to exclude the English and all other nations from the slave trade with Africa. The other was to raid the Spanish treasure fleets in the Caribbean (an effort at which they made good—in a few years their loot amounted to more than ten times the capital of the Company). To them, their colony in the New World on the Hudson River was as trivial as a peanut stand would be to a person who

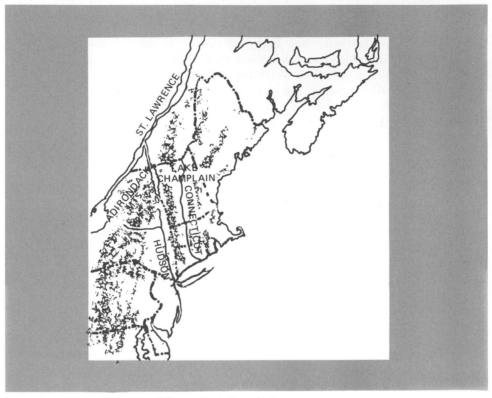

FIGURE 2-3. *The Hudson and Connecticut River Systems*

owned the oil wells of Texas. Their neglect of New Netherlands might have worked out well, as did English neglect of Virginia, save for a fatal difference in the two situations: Holland was so prosperous that spontaneous emigration from it was virtually zero.

Also unlike Virginia, power in New Netherlands was not divided; the governor had it all, and unfortunately each of the colony's successive governors was either incompetent or tyrannical. The Dutch colony had other weaknesses as well. Although it eventually exported some naval stores and farm products, its economic base was always the fur trade with the Indians. The consequence was widely scattered and highly vulnerable trading posts and hamlets. Another consequence was underpopulation; when New Netherlands fell to the English in 1664, it had only 7,000 people (many of whom were not Dutch), and the superb location of Manhattan Island, New Amsterdam, a mere 1,500. These were the fruits of trying to run a colony from the mother country, and of focusing on commerce rather than the growth of farming enterprises. New Netherlands was the eminent flop of an incredibly successful parent.

The earliest operations in New Netherlands were up the Hudson, planting a fur post in the area that became Albany. Although Manhattan had been discovered by Henry Hudson back in 1609, and although it offered as splendid a port as might be found on earth, the first settlement there was not made until 1626. Even then it did not thrive. Added to the indifference of the Company in Holland was the immersion of the governors of New Amsterdam in the interests of the huge Hudson riverbank estates held by "patroons" who planned to work them with hired labor and tenants. This effort to transplant a feudal setup to America was ill-adapted to the New World; only one patroonship was in good shape when the century ended. So the colony remained weak and in 1664, ironically during a period of "peace" between two Anglo-Dutch Wars, the English seized it without firing a shot. The Dutch governor Peter Stuyvesant had no choice but to surrender. His weaponry was in a miserable state; his fort had no gates at all, its walls were crumbling, and within those walls there was not one well or cistern.

There was another feature of Dutch rule that weakened the colony to hostile attack but had a favorable effect on the later growth of North America, and that was its disunity. The settlement had a tremendous diversity of religious and ethnic backgrounds resulting from the Dutch need to encourage lagging immigration with a policy of religious toleration. When New Netherlands became New York it held Dutch, Walloons, French, English, Portuguese, Swedes, and Finns. Religious diversity was equally great: besides the Calvinistic Dutch Reformed members there were Lutherans, Congregationalists, Mennonites, Quakers, Catholics. This conduct of affairs was continued by the new English governor, who insured the inhabitants of all ethnic groups not only possession of their property but also freedom of conscience. Such a policy may seem natural in the twentieth century, but not in the seventeenth. Spain held to the policy for her colonies that had been advocated as early as 1492 by Columbus writing to his sovereigns: "And I say that Your Highnesses ought not to consent that any foreigner do business or set foot here, except Christian Catholics, since this was the end and the beginning of the enterprise, that it should be for the enhancement and glory of the Christian religion, nor should anyone who is not a good Christian come to these parts." Similar conformity to the Roman Catholic faith was required by the French in their settlements in New France.

Another legacy from New Netherlands neatly shows both the conservatism of immigrants and the illogic of history. It seems they invented the front porch on homes. The tale goes as follows. Many immigrants had come from areas of Flanders that had no wood, so houses were made of a clay-straw mix. The region had heavy rains and strong winds. To protect the walls from damage by the downpours, builders extended the roof by a pronounced overhang. In the New World, houses were not made of a soluble compound but of wood or brick. Now that the need was gone, it would seem "logical" to save material by omitting the overhang. Not so. Perhaps to provide shade during the hot summers, builders pushed the flying gutters out farther yet and put posts at the corners. Thus the front porch. By the nineteenth century, no Midwestern home was complete without one. This change in building methods and designs furnishes a fine study in how technical innovations take place.

Many outstanding innovations do not deal with tangible objects at all. Due in great measure to a series of initiatives undertaken by John Winthrop, the development of Massachusetts took a far different course from either Virginia or New Netherlands. Winthrop was born in the year of the Armada, 1588, son of a London cloth merchant who had transmuted himself into a Suffolk landowner by purchasing confiscated monastery acres from the crown. John Winthrop was one of the solid gentry, a lawyer who presided over court on his father's manor at the age of 21. He inherited the manor and also came by sizable dowries from two marriages. In the vivid words of a recent historian, "He was a countryman of simple tastes who liked good food, good drink, and good company. He liked his wife. He liked to stroll by the river with a fowling piece and have a go at the birds. He liked to smoke a pipe. He liked to tinker with gadgets. He liked all the things that God had given him, and he knew it was right to like them, because they were God-given. But how was one to keep from liking them too much?" Here was no strait-laced, dour-faced Puritan. But Winthrop was a Puritan, and he was a leader of men.

When a man so well established in his homeland decides to emigrate, his reasons must be compelling. Winthrop could see daily that England was on a path to perdition. The decay of the textile trade in surrounding Suffolk was paralleled by a decay of morals at court and throughout England; one of his sons had become a notorious rakehell and the queen of the realm was a Roman Catholic. A group of gentlemen combined in 1629 to secure a charter for the Massachusetts Bay Company. Then Winthrop and eleven others agreed to an unprecedented scheme: they would take the charter to the New World with them. Members of the Company would be residents in the colony. The governor of the Company would be governor of the colony. Winthrop was elected governor, a rank that he held every year except one until his death in 1649.

Although Winthrop was energized by his secondary callings (landlord, lawyer, magistrate), he never mistook them for his primary calling. He sought a New World because he sought salvation. Before he decided to leave England, he declared, "If the Lord seeth it will be good for us, he will provide a shelter and a hidinge place for us and ours." During the voyage to America on the *Arbella* he spelled matters out in his speech "A Modell of Christian Charity": "Now the only way to avoid this shipwracke, and to provide for our posterity, is to followe the counsel of Micah, to doe justly, to love mercy, to walke humbly with our God. For this end, wee must be knitt together in this work as one man. . . . For wee must Consider that wee shall be as a Citty upon a hill. The eyes of all people are uppon Us, soe that if wee shall deale falsely with our god in this worke wee have undertaken, and soe cause him to withdrawe his present help from us, wee shall be made a story and a by-word through the world. . . . Therefore lett us choose life, that wee and our seede may live by obeyeing his voice and cleaveing to him, for he is our life and our prosperity." The aim was to create and maintain a Sanctified Commonwealth.

In governing the settlement that they founded at Boston, Winthrop and his fellow magistrates did not have a free hand. They had to abide by the Company's charter, and one of its clauses required annual elections. They must also follow the prescriptions of the Bible. But how were they to know what the Scriptures prescribed? Here Catholic and Protestant answers diverged. The great thirteenth-century scholastic Saint Thomas Aquinas had distinguished four types of meaning in the Holy Writ: historical, moral, allegorical, and analogical. The leaders of the Reformation scoffed at the need for interpretation; in Martin Luther's words, "The literal sense of Scripture alone is the whole essence of faith and of Christian theology." John Calvin was even more scornful: "It is better to confess ignorance than to play with frivolous guesses."

The Puritans were not so naive as to cleave to this brand of fundamentalism. The Bible, they agreed, must be construed by men who have been specially educated for the purpose; the aim of providing an endless flow of learned ministers led them to found Harvard College in 1636, a mere six years after they landed at Boston. Of course even trained minds can disagree, but the orthodox Puritans had a response to that fact too. As one cleric explained: "*As for New England,* we never banished any for their consciences, but for sinning against conscience, after due means of conviction, or some other wickednesse which they had no conscience to plead for." In brief, after the Bible has been properly explained by the "clearsighted," only a willfully wicked man will then fail to recognize its "clear" meaning.* As it happened, the minister Roger Williams dissented. Much of his faith was pure Calvinism: original sin, predestination, irresistible grace from God. But he rejected some of the more limited doctrines of orthodox Puritanism. He denied that his generation had inherited from Abraham any covenant with God; the Substitutionary Atonement of Christ Jesus, he said, had annulled it. He denied that state power and civil punishments could be used to uphold all of the Ten Commandments; he said that the state had no power affecting the First Table with its religious laws (as distinct from the Second Table with its secular doctrines). He avowed that oaths could not properly be administered in courts of law, since only the regenerate could be expected to honor an oath once taken. Perhaps most trying of all, he questioned whether the Company's charter was up-

---

*In varied forms this belief crops up repeatedly in American history, even from our more libertarian thinkers. For example, what can we make of Thomas Jefferson's claim that man has an "innate moral sense"? (See the middle of Chapter 6 on Jefferson and Locke.) Or of Ralph Waldo Emerson's rhetoric that life in the woods can convert man into a "transparent eyeball"? (See the end of the Emerson discussion, end of Chapter 14.) These doctrines tend to disallow any disputes about moral issues among right-thinking men.

right on the grounds that the king could not grant away lands belonging to Indians.

John Winthrop and his cohorts knew how to deal with troublemakers: they banished Roger Williams from Massachusetts. Their reasons were three. Williams was violating the true faith in matters of religion. He was disrupting the peace of society. And he was self-righteous, even feisty, in his obstreperousness; rumor had it that he said to his wife, "Not one soul in this commonwealth is regenerate save me and thee, and at times I have my doubts about thee." On his behalf it must be said that he leaned farther toward religious toleration than any other leader of New England in his time, but it must also be said that his toleration had limits. He believed in freedom of worship, no more, no less. No citizen could plead his faith as a way of evading his civic duties. After Williams founded the province of Rhode Island and became its governor, he was deaf to Quakers who urged their pacifism as an exemption from militia days; he told them in effect to go home for their muskets and their marching shoes.

If Williams was strict with the Friends, the elders of Massachusetts were far more so. They forbade Quakers even visiting rights in the colony. Some who defied the rule were hanged. One was publicly flogged—117 lashes on his bare back with a tarred rope. As he lay dying, a minister remarked, "He endeavoured to beat the gospel ordinances black and blue, and it was but just to beat him black and blue."* From the viewpoint of the Boston magistrates, the Quakers had only one good trait: they were few. Even that virtue was denied to another faction, the swarming Antinomians, who also believed in an Inner Light; that is, they thought they could get immediate messages from God. (The essence of Antinomianism is put succinctly in a recording made by George Lewis and his Dixieland band: "You can talk to Jesus on the royal telephone.") Not only was the doctrine inflammatory, but the threat was multiplied because its chief prophet was a woman, Anne Hutchinson. Summoned before the magistrates and examined by John Winthrop, she admitted that, yes, God did talk to her at times. Heresy: orthodox Puritans knew that every ordinance that the Almighty ever issued to man or ever will issue to man is contained in the Bible. Morever, if individuals go around acting on private screeds from God, how can we maintain order in Boston? They banished Mrs. Hutchinson.

The centrifugal propulsions arising from religion went along with other disruptive forces in society. As soon as Boston was established, the tiny colony

---

*It must be said that, given the Puritan premises, (namely that disruptive dissent from the state's church was tantamount to conspiracy to overthrow the state itself), the minister's attitude was reasonable. It might also be asked if it is reasonable for us to talk about "human nature" from our perspective until we have tried to adopt a bitingly historical stance, seeking to get inside the mentality of a seventeenth-century zealot.

at Plymouth began breaking up. Free land meant men on the move. The emergence of a growing market for foodstuffs just across Massachusetts Bay prompted men to seek more acres for their corn and cattle. In the plaintive words of Governor William Bradford of Plymouth: "And no man now thought he could live except he had cattle and a great deal of ground to keep them, all striving to increase their stocks. By which means they were scattered all over the Bay quickly and the town in which they had lived compactly till now was left very thin and in a short time almost desolate. And if this had been all, it had been less, though too much; but the church must also be divided, and those that had lived so long together in Christian and comfortable fellowship must now part and suffer many divisions. . . . And this I fear will be the ruin of New England, at least of the churches of God there, and will provoke the Lord's displeasure against them."

Not that the ideal of the leaders had changed: far from it. One minister phrased it concisely: "a speaking *Aristocracy* in the face of a silent *Democracy*." But it said a lot that this particular clergyman, speaking bluntly in favor of a community that was both hierarchical and stable, was acting in a way that eroded it; he lived in Hartford, Connecticut, a colony founded by a splinter group from Massachusetts Bay. In that very citadel, the walls were oozing away. During the Civil Wars in England, so John Winthrop wrote in his journal (1645), the flow of immigrant servants went down. Wages went up. Things got sticky. One gentleman called in a hired hand to dismiss him, explaining that the next year's payroll could not be met without selling off cows. The servant suggested that he should be kept on and that the master should sell cows if necessary. But what will I do, asked the master, when all of my cows are gone? Said the servant, Come to work for me and make enough money to buy other cows. Governor Winthrop was not amused by such strivings: beside this entry he wrote a word in the margin of his diary: "insolent."

Or chuckle over the cavortings of William Hubbard. He was part of the in-group: went to Harvard; studied medicine. He became—and he was not unique in combining doctoring with preaching—pastor to the Congregationalists of Ipswich. Listen to him: "That God who assumes to him self the title of being the God of Glory, is the God of peace, or Order and not of confusion. . . . He is so in his Palace of the world, as well as in his temple of his Church: in both may be observed a sweet subordination of persons and things, each unto other. . . ." And again: "It is not then the result of time or chance, that some are mounted on horseback, while others are left to travell on foot. That some have with the Centurion power to command, while others are required to obey, *the poor and the rich meet together, the Lord is the maker of them both,* The Almighty hath appointed her that sits behind the mill, as well as him that ruleth on the throne." So what happened? When his first wife died, William Hubbard, having already lived beyond his allotted span of three score and ten, despite his organic theory of the community, flabbergasted the community by taking in wedlock—his housekeeper. The American climate just did not beam down on hierarchies; it clouded up and rained all over them. But erosion is slow. The time-honored society of stratification lasted through the eighteenth century and well into the nineteenth and in some respects still exists in the twentieth.

The governing class did not retreat with grace. Wherever we look, at economics or politics or religion, they defended the parapets. Since not one—not one—prominent merchant immigrated to America, businessmen in the New World had to start from scratch. Or almost from scratch: their method was to use family connections. A brother went to London to make deals with government officials, a cousin went to Madeira to buy wine, and so on. Because it did not have a staple product for export, Massachusetts was in a more difficult spot than either Virginia with its tobacco or New York with its fur trade. New England never did develop a specialized commodity that could be sold abroad in unlimited quantities at a profitable price. We slide into supposing that the chief resource of the early colonies was farming land, but this notion is probably false if applied to the area eastward from the Connecticut River. What mattered most was wood (probably fish also brought more foreign revenues into New England than did agricultural produce)—not just timber to build ships and their gear, but also ashes to make soap or candles. Making what they could of these products, New England merchant families rose to power in the colonial carrying trade. And the job of being a merchant-shipowner has always been, by the standard of any given time, a large-scale industry dominated by those with capital. A few families ran the show.

And so it went in politics: the old guard was a stubborn rear guard. In the early years nobody could vote unless he was a member of a Congregationalist parish. The suffrage seems to have covered only one of five adult males. But this changed quickly; when John Winthrop died, most men in the Commonwealth could qualify to help choose his successor. Winthrop's best barricade against the rabble—and a sly one it was—proved to be another derivative from England: an American version of the common law. In technical language, he resisted all efforts at codification. In yet other words, he sought to keep discretion in the hands of magistrates, like himself, who would interpret and enforce the rules. When a Roger Williams or a Mrs. Hutchinson came along, he wanted to be free from shackles except for the Bible and the Company's charter.

But as to those shackles, he was adamantine. Winthrop, great man that he was, was a dogmatist. That is, he believed in dogma so long as it was his very own, to be perceived step by step, case by case, as he went along. Having said so much, we might go on to brush away some misconceptions. The Puritans have lately been lauded because they were pragmatic, "practical-minded." So they were, up to a point. Let us look at Bradford, Winthrop's fellow governor in what is now Massachusetts. His *Of Plymouth Plantation* tells about a crime committed by a lad of 16 or 17: "He was this year detected of buggery, and indicted for the same, with a mare, a cow, two goats, five sheep, two calves and a turkey." (What, no snakes?) So find the right verdict: "A very sad spectacle it was. For first the mare and then the cow and the rest of the lesser cattle were killed before his face, according to the law, Leviticus xx.15; and then he himself was executed. The cattle were all cast into a great and large pit that was digged of purpose for them, and no use made of any part of them." Practical-minded? In the year 1642 when a cow fetched a handsome price?

A few historians writing in our day have also argued that some Puritans had leanings toward egalitarianism; Roger Williams has been tagged "the irrepressible democrat." He was not that. Neither was anybody else in 1650. Surely Governor Winthrop left no room for doubt as to where he stood. Common folk might have, unfortunately, the legal right to vote magistrates into or out of office, but they certainly had no authority to tell an elected executive how to do his job (see Document 2–2).

As with civil states, so with ecclesia. No useful analogy can be made between the governance of a Puritan church and sovereignty in a modern republic. The members of a congregation did have the option of picking their minister, but they could not tell him what to do; his duties had been defined once and for all by Scripture. Anybody supping at the Eucharist had the "right and power" of admitting to or expelling from Communion, but the "administration" of that sanction was with the elders. According to the foremost minister in Boston at mid-century; "The Gospel alloweth no Church authority (or rule properly so called) to the Brethren, but reserveth that wholly to the Elders; and yet preventeth the tyrannie and oligarchy, and exorbitancy of the Elders, by the large and firm establishment of the liberties of the Brethren." No self-government there, not as the phrase would be understood in the twentieth century.

The Congregationalists could hold their flock only by warping the staff of their righteous origins. Enemies were all about: the cursed Antinomians with their skirted prophet, the bloody Arminians yapping about freedom of the will (where did Divine Grace go?). By 1648 the elders thought that the situation was urgent. Over the years their assemblages and their edicts had failed to destroy heresy, so now they called a synod of all the parishes. The convention got off to a glorious start; at its first session a snake crawled into the meeting house whereupon a man stomped on its head and killed it. Obviously a special providence: Satan had been crushed. In less than a fortnight the synod drew up the Cambridge Platform with its catalogue of eighty-two "errors," no less, all of which violated Scripture. By convoking this synod the Congregationalists went far toward scrapping one of their foundation beams; no longer was it true that each parish was sole lord and judge in its own domain. A synod could frown at a congregation that failed to acknowledge "that which is *evidently expressed, or infallibly collected* out of the Word." It

45

could even spin the erring away spiritually into the wilderness. And when the woods were so near and so ominous, that threat cut deep.* But after all, what did men deserve who were guilty of "the Gangrene of Heresie" or "the Leprosie of sin"?

If the device of synods or "consociations" was a major revision in the design of Puritanism, the Half-Way Covenant almost broke the ridge-pole. The problem related to the third generation of New Englanders: who should be baptized? The original members of Massachusetts churches had all testified satisfactorily to their conversion experiences; otherwise they could not enter into the Fellowship at all. Since they were full members of the church, their children were baptized. But some of those children had no conversion experience. What of their children? Should they, grandchildren of the original parishioners, be baptized? Would you want your progeny scratched off as eternally damned? So the grandchildren were sworn in. At this time, 1662, the dikes of Congregationalism were drenched with latitudinarianism; if the true faith had meant anything it had stood for the transcendence of that moment when the immanence of God was March sunshine reflected from snow, beautiful and vivid in its glare.

The Puritans should not be taken as a covey of innocents. They knew what they were doing. Their shibboleth was said clearly: "There is another combination of vertues in every lively holy Christian, And that is, Diligence in worldly businesses, and yet deadnesse to the world; such a mystery as none can read, but they that know it." They knew about double-dealing: "Hypocrites in outward profession and appearance, go for faithful and godly." They knew that the danger of deception was enhanced "in these places and times, where Church-fellowship is an honour, and drawes after it sundry out-ward and worldly advantages." Their greatest preacher, Thomas Hooker (who could not bear to be number two minister in Boston and so went with the group that founded Hartford), was deft in distinguishing those sheep who would be received on the Day of Judgment from those who conned their way into a congregation: *"These we call visible Saints* (leaving *secret things to God*)." They knew about self-deception, pointing out that we tend to park all our mishaps on God's doorstep (Divine Providence, "bad luck") while crediting ourselves with our triumphs. But despite the elders' vigilance, disintegration of the faith was steady. The ministers began to wail, in a splurge of sermons that have been labelled "jeremiads." They ventured into a variety of lamentation that might have come from a modern existentialist, from Kierkegaard or Sartre or Camus: "Doth not a careless, remiss, flat, dry, cold, dead frame of spirit grow in upon us secretly, strangely, prodigiously." But all

---

*Forests were at your stoop. Any reader who wants to risk their darks might go to Nathaniel Hawthorne's *The Scarlet Letter*. Or brood about the death of Governor Bradford's wife. Apparently she, after staring for six weeks at a view so menacing in contrast to her plowed and cultured England, killed herself. (Robert Frost recorded the progress of such a wilderness depression in his poem, "The Hill-Wife.")

the wind shook no corn. Backsliders went their carefree ways, until finally some of them made their degeneration official and public. At the end of the century, November of 1699, the new Brattle Street Church issued a manifesto. Applicants would no longer be required to give open testimony of their conversions; mere "visible Sanctity" was the only ticket needed. Baptism would not be refused "to *any* child." That was really leaving secret things to God. The Sanctified Commonwealth had perished.

What killed it? Well, there was the vacant land. And the ruling class in England. And Indians. Adding the three, we can begin to understand what happened. On the greed and the mobility that were afforded by the frontier, all thoughtful men could see what was going on; "I fear that the common trinity of the World—Profit, Preferment, Pleasure—will be here the tria omnia, as in all the world besides:" wrote Roger Williams to John Winthrop Jr., "that Prelacy and Popery too will in this wilderness predominate; and that God Land will be as great a God with us English as God Gold was with the Spaniard." The concept of a town as a densely populated organic structure was eroded by the wilderness; the idea of a community became the notion of a promotion; town planters became town boomers; in many towns, as public land was sold away to private speculators, the village common shrank until a lusty boy aided by a gale could spit across it.

The efflux of population might have obliterated urbanity if it had not been checked by Indians. The prejudice of whites against reds was not so severe as the prejudice of whites against blacks, but it existed. And vice versa. Indians left few if any written records, so we must look at matters mainly through English sources. What they show is, in the jargon of anthropology, extreme culture conflict. Consider three instances: What could any respectable English lady think of Pocahontas, stripped to the altogether, turning cart-wheels in the market place of Jamestown? Or, again, when whites in Virginia built a house for the local chieftain, they felt he wasted hours on end while standing in the street locking and unlocking his door. Such strange tendencies, which were an affront to Englishmen who worshipped the Gospel of Work, could even be expressed verbally: In 1643 a handful of sachems drifted into the General Court of Massachusetts to profess their allegiance:

Member of the General Court: Will you worship the only true God?

Indians: We do desire to reverence the God of the English, . . . because we see he doth better to the English than other gods do to others.

Member: You are not to swear falsely.

Indians: We do not know what swearing is.

Member: You are not to do unnecessary work on the Sabbath.

Indians: That will be easy; we haven't much to do any day, and can well take our ease on the Sabbath.

Vital to Indian-white relations through the earliest years of a colony was the balance of power, which was likely to be close, precarious, and easily tipped. When the tribes of Maryland were said to be harvesting their corn and abandoning their villages, men ran for cover. Virginia for a while forbade any sale of firearms to Indians, but merchants in other colonies moved into the market so that Virginians got neither safety nor profits; the act was repealed in 1659. Several white colonies made efforts at decency and accommodation, but none could be sustained. Obstacles, most of them self-created, were too great. In Massachusetts, for instance, the elders chattered about the need to save Indian souls. But whites wanted to farm on lands where Indians wanted to hunt. Further, the ecclesiology of the Puritan church taught that virtually the only obligations of a minister were to his own congregation, so missionary efforts were laggard. Conversions were rare; wars were frequent. New England had its Pequot War in 1637, King Philip's War in 1675. In Virginia a third of the whites were killed in 1622; another outbreak in 1644 wiped out 300 more. The governor of New Netherlands launched an onslaught against the Indians in 1643 that kept the colony in a commotion for three years. Twenty years later some warriors decimated the village of Esopus on the Hudson. Only at the end of the century could settlers go north or west of Albany with a feeling of safety.

While Indians might harm a man's body, they seldom tarnished his soul. But from England an American could get both outer and inner hurt. Massachusetts had repeated ructions about its charter—discord of importance in two respects. For one, a community might have trouble believing that it had a covenant with the Almighty if a mere king could void its birthright. For another, the magistrates made noises like the American Revolution a century and more in advance. As early as 1646–1647 they were defying England on the score that their charter gave the colony "absolute power of government." Prudence suggested that insubordination should be reserved for the thickets and the hills; one reason that Winthrop did not want to codify the laws of Massachusetts was that he preferred not to put in writing their deviations from the English statutes. But many Puritan officials were not prudent men. The General Court blurted that "our allegiance binds us not to the laws of England any longer than while we live in England, for the laws of the parliament of England reach no further, nor do the king's writs under the great seal go any further." The colony's agent in London declared, "If the Parliaments of *England* should impose Lawes upon us having no Burgesses in their house of Commons, nor capable of a summons by reason of the vast distance of the Ocean being three thousand miles from *London,* then wee·should lose the libertie and freedom I conceived of *English* indeed." When reports struck Boston that the English were planning to send a force to carry the Company's charter back across the Atlantic, the magistrates discussed girding for battle.

They got their come-uppance. By 1665 a royal commission was urging that the authority of the Duke of York should cover New England as well as

New York. While neighboring colonies gained rights—royal charters to Connecticut in 1662 and to Rhode Island in 1663 gave them even the power to elect their own governors and made them almost autonomous—Massachusetts was forced back. It did escape being brought under the new Act of Uniformity in 1662, which applied only within the realm, not overseas. But it lost the five hamlets constituting Maine; Charles II granted them to the Duke of York in 1664. Twenty years later it was subjected to the woeful indignity of having its charter revoked. After James II took the throne he tried to fuse all of New England with New York and New Jersey under a single governor as the Dominion of New England. The Glorious Revolution gave the Puritans a chance to gain a little solace by toppling the governor. But the comfort was slight: a new charter for Massachusetts in 1691 provided that the monarch would appoint the governor and even leaned dangerously toward religious toleration. The Holy Community had become a royal colony.

In Virginia the county magnates had long been flinching under the actions of royal appointees. William Berkeley had come over in 1642, younger son of an English family that had invested in the Virginia Company. As governor, he made his office and his plantation at Green Springs into headquarters for recent immigrants. He gave them civic jobs with good salaries. He granted them large tracts of land. Such villainies were resented by the old settlers (not a term to be taken precisely: they were men who had been around for a decade or two). In 1675 two of the gentry, Nathaniel Bacon and William Byrd, tried to get from the governor a monopoly of the Indian trade in Virginia. While he seemed sympathetic at first, he had his own interests in that area and ultimately refused. The next year a rebellion broke out—led by Bacon and his friends but powered by land-hungry frontiersmen at odds with local Indians. Inchoate and inconsistent resolves adopted by "Bacon's Assembly" show two distinct and even hostile factions represented in it: Bacon and his colleagues rebelling against the governor and his Green Springs crowd; and the meaner frontier planters who wanted special concessions and restrictions against gentry such as Bacon and his friends. Both bevies gained something from the royal governor: a residence requirement for public office was a concession to the old gentry: their poorer brethren got more generous provisions about voting. But the rebellion as such was crushed, Bacon died discredited, and royal authority was strongly reasserted. By the beginning of the next century the Burgesses could still agree that public affairs should be managed by "men of Note & Estates." Deference to the established order was far from dead.

In 1700, British America stood thus. For the first time, Englishmen had founded permanent settlements: New Hampshire, Massachusetts, Rhode Island, Connecticut, New Jersey, Pennsylvania, Delaware, Maryland, Virginia, the Carolinas. Colonizing efforts by Sweden and the Netherlands had been conquered by the English. The other two competitors for North America were France (in New France that became part of Canada) and Spain (in Mexico and the Floridas). The English colonies had become mainly agricultural, but with large differences among them. The Chesapeake colonies, having developed tobacco as a staple, were exporting large quantities to the British Isles. From the Carolinas and the Middle Colonies, the chief export was furs and skins. In those areas as in New England, most of the inhabitants were subsistence farmers, largely by necessity. In their commercial intercourse with Europe and the Caribbean, New Englanders had the most success with products of their extensive forests and with fish. Politically the colonies had evolved varying forms of self-government, shaped considerably by the vestiges, imported from England, of a hierarchical society. But the provincials had engaged in several confrontations when they felt that home-based Englishmen were trying to encroach on their privileges, and they had shown that they would carry resistance to the point of violence.

Religion was a consistent galvanic force as a stimulus for emigrating to America. Men wanted to found a new order where society as well as religion would be "purified." Original views on the relation of church to state were not terribly different in the two strongest colonies in the seventeenth century, Virginia and Massachusetts Bay. The aim of purifying society did not mean that men in either region were willing to abandon the hierarchical structures that they had known in England. Far from it. They sought to transplant their traditional mores into new and healthier soil, saving the practices of a deferential society. These goals were shared by the governing classes of all provinces until 1700 and far beyond.

But intentions cannot be equated with realities. Conventional modes were eroded badly in the New World. The worst erosive agent was unoccupied land that often could be claimed by simply moving onto it. Why endure exploitation and abuse by another man when you can strike out into the wilderness and set up for yourself? A second democratizing agent was the steady growth of representative government. Whether called the General Court in Massachusetts Bay, the House of Burgesses in Virginia, or the Assembly of Pennsylvania, province after province won some kind of elective legislature. These bodies, although far from perfectly democratic, struggled with royal governors and appointive governor's councils. A third influence was religious. Clerics and elders might use cruel punishments in their effort to preserve orthodoxy. But the demands of mundane life crept stealthily in upon them. Men would be rich if not happy, and the area of secular claims expanded. Chapters 3 and 4 will study how these trends were pushed yet further in the following seventy-five years.

SOME NOTABLE EVENTS

1609 Church of England established by law in Virginia; it never had a bishop.

1612 John Rolfe becomes first white man in Virginia to plant tobacco.

1614 First export of tobacco from Virginia to England.

1619 Virginia House of Burgesses convenes. Was it a "legislature"?
First blacks landed in Virginia.

1620 Pilgrims land at Plymouth.

1622 First great war against Indians in Virginia.

1624 Dutch plant New Netherlands.
Virginia becomes a royal colony.

1631 Law adopted in Massachusetts that only Congregationalist church members can vote.

1633 Foundation of Boston Latin, first grammar school in America.

1634 Freemen of each town in Massachusetts granted right to send representatives to General Court.
Plantation of Maryland founded by George Calvert, Lord Baltimore.

1635 Thomas Hooker leaves Boston area to found Connecticut (at Hartford).

1636 Roger Williams founds Rhode Island (at Providence).
Foundation of Harvard, first college in America.
Antinomian crisis leads to expulsion of Anne Hutchinson.

1637 Pequot War.
Foundation of New Haven; merged with Connecticut in 1643.

1638 First printing press in the colonies installed at Cambridge, Massachusetts.

1639 "Fundamental Orders of Connecticut," first constitution in the colonies.
Bay Psalm Book published in Cambridge.

1641 First codification of the laws of Massachusetts.

1642 John Winthrop, Jr. takes lead in forming iron-works at Saugus, Mass.

1642, 1647 Massachusetts Bay enacts compulsory school laws.

1643 New England Confederation formed for joint defense.

1644 Roger Williams, *The Bloudy Tenent of Persecution.*

1646 General Court in Massachusetts is petitioned for formation of a Presbyterian Church.

1647 John Cotton's answer to Williams: *The Bloudy Tenent Washed in the Bloud of the Lamb.*

1649 John Winthrop dies.

1651 Congregational synods get some formal jurisdiction over parishes.

1659– 1661 Four Quakers hanged on Boston Common for entering the colony.

1662 The Half-Way Covenant.

1663 The Carolinas granted by charter to eight proprietors.

1664 The Jerseys granted to John Lord Berkeley and Sir George Carteret.

1676 Bacon's Rebellion in Virginia.
King Philip's War in New England.

51

Ways to Study History II

Read widely and become wise. Edmund S. Morgan is surely one of the half dozen most accomplished historians to have studied the British colonies in the seventeenth and eighteenth centuries. Some of his achievements have come from an utterly comprehensive search for primary sources; his *Prologue to Revolution* (1959) reprints every resolution of every colonial assembly about the Stamp Act of 1765 and adds thereto a considerable sampling from newspapers. Morgan and his wife Helen M. Morgan worked the subject into a splendid narrative in *The Stamp Act Crisis* (1953). But it must be admitted that these volumes are on traditional subjects and that Morgan worked on them in a fairly conventional way. His distinction came from being more industrious than most of us—and from writing better than most of us.

But Morgan is a nonesuch, it seems to me, in his gift for asking questions that nobody had asked before. We simply do not allow the obvious to cross our minds. For his *The Puritan Family* (1944), Morgan did not have any mass of untouched documents dating from the seventeenth century. Quite the contrary, most of his information came from the neatly printed *Publications of the Massachusetts Historical Society.* Anybody could have gotten the data. But Morgan knew how to use it. He found for instance that many Puritan parents who clearly did not need additional income nevertheless apprenticed their children into other homes. This normally happened when the child was 12 or 13. "In explanation I suggest that Puritan parents did not trust themselves with their own children, that they were afraid of spoiling them by too great affection. . . . The child left home just as the time when parental discipline causes increasing friction, just at the time when a child begins to assert his independence. By allowing a strange master to take over the disciplinary function, the parent could meet the child upon a plane of affection and friendliness." The Puritans were not fools.

Document 2-1

The best way to feel the rhetoric of this sermon
by Thomas Hooker is to read it aloud, like a
Stentor. It was titled, "A True Sight of Sin."

There is great ods betwixt the knowledge of a Traveller, that in his own person hath taken a view of many Coasts, past through many Countries, and hath there taken up his abode some time, and by Experience hath been an Eye-witness of the extream cold, and scorching heats . . .; and another that sits by his fire side, and happily reads the story of these in a Book, or views the proportion of these in a Map. . . . The like difference is there in the right discerning of sin; the one hath surveyed the compass of his whol course, searched the frame of his own heart, and examined the windings and turnings of his own waies, he hath seen what sin is, and what it hath done, how it hath made havock of his peace and comfort, ruinated and laid wast the very Principles of Reason and Nature, and Morality, and made him a terror to himself, when he hath looked over the loathsom abominations that lie in his bosom . . .; Another happily hears the like preached or repeated, reads them writ or recorded in some Authors, and is able to remember and relate them. The ods is marvelous great. The one sees the History of sin, the other the Nature of it; the one knows the relation of sin as it is mapped out, and recorded; the other the poyson, as by experience he hath found and proved it. It's one thing to see a disease in the Book, or in a mans body, another to find and feel it in a mans self. There is the report of it, here the malignity and venom of it. . . .

Document 2-2

Governor John Winthrop was put on trial in 1645
for allegedly exceeding his rightful authority.
Acquitted, he lectured his fellow citizens.

I entreat you to consider that when you choose magistrates you take them from among yourselves—men subject to like passions as you are. Therefore when you see infirmities in us, you should reflect upon your own, and would make you bear the more with us and not be severe censurers of the failings of your magistrates, when you have continual experiences of the like infirmities in yourselves and others. We count him a good servant who breaks not his covenant. The covenant between you and us is the oath you have taken of us, which is to this purpose: that we shall govern you and judge your causes by the rules of God's law and our own, according to our best skill.

When you agree with a workman to build you a ship or house, etc., he undertakes as well for his skill as for his faithfulness, for it is his profession and you pay him for it. But when you call one to be a magistrate, he doth not profess nor undertake to have sufficient skill for that office, nor can you furnish him with gifts, etc. Therefore you must run the hazard of his skill and ability. But if he fail in faithfulness, which by his oath he is bound unto, that he must answer for. If it fall out that the case be clear to common apprension, and the rule clear also, if he transgress here, the error is not in the skill, but in the evil of the will: it must be required of him. But if the case be doubtful, or the rule doubtful, to men of such understanding and parts as your magistrates are, if your magistrates should err here, yourselves must bear it.

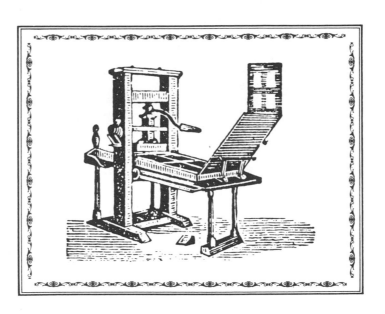

Patterns of Trade,
Patterns of Thought

Economic growth, speaking broadly, seems to result from two general processes. One is government policies that promote specific firms or industries or regions. Thus in Canada the actions of the Federal establishment at Ottawa and of the various provinces have in the last century hugely influenced the fortunes of business. Those actions have shaped both the tempo of the economy and also the sectors that would be given the bulk of the resources available. Similarly American history will furnish countless instances of the powers of government in directing, stimulating, and sometimes stifling the economy.

But the United States, from its origins until the latter nineteenth century, gives the best example known of the second mechanism of growth, the classical economic "free market" as described by Adam Smith (*The Wealth of Nations,* 1776). On the basis of a couple of historical facts, material progress in British North America developed as a spontaneous reflex of the total society.

One prerequisite was the type of Englishman who immigrated: ambitious, wanting to get ahead, wanting to pile up wealth, and carrying the technical know-how to use a wide range of the resources available in America. Under these conditions, Adam Smith's "invisible hand" had scope to operate, and competition among individuals trying to make it big really did result in a growing stock of goods and services for everybody. Further, it divvied up the products fairly equitably. Men were not equal, but they were more nearly so than in other countries. In consequence there was a rather large market for many more or less standardized goods. To cite Adam Smith again, the division of labor is dependent on the size of the market. In France, where concentrated riches and an exquisite taste provided a few customers for wares fine and unique, a craftsman might make hand-tooled silverware or lace tablecloths. One of a kind. In the New World he might make clodhopper shoes for use by slaves. All alike. Since he was turning out a uniform product, he could let machines do much of the job for him. (The interpretation here of a mass-production economy applies with increasing force to the centuries after 1700, but its germs can be detected even earlier.) Moreover, many laborers did not need any high grade of skill; machines furnished that. Dextrous and gifted men did not turn out products for quick consumption; they built tools and machines that would make consumer goods. Then they lowered their prices, and the market got bigger. And so on. Generation by generation this self-reinforcing process went on—to the marvel of European visitors. "Would any but an American have ever invented a milking machine?" asked an Englishman at the middle of the nineteenth century, "or a machine to beat eggs? or machines to black boots, scour knives, pare apples, and do a hundred other things that all other peoples have done with their ten fingers from time immemorial." This complex of processes came to be known as mass production.

These forces had an almost imperceptible impress on most Americans in the years around 1700. Of every ten men, nine were tilling the land. They were for the most part subsistence farmers, growing their own food, raising plants and spinning thread and hunting for skins to make clothing, erecting their own houses and sheds. Many might have wanted to be commercial farmers, but conditions did not allow it. Productivity was rising, but it remained so low that the use of child labor was ubiquitous because the man was rare who could produce a surplus beyond what was needed to sustain himself alone. The typical farmer sought out a few crops that he could cultivate in his climate, and thereafter he tended to do the same things in the same ways. This was even true of most tobacco planters. By about 1760 nearly all of them in Tidewater Virginia and Maryland were losing money. A few planters prospered by shifting to other crops such as wheat—or by selling off surplus slaves to meet the insatiable demands for fresh labor on the rice plantations of the Carolinas.

In this economy that seems so static in its products and methods, there were some innovators. They were merchants. Excluding shopkeepers and defining a merchant as somebody primarily engaged in overseas trade, there were a few dozen merchants in each of the coastal cities. In these terms, even at the end of the eighteenth century only about 150 persons in Boston would qualify as merchants. The numbers for Philadelphia and New York might be higher, but not by much. In the other busiest ports, Baltimore and Charleston, the numbers would be lower. Moreover, in days of peace these merchants did business by bits and drabs (in wartime, commerce could burgeon dramatically). Trade did not flow, it trickled. Look at Thomas Hancock, who was at mid-century one of the wealthiest men in America. Thomas made the fortune that his nephew and heir John Hancock would squander by poor judgment, casks of fine madeira, and revolution. In normal times, leaving aside for the moment the windfall gains of dealing in military victualling, Thomas Hancock thought it a good month if his gross sales totted to $4,000. But here, as we often must, we revert to the question of scale. What was the significance at the time of facts that we are pondering today?

Confronted with such a picayune business, the colonial merchant perforce dealt in a variety of goods. But the core of his task was clear. The American of the eighteenth century, like his descendants in the twentieth, was bound and determined to live beyond his means. He wanted to procure from foreigners more than foreigners wanted to buy from him. The merchant had to narrow the gap and to bridge what gap remained. He could develop or seek out any-old-where a commodity that could be vended at a profitable price in Europe. Or he could provide a service, such as oceanic shipping (the carrying trade), that foreigners would buy and pay for in their own moneys. Or he could borrow abroad. There was no fourth way to meet the needs of our spendthrift ancestors. The problem, bluntly, was to find exports or to get credit. In trying to cope with this question, traders arrived at a derivative set of queries. One recent historian (Bernard Bailyn) has summed up thus: "These were the fundamental interests of the New England merchants at the end of the seventeenth century: to maintain connections with highly placed individuals in England; to dominate the colonial councils; to control the English functionaries in the colonial service; and to find a solution of the money problem which had been created by the enforcement of the navigation laws and the imbalance of trade." Even so. And each of these aspects must be extended below. But beneath them all were the harrowing anxieties of spending less for imports and getting more for exports.

As to exports, the tobacco colonies came early to concentrate on "the dirty weed." But their geography betrayed them. Virginia especially was rife with navigable rivers, so that each planter could trade with shipowning merchants right at his own dock. No towns developed very much, and Virginians continued to buy from foreigners (whether in London or in New York, still foreigners) many of the goods and services that only a town could

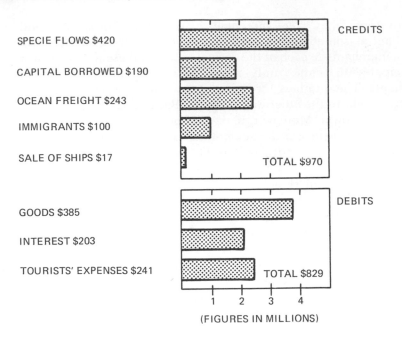

FIGURE 3-1. *An International Balance of Payments (1850–1860)*

Source: Adapted from G. R. Taylor, The Transportation Revolution (1951), p. 205.

An international balance-of-payments accounting can be a useful way to check indicators of the flow of economic activity, in various categories, between one region and the rest of the world. (One of the categories for international payment is of course created by trade, and a balance of trade for the colonial period is analyzed by region in Figure 5-4.) A balance of payments is run like any balance accounting, and even when there is a surplus or deficit in some category (signifying a problem somewhere, in an unbalanced flow of activity), this is recorded so that the debit and credit columns balance as equal. Thus the final count of payments flowing out of the region in exchange for goods from abroad, including goods and services bought by tourists, along with interests paid to foreigners, would be under the debit column above; the money coming in, either borrowed or paid in for purchases of goods and services, is under credits. Since the accounting above for America in the 1850's does not strictly balance, we should suspect it is not completely accurate somewhere— possibly in a missing or unreported category, or more likely in a misvaluation or distorted reporting in one of the listed categories. For example, what would happen to the above balance account if reports of import goods under debits had been undervalued by 10 per cent?

Our view of the economic activity indicated through this kind of account is greatly affected by how the various activities are classified and categorized. For the period after World War II the following six categories could be most useful: (1) goods (2) services (called "intangible trade") (3) military expenditures (4) long-term capital movements (investments in stocks and bonds) (5) short-term capital flows (changes in demand deposits) (6) specie movements (gold and silver). But for economic activity in the period prior to the Civil War (see Chapters 13 and 15) a different set of pigeonholes seems desirable, as shown in this graph. Even so, there are classification problems: Are tourist expenses and interest payments the most useful debit categories? For this or an earlier period, where should we classify expenditures for the import of slaves?

furnish. Virginia had also been laid out badly in that all of its rivers flowed into Chesapeake Bay. By simply patrolling the mouth of the bay, the English found it rather easy to enforce the Navigation Acts, much easier than in New England with its numerous inlets and beaches that made smuggling a cinch.

The purpose of the Navigation Acts was to procure to England—and to certain private interests within England—the maximum benefit from overseas possessions. Some rules for trade with North America had been laid down in Cromwell's time, but the chief laws were enacted right after the Restoration, in 1660 and 1663. It was provided that "noe Sugars Tobaccho Cotton Wool Indigoes Ginger Fustick or other dying wood" from the colonies could be shipped anywhere except to England or her other colonies. This was the so-called Staple Act, and it meant that even tobacco destined for the Continent had to pass through England, be taxed by the crown, and be further levied upon by English merchants. Whereas Virginia and Maryland seem to have suffered from the dabbling in colonial economies of the English government, other provinces benefited. The first staple to be exported from South Carolina was rice, regarding which England had no regulations. And finally, of course, there was the slave trade. Here is Henry Laurens, leading planter and merchant in Charleston, writing to a correspondent in Bristol, England: "I can venture to assure you there is a pretty good prospect for Sales of Negroes in that Colony as Rice promises to be a good Commodity the Quantity heretofore exported being lessen'd by the Planters attention to Indigo & from the success of the first attempt in that article we expect it will for the future make a very considerable addition in our remittances to Great Britain." Ah, exports. (See Figure 5-4.)

In the Middle Colonies, New York and Pennsylvania, a major resource until well on in the eighteenth century continued to be furs, mainly acquired from Indians. Still leaving aside the matter of provisioning English troops (see early Chapter 5), another crucial way by which these colonies earned foreign assets was by offering services: providing bottoms to haul goods owned by Englishmen or Europeans, being factors (middlemen, merchants) dealing with Southern planters. Some clauses of the Navigation Acts harmed them; for instance, they could not export their meats or cereals to England. But their chief surpluses—fish and meat and cereals and livestock and lumber—could legally be sent to foreign markets directly, that is, without going through a trade center in England. Further, American shipbuilders and shippers had the same rights in the entire British Empire as did their counterparts in the home country. They could keep ownership of an American-built vessel or they could sell it away to a London merchant; either way it could trade anywhere under the Union Jack. Taking one thing with another, the Middle Colonies did all right. On the eve of the Revolution, Philadelphia with its 50,000 inhabitants was the second largest city in the Empire, and Manhattan did not lag by much (see early Chapter 4 on the economics of trade).

Compared to the other colonies, the resources of New England were dwarfish; a wag would later remark that its only products that could be sold abroad were rocks and ice. "'Tis the Unhappiness of this Country indeed," commented a writer at mid-century, "to have no Staple-Commodity to send to England in lieu of the Merchandise they receive from thence, but what may be had cheaper from some part of Europe or other." So they scrounged. (John Brown, Congressman and lofty merchant of Providence, took part in the slave trade and did not care a whit who knew it.) Ignoring the Molasses Act of 1733 that laid a tax of sixpence a gallon on imports from alien colonies, they bought their molasses in the French West Indies as well as the British and did not bother to pay the duty. Back in Rhode Island they distilled the molasses into rum. This they might cart off to Africa to trade for blacks intended for the markets of the Caribbean and the Carolinas. Or they might carry rum to Newfoundland and swap it for codfish which could be sold in the Catholic countries of the Mediterranean (The golden cod on the dome of the Statehouse in Boston symbolizes many a fortune).

Of all the trades worked by the ships of New England, the busiest led to the West Indies. Business was done in piddling amounts. In the absence of large urban markets, the ship captain traded with an individual planter at his own wharf. Even a modest quantity of new goods could bring on a glut and disastrous prices. So the ships used were tiny, and each one carried a great variety in its hold. When the Brown brothers of Providence sent the sloop *Mary Ann* off for Surinam in 1776 to deal for molasses, she was carrying among other items

100 hogsheads tobacco
122 boxes of spermaceti candles
1,975 staves for barrels
433 hoops for barrels
4,000 bricks
8 horses
3,500 bunches of onions
62 shook hogsheads
$9\frac{2}{3}$ barrels of beef
$5\frac{2}{3}$ barrels of pork
50 kegs of oysters
12 barrels of flour
25 barrels of tar
8 barrels of oil

Surinam had a special spot in the New Englander's scheme. English law allowed Americans to buy only a few types of manufactured wares in the Continent. But they were permitted to carry provisions to the colonies of other European nations. Surinam became notorious for smuggling. By the 1730's Thomas Hancock was placing orders with Boston distillers for more than 5,000 gallons of rum at a time. He dispatched it to the tropics, and the return voyage would illicitly yield up its taffeta and velvet and French linen and raisins and gloves. Hancock knew what he was up to; he habitually saw situations in terms of maximizing his return. Starting out as a bookdealer, he wrote to a London publisher, "I can Improve my Money in other Goods from Great Britton to much better advantage. . . ." And again, "I can lay my Money out in any Goods to better Advantage than in books."

These merchants worked up several devices that foreshadowed the future. Take the problem of marine insurance. The colonies held no underwriters, and English firms asked prohibitive premiums to insure bottoms that they could not inspect. How to avoid the risk of your entire fortune going down in one storm? You bought not a ship but part of a ship. Robert Livingston of New York owned a quarter of the brigantine *Robert* after it was launched in 1694. A shipowner in Salem held shares in vessels, from as little as a sixteenth to as much as seven-eights. For some years Thomas Hancock bought only an eighth to a half of a ship. Often outright title was not involved: a group of merchants would join *ad hoc* to insure a bottom owned by one of their number.

Just as New Englanders had to improvise in respect to insurance, so did they make unusual arrangements in the payment of wages. Seamen often were compensated not in cash but by "privileges." A sailor shipping out to the West Indies might be paid the right to bring back to Boston on the vessel a keg of molasses as his private venture. Where an able-bodied seaman might get one such privilege, his captain might get twenty or thirty. On arrival back in Boston they would sell their personal property for whatever it would bring. Thus they were able to conduct business without any money.

Throughout the colonial period the dilemma persisted: How can you conduct a market economy without any gold or silver? The many devices will be described in some detail. But first we need to stake out an apparatus for analysis. "Money" has been defined (early in Chapter 1) as anything you can pay your bills with. In the eighteenth century in North America, the only money that you could be sure would be universally accepted was the precious metals. Today, in contrast, the most common form of money is checks; roughly 90 percent of all bills are paid by drawing against demand deposits in a commercial bank. Many of us are ill-fitted to comprehend the crucial function of such banks, for the reason that we have never drawn out funds that we had not earlier deposited. Thus our transactions merely transfer buying power from us to others. But the vital task of banks lies elsewhere—to create and destroy credit. When a bank gives a loan, it expands the volume of buying power; when it collects on the loan, it contracts the outstanding credit. This mechanism was far from novel in the eighteenth century; at least five hundred years earlier in Italian and Spanish towns, bankers had been creating deposits without the use of any cash.

But the colonies could not use it. English law forbade them. The other jaw of the vise was their own extravagance. They had never found any meaningful veins of gold and silver. They insisted on spending abroad more than they could sell to foreigners, so that the precious metals that came in, mainly silver from Mexico, promptly flowed out again to close up the international deficit. To evade the consequences of this condition, colonies experimented with three techniques. They tried to overvalue their few coins; that is, they set a higher nominal or legal value on a coin than the metal embodied in it would fetch on the open market. They founded, straight in the teeth of the English prohibition, banks authorized to issue a circulating medium. Lastly, the governments of some provinces put out their own paper money.

And of course they simply traded goods without using money—barter. In the mid-seventeenth century Harvard College had a yearly budget of £250, and most of its receipts were in "country pay," farm products. The town of Portsmouth, New Hampshire, in 1662 pledged a subsidy to the College of £60 a year for seven years, payable in pine boards and barrel staves. Lads paid for their room and board with shoats and rum. Already Massachusetts was overvaluing the shilling: "If our own coin be carried out of the country," said the mint-master, "it is a sign that it is not so light as it may be, and that it would be for public advantage to make it lighter, unless we had some public income from mines as the Spaniard hath." The same man, enviously eying Virginia where tobacco was deposited in government warehouses and where the resultant receipts circulated as money, posed the perplexity: "wee having no staple commodities to pass current in payments as in other Plantations, by which our Trade for want of money is much perplexed and decayed."

As master of the mint, he began in 1652 to stamp the little specie available into "Pine Tree Shillings." This practice continued until 1686, and some of these shillings were still in circulation at the time of the Revolution. But through the entire period from 1686 to 1775, the Bay did not issue any coins. A crisis came right after the minting was halted. Conflict broke out between England and France (King William's War). The colonies got into the fracas. Massachusetts put up £50,000 to send 2,000 militia and 34 ships to conquer Quebec, thinking to pay for the expedition by looting a prostrate city. The project flopped. How to pay? The answer, in 1690, was to print paper money—the first such issue anywhere in the British Empire. During the same year the name "dollar" (from the German *thaler*) was fastened to the Spanish peso or "piece of eight." Similar conditions in Carolina in 1702 led to identical tactics; the province emitted paper money to pay for a foray (also a failure) against the Spanish post at St. Augustine, Florida. Or take the affairs of the Pennsylvania Company, to which 200 Britishers subscribed the huge capital of £10,000. Money was so short in the colony that the firm had to sell on credit. That got it in trouble, and in 1723 it gave up the ghost and disappeared. Soon after, the aspiring Philadelphia printer Benjamin Franklin was earning considerable revenues by printing currency not only for Pennsylvania but also for Delaware and New Jersey.

Massachusetts tried another tack. In 1740 prices there were very depressed. A faction set up a so-called Land Bank to print money and lend it to borrowers against mortgages on real estate. The plan was that when the deflation had been cured, the Bank would receive back its own currency to retire the mortgages. To conservative merchants like Thomas Hancock, the notion of paper money was reprehensible, and to then go on to base it on unliquid assets such as land for which no dependable market existed was outrageous. They set up a rival bank that would try to keep a portion of its reserves in silver. This scheme might also have failed due to the lack of specie, but it never got the chance; Parliament declared both banks illegal.

What Boston merchants came down to was an ingenious array of accounting tricks. Behind them lay barter or credit. Thomas Hancock's father-in-law, also a bookdealer, paid a carpenter not only in books but also with a barrel of beef, cider, a gun, pencils, molasses, wood, and hogs. Hancock himself worked up an impressive panoply of arrangements. With some customers he used a series of offsetting entries in his ledger. Thus the account with a tailor shows what clothing Hancock received over about a year, and what he gave the tailor in return, and finally he strikes the balance. No cash needed to change hands. With other buyers Hancock would take payment in country pay. This mode could be extended with goods that were not perishable; pickled pork and molasses and corn all went on occasion through the assets of several men, serving in effect as commodity-money. The ledgers show triangular transactions; If Mr. A. owed Hancock £5 while Hancock owed Mr. B. £5, both entries are crossed out and a new one shows Mr. A. owing Mr. B. £5. Credit instruments were drafted that were payable not in money but in produce. Thus after John Hancock succeeded to his uncle's business he received this note: "Pleas to let Mrs. Mary Greenwood have Thirty shilling Lawfull Money in goods, and charge it to the Accot of yr Humble Servt Nath. Greenwood." This is a bill of exchange, virtually a check, but not a check redeemable in cash. That step came next. Reverting for a moment to England, we find a communication from a man who wanted to give a present to his wife:

Good Mr. Latouche
Pray open your pouch
and pay my soul's darling
One thousand pounds stirling.

This check was legal—and payable in cash. But only in Great Britain, not in the colonies. Merchants in North America understood well how to carry out the central job of commercial banks—the expansion and contraction of the supply of money. On their books they were frequently transferring credit from one correspondent to another. But under English regulations they could not found banks nor could they issue paper money. The best scholarship now holds that bickering over the currency may have been at least as important as the Stamp Act in fomenting the Revolution.

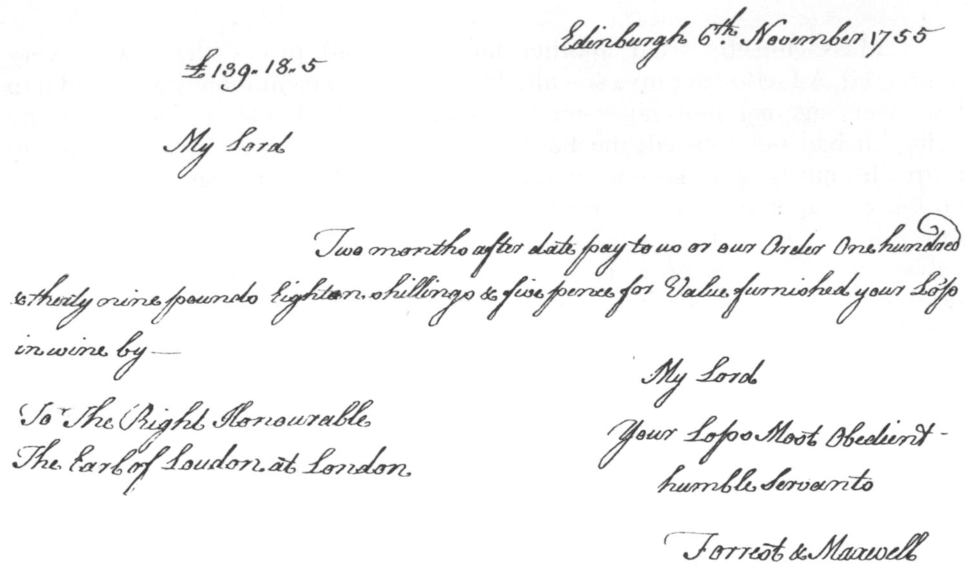

£139-18-5

Edinburgh 6th November 1755

My Lord

Two months after date pay to us or our Order One hundred & thirty nine pounds Eighteen shillings & five pence for Value furnished your Lop in wine by —

*To The Right Honourable
The Earl of Loudon at London.*

*My Lord
Your Lops Most Obedient -
humble Servants*

Forrest & Maxwell

FIGURE 3-2. *A British Credit Instrument*

The bridles on money and banking are one of the two ways that English rules seem to have curbed the commercial growth of the colonies. The other was the Staple laws on tobacco. With this brace of exceptions, the effects of imperial policy on the economic life of North America seem to have been indifferent or beneficial. This conclusion is not accepted by all historians. In discussing English ordinances having to do with manufacturing in the colonies, one authority has said that "English policies had a strong retarding influence. . . . British statutes restrained the American woolen, iron, and hat industries." But we may doubt it. England did try to keep America as a source of crude iron, with the intent of working it up into finished wares within her own boundaries. Imports of American pig and bar iron were essential to the hardware industry of the West Midlands; by 1738 it was estimated that at least 135,000 people in and around Birmingham were working in the iron trades. Americans could not lawfully, after 1750, found any new works to produce iron for nails, or bristle steel for tools, or sheet iron.

Such laws did little. The very next year one of the first rolling mills in North America began operations in Massachusetts—with a system of gearing that permitted the upper and lower rollers to turn at different speeds. Much earlier the same colony had seen the installation of trip hammers run by waterwheels to save the sweat from a blacksmith's arm. The mechanics of New England used sophisticated methods to produce a wide variety of hoops and bolts, scythes and bars, and clocks. In view of the techniques in use prior to the Revolution, it is rather silly to refer to a "take-off period" for industrial growth well along in the nineteenth century. "By the end of the eighteenth century," so we can read in a masterly article, "America appears to have been as far advanced as any country in the world in the basic applications of water power to mechanical movement, and was on the threshold of undisputed supremacy in the field of practical hydraulics." If England did not harm the colonies much if at all by her restrictions on iron manufacturing, she unquestionably helped them by the rules applying to some other trades. Among the beneficiaries can be listed the indigo planters, shipbuilders and shipowners, and suppliers of naval stores. Economically, up to the beginning of the French and Indian War in 1754, North America seems on the whole to have prospered through its inclusion in the British Empire.

Men came increasingly to believe that they could control their own destinies, and that if they could manage triphammers they could also create and manage governments. Many came to wonder if God had anything much to do with affairs on earth. Of this degeneration from the ideas of a Sanctified Commonwealth and of special providences, we can single out some signs. The most famous is perhaps the Great Awakening of 1740–1742. Before we look closely at that tangled episode, it may be appropriate to try to get the timing straight. According to Edmund S. Morgan "In 1740 America's leading intellectuals were clergymen and thought about theology; in 1790 they were statesmen and thought about politics." This remark culls out from the jumbled past a change of immense consequence. But a couple of warnings should be made. Millions of Americans (although perhaps not many prominent thinkers) continue to vibrate to religious currents right down to the present. Also the dates in the quotation seem too late; maybe it should say that in 1700 the powerful minds in North America were focused on the Divine but by 1760 they concentrated on earthly governors.

By 1740, a convenient date for the outburst of the Great Awakening, the one distinguished mind to be found in the ranks of clergymen was Jonathan Edwards. He deserved honor; he was probably one of the half dozen salient philosophers in American history. But accolades he has often not got. On the contrary, quite a few writers by their misguided fascination with one sermon, "Sinners in the Hands of an Angry God," have portrayed him as a sadistic ogre and accorded him notoriety. To understand the importance of Edwards in the American intellectual scene, we need to look carefully, not only at some major ideas developing in Europe during his time, but also at the struggles of his fellow American churchmen to keep the faith under new social and intellectual conditions in a society no longer dominated by a small group of Theocratic Saints. Thus Edwards, like his antitype the utterly secular Benjamin Franklin, must be seen in the context of the intellectual ferment of his times.

Wandering for a moment across the Atlantic, let us observe the greatest scientist of the early eighteenth century, Sir Isaac Newton. His formulae stating the attractions among physical bodies were of great interest to his contemporaries and were to be fundamental to later science, but they also were worrisome to serious thinkers as a challenge to the physics of Scripture and its accounts of the inevitable Apocalypse. But Newton was desperately anxious that he should not undercut Scripture. By saying he did not know the cause of gravity, and thus denying that it is any kind of self-determining or mechanical "inherent Power really existent within" the nature of matter, Newton avoided confrontation and showed himself a true believer. In 1693, six years after he had published his major book, he declined into a severe spiritual depression. He left his professorship at Cambridge University and went to London, where he became master of the mint. He was familiar at the clubs, always dining out, a gentleman. His spare time he spent pondering over the Bible. Especially was he bemused by two books: Daniel and Revelation. He was trying to fix a period for the end of the world, to pick the day of the Last Judgment. It seems plausible that his glimpse of the limitless spans of almost empty space in the cosmos had terrified him. What was man, after all, when confronted by infinity?* Due in considerable measure to Newton himself, Western civilization had arrived at one of the great hinges of history. Since the end of the Roman Empire nearly everybody had believed that religion could not be isolated from politics, that nature was a unity and that it cohered with the Divine Word because God had created all. Now these convictions were doomed to be pulverized. The world would split into segments. But the splintering did not happen overnight, and in its unfolding there would be vast differences in tempo for different men, in different cultures, brooding over various problems.

Certainly a lesser figure than Newton, but still worth considering as a predecessor of Jonathan Edwards, is John Wise, who was the Congregational minister in Ipswich up north of Boston. Some famous historians have promulgated the belief that Wise's ideas broke sharply from those of the seventeenth century—even that his *Vindication of the Government of the New-England Churches* was "in the spirit of the Enlightenment." But these pails of words won't hold much water. They exaggerate and oversimplify. Wise

---

*For an absorbing depiction of the impact of this vision on a fundamentalist minister in the twentieth century, see a short story by Wilbur Daniel Steele, "The Man Who Saw Through Heaven."

did sometimes write in terms of liberty and reason and nature in the fashion that men would use in the Revolution. But mainly he talked Revelation. The bulk of his argument in favor of the forms traditionally used in the governance of the Congregational churches is itself quite traditional; he says that they are prescribed by Scripture.

But the old modes were being widely subverted. A large influx of Scots-Irish with their Presbyterian synods occurred early in the eighteenth century; by 1730 there were 12,000 in Pennsylvania alone. There and in New Jersey the Congregationalists faced competition from the Anglicans. To fend off the threat they joined with ministers of other faiths to form the Presbytery of Philadelphia in 1706, seemingly regarding it as analogous to the consociations with which they were familiar. The same tendencies were working among the Congregationalists in New England, where the most potent federation was the Hampshire Association in western Massachusetts along the Connecticut River. The chief shepherd over this flock was Solomon Stoddard. Besides his centralizing animus he was boosting an "enthusiastical" mode of services: "the word is an Hammer, and we should use it to break the rocky hearts of men." A half dozen times he headed an emotional campaign of revival meetings endeavoring to bring everybody in a town to a state of repentence and declaring for Christ. This man was the grandfather of Jonathan Edwards. After Edwards graduated from Yale College in 1720, he eventually succeeded to Stoddard's pulpit in Northampton.

Unlike Benjamin Franklin, who could write toward the end of his long life that his only regrets were peccadilloes, Edwards brooded about his own defects and those of society. While a tutor at Yale in 1724 he wrote in his journal, "I have now, abundant reason to be convinced, of the troublesomeness and vexation of the world and that it never will be another kind of world." The concept of sin can only follow, not precede, a feeling of sin. That awareness springs up spontaneously in many ages; there is no reason to think that Edwards had to read John Calvin to know about sin, or that Calvin had to read St. Augustine. "Christians," wrote a minister in Connecticut, "have the most self-abasing Discoveries of their own Hearts, and the unspeakable vileness of their Nature."

The notion of original sin was in jeopardy. Quite a few men were no longer persuaded of their undying guilt; on the contrary they regarded themselves as great fellows who could remake the universe. It was said of Edwards' alma mater "that Y. Coll. was corrupted and ruined with Arminianism and Heresy." Arminianism, a point of view that would be held by nearly everybody by the middle of the nineteenth century, revolved on the notion that a man had freedom of the will, that he could even will himself into Heaven. Jonathan Edwards was certain that this position was impious; he knew in his heart that no man could be saved but through Divine grace.

Outwardly Edwards seemed the reverse of an evangelist. He was reserved, even chilly. His voice was flat and lacked expressiveness. He violated the axioms of oratory by staring over the heads of his audience. But in 1734 he set off a wave of revivals that swept the Connecticut Valley and lasted for three years. By a contemporary account: " 'Tis worthy of our Observation, that this great and surprizing Work does not seem to have taken its Rise from any sudden and distressing Calamity or public Terror that might universally impress the Minds of a People: Here was no Storm, no Earthquake, no Inundation of Water, no Desolation by Fire, no Pestilence, or any other sweeping Distemper, nor any cruel Invasion by their Indian Neighbours, that might force the Inhabitants into a serious Thoughtfulness, and a religious Temper by the Fears of approaching Death and Judgment." Then what was the propellant? Partly Edwards' personality; while he seemed cool without, his innards bubbled with passions (see Document 3-2). Partly the frontier perhaps; farmers and their wives were so isolated and lonesome that they grasped at reasons for a gathering. Maybe chief of all, a free-floating anxiety arising from the sense of betrayal of their forebears, of having strayed from the city on the hill. The very word "revival" implies going back to the past, means a degeneration from more sacrosanct antecedents and an attempt to recover them. Thus the outpourings of the mid-eighteenth century were an atavism, just as the splutterings of fundamentalism in the twentieth century have been an anachronistic fling at pretending that the devout "good old days" not only did exist but still do exist. They should not be read as a persistence of faith; they were rather a largely futile try to deny a decline of faith.

If it be true that the displays of 1734 to 1737 were not rooted in any visible disaster, so is it true that they did not breed tangible rifts in society. They were by and large decorous. The byways were not clogged with itinerant ministers who were journeying to try out their rantings on some strange congregation. A preacher tended to his own parish. Communicants did not use their doctrinal daggers on their fellows. Remarkably, considering the litigious nature of Americans, laws were not passed and lawsuits were not brought. And they petered out; in the words of Jonathan Edwards the revivals were "very much at a Stop" when the Great Awakening began.

That upheaval, however, did happen in 1739 far away in Williamsburg, Virginia, when George Whitefield stood on the dais in Bruton Parish Church and blurted at the parishioners: "What think ye of Christ?" Thereafter dignity was uncommon. Whitefield was a touring preacher from Great Britain. He had been educated at Oxford, where he and John Wesley were among the fellowship of the "Holy Club." (The obverse side of the age could be read in Benjamin Franklin's plan to launch a group in Philadelphia titled the "Free-and-Easy Club." However, anybody with insight into the labyrinths of Franklin's mind will realize that he was too canny to start the organization or even to make his idea public.) Whereas Wesley launched his own sect, which would have an imperial future in America as the Methodist Church, Whitefield was ordained in the Church of England and stayed there until death. But he was an enthusiastic, a Low Churchman, who abhorred hollow ritualism.

He was some talker. On 14 September 1740 he began a tour at Newport, Rhode Island. In two months he had gone north through Boston to Maine, then west to Northampton where he stayed at the home of Jonathan Edwards, south to New Haven, west to Stamford. On his second visit to Newark so many people wanted to hear him that the church nearly burst; they had to take out the window behind the pulpit so that he could preach to the masses in the graveyard. His sermon in Philadelphia apparently even conned Benjamin Franklin, not a reverent man. "I happened soon after to attend one of his Sermons, in the Course of which I perceived that he intended to finish with a Collection, and I silently resolved he should get nothing from me. I had in my Pocket a Handful of Copper Money, three or four silver Dollars, and five Pistoles in Gold. As he proceeded I began to soften, and concluded to give the Coppers. Another Stroke of his Oratory made me asham'd of that, and determin'd me to give the Silver; and he finish'd so admirably, that I empty'd my Pocket wholly into the Collector's Dish, Gold and all."

As the posture toward God of such men as Edwards and Whitefield became institutionalized, it was labelled the New Light. It stressed emotion—love of Christ—rather than the ceremonies of worship. It cautioned against "the danger of an unconverted ministry." It abjured icy formalism. It tried to breathe renewed life into awareness of that magical mystical instant of grace. (See Chapter 1 on Protestantism and later in this chapter on Edwards.) Clearly the appeal of these attitudes was widespread. But how much so? Was it not localized at all? Some pontificators have asserted that the Great Awakening was most intense on the frontier; others say that it was "great and general." Some argue that participants were likely to be members of the meaner sort; others say that it was not linked to any particular class. One minister in Boston declared how gratifying it was to his profession to see "in the weeks past, Old and Young, Parents and Children, Masters and Servants, high and low, rich and poor together, gathering . . . to the Doors and Windows of our Places of Worship." He entitled his pamphlet *Souls flying to Jesus Christ pleasant and admirable to behold . . .* The vision is charming, but is it accurate? Nobody knows yet. But it should be possible to find out. If twenty or thirty undergraduates made up a systematic sampling of parishes in the various denominations and then took a detailed look at the individuals in those congregations, they would be the dominant authorities on the subject. A study of Boston does tell a bit. The city's three Anglican churches apparently were not moved. In a reversal of what might be expected, the one Baptist church was hostile, while the sole Presbyterian group beamed. Of the fifteen Congregational clergymen, nine showed as New Lights, three stayed neutral, and only three stood as opponents. Significantly, however, one of the enemies kept quiet, one lost his church, and the third waited until 1743 to make frontal attacks.

The fruits of the Great Awakening were many. By 1745 a group of ministers in New Haven could declare: "Antinomian Principles are advanc'd, preach'd up and printed;—Christian brethren have their affections widely alienated;—Unchristian Censoriousness and hard judging abounds, Love stands afar off, and Charity cannot enter;—Many Churches and Societies are broken and divided; Pernicious and unjustifiable Separations are set up and continue. . . . Numbers of illiterate Exhorters swarm about as Locusts from the Bottomless Pit: We think upon the whole, that Religion is now in a far worse State than it was in 1740." Several years later a future president of Yale College would remark, "Multitudes were seriously, soberly and solemnly out of their wits."

Sectarianism flourished. The number of Congregational churches grew, partly by the schism of existing parishes between New Lights and Old Lights. The Baptists, with their emotionalism and their belief in the anointing only of adult believers by total immersion, got a mighty impetus. Connecticut saw a halt to the Presbyterianizing of its established churches. Although the New Lights were often wild and distinctly non-intellectual, they did found significant new colleges: Dartmouth and Brown in New England, the College of New Jersey that became Princeton.

Probably the Anglicans suffered the most from the Great Awakening. Their ceremonialism with its vestments and its set forms of worship repelled many people. They continued to be the established church in the Southern colonies, and their vestries may have equalled the county courts as agencies of local administration. But probably not even half of the population were participating members of the church.

Frontier dissenters made life especially difficult for Anglican priests. One in the heavily Scots-Irish and Presbyterian back country of South Carolina was repeatedly harassed. Although he was a stranger in the area, he had to visit several churches and many parishioners. If he stopped a man in the woods to ask his way, he might be sent off in the wrong direction. Local "Enthusiasticals" changed the dates on the notices of his sermons. They opened his mail, connived at robbery of his lodgings, and framed him on a morals charge. They stole the keys to his meetinghouse at Camden. Two hours before he was scheduled to preach they might dole out booze to get his parishioners drunk. He came to view the Presbyterians as "certainly the worst Vermin on earth." On one occasion they started fifty-seven dogs fighting outside the chapel while he was holding services. But he got back at them. Catching one bitch, he took her to the house of a deacon who was raucous among the enemy and suggested that she was one of the fifty-seven Presbyterians whom he had just wrangled into the true religion.

Thus far we have tried to winnow the institutional features of the Great Awakening. But what of its ideology? What of those intellectual aspects where Jonathan Edwards was the boldest advocate of all? It is vital to recognize the nature of the opposition that brought Edwards into the battle. They were Arminians, the peddlers of free will and good works as paths to salvation. One such minister near Boston preached a sermon that ignored the whole topic of Divine Grace and called blasphemous the practice of decrying personal virtue. Jonathan Mayhew, who became the foremost prophet among the Boston ministry of the Future American Revolution, defined the "one grand capital error." This fallacy, said Mayhew, boiled down to the erroneous idea of Calvinists like Edwards that "we are saved by grace." He ridiculed unreasonable "vain enthusiasts" like Edwards and the New Lights: "Whatever is reasonable, is with them carnal; and nothing is worthy of belief, but what is impossible and absurd in the eye of human reason."

Even at the risk of making the discriminations too sharp and too rigid, it may be desirable to lay down a new trinity:

Catholicism   redemption by faith (respect for symbolic ritual)

Calvinism   justification by grace (inner light)

Arminianism   salvation by works ("reasonable" good behavior)

Under this classification, Jonathan Edwards clearly belongs with the second category and his foes belong in the third.

Not until William James at the end of the nineteenth century would another American discuss the psychology of belief in words that came close to Edwards' profundity and power. Here is part of his description of his own conversion: "My experience had not then taught me, as it has done since, my extreme feebleness and impotence, every manner of way; and the bottomless depths of secret corruption and deceit there was in my heart. However, I went on with my eager pursuit after more holiness, and conformity to Christ. . . . The soul of a true Christian, as I then wrote my meditations, appeared like such a little white flower as we see in the spring of the year; low and humble on the ground, opening its bosom to receive the pleasant beams of the sun's glory; rejoicing as it were in a calm rapture; diffusing around a sweet fragrancy; standing peacefully and lovingly, in the midst of other flowers round about; all in like manner opening their bosoms, to drink in the light of the sun." This is the core of Edwards; perhaps his most fetching sermon is titled "The Excellency of Christ." The Lord Jesus is all good. He is perfection. The corollary—violators of His Word deserve eternal damnation— makes sense only in this context.

Edwards told at length the tale of Phebe Bartlet. When she was about four years old she spent endless hours in her closet brooding over the state of her soul. Saying that she could not find God, she was morbid in her melancholy. One day her mother heard these words from behind her door: "PRAY BLESSED LORD give me salvation! I PRAY, BEG pardon all my sins." Phebe came from the room weeping. She sat long, still in tears, by her mother. Finally she began to smile. Her mother was startled at the abrupt change. The child said, "Mother, the kingdom of heaven is come to me!" Presently Phebe returned to her room. That night while lying in bed she called a little cousin into the room. She told the boy that Heaven was better than this life. She agonized over the Afterlife and over guilt. One day she went with other children into a neighbor's lot where they helped themselves to some plums. When she got home with hers, her mother reminded Phebe that God had commanded us not to steal. She commenced weeping. The mother said they could feel free to eat the fruit if they had the owner's consent, and sent another child to ask it. The child returned and said it was all right. Still Phebe would not touch her portion. "BECAUSE IT WAS SIN." A report said that she avoided plums for quite some time.

These highly charged dramatizations, full of concrete impressions to heighten awareness of sin, were typical of Edwards' homiletic method in sermons and as published in his *Narrative of Surprising Conversions*. How did he reach his insight that a sense of sin and a sense of salvation are two aspects of one syndrome? To a great extent, obviously, from his observations of himself and of his contemporaries. He also picked up something from his grandfather who had said, "If men be thoroughly scared with the danger of damnation, they will readily improve their possibility, not stand for assurance of success." "Experience," declared Stoddard, "fits men to teach others." But much of his method was developed from John Locke's *An Essay Concerning Human Understanding*. Edwards came upon it in 1717, a lad who had not yet started college. The argument struck deep. A man, said Locke, is born *tabula rasa*, a blank page. He has no ideas, no beliefs, no sense of values. He picks up data from his surroundings by means of his sensory organs. He can reason about those data. He can endeavor to sort out the sense impressions that are true to nature from those that are illusions. He can try to systematize them. But ultimately all that he knows is based on what he has gleaned from his environment. These notions fed Edwards' thinking about the nature of a sermon; good preaching should beat at the parishioners with ideas that will move them emotionally to opt for virtue and not for vice. The stimuli of the services should make them seek God.

While Edwards tried to use his homilies as a pathway to holiness, he was also concerned to write decisive refutations of the Arminian contentions. They asked how—*if* God predestined each man at the Creation, and *if* man is created Free to sin or not—how can God be called just in dooming a man to everlasting Hell for committing sins that God Himself had decreed? Both premises are true, said Edwards, and still the conclusion is justice. Edwards' demonstration of this position, running to more than 300 pages, was published as *A careful and strict Enquiry into The Modern Prevailing Notions of that Freedom of the Will Which is supposed to be essential to Moral Agency, Vertue and Vice, Reward and Punishment, Praise and Blame* (1754). Through his habit of spending at least twelve hours a day in his study, he seemingly wrote it in about four months, and even working at that breakneck pace he fashioned proofs that are as inexorable as if they had been worked up by Spinoza.

A man can with justice be condemned for his actions if he chose them voluntarily, without being externally coerced as by a government or by a person stronger than himself. "Let the person come by his volition of choice how he will," wrote Edwards, "yet, if he is able, and there is nothing in the way to hinder his pursuing and executing his will, the man is fully free, according to the primary and common notion of freedom." Since he is free, he is responsible, and he can justly be punished. Where Edwards accused the Arminians of error was in their supposing that no limits existed for an individual's behavior, that his range of choices as to how he would act was unbounded, that his actions were often merely random. For Edwards, all comprehension of purposeful behavior had to proceed from the idea of cause-and-effect: A man acts on the basis of his current preferences, from inclinations which must themselves have causes. It is absurd to say that this chain of causes can be broken, and also it is absurd to say that it can regress infinitely. To Edwards of course the Final Cause was God, but there was a proximate final cause. Simply put, it was the character of the actor: A good man will behave virtuously, and a bad man will behave viciously. But then the virtue of a good man (or even of a vicious one) can be strengthened; the degree of virtue is the greater, according as "the *stronger,* and the more *fixed* and *determined* [is] the good disposition of the heart." It is ironical that within two centuries this line of attack would be fully secularized, as when John Dewey in *Human Nature and Conduct* (1922) analyzed the formation and operation of habits.

Edwards was high on intellectual rigor, and he did not blanch to follow through on his understanding. When his townsmen failed after 1742 to quicken into Life, he berated them with a phrase from John Winthrop: "No town in America is so much like a city set on a hill, to which God has in so great a degree entrusted the honor of religion." Then he sought to destroy the comforting notions developed since Winthrop's day. He talked down the entire Federal theology. He denied that God had made any promises to Massachusetts in the covenant with Abraham: the Divine power was without limits. He rejected the Half-Way Covenant, saying that only the children of full members of the church were eligible for baptism. He asserted that all men were born in sin and that no man could be sure that he was to be saved. His rigorous Calvinism was too much for his contemporaries. It had been hard enough to preach it to ordinary people in 1650; a century later they would not tolerate it. In the fattening economy of western Massachusetts, with its lively trade along the Connecticut, the case seemed clear. A man could gaze about and see that his society was prospering; he knew that he was getting ahead, and he took these bounties as evidence that God was smiling on him. So Edwards' parishioners ousted him from the pulpit once held by his grandfather. Within a hundred years famous preachers were to inflate the doctrine of free will to the extreme of saying that God could not save a person, that each person must save himself.

Thus the Arminians seized the bastions of faith. But they no more than Edwards were the harbingers of the future. The domain of religion in America was doomed to shrink before the onslaughts of men like Benjamin Franklin with their experimental science. Edwards (born 1703) was a mere three years older than Franklin, but they stood for two epochs. Franklin was too sagacious to admit that he might be an atheist or an agnostic; what he did was to exile God to some quadrant of the sky so remote that His ties to human affairs were severed utterly.

Franklin—rotund, wily, a man who went from wearing a leather apron in cobblestoned streets to sporting a coonskin cap around the salons of Paris—made scientific contributions of the first rank. Here lay the road to the new order. After the Leyden jar was devised in the Netherlands in 1746, he heard of it almost at once. He started tinkering. Everybody knows about his kite; in his experiments he used a variety of mundane gadgets such as a pump handle, a vinegar cruet, a saltcellar. He established that lightning was identical with electricity. He hypothesized that all substances contain electricity. It was he who proposed the terms that are still used to talk about charges, positive and negative (plus and minus), rather than the earlier "vitreous and resinous." He tried to use electricity to treat paralytics, and concluded that it did not work. He electrocuted animals (and he came close to electrocuting himself; see Document 3-3).

Surveying all his work in natural philosophy, as science was called at the time, two qualities can be discerned. It was experimental; theories had to be validated or disproved in terms of observable relationships. It was practical; nothing was worth fussing with unless it could be put to use. In the latter respect he was light-years away from the luminaries of science in the later nineteenth century who did not bother their heads with worries about the possible utility of their ideas. It may also be well to ask if Franklin did not share those two traits, experimental and practical, with Jonathan Edwards. Edwards even referred to "experimental religion" (we might term it "experiential religion"). Was not he too seeking a practical result when he tried to bring the masses into the church? If two Americans as divergent as Franklin and Edwards nonetheless shared some vital attributes, the convergence might say a good deal about what it meant to be an American in the mid-eighteenth century.

The matter of periodization is central to historical study. It is also complicated. For instance, the year 1898 might be taken as a new epoch in the history of foreign relations, but it marks no such sharp break in the story of immigration, or of painting. This chapter has tried to press the complications even further to explore interrelationships between two apparently distinct areas. In some eras, such as the eighteenth century, the closest ties of intellectual history were to the Atlantic economy. Every ship that brought English textiles to the New World also brought ideas. At other epochs, as will be seen in Part VI, new modes of writing and thinking were most influenced by social trends in society. The argument here has sought to summarize similarities and differences in these regards among the early colonies. How did Virginia differ from New England because the former had an outstanding export—tobacco—while the latter could not find one? What devices did Boston merchants innovate to circumvent their special problems? The concern for international commerce worked steadily if slowly to subvert the religious way of life. But men felt themselves sliding away from the beliefs of their fathers, and in 1739 a spasmodic reaction occurred which is customarily called the Great Awakening. Better it should be called a Reawakening. Symbolically, it was set going by George Whitefield, an Englishman. So, too, many of the ideas that were later to serve as banners in the War for Independence were imports from Europe, such as Montesquieu's from France or *Cato's Letters* from London (discussed in Chapter 6).

SOME NOTABLE EVENTS

1689–
1697 King William's War.

1690 Massachusetts issues first paper money in British Empire.

John Locke, *Essay Concerning Human Understanding.*

1692 Witch trials in Salem, Massachusetts.

1693 William and Mary College founded in Williamsburg, Virginia.

1694–
1696 Rice cultivation begun in Carolina.

1696 Board of Trade appointed by William III.

1701 Yale College founded in New Haven, Connecticut.

1702–
1713 Queen Anne's War; the War of the Spanish Succession.

1705 Newcomen devises the steam pump for mining.

1706 First Anglican parish in Connecticut formed at Stratford.

1707 Act of Union joins England with Scotland to form Great Britain.

1721 First smallpox inoculation in Boston is given.

1731 Benjamin Franklin forms first circulating library in the colonies.

1732 Franklin brings out first issue of *Poor Richard's Almanac.*

1733 Flying shuttle invented by John Kay in England.

Parliament passes Molasses Act.

1734–
1737 Religious revival in the Connecticut Valley.

1736 John and Charles Wesley found Methodism.

1739–
1748 War of Jenkins' Ear becomes War of the Austrian Succession.

1739 George Whitefield begins his tour of North America.

1740–
1742 The Great Awakening.

1742 Indigo introduced into South Carolina from West Indies.

1743 Franklin takes lead in founding American Philosophical Society.

1746 Leyden jar invented.

Jonathan Edwards, *A Treatise Concerning Religious Affections.*

1748 David Hume, *An Enquiry Concerning Human Understanding.*

Parliament votes a bounty of six pence a pound on indigo.

1752 Franklin's kite experiment.

1754 Jonathan Edwards, *Freedom of the Will.*

King's College (Columbia University) founded in New York.

1755 University of Pennsylvania chartered; first nonsectarian college in America.

Publication of first dictionary of English, by Samuel Johnson.

Ways to Study History III

Use unusual tools. Traditional approaches to the study of economic history are well illustrated by a series widely known as the Rinehart Economic History of the United States. Planned in ten substantial volumes of which eight have been published, the venture has produced some excellent works: I think especially of the studies by Fred A. Shannon, George Rogers Taylor, and Paul W. Gates. But even these outstanding books are, in their main contours, narrative histories of a conventional sort. The suspicion has persisted that the known sources could be made to yield additional and perhaps more precise conclusions if they were penetrated by a different set of weapons.

One breakthrough came in 1945 with the publication of *The House of Hancock* by William T. Baxter. The author was an accountant. Coming as a Commonwealth Fellow to the Harvard Graduate School of Business Administration, he was steered to the records of the Hancocks for the period from 1724 to 1775. Scholars had already delved into the monetary problems of the colonies, but Baxter because of his unusual training was able to pull out of the account-books a fine-grained depiction of the devices by which a merchant could do business in a society that had no bullion.

Computers are beginning to find applications in analyses of our former economies. For instance, the Massachusetts Register of Shipping for the years 1697–1714 exists in the Massachusetts Archives in the State House in Boston. Students had consulted it for specialized purposes, but no full-scale statistical dissection had been attempted. This job was done by Bernard and Lotte Bailyn using IBM tabulators and sorters. Their *Massachusetts Shipping* (1959) reveals for example that of the adult males in Boston, one of three owned some share in a vessel. In "A Note on Procedure" they describe some of the difficulties encountered.

Document 3-1

Colonel William Byrd II was the son of the founder of the family in America. Chiefly he was a Virginia planter, but he toyed with several types of enterprise. Here he tells how he investigated the possible profits of founding an iron works by the tactic of interviewing an experienced ironmaster.

He assured me the first step I was to take was to acquaint myself fully with the Quantity and Quality of my Oar. For that reason I ought to keep a good Pick-ax Man at work a whole Year to search if there be a Sufficient Quantity, without which it would be a very rash undertaking. That I should also have a Skilful person to try the richness of the oar. Nor is it great Advantage to have it exceeding rich, because then it will yield Brittle Iron, which is not valuable. But the way to have it tough is to mix poor Oar and Rich together, which makes the poorer sort extremely necessary for the production of the best Iron. . . . He told me after I was certain my Oar was good and plentiful enough, my next inquiry ought to be, how far it lyes from a Stream proper to build a furnace upon, and again what distance that Furnace will be from Water Carriage; Because the Charge of Carting a great way is very heavy, and eats out a great part of the Profit. That this was the Misfortune of the Mines at Fredericksville, where they were oblig'd to Cart the Oar a Mile to the Furnace, and after twas run into Iron, to carry that 24 Miles over an uneven Road to Rappahannock River . . . If I were Satisfy'd with the Situation, I was in the next place to consider whether I had Woodland enough near the Furnace to Supply it with Charcoal, whereof it wou'd require a prodigious Quantity. . . . That 2 Miles Square of Wood, wou'd supply a Moderate furnace; so that what you fell first may have time to grow up again to a proper bigness (which must be 4 Inches over) by that time the rest is cut down. He told me farther, that 120 Slaves, including Women, were necessary to carry on all the Business of an Iron Work . . .

Document 3-2

Jonathan Edwards delivered this sermon, "The Excellency of Christ," in 1734, based on Revelation v: 5, 6.

  . . . Fallen man is a mean, despicable creature, a contemptible worm; but Christ who has undertaken for us, is infinitely honorable and worthy. Fallen man is polluted, but Christ is infinitely holy: fallen man is hateful, but Christ is infinitely lovely: fallen man is the object of God's indignation, but Christ is infinitely dear to him: we have dreadfully provoked God, but Christ has performed that righteousness that is infinitely precious in God's eyes. . . .

  What is there that you can desire should be in a Saviour, that is not in Christ? Or, wherein should you desire a Saviour should be otherwise than Christ is? What excellency is there wanting? . . . Or, what can you think of, that would be encouraging, that is not to be found in the person of Christ? Would you have your Saviour to be great and honorable, because you are not willing to be beholden to a mean person? And is not Christ a person honorable enough to be worthy that you should be dependent on him? Is he not a person high enough to be worthy to be appointed to so honorable a work as your salvation? Would you not only have a Saviour that is of high degree, but would you have him, notwithstanding his exaltation and dignity, to be made also of low degree, that he might have experience of afflictions and trials, that he might learn by the things he has suffered, to pity them that suffer and are tempted? And has not Christ been made low enough for you? And has he not suffered enough? Would you not only have him have experience of the afflictions you now suffer, but also of that amazing wrath that you fear hereafter, that he may know how to pity those that are in danger of it, and afraid of it? This Christ has had experience of, which experience gave him a greater sense of it, a thousand times, than you have, or any living man has. . . .

Document 3-3

On Christmas Day of 1750 Benjamin Franklin wrote to a friend about a bungle he had committed.

  I have lately made an experiment in electricity, that I desire never to repeat. Two nights ago, being about to kill a turkey by the shock from two large glass jars, containing as much electrical fire as forty common phials, I inadvertently took the whole through my own arms and body, by receiving the fire from the united top wires with one hand, while the other held a chain connected with the outsides of both jars. The company present (whose talking to me, and to one another, I supposed occasioned my inattention to what I was about) say, that the flash was very great, and the crack as loud as a pistol; yet, my senses being instantly gone, I neither saw the one nor heard the other . . . Nothing remains now of this shock, but a soreness in my breast-bone, which feels as if it had been bruised. I did not fall, but suppose I should have been knocked down, if I had received the stroke in my head. The whole was over in less than a minute.

  You may communicate this to Mr. Bowdoin, as a caution to him, but do not make it more public, for I am ashamed to have been guilty of so notorious a blunder; a match for that of the Irishman, whom my sister told me of, who, to divert his wife, poured the bottle of gunpowder on the live coal; or of the other, who, being about to steal powder, made a hole in the cask with a hot iron. I am yours, &c.

                           B. Franklin

P.S. The jars hold six gallons each.

Deferential Society, Status Politics

After the eight proprietors of the Carolinas got their charter in 1663, the area was first settled largely from the West Indies. Conditions were not suitable for cultivation of either of the customary staples of the New World—sugar and tobacco—so a good many possibilities were tested: silk, olives, wine, flax and hemp, wheat and barley, indigo and cotton. The first great success came with rice, seemingly beginning about 1694–1696. The crop was confined to the flat coastal plain, particularly along the Cooper River and the Ashley River, which provided cheap transit to Charleston for the bulky and inexpensive product. Both rivers were named after one of the proprietors, Anthony Ashley Cooper, first Earl of Shaftesbury; Charleston, so parochial Carolinians held, is where the Ashley joins the Cooper to form the Atlantic Ocean. The proprietors had kept the right to appoint the secretary and the surveyor of the colony, and their chief duty was to issue and record land patents. That was the nub: the man who could gain title to rich acres in the right spot was on the way to a fortune. Exports of rice, a mere 3,000 barrels in 1713, soared to 100,000 barrels by 1724. Often a planter could get a profit of 50 per cent on his annual outlay. The situation of the Carolina gentry got better and better. The price of rice was depressed from 1744 to 1749, but by then the planters had found a second staple—indigo, which was introduced from the West Indies in 1742. To improve further an already posh situation, Parliament in 1748 voted to pay a bounty of sixpence a pound on indigo. The dyestuff sold in England at 3–6 shillings a pound, so here again the planter could frequently reap a net yield of 33 per cent or more. (See Figure 8-3.)

With an established and profitable staple, the Low Country grew quickly. The population of South Carolina in 1730 was only about 12,000 persons. By the time of the Revolution the Low Country had 110,000 inhabitants. Charles Town (to be Charleston) and Savannah together had 14,000 residents. In the three rice counties outside of Charles Town, slaves outnumbered whites by 18 to 1. Whites, sparse even in winter, disappeared almost entirely during the hot months; a common saw had it that the Low Country was heaven in the spring, hell in summer, and a hospital in the autumn. Newport, Rhode Island was a popular summer resort for Carolina gentry. Slaves did not have the same option to move about for seasonal reasons, and their mortality rates were high. But for the rice planters, the more blacks, the more profits, and they sought not only to replace but to expand their labor force. By 1770 the importation of slaves into Carolina was 3,000 or more a year.

Nobody alive today can fully grasp the horrors of the Middle Passage— so-called because the customary route of a slave ship was from its home port to West Africa, thence to the New World to sell the blacks, and back to its base. Even the inmates of prisons and concentration camps get a little fresh air, but on a slaver this benefice was scanty in all weather and unknown when the seas ran high so that the hatches had to be closed. The blacks were simply stuffed into the hold. Some captains were loose packers, but most were tight packers; it was said that a man did not have as much space as a corpse in a coffin. The only food might be some boiled grain. Disease was everywhere. Fatalities were frequent. Slavers were known to make the crossing without killing off a single captive; in 1679 when the *Sun of Africa* (the irony of that name) finished the run from the Gold Coast to Martinique she had lost only seven of 250. Such good fortune was providential. Ships were known to lose their entire "cargo," to the last man. Remaining records suggest that of every eight blacks driven onto slave ships, only seven lived to touch land again.

Ruling the black brigades of forced labor were the planters and their overseers. Of a white population in South Carolina in 1765 of perhaps 30,000, no more than 2,000 were planters. Few, but potent. Their sources of income were several. Many of them did not live on their plantations, which were managed by overseers while the owner resided in the city and had another career as merchant-shipowner. The colony continued to export large amounts of deerskins from the Indian trade. From 1740 to 1776 its output of indigo rose

FIGURE 4-1. *Westover, Home of William Byrd II*

Westover on the James River in Charles City County, Virginia was the chief residence of William Byrd II. This plantation had been in the family for three generations. William I, who inherited it from an uncle, had built a manor out of wood. When the property was devised to William II, probably after 1730, he rebuilt the mansion in brick. So it remains two and a half centuries later, one of the dozen or so most decorous and pleasing Georgian mansions in the New World. The Palladian design of the stately winged structure, with its gentle symmetry, was suggested by a house in Epsom, Surrey, England. Thus the house is another example of the migration of European culture to America.

In accord with a custom of the rich, destined to be revived much later in the "family room" of the less rich, William II had a billiard table where he whiled away the hours with visitors. He also frequently shot billiards in the evening with his wife. Matters stood differently with his library. He owned 3,600 volumes, a figure remarkable in our day and incredible in his. The Westover library included the classics: Homer and Lucian and Plutarch and Cicero. Byrd read the moderns like Machiavelli, Bacon, Erasmus, Thomas More. His diary notes an occasion when Mrs. Byrd wanted to borrow a book. He refused to lend it to her. Women may be all right in pool halls, but keep them out of libraries.

four times; rice exports trebled. Some of the fortunes were a scandal; Henry Laurens, himself a planter, commented in 1750: "The planters are full of money." One Carolinian owned 50,000 acres and 800 slaves. They were *nouveau riches* and their behavior showed it. So did their anxieties. According to the *South Carolina Gazette* on the eve of the Revolution: "Their whole lives are one continued Race; in which everyone is endeavoring to distance all behind him; and to overtake or pass by, all before him; everyone is flying from his inferiors in Pursuit of his Superiors, who fly from him, with equal Alacrity. . . . The better sort of Gentry, who can aim no higher, plunge themselves into Debt and Dependance, to preserve their Rank." In terms of wealth and income, South Carolina planters stood at the pinnacle of colonial society; nowhere else was the leisure class so numerous. But for more than one of them, the concept of culture extended no farther than powdering his wig before he went to Anglican services.

In Virginia some gentry had grown up with wealth and learned to use it well. William Byrd II (1674–1744) was the grandson of a goldsmith in London, son of a planter of the same name. Packed off to England for his education at the age of seven, he stayed there until he was twenty-two. He was tutored in business in the Netherlands as well as in England, and trained in the law at the Middle Temple. Once back in Virginia, he was chosen at once (it pays to have the right father) to the House of Burgesses. He was in London again when the elder William Byrd died in 1704, but he set in train a program aimed at capturing his father's public offices: member of the Governor's Council of Virginia, auditor for the colony, receiver-general of the province's taxes. He won in part. The last two offices were split up, and he became only receiver-general. He had to stand on the doorstep for five years to be named to the Council—but before he died he was its president.

In spite of his opulent and rustic existence, Byrd did not have a placid home life. He spatted with his wife daily, cheated on her weekly, and he may have sighed with gratification when she died in 1716. A sly footnote on his attitudes occurs in his journal for 1711, when the governor of Virginia was giving a ball in honor of Queen Anne's birthday. Mrs. Byrd wanted to pluck her eyebrows for the occasion: "My wife and I quarreled about her pulling her brows. She threatened she would not go to Williamsburg if she might not pull them; I refused, however, and got the better of her and maintained my authority."

The proper uses of both books and women are revealed in the entry for a single day in June 1718, when he was in London as the official agent for the government of Virginia:

16. I rose about 8 o'clock and read a chapter in Hebrew and some Greek in Lucian. I said my prayers, and had milk for breakfast. The weather was cloudy and warm, the wind southwest. About 10 o'clock Colonel came to see me but did

FIGURE 4-2. *Bruton Parish Church: The Governor's Pew*

The governor's pew in Bruton Parish Church, Williamsburg, Virginia serves well as an embodiment of deferential politics. The structure, of red brick, was built 1711–1715. A strange, although perhaps representative, addition came later. By 1769 the power of the Anglican church in the colony had been seriously eroded. The revenues of its clergy had been challenged and diminished. Thousands of members had deserted it to become Baptists or Methodists. But in that year Bruton Parish added a tower spire to its church.

By then, a related conflict was absorbing much energy. Since the Church of England had no bishop anywhere in America, every one of its priests had to go to the mother country for confirmation. A movement arose to have a bishop appointed to the colonies. Strong opposition arose, and it has been suggested that patriot leaders were influenced by this conflict in the period preceding the Declaration of Independence.

In province after province, the governor had been forced to yield before the legislature's power. The House of Burgesses in Virginia had been especially effective in swinging the whip of taxes and appropriations, but it had other weapons as well (see the end of this chapter on burgess appointments and elections). The governor retained considerable weight in regard to warfare; it was he for example who named George Washington to head the colony's militia. His formal authority in the Church of England was nil. But his status as the leading parishioner in Virginia is made obvious by this illustration. The pews occupied by the congregation do not appear in the photograph; they directly confront the pulpit. But to right of the priest sat the governor, in his personal stall, on his throne, almost majestic in his solitude. The private pews beyond the governor (toward top of picture) were used by his family and guests.

not stay because my chariot was come. About twelve I went to the Virginia Coffeehouse and saw Captain Randolph just come from Virginia. Then I went to Mr. Perry's and dined with Mike and ate some fish. After dinner I wrote a letter and then went and sat with Mrs. Cole, a milliner, and ate some cherries. Then I went to Chelsea and saw Mrs. A-l-c for the last time because she had played the whore. However I drank tea with her and about 8 o'clock returned to London and went to Will's where I read the news and then went to the Union Tavern to meet a young women who supped with me and I ate some roast chicken and then we went to the bagnio on Silver Street, where I lay all night with her and rogered her three times and found her very straight and unprecocious and very sweet and agreeable. I slept very little.

He was scarcely back at Westover in February 1720 before he wrote, "I began to kiss my girl Annie," and by May he would write: "At night I talked with my people and committed uncleanness with Annie." "My people" were of course the slaves. Of Westover he wrote: "I have a large Family of my own, and my Doors are open to Every Body, yet I have no Bills to pay, and half-a-Crown will rest undisturbed in my Pocket for many Moons together. Like one of the Patriarchs, I have my Flocks and my Herds, my Bond-men and Bond-women, and every Soart of Trade amongst my own Servants, so that I live in a kind of Independence on every one but Providence."

Patriarchs demand bowing and scraping. Byrd kicked a maid for lighting a candle before it was dark. He beat a cook who had not boiled the bacon long enough. Even white folks had to stay in their place: when a tailor in Virginia in 1674, the year of the birth of William Byrd II, presumed to enter a horse he owned in a contest, the court fined him a hundred pounds of tobacco because it was "contrary to law for a laborer to make a race, being a sport only for gentlemen." They demanded deference, and nearly always they got it. A biting bit of testimony was set down in the memoirs of his boyhood left by a Virginian, born in 1733 as the son of a carpenter and small landowner, who rose to take orders in the Anglican church and claim his own parish: "We were accustomed to look upon, what were called *gentle folks,* as beings of a superior order. For my part, I was quite shy of *them,* and kept off at a humble distance. A *periwig,* in those days, was a distinguishing badge of *gentle folk*—and when I saw a man riding the road, near our house, with a wig on, it would so alarm my fears, and give me such a disagreeable feeling, that, I dare say, I would run off, as for my life. Such ideas of the difference between *gentle* and *simple,* were, I believe, universal among all of my rank and age."

A Pennsylvania counterpart of Byrd was his exact contemporary James Logan (1674–1751). Just as the Virginian could read easily in Hebrew, Greek, Latin, French, and Italian, so the Philadelphian could handle all of those languages plus Spanish. Logan's library of more than 3,000 volumes included dictionaries and grammars of Anglo-Saxon, Portuguese, Polish, Magyar, German, Dutch, Arabic, Turkish, Syriac, Samaritan, Ethiopian, and Persian. Just as Byrd remodelled his home at Westover, so Logan at the same time built a brick country house five miles from Philadelphia on the Germantown road. He called it Stenton after his father's birthplace in Scotland. If Byrd nuzzled in the ambience of his household slaves, Logan kept at Stenton ten servants, blacks as well as whites. By handling the business affairs in America of the province's proprietor and by assiduous cultivation of the fur trade with the Indians, the son of a poor Quaker schoolmaster in Ulster had done right well by himself. When he died his estate measured 18,000 acres of good land and £8,500 in cash and bonds.

After Pennsylvania was founded in 1682 by its proprietor, it grew apace. This development seems paradoxical, for the founder of the Society of Friends, George Fox, had counselled, "My friends, that are gone, and are going over to plant, and make outward plantations in America, keep your own plantations in your hearts, with the spirit and power of God, that your own vines and lilies be not hurt." Pennsylvania's growth was in large measure due to its policy of toleration; "No man, nor number of men upon earth," declared William Penn, "hath power or authority to rule over men's consciences in religious matters." James Logan came to America in 1699 as Penn's secretary. When the latter went home, the former stayed. As commercial agent for generations of the founding family, he faced both eastward to England and westward to the frontier. Submerged in politics, he served straight through from 1702 to 1747 as a member of the Governor's Council. He gave the young Franklin his first large print order in 1731. He chatted often with the printer on scientific subjects, about which he had a voracious curiosity; he even served as a patient in Franklin's endeavors to cure palsy with electric shocks.

Increasingly he lived for his library, even though his efforts as a collector ran many perils, such as the time when one of his ships was wrecked and looted in Delaware Bay. The thieves were outraged when they came upon a trunk of "useless Latin Books," and in their wrath they tossed the volumes into the mid-winter tides. But in spite of hazards, he said, "Books are my disease." He owned seven editions of Homer, six of Horace, four of Virgil, three each of Aeschylus and Sophocles, several of Plato and Aristotle. He had two copies of the Koran and the works of Confucius and Moses Maimonides. Although he owned the first two editions of Newton's *Principia,* when a third was issued in 1726 he bought that too. He was disgusted to see that the author had deleted a passage in the earlier versions that gave Leibnitz equal credit with himself for discovering the differential calculus. He grieved over "the prevalency of human passions even in the greatest."

Logan ordered many of his books from London or bought at auction in New York, but he also patronized the local bookdealer, Robert Bell. This Scot had wicked habits: he publicly kept a mistress, he fathered a bastard. But he was an innovator when it came to merchandizing books. He brought out cheap reprints of many recent English works. He advertised in newspapers every-where in the colonies. He developed the auction, which had appeared in

Philadelphia by 1744, into a form of art; he would stand on the platform with a beer, tell jokes, act the clown, get the audience laughing. It was more fun than the theater, and it moved books at high prices. Bell was the man who auctioned away the holdings of William Byrd II, of which "perhaps as many as 40 waggon loads" arrived in Philadelphia.

The opulent merchants of Philadelphia were no levellers. One Quaker pundit was at pains to disavow such notions in his *An Apology for the True Christian Divinity* (1680):

> The several conditions, under which men are diversly stated, together with their Educations answering thereunto, do sufficiently show this: the *Servant* is not the same way Educated as the *Master*; nor the *Tenant* as the *Landlord*; nor the *Rich* as the *Poor*; nor the *Prince* as the *Peasant*. . . . *Let the Brother of high degree rejoice that he is abased, and such as God calls in low degree, to be content with their Condition, not envying those Brethren, who have greater abundance, knowing they have received abundance as to the inward Man*; which is chiefly to be regarded.

The Quakers did not yet enjoin the severe style of dress that would come later; they eschewed ruffles and other fripperies, but they liked to wear bright colors and the finest fabrics, and those who could afford it strutted around in velvet as like as not. No egalitarianism for them. They preached the same old hierarchical, organic society that William Hubbard had prattled about in the seventeenth century.

Conditions were against their ideal. Franklin and Logan were among the leaders in starting an English-language academy (it would become the College of Philadelphia, now the University of Pennsylvania). To publicize their intention Franklin wrote a pamphlet. It concluded: "Thus instructed, Youth will come out of this School fitted for learning any Business, Calling, or Profession, except such wherein Languages are required. . . ." Clearly this goal violated the received plan of variant educations for different social classes. But in the fluid society of Philadelphia, with its many openings for personal advancement, it was sensible. After all, it had taken Franklin a mere twenty-five years after he arrived in the city a penniless lad, to accumulate sufficient capital to retire from active business. Small wonder that he could write in his "Advice to a Young Tradesman": "Remember that time is money."

Not only was the content of education changing, but so were the institutions that provided it. Historically the foremost had been the family. Supplementary to this was the farflung device of apprenticeship, which had the master conveying both a craft and also more generalized precepts. These relations were massively conservative, with the adults seeking to pass on to their juniors the traditional lore. In the New World, especially in its cities, the old ways tended to crumble. Masters might still communicate a trade to their apprentices, but little more. The number of instructors outside the home became diversified: preachers, printers, professional teachers. Whereas the old society had used the "mysteries" of education as a way of controlling a man's station and thus of preserving the conventional order, in the new society the custody of learning was transferred to schools, where it was available to growing numbers.

Another corrosive of custom in Pennsylvania was the steady flow of immigrants. One spyglass through which to view developments in the province can be brought in focus with one phrase: Think Ethnic. Nearly all of the early settlers were English, but after 1720 a good many Scots-Irish began to arrive, and a decade later the influx of Germans became substantial. A smattering of Protestant French and Catholic Irish also came prior to the Revolution. The former homogeneity of background and manners disappeared. No longer could one say that a Philadelphian was a transplanted Englishman, and what became true in Pennsylvania had been true in New York ever since the days of Dutch rule. New England, in contrast, went on being exactly that—English.

Quite a few migrants remained in the few seaboard towns, but more invaded the hinterland. Writers have discussed this development in varying terms: The seventeenth century has been termed by some as "the deep-water period" of American history, when virtually all settlement was within ten miles or so of the Atlantic. The eighteenth century, when men started to make portages in order to push farther up the rivers, has been called "the shallow-water period." These ventures carried population above the "Fall Line"—an imaginary line connecting the most seaward waterfall on each river. In places it is ten miles from the ocean; in others, forty. Below it to the Atlantic is the Tidewater, a phrase applied particularly to the South and especially to Virginia, meaning the region below the waterfalls where the rivers still have a tidal flow. Above the Fall Line in the South is the Piedmont (literally from the French, the foot of the mountain), the foothills. The "back country" is a most imprecise expression meaning usually the Piedmont and what lies beyond it.

In the Middle Colonies and in New England, the penetration of the frontier took place first along such rivers as the Hudson and the Connecticut. Vast tracts between the coastal region and the river valleys would remain almost empty for decades. At the fall line it was necessary to transship goods from ocean-going vessels to shallow flat-bottomed boats, so along this line appeared a host of new towns:* in Virginia, Petersburg and Richmond and Fredericksburg; in New Jersey, Trenton and New Brunswick; in Massachusetts, Waltham on the Charles River. The presence of a falls and the resulting availability of water power would eventually make these towns into centers of manufacturing. Waltham, for instance, became the site of the first

---

*A definition. The U.S. Census defines an "urban" resident as living in a town of 2,500 or more inhabitants. Anybody who is not urban is "rural." These usages will be followed here.

integrated (both spinning thread and weaving cloth) cotton-textile mill any-where in the New World. We can also use Waltham to point up a potential danger in making historical inferences. In most instances the best opening move in understanding a historical event is to go to the site and see it for yourself, to get the lay of the land. But this strategy can be misleading: for example, the falls in the Charles at Waltham would originally have been fairly abrupt and would have generated much more power a hundred and fifty years ago than they could produce today when so much of the river's water is backed up into a polluted basin or pond. And our current increasing concern about pollution must remind us that man has been constantly revising his environ-ment. Often it is not possible to study a past episode by inspecting the location; it no longer exists.

The seepage of population into the frontier north of the Mason-Dixon Line is less dramatic by far than the rush into the Southern back country. As to people living above the Fall Line in 1776, the figures alone tell much of the story:

	Population	Per Cent of the Colony
Western Maryland	40,000	20
Great Valley of Virginia	53,000	11.8
North Carolina Piedmont	61,695	40
South Carolina Piedmont	82,942	49
Georgia back country	4,682	14.5

The surge into and finally beyond the Appalachians can be dated from 1716. Hoping to block the French incursions from Canada by seizing control of the mountain passes, Governor Alexander Spottswood of Virginia led an exploration by fifty gentlemen (plus slaves and Indian guides) over the Blue Ridge and down into the Shenandoah Valley. They knew it was a historic deed. The governor presented each of his peers with a horseshoe made of gold; they were known as the Knights of the Golden Horseshoe. But they were not emulated for several years. As late as 1730 the only whites in Virginia's back country were a few hunters and Indian traders. When the white intruders came, they were not moving westward at all, but southward from Philadelphia. They were not Americans, but Germans mainly from the Palatinate or Scots-Irish from Ulster. Having entered through the country's largest port, they turned south.

The Great Philadelphia Wagon Road could be navigated by Conestoga wagons for some 735 miles. It was made possible when the Iroquois in 1744 by the Treaty of Lancaster permitted use of their Great Warrior's Path down the Shenandoah Valley. Following the valleys, it ran for miles below Salisbury in North Carolina along the Cherokee Trading Path. This was the busiest thoroughfare in America; the Great Philadelphia Wagon Road in the last

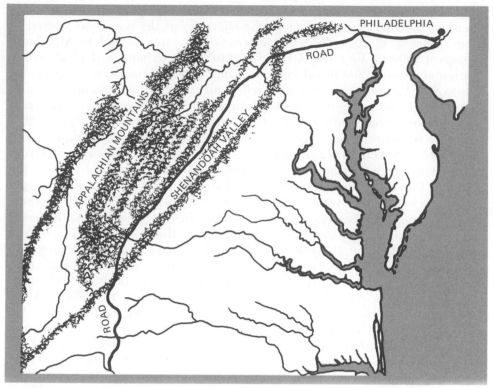

FIGURE 4-3. *The Great Philadelphia Wagon Road*

fifteen years before the Revolution may well have carried more traffic than all the other major roads combined. From 1730 to 1750 the flood of whites moved into the Great Valley and the Piedmont in Virginia. For the next five years, migrants hived into the upcountry of North Carolina. Until 1760 the Cherokees blocked entry into South Carolina, but then the gush began. By the Revolution the back country contained half of the people in South Carolina—and 79 per cent of its whites.

Most numerous among these migrants into the South were the Scots-Irish; next, Germans. Few had the skills they needed to pioneer; many could not use an axe or a hoe to good effect. The English and Scots-Irish were usually slovenly farmers. They cruised restlessly onto each new frontier. Instead of clearing land they lazily girdled the trees to kill them and planted their sparse crops among the stumps. Germans were different. Often they settled in their own agricultural villages where German would be the everyday tongue for generations. In regions like the northern half of the Great Valley, which they pretty much pre-empted, they actually cleared their land. Some farms would remain in the same family centuries later.

The emerging society was rough-and-tumble, partly because of its situation, perhaps more because of the character of the men who created it. From 1745 to 1775, some 9,000 convicts were transported to Maryland, perhaps 13,000 to Virginia. At least a third and perhaps half of all white immigrants prior to the Revolution were indentured servants, redemptioners, or convicts. They were a boozing bunch, at all ranks in the community. For all the recent hosannas about the comradeship manifested by cabin-raisings and corn-huskings, a contemporary said sourly, "things never go well at such a gathering for more time is spent in drinking brandy than in working." The daily beverages were hard cider and brandy made from peaches or apples; rum and rye whiskey were also consumed widely. Morality was loose (save in the tight-knit German villages). In the Great Valley a nabob might openly keep a mistress, while a major citizen was reputed to share his with his two brothers and his son, "tho these are the first people in this county." An observer remarked "nothing but whores and rogues in this country." The tavern supplemented the church as the two props of the backcountry. The grogshop might even supplant the chapel; it was said that some peckerwoods had never seen a minister, never heard a sermon or prayer, knew nothing of Scripture.

In some respects life was the same in the Low Country and the Piedmont. Diets were similar. The favored meats were beef and pork plus what wild game you could come by. Indian corn was the staple, but potatoes and peas were common. Children gathered wild fruits and nuts. Neither in Virginia nor in Carolina were men keen for growing vegetables (William Byrd would touch only asparagus and peas. Apparently he subsisted on little but meat or fish with wine. He was not for breads or baked desserts). In Virginia and Maryland the planters did not feud with the back country. They allowed it representation in the state capitols, provided law and justice, gave security to land titles. Matters sat differently in the Carolinas. Rancor against the seaboard was intense in the piney woods. Representation in the legislature was unfair. So were taxes. In South Carolina the only courts were in Charleston, so that a man might have to travel for days merely to get a marriage license or to register a transfer of real estate. These grievances help to account for the numerous Tories in the Carolinas during the Revolution (earlier the back country had rebelled as the Regulators). They had little love for the English, but still less for the Low Country grandees.

The flows of population meant shifts of power. (Let us define power as an ability to influence the behavior of others. Absolute power might be termed "control.") The tobacco planters of the Tidewater faced actual bankruptcy by 1765; the only men still prosperous were those like George Washington who turned to wheat as a cash crop. But as the seaboard aristocracy waned, a new governing group was forming above the fall line. The backcountry was never a classless Arcadia. From early days the Great Valley held so many gentry that a brisk market existed for indentured servants; "meere Irish" brought £15 to £24. In addition to their plantations the well-to-do might set up an iron mill. Some went into shipbuilding and trade. They trafficked in convicts and in slaves. But most of all they tried to amass huge tracts of land by getting grants from the government of the province. Riches meant status, and status brought privileges. "Important political positions," wrote one historian, "went first to gentlemen everywhere in the interior." As was said of the wellborn George Fairfax in Virginia, "Family, Fortune and good sense all entitle him to a place there."

The old edifices were being wrenched and strained, but they were not about to collapse. What we must understand is the tension, enduring for many generations, of permanence versus change, of stability versus fluidity, of hierarchy versus democracy. In the brief era when the New Sweden Company was trying to maintain its colony on the Delaware, one of its agents moaned "Here are as many who will scatter as there are who will hold things together." To keep his settlers the governor was forced to concede the Ordinance of 1655 which gave a measure of self-government. When a Puritan minister wailed "The cause of Christ in New Haven is miserably lost." and led his flock away to found Newark in 1666, his intent was to have close-knit agricultural towns. They slivered as men chose to build homes on their farms.

Similar processes acted from the earliest times around Boston.* A few examples might sweep away widely held illusions. For one, Northerners have a predilection for believing that racism is peculiar to prejudiced Southerners. In 1716 Samuel Sewall of Boston, who had served as judge in the Salem witchcraft trials in 1692 only to recant his role,** tried to prevent the taxation of Negroes and Indians on the same basis as hogs and horses. He failed. Late in the eighteenth century the Congress of the United States held no member who was more vocal in defense of the slave trade than John Brown of Rhode Island. But men felt counter urges. When a fellow judge was slated to preside at the trial of a man charged with killing his slave, Samuel Sewall wrote the magistrate: "The poorest boys and girls within this province, such as are of the lowest condition; whether they be English, or Indians, or Ethiopians. They have the same right to religion and life, that the richest heirs have. And they who go about to deprive them of this right, they attempt the bombarding of HEAVEN: and the shells they throw, will fall down on their own heads."

Faith in special providences lingered. Samuel Sewall, on the day after the coronation in 1661 of Charles II, left England for America. He was a boy of nine, and the weather on that occasion seemed prophetic: "The Thunder and Lightening of it." (Note also that the storm was equally an omen to the adult

---

*Here begins a brief backtrack to the 17th century. Readers might test it against a sentence from de Tocqueville: "If we carefully examine the social and political state of America, after having studied its history, we shall remain perfectly convinced that not an opinion, not a custom, not a law, I may even say not an event is upon record which the origin of that people will not explain."
**These trials have drawn far too much attention and have given Salem a bad name it did not deserve. Nearly everybody at the time, in England and on the Continent and in America, believed in witches.

and urbane Londoner Samuel Pepys.) The hurricane of witches that swept over Massachusetts Bay was taken as only one sign of God's displeasure with his wayward Saints. When a great fire roared through Boston, a celebrated divine gave a sermon: "Have not Burdens been carried through the Streets on the Sabbath Day? Have not Bakers, Carpenters and other Tradesmen been employed in Servile Works on the Sabbath Day? When I saw this . . . my heart said, Will not the Lord for this Kindle a Fire in Boston?"

If Southern rednecks were sometimes disorderly, so were Bostonians. The town book of the city for 1661 states: "It is ordered tht if any person shall discharge a gunn in the meetinghouse, or any other house without leave of the owner or house holder, hee or they shall forfeit five shillings for every such offense nor shall any person ride or lead a horse into the meetinghouse under a like penalty." If Pocahontas cavorted nude in Jamestown, a "young and tender chaste woman" in Boston topped her act. The lady withdrew from her congregation. Legally she could not do so, and she was summoned to explain her reasons. She refused. As a rebuttal to members who indicted her for teaching false doctrine, she appeared at the Sunday services naked as a jaybird. By order of court she was tied to a fencepost and flogged with "a certain twenty or thirty cruel stripes." Her judges, perhaps with relish, watched from a tavern.

North as well as South the chief vent for dissatisfaction—and the chief curb on oligarchic tyranny—was further migration. Boston had hardly existed for five years when secessionists went west, for example, to found Watertown. Originally from East Anglia (Norfolk, Suffolk) which had no tradition of open-field agriculture, the pioneers divided up Watertown into personal plots of twenty-five to fifty acres. With each man running his farm as he pleased, self-aggrandizement ruled. Then came more migrants from other parts of England (Derbyshire, Hertfordshire, Sussex). They did not admire what they found in Watertown, for they had known "open fields" and farming in common, and many of them did not own enough farm tools to work a tract independently. Also, after 1635 the municipality at Watertown was not granting any more allotments of land. But in Massachusetts they did not need to mire down. They got a piece of land below Concord from the General Court, and they named it Sudbury after an English town.

In Sudbury, Suffolk, England, the mayor and burgesses had a free hand and never bothered with town meetings; if they were incompetent or venal the commoners could only appeal to God and ask why He was punishing them. Businessmen ran the place. An election was not a public matter; none was ever contested. No disputes occurred over appointments to civic posts; no petitions were filed against official edicts. To challenge an act by the mayor was a criminal offense. An analogous scheme was revealed in an order by the vestry of Berkhamsted, Hertfordshire, in 1631: "That warning be given at some convenient time before the next communion . . . that the meaner sort of people do not press into that seat in the chancel where the minister dothe usually begin to distribute the holy bread and cup, but leave it free for the Bailiff and such others who are fit to sit with him and next after him."

Efforts were made to impose strata in Sudbury, Massachusetts. Fine discriminations were made in carving up the meadowland: the minister got seventy-five acres, another man only one. Division was made by either of two shibboleths or by a combination of them: by the number of people in the family, or by the value of property they had brought with them. No religious tests were used. Although he had been favored in allocation of real estate, the first minister griped that he was not treated with due respect; in the words of the pastor of adjacent Concord: "Shall I tell you what I think to be the ground of all this insolency, which discovers itself in the speech of men? Truly, I cannot ascribe it so much to any outward thing, as to the putting of too much liberty and power into the hands of the multitude, which they are too weak to manage, many growing conceited, proud, self-sufficient, as wanting nothing." In Sudbury any man could show up at the town meeting to "move any seasonable questions or to present any necessary motion or complaint." Most town ordinances proclaimed: "ordered and agreed by the inhabitants of this town of Sudbury." This was not the village in England, where the magistrates decreed all.

By 1656 officials feared that the town common was being overgrazed, so they apportioned pasturage. One man, who owned eleven acres of meadowland and thus was allowed to feed five and a half "beasts" on the public forage, complained, "That it was oppression. If you oppresse the poore, they will cry out; and if you persecute us in one city, wee must fly to another." Flight was the elixir that soothed many wounds. Twelve of the aggrieved in Sudbury asked the General Court for a new grant of land a bit farther west. They got it, and founded the town of Marlborough. One leader had moved four times in his life. From Suffolk in England he went to Hertfordshire, then to Watertown in Massachusetts, thence to Sudbury, finally to Marlborough. In England he had been toward the bottom of society. In the New World he became a landowner elected to several civic offices.

The spiral of men moving upward must not be made to seem more general than it was or more rapid than it was. Precise quantification is not possible, but the contours of politics give a crude index. Family counted for much. Of the ninety-one members of the Council in Virginia from 1680 to the Revolution, five were named Page and three each Burwell, Byrd, Carter, Custis, Harrison, Lee, Ludwell, and Wormley. One lady in the province was called "Grandmother Lucy" by a sixth of the members of the Council in this century. Married three times, she by a Burwell and a Ludwell was the direct forebear of seven Councillors and of the wives of eight others. When Governor Spottswood brought a Ludwell on charges in 1716, he could not press the trial before the Council; since a majority of its members were related to the defendant no quorum could legally be impanelled. When Richard Henry Lee on 2 July, 1776, moved that the Continental Congress affirm the freedom and independence of the colonies, or when Robert E. Lee in 1862 was "charged" with the Confederate armies, they were taking roles for which they had been cast not since birth but since before conception. Well might Governor Spottswood rail at the "hereditary faction of designing men" who repeatedly stymied him. When Thomas Jefferson was in the same position later he would protest that the network of county magnates foiled all constructive efforts by the governor—an office in which he achieved little.

Analogous conditions prevailed in other provinces. Seven families yielded a quarter of all Councillors in South Carolina before Independence. In Maryland a Tasker was named to the Council in 1699, his son in 1722, his grandson in 1742; Bordleys were chosen in 1721, 1759, 1768; Thomas Addison was son of a Councillor, son-in-law of another, a Councillor himself, father-in-law of two, uncle of one, grandfather of one. North of the Mason-Dixon Line the same phenomenon reigned. In New York the scintillating feats of Alexander Hamilton were proper for a person of his immense gifts, but they also owed a bit to his father-in-law, the wealthy landowner-politician Philip Schuyler. Of the twenty-eight Councillors from 1750 to 1776, at least twenty-five belonged to some great landed family. Looking at the 111 men who were uppermost officials of Connecticut between the charter of 1662 and Independence, the typical person was elected and re-elected fourteen times. One man held a top post for thirty-eight years; two others for thirty-six each. Thus the colony was called "the Land of Steady Habits." Perhaps most amazing of all are the Winthrops: John was governor of Massachusetts, his son John the Younger was governor of Connecticut as was his grandson Fitz-John.*

George Washington's initiation into public office will provide a clear picture of deference politics, but first some background figures must be brought into sharp focus. In the conduct of government, Virginians saw no clash in the co-existence of aristocracy and democracy. The common man was no doormat; he had a say. Property qualifications for the suffrage did exist, but most men could meet them. You did not need to live in a county to vote for its two members in the House of Burgesses, so long as you owned sufficient land there. Thus a man could have the suffrage in more than one place. Many today would regard this as an anti-republican attribute, and so were other political institutions of the time. The county courts, like the Council of Virginia, knew no checks and balances, no balance of powers. They exercised whatever type of governmental rule they wished. They were virtually independent self-perpetuating bodies. Legally they were appointed by the governor, but in practice they chose themselves; if an appointee as justice of the peace was disliked by the incumbents, they would all resign *en bloc* until the nomination was removed.

Charles S. Sydnor has charted the way to power in a lucid study

---

*A couple of marginalia. The power of these dynasties will explain the Southern practice of using family names as given names: Tasker H. Bliss, a general and member of the Supreme War Council, was a member of the peace commission to Versailles; the member of the Virginia senate from the Hampton district in 1966 was Hunter Booker Andrews, and so on. Likewise in the North, legactic oligarchies have not died out, as the makeup of the Corporation of Harvard University will reveal. Lamonts have had their seat, Shattucks theirs.

(published in 1952). He showed that to be named to a county court, you had to be one of the gentry, and also acceptable to that faction of your peers holding power at the moment. For election as a burgess, it was necessary further to be at least palatable to the voters—the freeholders. The common man had to pick. In Sydnor's words, "The House of Burgesses was made up of gentlemen, but only of gentlemen who were acceptable to ordinary men." Selection to higher place within the province (and ultimately to national office) depended almost entirely on the favor of your fellow burgesses. "The freeholders sent men to the Assembly, but only the Assembly sent men to higher places."*

Designation of two burgesses from each county was the only type of election that Virginia had. All other civic jobs were appointive. The mode of election was straightforward. All voters in the county met at the polls on a given day. As a freeholder heard his name called he stepped before the sheriff, was asked how he would vote, and replied. This *viva voce* method of public voting was a hobble on humbler men; if you were deeply in debt to a planter (or wanted to be) you were likely to speak while glancing apprehensively at him. We can see similar forces shaping the clique in Parliament called "the King's Men" during the days of George III, and again in many parts of eighteenth-century New England the town meeting operated similarly. Often vaunted as a "bastion of democracy," the town meeting in fact functioned much of the time as a way for the ruling group to mobilize consent to policies that it had already determined.

George Washington (1732–1799) did not build the stately mansion of Mount Vernon; his older brother did. Lawrence died in 1752, and a few years later George came into the estate. A man of property, he reached for power. On his first try at becoming a burgess, in 1755, he lost. The next time around, on 24 July 1758, he was better prepared. He used scarcely covert coercion. The military duties of Colonel Washington kept him away from the polls at Frederick Court House (now Winchester) but his friends were there. The first vote was by Thomas Lord Fairfax, prominent landlord and ranking magistrate of the Frederick County Court. He was for George. The next came from the Anglican pastor, the leading cleric in the county. He was for George. Then two colonels voted; two for George. Two more ministers, Baptist and Presbyterian, were for George. Four listed on the rolls as "gentlemen" were for George. Before any of the *hoi polloi* raised their sails, they knew how the tide had set and which way the wind was blowing. Washington's agent had another device: for the 391 voters plus the riffraff lounging about, he set up 160 gallons—50 gallons of rum punch, 28 gallons of rum, 46 of beer, 34 of wine, 2 of cider royal. It came to about a quart and a half per man. George finished at the top of the list of four contenders. He was a burgess.

---

*A generation that has seen as aspirants to the Presidency of the United States such men of inherited wealth as Barry Goldwater, Averell H. Harriman, John F. Kennedy, Robert F. Kennedy, Nelson Rockefeller, and Franklin Delano Roosevelt must understand the importance of family.

Look at another first family of Virginia, the Blands. The American founder of the line, Theodore, came from England in 1654. Before he died in 1671 he was a country squire, Speaker of the House of Burgesses, and for seven years a Councillor. His son Richard was a justice of the peace and a burgess. Theodore's grandson, Richard, Jr., was also a "j.p." and from 1742 until 1775 a burgess. Then for five years, 1761–1765, his son in turn was the other burgess from Prince George County.

Just as Chapter 3 argued a close relation of trade to changes in ideology, so has this one contended for the interaction of social structure with politics. In every province, a hierarchy existed. It was more fluid than in Europe, but the upper tier tried to keep distinct rigidity. The governing class consisted of the well-born who had wealth, prestige, and power. They monopolized the dominant offices of government. The richest and the haughtiest were in South Carolina, where the planters tended to live in Charles Town and to double as merchants or lawyers. But the oligarchs of Philadelphia and New York and Boston were not true believers in democracy either. Forces were working, however, to bite chinks into this pyramid. The ranks of the aristocracy were steadily infiltrated by meaner sorts who had made a lot of money. To switch the metaphor, the chief solvent of the organic society (Every man in his proper station) was free or cheap land. The historian who wants to understand the emergence of a relatively equalitarian American does not need the patience of a geologist who thinks in terms of millenia—but for some trends he does need to study his data in terms of centuries.

SOME NOTABLE EVENTS

1691 Crown government replaces the Calvert proprietorship in Maryland.

1702 East and West Jersey united to form New Jersey.

1704 Lower Counties of Pennsylvania split off to form the separate province of Delaware.

1710 Great German migration to Middle Colonies begins; by Independence it will bring 65,000 persons to Pennsylvania.

1713 North and South Carolina split apart.

1715 Maryland again becomes a Calvert proprietary, remains so until the Revolution.

1732 Scots-Irish migration into Southern upcountry begins.
North and South Carolina become royal colonies.
Charter for Georgia granted to 21 trustees.

1744 Treaty with Iroquois opens Great Philadelphia Wagon Road.

1752 Gregorian (New Style) calendar replaces the Julian (Old Style); henceforth the year begins on January 1 rather than March 25.

Ways to Study History IV

Find some new evidence. Occasionally a major source of information is found after it has been lost to view for decades, or even centuries. *Of Plymouth Plantation* by William Bradford, who died in 1657, was not published until 1856. By that time the manuscript had wandered into the library of the Bishop of London, England; as to whatever devious path it had taken to get there, we can only surmise some of the steps. The original was given to the Commonwealth of Massachusetts in 1897.

In 1648 the Bay Colony printed a compendium of its statutes as the *Book of the General Lawes and Libertyes concerning the Inhabitants of the Massachusetts.* Two centuries later not a single copy could be found. Then a copy turned up in a library in Rye, England. Sold in 1906, it then passed for a while from one to another of that select coterie of dealers who handle rare books and documents. At last a private collector bought it. He refused to let any historians look at it. Finally, by a special providence, he died. His heirs put the quarto volume up for sale, and it was purchased by a more generous tycoon. It is now in the Huntington Library, San Marino, California, available to scholars. A perfect duplicate was printed by the Harvard University Press.

Rembrandt Peale was a well-known painter of the early nineteenth century, but his portrait of Thomas Jefferson was out of sight for more than a century, and was only found recently. The Princeton University Press issued a handsome reproduction in color.

The only great poet to live in the American colonies was Edward Taylor of Massachusetts (1642–1729; see Document 4-1). He left 400 pages of verse, but his poems remained unknown for more than 200 years until they were collected and published in 1937.

Document 4-1

Nearly all of the significant literature from colonial America is prose: sermons, autobiographies, histories. The exception is Edward Taylor. A pious Puritan who emigrated to Massachusetts for religious reasons after the Restoration, he graduated from Harvard and ministered until he died to a congregation in the Connecticut Valley. He also farmed, and he served his town as physician. His poems make concrete what is mystical and holy by using images from everyday life. His poem "Houswifery" shows the need of every frontier household to make its own homespun. (Spelling and punctuation modernized. Courtesy of Princeton University Press.)

Make me, O Lord, thy spinning wheel complete.
 Thy holy word my distaff make for me.
Make mine affections thy swift flyers neat
 And make my soul thy holy spool to be.
 My conversation make to be thy reel,
 And reel the yarn thereon spun on thy wheel.

Make me thy loom then, knit therein this twine,
 And make thy holy spirit, Lord, wind quills.
Then weave the web thyself. The yarn is fine.
 Thine ordinances make my fulling mills.
 Then dye the same in heavenly colors choice,
 All pinked with varnished flowers of Paradise.

Then clothe therewith mine understanding, will,
 Affections, judgment, conscience, memory,
My words and actions, that their shine may fill
 My ways with glory, and thee glorify.
 Then mine apparel shall display before ye
 That I am clothed in holy robes for glory.

Document 4-2

This propaganda tract by Benjamin Franklin was probably written in 1782 while he was minister in France. "Information to Those Who Would Remove to America" was translated and widely reprinted in Europe.

Who then are the kind of persons to whom an emigration to America may be advantageous? and what are the advantages they may reasonably expect?

Land being cheap in that country from the vast forests still void of inhabitants, and not likely to be occupied in an age to come, insomuch that the propriety of a hundred acres of fertile soil full of wood may be obtained near the frontiers, in many places, for eight or ten guineas, hearty young laboring men, who understand the husbandry of corn and cattle, which is nearly the same in that country as in Europe, may easily establish themselves there. A little money saved of the good wages they receive there, while they work for others, enables them to buy the land and begin their plantation, in which they are assisted by the good-will of their neighbors, and some credit. Multitudes of poor people from England, Ireland, Scotland, and Germany, have, by this means, in a few years become wealthy farmers, who, in their own countries, where all the lands are fully occupied, and the wages of labor low, could never have emerged from the poor condition wherein they were born. . . . Tolerably good workmen in any of those mechanic arts are sure to find employ, and to be well paid for their work, there being no restraints preventing strangers from exercising any art they understand, nor any permission necessary. If they are poor, they begin first as servants or journeymen; and if they are sober, industrious, and frugal, they soon become masters, establish themselves in business, marry, raise families, and become respectable citizens.

Document 4-3

In seducing emigrants from Europe, Benjamin Franklin did not tell the full truth. Ships carrying indentured servants were often little better than slavers. In the peak year of the German flood, 1749, an estimated 2,000 German migrants died on the Atlantic. On one ship in 1752, only 19 or 200 survived. This account was written by an immigrant who returned to Germany after only four years in the New World.

But during the voyage there is on board these ships terrible misery, stench, fumes, horror, vomiting, many kinds of sea-sickness, fever, dysentery, headache, heat, constipation, boils, scurvy, cancer, mouth-rot, and the like, all of which come from old and sharply salted food and meat, also from very bad and foul water, so that many die miserably. . . .

The sale of human beings in the market on board the ship is carried on thus: Every day Englishmen, Dutchmen and High-German people come from the city of Philadelphia and other places, in part from a great distance, say 20, 30, or 40 hours away, and go on board the newly arrived ship that has brought and offers for sale passengers from Europe, and select among the healthy persons such as they seem suitable for their business, and bargain with them how long they will serve for their passage money, which most of them are still in debt for. When they have come to an agreement, it happens that adult persons bind themselves in writing to serve 3, 4, 5, or 6 years for the amount due by them, according to their age and strength. But very young people, from 10 to 15 years, must serve till they are 21 years old.

Many parents must sell and trade away their children like so many head of cattle; for if their children take the debt upon themselves, the parents can leave the ship free and unrestrained; but as the parents often do not know where and what people their children are going, it often happens that such parents and children, after leaving the ship, do not see each other again for many years, perhaps no more in all their lives. . . .

Warfare: Englishmen, Frenchmen, Indians

Armed conflict between national states has not been sufficiently studied. As for the wars that occurred from the sixteenth to the eighteenth centuries, a few men have done distinguished work in probing implications of the struggles: Sir George N. Clark, John U. Nef, Howard H. Peckham, Quincy Wright. But the bulk of the existing studies are "military history" in a very narrow sense—the sort of fretwork that makes students believe that the past is a dreary trudge of kings, dates, battles—and even as military history they do not explain anything. They deal mainly with specific days and specific clashes, rarely with campaigns, more rarely yet with the objectives behind the campaigns. Thus George Washington can be downgraded with the offhand slight that the only battle he ever won was the famous Christmas sally at Trenton. Thus it can be argued that the greatest military men of the Civil War were the Confederate commanders. But these conclusions will not stand up. The depth and determination of Washington's understanding of the main aims of the

Revolutionary War was equalled in his time only by Thomas Paine (a man he despised), and the Civil War's grand strategy was principally engineered by Lincoln with tactical help from Grant and Sherman. Thus few histories have explained how these and other wars were won even while the winners were losing most of the battles.

In the present chapter we face a similar problem in that we must deal on a rather low level of abstraction with particular battles and campaigns and with the inferences that some individuals drew from their experiences. Before roaming among the details, it is therefore expedient to state several generalizations. Warfare was becoming far more expensive. As late as 1500 no army in Europe included more than 12,000 men, and half as many comprised a large force. By the Thirty Years War (1618–1648) an army might tally 30,000 or more. Technology advanced: the machines of war became more complicated and military engineering became a profession. Each unit of munitions was more expensive, and a country needed more units. As shown in Chapter 1, the growing burden on the national treasury created calamitous social stresses even in England, but on the Continent matters were far worse. A popular saying held that each peasant had to carry an armed soldier on his back. From 1540 to 1640 England was relatively peaceful and became the center of science and technology but Europe knew those hundred years as a period of almost continuous warfare. The load was immense. France in 1690 had about twenty million people, of whom 446,000 were in the army. In fairly serene days after the Peace of Utrecht in 1713, French forces were never less than 130,000. Prussia, with two million inhabitants in 1739, had an army of 83,000. Meanwhile England was advancing quickly in peaceful occupations: in the decade after 1631 she mined nearly two million tons of coal a year while the rest of the world combined produced less than a fifth as much.

We can say that warfare in the eighteenth century was a courtly and sometimes a genial pursuit; certainly it was so by the standards of the preceding era or the succeeding one. Every sound thinker about military or naval strategy knows that the cardinal task is to destroy the enemy forces. But when war began between France and Holland in 1689, each side came to the conflict with a defensive outlook; nobody seemed thirsty for blood. These frays have been aptly called clashes "of forts against forts." The favorite tactic was the siege. Repeatedly in the century a besieged fort or town surrendered after giving little or no resistance.

The flavor of eighteenth-century conflict was captured nearly a century ago by Francis Parkman.* Louisbourg, the citadel by which the French

---

*Making a list of great historians must always make the writer's views seem *ex cathedra,* yet it is worth doing occasionally for the sake of reviewing professional standards. It cannot be said often enough that the two towering analysts of American history are Alexis de Tocqueville and Frederick Jackson Turner. Parkman must also be included in an enumeration of the dozen outstanding historians of the United States.

guarded the entrance to the St. Lawrence River, fell to Anglo-American forces under Jeffrey Amherst in 1758. During the antecedent siege the tone was convivial:

> Various courtesies were exchanged between the two commanders. Drucour, on occasion of a flag of truce, wrote to Amherst that there was a surgeon of uncommon skill in Louisburg, whose services were at the command of any English officer who might need them. Amherst on his part sent to his enemy letters and messages from wounded Frenchmen in his hands, adding his compliments to Madame Drucour, with an expression of regret for the disquiet to which she was exposed, begging her at the same time to accept a gift of pineapples from the West Indies. She returned his courtesy by sending him a basket of wine; after which amenities the cannon roared again. Madame Drucour was a woman of heroic spirit. Every day she was on the ramparts, where her presence roused the soldiers to enthusiasm; and every day with her own hand she fired three cannon to encourage them.

One diverting feature of such "civilized" trends in international conflict was the European preoccupation with esthetic values. Especially in such countries as France, Italy, or Switzerland, the advance of industrial civilization was not accompanied by much expansion of a free market, and so it consisted primarily of craftsmanship and quality of manufacture rather than of quantity production; (see the Chapter 3 introduction). As a further consequence, those countries did not develop an especially elastic supply of metals for munitions, but developed instead a refined sense of artisanship in manufacture. Thus the lure of the beautiful could reach the point of absurdity. For example, men had long been proud of the embellishments on their weaponry; armor was ornate, and in the early sixteenth century such great artists as Albrecht Dürer had been hired in Germany to design the leather-pricking for military saddles. In France by 1670 the production of artillery at the military foundry of the Arsenal at Paris was halted altogether, but it was reopened in 1684 to begin turning out statues for the new palace at Versailles and its surrounding gardens.

Among other dampers on militaristic savagery might be mentioned the reluctance of scientists to get entangled with dynastic ambitions; even in wartime many continued blithely corresponding with their counterparts in enemy states. The morale of soldiers, many of them serving only for the pay, tended to be low. Much of this shows in soldiers' responses to a visceral weapon such as the bayonet. It seemingly originated in hunting—a dagger to be fastened to a musket barrel and used to finish off a stag or a bear. It was cheap. After armor was no longer issued to troops, it was potentially the most lethal of the new weapons. By the 1680's it was being issued to Lord Churchill's regiment. But it created a strong urge to fight at long distance. "Since everyone carries it no one ever uses it," explained a French officer in

1775. Only after the French Revolution was it used widely, and then often against street mobs of radical working-class *sans culottes*.*

A development that gravely weakened the military-naval potency of Europe vis-a-vis North America was its shortage of lumber by the eighteenth century. Wood was vital to armies to make wagons for victualling, musket stocks, or gun carriages. To navies it was indispensable: no timbers, no ships. Advances had been made toward economizing the indispensable material. By 1700 in England coal was sometimes used instead of charcoal to extract tin, copper, and lead from their ores. But not until nearly the close of the century did the puddling process facilitate the widespread use of coal to smelt iron ores when an Englishman (in 1784) put together puddling and rolling into a coordinated new process. Four years earlier James Watt had made his remarkable breakthroughs—a condenser and valves—to design a new steam engine whose greater efficiencies brought marked savings of fuel.

The crisis of naval stores lingered through the eighteenth century. The situation was far worse for insular England, relying for so much on sea communications, than for continental France. When England began to enlarge her fleet in the reign of Henry VIII, who added twenty-four battleships to the seven left by his father, many of the masts and ship planks came from the sturdy oaks of her own southeastern reaches. These forests were heedlessly plundered. By the time of the First Dutch War (1652–1654) she leaned heavily on naval stores from the Baltic. When Denmark choked off this supply by barring The Sound to English vessels, Cromwell felt the crunch. He turned to America, and thenceforward until the Revolution nearly all English masts came from the New World. The naval authorities never had a high opinion of American oak; it was the white pine and spruce of northern New England that flowed out mainly through ports in New Hampshire and Maine. In regard to other necessaries—such naval stores as pitch and tar and resin—the American supply was insufficient, and England continued dependent on the Baltic. But New England had a staple to export; that relation did much to build her economic and military strength before the strike for independence came.

Thus straitened by deficiences of supply, England faced the power and ambition of France. The confrontation took place not only across the Channel but increasingly in the forests and on the waters 3,000 miles away. New France had never grown as had the English colonies; at mid-century twenty whites lived south of the St. Lawrence valley for every Frenchman living there or north and west of it. Much of the failure was due to official policy. Huguenots were denied the right to migrate to New France. All state power was in the hands of the governor and other royal officers; self-government was unknown. The aim was to have an administrative structure that told each man his place in

---

*Many American soldiers learned in World War II that the sole utility of the bayonet was to open canned rations.

James Watt's Steam Engine

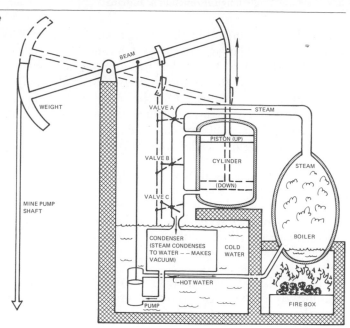

The basic principle of the early industrial steam engines (developed in the late seventeenth century as a device for pumping water out of mines) was to produce an alternating pattern of high and low pressure under a piston so as to move it up and down and run the pump. The early engines filled a cylinder with steam of moderately high pressure and then suddenly released that pressure by squirting in cold water for quick cooling and condensation of the steam. The suddenly condensed steam created a vacuum in the cylinder under the piston, causing it to collapse downward under air pressure from the other side of the piston. Unfortunately the rapid steam-heating and alternate cooling of the cylinder made the engine erratic and very inefficient in the use of heat and fuel. In 1769 James Watt patented important improvements shown here, in the form of a separated steam-condensing chamber (which allowed the cylinder and piston to remain steam-heated) and a set of valves to control the alterations of pressure above and below the piston in an efficient rhythm. (See Document 11-2.)

The solid lines in the drawing show Watt's engine in the "piston-up" position, with valves A and C open (valve B closed). In this position the open valve A is admitting steam into the cylinder chamber *above* the piston, exerting downward pressure on it. The open valve C is allowing all steam *under* the piston to expand into the condenser chamber (which is cooled by immersion in cold water) where the steam suddenly cools and condenses, with a vacuum effect that releases pressure under the piston and makes it collapse downward under pressure from above.

The dashed lines in the drawing show the engine in the "piston-down" position, with valves A and C closed but valve B now open. The steam previously pressing above the piston can now expand through open valve B into the chamber and cylinder below the piston; there is equal pressure of steam here above and below the piston. Now the piston is drawn upward by the counterweight on the pump beam, pushing steam down into the area below the piston. When the piston reaches the "up" position and valve B closes while A and C open, the steam under the piston will again condense via the consenser and the piston will collapse under steam pressure above to repeat the engine cycle. A smaller pump continually clears the condenser chamber of vapor and water, which is recycled back to the boiler for steaming up. In a later development, Watt devised a way of increasing power with direct steam pressure alternating on both sides of the piston, and other inventors then speeded up the process by putting the steam under increasing pressure.

the table of organization (much as a similar effort was made during the first years of Virginia; see early in Chapter 2). In striving to create a stable agricultural society, the authorities granted large tracts called "seignories" to a favored few. But the feudal modes that had been a natural growth over a millenium in France could not be transplanted to America without cracking. Men would not stay in their place and mind their betters.

As early as 1680 perhaps one man of three in New France was a *coureur de bois* roaming the backwoods in quest of furs. One priest lamented,

> One part of our youth is continually rambling and roaming about, and . . . it infects them with a habit of libertinism, of which they never get entirely rid; at least, it gives them a distaste for labor, it exhausts their strength, they become incapable of the least constraint, and when they are no longer able to undergo the fatigues of travelling . . . they remain without the least resource and are no longer good for anything.

As in the English colonies, increasing leeway for social mobility had to be granted. By 1733 the governor—a marquis—could moan: "The scarcity of men, and the high wages of both agricultural and urban labor, considerably diminishes the revenues of landlords and merchants." Already twenty-one years earlier, of the seventy-six secular seignories in New France, at least twenty-two were in the grasp of men whose origins were with the middle class or lower.

In all governments, military procurement was larded with graft.* A description of the economics of this colonial war (toward the end of this chapter) will show how some merchants in British North America used pay-offs to build their fortunes. For now let us take examples from two other countries: old England and New France. Soon after Henry VIII dissolved the monasteries, the Lord Admiral could be found trading widely in oak from monastic forests. Under the Restoration things were worse yet. In the words of a naval historian, "From the sixteenth to the nineteenth century the [ministry of] Ordnance enjoyed an unbroken reputation for procrastination and corruption, attracting the attention of Marlborough as of Hawkins, and of Wellington as of Pepys." The French administration was probably worse—a fact that may explain how they lost their empire in North America before the English contrived to lose theirs. The governor of New France, along with the intendant and the commissary general and forty other officials, was accused of fraud and peculation. Twenty-one of them stood trial in 1761 when France and her colony were still legally at war with England. The governor and seven others were acquitted, but his two ranking assistants were judged guilty. Victuals

---

*The point should not be misconstrued. Bagmen are universal; they flock like carrion around every bureaucracy. In some societies (Argentina, Kuomintang China) graft exists in pure form, for its own sake. But in others it may be a step in building such highways as the Massachusetts Turnpike. A fine dissertation topic would be "Economic Uses of Political Corruption."

intended for the army had been diverted to private speculators. Extortionate prices had been paid for supplies bought in Canada, and ships had been hired at inflated rates. Yet Canadian farmers had been forced to sell their grain at a fixed and artificially low price.

One authority on the colonial wars has pointed out that Englishmen in America had devoted their military efforts exclusively to frontier defense for their first eighty years on the continent. Whereas the ways of life in New France, based in large degree on the fur trade, did not always clash with the customs of the Indians, English ambitions did. (See Document 5-3). Rather in the style of the drunkard who fell into a mud puddle and emerged with his pockets stuffed with silver dollars, the original English colonists had stumbled into a fortunate setting; that is, the Indian populations along the coast were friendly, or sparse, or bemused by hostility to each other. For the brutal conflict that developed, the expansionist whites were the main culprits. As it turned out, a good deal of training for warfare could be gotten from the seemingly limited task of defending the frontier.

In Virginia the Indian-English antagonism flared soon; by 1610 we can read of the Jamestown fortification "it is true the Indian is as fast killing without as the famine and pestilence within." Pocahontas first came to the settlement in 1613 as a captive. In 1622 the Indians fell upon the tiny colony and killed 400 of its members. No matter what else should be said of that tormented episode known as Bacon's Rebellion (end of Chapter 2), it was set off by the Indian problem. Meanwhile through the years the whites made frequent forays into the woods lusting for redskinned game, destroying villages and burning crops. It is probably true that a united front among the Indians, at least until 1650, could have driven the invaders entirely out of North America—but nothing like a united front could be found.

In New England interracial diplomacy took a different course but reached the same genocidal end. Whites there had a rather easy time of it. In 1600 perhaps 25,000 Indians lived in New England, but fully a third of them were wiped out by an epidemic in 1616–1617. The disease was not smallpox or yellow fever or typhoid; it may have been bubonic plague or measles. Almost certainly the germs were brought in by European traders and explorers. In any event, some whites thought it a special providence: God was clearing His field for their divine mission. But for other Puritans the problem was not so simple. Far from touting some doctrine of racial inferiority, Puritan scholars thought Indians might be one of the lost tribes of Israel, and since these could be lost Jews descended to being "heathenish," efforts should be made to Christianize them. Thus missionary work was officially sanctioned and went on for decades in a few areas, supported by a few lone enthusiasts, but the total number of converts probably did not pass 2,500. The common fate was not salvation but decimation. In 1633 during their first rancor with the Bay colonists, thousands of Indians were killed by the worst epidemic in sixteen years. "God ended the controversy by sending the smallpox amongst the Indians." A far worse clash occurring in 1637 is called the Pequot War. Then in fairly tranquil decades a few ministers went around teaching the catechism and persuading some surviving groups of redeemed redskins to cut their hair in the white man's fashion.

The final mop-up, if a harsh word may be used, came in King Philip's War of 1675, when the last independent tribes of southern New England were virtually obliterated. The Narragansetts, Nipmucks, and Wampanoags were being ground to meal between two millstones: the Anglo-Americans driving westward, and an easterly push by the Iroquois Nations from central New York. The New England tribes rebelled under Chief Metacomet (Philip). He was killed, their food ran out, and they were suppressed. The last vestiges of the New England fur trade died when these Indians died or dispersed, but providentially the timber trade had emerged as a partial replacement. Meanwhile, elimination of the hostiles encouraged migration onto the frontier, especially in Connecticut. Colonists had learned that by playing on intertribal rivalries they could muster Indian allies. They had picked up some experience in military strategy and tactics. Most useful of all, they had seen that they could get best results if the provinces worked together rather than separately.

From an Olympian vantage, Indian warfare could seem almost a joke, and colonials did joke about it: "This fight is more for pastime, than to conquer and subdue enemies. . . . They might fight for seven years and not kill seven men." European styles in warfare were more bloody, and the exemption of Americans from the maelstrom of European broils ended abruptly late in the seventeenth century.

The conflict of France with England was far from new, but now it would be fought with increasing numbers of men, with more ships, with heavier artillery, and in a global arena. One site was North America. In the decades beginning with the Glorious Revolution, England was officially at war nearly half the time, and so were her New World colonies. Depending on where in the worldwide struggle we look, the series of conflicts can be labelled in various ways. Here is the list:

May 1689—September 1697. King William's War (also the War of the League of Augsburg). Ended by Treaty of Ryswick.

May 1702—11 April 1713. Queen Anne's War (also War of the Spanish Succession). Ended by Treaty of Utrecht.

March 1744—18 October 1748. King George's War (also the War of the Austrian Succession). Ended by Treaty of Aix-la-Chapelle. This fray actually began in the New World in October 1739 as a clash of England against Spain, and is further known as the War of Jenkins' Ear.

18 May 1756—10 February 1763. Seven Years' War. Ended by Treaty of Paris. This struggle too started in America, in 1754, and is called further the French and Indian War.

FIGURE 5-1. *A Beaver Dam Near Niagara*

"A New and Exact Map of the Dominions of the King of Great Britain on the Continent of North America . . . According to the Newest and most Exact Observations by Herman Moll Cartographer" was issued in 1711. This illustration appeared there as an inset. The caption to the panel read: "A View of the Industry of the Beavers of Canada in making Dams to stop the Course of a Rivulet in order to form a great Lake, about which they build their Habitations. To effect this: They fell Large Trees with their Teeth, in such a manner as to make them come cross the Rivulet, to lay the foundation of the Dam; they make Mortar, work up, and finish the whole with great order and wonderful Dexterity.

"The Beavers have two Doors to their Lodges, one to the water and the other to the Land side. According to the French Accounts"

The portrayal of beavers is not altogether accurate, and the background of Niagara Falls is not especially majestic. But within a century Americans were writing far more precise descriptions of their natural surroundings, witness Jefferson's *Notes on Virginia* (1784) and the journals of the Lewis and Clark expedition (1814).

In scale, King William's War was picayune; in consequence, it counted. Neither side ever had so many as 2,000 men under arms. But American losses were at least 650 dead, mainly in New England. Albany County, New York, pivot of the Indian trade, was especially hit; it had 84 killed and captured, prompting another 400 to move away so that population fell by 25 per cent. Some historians argue that the sources of the Anglo-French conflict were chiefly dynastic and strategic, but ripples of greed repeatedly surfaced. When it was proposed to set up an English colony in a part of America that was claimed but not yet occupied by Spain, a horrified official of the Board of Trade in London protested "that besides all other considerations the continuance of the present underhanded trade we have with them in those parts is highly advantageous to the Nation." The provinces jockeyed for gain, Pennsylvania particularly making its neighbors indignant. With Philadelphia in search of hands for a growing swarm of privateers, she lured seamen away from His Majesty's fleet as well as from Maryland vessels. Residents of the Pennsylvania proprietary paid no customs duties, protested the governor of New York, while his own citizens "pay Duty at 2% upon all Commodities"; he warned that the discrimination made his merchants "discontented and Mutinous": "The strange Neglect of these Plantations must in a short time occasion the Losse of them, and then the Nation will be exasperated beyond measure. . . ."

Despite such frictions, raids by French and Indians prompted a joint-security meeting in the spring of 1690, attended by Massachusetts Bay, Plymouth, Connecticut, and New York. Fine plans were made. However, of 855 militia pledged, only a third made an expedition against Montreal. It failed, but the first really serious intercolonial conference had been held, and this development fed the related notion that permanent peace could not be won for America until the French had been driven entirely off the continent.

Queen Anne's War brought new intramural fevers, new efforts to salve them. As officials in Britain clove to the idea that Americans should stand on their own martial feet, provincial governors begged in vain for regulars to launch against Acadia (Nova Scotia). Canada in turn foreswore sallies across the border for fear of annoying the neutral Iroquois. Thus for years the struggle was confined to New England in the north, to the Carolinas and Florida and the West Indies to the south. But by 1709 it seemed that spirits had been stirred for an Anglo-colonial onslaught against Quebec and Montreal. The project was approved by Queen and ministers. Never had the Americans of the North cooperated as they did now in mobilizing their militiamen. But where were the English troops and fleet? Not to be seen. After the irregulars had squandered the summer in gambling and brawling and brooding over the crops they would not reap, word came from London in October that the venture had simply been "laid aside." The cancellation had been taken in May, but the letter announcing it was not sent until August—and then by a ship that was not headed directly for America. Before the word came, the militia had been demobilized in September. From this fiasco the colonies learned a lesson that would

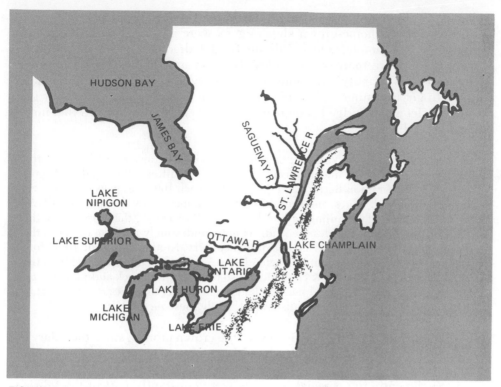

FIGURE 5-2. *The St. Lawrence River System and the Great Lakes*

become increasingly important—to keep agents at the British court so that they would get news promptly.

From Connecticut that winter came forebodings: "The disappointment We met with last Summer, which has issued in the death of neer one quarter part of the Quota detached from this Government, has struck a great damp upon our people; which will inevitably prevent such a forwardness in that Service, upon Second Orders, as generally attended the first." From Massachusetts came the lament that she had been at war for twenty years, that for the last six years she had spent nearly £30,000 per annum for that cause, "that other her Majesties plantations & Collonies—(Connecticut Excepted) have felt little of the War, either in charge or losses, but have been in a great measure quiet, being covered by our maintaining the Frontier." But few provincials as yet comprehended the incompetence, apart from the corruption, of the bureaucracy they confronted. Witness a letter from the Board of Ordnance in London replying to a request for supplies to be sent to North America: "As to the Stores, vizt 12 Cohorn Mortars with a proportionable number of Shells & materials for Fireworks, we being perfect Strangers to the Service, can't judge what is a proper Proportion, therefore the particulars should be expressed."

Meantime, home-grown shenanigans were a normal part of life in the colonies. For example, when William Byrd I died, he had been auditor of Virginia for more than two decades. His son and namesake was receiver-general of His Majesty's revenues for the province. William II immediately moved to get his father's place (See Document 5-1). Sensing that it may seem strange to let a man judge his own accounts, the job-seeker argued that no risk was involved:

> As the case stands in Virginia, there cant possibly be any fraud between the Auditor and any of the under officers. For as to the Quitrents the number of acres patented, appear upon Record, and the Sum that each 100 acres pays is certain. So it is likewise with Fines, and forfeitures, which appear likewise upon record. As to the Revenue of 2 shillings a hogshead, and Port Dutys, that appears by the Entry of each Ship. Besides the Audit is not clandestinely perform'd, but at the Public meetings of the chief People of that country. Neither is this all, for before the public accompts are sent to England, they are produced together with all the Vouchers, to the Governor & council, and so pass another check audit for several days together. Now the fraud must be laid much deeper than we are capable of in Virginia if it can escape being discover'd, while these methods are observd.

His sole purpose, said Byrd, was to save the crown money, since the salary of a separate and independent auditor would not attract "any person of Substance & Reputation".

Such conflicting special interests were constantly part of the fabric of war. In South Carolina Indian traders were inciting the tribes to war on each other, in hopes that any captives would be handed over to them as slaves. When a white led three hundred Indians against the Choctaws on the ground that they were allied to the French, he put up the ammunition in the hope that he would get fifteen Choctaw slaves. He got them. But the governor seized them with the claim that they had been meant as a gift for himself. The government of South Carolina meanwhile took as captives 118 French and Spanish. They were to be sent to England by means of the tobacco fleet from Virginia, but they did not reach the Chesapeake until three weeks after the fleet had sailed. The master of the prison-ship had orders, in that event, to turn the ship over to his captives with a month's provisions. Virginia, not eager to have potential privateers roaming its coasts, faced the prospect of subsisting the prisoners for the winter. She wanted South Carolina to ante up. In New Jersey the Council claimed financial inability to prosecute the war, charging that the Quakers in the Assembly, nearly a majority, would not vote funds for troops: "And with Humble Submission wee conceive, that unless the Quakers are Restrained from the management of Public Affairs, (as they are in Great Britain) and Obliged to Act conformable to the many Good Laws made for that Purpose: Your Majesty can never expect to see an end of the Confusions, & Divisions, which have so long Reigned amongst us; Nor Your Majestys Government Honourably Supported or Defended."

For a brief span hopes rose again. In 1710 a largely colonial force captured Acadia. The next June a convoy of sixty British vessels bearing 5,000 troops arrived in Boston. Although some Yankees worked on Sundays to get the expedition ready, local attitudes were generally hostile and grumbling instead of grateful. The fleet put to sea, but in the St. Lawrence eight transports were lost on the rocks, and 700 British regulars went under. The naval officers, not knowing the channels, decided to go back to England. When word reached the commander of the American troops planning to move against Montreal, he was so furious that he ripped off his wig and stamped on it. Word got to Boston concurrent with a terrible fire; a minister saw both disasters as Divine wrath toward Sabbath-breakers.* Whereas this kind of thinking was already almost an anachronism, a clearheaded French writer of the same era was more farsighted: he predicted that if Gallic government were expelled from Canada, the Americans "will then unite, shake off the yoke of the English monarchy, and erect themselves into a democracy."

Peace arrived in 1713 to last for twenty-five years while the rivals edged for position. The British colonies agonized over coordinating their defenses. At times the royal governors of New York and Massachusetts had been accorded military control over adjacent Connecticut and Rhode Island, and other larger schemes for coordination were advanced but not pressed. The Board of Trade in 1721 recommended a single commander of His Majesty's forces in North America. None was named; the blueprint remained merely that. French measures were more vigorous. By the Treaty of Utrecht she lost Acadia and Newfoundland, and thus had no harbor between France and the St. Lawrence. She responded in 1721 by starting what became a large garrison at Louisbourg on Cape Breton Island. Since it controlled the doorway of maritime access to the interior, this port was the fulcrum on which naval conflict would turn in the next two wars. The French also erected several forts to bar the St. Lawrence-Great Lakes routes, while the English built Fort Oswego below Lake Ontario.

In 1739 the English were at war again, this time against Spain. Their first major venture was a calamity. Sending a huge convoy under Admiral Edward Vernon carrying 9,000 soldiers, the British arrived at Cartagena, port of Colombia, in early March 1741. Vernon urged immediate attack. The general waited three weeks. At length he ordered an assault. His men were slaughtered. The rainy season hit the tropical region, bringing yellow fever. Then the British withdrew, dawdled away some months in Cuba, and went home. They had lost 55 per cent of their force. Of the surviving colonials, one was Captain Lawrence Washington. Broken in health, he returned to the Potomac where he named his plantation Mount Vernon after the admiral and willed it to younger brother George.

---

*See late in Chapter 4 on the New England social order and survival of beliefs in Special Providences.

The effects of the Cartagena disaster typified the significance of the conflict which became King George's War when the French took the field in 1744. Of small moment militarily or strategically, its effects on psychology, on politics, and on the economies were grave. The one major British victory was won by colonial troops at Louisbourg, and then tossed away by the King's ministers at the peace table. Two Massachusetts officials guided the venture: Governor William Shirley who raised the force, and William Pepperell, president of the Council, who led the campaign. Some 4,000 men were raised in New England. New York and Pennsylvania gave guns and supplies. The English furnished no land troops, only four ships. A rough trip northeast from Boston was only the beginning of hardship. They disembarked at Cape Breton Island on May Day, 1745:

> The landing of Provisions, ammunition & heavy artillery was attended with extream difficulty & fatigue; there being no Harbour there, the surf almost continually running very high, so that frequently for some days together there was no landing any thing at all, & when they did the Men were obliged to wade high into the Water to save every thing that would have been damaged by being wet, they had no Cloaths to shift themselves with, but poor defence from the Weather, at the same time the Nights were very cold & generally attended with thick heavy fogs, by means whereof it was near a Fortnight before they could get all their Stores ashore, & notwithstanding all possible Care to prevent it, many Boats and some Stores were lost.

All this at the beginning of a cold May in the North Atlantic had to be endured so that the siege of Louisbourg could begin. Then for six weeks the garrison was shelled relentlessly, with such devastation that the era of the impregnable fort seemed to be ended. When surrender came, the town held only one house that was "left unhurt." The Americans lost a mere 100 men to enemy action, plus 30 to sickness. (But the engagement was more benign than its sequel; nearly 900 New Englanders died of disease by the spring of 1746 while at Louisbourg.) Such a stirring victory at such low costs prompted the British admiralty to say it would hang anybody who thought of giving up the fortress. However, that is just what was done in 1748 when the Treaty of Aix-la-Chapelle returned Louisbourg to France (in exchange for a large slice of India). Meanwhile British-led efforts in the war had failed. In the spring of 1746 the provinces raised unprecedented numbers of troops, perhaps 8,000 men. Everything was ready in July, but the British were to put up eight battalions of regulars. They never came (they were used instead in a fruitless foray against the French coast). Not until the spring of 1747, long after the colonial troops had been disbanded, did royal authorities deign to say what had happened. Once again, as in 1709, American zeal had met with English indifference.

Another uneasy event was a fracas in Boston. The royal navy when at

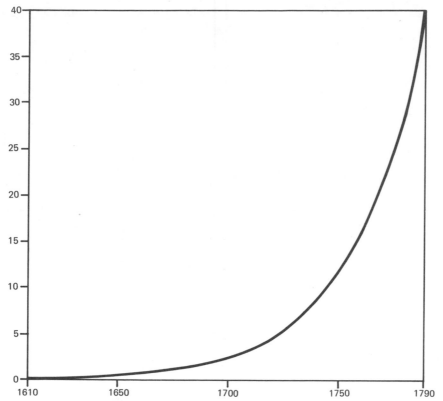

FIGURE 5-3. *Population of North American British Colonies to 1790 (in hundreds of thousands)*

home filled its vessels by sending press gangs to "persuade" any available drifters to make a crew. Why not in Boston? A commodore sent a gang to recruit seamen for his five ships. Angered by this tampering with free citizens, a mob seized some recruiting officers. Governor Shirley denounced the mob; a town meeting told it to free the officers. It did, and the commodore released the impressed Americans and sailed away. But the experience left a bad taste, as did others. America, so Shirley informed London, was "the best poor man's country on earth," and colonials were loathe to enlist for military duty. They particularly avoided British officers, whom the home officials repeatedly tried to shove down provincial throats. Some officers aggravated the resentments by abusing their men. A common joke held that no soldier in a colonial regiment ever died in action or deserted; once your name got on a company muster, there it stayed, and the captain palmed the pay of every man unable to claim his own. In their jargon, it was "vacant pay."

Inevitably, pious Yankees in the Louisbourg garrison were baffled or irked by Gallic customs and religion, as witnessed by a soldier's diary: "This Day I went into the Hospital to See the French People say Mass. I cou'd'ent

113

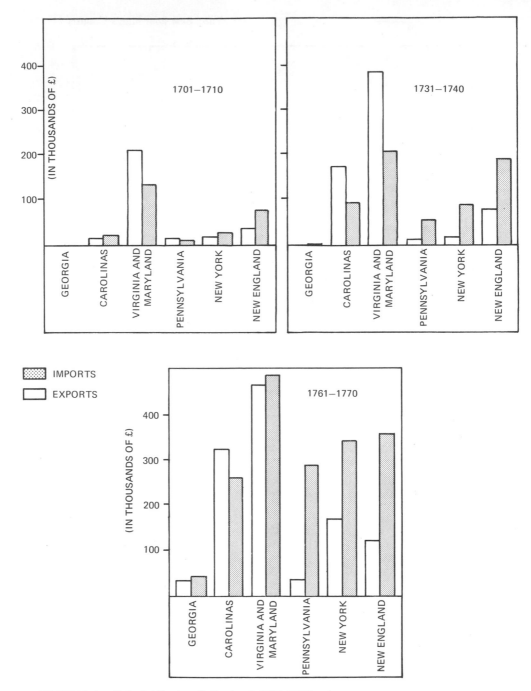

FIGURE 5-4. *Colonial Trade with England, 1701–1770*

Source: Ver Steeg, *The Formative Years* (1964). Adopted by permission.

help Wondring, to see Gent-men who were men of Lerning (I suppos'd, & Doubtless of good Natural parts also) so Led aside as to worship Images. to bow down to a Cross of wood. & to see so many of all Rank seemingly Devout. when we've Reason to think They never had any Communion with God— Through the Course of their Lives Being Ever So Strict in the Practice of their Religion." Any crusade against New France could draw on this religious fuel. Others knew less exalted motives for evicting France from the New World. The full roster was arrayed by Shirley in writing to the Secretary at War: It would bring huge savings for defense, since the Indians would come under English influence. It would mean a thriving fur trade, steady supplies of naval stores, an enhanced cod fishery to be a "nursery" of seamen for the Royal Navy, expanding markets for manufactured wares from England. Then came the kicker:

> That from the Increase of the Inhabitants of North America in less than a Century, such an Addition would probably be made to the subjects of the Crown of Great Britain, as might make 'em even exceed the Number of the French King's Subjects both in Europe and America, and thereby besides greatly contributing to maintain the Superiority of the British Naval power, strengthen the Crown upon occasion with such a Land force as might enable Great Britain most effectually to preserve the Ballance of Power upon the Continent of Europe.*

Parallel to these psychic and political strains were economic ones. The currency crisis was chronic. How to conduct business in a land with no coin? (See mid-Chapter 3 on New England trade balances.) Chesapeake planters for decades had been putting their tobacco in government depositories and the resulting warehouse receipts had then passed from hand to hand in payment of bills. As early as 1709 the governor of New Hampshire got a law that accepted casks of tar—above the market price—in payment of all provincial taxes. And the plaguey colonials would not leave off toying with paper money. The consequent inflations were a fine device for gouging creditors in England; Americans were constantly trying to pay off debts in money less valuable than what they had borrowed. The practice brought many protests into the Board of Trade. By a petition from merchants in London, Bristol, and Liverpool: "It has been, and is, manifestly Owing to the Creating and Issuing such Quantity of

---

*Seven years would pass before Franklin published a similar analysis: "Thus there are suppos'd to be now upwards of One Million English Souls in North-America, (tho' 'tis thought scarce 80,000 have been brought over Sea) and yet perhaps there is not one the fewer in Britain, but rather many more, on Account of the Employment the Colonies afford to Manufacturers at Home. This Million doubling, suppose but once in 25 Years, will in another Century be more than the People of England, and the greatest Number of Englishmen will be on this Side the Water. What an Accession of Power to the British Empire by Sea as well as Land! What Increase of Trade and Navigation! What Numbers of Ships and Seamen!"

Paper-Bills or Orders of Credit in the Several Colonies on the Continent of America, where Paper-Money only Prevails, and making it Obligatory on all Persons to take them in Payments, that all Gold and Silver-Coins have been and are Rated and Valued so much higher at this Time than they were in the Year 1700. . . ." The aggrieved said that whereas at one time the money of South Carolina had exchanged for gold at the rate of 1.33 to 1, this particular colonial currency had declined to 7.5 to 1. In North Carolina the rate had soared to 10:1.* They urged a policy that would drive all paper money from use, so that "Coins of Gold and Silver, of a known and fixt Standard of Value," should be the sole medium of circulation.

This goal was never reached. Uncertain rates of exchange were too useful to a handful of American merchants. The victualling of British troops in America had long been a prime source of revenue to a few fortunate colonials; not only did they make a profit on the transactions themselves, but since their bills were payable in London they thus acquired English money that could be used to buy goods for importation to the New World. In time of war, men who during peace had dickered for shillings could think on the scale of fortunes. One who was quick to improve his opportunities was Thomas Hancock of Boston (See early Chapter 3). He was engaged in 1745 as sutler to British forts in Newfoundland. The mechanics were simple: he used Massachusetts currency to buy foodstuffs and forage, delivered them to the army, and was paid in England in sterling. When colonials took Louisbourg, he set out to capture that contract too. Since the award would be made in London, he authorized his agent there to offer small bribes. When success came, the deals skyrocketed. By 1746 he was sanctioning payoffs of £1,000 at a crack. The venality was good business. He had a half interest in contracts that furnished more than £19,000 worth of supplies to His Majesty's forces in the twelve months beginning October 1747. The chief yield came not from the sale of goods but from the favorable rate of exchange he was allowed. The rate on the open market between Massachusetts money and sterling varied from 14:1 to 16:1, whereas Hancock and his partner were granted 9½:1 by the Board of Ordnance. It was thus that fortunes were made.

We can easily delude ourselves with the catchword that armies exist for purposes of national defense. Sometimes they do. But they may exist in order that a select few, career officers or commercial companies or whatever, can lap the gravy. The impression should not be left that it was solely, or mainly, colonials who benefited from favoritism. At the very beginning of the next

---

*I beg the reader not to close his mind in advance on the premise that he cannot understand international dealings in currencies. To say that £1 in British money would buy £10 in Massachusetts money is the logical equivalent of saying that £1 in British money would buy 10 watermelons. If you will sell me British money at 10 to 1, and I can sneak around the corner and sell it to somebody else for 20 to 1, I can make a profit. For present purposes exchange rates are no more complicated than that.

conflict, the French and Indian War, a contract was made between the Treasury in London and two local merchants. The entire payroll for the British army in North America was to be paid to the merchants. They would convert the sterling into Spanish or Portuguese coins, which they would deliver to paymasters in Williamsburg and in Boston. All of their expenses would be paid by the crown. In addition they would receive a "clear allowance" of 2 per cent of all funds they handled as a recompense "for their labour pains and Service herein. . . ." Patently their investment in these lucrative operations was—zero. Similar backscratching characterized the armed forces themselves. Commissions were not earned; they were sold or given. Of twenty-nine officers in one British regiment, ten were named Campbell. Officers in America received allotments to provide forage for their horses. The stipends were paid in cash, not in kind, and they were not proportioned to the expense. The colonel in a regiment got six rations as colonel, two more as captain; the lieutenant-colonel got four as lieutenant-colonel, another two as captain; the major got two as major, two more as captain; and so on.

Given the situation of 1748, a renewal of the war was inevitable. Indians goaded on by the French made bloody raids along the frontier. Perhaps equally important was the avarice of powerful colonials, especially in Virginia and Pennsylvania, for the ownership and development of new lands beyond the mountains. Much as the advent of World War I was spurred by the encounter in the Balkans between a German thrust eastward and a Russian encroachment southward, so did the rivals in America clash in the Ohio valley. The French, pushing south from Canada and north from New Orleans, turned east along the Ohio. To parry this threat, Virginia called up her militia in 1754 and placed it under the command of George Washington, who forged westward across Pennsylvania. While on the bungled campaign he got word of his promotion to colonel; it came just before he was forced to surrender to a French detachment and slink back home. The capitulation hurt his pride, but he had learned some lessons that he could turn to advantage later.

Now for the first time England, although nominally at peace with France until 1756, named a commander in chief for North America: Major-General Edward Braddock. Due to his talents the British nearly lost the war before they declared it. He got to Williamsburg in February 1755, and he did not like America. He was appalled by the deceitfulness and profiteering of colonial merchants and politicians (if they can do it, why not us?); Benjamin Franklin was almost the only person who proved reliable. He lamented that of his 2,000 men, 1,100 were "Americans of the Southern Provinces, whose slothful & languid Disposition renders them very unfit for Military Service;—I have employ'd the properest Officers to form & Discipline them, and great pains has and shall be taken to make them as useful as possible." In the event it was the British regulars who broke. By July 9 after a tortuous journey Braddock got his force to within ten miles of the French at Fort Duquesne

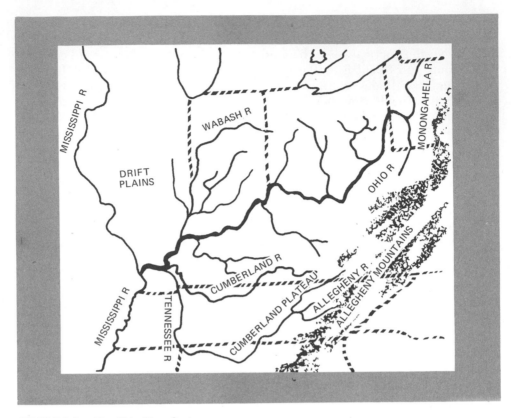

FIGURE 5-5. *The Ohio River System*

(presently Pittsburgh). Accounts vary, but some facts seem sure. An advance party of 1,300–1,500 men was ambushed (with the enemy known to be at hand). Some estimates place the foe at 300 French and 600 Indians; Colonel Washington, who was present, gave the number as "about 300 French and Indians." The English were not drawn up in line of battle but in line of march, so they were vulnerable to flanking fire from both sides. Their van cracked and fled, piling up on their comrades behind. Since they were not properly arrayed, they were shooting each other in the back; a guess reported by Washington said that two thirds of the casualties were inflicted by "our Own Cowardly dogs of Soldiers." He wrote:

> The Officers in generall behaved with incomparable Bravery . . . Our Poor Virginians behaved like men & died like Soldiers, for I beleive out of three Companies that were there that day scarce 30 were left alive. . . . In short, the dastardly Behavior of the English Soldiers, exposed all those who were inclined to do their duty to almost certain death, and at length in dispite of every Effort to the Contrary, broke and run like Sheep before the Hounds, leaving the Artillery,

Ammunition, Provisions and every Individual thing we had with us, a Prey for the Enemy; & when we endeavoured to rally them in hopes of regaining our Invaluable Loss, it was with as much Success as if we had attempted to Stop the Wild Bears of the Mountains.

The colonel got four musket balls through his coat and had two horses shot from under him. Braddock lost five horses before he took a fatal bullet. Of 83 officers involved, 26 were killed, and only 21 were unhurt. Total casualties were nearly a thousand men. A mortified George Washington declared: "We have been most scandalously beaten by a trifling body of men." His chief the governor of Virginia wrote a bristling note to the colonel who had succeeded to the supreme command. You still have 1,600 men, he urged, and I think I can raise another 400 in Virginia. Why not proceed with the attack on Fort Duquesne? "You have four months now to come, of the best Weather for such an Expedition." This colonel had no stomach for the task; he proposed instead to take up winter quarters at Philadelphia—in July.

The authorities in London did for a spell turn the helm over to an able and energetic man: William Shirley, who at least realized that European styles of battle were not wholly appropriate to the New World. (As a French general at Montreal phrased it in 1755, "les Canadiens sont plus propres pour la Petite Guerre que nos soldats"—Canadians are better at guerilla warfare than our regulars.) Shirley organized a group of New Hampshire woodsmen into a company of Rangers under Captain Robert Rogers, and this innovation would eventually bring a major change in the British army. Nonetheless Shirley was soon relieved of the command and ordered back to England. Why? Probably because the Earl of Loudoun wanted the job. (A hint of similar motivation can be discerned in a letter from a brigadier-general to a fellow officer in America, which looks apprehensively at the presence in the theater of another general, Lord Jeffrey Amherst: "I . . . cant help think that Mr. Amherst has come to lick the butter off both our breads." Sure enough, Amherst was promoted to the command.)

In spite of magnificent support from a new ministry headed by William Pitt, Loudoun achieved nothing. In May 1757 he left New York with a fleet from England; it carried 5,500 British regulars plus almost 4,000 colonials. By June 30 he was at Halifax, supposedly aimed at Quebec. For a month he was immobilized by fog and hostile winds. Then he learned that the French had naval forces available that were greater than his own. The British fleet returned to New York. Now it was Benjamin Franklin's turn to be disgusted; the campaign, he said, was "frivolous, expensive, and disgraceful to our Nation beyond Conception." A growing number of ranking provincials were coming to feel intense scorn for the military prowess of the British.

William Pitt, sure that the way to beat France was to peel away her colonies, hurled in resources. By 1758 he was raising 25,000 men to serve in North America. While subsidizing Prussia in hopes of a stalemate on the

Continent, he assembled the greatest fleet that had ever left Europe for the New World. They won back what had been given away: forty ships and 9,000 regulars led by Amherst forced the surrender of Louisbourg in July. In the next year other French strongholds surrendered or were abandoned. September 1759 saw a campaign against Quebec by General James Wolfe end in his victory over Montcalm, the death of both commanders, surrender of the city. Montreal now had no chance of getting effective supplies from her home government. She and all Canada capitulated in September 1760. Anglo-colonial troops had crushed the power of New France, and in so doing many American sons of the Protestant Reformation were happy also to have triumphed over a hated Church. But stresses remained. In December John Adams wrote in his diary: "The N. American War is not yet concluded, it continues, obstinate and bloody, with the Cherokees, and will be renewed probably, against the French in Louisiana. However with Regard to this Province, . . . it may not very improperly be called a Conclusion."

The protracted struggle against the French had seen changes in warfare. The siege of Louisbourg suggested that fortified cities were becoming obsolete; cannon balls could smash the enclosed buildings even if the surrounding walls were impregnable. Army-navy cooperation was mandatory; the last war alone had seen amphibious attacks on Louisbourg, Quebec, Havana, and Manila. The effective mode in the American future would be the new tactics pioneered by Rogers' Rangers armed with rifles. But Europeans were slow to take up the rifled barrels; the musket was still basic in the British army. And Braddock's folly would be repeated by Burgoyne in 1777, by Pakenham in 1815.

By the peace of 1763 Great Britain got title to all of Canada and Louisiana east of the Mississippi except New Orleans. Eviction of New France certainly mitigated but did not solve the problem of Indian "pacification." The tradition of bloody clashes did not end; it merely changed theaters. Subjugation of the tribes of New England had been largely finished in the seventeenth century, but telling raids were made in Massachusetts in 1697 and after, and in Maine in 1724. In 1755, with the Bay colony at war against all the Eastern Indians save the Penobscots, the government ordered the neutral tribe to bring in its old men, women, and children as guarantees of good behavior. The Indians refused, so Massachusetts declared war on them too. This, said William Shirley, "at a time when a fifth part of the Province's fighting Men, were engaged in other parts of the Kings Service." The Tuscaroras in North Carolina rose up and were smashed in 1711–1713. In South Carolina the Yemasees had to be subdued in 1715. The hegemony of Spain over Florida supported neighboring Creeks and Choctaws as a menace to the province of Georgia. In 1760, as John Adams' diary remarked, an English fort in Tennessee had to surrender to the Cherokees.

Some threads can be traced through these hostilities. Articulate whites in general often tried to treat the Indians fairly—by white man's standards. Roger Williams even denied that the charter of Massachusetts was valid, on the grounds that the king could not grant away lands of the Indians. The founding Puritan theologians, seeing the red man as a fellow child of God (if a poor candidate for the fellowship of Saints), had little color prejudice. The indecent repression of Indians that culminated in King Philip's War was forced on the magistrates by popular greed and bigotry. The deputy governor of Pennsylvania spoke an approximation of the truth when he told a conference in 1757: "The Proprietaries have never granted away any Lands, though within the Limits of this Province, without first purchasing them of the Indians." But, as an Onandaga chief had already said at another meeting: "Your Horses and Cows now eat the Grass our Deer used to feed on. . . . We know our Lands are now become more valuable. The white People think we do not know their Value; but we are sensible that the Land is everlasting, and the few Goods we receive for it are soon worn out and gone."

Sentimentality aside, it is doubtful that white-red relations in America could have taken a substantially different course. Culture conflict was sharp and not to be evaded (See Document 5-3 and late in Chapter 2). Europeans subverted Indians as much as they conquered them. The impact of European diseases and European liquor is widely recognized. But what of the impact of alien weapons on a Stone Age society? The demand for use of a white gunsmith was a common plank in Indian platforms. They could not repair firearms, nor could they make gunpowder. Muskets were easier to use and could be more effective than a bow and arrow, but reliance on them fatally weakened the Indian supply lines. It was like trying to use modern weaponry if you have no auto mechanics or gasoline dumps.

By the mid-eighteenth century the nub of Indian-white conflict lay in the Middle Colonies plus what became the territories of Ohio and Michigan. To keep the peace in this area the English relied mainly on the most powerful coalition, the Iroquois or Five Nations: Mohawk, Oneida, Onandaga, Cayuga, Seneca (references were common to the Six Nations, adding the Tuscarora). By King George's War they had learned to fear the European frays that swirled around their hunting grounds; a chief protested to the white combatants that "there was Room enough at Sea to fight." Due chiefly to British control of the Atlantic and Louisbourg, the *coureurs de bois* of New France had increasing difficulty procuring trade goods from home. They began to lose the fur trade to the English who could offer better prices to the Indians.

This erosion of alliances was offset by other events. Indian warfare came to Pennsylvania when Scots-Irish Presbyterians began to locate in the backwoods. Raiding parties from the Ohio country were striking at the farmsteads of German immigrants within 100 miles of Philadelphia. In the next war Braddock's defeat and other setbacks further tipped the balance against the English. Striking back at the red allies of the French, General Shirley ordered

FIGURE 5-6. *Seneca Maska*

These False Face masks were created by the Seneca. On left is a Beggar Mask, on right a Doorkeeper Mask, representing mythic personalities in various ceremonies. The Seneca were a component in the Iroquois Confederacy, which also included Mohawk, Oneida, Onondaga, and Cayuga. Although the power of this league extended at times from beyond the Ottawa River south to the Tennessee, it tended to center near the present Finger Lakes District in upper New York. The Confederacy known to the early white settlers is often called the Five Nations, and after incorporating the Tuscarora from the Carolinas in 1722, the Six Nations.

Inhabiting a heavily timbered area, these tribes used wood as a basic component of their cultures. Unfortunately for us, wood has a weakness to rot and decay, so that few ancient objects in this substance have survived. Some have, and they provide us with much of the best evidence about Indian civilizations. Iroquois long houses, for instance, provide glimpses into family structures. These buildings, some of them as much as 100 feet in length, were opened in the center by a longitudinal corridor, itself interrupted by fire pits. With separate rooms on each side, the structure served at once as dwelling and warehouse. Early white colonials found the design useful for some of their own buildings, although within a century they had worked out far different conceptions or they had put their European traditions into material form (Chapter 2).

For us, these masks can serve more than one purpose. They can remind us how we cheapen others when we refer to "the Indian." Hundreds of tribes existed until the invading whites obliterated some, and they differed greatly from one another; who could mistake these fluid shapes for those of a Navajo rug or a Sioux bunting or an Arapaho dress? The masks with their stereotypes and their grotesqueries effectively disrupt our own stereotype that aborigines were somber scoundrels lurking with scalping knives; they like whites sought a life of humor, order, and dramatic variety. Also the masks, with vivid contrasts of reds to blacks, can sharpen our sense of beauty.

that recruits to his cause from the Iroquois should be promised "a reward for Every Prisoner or scalp taken from the Enemy. . . ." The governor of Pennsylvania went further by declaring war against the Shawnee and Delaware and offering a bounty for scalps: $130 for males over age ten, $50 for females. The scales continued to move toward the French. A party of Ottawa surprised 350 English soldiers on Lake George; they killed 160 and took 151 prisoners. Indian losses, one brave slightly wounded. An English officer with 842 men tried to storm Fort Duquesne; his losses were 270 killed and 100 prisoners. (How did such disasters change American attitudes toward British troops?) Then came two years of British victories, and our focus must shift to Fort Detroit, which yielded to English troops in 1760. Here the spotlight shone on Pontiac, a chief of the Ottawa.

Few Indians wondered how the English regarded them: the disdain was clear enough. So long as European rivals had contended for Indian friends, their bargaining power had been high. Now, whereas the French as a matter of routine had given out presents in exchange for support, General Amherst refused them. He also ordered that sales of gunpowder to Indians should be only a minimal amount for hunting. These two ruptures of custom set off a series of rebellions. At Fort Detroit, Pontiac and his cohorts tried by a ruse to seize control in May 1763. Thwarted, they laid siege. Through an anxious summer the garrison held on. The engagement was broken off in November by the same propulsion that always frustrated an Indian siege; they had to quit to go get food for their families. Meanwhile Indian insurgents struck at scattered points from New York to the Mississippi River. For Britain, the losses were more than 400 regulars and provincial soldiers killed. Of civilians the toll ran higher; a contemporary estimated that Indians "killed or captivated not less than two thousand of His Majesty's subjects and drove some thousands to beggary and the greatest distress."

By the eighteenth-century Europeans' code of warfare, Indian practices were an affront; for instance some Indians, while not cannibals, would hack up a conquered foe and eat his flesh. At the same time, the sanguinary summer of 1763 released savagery in some European hearts. Of course nobody knew what caused smallpox, but yardgoods were known to be an effective carrier, and now the English turned to germ warfare. When a group of Delaware appeared with a warning at Fort Pitt (ex-Duquesne), a Swiss mercenary officer sent them home with two blankets and a handkerchief from his smallpox hospital. General Amherst agreed that any means were fair to wipe out barbarians! He wished to hunt "the vermin" down with dogs. He also wrote: "You will do well to try to inoculate the Indians by means of blankets, as well as to try every other method that can serve to extirpate this execrable race."

Pontiac made his peace with the English years before he was assassinated by another Indian in 1769. But he had set in motion the most formidable Indian resistance the English-speaking people had yet faced, or ever would face, on this continent.

By the eve of the Revolution armed conflict had permeated the lives of the provincial Americans. Clashes with Indians had taught them some techniques of wilderness warfare. These skills they would use against the English, as soon as there were reasons to do so that seemed sufficient. The colonists had also developed hostile attitudes toward their future enemies. The British had more than once failed to follow through on a military commitment (1709, 1746, 1757). When they did manage to arrive at an American battlefield, their leadership was incompetent (as at Cartagena or at Braddock's rout). The administration of their armed forces was even more corrupt and nepotistic than is common in such bureaucracies. In the French and Indian War their ineptitude had scandalized both Washington and Franklin, and the impression had spread in America that British power was vulnerable. One reason for the War for Independence (never noticed so far as I know) was that influential colonials thought they could win it.

SOME NOTABLE EVENTS

1608 Quebec founded by French.

1694 Foundation of the Bank of England.

1711–
1713 Tuscaroras crushed, North Carolina.

1713 Newfoundland, Acadia, Hudson Bay, and Gibraltar pass to England under Treaty of Utrecht.

1718 New Orleans founded by French. Yemasee driven by South Carolina into Florida.

1721 Louisbourg founded by French.

1730 Estimated population of colonies: 654,950. About 75,000 are slaves.

1744 The Iroquois by Treaty of Lancaster open their Great Warrior's Path through the Shenandoah Valley to become the Great Philadelphia Wagon Road (See Chapter 4).

1749 Halifax, Nova Scotia, founded by 2,500 emigrants direct from England.

1760 Treaty with Cherokees.

1763 The Floridas by Treaty of Paris pass from Spanish to British rule. Estimated population of colonies: 1,650,000.

Philadelphia	24,000
Boston	16,000
New York City	14,000
Charleston	10,000
Newport	8,000

Ways to Study History V

Develop a precise angle of vision. We all know the tale about blind men trying to comprehend an elephant: the man who felt its torso thought it a wall; the leg became a tree; the trunk, a snake. The anecdote clearly cautions against overgeneralizing our evidence. It also poses the problem of position. From what spot are you feeling? A historian needs to remind himself that no fact wears its meaning on its sleeve. Assessment of the meaning of an event starts with the question: To what end?

For instance, a noted specialist on French history recently wrote: ". . . the War of the American Revolution was a conflict in which France played the major part on the allied side and the American states a minor one." Yes and No. As to the worldwide "great struggle for the empire," the remark may be true, but in studying the evolution of America the focus must be on the colonies with other phenomena as an active backdrop. (What is "active"?)

Obviously our colonial history would not exist without immigration from Europe and Africa, and these movements of course had many consequences. Through the colonial period, probably the bulkiest item on the debit side of the international balance of payments of America arose from the importation of manpower, not only in the purchase and shipment of slaves, but also in financing the voyages of indentured servants; (see the graph for a later period near the opening of Chapter 3). But what was central to America seemed marginal to England. A Briton may have sensed that people were going to America, and it meant peanuts to him because it was having so little apparent impact on his own life.

To ask "What is my angle of vision?" raises questions of proportion of scale (if you can snare your prey before it slips past you). *Ways to Study History XV* looks at this related problem.

Document 5-1

Placemen of the eighteenth century used a delightful blend of circumlocution and candor in seeking income for their own (see William Byrd II's formulation above, in this chapter). When the Collector of the Customs for the ports of Salem and Marblehead quit his post, the ranking official in the service in North America chose his son to fill the job. Governor Shirley proposed instead, writing to His Majesty's chief minister on May Day 1744, that the Collector of Customs appointment, "of the value of about £150 Sterling per annum," be "annex'd" to the position of the Advocate General of the Vice Admiralty Court in the province which had the chief responsibility for enforcing the Navigation Acts.

. . . very much depends upon the good abilities, Diligence, and Integrity of the Advocate General, whose office in this province more especially, where there is a greater variety and larger extent of Business arising from Illicit Trade, the Destruction of his Majesty's Woods . . . captures of Vessells in time of War, and the maintenance of the Droits of the Admiralty, than in any six others of his Majestys Colonies, is extremely Difficult and Invidious, as the sole Direction and Conduct of prosecutions in all those Cases in the Court of Admiralty rest with him; and he bears the Brunt and Envy of the whole, which must sensibly afect him in that share of his private Business which depends upon the merchants, if he acts with that Vigour and Resolution in his post which his Majesty's Service requires here. . . .

I think it my Duty also to inform you of another circumstance, Sir, which is that the present Advocate Genl Mr. Bollan is my Son in Law; not as what I would mention in favour of the Case, which I have laid before you; for I am sensible that I have already receiv'd so large a share of the Favours of your Noble Family, that asking more may seem ingratitude for those already conferr'd, but, as what has rather given me some Satisfaction in the matter; and would induce me to be Silent in this Case, if I could do so with Justice to Mr. Bollan or to his Majesty's Service. . . .

Document 5-2

The urgent centripetal force for cooperation of several colonies was the need to cope with common enemies, including Indians. Of all the gestures toward this objective, the most ambitious was put forward on the eve of the French and Indian War as the Albany Plan of Union. Because of antagonisms among the colonies, the delegates at the 1754 conference proposed that Parliament should ordain a general government for specified purposes in the colonies. Even so, they underestimated the difficulties; the Plan was rejected by the authorities in England and it failed to win ratification by any of the provinces.

1. That the said general government by administered by a President-General, to be appointed and supported by the crown; and a Grand Council, to be chosen by the representatives of the people of the several Colonies met in their respective assemblies. . . .
10. That the President-General, with the advice of the Grand Council, hold or direct all Indian treaties, in which the general interest of the Colonies may be concerned; and make peace or declare war with Indian nations. . . .
12. That they make all purchases from Indians, for the crown, of lands not now within the bounds of particular Colonies. . . .
15. That they raise and pay soldiers and build forts for the defence of any of the Colonies . . . but they shall not impress men in any Colony, without the consent of the Legislature.
16. That for these purposes they have power to make laws, and lay and levy such general duties, imposts, or taxes, as to them shall appear most equal and just (considering the ability and other circumstances of the inhabitants in the several Colonies), and such as may be collected with the least inconvenience to the people; rather discouraging luxury, than loading industry with unnecessary burdens. . . .

Document 5-3

The Iroquois sold to the English a tract at the forks of the Delaware River. The Delaware continued to occupy it. In 1743 Pennsylvania asked the Iroquois to make them move. They resisted, saying that since they shared the Christian religion with the white man they should not be compelled to live among heathens. They lost the argument. The grievance rankled until 1757, when Little Abraham, a Mohawk sachem, explained matters to the authorities of Pennsylvania.

We must now inform you, that in former Times our Forefathers conquered the Delawares, and put Petticoats on them. A long time after that they lived among you our Brothers, but upon some Difference between you and them, we thought proper to remove them, giving them lands to plant and hunt on . . . But you, covetous of Land, made Plantations there, and spoiled their hunting Grounds; they then complained to us, and we looked over those Lands, and found their Complaints to be true. At this Time they carried on a Correspondence with the French, by which Means the French became acquainted with all the Causes of Complaint they had against you; and as your People were daily encreasing their Settlements, by this Means you drove them into the Arms of the French, and they took the Advantage of spiriting them up against you, by telling them: "Children, you see, and we have often told, how the English, your Brethren, would serve you; they plant all the Country, and drive you back; so that in a little Time you will have no Land: It is not so with us; though we build Trading-Houses on your Land, we do not plant it; we have our Provisions from over the great Water. . . . our advice to you is that you send for the Senecas and them; treat them kindly, and rather give them some Part of their Fields back again than differ with them. It is in your Power to settle all the Differences with them if you please.

FIGURE A. *Thomas Smith,* Self Portrait

The fine arts have been slow to develop in the new communities spun off from Europe. A common explanation for this retardation has been that pioneers had other things to do: plant crops to fill their bellies, fight off the aboriginal enemies. But questions remain unanswered. Why does one type of art win approval—and produce outstanding works—before another? In the English colonies of North America, architecture and household furnishings of the early settlers remain interesting today. Similarly prose literature of the Puritans is still readable today. Music was the last art form to attain stature in the United States, perhaps due to the relative expense of the materials with which it worked; not until the late nineteenth century was music being created and performed with a perfection that the nation can look back on with pride (see Chapter 27 on the rise of jazz). Another laggard was the visual arts, perhaps because of separation from classical works that could serve both to stimulate and to guide, lack of discerning patrons—our speculations could run for quite a while. Whatever the reason, most painting of the colonial period seems flat and dull. Its typical mode was the portrait, and the subject is offered down to posterity as a two-dimensional block of rectitude.

Exceptions, however, have survived. This self-portrait by Thomas Smith, done about 1675, is one. The hollows in his cheeks, the lines in his face—he seems solid flesh and bone. Little is known about the man. He had lived in Bermuda as well as Boston—he had fought at sea. Partly in love with death, his hand rests on a skull and on a manuscript that says:

> *Why why should I the World be minding*
> *Therein a World of Evils Finding*
> *Then Farwell World . . .*

FIGURE B. *John Singleton Copley,* Paul Revere

Everybody knows about the "Midnight Ride of Paul Revere," which was painted by Grant Wood in 1931 (Figure 25-3). But how many have heard of Revere as a great silversmith, whose bountiful creations can still be seen in the museums of New England? This portrait by John Singleton Copley (1738–1815) shows the craftsman surrounded by the tools of his trade. The picture also reflects Revere's relation to those tools, and hints of the problems he encountered in creating the product that he holds in his hand.

Probably no greater tribute could be paid to any painter of portraits than the one that John Adams paid to Copley's graphic studies of individuals: "You can scarcely help discoursing with them, asking questions and receiving answers." Born poor, Copley early became wealthy by depicting the wealthy, but he did not truckle to them; he depicted them. On the eve of the War for Independence, he took his Loyalist wife and repaired to England. He never came home again. Financially, he was still a success. Artistically, he withered. But he will remain as the first great American painter. Maybe he wanted no more; he said once that seeing is a sort of luxury.

FIGURE A. *Thomas Smith,* Self Portrait

FIGURE D. *Karl Bodmer,* Indian Chief

FIGURE C. *John James Audubon,* Passenger Pigeon

The subject of this painting demonstrates one trait in the American character which has been remarkably persistent: a belief that the abundance of the environment knows no limits. Almost every commentator on America in the 18th and early 19th centuries spoke of the incredible number of wild pigeons about. Audubon himself estimated one flock to consist of over a billion birds. The species is now extinct. Its demise must be laid to the discredit of the same kind of rapacious slaughter in the Kentucky squirrel hunt described early in Chapter 11. Audubon witnessed a hunt at Louisville. "The people were all in arms. The banks of the Ohio were crowded with men and boys, incessantly shooting at the pilgrims, which there flew lower as they passed the river. Multitudes were thus destroyed. For a week or more, the population fed on no other flesh than that of pigeons, and talked of nothing but pigeons." At another hunt, 300 hogs were driven to the site to feed on the residue of carcasses after the people had taken all they could possibly use.

But the painting shows another set of attitudes, admittedly more common among Easterners and Europeans than among frontiersmen. Not only a love of nature, but a concern for recording its components in painstaking detail seemed to have been increasing in the early nineteenth century. Whereas the engraving of the beaver dam (Figure 5-1) is sketchy and inaccurate, Audubon's paintings are marvels of precision. He saw his duty to be almost as much scientific as artistic. Travelling about America from 1821 to 1824, he made field drawings of all birds that he encountered. He then used these notes to compose paintings showing a species, often a male and female pair, located in its characteristic habitat. He also frequently portrayed behavior typical of the species: the feeding sequence shown here is part of the pigeons' courting ritual. His aim was to publish a series of color plates, accompanied by a descriptive text, which would include every bird native to North America, as well as certain common mammals. The publication of *The Birds of America* took twelve years (the last plate was engraved in 1838), required 435 plates, and cost $100,000 dollars.

FIGURE D. *Karl Bodmer,* Indian Chief

The best-known painter of trans-Mississippi Indians prior to the Civil War is George Catlin (1796–1872). Anthropologists will always be grateful for Catlin's renditions of life among many tribes, such as his depiction of a Mandan village in what is now North Dakota. But recently many critics have come to feel that his art is inferior to that of Karl Bodmer (1809–93), who also worked among the Mandans. Bodmer went even farther west than Catlin; he accompanied Prince Maximilian of Wied in 1832–33 on a trip through the northern plains. His bold watercolors of Blackfoot and Hidatsa were converted into plates by Rudolph Ackermann, and these eighty-one "elaborately colored" reproductions are the mainstay of Prince Maximilian's *Travels in the Interior of North America* (2 vols., 1839–41). Bodmer also left a visual record of the Yellowstone River and the Little Rockies. More than 400 of his works are now present in the Joslyn Art Museum in Omaha.

The original publishers of the book illustration made from this painting had to use skilled European artisans to produce a colored print; each page was tinted by hand, as also were the book engravings made from Audubon's paintings (Figure C). Today's multiple color printing requires precise alignment of press plates for each color, and careful work with a photographic light screen to separate the color for each plate so that its tone will balance faithfully with the others. The latter process often still requires skilled handwork, and until very recently these skills were more cheaply available in Europe than in America. Commercial color printing has always required a balance between extremes of cost and quality, and this particular print has been used as a sample of medium-difficulty color work in demonstrating what an American printer can accomplish economically.

PART II

The Struggle for Independence

1763–1815

The Enlightenment and the Republican Revolution

It is not easy to find a working definition of the outburst of optimism that is known as the Enlightenment. A recent work with pretensions to authority makes no precise effort either to date the epoch or to define its character, but parades some traits, not bothering to rank them in significance or to unravel their interactions. Of the influential French philosophes one learns only that they had almost nothing in common beyond critical attitudes toward orthodoxy, especially in religion. Such vagaries are metaphysical hairsplitting, not history; the reader deserves something solider to chew upon here.

The Enlightenment is a breathtaking deviation in western history. It lasted about three generations. It did not embrace anybody born before 1685. That year saw the birth of Bach and Handel; it saw too the final ghastly religious persecution in western Europe with the revocation of the Edict of Nantes and the ensuing purge of the Huguenots in France. The Enlightenment did not win thinkers born after 1760. The revolutions in America and France, the conquests by Napoleon, made it impossible for the contemplative to seize life with dewy-eyed ecstasy.

Western man through the centuries has been a gloomy chap. He has believed in original sin and eternal damnation. In our time Albert Camus has written: "There is but one truly serious philosophical problem, and that is suicide. Judging whether life is or is not worth living amounts to answering the fundamental question of philosophy." A relative and parishioner of Jonathan Edwards cut his own throat; it seems that Abraham Lincoln as a young man considered doing himself in; Theodore Dreiser returned often to the image of man drifting helplessly on the waves; Clarence Darrow loved to take the negative in debates on "Is Life Worth Living?" Instead of lolling in talk about innate depravity, the Enlightenment glorified man's ability to re-shape the world. Voltaire or Franklin would have thought Camus diseased to advance such a thesis; we may even doubt if they would have understood what he was talking about. The Enlightenment was a boisterously positive stance toward the human condition. It was *éclat, élan,* spirit, brilliance. It shouted that whatever is, is good (or can be improved with sweet reason).

The work of definition may be done by comparing an eighteenth-century philosopher to a predecessor. Thomas Hobbes, surrounded by the carnage of religious fanaticism (Cromwell captured Drogheda in Catholic Ireland and slaughtered the whole garrison), could write "My mother bore twins, me and fear." How different the posture of *The Social Contract* (1762). A passage talks of the two modes of selecting civil officers. You can do it by choice, whether by appointment by one man or election by many. Or you can do it by lot, simply drawing straws.

> When choice and lot are combined, positions that require special talents, such as military posts, should be filled by the former; the latter does for cases, such as judicial offices, in which good sense, justice, and integrity are enough, because in a State that is well constituted, these qualities are common to all the citizens.

Rousseau's blithe assumption may boggle the mind of a modern man, but to him it was normal, self-evident.

The preceding chapter deals with results of warfare. Save from 1713 to 1739, it was unusual for England and France to be at peace. But here was nothing resembling the rapine that laid barren all of Europe during the Thirty Years' War. Here was no counterpart to the civil wars in the British Isles. A man, a generation, a nation—all appraise their present state through the lens of past conditioning, and to many a citizen of the eighteenth century his days seemed basically placid, secure, and perhaps improvable. It is indispensable to realize that Rousseau and his fellows were not daft. The air of optimism rested on great and tangible achievements. Wars may occur, but man can control and civilize them. And as startling proof of such optimism, by the American Revolution a people did claim sovereignty for itself, did to an extent form its own government from the ground up, *de novo*. It must also be conceded that the ideas discussed below touched only a narrow segment of most societies in Europe. Vast changes are not synchronized across entire populations. Just as millions of Americans today hold to a religion that would be suitable to the sixteenth century, so did the average man two hundred years ago wend a customary but tedious round, oblivious to the conceptual hurricanes that knifed the air about him. Alongside the surge of science were superstitions and delusions. Thus one Englishwoman claimed that she gave birth to rabbits, and among the masses deceived was George II's personal physician, who intended to award her a pension. Then she was caught bribing a servant to buy the rabbits.

At the center of the Enlightenment was an emerging array of new answers to old questions. Where does God stand in regard to human affairs, particularly to government? Can politics be a science? How does a legitimate state begin, and what are its proper goals? Must a citizen accord passive obedience to the existing state even though it did not originate legitimately, or can rebellion be justified? If government begins with a compact, what is its nature? Who are the parties? Do we have only "positive" rights that take descent solely from the sanction of the government, or do we have from a pre-existing state of nature certain natural rights? If so, what are they? What other aspects of human nature should be taken into account?

The first task was to subvert the dogma that the king held his power from God, and for this there are some clear logical possibilities. One is to hold that the Almighty has nothing to do with civil government after he has created man with certain powers and rights. To an American cleric as the Revolution neared, government was *"the ordinance of men—an human institution."* John Winthrop would have repelled this apostasy with a second, opposite view: he knew that even if the selection of magistrates had been left to the citizens, the forms of the state had been decreed by God down to some details. The best man to fill a role might be open to question, but the content of the role was preordained. A third view reversed the second: God picked the ruler, and then the ruler defined the forms of government. That was the original dogma at issue, and it represented the Tory view: a king succeeded to the throne by divine right.

Major demolition was wrought by John Locke in England just prior to the dawn of the Enlightenment. He began with God: we are all His servants, even His chattels; He did not set one above others; in this sense each individual has a right to govern himself. We are free of each other, and we are equal to each other (as will be seen later, the ruler in certain respects is inferior to the ruled). Here is political theory that was conservative in taking God as the first premise, but rebellious in enrolling Him against passive compliance with a hereditary monarchy. Disputes about the links of God to civil government bit by bit dissolved the fetters entirely, with discourses on politics tending to reduce or omit the Divine plan. John Wise gave equal validity to the Bible with natural law, since each was decreed by God and discerned by human reason. But a contemporary bishop in the Church of England, taking as his text Christ's pronouncement that His church was not of this world, argued in continuation that the visible church had nothing whatever to do with mundane affairs.

Some would not go so far, but they juggled priorities. The authors of *Cato's Letters,* the English text that seems to have exercised the greatest influence in America, were as ingenious as anybody: "Were we not *rational Creatures,* we could not be *religious Creatures,* but upon a Level with *Brutes,* to whom God has made no Revelation of himself, because they want Reason to discern it, and to thank him for it. *Revelation* therefore presupposes *Reason,* and addresses it self to *Reason . . .*" In conclusion, "As we must judge from Scripture what is Orthodoxy; so we must judge from Reason, what is Scripture." They made an audacious retort to the brief for special training in the interpretation of the Holy Writ: "When God would have his Pleasure known to Men, it is agreeable to his Goodness to make it evident; when he would not, it is agreeable to his Wisdom to make it impenetrable." Who are these upstart ministers that they presume to make transparent what God Himself could not or would not clarify? Beliefs were wobbling. A Connecticut pastor in 1758 could wail that "the fear of God is amazingly cast off in this day"; a crying fault was the predilection for "exalting human Nature under all its Depravity to a situation equal to all its Necessities . . ." That was the break we call the Enlightenment, but change was far from total. During the Revolution John Adams could note humbly (to be echoed in the next century by Lincoln): "There is no such thing as human wisdom. All is the providence of God." Characteristic was the reversion of another New England preacher in 1750 to a straddle: "We may safely assert these two things in general, without undermining government: One is, that no civil rulers are to be obeyed when they enjoin things that are inconsistent with the commands of God. . . . Another thing that may be asserted with equal truth and safety is, that no government is to be submitted to at the expense of that which is the sole end of all government—the common good and safety of society." Jehovah had not been thrust altogether into the wings, but he could no longer upstage man, and He had not named any tyrannical kings as His understudies.

If God has ordained no rules and no rulers, where should modern man turn for guidance? He might look to the past, suggested *Cato's Letters*: "Mankind will be always the same, will always act within one Circle; and when we know what they did a Thousand Years ago in any Circumstance, we shall know what they will do a Thousand Years hence in the same. This what is called Experience, the surest Mistress and Lesson of Wisdom." This tack could be reversed, as was done by David Hume: "Mankind are so much the same, in all times and places, that history informs us of nothing new or strange in this particular. Its chief use is only to discover the constant and universal principles of human nature, by showing men in all varieties and situations, and furnishing us with materials from which we may form our observations and become acquainted with the regular springs of human action and behavior." Small matter whether we probe the past to shape the present or look at the present to understand the past; by either procedure politics to an extent, in Hume's phrase, "may be reduced to a science." It comes as no shock to find American colonials pottering about in classical ruins. They especially loved to catalog the moral blemishes that eroded the Roman Empire, with the implication that its vices would similarly undo the British.

The view of history that the Enlightenment produced was hypothetical history, an abstraction, theory, what a twentieth-century social scientist would call a model. No sensible person believed that any existing government in Europe had proceeded from a "state of nature" to its current state by means of a "social compact." But we must not ignore the true-to-life analogues for their conceptions. "In the beginning all the world was America," wrote Locke, making the false inference that Indian tribes had no government when the white man arrived and further postulating that the Europeans of Old Testament times had been in a similar condition. The ideologists could point to many instances in which contemporaries had banded together to form a voluntary association from thin air, as it were. Every joint-stock company was such a structure. So were Congregational churches. Emigrants on ships bound for the New World often set up an organization and chose officers for the duration of the voyage. The polity at Plymouth was so founded by the Mayflower Compact.*

So the idea of the covenant was a continuation, but it was modified. Permanance with change, that is history. In the Federal theology, the elect opted to live by God's decrees. The harshness of some of His commands was softened in some measure by mufflers imposed from England, largely from mercenary motives. When Maryland legislated against Catholics, English authorities in 1704 voided two measures on the ground that they tended "to depopulate that prosperous colony." Virginia a half century later was warned against religious bigotry because "Toleration and a free Exercise of Religion" were "essential to the enriching and improving of a trading Nation." With Jehovah at most a silent partner, the concord remained, but as a secular one. Men joined to create a state, to effectuate not Divine ordinances but their own. Sovereignty lay with the people, not with the mass together but with each as a stockholding individual. (Nor should we say that colonists acted on a belief that "The voice of the people is the voice of God." The voice of the people is

---

*Lazy, mankind almost never thinks up truly new patterns; he tries to cope with new situations by adapting and distorting traditional categories and models. To justify a state, why not reason from a stock company?

the voice of—the people; there is no higher sovereignty, and God cannot vote except when the people take the initiative in granting Him a special franchise when they revolt against their earthly ruler.) This mode of thought made two assumptions: First, that individuals exist and have the right to govern themselves. The view was atomistic; Jefferson, for instance (using a term from philosophy), was a nominalist: "Nature has, in truth, produced units only through all her works. Classes, orders, genera, species, are not of her work." But since as individual men we cannot cope with the complexities of nature as unrelated items, we must classify "arbitrarily on such characteristic resemblances and differences as seem to us most prominent and invariable in the several subjects, and most likely to take a strong hold in our memories." Second, covenant-thinking went on to a logically inconsistent secondary premise that the units labelled men could unite to form social structures or organizations which would exist and have real power.

The second axiom is, however, empirically true and was hardly an axiom at all, since it was inferred from observed realities. But the first axiom is palpably false. Man (as species or individual) cannot be neatly severed even from his physical habitat, and to regard him apart from his culture is to study phantoms; as John Wise said, man is a "sociable" creature. But let us argue from the absurd premise. To do so, we must jettison the vocabulary that referred to "the social compact" as a single act. Logic requires not one compact but two, although they might be simultaneous. Men as units must act, however unconsciously, on common customs to create a society. This "compact," involving a consensus of common cultural values, has an implicit existence, and we may term it the origin or precondition for what we may call the "state of society" (by another lexicon, that would be called Locke's "state of nature"). Here, with the people as a cultural group, and emphatically not with the government which may not even exist as yet, is the locus of sovereignty.

But the "state of society" is deficient because, in Locke's phrase, it is characterized by "want of a common judge." In such a situation "there is always Warre of every one against every one" (Hobbes); human life is "solitary, poor, nasty, brutish and short." "Whereas were all Men left to the boundless Liberty which they claim from Nature," said *Cato's Letters,* "every Man would be interfering and quarrelling with another; every Man would be plundering the Acquisitions of another. . . ." No mechanisms are available to enforce the laws, much less to revise them. To escape this anarchy, members of the society enter a second compact, erecting a government. The social contract, wrote Rousseau, is the deed "by which a people is a people." He denied that sovereignty was conferred on any select few by divine right. He denied that our ancestors had committed us to any arrangements whatever. All civic officials can be removed, and all forms of state can be altered. The past has no right to bind the present, would echo Thomas Paine and Thomas Jefferson, and the present none to shackle the future. No government can be legitimate except by the active consent of the living people.

Although he tried to escape the chains of history, Rousseau was held by them in ironic fashion. In a pluralistic society such as modern Canada or the United States, it is accepted that popular government means majority rule hedged by certain rights for minorities. That is not how Rousseau saw it. Under the social contract, no member would be coerced by the state, because laws would embody the "General Will." In effect, nobody would be a dissenter pummelled by the rival will of a transient majority; when he obeyed the law he was merely obeying himself. The idea of a General Will may seem fantasy, but it must be recalled that Rousseau was heir to the Middle Ages when the received analogy for a society or government was an organism. Indeed, several modern nations are posing sharply the question of whether a government can survive when the society knows no General Will, when some glorify as highest virtue what others spit upon.

In discussions of the proper goals of the state, much has been made of the transition from Locke's phrasing about protection of "life, liberty, and property" to the famous triad in the Declaration of Independence. The connections among these terms would be more clear if the uses writers made of them were less obscure. At times Locke seems to use *property* as indicating immediate and tangible goods or money that can be immediately converted into them. But is he close to Jefferson when he writes of "Lives, Liberties and Estates, which I call by the general name, *Property*"? *Cato's Letters* asked: "What is Government, but a Trust committed by All, or the Most, to One, or a Few, who are to attend upon the Affairs of All, that every one may, with the more Security, attend upon his own?" It argued that Happiness depends upon financial independence, which rests upon property, which can only be won by Liberty and protected by good government.

It is obvious today that the natural-rights philosophy and covenant-thinking of the Enlightenment should not be separated from the temporal zeal for profit-making. The tie was blatant in Locke's fripperies about private property. He began with a labor theory of value that might have won endorsement from Karl Marx. A man gains title to a natural object by mixing his labor with it so as to alter it. But if the man's servant or slave is the one to invest toil in the object, it is still the man who gets ownership. Why is it not "owned" by the servant or the slave? By evading this query, Locke came to a theory that was quite contrary to any concept of innate right to property. Since each man is God's property, (according to traditional theology), he would have no sanction for alienating any part of his personality even if he wanted to. But now, so Locke's thesis ran, he can alienate or keep for himself alone those things with which he has mixed parts of his personality. Instead of a natural right, property was a "positive" right operative by decree of the state. A century later Franklin took a mixture of the two positions in analyzing the duty to pay taxes. His language was so lucid and his viewpoint so representative as to deserve lengthy quotation:

All Property, indeed, except the Savage's temporary Cabin, his Bow, his Match-coat, and other little Acquisitions, absolutely necessary for his Subsistence, seems to me to be the Creature of public Convention. Hence the Public has the Right of Regulating Descents, and all other Conveyances of Property, and even of limiting the Quantity and the Uses of it. All the Property that is necessary to a Man, for the Conservation of the Individual and the Propagation of the Species, is his natural Right, which none may justly deprive him of: But all Property superfluous to such purposes is the Property of the Publick, who, by their Laws, have created it, and who may therefore by other Laws dispose of it, whenever the Welfare of the Publick shall demand such Disposition. He that does not like civil Society on these Terms, let him retire and live among Savages.

Well enough. But note the two qualifications. A man can justly yield his belongings only by his own consent, direct or delegated. And it can only be demanded for "the Welfare of the Publick."

The Enlightenment shilly-shallied toward the view that utilitarianism would embalm as "the greatest good of the greatest number." This creed may now be identified with Jeremy Bentham, but it was formulated earlier. We may be tempted to see it in a Boston election sermon of 1667 defining "the *Compass* that Rulers are to steer by" as "What is for or against the Public good." Not so: the minister meant that God would instruct the magistrates on this subject. The meaning was far different when *Cato's Letters* later said: "The Good of the Governed being the sole end of Government, they must be the greatest and best Governors, who make their People great and happy. . . ." Thomas Paine quoted approvingly a "wise observer on governments": "The science of the politician consists in fixing the true point of happiness and freedom. Those men would deserve the gratitude of ages, who should discover a mode of government that contained the greatest sum of individual happiness, with the least national expence." Scourging any notion of divine right, Paine also rebutted Hobbes' thesis that a subject should obey his ruler on the grounds of expediency because any government is superior to anarchy. A tyrant, said Paine, must always cause misery for his subject, and passive obedience cannot be defended.

A government originates by voluntary agreement. In talking about this pact, Locke skirted use of the word "contract," perhaps because at law it conveys a reciprocal obligation. He used another and one-sided legal term: "this express or tacit trust" and "the trust of prerogative." The beneficiary must have rights, the trustee may have only duties. If he violates the terms, the fiduciary relation is dissolved. Having thus imposed a moral hedge on rulers, architects of the state imposed institutional ones. Thence came the theory of checks and balances. The type known as the tripartite division of powers (legislative, executive, judicial) is frequently cited as a contribution initiated by Montesquieu, but in fact it had been a common institutional fact for decades in America. The French statesman might be better cited in connection with the division of the legislature into "upper" and "lower" chambers. Pointing to the frequency of barons' wars, he wanted to give noblemen a special weight in government; if they counted for no more than commoners, they would be rebellious. To this Rousseau answered: "It is precisely because the force of things always tends to destroy equality that the force of legislation should always tend to maintain it." John Adams put forth a reversal of Montesquieu's reasoning, but with a similar conclusion. He feared a unicameral legislature such as the one Franklin was defending in Pennsylvania. Adams wanted to segregate the rich and well-born into a senate where they would be less able to pervert the needy and numerous members of the assembly. Fence power in, split it up.

Whereas the Enlightenment faced life affirmatively as a good, it was not appreciative of man's needs as an individual, especially his spiritual needs. It was wary, even hostile; it could be cynical. Thus Benjamin Franklin, caring not a fig for salvation, urged support for churches by mentioning "how great a Proportion of Mankind consists of weak and ignorant Men and Women, and of inexperienc'd and inconsiderate Youth of both Sexes, who have need of the Motives of Religion to restrain them from Vice. . . ." Here was the spirit, if not the erudition, that Edward Gibbon was building into his corrosive chapters on Christianity in *The Decline and Fall of the Roman Empire*: with tongue in cheek, use the Holy Writ for social control. Thomas Paine was caustic against the muddleheads who could not tell society from government, the one coming from needs, the other from wickedness. If we could restrain our own vices, no state would be required to do it for us. "Here then is the origin and rise of government, namely, a mode rendered necessary by the inability of moral virtue to govern the world; here too is the design and end of government, viz. freedom and security." Alexander Hamilton allegedly thought men would move to two motives only: Interest, or Force. Buy 'em or beat 'em . . . The carrot or the club. The mood of the age taught that power corrupts, and that access to power would only feed a voracious appetite for more power. When Jefferson ascribed the above attitude to Hamilton he was seeking to discredit it, but even the most ardent exponents of popular government were prone to rely on a negative argument. Jefferson seems to glance over his shoulder as if to concede that a republic would be inept in running even a hotdog stand, and as for managing a nation—well! But his reply is: What better mode can you offer? No wild-eyed enthusiast wrote the Inaugural Address for 1801: "Sometimes it is said that man cannot be trusted with the government of himself. Can he then, be trusted with the government of others? Or have we found angels in the forms of kings to govern him? Let history answer this question."*

Seeming exceptions can be found. But notice that Rousseau, no matter how extreme his euphoria, stipulated (in the quote at the beginning of this chapter) "in a State that is well constituted." Snatches can be seen in the

---

*I realize that a prudent man's views are tempered to his audience, and I know too that they change with time, especially in Jefferson's case. With few exceptions, evidence used in this chapter is dated before 4 July, 1776, and if not, I think it represents matters as they stood prior to that day.

Enlightenment of Locke's seeming belief that "virtue" is a natural attribute common among men. The worst challenge comes from Jefferson's belief in an innate "moral sense":

> Man was destined for society. His morality, therefore, was to be formed for this object. He was endowed with a sense of right and wrong, merely relative to this. This sense is as much a part of his nature, as the sense of hearing, seeing, feeling; . . . The moral sense, or conscience, is as much a part of man as his leg or arm. It is given to all human beings in a stronger or weaker degree, as force of members is given them in a greater or less degree.

Was this idea just idle prattle to a favorite nephew entering manhood? Not likely; we must apparently take this idea seriously, since it was not in a private lecture but in a public opinion to President Washington that Jefferson referred to "the moral law to which man has been subjected by his creator, and of which his feelings or conscience, as it is sometimes called, are the evidence with which his creator has furnished him." But before Jefferson wrote this, Paine had already refuted him:

> For were the impulses of conscience clear, uniform, and irresistibly obeyed, man would need no other lawgiver; but that not being the case, he finds it necessary to surrender up a part of his property to furnish means for the protection of the rest; and this he is induced to do by the same prudence which in every other case advises him out of two evils to choose the least.

Sincere or not, Jefferson's dream for an innate moral sense was, to say the least, a poor foundation for politics. Mankind has long had a penchant for an "extrasensory" way of discovering the unexplainable through sense organs beyond the obvious five. When Jonathan Edwards endowed the sanctified with a "new spiritual sense," he had the gumption to say that it was "entirely above nature." Spokesmen for ESP (extrasensory perception) deny that it is supernatural. As for some innate moral sense that leads inevitably to good behavior, if man had it, the world would hold far less cruelty than it does. From one perspective we are all born little Hitlers, in that nobody understands at birth that other beings than himself can suffer pain. Morality must develop through learning, and this development is frequently flawed. The ultimate data of all we know, taught Locke, must come to us through our five senses. Jefferson agreed to the point of saying bluntly: "Our opinions are not voluntary." Whence come they? We can grasp ideas only by using our sensory organs—and alas they too are fallible. Our eyes like our brains may mislead; when we look at the same scene, what I am willing to see is not necessarily what you are ready to see. Since the finest wisdom is derived in the end from dubiously gathered evidence, all knowledge is provisional. By this route Americans came to a scorn for finespun speculations. No idea was sound until proven by practice. Wisdom was a law of averages applied to the accumulated perceptions of mankind. Anybody proceeding from this philosophical framework was bound to be a conservative unless he lost his wits. Samuel Adams, as flamboyant a patriot as any man in America, was not playing verbal tricks when he said the colonies sought merely to be "restored to their original standing."

Whatever may have led to the American Revolution, it was not a dispute about lofty principles. Thinking Britons would concede that the Americans were sound on such matters. To the theoretical issues posed by the Enlightenment, the Atlantic was a highway and not a moat. Englishmen and Americans had resolved them by 1763 on the same terms; it is noteworthy that after 1761 the very label "Tory" was not used in contemporary analyses of general elections in Britain. Whatever clashes would occur must come on a lower level of abstraction ("Can sovereignty be divided?" is less abstract than "What is sovereignty?" "Is virtual representation real?" is less abstract than "By what right should a man be represented at all?" And these were the only two theoretical contentions to be resolved after 1763.)

More remarkable yet, leaders on both sides of the water agreed in their conceptions of the ideal society. Granting that they took part in great changes, they did not so intend. American steps toward education for all were surely revolutionary, but the pedagogic blueprints were copies. The first provost of Franklin's Philadelphia Academy wanted three different kinds of education, one for "gentlemen," another for pupils "design'd for the Mechanick Professions," a third for "all the remaining People of the Country." Jefferson agreed (his vaunted faith in schools as the bedrock of the republic has not been examined any more sharply than has Roger Williams' advocacy of religious liberty; see mid-Chapter 2); he thought the common man needed nothing beyond the three r's. The colonial who leaned farthest toward democracy in education was Franklin (see early Chapter 4). But the man who helped to found the Academy was the same leather-apron who mourned the proliferation of taverns because competition among them would put the owners "under greater Temptations to entertain Apprentices, Servants, and even Negroes."

When they came to write a brief for rebellion, Americans had to phrase it in terms of the conservatism of mankind. Man was patient, easily abused, almost inert. But to earlier doctrine the Enlightenment gave a secular turn. Hamlet's famous soliloquy (III, i) raised the basic question:

> who would fardels bear,
> To grunt and sweat under a weary life,
> But that the dread of something after death,—
> The undiscover'd country from whose bourn
> No traveller returns,—puzzles the will
> And makes us rather bear those ills we have
> Than fly to others that we know not of?

The Declaration of Independence took a similar tack with no mention of any Hereafter: "Prudence, indeed, will dictate that Governments long established should not be changed for light and transient causes; and accordingly all experience hath shown, that mankind are more disposed to suffer, while evils are sufferable, than to right themselves by abolishing the forms to which they are accustomed." Rebellions are not too frequent but too rare. The urgent threat is not anarchy but tyranny. The final justification of any revolution is simply that it occurred.

The Founding Fathers looked in two directions; they fought on two fronts. With one hand they wrested new privileges from their erstwhile superiors. With the other they repelled urges toward egalitarianism that surged upward from the masses of their own society. They wanted no levelling, but neither did they want a replica of Europe. Their dual vision was perfectly said by a young Philadelphian who visited France after the American Revolution. Himself born to status (his father was descended from a founder of Pennsylvania and his mother was a Lee from Virginia), he was appalled by European extremities of condition, by the harsh specifics of rich and destitute. To his father he wrote "a *certain degree of equality* is essential to human bliss" and then added "without destroying the necessary subordination."

Through the Western world in the late eighteenth century the governing classes were rapidly gaining in wealth and power. So were their inferiors. The contrary impulses collided. Pandemonium ensued. Usually the question of universal suffrage was not the battleground. The fray in most jurisdictions swirled around the so-called "constituted bodies"; in the Anglo-American clash it involved Parliament and the provincial assemblies. The demand was not that these bodies be abolished but rather that they be hedged in and opened up. The foe was hereditary or privileged or self-perpetuating power. The guidons blazed: All power is delegated power. All officials can be sacked. These two maxims may not flutter us, but in the eighteenth century they were heresy.

The magistrates had been driven far from what they wanted. Governor Winthrop had no desire for a codification of the laws of Massachusetts, but he had to accept one. Early divines, convinced that man had the right to seek truth directly in the Bible, opposed man-made confessions on the ground that they "doth seem to abridge them of that liberty," but they had to issue a catalog of errors from the Cambridge Synod. The habit of spelling everything out and writing it all down had become so deepseated by the American Revolution that a great scholar can speak of "the single salient feature of American constitutionalism, viz., the binding character of the written constitution." Another great historian, Robert R. Palmer (see Ways to Study History VII), has pointed to "the essential revolutionary idea of the American Revolution: the idea of the people as a constituent power, working through a special convention conceived as outside and prior to government, and creating, by its sovereign action, the organs of state to which it grants a delegated authority."

But none of this was new in 1776, it was old. We need to stand back from the details and look at the drift of history from 1600 to 1850. Palmer has characterized the last four decades of the eighteenth century as "the age of the democratic revolution." The phrase is apt, but the dates cannot be made to fit the American story. Democracy was a much slower growth. Its development was jagged. Elements of the structure of politics were determined in many colonies before 1760: most white men could vote, legislatures had won hegemony over governors, and they were the most democratic assemblies in the Western world. Other elements, such as the conviction that all adult males are equally suited for public office, would not be popular until after 1800. What the Revolutionary generation achieved, according to one recent commentator, was to validate and stabilize and perhaps sanctify relations that were already accomplished.

This conclusion is so telling, its ramifications are so wide, that it must not be either brushed off or swallowed. Let us break it down. Take the abolition of primogeniture and entail in Virginia. Jefferson thought it one of his finest achievements; a modern student calls it "of little material consequence." Jefferson was proud of his law for religious toleration, but already the suffrage in civil elections was freed from sectarian tests, only the few Catholics in Virginia were barred from public office, and non-Anglicans often were exempted from the parish taxes to support the church. Property qualifications were still imposed on voting rights, but they meant little because where land was cheap almost all white males could pass them. No civic offices were hereditary.

These statements are by and large true—descriptive of conditions as they actually existed at the beginning of the Revolutionary era.* But was Jefferson then simply big-headed in boasting of his accomplishments? I think not. We should weigh his belief that the price of liberty is eternal vigilance. History knows regressions, reversions, atavisms. No civilized European in the late eighteenth century would have credited the use of genocide against other civilized Europeans, but it has happened in the twentieth. Monopoly of land was not a problem in Virginia in 1780, but it could have become one by 1830; the Louisiana Purchase was not foreordained. Belief in an established church may have atrophied by the Revolution but it had not died, and the modern epoch has seen more than one secular ideology decreed for a nation. The issue of democratic participation in politics has not been settled once for all; in 1970 the Association of Manitoba Municipalities could propose that nobody be allowed to run for public office who was receiving public-welfare payments or who owned less than $500 in property. The Revolution in America made clear commitments in most of these areas, and eventually established decisive ways of coping with the issues.

---

*We have learned a good bit on these matters in the last twenty years, but not enough to be complacent. We still have not even discussed seriously the question of whether a statistical approach is likely to be the most fruitful one (I suspect not). It is no help at all to cite figures for voter turnout in a single town in a single year, but reputable scholars still do it. Tactics must be devised for estimating how far the town and year speak for more generalized behavior.

To the extent that we are concerned with the growth of ideas, we could say simply that the Founding Fathers spelled out in workaday institutions some principles that were new to the Enlightenment. At the highest level of abstraction, they had no argument with educated Englishmen (see above), but at a lower level they did. Any republican government, the men of the American Revolution proclaimed, must be federal, with local sovereignty and limited levels of central authority. They added that any system of representation must involve several strata of delegation, in the sense that Mr. Jones is entrusted not only to name Mr. Smith to represent Mr. Jones; Mr. Jones can also name the same Mr. Smith to represent Mr. Powell. Thus neither of our questions about sovereignty (Can sovereignty be divided? Is virtual representation real?) can be answered on the level of abstraction on which it is asked. Each must be made more concrete. What level of government should be charged with which powers? (A businessman in the United States might be flabbergasted to hear that in Canada the federal minimum-wage law has almost no bearing on manufacturing.) Second, given a system of "virtual representation" in which Mr. Jones sometimes votes (through Mr. Smith) on behalf of Mr. Powell ("virtually" represented by Mr. Smith), how can the system guarantee that Jones' vote will produce results in the interest of Powell and not in the interest of Jones? On the first problem of dividing sovereignty, Great Britain accepted in practice the American view, but she did not admit to doing so. On the second problem, virtual representation, America accepted in practice the British view, but she did not admit to doing so.

These questions were not narrowly political. Setting out to elucidate "the wealth of nations," Adam Smith was faced with both. If Jones is the worst kind of self-seeker, what system will force him also to act in Powell's interests? The answer, said Adam Smith, is the "invisible hand" of competition. Confronted with thousands of other Joneses turning out a product similar to his own, this specific Jones will have to sell to Powell decent goods at a decent price. Thus, when we are blessed with competitive markets, no superior force need be invoked. Conflicting interests can be left alone with the laws of competition, and the great majority of possible powers should not be given away to any level of government.

Like his counterparts in American political theory, Jefferson and Paine, Adam Smith knew what he did not want. He did not want an arrangement by which a king could announce "I am the state." Even if monarchs were shackled, it was hardly better to let another organ of a massive central government interfere as it pleased with men's fortunes. Every power should be kept as near as may be to the grasp of each individual citizen. If he could not wield it effectively, give it to the precinct. If the precinct proved ineffective, let the ward have it. At all costs, block the leakage of power upwards. All this was consonant with the practices that had developed over generations in the American colonies. No governor of Virginia in 1763 would have dared to assert that he was the law, but we can easily imagine a justice of the peace named

Carter saying "I am the state in Charles City County." It was all counter to the theory that had developed in Europe. Kings had been striving to perfect mechanisms with which they could intrude on the smallest detail in the life of the scrawniest peasant in the most remote corner of the realm—and philosophers had been trying to anoint their efforts. Jean Bodin, Hobbes, Locke, all said that sovereignty could not be divided. Through the fog of ideology, some men could not see reality; on the eve of the Revolution, 1773, the Boston-born and Harvard-bred royal governor of Massachusetts was solemnly intoning, "It is impossible there should be two independent Legislatures in the one and the same state."

Poppycock. Right under his nose his fellow-citizens, while offhandedly allowing that Parliament could regulate trade for the entire Empire so long as no attempt was made to enforce the regulations, had worked up a complex of agencies to run matters within Massachusetts. Other evidence was ready at hand. Switzerland had survived since 1648 as a confederation of cantons. The Holy Roman Empire may have had a command post at Vienna, but it encapsulated some 300 semi-autonomous states and the command post did not control all. In Great Britain, sovereignty was not absolute and concentrated, even if theory did say that the King-in-Parliament was absolute. The Poor Laws and the successor Speenhamland system were run by the parishes, and central authority did not interfere. County courts and sheriffs lorded it over their own jurisdictions. Their weight could be crushing when London intruded. In 1616, for instance, a chum of the Duke of Buckingham was given a patent by which he could charge a license of £5 to each inn in the nation. This matter had formerly been controlled in each county by the justices of the peace. They instituted an investigation by Parliament. The Duke's chum found it advisable to flee the country. Was it federalism? Just say that it worked like federalism.

However matters stood in practice, guiding opinion in England on the eve of the Revolution was hellbent on principle. In 1775 the chief justice, a leading exponent of the North ministry in the House of Lords, declared of the American impasse: "We were reduced to the alternative, of adopting coercive measures, or of forever relinquishing our claim of sovereignty or dominion over the colonies. . . . the supremacy of the British legislature must be complete, entire, and unconditional; or on the other hand the colonies must be free and independent." To this view Americans might be deaf and indifferent, until England made efforts to apply it. Then most Americans would balk. As early as 1768 Richard Bland (see the end of Chapter 4) stated the case for his countrymen:

> They presume not to claim any other than the natural Rights of *British* subjects; the fundamental and vital Principles of their happy Government, so universally admired, is known to consist in this: that no Power on Earth has a right to impose Taxes upon the People or to take the smallest Portion of their Property without their consent, given by their Representatives in Parliament . . .

145

But did Americans have representatives in Parliament? Englishmen said yes, colonials said no. On this matter English and American thought have separated so widely in the course of three centuries that it is difficult for an American even to hear the argument for virtual representation. But, as hopefully will be shown, he should. Americans have reasoned from the existence of a pluralistic society. Different segments of the population have diverse interests. The more important ones are likely to be geographically concentrated. Therefore representation should be by area, and a burgess should speak for his home district. In the entire United States in the twentieth century, the only carpetbagger to achieve eminence was Robert F. Kennedy, and he was compelled not only to meet the requirement of the Federal Constitution that he must reside in the state that sent him to the Senate, he was compelled also to meet the more stringent requirement of convincing the voters in New York that he was *their* man. This is contrary to British tradition. To sit in Parliament as a knight of the shire, a man commonly lived in the county that returned him, but many members for boroughs ("for" not "from") did not reside among their constituents. After the party system arose in Great Britain in the nineteenth century, an M.P. might sit for several distinct ridings in the course of his career; if he were important to the party and lost his place in one district, the party would switch him to a safe seat. In Canada the practice has been between the English and the American models—rather closer to the American (This curiosity needs explanation, since the party system in Canada is nearer the British mode than the American).

A famous statement of the English view was made by Edmund Burke to the electors of Bristol just before the American Revolution:

> Parliament is not a *congress* of ambassadors from different and hostile interests, which interests each must maintain an agent and advocate, against other agents and advocates; but Parliament is a *deliberative* assembly of *one* nation, with *one* interest, that of the whole—where not local purposes, not local prejudices, ought to guide, but the general good, resulting from the general reason of the whole. You choose a member, indeed; but when you have chosen him, he is not a member of Bristol, but he is a member of *Parliament*. . . . We are now members for a rich commercial *city*; this city, however, is but a part of a rich commercial *nation,* the interests of which are various, multiform, and intricate. We are members for that great nation, which, however, is itself but part of a great *empire,* extended by our virtue and our fortune to the farthest limits of the East and of the West. All these wide-spread interests must be considered— must be compared—must be reconciled, if possible.

Stated thus, the theory sounds pleasant, and surely it is not absurd on its face as many Americans like to believe. Procedures in the United States have accepted several varieties of virtual representation. Nobody wants to give the suffrage to children, and their rights are protected reasonably well. For centuries it was assumed that husbands would vote as surrogates for their wives, with more or less tolerable results. Perhaps the most remarkable instance was the treatment of developing regions, which will be scrutinized closely below in discussions of the federal public lands. White inhabitants of federal territories were treated with splendid generosity by the United States even before they acquired the right to vote. In short, a trust can be honored.

But it need not be, as the experience of the Indians so tragically proves. The official pretension held that they were wards of the nation. Even as a principle it was vile, but the manner in which the custodian stole from his wards was worse, and the process has not ended. Let us look at one illustration in the last two decades. A tribe of Agua Caliente owned in common some land in southern California. It was warm there in winter, and the town of Palm Springs emerged as a resort for the wealthy from Beverly Hills and Hollywood. A ruling was obtained in Washington that divided up the tribal lands and parceled them out among members of the Agua Caliente. The next stop of the white pirates was Sacramento, where a law was secured that allowed a county court (read "judge") to appoint a "conservator" (a lovely word) over the property of any person who lacked experience in business affairs. The conservators sold off Agua Caliente land to developers. With the proceeds they paid themselves fees for their exertions in managing the estates.

This is the sort of relation that colonials in 1763 would not accept. They did not reject outright the device of virtual representation; it may have merit in some situations. But, they said, it does not apply here. It will result in equity only if trustee and ward share long-term commitments. That condition clearly is not met in the present arrangement. Quite the reverse. The more taxes that Englishmen can extract from us, argued Americans, the less they themselves need to pay.

Even a greedy king, if wise, will follow policies that promote the prosperity of his overseas subjects because it will build up the bounty that he will leave to his heir. But the royal placemen who swarm to the colonies have no such concern. They would not take foreign appointments at all unless they were needy and desirous of improving their estate. Once in America, their sole wish is to fleece us quickly and retire to the family acres in England. It remains to study next the means by which officials tried to gain their ends.

Apart from its dates and other generalizations ventured already, we might state a few conclusions about the Enlightenment. Among literate people, it undermined religion. Whereas the catchword for centuries had been Faith, by 1775 it was coming to be Science. The Enlightenment pushed even further the emphasis on individualism that had been promoted by the Protestant Reformation; with extremists like Thomas Jefferson, society seemed to consist of autonomous atoms. These convictions could be turned against many types of orthodoxy. The revolutionaries in America had no desire to create an egalitarian society. Neither would they concede that all power belonged to the King-in-Parliament. Some degrees of authoritarianism they would not accept. They still believed in a hierarchical society, but they sought to widen considerably the governing group. As they vehemently insisted, they were republicans but not democrats. When they rebelled against their sovereigns, they took usable rationalizations from the Enlightenment in Europe: rule by consent of the governed, natural rights, division of powers, federalism between nation and states.

SOME NOTABLE EVENTS

1651 Thomas Hobbes, *Leviathan.*

1690 John Locke, *Essay concerning Human Understanding.*
John Locke, *Two Treatises of Government.*

1717 John Wise, *A Vindication of the Government of New England Churches.*

1720–
1723 *Cato's Letters.*

1739–
1740 David Hume, *Treatise of Human Nature.*

1748 Montesquieu, *The Spirit of Laws.*

1750 Jonathan Mayhew, "Unlimited Submission and Non-resistance to the Higher Powers."

1762 Jean Jacques Rousseau, *The Social Contract.*

1765–
1769 William Blackstone, *Commentaries on the Laws of England.*

1776 Thomas Paine, *Common Sense.*
The Declaration of Independence.
Adam Smith, *The Wealth of Nations.*
Edward Gibbon, *The Decline and Fall of the Roman Empire.*
Jeremy Bentham, *Fragments on Government.*

Ways to Study History VI

Write fake documents. This precept is not intended to advocate fraud. It does not mean that we should deceive ourselves or others. It does suggest the uses on occasion of proceeding from a conjunction known to be false. In technical language, you make a counterfactual assumption. Opponents of this device have in their arsenal some potent weapons, especially ridicule; an old Yiddish proverb from Russia taunted, "If, if, if, if my grandmother had wheels she'd be a wheelbarrow". These "simulation games" (or role playing) are often used by today's psychologists.

But look at the possible gains. We can make ourselves try to think as our ancestors thought. We can test our comprehension of the strategies by which they characteristically approached various situations. Further, the technique can be used at many levels of sophistication: it is one thing to know "in general" how a person reckoned and quite another to conjure up the terms in which he would reckon. Some years ago, for a graduate seminar in intellectual history, I cooked up a sermon in the style of a seventeenth-century Puritan. Here is part:

> "Thou who are without life because dead in sin, when thou standeth before the God of Judgment, then shalt thou dance live enough. Then you will invent the infinite majesty of God. Dost thou think to stand still when the yellow flame licks at thee, even at the rim of the heat where the fire burns coolest? And if you dance in the yellow, how shall it be when you comest to the blue? And if the blue scorch, what when you come to the red? At the last, to the crucible of the heat, to the white flame, there is pure fire, heat with no touch of cold, where you will stay forever."

Does this passage have any attributes that might mislead you into thinking it genuine? See the Documents following.

Document 6-1

The authors of *Cato's Letters* were eager to discredit the councils that had issued so many tests of religious orthodoxy. Their tactic was derision, or just plain old name-calling. Even though their immediate target in this passage, published in 1720, was ecclesiastical reform, they reveal many of the assumptions that guided them in their comments on civil affairs.

> *And indeed, what better could be expected from Men so chosen, so unqualify'd, and so interested, as the Members of those general Creed-making Councils for the most Part were? They were chosen from several Parts by a Majority of Votes; and they were were most aspiring, factious or crafty, carried it. They sprung from the meanness of the People: They were bred in Cells: They popped into the world without Experience or Breeding: They knew little of Mankind, and less of Government, and had not the common Qualifications of Gentlemen: They were governed by Passion, and led by Expectation: And, either eager for Preferment, or impatient of missing it, they were the perpetual Flatterers or Disturbers of Princes.*
>
> *These were the Men, this their Character. When these Reverend Fathers were got together in a Body, by the Order of a Prince or a Pope; who, having his Necessities, or the Ends of his Ambition to serve, chose proper Tools for those Purposes; they were directed to form such Creeds and Systems of Faith, as his present Views or Interests made requisite for Mankind to believe. . . .*
>
> *Thus any Emperor or Pope might have what Creed he pleased, provided he would be at the Pains and Price of it. And for the rest of Mankind, they had this short Choice, to comply, or be undone.*

Document 6-2

This letter is bogus. So far as I know, its author has not been identified. The text has been in circulation for years around graduate departments of history in the United States, but some of my present colleagues who were formerly at Oxford University say that they never saw it there. Granted that the diction might not be a perfect copy of eighteenth-century prose (although I concede that perhaps it should get a higher grade than my flummery with the sermon), granted too that 1733 would be a better date for a protest against the English budget, does the letter tell us something important about the nature of British politics or is it merely a naughty joke? The supposed author is an M.P. named Anthony Lewis, and he is writing to some of his constituents who complained about the budget for 1714.

Gentelmen:

I have received your letter about the excise, and am surprised at your insolence in writing to me at all.

You know, and I know, that I bought this constituency. You know, and I know, that I am now determined to sell it, and you know what you think I don't know, that you are now out looking for another buyer, and I know, what you certainly don't know, that I have now found another constituency to buy.

About what you said about the excise: May God's curse light upon you all, and may it make your homes as open and free to the excise officers as your wives and daughters have always been to me while I have represented your rascally constituency.

Document 6-3

Mimeographed copies of this spurious address were passed from hand to hand along Madison Avenue for months before the perpetrator of the hanky panky became known. The implied comparison between two former Presidents is certainly cruel—but not unfair. The transition asks an important question: At what time, and why then, did Americans begin to elect to highest office men who could stand up in public only to jumble their syntax and mix their metaphors?

Gettysburg, Pennsylvania
November 19, 1863

AND NOW FOR A FEW CLOSING REMARKS BY PRESIDENT EISENHOWER

I haven't checked these figures but eighty-seven years ago I think it was, a number of individuals organized a governmental set-up here in this country, I believe it covered certain eastern areas, with this idea they were following up based on a sort of national-independence arrangement and the program that every individual is just as good as every other individual. Well, now, of course, we are dealing with this big difference of opinions, civil disturbance you might say, although I don't like to appear to take sides or name any individuals, and the point is naturally to check up, by actual experience in the field, to see whether any governmental set-up with a basis like the one I was mentioning has any validity, whether that dedication, you might say, by those early individuals will pay off in lasting values. . . . It was those individuals themselves, including the enlisted men, who have given this religious character to the area. The way I see it, the rest of the world will not remember any statements issued here but it will never forget how these men put their shoulders to the wheel and carried this idea down the fairway.

Our job, the living individual's job here, is to pick up the burden and sink the putt they made these big efforts here for. . . .

A Reluctant Revolution

Much as John Adams entered into the Enlightenment dragging his feet (See early in Chapter 6), so did the colonies sidle into their struggle for independence in the same spirit, or with the same lack of spirit. As late as 1778 John Adams heard that Thomas Hutchinson, former governor of Massachusetts and now a Tory refugee in England, had persuaded Parliamentary leaders that only one American in five supported Congress. Adams would say scornfully, "If there ever was a war that could be called *the people's war,* it is this of America against Great Britain; it having been determined on by the people, and pursued by the people in every step of its progress." While it is very likely that both Hutchinson's and Adams' statements are correct, we will never know for certain. It is futile to try to explain a revolution by counting hands. Quantity counts far less than quality: it is not the number of insurrectionists but their zeal that is measured at the barricades. What is needed is to analyze the specific measures by which strategic groups of colonials decided to unite in order to throw off British rule.

Predictions had been made long since that the expulsion of France from America would bring grave troubles for England. (See the early remarks by the Frenchman in mid-Chapter 5.) However prescient these remarks are in retrospect, they seemed clairvoyant at the time. During the French and Indian War, thoughtful men had tried to foresee the postwar era. For example, William Shirley in 1755 proposed a plan to conquer all of Canada, predicting huge benefits to Great Britain including all of the fur trade and the cod fisheries. Since the population of the colonies would continue to double every twenty years, they would form a steadily growing market for English manufactures. The Indians would be more tractable without French influence, and thus Americans would be relieved from devastation of their frontiers and from many expenses of defending them. This would enable the colonials to pay higher taxes to maintain an English army in the New World. Shirley estimated that a mere 3,000 troops could guard the whole continent from New Hampshire to South Carolina, "unless in the case of a formal Expedition from Europe with a very strong armament." Any apprehensions that the colonies might unite to declare their independence were certainly bugaboos, since their interests were in conflict, one with another, and their governments varied in constitution. At the end of his proposal Shirley put in a special plug for governors' prerogatives; he suggested that royal officials such as himself be made financially independent of the assemblies.

Benjamin Franklin would never have assented to the final suggestion, but his general analysis was the same. Even though in 1760 he stressed colonial disunity in trying to persuade British authorities to evict the French from Canada, his assertions should not be dismissed as mere propaganda. He denied that the fourteen colonies (including Nova Scotia) could ever join forces against England; they had "different forms of government, different laws, different interests, and some of them different religious persuasions, and different manners." They were so jealous of each other that they had never been able to agree on means of fending off the French and Indians; how absurd then to suppose that they could unite against their mother country:

> In short, there are so many causes that must operate to prevent it, that I will venture to say, an union amongst them for such a purpose is not merely improbable, it is impossible; and if the union of the whole is impossible, the attempt of a part must be madness: as those colonies, that did not join the rebellion, would join the mother country in suppressing it. When I say such an union is impossible, I mean without the most grievous tyranny and oppression.

This reasoning was compelling. Americans on the whole had benefited by their hundred and fifty years inside the British Empire. The Navigation Acts had worked in myriad ways for colonial prosperity. Enforcement of the Molasses Act and of the few restrictions on manufacturing had been so lackadaisical as to harm few if any. Trade routes did not go from one province to another; they went from each province or even from each plantation directly to London or Bristol. The colonies by deliberate policy built walls against the growth of intra-American commerce; rum distilled in Massachusetts was not welcome in Rhode Island or Connecticut.*

Patterns of trade became patterns of thought; (See Chapter 3). In religion Virginia might differ from Massachusetts, but each of them took its creed from England. So did the most numerous new sect—the Methodists. Even within each colony, the difficulties of travel walled Americans off from each other. After 1763 the exceptions to this statement would be increasingly important, and already they mattered a great deal. Discussion at the Raleigh Tavern in Williamsburg, with Jefferson seeking the counsel of George Wythe or Richard Bland, was equal to any in the civilized world, and John Adams honed his wits over many bottles of claret. But we must not bemuse ourselves with images of Southern gentlemen incessantly visiting from one plantation to another, or with the fact that Jefferson could build a sophisticated mansion at Monticello, a hundred and fifty miles from Williamsburg and even today a rather remote place. Most men were dreadfully isolated. Consider the typical case of two Virginians, each of whom had a keen interest in botany; they lived only forty miles apart but they never met.

Bonds among the colonies were frail; the bond of each to England was still tenable. But it was weakening. Americans commonly used the word "home" to refer to England, but we may wonder whether their hearts fluttered as they wrote it. Two thirds of them at least had been born in the New World. Most of the others were not English; they were German or Scots-Irish or French. The number of native-born Englishmen in the colonies was only a few thousand, and many of those were in Nova Scotia; even such an eminent royal official as Hutchinson was American. The Church of England itself, though still established in the Southern provinces, was but a fragile link to the mother country. No bishop was ever named for America. In 1771 a meeting was called of the Anglican ministers in Virginia to consider petitioning the king to appoint a bishop. Of more than a hundred parsons in the province, only eleven attended. Four of them were against the proposal. Two opponents objected "Because we cannot help considering it as extremely indecent for the Clergy to make such an Application without the Concurrence of the President, Council, and Representatives of this Province; an Usurpation directly repugnant to the Rights of Mankind." Richard Bland was more outspoken yet: "I profess myself a sincere son of the established church, but I can embrace her Doctrines

---

*We do not know nearly enough about intercolonial commercial contacts. Great justices of the Supreme Court, including John Marshall, Morrison R. Waite, and Felix Frankfurter, appear to have thought that the commerce clause (I, 8) was the most important single section of the Constitution. But we have no systematic study of its colonial background. Here is another splendid topic for a doctoral dissertation.

without approving of her Hierarchy, which I know to be a Relick of the Papal Incroachments upon the Common Law." The Church of England in the South became less episcopal, more congregationalized with each vestry veering toward autonomy. Meanwhile the Congregational churches of New England with their synods and consociations were being presbyterianized. A peculiarly American, homogenized, leaning toward nonsectarianism, brand of religion was emerging.

The notion that all was filial affection between English and colonials in 1763 simply will not wash. An especially fruitful source of frictions had been the widespread instinct of American merchants to cheat on their taxes. Customs officials, understandably despairing of gentler measures, sought to ferret out smuggled goods by the use of writs of assistance; that is, general warrants to search and seize. Thanks to the argument of James Otis in Boston, a matter of tariff collections was converted into a constitutional issue of widest scope. Having been in court to hear Otis, John Adams recalled: "Then and there, the child Independence was born." Certainly Otis's language was reckless in its espousal of judicial review:

> I will to my dying day oppose. . . . all such instruments of slavery on the one hand & villany on the other as this writ of Assistance is. . . . No acts of parliament can establish such a writ; tho it should be made in the very words of the petition 'twould be void. An act against the constitution is void.

Under British law, of course, no act of Parliament could possibly be against the British constitution, but Americans were not persuaded.

It is significant that this trial occurred in 1761 immediately following the war. Wartime had a way of drawing potential crimes into the open because, in addition to their proclivity for smuggling, colonials persisted in trading with the enemy. Every conflict with France brought the same disputes. As early as 1698 the royal governor of New York was complaining "my checking the Marchants of this town in their unlawfull trade, and preventing Pyrat ships from coming into this port, has drawn on me their most Inveterate hatred." Near the beginning of the French and Indian War an official in London wrote General Braddock that an admiral with seven ships of the line had been dispatched to the American station. Among other duties they were to be used to frustrate illegal trade with the enemy, "particularly with regard to the Inhabitants of Pennsylvania & New York, who are reported to be the most notoriously guilty of supplying the French with Provisions." The reports were probably false, not in being too harsh on the Middle Colonies but in being too generous about the others. The activities of Rhode Island merchants were a scandal. Many a ship left Boston allegedly bound for Newfoundland but really headed for trade with the French on Cape Breton Island. True ingenuity was shown in the commerce with the French West Indies. An American merchant could apply for a license to visit there in order to exchange prisoners of war. The game was, of course, to load your hold with trade goods, take on a couple of token French prisoners, and sail gaily away with no need to fear the British customs-men. Reportedly a lively black market in French prisoners of war developed in Boston.

On 14 March, 1755, an embargo was laid in New York. A British general had to send an urgent message to a commodore reporting that several merchant-men needed as military transports were planning to sneak away and urging that they be detained. Philadelphia was no better. A navy lieutenant on patrol in the Delaware River spotted a ship coming back from Honduras Bay with a cargo of logwood. He gave chase; the merchantman fired at him; he reported that the fort at Newcastle seemed ready to do the same "imagining me to be a French Privateer"; (so hard to tell who is a patrolman nowadays). "They are very Stubborn and Saucy in this Part of the World," reported the lieutenant. But they talked so sweet that butter would not melt in their mouths. "Your Excellency," wrote a Philadelphia firm to a general, "drop'd some words that intimated a suspicion, that Commerce had been carried on Past Embargo, under the Umbrage of supplying the Fleet. We can only answer for our selves, and do assure your Excellency, we never, by the smallest Article, infringed, or connived at the Violation of it. Such practices would very ill become Men of any Character."

In peacetime the typical colonial had little or no contact with Englishmen; he had no chance to like or dislike. But the armed forces rubbed the groups together, and the chafing was severe. In Great Britain no man went into the ranks in the royal army or navy if he could make good as a civilian—unless he was dragged into it by a press gang. Assuming that they were dealing with scum, officers traditionally treated everyone in the ranks like scum. Some stole mercilessly from their troops. An enlisted man was supposed to pay for certain of his supplies by means of deductions from his pay called "stoppages." The stoppages were made, but the rations were not forthcoming. Discipline when present at all was savage. One soldier in 1759 noted in his diary that another had been convicted of stealing "his Majesties arms and working tools." Sentence: 400 lashes. Nine others were convicted of the same offense but "as their crimes Dont appear so notorious" they received "only" 300 lashes each.

William Shirley repeatedly warned his superiors at home that customary methods could not succeed in America. Especially pernicious was the practice of sending over all officers from England; (it says a lot that on a list of seven officers up for promotion, four were being recommended by peers, a fifth by an M.P., a sixth by a colonel, and the last by a lady). Colonials simply would not enlist to serve under such imports. Even when it was decided to raise two American regiments (about a thousand men each), many of the officers were British. This infuriated the colonial officers who had served in Shirley's celebrated campaign against Louisbourg; they wanted higher ranks and more of them. The disaffected leaders might well try to persuade their soldiers not to re-enlist.

> . . . indeed in such a Country as this, which is called the best poor mans Country in the World, where Labour is much dearer and idle vagabond People more Scarce than in England, and they have a particular Disinclination to the Life of a Garrison Soldier, and a terrible apprehension of the Strict Discipline exercised by the British officers it seems a very easy matter to beget an aversion in the men to inlist into a Regiment under Captains, who are Strangers to 'em . . .

What Shirley wanted was more funds to pay bounties. He also wanted blank commissions to be sent to him from London, which he would then grant conditionally; viz., a captain would have to recruit fifty men, a lieutenant thirty, and so on. He was also concerned that no chaplains were included in the roll of officers for the two American regiments. This would impede enlistments "as the People of this Country are particularly scrupulous in the Observation of the Sabbath & Performance of Religious Duties. . . ."

With occasional exceptions, Americans labored zealously to shift military expenditures onto other shoulders, either onto another colony or England. In King George's War Massachusetts complained that because it buffered New England against the French and Indians, it was losing population to neighboring colonies and thus afforded protection to men who paid their taxes elsewhere. New York was ceaselessly eager that any contributions it might make to the common defense should be used to improve fortifications within its own boundaries. In 1754 the governor of Georgia, in requesting 150 regular troops, stressed that his province was "a Frontier Country." Another somber element was emphasized by merchants and planters:

> That the Inhabitants of So. Carolina & Georgia altho few in Number as to White people are by the Number of their Negroes of Greater Importance to Great Britain than any Colony on the Continent in respect to the number of Subjects, yet would be in a more dangerous Situation in Case of an Attack than any other, as their whole Domestick Force would be required to keep their Negroes in proper Subjection.

A British commander in chief lamented to William Pitt that the various assemblies "are but too apt to seize upon every Precedent that may countenance their Burthening the Mother Country & exempting themselves." He was right of course.

The Seven Years' War, piled on top of its predecessors, meant financial crisis to the governments involved. They responded differently. The routine answer was to impose new taxes or raise the rates. The Habsburg government was more imaginative, seeking to raise the productivity of its subjects by knocking down guild restrictions and tariff walls. But such a policy needed time to succeed, and the men at Britain's helm felt they had no time. Pitt's dauntless use of men and supplies had won the war, and it had also brought fiscal crisis. The national debt had nearly doubled:

1755	£72,289,672
1764	£129,586,789

Worse yet, no relief was in sight. The government's revenues sufficed only to meet its ordinary expenses and to pay interest on the debt; none could foresee how or when the principal could be reduced.

Nor could anybody know if the troubles in America were ended. Pontiac's rebellion seemed to say they were not. In this situation the king decreed that for the time being no white settlement would be permitted beyond the crest of the Appalachians; in other words, settlers were supposedly blockaded from crossing an imaginary Proclamation Line joining the sources of the rivers flowing into the Atlantic. The policy was meant to be a stopgap until a more permanent arrangement could be reached. In spite of statements then and later that settlement of the interior would harm England by depriving it of customers for its manufactures, the chief intent surely was to placate the Indians. Nor should we take overseriously the assertion that the Proclamation Line caused "acute discontent" in several provinces. Thousands of Americans ignored the law. In 1769 the Watauga settlement was started in Tennessee and Daniel Boone entered Kentucky, where six years later he founded Boonesborough.

The Grenville ministry also decided to maintain 10,000 regular troops in America. The estimated cost was £220,000 a year. Since the provinces were to be the beneficiaries, they should help pay the bill. The colonists demurred. During all the decades when France held Canada and was constantly inciting the Indians against us, said the Americans, you gave us very little help. Now that the threat has been greatly reduced, why do we need your soldiers at all? Moreover, you have no right to tax us without the consent of our representatives. The debate raged. A high official in London said that the colonials were virtually represented in Parliament, just as were men and districts in Great Britain that had not the franchise (See the end of Chapter 6). Daniel Dulany objected that the diversity of residence created not just a difference but a conflict of interest. The Virginia legislature referred emphatically to "the *British* Parliament where the Colonies cannot be represented. . . ."

The government proceeded to put its new financial system into effect. To it the justice of doing so seemed obvious. In Great Britain the annual tax per capita amounted to 26 shillings. A typical resident in Massachusetts or Pennsylvania or Maryland paid only 1 shilling, in New York only 8 pence, in Connecticut only 7 pence, in Virginia a mere 5 pence. Even if the margin of error in these estimates is 100%, the discrepancy is gigantic. In addition, the public debts of the various provinces were so trivial that they would all be paid off by 1770 or so. It is impossible not to hear the complaints from Great Britain:

> England labours under a great load of debt, and heavy taxes; England has a very expensive government to maintain; the Americans have a government of very little expense; and consequently we must dwindle and decline every day in our trade, whilst they thrive and prosper exceedingly. The consequence of this will certainly be that the inhabitants will run away as fast as they can from this country to that, and Old England will become a poor, deserted, deplorable Kingdom—like a farm that has been over-cropped. (1776)

On the eve of the Revolution (1775) an Englishman would grumble that eight million of his countrymen paid £10 million in taxes, while three million Americans paid only £75 thousand, "and this in a country where a labouring man gets three times the wages that he does in England, and yet may live on half the expense." Even if all of the proposed measures had been successfully enforced in the colonies, the resulting burden would have been light in comparison to England's. But an American, looking from a different angle, saw the schemes as more than doubling his tax load.

The Sugar Act of 1764 sought to increase revenues by cutting rates; it reduced the duty on molasses imported from non-English possessions from 6d to 3d per gallon (When New England continued to protest, it was lowered again in 1766 to 1d but applied to all imports of molasses whether from English possessions or foreign). More important, it tried to tighten up the collection of customs duties, with results that will be examined below. At the time probably more resentment was caused by the Currency Act of 1764. In 1751 the provinces of New England had been forbidden to issue paper money as legal tender; now this restriction was applied to all of the colonies. Earlier inflations doubtless brought hardship and injustice to creditors, but the new rules meant privation for nearly everybody. These laws of 1764 were the beginning of a train of English actions that one by one eroded the loyalty of some crucial segments of American society. Not only was British policy aimed against cohesive groups that could rally to defend themselves; it also vacillated, so that the government lost some important friendships without gaining the revenue. It got the worst of two worlds.

The Stamp Act of 1765 sparked the antagonism. If you want to get money, you must take it from those who have it, and this law struck the most potent elements in America. Chief victims would be merchant-shipowners, who would have to buy a stamp every time a vessel cleared a port. Lawyers had to buy stamps for every legal document. Any transfer of land recorded with a court needed a stamp. Finally, as if to ensure that opposition to the statute would get a public hearing, newspapers required stamps. How to make enemies: shipowners and merchants, lawyers, editors, land speculators. Although receipts would all be spent in America and thus would not bring a direct export of specie, the requirement that stamps had to be paid for with sterling would tighten the domestic supply of money. This would be a main point of protest: "That Money is already become very scarce in these Colonies, and is still decreasing by the necessary exportation of Specie from the Continent, for the Discharge of our Debts to British Merchants."

Most American rates were set lower than the equivalent taxes in England, but some were higher. Entry to the bar cost £6 there, £10 here. Registration in a college there cost 2 shillings, here £2. A treasury official explained the government's viewpoint, "the Duties upon degrees should certainly be as high as they are in England; it would indeed be better if they were raised both here and there in order to keep mean persons out of those situations in life which they disgrace."

Objections to the measure began while it was still being debated. A distinction emerged between external and internal taxes. The governor of Connecticut seemed to base his complaint on the fact that a stamp tax would be collected within the colonies, rather than at ports of entry as import duties were. The quibble became popular in London. Benjamin Franklin used it in appearing before a Parliamentary committee, but he was in the position of a lawyer representing a client who will seek to gain a practical result by using whatever argument seems likely to appeal to the court. After passage of the Stamp Act, the Rockingham ministry would use Franklin's testimony to seek its repeal. But with few exceptions the colonists rejected this line of argument. James Otis declared "there is no foundation for the distinction some make in England between an internal and an external tax on the colonies." Thomas Hutchinson agreed, asking in effect what difference it made whether you took a man's property away from him on the high seas or in his home town. Save for Connecticut, the official protests from the provinces flatly denied, without qualification, that Parliament could levy any tax whatever to raise revenue from them. Later Connecticut itself would resolve, "That in the Opinion of this House, An Act for raising Money by Duties or Taxes differs from other Acts of Legislation, in that it is always considered as a free Gift of the People made by their legal, and elected Representatives. . . ."

Here was a discrimination that Americans would accept: Parliament could not tax them, but it could legislate. It could regulate the trade of the Empire, but it could not raise revenue in the colonies. When the English asserted that Americans had been paying duties under the Molasses Act and that they had never objected to the Navigation Acts, Daniel Dulany of Maryland used Grenville's own figures to show that earlier acts had not been meant to raise revenue. Over a period of thirty years, collections of customs duties in the colonies had averaged less than £2,000, of which only £700–800 came from North America. Meanwhile the average expense of engrossing these duties had been £7,600. It would be a peculiar revenue measure that lost so much money for such an extended period.* The colonial position was stated by William Pitt in Parliament: "Taxation is no part of the governing or legislative power."

From Portsmouth, New Hampshire the Sons of Liberty wrote to their counterparts in Boston that, since the Stamp Act abridged the basic privileges of Englishmen, it was "Therefore void of all Lawfull Authority, so that depending upon Meer Force it may Lawfully be oppos'd by Force." The recipients were already acting on the message. By early summer of 1765 a group of commonplace men in Boston were calling themselves the Loyal Nine. They got in touch with Ebenezer Mackintosh, a shoemaker who reportedly had 2,000 followers. They were crude chaps. When a man accepted appointment as distributor of stamps for Massachusetts, a mob hanged him in effigy and wrecked his house. The governor reported to London in despair, "I sent a written order to the Colonel of the Regiment of Militia, to beat an Alarm; he answered, that it would signify nothing, for as soon as the drum was heard, the drummer would be knocked down, and the drum broke; he added, that probably all the drummers of the Regiment were in the mob." Two weeks later a mob broke into the mansion of Lieutenant-Governor Hutchinson, stole £900 in cash, and wrecked the place. When Mackintosh was picked up for leading the riot, the sheriff had to release him.

At the suggestion of Massachusetts, delegates from nine provinces met in New York on 7 October 1765. That the colonies could go so far toward joint action was radical enough, but the ground adopted by the Stamp Act Congress was a conservative appeal to the rights of Englishmen and "old Customs and Usages." Massachusetts took a loftier tone: "That there are certain essential rights of the British Constitution of Government, which are founded in the Law of God and Nature, and are the common Rights of Mankind. . . ." In Boston the regular government had lost nearly all authority. The courts reopened—without using any stamps. The press was prescribing a future for Grenville:

> To make us all Slaves, now you've lost Sir! the Hope,
> You've but to go hang yourself.—We'll find the Rope.

The same paper wished for all friends of the Stamp Act "a perpetual Itching without the benefit of Scratching." Disorder was everywhere. The governor of Georgia feared that if he called out the militia he would only be arming his

---

*This line of argument need not be facetious; taxes are levied for many purposes other than meeting the expenses of government. When Great Britain in 1846 repealed the Corn Laws (an import duty on grain), she kept a small impost. Its function was not even regulatory but statistical; it was a way to keep track of the movements of trade.

enemies, and he could not rely on ten men in Savannah. The governor of New Hampshire thought that no militia on the entire continent could be trusted "because the Militia are the very People on the other Side the question."

During the early stages of the agitation, in most communities the "better and wiser part" tended to support and even to lead it. In New York, according to the lieutenant-governor: "The whole Body of Merchants in general, Assembly Men, Magistrates, &c. have been united in this Plan of Riots, and without the influence and instigation of these the inferior People would have been quiet. Very great Pains was taken to rouse them before they Stirred. The Sailors who are the only People who may be properly Stiled Mob, are entirely at the command of the Merchants who employ them." Well-to-do merchants might shake their heads at riots and see them as menacing to the social stability that yielded so many benefits. Some felt themselves the hostility of a mob. For instance Henry Laurens, merchant and planter of South Carolina, was perhaps the wealthiest man in the South. Unwilling to abide actions that might rock his ships, he opposed sending delegates to the Stamp Act Congress. He was even rumored to have stamped paper in his house. One night he was awakened by a loud banging and shouts. Men in the crowd had tried to disguise themselves by wearing sailors' clothes and blackening their faces with soot. Nonetheless, Laurens could identify nine men by name.

Distressing as the tumults in America may have been, it is likely that the ministry was more influenced by protests at home. London merchants took the lead in circularizing other commercial cities for action to restore the former state of trade. Rockingham determined to repeal the Stamp Act, and this was done on March 18, 1766. At this point a splendid opening was let pass. If petitions originating with Great Britain could prompt Parliament to redress a colonial grievance, then the theory of virtual representation was indeed not "fantastical" as Americans had asserted; it was an operational reality. What Parliament did, also on March 18, was quite opposite; it issued the Declaratory Act, which said:

> That the said colonies and plantations in *America* have been, are, and of right ought to be, subordinate unto, and dependent upon the imperial crown and parliament of *Great Britain*; and that the King's majesty, by and with the advice and consent of the lords spiritual and temporal, and commons of *Great Britain,* in parliament assembled, had, hath, and of right ought to have, full power and authority to make laws and statutes of sufficient force and validity to bind the colonies and people of *America,* subjects of the crown of *Great Britain,* in all cases whatsoever.

Parliament had asserted that the constitution did not link taxation to representation. Worse, it had not even taken the trouble to draft a new statute, but had merely copied almost verbatim a law of 1719 proclaiming the subservience of Ireland to Great Britain.

The Declaratory Act did not help to ease the fiscal crisis. Grenville had estimated that the tax bills introduced in 1764, including the stamp tax, would bring in some £100,000 a year from America. Now a part of the package had been discarded. The Rockingham government fell, and William Pitt returned to the tiller, but he fell ill, and the effective head became Charles Townshend. Nearly a year elapsed before the ministry put through its own revenue measures in the summer of 1767. The new duties were ludicrous. (a) With one exception (tea) they taxed items in which trade was modest. The petition to Parliament of the London merchants had referred to exports of "very large Quantities of *British* Manufactures, consisting of Woollen Goods of all Kinds, Cottons, Linens, Hardware, Shoes, Household Furniture. . . ." None of these classifications got a new impost. (b) With the same exception, the items taxed—paper, glass, lead, paint—could be produced by the Americans for themselves, and soon were. Townshend projected that the new duties would yield £40,000 annually. From North America, omitting the Caribbean, the bill in fact produced about £13,000 in 1768, less than £3,000 in 1769. In 1770 it was repealed except for the tea tax.

More significant than the added duties was another section of the program. By it, additions to the revenue could be kept in America and used to pay the salaries of governors and other royal officials. Here was an innovation that the colonial assemblies would never accept. For generations they had struggled to gain financial suzerainty over the governors. By and large they had won. They would not at a stroke yield up their hard-won gains. Also ominous were provisions of the Townshend Acts to tighten up the procedures of the revenue service. They included the erection of a separate Board of Customs Commissioners for the Americas. It was to be quartered in Boston, and the three officials began operations there in November 1767.

To understand what happened next, we must move back for another wide-angle scan. If the British government had too little money, it had too many people; that is, it had too many people asking jobs from it. The fiscal crisis was reinforced by a population explosion. Say that the governing class numbered at most 50,000 families. The aristocracy and the gentry were growing in number: there were more families, and the families were larger. This segment of society assumed that its members had to be accommodated into some fitting station in the system. If a gentleman could not provide properly for his younger sons, then the Church must do so, or the government. The number of so-called civil servants soared, and the surplus income within the realm that could be siphoned off to support them could not keep pace. A throng of these placemen had to be dispatched out to the colonies, and the funds to sustain them had to be raised from within the colonies. One traveller from Connecticut (he was the son of a wealthy clergyman but in 1787 would sit as a delegate at the federal convention in Philadelphia) was appalled at the conditions that prevailed in Great Britain: "the Common people of England are a very different sett of Men from the people of America, otherwise they never would submitt to be taxed in the Manner they are, that a few may be loaded with places and Pensions and riot in Luxury and Excess, while they themselves cannot support themselves and their needy offspring with Bread; I thank God we are not such Jack Asses in America, and I hope in God we never shall be brought to submit to it. . . ."

Tightening the job squeeze (or "sinecure squeeze") on the hereditary elite was a growing inclination to throw some occupations open to talent. It remained true in the royal army that a general was likely to be a peer, that commissions and promotions were purchased, that your rank was largely dependent on your family's standing. But the Royal Navy was far more democratic, as revealed in a marvelous monologue in Jane Austen's novel *Persuasion* (1818); the speaker is explaining why the Royal Navy is not a suitable career: "Yes; it is in two points offensive to me; I have two strong grounds of objection to it. First, as being the means of bringing persons of obscure birth into undue distinction, and raising men to honours which their fathers and grandfathers never dreamed of. . . . A man is in greater danger in the navy of being insulted by the rise of one whose father his father might have disdained to speak to, and of becoming prematurely an object of disgust himself, than in any other line." This attitude said: By right (whether divine or not) the world belongs to us. They grabbed what they could. Grenville and Townshend were brothers to peers, Lord North was son of a peer, more than half of the members of Commons were related to baronets or peers. They became colonels or ambassadors or got government pensions. An anecdote will illustrate the attitude that the Americans were confronting—or thought they were confronting. One yarn of course proves nothing, and our authority for this one is not the best: Franklin as a very old man told it to Jefferson; Jefferson as a very old man wrote it in his autobiography. It concerns negotiations that Franklin was conducting with the North government soon before armed conflict began. Lord Howe and his sister were serving as go-betweens. North was unbending. At last he said to the mediators that "a rebellion was not to be deprecated on the part of Great Britain; that the confiscations it would produce would provide for many of their friends."

In this context the ministry moved to strengthen the customs service. Ostensibly the goal was to help the treasury. In practice the aim was to enrich some carpetbaggers. Again the turkeys to be plucked were those who carried the most fat—but unfortunately for Great Britain they also were the ones with the most muscle. The techniques used have been called "customs racketeering," and the term is apt. It is hardly too much to say that the colonies were lost in order that a few officials might become wealthy; Whitehall's inability and its unwillingness to control its subordinates was remarkable. The enemies to the crown created by a few placemen to the crown would prove the undoing of the crown. Among them were men whose initial bias was toward live-and-let-live, such as Henry Laurens. The regulations used against him stipulated that a cargo must be put under official bond before it was loaded and that it could not be broken before it had cleared through a customs house. In May 1767 Laurens sent his ship *Wambaw* carrying tools and provisions from Charles Town to supply his plantation on the Altamaha River in Georgia. The fifty-ton schooner delivered the goods, and took on some shingles as ballast for the return trip. This lumber might under the law need to be bonded. Since the nearest customs house was fifty miles away, the ship's master went nine miles to two magistrates and posted bond with them. The ship and cargo were seized and condemned by the admiralty court in Charles Town. Laurens was allowed to buy the ship back for £175. There is no need to enter further details and complications here—but two considerations are vital. Only a minor part of the yield from such proceedings went to ease the fiscal crisis of the Crown; by law most of it was divided among the royal officials involved. Second, this type of harassment and confiscation—repeated several times—served to convert Henry Laurens from a pacific planter-merchant into an insurrectionist.

Matters were fairly placid in the Middle Colonies and around the Chesapeake, and even in a way in Massachusetts. While the assembly did in February 1768 adopt the Circular Letter that repudiated the Townshend Acts as unconstitutional, Samuel Adams wrote into the document a disavowal of the charge that his countrymen were "factious disloyal & having a disposition to make themselves independent of the Mother Country." The letter, with its carefully limited contentions, was endorsed by the other assemblies. But it created fury in London, and the government made ready to send regular troops to Boston. Before they arrived, the most influential merchant in the city, John Hancock, had felt the greedy fingers of the placemen. Again, repeated efforts were made to pick his pockets (which admittedly were well filled). His ship *Liberty* was seized in Boston a month after she had legally entered. Suit was brought by the royal officials against Hancock and five other men for £9,000 each. If judgment had been rendered and collection made, the governor of Massachusetts would have received a share of one third. The £18,000 would have exceeded his regular salary for a period of ten years. Some nine months later the suit was dropped.

But judgment of another sort, in another court, had been rendered. Seizure of the *Liberty* set off a riot. The rioters were seamen. Quite possibly Hancock did not approve of their rambunctiousness. They had grievances of their own. When a sailor swaggered aboard in a foreign port carrying his "privilege" (a share of the cargo; see mid-Chapter 3) he did not post bond for it or enter it on a bill of lading. This practice was traditional. Now, customs officials, by unexpectedly enforcing the letter of the law for their own profit, were in effect stripping the seaman of his wages. British press gangs had made hundreds of enemies around the docks and the taverns (mid-Chapter 5). An untold number of colonial mariners were deserters from the brutalities of the Royal Navy; it was a common saying in British fleets as they entered American harbors that "from hell to heaven is a short swim." To the gathering array of enemies to the crown—editors, lawyers, merchant-shipowners, land specu-lators—the sailors would afford a mass base in the vital ports. It was not merely symbolic that one of the three Americans slain at the Boston Massacre in March 1770 was a ropemaker.

In the same month Parliament repealed the Townshend duties except on tea. At the time of the Circular Letter the colonials had organized an effective non-importation agreement, but enthusiasm for it had atrophied. Thomas Hutchinson, now governor, tried to heal another wound by asking the ministry to withdraw the British regulars ("Troops can be useful in case of actual rebellion only, when civil government ceases, and the military is at liberty to act independent.") His exhortations failed, but even so he thought that matters were going well. He refused to take alarm when Sam Adams and Joseph Warren founded at Boston the first of the Committees of Correspondence: "Such a foolish scheme that they must necessarily make themselves ridicu-lous." Within a few months he knew his mistake and was calling the Committees "very dangerous." The new agitation saw one town after another in the province vote an unqualified denial of the right of Parliament to levy taxes on the colonies.* Already neighboring Rhode Island had clanged an even louder cymbal of defiance: when the British revenue schooner *Gaspée* ran aground near Providence, a gang led by an eminent merchant had burned her into the beach.

The next explosion is both ridiculous and ironic. The Tea Act of 1773, a scheme for government controls and subsidies on the tea market (to bail out the British East India Company) would have lowered the immediate price paid by American consumers. Then why object? Because it might have taken much of the tea business away from the control of colonial merchants. They had been good boys since the repeal of the Townshend duties in 1770, importing sugar and molasses and tea and often paying the tax, but now they rediscovered their civic responsibilities. At Philadelphia the ship bearing East India Company tea met with an animosity that prompted its captain to go home without debarking. At Charles Town the tea in the original package (to use the phrase of a later judicial doctrine) was piled in a damp cellar and forgotten about. At Boston it was dumped in the harbor. The Boston Tea Party, 16 December 1773, accelerated the total confrontation. When the news reached London, the North ministry knew no response except coercion. The Boston Port Act legally sealed off that harbor altogether. The Quartering Act put troops back in Boston. The Administration of Justice Act provided that royal officials accused of crime could be sent for trial to Nova Scotia or Great Britain instead of facing a local jury. The Massachusetts Government Act was a cruncher. Some eighty years

---

*As a British diplomat would write a century later: In politics as in war, organization is all. Given the lamentable communications among the provinces, the rebels achieved a high degree of coordination. Their Loyalist opponents in contrast remained each in his splendid isolation.

earlier the freemen of the Bay had lost the right to elect their governor. Now the assembly was stripped of the power to elect the Councillors; henceforth they would be named by the governor. The Councillors lost the power to accept or reject the gubernatorial appointments to sheriff. Town meetings could no longer be convened at the will of citizens; one gathering a year was allowed, to elect town officials, unless the governor should summon a special meeting. To cap the Intolerable Acts, the commander in chief of His Majesty's forces in North America was named governor of Massachusetts.

Soon after came the Quebec Act, making a province of an area that had been under military rule since 1763. A civil government was decreed—but with no elected assembly. The widely despised Roman Catholic Church was given equal status ("and that the Clergy of the said Church may hold, receive, and enjoy their accustomed Dues and Rights, with respect to such Persons only as shall profess the said Religion."). The borders of Quebec were extended down the Mississippi valley all the way to the Ohio River. Here was a modification of the Proclamation of 1763 that might actually be enforceable.

More than a year earlier (March 1773) Virginia had proposed that the Committees of Correspondence in the various colonies should cooperate, rather than functioning merely within their own province. Now Massachusetts used this device to adopt a non-intercourse pact and invite the other colonies to join it. The merchants of New York, seeking to check radicalism because of the profitable trade with Britain, countered by suggesting another assemblage modelled on the Stamp Act Congress. Massachusetts had no choice but to agree, and the First Continental Congress met in Philadelphia in September. The problem confronting the Bay Colony was clear: she had to have Southern support. New York could not be counted on; throughout the War for Independence, perhaps as many as half of her politically active citizens were Loyalists.* In Pennsylvania and New Jersey the Quaker element was still powerful and was confirmed in its pacifism. So write off the Middle Colonies. New England had to look southward, especially to Virginia and South Carolina. The Massachusetts delegates to the Congress behaved with consummate skill. The effort may have caused deep anguish to temperaments like Samuel Adams and John Adams, but they realized that they had to let others run interference for them. They stayed out of the limelight. But they worked. A hostile observer said of Sam Adams, "He eats little, sleeps little, thinks much, and is most decisive and indefatigable in the pursuit of his objects." (He was tireless in his propaganda; a full two dozen pseudonyms in letters to newspapers have been identified as signifying Samuel Adams.) And they could till fertile soil. Earlier the Southern lords had not been inclined to seek trouble; they were conservatives with a fondness for minding their own business. But the image of a royal governor simply imposing a sheriff on a community must

---

*Throughout this work the men who did not abjure allegiance to King and Parliament will be called Loyalists rather than Tories.

have caused shudders in many a county magnate (see the end of Chapter 4.) After more than a month of discussion, the Congress adopted a resolution that John Adams shrewdly drafted to bring along the more reluctant delegations. While insisting that the provincial legislatures had the sole right to make laws "in all cases of taxation and internal polity, subject only to the negative of their sovereign, in such manner as has been heretofore used and accustomed," the Americans would "cheerfully consent" to Parliamentary rules for "the regulation of our external commerce." More important, the Congress unanimously adopted the Association—an oath to abide by the non-intercourse agreements which would be enforced by local Committees of Inspection. After agreeing to meet again the following spring, the Congress adjourned, and the Adamses went home to join their townsmen who were accumulating gunpowder to repel the army of occupation.

Resolved to impede this dangerous course, a British detachment marched out of Boston in April 1775 to seize a reported cache of munitions at Concord. The consequences are known to all. A month later the Second Continental Congress met; Washington was named general; a battle was fought at Breed's Hill; the Congress made another almost grovelling appeal to the king to restrain his wicked ministry, but the king refused even to receive the Olive Branch Petition. The war had begun. The events that led to the Declaration of Independence have been charted. Running through them all was a constant—the character of the British governing class. But American perceptions of it had altered drastically. Early in the century the colonials had joined in the hosannas to "the glorious English constitution." But while the praise swelled to a crescendo within Great Britain, capped off by Blackstone's fulsome self-congratulations in his *Commentaries,* Americans came to perceive the English ruling groups as decadent debauchees who would plunder anybody willing to submit. Just before leaving London in early 1775, Franklin wrote back to Pennsylvania his summary of the situation:

> When I consider the extream corruption prevalent among all Orders of Men in this old rotten State, and the glorious publick Virtue so predominant in our rising Country, I cannot but apprehend more Mischief than benefit from a closer Union. I fear they will drag us after them in all the plundering Wars which their desperate Circumstances, Injustice, and Rapacity, may prompt them to undertake; and their wide-wasting Prodigality and Profusion is a Gulph that will swallow up every Aid we may distress ourselves to afford them.
>
> Here Numberless and needless Places, enormous Salaries, Pensions, Perquisites, Bribes, Groundless Quarrels, foolish Expeditions, false Accounts or no Accounts, Contracts and Jobbs, devour all Revenue and produce continual Necessity in the Midst of natural Plenty.

From this system the preponderance of the American oligarchs had resolved to cut loose. Nothing could be gained here by launching into a detailed narrative of the six years of campaigning; the tactics of battles may well be left to specialists in military history. The Americans won because they had a sound policy and a brilliant strategy; (see the opening of Chapter 5). The policy was simple: the colonials were fighting the War for Independence. This was an objective that could awaken in many men a fanatical lust for Liberty and induce them to endure terrible hardships for long periods of time (Document 7-3). The strategy was also simple: the Americans could win if they could keep an army in the field. It was not necessary to win scintillating victories. It was enough to retreat, to endure, to hold out.* It is necessary to discard the common foolishness that the colonies were somehow "protected" by 3,000 miles of ocean. The reverse is true. Apart from financial problems, the British had little trouble in mobilizing men and supplies at home, in transporting them across the Atlantic, in capturing coastal cities in America; all four of the major ports were occupied at some time, and the occupation of New York lasted for seven years. But the British military was lost when it got away from navigable water; in other words, their navy was effective, their land forces, hardly at all.

This trenchant strategy is not something that historians have needed to discover in retrospect. It was apparent to several colonials early in the conflict. As far back as the Stamp Act riots, the governor of Massachusetts had corrected his original estimate that unruliness was limited to Boston. At last he said of the back country folk: "They talk of revolting from Great Britain in the most familiar Manner, and declare that tho' the British Forces should possess themselves of the Coasts and Maritime Towns, they never will subdue the inland." In early 1777 an American was explaining why the English had to play for a quick kill: "The expense of feeding and paying great fleets and armies, at such distance, is too enormous for any nation on earth to bear for a great while." A cogent explication of the strategy of space was given by Thomas Paine in *The Crisis* (second paper, published 13 January 1777). He jeered at the opposition, "You cannot be so insensible as not to see that we have two to one the advantage of you, because we conquer by a drawn game, and you lose by it. . . . I have no other idea of conquering countries than by subduing the armies which defend them: have you done this, or can you do it? . . . if you get possession of a city here, you are obliged to shut yourselves up in it, and can make no other use of it, than to spend your country's money in."

General Washington did not immediately come to these insights; indeed, perhaps he never came consciously to them at all. We can understand his blockages. A ferociously proud man, he had suffered two humiliating setbacks by the French and Indians in prior wars. Now he must have wanted to show that he could fight and win. But he did not. He mastered the art of giving

---

*This strategy was a splendid application of the modern theory of games, by which you must never make a move involving the risk that you may be put out of the game altogether.

ground. Of the two significant American victories in battle before Yorktown, one was not his. Washington's raid at Trenton had a crucial effect on colonial morale, but it did not destroy a major part of the opposing military strength. This result was won by the American defeat of Burgoyne at Saratoga, which also had a vital influence on the formal consummation of the alliance with France (Chapter 8), but it was directed by other generals than the commander in chief. Even the final surrender at Yorktown was accomplished not so much by Washington's forces as by a momentary naval superiority in the York River due to the arrival of a French fleet (although anybody who has paced those unprotected flat fields will not forget the flamboyant bravery of a sally against the entrenched British positions which was led by the general's young aide, Alexander Hamilton).

Actually the war, when it started, was not so uneven as it might seem. In regard to white, free inhabitants, the ratio between the combatant populations was about four to one. But this inequality was offset by some potent factors. The British were regulars fighting in a hostile land. The Americans were short-term volunteers fighting near home; often when a soldier became ill, he could repair to his fireside to recover. The weight of this consideration in the eighteenth century can hardly be exaggerated. In the Seven Years' War, some 1,500 seamen and marines were killed in action while nearly 100 times as many, 133,708, reportedly deserted or died of sickness. During the War for Independence perhaps 175,000 seamen and marines served at some time between 1774 and 1780 in the Royal Navy. Losses to disease were more than 18,000, battle deaths a mere 1,243, while more than 42,000 deserted. The melancholy truth was put forth in 1771 by Dr. Johnson:

> Of the thousands and tens of thousands that perished in our late contests with France and Spain, a very small part ever felt the stroke of an enemy; the rest languished in tents and ships, amidst damps and putrefaction. . . . By incommodious encampments and unwholesome stations, where courage is useless, and enterprise impracticable, fleets are silently dispeopled and armies sluggishly melted away.

The matter may be pressed further. Military historians have been fond of pointing to Washington's laments about the difficulties of fighting a war with militiamen who had volunteered for short terms only; the usual charges have been that colonial soldiers were inferior to regulars in fighting pitched battles on an open field or in enduring the boredom of garrison duty. Such allegations are almost irrelevant, since they amount to saying that Americans were not disciplined to fight in a fashion that in general they wisely chose to avoid. What may be relevant is the guess that, man for man, American militia were physically in much better condition than their opponents. As far back as King George's War we can read the complaint that British officers had been stealing too much from the regular troops under their command, and from there matters got worse, according to one army account: Recruiting had been made so difficult that men are kept in the service " 'till they become deaf, blind, or otherwise decrepit with Age." En route to America they are kept so long confined on board the transports and are fed so relentlessly with salt provisions that a third of them die before reaching their garrisons in the New World; (Compare sea voyage conditions on slavers; Chapter 4 opening). Even the survivors have contracted scurvy and "have their whole Mass of Blood so infected with that Distemper, that they can scarcely be deem'd effective Men. . . ."

The defects of British personnel are more apparent at higher ranks. Sir William Howe, who commanded until 1778, had opportunities to follow up a victory by seeking to decimate Washington's army. He never did so. Clearly he was more concerned with his duty to make peace than with his simultaneous duty to make war; it may not go too far to accuse him of secret sympathies with the Americans (See above on conditions among British army officers). His successor Sir Henry Clinton was lazy; in 1780 he sat with 20,000 men in New York City while Washington's 7,000 soldiers were camped only fifty miles away and freely roamed around in search of forage. The inadequacies of Burgoyne and Cornwallis are also a matter of record.

For the Americans, problems of supply were maddening but far from fatal. Lack of a brass industry and of gunpowder plants was remedied by imports from France and the Netherlands. The colonies by 1775 were producing a seventh of the world's supply of iron. Of the 7,000 ships plying in English commerce, a third had been built in American yards. Dependent on hunting wild game for the sustenance of their families, every colonial farmer was familiar with firearms to a degree that was unknown in Europe. Quite a few had rifles, whereas the common British gun was still the musket. Campaigning often among friends, they could draw much of their provender from the countryside. They had the advantage of protective coloration that any guerilla army has; they could simply dissolve into the civilian population. But we need not minimize the sufferings of the rebel troops, or blink aside the desperation behind the mutiny of the Connecticut line in 1780. Imagine yourself with the highest fever that you have ever run. Now add a terrible toothache. At the same time put yourself in a cold rain, and suppose that you have only raggedy clothes and perhaps a tattered blanket. Add chronic diarrhea. That begins to give the feeling. But they held out.

It is hard to believe that this result could have been gained without George Washington. For thirty years he was to me an enigma: How did it happen that the gaggle called the Founding Fathers—each man immensely able, pigheaded, several of them egomaniacal—was unanimous in deferring to Washington? I could not figure it out; he seemed so drab, lacking in color, stony-faced. The last word is the key. The best clue I know to the general occurs at the beginning of Emerson's essay on "Character." What does the term mean? "The largest part of their power was latent. This is that which we call Character—a reserved force, which acts directly by presence and without means." What impressed his fellows about Washington was perhaps the sense that no matter what hardships beset him, he would be equal to them. It is easy to picture his few thousands of tattered and homesick troops thinking to themselves: If the general can stick it out, so can I. Had he gone home to his beloved Mount Vernon, so might they have returned to their more humble hearths.

The War for Independence was the first modern struggle to set up a free national state. Just as the founding of the colonies in North America had been a pioneering venture, so was the revolution against British rule. But the path to it was tortuous. It was beset by thickets of doubts in the minds of the colonials. Ties to England were still strong for many Americans. The various provinces had no love for each other. Religious distinctions, conflicts over title to lands on the frontier, clashes over trade, over taxes on goods shipped from one colony to another—these were more stirring than any controversy with England. Besides, France had been thrown out of Canada, although this achievement had cost the United Kingdom enormous sums of money. So the King-in-Parliament resolved the ambiguity in the minds of Americans by imposing several new taxes. Many of the colonial arguments against these new imposts were highly sophistical, mere pettifogging. However, many rebels could unite on this proposition: they did not want higher taxation, with or without representation. When war began in 1775, the makeshift American army drew upon a brilliant strategy which might be summarized in the word *retreat* (or perhaps, *survive*). There were hundreds of thousands of square miles of empty wilderness or farmland into which the guerrilla army could withdraw. During the prolonged retaining action, General Washington played an essential role. Now the colonials had their freedom. How would they use it?

SOME NOTABLE EVENTS

1761 James Otis speaks against use of writs of assistance by British customs officials.

1763 Peace of Paris ends Seven Years' War, February 10.
Grenville ministry formed.
Proclamation Line of 1763 decreed, October 7.

1764 Sugar Act passed on April 5.
Currency Act of 1764 extends Currency Act of 1751 (New England only).

1765 Stamp Act passed, March 22.
Rockingham ministry formed in July.
Stamp Act Congress, October 7–24, at New York.

1766 Stamp Act repealed but Declaratory Act passed, March 18.
Pitt ministry formed in July.

1767–
1771 Regulator movements in the Carolinas.

1767 Townshend Acts, passed June and July, set new import duties.
Board of Customs Commissioners set up at Boston, November.

1768 Massachusetts Circular Letter, February 11.
Riots over seizure of Hancock's *Liberty*, June 10.
Vogue spreads for nonimportation agreements.
British troops occupy Boston, September 29.

1770 North ministry formed in February.
Boston Massacre, March 5.
Townshend duties except on tea are repealed, March.
Nonimportation collapses.

1772 British customs schooner *Gaspée* burned near Providence, June 9.
Boston is birthplace of first Committee of Correspondence, November.

1773 Virginia urges intercolonial Committees of Correspondence.
Tea Act passed, May 10.
Boston Tea Party, December 16.

1774 Coercive Acts ("Intolerable Acts") passed, March 31–June 2.
Quebec Act passed, June 22.
First Continental Congress at Philadelphia, September 5–October 27.

1775 America began producing more pig iron than England and Wales.
Battles of Concord and Lexington, April 19.
Second Continental Congress meets, May 10.
Battle of Bunker Hill, June 17.
Congress sends the Olive Branch Petition, July 8.

1776 British forces withdraw from Boston to Halifax, March 17.
Congress recommends formation of new state governments, May.
Declaration of Independence, July 4.

1776–
1779 Main theater of war is the Middle Colonies; New York and Philadelphia occupied by British.

1777 General John Burgoyne surrenders, October 14.

1778 United States and France sign treaties, February 6.
France enters the war against Great Britain in June.

1780 Anti-Catholic mob, in Gordon riots, terrorizes London for a week in June.

1779–
1781 Main theater of war shifts to the South, especially South Carolina.

1781 Articles of Confederation proclaimed, March 1.
General Lord Cornwallis surrenders at Yorktown, October 19.
Congress charters the Bank of North America.

1783 Treaty of Paris signed, September 3.

Ways to Study History VII

Do comparative studies. Two generations ago H. G. Wells brought out a massive set of works that purported to be the story of mankind. Others, slightly more modest, have offered us accounts of Western civilization. Conceived on so sweeping a scale, a project may, if the author has a sufficiently stimulating mind, produce interesting books, but it will not be history. In modern history especially, often the investigator cannot hope to use all of the primary sources; I shudder to think of the tons of documents pertaining to events in Washington in the last twelve months. But he can so define his problem as to be able to identify and master the best relevant secondary sources.

Using this approach, scholars recently have tried to break beyond the bounds of the old-fashioned studies that were conceived largely or solely in terms of national histories. Some categories of our conceptualizations have seemed especially promising as objects of this technique. Concern for the economic growth of underdeveloped countries has brought studies of the conditions for it in various areas. Urbanization has been the spur for distinguished work by Lewis Mumford, and series of books by several authors have been launched to analyze cities at different times and places. Our understanding of the westward movement in the United States has been sharpened as we have learned more about the frontiers of Australia and Canada.

Social conflict has drawn much attention. Here the most impressive achievement of the comparative method is Robert R. Palmer's *The Age of the Democratic Revolution* (1959, 1964). These two volumes aim to analyze political change throughout Europe and the Western Hemisphere from 1760 to 1800. Palmer was able to show that many nations had a simultaneous increase of the power of both aristocratic and democratic forces. Clashes were inevitable, with the balance going differing ways at different places. His measuring of each society against others helps to give us insight.

Document 7-1

Proceedings in the Virginia House of Burgesses in the spring of 1765 allegedly occasioned Patrick Henry's famous "If *this* be treason, make the most of it." But we do not have an official transcript; the several accounts vary, and none is above question. We do not even know infallibly just what the Virginia Resolves said. Several versions appeared. The first one to be printed was in the *Newport Mercury* on 24 June 1765, and it is reprinted here.

Resolved, *That the first Adventurers, Settlers of this his Majesty's Colony and Dominion of Virginia, brought with them and transmitted to their Posterity, and all other his Majesty's Subjects since inhabiting in this his Majesty's Colony, all the Privileges and Immunities that have at any Time been held, enjoyed and possessed by the People of Great-Britain. . . .*

Resolved, *That his Majesty's liege People of this Antient Colony have enjoy'd the Right of being thus govern'd, by their own Assembly, in the Article of Taxes and internal Police; and that the same have never been forfeited, or any other Way yielded up, but have been constantly recogniz'd by the King and People of Britain.*

Resolved, *therefore, That the General Assembly of this Colony, together with his Majesty or his Substitutes, have, in their Representative Capacity, the only exclusive Right and Power to lay Taxes and Imposts upon the Inhabitants of this Colony: And that every Attempt to vest such Power in any other Person or Persons whatever, than the General Assembly aforesaid, is illegal, unconstitutional and unjust, and have a manifest Tendency to destroy British as well as American Liberty. . . .*

Document 7-2

In New England hostility to the Stamp Act welled up from the towns. At a town meeting in Braintree, Massachusetts a committee including John Adams was appointed to write a document that would inform their representative in the state assembly of their views. Adams drafted these instructions, which were adopted without dissent by the town meeting.

Sir: In all the calamities which have ever befallen this country, we have never felt so great a concern or such alarming apprehension as on this occasion. Such is our loyalty to the King, our veneration for both houses of Parliament, and our affection for all our fellow subjects in Britain that measures which discover any unkindness in that country towards us are the more sensibly and intimately felt. . . . We further apprehend this tax to be unconstitutional. We have always understood it to be a grand and fundamental principle of the constitution that no freeman should be subject to any tax to which he has not given his own consent, in person or by proxy. And the maxims of the law, as we have constantly received them, are to the same effect, that no freeman can be separated from his property but by his own act or fault. We take it clearly, therefore, to be inconsistent with the spirit of the common law and of the essential fundamental principles of the British constitution that we should be subject to any tax imposed by the British Parliament, because we are not represented in that assembly in any sense, unless it be by a fiction of law, as insensible in theory as it would be injurious in practice if such a taxation should be grounded on it. . . .

Document 7-3

Albigence Waldo was born in 1750 in Pomfret, Connecticut. On Christmas Day 1765 the people of Pomfret convened to resolve "That God and Nature brought us into the world Freemen" and that the English constitution had made their natural rights into positive law, "nor shall it be in the Power of any to deprive us of them, but with our lives." Waldo took these sentiments to heart. Beginning in July 1775 he was intermittently in military service. On New Year's Day 1777 he was commissioned a surgeon in the First Connecticut Infantry Regiment of the Line. The next winter he spent with General Washington at Valley Forge, where he kept a diary.

December 9.—We came from within the breastworks, where we had been coop'd up four tedious Days, with Cloaths and Boots on Night and Day, and resumed our Hutts east of the Breastwork. The rest of the Army chiefly had their huts within the Lines. We are insensible what we are capable of enduring till we are put to the test. To endure hardships with a good grace we must allways think of the following Maxim: "Pain succeeds Pleasure, & Pleasure succeeds Pain." . . .

December 14.—. . . I am sick—discontented—and out of humour. Poor food—hard lodging—cold weather—fatigue—nasty cloathes—nasty cookery—vomit half my time—smoked out of my senses—the Devil's in't—I can't endure it—Why are we sent here to starve and freeze?—What sweet felicities have I left at home: A charming wife—pretty children—good beds—good food—good cookery—all agreeable—all harmonious! Here all confusion—smoke and cold—hunger and filthyness—a pox on my bad luck. There comes a bowl of beef soup, full of burnt leaves and dirt, sickish enough to make a Hector spue—away with it, boys!—I'll live like the chameleon upon air.

Poh! Poh! crys Patience within me, you talk like a fool. . . .

Zigzag toward American Federalism

The eighteenth century held to the quaint idea that war should be followed by peace, that an agreement should be reached to define and stabilize the new status quo. When serious talks began in Paris in 1782, the American spokesmen were top drawer: Franklin, John Adams, John Jay of New York. Their instructions from the Continental Congress told them to do nothing without the "knowledge and concurrence" of the French. The instructions were ignored. The Americans won in the conference room a good bit more than their compatriots had won on the battle field. Franklin typically started with a list of demands that might as well have included Heaven—a large indemnity, freedom of all British ports for American ships, British evacuation of "every part of Canada." What Americans got was a great deal. The Treaty of Paris recognized the Mississippi River as the western boundary of the United States; the northern and southern borders were left vague and provoked many subsequent disputes. At the insistence of that staunch New Englander Adams,

FIGURE 8-1. *Center of Population of the United States, 1790–1860*

the "liberty" of Americans to fish off Newfoundland was acknowledged. The Congress promised that British creditors would "meet no lawful impediment" in seeking to collect prewar debts owed by Americans. Further, the Congress would "recommend" to the states that they make restitution for confiscated Loyalist property. The British retained Canada but, by ceding the Floridas back to Spain, they sacrificed one blade of the scissors that might otherwise have been applied against the United States.

What changes had occurred during the war? The most vital is obvious: Independence had been won. Whole segments of the top layer of government had been cast off. No longer would a foreign authority tell settlers that they could not pass over the crest of the Appalachians. No more would London order a colonial entrepreneur to abandon his plans to build a mill for the production of finished iron products. Never again would American promoters be restrained by the Commissioners of Trade and Plantations from the establishment of commercial banks. Across the board, a new freedom from imperial regulations had been won, freedom to plan, to organize, to expand, to build.

Perhaps too much freedom had been won. Anarchy had been unleashed by the Stamp Act riots and their successors. As early as 1770 the would-be aristocrat Gouverneur Morris was warning in New York that the rabble "mob," or "mobility grow dangerous to the gentry, and how to keep them down is the question." Vigilantism and mob rule were fed by the internecine conflicts of Loyalist and Patriot. Many revolutionaries meted out reprisals against Loyalists without pity, turning over their privies, boycotting their businesses, driving them into exile, killing them. Especially in certain frontier areas where much of their strength was concentrated, as in western New York and the backcountry of North Carolina, the Loyalists could be equally savage, and late in the war General Clinton permitted them to organize freebooting raids into regions that were loyal to the Congress. The gentle French immigrant in Pennsylvania, Hector St. John Crevecoeur, who had loved America as it was prior to the revolutionary agitation, recoiled from the chaos he saw about him. He had thought that American grievances against Great Britain were largely fictitious; now he was appalled at the extremes of rancor:

The rage of civil discord hath advanced among us with an astonishing rapidity. Every opinion is changed; . . . every mode of organization which linked us before as men and as citizens, is now altered [This remark, as will be shown presently, is an exaggeration]. . . . When, from whatever motives, the laws are no longer respected; when . . . all the social bonds are loosened, the same effects will follow. This is now the case with us: the son is armed against the father, the brother against the brother, family against family.

The leaders of the Revolution would all have agreed that this picture was badly overdrawn. They would also have thought that it came dangerously close to the facts. While fighting a war, they wanted peace. Paradoxical as it may seem, they believed fervently in law and order. Even before the Declaration of Independence, the Continental Congress had advised the people of the states to set up formal governments. Here we might pause to ask what was going on. One expert has declared recently that by throwing off the British yoke the colonists had reverted to a state of nature. This view is too extreme. The political compact had indeed been revoked (see Chapter 6), but the antecedent agreement, the social compact, remained in effect. What was needed was to re-institute a political or governmental one. By the end of 1776, ten states had adopted constitutions; the other three by 1780. Whereas the articles of government in each colony had formerly rested on a royal charter, they now rested on the consent of the governed—with haunting specified restrictions as to sex, color, religion, and property. The degree of continuity from colonial times is particularly striking in those colonies where the electors had long held the right to choose their governor; properly modified because of full independence from Great Britain, the Connecticut charter of 1662 held sway until 1818; the charter of 1663 for Rhode Island until 1842.

The fabrication of new governments proceeded from shared beliefs. It must be based on voluntary agreement among the freemen. In writing the preamble for the constitution of Massachusetts (1780), John Adams declared: "The body politic is formed by a voluntary association of individuals: It is a social compact by which the whole people covenants with each citizen and each citizen with the whole people that all shall be governed by certain laws for the common good." Second, it must be grounded in a written constitution which will serve as supreme law. Here the states adhered to colonial ideas (the Bible, the charter of the province, the Fundamental Orders of Connecticut), but diverged from British ones, in which the constitution is a very loose bundle indeed that is nowhere formulated or codified. It must prescribe elections at fixed times. Again this was a departure from the emergent English mode, where the practice of a ministry responsible to a Parliamentary majority would permit the government to hold elections at its discretion within a certain period. While men agreed that the state should embody a separation of powers, and that each gear in the mechanism should check and balance others, they were far from unanimous on how these goods could best be fabricated. They would soon agree, by 1790, on a bicameral legislature, an independent executive, and a separate array of courts. The citizens of Pennsylvania were for a brief time the chief dissidents. Leaning farther toward a levelling attitude than the majority in any other state, they wrote into their constitution of 1776 a one-house legislature that was given the power to choose a plural executive. By 1790 these arrangements were junked.

A foremost principle of the republican revolution was equality in the eyes of the law. Clearly the War for Independence did not bestow this benefit.

Some women in the colonies (the dependents of freemen) had long enjoyed more legal rights than any European women: in land ownership, in conveying personal property, in marriage and divorce. But seemingly the American Revolution did little or nothing to enhance the degree of justice accorded to women. As to indentured servants, one reads of them less often after the war, but this reform was due less to statutory revisions than to changes in social conditions; more persons now had no compulsion to accept so degraded a status. Religious dissenters made some headway; only South Carolina kept a religious requirement for the suffrage. Overlooked nearly everywhere in passing out rights were the slaves. Only Delaware in its constitution saw fit to abolish the slave trade. When Virginia in 1782 authorized manumission by slaveholders, it did so in a statute. The effective abolition of slavery in Massachusetts the next year was even farther removed from constitution-making; it came in a decision by the Supreme Judicial Court.

Although Americans in 1776 agreed on many aspects of the machinery to be used in creating a state *de novo,* some features were yet to be learned. Some of the original constitutions were written by special conventions called solely for that purpose, but others were simply decreed by the legislature. Not one of the first twelve was submitted to the citizens for ratification; "consent of the governed" did not necessitate their direct acceptance even of the frame of government. When Massachusetts in 1778 pioneered in asking its electorate to vote a draft up or down, they voted it down, to be superseded by John Adams' document of 1780. A major innovation in some of these new constitutions was the clause specifying a procedure by which amendments could be made; the state should be stable, but it should not be rigid.

The difficulties in achieving politico-legal order were aggravated by ruptures in society and the economy. In the course of shedding the segments of colonial government that were located in England, the Revolutionaries had evicted segments of the provincial oligarchies as well. The available facts about the Loyalists are far from satisfactory. One recent study does not make any effort at all to do a statistical analysis, not even to the point of listing a few hundred prominent Loyalists and ascertaining where they were born, where educated, to what extent dependent financially on royal favors. Going from current guesswork, perhaps 30,000 Americans served at some time with the British forces. The number who went into exile can be reasonably estimated at 80,000 persons, but other speculations have it as high as 250,000. Since the population of the colonies at the end of the war was at most 3 million, the proportion of refugees was perhaps 24 per thousand. Thus Americans should never have become strident about "the Terror" during the French Revolution, where the émigrés numbered only 5 per thousand people. Consider another comparison. The exact value of confiscations from Loyalists cannot be known, but we do know that the British government paid them £3.3 million in indemnifications for American property they had lost. The compensations paid by the French government after the Revolution there were only twelve times as great. It has been surmised that Loyalists in the colonies tended to be persons who belonged to some minority in their home locality (as Anglicans in an overwhelmingly Congregationalist community) so that they needed external power applied by the British authorities to protect them against their neighbors. They seem to have been more prosperous and more urban than the generality of Americans. We have as a sample the 1,100 civilians who accompanied the British forces in the evacuation of Boston in 1776. Included were 102 councilors or other civic officials, 18 clergymen, 382 farmers, 213 merchants "and others," 105 from outlying towns. Probably most of the remainder were women and children. That is hardly a cross-section of the population.

The expulsion of a goodly number of oligarchs was one element in a decline in deference (see the end of Chapter 4). Complaints about it were everywhere. Wrote one Pennsylvania, "the most insignificant now lord it with impunity & without discretion over the most respectable characters." A Loyalist in Salem lamented, "Everything I see is laughable, cursable, and damnable; my pew in the church is converted into a pork tub; my house into a den of rebels, thieves & lice; my farm in possession of the very worst of all God's creation; my few debts all gone to the devil with my debtors." It was observed that "a nasty great cooper" could be seen on Sundays wearing clothes he had taken from a gentleman. A galling thought was that men "who had not money enough for shoes for their feet, are now riding in coaches of their own in Boston." Governor Hutchinson in London grieved that "Washington, it is said, rides in my coach at Cambridge." The coach was a luminous symbol: as a great American poet of the twentieth century would remark, nobody can play the duchess without a carriage as a stage-prop. The wife of the leading Loyalist in Pennsylvania, Joseph Galloway, was mortified: ". . . as I was walking in the Rain, My own Chariot Drove by. I own that I then thought it hard but I Kept Up pretty well but when I turn'd into the alley My dear child came into My Mind & what she wou'd say to see her Mamma walking 5 squares in the rain at Night like a common Woman . . . I dare not think."

What was disaster for many was opportunity for some. Spoils from privateering spawned a new governing group in Massachusetts to replace the Loyalists who had fled. Or look at New Jersey: in 1776 as Washington's army fled across the state, pandemonium prevailed. The legislature appointed a Committee of Safety to restore order, and one of its members was William Patterson, born a shopkeeper's son in Ireland. He was also the attorney general, in which role he aimed many arrows against the "pernicious class of men called moderates." He used his public connections to buy confiscated Loyalist property on good terms. Before he died, President Washington would appoint him to the Supreme Court of the United States.

Other forces can be seen behind the rising equality. One was the spread of written news. Just as printing had eroded the authority of the clergy by enabling more men to read the Bible themselves, so now did widespread literacy wash away deference. The facts are startling. *Common Sense,* published 10 January 1776, reportedly sold 120,000 copies in less than three months; comparable popularity in the United States today would mean sales of at least 10 million—of a serious work. The colonies had twenty-three newspapers in 1765, thirty-seven in 1776, probably over a hundred by 1789. A nobleman visiting in Massachusetts wrote, "All these people busy themselves much with politics, and from the landlord down to the housemaid they all read two newspapers a day." Another equalizing experience, perverse though the truth may seem, was military service. Clearly generals want to effect a strict maintenance of status, and with regulars they can usually do so. But not with militia, who in many instances even elected their own officers. It is easy to imagine a soldier swearing scornfully against his commander while standing by a campfire in Pennsylvania, when he would never dare to take the same attitude if both men were back in civilian life.

Independence aside, the main immediate effects of wartime had been economic. Crucial here was the concentration of liquid capital; further, it was concentrated under the control of men of enterprise who could be counted on to invest it in further profitable innovations. The process had several facets. In addition to the confiscation of Loyalist property, it involved the repudiation on a giant scale of private debts owed to British merchants. Take Aaron Lopez of Newport. Before the war he imported large amounts of dry goods from England. To balance his accounts he relied heavily on West Indies products, but he also borrowed as much as he could. In 1765 he owed £10,000 to a Bristol merchant. While this debt was being reduced hardly at all, he used his credit with a London house; in 1774 he owed it at least £12,000. Dozens of colonial merchants and planters were similarly in debt to Britishers when the War for Independence began. Charges were rife that the American desire to disclaim debts was a main motive for independence. A bard of Old England wrote thus about the knavery of Revolutionary Virginians:

> *Those vaunted demagogues, who nobly rose*
> *From England's debtors to be England's foes,*
> *Who could their monarch in their purse forget,*
> *And break allegiance, but to cancel debt.*

Repudiation of debts and confiscation of Loyalist property were dispersed widely through the states, but loot from profiteering was concentrated in a handful of ports. A major consequence of the entry into the war of France, Spain, and the Netherlands was that it made available to American privateers a plethora of ports both in Europe and the Caribbean where they could take captured prizes. The profits from this industry (I use the word deliberately) could be enormous, and part of the pattern was already established. Abraham Whipple of Rhode Island can serve as a case study. During the Seven Years'

War on one cruise (1759–1760) he took twenty-three prizes; their value was a million dollars. In the War for Independence he used a clever stunt. He simply sidled into an English convoy bound from the West Indies to Great Britain, and acted as if he belonged there. Each night for ten straight nights his men boarded an enemy merchantman, subdued the crew, and Whipple sent her off to Boston with a skeleton force. Eight of them reached their adopted home. Their cargoes brought more than a million dollars. As early as the beginning of 1777, the damage to the West India trade from American privateers had approached £2 million sterling, and the vessels captured on those routes totalled 250. In the course of the War perhaps 90,000 Americans served at some time on the more than 500 privateering ships commissioned by various states. In one month (May 1779) the minor port of New London received eighteen prizes. Salem alone in 1781 was home to 59 privateers, which carried 4,000 men. Although Massachusetts provided two thirds of the men who sailed on privateers during the War, the practice was common in other ports as well. Robert Morris of Philadelphia reportedly raised his fortune to more than £300,000 by such ventures. New York, occupied by the British throughout the War, and Charles Town, in foreign hands after May 1780, did not get their share of the bounty.

By these varieties of quasilegal theft, a few hundred merchant-ship-owners acquired large pools of liquid wealth. They promptly looked about for ways to make it even larger, and their earlier experimentation with credit pointed a path (see Chapter 3 on New England trade and credit). It was not accidental that the first commercial banks were located in the biggest ports. Congress granted a charter to the Bank of North America, promoted by the wealthy ex-privateer Robert Morris, and it opened in Philadelphia in 1782. The Massachusetts Bank was founded in 1784 under a charter from the state. A similar procedure resulted in the same year in founding the Bank of New York in Manhattan. These were the only three commercial banks to antedate the Constitution. Once established, the early banks devoted their resources to mercantile activities. A typical set of postwar transactions might see a Boston merchant dispatching a varied cargo, perhaps with emphasis on naval stores and whale oil, to his agent in England. He would be paid with a bill of exchange drawn against a London bank payable sixty or ninety days in the future (see Chapter 3 on New England credit). He would immediately trot off to the Massachusetts Bank and "discount" it or sell it to them, meaning that he could get nearly all of his money at once. He would then invest in another venture. By such tactics is the purchasing power of an economy expanded, with the frequently happy result that the volume of trade increases also. The ability of commercial banks to extend credit could find other uses; it could help to set up joint-stock companies for nonbanking enterprises. In the entire colonial period only a half dozen charters had been granted by the provinces to business firms. In 1781–1785 the number rose to eleven, in 1786–1790 to twenty-two.

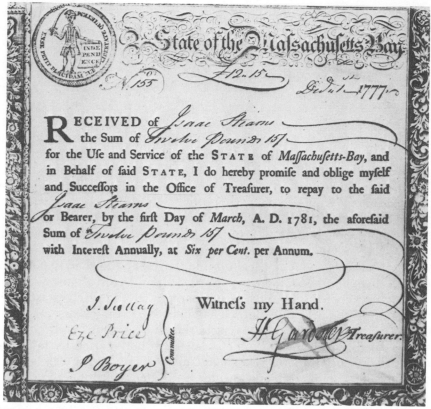

FIGURE 8-2. *A Continental Bill of Credit from Massachusetts*

A system of private credit will work only so long as most people believe in it; they must think that propping up all of the paper transactions is some commonly received token of value. That did not exist in 1783. The utilization of credit, especially in borrowing abroad, was vastly complicated by the deplorable state of public finances. The Continental Congress had no power to tax, and the War had been financed by (a) requisitions on the states, (b) borrowing from the public, and (c) subsidies and loans from foreign countries. Revenues from abroad were fitful. Sometimes the states did not come across. Despite efforts led by Robert Morris (now Superintendent of Finance for the Continental Congress) to sell bonds as widely as possible within the states, the yield did not suffice. While General Washington wrote an interminable series of letters imploring money and supplies, the Congress resorted to (d) printing paper money. The pace of the printing presses accelerated, with predictable consequences; the second column in the table shows the emission of bills of credit in given years (in millions of dollars); the fourth column shows the exchange ratio between Continental dollars and specie:

1775	$ 6 million		
1776	19		
1777	13	Oct. 1777	3 to 1
1778	63	Dec. 1778	7 to 1
1779	90	Dec. 1779	42 to 1
		Dec. 1780	99 to 1
		April 1781	147 to 1

Morris in 1782 wrote that the principal owed by the Congress would amount the following year to $30 million. Interest would be $2 million. This sum, he thought, could be raised by four types of tax that would yield about $500,000 each: import duties, a tax on land, a poll (on heads) tax, and excise duties on distilled liquors. "A public debt, supported by public revenue, will provide the strongest cement to keep our confederacy together." Here was the notion that would become eminent wearing the emblem of Alexander Hamilton, but the states in 1783 could not agree to grant Congress the power to levy the taxes.

The states also were in fiscal trouble. Together, they had issued treasury notes (call them bonds) for more than $200 million. Taxes, almost negligible in most provinces before the War (see Chapter 7), had risen drastically. In Virginia in 1765 the per capita burden had been 5d; twenty years later it was 10 shillings; in the same period in Massachusetts it rose from 1 shilling to 18 (all figures in English shillings). Problems were further snarled by the derangement of commerce. True, American merchants were no longer legally bound to market through a staple or market center in England for tobacco or any other product, but it is absurd to say, as has often been said, that they could roam at will; every European power preserved for its empire overseas a tangle of regulations. Cultivation of indigo in South Carolina was destroyed by the withdrawal of the British bounty. Tobacco planters, in spite of their statutory freedom, continued to find it wise to market their crops through Glasgow factors or agents who could give long-term credit and who could maneuver the markets in Europe. The most important of all colonial channels of trade—that to the British West Indies—was prohibited to Americans after they left the Empire. The former imperial advantages in Great Britain itself were also lost to Americans dealing in such wares as ships and naval stores. It was even said that in American ports British ships were close to gaining their own oligopoly to corner trade with the British Empire. By the spring of 1786 James Madison was spreading his gloom to Jefferson (who was serving as United States minister to France): "A continuance of the present anarchy of our commerce will be a continuance of the present unfavorable balance on it, which by draining us of our metals furnishes pretexts for the pernicious substitution of paper money, for indulgences to debtors, for postponement of taxes. In fact most of our political evils may be traced to our commercial ones, as most of our moral may be traced to our political."

FIGURE 8-2. *Indigo Drying*

Indigo Drying in Southern Carolina is an anonymous print, but it can be dated fairly closely, because the crop had such a short career in North America. Also it never expanded beyond a limited area in South Carolina. That colony grew rice in its moist lands along the coast. In the uplands it grew cotton. The intervening foothills, for a span that hardly exceeded three decades, was the site of indigo culture.

The plant, when it was dried and powdered and boiled, produced a blue dye. Whirlwind expansion of the English textile industry in the mid-eighteenth century brought a rapidly growing market for dyestuffs. The British West Indies could not meet the demand for indigo at a reasonable price, so in 1742 the crop was introduced into South Carolina. Its success there was due to subsidy from the United Kingdom; in 1748 Parliament voted a bounty of 6¢ a pound. When the War for Independence killed the British bounty, the cultivation of indigo in the United States died with it.

No reader should forget that it was largely the labors, under scorching heat, of slaves like those shown here that financed the construction of estates such as Westover—and bought its superb library (Figure 4-1).

To understand Madison's complaints, we must stand at the right spot and look from the proper angle. He was not speaking for most of his countrymen. A generation ago the fashion was to dramatize as "the Critical Era" the period when the new nation subsisted under the Articles of Confederation. But the typical citizen then was not conscious of being under any gun—quite the contrary. We can read about depressed conditions in certain ports in 1783, or about the misfortunes of localized regions as some indigo and tobacco districts. But we have little reason to doubt the overall accuracy of Franklin's portrait in November 1786:

> Our husbandmen, who are the bulk of the nation, have had plentiful crops, their produce sells at high prices and for ready, hard money. . . . Our working-people are all employed and get high wages, are well fed and well clad. . . . Buildings in Philadelphia increase rapidly, besides small towns rising in every corner of the country. The laws govern, justice is well administered, and property is as secure as in any country on the globe. Our wilderness lands are daily buying up by new settlers, and our settlements extend rapidly to the westward. European goods were never so cheaply afforded to us as since Britain has no longer the monopoly of supplying us. In short, all among us may be happy who have happy dispositions; such being necessary to happiness even in paradise.

A society living in quiet and moderate comfort was not enough for men of power. In a span of four years, 1783–1787, a half dozen flaws in their circumstances brought them to create a new national-federal government. Probably the worst failing of the Articles of Confederation was that the Congress could not cope with foreign relations. In modern language, the national security was shaky. Independence had been won, but nobody knew for sure that it could be held. In 1787 the British army still occupied several posts on the frontier in United States territory. As a justification for holding them it was pointing to the failure of American legislatures to make provision for compensating Loyalists who had lost property. The Congress, with no power to tax even for military expenditures, lacked the strength to expel the British. An amendment to the Articles that would give Congress some taxing powers needed the unanimous approval of the thirteen states represented in the Congress. Twelve said Yes; New York said No. Another irksome aspect of foreign relations lay in the money markets. The United States had borrowed heavily during the War, particularly in the Netherlands and in France. Unless arrangements could be made to honor those obligations, any American project, private or public, would carry a bad aroma at Amsterdam or Paris.

Domestic disorders continued to be common. Oligarchs in several states met with local challenges. Nobody could be surprised that unruly Rhode Island was flooding the territory with paper money, but what of usually law-abiding Pennsylvania, where insurgents in the legislature actually went so far as to revoke the charter it had granted to the Bank of North America. Then came Shays' Rebellion around Worcester County in western Massachusetts.

Although this uprising by a few thousand farmers inspired one of Jefferson's best-known hyperbolic squawls ("I hold that a little rebellion, now and then, is a good thing."), it seems in retrospect to have been a rather mild affair. A few courts were forcibly closed, but not for long. The significance of the episode is not chiefly that it achieved some reforms, as it did, but that it, like the tribulations of banker Morris in Pennsylvania, helped to scare some pivotal oligarchs into the belief that a stronger central government standing above the states might be needed at times not only to handle foreign affairs but also to intervene within a state to preserve order.

The Congress had already shown that, given the chance and the required authority, it could move with exemplary wisdom. It had also acquired assets—Western lands—that in time could be converted into financial resources. Under their royal charters, several colonies had held title to huge tracts beyond the mountains. In 1781–1785 three states, New York, Virginia, and Connecticut, had ceded part of these possessions to the Confederation. Eventually, but not overnight, funds could be raised by selling these lands to private buyers. As early as 1780 the Congress had prescribed that any federal acquisitions should be "formed into separate republican states, which shall become members of the federal union, and have the same rights and sovereignty, freedom and independence." A committee headed by Jefferson submitted a report to the same effect in 1784. With many modifications, the plan became the kernel of the Northwest Ordinance of 1787, under which were formed five new states that would serve as the heartland of the nation through much of the nineteenth century. Perhaps never has any expansive nation treated its conquests (always excepting of course Indians and blacks) with greater justice and foresight.

One sphere of activity over which the Congress had no power whatever was commerce crossing state lines. This defect was the immediate impetus that led to the Constitutional Convention. Each state simply acted as it saw fit in laying tariffs upon goods coming from its neighbors. The tangle of impediments to trade on Chesapeake Bay seemed especially wretched, so Virginia proposed an interstate conclave to discuss the mess. The New Jersey delegates came ready to talk over not only commerce but also "other important matters," and already James Madison had written to his confidante Jefferson in France, "Gentlemen both within and without Congress wish to make this meeting subservient to a plenipotentiary convention for amending the Confederation." When the Annapolis Convention met in September 1786, Madison was present; so was Hamilton for New York, as well as representatives of Pennsylvania, New Jersey, and Delaware. Here was the heartland of the United States in the late eighteenth century; of the strongest states, only peripheral South Carolina and Massachusetts were missing. The assemblage did not solve the commercial problem, but it did propose a general convention for the following May in Philadelphia.

Why was a convocation of all the states needed to revise the Articles of Confederation? The answer is simple. Under its terms, it could be amended only by unanimous agreement of all members. As New York had shown by its single-handed veto of a taxing power for the federal machinery, such harmony was impossible. So the advocates of a new national government simply by-passed the Congress altogether.

Some abstractions must be stated about the Federal Convention. First, the question before it was not what kind of national government the country would have, but whether the country would have any national government at all. Second, each delegate did have his own private financial interests and concerns, as all men do, but the evidence does not suggest that those interests controlled any major decision by the Convention. Ideas and convictions do matter. Third, it will not do to set off the Declaration of Independence as a "liberal" or "radical" document as against the Constitution as a "conservative" or "reactionary" one; the line of development from the one to the other was direct and straightforward. With few exceptions the individuals who led the War for Independence were the men who spearheaded the struggle for the Constitution. The continuity of leadership is startling to anybody who has looked at other revolutions, and the Founding Fathers had not suddenly adopted a whole new set of persuasions. To say (as used to be argued by some) that the Declaration spoke for "human rights" while the Constitution embodied "property rights" is nonsense; the protagonists made no such distinction and they were unanimous that one of the most sacred of human rights was the right to own and manage private property.

The Convention met in the State House behind closed doors. It issued no press releases. No official transcript was kept; the best record we have is the voluminous notes taken by Madison. Why had they met? There was no widespread or raucous dissatisfaction with the Confederation. Most Americans would have assented to Jefferson's remark of 1787, "with all the imperfections of our present government, it is without comparison the best existing or that ever did exist." The Continental Congress had authorized the Convention, but only "for the sole and express purpose of revising the Articles of Confederation." Clearly most of the delegates arrived in Philadelphia with more sweeping aims. George Washington, chosen on the first day as president of the assemblage, was moving around in the early going saying, "It is too probable that no plan we propose will be adopted. Perhaps another dreadful conflict is to be sustained. If to please the people, we offer what we ourselves disapprove, how can we afterwards defend our work? Let us raise a standard to which the wise and the honest can repair. The event is in the hand of God."

What they did, of course, was to run up a standard to which "the people" could repair far beyond the ranks of the wise and the honest. Fifty-five men served at some time during the summer as delegates to the Convention.

Average daily attendance was only about thirty, and most of those had little or no impact on decisions. It is no exaggeration to say that the Federal Constitution was the work of a dozen men. Rhode Island was never represented at all; Georgia had no weight; North Carolina, Delaware, to a lesser degree Maryland and New Jersey, and New Hampshire had mainly a negative influence. New York again revealed its peculiar position among the states. It had a strong itch to go it alone. Virtually dragooned into laggard support of the War for Independence, New York had later cast the black ball against the proposal that the Continental Congress be given a limited right to impose tariffs. Eventually, after the publication of the Constitution, it would be coerced into ratification. As late as the outbreak of the Civil War, its officials would still be toying with the notion of seceding from the United States. Now, in 1787, its representatives played almost no part whatever. Hamilton gave a speech that was reportedly brilliant ("the British government was the best in the world"), but he found no buyers. Massachusetts, with John Adams in England and both Hancock and Samuel Adams staying away, did not exert its due force.

In a fevered ambience of wheeling and dealing (Philadelphia in summer is favorable to fevers) the proficient manipulators came from four states: South Carolina, Virginia, Pennsylvania, and Connecticut. The able group from the Old Dominion led by Washington included Madison, Edmund Randolph, and George Mason. Apart from the president's personal standing, it acted a strong part in effecting the ultimate compromise about representation between the large states and the small ones. South Carolina's spokesmen complemented each other well: Charles Pinckney was eloquent when not flamboyant, while John Rutledge was a learned barrister who knew how to maneuver in the lobbies and boarding-houses. They had two special concerns, made urgent by the crisis in marketing products from their plantations. Since the South was then the chief exporting region of the country, they wanted to deny any new government the power to tax exports. They also wanted to be sure that government could not in the near future interfere with the slave trade. They got much of what they wanted—at a price. The federal government was denied the power to tax exports, but the South failed to win its goal of requiring a two-thirds vote in Congress for enactments affecting interstate or foreign commerce; a simple majority could carry these laws. The period within which Congress could not prohibit the slave trade was limited to twenty years, and even in that span it could tax incoming slaves. The South also favored Mason's idea that Americans should not be forced by a federal government into paying their pre-war debts to Englishmen. Here it won. From the North, Connecticut exercised disproportionate influence because it was served by two shrewd operators in Roger Sherman and William Samuel Johnson. Their state needed land. It had a tentative agreement giving it title to a large chunk of northern Ohio—the Western Reserve—but the arrangement would be safer if a general government existed to give it sanction. The Pennsylvanians too were fighting a rear action; they wanted security for the Bank of North America. Buoyed by Franklin's prestige, they also had the talents of Robert Morris, James Wilson, and Gouverneur Morris.

It is essential to grasp the history-making precedent that was set. As James Wilson wrote after the Convention adjourned in September, "America now presents the first instance of a people assembled to weigh deliberately and calmly, and to decide leisurely and peaceably, upon the form of government by which they will bind themselves, and their posterity." When debate began they agreed upon much, but they were not even clear that they wanted to create a tripartite structure with fairly complete autonomy of executive and judiciary from the legislative branch; for most of the summer they seemed to tilt toward a congressional dominance akin to the Continental Congress. They were agreed from the outset on a crucial innovation. Earlier forms of federalism consisted of a central organ that could act only on its subsidiary bodies and that did not act directly on individual citizens. (See Chapter 6 on divided sovereignty in America.) The Confederation had shown the debility of such schemes. What the Convention devised was a national-federal structure. But the Founding Fathers were also keen to avert a centralized power that could become tyrannical; they had lived in the age of absolute monarchs.

The first split in the Convention came with presentation of the Virginia Plan, mainly Madison's handiwork. It had little chance of being accepted. The issue was whether freemen or states should be represented in Congress; if the former, the populous states would dominate. The Virginia Plan called for voters in each state to elect a lower house, which would then choose members of the upper house from a list of nominees drawn by the state legislatures. The small states would never agree to any such arrangement. In the discussions it was meantime voted "that a national government ought to be established consisting of a supreme Legislative, Executive and Judiciary." After a fortnight of harangues and lobbying, the New Jersey Plan was submitted by William Patterson (the war profiteer; see above). It would leave untouched the method of electing the Congress and the basis of representation therein—one state equals one vote. The Congress would select a plural executive. The large states obviously found this scheme unacceptable.

The Great Compromise as to representation is also called the Connecticut Compromise because it was put forward by that delegation: "that in the second branch . . . each State shall have an equal vote." Thus in the Senate or upper chamber every state legislature would name two members. Representation in the lower house was distributed among the states by population. The Convention again used the so-called three-fifths rule, which had been used by the Congress as far back as the proposed revenue amendment of 1783; that is, in apportioning representatives in the lower house, each slave should count as three-fifths of a man. Otherwise the entire topic of slavery was almost ignored in the Convention apart from the ban of legislation on the slave trade for twenty years. Madison got little attention with his observation that "the great danger to our general government is the great southern and northern interests of the continent, being opposed to each other." This Great Compromise proved the chief cement of union; it was representation and not slavery that had been the grounds of division, and the cleavage had been between large states and small ones. As Pinckney drily remarked, "Give New Jersey an equal vote, and she will dismiss her scruples and concur in the National system." Of the powers accorded to the new national legislature beyond those held by the Continental Congress, two would prove to be crucial: the power to levy taxes directly on the citizens rather than to make requisitions on the states, and the authority to control interstate and foreign commerce.

Not until early September, after nearly four months of deliberations, was a method of picking an executive arrived at. At that time a committee brought in the outlines of what became the Electoral College; the president would be chosen by electors selected in a manner determined by each state's legislature and proportional to the state's number of Congressmen. The next step was to give the president the power to appoint judges to the Supreme Court of the United States, plus any subordinate courts that the future Congresses might erect, "with the advice and consent of the Senate." Prior to these decisions, a congressional government had seemed possible, perhaps even likely. Now the tripartite structure—division of powers, checks and balances—had been hardened. By making the president largely independent of the legislative branch, the Convention had made it almost inevitable that the judiciary would be autonomous also. The Founding Fathers had done a superlative job of building exactly what they wanted: a government that was most unlikely to become despotic. They had forged a machine in which the gears do not mesh—they grind. The contraption was fine in normal times when most Americans agreed "that government is best that governs least"; in modern vernacular, just stay off my back. But it was ill-conceived to cope with cataclysms in society such as the problems of slavery or the depression that began in 1929. In the summation of the historian Forrest McDonald:

> So cumbersome and so inefficient was the system that the people, however virtuous or wicked, could not activate it. It could be activated through deals and deceit, through bargains and bribery, through logrolling and lobbying and trickery and trading, the tactics that go with man's baser attributes, most notably his greed and his love of power. And yet, in the broad range and on the average, these private tactics and motivations could operate effectively only when they were compatible with the public good, for they were braked by the massive inertia of society as a whole.

Having drafted the Constitution, the delegates had to get it accepted by the people. Much of the effort of the Convention had gone into drafting an arrangement that would be palatable to the folks back home. But what did "consent of the governed" imply in practice? What forms should be used to test if such consent can exist? For instance, the Convention could have submitted its work for acceptance or rejection to the various state legislatures. Or to the Continental Congress. Or to the voters of the country as a whole. It did none of those. By its recommended procedure for ratification, it gave its answer to the question: Where does sovereignty reside? The Constitution was submitted to the freemen of the nation. But not to the freemen *en masse,* but to each of them as a citizen of a specific state. Here then was bedrock in the American polity.

In making the submission, the Founding Fathers did not play fair. They rigged the cards. The Articles of Confederation had taught them their lesson about unanimity rules. Article VII of their creation stated: "The Ratification of the Conventions of nine States, shall be sufficient for the Establishment of this Constitution between the States so ratifying the same." Several states were sure to ratify from the beginning. Of the first four, three did so by unanimous vote of their ratifying conventions: Delaware, New Jersey, and Georgia. Delaware had little choice; it was too small to survive on its own. New Jersey, in the scintillating phrase of James Madison, was "a cask tapped at both ends." Its imports from Europe came usually either to New York or to Philadelphia. The neighboring states, by imposing tariffs, could systematically drain off the resources of New Jersey. The state also had a substantial debt and heavy taxes. Any system that might help to ease these difficulties could only be approved. Georgia's prompt acclaim was also the result of geography; it was a frontier area. At the moment when the ratifying convention met, the militia was being mustered to fight off an expected attack by the Creeks. What Georgians wanted was a federal army to protect them. Early action by Pennsylvania was more a matter of economics; here was the state that came closest to being swayed by Charles Beard's "personalty interests." Pennsylvania had gone farther than any other state in developing a system of political parties, and Robert Morris's legions used it relentlessly to buttress the security of the Bank of North America. They won ratification by a vote in their convention of 46 to 23.

These four affirmations happened in less than a month, 7 December 1787 to 2 January, 1788. Connecticut followed two days later. Its economy was in bad shape. Many of its ships had been specially designed to transport horses for sale in the British West Indies, and that trade was now closed. The state was badly overpopulated and wanted a stake in western land. Taxes were crushing. But residents of the state did own considerable public securities. If those obligations could be fobbed off onto a federal government with taxing power so that the debts could be paid off and thus converted into liquid capital, Connecticut would benefit immensely. More than a month passed before Massachusetts joined. This victory was crucial—and somewhat comical. Business in the state, in spite of some dislocations that had attended Independence, was in good shape. The determining factor was not economics, as in Pennsylvania, but politics. When the 355 delegates to the convention met, probably a substantial majority were opposed to the Constitution. But vain John Hancock had many admirers. The rumor went out that he could be vice president of the proposed Union (maybe even president if Virginia did not ratify in time to qualify Washington). The pros took it, but only by 187 to 168.

Then Maryland came in. The United States now numbered seven. But the elements that had agglutinated so far represented weakness as much as they did strength. Of the large states, Virginia, South Carolina, and New York remained holdouts. South Carolina toppled in May. Loss of the bounty on indigo had hurt. For 1783, 1784, and 1785 the rice crop had been poor; never before in memory had it failed three years in a row. During the War for Independence the state had proven terribly vulnerable to invasion; of the 3,000 black slaves carried away by British troops at the end of the war, perhaps a majority were taken from South Carolina. On the other side, the state had confiscated valuable British and Loyalist estates, which it had then sold. Many of the payments to it had been made in Continental debt certificates. If a new federal government would redeem these securities at face value, the state could suspend all taxes for several years. Rutledge and Pinckney and their friends swung into the movement for ratification, but even so they were able to carry their convention only by a margin of 2 to 1. New Hampshire followed by an even closer tally.

When summer came, more than six months after the Constitution had been submitted, Virginia and New York were still outside. Some of the opposing arguments can only be called ludicrous. Article VI said "but no religious test shall ever be required as qualification to any office or public trust under the United States." This provision, it was charged, opened the door for election of the Pope as president. George Mason cautioned that another clause would enable Congress to decree that all elections for the entire nation should be held in New York. Congress could designate the site of a future national capital; this would let them place it in Peking. This capital was to be ten miles square and within it Congress would have sole jurisdiction; thus it could do as it pleased there, even, warned Patrick Henry, hang "any man who shall act contrary to their commands . . . without benefit of clergy." Surveying this catalogue of perils, in 1955 Cecilia Kenyon commented: "All in all, a terrible prospect: the Pope as President operating from a base in Peking, superintending a series of hangings without benefit of clergy! Or worse."

This sort of gibberish played a role in nearly defeating the Constitution in Virginia; also counting in the anti-Federalist opposition of course was the jealousy felt by many of the county magnates against any outside power that might conceivably infringe on their prerogatives. Even with the support of such figures as Washington and Madison and George Wythe, the Constitution was ratified only by 89 to 79. Thus on 25 June, 1788, with the most populous state in the fold, implementation of the new document became certain. But this assurance did not cause universal rejoicing. North Carolina in July rejected the Constitution by a margin of more than 2 to 1. This defection was hardly fatal to the Union—but New York almost took the same course. The faction in state politics led by George Clinton had become infatuated with their resources: a

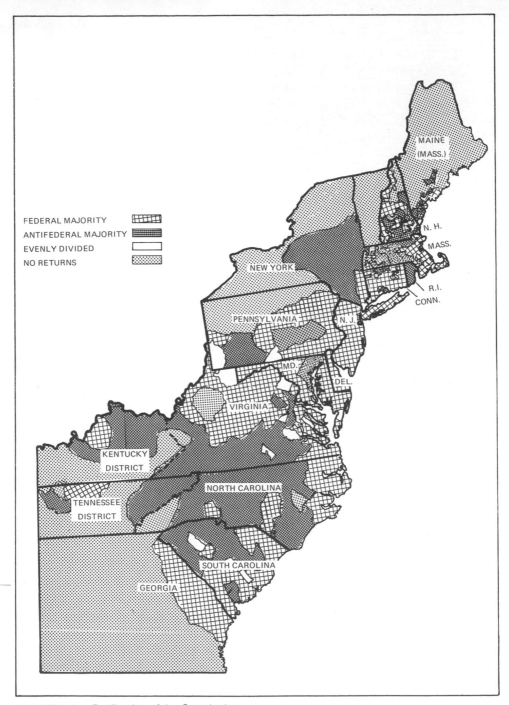

FEDERAL MAJORITY

ANTIFEDERAL MAJORITY

EVENLY DIVIDED

NO RETURNS

MAINE
(MASS.)

N. H.

MASS.

R.I.

CONN.

NEW YORK

PENNSYLVANIA

N. J.

MD.

DEL.

VIRGINIA

KENTUCKY
DISTRICT

TENNESSEE
DISTRICT

NORTH CAROLINA

SOUTH CAROLINA

GEORGIA

FIGURE 8-4.   *Ratification of the Constitution*

central location, good farm land, navigable rivers, a majestic port. They thought they would go it alone. In electing delegates to the convention, the Federalists could win only New York (Manhattan) and three other counties; their opponents carried nine. The delegates were anti-Federalist by 2 to 1. Then a lobby headed by Hamilton and his father-in-law Philip Schuyler went to work. If you do not join the Union, they said, Manhattan will secede from the state of New York. Even this blackmail won adoption only by 30 to 27.

North Carolina did not become one of the thirteen "original" United States until November 1789, months after the new government had begun operations. Rhode Island entered even later, May 1790, and then only because Providence had seceded from the state.

The Constitution of the United States has proven itself as the most enduring frame of government of any republican polity. That fact is amazing. When you look back to the events that resulted in that astounding blend of verbosity and terseness, you wonder how it got adopted at all. The process seems almost to have been accidental. Diversities among the states were immense. Most of the big ports had been occupied for years by British forces. Yet the inland regions in general had not suffered much. Some men had grown rich by the profits of war, especially from privateering. Others who lived in ravaged areas had seen their fortunes wiped out. Farmers had been coerced by the army quartermaster into selling their produce for pay in Continental dollars that turned out to be worth nothing. But after the war ended in 1781, much of the agricultural sector of the economy operated for several years in a sellers' market. Even so, many farmers still had grievances, particularly gripes about governmental discrimination against them. These complaints provoked much civil disorder, of which the most notorious case is Shays' Rebellion in New England. Out of this turmoil, and out of preliminary negotiations, came the Philadelphia Convention of 1787 which drew up the Constitution. The original thirteen states, each for its own reasons and in its own way, ratified a document that was then unique. A new stage in the history of the formation of nation-states had been reached.

SOME NOTABLE EVENTS

1779 First Universalist church starts in Gloucester, Massachusetts.

1780 Massachusetts adopts a constitution.

1783 Yale, with 270 students, is largest college in United States.

1783–
1784 Flood of imports at war's end, plus British banking crisis of 1784, contributes to disruption of trade in some states.

1784 Thomas Jefferson, *Notes on Virginia* (Paris, dated 1782).

1785 Edmund Cartwright in England invents power loom.

First state college, University of Georgia, is founded.

Virginia is first state to authorize a turnpike company.

Ordinance of 1785 for disposition of Federal lands in West, 20 May.

1786 Annapolis Convention meets to discuss interstate commerce, September 11–14.

1786–
1787 Shays' Rebellion in Massachusetts.

John Adams, *A Defense of the Constitutions of Government of the United States* (3 volumes).

1786–
1788 Land speculators start companies to promote settlement of Ohio valley.

1787–
1788 Madison, Hamilton, Jay, *The Federalist* (October–May).

1787 First American mill to weave cotton fabrics starts at Beverly, Mass.

Constitutional Convention, May 25–September 17.

Delaware accepts the Constitution, ratifying it, 7 December.

Pennsylvania ratifies Constitution, 15 December.

New Jersey ratifies, 18 December.

1788 Georgia ratifies Constitution, 2 January.

Connecticut ratifies, 4 January.

Massachusetts ratifies, 6 February.

Maryland ratifies, 26 April.

South Carolina ratifies, 23 May.

New Hampshire ratifies, June.

Virginia ratifies, 25 June.

New York ratifies, 26 July.

Convicts from England begin white colonization of Australia.

1789 North Carolina ratifies Constitution, 21 November.

1790 Rhode Island ratifies, 28 May.

Ways to Study History VIII

Be exhaustive. Probably the outstanding achievement of this generation in the study of American history is the publication of comprehensive editions of the writings of outstanding statesmen: Jefferson, Hamilton, Franklin, Adams, Madison, for a later time Henry Clay and John C. Calhoun. Until recently, scholars were using as standard editions the compilations of these works that had been issued around 1900. They were useful, and we thanked Heaven for them. But their defects glared. The principle of compilation was sometimes catch-as-catch-can; the editor simply seized whatever came readily to hand. Transcriptions of documents were slovenly. Explanatory glosses were seldom provided. An editor might even suppress a manuscript that in his opinion showed the author in a bad light or that was "too personal."

A new standard was set by Edmund Cody Burnett. Under the auspices of the Carnegie Institution of Washington, he brought together the *Letters of Members of the Continental Congress* (8 volumes, 1921–1936). By comparison with earlier efforts, Burnett seemed to have ransacked archives and attics to the ends of the earth. The level of accomplishment was carried higher yet by Julian P. Boyd in *The Papers of Thomas Jefferson* (1950–   ). This magnificent set will run to more than 100 volumes of 500 pages each. It will contain every item known that Jefferson wrote plus many letters he received. It is copiously annotated. In addition, Boyd has interspersed the primary sources with interpretative essays he has written on such topics as the evolution of the Virginia Statute of Religious Freedom.

Can the vacuum cleaner be too thorough? Reviewers have suggested that some of the new sets are going beyond reason, that important documents are being buried under a mass of lunch menus or bread-and-butter notes. Any message can be stifled by noise.

Document 8-1

J. Hector St. John Crèvecoeur (1735–1813) was born in France and served in the French army in Canada in 1758–59. He then travelled widely in the British colonies and lived in them for many years, mainly as a farmer in New York. His *Letters from an American Farmer* was published in 1782.

I wish I could be acquainted with the feelings and thoughts which must agitate the heart and present themselves to the mind of an enlightened Englishman, when he first lands on this continent. . . . If he travels through our rural districts he views not the hostile castle, and the haughty mansion, contrasted with the clay-built hut and miserable cabin, where cattle and men help to keep each other warm, and dwell in meanness, smoke, and indigence. A pleasing uniformity of decent competence appears throughout our habitations. The meanest of our log-houses is a dry and comfortable habitation. Lawyer or merchant are the fairest titles our towns afford; that of a farmer is the only appellation of the rural inhabitants of our country. It must take some time ere he can reconcile himself to our dictionary, which is but short in words of dignity, and names of honour. . . . What then is the American, this new man? He is either a European, or the descendant of a European, hence that strange mixture of blood, which you will find in no other country, I could point out to you a family whose grandfather was an Englishmen, whose wife was Dutch, and whose son married a French woman, and whose present four sons have now four wives of different nations. . . . He does not find, as in Europe, a crowded society, where every place is over-stocked; he does not feel that perpetual collision of parties, that difficulty of beginning, that contention which oversets so many. There is room for everybody in America; has he any particular talent, or industry? He exerts it in order to produce a livelihood, and it succeeds. . . .

Document 8-2

In October 1787, right after the Federal Convention, the newspapers in New York started to print a series of long articles signed "Publius." The eighty-five items ran to the following May. We now know that this remarkable advocacy of the Constitution was written by Madison, Hamilton, and Jay. Most of the numbers can be definitely ascribed to a specific author. This one was written by Hamilton. Note how his emphasis on foreign relations led to gloom, while Franklin by focussing on prosperity at home (see the quotation above) could be jubilant.

There is scarcely anything that can wound the pride or degrade the character of an independent nation which we do not experience. Are there engagements to which we are held by every tie respectable among men? These are the subjects of constant and unblushing violation. Do we owe debts to foreigners and to our own citizens contracted in a time of imminent peril for the preservation of our political existence? These remain without any proper or satisfactory provision for their discharge. Have we valuable territories and important posts in the possession of a foreign power which, by express stipulations, ought long since to have been surrendered? These are still retained, to the prejudice of our interests, no less than of our rights. Are we in a condition to resent or to repel the aggression? We have neither troops, nor treasury, nor government. Are we even in a condition to remonstrate with dignity? The just imputations on our own faith, in respect to the same treaty, ought first to be removed. Are we entitled by nature and compact to a free participation in the navigation of the Mississippi? Spain excludes us from it. Is public credit an indispensable resource in time of public danger? We seem to have abandoned its cause as desperate and irretrievable. . . .

Document 8-3

No analysis of American society and politics is better known or more trenchant than Federalist Paper No. 10, written by James Madison. When we put his remarks here in conjunction with his work in practical politics including the Constitutional Convention, Congress, his tenure as Secretary of State, and his Presidency, we can truly appreciate the comment by historian Marvin Meyers: "The boundary between significant thought and effective action is thinner here than in any other era of American history."

By a faction I understand a number of citizens, whether amounting to a majority or minority of the whole, who are united and actuated by some common impulse of passion, or of interest, adverse to the rights of other citizens, or to the permanent and aggregate interests of the community. . . . A zeal for different opinions concerning religion, concerning government, and many other points, as well of speculation as of practice; an attachment to different leaders ambitiously contending for pre-eminence and power; or to persons of other descriptions whose fortunes have been interesting to the human passions, have, in turn, divided mankind into parties, inflamed them with mutual animosity, and rendered them much more disposed to vex and oppress each other than to co-operate for their common good. . . . But the most common and durable source of factions has been the various and unequal distribution of property. Those who hold and those who are without property have ever formed distinct interests in society. Those who are creditors, and those who are debtors, fall under a like discrimination. A landed interest, a manufacturing interest, a mercantile interest, a moneyed interest, with many less interests, grow up of necessity in civilized nations, and divide them into different classes, actuated by different sentiments and views. The regulation of these various and interfering interests forms the principal task of modern legislation, and involves the spirit of party and faction in the necessary and ordinary operations of government. . . .

The Napoleonic Wars
and a New Nation

Of the nearly four centuries of American life, no decade is more fuzzy in our present comprehension than the ten years after 1789. What with patriotic rhapsodies about the early republic and all that, a good bit has been written about those times. But it does not fit together into a satisfying story. The epoch begins emphatically, with the inauguration of an unprecedented national-federal government. The epoch ends dramatically, with the moral courage of President John Adams as a major barrier to American involvement in a full-scale war against a European great power.

Several of the major developments of the years 1789–1799 can be charted firmly. Apart from considerable burnishing of the new federal machinery, probably no change meant so much as a remarkable prosperity. For reasons to be analyzed presently, a few port cities were the chief beneficiaries of this boom in the economy. Thirdly, the French Revolution and its sequels rent the American commonwealth. The United States was tied by treaties of friendship and commerce to France, and it had to decide in what ways and how far those obligations should be respected in a period when Europe was at war. In the process President Washington did not advance to his countrymen any new ideas, but he did formulate in memorable phrases a stance toward the outside world that the United States would maintain for a century. His foresight in diplomacy was matched by the cogency in economics of his long-time aide Alexander Hamilton. In a series of state papers as brilliant as any ever written by an American (perhaps ever written by anybody), Hamilton laid out with amazing prescience the range of policies that the federal government would follow in seeking to promote the economic growth of the new nation. While hatching devices for diplomacy and for business, Americans achieved a result that none of them wanted and that all of them originally abhorred: they developed political parties.

We do not know just how this change happened. A dozen studies of the last twenty years purport to cope with some sizable slab of the evolution, but we remain perplexed. The broad outlines are discernible, but many details remain clouded, and generalizations are likely to be the sort of wisdom that is not gratifying, such as "The growth of political parties is somehow related to the rise in newspapers," or, "James Madison probably had more influence than Jefferson in forming the Democratic-Republican machine." Rather than such sweeping abstractions, we ought to have precise surveys of daily events in limited areas, in towns or counties or states. Even so, clear patterns will not appear easily. One ambitious effort in this direction, a study of the state of New York, sets so many qualifications to its analysis that nobody can tell what conclusions are warranted or whether more evidence will necessarily lead to a clearer picture. It seems our understanding of the past will always have a few gaps, but we can get a good general view of the rise of organized factions in this chapter and the next.

European statesmen viewed the institution of the new federal government with hostility tempered by skepticism. They thought it was an attempt at the impossible. First, doubts were widespread that the United States could maintain its independence. Many Americans shared these doubts, and their apprehensions would sometimes prompt them to act as if they were an enclave beset by lethal enemies. Their fears seemed not fanciful as they contemplated the mighty British fleet, British control of Canada and continued occupation of frontier forts both along the Canadian border and along the Mississippi River, Spanish power in the Floridas and beyond the Mississippi, tribes of hostile Indians.* No European government was ready to make an all-out effort to topple the young nation, but they were all seeking out tactics that might whittle it down or split it up. Added to their gamble for independence,

---

*In making these remarks, I do not mean to concede any truth to the common assertion that the United States suddenly became "a world power" in 1898. There is no reason to dispute the conclusion by historian Thomas A. Bailey that the nation was a power as soon as it voted independence on 2 July, 1776, a world power after 1815, a great power by 1861. See Chapter 18.

Americans were so foolish as to try to survive as a republic. Europeans were not yet ready to believe that a country could be governed without a hereditary monarch. (See mid-Chapter 1 on the English Revolution.) Some Americans shared the skepticism, if we can believe the testimony of Washington. A year before the Federal Convention he had written to John Jay:

> What astonishing changes a few years are capable of producing. I am told that even respectable characters speak of a monarchical form of Government without horror. From thinking proceeds speaking, thence to acting is often but a single step. But how irrevocable and tremendous! What a triumph for our enemies to verify their predictions—what a triumph for the advocates of despotism to find that we are incapable of governing ourselves, & that systems founded on the basis of equal liberty are merely ideal & fallacious! Would to God that wise measures may be taken in time to avert the consequences we have but too much reason to apprehend.

This kind of anxiety produced the Federal Convention.

Now Washington was president, and the chief burden of activating the new instrumentalities was his. The federal officials who met in New York in March, 1789, had several assets. They did not need to create the entire structure from the ground up. Congress—modified of course by its enlarged powers, by its bicameral nature, and by the altered distribution of voting rights—could continue to work much as the Continental Congress had functioned. The key device was the committee. This splendid structure of representative government has the merit of combining the give-and-take of discussion in a small group with final responsibility to a larger delegated body. Committees were everywhere; in the Continental Congress, John Adams reportedly served on eighty.

Far newer and therefore more disturbing to harmony was the erection of an executive branch and determination of its relations to the legislative. In colonial times the assemblies had grown accustomed to antagonism to the governors; now presumably the two branches were to work together amicably. But what concrete arrangements would best conduce to this objective? For example, the president was given power to make treaties "with the advice and consent of the Senate." One day Washington visited that body to seek advice. A rambunctious member, fearing that "the President wishes to tread on the necks of the Senate," moved that the president's request for an opinion be referred to a committee for consideration. Washington was outraged. "This defeats every purpose of my coming here," he reportedly said, and as he left the Senate chamber he allegedly exploded that "he would be damned if he ever went there again." He never did. Nor did any of his successors ever seek prior consultation with the full Senate before a treaty was signed. In a practical sense, the word "advice" was deleted from that clause of the Constitution.

Another asset of the new government was that its leaders knew each other intimately, talents and pomposities, backgrounds and foibles. Hamilton, the president's closest associate since the early days of the War for Independence, became secretary of the treasury. Jefferson came home from his ministry in France to serve as secretary of state. Another ex-governor of Virginia and former delegate to the Federal Convention, Edmund Randolph, was attorney general. At the war department was another former Revolutionary general, Henry Knox. These executives did not have the worries of managing a swollen bureaucracy; the department of state consisted of the secretary and a half dozen clerks, not one of whom had any experience in foreign affairs. Moreover, this tiny staff had inherited some sound procedures. During most of the War for Independence the Continental Congress had intervened directly in the day-by-day management of foreign relations. The inevitable consequence was chaos. In January, 1781, the Congress set up a department of foreign affairs, and thereafter for slightly less than two years it had been headed by Robert R. Livingston as secretary. He did much to make the diplomatic service professional. He got the power to correspond directly with American agents abroad, without prior consultation with the Congress. No longer did the Congress persistently stick its nose into current affairs. The diplomatic staff overseas was put on a standardized scale of pay. Consulates, responsible for representing American individuals and business firms in alien countries, were split off cleanly from the diplomatic branch, and men in the latter were forbidden to engage in private trade.*

Nor did the federal judiciary occasion much grief in the early years. The Constitution made the Supreme Court mandatory and left lower courts optional. Although in the colonial period the legal profession had been weak—good law libraries were rare, well-trained attorneys even rarer—one result of the Revolution had been to raise the lawyers to power in politics and government, an eminence from which they have never been dethroned. Now at the formation of the new government, lawyers swooped in. John Jay, experienced on the bench of New York, was named by Washington to be chief justice of the United States. Congress by the Judiciary Act of 1789 provided a system of inferior federal courts. The limits to each of these jurisdictions were subsequently clarified by a series of statutes and decisions.

The federal government in its first decade had to function in a sharply divided society. Many of these rifts originated in American relations to the outside world. Before entering into specifics, we should take a panoramic look at some elements of the context in which the issues arose. At the beginning of the decade the foreign trade of the young republic was badly embarrassed. American tobacco, barred from Iberia altogether, paid heavy tariffs in England, France, and Sweden; rice likewise in England and Sweden; whale oil

---

*Diplomatic representatives of the United States were posted in 1792 at London, Paris, the Hague, Madrid, and Lisbon. They were called ministers or chargés d'affaires because it was thought that "ambassador" denoted the personal representative of a monarch. Not for more than a century would the republican United States adopt this royalist title for its agents to the more important governments abroad.

and fish could not legally enter England. In the West Indies the possessions of Great Britain, Spain, and Portugal were closed. American ships could not carry even American products to Canada, and they could not carry foreign goods to any British port in Europe. To the economic troubles were added diplomatic ones. British troops continued to occupy military posts on American soil. The matter grew increasingly touchy as American settlers flocked over the Appalachians to start farms and even towns near the forts. To American protests that the British action violated the Treaty of Paris, as it did, the British replied that Americans were violating the Treaty in regard to prewar debts owed to private British creditors, as they were. Another frontier—the ocean—provided additional grievances as the Royal Navy continued to impress seamen off American ships. By 1792 the United States seemed to be moving headlong toward a renewal of war against England.

And then, Providence took a hand. On Independence Day of 1790 the secretary of state wrote to a friend, "the new world will fatten on the follies of the old." This prediction now proved magnificently true. The French Revolution began with the storming of the Bastille on 14 July, 1789. In April, 1792, France declared war on the Habsburg Monarchy. Prussia joined Austria. England entered the First Coalition. Since citizens of neutral nations hold certain protections on the high seas (in theory, and sometimes in practice), the situation was made to order for a neutral country that owned a large merchant marine. American shipowner-merchants leapt to fill the bill. The effect on foreign trade was electric (figures in millions of dollars).

	exports of goods	re-exports	net earnings of carrying trade
1790	20.2	.3	5.9
1807	108.3	59.6	42.1

These figures can be fleshed out by others. By far the most important debit item in the international balance of payments of the nation (see Figure 3-1, Chapter 3 opening) was imports of goods. Imports that were consumed within the United States increased four times from 1790 to 1807. Rising incomes of many Americans caused them to indulge in higher standards of living, and many of the foreign wares that entered the country were luxury items. The figure for re-exports shows the foreign goods that entered the country, and then left it for sale abroad; often the cargo was not even transshipped. This trade, trivial in 1790 in peacetime, was bloated enormously by the European conflict. Nor did the benefits for Americans end there. Most of the re-exports were tropical products (sugar, coffee, cocoa, pepper). Due to absence of the normal competition among European buyers in Latin America, prices there of sugar and coffee were low. But in Europe due to wartime shortages, these commodities were unusually expensive. American merchants

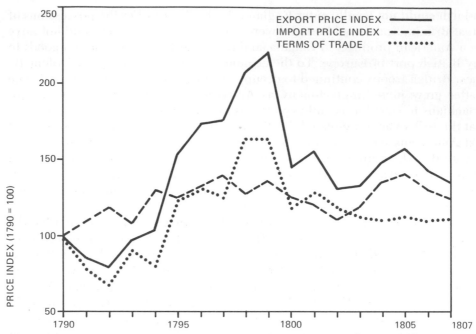

FIGURE 9-1. *Terms of Trade, 1790–1807* (data from North, *Economic Growth,* 1961)

were blessed by the yields from an ancient formula: Buy cheap and sell dear. Expressing this in technical language, we would say that the terms of trade of the United States swung sharply favorable; costs were low and selling prices were high. (See Figure 9-1.) This effect was concentrated in the years 1793 to 1798. If we measure a price index, starting arbitrarily with averaged prices in 1790, we would say the index rose from 100 in 1790 to more than 160 in 1798. It dropped sharply after 1799, and in 1807 it fell below 100.

In yet another way the Napoleonic Wars benefited American shipowners. American exports of goods were never in any year from 1790 to 1807 large enough to pay for imports of merchandise, although the fortunate rise in re-exports did help to reduce the import balance. Theoretically an outflow of gold and silver from the United States could have been used to offset the excessive imports, but practically of course this was not possible; flows of specie were slight. As it turned out, the other chief credit item in the international balance of payments came from the surge in net earnings of American deep-sea vessels. (See the adjacent graph on terms of trade.) Here again, the Wars were the key. Merchants in belligerent countries, seeking the added security of sending their goods in neutral bottoms, often chose to send them by American ships. Involved in this practice was a question that would arouse harsh contentions for the indefinite future: Do free ships make free goods? (The American answer was nearly always "Yes.") And once more, the United States profited from a highly advantageous shift in relative values:

freight rates for ocean shipping rose far more than other prices in the international market.

Alexander Hamilton had schemes for another way to offset the import balances of the young republic, namely, to restore the foreign credit of American governments so that the United States, including its private citizens and companies, could borrow still more money abroad. This can be stated in other phrases. What was happening was a rapid expansion in the pool of liquid wealth available to American businessmen, together with the concentration of this purchasing power under the control of a compact cluster of entrepreneurs. Privateering during the war had contributed heavily to this pool (see early Chapter 8 on the economic effects of the war). Foreign trade would in the near future make its own substantial donations. Standing in time between these two processes was the economic program of the secretary of the treasury.

He first tackled the problem of the public debts. Here his reasoning resembled the financial system worked out by Morris in 1781–1783 and endorsed by Washington. Hamilton's objectives were clear. He wanted to restore confidence in the good faith of Americans so that they and their federal government could borrow more money, especially in Europe. He sought to provide a stock of public securities with an active and stable market for them so that they could be bought and sold freely at face value. Thus they could be converted quickly into liquid capital and indeed by passing freely from hand to hand would virtually be an addition to the money supply. (He shrewdly remarked that this inflation would raise the value of Southern lands.) He had another, a political, aim. He wanted to bind the creditors, who were likely to be men of wealth and power, firmly to the federal government; he wanted to make them identify their welfare with the survival and growth of the new polity.

By Hamilton's estimates, the picture in January, 1790, stood thus:

	Federal Debts	
	owed abroad	*owed in U.S.*
principal	$10,070,307	$27,383,917
accrued interest	1,640,071	13,030,168
totals	11,710,378	40,414,085

Thus the federal debts totalled some $52 million. To this must be added the state debts for which the federal treasury finally assumed the burden—another $18,271,786. Hamilton's proposal was that the president be authorized to borrow $12 million to retire the federal debt owed abroad. For domestic holders of federal debt, they would exchange their old Continental Congress securities for two classes of new federal securities. As to the back interest due to them, the government would be empowered to borrow money at 3% interest to pay the arrears. If the federal government assumed responsibility for state debts that had been incurred to help finance the War for Independence, the various certificates would be exchanged for three classes of new federal securities.

No prominent official objected to retiring the federal debt owed in Europe. But objections to other features were vociferous. There was a sectional bias in Hamilton's plan: a disproportionate number of the debts had been incurred by Southern states, with a disproportionate number of the securities now owned in New England, and thus the funding scheme would transfer wealth from one region to another. Wanting to curb speculators, Madison proposed that owners who had bought their securities directly from the government should be compensated at one rate, while later buyers would receive a lower rate. Hamilton pointed out that this discrimination would be hellish to administer. Further, it would subvert his desire to establish quickly a public market for the new federal securities at a stable price. Since some states had already made strides toward retiring their own debts, they deeply resented the idea that they should now be taxed to meet the obligations of other states. Tempers in Congress grew so hot that no business could be transacted. It seemed clear that the assumption plan could not be passed. Jefferson later described what ensued:

> Hamilton was in despair. As I was going to the President's one day, I met him in the street. He walked me backwards and forwards before the President's door for half an hour. He painted patriotically the temper into which the legislature had been wrought; the disgust of those who were called the creditor States, the danger of the secession of their members, and the separation of the States.

Jefferson proposed that they dine together the next day, and he undertook to invite some friends. In this discussion a deal was made. It was clear that Manhattan, with only four states to the "east" (New England) and eight to the south, could not indefinitely be the national capital. Both Philadelphia and Georgetown on the Potomac had been suggested as sites. Now it was proposed that the former should have the honor for ten years, and then it should pass to the latter. As a result of this soothing "anodyne" for the South, two congressmen from Potomac districts changed their votes on assumption of state debts. The measure passed, and by the end of 1794 new federal securities of more than $63 million had been issued. Here was a fine increment to the country's pool of liquid wealth; now it was desirable to augment it still further.

Hamilton wanted Congress to charter a national bank as a supplement and support to existing private banks (See early Chapter 8 on postwar economics). The president asked his advisers whether such a measure would be constitutional. Jefferson said not: we have only limited and specified powers, and nowhere does the Constitution authorize Congress to charter a bank. To sustain the affirmative, Hamilton pointed to the "necessary and proper" clause (Art. I, Sec. 8). Arguing that a national bank could aid the government in many ways, including propping up the market for federal securities, he contended that the clause in question made a positive grant of power. Washington and Congress went along with Hamilton, and the first Bank of the United States started operations in 1791. We need not enter into details of its structure, but some features were notable. It was a mixed corporation: one fifth of its capital came from the federal government, the rest from private investors, and representation on the board of directors followed the same ratio. Given the scale of the economy, the Bank's size was huge; its capital was $10 million, and it was authorized to issue United States Bank notes (paper money, more liquid capital) to the same amount. How could the Bank be certain that its Bank notes would not depreciate as Continental bills of credit had done? (See early Chapter 8); since admittedly this measure was meant to be inflationary, how could it avoid starting a runaway inflation? This question was met by two provisions. Of the $8 million in stock available to private investors, it was required that they pay $2 million in cash. This would give the Bank a substantial reserve of specie so that it could redeem its Bank notes on demand. (The government's subscription to the Bank's capital is not relevant; by a complex set of maneuvers, it in effect borrowed from the Bank the funds it used to buy stock in the Bank.) Second, all taxes owed to the federal government could be paid with Bank notes. By thus setting itself up as a buyer that would take large quantities of the paper money at face value, the government underwrote the validity of the notes in general. Lest anybody think that the above remarks about the creation of a large fund of liquid wealth are exaggerated, be it said that the $8 million in stock offered to the public was oversubscribed within an hour, although, admittedly, the price could be paid in four installments over a period of eighteen months.*

The third major portion of Hamilton's program for the promotion of economic growth was contained in his *Report on Manufactures*. This study was requested by Congress in January 1790. Since the secretary was then engaged in a tumultuous and finally scandalous affair with another man's wife, he took nearly two years to submit his analysis, and it has been said that a good piece of it was produced by one of his assistants. No matter who wrote it, it is a masterpiece. Here were outlined all of the important policies that would be used by the federal government in the next century to stimulate the development of the nation's economy. As an application of foresight, the document can hardly be matched. In the use of the politics of persuasion, it is equally impressive. The *Report* seems guileless. Hamilton began by stating at length and fairly the argument that manufacturing could not be developed in the United States because of the shortage of capital and the scarcity of hands which meant "dearness of labor generally." He responded that division of

---

*It is no accident that the New York Stock Exchange was founded in 1792. Virtually its sole function was to provide a ready market for shares in the Bank of the United States.

labor and the substitution of machinery for labor could be pressed farther in manufacturing than in farming. Then he outlined the policies that had been followed by other governments to aid manufactures.

For all its brilliance, the *Report* fell on deaf ears. It mentioned the possibility of banning exportation of raw materials needed by a home industry, although the federal government would certainly never consider prohibiting exports of cotton or of wheat (nor would it have been wise to do so). On the other hand, some planks in the platform had already been put into effect. For example, as to "facilitating of pecuniary remittances from place to place," the Bank of the United States with its growing number of branches in cities other than Philadelphia was already meant to do that. But as to the report's prescription for "facilitating of the transportation of commodities"—for many inland areas a desperate problem, one that was soon to cause a civil war in western Pennsylvania—not until after 1800 would the federal government seriously consider subsidizing construction of roads and canals. As to tariffs, the law of 1789 had been meant as the principal source of revenue for the federal government, but it did provide a measure of protection for several industries. The nation already had a patent law to encourage inventions. Hamilton built a lucid case for the payment of bounties in some situations. They do not raise domestic prices as much as would import duties. For instance, if a tariff of 10 per cent is imposed on an item, and if the receipts are distributed among American producers, the effect on home prices is only 10 per cent but the stimulus to home production is equal to that of a 20 per cent tariff. While bounties may be useful to promote a new industry, payment of them to long-established industries is always "of questionable policy." Other qualifications were carefully stated. In paying bounties, the United States should recognize that freight charges from Europe act in effect as a tariff, "amounting to from 15 to 30 per cent on their value, according to their bulk."* Hamilton conceded that some citizens objected to bounties as being a device for enriching privileged groups "at the expense of the community." He replied magisterially: "There is no purpose to which public money can be more beneficially applied, than to the acquisition of a new and useful branch of industry."** Again, the course of subsequent events shows Hamilton's fore-sight and shrewdness. But his wisdom did not make him popular, and his economic program was the axe on which the nation soon began to split into hostile camps.

Further splits in American society were to come, and another axeblow

---

*Although this point is vital, many persons overlook it. The selling price to a consumer is the sum of (a) cost of production including the producer's profit, plus (b) transportation costs, plus (c) any taxes imposed by any government. Manufacturers beyond the Appalachians would be able to dominate their local markets because of a similar de facto tariff conferred by the high costs of transportation from the seaboard.

**Again, this policy had already been applied. Congress in 1789 had gratified Massachusetts by granting a bounty on all exports of codfish. The basis was changed in 1792; thereafter the bounty was proportional to the tonnage of any vessel engaged in the cod fishery four months in the year.

can be symbolized by the arrival of Citizen Genêt. With France at war against much of Europe, the president on 22 April, 1793, issued a Proclamation of Neutrality calling on his countrymen to "adopt and pursue a conduct friendly and impartial toward the belligerent powers." He warned that no American should give aid of any sort to a belligerent, not even "by carrying to any of them those articles which are deemed contraband by the modern usage of nations." Offenders would not be accorded the protection of the United States if they were brought to justice by a foreign power; indeed, they might be prosecuted by their own government. But when Genêt arrived in America as emissary from France in April, 1793, he had intentions that were grossly contrary to American policy. He so interpreted the Franco-American commercial treaty of 1778 as to give French privateers an automatic right to use American ports. Hoping to seize not only Canada but also parts of Spanish America, he carried blank military commissions to be awarded to any Americans who would fight the enemies of France. He landed in Charles Town, where he met frenzied enthusiasm. With the sympathy of the governor, he promptly outfitted privateers and established prize courts. While moving northward to the capital at Philadelphia he was surrounded by ecstatic welcomes. At last, Americans seemed to be rejoicing, the face of the earth knows a second republic.

Brashly, Genêt misjudged his situation. The responses he had seen in the South were not typical of the nation. The king and queen had been guillotined in January, and the Terror had started. Many Americans regarded French events with dismay or horror. A few, like Vice President Adams, were not surprised; he recalled those years in writing to Jefferson in 1813:

> The first time, that you and I differed in Opinion on any material Question; was after your arrival from Europe; and that point was the french Revolution.
> You was well persuaded in your own mind that the Nation would succeed in establishing a free Republican Government. I was as well persuaded, in mine, that a project of such a Government, over five and twenty millions of people, when four and twenty millions and five hundred thousands of them could neither write nor read: was as unnatural irrational and impracticable; as it would be over the Elephants Lions Tigers Panthers Wolves and Bears in the Royal Menagerie, at Versailles. Napoleon has lately invented a word, which perfectly expresses my opinion at that time and ever since. He calls the Project Ideology. [No crack-brained ideologies for John Adams]

Gouverneur Morris, as minister in Paris, sent home a running stream of inflammatory reports, often shortcircuiting Jefferson to write straight to Washington; the secretary of state objected that Morris "kept the President's mind constantly poisoned with his forebodings."

Genêt brought the crisis to a head by asking for advance payments on the debt owed France by the federal government. On Hamilton's advice, Washington refused. Genêt went berserk. He outfitted a French privateer in

Philadelphia and sent her to sea. Jefferson was disgusted; "Never in my opinion was so calamitous an appointment made, as that of the present Minister of F here. Hot headed, all imagination, no judgment, passionate, disrespectful & even indecent towards the P in his written as well as verbal communications, talking of appeals from him to Congress, from them to the people, urging the most unreasonable & groundless propositions." In August Jefferson asked France to withdraw Genêt, and although a replacement eventually defused that crisis, Jefferson's feelings on France had compromised his cabinet position. With a characteristic sense of symmetry, the secretary of state waited until December 31 to leave his own federal office and go home to Monticello. With this resignation we begin to suspect that one reason for the emergence of political parties (although little noticed by historians) was simply the character of George Washington. Nobody can doubt the depth and honesty of his attachment to republican institutions. But he believed in the old-style republicanism, when men accepted authority and recognized their betters. He could listen to and indeed sought out opinions contrary to his own, but he could not stand the antagonism of an organized group. He could not understand the meaning of, much less accept the desirability of, a loyal opposition. His hard-nosed demand for fealty might drive men into a hostile camp and fasten them there.

Further polarizing the nation was the Whiskey Rebellion of 1794. When the federal government in 1790 assumed responsibility for state debts, it needed more revenue, about $825,000 a year. In March, 1791, Congress levied an excise tax on distilled spirits (amended May, 1792). This tax bore with especial severity on transmontane farmers. Chapter 11 will take a protracted look at conditions of overland transportation; suffice it here to say that they were wretched. In southwestern Pennsylvania, where the uprising occurred, farmers could grow only a limited range of cash crops, particularly grains and livestock. Since no rivers flowed over the ridge to the seaboard, drovers took cattle and hogs to eastern markets by their own locomotion. With corn or rye the problem was harder; their value per pound was abysmally low. The solution was to distill the grain. If the rye crop was transported as grain, a packhorse could carry only four bushels; if as whiskey, 24 bushels. Thus the federal tax was an onerous bite into the farmers' yield. They rebelled, refusing to pay their taxes and strictly boycotting the excise officers. When James Wilson, a justice of the Supreme Court, notified the president in August, 1794, that federal laws could not be enforced by ordinary processes, Washington called for militia from Pennsylvania, New York, Maryland, and Virginia. The number reached 15,000, and Hamilton himself accompanied them westward. He hankered for a clash and longed to take a leader of the uprising, the Swiss immigrant and ex-legislator Albert Gallatin, back to Philadelphia in chains. Not surprisingly, since the militia were a larger force than Washington had commanded at any time during the War for Independence, there was no resistance. The authority of the federal government had been maintained. Two prominent insurgents were convicted of treason, but the president pardoned them both. He remained convinced that the rebellion had been fomented by the Democratic Societies that had been forming in support of the French Revolution, and he made a public attack on these "self-created societies" that threatened the federal administration and spread "suspicions, jealousies, and accusations, of the whole Government."

If the president and his friends (Jefferson and Madison were no longer of that number) had wished to win the favor of the West, they could have made better use than they did of two treaties that they soon negotiated. President Washington, in what would seem to be a clear contravention of the separation of powers between executive and judiciary, sent Chief Justice Jay (a former secretary of state) to England as envoy extraordinary to try to settle differences. Although the English were flushed with recent victories over France, they were cordial. For one thing, they already had been told that the United States would not join the Armed Neutrality being promoted by Denmark and Sweden; Hamilton, without Washington's knowledge, had leaked the news to their minister in Philadelphia. For another, as a British minister said, the Americans "are so much in debt to this country that we scarcely dare to quarrel with them." Jay's Treaty provided that the British would turn over the frontier posts on American territory that they still occupied by June, 1796. Three classes of questions—disputed segments of the boundary between the United States and Canada, pre-Revolutionary debts owed by Americans, and recent seizures of property—were referred to mixed commissions for settlement. No mention was made of the impressment of American seamen. No mention was made of black slaves abducted by British troops during the war. No mention was made of British intrigues with Indians. The most explosive provisions had to do with the British West Indies. American ships of less than 70-ton capacity were granted entrance. In return, the United States agreed that its own ports would be the only admissible destination for its vessels carrying sugar, molasses, coffee, cocoa, or cotton; Americans would abstain from shipping those commodities to any other spot on the globe.

Jay's Treaty was interpreted by Spain as marking an Anglo-American reconciliation. At the moment Spain was considering switching sides; that is, making peace with France and breaking off relations with Great Britain. Since she could not afford an Anglo-American or even an American attack on her possessions in Florida and Louisiana, it suited her to buy as much goodwill as possible from the new republic. Notified of her readiness to talk, Washington sent his minister in England, Thomas Pinckney, to Spain. He got the moon. Spain granted to American property the unrestricted navigation of the Mississippi River for its full length. She granted American goods the right of deposit and transshipment at New Orleans, for a term of three years and renewable. She promised not to stir up Indians, and the United States reciprocated in kind.

Pinckney's Treaty won universal acclaim at home; not so with Jay's Treaty. Probably no emissary could have won a better deal for his country, but his handiwork was spat upon in many circles. It won some friends in the West because of the provision about evacuation of British troops,* but in the ports it was anathema. Not only was it silent about impressment, it also granted to the Royal Navy the right to seize noncontraband goods such as foodstuffs off American bottoms if they were bound to a belligerent and if full compensation was made. Already the re-export trade was booming:

	coffee, lbs.	brown sugar, lbs.
1791	962,977	74,504
1793	44,580,049	4,539,809

Jay had signed that boon away. Many ships to the West Indies were larger than 70 tons; Jay had signed that advantage away. Seamen had another cause to riot over. When Hamilton tried to defend the treaty at a public meeting in Manhattan, few of his remarks reached the audience "on account of hissings, coughings, and hootings which . . . prevented his proceeding." Jay complained that he could travel at night from one end of the land to the other by the light of bonfires where he was being burned in effigy. Even with Washington behind it, a bare two-thirds majority of the Senate would approve the treaty; in June, 1795, the vote was 20 to 10, and only after the provisions dealing with the West Indies had been stricken. Then the president delayed two months before signing the ratification. When it came time for the House of Representatives to vote funds to carry out the agreement, they balked. Pressures were exerted: it was rumored that Spain, in her eagerness to curry favor with England, would not implement Pinckney's Treaty unless the United States implemented Jay's Treaty. At last the money—a picayune $80,000—was voted by a slight majority. It is often said that at this time the first party caucus of congressmen was held by Madison and other opponents of the treaty in the House. If this were said in connection with a legislative body of many members, this assertion might be useful, but in the context of the early Congress the distinction seems merely academic, since Madison and his friends had been meeting privately for years to coordinate tactics.

The president must have been gratified when the Senate approved Pinckney's Treaty unanimously in March, 1796, but he had many reasons to be disgruntled. Hamilton had followed Jefferson into retirement, and Washington had been unable to get replacements remotely comparable in quality. The

---

*In practice, this provision was a joke. When the appointed time of June 1796 arrived, the United States did not have enough troops to garrison all the posts, and it asked the British forces to stay on.

president was aging and ailing. He had wanted to withdraw to Mount Vernon back in 1792. Now, determined not to stand for re-election, the chief executive took up again a possibility that he had considered earlier—to give his countrymen some last advice before he left office. The result was his Farewell Address, the joint work of Washington and his longtime amanuensis Hamilton. The chief admonitions were two: Do not allow factions to develop in American politics. Do not make any long-term commitments that will involve the nation in the broils of Europe.

The latter attitude toward foreign relations had a considerable history that began in Great Britain. Three changes combined to make the eighteenth century "a landmark in the history of European diplomacy": The War of the Spanish Succession (1702–1713) was the last great clash between Bourbon and Habsburg; thereafter the Franco-Austrian conflict on the Continent slowly died out. Russia and Prussia intruded themselves into the European system. Most important for our purposes, France and England increasingly competed for overseas empire. For England this meant a re-orientation. She still sought to maintain the balance of power in Europe, but now she saw colonies abroad as a growing weight in that balance. By 1739 Robert Walpole, the first Englishman who can justly be called the prime minister, could declare in Commons, "This is a trading nation, and the prosperity of her trade is what ought to be principally in the eye of every gentleman in this House." William Pitt went far toward solidifying this dual attitude, especially during the Seven Years' War. On the eve of the American Revolution a British theoretician declared that his country had no reason "to intangle ourselves with the disputes between the powers of the continent."

The chief agent carrying to America this approach to foreign relations was Thomas Paine and specifically his *Common Sense* (1776). Here Paine asserted that there was not "a single advantage that this continent can reap by being connected with Great Britain." For America, the true "plan is commerce, and that, well attended to, will secure us the peace and friendship of all Europe; because it is the interest of all Europe to have America a free port."

> Any submission to, or dependence on, Great Britain, tends directly to involve this continent in European wars and quarrels. . . . As Europe is our market for trade, we ought to form no partial connections with any part of it. It is the true interest of America to steer clear of European contentions.

This doctrine innately was congenial to the colonials. From the earliest settlers, Americans had held a twin stance toward Europe. This bifurcation was rooted in the duality of their motives for immigrating to the New World. On the one hand, they wanted to benefit financially. On the other, they wished to create a new and purified social order. The first required the most intimate trade connections with England and Europe. The second was thought to require the utmost isolation from the Old World; John Winthrop's "city on a hill" (Chapter 2) was still an intensely functional image. When Vergennes, the French foreign minister, advised minister John Adams to make an adjustment to prevailing diplomatic customs, Adams lectured him: "The dignity of North America does not consist in diplomatic ceremonials or any of the subtleties of etiquette; it consists solely in reason, justice, truth, the rights of mankind, and the interests of the nations of Europe." (It is easy to imagine that Vergennes choked.) The United States had applied this dual policy in contracting the French alliance of 1778. The word *alliance* did not then imply some political and military commitments as it would later; the Franco-American treaty was confined almost entirely to matters of commerce and navigation. Washington's "Farewell Address" was meant to codify an existing approach to foreign relations and hopefully to unify his countrymen in its support (Document 9-1).

The warning against factions should have been phrased as a lament. By 1796 it was common, at least in some sections of the country and at the national capital in Philadelphia, to speak of Republicans versus Federalists. Continuity from the struggle over the Constitution was only fitful; the top Republican leaders had supported ratification, while a bitter opponent such as Patrick Henry ended as a Federalist. While Washington got ready to retire, factional whips were working to meld blocs of voters for the coming presidential election. Not only had the number of newspapers greatly expanded but many of them had taken a violent stand either for or against the French Revolution; their rancor and vituperation passed all bounds. Thus they joined the partisan press. But the two stand-out candidates would not soil their own hands. Adams rested on his dignity as vice president of the United States. Jefferson was reconciled that he might be drafted; Madison and other congressional spokesmen were working steadily in his behalf. He did not care to have the job; as he wrote to Madison, "There is nothing I so anxiously hope, as that my name may come out second or third." Another main figure behind the campaign was Hamilton, now practicing law in New York to patch his tattered finances. He and Adams despised each other. Seldom have two men had life-styles so contradictory. The one fancied himself in martial uniform, the other in brownspun. The one bespoke torrid romances, the other, in spite of his many years absent from home in the public service, represented domestic tranquility marked by lifelong devotion to Abigail and austere affection for his children. The one stood for wheeling and dealing, the other for sturdy rectitude (and, on occasion, for insufferable self-righteousness. Adams was sure that Franklin was a sharpie not to be trusted, and he referred in 1813 to the long-dead Hamilton as "a bastard Bratt of a Scotch Pedlar." No prattle about speak-well-of-the-dead for him). Hamilton entered upon a backstairs play. He reasoned that Adams could win nothing in the South, and that Jefferson could not get electoral votes from New England. If Thomas Pinckney, given the fabulous popularity of Pinckney's Treaty, could hold his own South Carolina and other parts of the South, he might get enough second votes from New England (under the then current system, the electors would not distinguish between their first or second choices) to make him president.

His assumptions both proved out true in the election, but he did not quite gain the result he wanted. An ill wind indeed was the extreme sectional schism. With each member of the Electoral College voting for two men, from New England Adams got 39 votes, Jefferson none. In the states from and including Maryland southward plus the two new Western states of Kentucky and Tennessee, Adams got nine votes, Jefferson 54. The tally stood thus:

Adams	71
Jefferson	68
Pinckney	59
Aaron Burr	30

Even in the Middle States, Jefferson could win only fourteen of the fifteen votes from Pennsylvania. The reality behind Madison's forebodings (Chapter 8; his fears on sectionalism at the Constitutional Convention) had shown itself. Another feature of the election was public apathy. In ten of the fifteen states, the electors were named by the legislature, so the voters had little cause to get aroused. The electorate did show more interest where it had a voice in the selection, but even in Pennsylvania, where the electors were picked by general ticket, only 25,000, perhaps one in four adult white males, bothered to vote.

From the day he became president, Adams faced a crisis with France. The French minister in Philadelphia had openly intervened in the presidential canvass on the Republican side. The Directory now ruling France had been seizing American ships and confiscating neutral cargoes. In March, 1797 as Adams took office, they decreed that Americans serving in the Royal Navy, even though they may have been impressed, should be hanged if captured. For once, Adams and Hamilton agreed that steps should be taken to mend the breach, and the president sent off to Paris a distinguished peace commission: John Marshall of Virginia, Elbridge Gerry of Massachusetts, and Charles Cotesworth Pinckney of South Carolina. Congress voted to create a separate department of the navy. Although the Senate voted to buy or build twelve frigates, only three were actually ready for launching in time to meet the crisis. For the first time since the War for Independence, these three ships bore the flag of the United States Navy onto the Atlantic during the summer of 1798. It was this policy of building up the navy that severed the last ties between Adams and Hamilton. The latter wanted to concentrate on the army. After the president successfully appealed to Washington to come back in command of the armed forces, Hamilton took effective control, and he set as a goal an army of 50,000 soldiers. That Washington averred that France could not invade the United States was not very pertinent to Hamilton's objectives. He thought that a war scare would help to build the electoral strength of the Federalists. Second, he believed that the "levellers" among the Republicans were on the verge of launching a violent rebellion, and he wanted a large army more to cope with domestic than with foreign enemies.

The president's peace commission gave the occasion for the next explosion. In Paris the commissioners were treated rudely. Then they were approached by agents of Talleyrand, the minister of foreign affairs, with the suggestion that negotiations might be oiled if they would pay a bribe of $250,000 to Talleyrand and the Directors, and if they would also grant the French government a loan of $12 million. When word of this proposal reached the president, he went before Congress on 19 March 1798 to say that France had refused to receive his commissioners. He asked authorization to arm merchant ships and to take other defensive steps. The XYZ proposals, as they became known, were given to the press, and their publication caused a turbulent public agitation. Adams seemed near the breaking point. Further negotiations, he said, would be "not only nugatory but disgraceful and ruinous"; he saw "no alternative between war and submission to the Executive of France." Hamilton was hot for hostilities, and even the secretaries of state and the treasury were more responsive to his promptings than to cues from the president.

And yet, in the ensuing year, and even as his party was shattering around him in an intense war fever, Adams failed to send a war message to Congress. Only a calmheaded and resolute man could have made such a display of moral courage, one of the finest cautionary moves ever to come from a chief executive of the United States. The president had even wanted to use some of the new military commissions to win over to his administration Jefferson's more moderate supporters, especially Aaron Burr in New York and Peter Muhlenberg in Pennsylvania:

> But I soon found myself shackled. . . . I could not name a man who was not devoted to Hamilton without kindling a fire. I soon found that if I had not the previous consent of the heads of departments, and the approbation of Mr. Hamilton, I ran the utmost risk of a dead negative in the Senate.

When he was thus balked in Congress, Adams did a slowdown for his own reasons, and he went on dragging his feet. Nearly a year after the XYZ disclosures, the Speaker of the House of Representatives complained, "The army and navy must be attended to. In regard to the former, the conduct of the Executive has been astoundingly dilatory. As yet not a single enlistment order has been issued."

While the war fever flared, the Federalists in Congress put through, and John Adams signed, a set of four laws usually referred to as the Alien and Sedition Acts (Document 9-2). While they seemed to many citizens to be essential to the preservation of the nation, clearly they were also meant to sap sources of Republican strength. One increased the probationary term for naturalization as an American citizen from five to fourteen years. Another provided for deportation or imprisonment of suspected aliens. A third provided stiff fines or prison for anybody guilty of disseminating material of a "false, scandalous and malicious" character against the government or any of its officers. Anticipating that the latter provision was dictatorial in intent, opposition strongholds in the South and West rose to combat this "Monocrat" repression, and the Republican-dominated legislatures of Virginia and Kentucky were explicit in their condemnation. The Kentucky Resolves offered a rationale for nullifying the Constitution (Document 9-3), and some Congressmen went further to speak of secession and a dissolution of the Union.

In March, 1799, President Adams made a decisive move toward stilling the hysteria. He announced that he was again sending a commissioner to Paris. Although the results made him unpopular with a war-crazed public, Adams never regretted his peace missions. "They were the most disinterested and meritorious actions of my life," he wrote later. (See the opening of Chapter 10.) For their own reasons the French did agree to a standoff, and Adams, by holding out against hysteria, gave the nation a few more years of continued peace and prosperity.

Wars in Europe have repeatedly rained down blessings on the American economy. This time the shower of wealth came after the French Revolution and Napoleon's rise to power in France. The entire Continent and the Atlantic Ocean were battlefields for twenty-five years. The United States was the most important neutral with a large merchant marine. For several reasons her merchants and shipowners profited in legitimate trade. Not overly scrupulous, they also made money by illicit means. They flocked into privateering, which might be termed legalized piracy. They also traded with the enemy, and smuggled goods through every crack. The returns from these ventures flowed chiefly into a few large port cities along the seaboard; not only Boston but also such lesser ports as Salem witnessed a host of fine new mansions. This prosperity helped to stabilize the new republic. The infant nation drew yet more strength from brilliant achievements in statecraft. Foremost of course was the Constitution. Then Alexander Hamilton put forward a number of solid policies by which the federal government bolstered the economy. President Washington in his Farewell Address advanced tenets that his country would follow throughout the nineteenth century. President Adams demonstrated that the United States could indeed be "too proud to fight." Those words were spoken more than a hundred years later by President Wilson, with far less happy results than Adams had won.

SOME NOTABLE EVENTS

1775 First American antislavery organization formed by Franklin and Benjamin Rush.

1777 Slavery abolished in Vermont by constitution (See Figure 11-2).

1780 Gradual-abolition law in Pennsylvania.

1783 Slavery in Massachusetts abolished by court decision (Figure 11-2).

1784 Gradual-abolition law in Rhode Island.

Gradual-abolition law in Connecticut, supplemented in 1797.

1787 Northwest Ordinance (mid-Chapter 8) abolishes slavery in future states north of the Ohio.

1787–
1790 Ship *Columbia*, leaving Boston 30 September, makes voyage that opens the Northwest fur trade, soon tied into Far Eastern trade.

1789 Bastille stormed, 14 July, marking start of French Revolution.

1790 First United States census: population 3,929,627.

Hamilton's debt plan adopted by Congress.

National capital will move from New York to Philadelphia, for a stipulated ten years; then it will move to Georgetown on the Potomac.

1791 Foundation of the first Bank of the United States.

Vermont admitted to Union as fourteenth state.

1792 Ratification of first ten amendments to Constitution (the Bill of Rights).

Kentucky admitted to Union as fifteenth state.

Foundation of New York Stock Exchange.

1792–
1797 War of the First Coalition against France.

1793 Cotton gin invented by Eli Whitney (patented 14 March 1794).

Louis XVI and Marie Antoinette executed in Paris, 21 January.

Washington's Neutrality Proclamation, 22 April.

Citizen Genêt embroglio.

Jefferson resigns as secretary of state, 31 December.

1793–
1794 Reign of Terror in France.

1794 Whiskey Rebellion, August–November.

Jay's Treaty with Great Britain, signed 19 November.

1795 Hamilton resigns as secretary of the treasury, end of January.

Pinckney's Treaty with Spain (Treaty of San Lorenzo), signed 27 October.

1796 Washington's Farewell Address, 17 September.

Tennessee admitted to Union as sixteenth state.

1796–
1798 General Bonaparte campaigns in Italy and Egypt.

1797 XYZ Affair brings crisis in relations with France.

1798 Thomas Malthus, *Essay on Population*.

Alien and Sedition Acts passed, June–July.

Kentucky and Virginia Resolves, November–December.

1799 Gradual-abolition act in New York, supplemented in 1817 (Figure 11-2).

1799–
1804 Napoleon Bonaparte First Consul of France.

1802 Slavery in Ohio is prohibited by constitution (Figure 11-2).

1804 Gradual-abolition act in New Jersey.

1816 Slavery in Indiana is prohibited by constitution.

1818 Slavery in Illinois is prohibited by constitution.

Ways to Study History IX

Define your problem clearly. The person who sets out to investigate the story of humanity is doomed to stand humiliated while others watch the ashes blow out of his palm. A problem can be defined so broadly that the mass of pertinent data becomes unwieldy or completely overwhelming. Further, most historians would agree that history is not a seamless web, that, while nobody ever makes a totally fresh start, at certain junctures the rules of the game are significantly revised. One mode of delineating these creases is chronologically (the Age of Jackson, the Progressive Era, and so on) and we will later confront the difficulties of periodization. The other mode is topically. Any university catalogue shows the standard "fields" into which American history is now parcelled: political, economic, social, diplomatic, constitutional, intellectual, the history of the West, urban history, immigrants and American life, black history. Indeed, when any historian sets out to find himself a job, probably the first question from a potential employer will be: What is your field? But in college courses, a rigid categorization is hurtful; in research, it is disastrous.

Felix Gilbert set out to study *To the Farewell Address: Ideas of Early American Foreign Policy* (1961) His topic could not be twisted into a conventional pigeonhole, but it defined its own ground. It involved diplomacy; it was intellectual history. The likely impact of a policy on American voters was often in view. Whereas a literary critic looking for precedents to a given document (say, *Mrs. Wiggs of the Cabbage Patch*) might have to be tedious in proving that the author was aware of the precedents, Gilbert avoids this. He just assumes that an alert Englishman like Thomas Paine was aware of Walpole and Pitt, or that Hamilton and Washington were aware of Paine, and he is right. By sticking to his problem and using methods suitable to it, Felix Gilbert wrote an amazingly concise and lucid work.

Document 9-1

President Washington's Farewell Address of 17 September 1796 set forth the maxim that the United States should avoid deep involvements in the dynastic scrambles of Europe. This so-called Great Rule would buttress American foreign policy for more than a century; indeed, it was scarcely broken until World War II. The other theme of Washington's message was the need to guard the Union that brought such great benefits to all. The thrust of his warning was not directed against class conflict so much as against sectional fissures, coupled with his concern about the intrigues of foreign governments in American politics (as described in this and the preceding chapters).

The alternate domination of one faction over another, sharpened by the spirit of revenge internal to party dissension, which in different ages and countries has perpetuated the most horrible enormities, is itself a frightful despotism. But this leads at length to a more formal and permanent despotism. The disorders and miseries which result gradually incline the minds of men to seek security and repose in the absolute power of an individual, and sooner or later the chief of some prevailing faction, more able or more fortunate than his competitors, turns this disposition to the purposes of his own elevation on the ruins of public liberty. . . . Why, by interweaving our destiny with that of any part of Europe, entangle our peace and prosperity in the toils of European ambition, rivalship, interest, humor, or caprice?

It is our true policy to steer clear of permanent alliances with any portion of the foreign world, so far, I mean, as we are now at liberty to do it; for let me not be understood as capable of patronizing infidelity to existing engagements. I hold the maxim no less applicable to public than to private affairs that honesty is always the best policy. I repeat, therefore, let those engagements be observed in their genuine sense. But in my opinion it is unnecessary and would be unwise to extend them. . . .

Document 9-2

A substantial objection to the Constitution as it was submitted to the states was its omission of any Bill of Rights. But the best scholarship today indicates that this defect bothered mainly intellectuals—Jefferson and Madison. Indeed, current evidence suggests that the presence or absence was not at all crucial to the question of ratification. The first ten amendments, most of which were designed to protect the rights of individuals from infringement by the federal government, were adopted in 1792. When the Alien and Sedition bills were introduced, such Republican spokesmen as Edward Livingston of New York and Albert Gallatin (himself thought to be a target of the legislation) denounced them as unconstitutional. Here is a portion of what is usually called the Sedition Act.

Sec. 2. That if any person shall write, print, utter, or publish, or shall cause or procure to be written, uttered or published, or shall knowingly and willingly assist or aid in writing, printing, uttering or publishing any false, scandalous and malicious writing or writings against the government of the United States, or either house of the Congress of the United States, or the President of the United States, with intent to defame the said government, or either house of the said Congress, or the said President, or to bring them, or either of them, into contempt or disrepute; or to excite against them, or either or any of them, the hatred of the good people of the United States, or to stir up sedition within the United States, or to excite any unlawful combinations therein, for opposing or resisting any law of the United States, or any act of the President of the United States, done in pursuance of any such law, or of the powers in him vested by the constitution of the United States, or to resist, oppose, or defeat any such law or act, or to aid, encourage, or abet any hostile designs of any foreign nation against the United States, their people or government, then such person, being thereof convicted before any court of the United States having jurisdiction thereof, shall be punished by a fine not exceeding two thousand dollars, and by imprisonment not exceeding two years.

Document 9-3

While the Alien and Sedition statutes were pending, Madison wrote to Jefferson: "The Alien bill proposed in the Senate is a monster that must forever disgrace its parents." But it passed. In October Jefferson wrote: "The X.Y.Z. fever has considerably abated throughout the country, as I am informed, and the alien and sedition laws are working hard. I fancy that some of the State legislatures will take strong ground on this occasion. For my own part, I consider those laws as merely an experiment on the American mind, to see how far it will bear an avowed violation of the Constitution. If this goes down, we shall immediately see attempted another act of Congress, declaring that the President shall continue in office during life. . . ." The two Virginians took the lead in legislative action. Madison's relatively mild Virginia Resolves were content to assert that the statutes were unconstitutional; the Kentucky Resolves drafted by Jefferson went further to claim for each state a right of nullification (see the end of this chapter).

I. Resolved, that the several States composing the United States of America, are not united on the principle of unlimited submission to their general government; but that by compact under the style and title of a Constitution for the United States and of amendments thereto, they constituted a general government for special purposes, delegated to that government certain definite powers, reserving each State to itself, the residuary mass of right to their own self-government; and that whensoever the general government assumes undelegated powers, its acts are unauthoritative, void, and of no force: That to this compact each State acceded as a State, and is an integral party, its co-States forming, as to itself, the other party: That the government created by this compact was not made the exclusive or final judge of the extent of the powers delegated to itself; since that would have made its discretion and not the Constitution, the measure of its powers; but that as in all other cases of compact among parties having no common judge, each party has an equal right to judge for itself, as well as of the infractions as of the mode and measure of redress. . . .

A Glorious Road to an Inglorious War

While the federal capital was being removed from Philadelphia to Washington, President Adams' commission was negotiating in Paris. The fruits of its efforts proved costly in money, but they were worth the price. Since 1793 American citizens had accumulated almost $20 million in claims for spoliations against their vessels and cargoes by French warships. The United States agreed to drop these claims against France, which left the federal treasury at least morally responsible for them. France on her part had been recently mauled by the British navy and now consented to a joint abrogation of the treaties of 1778 and 1788. In buying cancellation of pre-existing commitments in Europe, the young republic was pushing Washington's Great Rule even a step beyond what he had recommended.

The common assertion that the presidential election of 1800 marked a total revolution in American politics will be examined in the next few pages.

Although much was changed, much lingered on. A related misconception has held that Federalist responsibility for the Alien and Sedition Acts was vital to the Republican victory. By this contention, moral outrage at these laws was so widespread among the voters that they turned the rascals out. No way has yet been devised to quantify the impact of the four repressive statutes; the most malign form of censorship is self-censorship, and we cannot tell how many citizens learned to still their tongues. Some general comments can be made, however. For one thing, the Sedition Act was not really needed, since in the common law of England (still then operating in America), seditious libel was already a crime, and federal courts had previously been trying cases under this warrant. Not until 1812 would a divided Supreme Court rule that the common law of crimes did not confer any jurisdiction on federal tribunals. The Acts, then, were party measures passed for partisan advantage. At least two dozen persons were arrested, of whom ten were convicted. They were definite types: editors of Republican newspapers including the four main ones in Boston, Philadelphia, New York, and Richmond; other prominent persons including a Congressman from Vermont; also some obscure citizens. The opening to tyranny is shown by the trial of two men in Massachusetts for erecting these words on a Liberty Pole:

> *No Stamp Act, no Sedition, no Alien Bills, no Land Tax:*
> *downfall to the Tyrants of America, peace and retirement to*
> *the President, long live the Vice-President and the Minority;*
> *may moral virtue be the basis of civil government.*

One defendant who abjectly begged mercy was sentenced to six hours in jail and $5 fine. The other received eighteen months in jail and a fine of $400. Unable to pay the fine, he served more than two years. Although John Adams later asserted that he had not enforced the Alien Act in a single instance, clearly its adoption prompted quite a few immigrants, particularly Frenchmen, to leave the United States.

More weighty than suppression in tipping the presidential scales toward Jefferson were fiscal burdens. The army that had been voted during the war scare had cost a fortune. The total expenditures of the federal government, a mere $5.7 million in 1796, were $10.8 million in 1800. The Department of the Army spent $1.3 million in 1796, $2.6 million in 1800. The cost of the navy was $275,000 in 1796, $3.4 million in 1800. Meanwhile the federal debt scarcely rose at all, meaning that the extraordinary drains caused by armaments were being met by current taxes. Americans who had revolted against British taxation were not about to lie down supinely merely because domesticated tyrants had replaced foreign ones. The growth in taxes was a crucial element in alienating former Federalist voters in New England and in the all-important Middle States.

As the campaign approached, the president could count on New

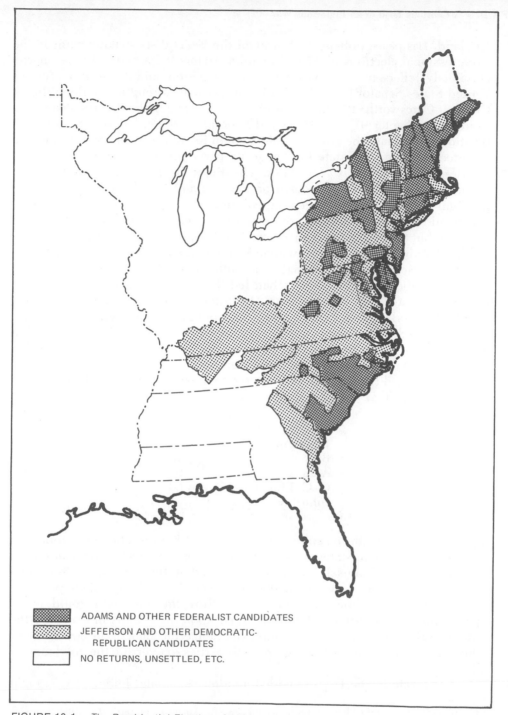

FIGURE 10-1. *The Presidential Election of 1800*

ADAMS AND OTHER FEDERALIST CANDIDATES

JEFFERSON AND OTHER DEMOCRATIC-
REPUBLICAN CANDIDATES

NO RETURNS, UNSETTLED, ETC.

England. His peace policies had brought the Federalists striking gains in the Congressional elections of 1799, but John Adams led a badly divided party. Obviously Jefferson would stand for the opposition, and Aaron Burr, former United States Senator from New York, was showing strength as a Republican. Charles Cotesworth Pinckney, brother of Thomas, (the treaty-maker and candidate, Chapter 9) was the second Federalist contender. We are now in a position to evaluate the alleged "Jeffersonian Revolution" of 1800. It must be reported that the only state to change its party preference in a presidential election since 1796 was New York. The Republicans won South Carolina because Charles Pinckney, cousin of Thomas and Charles Cotesworth, was prodigal with promises of federal appointments (which the successful Jefferson would honor). In Virginia the presidential electors had been chosen by districts, but the Federalists had elected five Congressmen from those districts. So the Republican legislature switched the method of selection to a statewide ticket. Jefferson was also fortunate that both George Washington and Patrick Henry had died in 1799; if they had led the Federalist cohorts in 1800, he might well have lost his own state. In crucial New York, the Republicans needed the workingmen's vote, so they came out in favor of high import duties. They also needed the businessmen's vote, so, while Jefferson lived in seclusion at Monticello, Aaron Burr in 1799 founded the Bank of Manhattan and began judiciously making loans in the right quarters. As the tally in the Electoral College mounted through the autumn, the two parties seemed to be running a dead heat. The final outcome stood thus:

Jefferson	73
Burr	73
Adams	65
C. C. Pinckney	64
John Jay	1

The deadlock threw the election into the House of Representatives. Support by nine of the sixteen states would be necessary to elect. Now Alexander Hamilton whipped himself into a frenzy to head off the selection of Burr, long a hated rival in New York. He loathed Jefferson ("a contemptible hypocrite," "tinctured with fanaticism") but beside Burr the Virginian could claim "pretensions to character." Hamilton urged upon his friends in Congress the judgment that Burr was "the most unfit and dangerous man of the community" who was sure to "employ the rogues of all parties to overrule the good men of all parties."*

The vote in the House yielded another stalemate. Jefferson won eight

---

*The tie in the Electoral College did produce the Twelfth Amendment, ratified in 1804, by which each member had to distinguish his choice for president from that for vice president. But this can hardly be counted a radical revision. The changes in political practices after 1800 happened apart from constitutional alterations and from formal institutional innovations.

states, Burr six, two split. At this point, if the Federalists had held firm, they could have prevented the election of a president. Thirty-five ballots were taken, without issue. Then a Federalist from Delaware seemed to waver, and later even wrote to Hamilton after a bitter session, "I came out with the most explicit and determined declaration of voting for Jefferson." His reconsideration seems to have broken the deadlock and forced some realignments, so that when the air cleared, Jefferson was chosen by the support of ten states, Burr got four, and two refused to cast ballots at all. It is pleasing to note that the decisive vote was cast by the one representative—from Vermont—who had been jailed for violating the Sedition Act. In the end the potential renegade from Delaware did not have to act on his "determined" resolve, but with many of his colleagues, cast a blank ballot so that Jefferson did not get a single Federalist vote.

The election did accelerate change in the structure of politics. Prior to 1795, although most adult white males in most states would meet the requirements for the suffrage, they usually did not bother to exercise their rights. Actual voting seldom rose above 40 per cent, and could fall as low as 15 per cent. A gradual rise in participation took place from 1796 to 1799. Then, from 1800 to 1816, it shot upward. In state elections, participation by two thirds of the electorate became normal, and the figure could reach as high as 98 per cent of adult males. It seems clear that changes in the suffrage requirements during the presidency of Andrew Jackson, (1829–1837) followed, rather than preceded, increased political activity by the ordinary citizen. Moreover, the growing concern of voters beginning in 1800 was a direct consequence of the emerging two-party system with its ferocious competition for votes. One index is the growth of the press, much of it fiercely partisan. Whereas all the colonies together had in 1765 only twenty-three newspapers (early Chapter 8), by October, 1800, Pennsylvania alone had 34, New York 30, Massachusetts 23. Many of them were strongly Federalist. The Washington-Adams party did not roll over and die, but it did alter its techniques.

Federalists, whether gentlemen of the old school or young innovators (see Ways to Study History X), believed that a sound republic must contain a proper degree of subordination. They thought that high public office belonged to persons of wealth and breeding, of good family and education. The elder generation also believed that while a gentleman might stand for election, he would never run for office. They despised men among their peers such as John Hancock who truckled to the mob. Even after the election of 1800, one of them could propose as a toast at a testimonial dinner: "Talents and virtue in individuals, and good sense in the community, properly to appreciate them." Among these older Federalists, two reactions to the election were common. One was to assert that the results were not tenable; Charles Cotesworth Pinckney declared that the Republicans would "proceed on their mad and wicked career, and the people's eyes will be opened." The other was to withdraw from civic affairs, perhaps with a sardonic joke about the Jeffersoni-

FIGURE 10-2. *Gore Place, Waltham, Massachusetts*

The benefits to America from the Napoleonic Wars still endure. A notable example is Gore Place in Waltham, Massachusetts, one of the finest examples of Federal architecture to be found anywhere. This style in domestic design—its symmetry, its dedication to brick as the basic material—was an improvisation on Georgian. But its deviations mattered: the fluted half-moon windows, the free-floating staircase in the main hall which leads to the second floor. Perhaps most enchanting is the two oval rooms, with even the doors curved to match the contour of the walls. Shown here is the dining room on the main level; identical above it is the study.

Christopher Gore was governor of Massachusetts from 1809 to 1811. His trade was the law, but he also invested wisely and well. Since he was one of the Young Federalists, he doubtless got many good tips. This mansion with its estate, covering nearly a square mile of grounds, was built at the ans' greed for office: "When these gentry find that there are more PIGS than TEATS, what a squealing there will be in the hog pen." Others broke camp quietly: Pinckney went to isolation on an island; George Cabot, Adams, John Jay, and later Gouverneur Morris cloistered their talents on country estates. One fugitive to a Berkshire mansion grumbled: "The aristocracy of virtue is destroyed; personal influence is at an end. I would never have abandoned the government personally, but from the most complete conviction that the people would make an experiment of democracy."

Young gentlemen likewise had two responses. They might never even enter politics, abstain from the beginning. Occupancy of public offices by eminent businessmen fell sharply. A letter written to John Quincy Adams by a younger brother in 1802 already bears that tone of rebuffed petulance that would characterize the Adams family two generations later: "I cannot endure that state of society wherein the men of talents, of mental endowments, 'whose hearts are pure and whose hands are clean,' are least in honor and estimation among us. When such men are awed into forbearance or stand mute through terror, it is time to despair for the commonwealth." Such men stuck to their counting houses. But others determined to treat politics like a body-contact sport and to whip the Republicans at their own game. By 1803, a Representative from New Hampshire was writing a friend, "Federalism can suit only a virtuous state of society. Don't flatter yourself that it is ever to have a resurrection." Significantly, this turncoat soon switched to the Republican party. Prior to his conversion he had seen that the Federalists' one chance was to "form a union with some of the better sort of democrats, and with some of the worst. We want the former to increase our numbers, and the latter to do our lying." A succinct formula came from a young Federalist in 1813: "You must get close to the people in order to manage them; there is no better way."

Amidst the uproar and turmoil there developed for the first time in America the recognition that a loyal opposition might have its uses. An early statement came in the House of Representatives in 1798 from Robert Goodloe Harper, a flashy but percipient South Carolinian:

---

staggering cost $23,000 although Gore wrote that it was constructed "with the greatest economy and absence of ornamentation." In a sense, he was right: Nothing about the dwelling seems ornate. But he had a huge pool table (like Byrd's at Westover—see Figure 4-1). He had a shower room on the first floor so that a servant could stand above him to pour water down. Being a civic official, he had to entertain often, and, caring for his own comfort, he had a horsehair cushioning inserted under the marble flooring in some public rooms. The floor gives. Hinges on certain doors are cut on the bias so that the door will rise to swing over the carpet.

Two further facts seem relevant. This house was built in 1805, before Gore became governor. Second, it was meant to be a summer home, although he later converted it for year-around occupancy. The rich enjoyed both cosmopolitan and bucolic life before the middle class invented suburbs.

While opposite parties in the Government struggle for pre-eminence, they are like persons engaged in an exhibition before the public, who are obliged to display superior merit and superior excellence in order to gain the prize. The public is the judge, the two parties are the combatants, and that party which possess[es] power must employ it properly, must conduct the government wisely, in order to ensure public approbation, and retain their power. In this contention, while the two parties draw different ways, a middle course is produced generally conformable to public good. Party spirit, therefore, and the contentions to which it gives rise, neither alarms nor displeases me. . . .

The extreme violence of party battles in America during this period should be viewed against the background of Europe. Not one major monarchy of 1789 seemed safe in 1815. The king of France had been guillotined; king of Sweden, shot; czar of Russia, strangled in bed. The rulers of Great Britain and of Portugal had gone crazy. In the United States, as intense concern with religion waned and as men removed from the seaboard to lonely lives on the frontier (Chapter 11), politics became a normal preoccupation as the most available source of excitement. The partisan virulence was incredible. Duels became frequent.* Two brothers fought each other—"a sad example of political enthusiasm." A Federalist editor in New York shot the Republican harbormaster dead. The same editor was attacked by a Republican doctor armed with a stiletto who sought to carry out a "surgical operation." Joseph Story, later to be a distinguished justice of the Supreme Court, had a fist fight in the streets of Salem with a Federalist opponent. Alexander Hamilton's son was killed in 1801 in a political duel. On 11 July, 1804, Hamilton met the same fate in an "interview" with Aaron Burr.

In South Carolina a gentleman remained passive while an enemy called him the vilest names imaginable. But when he was tagged "a damned Federal," the gentleman knocked his calumniator down. The Congregationalists of Connecticut were especially vehement Federalists. A lady fired her maid because the servant was a Republican. A man at Deerfield started building a new house before the 1800 election, but it was unfinished when Jefferson won. The man vowed that he would not finish the structure until the Federalists returned to power. That day did not come, and for almost twenty years the house stood empty. No rites remained sacred. In Massachusetts a man refused to go his brother's burial because Federalists had "snatched" the "putrid corpse" and featured it in a "political funeral." One death at least brought the growl: "Another God-damned Democrat has gone to Hell, and I wish they were all there."

---

*Early in the seventeenth century duelling was so common in the French army that it was decimating the ranks of officers. Therefore the king outlawed it. Having forbidden an abused man from seeking "personal satisfaction," he had to find a substitute. The ban on duels was an impetus behind the creation of the laws of slander and libel.

The president was an obvious target for canards. During the campaign he had been denounced as a Jacobin, an atheist, and a snake. Jefferson did not submit meekly. When excoriated by a newspaper, he urged upon the governor of Pennsylvania in 1803 a "few prosecutions" that might "have a wholesome effect in restoring the integrity of the presses." The First Amendment was no bar; as he wrote to Abigail Adams in 1803: "While we deny that Congress have a right to controul the freedom of the press, we have ever asserted the right of the states, and their exclusive right to do so." Although Jefferson did pardon victims of the Alien and Sedition Acts and although the laws expired early in his administration, in 1806 six men were called before the Federal Circuit Court in Connecticut and charged with seditious libel of the president.

Jefferson's chief defense was to build up his own political following. To be blunt, he used patronage to buy support. Bestowing public office on your kinfolk and friends was a hallowed custom in British government (see Chapter 5) and the colonists had carried the practice with them across the Atlantic. Jefferson's achievement was to make the arrangement systematic, indeed scientific. His First Inaugural was a shrewd initial try at conciliating his foes (Document 10-2). He was keenly aware that he was the head of a sectional party, limited to the South and West, and he set about transforming it into a truly national organization. The federal government had vacancies for cabinet officers, for ministers overseas, for judges, for postmasters, for customs officials; why not fill them with erstwhile foes who could be won over to the administration? Jefferson labored stoutly to build Republican ranks especially in the Middle States and New England. True, he went to the Old Dominion to recruit James Madison as his secretary of state, but the attorney general and the secretary of war were from Massachusetts, the postmaster general from Connecticut, the secretary of the treasury was Albert Gallatin from Pennsylvania, Justice Brockholst Livingston was from New York, and so on.

The first crisis to confront Madison was in the Mediterranean, where the problem was of long standing. The four Barbary states of northern Africa had been accustomed to plundering ships and enslaving their crews in a fashion indistinguishable from piracy. European nations had sought immunity for their citizens by paying annual tribute to the Barbary governments, and Americans prior to independence could crawl under this protective cover. The Washington and Adams administrations had signed humiliating treaties under which they paid annual ransoms. Matters came to a head in May, 1801, when the pasha of Tripoli declared war against the United States. Jefferson resolved to retaliate; he relaxed his policy of economy in government in order to build up the navy. The rather lackadaisical conflict lasted for four years, but the United States fought it with vigor for only one. When a settlement came, it was not by any means satisfactory in giving full security to American interests. In 1807 Jefferson, after another crisis with Britain to be examined presently, withdrew his naval squadron from the Mediterranean, and for the next eight years the Barbary pirates pursued their depredations unchecked. The situation was not resolved until after the War of 1812.

The other major sally into foreign relations of Jefferson's first administration—the Louisiana Purchase—was a luminous triumph. It was perhaps the best real-estate deal in history, and that facet of the episode was accidental. This is not to say that the president was just blundering around. Jefferson knew exactly what he wanted—New Orleans (Document 10-2)—and he got it. But that he got so much besides was happenstance. Toward the close of the Adams administration, rumors had circulated that by a secret treaty Spain would soon convey title in Louisiana to France. Transfer would put the expansionist Napoleon in a position to block egress to the oceans of every American product leaving the transmontane West (Chapter 11). More, the French could inflame Indians against the settlers; they might develop dreams of paring off chunks of the United States. As talk of a Franco-Spanish agreement persisted through 1801, Jefferson's worries grew. By May Day of 1802 Madison was instructing Livingston to ask what price France would set on New Orleans and West Florida (also reportedly to be transferred, although in fact Spain was never willing to relinquish any part of the Floridas). Matters became critical on October 16 when the Spanish intendant at New Orleans withdrew the right of deposit there for American goods. Resentment was bone-deep in the West. Demands for military seizure of the port were common. According to a British observer, "Scarcely any Thing has happened since the Revolution which has so much agitated the minds of all Descriptions of People in the United States as this Decree." Jefferson now reinforced Livingston's mission in Paris by sending as his associate James Monroe, who was popular both in France and on the American frontier.

Napoleon's fantasies for the New World had come a cropper. He sent an expedition to reconquer San Domingo, which had virtually won independence from white rule in 1795. The black inhabitants resisted bitterly. More serious still, the invading troops got yellow fever. In one year, San Domingo cost France 50,000 soldiers. Spain would not part with the Floridas. By the spring of 1803 it was clear that the Peace of Amiens was breaking down, that war against England would begin anew, and that Britain could easily launch a naval assault on New Orleans. American agents slyly fed Napoleon's fears. Jefferson persuaded Congress to vote an army of 80,000 men plus fifteen gunboats on the Mississippi. At last, on 11 April, 1803, Talleyrand put a question to Livingston—What would the United States give for the whole of Louisiana? Two days later Monroe reached Paris. The two envoys were in a dilemma. They were not authorized to buy such a huge tract, nor were they authorized to spend the requisite sum of money. Nonetheless, they resolved to go far beyond their instructions and to seize the bargain. On 30 April treaties were signed by which the United States agreed to pay $15 million in cash and claims (A British banking house later loaned the young republic more than $10 million toward the purchase price). Nobody knew it at the time, but the Louisiana Territory would turn out to be 828,000 square miles; the price was

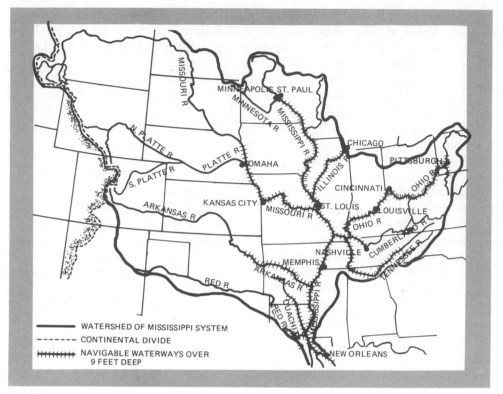

FIGURE 10-3. *Mississippi River System*

about three cents an acre, (no mean bargain for land of which one part is today downtown Kansas City). Livingston questioned Talleyrand about the vague boundaries to the cession. The foreign minister replied: "I can give you no direction; you have made a noble bargain for yourselves, and I suppose you will make the most of it"—which the Americans certainly did. "We have lived long," Livingston exulted, "but this is the noblest work of our whole lives." He was right too; the area of the United States had been expanded by 140 per cent. Settlements along the Mississippi had been freed from apprehensions about foreign agents stirring up Indian raids, from worries about hostile barriers to navigation along the Father of Waters, from uncertainties about land titles.

The president had no intention of repudiating the latitudinarian act of his agents. For a time he did wonder if a constitutional amendment might not be needed, because in his opinion the United States was a government of limited and specified powers and nowhere was it explicitly stated that federal funds could be used to buy a gigantic territory. In his dispute with Hamilton as to whether Congress was authorized to charter a bank, he had flatly denied that the "necessary and proper" clause could be used as a warrant to extend federal jurisdiction. But now he submitted the treaties with France to the Senate, where they won hearty consent in October (Perhaps Jefferson was an ideologue who babbled at times about equality and fraternity and the need for revolutions, but when pitch came to toss he was not going to bog down in what he termed "metaphysical subtleties").

Already had begun one of the finest adventures in American history: the Lewis and Clark expedition. As early as 1786 Jefferson had tried to promote explorations of the trans-Mississippi. At last succeeded. Fifty men left the East on 5 July 1803 and many of them did not return to St. Louis until 23 September 1806. Their instructions were to follow the Missouri River to its source, find passes through the Rockies and pick up a water route to the Pacific. They were to take copious careful notes on terrain, soils, minerals, flora and fauna. Since Jefferson was trying to confine the Indians in the East on small reservations, the fur trade was being obliterated, so Lewis and Clark were to seek new regions and contacts that might be exploited by American trappers and merchants. The expedition won through, until at last they looked upon the Pacific, "the object of all our labours, the reward of all our anxieties." They had surveyed many landscapes that no white man had seen before, fought eight Blackfeet and killed two, learned to eat horse meat. They had also made friends of a dozen Indian bands and collected invaluable scientific data (Document 13-1). Jefferson persuaded a reluctant Congress to finance a few other explorations of the West, the most notable being led by Zebulon Pike into Colorado and New Mexico. (It is almost funny that Pike tried to climb the peak now bearing his name, and failed.)

The state of the nation, with qualifications to be noted, can be described as soaring prosperity. Both the British and the French were seizing neutral ships and cargoes on the oceans, but the highjackings were far from lethal to trade. One American merchant estimated during the Napoleonic Wars that if he sent out three ships and one reached its port safely, he would still net a satisfactory profit. The presidential election of 1804 took place in this context. Jefferson's studied moves in building up the Republican press and in manipulating the federal patronage now bore fruit; in fact it is hard to understand why anybody accepted the Federalist nomination. Charles C. Pinckney did, again. He got 14 electoral votes: the 9 of Connecticut, the 3 of Delaware, 2 of the 11 from Maryland. Jefferson got 162. Only five other presidents have received such an overwhelming endorsement (Washington, Monroe, Franklin Delano Roosevelt, Lyndon Johnson, Nixon).

Still sparking the American boom were re-exports and earnings from the carrying trade (See early Chapter 9). From 1795 to 1800 American exports of sugar to Europe had more than doubled. In the same period, exports to the British Empire rose 300 per cent. Under Jay's Treaty, American bottoms could not carry foreign goods to any British port, nor could they engage in the coasting trade in India. Both prohibitions were ignored. Since 1801 American vessels had been transporting the goods of India to Europe as freely as did the ships of the British East India Company itself. It is worth while to take a

FIGURE 10-4. *Samuel McIntire, Chestnut Street, Salem*

While most of the profits from foreign trade during the Napoleonic Wars came to the major ports, merchant-shippers in outports could also do quite well. Chestnut Street in Salem, Massachusetts embodies one hundred and fifty years of American history. The construction of these houses was paid for by the profits from trading voyages. Having more than a dozen rooms, many of these dwellings can be supported today only by professionals who also use them as offices.

Chestnut Street, three blocks long, may well be the most distinguished street of houses in the United States. It quietly states its unity and its diversity: the fan windows, the symmetry—these are standard. Also hipped roofs, square sturdy lines, red brick. The builder, Samuel McIntire, knew how to build diversity into this integral design. Some of the houses are singles, some are doubles. There are those close up to the sidewalk, those far back. Main entrances may be toward the front, or toward the side. In spite of variations, the street seems to be "of a piece."

McIntire, like Nathaniel Hawthorne, was Salem-born and bred. Many of his townsmen praise him most for delicately carved woodwork in the interiors, but I do not agree. What makes his legacy distinctive is that he created an urban environment that was varied, intimate, and compatible with the surrounding rural setting.

235

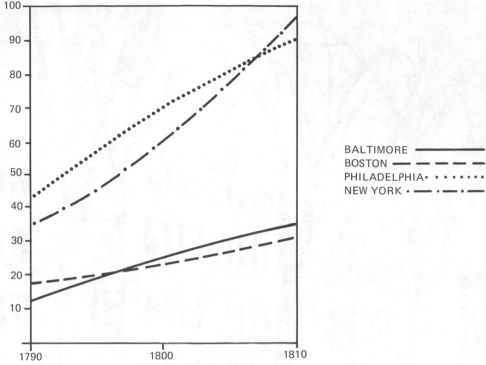

FIGURE 10-5. *Population Growth of Four Ports, 1790–1810 (in thousands)*

detailed look at one voyage in order to grasp the magnitude of the profits that could be made. When the *Pearl* left Boston, the combined value of vessel and cargo was at most $40,000. She rounded Cape Horn and stopped in the Pacific Northwest, where she traded for furs. Thence to Hawaii to take on a load of sandalwood. Then she sailed to Canton. There the captain could pay all expenses of the voyage and buy a return cargo valued at $156,000 on the local market: dining sets ("china"), tea, "Nankins" (cotton goods). The *Pearl* got back to Boston in 1810. Her cargo was sold for $261,000. Expenses for the return voyage were paid. The captain got a "primage" of 5 per cent of the remainder, which came to $13,000. The owners shelled out customs duties of $40,000. That left them with more than $200,000. Even deducting the full $40,000 of their initial investment, they had more than $160,000 or about 400 per cent on their capital.

By the nature of the situation, American plunder from the Napoleonic Wars was concentrated in a few port cities. Of the $60.3 million in re-exports in 1806, fully $52.9 million issued from four states: Massachusetts, New York, Pennsylvania, and Maryland. Exportation of domestic products was spread out more, but even so more than half of it emanated from the same four states.

Within those states, it flowed through the major cities. In 1790 only 5.1 per cent of the nation's population was urban (that is, residing in towns of 2,500 or more people); in 1810, 7.3 per cent. Most of the growth came in four ports:

	1790	1800	1810
Baltimore	13,503	26,114	35,583
Boston	18,038	24,937	33,250
New York City	33,131	60,489	96,373
Philadelphia	42,520	69,402	91,874

Here we can see the profundity of Adam Smith's argument that the productivity of labor depends upon specialization of function, and that specialization depends on the size of the market. The new cities could support many specialized enterprises that had been impossible with a rural dispersed population. Banks grew in number and size. Commission merchants could deal in a limited range of products, and so New York developed a number of cotton factors. Brokerage firms developed, and did a steady trade in the securities of the first Bank of the United States. The United States had a single marine insurance company in 1792, and forty by 1804. Docking facilities and warehouses multiplied. Manufactures, mainly of the domestic kind located in homes, grew to produce for the local market: baking, shoes, clothing.

The development of manufacturing (note that we do not say "origins"; they lie much earlier; see Chapter 3) will be examined in Chapters 11–13, but some remarks should be made here. First, the Constitution of the United States was crucial to the growth of trade. It forbade any state to impose legal barricades to the movement of goods across its borders; (in contrast, tiny Switzerland until 1798 had a hundred different tariff zones). It also barred the federal government from imposing duties on exports. These provisions created a legal framework within which Adam Smith's prescriptions could operate. Obstacles to trade remained, but they were not padded by statutes and taxes. The chief obstacle to long-distance transportation was the crunching cost of moving any article that had left the waterways (see Chapter 11). This charge operated as a *de facto* tariff. Its impact was reinforced during the Napoleonic Wars by the blockades and confiscations of the combatants. Gallatin in 1810 explained the changes in the American position; he started by discussing reasons for the earlier delays in promoting manufacturing:*

The most prominent of those causes are the abundance of land compared with the population, the high price of labor, and the want of sufficient capital. The

---

*The young republic was wise enough to bestow civic power on men who knew how to build and operate the institutions of a modern economy. In banking, the names of Hamilton, Gallatin, and Nicholas Biddle (until 1832) are majestic. As to transportation, so-called "internal improvements," Gallatin is pre-eminent along with John Quincy Adams and Henry Clay.

superior attractions of agricultural pursuits, the great extension of American commerce during the late European Wars, and the continuance of habits after the causes which produced them have ceased to exist, may also be enumerated. Several of these obstacles have, however, been removed or lessened. The cheapness of provisions had always, to a certain extent, counterbalanced the high price of manual labor; and this is now, in many important branches, nearly superseded by the introduction of machinery; a great American capital has been acquired during the last twenty years; and the injurious violations of the Neutral commerce of the United States, by forcing industry and capital into other channels, have broken inveterate habits, and given a general impulse, to which must be ascribed the great increase of manufactures during the last two years.

The increase had indeed been enormous. It can suffice here to glance at the accelerating construction of cotton-textile mills:

1791	1
1795	1
1803–4	2
1804–8	10
1809	89

These factories did spinning only; not until the Boston Manufacturing Company opened its mill in Waltham, Massachusetts during the War of 1812 would the New World hold an integrated plant that wove its yarn into cloth.

Ralph Waldo Emerson would later comment about his home state: "From 1790 to 1820, there was not a book, a speech, a conversation, or a thought in the State." He was wrong of course. Whereas the keenest talents of America in the seventeenth century had turned to religion, of the eighteenth century to statecraft, the best minds of the early nineteenth were focused on profit-making enterprise. Soon after the Republican victory in 1800 one man commented: "Many of our Gentlemen of Large Fortune take no part in the public affairs & hope to comprimise with the fury of democracy by their inactivity and even submission. It is true everywhere." A young Federalist in Boston lamented, "Talents among us are employed to get riches, and wealth is used only to buy distinction and pleasure. When property is threatened, its possessors are impatient to enjoy the present moment and careless of futurity." John Hancock had spent his adulthood squandering a fortune; the next generation would strike a diametrically opposed stance.

But businessmen were being harassed. Their ships were in daily peril. From 1803 to 1812 the British seized 917 American merchantmen; in the five years beginning in 1807 they took 389, while France was seizing 558. Within a year Napoleon confiscated American vessels and cargoes to a value of $10 million. Most Americans were even more incensed by impressments (as during the French war, Chapter 5, and the Revolution, Chapter 7). A British commodore had said bluntly in 1797, "It is my duty to keep my Ship manned, and I will do so wherever I find men that speak the same language with me." A few years later an English lord added: "The pretension . . . that the American flag should protect every individual sailing under it on board of a merchant-ship is too extravagant to require any serious refutation." Through the entire duration of the Napoleonic Wars, it seems likely that Great Britain impressed off American ships as many as 10,000 sailors. Not more than 10 per cent of them were British citizens. The British reply pointed to desertions from the Royal Navy, probably 20,000 men; Lord Nelson once put the total as high as 42,000. At a single moment in 1804, twelve of His Majesty's vessels were immobilized at Norfolk because of desertions; the scalawags were so impudent as to thumb their noses at their former officers in the streets of the town.

The clash of policy exploded in June of 1807. The *Chesapeake,* American frigate of forty guns, sailed from Norfolk bound for the Mediterranean. Expecting no trouble, she had her gun deck so cluttered that her weaponry was virtually unusable. Beyond the three-mile limit, but not by much, she was hailed by the British 50-gun *Leopard.* The British asked to board the *Chesapeake* to search for four deserters. They were refused. They then poured broadsides into the U.S. vessel, killing three men and wounding eighteen. The American commander struck his colors. Of the four men seized by the British, three were native-born Americans (two of them black). The battered *Chesapeake* limped back to port. Jefferson banned all British warships from American waters and ports. He called on the state governors to provide 100,000 militia. He put coastal defenses in readiness. "Never since the battle of Lexington," said the president, "have I seen this country in such a state of exasperation as at present, and even that did not produce such unanimity."

But armed conflict was not Jefferson's way. In April, 1806, Congress had passed a Non-Importation Act that would have excluded certain British manufactures from the United States unless American grievances were resolved, but the act had been repeatedly suspended. In December, 1807, it went into effect. A week later, prodded by the president, Congress enacted the Embargo. This statute prohibited any American ship from sailing to a foreign port. Coasters had to post sizable bonds that they would not put off to alien if profitable destinations. The administration tried to pretend that the measure was impartial as between Britain and France. Madison pointed out the French would lose luxuries from the West Indies, while Britain would "feel it in her manufactures, in the loss of naval stores, and above all in the supplies essential to her colonies." This was window dressing. Since England controlled the seas, she was the larger loser. One Federalist in Boston grumped, "Mr. Jefferson has imposed an embargo to please France and to beggar us!" From Dover, New Hampshire on 4 July, 1808, came a refrain:

> *Our ships all in motion*
> *Once whiten'd the ocean;*
> *They sail'd and return'd with a Cargo;*
> *Now doom'd to decay*
> *They are fallen a prey,*
> *To Jefferson, worms, and EMBARGO*

Along the docks in New York, according to a British observer, "The coffee-houses were almost empty; the streets, near the water-side, were almost deserted; the grass had begun to grow upon the wharves."

Napoleon was quick to move into the opening left for him; since no American ship could legally be in Europe, he decreed, the vessels there must be British. He seized them. Even with this blow, American efforts to counter the Embargo could sometimes become maniacal. Merchants who had smuggled to elude British customs could also smuggle to evade their own Embargo. New England especially heard talk of nullification and of secession from the Union. Federalists won some state elections (but this fact does not in itself prove that those elections were a referendum on the Embargo). Not wishing to will the Embargo to his successor, Jefferson supported a repeal measure that went through Congress three days before he left office. Most historians have agreed that the Embargo was a mistake, and some have thought it almost a disaster: it caused a depression; it did not stimulate industrialization; it did not force a change in British or French policy; it was politically unpopular. Still, it is worthwhile expressing some skepticism here about some counts in this bill of particulars, and their conclusion about the Embargo could very well be wrong. Jefferson wrote about the Embargo, just before its repeal, that it had "produced one very happy & permanent effect. It has set us all on domestic manufacture, & will I verily believe reduce our future demands on England fully one half." (See Chapters 11–12.) Perhaps more important, and certainly not to be shrugged off, it had bought a few years of peace. Those who opine that a war later is identical with a war now might well ponder the comment made by Jefferson in 1815, after the War of 1812: "For twenty years to come we should consider peace as the *summum bonum* of our country. At the end of that period we shall be twenty millions in number, and forty in energy, when encountering the starved and rickety paupers and dwarfs of English workshops." This projection of population growth proved to be a bit high; a reasonable guess at the number of Americans in 1835 would be 15 millions. (We shall confront an analogous question in evaluating the Compromise of 1850 and the Crittenden Compromise that was rejected by President Lincoln in 1860, namely: What is gained or lost by deferring the resolution of an issue?)

As to the alleged political unpopularity of the Embargo, it was still in effect when the presidential election of 1808 took place. James Madison, the Republican candidate hand-picked by Jefferson, was an exceptionally able man—but he did not exactly glitter with charisma. Even so he won 122 electoral votes to 47 for the Federalists. The opposition could carry only New England minus Vermont, plus Delaware and some electoral votes from Maryland and North Carolina. Of course this result must not be taken as a mandate on the Embargo. But the Jefferson administration had made out all right in foreign affairs, and its victories would be solidified by Madison. In 1810 the United States simply seized West Florida, on the flabby pretext that Spain had transferred it to France and that it had been a part of the Louisiana Purchase. A further step in opening the West came the following year when American forces under William Henry Harrison whipped Tecumseh's tribe of Shawnees at Tippecanoe, Indiana Territory.

Events on the high seas were less fortunate. A triangular series of thrusts and counterthrusts, edicts and retaliations was enacted by Great Britain, France, and the United States. No purpose would be served here by detailing the various decrees of the European powers. In a sense the British actions were more "legitimate" than the French. By international law, insofar as that term is useful at all, a blockade becomes legal if it is effective. Since the French could not enforce their "paper blockade" of the entirety of the British Isles, it was illegal. England by a sequence of Orders in Council closed the European ports held by Napoleon. After other jabs, including a Non-Intercourse Act that replaced the "dambargo" in 1809, the United States adopted Macon's Bill No. 2 in 1810. This monstrosity of a measure is beyond belief. It reopened trade with both belligerents. It also provided that if either Britain or France repealed its discriminations against American commerce, the United States would again impose nonintercourse against the other. Napoleon managed to trick the Madison administration into believing that he had revoked his hostile decrees, and in March, 1811, Congress once more suspended trade with Great Britain. Incidents accumulated: England sent over a minister who was as stupidly arrogant as Genêt had been; American and British warships fired in anger on the Atlantic.

Among the fruitless disputes engaged in by many historians, one argument that can never be resolved has to do with the relative weights to be assigned to the array of American motivations in declaring war against Britain in 1812. The list is long. Some Americans wanted to conquer Canada. But why? Again the subcategories multiply. This man wants to seize the rich agricultural land along the St. Lawrence; that one has been inflamed by his conviction that the English are stirring up Indian raids against the frontier. Southerners lusted to grab East Florida away from Spain. Everybody was furious about impressments. Confiscations on the oceans were damaging men of many trades and in many regions, not only merchants in New England but also planters of hemp in Kentucky, of tobacco in Virginia, of cotton in South Carolina, all of them dependent on foreign markets. On this score, of course, the two combatants were both culpable; as one congressman said, "the Devil himself could not tell which government, England or France, is the most

FIGURE 10-6. *Matthew Jouett,* Henry Clay

This portrait of Henry Clay (1777–1852) admirably suggests his character. When Matthew Jouett painted Clay about 1824, he recognized that his subject knew nothing and cared less about the emergent "puritanism" of the nineteenth century. Clay was not a Victorian, but a man of the Enlightenment. He loved dirty jokes, fine whiskey, beautiful women, and gambling. While the American delegation was negotiating the Treaty of Ghent, John Quincy Adams wrung his spiritual hands at the behavior of his fellow envoy; Clay would arrive at the bargaining table in the morning (promptly) having come straight from another table with a green baize cover. Clay's wife was a similar breed. Asked if she did not deplore her husband's lust for wagering, she replied: Only when he loses. In his devotion to funny off-color stories, Clay resembled the father of John Quincy Adams although he did not resemble the son. When Clay learned that Napoleon was having his marriage wicked." Henry Clay replied that Britain could be hit in Canada, while France could not be reached; in the words of *Niles' Weekly Register* England was "tangible in her tenderest points."

Clay had emerged as leader of the War Hawks. Only thirty-five years old, he had served out two unexpired terms in the United States Senate. He had then been elected to the House, and since 1811 he had been Speaker. Joined with him in flaunting martial banners was a band of some twenty-eight congressmen. They were Republicans, and most were from the South or West. Probably they could have been fended off if the president had held out against them, as John Adams had done fifteen years earlier. But in June, 1812, just as Great Britain was in course of revoking its Orders in Council as they applied to American vessels, Madison decided for war; he was especially incensed about maritime grievances. The division in the House was more a matter of party than of section, but the split between regions was pronounced. Most New Englanders voted against the declaration of war, most Representatives from the South and West for it. Of the Republicans from the Northeast, forty supported the president, but eighteen broke party ranks to oppose him. The final tally was 79 pro to 49 con. The result in the Senate was even closer: 19 to 13. Then, in a real fit of megalomania, the upper chamber spent four days debating whether the word *France* should be added to the war declaration. Fortunately the remark by Jefferson that it was silly "to fight two enemies at a time rather than to take them in succession" was heeded, but the vote to omit was only 18 to 14. After the vote the French minister reported to Paris:

> I can assure Monseigneur the bitterness which has developed against France is really such that if the policy of the Government had not arrested the movement in the Chambers, during the secret deliberations, war would have been declared against both Powers.

On land, the hostilities had little issue; in fact they were farcical. The adversaries did exchange insults by destroying each other's capitols; in 1813 an American force burned the upper Canadian parliament at York, and the

---

annulled because his wife had not produced an heir, Clay commented that there was nothing wrong with the woman that a strong-backed Kentuckian couldn't fix.

His wit and his flair alone would make the man memorable. But to concentrate on these traits would omit half of his appeal. Since the days of the Founding Fathers, perhaps only J. Q. Adams and Lincoln have been his peers in statecraft. He understood—and accepted—democratic government as few have done in the last two centuries. Although that scheme of polity involves far more than a willingness to meet your opponent halfway, it should be noted that Clay was the chief architect of three compromises that were needed to preserve the Union: the one over Missouri in 1820, the tariff act of 1833, the one in 1850. But he cannot be depicted as an opportunist. Speaker of the House of Representatives when he was only 34, he was a leader of the "war hawks" against Britain. He fought for the Second Bank of the United States when that cause was a political risk. He ran for President three times (1824, 1832, 1844) and should have been elected, but was not.

following year the British navy destroyed Washington. On the Atlantic there was no contest; the United States did not have the tools to put up an organized fight against the Royal Navy. Privateers were another matter: American buccaneers seized or destroyed more than 1,300 English merchantmen. Similarly on the interior lakes the Americans won two significant victories, by Oliver Hazard Perry on Lake Erie, and by Thomas Macdonough on Lake Champlain near Plattsburgh. These triumphs had lasting results. After peace returned, John Quincy Adams, minister to St. James's, suggested a mutual disarmament on the Great Lakes. The British Foreign Minister agreed that "everything beyond what is necessary to guard against smuggling is calculated only to produce mischief." The resulting Rush-Bagot Agreement (approved 1818) made it possible to avoid a costly Canadian-American arms race.

By the time of the first decisive engagement on land, gloriously won by Andrew Jackson at New Orleans, peace had been signed. The American delegation to the conference at Ghent included some of the ablest men in the United States: John Quincy Adams, Albert Gallatin, and Henry Clay. Adams was head of the commission. Quite possibly the greatest diplomat ever to bless his country, he managed simultaneously to be one of the least tactful of men. An Englishman who met him when he was minister to Russia declared that of all the men he had met in his life, Adams was "the most doggedly and systematically repulsive." Adams' judgment of himself was hardly more lenient: "I am a man of reserved, cold, austere, and forbidding manners; my political adversaries say, a gloomy misanthropist, and my personal enemies, an unsocial savage."

Adams and Clay both brought passion and intelligence to the assertion of their nation's interests. But each of them also had a sectional concern that ate at him. Clay did not want to renew the clause of the Treaty of Paris (1783) that accorded to British subjects the right of unrestricted navigation on the Mississippi. Adams was willing to barter that freedom away in exchange for British recognition of the rights of New Englanders in the cod fisheries along the Grand Banks of Newfoundland and Labrador. It was this clash that made Gallatin's presence vital. The oldest of the trio, the only native of Europe, expert in financial matters, urbane and flexible, he mediated. While Gallatin reasoned with his colleagues, military events were forcing both sides to moderate their demands. Back in 1810 Clay had boasted on the floor of the Senate "the militia of Kentucky alone are competent to place Montreal and Upper Canada at your feet." But invasions of Canada had achieved nothing, largely because the contiguous states in the North, especially New England, felt no enthusiasm for the war. Indeed, the New Englanders had felt enough common cause against the war to call a special assembly, the Hartford Convention, at the end of 1814 to consider action on their grievances, and rumors were afloat that many of its members favored secession. George Cabot, leader of the Massachusetts delegates, was constrained to caution: "The worst of all evils would be a dissolution of the Union." Happily the Convention was content to suggest several Constitutional amendments aimed at strengthening the position of minority sections.

The English also had toned down their initial arrogance. Before the negotiations *The Times* (London) had pontificated: "Our demands may be couched in a single word, Submission!" One American commissioner complained, "Their terms were those of a Conqueror to a conquered people." American naval victories on the Great Lakes stopped this foolishness. The Duke of Wellington ended the charade in November by writing to the foreign minister, "I confess that I think you have no right, from the state of war, to demand any concession of territory from America." The Treaty of Ghent was signed on Christmas Eve, 1814, a fortnight before Jackson's triumph at New Orleans. The pact amounted to little more than an agreement to stop fighting. All territory was restored, *status quo ante bellum.* What of Canada? Not mentioned. What of Florida? Not mentioned. The hostilities supposedly had started in defense of maritime rights, but the Treaty said not a word about impressment or the status of neutrals in wartime. "I hoped," declared John Quincy Adams, "it would be the last treaty of peace between Great Britain and the United States." And it was.

The presidential election of 1800 marked a quickened interest of Americans in politics. A typical white adult male anywhere in the land had long had the right to vote. But often he had not bothered to exercise it. The extreme virulence of the Adams-Jefferson contest, coupled with the tie between Jefferson and Aaron Burr, impelled men to the polls. Then began twenty-four years of the Virginia Dynasty: Jefferson, Madison, Monroe. Signal accomplishments of these years contributed to (1) continentalism and (2) manifest destiny (Chapters 11 and 13). The Lewis and Clark expedition lasted from 1803 to 1806, and found a workable route to the Pacific coast. Its practical results were given increased legal validity by the Louisiana Purchase. These two events were truly turning points in American history—far more so than, say, the Open Door Notes about China or President Franklin Roosevelt's speech about the Four Freedoms. The Purchase more than doubled the land area of the United States; the Lewis and Clark trip gave Americans their first hints about how to use the continent. Meanwhile American merchants were extending their commerce, formerly limited to Europe and the Western Hemisphere, to the Far East, especially to China. They were pouring westward over the Appalachians. As seaboard merchants became more aware of the promise of markets and materials to the West, they started to divert their capital into domestic industries. Textile manufacturing started. Attempts to push exports were instrumental in involving the Early Republic in a second war with the United Kingdom, which did not yield profit or glory for either side.

SOME NOTABLE EVENTS

1800 Convention of 1800 suspends Franco-American treaties of 1778 and 1788.

Federal capital moves from Philadelphia to Washington.

Spain, by secret Treaty of San Ildefonso, cedes Louisiana to France.

Alessandro Volta develops electric battery.

1801 Union of Britain and Ireland forms United Kingdom.

Jefferson's Inaugural, March 4.

1801–
1804 U.S. war against Tripoli.

1802 Peace of Amiens, in March, brings respite in war until May 1803.

U.S. Military Academy opens formally at West Point, N.Y., July 4.

Enabling act for Ohio introduces policy of giving each new Western state two townships to sustain a public university.

1803 Ohio becomes seventeenth state, February 19.

Louisiana Purchase more than doubles area of U.S., which takes formal possession, Dec. 20.

First Roman Catholic Church in Boston is dedicated.

1804 Lewis and Clark expedition leaves St. Louis, May.

Alexander Hamilton killed in duel with Aaron Burr, July 11.

Haiti shakes off France and becomes first Latin American nation to win independence.

Napoleon crowned Emperor.

1806 Non-Importation Act passed, April 18.

Napoleon's Berlin Decree, Nov. 21.

Non-Importation Act suspended, December.

1806–
1807 Zebulon Pike explores Colorado and New Mexico.

1807 Great Britain's Orders in Council, January 7, November 11.

Act of Congress, March 2, bans importation of slaves by 1808.

Chesapeake-Leopard clash, June 22.

Ex-Vice President Burr acquitted of treason, September 1.

1807 Napoleon's Milan Decree, Dec. 17.

Embargo Act becomes law, Dec. 22.

1808 Albert Gallatin's comprehensive report on internal improvements.

1809 Non-Intercourse Act replaces Embargo, March 1.

1810 Macon's Bill No. 2 passes Congress.

West Florida annexed, October 27.

1811 William Henry Harrison defeats Indians at Tippecanoe, Indiana, November 7.

Federal debt, $86 million in 1803, is reduced to low of $45 million.

1812 Louisiana becomes eighteenth state, April 8.

War declared against Great Britain, June 18.

Benjamin Rush, *Observations upon the Diseases of the Mind.*

1813 Yankee forces burn Canadian capitol at York (now Toronto), late April.

Oliver Hazard Perry guides American victory on Lake Erie, Sept. 10.

Boston Manufacturing Company at Waltham, Massachusetts becomes first integrated textile mill in the New World.

1813–
1814 Andrew Jackson fights Creeks in Alabama, Nov.–March.

1814 Napoleon exiled to Elba, April 11.

British forces burn capitol at Washington, August 24.

Americans win naval victory on Lake Champlain, September 11.

Treaty of Ghent ends War of 1812, December 24.

1814–
1815 Hartford Convention, December 15–January 5.

Congress of Vienna, September–June.

1815 Andrew Jackson defeats British at Battle of New Orleans, January 8.

The Hundred Days: Napoleon returns to France on March 1; defeated at Waterloo on June 18; interned on St. Helena.

Quadruple Alliance (Austria, Prussia, Russia, Great Britain) and Holy Alliance formed.

Steamboat *Enterprise* runs upstream from New Orleans to Pittsburgh.

Ways to Study History X

Refine your categories. Right after World War II graduate students were avidly reading V. L. Parrington's *Main Currents in American Thought* (3 volumes, 1927, 1930). But the work would not find many champions today. Parrington's technique was to dichotomize the nation's public life as a series of recurrent clashes between "liberals" and "conservatives." Such a gross discrimination has little or no cutting edge; it often stuffs into the same box men who differed on several significant subjects. When confronted with the artist Edgar Allen Poe, Parrington could only shrug his shoulders and admit that his method was not applicable. A similar obsolescence has overcome Charles A. Beard's *An Economic Interpretation of the Constitution* (1913) with its crude distinction between the commercial and the agrarian interests, between personalty and real property.

But we cannot think without schemes of classification; no human mind can cope with millions of individual data. The task is to devise categories that are more relevant and precise, that do not conceal or distort facts. An outstanding example is David Hackett Fischer's *The Revolution of American Conservatism* (1965). To analyze the changes in the Federalist party that began at the very end of the eighteenth century, Fischer wrote brief characterizations of the party's leaders in each state. The Appendix containing these biographies runs 185 pages. Each leader is sorted under Federalists of the Old School, or Transitional Figures, or Young Federalists. The device allows fine discriminations: for instance, Patrick Henry and Washington are both assigned to the first category, but the sizable differences between them are also revealed (Henry wanting a weak state, the President believing in a corporate society and strong government, and so on).

Document 10-1

Thomas Jefferson, like the other Founding Fathers, was not enthusiastic about the notion of a two-party system. He tended to regard his opponents as deceitful monarchists who were conspiring with foreign enemies. However, taking office in March, 1801, he recognized that he was presiding over a deeply riven nation. His First Inaugural was a deft and pliable attempt to pour oil on the waters.

During the contest of opinion through which we have passed the animation of discussions and of exertions has sometimes worn an aspect which might impose on strangers unused to think freely and to speak and to write what they think; but this being now decided by the voice of the nation, announced according to the rules of the Constitution, all will, of course, arrange themselves under the will of the law, and unite in common efforts for the common good. All, too, will bear in mind this sacred principle, that though the will of the majority is in all cases to prevail, that will to be rightful must be reasonable; that the minority possess their equal rights, which equal law must protect, and to violate would be oppression. Let us, then, fellow-citizens, unite with one heart and one mind. Let us restore to social intercourse that harmony and affection without which liberty and even life itself are but dreary things. . . . But every difference of opinion is not a difference of principle. We have called by different names brethren of the same principle. We are all Republicans, we are all Federalists. If there be any among us who would wish to dissolve the Union or to change its republican form, let them stand undisturbed as monuments of the safety with which error of opinion may be tolerated where reason is left free to combat it. . . .

Document 10-2

The hardnosed realism of early American diplomacy is nowhere more evident than in this letter from President Jefferson to his Minister in France, Robert R. Livingston, 18 April, 1802.

The cession of Louisiana and the Floridas by Spain to France, works most sorely on the United States. On this subject the Secretary of State has written to you fully, yet I cannot forbear recurring to it personally, so deep is the impression it makes on my mind. It completely reverses all the political relations of the United States, and will form a new epoch in our political course. Of all the nations of any consideration, France is the one which, hitherto, has offered the fewest points on which we could have any conflict of right, and the most points of a communion of interests. From these causes, we have ever looked to her as our natural friend, *as one with which we never could have an occasion of difference. . . . There is on the globe one single spot, the possessor of which is our natural and habitual enemy. It is New Orleans, through which the produce of three-eights of our territory must pass to market, and from its fertility it will ere long yield more than half of our whole produce, and contain more than half of our inhabitants. France, placing herself in that door, assumes to us the attitude of defiance. Spain might have retained it quietly for years. Her pacific dispositions, her feeble state, would induce her to increase our facilities there, so that her possession of the place would be hardly felt by us, and it would not, perhaps, be very long before some circumstance might arise, which might make the cession of it to us the price of something of more worth to her. . . . The day that France takes possession of New Orleans, fixes the sentence which is to restrain her forever within her low-water mark. It seals the union of two nations, who, in conjunction, can maintain exclusive possession of the ocean. From that moment, we must marry ourselves to the British fleet and nation. . . .*

PART III

Union or Sectionalism?
1815–1860

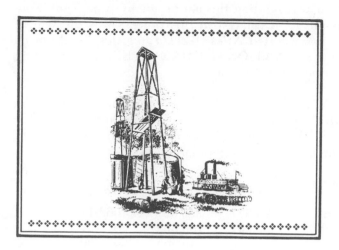

From Facing Eastward
to Looking Westward

From even before the first white settlers arrived, the future United States was already primed for blowing apart (See Chapter 2 on Puritan dissensions; Chapter 8 on Confederation sectionalism, etc.). A centrifugal force that existed prior to colonization of the New World was the Protestantism of the Reformation, which could allow one man to construe the Bible as well as another. America added another explosive element in its land waiting to be claimed by new settlers. As we saw (Chapter 4 on back-country settlement), by the middle of the eighteenth century families were infiltrating the Piedmont and spilling over the mountains. This geographical dispersion was merely one aspect of the disintegration of American society. There was also a polarization in politics. In April, 1812, it was widely believed, rightly or not, that a band of War Hawks led by Clay had informed the president that they would fight his renomination unless he announced for war. The harsh truth was that from Delaware northward, Madison did not win a single electoral vote except eight from

Vermont. In the next fifty years, divisive impulses would bring Civil War. But—the other side of the coin—the secessionists would lose the war. At the same time that sectionalism was rending the nation, many Americans were becoming intensely nationalistic. A catalyst in this process was the War of 1812: "war dreadful as it is," asserted *Niles' Weekly Register,* "will not be without its benefits in giving us a NATIONAL CHARACTER, and separating us from the *strumpet governments* of Europe."

Before we examine the regional division of labor that emerged in the era from the Revolution to 1830, we must watch some people migrate over the mountains. In this table, the date in parentheses shows when each territory was admitted as a state; the figures record population:

	1790	1800	1810
Kentucky (1792)	73,677	220,955	406,511
Tennessee (1796)	35,691	105,602	261,727
Ohio (1803)		45,365	230,760

Trying to peer through and behind these statistics, we can find a pattern even though it does have several variants and some downright exceptions. The first stage in penetrating a wilderness was likely to be (a) a military expedition followed by a permanent post, or (b) fur traders, or less frequently (c) hunters or trappers. Recent research indicates, rather surprisingly, that the next step might be the establishment of a town to import supplies for the soldiers or traders. Only then did farmers come with their plows to supply the already existent local markets. In other words, commerce often preceded agriculture. That venerable symbol—the subsistence farmer—was in this sense unknown on many frontiers from their very origins, and where he did exist he probably lusted to become a commercial farmer. Looking at five towns in the Ohio valley, Pittsburgh was established because of the fort there. Formally laid out in 1764, it had 1,500 residents by 1800. The growth of St. Louis was slower. It too was started in 1764, by an expedition sent north by a wealthy French merchant in New Orleans to seek a proper location for a fur-trading factory. The 14-year-old leader of the party picked a fine site for the venture, but it was hemmed in by an Indian scare. Lexington, Kentucky, was founded in 1775; by the century's close its status as chief distributing point for western Kentucky and Tennessee had brought to it nearly 2,000 citizens and it boastfully called itself "the Philadelphia of Kentucky." Over the entire route from Pittsburgh to New Orleans, the complex of the Ohio-Mississippi rivers contained only one obstruction so severe that goods had to be portaged—falls in the Ohio. There a military post was founded in 1778 to serve as a base for sallies westward, and the next year a fledgling Louisville began. Cincinnati was planted in 1788 by a congressman from New Jersey who was also a land speculator, but the town did not begin to boom until Fort Washington was built four years later as an Indian post. Soldiers eager to buy goods were constantly passing through. The items in local stores with the highest turnover are revealed in a comment by a future president, William Henry Harrison: "I . . . saw more drunken men in forty-eight hours succeeding my arrival at Cincinnati than I had in all my previous life."

If we stand back to scan the entire period from the Revolution to the Civil War, we detect a distinct reorientation of the dynamic segments of the American society. As late as 1810, even while new towns were developing beyond the mountains, the men who were the chief agents in remolding institutions were the merchants of seaboard cities. They stood squarely in the littoral, and their gaze was fixed eastward across the Atlantic. Their interests were commercial. The ensuing decades saw them turn as on a pivot. For the last century the merchant marine of the United States has been trivial, and largely confined to the coasting trade. Whereas the eighteenth century had seen entrepreneurs begin to forsake the deep water in order to forage up the rivers and lakes, in the nineteenth they put their capital in overland transportation, into factories, into the exploitation of the various hinterlands. The emerging attitude of American businessman and statesmen has drawn an apt label: continentalism.

One spur that drove Americans over the Appalachians was very old; it antedated the origins of white civilization in the New World. The polite term is land hunger; the nasty epithet is greed. During the first two centuries of the American experience, a striking impulse for change seems to underlie an equally strong urge to remain persistently the same. Let us take various dates as water-marks and ask: What word or phrase at that time would have infused the greatest emotional charge into Americans? In 1630 the word would be God. In 1776 it would be Liberty. But at both dates the next most potent word would be the same: Land. It was the road to wealth—the embodiment of status—the mechanism for playing a hunch, for taking a flyer, similar to gambling in corporate stocks in the twentieth century. To get more land, frontiersmen would subject their families to appalling risks. One morning a settler took the household's only gun and went into the forest to look for game. While he was gone a small war party of Indians came to the cabin. To protect her children the woman bolted the door. Some Indians chopped a hole in it with their hatchets. They then crawled inside. Others entered the shack by dropping down the chimney. When the white man returned he found that all of the intruders were dead. Their blood and brains bespattered the floor and the walls. The woman had killed them with an axe. Subjection to dangers of this sort was merely an aspect of daily routine to thousands of men who were desperate to gain title to a slice of wilderness. But while greed was a constant in the westering, other stimuli around 1800 were new: federal public-lands policy, the huge expansion of cotton cultivation and development of manufacturing, road construction, steamboats, the Napoleonic Wars and foreign markets.

In the epoch from 1789 to 1860, Congress spent more time considering the federal lands than any other range of topics. The sectional conflicts were pronounced. Although the alignments were shifting as the several regions acquired new sets of interests and attitudes, a few generalizations can be made. The rise of factories in New England caused spokesmen for that section to want to impede the westward flow so that they could keep a large force of cheap labor. Usually they sought to keep the price of public lands as high as possible. The South, heavily dependent on imports, understandably wanted to keep tariffs low; it too favored high prices for public lands as an alternate source of federal revenues. Westerners to a man wanted cheap land and a lot of it. Out of this welter of cross-purposes came a series of laws:

	Minimum Area in Acres	Minimum Price per Acre	Terms of Sale
1785	640	$1	no credit
1796	640	$2	$\frac{1}{2}$ down; $\frac{1}{2}$ in one year
1800	320	$2	$\frac{1}{4}$ down; $\frac{1}{4}$ each year
1804	160	same	same
1820	80	$1.25	no credit

When preparing its huge tracts of western lands for sale to private owners, the federal government marked off squares measuring a mile on each side. Each square was called a section, and the quarter section—160 acres—came to be the typical landholding through the Old Northwest. The chief fault of the system, with its total disregard of natural topography, was its visual monotony; the checkerboards of mid-America can still be seen in any aerial photograph or observed at ground level in boring cities like Indianapolis. The virtue of rectangular surveying was that it facilitated land deals. Even with it, the litigious settlers were forever in court over land titles. In spite of its defects, clearly it was superior to the practices followed by states in disposing of their public lands. When Virginia was disposing of land in what became Kentucky, two thirds of all grants were at least 1,000 acres. Or who could be sure of the location of a tract of 500 acres as it was described in the Kentucky survey of 1 May, 1781: "Beginning on David Vance's west line of his pre-emption at two sugar trees and an ash, thence north 30° 155 poles to three sugar trees then north 60° west 330 poles crossing two small branches to two ashes and sugar trees thence south 30° west 377 poles to a buckeye, hoop ash, and sugar tree, thence 60° east 330 poles to the beginning." Particularly allowing for the passage of time and the disappearance of vegetable landmarks, trying to use these directions would be similar to deciphering verbal instructions by a choreographer.

While the new frontier spawned legal disputes, it was also fertile in benefits. A man might come home to find his family slaughtered by Indians, but the survivors would not starve. A modern hunter would choke at one episode: on 17 May, 1796, a group of men got together at Irvine's Lick, Kentucky, and that day killed 7,941 squirrels. The name of the rendezvous (referring to a salt "lick" or surface deposit which drew game and nourished livestock) shows in strong accents the crucial significance of any sort of seasoning, any hint of variety in the frontier diet. (The "licks" were also often sources for saltpeter for gunpowder.) When one Hoosier heard the Biblical account of Lot's wife being converted into a pillar of salt because she turned to look back on the Sodomites, he remarked, "Had that happened to her in Indiana, the cows would have licked her up before sundown."

In addition to federal public-lands policy, the settlement of the Old West was hastened by two inventions. The last to be made but the first to be influential was the cotton gin. New techniques for spinning and weaving cotton goods had made them into a major fabric in Great Britain. A market for raw cotton already existed. Americans were desperate for a new cash crop. The South especially had been hit hard by Independence. Indigo had ceased to be profitable with the cancellation of the English bounty. The markets for tobacco had been glutted for decades. With the development of the cotton gin in 1793 (see the adjoining insert, How Did It Work? #3, for an explanation of this device) cultivation of cotton became practical throughout most of the South (Document 11-1).

As the South expanded westward, the ambivalent hostility of Southerners toward Europe was perhaps even intensified. Nearly everybody in Kentucky for instance would have agreed with Jefferson's 1796 characterization of the Federalists as "Anglican, monarchical, & aristocratical . . . timid men who prefer the calm of despotism to the boisterous sea of liberty, British merchants & Americans trading on British capital, speculators & holders in the banks & public funds . . . their heads shorn by the whore England." Planters in 1800 may have been parochial and domineering, but they had not yet acquired the rancor and spite that would typify many of their breed a half century later. A young divinity student from Harvard, William Ellery Channing, tutored for a time near Richmond and liked what he saw:

> Here I find great vices, but greater virtues. There is one single trait that attaches me . . . more than all the virtues of New England. They *love money less* than we do. . . . They are more disinterested. Their patriotism is not tied to their purse-strings. . . . Could I only take from the Virginians their *sensuality* and their *slaves,* I should think them the greatest people in the world. . . . They address each other and converse together with the same familiarity and frankness which they used to do when they were boys. How different from our Northern manners! There avarice and ceremony at the age of twenty graft the coldness and unfeelingness of age on the disinterested ardor of youth.

Cotton Gin

The matured cotton flower, or boll, consists of the cotton fibres and the seeds, which are buried in its midst. There are two basic types of cotton. Sea Island is characterized by long fibres, suitable for the most delicate textiles, and smooth seeds; it requires specific climatic conditions available in the United States only along the South Carolina and Georgia coasts. Upland cotton is hardier, and will grow throughout most of the American South. Its shorter fibres are suitable for making many different weights of cloth, but its seeds are covered with many small burrs which cling to the fibre. The smooth seeds of Sea Island cotton can be removed by merely passing the bolls through two rollers, set closely enough that the seeds cannot pass through. But if you try to treat upland cotton in this way, the closely adhering seeds will be crushed between the rollers before they will pass through. Before Eli Whitney devised the cotton gin in 1793, upland cotton had to be cleaned by hand, and it took a worker a full day to produce one pound. With the gin, he could do ten—fifty if he had a horse to turn the cylinder.

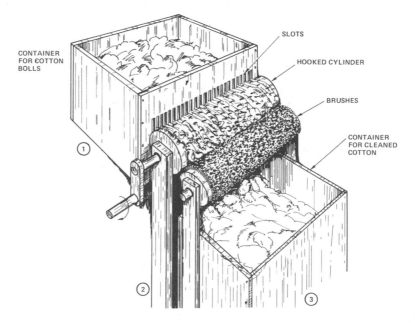

CONTAINER FOR COTTON BOLLS

SLOTS

HOOKED CYLINDER

BRUSHES

CONTAINER FOR CLEANED COTTON

(1) The cotton bolls are placed in a container, pierced by slots along one side. The slots must be narrow enough to prevent the seeds from passing through them.

(2) A cylinder, covered with small hooks, is turned by a crank. The hooks just pass through the slots, and pull the fibres loose from the seeds and onto the surface of the cylinder.

(3) A second cylinder, covered with brushes, and spinning in the other direction, cleans the cotton off the hooks. It drops into a container below. Both cylinders can be turned by the same crank, by means of a simple belting arrangement not shown.

It was only after the invention of the gin that cotton, formerly a luxury textile, became the world's cheapest, and the Southern economy, languishing for a cash crop, boomed. But Whitney himself reaped very little from his discovery. The gin was so simple that any home craftsman could make one, and Whitney's years of litigation in defence of his patents probably didn't even pay for themselves. In later years he made substantial sums in the gun business, where he is often credited as the "inventor" of the system of interchangeable parts. Although he was surely not that, he was the first to use them on a large and orderly scale.

The other big innovation in technology at the end of the century was the improved steam engine—with its soon-to-be offspring, the steamboat and the railroad locomotive. A sharp contrast is apparent between these innovations and the cotton gin. Whitney's invention seems almost to stand without antecedents, in splendid isolation, whereas mastery of the relations of heat to water was puzzled out in a prolonged series of steps. Robert Fulton is still widely regarded as the "inventor" of the steamboat, and the run of his *Clermont* up the Hudson in 1807 is lauded as epochal. The facts are otherwise. The crucial improvement in the efficiency of the steam engine was made in England, by James Watt when he devised a condensing chamber and a new set of valves. (See the insert in Chapter 5, How Did It Work? #2, and also see Document 11–2.) Even in the United States, Fulton was not the forerunner. That honor goes to John Fitch. Born in Hartford County, Connecticut in 1743, Fitch was apprenticed to watchmakers. He became a failure and a wanderer. In 1780 he drifted to the Ohio valley where he worked as a surveyor and speculated in land. Steam power, he perceived, was the key to transportation in the Mississippi basin. After 1785 he began to devote himself full-time to the project. By August, 1787, some members of the Constitutional Convention in Philadelphia could go down to the Delaware River and watch his 45-footer, with three paddle-wheels on each side. He made bigger boats. He worked up a scheme of screw propulsion. But he kept having trouble raising capital. He seemed to businessmen an unstable sort: deserting his wife, uncouth in manner, a noisy anti-Federalist, an extreme Deist like Tom Paine. His troubles ended when he killed himself in a tiny town in Kentucky in 1798. But by 1815, when the *Enterprise* docked at Louisville after a successful run against the Mississippi-Ohio currents, it was clear that he had been dead right.

Settlement of the Ohio valley had vastly increased the flow of goods. In 1799 about $1 million in commodities was received at New Orleans from upriver. By 1807 the figure had gone over $5 million. Nearly all the trade was one way. That year over 1,800 boats came downstream, but only eleven went up. The cost of overland transport was prohibitive for nearly all items. Away back in June, 1755, General Braddock was complaining that the charge for moving stores was "many times more than double the original cost of them. . . ." In the War for Independence it was logistics that swamped General Burgoyne and several other British commanders. The burdens and delays of overland transit lingered. As early as 1785 Virginia had chartered the first American turnpike company, but even on such relatively good roads, haulage cost some 15 cents per ton-mile. From interior Massachusetts it was advisable to wait for winter and ship your crops by sleigh eastward rather than drag them over the muddy trails. As late as 1814 Robert Fulton said that the "usual" charge for wagoning was 32 cents a ton-mile; two years later a Senate committee put it at 30 cents.

The same Committee Report declared: "A coal mine may exist in the

United States not more than ten miles from valuable ores of iron and other materials, and both of them be useless until a canal is established between them, as the price of land carriage is too great to be borne by either." A ton of merchandise could be brought 3,000 miles from Europe to America for $9; for that sum it could be moved only 30 miles overland. The situation can be stated in specifics. In 1816 prices were fairly high at Philadelphia. Wheat was $1.94 a bushel; corn $1.13. About 33.5 bushels of wheat weighed a ton. With wagonage at 30 cents, transport charges would devour the sales price of wheat shipped 218 miles, of corn shipped 135 miles. A committee of the New York legislature in 1817 noted that transportation costs from Buffalo to New York City were three times the value in Manhattan of wheat, 6 times for corn, 12 times for oats. Since farmers could not afford to ship their bulky products to market, they had no money to buy the lighter (more valuable per pound) manufactured goods. Even letters could not be sent easily; in 1800 the post office handled only about 3 million items—less than one per person.

Exorbitant freight charges combined with the Napoleonic Wars to give a temporary incentive to factories aimed at localized markets; a tariff wall would have had a similar impact. Pittsburgh, with nearby iron ore and coal, had the first plant in the nation to make glass using coal as fuel. In 1810 the town was producing glass worth $63,000; by 1815, $235,000. Iron mills were even bigger. The industry began as a rural trade, but very early the town's blacksmiths were getting iron bars from the countryside and forging them into tools and household utensils. They were sold to transient settlers headed farther west who had liquidated their heavy equipment before starting the arduous trip over the mountains. A nail factory was started in 1799; by 1812 there were five. The town had an air foundry, rolling mills. More than a quarter of all goods manufactured in Pittsburgh were iron products. Little capital to sustain this growth came from the East; industry was locally financed.

St. Louis got its impetus as a shipping center for lead from mines in Wisconsin or Missouri. The crude or smelted metal found two markets: glass works in Pittsburgh, or mills in Philadelphia that made gunshot. At Louisville iron manufacturing sought to exploit what contemporary accounts called the "advantage" of "working with slaves," and according to another local account a New England firm started a distillery "in a much more extensive mode than any hitherto established in the United States." The local Merchant Manufacturing Mill was six stories high and cost $150,000. The townsfolks' property, assessed at $90,000 in 1803, rose to $328,000 by 1812. By one early account, "For a length of time after the settlement of this place, lots on the principal streets were sold at from $700 to $1,400." By 1815 the same lots had gone over $4,000.

The base of Lexington was its status as emporium for a large area. Two men named Trotter did a wholesale business of $60,000 a month. In boom seasons, others grossed $100,000 monthly. "Men were tempted to engage in business with slender capital and fake and chimerical hopes." Mercantile profits were put into manufacturing. With abundant nearby supplies of hemp and wool, mills were started to produce bagging and rope and sails of duck. In 1810 a newspaper said that all 19 of the local ropewalks were profitable; the next year the output of hemp products was estimated at $900,000. At war's end *Niles' Weekly Register* reported that "*town lots* sell nearly as high as in Boston, New York, Philadelphia, or Baltimore, which shows that this is not a place in the wilderness, as some people suppose it to be." The same journal was lured into a bad prophecy: "the manufacturing establishments of this town, have reached an eminence which ensures their permanent prosperity and usefulness." Actually the steamboats, by diverting trade to Louisville with its favorable site on the river, left landlocked Lexington to stagnate.

To support its rapid if ill-starred surge of industrialization, Lexington had to rely on both slave labor and mechanization. "The want of hands excites the industry of the inhabitants of this country. This scarcity proceeds from the inhabitants giving so decided a preference to agriculture, that there are very few of them who put their children to any trade, wanting their services in the field." Here a standard of comparison is ready to hand between the newly opened West and France. A distinguished economic historian guessed that all of France at the end of the Napoleonic Wars did not contain more than fifteen enterprises having steam engines. Most of them were used to pump mines. In contrast, both Pittsburgh and Lexington had factories that themselves manufactured steam engines. By 1815 Lexington had six mills driven by steam: grinding grain, spinning and weaving cloth, making paper. In Pittsburgh a flour mill was run by steam. Instead of the customary trip-hammers powered by water wheels, its iron industry boasted a rolling mill that used steam. Visitors to Cincinnati admired its nine-story steam-powered mill down by the river. Rapid mechanization in the Ohio valley reached out even to smaller towns; for instance within six miles of Mount Pleasant, Ohio were located nine merchant mills (flour for export), two grist mills, twelve saw mills, a paper mill, a woolen factory with four looms, two fulling mills.

Prosperity was widespread. A merchant in Cincinnati, who said that he was "making money very fast," declared that another man who had come from New England six years earlier with a mere $300 had traded with New Orleans and now was worth $10,000 in cash. In St. Louis good times seemed boundless. Thomas Hart Benton, later famed as a United States Senator, arrived there in 1815 with $400; four years later he claimed to be "comfortably established," and wailed that if only he had started with $20,000 he could have made $250,000. Of Louisville we read: "The capital accumulation there is very respectable, and it is rising in importance with a rapidity never before excelled, even in the western country." During the War of 1812 many soldiers passed through Cincinnati, leaving behind them a needed supply of hard cash. An influx of civilians since 1810 had caused a housing shortage and driven prices above their normally high level. Meanwhile the Old Southwest benefited after 1812 by a rising trend in cotton prices.

The general ebullience of the expanding frontier did not stave off postwar collapse of the economy. Detailed discussion of two sets of causes for the depression must be postponed until Chapter 12 where they can be analyzed in a more tidy way, but they need to be mentioned here. They were financial maladjustments and renewed competition by imports from Europe, especially manufactures from Great Britain. The former in turn needs to be split into subcategories. Federal fiscal policies did much to restrain inflation prior to the war. When the charter of the first Bank of the United States expired in 1811, it was not renewed. States gave charters to many banks that were deficient in both capital and specie, and the federal government no longer had an effective agency to bridle them. Credit was expanded wildly. As the volume of bank notes in circulation grew, the issuing institutions could not redeem them in specie. The value of paper money dipped drastically. Federal fiscal policy in wartime zoomed the inflation. By 1814 the banks of all regions except New England had suspended specie payments. An effort was made to recoup the situation by chartering the Second Bank of the United States in 1816. But the network of credit relations was too unstable to endure; a blow at any vital fissure would have wide repercussions. A creeping recession began in some sectors of the economy soon after the return of peace. An abrupt and sharp tightening of credit brought financial panic in 1819. The ensuing depression was more or less protracted in different sections.

Cotton cultivation had become almost synonymous with expansion in the South. The phenomenal gross returns from the cotton crop of 1815— $18,526,589—gave planters the capital to buy more land and bring it into cultivation. With cotton bringing 30 cents a pound, wheat $2 a bushel, tobacco 14 cents, the public demand for federal lands soared. It was financed by a steady growth of paper money. The notes in circulation from all banks rose from $45 million in 1812 to $100 million in 1817. The second Bank of the United States within two years of its formation issued $8.3 million in its Bank notes and made loans of $41 million against the collateral of real estate and securities in state banks. As the price of cotton doubled from June 1814 to June 1816, the most intense scrambles around the federal public-land offices took place in Alabama and Mississippi. From 1814 to 1819 the American output of cotton more than doubled. Then the bubble broke. The weighted average price of cotton, 29.8 cents in 1817, was only 14.3 cents in 1819. One consequence was a collapse of land prices. Tracts that had been valued as high as $69 an acre were now sold for $2. Since banks had loaned so much money against the security of real estate, they now found themselves foreclosing on property that was severely devalued and they in turn were forced into insolvency (many of them of course had been *de facto* insolvent from the time they opened their doors). Another consequence of the Panic of 1819 was that Congress omitted

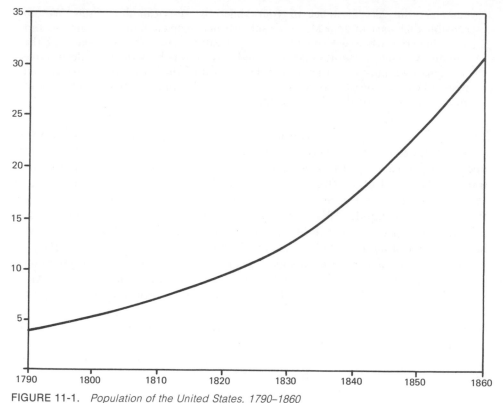

FIGURE 11-1. *Population of the United States, 1790–1860*

the provision for sales on credit when it passed a new public-lands act in 1820 (see above, the table on land values).

Settlement of the Gulf Coast is inseparable from the existence of slavery. The South had wallowed in this dilemma from the beginning. The more labor a planter could get, the more acres he could work and the more tobacco or cotton he could sell. But whites were not willing to migrate into the wilderness to work for wages. For decades indentured servants had been a stopgap, but by the nineteenth century this solution was no longer available. The only way to recruit more workers for the frontier plantations was physical coercion—slavery. To complicate matters further from the viewpoint of the plantation owners, the legal importation of slaves had been halted by Congress in 1808. Americans had been trying since colonial times to abolish the slave trade. In 1772 Virginia's House of Burgesses had sent a petition off to London:

> The importation of slaves hath long been considered a trade of great inhumanity and under its present encouragement we have too great reason to fear it will

261

endanger the very existence of your Majesty's American dominions. We are sensible that some of your Majesty's subjects may reap emoluments from this sort of traffic, but when we consider that it greatly retards the settlement of the colonies with more useful inhabitants and may in time have the most destructive influence, we presume to hope that the interest of the few will be disregarded when placed in competition with the security and happiness of such numbers of your Majesty's dutiful and loyal subjects.

The appeal went ignored. Virginia passed several laws itself for the suppression of importations; all were overruled by the King in Council. These vetoes became a grievance in the Declaration of Independence. Virginia banned the trade in 1778; all other states did so by 1807 (South Carolina reopened it in 1803). Many men in the South expected slavery to die out. In 1794 President Washington declared: "Were it not that I am in principle against selling negroes, as you would cattle in a market, I would not in twelve months hence be possessed of a single one as a slave. I shall be happily mistaken if they are not found to be a very troublesome species of property ere many years have passed over our heads." The Constitutional ban on congressional action (Art. I, Sec. 9) expired in 1807, and a federal prohibition took effect. In 1820 the importation of slaves was put on the same footing as piracy and made punishable by death. A substantial illegal trade continued, but for obvious reasons no reliable estimates of its extent can be made.

Even without legal importations, the slave population increased roughly in proportion to the growth of the population at large (in millions):

	national population	number of slaves
1790	4.0	.7
1800	5.3	.9
1810	7.2	1.2
1820	9.7	1.5
1830	12.9	2.0
1840	17.1	2.5
1850	23.2	3.2
1860	31.4	3.9

Though the ratio of slaves to general population declined, the slow rate of decline is remarkable in light of the surge of white immigration after about 1845.

Whitney's cotton gin and rising cotton prices had combined to swamp

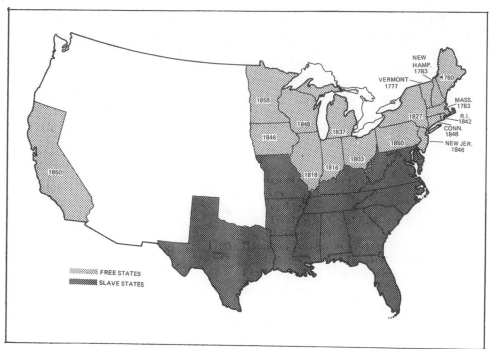

FIGURE 11-2. *Elimination of Slavery in the North*

the Southern conscience. Sectional conflict was nothing new in the United States: Madison had forewarned of it in the Federal Convention, and it had appeared in every presidential election since 1800. But it was the westward thrust of cotton culture that produced the first forthright assertions ever made in Congress that slavery was not a lamentable evil but was rather an absolute good. The sectional split on the issue was almost total. From Delaware northward, slavery had disappeared as an efficient organization of production. New England and the Middle States had never managed to develop a plantation staple such as tobacco or cotton or rice or sugar. Northern employers simply lost interest in slavery; as their business became increasingly urban and mechanized, they made no effort to buy and exploit blacks in factories. Ownership of slaves would have brought inflexible labor costs into complex relations where variable costs could be a key to survival. So Northern states enacted various schemes for the gradual abolition of the institution: a common policy was to provide that no person born henceforth should be a slave, so that within a generation, hereditary servitude would disappear. By 1860, slavery had simply vanished north of the Mason-Dixon line.

263

To the five seaboard states in the South, five more had been added by 1818. To these ten states, slavery was the livelihood of the upper classes. The non-slave states numbered twelve. But applications for admission by Alabama and Missouri were pending. Alabama's admission was certain. Therefore many congressmen from the North were unwilling to admit Missouri also if its constitution permitted slavery. The issues could be posed thus: What was the status of slavery in the Louisiana Purchase? How far could Congress go in imposing conditions on a Territory that sought admission as a state? Slavery had been legal in Louisiana Territory under both French and Spanish rule. When Congress was passing the fundamental laws for Upper Louisiana, none of them mentioned slavery. But the United States never disavowed certain pro-slavery regulations for the area involved, and the treaty of 1803 had guaranteed that the property of the inhabitants would not be molested. A senator from New York had argued that the word "property" did not include slaves, but James Monroe, who had negotiated the treaty, certainly thought it did. The forementioned senator asserted that Congress had plenary powers over slavery in purchased areas. A representative from Massachusetts pointed out that when Louisiana was admitted as a state in 1812, Congress had imposed conditions. Flak was heavy.

Before we take a look at the highpoints of the debates, it seems wise to record some predictions made at the time. James Monroe, now president, and his secretary of state, John Quincy Adams, talked about the slavery issue. Monroe said that it would be "winked away by a compromise." Adams replied that the problem was destined "to survive his political and individual life and mine." A month later Adams talked about the situation with John C. Calhoun of South Carolina, now secretary of war, and stated that if slavery caused a dissolution of the Union, universal emancipation would be inevitable. After the rhetoric in Congress had occupied nearly all of 1820, Adams thought that secession "for the cause of slavery" would mean a civil war and that "its result must be the extirpation of slavery from the whole continent."

In 1818 Missouri applied for admission as a state. A representative from New York moved that the act should prohibit further importation of slaves and that all slave children born after statehood should become free at the age of 25. Constitutional questions abound, for those who appreciate niceties. Congress is forbidden to tax an export from any state; if it bans importation of slaves into Missouri, is that equivalent to taxing their exportation from, say, Virginia? Certainly the effect on the market price would be similar. Take another. Article IV, Section 2 of the Constitution guarantees certain rights to "citizens"—Does the clause apply to blacks? The House contained one member who had been a delegate to the Federal Convention, and he now claimed responsibility for inclusion of the pertinent formula and defined what he thought it meant:

> I perfectly knew that there did not then exist such a thing in the Union as a black or colored citizen, nor could I then have conceived it possible such a thing could

ever have existed in it; nor notwithstanding all that is said on the subject, do I now believe one does exist in it.

A similar viewpoint would have enormous repercussions when it cropped up in 1857 in some opinions on the case of Dred Scott (near the end of Chapter 15). On this occasion the speaker went on to charge, with justice, that Northern states were trying to drive out their populations of free blacks "by treating them, on every occasion with the most marked contempt. . . ."

The constitutions and laws of existing states proved that neither North nor South thought a black fit for citizenship. No state had passed a statute making him a citizen or admitting him to the militia. The constitution of Kentucky explicitly laid down that "every white male (negroes, mulattoes, and Indians excepted) shall enjoy the right of elector"; the same provision was in the constitutions of Ohio and Connecticut. Vermont and New Hampshire barred blacks from their militias. Indiana and North Carolina would admit a black to the suffrage, but would not permit any black to testify as a witness in any suit against a white. Congress in May, 1820, made only free white males eligible for the office of mayor of Washington, D.C. Southerners gibed that many Northern states had laws against miscegenation. Their opponents replied that these statutes were not discriminatory since they impartially forbade intermarriage to both whites and blacks.

It is worthwhile to look at the extreme pro-slavery position, not because most Southern members of Congress endorsed it—clearly they did not—but because it was a view that would steadily win adherents over the coming decades. A senator from South Carolina made a passionate argument that slavery was a beneficial institution. Citing Greek and Roman precedents, when he turned to the Bible he relied especially on Leviticus xxv: 44–46: "Mr. President, the Scriptures teach us that slavery was universally practiced among the holy fathers." This senator was an extremist in other respects also: an all-out exponent of state rights, adamant upon the strict construction of the Federal Constitution and upon denial of implied powers. Another plank in the pro-slavery platform was an assertion that the Northwest Ordinance was not valid. The author of this thesis also was not typical. He was notorious for long-winded arguments; on one occasion when he was a member of the House, he proclaimed that he was not going to speak for the day only but for posterity, prompting Henry Clay to remark that he hoped the gentlemen did not intend to go on talking until his audience arrived. In regard to the Ordinance of 1787, he averred that the Continental Congress at that time had represented states rather than the sovereign people. Therefore the law was not binding in the new states of the Old Northwest: Ohio, Indiana, and Illinois.

The possibility of compromise arose when Maine, heretofore a part of Massachusetts, applied for admission as a state with the consent of its parent body. Clay took the lead in the complicated negotiations. The resulting package opened the door to statehood for both Maine and Missouri. By an amendment to the measure for the latter, slavery was banned from any lands acquired by the Louisiana Purchase north of 36 degrees 30 minutes (the southern boundary of Missouri) except the new state.

The hassle was not yet over. The very act of Congress that authorized Missouri to elect members of a constitutional convention limited suffrage in that election to white male citizens. When the delegates assembled, they enthusiastically went along with Congress. Their constitution sanctioned slavery. Further, it instructed the future legislature "to prevent free negroes and mulattoes from coming to and settling in this state, under any pretext whatsoever." Did this provision infringe Article IV, Section 2 of the Federal Constitution? The Missouri document reached Congress for sanction in November, 1820. For three months history became farce. Clay worked up another compromise, by which Congress sanctioned the state constitution but decreed that a certain clause in it should never be construed in any way that denied to any person a right or privilege which he could claim under the Constitution of the United States. Moreover, Missouri must affirm by "a solemn public act" that it accepted this condition. The state was as recalcitrant as it could have been; its spiteful retort was that Congress had no right to impose such a condition. Nonetheless, President Monroe the following autumn declared that the admission of Missouri as a state was complete. In 1825 Missouri by law excluded free blacks and mulattoes unless they were citizens of another state. To meet that qualification, they had to present naturalization papers. Since they had never been naturalized, the proviso was a malicious jest. And in 1847 came the ultimate: "No free negro or mulatto shall under any pretext emigrate into this State from any State or Territory."

Given the contours of white minds in 1820, no firmer move toward freedom and equality was possible than the Missouri Compromise. In retrospect, its significance was as a step in welding the South into a self-conscious minority. As late as the Federal Convention and after, a man identified with his province, not with his section; a reputable historian has denied that a "Southern accent" existed in the oral speech of that period. Further, bitter divisions within states were common; consider the rancor of the upcountry against the seaboard in the Carolinas. Now the slave states began to turn waspish toward critics and to form into an enclave. Worse, they were drawn together to justify their ugliest feature, one that could not be justified. Thenceforth in the South, the cause of state rights—a cause that had been and can be honorable—tended to fuse with rationalizations for the "peculiar institution." To cite one change, the large numbers of free blacks in Charleston had been relatively free from molestation by the authorities just previous to the debate; starting in 1822 (partly in reaction to a slave uprising), South Carolina began to wantonly toss free black seamen into jail.

So far no historian has made an exhaustive effort to correlate the public furor over Missouri with the concurrent business depression. We can guess that distraught farmers or unemployed workers were especially vulnerable to agitation over a political crisis. But it must be noted that hard times were much different in various places. Pittsburgh for instance was badly hit, and early hit. Several of its new factories could not stand against the postwar flow of British imports. The first drop was felt in iron products and textiles; by February, 1817, local manufacturing "has lately suffered the most alarming depression." Then glass and leather faltered. A pedestrian through the industrial district in 1821 reported "there used to be a terrible racket, and clattering of hammers in the two steam engine factories; now it is all over—you might rock a child to sleep in an unfinished cylinder." But by Christmas Day of 1824 a newspaper could boast:

> Three years ago, our population did not exceed eight thousand—it is now near eleven thousand. Many of our manufacturing establishments were then idle and vacant—they all now exhibit the pleasing bustle and busy hum of employment.

Since recovery in the town was not complete until 1825–1826, its depression had lasted about a decade. The shock to Cincinnati, a commercial rather than an industrial town, was far milder. As late as July, 1818, a local editor could write: "As yet we have felt little of it here. Our city is improving almost beyond example—we have no bankruptcies—no imprisonment for debt; but we need not expect to escape the general shock." He exaggerated. In that year imports into the town, many of them of course re-exported, were $500,000, less than a third of 1817. But the upswing came soon. Population more than doubled in the decade 1816–1826, to reach 16,000 (it rose to nearly 25,000 by 1830). In the latter year imports into Cincinnati went over $2,500,000. Their composition says much. Half was dry goods from the East. The balance included iron goods from Pittsburgh, rough timber from the Alleghenies, while upriver from New Orleans came Queensware, sugar, coffee, and tea. The chief product of the neighborhood was meat; the town shipped in that year 40,000 hogs.

The revival and further growth of western trade depended on steamboats. In 1817 the Ohio-Mississippi basin had 17 boats totalling over 3,000 tons. By 1830 it had 187 steamboats aggregating nearly 30,000. By that date steam tonnage on western waters roughly equalled the merchant steam shipping of the entire British Empire. To cope with the extreme seasonal fluctuations of water level, some western boats had amazing design. Although it dates from a little later, we may cite the *Orphan Boy*, 169 tons, built in 1841. It could carry 80 passengers along with 40 tons of freight. But it drew only 22 inches of water. Another engineering feature of early western steamboats was their cheap construction, resulting in a propensity to blow up; no sane carrier would have issued trip insurance along the Mississippi River. But of the steamboat's impact on western development there can be no doubt. According to a French official in 1824: "In the brief interval of fifteen years, many cities were formed . . . where before there were hardly the dwellings of a small town. . . . A simple mechanical device has made life both possible and comfortable in regions which heretofore had been a wilderness."

The first steamboat on the Great Lakes entered Lake Erie in 1818. She was destined to have many sisters. Their mother was the Erie Canal. This product of inspired statecraft was chiefly the work of DeWitt Clinton, former mayor of New York and, from 1817 to 1828, (usually) governor of the state. The idea was to secure for Manhattan the trade of the Old Northwest; the technique was to connect the Hudson River with Lake Ontario. Support could be rallied because farmers and townsfolk along the route would also benefit. But digging the ditch was a herculean prospect for an age that knew no steamshovels or bulldozers. Only 100 miles of canals had been built in North America; only three were more than two miles long; the longest, from Boston to the Merrimack River, was less than twenty-eight. From Albany to Buffalo was 364 miles. Begun in 1817, the Erie Canal was opened in 1825. It was 40 feet wide by 4 feet deep. Its success was instantaneous and stupendous. The cost of shipping a ton of merchandise from Buffalo to New York City fell more than 90 per cent (for instance, $100 in freight charges was reduced to $8). Within a decade, the legislature voted to enlarge it to 70 × 7 feet. Other results were manifold. The explosion of farming in the Midwest undercut the agriculture of New England, thus boosting alternative occupations in manufacturing and trade. Manhattan ensured its position as entrepot of the interior, and it outdistanced New Orleans in striving for the trade of the Ohio valley. New York state could reduce or abolish other taxes because of its revenues from Erie Canal tolls. Rival cities were lured into seeking fool's gold. An envious Pennsylvania built a crazy-quilt of canals and railroads called the Main Line. Any topographical map shows why the project was absurd (see Ways to Study History XI). The Erie Canal rose at most 650 feet above sea level, while the Main Line reached 2,200 feet. The Erie had only 84 locks, the canal sections of the Main Line had 174, and the route involved several transshipments from water to rail and back again. Other states made the same mistake as Pennsylvania. At its height in 1830, the canal-building outburst saw 4,000 miles finished or well advanced, another 7,000 started or under consideration. The waste of resources was huge. Since much of the capital was borrowed abroad, and then not repaid, the name "American" came to stink in many European noses. (See Chapter 12.)

Very early a clamor was made for the federal government to finance "internal improvements." Hamilton had alluded to the topic in his *Report on Manufactures* (mid-Chapter 9), but the first systematic appraisal came from another secretary of the treasury in 1808. The Senate asked Albert Gallatin for a report, and its reward was another masterpiece. He called for the expenditure of $20 million in federal funds. The use of each portion of such vast ventures depended on completion of the whole job; it was a lump investment. Voluntary associations or states or cities could not raise enough capital quickly to get the task over and done with. Most of the federal moneys would be spent to open up the interior. This achievement would yield disproportionate gains to a few cities (New York, Philadelphia, Baltimore). Therefore, in justice, equalizing appropriations should be made for some improvements in the South and New England even though they are more local in nature. The dividends from this project would not be only an enhancement of commerce. "No other single operation, within the power of government, can more effectually tend to strengthen and perpetuate that Union which secures external independence, domestic peace, and internal liberty."

President Jefferson was not fully convinced; as with the problems of chartering a bank or buying territory from a foreign government, he was not sure that the Constitution accorded the federal government the power to build roads or canals. He did approve expenditures on the National Road, meant to connect Cumberland, Maryland to Wheeling, Virginia (now West Virginia; this highway was also called the Cumberland Road), but only on condition of the approval of states transversed. When the second Bank of the United States was chartered in 1816, a measure provided that part of its profits should be spent on internal improvements. This bill was vetoed by President Madison on constitutional grounds. The same scruple was voiced by James Monroe in announcing a veto in 1822. An exactly contrary ground was taken by John Quincy Adams in his annual message to Congress in 1825 (Document 11-3). Andrew Jackson, a darling to many recent historians, has gotten much attention because of a veto message in 1830. Admittedly his language is forthright:

> If it be the wish of the people that the construction of roads and canals should be conducted by the Federal Government, it is not only highly expedient, but indispensably necessary, that a previous amendment of the Constitution, delegating the necessary power and defining and restricting its exercise with reference to the sovereignty of the States, should be made.

But since these remarks are mere footnotes on a bill that gave road funds to a private company building entirely within Kentucky, we cannot take them as serious indications that Constitutional scruples alone were inhibiting Republicans from interstate transportation projects. It seems that transportation funding, then as now, would depend more on special economic interests than on grand designs initiated by the central government.

From 1815 to 1860, businessmen in America did an about-face. From preoccupation with Canton and Bristol, they thought about the Old Northwest or the trans-Mississippi prairies. The westward movement sprang from discernible interlocking factors: prior occupation of the better lands in the East, growth of population that caused spurts of movement out of settled areas, construction of canals and better roads, introduction of the steamship, and, after 1830, the building of railroads. Some consequences are also clear. The spread of cotton culture meant an enormous increase in the volume of exports from the United States. This expansion overseas prompted a multiplication and diversification of service industries (shipping lines, banks, insurance companies, brokerage firms). The growth of slavery provided a stable market for standardized goods made in Northern factories such as cheap clothing and brogans. But it raised the fear that slaveholders would monopolize Western lands to the detriment of yeomen farmers. (See Lincoln's point at the end of Chapter 15). This menace was an indispensable element in the emergent sectional conflict (Chapters 14 and 15). In the event, the best solution the contestants could find was to fight it out.

Ways to Study History XI

Get thee to an atlas. The physical setting of an event is often influential in shaping its course; sometimes it is determinative. We have seen how the attributes of some states made it almost mandatory for them to promptly ratify the Constitution (end of Chapter 8). The flow of Americans across the Appalachians makes sense if it is studied with the aid of a good topographical map showing not only rivers but also other passes through the mountains. Yet many readers have only rudimentary knowledge of geography.

The accumulation of data about the earth's surface has called forth both patience and ingenuity. In the sixteen century the Italians dominated cartography; in the seventeenth the Dutch; by the eighteenth the English and French. The creative mapmakers were to be found in the leading commercial nations. Persons accustomed to consulting maps solely to learn the location of the relevant superhighway might be astounded to hear the variety of data contained in a good atlas. In studying the voyages of Columbus, for instance (see the opening of Chapter 1 and Ways to Study History I), it is useful to know the direction and approximate force of ocean currents, and maps showing these facts are readily available. It is also illuminating to know the direction and velocity of the winds in various places at certain seasons of the year; such data can be found in any decent atlas.

One problem in cartography is insoluble: the rounded surface of the globe cannot be portrayed on a flat sheet of paper without distortion. Many partial solutions to this dilemma have been devised; you must seek out the projection suited to your purposes in hand. The best atlas now available to English-speaking readers is *The Times Atlas of the World* (five volumes collected into one, 1968). This volume is too expensive for ordinary persons, but fortunately we have a usable desk atlas in *Goode's World Atlas* (revised frequently for many years by Edward B. Espenshade).

Document 11-1

Probably the single most important factor in the American economy from 1790 to 1860—looming above even the development of factories or the Erie Canal or the origins of railroads—was the growth of cotton plantations and exports. Some aspects are summarized here.

	Exports of Cotton (100,000 lbs.)	Price Wholesale of Cotton (cents)/lb.	Terms of Trade (1790 = 100)
1791	1.89		78
1792	1.38		69
1793	4.88		90
1794	16		80
1795	62		124
1796	61		130
1797	38		125
1798	94		163
1799	95		163
1800	178	.24	117
1801	210	.44	129
1802	280	.19	118
1803	411	.19	113
1804	381	.20	110
1805	403	.23	112
1806	375	.22	109
1807	662	.215	109
1808	120	.19	93
1809	532	.16	90
1810	939	.16	99
1811	621	.155	106
1812	289	.105	97

Document 11-2

In Great Britain by the late nineteenth century the accessible waterfalls for industrial power had been pre-empted. This deficiency might have seriously impeded the further development of cotton-textile manufacturing had it not been for James Watt's inventions that made possible the use of coal as a power source. Watt, trained in Glasgow and London as a maker of scientific apparatus, greatly improved the efficiency of the steam engine. This account of his achievement was published in London in 1835. (See also this chapter's discussion of rising western industry, and How Did It Work? # 2 in Chapter 5).

It is not a little remarkable that his patent, "for lessening the consumption of steam and fuel in fire engines," should have been taken out in the same years as Arkwright's patent for spinning with rollers, namely, 1769—one of the most brilliant eras in the annals of British genius . . . .

Watt laboured incessantly to perfect this important and complicated engine, and took out three other patents in 1781, 1782, and 1784, for great and essential improvements . . .: 1st. The condensation of the steam in a separate vessel: this increased the original powers of the engine, giving to the atmospheric pressure, and to the counter-weight, their full energy, while, at the same time, the waste of steam was greatly diminished. 2d. The employment of steam pressure, instead of that of the atmosphere: this accomplished a still further diminution of the waste, and was fertile in advantages, as it rendered the machine more manageable, particularly by enabling the operator at all times, and without trouble, to suit the power of the engine to its load of work, however variable and increasing. The third improvement was the double impulse, which may be considered as the finishing touch given to the engine, by which its action is rendered nearly as uniform as the water-wheel. . . .

Document 11-3

As part of his expansive view of the scope of federal powers, John Quincy Adams requested a national university and a national astronomical observatory. He also wanted enlarged expenditures on canals, roads, and harbors. In his first annual message to Congress in 1825, he reported that the Board of Engineers for Internal Improvement had been busily at work.

They have completed the surveys necessary for ascertaining the practicability of a canal from the Chesapeake Bay to the Ohio River, and are preparing a full report on that subject, which, when completed, will be laid before you. The same observation is to be made with regard to the two other objects of national importance upon which the Board have been occupied, namely, the accomplishment of a national road from this city to New Orleans, and the practicability of uniting the waters of Lake Memphramagog with Connecticut River and the improvement of the navigation of that river. . . .

The acts of Congress of the last session relative to the surveying, marking, or laying out roads in the Territories of Florida, Arkansas, and Michigan, from Missouri to Mexico, and for the continuation of the Cumberland road, are, some of them fully executed, and others in the process of execution. . . . The continuation of the Cumberland road, the most important of them all, after surmounting no inconsiderable difficulty in fixing upon the direction of the road, has commenced under the most promising auspices, with the improvements of recent invention in the mode of construction, and with the advantage of a great reduction in the comparative cost of the work. . . . The great object of the institution of civil government is the improvement of the condition of those who are parties to the social compact, and no government, in whatever form constituted, can accomplish the lawful ends of its institution but in proportion as it improves the condition of those over whom it is established. Roads and canals, by multiplying and facilitating the communications and intercourse between distant regions and multitudes of men, are among the most important means of improvement. . . .

Politicians and Bankers

Earlier, say in the sixteenth century, European powers often made foreign policy without much heed of business relations. Diplomacy was shaped by dynastic rather than by economic considerations. But by the mid-seventeenth century the promotion of foreign trade had become vital; one eminent scholar has labelled the Anglo-Dutch wars of that epoch the most "purely commercial" conflicts in modern times. By the early nineteenth century the contours of Great Britain as the workshop of the world were increasingly clear. The Industrial Revolution had vastly increased the efficiency particularly of the textile and iron trades. A swelling supply of products from factories was not matched by the growth of domestic demand. To safeguard the stability of sterling, the British government after 1815 followed a harsh deflationary policy of retiring the huge public debt. The result was falling prices and flaring social unrest, which manifested itself in such ugly episodes as riots leading to the Peterloo massacre of 1819. The next year London merchants, the Chamber of Commerce in Glasgow, woolen manufacturers in Howick—all were beseeching Parliament to lower the barriers to trade so that they could sell more goods abroad. Clearly the most alluring target was the United States. But Congress too was subject to pressures. Since 1815 marginal manufacturers, created and nourished by wartime scarcities and the Embargo, had been damaged or destroyed by the inflow of cheap British goods. Some distressed industrial districts such as Pittsburgh had come to the high-tariff protectionist position that would typify them for more than a century. Congress had responded in 1816 by passing the first frankly protective (as distinguished from revenue-producing) duties against some imports. The British government was desperately eager to stimulate the sale of British goods in American markets. Thus the new age was characterized by a complex interplay of economics with politics and diplomacy; the nature of the web is suggested by the very phrase that was used for the classical theories of Adam Smith and David Ricardo: "political economy." It was in this context that the United States arrived at a signal monument in its foreign policy, the Monroe Doctrine—and then used the Royal Navy to make it effective.

Questions of Anglo-American trade were tangled with independence for Latin America. Since 1809 a series of revolutions had deposed Spanish rule in many areas. If it could be re-established, those potential markets might be closed to American and British ships. The English could not well bear further losses in 1820. They were suffering a disastrous decline in exports, and the prime minister reported that it was due "principally, if not exclusively" to a decline in shipments to the United States (Document 12-1). Another lord arguing for freer trade summed up the situation:

> Their Lordships, he was sure, were well aware that in the year previous to the commencement of the unfortunate war which terminated in the establishment of American independence, our exports to the United States did not amount to more than £3,000,000, whereas at present they amounted to no less a sum then £30,000,000. Was this great and amazing increase the result of restrictive laws and provisions? Certainly not: *it was the result of the increased prosperity and population of those states, and of their becoming, in consequence of it, great consumers of our produce and manufactures.*

The truth of this appraisal was obvious, but nonetheless the British still barred American ships from their West Indies. In retaliation Congress in 1820 ordained total nonintercourse with British ships from all British colonies in America. Then the bargaining started. When the English minister called at the State Department, the secretary told him that the United States had "no disposition to encroach upon" any British possession in the Western Hemisphere. Adams gave an adumbration of the Monroe Doctrine: "Keep what is yours, but leave the rest of the continent to us." In a public address on the Fourth of July, 1821, the secretary of state gave a bad pummeling to the English lion.

Adams knew how to keep the heat on. In 1822 Parliament opened certain "free ports" in the West Indies to American vessels on the same terms as British vessels, provided the United States gave reciprocal privileges. A few months later America rebuffed the gesture. Congress decreed that British ships from the specified free ports should be treated like American bottoms from the same harbors, on condition that American ships *and goods* at those ports were treated like carriers and cargoes "from elsewhere." The British minister called at the State Department to ask what "elsewhere" meant. It meant, replied Adams, from anywhere else. Here was a head-on assault against imperial preference. An English official asked how Americans would react if Britain demanded that West Indies sugar be admitted to New York on the same terms as sugar grown in Louisiana. But rhetoric could not alter facts. About a sixth of all British exports were being sold in the United States. About 90 per cent of all American imports of textiles came from the British Isles. England hoped to build these markets further, but factory construction in New England and the Middle States threatened to reduce them drastically. (See the end of this chapter and Document 12-1).

Here Spain and France intrude on events. A constitutionalist rebellion was under way in Spain. The French king, having publicly affirmed the most extreme doctrines of monarchy and legitimacy, in April, 1823, sent his armies sweeping over the Pyrenees to smash the revolt. This fanned the old fears that European powers would help the Spanish monarch restore his rule throughout Latin America. The English foreign minister was disturbed. He received the American minister, Richard Rush, who commented that he took comfort in knowing that Great Britain would not allow France to reinstate Spanish rule in the New World. In reply, the English minister asked: How would your government like to announce such a policy jointly with mine? Diplomats have a way of agreeing "in principle" while making no commitments, and wily hedges by the two men consumed the summer. Spanish loss of Cadiz to French armies in late September forced the British hand, and she took other steps to safeguard her interests.

But Rush had already forwarded the British proposal to Washington. It precipitated a hot debate in the cabinet. President Monroe while in Virginia showed the dispatches to Jefferson and to Madison. Both ex-presidents advocated the joint declaration. The cabinet was for it unanimously—almost. Secretary of War Calhoun wanted to give Rush discretionary power to issue it, even if the United States had to concede that she would never annex Cuba or Texas. John Quincy Adams, the secretary of state, warmly disagreed. Most members had drawn gloomy inferences from a communication by the Russian minister congratulating the United States on its *neutral* stand toward Latin America. Adams dissented, arguing that the Russian note gave the administration a chance to avow American principles while spurning the English seduction. It was more manly to oppose France and Russia face-to-face "than to come in as a cock-boat in the wake of the British man-of-war." Although his remarks greatly impressed the president, the lineup remained lopsided. At this stage the odds were clear: Adams against the field. News of the French victory at Cadiz arrived on November 13, so alarming Monroe that he wavered. When Calhoun urged preparations for war, Adams ridiculed him. Calhoun said that the Holy Alliance with 10,000 men could reinstate Spanish hegemony over all Latin America. Adams replied, "They will no more restore Spanish dominion on the American continent than the Chimborazo will sink beneath the ocean" (this peak in Ecuador has an altitude of 20,557 feet and is 100 miles from the Pacific). Two days later a dejected Monroe again mentioned a joint declaration, and again Adams fought it. Then it just died.

Now the president made his one major contribution. Adams had been assuming that the American attitude would be circulated to the powers in a diplomatic communiqué. Monroe decided to include it in his annual message to Congress. He read a draft to the cabinet, in which he denounced the French invasion of Spain and recognized independence for the rebellious Greece. Adams objected, on principles that went straight back to the doctrine of the Farewell Address:

> The ground that I wish to take is that of earnest remonstrance against the interference of the European powers by force with South America, but to disclaim all interference on our part with Europe; to make an American cause, and adhere inflexibly to that.

Two days later Monroe produced a revision that to Adams seemed "quite unexceptionable." The Doctrine consisted of three precepts: (a) no future colonization by Europe in the Western Hemisphere, (b) no colony in the Americas should be in future transferred from one European power to another, (c) no meddling—by Europe in the Americas, or by the United States in Europe. John Quincy Adams had reached the pinnacle of statecraft (and of pugnacity). But his countrymen did not know it; the reaction to Monroe's message was placid. Britain soon recognized the new governments of several Latin American states. The best-known phrase from the whole episode was spoken later by the English foreign minister: "I resolved that if France had Spain, it should not be Spain 'with the Indies.' I called the New World into existence to redress the balance of the Old."

This boast reversed reality. In truth the United States was using Europe to rectify many of its own imbalances, most notably some important financial ones. To grasp the fiscal situation at the end of the 1812 war, we must backtrack. Alexander Hamilton's program had begun to regularize the nation's finances. Gallatin, Secretary of the Treasury from 1801 to 1814, carried on. Of central importance was reduction of the federal debt. At a time when foreign demand for goods was an inflationary pressure on prices, surplus financing by the federal government was a desirable counterforce. The procedure was simple: in order to pay off its outstanding securities on the debt, the Treasury had to draw out of the economy by its taxes more purchasing power than it inserted by its expenditures. The result was a deflationary seepage. The federal debt exceeded $83 million in 1801; by 1812 it had been cut to $45 million. In 1811 the charter of the first Bank of the United States came up for renewal. By the margin of a single vote in each House of Congress, the application was turned down. Thus when war came, the government had no central bank by which to conduct its own finances or to control credit in the private sector of the economy. At that point federal policy served not to muffle but to reinforce inflation. It pumped into the markets in expenditures more than it took out in taxes. The federal debt rose to $127.3 million by 1816. The increase of $80 million in indebtedness had brought the Treasury only $34 million in specie values.

The acceleration of the private sector was lopsided. Although the British during the war had an effective blockade of American ports, they did license certain exports, especially flour bound to Wellington in Iberia. In 1814 when they could once more get grain from the Baltic, they stifled this trade again, but much smuggling continued from New England to Canada. New England had also transferred considerable capital into manufacturing, and it sold on favorable terms to the rest of the United States. It took payment in hard coin; from 1812 to 1814 the specie reserves of banks in Massachusetts almost doubled. Then came the British raid on the nation's capital in August, 1814, followed by an invasion of Maryland. Banks in the region hastily seized the excuse to suspend specie payments. Other areas followed suit. Only in New England were banks still redeeming their notes. The number of banks in existence had increased enormously:

1791	3
1800	29
1811	90
1816	246
1820	over 300

By Gallatin's calculations, the volume of bank notes in circulation went from $28 million in 1811 to $68 million in 1816. The price level rose to the highest peak it would reach in the entire nineteenth century. As to the reasons, under the conditions of the War of 1812 the quantity theory of money (see early Chapter 1) would hold that increased volumes of money in the economy should produce inflationary prices. This could be approximately true when other factors are constant. With the full employment of wartime, the quantity of goods and services produced (P) could not rise yet, given the soaring foreign demand for goods and services, the velocity of circulation of money (V) would not slow down. With few savings or long-range investments and everything at peak production, there would be inflation. (A chart of these relationships is shown in Figure 26-5 in Chapter 26.)

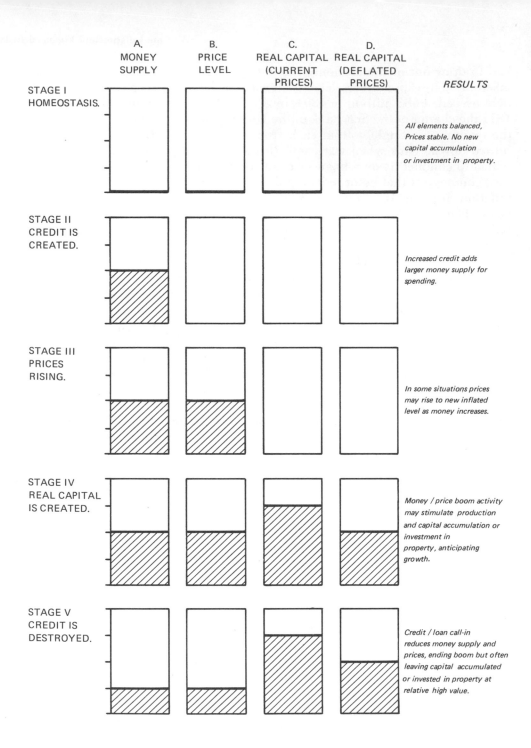

FIGURE 12-1. *Credit Expansion, Price Level, and Real Capital*

West of the Appalachians the growth of banking was swift and shaky. Firms founded for other purposes, insurance or exporting or general commerce, took on the task of issuing notes. Leading merchants wanted a looser currency, more credit. In 1814 the Pennsylvania legislature chartered 41 banks. Ohio had 26 by 1818. The legislature of Kentucky set a record by chartering 33 in a single session. A Cincinnati editor remarked in 1818: "A new idea seems to have sprung up that the only way to destroy the monopoly of banking, is to make it universal." To meet its own fiscal functions if for no other reason, the Treasury clearly needed a national bank. Congress voted the charter in 1816 by avoiding some of the issues of 1791 and 1811; the question of constitutionality was quietly waived. As in 1791, sectionalism ruled the vote, but the two blocs had reversed position. Now the West and the South voted for the second Bank, while the North opposed it. Taking the vote in the House, the nine Northern states were 45 to 35 against charter; only New York, New Jersey, and Rhode Island showed majorities in favor. The nine Southern and Western states were 45 to 26 pro; only Virginia was anti. Recognizing that the economy had grown since 1791, Congress authorized a much larger national bank. The gross capital was $35 million. Liabilities (demand deposits plus notes in circulation) could not exceed gross capital. As a further prop to solvency, 20 per cent of the capital was to be paid in specie, but this provision was not enforced. Receipts to the Bank from the original sale of stock were as follows (in millions): specie $2, government securities $14, personal notes $12. Picking as its first president a Philadelphia politician-merchant who had just gone through bankruptcy, the Bank at once started branches in major cities. The behavior of the Bank was reckless in the extreme. Already many manufacturers were in bad straits. The credit structure of the mercantile world was strained. The Bank fed the inflationary flames. In the single month of June, 1818, the Cincinnati branch discounted over $1.8 million, the Lexington branch over $1.6 million.

The collapse began in 1818. Good crops in Europe curtailed the market for American foodstuffs. By 1818 the second Bank had specie of only $2.36 million against demand deposits of $22.3 million (a safe ratio might have been 3 to 1). Then the Treasury called on the Bank for $2 million in specie to meet certain of its commitments incurred during the Lousiana Purchase. This crisis was fended off, but the Bank panicked. To reduce its liabilities the Bank began to call in loans right and left. Having foolishly helped to spur inflation, it now forced a drastic cut-back in credit. As one man put it, "The Bank was saved, and the people were ruined." From Philadelphia, one of the cities hardest hit, came this report:

> that the enlivening sound of the spindle, the loom, and the hammer has in many places almost ceased to be heard—that our merchants and traders are daily swept away by bankruptcy one after another—that our banks are drained of their specie—that our cities exhibit an unvarying scene of gloom and despair—that

confidence between man and man is almost extinct—that debts in general cannot be collected—that property cannot be sold but at an enormous sacrifice—that capitalists have thus an opportunity of aggrandizing themselves at the expense of the middle class to an incalculable extent—that money cannot be borrowed but at extravagant interest—in a word, that with advantages equal to any that Heaven has ever bestowed on any nation, we exhibit a state of things at which our enemies must rejoice—and our friends put on sackcloth and ashes.

Philadelphia, admittedly, was not typical. The bustling prototype of a century earlier was enshrined in the very name of the Franklin Institute, created in 1824 as a clearinghouse for technological information. Capital was abundant, and so was a skilled labor force. But these assets had a fitful impact. The spinning jenny had been brought to the city as early as 1776, and by 1811 some 4,000 hand-loom weavers were at work locally. A modern carpet factory was started in 1815. It drew no imitators. The power loom was twice introduced in the five years after 1837, but it did not take hold. Power weaving did not invade the Philadelphia rug industry until after the Civil War. The well-organized weavers were able to impede innovations in machinery, but the cordwainers (shoemakers) had no such luck. Even though their industry did not undergo any major technological change until the improvement of the McKay sole-sewing machine in 1866, the structure of the business was altered so that workers lost control of their fees.

This shift was due mainly to improvements in transportation, which greatly enlarged the potential market-area. The conquest of these markets made possible the further substitution of machines for men in some mills. In this process the pathfinder was the Boston Manufacturing Company of Waltham, Massachusetts. This momentous venture began when Francis Cabot Lowell took his sons off to Great Britain to get a proper education. Exportation of textile machines from England was forbidden, but Lowell visited several mills and left with some visual patterns. Back home in Boston in 1812 (good timing) he got the tinkerer Paul Moody to make his images manifest in a plan for a working model. By a piddling waterfall in the Charles River they erected the first integrated textile mill in the New World. Here cotton was spun into thread, and under the same roof the threads were woven into sheetings. Rewards were ample. While other manufacturing concerns were failing on every hand, this one from 1817 to 1824 paid to its few investors a total of 154 per cent of its capital—an annual average of 19 per cent. In 1816 it successfully pushed for a protective tariff from Congress. The next year it began to manufacture machine tools for sale to other companies. By 1821 its needs for power had surged over and beyond the waterfall in Waltham, and it moved north to a bigger river to begin fabricating the textile mills and boarding houses that conglomerated into what the proprietors named Lowell. It was only the first of many mill towns thrown up by the Boston Associates. Perhaps we should say that now the Industrial Revolution, properly so-called, was under way in America. But it could never have occurred without the prior acquisitions of capital and technical skills and organizational understanding (mid-Chapter 3 on colonial trade and industry), and we must not lose sight of the interstate commerce opened up by the Constitution of the United States, which did so much to facilitate the division of labor and the rise of manufacture (mid-Chapter 10).

This period has been denominated by historians of American politics as the Era of Good Feelings. Can this label be apt? Economic changes were occurring that were cataclysmic. Each section was becoming what it had not been. Along with its cultivation for market of tobacco and rice and indigo the South had formerly produced a wide variety of foodstuffs: now it concentrated on the single crop of cotton. Leadership of the region in national politics, traditionally the hallmark of Virginia, had by 1830 passed to South Carolina. By then, lands beyond the mountains had been thickly settled and the West was pouring out provisions for sale to Europe or to the cotton-dominated plantations. Farming in the Middle States and even more in New England was losing out to cheaper products from the Midwest, and the resources of Eastern areas were being diverted into manufacturing and into a widening range of tertiary occupations such as banking and other service industries. Is it possible that economic transformations of this magnitude could take place without generating strident conflicts in politics? No.

The notion of an epoch of benign consensus stems from a myopic perception of politics as being nothing but presidential elections. Local clashes at the polls could be almost fratricidal. After the war the Federalists could not assemble into a unified national party but in many states they remained strong, controlling Maryland until 1820, Delaware even longer, Massachusetts until 1823, and still playing at that time a meaningful role in Pennsylvania. Scholars love to talk about the great "national issues" because this vision yields a neat and tidy picture, even though the voters of the time were more concerned with local problems. Concentric frays brought more voters into politics. From 1804 to 1816 the use of the suffrage soared, reaching as high as 98 per cent of the qualified voters in some elections. The electorate in 1830 was double what it had been a decade earlier. No longer did men "stand" for office, they "ran" for office. The times were spawning new words to describe new patterns of behavior. It seems that the phrase "self-made" was introduced in a Senate speech by Henry Clay in 1832. By then the term "lobby-agent" and its contraction "lobbyist" were in general use.

The new vocabulary emphasized the interaction of economics and politics. References to the "industrial revolution" seemingly start in France around 1810. Since the phrase is a cliché, few bother to appraise it. It suggests a connection between power tools and democratization, between technological growth and political equality. The very word "technology" was coined by a Harvard professor, Jacob Bigelow, in 1829. Other meanings were shifting or even flipping onto their heads. A "factory" had been a store run by a factor who bought and sold; quickly the word acquired its twentieth-century meaning. "Manufacturing" had been a transformation wrought by human muscles; it came to imply water wheels and steam engines. Modern meanings must not be read back blandly into the rhetoric of our ancestors. The "working class" that fought for power during the Great Depression after 1929 was a far narrower group than was connoted by the phrase a century earlier. (Even in 1885 when the Knights of Labor tried to organize the working class it excluded from membership only publicans, bankers, and attorneys.) We should not be bamboozled because the polemics of politics shrieked that all men are brothers. Jefferson had found a winning theme, and his successors in the Virginia dynasty preserved it; of James Monroe Secretary Adams said that "the pole-star of his policy" was tranquillity. So also, in terms reminiscent of Rousseau's *The Social Contract,* President Jackson prattled about "all classes of the community" and appealed to a general "will of the American people." But when he got around to specifying "the real people" he mentioned only four occupations: farmers and planters, mechanics and laborers. These men, all of whom produced tangible goods, things that a body could hold in his hands and sink his teeth into, were "the bone and sinew of the country." Fops who supplied mere services, and especially those such as bankers who fiddled with monetary values, were beneath contempt. These shifts in activity and in language point to alterations in the structure of politics.

Whether we see stagnation or flux depends on where we look. The presidential election of 1816 whispers the former. Succeeding to an eminence that had been held only by Virginians since the beginning of the century, James Monroe got 183 electoral votes to only 34 for Rufus King of New York. But looking at federal control of business gives a different impression. The Federalists before 1800 had never questioned federal regulatory powers. But Republican dominance, especially the Embargo, brought a reversal. One of the young Federalists, Josiah Quincy, said in Congress in 1808:

> The best guarantees of the interest society has in the wealth of the members which compose it, are the industry, intelligence and enterprise of the individual proprietors, strengthened as they always are by the knowledge of business, and quickened by that which gives the keenest edge to human ingenuity—self-interest.

When the tariff bill of 1816 came to a vote in the House, Daniel Webster of New Hampshire opposed it because he thought its protective features would harm the mercantile and shipowning interests of the seaboard. Calhoun supported it because South Carolina was dreaming of becoming a major manufacturing state. Within a decade—as the economic commitments of the two regions were transformed—each man would switch sides. Webster moved to Massachusetts and was sent to the Senate, where he was as florid a protectionist as any. Calhoun by 1832 was so dedicated to cheap imports for the South that he verged on destruction of the Union even though he was its vice president at the time. But with these tensions and metamorphoses in the society, presidential elections appeared placid. In 1820 there was no contest at all. Monroe very nearly followed Washington's precedent of getting every vote in the Electoral College; only the unruly William Plumer of New Hampshire cast a dissenting ballot. But this was the unanimity of indifference. In Philadelphia, where 4,700 voters had recently taken part in a gubernatorial contest, only 2,000 voted for the president in 1820 even though he was challenged in the Quaker city by an antislavery slate headed by everybody's hero, the canal-builder DeWitt Clinton. In Richmond, Virginia, it was reported, only seventeen men went to the polls.

The disintegration of the (largely illusory) monolith came soon. Thus the legislatures had chosen the presidential electors in most states. Moreover, the nominees had been put forward by caucuses in Congress. As 1824 approached, it was clear that William Crawford of Georgia would be the administration candidate. (If Virginia could not keep the presidency for her very own, at least she could exalt a cordial neighbor.) Many voters found the choice unpalatable, and they also objected to the "old and tried mode" of nomination by congressional caucus. As early as 1822 the Kentucky legislature announced for Clay. Several county conventions, beginning in his native Tennessee in June, 1823, came out for Andrew Jackson; he had been a popular idol since the Battle of New Orleans and had further burnished his image campaigning against the Indians in Florida. Calhoun was put up by South Carolina, Crawford by Virginia, J.Q. Adams by New England, Clinton by some Ohio counties. The candidates agreed that Calhoun should be vice president, so he dropped out of the race for the top office, and so did Clinton. But when the congressional caucus assembled in February, 1824, four prominent names remained. Only 66 of the 261 congressmen appeared for the meeting. Most of those present came from four states, and eight of the twenty-four states were not represented at all. They nominated Crawford, but it meant nothing—King Caucus was dead, and so were the days of deference politics.

The election was apathetic. Six states did not bother with a popular vote at all. Of 360,000 ballots cast, Jackson led with 152,000. But he lacked a majority in the Electoral College, so under the Twelfth Amendment the contest was thrown into the House of Representatives. No more than three names could be considered. Clay was out. The stage was set for the events that Jackson partisans would always call "the Corrupt Bargain." Clay gave his support to Adams. The delegations voted by states. Adams won thirteen, Jackson seven, Crawford four. As to individual representatives, Adams got 87, Jackson 71, Crawford 54. On taking office the new president appointed Clay to be secretary of state. Had there been a prior agreement? Since an absence of evidence can never prove a conclusion, nobody can document his judgment in this instance, but surely we should say "No." In terms of national issues, Jackson and Clay were diametrically opposed. Clay was a duellist like Jackson but in public affairs he was a cool head. Adams was different in life-style from both of the Southerners, but he had had innumerable opportunities to appraise and appreciate Clay's ability. And he and the Kentuckian were in close concord as to the desirable course for their country.

The achievements of the Adams administration were zero. The president had incredible experience in foreign relations; prior to taking over the State Department he had served in France, the Netherlands, Sweden, Russia, Prussia, and England, and from 1778 to 1817 nearly half of his time had been spent abroad. But diplomacy during his tenure brought no triumphs and few challenges. He was unable to open the British West Indies to American commerce. His effort to take part in a Pan-American gathering was thwarted by Congress. The big battles were on the home front, and he lacked the talents for the new-style politics. His bold program for federal initiatives brought the country no good and gave him only grief (Document 11-3). As his term neared its terminus, his chances for re-election did not look good. Officially he and Jackson were both Republicans; as a national body the Federalists were dead. But the two Republican factions were acquiring subtitles: the National Republicans vs. the Democrats. In a campaign that turned mainly on personalities plus the allegation that Jackson had been "wronged" in 1824, the advantages were all with the Tennessean. Adams' unpopularity should not be exaggerated. Outside the six New England states he won only New Jersey and Maryland, but his half million votes were far more than the total cast for all candidates four years earlier. Jackson got 650,000, and in the Electoral College his margin was more than 2 to 1. The popular vote had more than trebled since the preceding presidential tally. Calhoun, with major consequences, kept office as the vice president. When Jackson was inaugurated, Joseph Story lamented from his post on the Supreme Court, "The reign of King 'Mob' seemed triumphant." John Randolph was beside himself: "The country is ruined beyond redemption; it is ruined in the spirit and character of the people." He wailed, "Where now could we find leaders of a revolution?"

Tocqueville made particular note of the decline in quality of public leadership:

I attribute the small number of distinguished men in political life to the ever increasing despotism of the majority in the United States.

When the American Revolution broke out, they arose in great numbers; for public opinion then served, not to tyrannize over, but to direct the exertions of individuals. Those celebrated men, sharing the agitation of mind common at that period, had a grandeur peculiar to themselves, which was reflected back upon the nation, but which was by no means borrowed from it. . . . In that immense crowd which throngs the avenues to power in the United States, I found very few men who displayed that manly candor and masculine independence of opinion which frequently distinguished the Americans in former times, and which constitutes the leading feature in distinguished characters wherever they may be found. . . .

Under the new dispensation, able men were loathe to risk the indignities of the polls. Too much was changing too fast. Nobody was certain what ground rules applied. Paradoxically, the conventional frontier lifeways were themselves of a type that bred changes. A traveller on the frontier reported that it would coerce the most traditional English immigrant into realizing "that he has got to a place where it answers to spend land to save labour; the reverse of his experience in England; and he soon becomes as slovenly a farmer as the American, and begins immediately to grow rich." The American way was to squander resources. New World attitudes toward time were equally puzzling to Europeans. Away back in *Poor Richard's Almanac* readers found the maxim: Time is money. A Yankee seldom had fun for the reason that he was never involved in the present, he was chronically afflicted with anxieties about where he needed to go next. A visitor from France wanted to explain how far Europe diverged from the United States in setting no economic value on time. He cited the company that sought to establish a steamship service between Naples and Sicily. The Neapolitans countered, "Your boat takes us over in one day, and yet you demand the same fare as a sail vessel which is three days. That is absurd; how can you expect that we will pay as much for one day as for three?" For an American to look at his watch was habitual, and that obsession has lasted for centuries.*

In this maddened hurly-burly, Andrew Jackson spoke for the past. Streamers of nostalgia floated around his polemics. He stressed the need to "dismantle" the fake world of credit. He urged the "restoration" of the Old Republic. A cardinal virtue of bygone times was their abjuration of banks. Paper notes were not real money; only specie would suffice. With this cast of mind, the president had to see Nicholas Biddle and the second Bank of the United States as arch-fiends, as the spearhead of the immoral rush toward paper money and inflation. The indictment could hardly have been more unjust, but from the day he became president, Jackson was determined to undercut the Bank. Ironically Biddle, in spite of repeated warnings, continued for years to think that he could conciliate the administration.

If we adopt a static perspective and fix our gaze on the structure of society, much can be said for Jackson's hostility to the Bank. It was endowed

---

*Some examples: the timepiece could serve as central symbol in Henry James' novel of 1903, *The Ambassadors*. An anecdote: after World War I a New Yorker was conducting a Japanese guest uptown by subway; they caught a local train, soon changed to an express, changed back to another local; at their destination the American explained that the transfers had saved three minutes. A wry query came: "Now that we have saved them, what are we going to do with them?"

FIGURE 12-2. *John Frazee, Bust of Thomas H. Perkins*

Although it could hardly be acclaimed as a great artistic work, this bust by John Frazee deserves notice on more than one count. Its subject, Thomas Handasyd Perkins, was a pioneer in the Far Eastern trade and also in large-scale private philanthropy. Perkins (1764–1854) was the son of a Boston merchant. After he had participated in a firm in Santo Domingo which aborted, the majority of his ventures were in China but he sent ships and goods to any port that promised a profit. He took a lengthy stride in the development of railroads by building a tramway that worked by gravity to carry stone from a quarry down to dockside in Quincy, Massachusetts. He served as president of the Boston office of the Second Bank of the United States. Several times he was used as a semi-official envoy in Europe of the Federal government. In 1839 he donated his residence to the New England Asylum for the Blind; that institution now bears his name.

with a huge concentration of power that a republic had best not put into private hands that are charged with earning a profit for stockholders. But if we take a dynamic view and focus on strategies for economic growth, Biddle was right. Becoming head of the Bank in 1822 as the nation was recovering from the financial panic of 1819, he had brilliantly improvised the techniques that are proper for a central bank. With no intention of begging the issue by using loaded terms, we can say that Biddle tried to steer a middle course between the hard-money men represented by Jackson and the hundreds of private banks chartered by states which wanted to inflate the currency as fast as printing presses could produce notes. To use the trite phrase, the Bank acted as the "lender of last resort." When inflation threatened, Biddle would collect the notes of offending banks and send them home for redemption in specie.* This procedure would check expansion of the money supply. Conversely, when a credit stringency impended so that interest rates rose, Biddle would buy some of the less liquid assets of straitened institutions. Now, equipped with specie reserves that would enable them to carry more liabilities in the form of demand deposits, the state banks could expand their loans to businessmen. By such means the Bank stabilized the economy. Shifting the metaphor, the Bank helped to keep the volume of money on the road by imposing curbstones that it could not jump. Its services, however great, were not popular. The coalition that destroyed it had two wings directly contradicting each other in their monetary prescriptions and agreeing in nothing except animosity to the Bank. This fusion of enmity found other allies: Wall Street's jealousy of the Philadelphia giant; politicians' rancor at encroachments on states' rights; native speculators resentful of the Bank's foreign stockholders (which was slyly appealed to by Jackson; see Document 12-2). Perhaps most justifiable of all, also inflamed by the president, was a general fear that the Monster Bank might subvert the most cherished ideals of the populace—a fair field in business, equality in society, democracy in politics.

---

*Remember that the Bank and its branches were the depository for most of the funds that the Treasury collected in taxes. Thus a high proportion of the total circulation of bank notes passed through its hands.

Perkins also was a benefactor of the Boston Atheneum and other cultural foundations. The interplay between business and the arts was still highly virile and it worked in both directions. Merchants like Perkins and his friends could subsidize beauty. Conversely, it seemed appropriate to plan a highly successful trading voyage to the Orient at the home of architect Charles Bulfinch.

The style of this statuette is also distinctive: the Boston speculator as Roman senator. References recur often to the Greek Revival and the Roman Revival. Admittedly, Americans rediscovered the virtues of classical precedents, but this accession took place in a ragged chronology. The Founding Fathers had often appealed to ancient authority when discussing political philosophy. Jefferson and Bulfinch had used archaeology for help in designing buildings. But widespread reliance on the classics did not occur in some visual arts until after the War of 1812 (see Chapter 12).

FIGURE 12-3. *Biddle's Home, Andalusia, near Philadelphia*

Although the culture of Greece was the ancestor of Roman art, their heydays in the United States reversed the sequence. George Washington before his death was being depicted in Augustan toga, but the peak of Greek Revival architecture came in the decades from 1820 to 1850. In 1811 Nicholas Biddle gained possession of the country estate near Philadelphia, Andalusia, through his marriage to the daughter of one of the wealthiest men in the city. He hired an eminent designer to work it up in the classic mode. Completed in 1833, the remodeling had added the Doric columns rising from a stepped platform, the portico that commands them, and other rather austere features.

Biddle's attachment to the Mediterranean and to its cultures old and new were of long standing. As a young man he had travelled the area studying ruins, recording inscriptions, measuring buildings. He learned ancient and modern Greece well enough to discuss the differences with leading scholars of the day in England.

From 1829 to 1831 Biddle, ignoring many provocative remarks from the administration, stood above politics and did his banker's duty to the nation. He was on thin ice without knowing it. The confused or schizophrenic attitudes toward banking had shown already,* and of course the president had only contempt for financial tinkering. Then Biddle took terrible advice. The chief culprits were Clay and Daniel Webster. The latter, a lawyer for the Bank as well as a senator, had largely political motives. Although the charter of the Bank would not expire until 1836, a decision was made to press for recharter in January 1832. If Jackson dared to veto the bill, he could be beaten for re-election in the autumn. Webster had won great glory by his rebuttal in the Senate to a South Carolinian who rationalized nullification; a public contest over the Bank might make him chief executive. Clay may have been moved by personal pique also; since 1824 Jackson's aides had called him most of the vile names in the language. Biddle's judgment failed. Doubtless the president's wrath against the Bank was sincere; he termed it a "hydra of corruption" that was "dangerous to our liberties by its corrupting influences everywhere and not the least in the Congress of the Union." The administration was firing volleys of propaganda against the Bank. To offset the attacks, Biddle's friends set up hearings by congressional bodies. Biddle appeared before the Senate committee. Asked if he had ever oppressed state-chartered banks, he said "Never." Then he explained: "There are very few banks which might not have been destroyed by an exertion of the power of the Bank. None have ever been injured. Many have been saved. And more have been, and are, constantly relieved when it is found that they are solvent but are suffering under temporary difficulty." This argument, while true, was a startling indiscretion in asserting the Bank's apparently arbitrary power over the nation. Thomas Hart Benton, who was leading the Senate opposition, aptly observed that the statement "was proving entirely too much."

Recharter cleared Congress in early July. On July 10 Jackson vetoed it. Then he ran for re-election, with Clay as the National Republican luminary. Amidst the haze of campaign hubbub, disputes over policy were clear. Clay's

---

*In February 1819 Maryland enacted a law against banks that would not redeem their bank notes. Two days later it adopted a law against any person who presented a bank's notes for redemption.

He was surely one of the half-dozen greatest bankers the United States has ever had. He had a feel for it; he knew what to do and when to do it. However, as a young man he also ventured into politics. He had no feel whatever for that. Ironically, since he was finally victim to a Democratic president, his attachments were always to the Jeffersonians. After his Greek exploits he served as secretary to the American minister in England, James Monroe. In 1810, the same year his father was chosen to the Pennsylvania senate, Biddle went to the lower house. He withdrew from public affairs for a few years, but in 1819 President Monroe named him a director of the Second Bank of the United States, and within four years he was president. He did splendidly in that job for ten years. Then he tangled with Andrew Jackson and got kicked in the pants. One astute critic, recognizing the difficulty of pioneering a central bank in an era of wild economic expansion, noted that Biddle was superbly qualified in "everything he needed except what he needed most." (See also Chapter 26.)

"American System" had consistently for fifteen years meant four planks: federally chartered central bank, high to moderate protective tariffs, federal support for internal improvements, strengthening of the Union. On none but the last did Jackson agree. His own appeals emphasized hostility to foreign capitalists and to government-bred monopolists. He won a smashing victory, getting more than four times as many electoral votes as Clay. With his mandate from the common people, he took a decisive step in September, 1833. When two successive secretaries of the treasury refused to divert federal deposits from the Bank and its branches, Jackson replaced the last with a man soon to become famous on the Supreme Court, Roger B. Taney. Taney transferred all federal funds to favored state banks. As Gallatin pointed out later, Biddle ceased about 1832 to regulate the currency, with consequences for the economy that will be examined in a moment.

The destruction of the central Bank meant the annihilation of one of the bonds—all too few in the first place—that held the nation together. The most important trend toward interdependency had been a decline in local self-sufficiency. Regional specialization was growing rapidly: cotton from the South, foodstuffs from the Midwest, manufactures and services from the East. The flows of internal commerce were so many chains that held the Union as an entity. Other ties were political and governmental. Many of these were woven by the Supreme Court presided over by another great Virginian, John Marshall, from 1801 to 1835. Marshall was particularly effective in clarifying the precise meanings of the separation of powers in the federal structure. In *Marbury* v. *Madison* (1803) the Court for the first time declared unconstitutional an act of Congress. Especially since the early New Deal when the Supreme Court was guilty of moving beyond its proper role into deeds of usurpation, much wrath has been directed at judicial review. The courts have been accused of "legislating." More than a century ago travellers from England and France were expressing their surprise at the American mode. In Great Britain the problem did not arise: the nation had no written constitution, and the supremacy of Parliament was recognized as absolute. France had a written constitution, but it specified that the legislature should be final judge of the validity of bills. Given the proclamation by the Constitution that it shall be "the supreme Law of the Land," it is hard to see an alternative to the system that evolved by which the authority of each of the concurrent branches—the congress, the president, and the courts—would pass independently on the constitutionality of each law. For any of the branches to do less would be to violate every oath of office. Judicial restraint is clearly desirable, but judicial review is a necessity.

Decisions by the courts (and of course by others; see the beginning of Chapter 9 on Washington) to apportion authority among various federal bodies were imperative. It was even more urgent to resolve some aspects of the separation of powers between the federal government and the states, for on these resolutions depended the very survival of the Union. For example, the case of *Martin* v. *Hunter's Lessee* (1816) involved part of the estate of the late Lord Thomas Fairfax, patron of the late President Washington. During the War for Independence, Fairfax had been a Loyalist, and Virginia had confiscated his property. When a British heir sued, the state courts rejected his petition, and he went to the Supreme Court of the United States, which upheld his claim. The court of appeals of Virginia responded by declaring unconstitutional a federal law that gave federal courts jurisdiction over its decision. If this view were allowed to stand, the United States would be no more. Marshall for the Court rejected it with a resounding lecture on the origins and nature of American federalism.

Another state effort to hamstring federal powers arose in regard to the second Bank of the United States. In 1818 Maryland imposed an annual tax on all banks or branches that it had not chartered. Five other Southern and Western states enacted similar levies. It is an irony of the Panic of 1819 that one of its chief incendiaries should have won immortality. James W. McCulloch was the cashier (chief operating officer, or manager, in effect) of the branch of the Bank at Baltimore; with no personal assets worth mentioning, he loaned himself more than $500,000 in the Bank's funds. But when the Bank moved legally against the state, suit was brought in his name, and it will be known forever as *McCulloch* v. *Maryland* (1819). The Supreme Court disallowed the Maryland tax. Marshall proceeded from a dogma that would become a watchword to generations of jurists: "the power to tax involves the power to destroy" and "the power to destroy may defeat and render useless the power to create."* Marshall had no doubt that the charter issued by Congress was valid:

> Let the end be legitimate, let it be within the scope of the Constitution, and all means which are appropriate, which are plainly adapted to that end, which are not prohibited, but consist with the letter and spirit of the Constitution, are constitutional.

Here was sweeping affirmation of the "necessary and proper" clause as the foundation of implied powers.

To watch a juristic statesman at work, we can follow the series of cases in which John Marshall worked out—by ax smashes and by pin pricks—the meaning of the interstate commerce clause. Historically this has been the most important single provision of the Constitution. And the most important single decision was handed down in *Gibbons* v. *Ogden* (1824). The complicated facts need not be detailed. New York had granted a monopoly to a ferry line operating to New Jersey, and when a competitor brought suit, the Supreme

---

*Decades later this prompted a witty retort from another great justice: "The power to tax is not the power to destroy while this Court sits." J. Holmes in *Panhandle Oil Company* v. *Mississippi ex rel. Knox* (1928).

Court invalidated the monopoly insofar as it involved traffic between states. Another embarrassment to trade was removed by the "original-package doctrine" in *Brown* v. *Maryland* (1827). The state required certain importers to be licensed. At what point does federal control over imports give sway to a state's control over goods within its borders? At the point, decided the Court, when commodities have been uncrated. Crucial to Marshall's genius was his instinct for leaving himself safety valves, so that any decision that drew too much hostility could be qualified and hedged in later cases. Thus, having asserted the broad powers of Congress under the commerce clause, he went on to rule that those powers should be accommodated to local needs. One lasting device appeared in *Willson* v. *Black Bird Creek Marsh Co.* (1829)—the "police powers" of states. Delaware had authorized construction of a dam across a navigable tidal creek that emptied into the Delaware River. Under the federal coastal licensing act, vessels could ply the Delaware and its tributaries, and the dam was a complete barrier to some interstate commerce. But Marshall sustained the Delaware law: "We do not think, that the act empowering the Black Bird Creek Marsh company to place a dam across the creek, can, under all the circumstances of the case, be considered as repugnant to the power to regulate commerce in its dormant state, or as being in conflict with any law passed on the subject."

Assertions by state courts of their power to overthrow an act of Congress were ominous; even more so were similar assertions by legislatures, because the latter were more likely to project the emotions of the dispute among large groups of citizens. By 1832 South Carolina had displaced Virginia as the most powerful and most aggressive congressional spokesman for the South. The section henceforth would be ambivalent. Sometimes it followed its longtime strategy of combining with the West to restrain the centralist policies of the East (high tariffs, internal improvements, high prices for federal public lands). Sometimes, despairing of wooing the West, it resorted to bizarre constitutional fancies aimed at saving the interests of a permanent minority. A crisis followed the 1828 "Tariff of Abominations," whose protective duties clearly discriminated against a region dependent on cotton exports and manufactured imports. The law had resulted partly from a tactic in Congress that backfired, and in 1832 New England was mollified by revisions bringing down rates on raw wool and hemp. The South got no concessions. For the second time a vice president broke vigorously but furtively from his chief. As Jefferson had drafted the Kentucky Resolves (see Document 9-3), now Calhoun wrote a Nullification Proclamation that was voted by a special convention in South Carolina. Not only did the Ordinance of Nullification proclaim the recent tariff acts "null, void, and no law," but it announced that any federal effort to execute them by force would be "inconsistent with the longer continuance of South Carolina in the Union. . . ."

Within a fortnight the president answered this challenge:

If this doctrine had been established at an earlier day, the Union would have been dissolved in its infancy. . . .

I consider, then, the power to annul a law of the United States, assumed by one State, *incompatible with the existence of the Union, contradicted expressly by the letter of the Constitution, unauthorized by its spirit, inconsistent with every principle on which it was founded, and destructive of the great purpose for which it was formed.* . . .

The message as a whole took the superior tone of a parent chiding his child, and Clay thought it was "too strongly biased on the side of consolidation." Meanwhile the administration put forward a Force Bill to implement collection of the customs. Simultaneously an olive branch was offered in the form of bills to lower the tariff; the one ultimately passed was the Compromise Tariff of Henry Clay. The Force Bill and customs act were signed by the president on the same day, March 2. South Carolina promptly nullified the Force Bill. The Compromise Tariff provided for a sliding scale reduction of tariff rates in each passing year, with the object of bringing the maximum duty down to a future level not to exceed 20 per cent ad valorem of the price of goods by 1842.

Jackson's message on the Ordinance of Nullification—his famous toast at a Jefferson Day Dinner in 1833: "Our Federal Union. It must be preserved."—brought him unwonted popularity in New England. But he soon threw it away by removing federal funds from the second Bank. In any case, Jackson always seemed to be courting hatred from some quarter. In a more sensitive atmosphere people might have gone blue from shock at the frequent sulphuric accusations that the president was a tyrant. Valid charges against the man would be enough to earn him animosity: He understood nothing of a modern monetary-banking system. His devotion to an agrarian past blotted out any perception of an industrial future for his country. He did not confine his passions to his personal affairs but allowed them to taint his nation's reputation; his acquiescence in the hanging of two British subjects in Spanish-ruled Florida in 1818 was immoral, illegal, and an affront to two empires.

But two frequent allegations seem unjust to Jackson. One holds that he created or exaggerated the "spoils system" in filling posts in the executive branch. But as we have seen, nepotism was one of the earliest exports from England to America. The first president to represent a change of administration, Jefferson, put friends in office and fought many hostile incumbents; the event that triggered *Marbury* v. *Madison* was his refusal to deliver their rightful commissions to Adams' newly appointed Federalist judges. Madison and Monroe inherited a friendly bureaucracy. While John Quincy Adams refused to remove a postmaster general who was working for his defeat, we must remember that he was an Adams. Jackson had direct control of about 600 posts; some 252 incumbents were removed. Of the 8,000 deputy postmasters in the country, only 600 were replaced. Perhaps some critics were beguiled because during Jackson's tenure another Democratic politician, William L. Marcy of New York, gave them a label in 1831 that they could tender in place of insight:

> It may be, sir, that the politicians of New York are not as fastidious as some gentlemen are, as to disclosing the principles on which they act. They boldly *preach* what they *practice*. When they are contending for *victory*, they avow their intention of enjoying the fruits of it. If they are defeated, they expect to retire from office. If they are successful, they claim, as a matter of right, the advantages of success. They see nothing wrong in the rule that to the VICTOR belongs the spoils of the ENEMY.

Another unfair charge stems from Jackson's use of the veto. He was more lavish than all predecessors combined; they had vetoed altogether nine bills, while he disallowed twelve. He upset schemes of major import such as the Maysville Road bill in 1830, recharter of the second Bank in 1832, distribution of the federal surplus to the states in 1833. In the last instance he used the first "pocket veto" in American history. Henry Clay was working harder than usual at politics that year. The Compromise Tariff was one instance. He saw another opening that might combine several goals. Since 1815 the Treasury had been reducing the federal debt; it had fallen from $127 million to a mere $7 million. A federal surplus was piling up. Clay proposed to give it to the states to be spent by them for internal improvements. If the Treasury were decimated, perhaps at some future date the need for funds could become an excuse for raising import duties or at least for revoking the scheduled reductions. The bill passed by more than a two-thirds majority in each House, but less than ten days remained in the session of Congress. The president is allowed ten days to consider a bill. Refusing either to sign or to veto, Jackson killed it by putting it in his pocket. In his vetoes the president clearly acted within the constitutional limits of his office. Jackson also worked a metamorphosis, even a reversal, in public opinion. Always the legislature had been regarded as the voice of democracy, the spokesman for the sovereign people, while the other branches were seen as potential despots. Now the president emerged as the popular champion against the menace of transitory majorities in a legislature swayed by corrupt and corrupting lobbyists. Each congressman spoke only for local and "vested" interests but the president represented the whole people. The opposition fought for its life against Jackson's popularity. Striving to appear democratic, the National Republicans in May 1832 adopted the first national platform of any political party. Still losing ground, they intensified the clamor against the president's "tyranny." He became King Andrew. The opposition took the next step in demagogy by assuming the name of the English enemies of divine right of kings—the

Whigs. This designation appeared in *Niles' Weekly Register* in April 1834, when it was already being used by anti-Jackson parties in New York and Connecticut. The Democrats came back at them with a campaign song:

> *Mechanics, Carters, Laborers*
> *Must form a close connection*
> *And show the rich Aristocrats*
> *Their powers at this election.*
> *Yankee Doodle, smoke 'em out*
> *The proud, the banking faction.*
> *None but such as Hartford Feds*
> *Oppose the poor and Jackson.*

Starting in 1832 the banking system went insane. By 1836 the number of banks had doubled since 1828, as had the volume of bank notes in circulation. Even though the size of the cotton crop nearly doubled in the five years after 1833, the price rose from 11 cents to 16 cents. Many banks had negligible reserves; bank A might include in its reserves its deposits in bank B, which of course left bank B free to count its deposits in bank C (or in bank A, for that matter). The phrase "wildcat banking" seems to date from this era; when you went to redeem banknotes in specie, you learned that the bank's only office was back in the piney woods where the bobcats lived. Although New York and Massachusetts worked out restraints of their own, through most of the nation a huge structure of credit was built upon air. Critical here was the absence of the earlier efforts at regulating the currency by the second Bank. Biddle's behavior had become erratic, irresponsible. After losing his federal charter he continued under one from Pennsylvania; when the price of cotton broke late in the decade, he fell to the folly of supposing that his bank could peg cotton values.

Perhaps no group of executives, whatever their financial resources, whatever their genius, could have held back the runaway impulses. The economy was spurred by extreme hopes—and by equally extreme fears. Prevailing tempers were described by a lawyer who practiced among the booming new plantations of Alabama and Mississippi:

> An emigrant community is necessarily a practical community; wants come before luxuries—things take precedence of words; the necessaries that support life precede the arts and elegancies that embellish it. A man of great parts may miss his way to greatness by frittering away his powers upon non-essentials—upon the style and finish of a thing rather than upon its strength and utility—upon modes rather than upon ends. To direct strength aright, the aim is as essential as the power. But above all things, success depends more upon self-confidence than anything else; talent must go in partnership with will or it cannot do a business of profit. . . . And where can a man get this self-reliance so well as in a new country, where he is thrown upon his own resources; where his only friends are his talents; where he sees energy leap at once into prominence; where those only are above him whose talents are above his; where there is no *prestige* of rank, or ancestry, or

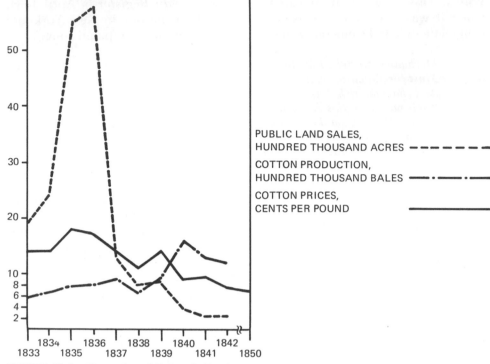

FIGURE 12-4. *Expansion of Cotton Cultivation*

wealth, or past reputation—and no family influence, or dependants, or patrons; where the stranger of yesterday is the man of mark to-day; where a single speech may win position, to be lost by a failure the day following; and where amidst a host of competitors in an open field of rivalry, every man of the same profession enters the course with a race-horse emulation, to win the prize which is glittering within sight of the rivals. There is no stopping in such a crowd: he who does not go ahead is run over and trodden down. . . .

Implications leap in several directions from this portrait. It suggests a French proverb that was even more true for the United States: "From shirtsleeves to shirtsleeves in three generations." And the lawyer's final sentence preaches that your competitors will eat you alive unless you rend them first. This suggests the futility of Nicholas Biddle's efforts to restrain his countrymen; men intent on self-preservation will not be curbed.

The phantasmagoric flights of credit must not divert us from the growth of real capital. This investment can conveniently be considered in four categories: internal improvements, other social overhead, manufacturing, growth of arable land. From 1816 to 1840 some $125 million was spent on canal construction. Steamboat construction more than doubled from 1832 to

1837; the tonnage built in 1837 alone was more than the total in the Ohio-Mississippi basin in 1830. Most regions boasted new turnpikes and bridges. An accelerating start was made by railroads; about 3,000 miles was in operation by 1840 (Chapter 13). The growth of Eastern cities and settlement of the West meant more homes, more schools, more stores, courthouses, churches. The new town of Lowell, Massachusetts was founded only in 1822, but by 1839 the capital invested in its mills was greater than the original cost, $10 million, of the Erie Canal. Spindles in cotton manufacturing in the nation rose sharply:

1820	$200,000
1825	800,000
1835	1,750,000

Capacity grew substantially in iron, machinery, woolens, shoes and leather products. Sales of federal public lands soared from $2.6 million in 1832 to $14.8 million in 1835 to almost $25 million in 1836—the all-time high in our history.

The inflation should not be regarded as a domestic affair; it paralleled a similar phenomenon in Europe. But seemingly it was less extreme in parts of Europe. In the United States by 1836 interest rates of 2–4 per cent per month were not unusual.* These high yields drew capital from abroad. Then foreign investors became leery and started withdrawing funds. The first shock was multiplied by the federal government. Its Specie Circular in the summer of 1836 required that all sales of federal public lands should be financed in hard coin. The nation showed an import surplus for the year of $61 million, so that specie was being drained from Eastern banks in both directions—to go to Europe and to go to the frontier for public-land purchases. On 10 May, 1837, the New York banks ceased to redeem their notes in specie.

Although the West got some relief from the eventual success of Clay's Distribution Act, which took effect 1 January, 1837, the East was harmed as much as it was helped by that policy. The ensuing depression did not abate in many regions until 1842–1843. By imposing severe hardship on countless numbers, it advanced two desirable reforms: the abolition of imprisonment for debt, and a federal bankruptcy law. As to the latter, English precedents were not suited to American needs. Bankruptcy had applied only to men engaged in

---

*This inflation, lasting almost without break from 1823 to 1837, is a classic case of the redistribution of wealth from one part of a society to others—thereby changing the rate of economic growth. A rise in the price level means that persons receiving a fixed income must curtail their consumption. This development frees resources that can be used to increase investment, be it for roads, canals, factories, or whatever. In short, spending power is transferred from a quiescent segment to active entrepreneurs.

trade, to merchants, not to such classes as farmers or laborers. The action was often involuntary, being brought by creditors eager to recapture at least a portion of the debt. There was no way under federal law for an ordinary citizen to voluntarily turn his assets over to his creditors so that he would emerge a free man without onus. In an age that was coming to believe fervently in the Religion of the Second Chance (or the Fifth; see Chapter 14), the omission seemed unjust, unChristian. Moreover, not only was imprisonment for debt foolish in its results for all parties directly concerned, it was a serious drain on the economy because it converted debtors from productive members of society to burdens on taxpayers.

If we forswear sentimentality, we will find it hard to credit how dire for the nation was the jailing of debtors. Most debts were incurred by business-men who hoped to invest the funds at a profit. Sometimes they failed. Robert Morris with debts of $12 million spent almost three years in a Philadelphia cell; Justice James Wilson fled to North Carolina to avoid a jail in Penn-sylvania. During 1809 in New York alone, 1,300 men were imprisoned for the crime of having been defeated by the Embargo. Exalted merchants were not the only ones to suffer. Pittsburgh in 1819 had some 8,000 residents. In six weeks that summer, 115 people were imprisoned for debt. Two thirds of them owed less than $10, only three more than $100; one man was jailed because of an obligation of 18¾ cents. In Philadelphia from June, 1829, to February, 1830, (not a depressed period by any standard) 817 persons were sentenced for their insolvencies. Only 98 owed more than $100 each, 263 less than $5, 30 less than $1. In 1833 it was estimated that 75,000 persons a year were going to jail for debt: New York, 10,000; Pennsylvania, 7,000; Massachusetts and Mary-land, 3,000 each. The stupidity of the practice was becoming obvious. Kentucky abolished it in 1821. Although New York followed ten years later, most of the early repeals were effected in noncommercial states. At last in 1857 Massachusetts decreed that "imprisonment for debt except in cases of fraud is hereby abolished forever"; by then nearly all states had acted.

The Federal Convention with almost no debate had empowered Con-gress to "establish uniform laws on the subject of bankruptcies." The Consti-tution also said: "No State shall . . . pass any . . . Law impairing the Obliga-tion of Contracts. . . ." Did these provisions render invalid all state insolvent laws? Congress passed its first bankruptcy act in 1800. In the English fashion it applied only to traders. It had no voluntary clause; any proceeding had to be brought by a creditor against a debtor. Dissatisfaction was common for several reasons, and the law was repealed in 1803. The Panic of 1837 thrust the question forward, and the Whigs put up a bankruptcy bill. The background for it was explained in the Senate: "A sort of mania had seized upon our community, and by a course of untoward adventures and speculations had involved in one common deluge of disaster the fortunes of the rich and the hard earnings of the industrious. . . . There was improvident, wild, and unwarrantable use of individual credit." In June 1840 the Senate passed the bill, but it was blocked in the Democratic-controlled House. The election that fall reflected the issue. The Whigs won—thanks, so the opposition charged, to the votes of 400,000 bankrupts. Allegedly these votes had tipped the scales in five states with 89 electoral votes. Those five states included New York and Pennsylvania and had a combined total of 900,000 voters while the aggregate Whig majority was only 18,000.

The need for the immoral statute was clear. As one representative explained: "The country is covered with debt, contracted when currency was worth not more than half its values, when banknotes were plenty as the leaves in autumn. The exact payment now is in truth to exact two dollars for one." Undoubtedly the deflation from 1837 to 1841 bore hard on debtors. Even so the House rejected the bill. It was logrolling that saved the situation. A New Distribution Bill had been introduced; this one would apportion among the states certain federal public lands and receipts from their sale. Within two days, votes for it had been swapped for votes in favor of the Bankruptcy Act and the latter was passed. The law lasted only a little more than a year before it was repealed. But it did its work. By subsequent report, 33,739 persons sought relief under its provisions. Only 765 petitions were rejected. The debts absolved were the gigantic sum of $440,934,000; the property surrendered by debtors brought $43,697,357. Thus quickly could Americans weasel through an escape hatch if it was left ajar.

Prior to the War for Independence, portions of America had undergone what has been aptly dubbed the Pre-industrial Revolution. But only after the War of 1812 did the Industrial Revolution strike like a tornado. The dramatic economic growth of the Early Republic was marred by a financial crisis in 1817 that led to a depression that was especially severe in such manufacturing centers as Pittsburgh. But within five years or so, the boom was going again. While the population and purchasing power of the United States grew mightily, Great Britain was becoming increasingly dependent on foreign markets to buy her manufactures. This setting made possible the Monroe Doctrine, which ranks with the Farewell Address (Chapter 9) as one of the two master tenets of American foreign policy in the nineteenth century. A decade later came the two most ghastly domestic conflicts of the period 1815–1837. President Jackson was a central figure in both. Due to his distrust of banking and of paper money—a hard-money man he—he led the successful fight to destroy the Second Bank of the United States. Second, when South Carolina (in a paper secretly written by Vice President Calhoun) asserted her sovereign right to secede unilaterally from the Union, Jackson was quick to assert the power of the federal government to enforce its laws in all areas of the United States. Calhoun won a compromise tariff, which was the original point of contention, and Jackson maintained federal jurisdiction. But the New Republic was beginning to fissure, feeding the hopes of its worst enemies and forewarning the divisions that would lead to civil war in 1861.

SOME NOTABLE EVENTS

1803 *Marbury* v. *Madison*; First congressional act declared unconstitutional by Supreme Court.

1809–
  1825 Latin American colonies win independence from Iberian nations.

1810 *Fletcher* v. *Peck*; Supreme Court forbids state legislature from cancelling a contract, even through fraudulently made in Georgia land grab.

1816 Second Bank of the United States chartered.

  Tariff Act is the first obviously protective set of import duties.

  Martin v. *Hunter's Lessee*; Supreme Court asserts supremacy of federal law on constitutional issues.

1818 *McCulloch* v. *Maryland*; Supreme Court denies state power to tax arbitrarily.

1819 *Dartmouth College* v. *Woodward*; Supreme Court upholds basic contract obligations.

  University of Virginia opens—the first American college not to require a profession of religion or attendance at chapel.

  Unitarian Church started by William Ellery Channing.

1820 U.S. census: 9,638,453 (7.2% urban).

1820–
  1821 Massachusetts constitutional convention.

1821 New York constitutional convention.

  Greece proclaims independence from Turkey.

  Cohens v. *Virginia*; Supreme Court reasserts power to rule on constitutionality of state laws.

1823 Monroe Doctrine, December 2.

1824 *Gibbons* v. *Ogden*; Supreme Court invalidates monopolies in interstate commerce.

1825 Erie Canal opens, October 26.

  England opens the world's first railroad.

1827 *Brown* v. *Maryland*; Supreme Court defines the limits of interstate commerce.

1828 Tariff of Abominations means highest general level prior to Civil War.

1829 *Willson* v. *The Black Bird Creek Marsh Company*; Supreme Court defines state powers in regulating interstate commerce.

1829–
  1830 Virginia constitutional convention.

1830 Jackson vetoes Maysville Road bill, May 27.

  U.S. census: 12,866,020 (8.8% urban).

1831 *Cherokee Nation* v. *Georgia*; Supreme Court defense of Indian rights rendered powerless by President Jackson's refusal to enforce with federal troops.

  Nat Turner slave rebellion in Virginia.

1832 Jackson vetoes recharter of the second Bank of the United States, July 10.

  Ordinance of Nullification by South Carolina, November 24.

  Jackson replies to South Carolina, December 10.

1833 South Carolina nullifies the Force Bill, March 18.

  Jackson notifies his cabinet of the witholding of federal deposits from the second Bank of the United States, September 18.

1835 Jackson justifies the forced relocation of Southern Indians; federal land sales moving to all-time high.

1836 Specie Circular, July 11.

1837 Distribution Act takes effect, January 1.

  New York banks suspend specie payments.

  Charles River Bridge Company v. *Warren Bridge Company*; Taney for Supreme Court defends government limitations on monopolies.

1841 Second federal bankruptcy law, August 19.

Ways to Study History XII

Exploit visual aids. The typical map demands careful study. Any effort to portray three-dimensional realities in a two-dimensional schema is bound to encounter dilemmas. Most maps of military campaigns and battles are disappointing or even misleading for their failure to show the terrain on which the encounters were fought; see for example the depiction of engagements during the War for Independence in the volume by Clifford L. and Elizabeth H. Lord (1944). These deficiencies can be seen in the military maps of nearly all textbooks about the United States.

The general-purpose atlases of American history are treacherous in their failure to face squarely the limitations of their medium. A recent atlas by Martin Gilbert (1968) declares that it wants to be "as comprehensive as possible, consistent with clarity. . . ." But the attempt to map "Social Problems 1792–1860" was a foredoomed venture. While the map of the Cumberland Road is helpful, the accompanying one of railroads in 1860 gives a false impression.

A solution to the three-dimensional problem which is not often available is the relief map. (Banff, Alberta features before its museum a large map of the town on which the topography is shown to scale.) Another answer is the isometric projection; a continuous-line connects all points having the same elevation above sea level.

The most promising approach would seem to be the special-purpose atlas. The aim here is to select a topic about which quick glances at maps can convey much information. Two recent works merit special commendation. George Rogers Taylor and Irene D. Neu in *The American Railroad Network* (1956) use vivid maps in showing how variations in gauge were eliminated between 1861 and 1890. Randall D. Sale and Edwin D. Karn, *American Expansion: A Book of Maps* (1962), yields more insight into some aspects of the subject than could be gleaned from reading hundreds of pages of prose.

Document 12-1

Robert Banks Jenkinson, second Earl of Liverpool, was Prime Minister from 1812 to 1827. In a brilliant speech to the Lords in 1820, he analyzed the consequences for the United States of the Napoleonic Wars and also the economic needs of his own nation that enabled the United States to count on British support for the Monroe Doctrine. Referring to the current business distress in the Atlantic world, he explained that of all countries the deleterious effects of peace were being felt most keenly by the United States.

And how has she felt it? During the whole of the late war, America was the principal neutral power. During a part of that war she was the only neutral power. She enjoyed the most extensive carrying trade. She supplied this country, and she supplied other countries with many articles, which, neither this country, nor other countries could at that time obtain elsewhere. What was the natural consequence? That America increased in wealth, in commerce, in arts, in population, in strength more rapidly than any other nation ever before increased, in the history of the world. In twenty years, the United States of America made a greater progress than the same nation, in the ordinary and natural course of events could have accomplished in forty years. But now all the world is at peace. . . . The state of America, my lords, at this moment is not so much the effect of present positive distress, as of extraordinary past prosperity. She must retrograde to a certain point. . . . I am far from saying this invidiously—On former occasions I have sufficiently stated my conviction that there is no country more interested than England is, that the distress of America should cease, and that she should be enabled to continue that rapid progress which has been for a time interrupted; for, of all the powers on the face of the earth, America is the one whose increasing population and immense territory furnish the best prospects for British produce and manufacturers. Everybody, therefore, who wishes prosperity to England, must wish prosperity to America. . . .

Document 12-2

Although the charter of the second Bank of the United States would not expire until 1836, Nicholas Biddle allowed its petition for renewal to come before Congress in January 1832. Everybody knew the application would pass, and it did. But President Jackson vetoed it.

Among the reasons he cited the bill's grant of a monopoly. In addition to its denunciation of governmentally bestowed privileges, the President's message skillfully appealed to xenophobia.

The present corporate body, denominated the president, directors, and company of the Bank of the United States, will have existed at the time this act is intended to take effect twenty years. . . . The powers, privileges, and favors bestowed upon it in the original charter, by increasing the value of the stock far above its par value, operated as a gratuity of many millions to the stockholders. . . . It is not our own citizens only who are to receive the bounty of our Government. More than eight millions of the stock of this bank are held by foreigners. By this act the American Republic proposes virtually to make them a present of some millions of dollars. For these gratuities to foreigners and to some of our own opulent citizens the act secures no equivalent whatever. . . .

Is there no danger to our liberty and independence in a bank that in its nature has so little to bind it to our country? The president of the bank has told us that most of the State banks exist by its forbearance. Should its influence become concentrated, as it may under the operation of such an act as this, in the hands of a self-elected directory whose interests are identified with those of the foreign stockholders, will there not be cause to tremble for the purity of our elections in peace and for the independence of our country in war? . . .

If we must have a bank with private stockholders, every consideration of sound policy and every impulse of American feeling admonishes that it should by purely American. . . .

Document 12-3

By general consent, Alexis de Tocqueville is the most profound of all commentators on American society. Perceiving that his own France was taking the road to human equality, he visited the United States in 1831–1832 to get a preview of what awaited his homeland.

The nearer the people are drawn to the common level of an equal and similar condition, the less prone does each man become to place implicit faith in a certain man or a certain class of men. But his readiness to believe the multitude increases, and opinion is more than ever mistress of the world. Not only is common opinion the only guide which private judgment retains among a democratic people, but among such a people it possesses a power infinitely beyond what it has elsewhere. At periods of equality men have no faith in one another, by reason of their common resemblance; but this very resemblance gives them almost unbounded confidence in the judgment of the public; for it would seem probable that, as they are all endowed with equal means of judging, the greater truth should go with the greater number.

When the inhabitant of a democratic country compares himself individually with all those about him, he feels with pride that he is the equal of any one of them; but when he comes to survey the totality of his fellows and to place himself in contrast with so huge a body, he is instantly overwhelmed by the sense of his own insignificance and weakness. The same equality that renders him independent of each of his fellow citizens, taken severally, exposes him alone and unprotected to the influence of the greater number. The public, therefore, among a democratic people, has a singular power, which aristocratic nations cannot conceive; for it does not persuade others to its beliefs, but it imposes them and makes them permeate the thinking of everyone by a sort of enormous pressure of the mind of all upon the individual intelligence. . . .

Continentalism as a Foreign Policy

Two Boston merchants can be seen as symbols of the re-direction of American aspirations in the nineteenth century. John Perkins Cushing began withdrawing his capital from foreign trade after 1828. But in 1832 he was still using $454,500 in foreign ventures and only $356,129 at home. By 1837 the first category had fallen below $10,000 and he had more than a million dollars in the United States. His holdings of manufacturing stocks reached $150,000 by 1835 and to nearly twice that sum in 1851. The interests of John Murray Forbes were even more migratory and more concentrated. Born in 1813, he made his first fortune as a young man in the China trade. Back in Boston he managed his own money and served as private trustee to the estates of others. Until about 1850 he was heavily involved in textile stocks and took an active part in overseeing the companies. As this branch of manufacturing became overbuilt in New England, he looked for a new growth industry. He found it—Midwestern railroads. At the time of his death in 1898 his lines stretched from Chicago to the Twin Cities to Denver.

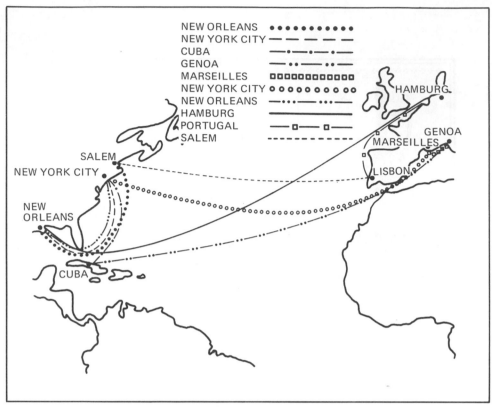

FIGURE 13-1. *Voyage of the* Forrester, *1826–1828*

This reorientation was dramatic and it was conclusive for the future. But its degree and speed must not be exaggerated. Foreign markets continued to loom large in American hopes. Moreover, much oceanic commerce went on in the haphazard ways of the old-style tramps, as in the typical voyage of the *Forrester* of Salem, shown in Figure 13-1. (We could hazard some interesting guesses as to her cargo on each leg of the voyage.) But of growing importance were the packet lines that met definite schedules. The first from New York was started in 1818; that port by 1845 was serving fifty-two packets and its docks offered three regular sailings a week.

Due to the gross inefficiency of available engines, steamships were much slower to conquer the high seas than the inland waterways. The first to cross the Atlantic was the *Savannah,* which in 1819 made a run from her namesake city to Liverpool in twenty-seven days. When the *British Queen* was launched twenty years later, she was designed to carry 750 tons of coal and a mere 500 tons of cargo. Only at the end of the century (1899) did the White Star Line put on the Atlantic a steamer that carried no sails. But the dimensions of merchant vessels grew spectacularly. In the decade beginning with 1820 a cargo ship of 500 tons was substantial; by the 1850's bottoms three times that large were common. Speed soared. In 1820 a packet crossed in 40 to 60 days; by 1860 the trip might be made in less than ten days and more than two weeks was thought slow. Freight charges fell. To ship cotton to Liverpool or Le Havre in 1856 cost less than half what it had cost thirty years earlier. As we shall soon see, this mighty American merchant marine almost disappeared from the oceans after the Civil War. American ships had always paid higher wages than other navies, but they could compete because they carried smaller crews. A British vessel of 1,000 tons required 40 men plus 10 boys, whereas an American ship of the same size had a different design to its rigging and needed only 20–30 hands. Also American ships were built better and lasted longer. But when wooden vessels were superseded by iron hulls, shipbuilding in the United States became untenable. By then most of the nation's resources, including steel mills, were inland, and thereafter only two branches of the merchant marine could survive. A few passenger vessels were given federal subsidies for carrying the mail, the first subsidy being granted in 1845. Also since foreign ships were banned from the coastal trade, American ships continued on those usually short runs.

Segments of the merchant marine had withered before the Civil War. A prominent casualty was whaling. Its early capital on Nantucket declined as vessels had to go farther afield for their prey. The larger ships could not be handled by the shallow harbor on the island.* Then the trade centered at New Bedford on the mainland. Here one blacksmith in his career made 58,517 harpoons. The town stood on the west bank of the Acushnet River, which gave its name to the whaler that carried Herman Melville to the South Pacific in 1841 (see the end of Chapter 14). Later these entries were made in the *Acushnet's* log: "December 16, 1845—Busy Doing nothing—nothing to do it with . . . Friday, January 23, 1846—Doing nothing special. Dull as you please." Although the job was usually monotonous, sounding a pod of whales would bring incredible thrills, and subduing a whale meant great gains. One ship that was only two-thirds full on its return nonetheless yielded its owners $850 for every $500 they had invested. New Bedford peaked in 1857. Ten thousand men were engaged in whaling, and a fleet of 329 ships brought home oil and bone that sold for $6,178,728. The discovery of petroleum in 1859 meant the displacement of whale oil by kerosene as an illuminating fuel, and the industry atrophied after the Civil War.

A general view of the place of the United States in the world economy seems appropriate at this point; (see Figure 3-1). Fluctuations in American prices and price levels tended to correlate with those in Britain and western Europe. Second, the growth of foreign trade was proportionate to the rise of

---

*Other ports suffered the same doom for the same reason. Salem, which had been after 1790 the international mart for pepper from Sumatra, could not accommodate the bigger bottoms after 1815. Cotton was collected in modest ships along the Gulf coast and brought to New York for transshipment into larger vessels for the transatlantic crossing to Liverpool.

domestic population; each quantity slightly more than tripled from 1820 to 1860. Third, the value of alien investments in the United States was amazingly low, the accumulated total being a mere $400 million in 1860.* This sum was just slightly greater than the value of merchandise imports for that single year. As to exports, three declined in relative importance—tobacco, rice, lumber products. Wheat and flour in 1860 stood about where they had in 1820. The great change came in exports of cotton. They provided 39 per cent of the total value 1816–1820, and rose to 63 per cent 1836–1840. Although they declined thereafter, they were more than half of the value of all exports in every year until the Civil War. Southern planters approached the conflict with the jeer COTTON IS KING.

From 45 per cent of the nation's population in 1820, the South had declined to 35 per cent by 1860. Within the section the proportion of blacks had fallen: one person of every 5½ in 1820, only one of 7 in 1860. Urbanization lagged behind the pace of the Northeast. Due mainly to the steamboats but also to the need of cotton and sugar planters for some localized services, it was river towns that grew most rapidly in the South. In the decade after 1850 New Orleans grew 45 per cent, Louisville 55 per cent, St. Louis nearly doubled. It is true that Mobile on the Gulf had multiplied twenty times since 1820, reaching 30,000 inhabitants by 1850, but look at what happened in Memphis. This river town was not founded until 1819 and in 1826 it had fewer than 500 residents. But by 1850 it reached 8,839 and then bounced to 22,263 in 1860. But the South Atlantic cities foundered. A Southern novelist wrote of Savannah: "Like most of our Southern townships and depots it remains stationary and has an air of utter languishment." That was 1831; by 1850 the town revived a bit and grew 45 per cent in the next decade. Charleston had no such luck; its population was less in 1860 than twenty years earlier.

These processes need a closer look later (Chapter 15). For now, we can say that capital spent on slaves and on land for cotton cultivation yielded such a high rate of return that other types of investment were inexpedient. The South as a section preferred to buy such services as banking, insurance, shipping, marketing, and even food and clothing from outside its own borders—from the North or Europe. Thus it never sustained those secondary and tertiary industries that result in the growth of cities.** Above the Mason-Dixon Line (say, the Ohio River) the story was different. The rate of urban

---

*This figure takes no account of prior repudiations. Nobody has tried to estimate the value of obligations to foreigners that were written off—many times in circumstances that condemn the action—by American citizens and governments: confiscations of Loyalist property, reneging by states and cities on bonds they issued during the public-improvement craze of 1830 to 1860.

**Primary industries, meaning the direct exploitation of natural resources, involve such extractive operations as lumbering, mining, farming. Secondary ones—manufacturing or ore refining—process these crude materials. Tertiary ones deal in the intangibles usually labelled services. An incisive way to see the history of any economy is to watch the replacement of one category by another.

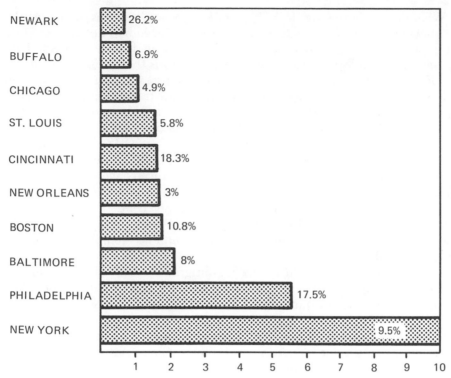

FIGURE 13-2. *Population of American Cities, 1860 (hundred thousands)*

growth (of towns bigger than 2,500) was greater during 1840–1850 than in any other period in American history. The population of cities almost doubled. Whereas only twelve towns exceeded 10,000 people in 1820, the number was 101 by 1860. The score then stood thus:

	1860 Population	Per cent of Population in Manufacturing
1. New York City	1,080,330	9.5
2. Philadelphia	565,529	17.5
3. Baltimore	212,418	8.0
4. Boston	177,840	10.8
5. New Orleans	168,675	3.0
6. Cincinnati	161,044	18.3
7. St. Louis	160,773	5.8
8. Chicago	109,260	4.9
9. Buffalo	81,129	6.9
10. Newark	71,941	26.2

What do the figures signify? Every one of these cities was on navigable water. Their rate of growth was extremely rapid. Chicago had not even existed in 1830; she got a rapid start as a lake port and railroad center, but she had hardly begun to develop the stockyards and steel mills that would make her a center of manufacturing. New Orleans had almost skipped the stage of secondary industries and relied on mercantile and transportation services. Buffalo was dependent on the initiative that had brought the Erie Canal, as was Albany (twelfth). Washington (thirteenth) was built on a single service: government. Due to the gold rush that had started in 1848, San Francisco (fourteenth) had more than 50,000 people of whom only 2.6 per cent were in factories. As a contrast, the mill towns of Massachusetts were more deeply rooted in secondary industries even than Newark; Lowell had 36 per cent of its population in manufacturing, and Lynn all of 45 per cent. In other respects these textile villages had a skewed demography.* An abnormal part of their population was of working age, and a high proportion was female (see Ways to Study History XIII).

The rise of cities was fed by mass immigration. Only in 1825 did the influx from all countries first top 10,000. But in 1842 it was ten times that figure, and by 1854 it had quadrupled again. The chief source was Ireland, where famine began in 1845 and then ground its pitiless course. Most Irish fugitives could barely limp to the American seaboard where they piled up as destitute masses in the largest cities. By 1855 the once English-stock Boston held 55,000 Irish—with strains on the social structure to be examined presently. Congestion near each metropolitan core became grotesque; the first multi-family tenement building was erected on Cherry Street in Manhattan in 1835. At mid-century conditions had deteriorated further. The few studies that have been made of Massachusetts textile mills suggest that wage scales actually declined after 1840 under the impact of mass immigration. In New York City although such skilled crafts as blacksmiths and carpenters may have earned as much as $12 a week, the employee who could command more than a dollar a day was rare. At the bottom of the heap were seamstresses who worked at home (fine word for a wretched hole) in the putting-out branches of the needle trades; a day's work often brought a mere twenty-five cents. Some skills tried to organize collectively to guard both their craft and their income, but these sporadic efforts at trade unionism frequently met with trouble from the law. A New York court in 1835 ruled that a combination of laborers to maintain wages was *per se* a criminal conspiracy, while seven years later the Supreme Court of Massachusetts under Chief Justice Lemuel Shaw reached the contrary view. The issue remained for future decision.

---

*Demography, a growing and exciting branch of historical studies, deals with changes in population and the factors that underly those changes: birth rates, death rates, average age at marriage, life expectancies at various ages, the distribution of a given population by age and by sex, differences in these variables over space and time.

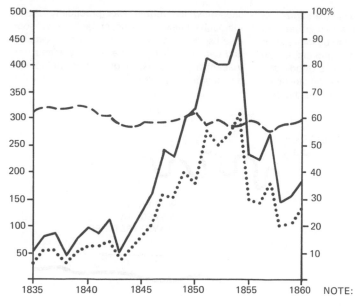

TOTAL IMMIGRANTS ————

NUMBER AGED BETWEEN
15–40 YEARS •••••••••••

PERCENT MALE — — — —

FIGURE 13-3. *Immigration, 1835–1860*

NOTE: RETURNING US CITIZENS
ARE INCLUDED IN THE
FIGURES. THE FIGURES
FOR 1843 INCLUDE ONLY
THOSE IMMIGRANTS WHO
ENTERED DURING THE
NINE MONTHS WHICH
ENDED SEPTEMBER 30.

Cities grew only by facing and trying to conquer grave obstacles. Urban sanitation was hideous. In New Orleans in 1853 some 40,000 persons, one resident in four got yellow fever; 8,000 died. A report on pollution of air and water in Boston reads as if it had been written more than a century later (Document 14-2). Another problem was to feed a concentrated population and to keep it warm in winter. Even before the War for Independence the growth of Boston had been reversed by a shortage of firewood; this impediment was overcome by the exploitation of deposits of anthracite coal. The figures are startling: from one ton a day, 365 tons for the year, in 1820, to 175,000 tons in 1830. The growth of cities also meant a rapidly growing market for manufactures. Only after 1850 was this new demand being typically met by factory-produced goods. Earlier suppliers were (a) an enlarged handicraft or shop production, and (b) spread of the domestic or putting-out technique. But the encroachments of factories were inexorable. The woolen mills of New England produced less than $1 million worth in 1820, more than $11 worth in 1831. As a swelling tide of cloth poured from nascent factories, manufacturing in households declined. Spinning wheels and handlooms in the homes of New

Vulcanized Rubber

Crude rubber, or latex, is the sap of the rubber tree. When dried, this sap possesses limited qualities of elasticity, can be formed into a bouncing ball, and will erase (rub out, hence rubber) pencil marks. Until Charles Goodyear's almost accidental discovery of the Vulcanization process in 1839, the last function was the only one for which rubber was practically useful. Although somewhat elastic, crude latex will soon lose its resiliency; it will crack in cold weather and become gummy in the heat of summer. The Vulcanization process made rubber available for a wide variety of uses.

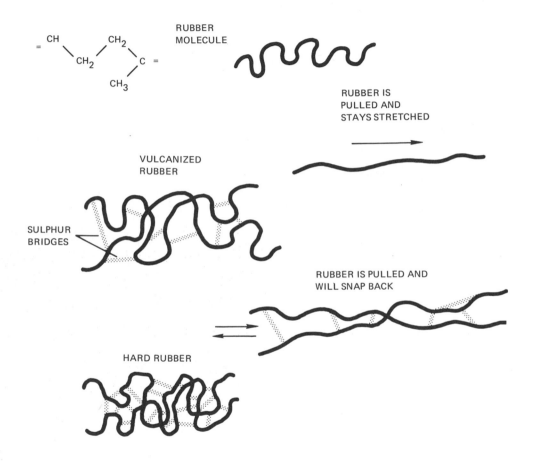

(1) Raw rubber consists of carbon and hydrogen atoms, arranged as shown. A chain of more than 2000 of these units makes up the rubber molecule. The molecules are not interlocked.
(2) When rubber is mixed with sulphur and heated to 200° F, the sulphur molecules form bridges between the rubber molecules. Now when the rubber is stretched and released, the sulphur bridges will pull it back to its original position. It has also acquired a much greater resistance to heat and cold.
(3) Hard rubber contains a great many sulphur bridges and consists of 15 to 30 per cent sulphur, compared to 1.5–5.5 per cent in softer elastic rubber.

York State produced 8.97 yards of textiles per capita in 1825, less than a foot in 1855.

From Massachusetts came a clear statement: "Labor-saving machinery bringing the articles so much lower than can be made in houses, it is found most profitable to purchase. The same time spent in a factory will produce at least ten times as much as in household manufacture." The American genius ran to speeding up machines and making them so automatic that the operators needed little skill. A new American spindle would run three times as fast as the Arkwright spindle used in Britain. Costs of production fell rapidly. Cotton sheeting cost 18 cents a yard in 1815, only 2 cents in 1860. In the United States the pressure to mechanize was felt even by industries that did not turn out a truly standardized product. Watches were not composed of really standardized parts and needed considerable fitting by hand. The number of man-days needed per watch in Switzerland was falling hardly at all. But Waltham Watch, opening its doors in 1854, within five years had cut the requirement from 21 man-days to 4.

Such gains in output by factories could not have occurred without concomitant improvements in transportation. The emergence in rural areas of a market for fabricated wares depended on a reduction of freight charges so that farmers distant from urban buyers could deliver their produce there at profitable prices. Conversely a factory had to be able to deliver its goods to the farmer at a price he could afford to pay. The drastic decline in shipping costs began with the Erie Canal. The average ton-mile rate to all freight carried by it in 1857–1860 was .8155 cents—less than a penny; this was a reduction of more than 95 per cent from the Buffalo to New York City charge in 1817. It is no surprise that the atrophy of household manufactures in New York State happened fastest in counties along the Hudson River-Erie Canal route. A similar drop took place on the Ohio-Mississippi. On the eve of the Civil War, although downstream rates were still 25–30 per cent of what they had been right after the War of 1812, the upstream charges had fallen all the way to 5–10 per cent of the base period. On the run from Cincinnati to New Orleans, competition at times knocked the costs down to .27 cents per ton-mile. Railroad construction beginning in 1830 almost universalized these reductions. In New York State as late as 1848 the average ton-mile rate of all railroads for first-class freight was 9.04 cents, for second-class 5.79 cents. Within three years the general average became 4.05 cents, and by 1860 it was 2.2 cents. By then an all-rail shipment of wheat from Chicago to New York could go for 34.8 cents a bushel, about 1.2 cents a ton-mile. (On the reverse runs the trains, with crude benches installed in box cars, carried immigrants for about a penny a mile.) A sound generalization is to say that in forty years the cost of sending bulky products in the American interior had fallen by 95 per cent. Speeds increased. The time from Cincinnati to New York declined from fifty days to as little as six days. Steamboat and railway could move freight five times as fast as canalboat and wagon.

The railroad was made technically feasible by the improved efficiency of steam engines (see early Chapter 11 on key inventions); tramways on rails operated by gravity or horses had long been used around mines. Its profitability under some conditions had been proven in England. The first American line, the Baltimore & Ohio, was promoted by leading merchants who sought "the best means of restoring to the city of Baltimore that portion of the western trade which has recently been diverted from it." This stimulus typified the early railways. They were devised by merchants of a city as feeder lines to capture from rivals the trade of a hinterland. Thus they were short nonconnecting roads. For instance, Charleston promoters hoping to beat nearby Savannah to the business of a rapidly growing cotton district built a line to Hamburg on the Savannah River. When finished in 1833, its 136 miles made it the longest road in the world under one management. Even with limited objectives the early companies had grave problems. They tried to copy the past in ludicrous ways. Railroad coaches copied stage coaches in design, including an elevated seat for the coachman. Executives thought they could copy toll roads and make each shipper provide his own motive power. The width customary in England for wagons had been 4 feet 8½ inches so the first tramways had been built to that gauge. It was simply copied for railways. This "standard gauge" did not become universal in the United States until 1886; the Erie used a 6-foot gauge to prevent diversion of its traffic to other lines, while a 5-footer was common in the South.

Railroads were forced to innovate on a dozen fronts. Unprecedented quantities of capital had to be raised, far more than was needed by any previous mode of transportation. Construction costs varied with terrain and with the quality of the product desired, but generally they were lower than for European railroads. Costs per mile in early transport construction were as follows; (convert British pounds to U.S. dollars at the rate of £1: $5):

railroads in Germany	£11,000
railroads in Belgium	£16,500
railroads in England	£30–40,000
stone turnpikes in U.S.	$5–10,000
canals in U.S.	$20–30,000
Georgia Railroad	$17,000
Baltimore & Ohio R.R.	$54,000
Boston and Lowell R.R.	$71,000

Such immense sums could not have been raised without government help. As early as 1838 an estimated $43 million in the public debts of states could be attributed to aid to railways. In the fifteen years after 1845 the states borrowed for this purpose more than $90 million.* It seems likely that municipalities and other local governments furnished even more assistance than did states. The first notable federal grant of public lands to assist railroad construction was not made until 1850. Prior to then the national government had given only two types of help. Its engineers had made free surveys of proposed routes. From 1830 to 1843 a differentially low tariff was set on imports of iron meant for railroad use.

American railroad building outpaced the rest of the world combined. By 1840 about 2,200 miles of track had gone into operation, by 1850 another 6,000, and in the next decade an astounding 22,000. The total bill for construction by 1860 was about a billion dollars. But note that by 1868 the total cost of railway construction was less than the English companies had spent for a single purpose—the purchase of land. Here is yet another way that American governments, mainly the states, helped the railways. History furnished little or no precedent for dozens of legal problems posed by the railroad. The chief innovator in a creative adaptation of the law was, again, Lemuel Shaw. Whereas the British gentry engaged in a form of legalized piracy in selling rights of way (virtually doling them out at so much a rod), Massachusetts under Shaw's guidance pioneered the doctrine of eminent domain. A company, by getting a charter from the state, had taken on certain responsibilities. But it had also acquired unusual rights. If it needed a piece of property, it could ask the courts to set a fair price. Barring reversal on appeal, the owner had to sell at that figure. This privilege could be and often was abused, but without it the railroads would not have been built. And reciprocally, the state supreme court in 1852 held that public commissioners could examine a schedule of rates on its merits and make equitable adjustments.

To what degree is a railroad liable for goods that it hauls? Liability was lessened by abrogating all requirements that a consignee had to be notified of the arrival of his shipment; this "Massachusetts doctrine" was followed as far afield as Georgia and Illinois. A rule covering transshipments held that a railroad was not responsible for damages unless the item was physically in its custody at the time of the injury. Is a railroad culpable for the destruction of goods that have reached their destination but that are still in its care? No. In an 1854 decision, Shaw considered a consignment that had reached its intended station. Uncalled for, it was placed in a warehouse owned by the railroad. The building burned, and the goods went up in smoke. Shaw held that the railroad's special liabilities had ended when the shipment reached the ter-

---

*Eight states, particularly in the Old Northwest and the South, disavowed in whole or part the obligations incurred to aid canals and railroads. One result was to give the young republic a bad name among British and European investors. Inexplicably, foreign capitalists later provided even larger sums to the trans-Mississippi lines.

minus of its route, and that thereafter the company had only normal responsibilities in caring for the property.

Encouraged by such friendly rulings, larger capitalists began to invade the railroad field about 1850. A favorite technique was to scoop up several short roads and combine them into a trunkline. Erastus Corning in 1853 headed a group that forged seven local companies into the New York Central from Buffalo to Albany. When the Civil War started, the Pennsylvania was a unified line from Philadelphia to Pittsburgh. Even more momentous in the decade after 1850 was the railroad construction in the Old Northwest. By 1860 the two states with the most railway mileage were Ohio and Illinois, with Indiana not far behind. Within the decade Ohio saw twenty combinations of railroads effected, by lease or sale or consolidation. (The state until 1852 did not tax the general property of railroads at all and not effectively until after the Civil War.) These Midwestern developments had a revolutionary impact on the sectional politics of the United States, which must be examined in Chapter 15.

The railroad boom spurred the whole economy. With two brief interludes, 1847–1848, 1854, the ebullience of business was unchecked from 1843 until the financial panic of 1857. In degree, in ubiquity, in duration, this prosperity has probably been matched only by the upsurges of 1898 to 1907 following the Spanish-American War and since 1955 following the Korean War.

Consider, for example, the telegraph. The first demonstration of the device did not come until 1844. But by 1852 there were 23,000 miles of wire in operation, and this figure more than doubled by the Civil War. This economic boom must not be reduced to technology alone. It fed on ingenuity and gumption, and nowhere were they more apparent than in New England. A truism held that the region had only two assets that it could export: ice and rocks. One proof that this deprivation could be transmuted into an asset was provided by Frederic Tudor the Ice King. About 1805 he started an operation to mine ice from New England ponds in winter and sell it in warm climates. Everybody else in Boston thought he was crazy, but the first entry in his notebook, 1 August, 1805, reads: "He who gives back at the first repulse and without striking the second blow despairs of success has never been, is not, and never will be a hero in war, love or business." In fifteen years he was making money. His manager invented an ice-cutter that brought the price of harvesting down to 10 cents a ton. He invented a scraper to clean the surface. He learned to use sawdust as insulation, thus utilizing what had been a worthless by-product of Maine lumber mills. In May, 1833, deciding to branch out from the West Indies, Tudor made his first shipment to Calcutta, where he later built a large depot. In 1846 Boston shipped 65,000 tons. Ten years later it sent more than twice that amount to spots as distant as China and Australia. Already Thoreau had written about ice harvesters in *Walden*: "They told me that in a good day they could get out a thousand tons, which was the yield of about one acre. . . . . They told me that they had some in the ice-houses at Fresh Pond five years old which was as good as ever. . . ."

Doubtless the westward surge of the iron rails did much to encourage ordinary men to dream of settling in the trans-Mississippi West. Those sprawling domains had known no white face except an occasional fur trader or trapper or soldier. An essential step in conquering this frontier was to establish the sovereignty of the United States by extinguishing all European claims to any part of the area. The Louisiana Purchase had been a magnificent beginning; thenceforth France would be out of the game. But Great Britain, Spain, and Russia were still in it. One contest was postponed by the Convention of 1818; Britain and the United States agreed for ten years to share the Pacific Northwest. Under this joint occupation the citizens of either nation could roam the territory at will. In 1827 this agreement was extended without term; repeatedly when confronted by a strong rival the American policy was stall. But against weak opponents we were not dilatory. One was Russia. In 1821 the Czar had prohibited all foreign ships from approaching the American mainland anywhere north of the 51st parallel. This ukase clearly encroached on the Oregon Country that the United States and Great Britain had agreed to occupy jointly. Secretary Adams was blunt to the Russian minister in Washington:

I told him specially that we should contest the right of Russia to *any* territorial establishment on this continent, and that we should assume distinctly the principle that the American continents are no longer subjects for *any* new European colonial establishments.

(Here was the Monroe Doctrine, four months before its statement by the president; see the opening of Chapter 12.) By a treaty of 1824, Russia withdrew its claims to the area south of 54° 40′.

Even more helpless than Russia was Spain. By the Adams-Onís Treaty of 1819 she acknowledged American title to all of the previously disputed Florida territories. The document also drew a transcontinental line that began on the Gulf of Mexico at the boundary of Texas and wandered northwestward all the way to the Pacific. Spain surrendered all claim to any territory west of the Rockies that was north of the 42nd parallel—the present northern boundary of California. John Quincy Adams was proud of his achievement: "It was, perhaps, the most important day of my life."

Americans were arriving at an expansive dream, which became an expansionist foreign policy. It was encouraged by the Lewis and Clark expedition, and fleshed out by the Adams-Onís Treaty. Its objective was clear: continentalism. By this creed, it was the "manifest destiny" of the United States to hold dominion over the entire continent of North America. No other sovereignty, not British-Canadian nor Spanish-Mexican nor tribal council of the Indians, had a right to thwart the American fate.

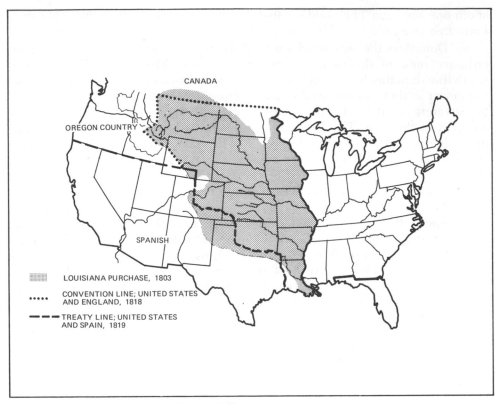

FIGURE 13-4. *The Adams-Onis Treaty, 1819*

The dominion to be drowned by the next Yankee wave was Mexican, and the United States government never appeared on stage at all. Coahuila-Texas was the northeastern state of Mexico. The new Mexican president, General Antonio Lopéz de Santa Anna, in 1834 dissolved the Mexican federal congress. Then he wiped out the states and declared himself dictator of a centralized government. It was rumored that he meant to disfranchise all Americans and drive them back to the United States. The Yankee intruders were in no mood to tolerate such foolishness. In the totality of Coahuila-Texas they were only 10 per cent of the population, but in their own locality they were a great majority. In January and February of 1835 some 2,000 Americans debarked at the mouth of the Brazos River; that brought their tally in Texas to nearly 30,000 while there were only 3,500 Mexicans. Prior to Santa Anna's usurpations the Americans had already felt abused. The legal system of Mexico short-circuited the right of trial by jury. Government, an offspring of its Spanish forebears, was absolutist, while Texans were strident for individualism and political liberty. Whites had contempt for browns: "five Indians will chase twenty Mexicans, but five Anglo-Americans will chase twenty Indians." This was the situation when the Mexican president founded more military garrisons to tighten the collection of customs duties. In a mode reminiscent of the customs racketeering that helped provoke the American War for Independence, the officials gouged for bribes and outrageous fees.

Armed clashes with the Mexican army began in the autumn of 1835. The following March 2 a "consultation" of delegates proclaimed independence. Then they had to fight to sustain the Republic of Texas. A major battle took place at San Antonio where the Texans sought refuge in a deserted mission. On March 6 the defenders of the Alamo were annihilated—but they exacted from Santa Anna a ferocious price. The Texas dead numbered 187; the Mexican, 1,544. After another massacre near Goliad, the Republic of Texas gave full martial powers to Sam Houston. This resolute general explained: "Had I consulted the wishes of all, I should have been like the ass between two stacks of hay. . . . I consulted none—I held no councils of war. If I err, the blame is mine." Again vaguely reminiscent of the War for Independence, Houston for six weeks followed a strategy of retreat. Then he struck. At the San Jacinto River on April 21, with an army of fewer than 800, his force killed or captured everybody in a Mexican army nearly twice as large. The war was over. Although Mexico did not legally concede the independence of the rebellious state, France in October, 1839, recognized the Republic of Texas. Great Britain followed suit in November, 1840, and Belgium and the Netherlands soon after.

The next important step in expanding the American sphere of influence was also achieved without any official action by the federal authorities. Russians had first come to the Pacific Northwest in 1742. A half century later the Russian American Fur Company was chartered, and in 1812 it established Fort Ross some 100 miles north of the Golden Gate. But in 1839 after many peregrinations a Swiss immigrant named John A. Sutter reached California. Two years later he bought Fort Ross, and the Russians retired all the way to Alaska.* The Mexican challenge had now been pushed back in the Southwest, the Russian one in the Northwest.

The next important development came in the Northeast, and involved Britain and Canada. A comprehensive American-Canadian boundary had never been agreed to. Friction was especially sharp along the line between Maine and New Brunswick. While tensions rose in New England, they were reinforced with a grievance against England by Southern slaveholders. Whereas the United States had never acted vigorously to enforce its own ban on the slave trade, Britain had done so and had also in 1832 abolished slavery everywhere in the Empire. A blow-up came in November 1841 when a cargo of slaves bound from Virginia to New Orleans seized the crew, killed a white man, and headed for the Bahamas. British officials there hanged the murderers,

---

*This power-hungry and amusing promoter in 1843 completed, at the head of navigation on the American River, a sizable town enclosed by the walls of Fort Sutter. Before the decade ended he would take a major role in the California gold rush.

FIGURE 13-5. *George C. Bingham,* The Wood-Boat

James Watt's improvements and later innovations vastly reduced the amount of fuel required by steam engines. But their maws remained hard to feed. Railroad locomotives could not have crossed the Great Plains without bringing along their own power, and it was in a new form—coal. Between 1790 and 1850 the mobile vehicles that were driven by steam engines were the steamships on inland waters, and their fuel was wood. This brief epoch in American westering was captured by George Caleb Bingham in *The Wood-Boat* (1850).

Bingham (1811–1879) was born in Virginia, but his parents took him to Missouri when he was eight. There he stayed. His exposure to European art was slight: his schoolteacher mother showed him some engravings; he went to Philadelphia in 1837 and stayed about a year. He was largely self-taught, and his products resulted from direct exposure to their subjects. But the pyramidal structure of this painting, embodied in the three men in the foreground and employed by Bingham in several other works, has its prototypes in earlier Continental art.

but refused to surrender the now free blacks. American-British relations clearly were getting out of hand.

But the English had friends in Washington. The Whigs were now in power, and Daniel Webster was the secretary of state. His friends were merchants, and their trade with England was quite profitable. So his view was simple: "no difference shall be permitted seriously to endanger the maintenance of peace with England." Because she had kept a half interest in the public lands of Maine when that state became separate in 1820, Massachusetts was keenly interested in the location of the boundary. In dispute were 12,000 square miles. By the Webster-Ashburton Treaty (1842), Maine got 7,000, New Brunswick 5,000. Evidence later made public showed that the United States was probably entitled to all of the disputed zone, but by considerable skullduggery with maps Webster got the agreement ratified. Since the document also set a boundary west of Lake Superior that gave the United States the eastern Mesabi Range, soon to prove indispensable for its iron deposits, the secretary in retrospect seems to have made a good deal. Then, too, on the slave trade he had not conceded the "right of visit" that the British wanted.

An abortive effort to stabilize another boundary was made in 1825. At that time Congress decreed that the present-day western boundary of Missouri and Arkansas should be the Permanent Indian Frontier. Beyond would be an eternal refuge for the tribes that were being so ruthlessly expelled from Eastern states. Even as the policy was promulgated it was being violated, although at first only in small numbers. These early intruders were the Mountain Men— trappers and fur traders. Most of the romantic legend that gathered about them was false. Perhaps a thousand men followed this trade between 1805 and 1845. The latter careers of 446 men, or nearly half, have been traced. Death in the Rockies was the destiny of 182; another 147 seem to have dropped out of sight or continued trapping. The post-trapper careers of another 117 are known. A third of them found a calling that was connected with agriculture including ranching. Seven got into politics and one went to Congress; three others founded Denver; most took up a mercantile pursuit. From this it seems that the Mountain Man was not devoted to a wild and free life, but carried west with him a definition of success and respectability that he had learned in the East. While some loved adventure, they were ready to abandon it as soon as they had earned a grubstake that they could turn to advantage back in settled society.

Partly because their migratory lives did not clash sharply with Indian

In addition to his creations that focus on the human experience with nature in the Missouri-Mississippi valley, Bingham was keenly interested in the political life of his environment. More than anybody else, he left behind the visual depiction of the street meetings and stump speeches that were the settings for Lincoln's back-home career. At his peak as an artist, Bingham deserted art for civil office, serving as legislator, state treasurer, and adjutant general of Missouri. Besides his canvases, he left a forthright declaration of his aims as a painter: "I have no hesitation in affirming that any man who does not regard the imitation of nature as the great essential quality of art will never make an artist."

319

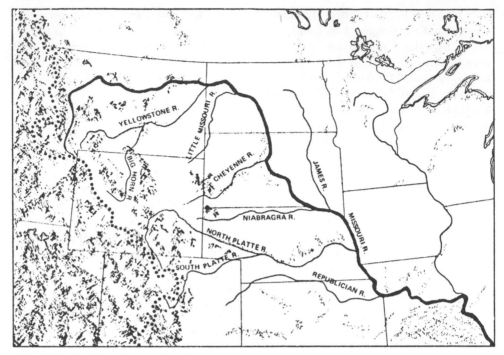

FIGURE 13-6. *The Missouri River System*

cultures (Document 6-1), Mountain Men usually found the Indians friendly. This amity persisted for a while after permanent settlers began to cross the Mississippi; historians seem to have little noticed that the sanguinary clashes with Indians in that region are concentrated after the Civil War, not before it. But there were apprehensions. Some early settlers' fears of "hostiles" could reach beyond paranoia into farce. One such incident seems nearly as funny as the war of big enders against little enders in *Gulliver's Travels*. Some members of a wagon train in 1842 claimed that the accompanying hounds were a menace because they not only scared away game but also attracted hostile Indians. The dog owners were fervent but not alert. Anti-canines undertook to slaughter their enemies. Dog owners set out to execute the villains who would kill helpless animals. Fortunately the two factions parted company before they butchered each other. Then the next year another mass movement began to germinate; it was reported that some Plains Indians considered taking their families to the East because they were sure the westward migration of "the whole white village" had depopulated that area. As whites came in greater numbers, troubles grew disproportionately. The Pawnees in Kansas acquired a name as unscrupulous thieves. An uprising in 1855 by Yakimas in the Northwest was not suppressed for three years. In the single year 1859 ten stagecoach drivers were killed in the Southwest by Apaches and Comanches.

Much as the emigrants of the seventeenth century had adopted covenants for the transatlantic crossing, so did each wagon train set up an *ad hoc* government and elect leaders. Although many a pilgrimage saw disputes over which it could splinter, the demand for cooperation was compelling. Besides danger from Indians, engineering obstacles could only be met by mutual aid. Several ox teams might be needed to get one wagon across a deep river or up a mountain. On one 35-degree slope in the Sierra Nevadas, fifteen pairs of oxen up on the ridge drew a chain over a roller, thus providing a home-made winch. Going downhill could be just as perplexing as getting up. Brakes could not be trusted; a runaway vehicle could overtake its motive power and smash bones. In timbered country a heavy log could be dragged downhill behind the wagon, but often this resource was not available. It became common to convert one wagon in each company into a windlass to help the others on steep grades.

In discussing Christopher Columbus we noted the fusion of courage with greed that has been so prominent in American history. Nowhere is this merger more glaring than in the conquest of the trans-Mississippi West. For motives of land hunger, men exposed their families to the gravest perils—on a trip that can be difficult even in the era of expressways and 350-horsepower engines. The possible torment is revealed by the Donner catastrophe. When it headed west from Fort Bridger (now southwestern Wyoming) on the last day of July in 1846, the party seemed exceptionally suitable. More than half of its 89 members were adults, more than a third were men. Some, including the two Donner brothers, were well-to-do. They had even read about what to expect— but they had been misled. The traditional route to the Pacific made a great loop north of Salt Lake, but a promoter had convinced the Donner company that it could shorten its trip some 400 miles by going south of the lake and heading almost due west. An earlier party that same summer had narrowly missed disaster going through the Upper Weber Canyon; the present highway by this route has in many places been blasted out of rock. But the Donner company set out. Their grave troubles began in the Wasatch range, when in 15 days they made about 40 miles. Then they came to the Salt Desert. Their informant had reported that it was 40 miles wide and could be crossed in one day; next he said two days. In fact the Bonneville flats are some 80 miles wide. By traveling nearly all of every night, the wagon train made the crossing in six days. The date was now September, and morale in the company had collapsed. It creaked and staggered and bled onward. At the beginning of November it had barely crossed the line into California north of Lake Tahoe. Four times the company essayed the divide; four times it failed. More snow fell. The party was tied down for the winter. People died. Others ate their flesh. It seems probable that some desperadoes tired of waiting for their fellows to die from natural causes, and helped to hasten them along. This is perhaps the best authenticated instance in American history of cannibalism by white Anglo-Saxon Protestants. Only 49 members of the party—barely more than half—survived. The episode gave its name to an awesome pass and to a lake as beautiful as any in the United States.

If the Donner calamity is the nadir of the westward movement, the general experience of the Mormons is the zenith. Doubtless self-reliance is a valuable trait in settling a wild country; at the century's close Henry Demarest Lloyd would label individualism as "frontier ethics." But the Mormons proved that religious communalism could create fecundity in a barren land. (See early Chapter 14 for discussion of their background.) Each sectary of this exiled and abominated group paid a tenth of his income to the Church of Jesus Christ of Latter-Day Saints. This tithe plus a highly organized, communalized society and centralized administration of the funds was the key to survival and growth. Part of the money was used for ecclesiastical purposes; to build their tabernacle the Mormons had neither stone nor metal, but they built a structure using nothing but wood that still majestically stands. Part went for civic uses; they laid out a city on the grid pattern with boulevards so wide that Salt Lake City today has no serious traffic problems. Part went into paramilitary uses, and for decades the Mormons fought off the United States army. A portion was spent in a planned fashion to develop the economy of the area, and soon the prosperity of Utah became the envy of the West.

The new Zion had its ugly side. Apart from their function as mothers, women were scorned. They took no role in civic affairs; and a Mormon with self-respect would never ask his wife's opinion on any question. He might be so bigoted as to treat all outsiders contemptuously or indeed savagely. No sane person could condone, for example, the Mountain Meadows Massacre of 1857. A company of 140 persons bound for California was passing through southern Utah. Its disreputable members had made some enemies along the way, but most of the emigrants were God-fearing folk. They were attacked by Indians. A party of fifty Mormons arrived at the encircled wagons. By a trick the travellers were lured out of their makeshift stockade. The Mormons joined with the Indians to butcher them. The toll was 120 corpses.

In spite of hardships and carnage, the cohorts of civilization flocked westward. A few sweeping remarks may be hazarded. The tempo of occupation would not have increased as it did had it not been that most migrants in fact bettered their condition. Second, such costly relocations were always greatest, for obvious reasons, in prosperous times; therefore the economic boom of 1843–1857 brought a massive surge into the West. Third, although the settlement of the trans-Mississippi regions has seemed to capture most observers, the bulk of population growth from 1840 to 1860 occurred east of the great river. True, New England was fairly static, while the South Atlantic and East South Central blocs lagged behind the national average. But fully half of the population increase for the entire country took place in the Middle Atlantic and East North Central sections. Fourth, up to 1845 the westward movement had been almost exclusively the result of personal initiatives by private individuals. But action by the federal government was needed to resolve the legal-international questions of disputed sovereignties.

After Whigs and Democrats had crystallized as the two major parties in the United States, Martin Van Buren had presided over four years of business decline. The first Whig president was elected in 1840 for no reason that most voters could explain, except that he had earlier won a battle against Indians at Tippecanoe. Immediately upon taking office, William Henry Harrison died, and his successor could not even get along with his own party. The equal strength in the nation of the two parties was shown in 1844 when Henry Clay, the ablest public figure in the country, was narrowly beaten by the Democratic nominee James Knox Polk. Then the eagle really began to scream. Just before Polk took office, delays of nine years were ended by the annexation of Texas. Now the president was free to nail down the American title to the Pacific slope, where it was contested by both Great Britain and Spain.

Here we meet again a persistent dream of Americans—the passage to India, access to the wealth of the Orient. This flame was re-ignited by the journey of Lewis and Clark. It inspired a poem by Whitman and brought Thoreau to the study of Hindu philosophy. It lured American clippers to China and brought about the Treaty of Wanghia (1844) that opened the Celestial Empire to American merchants. It prompted the doughty spokesman for Massachusetts business, Daniel Webster, to assert early in 1845, "You know my opinion to have been, as it now is, that the port of San Francisco would be twenty times as valuable to us as all Texas." And it guided the territorial aims of every president from John Quincy Adams to Polk. They were not the least averse to gaining rich agricultural lands that might appeal to rural voters in the Midwest. But Polk at least was more concerned with conquering some stepping stones to the Pacific which were being demanded in the East. Specifically he wanted three ports: San Diego, San Francisco, and the Juan de Fuca Straits. All three objectives, and more besides, were won in 1846.

In some minds the issue had shaped up several years earlier. In 1841 the English minister to Mexico had urged British colonization of California with the hope of eventually gaining sovereignty there. At the same time a Mountain Man had urged a party of 700 American citizens to "join the standard of their country, and make a clean sweep of what is called the Origon Territory; that is clear it of British and Indians." The public in the United States was more interested in Oregon than in California; extremists were insisting that the international boundary should be 54° 40′. Until Polk became president neither government was inclined to force a resolution. Then in July, 1845, he suggested a settlement at the 49th parallel. Great Britain rejected the proposal. *The Times* (London) in the autumn exhorted about California: "England must think of her own interests and secure the Bay of Francisco and Monterey . . . to prevent those noble ports from becoming ports of exportation for brother Jonathan for the Chinese markets." By then Americans cared as much about California as about Oregon. The United States had its own exponents of continentalism—"manifest destiny" (Document 13-2). It was fear of England more than any other single consideration that spurred American rule all the way to the Pacific in 1846.

Fortunately each nation was subject to pressures for compromise and

323

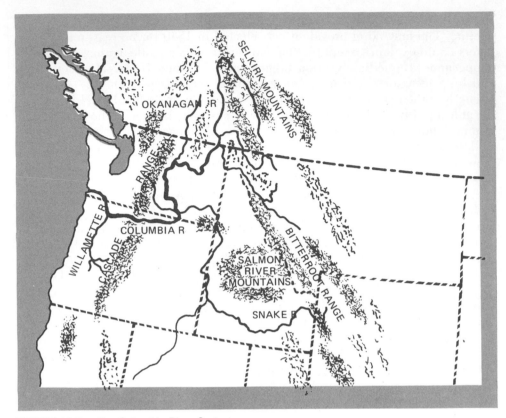

FIGURE 13-7. *The Columbia River System*

peace. In December the president asked Congress to authorize the required notice to Britain of cancellation of the 1827 agreement for joint occupancy of Oregon; Congress passed the resolution in April 1846 and it would take effect in one year. Meanwhile much else had happened. One set of influences was stated in January by a Massachusetts Congressman: "We need ports on the Pacific. As to land, we have millions of acres of better land still unoccupied on this side of the mountains." Albert Gallatin, still alive and right as usual, argued that agreement on the 49th parallel would satisfy the chief American need. By February war against Mexico seemed almost certain, and it seemed unwise to fight two enemies on several fronts simultaneously. On the other hand, Britain was bedeviled in the Middle East, in India, in Ireland, and at home. But the chief coercion came from the Pacific slope. Migrants into Oregon numbered 3,000 in 1845. This flow doubled the population of the Willamette valley; anybody who has ever seen this area will understand their choice of destination. And so it happened that Oregon and Washington were secured by American settlers; the 49th parallel became the international boundary, with guarantees of protection to British property in the American

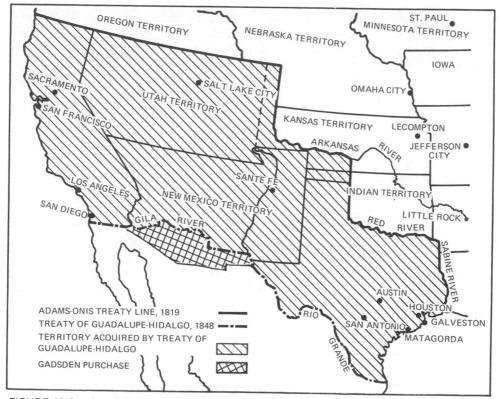

FIGURE 13-8. *Acquisitions from Mexico, 1848–1853*

zone and with assurance of free navigation on the Columbia to Hudson's Bay Company employees.

Events in California seemed almost copied from Texas precedents. Americans centered on Monterey had long been prominent in the region's trade, from hides to whales. Before 1845 ended some 400 of their countrymen had settled at San Francisco. But Texas provided the site where major conflict began. Under suspicious circumstances that drew endless Whig charges of mendacity, American troops clashed with Mexican forces along the Rio Grande. Prompted by the president, Congress on 13 May, 1846, declared war. Within a month Americans in Monterey had seized the town by the Bear Flag Revolt; they took San Francisco; a force led by John C. Frémont took Los Angeles; by January, California was ours. But the subjugation of Mexico was not the pushover that most Americans had expected, although in fighting a more populous and more industrialized neighbor Mexico was simply outgunned. After prolonged harassment and a few severe battles, a Yankee army took Mexico City in September, 1847. Some months later the Treaty of

Guadeloupe Hidalgo fixed the southwestern boundary of the United States (except for a strip added by the Gadsden Purchase in 1853) at its present line.

From today's perspective, three other facets of the Mexican War obtrude. First, it sustained the national itch to name generals as president: Washington, Jackson, Harrison; in 1848 it would be the first American commander in Mexico, Zachary Taylor. Second, it gave combat training to numerous young officers who would guide the rival armies in the Civil War, including Grant and Lee. Third, it splintered the political structure of the nation, and in the end would split the federal polity. In his annual message of December, 1847, Polk had rejoiced that the Pacific harbors "would afford shelter for our navy, for our numerous whale ships, and other merchant vessels employed in the Pacific ocean, would in a short period become the marts of an extensive and profitable commerce with China, and other countries of the East." He wasn't listening. A Whig from Ohio had told the Senate: ". . . if I were a Mexican I would tell you, 'Have you not room enough in your own country to bury your dead men? If you come into mine, we will greet you with bloody hands, and welcome you to hospitable graves." Almost equally virulent were such anti-slavery Democrats as Representative David Wilmot of Pennsylvania. In the summer of 1846 he offered the House a resolution that would ban slavery from all territory gained from the Mexican War. The House passed it, as it would do many times again.

The Mexican War cost 13,000 American dead. It also hurried along events destined to culminate in a conflict that would kill many, many more.

A tendency among American merchants to divert their capital from overseas trade into domestic ventures was noted in Chapter 10. This trend accelerated noticeably after 1815, as the frontier surged westward. It took place, remarkably, in the face of vastly improved oceanic shipping: size of vessels increased, costs came down, packet ships worked on regular schedules between the major ports. Even more striking were the results of building railroads after 1830. But the new fire-spitting demon brought a huge array of problems. Its technology at first was very crude, though it was incessantly improved; its legal position was obscure and ambiguous, though jurists (many of them investors in railroads) worked hard to tidy up the scene; struggles for rights-of-way were strenuous. However, if a railroad promoter had been asked on his death bed in 1860, "What was your sorest headache?" he would probably have answered "Money." Finance—the ability to raise the gigantic amounts of cash needed to buy rolling stock and to run track through unsettled territory—was the key to survival. Thousands of Americans went west in advance of railroad construction. Their sprawl brought on the conflict of white Texans with Mexico, then of the United States with Mexico. It brought acquisition of Texas, supplemented by the Southwest and California, from the "brown-skinned neighbors" to the south. A large chunk of the Pacific Northwest was gained by agreement with the United Kingdom. The spread eagle was on the wing.

SOME NOTABLE EVENTS

1742 Russians led by Vitus Bering, a Dane, become first Europeans to discover America from the west.

1769 As defensive measure, Spaniards establish first mission in California.

1799 Russian American Fur Company established.

1811 American Fur Company (John Jacob Astor) and Canadian North West Company agree to divide the trade of the Pacific slope.

1818 First New York-to-Liverpool packet line established in January.

Convention with Great Britain for joint occupation of Oregon, October 20.

1819 Transcontinental Treaty with Spain (Adams-Onís Treaty), February 22.

1821 Hudson's Bay Company, founded in 1670, merges with North West Company which had acquired American Fur Company in 1814.

1825 Suffolk system begins to regulate banking in Massachusetts.

1829 New York Safety Fund set up for banks.

1830 Baltimore and Ohio, first railroad in United States, opens 13 miles of track. (First in England, 1825; see "Events," Chapter 12.)

Massachusetts accords limited liability to stockholders in corporations.

1831 William Lloyd Garrison publishes first issue of *The Liberator*, January 1.

Cyrus McCormick develops the reaper.

1832 First American clipper ship.

Abolition of slavery everywhere in British Empire.

Reform Act in Great Britain extends the suffrage.

1833 Charleston to Hamburg railroad, 136 miles, is longest in world under one management.

British Factory Act regulates child labor.

American Anti-Slavery Society issues its Declaration of Sentiments, December 4.

1834 *Zollverein* reforms import tolls among German provinces.

1835 New York decision on trade unionism, *People* v. *Fisher*.

1836 Texas declares its independence, March 1.

1837 Steel plow reaches U.S.

Charles River Bridge Company v. *Warren Bridge Company* (limits monopoly; see "Events," Chapter 12).

Connecticut passes first sweeping law for general incorporations.

Abortive Canadian rebellion leads to controversy over the *Caroline*.

1838 New York Free Banking Act.

1839 Charles Goodyear vulcanizes rubber.

1840 U.S. census: 17,120,000 10.8% urban).

About 2,200 miles of railroad in operation.

First English settlers reach New Zealand.

Union of Upper and Lower Canada forms United Provinces of Canada.

1841 Russians sell Fort Ross, California, to John A. Sutter and withdraw to Alaska.

Pre-emption Act permits prospective claims on unopened federal lands.

1842 Massachusetts decision on trade unionism, *Commonwealth* v. *Hunt*.

Hong Kong ceded to Great Britain by China.

Webster-Ashburton Treaty, August 9.

1844 Samuel F. B. Morse develops practical telegraph.

Clay publishes his "Raleigh letter" on Texas, April 17.

Treaty of Wanghia with China, July 3.

1845 Texas annexed by U.S., March 1.

Ireland stricken by famine.

1846 Great Britain repeals its Corn Laws.

President Polk sends his war message to Congress, May 11.

Elias Howe invents sewing machine.

Bear Flag Revolt in California, June.

Oregon Boundary treaty with Great Britain, June 15.

1846	David Wilmot introduces his Proviso in Congress, August.		Revolutions in France, Germany, Austria, Italy.
1847	Mormons led by Brigham Young found Salt Lake City.	1850	U.S. census: 23,261,000 (15.2% urban).
	Liberia established as a republic.	1854	Perry opens Japan to trade.
1848	London Working Men's Association issues the National Charter.		10,000 miles of railroad in U.S.
		1867	Dominion of Canada founded.
	Treaty of Guadeloupe Hidalgo with Mexico, February 2.	1870	Hudson's Bay Company surrenders its gubernatorial powers.

Ways to Study History XIII

Find sources that suit your needs. The study of "labor history" had long been strictly defined by the kind of documents unearthed by one prominent graduate school, the University of Wisconsin, which long maintained almost a stranglehold on its field. Copious use was made of standard published documents such as law statutes and court decisions, though most scholars today would see but slight connection between laws and actual patterns of human behavior. Also used were commercial and trade-union papers, taken more or less at face value, though almost everyone today knows how to discount for bias in any newspaper's account of a strike. The result of such narrowminded use of sources was a narrow view of many complex social patterns that underlie the growth of industries, trades, and labor resources.

Generalizations from such sources as this (so I argued in 1954,) can yield contradictory conclusions and oversimplify our view of a number of significant problems. Seeking to break out of the trap, I started with more concrete evidence that needed careful sifting and analysis: a box of letters dated a century earlier which related to the enlistment of female weavers in Scotland to work in a cotton mill in Holyoke, Massachusetts. The same manuscript collection held the payrolls for the factory. Since the company paid the transatlantic fare for every recruit, to be repaid from earnings, it was possible to compute a rate of savings for each employee. The figure was a startling 50 per cent. This finding, we must remember, is for workers who were (a) single, and (b) skilled. The very great turnover among these mill-hands highlights a conundrum that was faced by every American manager. The task of tracing each individual through erratic monthly records was tedious and involved several perils. Morever, the degree to which these women were representative of other segments of the working class cannot be known without other studies from reliable sources.

Document 13-1

The Lewis and Clark expedition was the first and most important of many Federal explorations into the trans-Mississippi West (mid-Chapter 10). Here is Meriwether Lewis' description of the awesome waterfall that he saw in the Missouri River. The beauty of this sight has been erased by hydroelectric facilities, and Great Falls, Montana now boasts that it has the largest shopping plaza west of St. Louis.

. . . immediately at the cascade the river is about 300 yds. wide; about ninety or a hundred yards of this next the Lard. [larboard, i.e. left] bluff is a smooth even sheet of water falling over a precipice of at least eighty feet, the remaining part of about 200 years on my right formes the grandest sight I ever beheld, the hight of the fall is the same of the other but the irregular and somewhat projecting rocks below receives the water in it's passage down and brakes it into a perfect white foam which assumes a thousand forms in a moment sometimes flying up in jets of sparkling foam to the hight of fifteen or twenty feet and are scarcely formed before large roling bodies of the same beaten and foaming water is thrown over and conceals them. in short the rocks seem to be most happily fixed to present a sheet of the whitest beaten froath for 200 yards in length and about 80 feet perpendicular. the water after decending strikes against the buttment

before mentioned or that on which I stand and seems to reverberate and being met by the more impetuous courant they roll and swell into half formed billows of great hight which rise and again disappear in an instant. . . .

Document 13-2

In 1845 during the controversy about the annexation of Texas, John L. O'Sullivan, editor of the *United States Magazine and Democratic Review*, argued that American expansion was inevitable. It was, he asserted, "our manifest destiny to overspread the continent allotted by Providence for the free development of our yearly multiplying millions." He found an ingenious twist to justify Polk's policy for Texas.

Nor is there any just foundation for the charge that Annexation is a great pro-slavery measure—calculated to increase and perpetuate that institution. Slavery had nothing to do with it. . . . That it will tend to facilitate and hasten the disappearance of Slavery from all the northern tier of the present Slave States, cannot surely admit of serious question. The greater value in Texas of the slave labor now employed in those States, must soon produce the effect of draining off that labor southwardly, by the same unvarying law that bids water descend the slope that invites it. . . .

No—Mr. Clay was right when he declared that Annexation was a question with which slavery had nothing to do. The country which was the subject of Annexation in this case, from its geographical position and relations, happens to be—or rather the portion of it now actually settled, happens to be—a slave country. But a similar process might have taken place in proximity to a different section of our Union; and indeed there is a great deal of Annexation yet to take place, within the life of the present generation, along the whole line of our northern border. Texas has been absorbed into the Union in the inevitable fulfillment of the general law which is rolling our population westward; the connexion of which with that ratio of growth in population which is destined within a hundred years to swell our numbers to the enormous population of two hundred and fifty millions (if not more), is too evident to leave us in doubt of the manifest design of Providence in regard to the occupation of this continent. . . .

Document 13-3

When the transcontinental railroad was completed to Utah in 1869, some 80,000 Mormons had already migrated there. From 1856 to 1860 nearly 3,000 took the advice of Brigham Young: "Let them come on foot with handcarts or wheelbarrows; let them gird up their loins and walk through and nothing shall hinder or stay them." He was wrong. Two companies totalling 400 new immigrants from Europe set out in 1856 from Florence, Nebraska. They intended to cross the high plains of Wyoming to Salt Lake. More than three score did not finish the trip.

The emigrants were entirely ignorant of the country and climate—simple, honest, eager to go to "Zion" at once, and obedient as little children to the "servants of God." Under these circumstances it was natural that they should leave their destinies in the hands of the elders. . . . These men prophesied in the name of God that we should get through in safety. Were we not God's people, and would he not protect us? Even the elements he would arrange for our good, etc. But Levi Savage used his common sense and his knowledge of the country. He declared positively that to his certain knowledge we could not cross the mountains with a mixed company of aged people, women, and little children, so late in the season without much suffering, sickness, and death. He therefore advised going into winter quarters without delay; but he was rebuked by the other elders for want of faith, one elder even declaring that he would guarantee to eat all the snow that fell on us between Florence and Salt Lake City. Savage was accordingly defeated, as the majority were against him. . . .

Death was not long confined in its ravages to the old and infirm, but the young and naturally strong were among its victims. Men who were, so to speak, as strong as lions when we started our journey, and who had been our best supports, were compelled to succumb to the grim monster. . . .

In Search of Equality with Order
—plus Salvation

Religion permeated all aspects of life in America in the nineteenth century. Not only was almost everyone frequently engaged in searching for the "signs" of his own salvation, grace granted by a personal God, but a desire to promote faith sparked almost all the reforms and appeals to social consciousness of the time. Samuel Gridley Howe, the first notable teacher of the blind in America, believed that helping them learn to read the Bible was his most important contribution to society. Religious concerns influenced the outcome of elections. In 1832, when Henry Clay was the Whig candidate for the presidency, the election of a Jacksonian to the Kentucky governorship humiliated him. Clay was a Presbyterian, and members of that church were not popular in Kentucky. He estimated that anti-Presbyterianism gave the Jacksonian 3,000 votes.

Americans of the Enlightenment would have been surprised by the importance of religion to their descendants. These men, involved with

331

questions of political philosophy and scientific investigation, content to let a mild deism explain the unknown, optimistic about man's nature and his future, must have been dismayed to see the guilt, the fear and trembling and shouting which characterized the numerous revival meetings of the first half of the new century. Several causes of the change are evident. Many Americans were greatly disturbed by the "atheism" of the French revolution, and by the many bloody years which followed. But those who saw the hand of God in events abroad were always more intently concerned with derilictions at home. Thus in 1795 the Methodist Church could exhort its members to observe a day of fasting, not mentioning France, but concentrating on the sins of America, profanations of the Sabbath, disobedience to parents, increase of drunkeness. In 1798 the Presbyterian General Assembly did briefly consider the war in Europe, but the evil abroad in America engrossed their serious attention. There is no reason to think that Americans were any worse than they had been and later became, or than other people were. Perhaps the American conscience was suffering from a surfeit of good fortune. The country had won Independence without undergoing the upheavals of France, the economy purred when it did not boom, and the possibilities of the frontier and a continent beckoned. When God so obviously smiled, it might have become increasingly important not to risk losing His favor.

Furthermore, boredom and hard work characterized most people's lives. Roads were bad, neighbors distant, and opportunities for emotional expression scarce. None of these things were new, but the extension of the frontier made them worse. Thus it is not surprising that when the Second Great Awakening began in 1800 (see mid-Chapter 3 on the first), the fires burned strongest on the edges of settlement. In 1801 one of the first camp meetings, at Cane Ridge, Kentucky, excited the nation. There, to the exhortations of a group of preachers of several denominations, the violent emotions of the converted erupted in barking, falling, trances, running. Peter Cartwright, himself responsible for many revivals, said that the news of Cane Ridge "spread through all the Churches, and through all the land, and it excited great wonder and surprise; but it kindled a religious flame that spread all over Kentucky and through many states."

The Awakening of 1800 heralded the events of the next half century. Revivals of religion, interspersed with what the preachers were to call "declensions," were to be a dominant fact of life.* The word "Revival" is significant. For the most part, the wailing sinners at the camp meetings were not people who were being converted for the first time, but believers who had backslid. Faith was not created, but "revived." As one Methodist Bishop put it, the conversion of sinners was secondary to "the quickening of the people of

---

*One frontier area, in western New York State, was seared by so many waves of religious emotion that it came to be called the "burned over" district.

God to a spirit and walk becoming the gospel." A revival preacher aimed at the conversion of an entire community; joint participation in religious terror and ecstasy became the last refuge from the cult of individualism.

While the religious feeling of the nineteenth century resembled that of the first Awakening (mid-Chapter 3), the religious beliefs it encouraged had changed. The cold, pure, Calvinism of Edwards would not be accepted by the new Brother Jonathan (as the typical Yankee was now titled). The theology of the most successful preacher of the middle of the century, Charles Grandison Finney, illustrates the new faith. He believed in free will; everyone had the power to come to God if he tried. Finney did make the distinction between "willing" and "wishing." Just wishing for salvation was not enough, but really willing something meant doing it. Since God was just, He would not ask man to do something beyond his powers. Thus it was within everyone's capabilities to repent and be saved. "Sinners ought to be made to feel that they have something to do, and that is to repent; that it is something which no other being can do for them, neither God nor man, and something which they can do and do now. Religion is something to do, not something to wait for." Only an American could have made a statement in such terms. The American's sense of optimism, of personal responsibility for his own destiny, could not allow him to be a passive recipient of salvation; his faith in equality made abhorrent the tenet of the elect.

But if these beliefs harmonized with the developing national character, they could only increase the guilt of the frightened sinner. Although it was a Calvinist's duty to try to find God, it also behooved him to accept his fate should God choose to damn him. A Calvinist's salvation was not, finally, his own responsibility. But a sinner who listened to Finney and was left without conviction and repentence could only conclude that it was his own fault. A community which did not periodically recharge its faith by emotional up-heavals was more than wicked, it was lazy. Fortunately for the national sanity, it is unlikely that many, if they recognized these implications, dwelt upon them. Although concern with religion was increasing, its influence on most of the other aspects of life had declined. From the first generation Puritan, seeking salvation through all the activities of his life, including his secondary calling (see mid-Chapter 2 on Winthrop) the American had become a man occasionally gripped by religious frenzy, going to church on Sunday if he were lucky enough to live someplace large enough to have a church, but rarely willing to let his faith interfere with important, secular matters.

Two aspects of religious life in the first part of the nineteenth century are evident: evangelical, emotional sects were swamping the rational, ritualis-tic ones, and the number of sects was greatly increasing. Although most of the new sects differed from each other only in trivial ways, some adhered to remarkably innovative religious and social beliefs. Most of the more startling new churches, like strange mutations, soon became extinct. But one, the

Church of Jesus Christ of the Latter Day Saints, the Mormons (late in Chapter 13 and Document 13-3), deserves closer examination. Originally but another splinter group, the Mormons were to become a remarkable semi-theocratic state. They had a net of missionaries converting the infidels of Europe, a distaste for the United States government, and skill at desert taming.

In 1840 they were consolidated in the settlement of Nauvoo, Illinois. By voting as a bloc and playing the candidates in that year's election against each other, they managed to win an extraordinary charter from the state, which gave Nauvoo virtual independence. The town made its own laws, kept its own militia, maintained its own courts. But the ensuing prosperity was short-lived. Their neighbors feared the Mormons' political power, detested their spiritual arrogance, and were horrified at rumors of polygamy. When a mob attacked Nauvoo in 1844 the authorities conveyed its prophet, Joseph Smith, to a nearby jail for "protection," where he was shortly murdered.

All of the Mormons had been forced out of Nauvoo by the following spring. Most of them were destitute, since they had sold their land and improvements to their Gentile neighbors at bargain rates. But within a few years, under the leadership of Brigham Young, they were solidly established in the valley of the Great Salt Lake. The task they faced in 1845, crossing the plains and mountains with whole families, and bringing some of the most inhospitable country on the continent under cultivation, seems Herculean in retrospect. The Mormon's success can be partially attributed to their social organization and religious beliefs.

Communal societies are very good devices for pioneering, yet have had scant success in the United States. They soon disintegrated, fractured by the opportunities for individual advancement available to their members. The Mormon organization, while providing for centralized control under the President of the Church and his twelve Apostles, permitted, encouraged, Church members to become rich on their own account. Thus, while a man had to tithe, had to go off on missionary work if ordered, and, later, had to shop at the Church-owned cooperatives, he still could fulfill his personal ambitions. Meanwhile, the poor and the sick were tended, and personal rivalries were not allowed to endanger the safety and stability of the community. For example, the Salt Lake settlement profited in the sale of food, clothing, and implements to miners passing through on their way to the California goldfields. When some of the Saints proposed searching for precious metals nearby, Brigham Young forbade the enterprise, saying that establishing self-sufficiency in agriculture was more important. Another community, which lacked the centralized authority of the Church, would have ignored this wise counsel.

The Mormons' most peculiar practice, polygamy, had functional uses. The Church alleged that a single person would be a servant in Heaven, a married couple respectable but insignificant, and a polygamous family of great repute. Not only did this practice keep the birth rate high, but it must have encouraged many men to work hard so that they could afford a second wife.

Most of the important characteristics of the Mormon faith were not so odd as they appeared to contemporaries. They believed in emotional religion, in grace as a prerequisite to conversion. They believed in salvation for everyone—who had the sense to join the Church. They believed in personal responsibility. They believed in a shining future, here on earth. All of these beliefs, including the final, secular, faith, they shared with most other Americans.

The first half of the nineteenth century was a time of immense optimism. The typical American believed in a great many things: the United States was the best country on earth, and getting better all the time; his section was going to become the most important, the richest, the noblest, part of the country; his town should be the state capital, or at least the county seat; and he, himself, personally, would eventually be a rich man. Although these aspirations were more reasonable than they had ever been before, it was obviously impossible for the dream to materialize for everyone. But failure didn't often dim the American's hopes. The man who was but marginally successful on a farm in Ohio would cheerfully hack a new one out of the forest and swamp in Indiana, then live in a sod dugout in Kansas, perhaps even undergo the incredible hardships of a journey to California or Oregon. He was always looking for something better, and convinced that eventually he would find it.

The American circumstances that formed these traits helped to assure their durability. As De Tocqueville said,

> In Europe we are wont to look upon a restless disposition, an unbounded desire of riches, and an excessive love of independence as propensities very dangerous to society. Yet these are the very elements that ensure a long and peaceful future to the republics of America. . . . such is the present good fortune of the New World that the vices of its inhabitants are scarcely less favorable to society than their virtues. These circumstances exercise a great influence on the estimation in which human actions are held in the two continents. What we should call cupidity, the Americans frequently term a laudable industry; and they blame as faint-heartedness what we consider to be the virtue of moderate desires.

As a companion piece to his personal optimism, the American believed in a general way in the glories of the future. As one English traveller put it in 1836, "Americans loved their country not for what it then was, but for what it was to be—not the land of their fathers, but the land their children were destined to inherit." Not surprisingly, this concern for the next generation was reflected in a faith in the values of education. In 1840 more than 47,000 primary schools contained 2,000,000 pupils, and 16,000 students attended 173 colleges and universities. Nor was adult education neglected. The lyceum movement was begun in 1829, as an attempt to improve the mind by study, encourage libraries, promote the public schools, and compile local histories and surveys. By 1834 3,000 local lyceums existed in the United States. By 1853 three Midwestern states had established compulsory public education, and in 1848 the movement for special teacher-training ("normal") schools had begun. By 1840 only one adult white in thirty-one was illiterate, and twenty per cent had some education beyond the primary grades. If most schools were not very good, at least the dream of education for all was much more advanced in the United States than anywhere else in the world.*

But the relatively high level of American literacy made it unstable. Every important immigrant group was less educated than the native-born, and many of them came to the United States without the respect for formal learning which had become ingrained here. The influx of the Irish after 1845 provides an example. The failure of the potato crop for two consecutive years had reduced hundreds of thousands of Irish peasants to starvation; they were forced to emigrate or die. In lives so near the brink of extinction there is no room for the frills of book learning. Very few in the flood of Irish immigrants were even minimally literate, very few could acquire better than the meanest jobs. And since they had not been taught to honor schooling, and needed their children's labor, this condition echoed down through the generations. Although there are no reliable statistics available, the rosy picture of nearly universal literacy in 1840 had darkened considerably by 1850, and was to stay gloomy until well into the twentieth century.

The future was important to the American; the past, of both ideas and objects, he thought old and fusty. The love which most Europeans felt for the familiar and the ancestral had become attenuated; sentiment had been downed by progress. De Toqueville expresses the shock (and the awe) most foreign observers experienced at this phenomenon:

> In the United States a man builds a house in which to spend his old age, and he sells it before the roof is on; he plants a garden and lets it just as the trees are coming into bearing; he brings a field into tillage and leaves other men to gather the crops; he embraces a profession and gives it up; he settles in a place, which he soon leaves to carry his changeable belongings elsewhere.

Respect for the virtues of quality and craftmanship was being supplanted by admiration of quantity and speed. The Paul Bunyan legend illustrates this. Paul was a logger, a destroyer. (This association is much more readily apparent now than it would have been 150 years ago.) Paul is enormous, a giant; his virtues become more admirable by being larger. To complete his association with the emerging American type, he was a great inventor. Numbers, counting, "figurin'" are important in almost all his exploits. But it would be unjust and ahistorical to sit, coughing, in the midst of

---

*The "gab school" was characteristic in rural areas: each pupil read aloud, simultaneously. Country schools were rarely in session more than a few months in the year, and the teachers had scarcely more education than their students. Such schools could not attempt to impart much more than elementary "readin', writin', and 'rithmetic."

a smog ravaged city and rap the past on its knuckles. Preoccupation with size and quantity, willingness to ignore the past and to subdue affection for any given place, and optimistic hopes about the future were all functional in American lives, and requisite to the settlement of the country. Further, given the kinds of Europeans who emigrated and the circumstances which they found in North America, it is difficult to imagine a different kind of man evolving.

If the American's character fitted his circumstances, his myths often did not. The first visions of the trans-Appalachian west, the idealized Daniel Boone, Natty Bumppo, were important chiefly as they presaged the later, more enduring dream which has been formalized in the Western novel. But the land was shortly fictionalized again, and more enduringly, in the Myth of the Garden and the yeoman. This vision characterized the Mississippi Valley as a homogeneous land of independent proprietors planted firmly on family farms. Solid, virtuous, self-reliant, they had no truck with cities or machines and were the nation's bulwark against the corruptions of the East, which was populated by ignorant, immoral immigrants and controlled by cold-eyed bankers and factory-owners. This visualization, which was of course nonsense (see Chapters 11 and 13 on Western industry), has in modified form persisted until the present day, and had extraordinary strength in the years before the Civil War. Even Ralph Waldo Emerson, who in his private journals was ready enough to admit that he found the Middle West ugly and uncomfortable, felt compelled to yield to the myth in his published work. In 1846 an Illinois editor could still say, however untruthfully, "The West is agricultural; it has no manufactures and it never will have any of any importance."

Alongside the Creed of the Farmer the newer Gospel of Work and its corollary, the Canon of the Self-Made Man, gathered strength. These ideas, which were to become more influential throughout the century, and of which such books as *How to Win Friends and Influence People* are modern examples, concerned the opportunities for wealth which were to be found in the cities, particularily the Eastern cities. In its moderate form this myth was a reasonable one. The opportunities available to a poor man who was willing to think and work hard, take chances, and dedicate himself wholly to the task of "getting on" were enormous. Many rich men and many more who were merely comfortably prosperous were indeed "self-made."

But the myth went beyond these facts. Many people believed that wealth was the result of virtue, the virtues of prudence, diligence, thrift, industry, etc. Also, the creation of virtue was supposed to be the particular province of the farm (the Myth of the Garden again). Thus, to have a good chance to become a millionaire, a boy should be raised on a farm, by honest, strict, poor parents. Then he should leave the farm and put his noble traits to work in the city. According to the legend, it was a disadvantage to be born of wealthy parents, or to grow up in an urban environment.

Despite its divergence from reality (see Chapter 17 on "self-made" men), the myth persisted and grew. Self-help manuals sold widely, and children were early taught that getting ahead should be their first ambition. One explanation for the special durability of this ideal lies in what Tocqueville called the Americans' most distinctive characteristic—their "equality of condition." In a society of perfect equals, which America never was, but which most Americans wanted it to be, wealth was the only permissable distinction between man and man. Money could buy, among other things, privacy. Therefore seeking to become rich was a reasonable and legitimate occupation. But a hereditary class of rich men must not be allowed to develop, as such a class would destroy the principle of equality. If such a group does evolve, one must ignore it, perhaps by insisting that the poor and virtuous have the best chance of becoming rich.

Since wealth was equated with virtue, it followed that poverty must result from evil and laziness. The struggle for economic salvation became associated in many minds with that for spiritual salvation. Since virtue brought riches, it must be assumed that the employer could infallibly recognize the spiritual nature of his employees; for the poor man to rail at his misfortunes was as pointless and almost as sacrilegious as for the damned to stand on a hilltop and rant at his God. This attitude went beyond a contempt of poverty. Anyone who did not "progress" quickly was the object of at least veiled disdain; a man's moral worth came increasingly to be measured by the length of his purse. Moreover, the "failure" assessed himself by the same criterion; he knew in his heart that he deserved his ignominy.

But what about equality? An analogy can be drawn between the theology of Charles Grandison Finney and the nineteenth century doctrine of equality, and seventeenth century Calvinism and the deferential society (Chapters 1 and 2). Finney believed that every man was endowed with an equal ability to be saved; if he did not use it, his damnation was no one's fault but his own. "Equality" signified every American's right to start life with an equal chance at success; a man's failure to overcome later obstacles indicated nothing but his own sloth. In the earlier Calvinist scheme, this problem was not so intense. The Calvinist believed in the elect; everyone's salvation was predetermined. And in a deferential society, social position was predetermined also—the magistrate was "better" than the baker. But the baker's self-respect was not lessened because he had not become a magistrate, his calling did not affect his chance of salvation at all. At least, so was the theory. As we have seen, American circumstances started to break it down almost from the beginning. By the nineteenth century the theory of society as interrelated and cooperating hierarchical groups, had fallen before that of society as equal individuals, competing.

The preceding congeries of ideas can help interpret the reform movements that proliferated in the second quarter of the century. It seemed that almost every unfortunate had some organized group striving to help him.

Prisoners, the insane, the deaf, the blind, the uneducated, the drunkard—all were the subject of "improvement." But certain patterns can be seen. First, religion permeated all reform movements; to improve a man's condition, one had first to save his soul. For example, an applauded change in prison management took place in Philadelphia: each prisoner had a private cell and tiny exercise yard, where he worked, alone, at certain tasks which the prison had contracted to perform; conversation was forbidden. The idea was to give the sinner plenty of opportunity to meditate upon his sin, repent, and (necessarily) reform. The many approving observers of this system noticed its one apparent drawback, the high suicide rate, but some felt that this only indicated its success, as those who killed themselves must have been overwhelmed with a sense of guilt and sin.

Second, the majority of reforms which met with popular approval were designed to remove blocks to equality of opportunity. (Remember, poverty was not held to be such a barrier.) Reforms designed to help the blind and the deaf, and the campaign for better free education, fit into this category. Then as now, "charity" towards those who are clearly unfit for equal competition through no fault of their own received the widest public support, and the physically handicapped provide the most obvious example. Reforms which aid individuals to advance were second in respectability, while radical changes in society which would involve whole classes appalled all but a handful. Most Americans could think only in terms of individuals, and were blind to the problems of groups. They might think it unjust that a poor boy should be uneducated merely because his family could not afford his schooling, but rejected the possibility that his father might unite with other workers to seek higher wages. That would be an affront to "individualism." The emphasis was always upon mobility between classes, rather than upon improvement of the conditions which spawned poverty. Direct aid, when occasionally given, resulted from the kindness of the rich, and was a humiliation for the poor to receive.

Third, optimism underlay all projects for improvement. Very few reformers doubted that the world was getting better; its defects could be remedied with but a little tinkering. Utopia was just around the corner. The evils which must be eliminated could be cast out, and quickly.

Fourth, reform movements were an urban phenomenon, and their growth paralleled the increasingly urban character of the United States. In 1830 the almost thirteen million inhabitants of the country were 8.8 per cent urban; in 1860 19.8 per cent of the thirty one million residents were urban dwellers. Perhaps some people at the time, if they had noticed the city bases of reform, would have said urbanites have more need of uplift to withstand the corruptions of the city (the Myth of the Garden). But it is doubtful that the city was any less pure, or any poorer. Contrasts between rich and poor were more evident in the city; human misery was more apparent because more concentrated. Most important, the frequent contact with others of like opinions which the city provides permitted the organization which a reform movement

339

The leopard with the harmless kid laid down,
And not one savage beast was seen to frown.

The wolf did with the lambkin dwell in peace.
His grim carnivorous nature there did cease.

The lion with the fatling on did move.
A little child was leading them in love.

When the great PENN his famous treaty made,
With indian chiefs beneath the elm-trees shade.

New York State Historical Society, Cooperstown

FIGURE 14-1. *Edward Hicks,* The Peaceable Kingdom

The Peaceable Kingdom by Edward Hicks was painted 1830–1835. Born during the American Revolution into a Tory family, Hicks lavished his adolescence on the role of wastrel. Living as he did in Bucks County, Pennsylvania, it was natural that when he saw the light at about age 20 he should have joined the Society of Friends. Although the Quakers do not have professional pastors, Hicks took to preaching at a meeting house next door to his home, and at many other places where he could find fellow communicants. He studied the visual arts briefly with a well-known teacher in Paris, but his own living was earned by lettering mile-posts, doing up signs for taverns, painting carriages. This painting is one of as many as a hundred versions on the same that he did, taking his theme from Isaiah XI: 6.

requires. There were doubtless many country folk who regretted whatever poverty and ignorance they saw about them, but, isolated from one another, individuals could do little. Communication and joint action were crucial. Realizing this, the reform movements of the early nineteenth century developed two new institutions which have now become entrenched in business as well as in voluntary organizations: the periodic convention, and the organizational newspaper.

Communication among as well as within reform movements was valuable and made easier by the fact that most of the leaders not only knew each other, but participated in each others' causes. There developed almost an interlocking directorate of improvement. For example, Horace Greeley, an important exponent of abolition, was involved in Fourierism (an infant socialism), Brook Farm (a transcendentalist experiment in communal living), the temperance, peace, and women's rights movements, and supported both spiritualism and the Shakers. The extent of this interrelatedness startles. Most liberals were fundamentally perfectionists. They believed all evils could be eliminated, and duty required that all be attacked.

Reform activities were almost completely limited to the middle and upper classes. While altruism ranked high among the virtues, only individual, not class, self-help was respectable. Farmers, workers, and the poor were expected to advance their personal interests, and not "waste time" trying to improve the position of their groups. Since America at this time was very much an open society, those individuals who might have led labor unions or farmer's cooperatives usually left their class. Organizations of free blacks were a partial exception. Those leaders who later moved into the middle class were unable to dissociate themselves (some tried) from the whole black population. They came increasingly to realize that their interests were tied to their caste, not their class, and the advancement of the status of all blacks became their goal.

An exception to other reform patterns lies in the temperance movement, which was much more important among the working class than any other reform. Moral and religious fervor, and a certain amount of meddlesomeness, characterized all the social reform activities of this time, but in the crusade for

His painting was pointing toward a minor but interesting trend in twentieth-century art. The flat forms and stylized figures of *The Peaceable Kingdom* typified what has come to be called "primitive art." Modern practitioners would include Horace Pippin (Figure 28-1) and the better known Grandma Moses. Hicks' infatuation with carnivores in quiescent poses has been shared by the French primitivist Henri Rousseau—illustrating how fatuous is any attempt to discuss current art solely within the boundaries of one country.

This painting can profitably be seen as part of the religious history of the mid-nineteenth century. Hundreds of thousands of the devout in the United States were seized by millenarianism. They were transported by the faith that the Day of Judgment was at hand. They believed that Christ Jesus was scheduled to arrive again. Some even made up his time table. Hicks was far from sure that his avocation would bring him salvation. Painting on a canvas, he pined, was "one of those trifling, insignificant arts which has never been of substantial advantage of mankind."

prohibition these aspects were all-important. Some temperance tracts contained references to the expense of alcohol, the working time lost by its use, or the sufferings of innocent wives and children, but the emphasis in almost all was the inherent sinfulness of Demon Rum. I suspect that many prohibitionists only discussed the impracticalities involved in addiction to alcohol because practical questions come quickly to the American mind; to them the evil was in the thing itself, not in its results. Furthermore, while a branch of the movement did in fact advocate temperance, its most vociferous element campaigned for total abstinence. They worked in three ways. First, they propagandized, picturing the horrible life of the drunkard, and often equating anyone who "touched a drop" with the alcoholic. Second, they campaigned for local or state prohibition laws, succeeding in getting such a law adopted in Maine in 1851. But their most important activity was closely tied to religion. They attempted to get people to pledge to drink no alcohol. This campaign was a feature of many revival meetings, and "taking the pledge" always resembled, emotionally, the conversion experience. Further, the prohibitionists saw their activities in the light of a religious campaign. They no more conceived of themselves as busybodies interfering unjustifiably with the lives of others than a minister would so perceive himself when he tried to convert the damned. The minister himself came to be an agent of prohibition, as the influence of the churches importuned against alcohol, and a few of them (notably the Methodists) made the "pledge" a precondition of membership.

After successes in the 1820's, the temperance movement declined in the South. Most of its nationally known leaders were also prominent abolitionists; Southerners came to associate the two movements. Actually abolition always rested on a much narrower base than temperance, and the identity of leadership resulted from one small group of humanists' tendency to lead everything. A more rational association of reform and sectionalism came in the middle forties, when the Methodist and Baptist churches split into Northern and Southern Branches. The national conventions of those churches (by far the largest in the South) felt compelled to denounce slavery as a sin at a time when the mystique of slavery as a good was being formulated, and Southern ministers, for their safety if not for their convictions, had to break away.

Although only a minority of ministers were abolitionists, the influence of religion on the movement was strong. Charles Grandison Finney was particularily influential. He said in 1835, "Revivals are hindered when ministers and *churches take wrong ground in regard to any question involving human rights.* Take the subject of SLAVERY for instance. . . . this monster is dragged from his horrid den, and exhibited before the church, and it is demanded of them, 'IS THIS SIN?'. . . Consequently, the silence of Christians upon the subject is virtually saying *that they do not* consider slavery as a sin. The truth is, it is a subject upon which they cannot be silent without guilt." Finney's preaching converted several of its·leaders to the abolitionist cause, and probably led a larger number of people, not actually abolitionists, to the conviction that slavery was repugnant.

The association of slavery with sin was possibly a more important part of abolitionist thought than concern for the slave. The proposals of the most extreme abolitionists, represented by William Lloyd Garrison, would indicate that this was so. Garrison advocated the abolition of slavery in the South, but if that could not be attained, he believed that the North should secede. If evil could not be stopped, then it was the duty of the righteous to dissociate themselves from it. Abolitionists deplored slave illiteracy—because slaves could not read the Bible. They ranted against the illegality of slave marriages —less because families could be broken up than because the slaves were necessarily "living in sin." Some abolitionists were flamboyant, a trait which was more effective in reassuring the abolitionist of his own unimpeachable morality than in fighting slavery. Frederick Douglass, escaped slave and surely one of the most trenchant intellects of his time, saw some of the activities of the underground railroad in this light. Douglass said in his *Autobiography,*

I have never approved of the very public manner in which some of our western friends have conducted what they call the *underground railroad,* but which I think, by their open declarations, has been made most emphatically the *upper-ground railroad.* I honor those good men and women for their noble daring, and applaud them for willingly subjecting themselves to bloody persecution, by openly avowing their participation in the escape of slaves. I, however, can see very little good resulting from such a course, either to themselves or the slaves escaping; while, upon the other hand, I see and feel assured that those open declarations are a positive evil to the slaves remaining, who are seeking to escape.

Although the abolitionists realized that the unequal treatment which free blacks met in the North provided the Southern apologists with useful arguments for slavery's benificence, (and therefore worked for the improvement of Northern conditions) freedom, not equality, was their goal. Even the most radical of the slave's friends did not think the black man his equal; after the war the abolitionist organizations broke up, and did not continue working for a less prejudiced society. There can be no doubt that, in both intellect and character, Frederick Douglass was the superior of William Lloyd Garrison, yet Garrison felt it natural to write a patronizing introduction to Douglass' *Autobiography.* Garrison said, "considering how long and dark was the career he had to run as a slave,—how few have been his opportunities to improve his mind since he broke his iron fetters,—it is, in my judgement, highly creditable to his head and heart." The book does not need Garrison's special pleading.

While abolitionists gave lip service to equality in the name of freedom, most Northerners were frank white supremacists. Equal suffrage was anathema almost everywhere. In 1860 only five states, containing 6 per cent of the Northern black population, allowed it. Prejudice was strongest in those states where slavery had never existed at all, in the Mississippi Valley (see Chapter

FIGURE 14-2. *Suzanne Hodes*, Frederick Douglass

    Frederick Douglass was born a slave in Maryland in 1817. He never knew who his white father was. As a house servant in Baltimore he learned to read and write. In 1838 he escaped to the North. Three years later he addressed a meeting of the Massachusetts Anti-Slavery Society, whose leaders were so impressed by his rhetoric that they hired him as a lecturer. While carrying out his duties he was often assaulted by mobs. Fearful that he might be returned to slavery, he spent two years (1845–47) in Great Britain and Ireland; the money he earned there giving public speeches enabled him to buy his freedom when he returned to the United States. He then founded the weekly *North Star* in Rochester, New York, which was published from 1847 to 1864. After the Civil War he held Federal

15 on "free" blacks, free land). Education was an explosive issue everywhere. In most Eastern states the right of black children to public (segregated) primary schools was acknowledged. But in Troy, Ohio, in 1840 a mob nearly demolished a school because a white man had engaged to teach the black children of the neighborhood. Further, the segregated public schools were uniformly abysmal; even in New England public opinion censured "higher" (i.e. anything more than the rudiments of reading and writing) education for blacks. The most frequent argument against such training insisted that providing educational facilities would tend to attract black residents, but a sense of the unfitness of "educated Negroes" surely influenced many whites. Nonetheless, 28 blacks by 1860 had earned degrees from "recognized" colleges, the first graduating from Bowdoin in 1828.

Exclusion from the polls and the schools were the most important legal disabilities under which the Northern black labored; extralegal norms reinforced his inferiority. He was either excluded from or segregated within most forms of transportation, theatres, lecture halls, hotels, restaurants, churches, and hospitals. Almost all the "better" occupations were closed to him. When Frederick Douglass escaped from slavery he was a skilled caulker, and attempted to continue his trade in New Bedford, Massachusetts. He was forced to support himself by common labor, because all the white caulkers would have walked off the job rather than work by the side of a black man. After the Irish influx of the 1840's the Northern black found himself pushed out of even those menial occupations which had been traditionally his. Segregation did encourage the rise of a small group of black professionals—ministers, teachers, doctors, undertakers—who received the custom of members of their race which whites would not accept.

The antipathy with which it was regarded, and the treatment which it met, not only impoverished many aspects of the black community, but reduced its self-esteem. Doubtless many blacks believed that they were really as worthless as the white folks said, and made no effort to change. But a bitter irony lies beneath the whole grim tale. When whites were asked what the blacks could do to improve their circumstances, and to gain the good opinion of the rest of society, they preached the ideology of self-help. Be industrious and frugal, sober and religious, become educated, they pronounced. But industry and frugality, though admirable, avail little on wages of a dollar a

appointive jobs under Republican administrations. His slender *Narrative of the Life of Frederick Douglass* is one of the finest autobiographies by an American in the century. Published in 1845, it was reissued in expanded versions in 1855 and again in 1892. (See also Document 16-3.)

This etching of Douglass by Suzanne Hodes was commissioned especially for this book. Hodes' works are held by many public and private collections. She was born in 1939 in New York City and educated at Radcliffe, Brandeis, and Columbia. Her paintings and prints, in several media and techniques, have been exhibited in New York, Boston, Paris, Salzburg, and Israel. Hodes' creations, while diverse, have aimed at characteristic elements of contemporary American life—the urban world, the Kennedy assassinations (in a series of paintings entitled *American Rituals*), jazz music, drag racing, and the Maine landscape (Figure H).

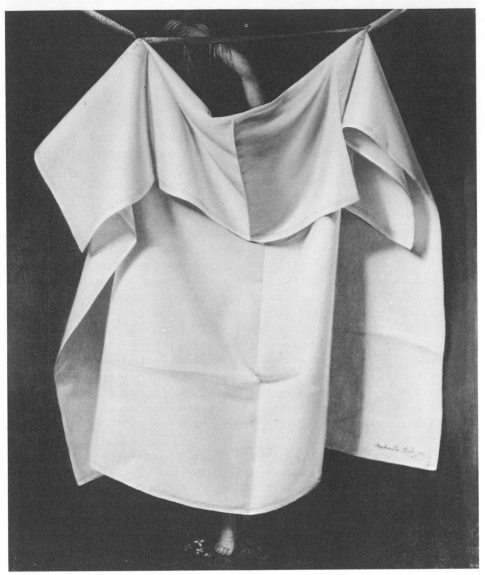

FIGURE 14-3. *Raphaelle Peale*, After the Bath

The fake nude did not originate with Hollywood movies and the Hays Office that censored them. This oil painting, one of the wittiest ever done in the United States, was made in 1823. The artist was Raphaelle Peale. Both picture and painter deserve some attention.

Raphaelle Peale was the son of Charles Willson Peale. That remarkable man had sixteen other children (plus three adopted ones), among whom were three other notable painters named Rembrandt, Rubens, and Titian. The father, a friend of President Jefferson, used a mastodon skeleton to draw visitors to his exhibition in Philadelphia—the first natural history museum in the nation, which opened in 1802 and three years later he opened the first public art gallery in America. As for his talented son Raphaelle, while he was a wit, he was also an alcoholic.

Perhaps in that era, the two naturally went together. The United States had turned against the day; sobriety and piety were within the black man's grasp, but could not change his condition. The education which the whites told him to achieve they denied him the means of acquiring. Some blacks did manage to follow instructions, often bringing down upon themselves yet more hatred and contempt. A white man who could look upon an ignorant, shiftless, shuffling "boy" with affectionate disdain, could find no place in his scheme of things for an educated, sober, pious, industrious black professional. Precisely because such a man confuted the prevailing mythology of race superiority, his achievements had to be ridiculed.

While the reformers crusaded, the farmers pushed westward, and the American character defined itself, a lush new flower of literature and philosophy bloomed, especially just outside of Boston. In the forties and fifties Ralph Waldo Emerson, Henry Thoreau, Edgar Allan Poe, Nathaniel Hawthorne, Walt Whitman, and Herman Melville were all writing. Most importantly, the masterworks that these men produced were all distinctly American—in image and symbol, in content, and even, often, in form. Earlier, James Fenimore Cooper and Washington Irving wrote within an American setting, but their ideas, ideals, language, and most of their characterizations followed the standard European model. The intellectual blooming of the twenty years before the war was new.

In 1837 Ralph Waldo Emerson lectured to the Phi Beta Kappa society at Harvard. Topic: the American Scholar. Emerson said that the thinker in America had to stop slavishly duplicating his colleagues in Europe; cease turning out slick copies and begin fashioning his own work, out of his own, not the European, experience. He called on Americans to concern themselves with "the near, the low, the common . . . the meal in the firkin; the milk in the pan." Only then could they be something other than hacks; only then could they receive the respect due to independent minds. This address was received with great enthusiasm. Ironically enough, Emerson responded to the man who most explicitly followed his instructions, Walt Whitman, with confused

---

flesh. This change should be seen as a landmark. The Puritans had favored sensuality, as long as it was exercised in moderation. Many Americans of the Enlightenment had embraced it with delight: wine and women and song. But now the sober bourgeoisie was offended by such mild titillations as naked statues. This reversal in public attitude has not been satisfactorily explained. One speculation might be that it was linked to the ascending emphasis on money-making, on duty, on thrift. Another view might see it related to the Temperance Movement as a reflection of the growing influence of women who could impose their standards on the once lustier males. We can speak a bit more confidently about the consequences of nineteenth-century squeamishness than about its causes, although both aspects need much more study. It decreed that certain topics were taboo to all forms of art. To countless persons, in England as well as America, it brought the phenomenon in early adulthood that was euphemistically called "a nervous breakdown": Carlyle, Ruskin, the Bronte sisters, William James, his sister Alice, Abraham Lincoln. Here is another enticing subject for exploration.

Thus when Raphaelle Peale chose to call this painting *After the Bath* and to expose only the girl's feet and arms, he was parodying his entire culture. He also painted a large expanse of cloth with realism that any great modern might admire. Is the picture a portrait, or is it a still life?

feelings. Whitman was *too* low and common. Although Emerson wrote Whitman an enthusiastic letter upon the publication of *Leaves of Grass,* he was embarrassed when Whitman published the letter in the preface of the next edition.

The flowering of American letters had its roots in a small, vaguely defined and constantly shifting group of people centered in Concord, Massachusetts, the Transcendentalists. In the beginning they were in revolt against the dominant religion of intellectual Boston, the sterile, sober, Unitarianism of William Ellery Channing. The final product of the "Old Lights" of the Great Awakening, this faith had expunged itself of all sensationalism, and had become devoid of vividness and vitality. The Transcendentalist group wanted to forge an intellectual life which did not preclude emotion. Most of the thinkers of the time had some contact with this circle; all of them were influenced by ideas which it promulgated. Emerson was unquestionably at its center, and his ideas can be taken as a norm of Transcendentalist thought. In some ways it was a late offshoot of European romanticism, and its members were young cousins of Keats and Wordsworth, Coleridge and Shelley. In their optimism they were very American; in the forms they expected progress to take they were not. Emerson partially defined this aspect of the Transcendentalist: "He believes in miracles, in the perpetual openness of the human mind to the new influx of light and power; he believes in inspiration and ecstasy. He wishes that the spiritual principle should be suffered to demonstrate itself to the end, in all possible applications to the state of man."* Casting out original sin, rejecting guilt, the Transcendentalist believed the human soul a shining thing, which the physical world often soiled. While the soul must not on that account isolate itself from the tangible world, it had a responsibility to regard it as merely a part of a spiritual whole, demolishing its "apparent" evils. Emerson once wrote that the poet (all men should be poets) "disposes very easily of the most disagreeable facts." Herman Melville wrote in the margin, "So it would seem. In this sense, Mr. E is a great poet."

The Transcendentalists were idealists. They believed in the reality of a mental "ideal form" which united all physically similar things, and which was more important than any specific actuality. This conceptualization enabled them to ignore "disagreeable facts," and, more importantly, to strive for an understanding of the world as a whole. At this time scientific rationalism was becomingly increasingly important in America. It consisted of classifying physical things, of slicing the accessible universe up into smaller and more discrete chunks. The Transcendentalists rejected this method of dealing with reality, and insisted that the spiritual whole, more important than its concrete

---

*Continuities with the Arminians of the seventeenth century are clear. The first two sentences of the next paragraph descend from Plato.

parts, was lost by fission and discovered by fusion. Although they are easy to ridicule, this vision of life as an indivisible whole proved fruitful in American thought, and provided a counterweight to the particularizing tendencies of the era.

Although Emerson called for personal self-reliance, transcendentalist belief rejected the cult of individualism. Human thought was only important when it went beyond merely personal quirks; a man became great only when he nurtured those aspects of himself which he shared with every man. The surest way for him to do this was to study nature. While the Transcendentalists refused to grant the existence of evil, they admitted that in human beings one could suppose he saw traces of evil. But nature "never wears a mean appearance." These people all lived in the settled, but not urban, parts of New England. Their devotion to nature could cause them no greater harm than an occasional pair of muddy shoes; undoubtably the charms of this unquestionably lovely part of the country inspired them. But their inability to comprehend the much harsher and more devilish "nature" with which their Western countrymen had to contend denotes a serious failure of the imagination. Emerson, in particular, often sounds like a fool. He made frequent journeys to the Mississippi valley on lecture tours, and should have been able to readjust his categories upon receiving conflicting evidence. But he could only write in shocked amazement, "all the life of land and water had distilled no thought."

On rejecting traditional Unitarianism the Transcendentalists embraced a "religion" which was simultaneously less theistic and more emotional. The only "God" which they recognised they called the "Oversoul." This was not a particular or a sentient being, but the union of all souls, of all thought. Everyone was part of the Oversoul, and achieved his finest moments when he submerged himself into the All. This idea was in large part derived from Far Eastern mysticism. But while the Eastern mystic tried to achieve the transcendent state through ascetic practices, the Transcendentalist believed that it could be found by becoming one with nature. Emerson described the process as becoming a "transparent eyeball":

> In the woods, we return to reason and faith. There I feel that nothing can befall me in life—no disgrace, no calamity (leaving me my eyes), which nature cannot repair. Standing on the bare ground—my head bathed by the blithe air and uplifted into infinite space—all mean egotism vanishes. I become a transparent eyeball; I am nothing; I see all; the currents of the Universal Being circulate through me; I am part or parcel of God.

Herman Melville, in *Moby-Dick,* described this state as it occurred to a sailor up in the crow's-nest watching for whales. But he insisted that it was a dangerous condition. The sailor might, in his revery, fall off and drown, and anyone was vulnerable to the dismaying shock of returning identity. The only

FIGURE 14-4. *Emily Dickinson, 1847*

The soul selects her own society,
Then shuts the door;
On her divine majority
Obtrude no more.

Unmoved, she notes the chariot's pausing
At her low gate;
Unmoved, an emperor is kneeling
Upon her mat.

I've known her from an ample nation
Choose one;
Then close the valves of her attention
Like stone.

real unity comes in death; while alive, we must cope with reality from within the shells of our separate personalities.

Henry David Thoreau, like Emerson, lived in the core of the Transcendentalist group about Concord. But the most enduring aspects of his work are not particularly "Transcendental." He searched for ways to simplify human life, believing that material complexities unnecessarily consumed the soul. He insisted that the claims of conscience superseded those of society and law. While Emerson agreed with him, Thoreau's emphasis differed, as indicated by the following incident: Thoreau disapproved of the Mexican War, and in protest refused to pay his taxes. When he was jailed, Emerson bailed him out, whereupon Thoreau informed him that in conscience he should have been in there too. Although the other Transcendentalists declared that the spiritual aspects of life were more important than the material, they lived upper middle class lives, and were willing to work to get the money to do this. Thoreau thought that almost all worldly goods were a clutter, and "getting ahead" a waste. He did not share the American optimism that came with prosperity; it seemed to him that increasingly efficient exploitation of the environment cost too dear in human terms. "Most men . . . through mere ignorance or mistake, are so occupied with the factitious cares and superfluously hard labors of life, that its finer fruits cannot be plucked by them . . . the laboring man has not leisure for a true integrity day by day. . . . He has no time for anything but a machine." The image of the machine, particularly the railroad, haunted Thoreau as it did others. When he was experimenting with simplicity on the shores of Walden Pond, he daily saw the trains between Boston and Chicago go by. But this symbol of progress was to Thoreau but "an improved means to an unimproved end." His vision of progress consisted of improvement in

---

This daguerrotype of Emily Dickinson (1830–86) is the only known portrait of her since her childhood; it was made when she was seventeen. It is appropriate that she should present a shadowy figure in adulthood, since she spent the last half of her life as a virtual recluse, rarely venturing outside her father's house in Amherst, Massachusetts. But if her experience was not wide, her vision cut deep. Most of her poems are, like the one above, about the universals of the human condition—love, time, death—or about nature. And her powers of imagination were great enough that even when she speaks of things she never encountered—the sea, for example—her message rings true.

Dickinson's physical isolation was paralleled by her complete separation from poetic fashions. She belonged to no school, followed no patterns. It is impossible to "place" any one of her poems except as being, simply, hers. But the body of her work has great internal continuity of style. Her imagery is usually taken from nature, and her metaphors are often both apt and startling. She speaks, for example, of a railroad train which "laps the miles up", of a snake causing its observers to feel "zero at the bone." Note in the above poem the image "valves of her attention." Also note another pervasive quality of her poetry which became a common device but which was unusual in her era, the way some of the rhythms (and elsewhere the rhymes) break loose from the usual strict formal patterns. The short, abrupt, last line suggests a trap, snapping shut.

human lives, and he did not consider mere material advantages any such good.

Nathaniel Hawthorne associated with the Transcendentalists, and even lived for a time in their experimental Utopia of Brook Farm, but he was not of them. The Oversoul he found nebulous, faith in the future seemed to him misplaced, and the persistence of evil he confirmed. Hawthorne has been called a Puritan; certainly he appears to have found New England's past more gripping than its future. Unable to accept the new faith, either in Transcendental optimism or the cult of the machine, he satirized one through the means of the other in a parody of *Pilgrim's Progress* entitled "The Celestial Railroad." The modern Christian travels to heaven by modern means, finding the Slough of Despond bridged, with its foundations well anchored in "French philosophy and German rationalism." The burden which Bunyan's pilgrim had carried on his back is now neatly stowed in the baggage car. Unfortunately the train arrives at the wrong destination, as the guide is in league with the devil. To Hawthorne, the easy road was the wrong one, the harsh acceptance of sin and guilt more fruitful than Transcendentalist wishful thinking. The worst sin was that of pride—intellectual, spiritual, physical—because it separates man from his fellows. Only love and humility can save him from the evil which his soul dictates; only through the recognition of the pervasiveness of evil can he become wise.

Herman Melville's contact with the Transcendentalists was marginal, although he had read them. They knew him, if at all, as a pleasant writer of romantic tales of the South Pacific; it would be three-quarters of a century before his masterwork, *Moby-Dick,* would be recognised as anything other than another unimportant, unsuccessful novel. This disregard is in a way suitable, as Melville can be described as the first American whose ideas are those of the twentieth century. He was out of step with his time, and sometimes frighteningly relevant to ours (Document 15-2). Melville rejected optimism and individualism, and saw nature to be evil, the universe to be indifferent, and things rarely to be what they seem. He did not believe that his country had God on its side. These ideas, which many people can accept comfortably today, were profoundly disturbing to a man in the middle of the last century. Surrounded by believers, all striving busily for things that he believed were destructive, his unbelief could only distress Melville without indicating any way for him to improve the circumstances in which he found himself. He was probably the first American to recognise openly the nightmare of loneliness and potential failure which was one of the conditions of belief in the American Dream. Competition separated man from his fellows even when miles of prairie did not isolate him; union within the Oversoul seemed to Melville a mere narcotic. But the man who realized this, in the nineteenth century, must himself experience dreadful loneliness, for his scepticism of the faith of other men dug an abyss across which he could not meet them.

By 1850 it was clear to any thoughtful person that religion was not and would not become the overbearing concern of everyday life in the United States. But its elixir remained to saturate many aspects of the American mind. This rejuvenation is a splendid illustration of the meaning of "revival." Men of the Enlightenment had backslid; their descendants sought to return to the true faith. Thus began the tradition of the camp meeting, which lasted into the twentieth century. It was fed by the ubiquitous optimism and individualism, so prominent in the success of Jacksonian democracy. These same qualities fed the great reform movements of the era: women's rights, temperance, equality in politics, and, greatest of them all, the abolition of slavery. Here we come full circle. Many Americans hated slavery, not because it was wasteful or because it was anti-human, but because it involved *white* people in sin. The majority of whites, of course, hardly thought about black bondage at all. When they did, they regarded it favorably. The nation to them was emphatically "a white man's country." Strident assertions of progress and the "strong man" acting on his own were heard not only from ordinary citizens but also from the eminent writers of the period, who were perhaps all too conscious (even if they didn't understand it) of the rapid conquest of the frontier. There were exceptions. Herman Melville wrote about that eternal frontier—the ocean—and he was a freak who did not sound optimistic at all. He also wrote about that horrible ordeal that would round off the epoch, the Civil War.

SOME NOTABLE EVENTS

1816 American Bible Society organized.

1817 Thomas Hopkins Gallaudet founds the "Connecticut Asylum" for the care and education of the deaf.

1825–
1827 Robert Owen's socialist experiment at New Harmony.

1826 Lyceum Movement begun in Milbury, Massachusetts.
American Temperance Society founded.

1827–
1832 Anti-Masonic Party (Whig splinter group opposed to government "conspiracies") important in national politics.

1830 Joseph Smith founds the Mormon Church.

1831 William Lloyd Garrison begins the *Liberator*.

1836 First *McGuffey's Reader* published.
"Transcendental Club" begins as a casual discussion group.

1837 Ralph Waldo Emerson, "The American Scholar."

1840 Richard Henry Dana, *Two Years Before the Mast*.

1840–
1844 The *Dial*, Transcendentalist magazine, is issued.

1841 First series of Emerson's *Essays* published.

1841–
1846 Brook Farm near Boston, utopian community of Transcendentalists.

1842–
1856 Hopedale Community southwest of Boston, Christian communistic community.

1843 The year that the Millerite Millenialists believed the world would end.
Dorothea Dix presented a Report to the Massachusetts legislature on the condition of the insane in that state.

1845 Edgar Allen Poe, "The Raven."
Frederick Douglass' autobiography published.
Margaret Fuller, *Woman in the Nineteenth Century*.

1845–
1880 Perfectionist Community at Oneida, New York.

1846 World Temperance Convention held in London.
Congress establishes the Smithsonian Institution.

1847 Foundation of Salt Lake City.
American Medical Association begun.
Frederick Douglass begins publication of the *North Star*.

1848 Convention on women's rights held at Seneca Falls, New York.

1850 Nathaniel Hawthorne, *The Scarlet Letter*.

1851 Prohibition adopted in Maine.
Herman Melville, *Moby-Dick*.

1852 Harriet Beecher Stowe, *Uncle Tom's Cabin*.

1854 Henry Thoreau, *Walden*.

1855 Walt Whitman, *Leaves of Grass*.

Ways to Study History XIV

Brood over novels. It is a truism to say that *Moby-Dick* can be read on many levels, as a concrete description of American whaling or as a symbolic account of the tensions among the id, ego, and super-ego. Between these limits of abstraction, a close reading of this book reveals a conception of nature which is more useful in understanding the American experience, both on the sea and on the frontier, than Emerson's specialized optimism.

Melville perceived the universe as indifferent to man, and nature as a fearsome thing, the more dangerous because it was often beautiful. Lulled by beauty, man was more vulnerable to peril; he must be constantly on guard. "These are the times of dreamy quietude, when beholding the tranquil beauty and brillancy of the ocean's skin, one forgets the tiger heart that pants beneath it, and would not willingly remember, that this velvet paw but conceals a remorseless fang." European visitors to the West remarked on the frontiersman's obliviousness to the beauties of the land. Perhaps the Westerner, conscious of the threats about him, could not afford to let his senses be dulled by "appreciation" of the charms that could so easily kill them.

Although realizing that nature concealed a snarling face behind a shimmering veil, Melville nonetheless could not resist describing it in its happier moments. In *Moby-Dick* he invariably uses images which are not merely civilized, but of the highest sophistication. He speaks of days which were "as crystal goblets of Persian sherbet," of "starred and stately nights" which "seemed haughty dames in jeweled velvets," of "absent conquering Earls, the golden helmeted suns." The sea and the land were often magnificent; a man needed to be clothed in some of the protections of society to savor them, or even often to see them. Naked, he must freeze.

Document 14-1

In July of 1848, at Seneca Falls, New York, American women convened for the first time to discuss the question of their rights. They produced a "Declaration of Sentiments" modeled on the Declaration of Independence, which concluded with a list of resolutions. All of them passed unanimously except the call for equal suffrage.

Resolved: That such laws as conflict, in any way, with the true and substantial happiness of woman, are contrary to the great precept of nature and of no validity; that all laws which prevent woman from occupying such a station in society as her conscience shall dictate, or which place her in a position inferior to that of man, are contrary to the great precept of nature; that woman is man's equal; that the women of this country ought to be enlightened in regard to the laws under which they live; that inasmuch as man, while claiming for himself intellectual superiority, does accord to woman moral superiority, it is preeminently his duty to encourage her to speak and teach, as she has an opportunity, in all religious assemblies; that the same amount of virtue, delicacy, and refinement of behavior that is required of woman in the social state, should also be required of man; that the objection of indelicacy and impropriety, which is so often brought against woman when she addresses a public audience, comes with a very ill-grace from those who encourage, by their attendance, her appearance on the stage, in the concert, or in feats of the circus; that woman has too long rested satisfied in the circumscribed limits which corrupt customs and a perverted application of the Scriptures have marked out for her; that it is the duty of the women of this country to secure to themselves their sacred right of the elective franchise; that the equality of human rights results necessarily from the fact of the identity of the race in capabilities and responsibilities; that it is demonstrably the right and duty of woman, equally with man, to promote every righteous cause by every righteous means; that the speedy success of our cause depends upon the zealous and untiring efforts of both men and women, for the overthrow of the monopoly of the pulpit, and for the securing to woman an equal participation with men in the various trades, professions, and commerce.

Document 14-2

In 1855 Lemuel Shattuck, a Boston bookseller, issued a report on conditions of sanitation and public health in that city, which included recommendations for the whole state. The Shattuck Report was in some respects generations ahead of its time; not until 1869 would Massachusetts even set up a Board of Public Health.

We believe that the conditions of perfect health, either public or personal, are seldom or never attained, though attainable;—that the average length of human life may be very much extended, and its physical power greatly augmented;—that in every year, within this Commonwealth, thousands of lives are lost which might have been saved;—that tens of thousands of cases of sickness occur, which might have been prevented;—that a vast amount of unnecessarily impaired health, and physical debility exists among those not actually confined by sickness;—that these preventable evils require an enormous expenditure and loss of money, and impose upon the people unnumbered and immeasurable calamities, pecuniary, social, physical, mental, and moral, which might be avoided;—that means exist, within our reach, for their mitigation or removal;—and that measures for prevention will effect infinitely more, than remedies for the cure of disease. . . .

We recommend that a General Board of Health be established, which shall be charged with the general execution of the laws of the State, relating to the enumeration, the vital statistics, and the public health of the inhabitants.

We recommend that the laws relating to the public registration of births, marriages, and deaths, be perfected and carried into effect in every city and town of the State.

We recommend that measures be taken to ascertain the amount of sickness suffered, among the scholars who attend the public schools and other seminaries of learning in the Commonwealth.

We recommend that every city and town in the State be REQUIRED to provide means for the periodical vaccination of the inhabitants.

We recommend that measures be taken to prevent, as far as practicable, the smoke nuisance.

Deadlock and Division

Slavery has been considered in several aspects: the origins of black slavery in America (early Chapter 2), the slave trade (early in Chapters 3 and 4), the growth of slavery (early Chapter 3; mid-Chapter 7; late Chapter 8), the geographical expansion of the institution and the attendant controversies (Chapter 11 on the cotton gin, and cotton land boom; end Chapter 13). It remains to depict the class structures of slave-plantation culture in its most mature form.

Numerically, the yeoman farmer dominated white society. In late ante-bellum days, three white families in every four in the South owned no slaves at all. The approximate percentages of slaveholding families varied widely from region to region (see Figure 15-1). The late Frank L. Owsley worked out far more detailed descriptions of patterns of land- and slaveholding for many Southern counties that he took to be representative. He concluded that, save in Virginia and the Carolinas, 80 per cent of white farmers

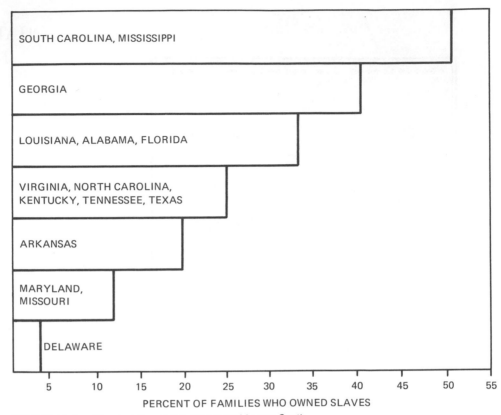

FIGURE 15-1. *Slaveholding in the Upper and Lower South*

owned the acres they worked. By hard work the yeoman lived in austere comfort. Relying on the labor of his family with perhaps a hired hand or two, the owner of no slaves merges almost imperceptibly with those slaveholders who had only a few, say, up to twenty. Jefferson's father illustrates those farmers who worked in the field with their slaves. So does Jacob Eaton, who in 1860 had 160 acres in the Piedmont of North Carolina. His seven slaves were man, woman, and five children. A pious Methodist with eight children, Eaton rejoiced in his self-sufficiency, which included wearing homespun and burying his dead in the family cemetery.

Of the 385,000 families that owned slaves, only 12 per cent owned twenty or more. The aristocracy owning fifty or more were some 10,000 families. Of nabobs, namely those possessed of 200 slaves or more apiece, a mere 312 existed in 1860. These grandees were concentrated in zones that produced rice or sugar and in the newer cotton areas. William Aiken of South Carolina cultivated 1,500 acres of rice and 500 of corn. His investment in land and 700 slaves came to $380,000. Nathaniel Heyward of the same state owned seventeen plantations and 2,000 slaves. When he died in 1852 his human chattels, valued at a million dollars, were only half of his estate; he was "the largest planter of his day." In sugar-growing Louisiana, Colonel J. A. S. Acklen owned 700 slaves and 20,000 acres organized into six plantations. Joseph Davis, whose brother Jefferson Davis would be president of the Confederacy, did so well with fresh cotton lands in Mississippi that he was accounted a millionaire.

Roughly comparable in status to the yeoman was an amorphous group that was largely urban. Few students have noticed the existence of white craftsmen and shopkeepers, but this segment of the white labor force was nearly 10 per cent in Georgia and ran to 26 per cent in Louisiana. Overseers frequently were scorned, but by some criteria they could be quite respectable; the forenoted Aiken paid his overseer $2,000 a year. Sidling upwards from these categories were the professional men: preachers, doctors, lawyers who were not also planters and merchants. These were the city folk, properly so called. For the lowest class of whites many terms were coined—"poor white trash," "peckerwoods," "piney woods folks," "crackers," "sandhillers." They were hardly part of the white culture at all; they had been shouldered aside by the main stream into gullies and backwaters and byways. One of the few manifestations of subsistence farming in American history, they scarcely impinged on the market economy. Indeed, many did not subsist by agriculture but by the primitive methods of gathering and hunting and fishing. Cloistered into the mountains of east Tennessee or the piney barrens of north Georgia and Mississippi, they might continue for decades to eke a deprived (and often depraved) life.

The class divisions in Southern society are obvious. But class-consciousness hardly existed before about 1845 or 1850. The fluidities of a frontier were still alive; nabobs had brothers who were yeomen. Few whites were directly exploited; instead they were merely edged onto poorer lands. Capable yeomen could still rise rapidly, and in a semi-wilderness virtues like courage and strength could count for as much as inherited wealth. Of eight governors of Virginia from 1841 to 1861, only one was a gentleman by birth. Advancement of gifted yeomen both deprived their peers of leadership and also persuaded them that they could get ahead and become successful slaveholders on their own. Finally, the behavior of many grandees had two sweeping consequences. Toward all whites down to the meanest they might exhibit a free-and-easy camaraderie. And they spread the instinct that the lowest white stands taller than the most exalted black. But in the decade or so before the Civil War, this harmony among classes in the white South seems to have changed. The problem is another that needs more study. Present evidence suggests that the rupture was made from both directions—the middling classes thrusting upward, the upper classes stomping down. When boys without standing like Joseph E. Brown in Georgia and Andrew Johnson in Tennessee won high office, the Old South had moved a good distance from the deferential society that George Washington admired. Available facts do not afford a firm conclusion, but it is easy to imagine that other Georgians (Alexander Stephens) panicked when a nobody like Brown became prominent in politics. Also pressing the self-appointed aristocrats was an obsession with their own eminence. This trait was not new among them. Thomas Dabney, a Virginia planter, removed to Mississippi in 1835. Arrived there, he showed up one day with a gang of black slaves to help a neighbor. He wore his gloves while he sat on his horse and ordered his crew about. He made no friends that day, neighborly aid or not. By late ante-bellum times this arrogance had become ingrown. Just listen to James H. Hammond of South Carolina, who served as both governor and senator: "Planting . . . in this country is the only independent and really honorable occupation. . . . The planters here are essentially what the nobility are in other countries." Perceiving that a class rift might become a chasm, the 1856 governor of South Carolina proposed a plan to make every white a slaveholder. He wanted to reopen the slave trade, thus lowering the price of a slave. For three reasons the scheme got nowhere in the South. The Upper South, for reasons that will be promptly stated, opposed it. The nabobs in the Lower South, for reasons that should be apparent from their heavy investment in slaves, were not warm. (But of course they would and did smuggle Africans into the country.) Finally, the idea violated a federal law which held that the slave trade was piracy, and to adopt it was to secede from the Union. Times were not quite ripe.

As the white South had a class structure, so did the South of the black slave. It rested on many variables: (a) tenure of his family in the United States, (b) dexterity with English, (c) color of skin, (d) household worker or field worker, (e) occupational skill, (f) amount of power delegated to him by white masters, and so on. Do not imagine that these gauges always jibed. If a master in the border states was choosing a domestic servant, he would plunk for a light skin. But if he was selling off the same slave, a light skin brought a lower price because it facilitated escape. The outlines of stratification among plantation slaves seem clear. Duties in the master's house were best. If you had to work in the hot sun, it was better to be a driver with a whip than to be one of those driven. It was better to be in the Upper South than in the Lower. It was better to be slave to a rich master than to a poor one.

We can read many generalizations by modern writers about slavery. Some may mislead or oversimplify, such as the basically ethnocentric assumption that black slaves were merely ordinary human beings, (that is, as one writer says, "innately Negroes *are,* after all, only white men with black skins, nothing more, nothing less")—an assumption that ignores a unique history stretching through many centuries and untold anguish (and what does "innately" mean?). Another view holds that black children grew to be obsequious "Samboes" because plantations seemed to offer them no really satisfactory father-image other than the master. But most such generalizations are made from distorted assumptions and negligible evidence. Whether many slaves became stereotyped Samboes, for example, would be a question best studied by analyzing the surviving evidence about slaves, not by making coarse analogies to the inmates of Nazi concentration camps. Even about the external behavior of slaves, precious little evidence has been gathered. Their work was physically taxing, but probably no more so than that done by most whites at the time. Looking only at their tangible standard of living—food, clothing, housing—their lot often compared well with the station of millions of European peasants (Document 15-2). But there are three overriding facts: They had no hope for advancement for themselves or their children. Also, white society wanted nothing from them except the equivalent energy of a water-wheel or a steam engine; they were regarded as merely a form of animal power. (It does not answer to say that most masters were kindly; horses and oxen are treated well by wise masters.) Third, their every known action (needless to say, many of their actions were not known to their masters) was dependent on the will of another.

Slavery was older than Christendom, and many Western societies had evolved elaborate codes to regulate it. The late Roman Empire held so many avenues of manumission that of those born into slavery perhaps one in five died a free man. In Africa among the Ashanti, the tribe from which many American slaves derived, a slave could marry, own property, testify in a trial. The Roman Catholic Church insisted that a slave of whatever color possessed an immortal soul. In consequence the Spanish and Portuguese colonies of the New World knew many limits to the power of slaveholders. Sexual pairing among slaves had to be consecrated by clergy. Cuba allowed its magistrates to emancipate slaves who were unjustly punished. Brazil permitted any slave who had sired ten children to demand his freedom. As one Catholic prelate stated matters in the eighteenth century: "Slavery is not to be understood as conferring on one man the same power over another that men have over cattle. . . . For slavery does not abolish the natural equality of man. . . ."

But at the time of English settlement of America, slavery was not known to English law. Thus masters knew no restraint from church or state. In very early Maryland the status of a black child was derived from his father, but by the beginning of the nineteenth century a Kentucky court could rule, "the father of a slave is unknown to our law." Obviously patrilineal descent in the United States would have meant the creation of a huge group of free mulattoes, and such a result could not be permitted. A North Carolina judge in 1829 gave a tart summation:

> The power of the master must be absolute to render the submission of the slave perfect. I must freely confess my sense of the harshness of the proposition. I feel it as deeply as any man can. . . . But it is inherent in the relation of master and slave. . . . We cannot allow the right of a master to be brought into discussion in the Courts of justice. The slave, to remain a slave, must be made sensible that there is no appeal from his master. . . .

Kindness or no, physical coercion was never farther from a slave than a white arm could swing. In 1831 came a report about a runaway in a Louisiana jail: "He has been lately gelded, and is not yet well." Admirers of Andrew Jackson as the avatar of modern democracy should know that he offered a reward of $50 for a runaway, "and ten dollars extra for every hundred lashes any person will give him to the amount of three hundred."

Not only do we hear it argued that most masters were genial chaps, as perhaps they were, but we also meet the contention from a generation ago that the institution was withering because it had ceased to be profitable. Recent careful studies agree on the contrary conclusion. The argument of unprofitability notes that in the long upswing after 1842, the price of slaves rose more rapidly than cotton prices. But this change proves nothing because it ignores the rise of output per manhour as slaves were transferred to more fertile soil. The argument also takes no account of the human crop that plantations added to their farm produce. Developing areas turned out a profitable crop of cotton or sugar or rice. But nearly every region also gave its planters a capital gain by the natural rate of increase of their slaves. Only in the sugar district of Louisiana did the black population fail to reproduce itself. Moreover, the stock of slaves in the Old South was not depleted by exports of blacks to the Lower South; only the natural increase was sent away. From 1790 to 1850 the slave population of the Atlantic states grew an average of 2 per cent a year, while for the Gulf states plus Arkansas and Tennessee the rate was 18 per cent. The number of blacks from the border states who emigrated with their masters to growing sections or were exported there has been estimated:

1820–30	124,000
1830–40	265,000
1840–50	146,000
1850–60	207,000

Although some slaveholders did offer baby bonuses to black mothers, it would be fruitless here to make guesses about the degree of slave breeding that was practiced. What is certain is that tobacco planters in Virginia and Kentucky depended for their survival on the sale of surplus laborers to the Lower South. Further, we have no reason to think the planters would have voluntarily scrapped their peculiar institution. It has been argued that slave capital earned returns at least equal to those earned by other forms of capital. Thus a slave system could be so well supported and encouraged by economic forces as to require a harsh political move to stop it, and such was the American experience.

The eminent Allan Nevins suggested that the Civil War resulted from the interplay of an institution with a passion: slavery plus race prejudice. The latter can be seen in regard to free blacks in the North and to all blacks whether free or slave in the urban South. In cities below the Mason-Dixon Line, slavery had been integral to the culture until about 1840; then it atrophied. Numerically the decline was relative rather than absolute. In 1820, 37 per cent of city residents were black; by 1860, less than 17 per cent. For New Orleans the figures are more extreme; one resident of every two was black in 1820, only one of seven in 1860. Perhaps more important was a decline of the spirit of the institution. It was too bothersome for an urban master to keep his slaves under strict control. Slaves might be allowed to board themselves away from their owner. Some could find their own work and hire out for wages, on condition that they paid their master a fixed sum per year. Disintegration reached the point that Charleston held hundreds of nominal slaves for whom the owner was listed as "unknown." As slavery withered in the cities, segregation was instituted. New Orleans subjected blacks to "careful and complete" segregation on streetcars, in jails, hospitals, cemeteries, "at any public exposition or theatre." It excluded free Negroes from schools. In two institutions the segregation brought some benefits. Richmond whites began to exclude blacks from their churches. A consequence beginning in 1823 was independent congregations; by 1856 there were four. These can be called the first training grounds for black leaders. Reinforcing them were the "bands" that provided fitting funerals; one white minister complained that "they have been perverted and abused." A group launched for one function can serve many.

Bias against blacks was universal among whites (see mid-Chapter 14 on abolitionism, etc.). After the admission of Maine in 1819, every new state by its constitution limited suffrage to whites. New Jersey, Pennsylvania, and Connecticut, which had allowed Negroes to vote, now disfranchised them. Not until 1843 did Massachusetts repeal its miscegenation law. Illinois in 1847 banned further migration of Negroes into the state. New York City had its race riots, but the City of Brotherly Love was worse. Five times from 1832 to 1849 did mobs there stage major outbursts against black residents.

Despite daily proof that all whites joined in the belief that Negroes were inferior, slaveholders were wracked by fears. Chapter 14 briefly depicts the demands for abolition by free Americans—white and black. At least equally worrisome were subversions by slaves. Of these, the kind slaveholders found most worrisome are now the hardest to study because they were clandestine. Who can tell how much effort was deliberately withheld, how much of a slave's thought went to devise forms of what the Army would later call "dogging it" and "goldbricking"? Conscious destruction of equipment was doubtless common. Who today can count the blades on hoes which were broken? the plowshares that were bent? In contrast, flight was painfully overt, and from reward notices we can calculate that it occurred thousands of times a year. But, even though the statement by a Southern judge in 1855 that "upwards of 60,000 slaves" had by that time escaped to the North has lately been called "a reasonable estimate," we cannot know with certitude whether or not this guess is roughly true. We can surmise that nearly all escapes were made by one or two people and that they lasted only days or weeks before failing; on the other hand, the indomitable ex-slave Harriet Tubman conducted some sizable groups to safety.

Most terrifying of all was the slave revolt because it was directly revolutionary. Rumors of insurrections were far more frequent than insurrections. A slave rebellion in Santo Domingo in 1795 brought panic to the American South. The slave Gabriel led a conspiracy in Virginia in 1800 that allegedly involved a thousand rebels. A reputed plot led by Denmark Vesey in Charleston in 1822 resulted in many confessions, 35 executions, and 31 exiles from the region.* The most savage was headed by Nat Turner in Virginia in 1831. After the rebels had run amok and butchered whites with axes, authorities engaged in equal barbarities while putting down the revolt.

After 1831 no serious slave revolt took place. But reduction of the threat did not imply a diminution of panic; on the contrary the jitters seemed to increase. Just as the slaveholders crushed any violent uprising by blacks, so did they crush peaceful dissent by whites. Until 1830 the mass base of abolitionism was to be found not in New England but in the evangelical churches of the Ohio valley, especially the Upper South. This was ruthlessly put down. For the last twenty-five years before secession, no Southerner dared to question publicly the wisdom and justice of slavery. In 1837 Calhoun rose in the Senate to say of the peculiar institution: "We see it now in its true light and regard it as the most safe and stable basis for free institutions in the world." For this blessed conversion the demon opponents received credit; as the chief justice of Georgia expressed it in 1848: "Had the abolitionists let us alone we should have been guilty, I verily believe, of political and social suicide, by emancipating the African race, a measure fatal to them, to ourselves, and to the best interests of this Confederacy and of the whole world." Not content to suppress internal dissent, slaveholders sought to chain the federal apparatus throughout the nation. They tried to keep all abolitionist tracts from entering the South via the United States mail. They inaugurated a rule in the House of Representatives saying that petitions about slavery should be tabled without being read aloud. Many a proud moment came to Representative John Quincy Adams as he strode down the aisle to move rescission of the Gag Rule; he was elated when he succeeded in 1844: "Blessed, forever blessed, be the name of God!" Countless white moderates with no love of abolitionists were brought to a limited cooperation with them because of resentment at the slaveholder onslaught against civil liberties.

Yet other attacks were being mounted against those cherished American freedoms. Deep veins of hate were welling up against alien ways. The anti-Papist heritage from colonial and Revolutionary days dominated these xenophobic fears until about 1835. Revolution in France in 1830 heightened American paranoia; if Catholicism was overthrown in Europe, where could it flee but to America? Proscription of the Jesuits in Spain in 1835 prompted the

---

*A modern study denies that any mechanism resembling an organized Underground Railroad to help runaways ever existed at all. Another recent work, averring the undeniable truth that many confessions are false, suggests that there was no Denmark Vesey conspiracy. These conclusions seem to me extreme.

same question. As with planter terrors about slave revolts, so here: the less palpable the menace, the worse the nightmare (Document 15-1). At the same time nativist agitators were linking anti-Popery to the resentment against immigrant competition felt by native-born workers. No trash was too intellectually sleazy to find an audience. The highlight was the alleged confessions of Maria Monk, incarcerated in a Montreal nunnery. Her Mother Superior tells her to "obey the priests in all things"; her intended fate, to her "utter astonishment and horror, was to live in the practice of criminal intercourse with them." Bastards derived from these unions were at once baptized and then strangled. Says the Mother Superior: "This secured their everlasting happiness, for the baptism purified them from all sinfulness, and being sent out of the world before they had time to do anything wrong, they were at once admitted into heaven." Published in 1836, this book sold 300,000 copies before the Civil War.

Called Know-Nothingism because the members pledged secrecy, the movement had a special appeal in Southern cities. Old Whigs, headed by merchant-planters long accustomed to power, could use it to fight immigrant voters being enfranchised by Democrats, but also some saw it as a diversion from the troublesome conflicts about slavery. This kind of xenophobia and hatred had a political function, since immigrants were such a high proportion in several Southern cities:

St. Louis	60 per cent foreign-born
New York	50
Chicago	50
Milwaukee	50
New Orleans	40
Boston	36
Memphis (of whites)	36

While we can acknowledge that American society held many other fissures and clashes, it is most certain that the worst problems arose from territorial expansion as complicated by the status of slavery.* Oregon was organized as a Territory in 1848 and the principle of the Missouri Compromise was applied. But a deadlock developed over the standing of New Mexico and California. The latter, enjoying a tremendous boom from the gold discoveries, was in no mood to be patient. In 1849 its citizens took matters in their own hands by adopting an independent frame of government. It banned slavery. Already segments of Northern opinion had taken an intractable stand; the Cleveland *Plain Dealer* had announced, "Rather than see slavery extended one

---

*In retrospect, Tocqueville once more seems uncanny in his prognostication: "If ever America undergoes great revolutions, they will be brought about by the presence of the black race on the soil of the United States; that is to say, they will owe their origin, not to the equality, but to the inequality of condition."

inch beyond its present limits we would see this Union rent asunder." Southern fire-eaters had their reply ready. A South Carolina newspaper had stated "the only remedy" to protect the planters "from Northern oppression, from the Wilmot Proviso" with its evil intentions: "the *secession of the slaveholding states in a body from the union and their formation into a separate republic.*" The position of the South within the nation was deteriorating rapidly. Since Missouri joined the Union in 1821, four new states had been admitted. The prior two were slave, but the recent two were free: Arkansas (1836), Texas (1845), Iowa (1846), Wisconsin (1848). Already the slave states were badly outnumbered in the House of Representatives. South and North still had an equal number of Senators, but admission of Oregon and California would destroy the balance. The slave interest might soon become a permanent minority in Congress. As 1850 opened, John C. Calhoun reported from Washington: "The Southern members are more determined and bold than I ever saw them. Many avow themselves to be disunionists, and a still greater number admit, that there is little hope for a remedy short of it."

Again, Clay brought his parliamentary skills to bear. He needed them all. His final package provided for the admission of California as a free state and for settlement of the boundary between New Mexico and Texas. The rest of the Mexican acquisitions were organized into Territories without mention of slavery. The slave trade would be abolished in the District of Columbia, but slavery there would not be tampered with unless Maryland consented. Most explosive of all in Northern opinion was a strong Fugitive Slave Act. The Supreme Court in 1842 had ruled that Congress had exclusive control of the problem of runaway slaves but it had simultaneously denied any federal authority to compel state officials to enforce any such statute. The new law would be administered by federal officers. These provisions incited the most famous debates in the history of the Senate. William Seward of New York rose to declaim "there is a higher law than the Constitution. . . ." Clay replied that this theory was one of the "wild, reckless, and abominable theories, which strike at the foundations of all property, and threaten to crush in ruins the fabric of civilized society." When Daniel Webster gave his Seventh of March speech advocating the Compromise, a common reaction in Massachusetts was expressed in Emerson's comment that the word honor in the mouth of Daniel Webster was like the word love in the mouth of a whore. Of the Fugitive Slave provision Emerson said, "I will not obey it, by God." Senator Salmon P. Chase of Ohio averred, "Disobedience to the enactment is obedience to God." Senator Jefferson Davis of Mississippi denied all federal power to ban slavery from a Territory; the Missouri Compromise had "derived its validity from the acquiescence of the States, and not from the act of Congress."

The rancorous rhetoric continued through the spring and summer of 1850. In spite of Clay's management, it seemed doubtful that the Compromise could be effected. President Taylor seemed to be taking his lead from Seward, who was demanding firm adherence to principle. At this time the Southern

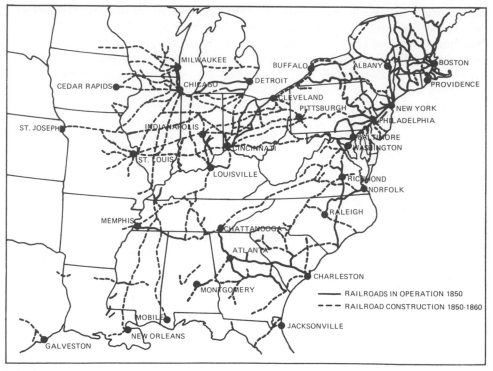

FIGURE 15-2. *Railroad Construction, 1850–1860*

secessionists missed the best opportunity that they would ever have. Without the Compromise of 1850, they might have persuaded the bulk of their section to leave the Union. Had they done so, the North would probably not have interposed serious armed opposition. But they did not push their aims to consummation. In the next ten years, due largely to railroad construction in the Old Northwest, the commerce of that section was re-oriented away from the South and toward the Northeast. Not only were the ties between sections altered, but industrialization and immigration gave the North a preponderance in those resources that influence the outcome of a war. In 1850, Clay's statecraft was saved partly by fortune. On July 9, while the struggle over the Compromise flared in Congress, Zachary Taylor died. His successor, Millard Fillmore, used the power of the presidency to force passage. Even so, the results in September were helter-skelter. All of the bills passed easily, the closest result being a 2-to-1 margin for the admission of California as a state. But only four Senators voted for every one of the medley of measures. Some had solid Southern support while getting a mere sprinkle of assent from the North. When the slave trade in the District of Columbia was abolished, every negative in the Senate was Southern. When the Territory of New Mexico was organized without the Wilmot Proviso, every negative in the Senate was Northern. Henry Clay had made his greatest single contribution to his homeland. What he had bought was time. Perhaps not much of that; as a Georgia newspaper noted: "It is the calm of preparation, and not of peace; a cessation, not an end of the controversy. . . . There is a feud between North and South which may be smothered, but never overcome."

Some aspects of the presidential election of 1852 suggested that the damper was working. The Free Soil party, the splinter group speaking for anti-slavery principles that had done so well in 1848 (see Document 15-3), was virtually obliterated. The Democrats put up a weak candidate, Franklin Pierce of New Hampshire. Even so they won a smashing triumph over the Whig Winfield Scott, the other American general who had won prominence during the Mexican War. Both major parties had affirmed that the Compromise of 1850 should be a final and irrevocable settlement of the issues of expansion and slavery. Each continued to be national rather than sectional; although two of the four states won by Scott were in New England, the others were Kentucky and Tennessee. But as auguries, these final results were less reliable than the path that led to them. The Democratic national convention, employing a rule that required two thirds of the delegates to support the successful nominee, took 49 ballots to put up Pierce. Superficially, the Whigs should have had an easy time of it with at least two attractive candidates and with no two-thirds rule to overcome. But incumbent President Fillmore running for re-election, although the early leader, could never get a majority, and the convention took 53 ballots to choose Scott. Endorsement of the Compromise of 1850 was passed by nearly three to one, but all of the negative votes were by Northerners who had supported Scott against either Fillmore or Webster. Perhaps presidential campaigns were not so good a thermometer to American society as were the religious developments. Churches had split along regional lines; now political parties were doing the same.

Another wedge to split society was the emerging dichotomy about the nature of the American dream. Apart from the spread of the plantation system, the westward movement had encouraged the kind of egalitarianism that so bedazzled Tocqueville. According to the famous thesis of Frederick Jackson Turner, the Frontier experience is the shaping force in American democracy. Dozens of scholars have pointed to flaws in the Turner thesis, but its central core of truth is unshaken. In a masterly study, Ray Allen Billington has pointed to several ways in which the economic equality of available lands encouraged political democracy. Wrote one Westerner, "The price of land is the thermometer of liberty—men are freest where lands are cheapest." (a) The very poor in settled areas could not afford to move westward, and the rich had no need to do so. Migrants tended to come from the middling sort, so the process was a leveller even before anybody struck roots in a new place. (b) Since nobody had inherited status in the community, leadership was decided by competition. It went to the man who could persuade his neighbors that he was akin to them and would follow their wishes. (c) In an era when self-rule was waxing throughout the Euro-American world, newer polities had scope to adopt the more democratic devices that had emerged in older jurisdictions. Of course they did not always do so: The first constitution of Kentucky prescribed an electoral college far removed from the populace to select not only the governor but also senators. In Tennessee the legislature elected justices of the peace for life. As has been said, immigrants lean toward conservatism. (See Chapter 2 on migrants and society.)

But each of these men wanted to better himself. A splendid device had come from their forefathers. Early cessions by Atlantic seaboard states had created 200 million acres of federal public lands. The Louisiana Purchase had greatly increased the total; after 1846 it stood at a billion acres (Think: Twenty times Kansas). No barrier could exclude land-hungry men from these tracts. By 1830 Congress had passed 33 special pre-emption laws that enabled squatters to move into certain areas before they were opened for sale. Then began general pre-emption statutes. Since 1841 a man had been allowed to squat on any portion of the federal domain that had been surveyed. This was only one stimulant in a land rush, beginning almost simultaneously with the Compromise of 1850, that "surpassed anything in previous history." Many of the boomers were immigrants from Germany or Scandinavia who scorned the life of an Eastern wage laborer and who had the resources to reach Illinois or Missouri. Newly built railroads helped them to get there and to ship their crops to market. They could get additional help because more credit was being offered by more banks. An English spectator later described the situation:

> Speculation in real estate has for many years been the ruling idea and occupation of the Western mind. Clerks, labourers, farmers, storekeepers merely followed their callings for a living, while they were speculating for their fortunes.
>
> The people of the West became dealers in land, rather than its cultivators. . . . Millions of acres were bought and sold without buyer or seller knowing where they were, or whether they were anywhere; the buyer only knowing that he hoped to sell his title to them at a handsome profit.

True enough, but behind the alchemist toying with his paper titles could be found one of the most ancient and intense of all American visions— the Myth of the Garden (Chapter 14). In the West, especially in settled areas just behind the receding frontier, free men would subdue the virgin continent until it was the Garden of the World. But now an ominous shadow descended. The Myth of the Garden bifurcated. Was the soil to be divided into tracts of 160 acres, or of 16,000? Should the central figure in the pastoral be a sturdy yeomen owning a family farm and earning his bread by the sweat of his brow? Or should the hero be a planter sitting on his veranda sipping his bourbon?

Almost—but not quite—equally hateful in the second image were black faces and black bodies, their vileness not quite concealed by the red blood pouring down their backs. To people who felt in these stereotypes, *Uncle Tom's Cabin* spoke truth. But to Jefferson Davis in Mississippi the aspirations of the Cavalier were holy; the trance holding him and his fellows had no roots in westering but was imported in finished form from the Tidewater.

Impinging violently on this conflict of ideologies came the ambitions of an adolescent cluster of businessmen—the railroad promoters. Especially since the gold discoveries and the boom along the Pacific slope, men had schemed to throw iron bonds across the trans-Mississippi West. Congress had sponsored surveys of possible routes. Two principal plans had emerged: a Northern railway to terminate at St. Louis (perhaps in Chicago), a Southern one to New Orleans. The chief Senatorial sponsor of the Northern alternative was Stephen A. Douglas of Illinois. The plot could hardly go forward until Kansas and/or Nebraska had been given Territorial rank, a step that would solidify settlement and thus help greatly to remove the Indian threat. As early as 1848 Douglas had publicly claimed for the people of any Territory the right to manage their own affairs, including determining the status of slavery. In January, 1854, he moved to incorporate Nebraska along these lines. The Kansas-Nebraska Act as amended came to organize also a Territory of Kansas. The bill explicitly repealed the Missouri Compromise in favor of the principle of "squatter sovereignty." Originally the preponderant Southern reaction was hostile. The measure, by offering an alternative, menaced the South's favored scheme for a Western railroad. Part of the Southern press saw squatter sovereignty as giving unfair advantage to free settlers who could move to the prairies long before a slaveholder could move his chattels there. The two most eminent Southern newspapers were the Charleston *Mercury* and the Richmond *Enquirer*. The latter said in March of the bill:

> All agree that slavery cannot exist in the territories of Kansas and Nebraska. . . . It is not, therefore, because of its effect in extending the sphere of slavery that the South advocates the repeal of the Missouri restriction, but solely for the reason that it would indicate the equality and sovereignty of the States. The single aim of the Nebraska bill is to establish the principle of *Federal non-intervention* in regard to slavery.

The *Mercury* reported approvingly that the majority of Southerners regarded the law, passed on May 30, "as a thing of so little practical good, that it is certainly not worth the labor of an active struggle to maintain it."

Douglas concurred that slavery would never invade the disputed area. Some historians have seized on this as a postulate and gone from there to momentous conclusions: that the question of slavery in the Territories was a trumped-up issue; that the Civil War need not have happened at all; that for its origins we must look not to a conflict of cultures but to the irresponsible demagogy of rabble rousers. These judgments rest on the premise that there were natural limits to slavery expansion. Let us look closely at this idea. Many planters looked to the west and south, wishing to expand the national boundaries even farther as a safety valve for the peculiar institution. In 1846 Robert J. Walker had argued that one benefit of war with Mexico would be that slavery would quietly drain away into Latin America. Others saw the Caribbean as more promising. Polk offered $100 million for Cuba, and private citizens organized filibustering forays against that island and Central America (1855, 1857, 1860). But could slavery have been transplanted to moderate nontropical climates? A negative answer rests on some false assumptions. Other crops than the Southern staples can use semiskilled farm labor; what of the gangs of migrant workers in the cotton fields of California, the truck farms there, the orchards of the Pacific slope and of Michigan, the sugar beet plantations of Colorado or southern Alberta? Nor was it true that slaves could not learn the skills that would equip them for manufacturing or lumbering or mining. Before the eighteenth century ended they were being used in large numbers in the ropewalks of Lexington. They worked in textile mills in the Carolinas; the expansion of these industries was impeded not by shortage of suitable labor but by the greater profitability of that labor in raising cotton or rice or cane. After the Civil War, black convicts were common enough in the sulphur mines and the turpentine camps of many Southern states. Slavery could adapt itself to new areas.

The sole means to deny it that chance was political and governmental, and the central figure in the obstruction came to be Abraham Lincoln. It was during the Kansas-Nebraska struggle that his reputation became more than just parochial. He had been active in local politics for decades. He could speak brilliantly at least as early as 1838. He served one term in Congress during the Mexican War and made a witty and harsh indictment of some of Polk's pretensions. But few knew his name. As he now began to emerge from the shadows he carried attitudes long established among his class and his region. In 1850 Senator James Shields of Illinois in his maiden speech had scoffed at secession: "Does any sane man suppose that the great Northwest, with all its millions—that world that is growing up between the headwaters of the Ohio and the headwaters of the Missouri, . . . will ever peaceably submit to see the mouth of the Mississippi River in the possession of a foreign Government? Never, sir, never." Adamance on this point was as old as the foreign policy of Thomas Jefferson (Document 10-2), and it would not be reduced when Lincoln entered the White House. In 1862 he would appeal specifically to the residents of the Mississippi valley:

As part of one nation, its people now find, and may forever find, their way to Europe by New York, to South America and Africa by New Orleans, and to Asia by San Francisco. But separate our common country into two nations, as designed by the present rebellion, and every man of this great interior region is thereby cut off from some one or more of these outlets, not, perhaps, by a physical barrier, but by embarrassing and onerous trade regulations. . . . True to themselves, they will not ask *where* a line of separation shall be, but will vow, rather, that there shall be no such line.

While Lincoln espoused concerns that were habitual to the Midwest, he also championed social groups that were new there. It is a safe guess that he would never have become president without the heavy immigration of Germans into the area from 1848 to 1860. They were anti-slavery almost to a man. They were also drawn to other planks in what came to be the platform of the new Republican party. The coalition that carried Lincoln to the presidency stood by and large on the American System: a protective tariff, federal grants to internal improvements, a national banking system of some type, and—the demand of the Republicans that showed the victory of the West over Eastern industrialists—a free grant of 160 acres of federal land to each settler. (See Document 15-3.) All of these proposals were congenial to most German and Scandinavian immigrants.

Newcomers to America needed every ally they could get, because they were surrounded by enemies. Indeed, in 1854 there was no reason to believe that the emerging Republican party would be the major party opposed to the Democrats. The Whigs clearly were breaking to pieces, but the Republicans were slow to gain after they began to coalesce from the first organizing conventions in the spring of 1854. Their showing in the autumn elections was much less impressive than that of the ferociously nativistic American party. Virtually unknown a year earlier, the Know-Nothings of Massachusetts won the governorship, every seat in the state senate, 376 of 378 in the lower house. The American party won Delaware, and shared with the Whigs control of Pennsylvania. The following year it came to power in Rhode Island, New Hampshire, Connecticut, Maryland, and Kentucky. In New York and California most state officials were Know-Nothings. In the South east of the Mississippi (including Louisiana) the movement came within 16,000 votes of matching its opponents. But by 1856 the Know-Nothings declined drastically. They had drawn hot denunciations from Lincoln and other politicians who looked toward the immigrant vote. Worse yet, they had been ridiculed mercilessly. Worst of all, their brand of hatred was eclipsed by the unrelenting tensions about slavery. But the speed of their demise should not be exaggerated. With the former Democratic President Millard Fillmore as its standard bearer, the American party won nearly 900,000 votes in 1856. The Republicans behind John C. Frémont ("The Pathfinder of the West" who was regarded as the conqueror of California) went over 1,300,000. The Democrats topped that figure by a half million. But the fractionizing was ominous. Even running the "doughface" James Buchanan of Pennsylvania, "a Northern man with Southern principles," the Democrats could not get a majority. The results were intensely sectional. Frémont won only a few hundred votes in the South.

Outside that region, Buchanan won only five states. In Illinois he got a narrow plurality thanks to the support for Fillmore. Two thirds of the tally for the American party was also in the South. The Whigs, who had teeter-tottered with the Democrats for over twenty years, simply disappeared.

During the campaign the South was anxiety-ridden from rumors about impending slave insurrections. A similar emotion in the North, resting on more solid ground, was generated in the Supreme Court soon after Buchanan took office. Never has that bench handed down a more confusing and tormented judgment than the Dred Scott decision. Each justice wrote a separate opinion. In law all that was decided was that the black appellant should not go free but was still a slave. But Chief Justice Roger B. Taney, and on this point he seemed to speak the sentiments of the majority, ruled that Congress did not have, had never had, and could not have the power to exclude slavery from a Territory (Chapter 11). At last, Lincoln had found his issue. Already in challenging the Kansas-Nebraska Act he had warmed up to it:

> The whole nation is interested that the best use shall be made of these Territories. We want them for homes of free white people. This they cannot be, to any considerable extent, if slavery shall be planted within them. Slave States are places for poor white people to remove from, not to remove to. New Free States are the places for poor people to go to, and better their condition.

Over this proposition, more than any other save one, the Civil War would be fought. The other proposition was: Our Federal Union, it must be preserved.

The propaganda from all factions became a barrage. Lincoln gleefully seized upon extremist sallies such as the one in a small Southern newspaper: "Free society! We sicken of the name! What is it but a conglomeration of greasy mechanics, filthy operatives, small fisted farmers, and moon-struck theorists? All the Northern and especially the New England States, are devoid of society fitted for well-bred gentlemen." Senator James H. Hammond of South Carolina scoffed at Northern laborers as "the mud-sills of society." George Fitzhugh of Virginia issued two quasischolarly tomes contending that all labor, white as well as black, should be enslaved. When financial panic struck in the summer after the election, it hardly hit the South. Planters at once seized upon their relative exemption as another proof of the superiority of their institutions over the decadent North. The depression was neither severe nor prolonged, but it did give Buchanan the occasion to drive voters away from his party. For some time the national government had moved toward a policy of withholding federal lands from settlement during hard times. Now the president, distressed by the decline in public revenues, dumped onto the market huge tracts on the trans-Mississippi prairies—this when wheat was so cheap that it hardly paid to ship it to market. The Republicans accused the president of having said that an employee needed no more in wages than a dime a day, and he was excoriated as "Ten Cent Jimmie." But it was the land question rather than the situation of urban labor that would carry the Midwest by 1860. Typical of the agitation was the Illinois editor who denounced the "demon of land speculation . . . that seizes the choice spots . . . in advance of the emigrants' arrival, separates the settlers' cabins by wide tracts of un-reclaimed wilderness, and encircles every embryo town and populous city with leagues of waste land as absolutely wild as when the deer and the Indian were its only inhabitants."

In this context the yeoman image and the planter ideal fought for supremacy. Adherents of both sides spilled across the Mississippi, and some of them immortalized the phrase "Bleeding Kansas." The epithet was badly exaggerated. Men dashed around madly and fired their guns quite a bit, but they seldom aimed at anybody. Casualties were amazingly low. Perhaps the only instance of true ferocity was the massacre perpetrated by old John Brown and his band. Fittingly, it was the same unbalanced zealot who in 1859 would stage the one serious effort to stimulate a slave uprising (and be hanged for the attempt). For the moment the war with weapons counted for less than the clash of words. Perhaps few contemporaries recognized the fact, but the chief encounter in the contest was the Lincoln-Douglas debates. Although these public forums could not directly influence the appointment of a new Senator, which would be made by the legislature, the series of seven debates has won numerous close readings. Ferrets have duly noted that Lincoln's anti-slavery sentiments became regressively muted as the disputants moved southward through Illinois. But no allegations of inconsistency should obscure the theme from which Lincoln did not depart: Slavery must be barred from the Territories so that they shall be the domain of free white people:

> We have no power as citizens of the free States or in our federal capacity as members of the Federal Union through the general government, to disturb slavery in the States where it exists. . . . What I insist upon is, that the new Territories shall be kept free from it while in the Territorial condition.

Thus spoke Lincoln in the final exchange at Alton on October 15, but he had used the same refrain throughout the debates. It did not win the Senate seat for him in 1858, but he held steadily to it until 1860.

In that year the Democrats were earliest to hold their national nominating convention. Fire eaters demanded that the platform be adopted before candidates were chosen, and they wanted a forthright insistence that Congress should declare in favor of slavery. Disappointed if not infuriated by the planks that were adopted, they bolted the convention. The remaining delegates then voted that two thirds of the original number should be needed for nomination, which meant an overwhelming majority among those remaining. This made the situation hopeless. Douglas consistently ran first, but after 57 ballots he had not gained the required number. The gathering then suspended, to reconvene six weeks later. Then they advanced Douglas by a vote of two thirds

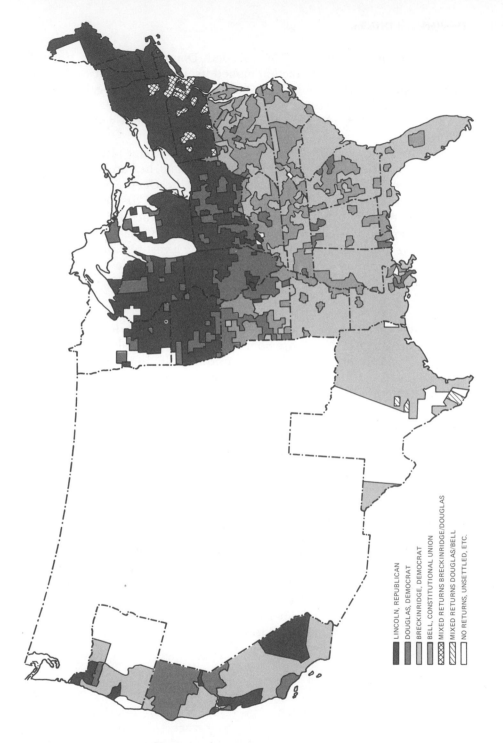

LINCOLN, REPUBLICAN
DOUGLAS, DEMOCRAT
BRECKINRIDGE, DEMOCRAT
BELL, CONSTITUTIONAL UNION
MIXED RETURNS BRECKINRIDGE/DOUGLAS
MIXED RETURNS DOUGLAS/BELL
NO RETURNS, UNSETTLED, ETC.

FIGURE 15-3.   *The Presidential Election of 1860*

375

of the members in attendance. The seceded Democrats put up John C. Breckenridge. Then a moderate faction named itself the Constitutional Union party with a slate headed by John Bell. At the Republican meeting, held before Douglas had won the Democratic nod, Seward led on the first ballot with Lincoln a strong second. Then the shifts began, and Lincoln was selected on the third round.

None of the four candidates turned out to be a paper tiger. Although Lincoln gained a solid majority in the Electoral College, he barely exceeded 40 per cent of the popular vote. Breckenridge swept the Deep South. Bell won three border states: Virginia, Tennessee, Kentucky. Most distorted of all was the Douglas vote. Only a half million votes behind Lincoln in the popular ballots, he got a mere 12 electors. The new chief executive had been picked by a minority of the citizens. Emphatically rejected by a vast region of the nation, he would be a sectional president. Would he also preside over a greatly reduced commonwealth?

Voters in all sections may well have asked themselves: What does the election of Abraham Lincoln mean? To those Southerners who were rabid in defense of their peculiar institution it showed that compromise had failed and that they were overwhelmed within the federal establishment. Their best chance was to pressure moderate Southerners to withdraw, to bow out, since they could not hope to maintain their economy or expand slavery when they were domineered over by the white House and by both branches of Congress. To abolitionists it was a pallid victory: he was the best choice available, but what did that amount to? (And of course, his election did not reflect any variations in the universal bias against blacks.) Northern businessmen saw him as a possible threat to their commercial ties with the South; his encouragements to the land-rush might drain their supply of immigrant labor; he was an unknown element, therefore a risk, and moneyed men do not like risks. To those (mainly Midwesterners?) who saw him deeply, he was governed by the Gospel of Work and a sense of Duty. In doing his job, he would be exasperatingly stubborn. He would hang in there. He would be compassionate when his task allowed it, ruthless when his task demanded that. Lincoln would bumble along, nearly always aware of his fallibility. He would seek out generals by trial and error, and his mistakes cost thousands of lives. But when he turned up a winning team he would recognize it and stick to it.

SOME NOTABLE EVENTS

1842 Tariff Act, which will raise duties, takes effect, August 30.

1846 Walker Tariff reduces rates.

1848 Gold at Sutter's Mill, California.

1850 Congressional land grant to Illinois Central is first substantial federal subsidy to a railroad.
Clay proposes resolutions to compromise the sectional dispute, January 29.
Compromise of 1850 passed after much debate, September 9–20.

1851 Maine is first state to adopt prohibition.
Gold found in Australia.

1853 Chicago linked to New York City by railroad.

1854 Kansas-Nebraska Act, 30 May.
Republican party founded, February–July.
Sweeping electoral successes by Know-Nothings.

1855 Soo Canal ties Lake Superior to Lake Huron.
Massachusetts Personal Liberty Act, May 21.

1855–
1856 Guerrilla warfare in Kansas.
John Brown leads massacre of five men at Pottawatomie, May 24, 1856.

1856 American party gets 872,000 votes for president.
Slave insurrection panic grows acute.

1857 *Dred Scott* v. *Sandford* decision on slavery in the territories, March 6.
Tariff Act cuts duties to average of less than 20%.
Financial panic begins August 24.

1858 Silver found in Nevada.
Lincoln's "House Divided" speech, June 17.
Lincoln-Douglas debates, August 21–October 15.
Hammond's "Mudsills of Society" speech, October 29.

1859 John Brown raids Harper's Ferry, Virginia, October 16–18.
John Brown's last speech, November 2.
Oil: Edwin L. Drake brings in first successful well, Titusville, Pa.

1860 U.S. Census: 31,443,321 (19.8% urban).
Lincoln elected, September-October.

Ways to Study History XV

Get the perspective right. A recurrent and baffling task in American history is to make proper adjustments of scale. The determination of an appropriate yardstick can be the key to understanding a past episode. This task is repeatedly taxing, and it can pose a true dilemma. The late Admiral Richard E. Byrd told of his troubles in Antarctica. Often the landscape was uniform and held only horizontals. It was devoid of man-made objects of which he knew the dimensions. Since he knew no sizes he could not estimate distances; since he knew no distances he could not guess sizes. The circle was closed. A story from the Arctic describes two hunters who spotted a brown bear. Expecting a long trek, they set out to stalk it. Soon almost under their feet they flushed a ground squirrel.

Ways must be found to break out of this prison. For colonial America, any figure we find seems paltry. When we read of the trifling munitions available to a Pequot band in 1637 (sixteen firearms and little gunpowder) we might laugh, but Puritans were justly alarmed. The problem of scale is vital in interpreting statistics about money or about land. Here are two useful gauges. Through the nineteenth century, by and large, common labor earned a dollar per day without fringe benefits. Anybody who has crossed the continent by automobile will appreciate the measure that Kansas holds almost precisely 50 million acres.

The figure for casualties in the Civil War—618,000—takes on meaning as we realize that the population of the entire country was only 31 million; a comparable proportion in World War II would have meant nearly 3 million dead. The Battle of Gettysburg cost the two sides 52,000 fatalities. That roughly equals the population today of Arlington, Massachusetts. To apprehend that the town and the battlefield are comparable in area will give a vivid picture of the holocaust that was Gettysburg.

Document 15-1

Even before famine struck Ireland in 1845, the immigration of Irish Catholics was fluctuating around 25,000 a year, and most of them settled in Eastern cities. Their arrival helped to reactivate a venerable Boston tradition—the mob. This account was written by Michael Chevalier, a French visitor.

The intolerant spirit of a part of the Protestant population was offended by the sight of the Ursuline Convent on Mount St. Benedict, within the limits of Charlestown, a town adjoining Boston. The sisters devoted themselves to the instruction of young girls, and many Protestant families had confided daughters to their care. Every thing proves that they were by no means devoured by a spirit of proselytism. In the beginning of August, 1835, a report got about in Charlestown, that one of the sisters, a young woman, was detained in the convent by force. The Selectmen of the town had a meeting, five of them went to the convent, which they examined from cellar to garret, had an interview with the sister who was represented as a victim of Catholic discipline, and became satisfied that she was there of her own free will. This conviction was made known to the public. But on the night of August 12th, the convent was surrounded and attacked by a handful of ruffians, at the head of whom was one John Buzzell, a brickmaker, noted for his brutal character. The sisters were driven from the convent with violence; every thing was plundered; the tombs of the dead were forced open. The building was then fired; it was burnt in sight of the Selectmen; the Boston firemen hastened to the spot, but were repulsed by the populace by main force. . . . On the anniversary of the outrage, the populace of Charlestown celebrated it as a day of rejoicing, and got up a shooting match, the target being a representation of the lady superior of the convent. . . .

Document 15-2

The eminent Scottish scientist Sir Charles Lyell in 1845 visited the South to study its geology. Among the many estates reached on his random travels was a large rice plantation near Savannah.

>	*To one who arrives in Georgia from Europe with a vivid impression on his mind of the state of the peasantry there in many populous regions, their ignorance, intemperance, and improvidence, the difficulty of obtaining subsistence, and the small chance they have of bettering their lot, the condition of the black laborers on such a property as Hopeton, will afford but small ground for lamentation or despondency. . . .*

>	*There are 500 negroes on the Hopeton estate, a great many of whom are children, and some old and superannuated. The latter class, who would be supported in a poor-house in England, enjoy here, to the end of their days, the society of their neighbors and kinsfolk, and live at large in separate houses assigned to them. The children have no regular work to do till they are ten or twelve years old. . . . The laborers are allowed Indian meal, rice, and milk, and occasionally pork and soup. As their rations are more than they can eat, they either return part of it to the overseer, who makes them allowance of money for it at the end of the week, or they keep it to feed their fowls, which they usually sell, as well as their eggs, for cash, to buy molasses, tobacco, and other luxuries. When disposed to exert themselves, they get through the day's task in five hours, and then amuse themselves in fishing, and sell the fish they take; or some of them employ their spare time in making canoes out of large cypress trees, leave being readily granted them to remove such timber, as it aids the landowner to clear the swamps. They sell the canoes for about four dollars, for their own profit. . . .*

Document 15-3

The Free Soil party, formed at Buffalo on August 9, 1848 put up ex-President Martin Van Buren and Charles Francis Adams, son of John Quincy. The ticket drew enough votes in New York to deprive the Democrats of that state and put Zachary Taylor in the White House. The platform advanced several of the planks on which Lincoln would later ride to power.

>	*Resolved, That it is the duty of the Federal Government to relieve itself from all responsibility for the existence or continuance of slavery wherever that Government possess constitutional power to legislate on that subject, and is thus responsible for its existence.*

>	*Resolved, That the true, and, in the judgment of this Convention, the only safe means of preventing the extension of Slavery into territory now free, is to prohibit its existence in all such territories by an act of Congress.*

>	*Resolved, That we accept the issue which the Slave Power has forced upon us, and to their demand for more Slave States and more Slave Territory, our calm but final answer is, No more Slave States and no more Slave Territory. Let the soil of our extensive domains be kept free, for the hardy pioneers of our own land, and the oppressed and banished of other lands seeking homes of comfort and fields of enterprise in the New World. . . .*

>	*Resolved, That the Free Grant to Actual Settlers, . . . of reasonable portions of the public lands, under suitable limitations, is a wise and just measure of public policy, which will promote, in various ways, the interest of all the States of this Union; and we therefore recommend it to the favorable consideration of the American People. . . .*

>	*Resolved, That we inscribe on our banner, "Free Soil, Free Speech, Free Labor, and Free Men," and under it we will fight on, and fight ever, until a triumphant victory shall reward our exertions.*

PART IV

Sectional Smiles, but Social Strife:
1860–1898

Civil War and (Non-) Reconstruction

The Civil War can be seen from several vantages. It might be viewed as a campaign for Southern suicide. It affirmed Herman Melville's vision of the implacable cruelty in the world (Document 16-1). For those few thoughtful persons who were still trying to rejoice with the Enlightenment, it stomped on the jaunty faith that progress was inevitable.

The secession process needs no close-grained treatment here, but some generalizations about it can be ventured. As one might guess, the first state to leave the Union was South Carolina on 20 December, 1860, by unanimous vote of a specially elected convention of 169 members. By 26 January, 1861, all of the Gulf states from Florida to Louisiana had seceded. These were the six states that convened to establish the Confederate States of America. Before they completed their constitution on March 11 they were joined by representatives from Texas even though Governor Sam Houston of that state opposed secession and was deposed from office for his loyalty. Texas was further distinguished by being the only state to submit its resolution of secession to a popular vote; elsewhere the matter was carried by a newly chosen convention.

Soon, of the fifteen slave states another four would join the Confederacy: Arkansas, Tennessee, North Carolina, Virginia. The new federal government had a constitution that was largely modelled on and often copied from the basic document of its parent. But, again as one might guess, the Confederate constitution placed even more weight on the rights of states. During the brief existence of the new government it was chronically beset by separatist movements.* The center of white disaffection was the same upcountry zone in the Carolina Appalachians that had spawned the Regulator movements (Chapter 4) a century earlier. From the peckerwood districts of the Carolinas and Georgia came a good many volunteers for the Union armies. East Tennessee produced a president of the United States, if not a distinguished one. These centrifugal impulses in the Confederacy came to their ultimate in Virginia when the mountainous western reaches split away altogether to form a new loyal state admitted to the Union in 1863.

The difficulties of the rebellion involved not only institutions but also personalities. The emergent polity erred badly in its choice of leaders. Jefferson Davis had graduated from West Point and had served in the army for several years. He had been secretary of war and a senator. But one suspects that he was elected president of the Confederacy because he and his brother owned as many slaves on their Mississippi plantations as did any family in the South. Along with (because of?) his elegant airs he was crude and imperious. He was repeatedly embroiled in quarrels with his congress. He chronically interfered in unwise ways with his field commanders, to the point of sending them detailed instructions about battlefield tactics when he could not possibly know what the specific situation was. Lincoln too had troubles with his Congress; he too spent years of trial and error seeking generals on whom he could rely. But when he found them—particularly Grant, Sherman, George H. Thomas—he left them to manage the conduct of campaigns.

Perhaps it is inevitable that the typical human will downgrade the difficulties he faces; if we did not, we might be inert. This self-deceit is especially apparent at the onset of war. An illustration can be given almost at random: in October, 1776, a British officer wrote from Westchester County, New York "I think that June next will bring us back to London. . . ." But the next May he wrote that he hoped "to visit you before Christmas." A bare three months later he amended: "I hope our Son and Daughter are in perfect health, they will have grown so tall & so old, I fear, before this War is over that we shall be greater Strangers when we meet than, I trust, we shall be ever after." But even if we try by such analogies to keep matters in perspective, who today can avoid a macabre smile at the reactions of American statesmen to the outbreak of hostilities in 1861? The Confederate hawks were confident that the

---

*A central theme of American history from the beginning has of course been the conflict of tendencies toward union and toward separatism. The latter urges can be traced at least back to the Reformation and would embrace, among other things, everything from Antinomianism to our contemporary divorce courts.

superior valor of their cavalier gentry would quickly ride over the mudsills. Similarly Lincoln, three days after the enemy on April 12 had fired on the Union's Fort Sumter in Charleston, South Carolina, called forth "the militia of the several States of the Union, to the . . . number of seventy-five thousand." He might have expected that the doughty yeomen of his free society could waltz into the Confederate capital at Richmond, but he would live to smell

> the patriotic gore
> That flecked the streets of Baltimore.

A fashion has persisted for speculating that Lincoln, by his efforts to supply the garrison at Sumter, deliberately provoked the secessionists into cannonading the fort and thus starting the war. This fad should stop. It is even more obscene than the speculations that Roosevelt wanted the Japanese to attack Pearl Harbor. The circumstances are clear. Lincoln had taken an oath to maintain federal property. The fort belonged in that category. He had no alternative to what he did. But a similar claim cannot be made for another decision he took. President-elect Lincoln made his worst judgment about policy—possibly his only serious blunder about policy—before he entered the White House. On 18 December, 1860, the Crittenden Compromise was put forward by a senator from Kentucky. This proposal for Amendments to the Constitution of the United States was a sober try at reconciliation.* It would have reconstituted the line of the Missouri Compromise at 36° 30′ in the federal Territories, with slavery allowed below, banned above. Each state would be allowed to set its own provincial policy on the question. Northern states would be asked to repeal their personal-liberty laws that conflicted with the Fugitive Slave Act of the federal government. It seems likely that Congress could have been persuaded to vote this package. But the personal intervention of Abraham Lincoln killed it.

His line of argument in reaching this verdict is not known for sure. Many historians have asserted that the Crittenden Compromise was merely a stopgap, that it could not have survived, that war was bound to come. This is almost certainly true, but at times it is wise to defer a war, if only for five or ten years. If compromise was useful to the Union in 1850, it would also have been useful a decade later. Crittenden's proposals were manifestly perpetuating an injustice to 4 million slaves, but we may doubt if that was Lincoln's reason for rejecting them. Vital to his opposition was the proposal to allow slavery expansion south of 36° 30′. A hunch whispers that he thought the showdown had come, and that it had best be faced when Abraham Lincoln was commander in chief rather than another doughface like Pierce or Buchanan. Even so, it seems that rejection of the Crittenden Compromise was at best

---

*One clause in the proposition still seems gravely defective: Article Six provided that the preceding Amendments could not themselves be amended. Sound reasons still exist for adhering to the creed of Paine and Jefferson that no generation in a republic can legitimately exercise the power to bind its successors.

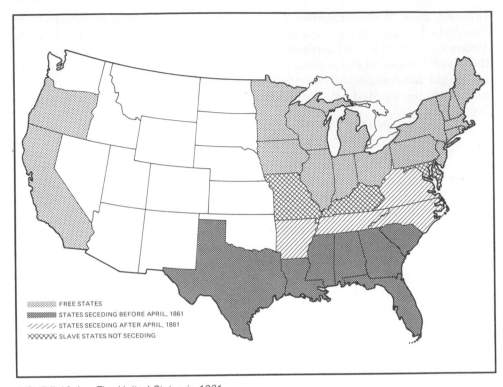

FIGURE 16-1. *The United States in 1861*

dubious statesmanship. Another mode of averting a civil war was also suggested. Lincoln's secretary of state, William H. Seward (appropriately on April Fool's Day, before the clash at Fort Sumter) proposed that he start a donnybrook with European powers that would hopefully lead to a foreign war, thus healing the domestic cleavage. The president spurned this option.

We must try to confront problems as they came upon the president. He quickly learned that 75,000 militia would not be adequate to the job. After two demoralizing defeats at Bull Run, the Union settled in for a wearing attrition. An inefficient but *de facto* draft was established by the militia act of 1862. In that same year, 27 September, the Confederacy passed its second conscription act, but the Northern Congress did not enact a similar measure until 3 March, 1863. It was immediately and violently resisted. The worst anti-draft riots occurred in New York City, especially by Irish immigrants. Hatred of conscription undoubtedly was a factor, but the explosion was aggravated when paddy longshoremen went on strike and were replaced by blacks as scabs. A provision by which the wealthy could buy their way out of the army was a further contribution to resentment. The Confederacy had an analogy: any overseer of twenty slaves (later fifteen) was exempt from conscription.

Mobilization of manpower by the Union must include the recruitment of leadership. In spite of Seward's lapses into miserable advice, he was an able man, and so were other members of the cabinet. While the civilian slots were filled with expedition and judgment, the military command was a persisting headache. For nearly three years President Lincoln experimented with field commanders in the East. He tried five—McDowell, McClellan, Burnside, Hooker, Meade—and found all deficient. But it is hard to see what alternative to trial and error the president had. He inherited a peacetime army plus a tradition of anti-militarism, of a civilian army. But slowly, while great masses of stolid soldiers were slaughtering each other in the brief march between the rival capitals at Richmond and Washington, the three generals who would do the most for the Union cause were rising to prominence in the Mississippi valley. It is gross error to assume that the South had the more competent generals: Grant, Sherman, and Thomas could rank with any trio of the Confederacy (Lee, Jackson, and Joseph E. Johnston?).

Such fallacies can become popular because few of us have bothered to think about warfare as an institution. An honorable exception to this aspersion is historian T. Harry Williams. In his masterly *Americans at War* (1960) he underscores the need to distinguish among the (a) tactics that determine battles, the (b) strategies that influence campaigns, and the (c) policy that often determines who will win the war. Considering the American War for Independence in this schema, for instance, it would have availed the British little if their strategy and tactics had been brilliant (they were not) because their policy was so bad.* Williams goes on to argue that the military genius of the Civil War was the president of the United States. This contention, while true, is so startlingly unusual as to need explication. Everybody knows the pointed maxim of Karl von Clausewitz that war is the continuation of politics by other means. So far, all right. But Clausewitz also wrote: "The *offensive* . . . has for its absolute object not so much *combat* as the *taking possession of something.*" We have all seen the United States generally accept this formula whereby the key to national security allegedly is to hold strategic points in the world. Lincoln promptly and decisively rejected this approach. His objective was not to capture Southern soil but to destroy Confederate armies.

Apart from Clausewitz, the reigning theoreticians of warfare in 1861 were Frenchmen such as Napoleon I and Antoine Henri Jomini. From their battles and treatises American officers had drawn the preachment that military force should be concentrated at a single point. But this principle had been derived in the relatively limited geographical areas of Europe. Lincoln swiftly saw that it did not apply to his problem. His strategy was to take the offensive simultaneously in many different theaters, to hit and hit and hit again, almost heedless of cost. And the cost was terrible. With the invention of the Gatling gun and the improvement of artillery, the advantage in battle had swung to defensive alignments, and attempts to dislodge enemy positions cost both

---

*The same conclusion applied with equal force to engagement of the United States in Viet Nam.

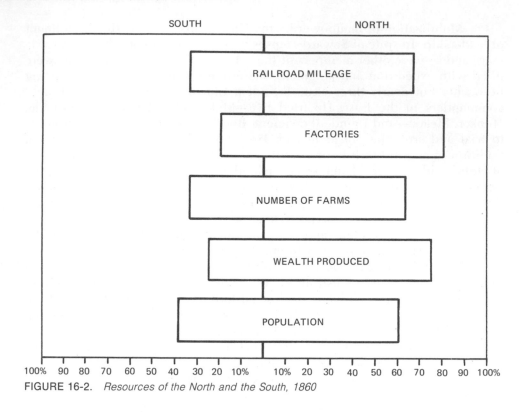

FIGURE 16-2. *Resources of the North and the South, 1860*

sides dearly in blood. Even today the figures are numbing: in a nation of 31 million souls, 600,000 lives came to a stop.

But the president knew that his cause could pay the ghastly price. When the war started the distribution of power was dreadfully lopsided. In man-power, in transportation, in its ability to produce uniforms as well as guns, the greater heft was in the North. The president, intuitively grasping the importance of economic warfare, wrenched the balance further by imposing a total blockade on Southern ports. Soon the South was deficient in vital supplies; a fascinating book tells how the shortage of salt prevented her from preserving meat. It has been common to argue that since the South had the interior position, she was benefited by having shorter lines of supply. Logistically the point should be heard, but it does not take full account of the facts. The chief iron and munitions factories of the Confederacy were in Richmond. Six railroads entered that city. No two of them connected. For rail and road communications the North had far better facilities.

Which brings us to another frequent distortion of the situation during the war. Lincoln's desire to hold the loyalty of the border states, particularly Kentucky and Missouri, is widely known, but a crucial reason for that desire is often ignored. More vital to the Union than any other pathway for moving men and matériel was the Ohio-Mississippi basin. He had to keep this channel open. Thus when John Charles Frémont, the general commanding in St. Louis, proclaimed on 30 August, 1861, that all slaves within his command were emancipated, the president at once revoked the order. A Republican senator from Maine called Lincoln's action a "weak and unjustifiable concession to the Union men of the border states." A concession it was, but we question the epithetical adjectives. The president said, "I hope to have God on my side, but I must have Kentucky." It is relevant too that more than 250,000 Union soldiers were recruited from the border slave states during the war.

On the question of slavery the president was caught in an incessant crossfire. Probably Lincoln knew from the start that the issue of emancipation could not be evaded forever. But he could not afford to admit that, so he presented his every action as a war measure done to save the Union (Document 16-2). Snide remarks have also been made that the Emancipation Proclamation, when it took effect on New Year's Day of 1863, did not free a single slave since it applied only in still rebellious areas where it could not be enforced. Such comments show little charity to a great statesman. Lincoln's task was literally impossible: to lead a self-contradictory nation to fight a bloody war for a revolutionary objective that nobody believed in. Yet he achieved it. In one sense he was probably lucky: he was assassinated at the right moment. Speculations have been rife about whether the troubled era of Reconstruction would have gone better if Lincoln had lived to tackle its problems. The answer clearly is No. The nation was hopelessly divided on many questions, and these rifts were concentrated in Washington. Congress had been at the president's throat from the moment he took office, and this internecine fray was not about to cease at the request of any chief executive.

The full extent of these antagonisms became clear between December, 1863, and July, 1864. First Lincoln announced his plan. It assumed that the rebellious regions had not left the Union at all. When the residents of a state equal in number to 10 per cent of the electorate in 1860 had taken an oath of loyalty, they could elect new members of Congress. A crucial feature of the procedure was the pardoning power of the president. But in Congress, where each house has the power to determine whom it will seat, the new men returned from the South were rejected. Congress summed up its opposition to the president's plan in the Wade-Davis bill. Here was what is called "Congressional Reconstruction." Whereas Lincoln's proposal had referred to a decimal of the electorate, this measure was predicated on a majority. Moreover, it barred from the polity all who had held office "under the rebel usurpation" or who had carried arms against the Union.

While politicians squabbled, some Union armies ground forward. The war was decided by two crucial events that occurred in the first four days of July in 1863. The difference between those two events illuminates the war's true nature, so often concealed by microscopic accounts of this battle and that battle. The first decision was made at Gettysburg where the clash killed 50,000 men in three days and ended a stalemate. The entire war in the East, over those dreadful bloody miles—a mere hundred—between the rival capitals, had been a stalemate. Nobody won; both sides lost in appalling measure. Since the North could better afford to waste men as well as matériel, these wicked engagements tilted the sectional balance still further. Second, the war was won in the Ohio-Mississippi valley. On Independence day, after a siege of six weeks, the Confederates at Vicksburg surrendered to Grant. Soon a decisive win by Thomas at Chattanooga opened the way for Sherman's subsequent invasion of Georgia. From this day forward the Confederacy had no chance for victory in the field.

By now, too, the schism within the North about the nature of the war had been stoutly expressed. Sherman took Atlanta on 2 September, 1864. Fearing a counterattack and desiring to shorten his lines, he ordered the city cleared of all civilians. The mayor protested that, with winter approaching, the evacuation would be inhumane to the aged and the ill. Sherman would not bend.

> We must have peace, not only at Atlanta, but in all America. To secure this, we must stop the war that now desolates our once happy and favored country. To stop war, we must defeat the rebel armies which are arrayed against the laws and Constitution that all must respect and obey. . . . I cannot discuss this subject with you fairly, because I cannot impart to you what we propose to do, but I assert that our military plans make it necessary for the inhabitants to go away, and I can only renew my offer of services to make their exodus in any direction as easy and comfortable as possible.
>
> You cannot qualify war in harsher terms than I will. War is cruelty, and you cannot refine it; and those who brought war into our country deserve all the curses and maledictions a people can pour out. I know I had no hand in making this, and I will make more sacrifices to-day than any of you to secure peace. But you cannot have peace and a division of our country. . . .
>
> We don't want your negroes, or your horses, or your lands, or any thing you have, but we do want and will have a just obedience to the laws of the United States.

Having departed from the benign eighteenth-century code of combat (Chapter 5), Sherman approached the doctrine of total war that has haunted mankind in modern times. But his commander in chief continued to advocate mercy, as he had exemplified in his Proclamation of Amnesty and Reconstruction.

Probably Grant in his attitude stood closer to Sherman than to Lincoln. But recognizing the differences among these three men should not blind us to their similiarities. In a revealing passage published in 1952, Benjamin P. Thomas focused on the conference among them at Hampton Roads, Virginia on 28 March, 1865. In a quiet way, Thomas came as close as anybody to defining what the Civil War was all about: "All three were Midwesterners, though Lincoln came of Southern origin. None of them could have come close to the top except in America. War had made them comrades of a sort; each trusted the others to do their job." While the conjunction of these men on this occasion might well symbolize the American experience, two of them saw the immediate future as forbidding: Grant and Sherman thought that another bloody battle must be fought. The president hoped not. As often, Lincoln was right. Lee surrendered on April 9; Johnston conceded for the other main Confederate army on April 18. In the interim the president was shot to death.

He was succeeded by Andrew Johnson of Tennessee. The very selection of a loyal senator from a Confederate state as the vice presidential nominee on the Union ticket in 1864 tells how perilous the president thought his position was. It also reflects how much importance he attached to the border states, and it shows his outlook toward getting the secessionists back into the Union. But because of his temperament, Johnson was not a happy choice. Some historians have emphasized his upbringing in the lower middle class (he was a tailor by trade), his fondness for booze, his crabbed mentality. He was fuzzy both intellectually and emotionally. He envied the deposed planters, which is to say that he both hated them and looked up to them. Looking always backward, he found his idols in Jefferson and Jackson, who had also looked backward.* Earnestly trying to improve the status of the white yeoman, he did not realize how many of his pets shared his sympathy for the old social order incarnate in the ex-slaveholders. About the blacks, free or slave, he cared nothing.

The new president did want to abolish slavery as a legal institution. But he did not seek to revamp the total structure in which slavery was the linchpin. Several congressmen disagreed. They deemed it essential that Union force should be used *promptly* to *reconstruct* the South. Any realistic chance for this kind of accomplishment was always most unlikely. It could not be achieved without use of the army, and the commander in chief was the hostile president. Not only was Johnson at best indifferent to any use of military strength to enhance the position of Southern blacks, he also regarded the status of the erstwhile governing class in the defeated provinces as a personal rather than a political problem; he wanted the subjugated to feel indebted to him as an individual rather than to a benign government. Lincoln would have granted a general amnesty; Johnson insisted on private applications to the president for a pardon. By September, 1867, he had granted about 13,500 such pardons, each signed personally.

Going further yet, he appointed many former Confederates to Union offices. The ex-foes heard their cues distinctly. In the summer and autumn of 1865, secessionist states seriatim passed their Black Codes. The intent was clear: to keep all blacks in a condition of servitude. Perhaps they would no longer be slaves at law, but in fact they would be suppressed, repressed, and depressed. Each slaveholder had lost his private property, but, as one senator said, "the blacks at large belong to the whites at large." The president made no protests.

---

*Here is another superb unexploited subject for a doctoral dissertation: the role of nostalgia in shaping the values of successive generations of Americans. Two facets of the topic are treated with insight by Henry Nash Smith, *Virgin Land* (1950) and by Marvin Meyers, *The Jacksonian Persuasion* (1957).

But a potent faction in Congress stood for a radically opposed policy. By the end of 1865 Johnson had given up hope of reconstituting the South; six months earlier some percipient congressmen had given up hope that he would do otherwise. The most forceful spokesman for this position was Thaddeus Stevens, Representative from Pennsylvania, although Senators Charles Sumner (Mass.) and Benjamin F. Wade (Ohio) held higher official positions. It is worth while to compare Stevens to Lincoln. The former was guilty of unfortunate rancor. The two differed not only in temperament but also in position: a representative can opt for an extreme that is denied to a president. But the two agreed in devotion to the welfare of the ordinary, aspiring citizen. Maybe the chief disparity is that Stevens was more willing to extend his dedication to all commoners, regardless of color. He left a clear testament; his will, decrying the ubiquity of all-white cemeteries, provided that he should be buried in a graveyard with blacks.

The irreconcilables in Congress seldom wield a majority. Even when he voted with his peers, Stevens was a far-out voice in a much broader chorus. They won some victories. The Freedmen's Bureau and an accompanying bank were created by Congress in 1865 and played a useful part for four years (see below on changes in the South). From 1865 to 1870 three Amendments were added to the Constitution, ostensibly to advance the rights of black people; their application was never more than haphazard. The reasons for this ambivalence will be viewed promptly below, and the tortuous course of judicial constructions will be examined at appropriate places thereafter. The Reconstructionists also carried Civil Rights Acts in 1866 and 1875 that would serve for a century as the main platform in federal courts for legal efforts to elevate the station of blacks. Repeatedly the insurgents had to carry their reforms by two-thirds majorities following a veto by the president. This fact may suggest that Andrew Johnson should carry much, perhaps most, of the blame for the failure of Reconstruction.

But to argue so would be mistaken. In his views of blacks, the president was undoubtedly closer to most voters than was Stevens. The latter might well declare, "This is not a 'white man's government.' To say so is political blasphemy, for it violates the fundamental principles of our gospel of liberty. This is man's government; the government of all men alike." This rhetoric was merely stating an ideal, an ideal that he held almost alone. The reality was put bluntly by a Republican representative from Indiana: "The real trouble is that *we hate the negro*. It is not his ignorance that offends us, but his color." That tells the story. American blacks had no keener white friend in 1865 than Thomas Wentworth Higginson of Boston. He was one of the Secret Six who financed John Brown's venture at Harper's Ferry. When the other conspirators tried to weasel out of their complicity, Higginson publicly avowed his. He was colonel of a black regiment during the war. But his reminiscences of that experience are larded with a condescending tone.

The vast majority of whites would not accept any black as equal socially, neither for a friendly beer nor for the connubial bed. But political rights were another matter. The Republicans won sweeping gains at the congressional polls in 1866, and they had an obvious interest in enfranchising the freed blacks. Whether their policy was supported by most Northern whites still seems a moot question. Ulysses S. Grant, even though he was a conquering general, won the presidency in 1868 only by reason of 700,000 black votes. Two years later the Fifteenth Amendment forbade discrimination in the suffrage at federal elections "on account of race, color, or previous condition of servitude—" But the issue had already been resolved in the negative. At various times in human affairs, one type of relation dominates others and in the postwar South economics would undermine politics.* At least a billion dollars in property, the slaves, had been cancelled. Major cities had been flattened. Railroads were disrupted. One farm animal in three had been killed. The labor force, particularly the managerial segment, had been greatly reduced, and what remained was chaotic. In such circumstances, the man who could first gain an independent livelihood would rule over the polity.

Contemporaries understood this. When black leaders met in Savannah just before the war ended, their word was "The way we can best take care of ourselves is to have land, and . . . till it by our own labor." Even earlier, a member of a commission appointed by the secretary of war to investigate the South had counselled: "No such thing as a free, democratic society can exist in any country where all lands are owned by one class of men and cultivated by another." Here too Thaddeus Stevens was clear. The plantations had been "nurseries of the Rebellion"; they "must be broken up and the freedmen must have the pieces." His plan envisaged confiscation of about 400 million acres (eight times Kansas) owned by 70,000 slaveholders, only 5 per cent of the South's white families. "The whole fabric of southern society *must* be changed," he declared, "and never can it be done if this opportunity is lost. How can republican institutions, free schools, free churches, free social intercourse exist in a mingled community of nabobs and serfs? . . . If the South is ever to be made a safe Republic let her lands be cultivated by the toil of the owners, or the free labor of intelligent citizens. This must be done even though it drive her nobility into exile." But the president opposed any redistribution of land among the freedmen. On the Sea Islands along the Georgia-Carolina coast General Sherman launched a program of granting not more than forty acres per black family; "40 acres and a mule." Johnson restored most of these lands to their former owners. He invalidated another program in Mississippi. By the time Stevens died in 1868, land reform and the economic independence of blacks were dead also.

But the spats of president with Congress had not abated. Quite properly, the Reconstructionists were provoked by the flagrant prejudice of Southern

---

*I have no desire here to lay down any universal law of history. The reverse may be true in other circumstances. The campaign for school integration, in spite of its prominence, did not accomplish much in the twenty years after 1954. The true revolution of that time was the enfranchisement of black voters. Political power can be a necessary prerequisite to economic power, as well as the reverse.

conservatives. The Black Codes were vainglorious in their bias: the South Carolina law, for instance, defined a vagrant as a person lacking "some fixed and known place of abode, and some lawful and reputable employment." A vagrant "of color" could be apprehended by a magistrate, tried by him in conjunction with five freeholders, and sentenced to a maximum of one year. He could then be hired out for the length of his term to do hard labor for any landholder. Thus originated the convict-lease system that, as shall be seen, produced some of the vilest crimes in American history. But even this was not the ultimate evil. The Black Codes at least were adopted under color of law, and some effort was made to administer them by judicial processes. But they were quickly supplemented by the extralegal Ku Klux Klan, by floggings and murders, by race riots in urban centers.

Congress met force with force. By the First Reconstruction Act it established a military occupation of the South, which was divided into five Army districts. Adult males, regardless of color, not disqualified for participation in the rebellion, would elect delegates to write a new constitution in each state and to form a new government. Johnson vetoed the bill, and Congress then passed it over his opposition. Congress promptly curbed the president in two other respects. The Tenure of Office Act forbade him to dismiss members of the cabinet without senatorial consent. A second statute hobbled the president's control of the armed forces. Johnson understandably was infuriated. These Congressional measures brought a showdown. The president sought to replace the secretary of war. The Senate declined its assent. Johnson persisted. In 1868 the House of Representatives for the first time exercised its power to impeach the chief executive for "the violation of a law of Congress and other offenses."

Although the trial of Johnson continues to create sensations, it had meager results. The evidence leading to this conclusion is varied. The Senate required a two-thirds majority to remove the president from office, and it failed of this margin by only one vote: 35 for conviction against 19. In spite of frequent assertions to the contrary, postbellum presidents were not "intimidated" by Congress: Grover Cleveland for instance distributed vetoes like confetti—as some deserved to be. The failure of Reconstruction was already clear, so the trial could hardly determine that topic. Congress had already stipulated the terms on which members of a seceded state would be seated: ratification of three Amendments to the Constitution of the United States, plus the Civil Rights Acts. By the end of 1868 six former Confederate states had been re-admitted to Congress.

In any case, the impeachment of Johnson, whatever its outcome, was trivial compared to realignments in society and its politics. The nation underwent a colossal shift in its political configuration. From 1875 to 1889, there was not an instant when the same party controlled the White House and both branches of Congress. Presidential elections were determined by a handful of votes. Thus if we focus on Washington we can talk seriously about a two-party system. But in most localities one party or the other had a stranglehold. Up to 1876 the Republicans needed the votes of Southern blacks to check Democratic challenges for the presidency. But the soaring population of the Old Northwest (the seven states from Ohio to Minnesota) altered the situation. Prior to the Civil War this area had rather consistently been Democratic. During the War its southerly portions had bristled with Copperheads, as the Confederate sympathizers in the North were called. But Republican strategists (think of Lincoln) helped to effect a massive switch. They had new groups of voters to appeal to: especially immigrants from Germany. They could impugn the opposition for disloyalty. The secessionist departure from Congress made it possible for them to enact some vote-getting laws to be examined later—the Homestead Act, a protective tariff, appropriations to improve rivers and harbors, a measure to establish land-grant agricultural colleges. In eleven presidential contests beginning with 1868, these seven states were all Republican eight times. Four of the states did not vote · Democratic a single time, Illinois and Wisconsin once each, Indiana thrice.

The meaning of such developments in the North was obscured until recently because historians of the late nineteenth century were preoccupied with politics, either in Washington or in the state capitals during (non) Reconstruction. Most overviews of the United States during that epoch halted abruptly with "the end of Reconstruction" in 1877 and resumed, also abruptly, with "the farmers' revolt" of the 1890's or even as late as the twentieth century and "the Progressive movement." The ascribing of categories is doubtless essential, but ill-chosen and loose rubrics can mislead historical understanding for generations. And surely nothing is gained by minimizing three of the most volatile decades in American history: the years from 1865 to 1895.

Surprisingly, the section of the country that has received the most study was the one where the least was changing—the South. Too much attention has been paid to governments, not enough to social structure, to economic life, to the daily routines that claimed the multitudes. Prosecutors and champions of the new black-white states have alike offered unbalanced judgments. Let us begin with two topics: schools, and venality. Only in this century have scholars generally recognized that public schools in the region had their origins during Reconstruction; Georgia, for example, by its constitution of 1868 declared for a "thorough system of general education to be forever free to all the children of the state." This ambition was not achieved anywhere in the former Confederacy. The dreadfully impoverished area could not afford teachers or classrooms or books. Parents could ill afford to release their children from productive labor, usually in the fields. The Freedmen's Bureau did start 4,000 schools to educate blacks. Many teachers were white imports from the North who hastened to meet the hunger of Southern blacks for learning. Few black teachers were available to be hired even where money was available to hire them; at the end of the century the historian W. E. B. DuBois would point out that black colleges to train black teachers had to precede primary and secondary schools in building an educational system for the South. The total funds granted to higher education in nine Southern states in 1903 did not equal the income that year of Harvard University.

On the other hand, until about forty years ago the received tradition among scholars amounted to a gross distortion of the nature and degree of peculation in the Reconstruction states. Crookedness among black office-holders, carpetbaggers (Northern whites who held Southern posts), and scalawags (Southern whites who endorsed the Northern occupation) was unquestionably common. But insight cannot be gained unless the phenome-non is seen in comparative terms. How typical was jobbery besides that in ante-bellum Southern regimes? How typical in postbellum Northern states and cities? in the federal government? in the post-Reconstruction Southern oligarchies commonly known as the Bourbons or the Redeemers (suggesting the restoration of local rule)? These questions must be asked, but they cannot now be answered with precision. Thieves notoriously like to work in the dark; bagmen do not demand receipts; the surviving evidence is perhaps no more than a fragment of what once existed. Incidents have lately been produced to suggest that many Redeemers did not earn a reputation for purity. In 1873 a Bourbon state treasurer in Virginia was indicted for embezzlement; he escaped trial on the grounds of insanity. The equivalent official in Georgia in 1879 was impeached for defalcation; he restored the funds and avoided punishment. The state treasurer of Tennessee skipped with $400,000 in 1883. The treasurer of Alabama dropped from sight only three weeks later, but he took only half as much.

These cases do not demonstrate individual culpability so much as social calamity. Whether white or black, a Southerner after the Civil War could hardly inherit wealth or marry it; the stuff was not there. So if he wanted it he had these choices: work for it, or steal it. Perforce, most of the available loot was in the public coffers. When blacks had access to the civic till—and let us never forget that these occasions were seldom—some dipped their fingers. With whites, who had the chance more often, likewise. Nothing is likely to be learned by trying to make distinctions here. But in other respects, discrimina-tions can be made. Blacks might sell, but they could not buy, railroad franchises. Perhaps even more significant in the short run for the acquisition of wealth in an impoverished society, they could be victimized by, but they themselves could not victimize by use of the convict-lease system. In the exploitation of prisoners the collusion was statewide rather than federal, as four jurisdictions will illustrate. In Georgia a senator (sometime redneck, sometime governor) owned coal mines. He paid the state for a 20-year lease that guaranteed him 300 able-bodied laborers. He paid the treasury about 8 cents a day for each man. In Alabama the warden of the state penitentiary "grew rich in a few years on $2,000 a year." In Arkansas in 1881 the death-rate among convicts was said to be 25 per cent. Thus it seems that one result of the prisoner-lease arrangement was to wipe out the prisoners. But that was not so beneficial to taxpayers as to wipe out the prison but keep the convicts. In 1883 the Tennessee Coal, Iron, and Railroad Company leased from that state all 1,300 state inmates, for a charge approximating 20 cents a man per day. It will not do to underestimate the degree to which an entire society can be lured into iniquity.

The procedures of selling or hiring your own chain gang had beneficiaries both north and south of the Mason-Dixon Line. Similarly with the purchase and sale of licenses to build railroads. These were various, from a mere authorization to operate a line, to grants of so many acres of land for each mile of track installed, to guarantees by cities and states of bonds sold to private investors. The last arrangement approached in fact if not in form the outright grant to the Canadian Pacific by the new Dominion of Canada of $25 million in addition to 25 million acres. This resemblance should be especially remarked, along with the reasons for it. Whether in Canada or in the former Confederacy, transportation could be improved only by seducing in capital from the American North; neither region had private funds within its confines to do the job. The handicaps of the slave states have already been summarized; the handicap of Canada was a population in 1881 of 4.3 million versus the projected line of 2,500 miles, through almost unpopulated territory, over often impassable terrain. The goal in one region was to rejuvenate a war-raped land, in the other to extend and preserve a foundling nation. Each found, as have many other peoples, that its noble aim did not reduce the high price to be paid for outside help. The perspective being underscored here is entwined in the essence of economic growth. If the ex-Confederacy or Canada wanted railroad development from 1870 to 1880, it would have to barter in a vicious market. Every culture at certain times has been forced to rely heavily on child labor; what then of free public schools? The existence of company towns and company stores need not mean that the company is fiendishly gouging; perhaps in a capital-rare district it had to use these devices to remove the timber or the minerals at all.

All of this leads us to the economic institutions of the postbellum South; here are some:

convict-lease system
crop-lien or crop-mortgage system
landlord-owned stores giving credit at high rates
sharecropping

The sole alternative to this infernal machinery had disappeared within three years of war's end: Forty Acres and a Mule. When that was gone, only sin was left. Except for the convict-lease system, the modes listed above can be described superficially as varieties of free contract. But they were only the flinty fragments—the talus, scree, and detritus—of the Enlightenment.

When one party to a negotiation has almost no bargaining power, the agreement is not free. The South had no money with which to lubricate its own economy. To get it, Southern businessmen were forced into onerous terms by Yankees; in Arkansas, for instance, the commissioner of immigration was given control of publicly held lands and instructed to use them to attract "northern capital and labor to the state." Six months after the war ended it was estimated that half of the stores in downtown Charleston were controlled by Northerners. Two men from Ohio, both Union soldiers, went into business in Tennessee after they were dismissed from service. They became prominent in coal and iron mining, iron furnaces, a portland cement plant, a cotton mill, a bank. Yankees did not need to invade the South in order to tap its economy: even in New York they could sell the shipping services and insurance and warehousing needed to move the cotton crop to Fall River and Liverpool. In the words of C. Vann Woodward, "The merchant was only a bucket on an endless chain by which the agricultural well of a tributary region was drained of its flow."

Southern promoters, then, could hire the funds of Boston and of Europe by pawning part of the future of their economy. But how could they hire workers? Even blacks were no longer vulnerable to the crude coercions of slavery. Would-be employers had no cash to pay wages. The ensuing accommodations involved a medley of barter, credit, and governmental manipulations. Sharecropping could involve a huge range of divisions of the product between landlord and tenant; if the cropper furnished his own tools and perhaps a draft animal he might get half of the proceeds. Under the crop-lien system the landlord in his turn might go into hock, mortgaging off a crop that was not grown in exchange for working capital. Then he might try to grab back a portion of what he had spent but not yet earned by requiring his sharecroppers to buy their provisions at a store that he owned and where he got inflated prices in exchange for the credit he granted. Crucial to the survival of this maze of credit was the overpowering fact of the state: judges and sheriffs would enforce the inequitable contracts. Historians of generally Marxist persuasion have done more than any other group in analyzing the role of government in what they call "the primitive accumulation of capital." In a poor culture, normal patterns of trade simply do not yield substantial profits. The sanctions of the state must be invoked to tip the balance of price-bargains, whether the precise shape be the war contracts of Thomas Hancock, licensed privateering and the courts of admiralty that passed on naval prizes, or the new weapons of exploitation that replaced slavery in the South.

Freedmen were badly fitted to survive in this competitive milieu; that they did so is a marvel of fortitude and adaptability. Subject at every turn to written words, to contracts and laws, most could not read. Subordinate to the rights of property, most owned none. Seeking to sustain themselves in a society ruled by political power, they had little. They knew their weakness. At the constitutional convention of South Carolina in 1868, an ex-slave declared: "I believe, my friends and fellow-citizens, we are not prepared for this suffrage. But we can learn. Give a man tools and let him commence to use them, and in time he will learn a trade. So it is with voting. We may not understand it at the start, but in time we shall learn to do our duty." But in the next thirty years the opportunity to learn civic responsibility be exercising it was stripped away from Southern blacks.

A good deal is now known about economic institutions and political realities in the postbellum South. But when we turn to social relations we find ourselves on uncertain ground. For decades the body of lore about the family patterns of blacks was unchallenged. Since man-wife ties under slavery were unstable both legally and factually, so the received argument ran, the black family after emancipation tended to be dominated by a matriarch. Recent research has at the very least forced us again to question this conclusion. A similar doubt surrounds another vital problem: the personal backgrounds of the whites who ruled the South after the war. Was the ruling class ex-slaveholders and their descendants? Or was it a new medley of self-made men who had pushed forward through virtual anarchy? A question of this sort can be studied systematically; we have revealing surveys of several other groups: leading executives in various industries, for instance. Somebody should take the 300 eminent citizens of each Southern state in 1880 or 1900 and tell us where they came from. Only by such methodical techniques will we improve our understanding of the processes that operated in the past.

To secede from the United States, the rebellious South followed procedures copied from those that had originated the Union seventy years earlier. Only Texas of the eleven departing states submitted the issue of secession to a popular vote; the others decided the matter by specially formed conventions. For the first two years of the War, the Confederacy seemed to be holding the Union to a stand-off, at times doing better than that. The superiority of the North then began to tell. This dominance had several facets. It was quantitative: more soldiers, more war matériel, more free productive workers. It was qualitative: better transportation networks, and, on balance, better leadership. If the two contestants were equal in terms of their generals, they were far from equal in terms of statesmen; a decided edge lay with the Union. The fray was the bloodiest by far in American history, and it taught parts of the nation the meaning of "total war." Although four years of conflict did preserve the United States and abolish slavery, they did not result in a social revolution in the defeated section. No white man was willing to accord sweeping equality to the freedmen. Congress would not even grant to blacks the chance that might have come from confiscating the plantations of slave-holders and using them to give each former bondsman forty acres and a mule. Indeed, from a longer view of postbellum society we might argue that the Civil War wrote more alterations in the structure of Northern culture than of Southern.

SOME NOTABLE EVENTS

1860   South Carolina secedes, Dec. 20.

1861   Confederacy formed, Feb. 4, at Montgomery, Alabama.
       Morrill Tariff Act passes, March 2.

Fort Sumter fired on, April 12.
First federal income tax.
First transcontinental telegraph.
Frémont's proclamation emancipating slaves, Aug. 30.

397

1862　U.S. government issues greenbacks.
Homestead Act passes, May 20.
Morrill Act passes to establish land-grant colleges, July 2.
Congress abolishes slavery in District of Columbia and the Territories.

1863　Emancipation Proclamation, Jan. 1.
National Banking Act, Feb. 25.
Battle of Gettysburg, July 1–3.
Grant takes Vicksburg, July 4.
Lincoln's Proclamation of Amnesty and Reconstruction, Dec. 8.

1864　National Bank Act, June 3.
Wade-Davis bill passes Congress; Lincoln vetoes it, July 8.
Sherman, May–Dec., sweeps from Tennessee through Atlanta to Savannah.

1865　Hampton Roads Conference, Feb. 3.
Freedmen's Bureau created; Freedmen's Savings and Trust Co. chartered, March 3.
Lee surrenders, April 9.
Lincoln dies; Andrew Johnson becomes president, April 15.
Johnson's Proclamation of Amnesty and Reconstruction, May 29.
Blacks convene at several sites to protest their treatment, May–Oct.
All-white legislatures in ex-Confederate states adopt Black Codes, summer–autumn.
Ku Klux Klan formed, Pulaski, Tenn.
13th Amendment to Constitution.

1866　Fisk University chartered for blacks, Jan. 9.
Civil Rights Act passes over president's veto, April 9.
ex parte Milligan case limits power of military courts over civilians.
Riot in Memphis, May 1.
Report of Joint Committee on Reconstruction, June 20.
Tennessee restored to Union, July 24.
Riot in New Orleans, July 30.

1867　Congress starts investigation of the president, Jan. 7.
First three Reconstruction Acts, March 2, March 23, July 19.
Union League begins to organize Republican politics in South, spring.
Constitutional conventions meet in former Confederate states, fall.

1868　Impeachment of Johnson begins, March 4.
Fourth Reconstruction Act becomes law, March 11.
Impeachment vote taken in Senate, fails to convict, May 16.
Arkansas restored, June 22.
Omnibus Bill restores North Carolina, South Carolina, Alabama, Florida, and Louisiana.
14th Amendment added to Constitution, July 28.
Thaddeus Stevens dies, August 11.
Georgia legislature expels its black members, Sept. 3.

1869　Conservatives win Tennessee, Oct. 4, and Virginia, Oct. 5.
Texas v. *White.*

1870　Virginia restored, Jan. 26, and Mississippi, Feb. 23.
Hiram R. Revels of Mississippi, first black senator, takes his seat, Feb. 25.
15th Amendment added to Constitution, March 30.
Texas restored, March 30, and Georgia, July 15.
Conservatives win North Carolina, Nov. 3.
Joseph H. Rainey of South Carolina, first black representative, takes his seat, Dec. 12.

1871　Conservatives win Georgia, Nov. 1.

1872　Colored National Convention, at New Orleans, Frederick Douglass presiding, April 15.

1873　Conservatives win Texas, Jan. 14.

1874　Conservatives win Arkansas, Nov. 10, and Alabama, Nov. 14.

1875　Civil Rights Act, March 1.
Conservatives win Mississippi, Nov. 3, and South Carolina, Nov. 12.

1877　Conservatives win Florida and Louisiana, Jan. 2.
Electoral Commission rules for Hayes, sets stage for troop withdrawal from South, Feb. 8.
Wormley House bargain, Feb. 26.
U.S. troops withdraw from South Carolina as arranged, officially ending reconstruction, April 10.

Ways to Study History XVI

Take a world view. Too often American history has been looked at with provincial or even parochial spectacles. We have already seen ways in which the Civil War has been distorted because some of its major aspects have not been taken into account: the vital importance of the Ohio-Mississippi river basin, the significance for military events of policy in addition to strategy and tactics. That event has also been interpreted largely in terms of its significance for the United States and for Americans. In point of fact the Civil War was "the last best hope" of all mankind.

David M. Potter, arguing along lines anticipated by Alexis de Tocqueville and Abraham Lincoln, emphasized that developments in the United States have revealed several paths that civilizations would come to follow in other parts of the world. In a brilliant essay, Potter wrote, ". . . here are two things which the Civil War did: first, it turned the tide which had been running against nationalism for forty years, or ever since Waterloo; and second, it forged a bond between nationalism and liberalism at a time when it appeared that the two might draw apart and move in opposite directions."

The war preserved the nation *unum,* but it likewise left it *pluribus.* To exemplify his thesis, Potter contrasts Lincoln to Otto von Bismarck, Chancellor of Prussia. While we could argue whether Lincoln created a national state or merely saved one, undoubtedly Bismarck was head architect in the fusion of German sovereignty. But conversely, in spite of wartime infractions against civil liberties, the United States that emerged from the war was a country where individual citizens had personal freedoms which never appeared in the centralized Germany of the Hohenzollerns.

Thus one merit of Potter's essay is that he underscores what might be called the global meaning of our Civil War. Another is that he does so in a form that is lucid, without pretensions, and takes only eleven pages.

Document 16-1

Herman Melville published "Shiloh" in 1866 in *Battle-Pieces and Aspects of the War.* This first horrendous clash on the Western front involved a Confederate force led by Albert Sidney Johnston and a Union army commanded by Ulysses S. Grant. In two days of fighting (April 6–7, 1862), over 23,500 men were killed or wounded.

Shiloh   A Requiem   (April, 1862)

Skimming lightly, wheeling still,
The swallows fly low
Over the field in clouded days,
The forest-field of Shiloh—
Over the field where April rain
Solaced the parched ones stretched in pain
Through the pause of night
That followed the Sunday fight
Around the church of Shiloh—
The church so lone, the log-built one,
That echoed to many a parting groan
And natural prayer
Of dying foemen mingled there—
Foemen at morn, but friends at eve—
Fame or country least their care:
(What like a bullet can undeceive!)
But now they lie low,
While over them the swallows skim,
And all is hushed at Shiloh.

399

Document 16-2

Clearly Lincoln's two most famous speeches are the Gettysburg Address and the Second Inaugural. They deserve fame. But in being succinct, lucid—and humane—this open letter to Horace Greeley, editor of the nation's most influential newspaper, approaches them in quality. The date is 22 August, 1862, just before the battle of Antietam.

I have just read yours of the 19th. addressed to myself through the New-York Tribune. If there be in it any statement, or assumptions of fact, which I may know to be erroneous, I do not, now and here, controvert them. If there be in it any inferences which I may believe to be falsely drawn, I do not now and here argue against them. If there be perceptable in it an impatient and dictatorial tone, I waive it in deference to an old friend, whose heart I have always supposed to be right.

As to the policy I "seem to be pursuing" as you say, I have not meant to leave any one in doubt.

I would save the Union. I would save it the shortest way under the Constitution. The sooner the national authority can be restored; the nearer the Union will be "the Union as it was." If there be those who would not save the Union, unless they could at the same time save slavery, I do not agree with them. If there be those who would not save the Union unless they could at the same time destroy slavery, I do not agree with them. My paramount object in this struggle is to save the Union, and is not either to save or to destroy slavery. If I could save the Union without freeing any slave, I would do it; and if I could save it by freeing all the slaves I would do it; and if I could save it by freeing some and leaving others alone I would also do that. . . .

I have there stated my purpose according to my view of official duty; and I intend no modification of my oft-expressed personal wish that all men every where could be free.

Document 16-3

Seventy years after the Civil War ended, the Federal Writers' Project of the WPA (Works Progress Administration; see mid-Chapter 27) interviewed hundreds of ex-slaves. An old person's memories of childhood are often inaccurate, but they can also be quite vivid about some episodes. The lad has accompanied his father to a hamlet in South Carolina in December 1864 to pick up the mail for the plantation. They watch a Confederate troop train en route to Savannah to help defend against Sherman's army.

I stand wid my pappy near de long trestle, and see de train rock by. One enjine in front pulling one in de back pushing, pushing, pushing. De train load down wid soldier. They thick as peas. Been so many a whole ton been riding on de car roof. They shout and holler. I make big amaze to see such a lot of soldier—all going down to die.

And they start to sing as they cross de trestle. One pick a banjo, one play de fiddle. They sing and whoop, they laugh; they holler to de people on de ground, and sing out, "Good-bye." All going down to die.

And it seem to me dat is de most wonderful sight I ever see. All them soldier, laughing light, singing and shouting dat way, and all riding fast to battle.

One soldier man say in a loud voice: "Well, boys we going to cut de Yankee throat. We on our way to meet him and he better tremble. Our gun greeze up, and our bayonet sharp. Boys, we going to eat our dinner in hell today." . . .

De train still rumble by. One gang of soldier on de top been playing card. I see um hold up de card as plain as day, when de luck fall right. They going to face bullet, but yet they play card, and sing and laugh like they in their own house . . . All going down to die.

De train pull 'cross de trestle. I stand up and watch um till he go out of sight 'round de bend. De last thing I hear is de soldier laugh and sing . . . All going down to die.

Capitalists, Workers, Farmers

The effulgence of the American economy after the Civil War suggests several theses, but perhaps we should begin with a protagonist. Andrew Carnegie admitted as a young man that he was pushy. Brought by his parents from Scotland to Pittsburgh when he was only twelve, he learned to send teletype. This craft, plus charm, made him personal secretary to Thomas A. Scott, who was superintendent of the Pennsylvania Railroad in the area. Railroad construction was the chief outlet for iron products at the time, so Carnegie's contacts here were indispensable later. As Scott climbed the ladder, so did Andy, becoming division supervisor himself. Early in the war he was an administrator of transport for the Union. Back in Pittsburgh, he worked for the railroad while also investing in the new oil fields of northwestern Pennsylvania. His investment in that sphere, $11,000, showed a profit of nearly $18,000 in the first year. He entered a syndicate that bought drilling rights on a specific farm for $40,000; their ultimate take was over $5 million. Andrew

Carnegie was only 27 years old when he was conscripted for the Union army, and he had to pay $850 for a substitute to go in his stead. He could afford to pay.

The juxtaposition of a popular tune with the financier's own words will emphasize the context in which Carnegie made his fortune. As a boy in Scotland he heard his father, a weaver, sing:

> To the West, to the West, to the land of the free,
> Where the mighty Missouri rolls down to the sea;
> Where a man is a man even though he must toil
> And the poorest may gather the fruits of the soil.

Before he was eighteen, Carnegie had written from America: "Our public Lands of almost unlimited extent are becoming settled with an enterprising people. . . . Pauperism is almost unknown. Everything around us is motion—mind is freed from superstitious reverence for old customs, unawed by gorgeous and unmeaning shows & forms. . . ."

If everybody was in motion, and the number of bodies was growing swiftly, obviously the transportation net would be both thickened and stretched. Carnegie could have settled down to grow with the Pennsylvania Railroad. But he did not. He went, so to speak, behind and beneath the operation of trains, into bridge building, telegraphy, manufacture of sleeping cars. In 1872 he embarked upon the construction of a completely new steel mill. His formulas for managing a company were precise. He emphasized a steady reduction in costs of production: if you succeeded in that sphere, profits were certain. Knock down the charges you paid to railroads for hauling your iron ore and coal and finished steel. Be ready to scrap any equipment, however new, if a tool becomes available that will cut costs per ton of output; in 1898 it was estimated that Carnegie's steel mills were replacing their entire capital plant every three years. He kept the salaries of his executives low, rewarding them by giving out small shares in the ownership. But he always kept a majority interest for himself. If any other administrator tried to thwart his policies, he was forced to withdraw from the firm.

He also had good luck. An omniscient executive might have embarked in the 1870's on a policy of vertical integration, by which a steel mill would have become self-sufficient by owning ore fields and fabricating its own finished products and so on. But Carnegie came to this strategy late and accidentally. He also profited immensely from the boom of the American economy at the close of the century. As late as 1898 the profits of Carnegie Steel were only $10 million. Then came the Klondike gold rush and the Spanish-American War. For 1899 the profits more than doubled. The projected figure for 1900 was $40 million. When Carnegie sold the company as the basis of the new United States Steel in 1901, his 58.5 per cent share brought him $255,639,000. He insisted that it be paid to him in 5 per cent first-mortgage gold bonds.

This concern for payment in *gold* became an obsession with groups of Americans in the last third of the nineteenth century. The preoccupation began during the Civil War. Americans have never been willing to pull their belts tight enough to finance a war while they are fighting it. An inevitable consequence was massive deficits because the federal government was spending more than it collected by taxation. A further result was inflation. Often after a war it has happened that the cost of living has achieved some degree of stability rather quickly. But after the Civil War this did not happen. The runaway inflation was reversed into a sharp drop in the value of goods and services; that is, into a rise in the value of money. In contrast to other postwar epochs, the deflation persisted for decades. Allowing for the fluctuations around this long-term trend—the shorter swings are usually called business cycles and last seven-ten years from trough to trough—the drop in prices continued for about thirty years: 1866–1897.

Part of the explanation of this secular trend lies in the monetary policies of the federal government. The justification of those policies was the need of the wartime Treasury for funds to pay soldiers and buy matériel. Conditions were indeed grim. Two slaughters of Union troops at Bull Run were strong warrant that the conflict would not be brief or easy. So Congress, unwilling to raise taxes to the level necessary to support military procurement, sought for a palatable bundle of fiscal devices. Government became entangled with politics.* The Republicans came to power in 1861 as a fledgling party and a minority party. They had to reach out vigorously to a diversity of groups, while also confronting the fiscal requirements of the sectional division. Even before Lincoln took office, Congress seized on the departure of its Southern members to pass a high protective tariff. The measure can be defended as wartime finance, but it was more than that; it enticed into the Republican fold both managers and workers of the iron industry in Pennsylvania. Having tossed a plum to that sizable voting bloc, the party proceeded to take apples away from them in order to placate other interest groups. The Homestead Act, by which any head of family could receive free 160 acres of federal land if he could meet simple tests, had long been blocked by a coalition of Southern congressmen (who wanted to sell the public lands to raise federal revenue so that the import duties could be kept low) with Eastern industrialists (who wanted to keep a large labor supply in their home counties). In 1862 Congress passed the bill. Giving away public assets instead of selling them was a peculiar way to finance a war, but it was an effective way to build a party.

It was a time of slippery alliances. Search as we may, we cannot see any majority in the entire land that could agree on the urgent issues of the period. Consider the desires for instance of the congressional delegation from Pennsylvania. In general they wanted

---

*Politics and government are always related in a republic, but it is not wise to confuse the two. A statesman as distinguished from a placeman may take an action that will hurt him at the polls. Conversely a deed may be done to help a party even though it will harm the nation.

high tariffs
easy or cheap or soft money
Radical Reconstruction

On the first they had their way; on the other two they did not. Their significance in the Republican party, while great, was not overriding. Or consider the Midwestern Democrats. From the days of Andrew Jackson their party had stood for hard money: now they drifted into the opposite stand and shouted for paper money, "shinplasters."

Paper money there was during the war; the Treasury required it to pay its bills with. True, the federal debt in 1865 that can be laid against the war came to $2.6 billion, whereas the issue of greenbacks was only a sixth of that amount. But this ratio tells nothing about whether the specific purchases made with the paper money were essential to the Union cause, and of course once put in circulation the bills were spent many times. We do not know, but a guess seems plausible. We do know that military necessity swayed many congressmen into voting for the issue of greenbacks which passed as legal tender; that is, sellers were required by law to accept them at their face value, and prices quoted in greenbacks could not legally be higher than prices quoted in gold. Many of the legislators who voted for the measure did so reluctantly. On principle they despised the idea of any paper money that would not be redeemed in solid coin, either gold or silver. Paper money (and the bank or government that issued it) was *per se* crooked. To this type of mind, money could not be separated from morality. Greenbacks were sterile. Decades earlier, a correspondent of Andrew Jackson had condemned the Second Bank of the United States on the grounds that it "had never raised a single bushel of wheat, nor even a single head of cabbage nor a single pumpkin, potato or turnip during its whole existence, nor never will." The Civil War greenbacks continued in circulation until 1879, while the metaphors mounted. Wrote one man: "Paper money is the sum of all iniquity: specie is philosophy, morality and religion." A prominent weekly financial journal fulminated about "a connection between irredeemable paper money and the growth of financial dishonesty since the war."

Clearly, thought congressmen of this ilk, a source was required that could emit money that would be stable in value and redeemable in specie. The result was the National Banking Act of 1863, amended a year later. This structure would be the essence of the country's monetary system for the next half century. Its details are not our concern, but the grave defects must be noted. One was its sectional inequities. To secure a federal charter, a bank had to have at least $100,000 in capital, and twice that in large cities. These conditions were far easier to meet in the East than in Midwest or South. In consequence the volume of bank notes in circulation—and therefore the degree of deflation—varied greatly in different areas. For 1863–1865, the dollars per person circulated in seven Midwestern states averaged $6.36, whereas in New England and New York the circulation was about five times as

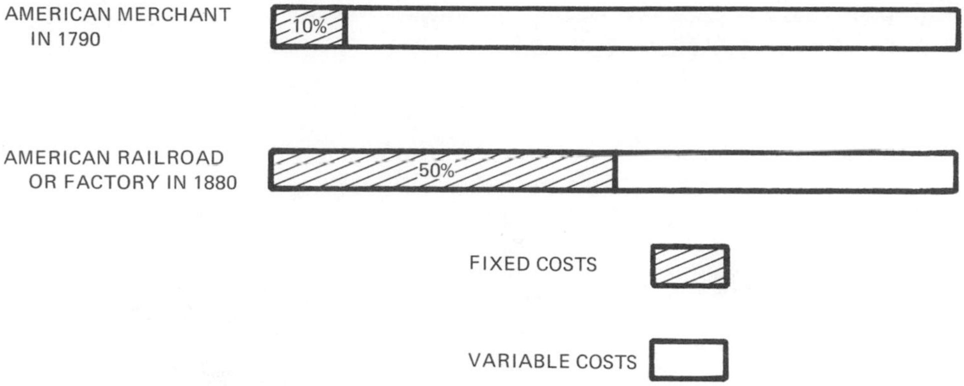

AMERICAN MERCHANT
IN 1790

10%

AMERICAN RAILROAD
OR FACTORY IN 1880

50%

FIXED COSTS

VARIABLE COSTS

FIGURE 17-1. *Fixed and Variable Costs*

The relations charted here are meant to be representative and to signify a shift in proportions (a) over time, and (b) from one type of activity to others. These percentages emphatically do not speak for any specific company, but my researches lead me to think that they are broadly typical of the type of enterprise named. Strangely enough, it is easier to give precise figures for the merchant in the late eighteenth century than for an industrialist in the late nineteenth. Merchants left ledgers that clearly distinguish office expenses and value of ship from value of cargo and pay to crew. In contrast, Standard Oil put up huge refineries and wrote off the entire expenditure as an operating expense; in modern language, the firm did not keep a separate capital account.

Variable costs are those that fluctuate as the output varies. For instance, under slavery the purchase and maintenance of the slaves was not a variable cost; it was a sum that had to be paid no matter what happened to the price of cotton or to the produce of a plantation. But with free labor, wages became a variable cost. Purchase of certain services such as banking and insurance and transportation might also come in this category. Conversely, fixed (otherwise called sunk or overhead) costs must be paid even if the level of production falls to zero. In the early railroad systems, interest on borrowed money was the vital element; repeatedly a company could not pay it and thus was forced into bankruptcy. But salaries to valued managers or indispensable maintenance of physical property are also normally an overhead cost.

The shift from variable to fixed costs is a clear index of the changing structure of business. The importance of the transition was aggravated by improvements in transportation; see Figure 17-4.

FIGURE 17-2. *Frederick Remington,* Fight for the Waterhole

Fight for the Waterhole by Frederic Remington imparts a curiously nostalgic aroma. Done in 1908, the painting seems to be a recollection of glorious days when giants roamed the earth. Partly this effect derives from almost unworldly chiaroscuro contrasts of light and shadow. (The desert indeed can be eerie with such stark lighting.) Also the artist used a large canvas, 27″ × 40″, perhaps to contribute to awareness of the vastness of the landscape.

This interpretation seems to fit the shape of Remington's brief career (1861–1909). Born to a well-to-do family in upstate New York, he was sent to military school and then sent to Yale to study fine arts. A college drop-out at nineteen, he headed for the Great Plains. He worked with trail crews and became adept with horses. The advent of railroads chilled his sense of romance. "I knew the wild riders and the vacant land were about to vanish forever, and the more I considered the subject, the bigger the *forever* loomed. . . . I began to try to record some facts around me, and the more I looked, the more the panorama unfolded." His attempts to immortalize facets of his transient present resulted in more than 2700 pictures. He had been a crony of Theodore Roosevelt, Rudyard Kipling, and Owen Wister, author of *The Virginian* ("When you call me that, smile."). When publisher Hearst sent him to Cuba to portray the Spanish-American War, he wired back that he couldn't find any war. Hearst's answer proved out for both men: "You furnish the pictures; I'll furnish the war."

The subject of this picture is also of special interest. Perhaps no Easterner can truly understand what water means in the West. For a rancher, even the federal land policy that had been devised for great. Seemingly by 1866 the disparity had become worse: $77 for Rhode Island, less than $6 for Illinois. The injustice of the situation was exaggerated because the newer areas needed more national bank notes than the seaboard, not less; the Midwest had not yet progressed nearly as far as the East in using bank deposits and checks as a form of money.

Another defect of the National Banking Act was its class inequities. Discussion of this topic can be subjected to many refinements that are not advisable here, but some usable angles can be suggested. Let us start with two groups within the business community: manufacturers, and bankers. The former had benefited immensely from the wartime inflation; they repeatedly bought raw materials and hired their laborers at a lower level of prices than the one prevailing when they sold their output. Their profits soared. For bankers, this situation might even be reversed; they often made loans in more valuable money than the form that was later repaid to them. After the war, when the level of prices was falling, we encounter a turnabout: bankers win, industrialists lose. Now the latter must buy their inputs at higher prices than what they can get for their outputs. In consequence, as the example of Andrew Carnegie illustrates, they faced a remorseless pressure to cut their costs of production. But for them this strategy became ever harder to implement because a growing percentage of their costs were fixed costs rather than variable costs (see Figure 17-1).

Meanwhile the bankers were in clover. With prices falling, loans they had made earlier were constantly being repaid in more valuable dollars than those they had loaned. Naturally they wanted to preserve this situation. They proclaimed: No repudiation of public debts. No cheap money. All the while, money became more dear. The bankers needed a line by which they could sell to millions of voters a policy that violated the interests of millions of debtors. So the fatcats talked about morality. Listen to a New York banker, son of Albert Gallatin, himself a New York banker who had been a great statesman:

> The demoralization of society progresses steadily under the blighting influence of an irredeemable legal tender paper money. Religion, virtue, and honor decline. Vice becomes fashionable. Gambling prevailes in the marts of trade and the financial centres, from the very necessities of the case, because the slow process of honesty, prudence, forethought and plodding industry are impracticable in occupations subject to the licentious reign of such paper money.

The Gospel of Work was virtually unchallenged in the nation. Man was born to do his duty, and his chief obligation was to drive himself relentlessly.

---

the prairies would not suffice on the plains—not enough water, not enough forage. New federal laws were enacted; a full section of land (640 acres) was taken to be a minimum. Colorado in 1862 had already put through a law regulating the diversion of water from streams into irrigation ditches; other states soon followed. Wyoming in 1888 hit the nail on its head: the water goes wlth the land.

The sanctified traits were three: be industrious, be sober, be frugal (Save). The original sin was sloth. This was the true American creed of our great-grandparents. Before we proceed with an explication of other major features of American industrialization, it might be well to confront some misleading notions. One is embodied in the phrase "social Darwinism." It implies that significant numbers of people thought of society in the vocabulary of biological evolution, thought in terms of the "survival of the fittest," believed it was right that weak people should be stomped under, and disapproved of any public program aimed at aiding the helpless. No evidence has been found to show that many businessmen reasoned in this way. Their self-justification was the right of private property: This company is mine and I'll manage it as I please. It is true that countless Americans regarded poverty not as a social maladjustment but as a penalty for personal vice; this creed, by no means extinct today, did not require an elaborate conceptual apparatus stemming from the evolutionist Charles Darwin.

Another, more complex, question is posed in the title of an article by Thomas C. Cochran: "Did the Civil War Retard Industrialization?" The literature bearing directly on this problem is extensive, and after perusing it I think the answer is definitely No. This judgment applies strictly to the United States as a whole. For the South the war clearly had a negative effect. Much of its productive capacity in farming was nullified. Its labor system was disrupted. Many of its workers, including a sizable segment of its managerial talent, were killed or wounded. Railroads and factories were smashed. Not until the new century would the South overcome the adverse consequences of the conflict. But in North and West the results generally were the reverse. There physical damage to resources was marginal. Secession freed the federal government to launch a series of policies that immensely aided large-scale private enterprise: the National Banks, improvements to rivers and harbors, protective tariffs, subsidies to trans-Mississippi railroads, the Morrill Act for providing research and scientific training to agriculture. But even these policies of the federal agencies seem to pale beside one overwhelming influence: The Civil War produced an unprecedented concentration of liquid capital in the hands of a small number who were determined to make it multiply. They were far from the first who wanted to make a dollar grow into two: it was the scale of their breeding program that commands attention. Today a few connoisseurs may think of the late nineteenth century by recalling outstanding writers or painters, but most Americans will think of Rockefeller's oil refineries and Carnegie's steel mills. Even these titans do not symbolize the age until we take account of Standard Oil profits grasping out in countless directions toward the end of the century. The symbol is J. P. Morgan's access to liquid wealth, to countless numbers of paper counters, to money. Large-scale production needs large-scale investment, and it was a few investment bankers like Morgan who could raise the funds.

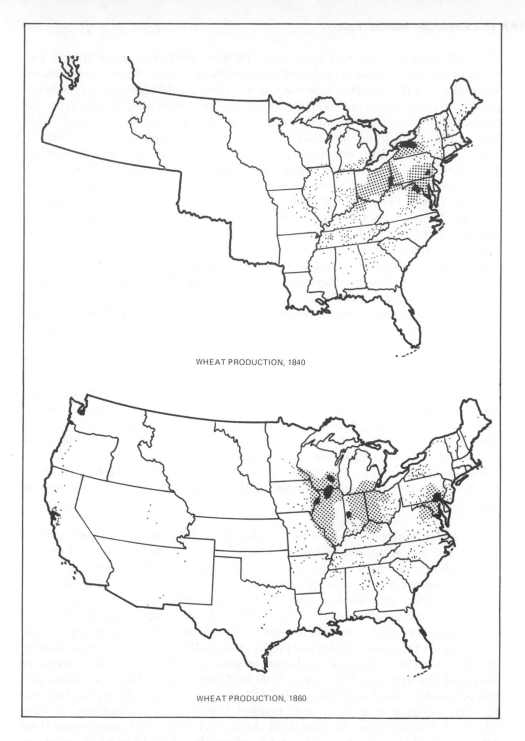

WHEAT PRODUCTION, 1840

WHEAT PRODUCTION, 1860

FIGURE 17-3. *Major Wheat-producing Areas, 1840 and 1860*

Considering the full span from 1865 to 1897, the main groups victimized by the economic-political developments were clusters of farmers.
Exceptions to this generalization might well be noted before we diagnose the
plight of most agrarians. Well-to-do owners of substantial holdings in the
Midwestern area from Pennsylvania to Iowa, for instance, did well right
through the hard times; the diary of the proprietor of a mixed farm (mainly
corn and hogs) in Illinois reveals him gaily junketing to the Chicago World's
Fair during the bleak days of farm depression in 1893. Also, as Henry Nash
Smith has demonstrated, Americans remained committed to the ideal of the
"family farm" long after it had ceased being practical. This commitment
produced some favorable legislation. In spite of all the abuses that occurred,
the Homestead Act did enable thousands of men to better themselves on the
land. But probably few of these beneficiaries had been poor earlier; they were
solid Ohio types who moved to Iowa and became more solid. Likewise the
already privileged were those most likely to use the facilities of the new
agricultural land-grant colleges.

The dilemma of many farmers began during the Civil War, when the
normal American reasons for mechanization were aggravated by the wartime
shortage of labor. Operations that could not raise the capital to buy a reaper
felt they had to buy one anyway, on credit. The axe did not immediately fall on
these downcoming victims at war's end. In 1868 the Democrats sought to win
power by appealing to the farm vote. That they did not win was due in part to
hatreds lingering from the conflict, in part as already noted (Chapter 16) to the
votes of blacks, but also in part to their failure to win enough rural districts.
The price of wheat in the election year was $1.46 a bushel—a peak never
reached again until 1914. Buoyant prosperity could mitigate where it did not
conquer the grievances of the yeomen: concentration of National Bank notes in
the East, the power of grain elevators and railroads that reached monopoly in
some districts (see Figure 17-4).

If the National Banking policy played a vital part in the long waves of
prices, the fluctuations in railroad construction were the chief single factor in
the shorter-run business cycles. Wherever a railroad was built, it wrenched the
local economy into a new set of occupations. In certain areas it cut sharply into
the profitability of what had long been a staple crop; in others it immensely
stimulated the production of a crop relatively new to the locale. The first
phenomenon can be diagnosed in western New York, where wheat was a staple
by the time of the Revolution. But the Genesee valley lost out when the prairies
of Minnesota and the Dakotas began to pour into Eastern markets swelling
floods of cheap grain. A farmer in Monroe County, New York, estimated that
the value of his land had fallen at least 25 per cent in about four years because
the rate policies of the railroads favored his Western competitors; to ship
identical freight from Rochester to New York City cost more than from
Chicago. Bell County, Texas shows how the railroad could virtually create an

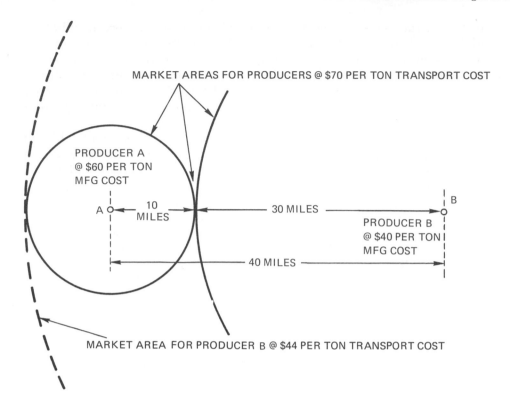

FIGURE 17-4. *Transportation Costs and Scale of Production*

This chart will illustrate the revolutionary effects of the railroad (as a great reducer of shipping costs) on other industries, whether in agriculture or manufacturing. Suppose that independent steel mills are located at A and B, forty miles apart. Since both are located within the United States, we need not allow for tariff or import duties. For mill A the cost of production is $60 a ton, for mill B $40, including a satisfactory profit for each. Transportation is by wagon, and the cost is $1 per ton-mile. The market areas will meet ten miles from mill A, for at that spot each mill can deliver steel at a price of $70 per ton.

Now imagine a railroad built, with the result that shipping costs for iron fall at once to ten cents a ton-mile. Now for only $44 a ton mill B can deliver steel at the doorstep of mill A. The market area of mill B will extend westward even beyond mill A, engulfing almost all A's market area. The latter is driven out of business. But the expansion of mill B will go further yet. Now it is selling more steel. This may open to it what are technically called economies of scale. Perhaps it can afford to buy more efficient machinery, as Carnegie did. Perhaps it can hire higher-priced but more competent executives, as Carnegie did not. Certainly it can drive better bargains in procuring raw materials and workers. Then it might begin to cut its prices. Then it might benefit from what economists call elasticity of demand; that is, as price per unit falls, volume of sales rises more than proportionately. By such processes a world market for steel was created.

411

industry. In the late seventies the farmers there grew what breadstuffs they used, having them ground into flour at local gristmills. Their cotton crop was small—too expensive to haul by wagon to ports on the Gulf since their community was some 115 miles northeast of Houston. Then came the railroad. In ten years the county's production of wheat fell 75 per cent. To buy flour milled in Minneapolis, the farmers grew and sold cotton; output grew four times in a decade.

No mileage would be gained by clogging this discussion with tables of figures, but it is valuable to show as precisely as may be the wild deviations in the pace at which the railroad network was extended. Here is the rundown on miles of track in operation:

1866	36,801	1879	86,556
1867	39,050	1880	93,262
1868	42,229	1881	103,103
1869	46,804	1882	114,677
1870	52,922	1883	121,422
1871	60,301	1884	125,345
1872	66,171	1885	128,320
1873	70,268	1886	136,338
1874	72,385	1887	149,214
1875	74,396	1888	156,114
1876	76,808	1889	161,276
1877	79,082	1890	166,703
1878	81,747		

Note especially the rate of construction fell markedly when the Philadelphia bank of Jay Cooke overextended itself in promoting the Northern Pacific Railroad and was forced to close in 1873 (Document 17-2). The ensuing depression lasted five years. Then came a huge surge forward: nearly 5,000 miles of new line in 1879, more than 6,000 the next year, 10,000 the next, a record 11,000 the next. Given the resources then available to American society, this table summarizes an unbelievable achievement.

The problems that had been solved were many. Routes had to be located. In this regard the federal government helped; many of the early surveys were done by the Corps of Engineers of the army. Then ownership of those routes had to be contested; the supply was small, and the avenues staked out then across desert and mountain are the ones used now by interstate highways and piggyback trains. The worst bottlenecks were the passes through the Rockies and the Sierras, and a company that seized one in strength could exclude everybody else. Right of way had to be set and rails to be laid, using human muscle rather than bulldozers and jackhammers. Readers who have driven across those arid reaches and craggy ranges in their 300-horsepower cars on freeways that afford them each hour a strawberry soda or a cup of coffee should still entertain a vague appreciation of the skill and valor shown by their forebears a century ago.

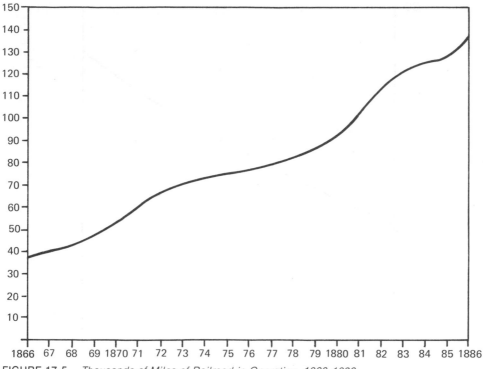

FIGURE 17-5. *Thousands of Miles of Railroad in Operation, 1866–1886*

The task of building railroads could probably not have been accomplished without the twice-blessed immigration from Europe from the Civil War to World War I. This matter will be discussed again in Chapter 19, but one consideration might enter here. Repeatedly these pages have asserted that the economic development of the United States was inevitable, given the psychology of the Europeans who emigrated plus the resources of their new environment. We must push this assertion further. Immigration from the Old World in the late nineteenth century constituted an immense annual subsidy to the growth of the New. In 1877 the population of the nation was 47 million; by 1893 it had grown by 20 million backs, 40 million hands (see Figure 17-6). In most years at least a third of the increase was immigrants. These newcomers were not a cross-section of their homelands, nor of their adopted country either. Year after year more than 60 per cent of the arrivals were male, more than two thirds were aged 15 to 40 (see Figure 21-3). The United States did not receive aged, infants, infirm. It got hearty workers who had been nurtured and educated for years at the expense of some other economy, and had then fled from their patrons to do the bidding of American employers. Socially and

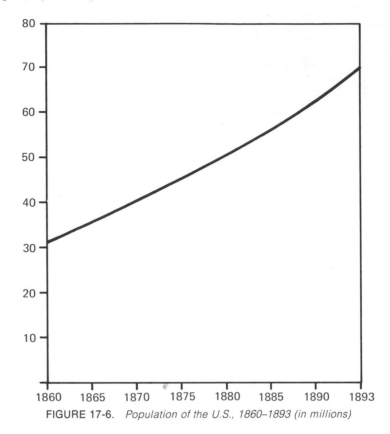

FIGURE 17-6. *Population of the U.S., 1860–1893 (in millions)*

psychologically there are handicaps in being a nation of fugitives, but as a formula for economic growth this pattern cannot be beaten.*

The matter should be stated carefully. Many economists have written as if the phrase "labor shortage" was simply meaningless. By this contention the ultimate reality that could be measured was relative levels of wages; if the hourly or daily rate was increased, the supply of workers would rise. But obviously this argument is silly if we want to consider specific skills; for example, no society early in the twentieth century had any supply of television repairmen, at any level of wages, and so at mid-century workers for the new electronics industries would be hard to find. We also know now by evidence from other cultures that any increase in the hourly wage may be followed by a reduction in the number of hours worked; many a laborer earns what he regards as a traditional day's wage and then goes fishing. Probably the most sweeping generalization that is valid is this: until about the Civil War, the

_____

*The gains are greater if your immigrants are above the average in education, as with West Germany since World War II.

chief impact of expensive labor in the United States was to stimulate the substitution of machinery for men, a so-called deepening of capital. Thereafter a cumulative change occurred in the comparative costs of labor and capital, with immigration driving down the value of labor, while massive expenditures in railroads and building construction drove the value of capital upward. This process encouraged a widening of capital; the new facilities being built were identical with the old in that the capital-labor ratio of inputs remained fairly fixed.

In fabricating the railroad net, it was not topography or climate or governmental obstacles or manpower shortages that was most likely to prove lethal; it was usually capital droughts and organizational defects. The business cycles in railroad building recorded above are attributable mainly to attitudes on Wall Street, on State Street (Boston), in the City (London), and in Hamburg and Amsterdam. The collapse of empires like Cooke's could turn the financial markets into dust bowls. New expansions could not be undertaken in panicky times like 1873–1878; the continuation of any construction at all was rather a febrile dance to gain some profit from investments already made. In retrospect, it is clear that most trans-Mississippi trunklines never had a chance to show a profit. There were exceptions. John Murray Forbes with his group based on the Burlington and James J. Hill with his Great Northern showed their genius in creating stable companies that helped to develop countless resources. Hill stated the core problem: You cannot make money hauling empties. The transport web of North America faced difficulties that did not confront the ones of Europe; it built into regions that had no people. Forbes' solution was to link cities: Chicago to Minneapolis, Chicago to Denver. Hill's solution was virtually to return to the technique of the American railroad promoters before the Civil War: to see his roadbed as a feeder into the Twin Cities and to push it forward foot by foot while he was toiling to aid farmers in the regions it serviced. But the exceptions were that. If we added together the interest and dividends paid by all American railroads, and subtracted from that all funds spent by citizens to buy bonds and stock, we almost surely would end with a negative figure. Why were investors so loony, not once, but over and over? Some railroad companies went into receivership a half dozen times, repeatedly writing down the book value of their "securities" (how is that for an ironical word?), not only in the United States, but in the "sophisticated" exchanges of Europe. The best answer now available to us points to the New World as incarnating the Myth of the Garden—an infinite market, beckoning from an idealized world of infinitely expanding frontiers for the rugged-individual family farmer (Chapters 14 and 15).

A major innovation of the railroads, then, was to raise unprecedented amounts of capital, and to tie much of it up in fixed costs (see Figure 17-1). But how could you put together an operation that could meet the claims against that capital, able to pay those fixed costs? Answers devised in other industries

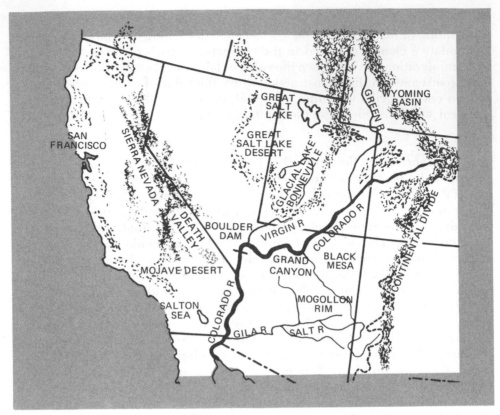

FIGURE 17-7. *The Colorado River System*

were not suitable for enterprises stretching over thousands of miles. Carnegie, for instance, had his producing facilities concentrated around Pittsburgh. He lived in New York where he got detailed reports often; he also made frequent visits to his factories. Seemingly only two of his ranking subordinates had exceptional talents. Standard Oil was at the other pole from this one-man rule. Certainly John D. Rockefeller was the first among equals, but he had a dozen partners who specialized in a phase of the business. An indication of their individual competence is that several of them went on to form their own empires that had nothing to do with petroleum (see mid-Chapter 21 on trusts and conglomerates). For one thing, the geographical sprawl of the company got to be immense, with the site of the oil fields leaping westward from Pennsylvania to the Lima fields in Ohio to the Spindletop well that inaugurated the Texas strikes in 1901. For another, the chief product of the organization was kerosene for lighting—goodbye to whale-oil lamps—and most of it was sold abroad (Document 20-1). Refineries migrated to the seaboard, and a distribution mechanism had to be maintained in Europe and China (Document 21-2). Standard Oil came to be run by a galaxy of committees. But in a significant respect it was not yet "modern"; by current standards its system of accounting must be labelled primitive. In the typical manufacturing firm, the managers still did their jobs by making on-the-spot inspections of the operation.

Even the railroads tried to preserve this principle. But a large system might be running thousands of miles of track. What to do? It was the railroads that pioneered in large-scale organization, and more specifically it was the Pennsylvania that first tried to tackle the problems systematically. One step was to divide the system into geographical divisions about 100 miles long. A superintendent was set over each. No employee could be given instructions by anybody except his immediate superior. Next an adequate breakdown of costs had to be achieved, in terms described by a railroad manager of the time:

> In the consideration of the subject of the cost of railroad transportation it is of the greatest importance to discriminate between the expenditures which vary with the amount of work performed and those which are entirely independent thereof. The latter form so large a proportion of the total operating expenses of railroads that it becomes impossible to make the *amount of work performed* a criterion or measure of the cost.

Thus emerged, but ever so gradually, such crucial ideas in accounting as the discrimination of fixed from variable costs, of capital budget from operating expenses (Figure 17-1). Further innovations in corporate organization and the correlate accounting will be examined in Chapter 21.

The myth of rags to riches has also been subjected to solid investigations. This problem has been studied from two perspectives: How far was the myth believed? How far was the myth an accurate rendition of reality? The answer to the first question is clear: Very far. Unless we are willing to believe that most people are fools, and I am not, the fact of its currency suggests that the desire to become a self-made man had considerable foundation in fact. But the research of the last twenty-five years shows that we should not exaggerate this substance. The poor lad from the farm was far less likely to make good than the middle-class boy in the city. One study took 190 corporate executives of 1900. When these men were born, about 1850, 83 per cent of all Americans lived in rural areas, but only 40 per cent of the executives were born and reared in that setting. Businessmen or professionals had been the parents of 86 per cent of the leaders of 1900. Nearly one of two in the general population had at least one foreign-born parent; among the sample, one in five. Four of every five business leaders were of British ancestry, and the majority were of old American families. Another survey treats only of the presidents of textile firms (note that this office was usually honorific, as the chief executive officer was normally the treasurer). The Civil War marks a rather sharp break. Before the conflict, if a man did not become president of a company by age 45, he was not likely to reach that goal at all. He was probably a rich Boston merchant who had diverted some of his capital into textile stocks, and the chances were that he stayed active in other forms of enterprise—in short, he was a general entrepreneur. For this industry at least, the postwar pattern was changed. Half of the presidents after the war did not gain that eminence until they had passed age 55. Often such men had inherited their fortunes. They were not smuggled into textiles from the general business community but had risen within the industry. Typically they had retired from active business concerns, and did not often take a hand in managing the firm over which they honorifically presided.

Many companies could ride favorably through stormy economic forces if they enjoyed crucial counterbalances in the struggle against the sagging level of prices. On the supply side, probably the two most important forces driving prices downward were the rapid advance of technology and the growing number of firms that competed fiercely. But on the demand side, consumers were present in growing numbers. More important, they not only had money but they were accessible because they were concentrated in cities as never before. Metropolises in the East grew rapidly: Manhattan from 1,911,692 in 1880 to more than 2.5 million in 1890; in the same decade Philadelphia from 847,170 to 1,046,964. But the real boom towns were in the Midwest:

	1880	1890
Chicago	503,125	1,099,850
Minneapolis	46,887	164,738
St. Paul	41,473	133,156
Kansas City	55,781	132,710
Denver	35,029	106,773

In ten years each of these cities except Chicago approximately tripled, while that metropolis doubled and would do so again by 1900.

We still do not have an adequate conceptualization of the processes involved in such headlong urban development. But we might hazard a few guesses, partly to illustrate how the Turner thesis—that the frontier experience has been the dominant theme in American history—does not limit its application solely to rural areas and farmers. What confronts us here is a phenomenon that has been aptly labelled "sequential growth." Many areas were opened long before a sturdy yeoman went near them, by a military post, by a mining venture, a lumber camp, a railroad junction point. A commercial-residential town appeared to sell goods and services to these first settlers. Then, and perhaps only then, farmers moved in to provision the town. Any new region offers quite a few opportunities for "one-for-all investment": roads and civic buildings, business centers, housing subdivisions. Opportunities are present for bankers and real-estate men, doctors and lawyers, scoundrels eager to dip to their elbows in any old public coffers. Land values might grow even more rapidly than population, and consequent profits can be reinvested in processing plants. This company builds a sawmill, that one a smelter; another begins to package oatmeal. Extension of job options will suck in more people. The sequence feeds on itself. Literally, a city reaches the stage when it grows because its inhabitants take in each other's washing. How do we identify that stage? Again, we do not yet know. For the late nineteenth century, my hunch whispers that about 50,000 people was the starting point for "take-off."

The expansion of demand was also spurred by what today's economists call the multiplier. Some students claim to have a hard time grasping the idea, but it is quite simple. Start from a government that spends money to buy goods and services (Government Expenditures, GE) or a company that buys new plant or equipment (purchases of second-hand goods do not count; Investment, I). These outlays will be income for others. They will spend in turn a portion of their increased receipts. So will the next round of recipients, and so on. Before these increments have flattended out to zero, the first I or GE will have been multiplied several times through a number of transactions. For the United States since World War II, a consensus holds that the multiplier has fluctuated around 3. This figure is probably valid for the late nineteenth century also. To comprehend how this statement can be made, an additional consideration must be introduced. Statisticians define Savings (S) simply: if you take Income (Y) and subtract from it the portion spent in the current time period for consumer goods and services (C), the balance is S (note that if your grandfather leaves a bequest that you put in your savings account, this is not a saving of personal income over consumer expenses, and so you have not committed S). It seems reasonable to assume that as income is distributed more equally, C will increase and S will decrease: poor people do not save as high a proportion of their income as do rich people. The best available studies conclude that in the United States, the distribution of personal incomes after taxes has not changed much if at all in the last fifty years. Maybe this ratio cannot be projected backwards in time indefinitely, but the proposition remains to be proved, and it is likely that the raw materials do not exist to reach a conclusive answer—ever. We can say this: in dollar terms, even the spending for railroad extension was less than that for construction of buildings. As these initial payments worked through the economy, their impact multiplied.

What is vital here is to grasp for a hold on the interaction of these processes, one with another. Manufacturers, for instance, would have been in a tighter vise without the rapid multiplication of urban buyers. So would farmers: the 10,000 acre bonanza farms growing wheat in the Dakotas would have made no sense whatever in an economy of self-sufficient yeomen (Figure 29-3). Each of these segments was affected in a contradictory way by the inauguration of a national railway network. The fall in transportation costs enabled an industrialist to reach out farther for more customers; it also exposed him to new competitors from distant locations. A Texas planter could specialize in cotton, at great economies of scale, but he also had to fight in the markets of the world against cotton from several other countries.

419

It remains to look at some effects of these developments on employees, especially industrial workers. Again, a couple of preliminary generalizations seem advisable. Although some solid investigations have been made, particularly since World War II, the study of the history of American laborers has been rather wretched. Basic difficulties stem from the influence of the so-called Wisconsin School, at the state University there. Some of their work is still useful; no scholar in the field can ignore the ten-volume *Documentary History of American Industrial Society* (1910–1911), but their efforts to theorize were deplorable. First, they concentrated on the history of trade unions, even though the significant question about American labor until the last forty years is the reverse: Why were so few unions organized? Then too, though substantial impediments lay in the path of industrialists' desires, they wrote of fifty years as if they were an unrestricted "age of the employers." In this milieu, they argued, the watchwords of the unions were three: More. Here. Now. They contended that this "business unionism" with its narrow focus on higher wages and shorter hours and job security was the ultimate in wisdom; never think of tomorrow, only of today. In plain truth, such business unionism before World War II had nothing to offer to the great majority of employees.

It is true that in times of crisis, capitalists could sometimes invoke the overpowering force of some government. We might begin with a famous episode—the Haymarket bombing in Chicago, because it was both sensational at the moment and also had repercussions that resounded for decades. The city, as the railroad hub of the nation, was also a booming industrial center. Its magnates tended to be hard-nosed; its laboring elements had a vociferous anarchist wing. Labor relations were tense and often approached violence. In 1886 a lockout occurred at the huge McCormick Harvesting Machine (reapers) factory. It reopened with new, non-union labor. Former employees continued to picket the gates. A widespread movement was trying to win an eight-hour day and had set May Day as the deadline for enforcement of the demand; it was estimated that one of every eight residents of Chicago was participating in the campaign. At the McCormick plant on May 3 a riot started. Police came. Two men were killed. A meeting to protest the police action was called to assemble at a square near downtown, the Haymarket. Affairs were peaceable. But nearly 200 police marched up in serried ranks. Somebody tossed a bomb among them. The police then fired into the crowd. Of the officers, the bomb killed seven, wounded 67. The toll among the audience is not known. Subtle discriminations are not made in times of panic. A police dragnet hauled in every anarchist to be found, plus many who were quite innocent. Eight men were brought to trial for the bombing. All were convicted. One committed suicide in his cell. Four were hanged. Three were imprisoned, and of them I shall tell more later (early Chapter 20 on Governor Altgeld).

This stark recital of a noisy and tragic episode should not obscure the fact that urban workers were not being ruthlessly crushed by some juggernaut of capitalists allied with governments. Laborers had their defenses, ways of fighting back. Also they had ways of evening the score; probably the most important of these was theft. Doubtless many employees at all times and places have stolen from the boss. This topic so far as I know has not been systematically studied, but there are many areas where it could be. We find numerous instances in the putting-out system of eighteenth-century Britain; slaves indulged in it; a famous book told of *White Collar Crime* in the United States (How was anybody ever so naive as to think that you are more likely to steal if you have a black face, or a blue collar?); soldiers have always thought that public property was fair game; the incentive to pilfer becomes more intense when a small electronics part can be sold in the black market for hundreds of dollars; in two major cities a ring of police has been caught with a warehouse filled with television sets.

Workers had more public weapons. The researches of Herbert Gutman have revealed their variety, especially in smaller industrial or mining towns. A case study is presented by Paterson, New Jersey. In 1877, after four gruelling years of depression, the silk-ribbon mills announced a 20 percent wage cut and other irritating stipulations. This brought the largest strike in the record of the town; 2,000 workers shut down the plants. The local Board of Trade, controlled by the biggest owners, screamed that "the laws of the land are treated with contempt and trampled upon by a despotic mob." One employer offered to pay for a private militia; another proclaimed that the strike leaders should be "taken out and shot." This bluster availed little. Shopkeepers gave credit to strikers and raised funds for them. While the newspapers were critical of the strikers also, they urged the employers to use "conscience as well as capital." With this tone in the community, public officials did not yield to the demands of the owners. The mayor with exemplary discretion used his police force only to prevent open violence. He owned a small spindle factory himself, and headed a local bank. The aldermen were skilled craftsmen, professionals, retailers, no workers or big owners. Even though they were mostly Democrats while the mayor was a Republican, they commended his "wise and judicious course." Similarly local courts stalled in deciding cases brought against strikers. After the shutdown had lasted for ten weeks, it was settled by a compromise in which the companies rescinded the wage reduction. Likewise in many other towns, owners could not always have their own way.

Especially fortunate workers did not even need to form a trade union in order to find a hothouse within which they could grow. Let us take as an example again the McCormick works in Chicago. Save for a brief period when the Knights of Labor penetrated its walls, the only organization was among the molders who were a mere 10 per cent of the labor force. This small band with a developed skill won repeated advances in their conditions. Remarkedly, these gains spread to the less skilled, unorganized employees. Just before the Haymarket episode the molders' union was destroyed in a strike, and the craftsmen were replaced by common labor using automatic molding machines. But the wages of unskilled employees did not fall; just the contrary. Their hourly rate remained at 15 cents while the cost of living declined. Real wages in 1896 for this group were more than double what they had been in 1860. Two influences seem to explain this notable result: The firm's executives feared that pay cuts might bring a return of unions. Perhaps more vital were the attitudes of the founder's widow, who held a major interest in the company. She feared that an earlier series of violent strikes had harmed her family's "good name" in the community; she wanted no more. Her pressure was frequently toward peace.

The above case studies should be taken as indications that local conditions could vary greatly. But they must be seen as qualifications. The generalization is simple: The late nineteenth century knew an enormous disparity in bargaining power. Speaking of collective disputes as a genus, employers nearly always had the upper hand, a topic to which we will return in Chapters 20 and 23. Even the gradations we have outlined show only that employees could often neutralize the power of the state; almost never could they use it to serve their own ends.

Nor should the relation of molders to semiskilled at the McCormick factory be understood as typical. In the sphere of labor history that I have studied the most closely—the railroad brotherhoods—the companies consistently pinched back from the pay envelopes of the less skilled what they had previously bestowed on the "aristocrats of labor." This label was applied to the locomotive engineers, who in many junction points strutted about with their gold chains across their serge vests, ranking with the banker and the lawyer and the doctor as the leading citizens in town.* At the other pole, the switchmen and the gandy dancers often did not earn enough to maintain their families in decency. Another useful insight into the railroad brotherhoods is to remember that they did not begin as collective-bargaining agents at all; they originated as fraternal and burial societies. They are classic instances of associations that originated for certain purposes and later were diverted to another function altogether. An analogy will be seen in the Patrons of Husbandry, commonly called the Grangers (see Chapter 20). Burial societies were likewise common in black neighborhoods: if a person cannot live with dignity, he should get some when he dies.

By this devious route we return to the central if usually ignored question raised above: Why were so few unions organized? (Dissenters can wave airily at the brotherhoods and the cigarmakers and the carpenters, but the staggering truth remains.) The core of the answer is surely that ancient cliché: the opportunities of American life. Most men, given a plausible chance to make good on their own, see no reason to make personal sacrifices in a common

---

*The shortage of many skills coupled with the new superabundance of unskilled workers brought immense differences in pay. At the Homestead works, the typical laborer got at most $1.50 a day, a puddler got $17. I do not mean to denigrate either the skill of or the health hazards to puddlers—in Sheffield, England, they could expect to die by age 31, and the life expectancy in the United States was probably little better—but common laborers also were working in a hazardous industry.

cause. They will go it alone, as individuals; they downright refuse to unite, and no amount of rhetoric matters.

These considerations bring us to a seeming conundrum: Why has it so often been the skilled workers who have taken the lead in organizing trade unions? I think this enigma can be dissolved. Many commentators have been misled by their attachment to the phrase "occupational ladder." By and large, this metaphor is false; a happier term would be "occupational tree." Just as it is nearly impossible to move from noncommissioned to commissioned rank in the army, so was it nearly impossible to move from a blue-collar to a managerial job. Imagine a tree with the branches inclined upward from the trunk; call the lowest branch I, the next highest II, etc. On each branch call the lowest job (nearest the trunk) A, the next highest B, etc. Promotion along any branch is largely automatic and depends on seniority (unless you grossly offend your superiors). But to move from I-Z to II-A is a dreadful task; you will probably need a patron on branch II to drop a rope and pull you up. How does this schema apply to the formation of trade unions? The workers at point Z are the most skilled workers on that limb. They can no longer hope to advance as individuals; they expect to live out their lives at point Z, and none will get ahead unless point Z moves upward. So they form a craft union, which is concerned solely with the position of point Z. They do not aim to lift the entire branch, but only to tilt its end upward. This may force the rest of the branch downward; sometimes, however, (see Chapters 20, 26), skilled workers may make common cause with unskilled to improve working conditions in a whole industry.

Although the impact of the Civil War on the South was in time moderated, the four years of battle had lasting consequences in the North that can fairly be called revolutionary. The inflated prices of wartime, added to the swelling market for foodstuffs, uniforms, and munitions represented by the Union military purchases, resulted in giant pools of liquid capital. These funds could be multiplied further by the growing number of commercial banks. Aggressive capitalists, with their enlarged resources, were not long to push railroads across the Mississippi and over the plains to the Pacific. While bankers supplied the funds for these ventures, new iron and steel mills produced the rails and locomotives and freight cars. Other entrepreneurs seized on the discovery of petroleum to start refineries for producing kerosene for lamps. As for tobacco, whiskey, wheat, sugar—processors of these farm products reached toward monopoly and gained huge profits. But the men who grew those raw materials, the farmers, were the most numerous group of victims of the total process. Prices of agricultural crops, especially the great staples of wheat and cotton, fell steadily from 1865 to 1896. Many farmers were ground down against the anvil of their fixed debts. The squeeze was aggravated by the monetary and banking policies of the federal government.

Business interests were the guiding force in the national capital, in state governments, at city halls. This interlacing of commerce with politics was particularly glaring during some of the violent labor strikes that rocked the period. In response, trade unions in many industries were likely to begin with the most skilled craft. It would hardly exaggerate to say that capitalists, including thousands of small owners, got ahead rapidly at the expense of other segments of the society.

SOME NOTABLE EVENTS

1864 George M. Pullman builds first sleeping car for railroads.

1865 Union Stockyards in Chicago open, Dec. 25.

1866 National Labor Union organized, Aug. 20.

1868 George Westinghouse patents air brake for railroads.

1869 First transcontinental railroad: Union Pacific and Central Pacific connect near Ogden, Utah, May 10.
Black Friday on New York Stock Exchange, Sept. 24.

1870 Standard Oil founded, Jan. 10.

1871 Chicago fire causes losses estimated at $196 million.

1873 Slaughterhouse Cases.
Jay Cooke & Company closes, Sept. 1 (Document 17-2).

1874 National Grange issues Declaration of Purpose, Feb. 4.

1875 Resumption of specie payments, Jan. 14; (see mid-Chapter 18).
Bessemer steel making at Pittsburgh initiated by Andrew Carnegie.

1876 Telephone patented by Alexander Graham Bell.
Munn v. *Illinois* asserts state power to regulate railroads for the public interest.

1877 Railroad strikes paralyze area from Baltimore to St. Louis.

1878 Knights of Labor adopt constitution.
F. W. Woolworth opens his first successful 5 & 10.
Bland-Allison Act, Feb. 28; vetoed by Hayes.

1880 U.S. census: 50,155,783 (28.2% urban).
Incandescent light patented by Thomas Alva Edison.

1886 Haymarket Square riots in Chicago.
American Federation of Labor is founded.

1887 Daimler develops first functioning automobile.

1890 Ocala Demands of the farmers' protest movements, December.

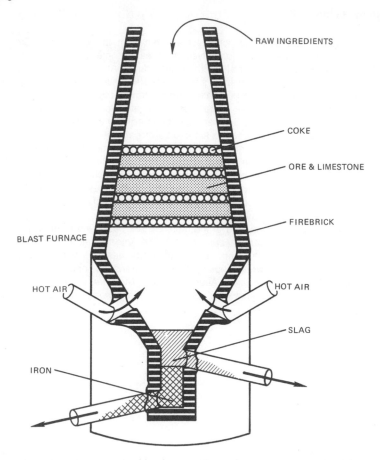

RAW INGREDIENTS

COKE

ORE & LIMESTONE

FIREBRICK

BLAST FURNACE

HOT AIR   HOT AIR

SLAG

IRON

To make steel it is necessary first to convert iron ore to solid, or pig, iron. This is done in the blast furnace. Iron ore, limestone, and coke (a coal product, almost pure carbon) are placed in the furnace, and a blast of hot compressed air is forced through the mixture. This ignites the coke. The heat then melts the iron which slowly trickles down to the bottom of the furnace. But iron ore is not pure iron; it is necessary to rid it of foreign matter. The hot furnace does this by burning the impurities, and forcing them to unite with the oxygen in the compressed air. They thus become oxides, which are lighter than the molten iron, and float on top of it in the form of slag. The slag is skimmed off, to be used for a number of purposes, before the iron is discharged from the bottom of the furnace. The whole process takes from three to six hours, and a modern furnace will produce 500–1200 tons of pig iron and 200–500 tons of slag each day.

Pig iron has a 3–4 per cent content of carbon, which makes it brittle and inflexible. Steel-making is the process of removing this carbon, as well as certain other impurities, most commonly sulphur and phosphorus. In the open hearth furnace, a mixture of gas and air is forced over the pig iron and burned. At a temperature of 1800° C the iron will melt, and the carbon will "burn." When a substance "burns" it combines with oxygen, and becomes an oxide; oxides of the impurities found in pig iron are light, and will float on the iron, which has now become steel. They can then be skimmed off, just as the slag was skimmed off the pig iron, before the steel is discharged from the furnace.

Ways to Study History XVII

Trace a family. Quite apart from the schools that stem from the theories of Sigmund Freud, psychologists for decades have sought to analyze child-rearing, interplay of heredity with environment, effective modes of schooling, social control of individuals. At the other extreme of the range of levels of abstraction, genealogists have spent a zillion years trying to prove that a certain person had seventeen eminent ancestors. Although the latter approach might have its occasional uses, nearly always it is just antiquarianism or, worse, pride. Most efforts at melodramatic psychohistory, such as a recent biography of Senator Charles Sumner, have been equally childish.

But solid reasons exist for pondering the course of generations. In perusing the economic history of North America, I think of a good friend of mine. His grandfather was a Canadian farmer north of Toronto. His father left home at 15 and went to Providence, Rhode Island, where he took work as a machinist. When the automobile boom started he was prepared; he became president of a parts plant. My friend went to a progressive college, then shifted to a business education in graduate school. After founding a successful company he became chairman of the Management Department of a large state university. His daughter is a pure intellectual.

Similar patterns can be uncovered in the more distant past. One of my favorite books was edited by F. O. Matthiessen, *The James Family* (1947). The American founder was a poor boy who became one of the richest men in the land: fast freight companies, railroads, land speculation; the son made no money whatever and wrote religious tracts; two grandsons became a great psychologist and a great novelist. To me another gem is Aubrey C. Land, *The Dulanys of Maryland* (1955), which does as much as a book could do to show how political power and wealth were used to escalate each other in colonial America.

Document 17-1

About a decade after the war ended, a growing number of blacks emigrated from the Deep South to such states as Kansas. Frederick Douglass, while asserting the full right of Negroes to live wherever they chose, in 1879 questioned some qualities of this movement.

It does not appear that the friends of freedom should spend either time or talent in furtherance of this exodus as a desirable measure, either for the North or the South. If the people of this country cannot be protected in every state of the Union, the government of the United States is shorn of its rightful dignity and power, the late rebellion has triumphed, the sovereignty of the nation is an empty name, and the power and authority in individual states is greater than the power and authority of the United States. . . .

The colored people of the South, just beginning to accumulate a little property, and to lay the foundation of family, should not be in haste to sell that little and be off to the banks of the Mississippi. The habit of roaming from place to place in pursuit of better conditions of existence is never a good one. A man should never leave his home for a new one till he has earnestly endeavored to make his immediate surroundings accord with his wishes. The time and energy expended in wandering from place to place, if employed in making him a comfortable home where he is, will, in nine cases out of ten, prove the best investment. No people ever did much for themselves or for the world without the sense and inspiration of native land, of a fixed home, of familiar neighborhood, and common associations. The fact of being to the manor born has an elevating power upon the mind and heart of a man. It is a more cheerful thing to be able to say, I was born here and know all the people, than to say, I am a stranger here and know none of the people.

It cannot be doubted that, in so far as this exodus tends to promote restlessness in the colored people of the South, to unsettle their feeling of home, and to sacrifice positive advantages where they are or fancied ones in Kansas or elsewhere, it is an evil. . . .

Document 17-2

As the Civil War financier Jay Cooke learned to his detriment, it was perilous to allow your personal fortune to become entangled in the financing of a railroad. The winning gambit was to use somebody else's money, whether federal funds that you borrowed or grants given outright by a local government or receipts from selling bonds to outside investors. This description was given in a speech in San Francisco as early as 1873.

For many years it has not been the American fashion for the owners of railroads to put their own money into their construction. If it had been it would have insured a more conservative and businesslike use of that species of property. The favorite plan has been to get grants of land, and loans of credit from the General Government; guarantees of interest from the State governments; subscriptions and donations from counties, cities and individuals; and upon the credit of all this, issue all bonds that can be put upon the market; make a close estimate as to how much less the road can be built for than the sum of these assets; form a ring . . . for the purpose of constructing the road, dividing the bonds that are left; owning the lands, owning and operating the road until the first mortgage becomes due and graciously allowing the Government to pay principal and interest upon the loan of her credit, while "every tie in the road is the grave of a small stockholder." Under this plan the only men in the community who are absolutely certain not to contribute any money are those who own and control it when it is finished. The method requires a certain kind of genius, political influence, and power of manipulation, and furnished one clew to the reason why railroads "interfere in politics." The personal profit upon this enterprise is not a profit upon capital investment, but the result of brain work—administrative talent they call it—in a particular direction.

Document 17-3

This payroll from the carding room of a cotton mill in Holyoke, Massachusetts, is interesting in several respects. The list of names (portions omitted) shows that the so-called New Immigration from southern and eastern Europe had begun to flood New England towns by 1889, the date of the ledger, that supervisory personnel and craftsmen were commonly of northern European stock, that a large discrepancy existed between pay of skilled and unskilled. All employees worked ten hours a day; most earned less than a dime an hour. This is considerably below the earnings of the average worker in the nation's industries, who is reported to have gotten $486 in 1890.

Names	Total Hours	Price	Amounts
Overseer			
J. W. Doran	*60*	*40*	*24.00*
		. . .	
Grinders			
J. Danforth	*60*	*15*	*9.00*
G. Meinay	*60*	*15*	*9.00*
J. Manning	*60*	*15*	*9.00*
F. Downie	*60*	*15*	*9.00*
M. Morrison	*60*	*15*	*9.00*
Geo Pray	*60*	*15*	*9.00*

Names	Total Hours	Price	Amounts
Railways and Drawing			
J. Laternak	60	7	4.20
P. Yourka	60	8	4.80
J. Lapoint	60	7	4.20
A. Garcoa	60	7	4.20
M. Wodjikoski	60	7	4.20
N. Ash	60	7	4.20
D. Chomerni	60	7	4.20

Document 17-4

Modern retailing took its origins in the decades after the Civil War. The spate of goods emerging from farm and factory was screaming to be sold, with the result that new institutions were devised. Urbanites got the department store, Macy's in New York and Marshall Field in Chicago. Rustics got mail-order merchandising as symbolized by the Sears Roebuck catalog. Indispensable to these drives was advertising. Earlier merchants had posted simple notices in the newspapers, but they had not known the hard-sell except by word of mouth. Now it appeared in print, and spearheading the innovation were patent-medicine producers. This ad is a manifestation of do-it-yourself, the American way. It also reveals a lack of historical knowledge among those who speak of the "new" drug usage.

ERRORS OF YOUTH

Sufferers from
Nervous Debility,
Youthful Indiscretions,
Lost Manhood,

BE YOUR OWN PHYSICIAN

. . . Perfectly pure ingredients must be used.

Cocain (from Erythroxlon coca) 1 drachm.
Jerubebin 1-2 drachm.
Hypophosphite quinia, 1-2 drachm.
Geisemin, 8 grains
Ext. igratiac amarac (alcoholic), 2 grains
Ext. Septandra, 2 scruples
Glycerin, q.s.
    Mix

. . . by remitting us $3 in post office money order, or registered letter, a securely sealed package in its pure state will be sent by return mail from our private laboratory. . . .

The Politics and Foreign Relations of a World Power

Half of this chapter will state some reasons for regarding the United States already by 1850 as a world power. But the point in contention might well be exposed here, before we observe the jousts between the national parties. The argument that economic self-interest had little to do with American policy abroad in the waning years of the century has usually had a corollary: that suddenly in 1898, as from the brow of Jove, the United States appeared on a global stage as a lusty infant. Indeed, a recent book with the subtitle *The Emergence of America as a Great Power* advances just this theme. It would be hard to miss the mark by more. Allowing for personal preferences in terminology, the argument below will resemble that given above opening Chapter 9. The United States was a recognized power as soon as it voted for independence on 2 July, 1776. (How can anybody doubt it who has read the correspondence of Vergennes at the time?) It was a world power by the Oregon Treaty of 1846. Only a great power could have forced France out of Mexico at a time when the United States had just finished the Civil War. In the years from

1850 to 1892 the United States had a confrontation on alien shores with every other strong nation in the world—and never came off second-best.

Without much distortion, federal politics in the postwar era could be summarized in one word: stalemate. However, the topic needs more explication than one word. The quadrennial (mock?) battles between the national parties were not all of politics. An informed study of politics at the state level in New York shows that the issues that swayed voters were not those great problems of monetary policy or the tariff or anti-monopoly. They were purification of elections and the stifling of alcoholic beverages (see Document 17-4). Most jurisdictions before about 1890 had no secret vote (the Australian ballot); the polls were still conducted by openly declaring your choices. The virtuous Protestant citizens, and for once they were right, thought this procedure abetted corruption. They also thought that liquor was evil. The extremists wanted prohibition; that is, illegalization of all alcoholic drink. Way back in 1851 Maine had taken the lead in banning the sale of liquor; twelve states did the same in the next four years. This mania for sanctifying your neighbors swept the nation. But to a great degree it was sham. As hooch was suppressed, patent medicines thrived, and some were highly alcoholic. One nostrum vender was informed by the Commissioner of Internal Revenue in 1883: ". . . to draw the line nicely, and fix definitely where the medicine may end and the alcoholic beverage begin, is a task which has often perplexed and still greatly perplexes revenue officers, and especially where a preparation contains so large a proportion of alcohol as yours does." One especially popular brew, Peruna, was 28 per cent alcohol; at least one Peruna alcoholic was reported to be a respected member of the Women's Christian Temperance Union. As one aspect of their high-powered merchandising, manufacturers put their swill in ornate bottles; you could drink out of a bust of George Washington or a log cabin or an Indian maid. Few of these bottles remain; one researcher speculates that people destroyed them so that they could buy new, full, replacements without having their neighbors see the incriminating relics. On such foolishness as this did the fate of office-seekers depend.

The emergence of new, often local or regional, issues caused a fragmentation of national politics that seemed as severe as that which preceded the Civil War. The Prohibition (of liquor) party put forward a presidential candidate for the first time in 1872. Four years later the Greenback party had its maiden run for the office. Greenbackers were often farmers, and in the Old Northwest they often belonged to the Patrons of Husbandry. One consequence was the so-called Granger laws, enacted by states to set maximum prices that could be charged by such companies as railroads and grain elevators. The fracas brought one major and enduring benefit: it produced a decision by the United States Supreme Court as incisive as any that tribunal has ever handed down. A recurrent problem in American history has been to fix the role of the federal judiciary in the national polity. That question was faced squarely by Chief Justice Morrison R. Waite in *Munn v. Illinois* (1876). His opinion has been crystallized in a phrase—judicial restraint. At issue was a statute that placed a ceiling on rates levied by grain elevators. One firm protested that the regulation took away its property without due process of law and thus violated the Fourteenth Amendment. The Chief Justice replied in quiet and unpretentious terms:

> . . . When one becomes a member of society, he necessarily parts with some rights or privileges which, as an individual not affected by his relations to others, he might retain. . . .
> Common carriers exercise a sort of public office, and have duties to perform in which the public is interested. . . . Enough has already been said to show that, when private property is devoted to a public use, it is subject to public regulation. . . .
> We know that this is a power which may be abused; but that is no argument against its existence. For protection against abuses by legislatures the people must resort to the polls, not to the courts. . . .

Bravo! But, at the time, inspirations were few, tensions were many.

Every area had its localized causes of unrest. Southern whites had to grapple with the failure of their lost cause, their war for sectional independence, their struggle to sustain slavery and injustice. The effort, not easy, has not ended; as a boy in Memphis I was nurtured on horror stories of Sherman's soldiers stealing chickens and ripping up featherbeds (Why so many decades of preoccupation with cheap cotton ticking?). A fine essay that tries to differentiate "the Southern character" from that of other white Americans gives four differentiae. Of the four, two originated with the Civil War. One is a visceral sense of what it feels like to be poor; prior to the conflict, a typical Southron was not impoverished below his counterpart in the North. Another was personal knowledge of what it means to lose a war.* In addition to the economic and social and psychological strains of the postwar years, secessionists had to put up with legal stresses. Thousands were forced to endure oaths of loyalty to the United States. They had to meet the accusation that the Confederacy was a bastard, illegitimate from its conception. This matter became explicit in the highest court, *Texas* v. *White* (1869). During the war the state government had owned some federal bonds. It sold them to raise funds to pay for Confederate supplies. After the war, the Reconstruction government brought suit against the buyers on the grounds that the secessionist government was not sanctioned and the sale had been therefore illegal. The Chief Justice agreed, pointing out that as rebels during the war, Texans had claimed no interest to participate in Washington's Congress, nor in its courts. In his words: "All admit that, during this condition of civil war, the rights of

---

*It is trite, but important, to mention that several million Americans in all reaches of the land have had some insight into the meaning of being conquered. Some forms of education are much more costly than others.

431

the State as a member, and of her people as citizens of the Union, were suspended. The government and the citizens of the State, refusing to recognize their constitutional obligations, assumed the character of enemies, and incurred the consequences of rebellion." Here is the authoritative doctrine on secession. The wartime regime in Texas had no legal authority to sell the bonds or to do any act whatever; it had no constitutional validity.

Southern blacks also had legal problems. The Civil Rights Act of 1875 had seemed to prohibit inns, public conveyances, and places of public amusement from discriminating against Negroes. Some believed that the law meant what it seemed to say. But when the issue emerged from the Supreme Court, the decision was that the Thirteenth Amendment had dealt exclusively with slavery: "Mere discriminations on account of race or color were not regarded as badges of slavery." As to the Fourteenth Amendment, it merely banned "state action of a particular character. . . . Individual invasion of individual rights is not the subject-matter of the amendment." The sole dissenter from this sophistry came from Kentucky, Justice John Marshall Harlan, who will merit further mention below (Chapter 29). He expostulated that the ruling rested "on grounds entirely too narrow and artificial." *Munn* v. *Illinois* had determined that institutions charged with a public function were subject to public regulation. Congress had, legitimately, imposed rules.

> The supreme law of the land has decreed that no authority shall be exercised in this country upon the basis of discrimination, in respect of civil rights, against freemen and citizens because of their race, color or previous condition of servitude. To that decree—for the due enforcement of which, by appropriate legislation, Congress has been invested with express power—every one must bow, whatever may have been, or whatever now are, his individual views as to the wisdom or policy, either of the recent changes in the fundamental law, or of the legislation which has been enacted to give them effect.

Or take another regional manifestation of prejudice. On the Pacific slope, the worst explosions were against Chinese immigrants. But before going forward, it may be best to retrace some steps. A theory of prejudice has already been advanced in foregoing chapters with the argument that nearly everybody fears an alien whom he perceives as different from himself in ways that are, to him, significant. To a white, some peculiarities of a Chinese were as immediately obvious as the distinctions of the Negro. Probably in his hostility to Asians, the typical Easterner was just as bad as the Westerners. But since few Chinese ever got to the East, the tension can properly be regarded as sectional. Like some other American racial prejudices, it also was tinged with class antagonism through labor competition. For some years after the Civil War, the federal government legalized the importation of labor on contract. The result was an anachronism—indentured workers a century after their day was done. For the nation as a whole, this measure had little effect. But under its provisions, Chinese were brought into the Far West, in gangs, virtually in bound servitude. By about 1880, at least one fifth of the wage earners in California were Chinese. And in plain fact, they did work for less pay than whites. In addition to this rational grievance, true-born Americans had irrational ones; during the long depression after 1873 they were unemployed, idle, desperate, anxious to find somebody they could kick in the ribs. One book explores the complexities of this ethnic encounter, with concentrated regard to the white trade unions of California. As the author points out, the Europeans transplanted to the New World have been confronted by three nonwhite groups: the aboriginal Indians, the conscripted blacks, and Asians. The record of those who deemed themselves civilized was, to speak kindly, nauseating.

> Central to each transaction has been a totally one-sided preponderance of power, exerted for the exploitation of nonwhites by the dominant white society. In each case (but especially in the two that began with systems of enforced labor), white workingmen have played a crucial, yet ambivalent, role. They have been both exploited and exploiters. On the one hand, thrown into competition with nonwhites as enslaved or "cheap" labor, they suffered economically; on the other hand, they benefited [through relatively higher status] by that very exploitation which was compelling the nonwhites to work for low wages or for nothing. Ideologically they were drawn in opposite directions. Racial identification cut at right angles to class consciousness.

The clash against most of the Indian cultures was more acute yet, and the resulting oppression was more horrendous (Document 18-3). But we today must try to confront this situation honestly; what would we have done? Without implying anything about "progress," about advanced or retrograde societies, it must be said that many tribes were still in the Stone Age; they were hunting and fishing societies or migratory agriculturalists. Even now many whites who are generally decent in their outlook find it hard to understand that some Indians want to be fundamentally different and resent the notion that white mannerisms are superior—if indeed they are. Among the Saks and Fox in Iowa, for instance, conventional modes of education are a failure; when children are called on in class, they stolidly refuse to compete with each other. In spite of such evidence, the federal government in Canada is trying to wipe out the treaty rights of Indians. Its justification is that Indians should be treated just like everybody else; they say they want to end discrimination. And in the United States, public policy can be worse than hypocritical, it can be genocidal (Document 18-3).

Social tensions were aggravated by the faultlines in the economy. As an example, we might return to a theme that has recurred often in these chapters—the medium of exchange; that is, money and banking. The subject really is not particularly complicated, but many persons simply turn off their minds when they hear "foreign exchange rates." They need not. The situation

FIGURE 18-1. *Cartoons and the American Character*

One of the brightest channels into the study of American history is lit by the cartoonists. Perhaps the United States has not produced an individual who could rank with Honore Daumier, but it has had several draftsman who provide illumination along with their wit. This is especially true in political and diplomatic history. Counting by generation, the country has held Art Young, Bill Mauldin, Herblock, Jules Feiffer.

Other spheres of interest have attracted genius. Who can forget the gibes at national character or the rakish displays of whimsy printed in *The New Yorker*? A more sardonic tone has typified the cartoons on economic and social questions—and in general they have taken the side of the underdog, striking out at the Establishment. But the downtrodden have taken their share of the abuse. This visual attack against Chinese immigrants appeared in *The San Francisco Illustrated Wasp*, 8 a century ago was similar to the one that developed after President Nixon announced in August, 1971, that a fixed amount of gold would no longer be paid for any dollar in United States paper money. At the beginning of 1873 the Treasury would redeem existing greenbacks in either gold or silver. Then came the "Crime of '73," when Congress dropped all silver coins from the emissions by the mint. Until this time a dollar could be exchanged for 412.5 grains of silver, 90 per cent pure. Now the value of silver was no longer guaranteed by the federal government. The legal (at the Treasury) ratio of gold to silver had been 1:16; now the value of the baser metal fell. By 1876 a dollar's worth of silver would buy only 90 cents' worth of gold. In technical terms, there was a premium on gold for international transactions, but the ramifications run farther. Suppose that a British exporter made a sale in the United States. He might be paid in American greenbacks. He would then use the paper money to buy gold, and ship the gold to England where he would spend it to buy pounds sterling. But because he had to pay a premium in New York to buy the gold, his income in British funds was lessened. These disparities functioned as a supplementary tariff, just as an increase in American continental freight rates would have done. Thus, for much of manufacturing, the monetary fluctuations of the times had a mixed effect: reduced prices for their goods on one hand; elevated tariffs on the other. But too much should not be made of the tariff influence. For industrialists by and large, the trend that overwhelmed all others was falling costs of production coupled with vanishing receipts per unit through reduced prices. Some years ago I wrote a book about this era entitled *Age of Excess*; now I will label it the era of cheap wares, with the proviso that many of the cheapies were also goodies. The quality of goods in general clearly did not decline, and countless Americans became the first people ever to enjoy so elegant a variety of consumables.

This phenomenon leads us partway toward unravelling an apparent tangle. Several social and economic grumbles have been recounted, but in the political sphere, the historian of a republic such as the United States ordinarily would expect that its more able citizens will enter national politics. But, until 1890, they did not. It is hard to imagine a less potent bunch than the presidents of that period. To validate this statement, an easy battery of tests can be run.

December, 1877. A fine study by Alexander Saxton, *The Indispensable Immigrant: Labor and the Anti-Chinese Movement in California* (1971) reminds us that agitation against Asians was a continuation of a racist impulse that had existed in America from its origins. Saxton also underscores the most extreme form of that racism. Having stated that Easterners carried the cancer to California with them, he states:

Their responses were largely shaped by previous responses to Indians, to immigrants, and especially to Negroes and Negro slaves. The numerous expulsions of Chinese from mine camps and the anti-Chinese ordinances written into the codes of local mining districts duplicated actions already taken against blacks.

For example, the Center for American Civilization, Brandeis University, had a gallery of the nation's chief executives. Most of the early ones there have a lean and hungry look, although John Adams, Andrew Johnson, and Grant had some tendency to be portly. But they were nothing like the mast-fed 300-pounders who succeeded them. But looking at more objective evidence in *The Congressional Record,* we learn that almost no laws of consequence were enacted for a decade after 1877. This conclusion will not be universally conceded. Some historians have eulogized Cleveland and Theodore Roosevelt as "virile Anglo-Saxons," whatever that might mean; others have written of the Civil Service Act of 1883 as a milestone on the road to human liberty. The two presidents will be discussed below; the statute needs a brusque rebuttal. It is certainly true that unleashed ferocity of a public official against his subordinates should be put in harness, but the measure in question had another effect in giving all the lesser bureaucrats the power to stamp on the faces of ordinary citizens. Nor did the evil end there. In specific school districts in several cities, employment of a teacher continued to be open to covert bribery, and the post of court probate officer in New York County is much coveted; it is not always raffled at a low price. But the ordinary customs officer probably was no longer subject to a party excise under the Civil Service Act. Since the political machines could no longer tax their placemen, they had to raise campaign funds by other methods. The obvious resource was the fat cats. Can't you hear a senator, aspiring to the presidency, implying to a businessman: "I will introduce a bill that would save you $3,000,000 in taxes next year, if you will contribute liberally to my race for re-election."

To date, so far as I know, satisfactory hypotheses that might apply to American political history in all periods do not exist. Conjectures about interest groups are doubtless helpful, as are some remarks about sectional differences and about ethnic variations. But no hard-and-fast conjuncture of social or economic pressures with political behavior can be assumed. Perhaps the Latin maxim should be revised to read "give them bread or circuses." Certainly the federal elections of the late nineteenth century offer hints that millions of citizens knew how to vote against their own well-being. But, in this political madhouse, a few patterns can be seen. A list of presidents reveals the states that the professionals regarded as crucial, the swing vote:

1876	Hayes—Ohio
1880	Garfield—Ohio
1881	Arthur—New York
1884	Cleveland—New York
1888	Harrison—Indiana
1892	Cleveland again—New York

So for twenty years three states contributed—might a poker player say "threw in"—every chief executive. Physically the presidents had much weight, politically they had little. No color; a drab bunch. Their meager distinctions tell the story: one fathered an illegitimate child, another got assassinated. Such deeds do not ease the turmoils of a nation.

These gloomy reflections are a help in understanding how brilliantly the Founding Fathers had carried out their aims. They wanted a government of checks and balances, and they created it. During the Civil War the president had refused to execute writs issued by the Supreme Court. After the war, Congress impeached the president. Later yet, a president, Cleveland, repeatedly vetoed the measures of Congress. However, he did not have as many opportunities as he might have wished, for Congress did not send him many measures. Pursuing our argument beyond the District of Columbia and into the electoral districts, the sagacity of James Madison in the Tenth Federalist Paper becomes pungent. In a republic so large and so diversified, he declared, no tyranny can exist because no majority can be formed. He was almost right. For three decades, it was virtually impossible to weld an electoral, or a congressional, majority. Few Americans have occasion to realize how different their federal government is from the parliamentary modes of other republics. In Canada the bills put forward by the cabinet are binding on every party M.P. If a member chooses not to support a party measure, he is expelled from the caucus. In distinction, Congress knew very little party solidarity. Votes were more likely to split regionally than along factional lines. One illustration can be given from 1893, when an amendment was offered to provide for unlimited coinage of silver with the old ratio to gold of 1:16. The nine Atlantic states from Maine to Pennsylvania had 99 representatives, 45 Democrats and 54 Republicans. The vote was 98 Nays, one Aye. Conversely the representatives of the eight states from Colorado to the Pacific were nine Republicans, a Populist, and seven Democrats. They voted 13 to 4 in favor of the amendment. Party lines meant little. The Democratic president who wanted to defeat the measure had to rely mainly on Republican votes.

But if we want to find men who could think incisively about civic problems, we should look not to the White House but to Congress, particularly to the Senate. Nelson M. Aldrich of Rhode Island, who became the father-in-law of John D. Rockefeller, Jr., was in my judgment a scoundrel, but he knew precisely how to use import duties to promote the causes that he wanted to promote. Even slicker was Orville Platt of Connecticut. Once he was back home mending his political fences. He drove his buggy past a field where a farmer was working, and stopped for a chat. A herd of sheep came along a cross-road. Said the farmer, "Them sheep been shorn." Said Platt, " 'Pears so. At least on this side." The anecdote shows only that he was canny; he was also wise. In one brief speech on the Senate floor in 1890, he acutely predicted more than two decades of judicial interpretation. Under debate was the Sherman Anti-Trust Act. Platt said that as submitted it applied to virtually all of the nation's business, and was unconstitutional because it wiped out state rights under the federal system. It could properly apply only to interstate "transportation." Five years later the Supreme Court accepted Platt's doctrine (discussed below, Chapter 20). His lucidity carried beyond; he also anticipated the Court's ruling in the Standard Oil Case of 1911 (Chapter 21). The course of his reasoning must concern us here, because it was crucial not only to domestic federal policy but to foreign relations as well. Platt talked about "eight representative woolen establishments" in his state that together employed 2,000 men. Even in the relatively prosperous year 1887, they had jointly taken a loss of $50,000. He went on: "They are running their business at a loss; they are making articles to which this bill refers; and this bill says that if those eight men should combine to get a fair, living profit upon their manufacture, that contract, that agreement is against public policy, unlawful and void." This theory he decried as "utterly unreasonable" and "immoral."

The problem posed must be seen from various perspectives. One surely is the cupidity of business, as Adam Smith had explained more than a century earlier: "People of the same trade seldom meet together, even for merriment and diversion, but the conversation ends in a conspiracy against the public, or in some contrivance to raise prices." On this matter, time and space have changed nothing; the Glasgow of then was the Gary, Indiana, of now.* But the public's angle of vision is not the only one; think of the poor manufacturer. The crucial lubrication in promoting worldwide competition for many commodities was provided by railroads (early Chapter 17) and also by steamships on rivers, canals, and oceans. For reasons already discussed, the supply of goods in the United States was growing more rapidly than demand, which was restricted by the inequalities of income distribution. Several labels have been used to summarize this condition; reputable scholars have chosen to call it unconsumption, but my own favorite appellation is excess capacity. Whatever the tag, businessmen sweated with the burden as if they were starred in the myth of Sisyphus, hopelessly rolling a rock uphill.

Thus we swerve toward a consideration of American diplomacy. However, it seems desirable to grasp at that topic before the difficulties of excess capacity became real. Chronologies become tangled, but we will not twist events too far in saying that the first nation to be put down was the United Kingdom. This suppression obviously had been going onward since the origins of British America. We have caught glimpses: the rancor by the Puritan fathers during the Commonwealth in England, obstructionism against royal governors, the War for Independence, the semi-farcical War of 1812 that nonetheless beat down British naval power on the Great Lakes, the struggle for predominance in Texas and Mexico and Oregon. By 1850 the American thrust was reaching farther. In that year, by the Clayton-Bulwer Treaty, it reached Central America. Space cannot be found here for the morass of maneuvers

---

*It may seem strange to those historians who believe that the "benefits of hindsight" are indispensable to their trade, but I will make a simple assertion: the best interpretations of the circumstances being described were those that issued from eye-witnesses.

FIGURE 18-2. *Alexander Gardner, The Overland Stage for Denver*

After the Civil War, the practice of having a staff artist with a transcontinental exploring or survey party was commonly revamped; the sketch or painting was replaced by the photograph. The accompanying picture was taken by Alexander Gardner, and was part of the first large-scale effort at a photographic rendition of the mystical terrain that lay beyond civilization. Americans had only hazy ideas of what the West was like; most still do. Those with proper skepticism might well look at a painting of the High Country by some noodle-head and scoff "Pure romanticism." But Gardner's photographs have a graininess and a calm that can turn bleak. They *feel* authentic and thus impart conviction. In the medium of the stereographs, Americans found a new technique through which they could learn about their country.

Born in Paisley, Scotland in 1821, Gardner came to the United States as a youth to help build a Utopian colony in Iowa. Within a decade he was back in New York. During the Civil War he worked out of Washington as a military photographer for that eminent entrepreneur Matthew B. Brady. In the autumn of 1867 Gardner moved westward with the extension of the Kansas Pacific Railroad, intended to link St. Louis to the Union Pacific. Along the way he took his flat, dead-pan photographs. Although their emotionality is not apparent at once, they are highly revealing.

This one, of a United States Overland Stage leaving Hays City, Kansas for Denver, recalls several major themes in American history. It suggests the barrenness at the time of that country, "289 miles west of Missouri River." It shows how primitive transportation was before roadbed was laid and rails placed. The military guard on top of the stagecoach reflects the still much present Indian antagonists. Finally, and you may need a magnifying glass to detect this, all of the soldiers are black. Evidence produced in the last few years suggests that blacks played a large role in subduing the Great Plains. One study tells of the significance numerically—and in other respects—of the "Negro Cowboy." Certainly the black as soldier was no longer new; when the Civil War ended, almost 200,000 were in Union armies.

about the Mosquito Coast and such like, but the quarrel about an isthmian canal was vital. Nobody yet could be exact as to the route that would be most advantageous. So the game was to leave all doors open. Hostilities between Great Britain and the United States became so great that the secretary of state said a "collision will become inevitable if great prudence is not exercised on both sides." However, in the negotiations he shot from the hip:

> There is not one of these five Central American states that would not annex themselves to us tomorrow, if they could, and if it is any secret worth knowing you are welcome to it—*Some of them have offered and asked to be annexed to the United States already.*

Note the context. America had recently fought a bloody war against Mexico. Her Congress was torn with anger about slavery, anger soon to be fended off by the Compromise of 1850. Even so, her diplomats felt able to bluster against the strongest naval power on the Atlantic. The diplomats, as so often, resorted to a stall. The two powers agreed that neither would "occupy" or "exercise dominion" over any part of Central America. Nobody knew what it meant, so the Senate gave its consent.

When the Civil War started, the Foreign Minister of the United Kingdom saw a chance to whittle down a rival. He wanted secession to win. In pursuit of that policy, the British government permitted shipyards there to build warships for the Confederacy. But its gauge of the balance of power was squinty. Large elements of its own working class resisted the pro-Southern policy. Also the British authorities were pitted against two of the toughest-minded statesmen the United States has produced, the president and Charles Francis Adams. Lincoln was adamant that any construction of vessels for the Confederacy was a belligerent act against the Union. British shipbuilders sought to sidestep this assertion by an evasion. The bottoms were constructed in the United Kingdom, but they picked up their armaments elsewhere; therefore, so it was contended, they were not warships at all. Adams, the Minister at St. James's, was not put off. These Confederate commerce raiders built in Britain captured or disabled more than 250 American merchant ships. The most notorious of the raiders was the *Alabama*. Adams kept his son and secretary, Henry (Chapter 19), working overtime to copy documents attesting to the nature of the *Alabama*. At last the evidence was delivered to the Queen's Advocate. Meanwhile that gentleman had gone insane. For five days the documents were unnoticed. Then the strain became worse when a shipyard began to build the so-called rams. These ironclad steam warships were designed for the obvious purpose of blasting through the blockade being maintained by Yankee wooden hulls. Fortunately at just this time in the summer of 1863, Union armies triumphed at Gettysburg and Vicksburg. The English Foreign Minister had second thoughts about the wisdom of his course. At last, on September 3, he ordered that the rams be detained. The order was secret, and Minister Adams knew nothing of it. Two days later he wrote a formal note: "I trust I need not express how profound is my regret at the conclusion to which her Majesty's Government have arrived. . . . It would be superfluous in me to point out to your Lordship that this is war." This matter usually called the *Alabama* claims dragged along for years after the war. At last the British government took the unusual, almost unique, step of making a public expression of regret for having allowed the ship to leave its waters. An arbitration commission finally in 1872 awarded the United States damages of $15,500,000.

The France of Napoleon III was confronted over the same issue. In 1864 he had to back down, even though he had tried hard to keep his conspiracy secret. The vessels intended for the Confederacy were sold to other buyers, and none reached the South in time to count for anything in the War. Even more humiliating to France was the course of events in Mexico. The invasion of that country began in 1861 as a Franco-Anglo-Spanish venture, with the normal justification that the expedition was meant only to collect just debts owed to Europe. The latter two nations soon withdrew, leaving Napoleon to pursue the project on his own. His armies conquered the country, and he installed an Austrian archduke as the emperor of Mexico. Here was a direct challenge to the Monroe Doctrine. The thrust never had a prayer of success, but the Union could not thwart it until the Civil War had ended. No American was furtive about what would happen then. One Bostonian wrote to his sister: "I mean to go to Mexico and fight the French after this war is done. It . . . would certainly be good fun to cut off those little red-legged sinners, who have been swelling about their fighting and victory." By January, 1864, the New York *Herald* was sneering:

> As for Mexico, we will, at the close of the rebellion, if the French have not left there before, send fifty thousand Northern and fifty thousand Southern troops, forming together a grand army to drive the invaders into the Gulf. That is the way we shall tolerate a French monarchy in Mexico.

In the spring of 1867, Napoleon withdrew his armed forces from the "arch-dupe" on the Mexican throne. That worthy died before a firing squad. There would be no francophile monarchy in North America.

The United States also got the best of Russia, although only with the exploration of Alaskan oil fields a century later did the dimensions of that triumph begin to emerge. By 1867 the Russians had controlled Alaska for more than two centuries. Apart from a rather modest fur trade, they had found nothing there to interest them. They had tried to exploit some mineral properties, but by 1854 that effort had died. Trade gains fell badly, the Russian-American Company declined steadily, and at last collapsed. The Czarist government was in serious fiscal troubles. And there was the glaring outward push of the United States. Already by 1860, according to a paraphrase memorandum to the Russian court: "They have taken California, Oregon, and sooner or later they will get Alaska. It is inevitable. It cannot be prevented; and it would be better to yield with good grace and cede the territory." So they did. The treaty of purchase in 1867 set a price of $7.2 million—for a domain that would become the most extended state in the Union. A story holds that Secretary of State Seward was so eager to conclude the deal that he, in the middle of the night, tossed in a whist hand, called some aides, and signed the documents at 4 in the morning.

Step by step the United States was building a Pacific empire (ah, those 300 million potential customers in China). In the year it acquired Alaska it also occupied Midway. This island, 1,134 miles west of Hawaii, would prove to be a handy coaling station in the age of the steamship. The Yankees, partly by muscle, partly by tact and charm, secured entry into major ports of Japan (Document 18-2). Perhaps the slickest operation of them all was in China. In 1858–1860, Britain and France had twice used armed might there, once to secure concessions, then to get them ratified. America took no part in these adventures and paid no bills. But after the Europeans had made their points, the United States pointed out that because of a most-favored-nation clause in a treaty with China, Americans were entitled to all concessions that had been made to anybody else. Anybody who has studied American foreign policy, especially since the Monroe Doctrine, will wonder at the contention that the Yankees were "innocents," ripe for exploitation; most often they were the exploiters of other major powers.

Relations with Germany were less decisive. But the blur should not detain us unduly, because the country at issue, Samoa, was not at all central to American purposes. Probably today the typical reader of these pages could not go to a globe and locate those islands to within a thousand miles. American intercourse with the archipelago reached back as far as 1838. But Germany acquired a privileged position there. Then in 1872 the United States negotiated a treaty giving it exclusive rights to a naval station at Pago Pago. This gain was upset when the Senate refused to ratify the treaty—a frequent recurrence to which we will return soon. A muddle ensued that lasted for twenty-seven years. In 1878 the United States gained a naval station—not exclusive—at Pago Pago. Germany began to push harder for privileges. Britons were in the scramble for land grants, trade concessions; one politician said of a leading seaport, "I never saw so good a place as this Apia; you can be in a new conspiracy every day." The situation was so edgy that the United Kingdom and Germany allowed their envoys in Washington to explore a resolution. Germany suggested that the commercially dominant nation in Samoa, herself, should control the islands. Britain, for a price to be paid elsewhere, endorsed the scheme. The United States spoke firmly for the autonomy of the archipelago, so the meeting broke up without issue. In these maneuvers, none of the powers cared a whit about the Samoans.

The next year, 1888, the Germans declared war against Samoa and deposed the king. America strengthened its fleet in adjacent waters—she had three warships there, Germany three, England one. Then the Almighty intervened with a hurricane—the British ship survived, but the other six all went under. One American newspaper revived the old doctrine of special providences: "Men and nations must bow before the decrees of nature. . . . Surely the awful devastation wrought in the harbor of Apia makes our recent quarrel with Germany appear petty and unnatural." As Chancellor, Bismarck acted reasonably. Secretary of State Blaine, often a sword-rattler, became a dove. Everybody liked everybody, except the Samoans. The outcome was a three-power protectorate over the archipelago. It did not work out. At last after the Spanish-American War it was abandoned; Germany took the two largest islands, and the United States took the others.

After this survey of American policies abroad, a few generalizations seem proper. First, virtually around the world, in regard to a wide range of conflicts, the United States had either won over or beaten off nations already great plus some destined to become so:

United Kingdom
France
Germany
Russia
Japan
China

We should abandon the illusion that the expansionist republic suddenly became a world power at the very end of the century. Second, the nation's negotiators were still negotiating, and they were careful not to lean too hard. America's aims were proportioned to her strength. In China she wanted what Britain and France got, but no more. In Samoa, she was willing to split the spoils with Germany. She did not try to seize Alaska, she bought it. In Japan her agent was most polite. The time of American belief in her omnipotence had not quite arrived. Third, the nation's objectives abroad were related to her domestic situation. Although it may seem silly to us to think that we can understand diplomacy merely by reading the formal communications between governments, a whole generation of diplomatic historians worked on that assumption. You went to the archives of a half-dozen foreign offices, you made (often inaccurate) copies or translations of the documents, and—presto—truth. No sense can be made of the doctrines advanced by American officials without realizing two salient facts about the internal situation in the nation: that many businessmen, including farmers, were harassed by a belief that additional markets for their products had to be found overseas; and that Americans, including missionaries, had an inflated sense of their own power and righteousness.

Finally, and this reflects on all the preceding assertions, the chief difficulty of the United States in dealing with other nations was to get agreement at home. Part of the trouble here arose from clashes within the economy or within the society, but much came from the political institutions.

Only tremulously can we refer to "the" foreign policy of the United States. The president may be launched on one course, the State Department on another, the Navy embarked on a third, the War Department on a fourth, a foreign ministry on a tack of its own. Normally the president can come close to working his will, but often not. In the nineteenth century, Congress, particularly the Senate, often blocked him. We have seen how it failed to act on a treaty with Samoa. In 1867 Secretary Seward obtained a treaty with Denmark to buy the future Virgin Islands for $7.5 million. It died in the Senate. President Grant in 1870 submitted a treaty annexing Santo Domingo to the United States. In spite of his assertion that the agreement was "an adherence to the Monroe Doctrine," the Senate voted it down. For all that, even though the nation did buy Alaska, the purchase continued to be known as "Seward's folly."

American politics at the national level from 1865 to 1890 was a stalemate. The presidency switched often from one party to the other. Only Grant served two consecutive terms. The chief executive, usually a Republican, was likely to be confronted by at least one house of Congress controlled by the other party. Even within his own ranks he could not sway the members of Congress. No significant federal laws were enacted except a series of Civil Rights Acts ostensibly to benefit freedmen, and even they had little effect for seventy years. Some changes were effected at the state level: regulation of rates for railroads and grain elevators, reform of elections, temperance measures for alcoholic beverages. Probably the most influential agency of government in the nation was the Supreme Court, which handed down some of the weightiest decisions in its history. But even though the customary political processes were proving impotent to resolve the internal problems of the United States, a federal government that seemed helpless on domestic matters was exerting a powerful thrust outward from American shores. In the four decades after 1846 the our eagle had clawed at the interests of the United Kingdom, Mexico, France, Germany, Russia, Japan, and China. In all those contests, the worst result for the United States was a draw.

SOME NOTABLE EVENTS

1850 Clayton-Bulwer Treaty, April 19.
1850–
  1854 Taiping Rebellion in China.
1852–
  1870 Napoleon III is emperor of France.
1853 Gadsden Purchase from Mexico, Dec. 30.
1853–
  1856 Crimean War between Russia and English-Turkish allies.

1854 Commodore M. C. Perry secures from Japan the first treaty of friendship she signed with any Western nation, March 31.
  Marcy-Elgin Treaty with Canada, June 5; first treaty signed by U.S. providing reciprocity in tariff concessions.
  Ostend Manifesto, Oct. 18, tries to assert U.S. interests in Cuba.

1855 Newfoundland given virtual self-government.

1857 Japan signs with U.S. her first commercial treaty with any Western power, July 29.

1857–
1858 Sepoy Rebellion in India against British.

1858 Treaty of Tientsin with China, June 18; Britain and France force trade concessions.

1860 Garibaldi's Red Shirts conquer Naples and Sicily, which are annexed to Sardinia-Piedmont, initiating Italian unification.

1861 Kingdom of Italy proclaimed, a united nationalist regime.

Russian serfs emancipated by Alexander II.

1862–
1890 Bismarck is chancellor of Prussia; proceeds with German unification, expansion.

1863–
1867 Maximilian is emperor of Mexico.

1864 International Red Cross founded.

1865–
1866 Atlantic Ocean is first spanned by cables, laid by Cyrus W. Field.

1866–
1867 U.S. pressure helps to force French troops out of Mexico and to topple Maximilian's puppet government.

1866–
1870 Fenian Irish-independence raids from U.S. into Canada opposed by U.S. Army.

1867 Dominion of Canada formed by British North America Act, July 1.

Second Reform Bill in Great Britain further widens the suffrage.

U.S. buys Alaska for $7.2 million from Russia.

1868 Ten Years' War in Cuba begins; first of rebellions against Spain.

1869 Suez Canal opens, dominated by Britain.

1870 Franco-Prussian War won by Bismarck, who annexes two French provinces.

1871 Tweed Ring overthrown in New York City; turnover in urban political machinery.

Treaty of Washington settles *Alabama* claims, May 8.

German Empire formed under Wilhelm I.

Third Republic of France replaces Louis Napoleon's Empire; it lasts until 1940.

1872 Crédit Mobilier exposed (congressional railroad subsidies bought with kickbacks).

Prohibition party for first time puts up presidential candidate.

1873 Silver demonitized by Coinage Act.

1875 Spain apologizes and pays indemnity for *Virginius* seizure.

1876 Greenback party for first time puts up presidential candidate.

1877–
1878 Russians win war against Turkey.

1878 Serbia, Rumania, and Montenegro become independent by Treaty of Berlin.

Bland-Allison Act, Feb. 28

Democrats win Congress for first time in twenty years.

1882 First Chinese Exclusion Act to block immigration.

1883 Pendleton Act (federal civil service).

Germany, Austria, Italy form Triple Alliance, eventual preliminary lineup of World War I.

1884 Berlin Conference on African colonies.

1885–
1886 British seize Burma.

1887 Interstate Commerce Act.

1888 Australian (secret) ballot introduced in Louisville; first use in U.S.

1889 U.S., Britain, Germany agree to condominium over Samoa, June 14.

1890 Sherman Anti-Trust Act against monopolies.

Sherman Silver Purchase Act.

McKinley Tariff Act.

1891–
1892 Chile humiliated in *Baltimore* dispute with U.S. and its "gunboat diplomacy."

Ways to Study History XVIII

Take a fresh look. Several exciting schema have been advanced in the last twenty-five years for understanding particular facets of American history. Perhaps none was more needed or more overdue than the new conceptualizations about foreign policy leading to the Spanish-American War. For decades the fashion was to emphasize the ambitions of public officials and the dreams of missionaries—the White Man's Burden revisited. Anybody who questioned whether the search for markets abroad was also involved—well, he was written off as a dirty Marxist. Thus skeptical lines of thought were vulgarized into some absurd theory that all businessmen were conspirators, which was of course ridiculous: ha, ha. The simple fact is that all segments of the labor force have special interests, whether employers, employees, or college professors, and each is sensitive to its own interests. The formulation of diplomacy is often a very complex matter, and I doubt if anybody today would want to deny that Protestant ministers had a hand in Washington in the late nineteenth century, but so did other groups.

Three scholars deserve notice for their contributions to this topic since 1955. In that year Norman Graebner demonstrated that perhaps the policy-makers of the ante-bellum years are best perceived in terms other than "continentalism"; what they wanted was not more agricultural land but three ports on the Pacific aimed at the markets of China. This thread ran unbroken for the next fifty years, as Charles S. Campbell showed in *Special Business Interests and the Open Door Policy* (1951). A painful strike at the traditionalist view was administered by Walter LaFeber in *The New Empire* (1963). By his showing, such diverse forces as politicians and financiers and industrialists and trade unions saw their problem as a glut of domestic markets and they saw their saviors as foreign buyers. Even LaFeber does not push this analysis far enough; he says little about farmers. My suspicion is that producers of staple crops such as cotton and wheat saw their own difficulties in the terms just stated. This further extension was made by William Appleman Williams with considerable detail in *The Roots of the Modern American Empire* (1969).

Document 18-1

President Grover Cleveland in 1889 was presented with a bill that appropriated $10,000 to provide seeds to farmers in a drought-stricken area of Texas. He vetoed it. The message below brings up two significant trends. One is the growing ideology of *laissez faire,* the notion that governments should not meddle with the economy. But this doctrine was applied selectively.

Although federal agencies were giving considerable aid to railroads, to the merchant marine, to manufacturers through protective tariffs, Cleveland here denies an extension of aid to farmers. Thus his words also mirror a pronounced shift in the balance of power within the country, away from agriculture and toward the commercial-industrial interests.

. . . I can find no warrant for such an appropriation in the Constitution, and I do not believe that the power and duty of the General Government ought to be extended to the relief of individual suffering which is in no manner properly related to the public service or benefit. A prevalent tendency to disregard the limited mission of this power and duty should, I think, be steadfastly resisted, to the end that the lesson should be constantly enforced that though the people support the Government the Government should not support the people.

The friendliness and charity of our countrymen can always be relied upon to relieve their fellow-citizens in misfortune. This has been repeatedly and quite lately demonstrated. Federal aid in such cases encourages the expectation of paternal care on the part of the Government and weakens the sturdiness of our national character, while it prevents the indulgence among our people of that kindly sentiment which strengthens the bonds of a common brotherhood.

It is within my personal knowledge that individual aid has to some extent already been extended to the sufferers mentioned in this bill. . . .

Document 18-2

Commodore Matthew B. Perry in 1854 secured a treaty of friendship with Japan, but it was little more than a covenant for shipwrecked seamen, the traditional "wood and water treaty." The true breakthrough was effected by an American consul general in 1858, who secured a sweeping commercial agreement. In his phrasing, "The pleasure I feel in having made this treaty is enhanced by the reflection that there has been no show of coercion, nor was menace in the least used by me to obtain it. There was no American man-of-war within one thousand miles of me for months before and after the negotiations. I told the Japanese at the outset that my mission was a friendly one; that I was not authorized to use any threats; that all I wished was that they would listen to the truth that I would lay before them." The following statement by the prime minister of Japan confirms this version—and contains sobering adumbrations (see Chapter 28).

> When our power and national standing have come to be recognized, we should take the lead in punishing the nation which may act contrary to the principle of international interests; and in so doing, we should join hands with the nations whose principles may be found identical with those of our country. An alliance thus formed should also be directed towards protecting harmless but powerless nations. . . . Our national prestige and position thus ensured, the nations of the world will come to look to our Emperor as the Great Ruler of all the nations, and they will come to follow our policy and submit themselves to our judgment. . . . now is the opportune moment offered us by the changed condition of the world to throw off the traditional policy three centuries old, and make a united national effort to seize the opportunity for realizing the great destiny awaiting our country, as stated above. For this purpose, speedy permission is respectfully and humbly solicited for opening intercourse with foreign countries.

Document 18-3

The Commissioner of Indian Affairs in 1871–1872 was an educated man, a scholar. But he shared the bias of most of his contemporaries. Few Americans at that time realized or admitted that the constant pressure of the advancing frontier and the repeated failure of the government to honor its treaties made the Indian uprisings nearly inevitable. By 1890 all of the western tribes had been herded onto reservations, but the process was not as quick and easy as this document predicts.

> It belongs not to a sanguine, but to a sober view of the situation, that three years will see the alternative of war eliminated from the Indian question, and the most powerful and hostile bands of to-day thrown in entire helplessness on the mercy of the Government. Indeed, the progress of two years more, if not of another summer, on the Northern Pacific Railroad will of itself completely solve the great Sioux problem, and leave the ninety thousand Indians ranging between the two transcontinental lines as incapable of resisting the Government as are the Indians of New York or Massachusetts. . . .
>
> No one will rejoice more heartily than the present Commissioner when the Indians of this country cease to be in a position to dictate, in any form or degree, to the Government; when, in fact, the last hostile tribe becomes reduced to the condition of suppliants for charity. This is, indeed, the only hope of salvation for the aborigines of the continent. If they stand up against the progress of civilization and industry, they must be relentlessly crushed. The westward course of population is neither to be denied nor delayed for the sake of all the Indians that ever called this country their home. . . . And it is because the present system allows the freest extension of settlement and industry possible under the circumstances, while affording space and time for humane endeavors to rescue the Indian tribes from a position altogether barbarous and incompatible with civilization and social progress, that this system must be approved by all enlightened citizens. . . .

Society and Ways to Understand It

While most Americans were revelling in the country's increasing power in the international arena, more thoughtful observers began to be disturbed by the divisions and tensions within the nation. Henry George, anticipating a concept made famous by the great historian Frederick Jackson Turner, blamed the fissures in part upon the rapid disappearance of the frontier. "The general intelligence, the general comfort, the active invention, the power of adaptation and assimilation, the free, independent spirit, the energy and hopefulness that have marked our people, are not causes, but results—they have sprung from unfenced land. . . . The great fact which has been so potent is ceasing to be. The public domain is almost gone—a very few years will end its influence, already rapidly failing." The increasingly mixed ethnic nature of the country worried others. In 1880 6.5 million of the 50 million Americans were immigrants, most of whom chose to live in the rapidly growing cities. (Twenty cities reported populations of more than 100,000 in that year.) Although many hoped that eventually the melting pot would eliminate the immigrants' diverse cultures, in the meantime a substantial part of the population either could not or would not abide by American values (discussed below). Another 6.5 million people were black. More than 1,500 of them were to be lynched in the next ten years. Political corruption, the coagulating power of certain big businesses, rural and urban poverty, the impersonality of big cities—all these could be perceived as either the causes or symptoms of a growing malaise. Even a man who presumably had everything going for him could feel this illness (Document 19-1).

Although many of the pre-war reform movements continued in the seventies and eighties, the moral fervor and the optimism which had characterized them earlier had evaporated. Few people could any longer believe in the imminent perfectibility of American life, and certainly not in theoretical utopia. The practical, the concrete, and above all, the personal, reigned. Religion continued to be important, and its stress was laid even more restrictedly upon personal salvation. The bonds between sanctity and philosophy had atrophied, and the churches only attempted to influence the most private aspects of morality. Slavery no longer existed to prick the ministerial conscience, and abolition had been the only important political issue on which religious opinion had spoken.

A (possibly apocryphal) story about Dwight Moody, the most popular revival preacher of the last part of the century, illustrates the depths to which revealed religion had fallen. A lady approached Moody after one of his sermons, saying that she loved his preaching but was not sure whether she agreed with his theology. "My theology?" he supposedly queried, "I didn't know I had one." Indeed the glutinous soothing syrup which Moody dispensed bore no relation to Jonathan Edwards' chill Calvinism, and not much to the sturdy self-reliance of Charles Grandison Finney. (See early Chapter 14 on revivalistic religion.) And where Finney fought for abolition, Moody's social doctrines reflected the prejudices and interests of his audience, drawn from the business middle class. A national magazine could say of him in 1896, "He is the enemy of sectionalism and all hostility of class to class. His mission is to arouse the conscience and awaken the spiritual side of men, to make them patient, long suffering, diligent."

Another form of personal religion became prominent in the latter part of the century. The Church of Christ, Scientist, founded in 1879, maintained that physical health (and general harmonious well-being) could be achieved by a proper spiritual attitude and alignment with the forces of good. Its adherents believed that the physical world didn't really exist, that it was just a reflection of mental realities. This belief recognizes the importance of psychosomatic ailments, but the growth of Christian Science as an organized credo must be credited to the personality of its founder, Mary Baker Eddy. Of a strictly Calvinist New England family, Mrs. Eddy was a chronic invalid most of her life, and during her middle years both poor and unhappy. From her childhood she seems to have been searching for a sense of harmony, as well as for fame and attention. After a series of mystical experiences, many of her physical symptoms evaporated, and she set about forging a systematized creed of spiritual control over health. Her greatest talent seems to have been as a teacher. One former student affirmed the "Spiritual or emotional exaltation which she was able to impart in her classroom; a feeling so strong that it was like the birth of a new understanding and seemed to open to them a new heaven and a new earth." Everyone who knew her, even those with whom she quarreled, agreed that her very presence implied that something exciting was going to happen. By 1889 Mrs. Eddy had personally taught more than 600 pupils, who then spread across the country disseminating her message. Although, given the miserable state of medical practice at the time, Christian Science probably made a real contribution to the health of many people, Mary Baker Eddy's religion stressed the individual over the group as much as that of Dwight Moody.

Religious opinion was silent about poverty, about exploitation of labor, about cut-throat competition, about racism. But it shouted loudly about the evils of liquor and any deviation from a unworkably rigid standard of sexual morality. The churches, and such non-sectarian groups as the Women's Christian Temperance Union, were adamant on these questions. In accordance with the prevailing belief that any vexing problem could be legislated out of existence, they worked hard for strict censorship and the prohibition of alcohol, and against the legalization of prostitution or divorce.* No play could depart from the strict rules of romantic sentimentality, or portray a woman who was not pure without showing her retribution immediately and obviously. The guidelines for printed literature were not so tightly drawn, but they were growing increasingly restrictive. Chicago maintained one police officer whose sole duty was to go about the city ferreting out "obscene" works of art. His test was simple: if a painting or sculpture cost more than $50, it was unquestionably not pornographic.

Although the more assiduous guardians of other people's morals would not have consciously adhered to the policeman's standard, hard cash was fast becoming the only viable standard by which to gauge right and wrong. The immensely popular Horatio Alger books of the era illustrate this tendency. Typically, a poor boy would do a minor sort of good deed, or show character in a trivial way. Unbeknownst to him, a rich man was benefitted, or observed him, and the virtuous lad would be rewarded out of all proportion to his deserts with eventual great wealth, or the boss's daughter. Virtue was plainly not a substantial enough reward for itself. McGuffey's Readers, of which 100 million copies were sold between 1850 and 1900, promulgated the same idea. A chimney sweep found himself in the fireplace in a lady's bedroom. He spies

---

*Belief in the efficacy of the law was not confined to "moral" questions. During these years the Indiana legislature decreed, by fiat, the value of pi (3.1416) to be four.

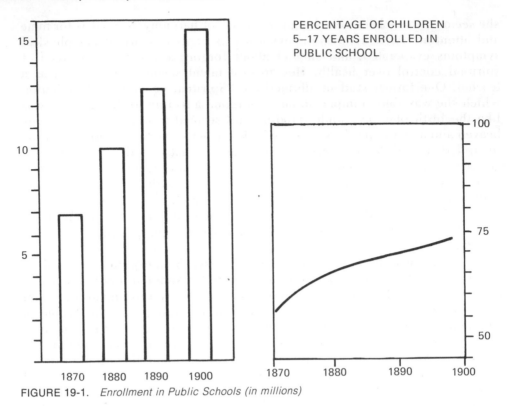

FIGURE 19-1. *Enrollment in Public Schools (in millions)*

a "fine gold watch." Although he wants to take it, his conscience forbids him. The next day the lady summons him, and rewards his honesty by adopting him. Disproportionate punishments could result from petty misdeeds as well: when a small boy snitches a piece of cake his mother threatens him with everlasting Hell, because "no liar can enter the kingdom of Heaven."

Americans wanted to believe that virtue would bring wealth; they also wanted to believe that the rich were good. A Philadelphia minister presented a talk on this theme more than 6,000 times, becoming rich himself. "Ninety-eight out of one hundred of the rich men of America are honest. That is why they are rich. That is why they are trusted with money. That is why they carry on great enterprises and find plenty of people to work with them. It is because they are honest men." Although this theme was self-deceptive in many ways, it carried a socially useful corollary. To become rich was a man's first duty, but his money brought the responsibility to use it unselfishly. The old doctrine of the stewardship of wealth had never entirely died, and the self-help lecturers were helping to revitalize it. When they preached for "success" they also exhorted their businessman listeners to behave in an honorable manner, to spend their money for the good of the community, and to treat their employees justly. While this advice was often ignored, it did help to alleviate the harshness of a relentless pursuit of profit (see late Chapter 17 on labor conditions).

Many Americans would have agreed that "to make money honestly is to preach the gospel," and that the desire for wealth was utterly normal, if not always entirely benign. But Henry George told them that thirst for money stemmed from fear of poverty. "And thus the sting of want and the fear of want make men admire above all things the possession of riches, and to become wealthy is to become respected, and admired, and influential. . . . Men instinctively admire virtue and truth, but the sting of want and the fear of want make them even more strongly admire the rich and sympathize with the fortunate." Perhaps the same fear made them despise the urban poor, who were often marked with the stigmata of foreignness as well as that of poverty.

Middle America feared the great cities, which they believed to be the breeding grounds for all manner of vices and corruptions. In some respects the country was correct in thinking the cities unwholesome. In 1870 the infant mortality rate in New York was 65 per cent higher than it had been in 1810. Polluted water made typhoid fever endemic in some cities; old tenement houses bred disease-carrying rats. But the squalor of the slums was often credited to their inhabitants' moral turpitude. Small-towners and the urban middle class feared that the cities would destroy democracy and morality. They believed political corruption was an exclusively urban phenomenon, and that the immigrants—ignorant, anarchic, "wet"—were to blame.

With a few exceptions, scholars have not paid much attention to the effects of population densities. The psychology of individualism, which was essential in frontier areas, became irrelevant or harmful in thickly settled cities. It might be permissible to throw your garbage out the door in Barrio Morcelo, Puerto Rico, but the same expedient does only damage in Spanish Harlem. If the population density of parts of Manhattan was ubiquitous in all parts of New York City, the 200 million people of the United States could be placed in three of the five boroughs of that one urban incorporation. Bombay and Calcutta were never so jammed together. What is more appalling, districts of New York were almost surely more crowded seventy years ago than they are now. The idea of the pure country and dirty city was stimulated by racism and ethnic intolerance. Although this antipathy was expressed most strongly against blacks, the new—and even the old—immigrants felt its sting. Asked "You don't call . . . an Italian a white man?" a western construction boss replied, "No, sir, an Italian is a Dago." In Minnesota and the Dakotas there were self-segregated Swedish districts and Norwegian districts; the Anglo-Saxon merchants who fattened off them despised both nationalities impartially. We have seen (early Chapter 18) how the Chinese were mistreated in California; in 1883 Congress suspended Chinese immigration for ten years.

The United States has been called a melting pot. It seems to me that this image is misleading. Scattered ethnic enclaves endure to this day, mostly in rural areas, such as the Amish. Others which have now disintegrated managed to preserve their cultural distinctness for generations after their founders came to America. But this conservatism was much easier to sustain in the isolation of a relatively self-sufficient rural village than in a diverse city, and by the end of the nineteenth century almost all new immigrants were living in an urban environment. Even in the city a few ethnic groups managed to create a stable neighborhood in which their culture could be passed along almost intact. The distinction between an ethnic neighborhood and a slum is crucial. In an ethnic neighborhood those individuals who can afford better housing than is available will often refrain from moving out. Instead, they might buy the tenement in which they live and renovate it. A slum offers no human advantages to balance its physical decrepitude; an ethnic neighborhood does. In the North End of Boston the Italian immigrants who came in the late nineteenth century found a slum and created an ethnic neighborhood; it has been stable for generations. Although its residents have certainly adapted to the United States, they have also preserved much of the culture that accompanied their ancestors. But this experience was far from common. Much more frequently only a few trivial parts of European tradition persisted into the third generation. The first generation would be unable to become "American," and would not try. Although proud of their children's greater adaptability, the first generation would nonetheless attempt to bring them up in accordance with tradition. But the second generation was often ashamed of their parent's "foreignness," embarrassed to be unable to quite escape the chains of the past, and determined that their children would do so. The third generation thus became completely homogenized. A few words of the Old Country language, a taste for a few unusual foods, were all that remained to them out of a complex tradition. Thus the immigrants were "melted," in the sense that their ethnicity was broken down, but the traits that they brought to this country never went into the pot to influence others. America chose to discard them, and few Americans regretted their loss.

Jane Addams, the founder of Hull-House, was one of the few. She recognized the merits in the Old Country traditions which she saw in the ethnic neighborhoods of Chicago. But as a well-to-do, educated young woman, she was horrified by the congested, filthy conditions there. On a trip to Europe she had seen a settlement house in London, and in 1890 began the first such facility in the United States. The residents of Hull-House provided a varied assortment of services to the sweatshop district in which they lived, and to the city as a whole. They offered hot lunches to factory workers, sponsored courses in cooking and hygiene as well as a University Extension, provided a gymnasium, an assortment of social and debating clubs, concerts, and art exhibits. They got the state to pass a law for the safety inspection of factories—and one of them became the first inspector. They fought against child labor and for compulsory schooling and better sanitation facilities.

The women of Hull-House were a remarkably effective group, who were often able to get what they wanted by guile when persuasion would not suffice. Most of them came from the same background as Jane Addams—prosperous families in midsized towns in Middle America who had been able to give their daughters a much better education than was at all common for women at that time. At college the girls had wanted to make the world a better place, to be publicly useful at a time when the private utility of marriage and motherhood was the only respectable avenue open to female talent. There is reason to believe that Jane Addams was desperately unhappy for a while before she began her experiment at Hull-House. With enough money to travel, to do almost anything she might choose, she could find no occupation to engross her capabilities. Her contemporaries often found themselves in the same quandary; some of them seized on the alternative of settlement work with fervor.

With varying degrees of ambivalence, Jane Addams' fellow-workers shared her respect for the virtues of the immigrants; they were powerless to halt the rush to exchange those virtues for American traits. The only people whose values today are substantially different from those of the rest of the country are neither immigrant nor more than marginally urban. Despite efforts to assimilate them for more than 300 years, many Indians still cling to a distinctively Indian cluster of attitudes—and this despite the total destruction of the economic system out of which those attitudes had arisen.

In a sense it is pointless to speak of "the Indian." The warlike Iroquois did not much resemble peaceful agriculturists of the Southwest; the settled fishing people of the Northwest differed from the nomadic hunters of the plains. But all the Indian peoples shared two qualities which they refused to abandon and to which the rest of the country has not been able to accommodate itself. First, they disapproved of Western European economic competition and regarded niggardliness as a disgrace second only (in some tribes) to cravenness. In the hunting economy that dominated many tribes, generosity was essential to the survival of the group. Not every hunter could be lucky all the time, and any possession could be quickly replaced from the surrounding environment. Furthermore, in many tribes the animals and the land belonged to everyone; an individual only "owned" something when he had caught it or made it. It was then his pride to be able to give it away.

The second belief which the Indians shared was even more un-American than their unwillingness to accumulate and consume. Each group felt a sacred relationship between themselves and a particular piece of land. Even the buffalo-hunting plainsmen, who seemed like aimless nomads to white eyes, considered specific places to be their own, by religious right. In recent years a group of Indians in the Southwest has been carrying on a

455

running skirmish with the Forest Service over their right to such a place. The officials say that this area, a mountain side which contains a remarkably beautiful lake, should be turned over to multiple uses—cattle grazing permits should be issued, and hikers and fishermen should be allowed in. The Indians reply that this lake and the land around it is sacred to them, that life began there. Their religion involves reaffirmation of man's unity with the earth and the sky, and certain rites are performed by the lake. Aside from participants in these, no one should enter this area at all.

A Nez Percé chief reminded his son (to become Chief Joseph) of the ties between the people and the land:

> Always remember that your father never sold the country. You must stop your ears whenever you are asked to sign a treaty selling your home. A few years more, and the white man will be all around you. They have their eyes on this land. My son, never forget my dying words. This country holds your father's body. Never sell the bones of your father and your mother.

Joseph buried his father in the Wallowa Valley in northeastern Oregon, saying at the time, "I love that land more than all the rest of the world." Nonetheless, he could not keep it. After being given 1,200 acres of reservation land in "exchange" for their million acre valley, Chief Joseph's band eventually attempted to flee to Canada, were caught after a retreat of extreme hardship, and shipped off to the Indian Territory (Oklahoma).

Another group of Indians became a cause célèbre in 1879. The Poncas, a small band from Nebraska, had been sent to the Indian Territory, where many of them died and all were living in extremely unwholesome conditions. About 30 returned to their old home, because the last son of their chief had begged to be buried by the Niobrara. They were bringing his body home. The Indian agent in Oklahoma called for their forcible return, since they had left the reservation without permission. In a court decision which gave the Indians the right, as individuals, to the protection of the courts under the Fourteenth Amendment, they were permitted to stay in Nebraska, but lost all treaty rights.

This case and others like it, aroused a good deal of sympathy for Indians and anger at the machinations of the "Indian Ring" in Washington. But much of the sympathy came about for the wrong reasons, and many of the measures proposed by those who considered themselves the Indians' best friends have only made things worse. "Crooked Indian Agents" aroused much ire. There probably never were very many of those, but it seemed to assuage the consciences of people who had stolen a continent from its owners to rant at those who deprived them of a few cattle or bolts of cloth. Eastern supporters of Indians cherished a romantic, sentimental view of Indian life. *Hiawatha* was required reading, and an extremely sentimental contemporary novel about an Indian princess, *Ramona,* became a best-seller. At the same time, most well-meaning Americans believed that the only way for the Indians to survive

FIGURE 19-2. *Charles M. Russell, An Indian Old Man*

This drawing by Charles Marion Russell symbolizes both the final destruction of the old Indian way of life, and the desperate efforts made by some groups to stay off reservations, to preserve their freedom. Chief Joseph of the Nez Percé led his people on a desolate 1,300 mile trek towards the sanctuary of the Canadian border, to be slowed by cold and starvation, and finally captured before he crossed it. Sitting Bull did manage to escape to Canada, and stayed for several years. When we consider the love which Indians had for their own land, such flight indicates that liberty was valued yet more. But even life itself was not secure under reservation bonds. On December 29, 1890, the 7th Cavalry (George Armstrong Custer's old outfit) murdered hundreds of Sioux at Wounded Knee on the Pine Ridge Reservation in South Dakota. When terrified women tried to save their children by running into nearby gullies, they were pursued and cut down. The figure in this drawing might well have been a survivor of this massacre, a man whose way of life has been destroyed, and who is forced to walk alone.

Russell (1864–1926) went to Montana at the age of sixteen, and worked there as a cowboy. Entirely self-taught, he amused himself and his friends by sketching the life around him, and thought he was a pretty sharp trader when an Eastern dude paid $100 for two paintings. Although he supported himself as an artist from the time he was thirty, he never lost his feeling for the open spaces and a cowboy's life. Like Frederick Remington (Figure 17-2), much of the power of Russell's art derives from his precise observation and empathy with his subject matter.

was to become like white Americans as quickly as possible. They failed to see that even if this would work for more than a tiny minority of individuals, it would mean the extinction of the groups *as Indians*. They worked to have tribal reservations broken up and assigned to individuals in severalty, a move that was disastrous for several reasons. First, individually owned land can be sold; much of it quickly passed into white hands. Second, individual ownership contradicts both qualities of Indianness discussed above. To prosper under this system, a man must learn to be personally acquisitive. Almost to live at all he must abandon the idea of a sacred relationship to a specific place. This the Indians have steadfastly refused to do.

Indians wanted to remain in their ancestral homelands; white men wanted to move whenever they could turn a profit. Even the profit was not always necessary. For some families the lure of opportunities farther west became a goal in itself, and they needed no specific spur to make them move. Hamlin Garland's family moved from Ohio to Wisconsin, to Iowa, and then to the Dakotas. When he returned to the Midwest after six years in Boston, and found them living quite pitifully on the high plains in a sod dugout, he declared, "I clearly perceived that our Song of Emigration had been, in effect, the hymn of fugitives." In some areas land prices rose so rapidly that farmers could turn a tidy profit by staying just ahead of the main line of settlement—clearing a tract, selling it in a year or two, moving west, and repeating the process. But even when it was profitable, the effect of this process on the minds of the people and the quality of life was lamentable.* (See Document 17-1.) Newness, bigness, growth were all, ripeness nothing. Even the churches defined prosperity in terms of change—a new building, more members. The hoopla of town boosterism replaced a feeling of community, while informal village rituals began to yield to formal social organizations—lodges, church "circles," clubs. Nostalgia for uptorn roots fostered the growth of genealogical, patriotic, and historical societies.

Climatic differences complicated the hazards of mobility. Farming methods which worked in Illinois were disastrous in western Nebraska—or anywhere west of the 100th meridian. (This line cuts Kansas, Nebraska, and the Dakotas almost in half. West of it, annual rainfall is less than twenty inches.) Unfortunately, by the time the Homestead Act was passed in 1863 most of the wetter land, which could be cultivated by methods and tools familiar to the midwestern farmer, had been taken up. To farm the Western wheat lands successfully a man needed much more land than 160 acres, and he needed a heavy capital investment in machinery (Figure 29-3). Aside from the ever present spectre of drought, residents of the trans-Mississippi West had to

---

*This same mobility, and its ill-effects, can be seen in many modern suburbs. All houses must be substantially the same, to facilitate resale. Everyone expects to move in a few years time, so they neither make real friends nor are especially concerned about the good of the community.

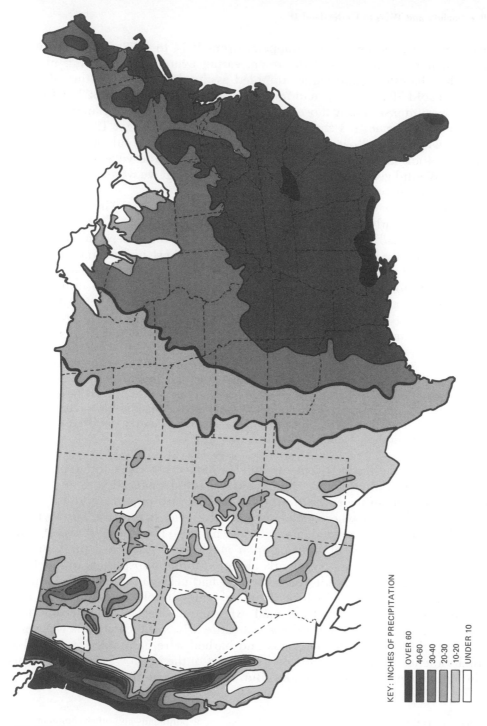

KEY: INCHES OF PRECIPITATION

OVER 60
40-60
30-40
20-30
10-20
UNDER 10

FIGURE 19-3. *Rainfall Belts*

face periodic invasion by grasshoppers. From 1874 to 1877 they came every year when the crops were half-grown, eating everything—growing plants, cloth, hoe handles. Land values tumbled as the disheartened returned east. One man sold 80 acres, a span of mules, a wagon, and a cow for $225. Human misery was intense among those who could not leave. A Norwegian immigrant woman wrote home in February of 1877, "This fall we got 124 bushels of wheat, 224 bushels of oats, and 11 bushels of barley. This is all the locusts left us. They took all the corn, all the potatoes, and all the vegetables we had planted. We did get enough for our needs this year, but we were not able to pay off any of our debts."

Why did they come? In part, out of sheer optimism. The Myth of the Garden—the nearly nonexistent infinite-ideal frontier of the family farm (Chapter 14)—had become too deeply imbedded in the American consciousness to be easily refuted by a few facts. Going West had meant increased opportunities for so long that it was hard to believe that it might have come to mean destitution. But town promoters and land speculators, the railroads in particular, did all they could to encourage the credulous to move west. Many Easterners were wary of "The Great American Desert"; speculators countered with the dictum, "rain follows the plow." One wrote of western Kansas,

> Just in the same proportion as the country has been opened up to cultivation the rainless limit has receded. We are not yet prepared to believe that it will during this generation recede beyond the western limits of this state. But we believe that the entire state will some time be settled. We are satisfied that the rainless belt has retreated before the march of civilization and that wherever civilization has pressed hardest there the limit is farthest west.

By 1890 these advertisements, and the pioneering urges of the American people, had done their work. The Census Bureau declared that there was no longer a line of settlement, a frontier. Henceforward opportunity was to be restricted to the place where it had always been greatest, the city. The Myth of the Garden and of the rugged family farmer had also been sadly shaken.* The increasing dependence of farmers upon machinery, Eastern capital, and a sophisticated transportation network, along with the inhospitality of much of the West to agriculture,—all this combined had nearly toppled it. But a new Myth was arising, one which could persist indefinitely because it did not require the reinforcement of personal experience. The Cowboy became the new American Adam. Actually the era of cattle drives and cowtowns was very short. By the mid-eighties railroads and barbed wire had ended it. And the ritual violence which is an indispensable part of the Myth was more a part of mining frontier than cattle frontier. But just at the time that the cowboy was

---

*It has not entirely fallen even yet. Observe the concern of politicians and other commentators over "preserving the family farm."

becoming nothing other than an unglamorous farm laborer, dime novels were establishing the Cowboy as the ultimate American Hero.

He was free, he was strong, and he would brook no challenges to his unrestrained individuality. He lived by a simple code of honor, was quick to resent any affronts to his dignity, to punish his insulter with his trusty Colt. His best friend was his horse; no man, and especially no woman, could order him about. This combination of traits was to become extraordinarily appealing to the American people. While the nation still believed in the cult of individualism, its exercise had become impossible for all but a very few—the very rich and the resigned poor. Practically everyone had to cooperate, to constantly compromise their desires. Most people, in the pursuit of success or even stability, had to compromise on honor and dignity as well. In an age when "morality" was fast becoming synonymous with abstention from sex and liquor, standards of behavior in almost every other aspect of life were cloudy. But the Cowboy was free. He carried everything he needed to earn his living within himself, and he did not want to "make money," so he could meet with his fellows as equals, and judge them on the basis of a few uncomplicated personal traits. Their money and power were simply not relevant.

This myth eventually came to be soothing even to the real victims of the westering urge—the small farmers. Their lives had long been pictured as the quintessence of bucolic joy. They might have few urban sophistications, but they possessed great security, ample food, and a kindly joviality that more than made up for it. Hamlin Garland, who came of such folk, was much upbraided when he helped to puncture this pleasant fiction. His writing portrayed small farmers as people living with the insecurities of great poverty, brutalized by boring, endless labor, and quenched by loneliness and a narrow society. Garland's people, particularily his women, are permitted a brief adolescent interlude of hope and joy, and then spend their lives struggling through an unremitting round of hard work that never gets them anything but more of it. Garland's portrayal was probably too unrelievedly harsh to be accurate, and its realism is marred by sentimentality. But undoubtably many rural people (East as well as West, South as well as North) did live lives as sullen and hopeless as those he describes. His work served as a useful antidote to the doses of optimism with which Americans had been periodically injected.

Indeed, it was not at all unusual for American writers of this era to project a feeling of depression about the state of America, as a glance at the work of a few of them will show. Henry Adams, writing about the upper classes of society, was similarly pessimistic in his one novel, *Democracy*. He despaired not over the circumstances of people's lives, but over their moral and esthetic insensibility. Mrs. Lightfoot Lee, young and charming widow, is bored by New York and Boston, and goes to Washington in the hope that the nation's political center will possess vitality. From the first the banality of the city's formal social functions horrifies her. Everything to do with political life seems ugly and meaningless. But then she meets Senator Silas Ratcliffe, an immensely powerful man. The possibility of sharing that power as his wife appeals to her, even though Ratcliffe does not share her views on certain ethical niceties. As governor of Illinois during the Civil War, Ratcliffe had feared that the "peace party" would carry the state, and that disunion would follow. He accordingly held back the Chicago vote until the returns from the southern part of the state were in, and made sure that the Union majority in the northern counties was sufficient to carry the state. This situation poses a neat moral dilemma, but Ratcliffe's action appalls Mrs. Lee, and Henry Adams. I doubt that his great-grandfather or grandfather would have been especially shocked. From henceforward Adams contrasts the corruption of Ratcliffe and other exponents of democracy with the virtues of Carrington, another archetypal "Southern Cavalier." It is he who finally breaks up Madeleine Lee's intended marriage to Ratcliffe by revealing that the man had accepted a bribe, but as an admirable model Carrington is no more appealing than the Senator. Possessing the capacity for fine moral judgments, he chose to pose on the sidelines and make them, disdainfully, like Adams himself. *Democracy*'s chief failing as a novel lies in this attribute of the author's: he was seldom willing to let characters reveal their nature by actions, but was constantly assessing them from afar, playing the aloof observing author.

Henry James' work does not fail in this respect, but his novel *The Bostonians* resembles *Democracy* in several ways. Both books satirize honored features of American life. Adams chose democratic institutions, James philanthropy, particularily feminine philanthropy. Both contain a Southern hero, although James' is much more realistically drawn. Most importantly, both stress the mechanically ugly, the greedily heartless nature of America. The country has no grace—it hasn't the time. It has no beauty—money that might go for beauty is squandered on display. Both James and Adams drew their inferences from an examination of the urban monied class, and concluded regretfully that it wasn't as leisured or as cultured as its opposite number in Europe. This was doubtless true, but to judge "America" without even glancing at ninety per cent of its citizens is acting on frail evidence.

James found the feminist movement in America ridiculous; he believed its proponents to be cold-hearted and self-seeking. Certainly the ones he portrayed were both. He didn't think that they could possibly be sincerely working for the good of other women, since to him feminine happiness lay in the traditional roles of wife and motherhood. However, in *The Bostonians* he indicates that this activity is likely to be unsatisfactory as well. Perhaps he believed that no contentment was possible in a society as warped as the American.

William Dean Howells, editor of *Harper's* and for thirty years the dean of American fiction, agreed with James that male-female relations were likely to be unsatisfactory. He ascribed many of their pitfalls to unrealistic expectations and adolescently romantic misconceptions. In *A Modern Instance* the heroine, Marcia Gaylord, is maniacally delighted when Bartley Hubbard asks her to marry him. Having decided to be in love with him, she has deluded herself into believing that he is a worthwhile man. Her father knows differently, but would not dream of interfering with his daughter's choice. Because of an imagined infidelity, she shortly afterward breaks with Bartley as violently as she had clung to him. Perfection or filthiness, passion or hate, are the only choices Marcia thinks are possible. Soon Bartley decides to leave for Boston, upon which Marcia decides to become passionate again, and they marry. Over the next few years Bartley's morals, flimsy enough to start with, steadily decay. Although his worthlessness is apparent enough to everyone else, Marcia steadfastly ignores it. She cannot allow herself to recognize that she might have made a mistake. Bartley's heedlessness and Marcia's hot temper have made for repeated scenes between them, which, while not lessening her jealous devotion, have cooled his slight affection. Finally he deserts her. Her response is to refuse to believe it. She insists to herself and to others that he is coming back to her. Eventually she rids herself of deluded passion by substituting neurotic hatred, but her feelings for Bartley remain the most important thing in her life, and aside from her child, the only thing. Howells scorned the sentimental romanticism which American women delighted in, but he was able to sympathize with those whose lives were ruined by it. Marcia, who could have been a simple, gentle woman, was destroyed by her belief that romantic love atoned for a multitude of evils, and by her refusal to face any reality which contradicted her faith.

Mark Twain viewed female sentimentality with a much harsher eye than Howells'. In the *Adventures of Huckleberry Finn* it is linked with an underlying rapacious cruelty. The women of the Grangerford family moon over a dead daughter, whose specialty had been crayon drawings which sentimentalized death. They are interrupted in this pursuit by the need to round up the menfolks to go shoot members of another family with whom they are feuding. A small Missouri town reveres an old lady for her piety—but she sells a slave "down the river" because the price was too good to pass up.

Women's cruelty was often the more vivid because of the contrast with their view of themselves as creatures both gentle and genteel, but men were vicious too. Shootings, lynchings, tar-and-featherings are almost daily occurences. Men attacked each other to defend their honor, to protect their property, or simply to break the monotony. The sleepy surface of life often cracked, and revealed violent impulses that were usually acted upon. When no excuse for hurting another person appeared, animals provided a handy substitute. Huck speaks of the residents of a small Arkansas town, "There couldn't anything wake them up all over, and make them happy all over, like a dog-fight—unless it might be putting turpentine on a stray dog and setting fire to him, or tying a tin pan to his tail and see him run himself to death."

Only Huck and the escaped slave, Jim, feel no need to go berserk. They are not bored, because they are able to enjoy the simple physical things around

463

FIGURE 19-4. *Winslow Homer,* Eight Bells

Winslow Homer (1836–1910) was a graphic artist throughout his adult life. During the Civil War he was an illustrator for *Harper's Weekly,* limited to drawings that could be turned into wood-cuts. He was an ardent fisherman and hunter, and many of his paintings depict the outdoors of New England and Canada. The Caribbean, especially the Bahamas, provided the subjects for many works of his later years. In these final efforts Homer revealed, more than any earlier American artist, the potentials of water colors as a medium. The plastic vigor of his water colors from the tropics also marks a departure from the stoic majesty of such canvasses as the one shown here, *Eight Bells* (1886).

Homer never stayed away from the ocean for long. Born in Boston, he later made his them—the ripples on the water, the sound of the wind, the taste of catfish and pone. Real life is more important to them than defense of a stylized code of honor or their self-importance. But this "reality" does not exist for others, and Huck and Jim are only able to have it when they are isolated from the rapacity of the rest of the human world. And the world won't let them alone. It sees Jim as its rightful prey because he is a slave, and Huck because he is a boy, whom adults can justly hound and mold. But even if they were not particularily vulnerable, their very apartness, their willingness to ignore the scrabbling and the self-puffing which consume everyone else would make them dangerous. Their society flaunts individualism, but cannot tolerate actual differentness. Significantly, at the end of the book Huck cuts for the hills, hoping to find some peace in a place where people are not. But even this sanctuary can be at best short lived.

When *The Adventures of Huckleberry Finn* appeared in 1885 it was widely criticized for its lack of gentility. Although it was not blemished by the demon sex, its characters were considered too coarse, and its language too vulgar, for it to properly fulfill the main function of literature, to uplift and to inspire. It is then no wonder that the following year the nation's foremost painter, Thomas Eakins, created a scandal by requesting a male model to remove his loincloth in an art class which included women students. Although in the preceding 10 years Eakins had helped turn the Pennsylvania Academy of Fine Arts into a source of serious artistic discipline, prudery easily overcame beauty, and forced his resignation (Ways to Study History XIX).

Although most Americans' artistic imagination stopped at advertising calendars and samplers extolling home sweet home, great changes were being made in the visual arts. The possibilities of the portrait were expanding. Some painters were departing from the stiff, "posed" portrait to show people in activity—boxers boxing, housewives cleaning. Albert Pynkham Ryder was experimenting with new techniques of color and line, and creating pictures whose symbolic meanings were more important than their representational ones. Winslow Homer, although not as profound an artist as Eakins or Ryder, was enraptured by the raw beauty of the Maine coast, and was painting landscapes that bore little relation to the manicured romances, derivatives of

---

permanent home on the coast of Maine. The whaling industry was in its dying years when he was an adolescent, but seafaring and the fisheries continued to loom large in the port towns of the northern Atlantic coast. Homer's appreciation of the workaday tensions between man and the sea both diminished and exalted the human dimension; individuals have no character in this painting except as they cope with the elements. He exulted in the external world: "The Sun will not rise or set without my notice, and thanks."

His verbal statement of his aims approximates that of Bingham in the preceding generation (Figure 13-6): "When I have selected the thing carefully, I paint it exactly as it appears." He did not, but the slant of his bias was clear.

Courtesy of the University of Kansas Museum of Art, Gift of the Arthur F. Enger Estate

FIGURE 19-5. *Albert P. Ryder,* White Horse Grazing

Albert Pinkham Ryder (1847–1917) may well have been the first major American painter to break with the Gospel of Work. Undoubtedly he brooded over each canvas, and he toiled over it—often too much. He never did master the craft of painting; his thickly caked pigments were so badly mixed that already many of his works have darkened and deteriorated. Also, although he differed from Thomas Eakins in that he became a financial success in his middle years, the two were the same in not caring about money. (See "Ways to Study History XIX" and Figure 19-6.)

Ryder was born in the erstwhile whaling center of New Bedford, but he spent his adult life in virtual solitude in a congested Manhattan. Here he helped to invent the life style of the bohemian. He the Barbizon School, which had heretofore been the standard product of American landscape painting.

In architecture, Henry Hobson Richardson was proving it possible to be both a creative and a financial success. Fascinated by the Romanesque style, he did buildings of massive red sandstone, with heavy piers and rounded arches. Trinity Church in Boston is a typical and felicitous example of his style. Although some of his buildings are drab, and others chaotic, the best are both graceful and integrated. One of his finest was the Marshall Field wholesale store in Chicago. Although much of the wall space consisted of windows, grouped in fluidly rhythmic patterns, the heavy sandstone and granite supporting piers bespoke solidity, while their seven-story sweep pointed upwards.

Richardson's Chicago store was a great success, both artistically and publicly, but skyrocketing urban land costs were making the large masonry building obsolete. The same high costs were forcing buildings to become taller, but as a masonry structure grew higher it required more and more massive supporting pillars at ground level. These in turn took up expensive space, and reduced the amount of window space which could be used for display purposes. Steel skeleton construction posed no such dilemma. Combined with the recently developed mechanical elevator, it imposed no practical limits on height, and since the external walls were a mere shell against the elements, bearing no weight, they could consist almost entirely of glass wherever that seemed desirable (Figure 29-4). But until Louis Sullivan attacked the problem, no architect perceived the artistic possibilities of this type of structure, probably because most architects were degenerates, content to apply the styles of past "periods" to new construction. Since the tall office building had no direct progenitor, they could only try to disguise it. Its increasingly elongated proportions made that increasingly difficult. Sullivan saw no reason for the disguise; he was fascinated by the possibilities for beautiful innovation provided by skeletal steel. In the Monadnock Building in St. Louis he provided an almost unbroken wall of glass at ground level for display (others had attempted to ape the heavy piers of masonry construction) and emphasized the structure's height by graceful vertical pillars, another new idea.

The Monadnock Building was acclaimed, but much of Sullivan's work

---

lived in a garret. His floors were littered with garbage, old newspapers, unwashed dishes. Amid the squalid rubble an alert visitor might detect a check for $500 which he had neglected to deposit. The division of artist from philistine was becoming visible. How unlike Charles Bulfinch, the great Boston architect of a century earlier, whose home provided a meeting-place for great merchants (Figure 12-2).

Ryder's canvas. *White Horse Grazing* cannot be precisely dated because he often worked at a single conception for a decade or more; the year 1885 should be close. Perhaps the best label for his vision would be mystic. Records show that he was capable of prolonged and close observation of the external world, but his paintings seem to be a controlled fling outward from internal passions.

was too innovative to have a broad appeal. Few people were yet able to escape the honeyed trap of the traditional, or able to see beauty except in terms of adornment. Nonetheless, American architecture seemed on the verge of a breakthrough to new forms. But in 1893 the Columbian Exposition set it back. This World's Fair drew more than 27 million visitors, more than any before. Its attractions ranged from prize livestock to a 150-ton cannon to a map of New York State made of pickles. The "White City" in which the Fair was housed enthralled visitors as much as its contents; the buildings had been designed as an integrated whole in the Greek Revival style (Chapter 12). Except for Sullivan's Transportation Building, none had any merit. The Exposition grounds were dazzling, but inane. Sullivan recognized the damage the Fair had done: "Thus architecture died in the land of the free and the home of the brave—in a land declaring its democracy, inventiveness, unique daring, enterprise and progress." Soon no one with any pretensions to gentility would consent to live in a house undecorated with pillars and portico, and businessmen who could afford it were having their commercial structures embellished the same way. The incongruities and inconveniences of this design made no dent in its fashionableness for years.

In 1883 Matthew Arnold, esteemed English poet and critic, wrote a short analytic essay on the United States, in which he said that the country was not "interesting." His two criteria were beauty and distinction. He said that America lacked beauty because of the absence of the patina of antiquity, the layered look of history. No one cherished any particular patch of ground, and consequently everything was ragged at the edges. Its citizens were hardly ever distinguished, because the cult of the "average man" dominated the popular imagination. To be different was not to be honored. The frenzy over the Columbian Exposition illustrates some of the reasons for this phenomenon. Despite boosterism, Americans did not trust themselves to develop their experience into its own artistic expression. Imitation of the European was safer. Public indifference and contempt drove most American artists into exile—either physically or mentally. Their isolation from American life then made their work less telling than it might have become.

In the 1850's only Herman Melville publicly despaired at the human future. By the 1890's no thoughtful person remained optimistic. Modern man, capable of enduring without believing, had arisen in those fifty years. So many successes had turned out to be failures. The ambitions of continentalism had been achieved, the folk with a manifest destiny had reached the Pacific, but now Henry George and Frederick Jackson Turner warned them that the old game had ended. The economy seemed deranged, in spite of the massive inflow of Europeans who contributed so much to the material growth of the nation. Unfortunately, as it seemed to the old-stock Americans, those very immigrants brought antipathetic folkways. Perhaps the best summary to this chapter is a book by Michael Lesy, a documentary dramatization of life during a farming depression in a town in Jackson County, Wisconsin. News stories of 1885 to 1900 from the local newspaper, plus artfully juxtaposed photographs, comprise *Wisconsin Death Trip*. The title is apt. Elsewhere I have called attention to the prominence of suicide in the works of great American writers of this period (Document 19-1), and Lesy's book fleshes out the literary evidence with the stark stare of documentary images. Rural life was not happy. Our great-grandfathers were not exuberant men. Through their ears and into their minds, while they were thrashing about desperately, they were listening to a daily litany of disaster.

SOME NOTABLE EVENTS

1865 Yale opens first fine arts department in any U.S. college

Mendel unveils his laws of heredity.

1868 University of California chartered.

1869 Wyoming grants the first women's suffrage in the U.S.

1870 The Vatican adopts the dogma of Papal infallibility.

Graduate work organized at Harvard and Yale.

1872 *Scientific Monthly* founded.

1874 Women's Christian Temperance Union founded.

1876 Thomas Eakins begins teaching anatomy at the Pennsylvania Academy of Fine Arts

Dr. Felix Adler founds the Society for Ethical Culture.

Johns Hopkins founded as a purely graduate school.

American Library Association formed.

1877 Thomas Edison patents the phonograph.

1878 Church of Christ, Scientist, formed.

1879 Henry George, *Progress and Poverty*.

1880 Salvation Army begins in the U.S.

1881 Wharton School of Finance and Economy founded.

National Red Cross founded.

1882 Chinese immigration suspended for 10 years (Chinese Exclusion Act).

1883 New York *World* under Pulitzer launches "yellow journalism" in U.S.

1885 Mark Twain, *The Adventures of Huckleberry Finn*.

William Dean Howells, *The Rise of Silas Lapham*.

Henry James, *The Bostonians*.

1887 Edward Bellamy, *Looking Backward*.

1889 Hull-House founded.

1890 Congress adopts its first international copyright law.

William James, *Principles of Psychology*.

1891 Cal Tech and the University of Chicago founded.

Ways to Study History XIX

Pore over portraits. Several years ago I devised an exercise for a graduate seminar in American biography and autobiography. Having picked a dozen slides, mainly in color, I projected them for the class. The students were told that each subject was an American, that each picture had been made by an American, and the date of creation of each. The assignment was then to write an imaginary biography of the subject up to the time the portrait was made. What traits of character are shown by his face, his stance, his expression? What social class did he represent? Where in the nation did he live? What typical experiences had he had? This assignment was frankly experimental, but the results were surprisingly rewarding; many students produced sagas that were highly inventive and also historically precise.

You might want to try the game with this depiction of *Mrs. Edith Mahon* by Thomas Eakins (Figure 19-6). The painter lived in Philadelphia, 1844–1916. His works are truly a gallery of his countrymen: opera singers, clerics, pugilists, men rowing on the Schuylkill. He also did a haunting Crucifixion. His effort was always to depict the thing as it was, while giving to the canvas a vividity that seemed to reach into nature. It says much about the esthetic standards of the late nineteenth century that he was never a success; the finest collection of his works is in the Philadelphia Museum of Art where it was lodged gratis by his widow.

Eakins' methods were painfully painstaking. If ever a man was infected by the Gospel of Work, it was he (yes, it even invaded art). The better to depict the human body, he studied anatomy and went to autopsies. He profited from photography. Planning to paint a carriage drawn by four horses, he worked with a photographer on countless rapid-action shots of the event. Then he made a small statuette of each horse. Then he began to paint. Never intended for public view, the other products were mere preliminaries.

Document 19-1

Walt Whitman stopped writing in 1873, and for more than twenty years afterwards American poetry did not exist in any serious sense. Edwin Arlington Robinson (1869–1935) began a new era with his first volume of verse, published in 1897. Notice the simplicity of the language, and the ease, the naturalness, of the expression in this poem. Robinson was one of the first Americans to realize that language need not be flowery to be "poetical." Also, he seems to have recognized what the psychologists now call "free-floating anxiety," an anguish which has no discernable cause.

> *Richard Cory*
> *Whenever Richard Cory went down town,*
> *We people on the pavement looked at him:*
> *He was a gentleman from sole to crown,*
> *Clean favored, and imperially slim.*
>
> *And he was always quietly arrayed,*
> *And he was always human when he talked;*
> *But still he fluttered pulses when he said,*
> *"Good-morning," and he glittered when he walked.*
>
> *And he was rich—yes, richer than a king—*
> *And admirably schooled in every grace:*
> *In fine, we thought that he was everything*
> *To make us wish that we were in his place.*

FIGURE19-6.   *Thomas Eakins*, Mrs. Edith Mahon *(Ways to Study History XIX)*

So on we worked, and waited for the light,
And went without the meat, and cursed the bread;
And Richard Cory, one calm summer night,
Went home and put a bullet through his head.

Document 19-2

One of the leading American novelists for forty years, William Dean Howells also encouraged the development of younger writers. When Stephen Crane interviewed him for the New York Times in 1894 Crane's career had hardly begun, and Howells' reputation was very high. Here Howells discusses the function of the novel and the novelist.

I believe that every novel should have an intention. A man should mean something when he writes. Ah, this writing merely to amuse people—why, it seems to me altogether vulgar. A man may as well blacken his face and go out and dance on the street for pennies. The author is a sort of trained bear, if you accept certain standards. If literary men are to be the public fools, let us at any rate have it clearly understood, so that those of us who feel differently can take measures. But, on the other hand, a novel should never preach and berate and storm. It does no good. . . .

It is the business of the novel to picture the daily life in the most exact terms possible, with an absolute and clear sense of proportion. That is the important matter—the proportion. As a usual thing, I think, people have absolutely no sense of proportion. Their noses are tight against life, you see. They perceive mountains where there are no mountains, but frequently a great peak appears no larger than a rat trap. An artist sees a dog down the street—well, his eye instantly relates the dog to its surroundings. The dog is proportioned to the buildings and the trees whereas, many people can conceive of that dog's tail resting upon a hill top. . . .

[The novel] is a perspective made for the benefit of people who have no true use of their eyes. The novel, in its real meaning, adjusts the proportion. It preserves the balances. It is in this way that lessons are to be taught and reforms to be won. When people are introduced to each other they will see the resemblances, and won't want to fight so badly.

Document 19-3

Although Mark Twain had little in common with Henry Adams and claimed he was unable to read Henry James, he shared their ironic distrust of human nature and the democratic process. "Purchasing Civic Virtue" illustrates his pessimism.

Every man is a master and also a servant, a vassal. There is always someone who looks up to him and admires and envies him; there is always someone to whom he looks up and whom he admires and envies. This is his nature; this is his character; and it is unchangeable, indestructable; therefore republics and democracies are not for such as he; they cannot satisfy the requirements of his nature. . . .

At first we granted deserved pensions, righteously and with a clean and honorable motive, to the disabled soldiers of the Civil War. The clean motive began and ended there. We have made many and amazing additions to the pension list but with a motive which dishonors the uniform and the Congresses which have voted the additions, the sole purpose back of the additions being the purchase of votes. . . . We have the two Roman conditions: stupendous wealth with its inevitable corruptions and moral blight, and the corn and oil pensions—that is to say, vote bribes, which have taken away the pride of thousands of tempted men and turned them into willing alms receivers and unashamed.

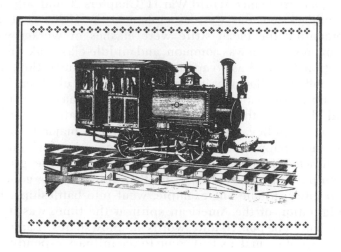

The Great Faultline, 1893–1898

This is a good point for some blunt assertions. With the possible exception of the years 1786–1788, the worst peacetime crisis in American history began with the financial panic of 1893 and culminated in the Spanish-American War. This remark may well be resented by many, especially by students and by blacks; these groups can with justification speak of the nuclear weapons, the threat of mass annihilation, the continuing oppression of blacks, the palpable insanity of the war in Viet Nam, the defects of the educational system, the lack of good jobs for young people—of any jobs. These grievances will be confronted below. But my initial statement should stand. In the closing years of the last century, American voters and American institutions were faced with several showdowns. They did not deal wisely with a single one of them. The price for those failures is still being paid, and the end is yet to come.

Before laying out some specifics, more assertions. Due in large part to the maldistribution of income, the economy was in a worse condition than ever before. Dislocations in the business world aggravated the ruptures in society. We have looked at some of the earlier race riots (early Chapter 15) and we will look at some that have occurred since World War II (Chapters 29 and 30); be it noted here that white-black tensions were as violent in the 1890s as at any other time. Complementing the racial strife were clashes of worker with employer. Talk of actual revolution was common, and middle-class folk valued the Army and the National Guard as weapons to suppress insurrection. The social and economic conflicts boiled over into politics. Probably elections have never been more corrupt, more violent, dirtier. The judiciary has never been more prejudiced. And all this seething mass spilled over the nation's borders and called itself a foreign policy. The consequence was a major break in American diplomacy. An unhappy land sought solace in grasping for commitments abroad that inflicted injustice on millions of others while grossly wasting American output; productive capacity that might have gone to improve sanitation in cities, to cite one example, went into battleships. But then, given the configuration of the American spirit at the time, was it not inevitable that wealth would be poured into swords not plowshares? Lament it as we may, the country's policy-makers had come to see military expenditures as the handiest solution for the glutted state of the economy that had been developing since as early as 1873. Businessmen and politicians seldom look for any answer which, even though it might promise to be lasting, is for the moment difficult; they want a quick way out of the box. They seldom look beyond the next balance sheet, the next election.

But it will not do to exaggerate the abruptness of the changes. The underlying difficulties of the economy had originated decades earlier, but they had grown worse. More important, people had become more aware of them. In addition to the ugliness of the Haymarket outburst, other eruptions had burst out. One focus of discontent was the favoritism by governments. A great commentator on the events of the period, Henry Demarest Lloyd, remarked: "The Standard has done everything with the Pennsylvania legislature, except refine it." The five railroads from the East Coast to Chicago were a glaring case of excess carrying capacity, and Standard Oil had also used this circumstance to get huge concessions in the freight rates charged to it; the so-called rebates. Here was another focus of animosity—the railroads. Thousands of farmers and other shippers were convinced they were being cheated; if you were unfortunately located in a spot that was served by only one trunkline, you might pay twice as much as a competitor paid to ship his product twice as far. That could mean your death. To quote Lloyd again: "The movement of the railroad trains of this country is literally the circulation of its blood." (See Document 20-1.)

The truth of that remark was underscored by strikes. Beginning in 1876, the span of one year saw eight important walk-outs; the next summer the series culminated in a tie-up of lines from the Atlantic to St. Louis. Railroads, burdened with gigantic fixed costs, could not tolerate such disruptions. So the

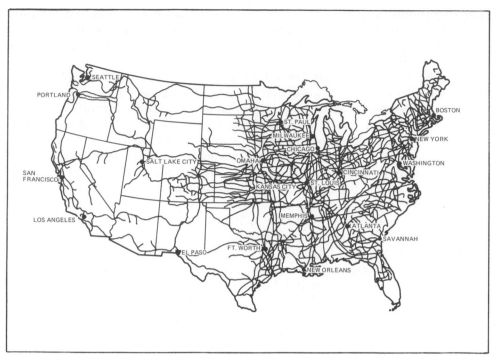

FIGURE 20-1.   *Railroads in the U.S., 1890*

companies felt compelled to wipe out all unions. Simply to report that would be far too facile, for they also worked toward quite detailed tactics for achieving the aim. A show-piece here is the Burlington strike of 1888. Establishment of the Interstate Commerce Commission in 1887—partly at the behest of some major railroads—had not instituted any machinery that could stop a strike by the Brotherhood of Engineers and by the Firemen, the two strongest unions. About 2,000 men hit the bricks. The strike lasted nearly ten months. Union sympathizers were convicted of planting dynamite to blow up track. Federal circuit courts issued injunctions to halt the walkout. Most crucial, strikebreakers could be hired. One company executive put it thus: "The result has demonstrated the fact that an abundance of labor will break up any strike, no matter how strong the striking party may be. We can easily get two thousand engineers if we need them." While goods were redundant, so were workers. This condition existed throughout the country.

Other examples will shortly be given, but they should not obscure the general situation. You will read of the Homestead strike, of the pardon of the Haymarket defendants. These episodes contributed to the existing malaise. But a couple of celebrated events do not create a ubiquitous state of mind. Thousands of shoot-outs, many of them in obscure mining towns or at lonely

475

junction points, were built into a gestalt pattern that some psychologists would call "free-floating anxiety," or a general state of mental depression. Even they did not know what they were afraid of, but they were very afraid (See Document 19-1).

The Homestead strike of 1892 illustrates several major developments. Carnegie's decision five years earlier to convert this giant mill from production of rails to structural steel reflects the growth of cities, the origins of the skyscraper, rising land values. The strike shows the invention of techniques for smashing a trade union. In 1889 a contract was signed, to last for three years, covering the 4,000 workers at Homestead; at that time the Amalgamated Association of Iron and Steel Workers had more than 20,000 members in the nation. With a large fraction of its organization composed of skilled workers, it was one of the strongest unions in the country. The contract with Carnegie gave widely differential treatment to the assorted occupations. Due to the shortage of skilled workers and the growing glut of unskilled immigrants, the hourly rate for common labor was 14 cents while other employees got as much as $14 a day. A newspaper reported on a "sober and thrifty" Welsh immigrant in Homestead whose family lived in "a large, handsome cottage in the Queen Anne style, gaily painted," with a parlor organ, electric lights, upholstered furniture, and deep carpets.

As the expiration date of the collective-bargaining agreement drew near, a board wall topped by barbed wire was built around the mill. At regular intervals, three inch portholes were cut. At this point some of the conflicts within the entrepreneurial class become manifest. Carnegie was in Scotland; the top executive on the spot was Henry Clay Frick. The two agreed that the union had to be destroyed. But it seems that Carnegie wanted to close down the plant and wait the opposition out. Frick chose a different course, and it says a good deal about the period to note that it was the hard-nosed antagonist who had his way. He locked out 800 men, prompting a strike by the entire labor force. He hired 300 armed guards from the Pinkerton detective bureau. When they arrived at Homestead, an all-day battle ensued. Ten strikers and three Pinkertons were killed. The governor of the state sent 8,000 militia to the town. But the walkout dragged along for more than three months, because the company had trouble getting skilled recruits to act as strikebreakers. At last production resumed with 2,000 workers, of whom only 400 had been employees before the strike. The union at Homestead had been crushed.

Another noteworthy product of labor strife was the decision by Governor John Peter Altgeld of Illinois to pardon the surviving defendants in the Haymarket case. Had he been prudent, he could probably have taken this action without arousing great controversy; since the trial six years earlier, hundreds of citizens had circulated petitions for amnesty. The common argument was that the men had expiated their guilt. But Altgeld did not take this ground. Far from conciliatory, he charged that the men had been unjustly convicted. His message pulsated with indignation at the conduct of the trial. He insisted that the jury had been deliberately packed, its members biased, the judge prejudiced, and the verdict founded on a rule of law that was ridiculous. That these rebukes should come from a prominent statesman was remarkable, but even more extraordinary was the reaction to the pardon. Almost the entire press responded with frenzy. They shouted apoplectically that Altgeld was not a Democrat at all but an outright anarchist. The republic was losing its nerve.

Psychic stress was exacerbated by the state of the economy. At the beginning of 1893 a large railroad went into bankruptcy—it had short-term debts of $18.5 million and liquid assets of about $100,000. Banks started to crumple:

January—April	28 suspended payment	
May	54	"	"
June	128	"	"

Worried foreigners began to unload their American securities and pull their capital home. It flowed out in gold. Drains on the treasury's gold stocks were more acute because of the Sherman Silver Purchase Act of 1890, which masqueraded as an effort to more than double the volume of silver bought and coined by the treasury. (With the expansion of silver mining in the West, the price of that metal had fallen: $1.15 an ounce at the passage of the Bland-Allison Act in 1878; in 1890 it was only 94 cents.)

The monetary stringency was felt especially keenly by farmers. In consequence, the small farmers, especially of the Midwest and South, began to focus their needs politically through a newly strengthened third party, the Populists (see Document 20-2). In 1892 they put forward some novel demands. Again, as in the reaction to the Haymarket pardon, the response to their audacity was extreme, even though the proposals were reasonable enough. One plank of their platform called for government ownership and operation of railroads, telephones, telegraphs. Acceptance of this policy would have saved the nation a lot of grief from that day to this. Another plank was the so-called subtreasury plan, under which a farmer who deposited his crop with a federal agency could get from the government up to 80 per cent of the cash value of the collateral. This is in essence the procedure later adopted under the New Deal, with rhetoric calling it the "ever-normal granary" and with bureaus called the Agricultural Adjustment Administration, the AAA. In the 1890s when it made considerable sense, it was not adopted; in the 1930s when it made little sense, it was picked up as a desperate panacea (Chapter 26).

In the presidential election of 1892, the People's party tallied more than a million votes in the nation. The most interesting area to study here is the South, which Vann Woodward and others have shown to be the fulcrum of Populist strength (see Ways to Study History XX). Faced with a new challenge to their traditional voting strength the national Democratic Party felt cornered. If they espoused free coinage of silver in order to win the Mountain states and the prairies, they would lose the conservatives whom they needed to win the East. But the Atlantic seaboard would not suffice, they must have the South

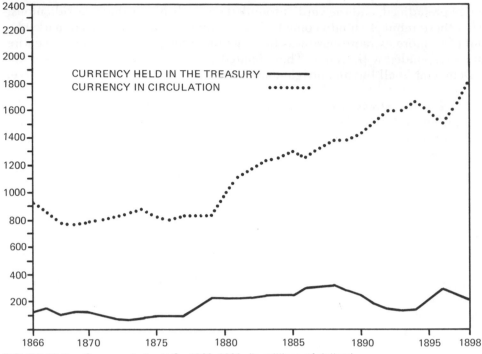

FIGURE 20-2. *Currency in the U.S., 1866–1898, (in millions of dollars)*

also. As it turned out, the Populist vote in the latter region was limited to 362,000. To achieve this outcome, the Democrats held off their challengers mostly with physical coercion. Look at Georgia, where in October of 1892 the Populist candidate for governor lost by a 2-1 margin, and a month later the party's nominee for president was credited with less than 20 per cent of the votes and ran third behind the Republican. The landed classes in Georgia feared that their entire system was toppling. Hadn't that rabblerouser, Representative Tom Watson, been telling both whites and blacks: "You are made to hate each other because upon that hatred is rested the keystone of this arch of financial despotism which enslaves you both"? Fear begets repression, and in the campaign an estimated fifteen blacks were killed by Democrats. The Democratic governor was heard to say "Watson ought to be killed and it ought to have been done long ago." In one county the Democratic chairman sent around to planters a flyer, "It is absolutely necessary that you should bring to bear the power which your situation gives over tenants, laborers and croppers." Negro field hands were carted to the polls packed like sardines, and voted like sardines. Voters were paid off in cash while the whiskey flowed from barrels. Impostors were brought into the state across the Savannah River to stuff ballot-boxes with fake votes. In Watson's congressional district, around Augusta, the vote was about twice the number of legal voters. While it was not the first time in American history that an election had been rigged, and it was not to be the last, this instance was extreme. White Populists began to get the impression that the power structure would never permit them to unite with blacks in order to gain power. This impression was hammered home by later elections. At length, in despair, the radical whites reverted to reaction, by returning to the old convention of white solidarity to stamp on the blacks. It was an atavistic spasm, and Tom Watson joined in.

Another effort at unified opposition among disinherited groups was launched among railroad workers. The kingpin was Eugene Debs, and the organization was the American Railway Union (ARU). Its structure, unprecedented on the railroads, was advanced for any portion of trade unionism in the United States. The technical term would be industrial unionism; that is, a single agency to bargain for all employees of companies turning out a given line of products, whether rubber or steel or automobiles or whatever. In the contrasting system, craft unionism, the workers are subdivided by skill or trade, so that one employer might deal with a dozen or more separate unions. This latter scheme had been habitual with the railroad Brotherhoods, and to some skilled workers it had brought benefits. For the semiskilled it had failed miserably. The task, as Debs saw it, was to weld together these disparate groups so they could bargain collectively. His venture had only two assets: the talents of a handful of organizers, and the grievances of legions of railway hands. It had no traditions, no structure, no experience, no money, and it faced the combined opposition of dozens of the strongest corporations in the world.

This hostile power proved overwhelming, and in the Pullman boycott we can watch it work. The initial successes of the ARU had been amazing. In a year it organized 150,000 men and became the largest union in the nation. In a strike against the Great Northern, the best managed of all large American railroads, it won nearly all of its demands. Then it encountered the collaborative enmity of a phalanx of companies. The union, to aid strikers against the company that made and operated Pullman sleeping cars, decreed a boycott against the cars. To speak gently, this move was not wise, and Debs did what he could to prevent it. The union would not move any train hauling Pullmans, and the railroads would not cease attaching Pullmans to trains. From Chicago westward, the blood of a nation stopped circulating. Now the massed power came into play. The twenty-four railways centering or terminating in Chicago were joined into the General Managers Association. These companies together had

a capital of 818×10^7
41,000 miles of track
221,000 employees

That monolithic (for the moment) Goliath would be a match for any David. But next the parasites began to bleed their host.

The ARU had appealed to other unions for help. Most answers were evasive. Only one promised full help. The national officers of most of the Brotherhoods worked against the strike. On one railroad where 400 Locomotive Engineers joined the strike, the president of the order denounced their action as a violation of his union's rules, and proclaimed that unemployed engineers could legitimately take the jobs of their "brothers." The head of the Conductors said that he had "neither authority nor inclination" to help the ARU. Later he explained that any industrial union like the ARU had to be opposed by a craft union like his own, "no matter what the conditions at Pullman were."* Debs' reply to this hostility was bitter: "Every concession the railway companies have ever made, has been wrung from them by the power of organized effort." He was right. In this instance the union, supported by many civic leaders, had asked that the original dispute be submitted to arbitration. A spokesman for the company answered that there was "nothing to arbitrate" (The spokesman was not George M. Pullman; he was on vacation. It was uncanny how the corporate autocrats managed to become unavailable when a strike was imminent.).

In spite of these handicaps—the combined opposition of the Pullman Company, two dozen railroads, virtually every commercial newspaper and magazine—for the first ten days of the boycott the union seemed on the road to victory. Subsequently Debs claimed that the railroads were hanging on the ropes: "Their immediate resources were exhausted, their properties were paralyzed, and they were unable to operate their trains." Then came the cruncher; the federal government, instead of being the referee, became a giant pugilist in the opposition corner. From this round forward, the tactics used were a series of low blows. They were ostentiously dirty, and designedly so. Since President Cleveland at the time had his hands full with a tariff bill in Congress, federal policy was made largely by the attorney general of the United States. But he needed deputies on the spot in Chicago; his solution was to appoint as special federal attorney to handle the situation the same man who was counsel to a large railroad involved in the boycott. The attorney general made no bones about his objective: "I feel that the true way of dealing with the matter is by a force which is overwhelming and prevents any attempt at resistance." His reasoning went thus. (1) Any national railroad strike was

---

*These conditions need not be detailed here; a few specifics will suffice. In less than a year beginning in July, 1893, the number of employees fell from 5,500 to 3,300. Dividends were actually increased, while payrolls declined 38 per cent. Rents in the company-owned houses were not reduced. Perhaps worst of all was the omnipresence of that would-be dictator, Mr. Pullman. One resident explained: "We are born in a Pullman house, fed from the Pullman shop, taught in the Pullman school, catechized in the Pullman church, and when we die we shall be buried in the Pullman cemetery and go to the Pullman hell."

automatically illegal.* (2) The causes of the strike in the town of Pullman were not relevant to the legality of the boycott. (3) Local and state officials could not be trusted to police the dispute. The second point may be conceded. The first may be technically accurate on the basis of the precedents then existing, but it was not a constructive approach to the problem. The third was simply absurd; in retrospect we must shake our heads sadly and say that Altgeld's image stemming from the Haymarket pardon had come home to haunt him.

However deceitful, the third postulate was needed for the attorney general's full program. First his agent procured from two federal judges an injunction against the boycott on several grounds, including interference with the mails and obstruction of interstate commerce. Its terms were amazingly sweeping; it forbade any person to do or say anything to promote the walkout. Next, ironically on Independence Day, the president rushed onward to a tragic climax by sending the United States army into Chicago. This act brought heated protests from Governor Altgeld, who pointed out, correctly, that the president could under the express words of the Constitution send federal troops into a state only to remedy certain evils and by certain procedures. The stipulated evils were not present. Nor were the proper procedures followed: "local self-government is a fundamental principle of our Constitution. Each community shall govern itself so long as it can and is ready and able to enforce the law." The response from the White House was haughty:

> While I am still persuaded that I have neither transcended my authority nor duty in the emergency that confronts us, it seems to me that in this hour of danger and public distress, discussion may well give way to active efforts on the part of all in authority to restore obedience to law and to protect life and property.

The strike was dead. The union was destroyed. Debs went to jail for contempt of court. But the episode cannot be abandoned without more analysis; it raised issues that have persisted to the present. One preacher made this contribution to the discussion: "the Anarchist is a savage in a civilized country who is trying to turn civilization into barbarism." How often has it happened in American history that the propertied classes and their pensioners, such as college administrators, have blockaded all the water taps through which justice might flow and then denounced anybody who tried to tap the water main as a saboteur?

Then, too, Altgeld was speaking sound doctrine when he called for the widest possible application of Jefferson's dictum that the government is best

---

*In no way do I intend to minimize the gravity of similar situations; recent strikes by postal employees and sanitation workers have reminded us that some functions are indispensable. But if the right to strike is to be denied, another mechanism to insure equity must be substituted. I doubt if compulsory arbitration is the answer. Why not tie the wages of essential civil servants to those of carpenters and steelworkers?

that governs least. Supporters of the New Deal and its successors have hailed every growth in federal power as an advance of human welfare (Chapter 26). Today, when the bureaucracy in Washington and elsewhere has reached an appalling stage of rampaging elephantiasis, we can have a keener appreciation of Altgeld's protests. We can see better why as much control as possible should be returned to the neighborhoods. And of course we can now see better how the matter touches on the division of power among the branches of government. For decades many liberal historians wrote as if the "great presidents" were synonymous with "the strong presidents," and wrote scornfully about weak executives like Harding (Chapter 24). Events have reminded us that a president can be too strong; it is more than ever true that absolute power corrupts absolutely. Finally, it might be remarked here that we hear the phrase "law-and-order" so often linked that we unfortunately think as if it were all one word. This is by no means so. Many Americans have always been ready, when they feared for the maintenance of order, to forego the rule of law. Thus we get arrests without warrants, detention without trials, suppression by the authorities of peaceable public meetings. Observing in a few months the Great Northern strike, the Pullman boycott, a farflung coal strike, one periodical lamented: "It is probably safe to say that in no civilized country in this century, not actually in the throes of war or open insurrection, has society been so disorganized as it was in the United States during the first half of 1894; never was human life held so cheap; never did constituted authorities appear so incompetent to enforce respect for the law." To this the republic had fallen.

As this passage suggests, the influence of government can also be too weak in respect to certain issues. For instance, Grover Cleveland had been re-installed in the White House after making powerful pleas for tariff reduction. But he was balked by Congress. The Wilson-Gorman bill aimed to reduce import duties from an average of 49 per cent of value to 30 per cent. The measure was passed by a large majority of representatives. But the Senate adopted more than 600 amendments. After months of haggling and log-rolling and back-scratching, the bill became law without Cleveland's signature; the defection of eight Democratic senators who voted for their constituencies (oh, those sugar states such as Louisiana and Maryland) rather than with their party proved to be the margin. The recurrent gold crises also highlighted the limitations of federal power. Cleveland simply did not have tools with which he could block the steady drainage of gold out of the country; as fears heightened abroad that the United States might leave the gold standard, investors in Europe sold their American securities and brought their capital home. Pressure against the gold standard was intense, and the only way that Cleveland could fend off a departure from "sound money" and "fiscal honesty" was to borrow from private agencies frequent injections of gold. This policy depended on the cooperation of investment bankers, and they dictated the terms of the loans. In simple fact, the most powerful man in the nation was not the president but rather the private banker J. P. Morgan, who could reach large supplies of capital (Chapter 21).

Other impediments to remedial actions by the federal government were interposed by the courts. The class bias of the Supreme Court was blatant. Perhaps its holdings in the various cases arising from the Pullman boycott can be justified by existing precedents. But the same argument cannot be made for three other decisions. One involved the meaning of the Sherman Anti-Trust Act of 1890. The constitutional basis of this statute was the power of Congress over interstate commerce. But ruled the Court: "Commerce succeeds to manufacture, and is not a part of it." Even if we concede that the defendant, a sugar refiner, was a manufacturer, it does not follow at all from the quoted edict that manufacture is not a part of interstate commerce. The next major decision was, if possible, worse. A tax of 2 per cent on personal and corporate incomes of more than $4,000 had been imposed by the Wilson-Gorman Act. A petitioner appealed that the tax violated the constitutional provision that all "direct taxes" had to be apportioned among the states according to population, and also that it breached the requirement "all duties, imports, and excises shall be uniform throughout the United States." A lawyer for the appellant warned that validation of the statute would lead to graver abuses until the nation would see "finally a provision that only the twenty people who have the greatest estates should bear the whole taxation, and after that communism, anarchy, and then, the ever following despotism." Outside the judicial chambers the rhetoric was equally florid, and equally irrelevant. As the proposition was put by the leading law journal in the East, it was the job of the Supreme Court to deliver "a crushing defeat of the pet schemes of the scum of Europe." After some legal complications, plus appeals to protect "thousands of widows and orphans" from an unjust exaction, a bare majority of the Court voted to disallow the income-tax clause.

A third judgment was as abhorrent as the second. An appeal came to the Supreme Court against a state law requiring separate coaches on railroads for blacks and whites. The statute did not violate the Fourteenth Amendment, ruled the Court, if the coaches were equal in quality. Only one justice dissented, and he composed a model of concision: "Our Constitution is color-blind." To this subject we will return (Chapter 29).*

In the field of diplomacy, American policy had been founded on a careful assessment of means against ends. It had studied the balance of power, and then sought precise and limited goals. Now it became grandiose. In

---

*A comment, to be expanded below, seems appropriate. Here was a blanket endorsement by the highest bench of the "separate but equal" doctrine. When it was rejected by a successor Court in 1954, that body most unwisely ventured on elaborate non-judicial exhortations. It might have simply reiterated, "Our Constitution is color-blind."

seeking to use braggadocio to win the reputation of being a world power, the nation's power became more unstable.

Hawaii gives an introduction to this theme. Americans in the China trade had become involved there before the eighteenth century ended, especially to buy sandalwood that they carried to the Asian mainland. American officials made several efforts at closer relations with the archipelago: a treaty of intended annexation in 1854, a reciprocity treaty (mutual reduction or elimination of tariffs) in 1855. But these efforts were blocked by opposition within the United States. Then recurrent crises hit the islands' biggest industry—sugar growing. The first reciprocity agreement between the two governments, made in 1875, was renewed until the McKinley Tariff Act of 1890. This statute pulled a cute trick: not only would domestic planters get a bounty of 2 cents a pound, but henceforth all foreign sugar would enter duty-free. To sugar planters in Hawaii, many of them transplanted Americans, the measure was disastrous to their market position. The revolution they organized in 1894 won without bloodshed, and it won with the aid of the United States. Several strands of influence can be seen. The influence of paleface planters was undoubtedly vital; they wanted to become a territory of the republic in order to regain their markets for sugar. They had the support of the American envoy, who proclaimed that "the Hawaiian pear is now fully ripe, and this is the golden hour for the United States to pluck it." The merger was encouraged by new strategic-mercantile concepts that were current; in 1890 Alfred T. Mahan had published the most compelling work in this vein. His book was entitled *The Influence of Sea Power upon History, 1660–1783,* but its message to contemporaries was urgent: it argued that no nation could succeed in the worldwide struggle for markets unless it had ports around the globe, plus a strong navy. The latter objective was advanced when, from 1890 to 1892, Congress voted funds for four warships. For a few years, however, the Hawaiian annexationist movement was stalled. Its most effective opponent was Grover Cleveland, returned to the White House in 1893. At that time a treaty to annex Hawaii was pending in the Senate. But it had not been ratified. The new president withdrew it, saying: "The mission of our nation is to build up and make a greater country out of what we have, instead of annexing islands." This should not be taken to mean that Cleveland was cautious in the assertion of American power; far from it.

A telltale episode is known as the Venezuelan boundary dispute. Although Great Britain way back in 1814 had taken over a portion of Guiana from the Dutch, the limits of its sovereignty there had not been settled. Many persons believed that the contested area held rich mineral deposits. Also the multiplication of Irish and German immigrants within the United States brought a growth of anglophobia. The American government, engaged since 1887 in trying to resolve the Venezuelan boundary with Great Britain, decided in 1895 to force the issue toward arbitration. It had a rapacious terrier to do the job; the man who had been attorney general during the Pullman boycott had moved up to the Department of State, and his message to England read in part as follows:

> Today the United States is practically sovereign on this continent, and its fiat is law upon the subjects to which it confines its interposition. Why? It is not because of the pure friendship or good will felt for it. It is not simply by reason of its high character as a civilized state, nor because wisdom, justice, and equity are the invariable characteristics of the dealings of the United States. It is because, in addition to all other grounds, its infinite resources combined with its isolated position render it master of the situation, and practically invulnerable as against any or all other powers.

Although this statement was so self-righteous and domineering as to be intolerable, Great Britain had to tolerate it, because it was true. During the entire life of the Monroe Doctrine, no American diplomat had claimed that it required arbitration of every dispute in Latin America that involved a European country. The expansive doctrine revealed a changing temper in the United States toward its relations abroad. Cleveland himself called the obstreperous communique "the best thing of the kind that I have ever read."

Responsible British officials were almost as irresponsible as the Americans. More than four months passed before they replied at all. The answer came by mail, not by cable. It was a peremptory rejection. The president got Congressional approval to name a commission to fix the boundary. Then the United States should employ "every means in its power" to maintain that line. To the hazard of war was added the threat of renewed financial panic; British investors hastily pulled their capital away from Wall Street, while bankers and brokers denounced Grover Cleveland for his impetuosity. But the fall in the stock market lasted less than a day; American investors took up the slack that Europeans had created. Just as there was no acceleration of the depression, there was no war. Great Britain was in no condition to fight the United States. She did not have one strong ally in the entire world. Her relations with France over African territory were so strained that they would verge on war by 1898. Germany had built up a steel industry that greatly enhanced its capacity for naval construction and other munitions. England initiated friendly talks, and in the event the Venezuelan border was indeed arbitrated. American assertiveness had its way.

These thrusts and counterthrusts, plus others, comprised the field of force for the election of 1896. From the formal opening of the campaign, remarkable events ensued. Normally a president controls the national convention of his party. Exceptions, some of them marginal, can be noted: John Adams in 1800, the other Adams in 1828, John Tyler in 1844, Lyndon Johnson in 1968. But the repudiation of Grover Cleveland by the Democratic nominating conclave in 1896 was unmistakable. Although he had allies, the pre-eminence of Governor Altgeld at the meeting in Chicago was clear. On point after point, the platform was a decisive rejection of the administration. Whereas the president had been struggling to sustain the "single monetary standard" of gold, his party now declared for the conversion into coin of all silver presented at the mint, with a ratio to gold of 16 to 1. It denounced the Supreme Court's judgment on the income tax in tones as stern as those that Lincoln had used about the Dred Scott case. It condemned "government by injunction" in the Pullman boycott. The document declared that "as labor creates the wealth of the country, we demand the passage of such laws as may be necessary to protect it in all its rights." In the perspective of time, these planks were surely more significant than the nomination for the presidency of a ninny named William Jennings Bryan. In spite of the contrary pretensions of some historians, Bryan was a nobody who would never become a somebody. Listen to him talk at the convention in Chicago:

> You come to us and tell us that the great cities are in favor of the gold standard; we reply that the great cities rest upon our broad and fertile prairies. Burn down your cities and leave our farms, and your cities will spring up again as if by magic; but destroy our farms and the grass will grow in the streets of every city in the country.

He did not see how the cities had been superseding rural areas for decades. In his boyhood he learned little, and in his adage he forgot most of that.* Even though he managed to secure the Populist nomination also, even though he would be put forward two more times by the Democrats, he did not fool all of his contemporaries; after that famous Cross of Gold oration in Chicago, Altgeld turned to his friend Clarence Darrow: "I have been thinking over Bryan's speech. What did he say anyhow?" Bryan lived in Lincoln, Nebraska. Readers who have never seen the River Platte should still enjoy the pungency of the comment that he was like that stream: an inch deep, and a mile wide at the mouth.

The Republican was no bargain either. William McKinley was the dreary sort who drones along about the virtues of God and motherhood. After he sponsored the tariff act of 1890 he was beaten for re-election to the House of Representatives. But he soon recovered to serve two terms as governor of Ohio. As against Bryan, he had advantages: brains and money. The first belonged to Mark Hanna, an industrialist who was notorious for buying votes at the polls in Cleveland. Hanna also saw to the money. Standard Oil and J. P. Morgan gave $250,000 each. Hanna and James J. Hill were seen daily in a buggy going from one corporate office to the next in Manhattan. Republican campaign funds mounted to at least $3.5 million; one estimate from a sympathizer put

---

*But note his role in forestalling war as Wilson's secretary of state, Document 22-1.

the total at twice that. The Chicago office alone spent almost $2 million, of which 75 per cent came from New York; at last the "usury states" were sending back part of the booty. The G.O.P. distributed five throw-aways for each voter, 100 million of them. Publicity was not the only Republican tactic. Altgeld, admittedly no impartial witness, claimed later that they stole 100,000 votes in his state. Our evidence is spotty as to the amount of economic coercion that some corporations exerted on their employees, but clearly there was some: a contract with a shipyard in Wilmington, Delaware, provided for cancellation if the Democrats won the election.

They didn't. The major consequences, ironically, were not those expected. Most Americans thought that the crucial contest in the campaign was whether the federal government, by re-instituting the unlimited coinage of silver, would boost the level of prices. Inflation did come, but the remonitization of silver had nothing to with it, and neither did the switch from Democratic to Republican control in Washington; it came with an enlarged supply of gold from the Rand fields in South Africa and the Klondike strikes. The chief results of 1896 lay in two other directions. One was the emergence of the Republicans as a (semi-) permanent majority in the nation. In a presidential tally of 14 million, McKinley's plurality topped 700,000. His party did not lose a single county in New England. He swept the East. Bryan won the South, and the silver-mining states, and most of the prairies, but that was all and it was not enough. Excepting the unusual circumstances of 1912 and 1916, the Republicans would not lose another federal poll until the New Deal (Chapters 22, 26).

It is not clear whether the second major shift was due to the political flopover at the capital. Perhaps the changes in America would have brought it anyway, no matter which party had held power.* But the import of the switch can hardly be doubted. The United States altered drastically its stance toward foreign relations. In an earlier period America's world power had been born and consolidated because it had been careful not to make commitments that exceeded its resources. Insofar as possible, for instance, it hid (not always gratefully) behind the British navy. To summarize the transformation in a different way, American foreign policy since 1789 had meant a careful measuring of aims against means. One recent writer has characterized the transition as going from realism to romanticism. Thus on the one hand we have President Jefferson averring that New Orleans must not become the possession of a strong European nation; on the other, President Wilson declaring that we must make the world safe for democracy. The former objective could be attained, and was. The latter was not, and could not have been.

It was Cuba (ninety miles from home) that galvanized the growing

---

*Granting a few honorable exceptions, questions of this rank have not been studied astutely. In 1961 a historian-politician said to me about a pure historian: "He thinks it still matters who is president." The proposition is worth some thought.

SECULAR BUSINESS TRENDS VS BUSINESS CYCLES, 1790-1900

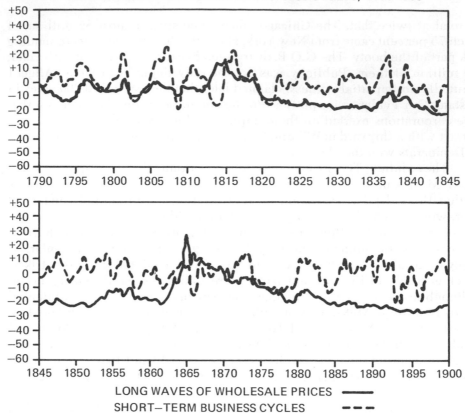

LONG WAVES OF WHOLESALE PRICES ▬▬▬
SHORT—TERM BUSINESS CYCLES ▬ ▬ ▬

FIGURE 20-3. *Secular Business Trends vs. Short-run Cycles*

Statistics is commonly said to have begun with the English economist W. Stanley Jevons a century ago. The emerging techniques can be remarkably useful, but many historians are still ignoring them or making a muddle of them. The applications of statistics can deal with a range of problems that goes far beyond economic history: Did immigration influence voting patterns? Did religious affiliations affect the kinds of books that were popular? A person can go a long way by knowing a little about correlations and linear regressions. Several superb books exist, but I do not know of any 25-page introduction that surpasses the first chapter of H. T. Epstein, *Elementary Biophysics* (1963).

The above chart illustrates one way that statistics can be helpful in separating elements that in reality are entangled. The great man in initiating this type of analysis of the American economic story was the late Wesley Clair Mitchell; among his successors the biggest name is Simon Kuznets. The above chart is an effort to distinguish the secular trends (long waves in prices) from the shorter run business cycles that usually last seven to ten years. In actuality the two phenomena are going on simultaneously, but, by refined manipulations, scholars have made at least approximate differentiation.

In seeking to understand the political history of the last third of the nineteenth century, a crucial consideration is the effect of the constantly falling level of prices on farmers who were also debtors. Some of the implications for other interest groups have been discussed above in Chapter 17.

American jingoism. After Cubans rebelled against Spanish rule in 1868, President Grant wanted to sustain the insurgents. He was held back. But in the next three decades the restraints weakened. Also an innovation by the German government—the payment of a bounty on exports of beet sugar—drove Cuba's cane sugar planters to desperation. The main market for Caribbean cane sugar had always been Britain; now Germany with its beet sugar became a strong competitor for the British market, and the price in London of unrefined cane sugar fell 50 percent. Revolution in Cuba began in February, 1895. Intrigue became elaborate within the United States. A Florida senator secured the appointment of his son as agent for Cuban insurrectionist bonds in England. Senator Henry Cabot Lodge of Massachusetts raved against Spanish "butcheries" and, quite properly, denounced the occupying army for herding Cuban civilians into concentration camps. Not so properly, he emphasized that a free island "would mean a great market to the United States; it would mean an opportunity for American capital." The atmosphere in Washington became fervid. But within the Democratic ranks, resistance remained strong. One party leader wrote in his diary, "The jingoism in the air is a curious thing, and unaccountable, except on account of the unrest of our people, and the willingness to turn from domestic to foreign affairs, always making greatest allowance for political maneuvering, and the ridiculousness of conducting foreign affairs by such town meetings as the Senate and House have become." When Congress resolved that the Cuban rebels should be recognized as belligerents, the president still refused to take that step.

The balance between the contending forces was tilted by the 1896 election, which added to the strength of the party that held the highest concentration of expansionists. That McKinley became president was also a change, but not a vital one. He would do whatever he thought was popular; Joseph G. Cannon commented that McKinley kept his ear so close to the ground that he got it full of grasshoppers. The crucial factors in rallying militaristic sentiment were a few politicians, missionaries, and commercial periodicals. The press fabricated a vogue in favor of the late Emperor Napoleon, of all people. Clerics explained that we must free the world from paganism; seemingly this slop played a large role in McKinley's behavior (Document 20-3). All this registered deep on a widespread sense of anxiety and depression. Just read Theodore Roosevelt writing to his friend Senator Lodge during the Venezuela boundary dispute: "Let the fight come if it must. I don't care whether our sea coast cities are bombarded or not; we would take Canada." Probably the strongest wind to fan the flames came from part of the urban press. As cities grew, circulation of newspapers grew with population. Some dailies had outgrown the staid mold of the past; they sent special correspondents to Cuba to telegraph regular stories about Cuban babies being bayonetted by Spanish villains. They instituted red headlines. All of this paraphernalia was put to lurid use when the American battleship *Maine* exploded and sank in Havana harbor, 15 February, 1898. Two hundred fifty

489

sailors were killed. Why the ship was there is irrelevant here. Why the explosion occurred is not definitely known and never will be. What was determinative was the American reaction, which can be illustrated from the front page of the Kansas City *Star*:

HE SAW THE TORPEDO

MAIMED SEAMAN'S STORY

Senator Lodge thought that, apart from the businessmen of Boston, the voters of his state were nearly unanimous for war. As a correspondent wrote to him, "I have not met a man . . . in the aristocratic upper crust in which you and I are imbedded, who considers that we have any justifiable cause for war. Below that crust . . . the wish for war is *almost* universal." Theodore Roosevelt, Assistant Secretary of the Navy, wrote to a New York banker: "We here in Washington have grown to feel that almost every man connected with the big business interests of the country is anxious to court any infamy if only peace can be obtained and the business situation be not disturbed." The city editor of a Manhattan newspaper wrote to the president: "Big corporations here now believe we will have war. Believe all would welcome it as a relief to suspense." This seems plausible. Standard Oil and other giants wanted to expand their exports, and Asia seemed the most promising goal. Some executives thought that hostilities would conduce to this end. Most religious sects were expansionist. Doubtless many Americans were outraged by Spanish brutalities in Cuba. By the end of March, 1898, the French ambassador was reporting home, "A sort of bellicose fury has seized the American nation." Perhaps it would be too glib to say that McKinley lacked the courage to stand up to pressure; his conception of politics in a republic was that the majority of the moment should not only have its way but also that its inclinations should not be questioned. He wrote a message to Congress asking authority to use American might to restore peace and stable government in Cuba. It did not call for Cuban independence. Not daring to make this demand publicly for fear it would offend conservative senators in his own party, he presented it privately to Spain. Spain refused. By now the president was out of control on Capitol Hill. After some tangles in Congress, a war resolution was passed on 25 April. A Republican congressman tried to summarize the development: ". . . possibly the president could have worked the business out without a war, but the current was too strong, the demagogues too numerous, and the fall elections too near."

Once the United States was at war against Spain, the scope of its operations grew at once. A fleet was sent immediately to the Philippines where it destroyed ten moribund Spanish vessels. Not one American life was lost, no American ship was seriously damaged. The acquisitive atmosphere of wartime facilitated the annexation of Hawaii. Again there were delays because the president was timorous, but at last he committed himself: "We need Hawaii just as much and a good deal more than we did California. It is manifest destiny." A joint resolution annexing Hawaii and making it a Territory passed through Congess. By that time the largest expeditionary force in American history put out to sea for Cuba—17,000 men. It was badly commanded; a sane general does not land his troops in an open roadstead and send them ashore in heavy surf. Fortunately the Spanish leaders were none too efficient either, but their soldiers were brave and some battles were bitter. More than one historian has been bemused by the sentence of Secretary of State John Hay: "It has been a splendid little war." It did not seem so to the men on the battlefields. In the words of Theodore Roosevelt after the famous charge up San Juan Hill, "Tell the President for Heaven's sake to send us every regiment and above all every battery possible. We have won so far at a heavy cost, but the Spaniards fight very hard and charging these intrenchments against modern rifles is terrible. . . . We *must* have help—thousands of men, batteries, and *food* and ammunition." Colonel Roosevelt may have been a coward morally, but he was not a physical coward, and he knew the odds.

The cause of Spain was of course hopeless. But she was not conquered on land anywhere in the Caribbean. Obliteration of her fleet there forced her to yield. The war was ended by a treaty concluded at Paris on 10 December, 1898. Spain gave up all title to Cuba, and ceded to the United States both Puerto Rico and the Philippines.

In the middle five years of the last decade of the nineteenth century, any interpretation of the United States as "the land of consensus" would have met with scorn. Millions of Americans feared that the nation would be torn by its second civil war within forty years. But this time it would not be North versus South. The conflicts could not be pigeonholed so neatly. It was black against white, employers against wage earners, farmers against Wall Street, Italians or Poles against Anglo-Saxons, Protestants against Catholics, gentiles against Jews. The contradictions within the nation were revealed in a setting of financial panic, devastating depression, race riots, labor strife, the culmination of the long struggle over the currency. The depression can be seen now to have been caused chiefly by the lopsided and self-destructive structure of personal incomes. But the years of hard times did not bring adjustments; the distribution of rewards was as unjust and as unworkable in 1903 as in 1893, in spite of attempts to enact a federal income tax and other corrective laws. The shedding of red blood did not improve black-white relations. Only the monetary situation found a corrective. Even that did not come from the wisdom in Washington. It came from gold strikes in South Africa, Alaska, the Klondike. The manifold frustrations of countless citizens primed them for the release that "a splendid little war" might bring.

SOME NOTABLE EVENTS

1890 Sherman Anti-Trust Act, 2 July.
Sherman Silver Purchase Act, 14 July.
McKinley Tariff Act.
Pension Act.
Ocala Demands issued in Florida by farmers' organizations, December.
Arthur Thayer Mahan, *The Influence of Sea Power upon History.*

1892 Homestead strike, June 28–mid-October.
People's party (Populists) gets more than 1,000,000 votes.

1893 Financial panic begins in January; becomes severe depression.
U.S. begins to appoint "ambassadors," 1 March.
Columbian Exposition in Chicago, May–October.
American Railway Union organized, 20 June.
Altgeld pardons Haymarket defendants, 26 June.
Repeal of the Silver Purchase Act, 1 November.
More than 600 financial institutions have gone bankrupt in the year.

1894 ARU strikes against Great Northern, 13 April–1 May.
ARU boycotts Pullman cars, 26 June–19 July.
House of Representatives opposes the annexation of Hawaii.

1895 *U.S.* v. *E. C. Knight Company*, 20 January, decision limiting Sherman Anti-Trust Act.
Gold outflows from Treasury in January total $43 million—a record.
Pollock v. *Farmers' Loan and Trust Company*, 8 April.
National Association of Manufacturers formed.
In re Debs, 27 May, conviction as outgrowth of Pullman strike.
U.S. intervenes in Venezuela boundary dispute, July.

1896 Presidential vote is 14 million; McKinley's plurality is 700,000.
Senate resolves in favor of recognizing Cuban rebels as belligerents, 28 February.

1897 Exports rise; economy begins to revive.
European powers seize territory in China.

1898 De Lome letter published, 9 February; public outcry against Spanish ambassador.
Maine sunk at Havana, 15 February.
McKinley submits his war message, 11 April.
Congress resolves for independence of Cuba, 20 April.
Congress resolves for annexation of Hawaii, 7 July.
Paris Peace Treaty with Spain, 10 December.

Ways to Study History XX

Let your sympathies flow. No scholar would question the ability of C. Vann Woodward to be patient; he did a study of the Wormley Conference of 1877 that rests on a sweeping exploration of the sources and that catches hold of a vast panorama of American economics and politics. Woodward has advanced some interpretations that seem to me, perhaps even in a few instances to him, mistaken. But besides his industry he has shown wide range and acute imagination (an oft-misunderstood word the definition of which will be probed in Chapter 27).

Admirable though these qualities are, they are not the key to Woodward's greatness as a historian. He was born and reared in Georgia, and he has not forgotten the agonies and the joys of poor farmers, whether white or black, in the South. This empathy was palpable in his doctoral dissertation and first book, *Tom Watson* (1938). The biography is not flamboyant, but in it the human passions surge and roar. Where the author is describing a young congressman risking his career by orating that all poor Georgians regardless of color must stick together, every reader can perceive his exultation in his hero. But he does not gloss over Watson's evils. As the aging senator becomes a bigot spewing hatred against blacks and Jews and Catholics, we realize Woodward's horror. In this reversal, the author seems to imply, lies an enigma that I cannot fully comprehend. If we could understand it, we might approach the core of the Southern contradictions as they have worked out over time.

The most ambitious effort to return to this problem, among Woodward's subsequent works, was *Origins of the New South, 1877–1913* (1951). Here again are diligence in research—and the same old sympathy. No study trying to cope with so broad a theme can be called definitive, but this one will survive as a monument, and every future student will have to pay homage to it.

Document 20-1

Henry Demarest Lloyd (1847–1903) published his "Story of a Great Monopoly" in 1881. Readers may be surprised to learn that the early power and prosperity of Standard Oil stemmed from its marketing of kerosene as an illuminant. Gasoline, before the automobile, was virtually a waste product called "stove naphtha."

Kerosene has become, by its cheapness, the people's light the world over. In the United States we used 220,000,000 gallons of petroleum last year. It has come into such demand abroad that our exports of it increased from 79,458,888 gallons in 1868, to 417,648,544 in 1879. It goes all over Europe, and to the far East. The Oriental demand for it is increasing faster than any other. . . . Very few of the forty millions of people in the United States who burn kerosene know that its production, manufacture, and export, its price at home and abroad, have been controlled for years by a single corporation, the Standard Oil Company. The company began in a partnership, in the early years of the civil war, between Samuel Andrews and John Rockefeller in Cleveland. Rockefeller had been a bookkeeper in some interior town in Ohio, and had afterwards made a few thousand dollars by keeping a flour store in Cleveland. Andrews had been a day laborer in refineries, and so poor that his wife took in sewing. . . .

The contract is in print by which the Pennsylvania Railroad agreed with the Standard, under the name of the South Improvement Company, to double the freights on oil to everybody, but to repay the Standard one dollar for every barrel of oil it shipped, and one dollar for every barrel any of its competitors shipped. . . . Ostensibly this contract was given up, in deference to the whirlwind of indignation it excited. But Rockefeller, the manager of the Standard, was a man who could learn from defeat. He made no more tell-tale contracts that could be printed. . . .

Document 20-2

William A. Peffer, member of the United States
Senate from Kansas, became a leading Populist.
This exposition appeared in his *The Farmer's
Side* (1891).

*The American farmer of to-day is altogether a different sort of man from his ancestor of fifty
or a hundred years ago. A great many men and women now living remember when farmers were
largely manufacturers; that is to say, they made a great many implements for their own use. Every
farmer had an assortment of tools with which he made wooden implements, as forks and rakes,
handles for his hoes and plows, spokes for his wagon, and various other implements made wholly
of wood. Then the farmer produced flax and hemp and wool and cotton. These fibers were
prepared upon the farm; they were spun into yarn, woven into cloth, made into garments, and
worn at home. . . .*

*Coming from that time to the present, we find that everything nearly has been changed. All
over the West particularly the farmer thrashes his wheat all at one time, he disposes of it all at
one time, and in a great many instances the straw is wasted. He sells his hogs, and buys bacon
and pork; he sells his cattle, and buys fresh beef and canned beef or corned beef, as the case
may be; he sells his fruit, and buys it back in cans. . . .*

*Besides all this, and what seems stranger than anything else, whereas in the earlier time
the American home was a free home, unincumbered, not one case in a thousand where a home
was mortgaged to secure the payment of borrowed money, and whereas but a small amount of
money was then needed for actual use in conducting the business of farming, there was always
enough of it among the farmers to supply the demand, now, when at least ten times as much is
needed, there is little or none to be obtained, nearly half the farms are mortgaged for as much as
they are worth, and interest rates are exorbitant. . . .*

Document 20-3

On 21 November, 1899, a delegation from the
General Missionary Committee of the Methodist
Episcopal Church came to see President McKinley. One delegate reported that McKinley spoke
to the group as follows.

*Gentlemen, just a moment. I have something I would like to say. And first, just a word with
you, esteemed Bishops. Last winter Congress increased the army by several regiments, but
provided no chaplains for them. Now I believe in army chaplains. . . . But some time ago I
appointed a Methodist chaplain, who came to me with letters and recommendations from half a
dozen presiding elders, doctors of divinity, etc., as well as members of Congress and senators,
and recently they have had to court-martial him for various misconduct, and I suppose we shall
have to cashier him—greatly to my regret as a brother Methodist. . . .*

*Hold a moment longer! Not quite yet, gentlemen! Before you go I would like to say just a
word about the Philippine business. I have been criticised a good deal about the Philippines, but
don't deserve it. The truth is I didn't want the Philippines, and when they came to us, as a gift
from the gods, I did not know what to do with them. When the Spanish war broke out Dewey was
at Hongkong, and I ordered him to go to Manila and to capture or destroy the Spanish fleet, and
he had to; because, if defeated, he had no place to refit on that side of the globe, and if the Dons
were victorious they would likely cross the Pacific and ravage our Oregon and California coasts.
And so he had to destroy the Spanish fleet, and did it! But that was as far as I thought then.*

*When next I realized that the Philippines had dropped into our laps I confess I did not
know what to do with them. I sought counsel from all sides—Democrats as well as*

Republicans—but, got little help. I thought first we would take only Manila; then Luzon; then other islands perhaps also. I walked the floor of the White House night after night until midnight; and I am not ashamed to tell you, gentlemen, that I went down on my knees and prayed Almighty God for light and guidance more than one night. And one night late it came to me this way—I don't know how it was, but it came: (1) That we could not give them back to Spain—that would be cowardly and dishonorable; (2) that we could not turn them over to France or Germany—our commercial rivals in the Orient—that would be bad business and discreditable; (3) that we could not leave them to themselves—they were unfit for self-government—and they would soon have anarchy and misrule over there worse than Spain's was; and (4) that there was nothing for us to do but to take them all, and to educate the Filipinos, and uplift and civilize and Christianize them, and by God's grace do the very best we could by them, as our fellow-men for whom Christ also died. And then I went to bed, and went to sleep, and slept soundly, and the next morning I sent for the chief engineer of the War Department (our mapmaker) and I told him to put the Philippines on the map of the United States, and there they are, and there they will stay while I am President! . . .

Don't go yet, please! Just a word more, friends; there's no hurry! . . . And before we part I just want to say to you, whatever men may think about me, or not think, I am a Methodist, and nothing but a Methodist—a Christian, and nothing but a Christian. When I was a little child my dear old mother used to take me to Methodist prayer meeting and class meeting. When I grew older I early joined the Methodist Church and Sunday school, and then became a Sunday school teacher, and afterward a Sunday school superintendent, and member of the Epworth League. . . . And by the blessing of heaven, I mean to live and die, please God, in the faith of my mother!

FIGURE E. *William Sidney Mount,* The Banjo Player

A native of Long Island, William Sidney Mount lived from 1807 to 1868. He got some formal training at the National Institute of Design, but illness drove him back to his rural habitat, fortunately for his art and for posterity. The son of a prosperous inkeeper, Mount delighted in music and in a cool draught of beer. His approach to art was to hang loose; his work seems easy and relaxed. He opined, "I never paint on a picture unless I feel in the right spirit." The tone of his art is expansive, the palette is founded on grays and browns, but accented by exhilarations that burst from an unerring sense of the texture of light at different hours of the day. Toward the end of his life he believed that Rembrandt was giving him personal messages about how to cope with the mysteries of optics.

His outlook was relentlessly democratic. "Paint pictures that will take with the public—never paint for the few." Mount's ebullience extended to his subjects as well as to technique; Walt Whitman applauded him for his portrayal of a black man who had won a goose at a raffle. This specific Negro, so Whitman said, was an individual American and not an insipid stereotype. The plaudit was deserved. Of all outstanding writers in the United States, Whitman, Emily Dickinson, and Mark Twain seem closest to Mount in a fervor to record the nobilities of everyday life.

FIGURE F. *John Singer Sargent,* Robert Louis Stevenson

Robert Louis Stevenson (1850–94) is remembered as the author of *Treasure Island* with its pegleg Long John Silver. But that and *A Child's Garden of Verses* are only two of his many works on which Americans doted for generations. The Scottish writer can epitomize for us the idolatry that the United States lavished on British culture toward the end of the nineteenth century. Self-esteeming Americans preferred British writers to their countrymen, British painters to their compatriots.

Thus it is fitting that this portrait of Stevenson was done by John Singer Sargent (1856–1925). Begotten by a Philadelphia doctor who had retired to Europe, Sargent was born in the citadel of Renaissance painting—Florence. His archetypes were the portraits done centuries earlier by Frans Hals and Velásquez. He painted people, for fees running as high as $5,000. He delighted in his work, but we must wonder if he respected it. Stevenson, who sat for this picture in 1884, called Sargent "a person with a kind of exhibition manner and English accent. . . ." The painter himself called portraiture "a pimp's profession." When a subject asked prior to his first sitting if Sargent did not want to chat with him a while to find out what sort of man he was, the reply was doubtless languid: "No, I paint what I see." If Bingham or Eakins (Figure 13-6; Figure 19-6) used those words, we could guess what he meant. But Sargent went on: "But I don't dig beneath the surface for things that don't appear before my eyes." When a female subject objected to the way he painted her mouth, he suggested that the feature should be omitted altogether. Another woman complained of the way he had depicted her nose. He hastily replied that she could easily fix "a little thing like that" after she got home.

His mastery of surface texture was supreme, and for that his age respected him and paid him well. To drop the subject there should speak volumes about the age of John Singer Sargent. The protagonists of his paintings are exposed only to the degree that is socially useful to them.

Courtesy of the Suffolk Museum & Carriage House at Stony Brook, L.I. Melville Collection.

FIGURE E. *William Sidney Mount,* The Banjo Player

Courtesy of The Taft Museum, Cincinnati, Ohio

FIGURE F. *John Singer Sargent,* Robert Louis Stevenson   (above)

FIGURE G. *Rafael Tufino,* Fiesta Poster   (right)

III FIESTA DE LA MUSICA PUERTORRIQUEÑA
TEATRO TAPIA NOV. 1968
INSTITUTO DE CULTURA PUERTORRIQUEÑA

To Vicky and Ray with love, to free persons like you are.

FIGURE H. *Henry Linschitz,* Maine Tidepool

FIGURE G. *Rafael Tufino,* Fiesta Poster

When critics think of posters as a legitimate form of modern art, they are likely to think first of the playbills of the Frenchman Henri Toulouse-Lautrec (1864–1901). Perhaps the highest that this genre has reached in the contemporary United States is the best of the sleeves (jackets) for LP records. Advertising posters for movies, to cite one example, are invariably sensationalistic and have no visual grip at all.

This defect does not characterize all countries. Several nations in Latin America have raised what might be called public—non-easel—art to a range far above what Americans have reached. Again the immediate images are the murals of Mexico. In spite of the exciting work in this mode that has been done by men like Ben Shahn (Figure 26-3), perhaps the two greatest murals existing in the United States were created by Diego Rivera (Detroit Institute of Arts) and Jose C. Orozco (Dartmouth University).

Puerto Rico shows a far different face from the mainland. Although the island had no tradition in the visual arts to compare with that of Mexico, it has become since World War II a breeding ground for graphic innovation. This creativity rests heavily upon institutional sponsors, whether the government of the Commonwealth or private organizations; either might print a thousand copies of a billboard to entice customers to come to an outdoor film or to eat fresh fruit. Although Rafael Tufino, one of whose advertisements is shown here, approaches middle age, his productivity does not dwindle. Besides dozens of silkscreens for public display, he has done lithographs for sale to tourists (some of which mock tourists) as well as a mural for the Hilton hotel in Mayaguez, the third largest city in Puerto Rico.

The island may or may not be a part of the United States, so this illustration may or may not belong here. Puerto Ricans are exempt from United States income taxes, but they are subject to conscription into the American army. Officially the island is an *Estado Libre Asociado*—the only one.

FIGURE H. *Henry Linschitz,* Maine Tidepool

Probably most observers would agree that photography with its ofshoots is the most significant new form of art to emerge in the last 150 years. Much of this book (especially its "Ways to Study History") has tried to show new angles of vision, new windows through which we can peer into the past. Now here is a question that might allow us to be another type of Peeping Tom: Which artistic media have been embraced most passionately at specific times and places in the American past? For alert Americans at the beginning of World War II, literature would have held the first rank. Perhaps many of the problems of universities in the United States derive from their continuing emphasis on the written word, while their students have been shifting focus to other (and equally legitimate) types of expression. The regnant mode of the last two decades has surely been music; in a popularity race of the 1960's the Beatles would have beaten Ralph Ellison if they were walking. Second only to music would be the movies.

But the arrival of motion pictures, first silent and then with sound, is not the only innovation in photography in the twentieth century. Consider this illustration, which was not meant to be printed on a page at all; it was intended for projection in color onto a screen. The resultant luminosity can only be called overpowering. Equally remarkable, this image was captured by an amateur photographer, Henry Linschitz, whose interests reveal the interpenetration of occupations that typifies the best products of the contemporary world. He worked at Los Alamos during World War II, and he has since taught at universities and done research in physical chemistry and biophysics. How did such a person come to have so much delight in the abstractions supplied by rocks, by sea, by living creatures? In his professional world, he has a special concern with photobiology, the manifold responses of living things to light. In his private world, he is married to artist Suzanne Hodes (Figure 14-2). This color slide of a tidepool on Monhegan Island, Maine, was taken from a height of approximately two feet.

PART V

How Successes Can Be Frustrating
1898–1929

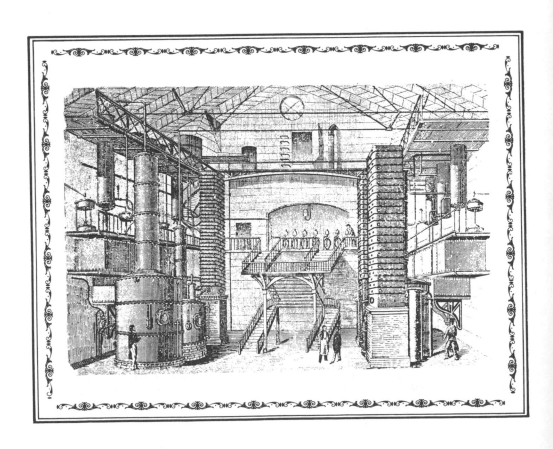

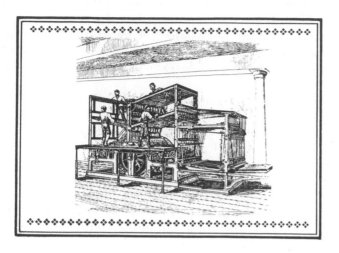

The Economy Surges—and the Fog Descends, 1898–1907

Both among the populace and in the Senate, the treaty ending the Spanish-American War provoked debate. A startling switch had occurred since the war began. Prior to that, many businessmen had been extremely cautious; they were skittish when mention was made of armed conflict. Commercial interests become jittery at any uncertainty, and wartime by definition is a period of dislocation and risk. Contrariwise, the self-proclaimed libertarians had joined the clamor to oust the Spaniards from Cuba; in Chicago, for instance, Altgeld and Lloyd and Darrow were noisy agitators in the cause. But with the appearance of the treaty, the two factions in a sense exchanged positions. Some industrialists could see no reason why, having endured the trials of war, the nation should not keep advantages to be gained by legal dominion over foreign markets. Conversely, advocates of the war now found that they did not want to taste some of its fruits. Their reasons varied. For most, the particular sticking point was the clause providing for acquisition of the

Philippines (Document 20-3). Some arguments used were perilously close to racism: that brown-skinned peoples could not learn the democratic way of life (Document 21-1). Altgeld on the other hand denounced these skeptics who claimed that "this people or that people are incapable of self-government."* Darrow told a mass meeting that he would not swap "the republic of Jefferson" for "the empire of McKinley." He demanded that the president "take away his lawless crew, remove his Christian cannon from those far-off shores. . . ."

The appeals to Christian forbearance and the Declaration of Independence did not prevail. The forces that vanquished them can be reviewed. Religious spokesmen were almost unanimous; of all denominations that declared themselves, only Quakers and Unitarians fought against imperialism. Politicians great and small flew the ensigns of rampant nationalism. It would be extreme to regard these appeals as mere stalking horses for material greed. But the desires of Americans for added sales in foreign markets were as weighty as the other pressures put together. Albert J. Beveridge, blunt for a man campaigning successfully in 1898 for a seat in the United States Senate, explained: "American factories are making more than the American people can use; American soil is producing more than they can consume. Fate has written our policy for us; the trade of the world must and shall be ours." After the war John Jacob Astor, great landowner and railroad pirate, came back from Europe with predictions of huge orders there for American electrical products and machinery. President McKinley a year later tried his own summary: "We want to send the products of our farms, our factories, and our mines into every market of the world; make the foreign peoples familiar with our products; and the way to do that is to make them familiar with our flag." Americans wanted to sew up not only foreign markets for our products but also sources of the raw materials to fabricate them. Thus Mexico was invaded by crews prospecting for crude oil. Mammoth forests in Canada were bought for woodpulp. Since the Mesabi fields in Minnesota were tied up by competitors, Bethlehem Steel looked for iron ore in Chile as well as in Cuba. Prognoses by businessmen are often faulty. Probably the main significance of overseas areas for the United States in the next three decades was not as markets, nor as providers of raw materials, but as outlets for American funds.

It is opportune to glance at the history of capital markets in this period. To do so sagely, we must backtrack fifty years. In the decade before the Civil War, the center of security flotations had migrated from State Street in Boston to Wall Street. The reason is easy to grasp: a slow rate of population growth in Boston went parallel to a slow pace of capital accumulation, and did not have

---

*Illinois citizens had reason to doubt this argument; trickery was open at the 1896 election in Chicago. Corruption among politicians there would rival any practitioners in Manila. The late John F. Kennedy repeated an appropriate joke about meetings of the Chicago common council at this time: You could empty the room by shouting: "Alderman, your saloon is on fire."

the resources to finance a majority of the long-distance railroads. But this relocation of investment banking had not brought about a change in the function. Only a narrow range of securities were traded publicly: federal and state bonds, railroad bonds often guaranteed by some civic authority—that was about it. The lack of quickly available liquid capital became critical. At the beginning of the century, most investments had been commercial, and involved consumer goods which could be quickly converted into cash. But by century's end, fixed costs could be preponderant in a steel mill or an oil refinery, while many companies continued to be owned by a family or by a limited number of partners. These sunk investments had to be made fluid or convertible into other forms of capital. One attempt at a solution after the financial panic of 1893 was the expansion to an "outside" market on securities not officially up for public trade, *i.e.*, a streetcurb market around the New York Stock Exchange. During the four years of the depression, the number of issues traded thus rose from about 30 to 200 or more. But this quasi-underground technique was not adequate. More creative was the device of issuing a wider variety of security or stock certificates, and of linking that innovation with the amalgamating of several former competitors to form a larger corporation that would be better known. Often an operation of this type hinged on an independent promoter who might weld an agreement among several erstwhile competitors and then issue several kinds of securities. (Bonds would have first claim on all earnings, with an interest rate of 6 per cent or so; preferred stocks were not a legal liability on the owner, but hopefully they would yield 7 or 8 per cent dividends; common stocks might not get anything at all, but often they were expected to earn 12 per cent.) Frequently these shenanigans brought grief to those who bought stock, or even bonds, even though the promoters usually came out well ahead.

The central purposes of these maneuvers merit repetition. First, to form by mergers some larger companies that would therefore have broader reputations. Second, to appeal to more investors by issuing different classes of securities, some offering a secure income, others hinting at higher incomes for persons willing to take risks. The whole idea was that this variety of issues could attract investors for a greater totality of liquid capital, and although neither material assets nor earning power had been increased, this produced more capital than could be drawn by the more limited range of issues beforehand. This scheme was greatly advanced during the depression of 1893 when preferred stocks of the industrial concerns did better than those of the railroads. Of the latter, one (Northern Pacific) had to scale down its capital values,* while the other that was most actively traded (the Wabash) paid no dividends. Turning to the largest industrials, only two preferreds failed to pay dividends, and one of the two (General Electric) did so to conserve its cash, not because it was losing money. Such new giants as American Tobacco and U.S. Rubber paid dividends throughout the depression. The public standing of

---

*The great theorist on this resolution was Thorstein Veblen, about whom see Chapter 25.

Sewing Machine

The sewing machine works by interlocking two threads. The needle's eye holds one, and the other is held in a bobbin under the throat plate, and passed through the upper thread by means of a shuttle. Both threads must be kept under a constant tension. Also required is the presser foot, which holds the fabric firmly against the throat plate, and the feed dog, which moves the fabric along under the stationary needle, one stitch at a time.

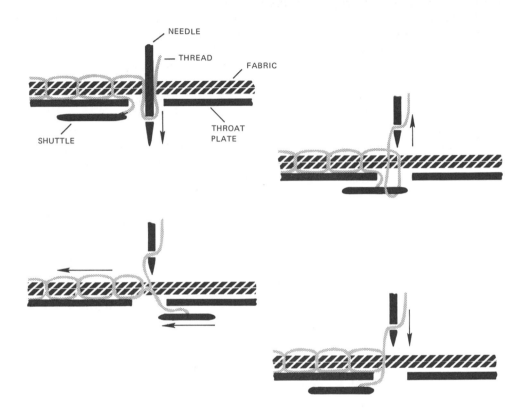

(1) The stitch begins when the needle pierces the fabric, and passes below the throat plate.
(2) The needle rises, leaving a loop of thread on the underside of the fabric. The shuttle passes through this loop.
(3) The feed dog (not shown in the diagram) moves the fabric forward one stitch length. During this process the needle remains stationary, and the shuttle returns to its original position. Since both threads are under tension, this pulls the slack loop taut.
(4) The mechanism is ready to begin another stitch.

This invention certainly eased the burden of the domestic seamstress. More importantly, it revolutionized the clothing industry. When all tailoring had to be done by hand, every garment was made-to-measure. Ready-to-wear clothing would have to be almost as expensive as custom tailored, and consequently there was no market for it. Except for a few expensive men's suits, all clothing was made in the home, consuming great amounts of the housewife's time. Thus only the rich, who could pay a seamstress to make their garments, could afford to have more than a very few.

securities in industrials was much enhanced in 1898 when the Morgan partners underwrote offerings by a steel merger. Again we must be sure not to exaggerate: Morgan too could make mistakes. In 1902 he promoted the International Mercantile Marine, which merged the two largest American transatlantic steamship companies with two British firms. He advanced $11 million in cash, and formed a syndicate to raise another $50 million cash. He got skunked, and so did investors. The latter took a combined package of commons and preferreds at $100, thinking that they could sell the common at $35 and the preferred at $85. It did not happen. Even Morgan had to wait years before he could recoup his stake; when he got out, he probably lost at least a million dollars.

Now some further oddities appeared. Just at the moment when a broader market for securities in industrial corporations became visible, that addition to liquidity paled in importance beside a new phenomenon that deserves to be explained. The chief innovation that was occurring at the turn of the century was the emergence of the giant corporation. Change was organizational more than it was technological (Chapter 23). However, paradoxically, the firms that were expanding most quickly and reorganizing most dynamically were likely to be following a timeworn strategy that had been stated explicitly by Carnegie: Put all your eggs in one basket, and watch that basket. In today's language, such firms were the opposite of diversified conglomerates. The businessman of 1900 was not the general entrepreneur of fifty or a hundred years earlier. He was a specialist. And although it is important to ask why this was true, I cannot give an answer that seems convincing—only guesses that seem plausible.

One scholar has presented a list of the fifty largest industrial firms in 1909. Only thirteen of them produced goods aimed at the ultimate consumers, you or me, and these produced tobacco, or meat, or whiskey, or petroleum products, or tires, or sewing machines.* The other thirty-seven corporations had few customers because each made semi-finished commodities; they produced structural steel for sale to big contractors, or locomotives for sale to railroads, and so on. In technical lingo, they turned out producers' goods. Thus in several senses they were not participants in the "distribution revolution" that was so critical to the period. They were not shooting *directly* at a mass market, and such businesses would tend to stress specialized trade relationships rather than broad or diverse ones. The picture is further confused. Many of the big mergers at the end of the century were initiated by industrialists, not by investment bankers.

Furthermore, a whole new element was emerging. Advertising was

---

*Here we have the problem of categories again. Most sewing machines were probably being sold to housewives, but many were going to the garment districts because the manufacture of ready-made garments had already become significant.

nothing novel, but display advertising was. National circulation magazines first began to depend on display ads late in the century. Then another step was taken: institutional advertising. We have already pointed to the "catalytic phrases" as an indicator of the emotional climate of a given generation("God"; "Liberty"; above all, "Land"; see early Chapter 11). One easily remembered index of the business climate of an era is to identify the tallest building on Manhattan Island. When the 47-story Singer Building was completed in 1908, it was twice as tall as any other structure in the United States. Its suzerainty was short-lived. It was surpassed in 1912 by the Woolworth Building, 60 stories, 792 feet. Singer's product was oriented to both consumer and producer; Woolworth's only to consumer. Then the latter was overtaken by the Chrysler Building after the war. Again the matter of scale is crucial. With no intention of making a play on words, it might be said that Woolworth dealt in units that were measured in nickels and dimes, Chrysler in hundreds of dollars. But Chrysler turned out to be too specialized to own the highest building. It in turn was outranked in 1931 by the Empire State, 1,472 feet. It has housed as many as 25,000 companies, ranging from magazine publishers to real-estate developers to clothing distributors.

This reversal is crucial, but not easy to explain. We might call it the faint beginnings of the diversified conglomerate firms. Several facets can be distinguished. First, even while J. P. Morgan was financing corporations on an unprecedented scale, he was losing his monopoly in this realm. Second, investment banking as a specialty was destined to decline, as more companies became able to reinvest their profits and thus became independent of all external capital. Third, the substitution effect must be considered. Some new organizations began to turn in a massive way into research and development. Over the next few decades the result was an extension of alternatives. It became almost meaningless to talk about "steel"; what kind of steel? You could not talk about transportation in terms of trains: trucks and new forms of water transportation had also to be considered.

These developments were so multifoliate and varied that it is hard to look at them systematically. Looking at only one contingent in a brigade, consider how the partners in Standard Oil took their winnings in several directions. One went to Florida, where he developed Key West, built railroads and hotels, got the main street in Miami named for him. Another helped to found the Amalgamated Copper Company, which was in a growth market with the expansion of telephone communications. Others muscled their way into American Tobacco. Perhaps most important of all, the Rockefellers had their own bank in New York, and competed with Morgan for contracts in the launching of big-time ventures. Then there was that dastardly combination of the bankers, the Kuhn, Loeb group with Edward H. Harriman. Harriman almost defies belief. At the beginning he was a stock speculator. Out of one operation, which involved issuing $75 million in additional securities while spending only $18 million on improvements, he and his associates took a profit of $23

FIGURE 21-1. *Frank Lloyd Wright, F.C. Robie House*

Economic booms can do wonders for domestic architecture, as the newly rich seek to make manifest their wealth. In doing so they may not only chagrin their neighbors but also provide themselves with uncomfortable housing, as at Hyde Park. But under proper tutelage from an architect, they can enrich the community as well as their family. More than any American designer since Samuel McIntire (Figure 10-4), Frank Lloyd Wright knew how to create homes for the wealthy.

The urban home shown here was done for F.C. Robie. When finished in 1908, it was just off the campus of the University of Chicago on the city's south side. It can be taken as the archetype of Wright's "Prairie House": low horizontals, sweeping eaves, as much interflow of interior with exterior as the climate and setting will permit. The first floor is one huge room, with dining area in the rear divided from the living room by a giant brick fireplace. One's eyes move naturally around both sides of the fireplace and through an aperture between the chimneys. To look through the continuous banks of windows onto the sweeping porch is like looking from a stateroom onto the deck of a ship.

Wright's incredible life began in 1868 and lasted nearly a century. Besides houses, he created the Guggenheim Art Museum in New York, office buildings, research centers, the first church of cast concrete, a night club, a mile-high structure for the Chicago World's Fair of 1933 that was never erected, and the Imperial Hotel in Tokyo. He was responsible for dwellings that could be built in the 1930's for $6,000, including his fee. He stooped to designing individual pieces of furniture to fit in specific places in specific rooms. His offhand remark was, "In a work of art, there are no trivial details."

million. Before he was finished he had direction of 25,000 miles of track with 70,000 employees—Union Pacific, Central Pacific, Southern Pacific. He did not fudge on expenditures to improve the physical facilities of his roads: where other lines needed a locomotive to move each ten cars or less, he used one for every 35 or 40. His ambition was boundless. Joining with his trans-Mississippi railroads, he controlled 35,000 miles of steamship routes on the Pacific. He began manipulations to get railroads in Manchuria and Siberia. Presumably if these had succeeded, he would next have sought oceanic lines on the Atlantic. What inspires awe is his ability to find lieutenants who were so expert in carrying out his intentions. His railroad empire was divided into seven systems, on a geographical basis, and thus got seven possible solutions to a problem. It could choose the best. A few examples must suffice here. It proved possible to reduce the volume of correspondence by more than 30 per cent. Many routine reports could be done away with. (The problem of intra-office memoranda will be perused in Chapter 28; every employee of a public university must sometimes hope that a shortage of paper will save us.) Harriman like James J. Hill realized that you can't make money hauling empties. So the 75,000 freight cars in the empire were pooled. Ton-mile and passenger-mile figures were studied closely. Within two years the passage of empty freights on the system had been cut by 54,000,000 car-miles. But for all these efficiencies, Harriman never reached his purpose of an around-the-world transportation system using both land and water; world politics had frustrated his aim until he died in 1910.

At this juncture it would be easy to leave a false impression. The glitter of the mighty can bemuse us. So can the miseries of the humble. But a crucial fact is the presence of a chance to get ahead. An adolescent immigrant from Italy has left us his memoirs. His first job was on a gang that was digging a sewer in Brooklyn. The padrone said that if the men did not work for him, police would come and put them in jail. But one day the immigrant went off to Newark and got "work on the street." That was better, until it stopped. He went back to Brooklyn where he met a bootblack "and learned the business."

> We had said that when we had saved $1000 each we would go back to Italy and buy a farm, but now that the time is coming we are so busy and making so much money that we think we will stay. . . . There are plenty of rich Italians here, men who a few years ago had nothing and now have so much money that they could not count all their dollars in a week.

Several times these pages have discussed the consequences of cuts in transportation costs. The implications of these changes for the location of certain industries might now be discussed. In spite of numerous exceptions, a principle can be stated: Usually a prosperous firm was so situated as to minimize its freight charges. For instance, the factor of cheaper labor will go far to explain the migration of cotton-textile manufacturing from New England

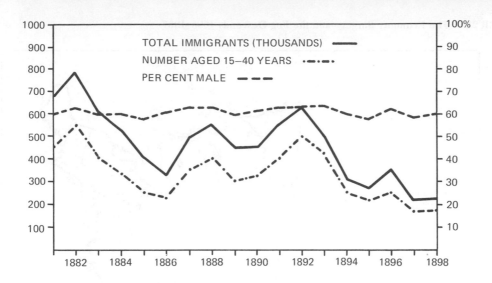

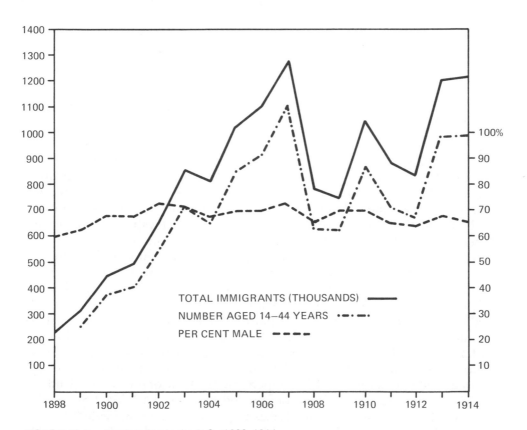

FIGURE 21-2. *Immigration in the U.S., 1899–1914*

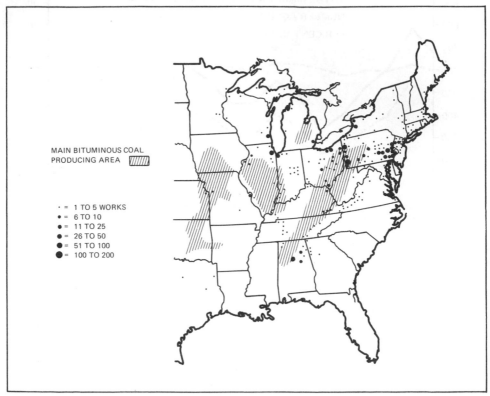

MAIN BITUMINOUS COAL
PRODUCING AREA

· = 1 TO 5 WORKS
• = 6 TO 10
• = 11 TO 25
● = 26 TO 50
● = 51 TO 100
● = 100 TO 200

FIGURE 21-3. *Main Bituminous Coal-producing Areas*

to the Southern Appalachians, but this differential will not account for the transfer of the center of shoe manufacturing from Lynn, Massachusetts to St. Louis. In both these manufactories, the charge per ton of shipping the raw material is not much different from the charge of shipping the finished product, but the shoe industry found a Midwestern location would place it closer both to its raw materials and to a focal point in its market. The circumstance is otherwise when a large part of the weight or bulk of the raw material is lost in processing it. Obviously an oil well must be located where the deposits are. But a marked shift occurred in the placement of refineries. The first primary locus was in Cleveland, partly because it was near the fields, partly because Rockefeller and his partners lived there. When they realized that most of their sales were overseas, they bought or built refineries along the Eastern seaboard. The location of iron and steel mills shows graphically the determinants of a processor of weight-losing minerals. A treaty had drawn an international boundary from Lake Superior to the Lake of the Woods. Under it, the Mesabi iron range in Minnesota proved to lie in the United States. The Sault Sainte Marie Canal, joining Lakes Superior and Huron, made it feasible to move Mesabi ore to the southern shores of the Great Lakes where it could be fused with coal from the Alleghenies. For decades the Soo Canal moved more tonnage than any other canal in the world, including Suez and Panama. From it sprang the $50-million mill of U.S. Steel at Gary, Indiana, plus several other mills along the shores of the Lakes.

The spurt in the economy produced its own kind of politics. While the emperors of antiquity held the masses in check with the reliable combination of bread and circuses, in the early years of this century, that ancient formula was split two ways. For most of the urban poor, the power structures of local neighborhoods produced the bread, while national politics offered the circuses. At the time, enough people were still in want that bread came first, so it belongs first here. The stream of immigrants needed special help. A million a year were arriving. The great majority were young and hearty, but many lacked money, lacked skills that could be sold in America, could not even speak English. The opportunity to rise in society was there, surely, but it cost the newcomers both sweat and years. Employers deliberately pitted them against one another. Policemen did not like them, especially when a cop was of a different nationality. They had trouble finding a job. So they were at odds with each other, with their bosses, with the police and the courts. Every immigrant was desperate for a friend, any friend. The lucky ones found help from three types of people: their fellow countrymen, social workers, and political bosses. Some studies have been made of urban social groups, but the one to pay most attention to mutual help among immigrants has to do with the Chinese.* Historical works make reference to burial societies among Negroes and among immigrant groups, but not much is really known yet about these institutions that must have touched the hearts of many displaced persons. For that matter, few historians have heeded how appropriate the phrase "displaced person" is, not just for immigrants from Greece or Poland but also for migrants who had never crossed a national boundary. A boy from Mississippi who wound up in Detroit was almost sure to feel that he did not belong there at all. Moving on to social workers, some of them served a very useful function. So far as I know, the most remarkable battalion of women in American history lived at Hull-House, Chicago in the early years of this century. But then, we have already had an introduction to these ladies (early Chapter 19).

The foregoing leaves the third group of patrons of the poor. These benefactors were the professional politicians, scornfully called in some circles "the old-line pols." It is rash to scorn them. One reason is that they were so numerous. A qualified English observer tried to take a frequency count for his country compared to the United States. The population ratio was about 1:2. However, England had only 4,000 men whose chief trade was politics, whereas in America the estimate was 500,000. The same commentator remarked that in politics as in war, organization is everything, and these professionals formed into phalanxes. They were likable; they liked others in

---

*Today, in Calgary and probably elsewhere, it is a justified boast of leaders in Chinatown that "our people do not go on welfare." The community takes care of its parishioners. In this respect, but with critical distinctions, the relation might be compared to slavery in the United States.

return; and they wanted to help their neighbors. We should not romanticize them; they were thieves. But they stole in a relatively gentle way, and they gave back part of their gains. The fixers flourished in a day when the phrase "social welfare" did not even show in the lexicons of most governments in the United States; the typical well-to-do citizen thought the whole notion was immoral because it would encourage indolence and alcoholism. For voluminous information about sub-national governments in the United States, the journalist Lincoln Steffens had no peer. Philosophizing about political bosses he had known, he found that, by and large, they were a good bunch. But he distinguished this group of "principals," men who could think and act for themselves, from the "heelers" who could do nothing but take orders (for illustrations of how a heeler worked, see Document 21-4). It can be noted in passing that this last distinction has been a common belief among Americans. Steffens' contemporary Clarence Darrow, when approving jurors in a criminal trial that involved strikers, would always take a corporation president in preference to a shop foreman, because he thought the former would have more independence of mind to follow the evidence. Or one could reach all the way back to the words of the Essex Result (1778): "all the members of the state are qualified to make the election, unless they have not sufficient discretion, or are so situated as to have no wills of their own." Two further statements about junior governments and their politics seem valid. First, they had little power beyond the maintenance of public peace, and even there the strains in the society were often too severe for them to cope. Municipalities were the frail creatures of the states, with only delegated powers that could be suspended or removed at the whim of the senior government; a major struggle of the period was the effort to get Home Rule for the metropolis. The status of the states was better, but not by much. They could and did pass a few types of humanitarian legislation: factory-inspection, minimum wages and maximum hours, laws to benefit female and child workers, but the limits on their accomplishments were stringent. Note for instance that at least a dozen states elected as governor a man of considerable ability and broad views. Altgeld may be taken as representative of these executives. In retrospect, his achievements seem almost entirely negative. He could veto evil bills. He could pardon prisoners who had been falsely convicted. He could try to restrict injustice, but he could do little to promote equity. Part of the defect lay in his own ideas of public authority: even when the depression of 1893 was at its worst, he would not endorse the idea of public works to relieve unemployment. The fight for livelihood was up to the individual, while the state could only stand by and wait for the hard times to go away.

Second, the "great issues" being debated in Washington were seldom the issues that swayed the average voter. Congressmen and presidents argued about the tariff, about revision of the National Banking Act, sometimes about conservation of natural resources. The common man worried about whether the ward boss would help him to get a job with the streetcar company or would provide him with a free turkey for Thanksgiving or would wangle his son out of jail. National politics and precinct politics were related to each other, but the relationship was not simple or direct. But while seeking to particularize and to make concrete, we should not go too far in atomizing the electoral scene. A careful study of state politics has parceled out two areas of concern where a candidate, if he were to succeed at the state level, had to find a workable straddle: election reform, and alcoholic beverages (Chapter 18 opening). These two reforms, if they deserve that name, tended to merge because the clamor for both of them came generally from the same group—white Anglo-Saxon native-born Protestant rural voters.

Anybody today knows that the cities are not Utopias. But the country-side did not and does not deserve that rank either. No convincing picture has been made to show that bucolics have been more upright that urbanites. The bias against city folk, however, was persistent, and often it oozed forth from racial prejudice. Describing his colleagues in the New York legislature in 1885, Theodore Roosevelt sermonized that the worst of them were from cities. A few from that locale were educated and ethical, "but the bulk are very low indeed. They are usually foreigners of little or no education, with exceedingly misty ideas as to morality, and possessed of an ignorance so profound that it could only be called comic, were it not for the fact that it has at times such serious effects on our laws." But the evidence of similar abuses among other segments of the electorate is strong. Adams County, Ohio was a farming district. Nearly everybody was native-born Protestant white. The county seat was the only one in the state with neither railroad nor telegraph, so it could not easily be polluted by outsiders. Most people were poor. After the Civil War the two parties were evenly balanced. One of the few commodities that these rural folks had to sell was their votes, so they did. The system persisted, openly, for decades. Under a law saying that anybody convicted of selling his vote should be disfranchised for five years, prosecutions were started after the 1910 election. One name in four was stricken from the registration lists. To a woman who is hungry, virtue seems trifling; to a man who is poor, so does honor. The condition was summarized by a rhymester:

> Many people sold their vote
> For to buy an overcoat,
> Or to buy a sack of flour,
> Thinking it a prosperous hour.

But Theodore Roosevelt, exposed to these exposures of the social roots of scandalous politics, could write that neither "capital" nor "labor" but the individual must bear the guilt for crooked government.

Roosevelt will do as a symbol for the epoch of national politics that we are now reviewing, since he was president virtually throughout its duration. He shouted and waved his arms, but his feet never moved. Some historians still refer sweepingly to "The Progressive Era." But the federal government in this period did little. There were crying abuses of federal legislation in the

By permission of Edward Steichen

FIGURE 21-4.   *Edward Steichen, J. Pierpont Morgan*

import duties and in the National Banking Act. Laws in both realms were highly discriminatory against the agricultural sector of the nation. Because the men who raised staple crops such as cotton or wheat perennially had an export surplus, no tariff could possibly protect their market, so it could not raise the price of the items they were selling. But it could raise the price of the manufactured goods they were buying, and it did. In this regard, matters had not changed much since the times of John C. Calhoun. The "hard money" monetary statutes, as has been noted, also were unfavorable to rural areas. But Roosevelt never thought it opportune to review the laws in either of these fields of policy. His concern was not with justice but with the retention and expansion of office. He came to high power due to his birth, due to his courage in warfare, due to his frenetic energy, due to his speechifying loquacity. He never understood that huge numbers of Americans were being treated wrongly by the federal government. His analytic mind might have been as dense and amorphous as potato chowder, but he had cunning; he gave to voters a few dreams in which they could get lost. As Roosevelt expanded, the fog grew denser, with himself revolving in the fog; he became a master of cant. One of his closest advisers is known to have said to him, "What I most admire about you, Theodore, is your discovery of the Ten Commandments."

Henry Adams observed that Roosevelt was "pure act." Steffens charitably wrote that "Roosevelt's lies were unconscious" and further noted the president's "old rule": "Never to deny anything unless it is true." The most caustic evaluation of all contemporaries might be the one made by Mark Twain

---

This photograph of the domineering investment banker must rank as one of the greatest portraits ever done. It reflects not only the advances in materials but also the expanding conceptions of what could be done with camera and film (see Figure 18-2). Perhaps Morgan never realized how devastatingly he had been pictured by photographer Edward Steichen. Seventy years after this print was made, many viewers see the subject as holding in his left hand a dagger, whereas the actual object is merely the burnished arm of a chair. Morever the dagger appears to be a bowie knife that a sadist might use to butcher his enemies; it is not a subtle stiletto. The characterization calls to mind a frontier mode of fighting duels; the officials gave to each combatant a bowie knife and locked them together in a room. Then they waited until one knocked on the door to come out.

Morgan was an aggrandizer. He could be polite when that seemed the shrewd tactic to improve his opportunities, but his impulses were the reverse. He was the fulcrum around which grew the biggest American organizations of his time. Occasionally he miscalculated, as with the International Mercantile Marine; but usually not, witness United States Steel and International Harvester. Living in an age when access to liquid capital was vital, he was born floating in it and quickly learned how to make more flow into his pond. His father was an investment banker in London; J. P. was born in the insurance capital, Hartford; he was educated genteely in Boston and at the University of Göttingen. Yet he was coarse and ruthless. As an aging man he took his mistress on his yacht to the fashionable resorts of the Atlantic. He was a stalwart of the Episcopal Church and expressed concern that his immortal soul should ascend to Heaven.

His dominant urge was not to create but to control. He owned perhaps the finest private art collection in existence. Some of his manuscript collections were housed in a rare book museum which eventually became a magnet for scholars. But other collections seem to have been guarded like dragon hoards, such as the fossil horse collection in the Museum of Natural History to which a famous scholar of evolution was recently denied access, apparently through some restrictive intention of the long-dead financier. Even in the grave, his grasp stayed firm.

to Andrew Carnegie: "Mr. Roosevelt is the Tom Sawyer of the political world of the twentieth century; always showing off; always hunting for a chance to show off; in his frenzied imagination the Great Republic is a vast Barnum circus with him for a clown and the whole world for audience." Another perceptive contemporary philosophized: "Americans have no political ideas; they follow leaders who attract them or who know how to manage them. The kind of political leaders they like are human circuses."

Confronted with the perplexities of anti-trust enforcement, the chief executive went from one foot to the other, much in the fashion of the other President Roosevelt a generation later (Chapter 26). The Northern Pacific Case shows one extreme, and to explain it the facts must be pared down a bit, without distorting the problem or its resolution. Two railroad magnates, Harriman and James J. Hill, wanted the same railroad to give their other lines an entry into Chicago. Their struggle drove the market value of stock in the desired company up 1,000 per cent. The stock exchange became so unsettled that Morgan stepped in. His answer was to form a holding company, Northern Securities, in which Hill and Harriman had representation. At this stage, Roosevelt decided that the federal government should act in accord with the anti-trust laws. The attorney general brought suit under the Sherman Act. The next parry was for Morgan to pay a social call to the White House, where he reportedly said to the president, "If we have done anything wrong, send your man to my man and they can fix it up." Finally, on 14 March, 1904, the Supreme Court ordered the dissolution of the holding company by a vote of 5 to 4. This episode posed a problem vividly, for the two best judges on the Court disagreed. Harlan wrote the decision for dissolution of the trust. But Holmes dissented, with the acid comment that Harlan's interpretation of the Sherman Act "would make eternal the *bellum omnium contra omnes* [Hobbes' "war of all against all"] and disintegrate society so far as it could into individual atoms." Holmes was quite possibly right, but his wisdom did not prevent the president from being annoyed at what seemed to him the treachery of his protegé, whom he had recently named to the Court. Roosevelt, in plain truth, did not want to have the problem posed vividly.

For a vignette of the president standing on his other foot in regard to the nascent trusts, the Tennessee Coal & Iron episode in 1907 provides one. Whereas in the Northern Securities incident the catalyst had been an excessive demand on the exchange for a specific stock, the difficulty here was an absence of demand. A large brokerage firm had made sizeable loans against the collateral of Tennessee Coal & Iron stock. The brokers needed cash, and they could not market the securities. So a proposal was made that U.S. Steel should buy the stock in question, giving in exchange its own bonds that could be sold on the open market. But would the federal government intervene again on the grounds that the effective merger of two large competitors violated the Sherman Anti-Trust Act? The head of U.S. Steel went to Washington to find out. Roosevelt did not object, and so J. P. Morgan's choice firm got control of another billion tons of coal and 600 million tons of iron ore.

From this muddled thinking, little good could come. To make a fast summation, we might note that the Roosevelt administration, with nearly eight years of power, proffered 44 indictments under the Anti-Trust Act. The Taft government, which lasted only four years, brought 65. Obviously the difference in quantity should not be regarded as decisive. But a glance at the impact of specific allegations confirms the impression given by the numbers. One indictment under President Taft was against the imperialistic Du Ponts (Chapter 23). Another was against U.S. Steel for its purchase of the Tennessee Coal & Iron stock. It says a good deal about the rank of William Howard Taft as chief executive (Chapter 22) that he did not know about this charge before the general public could read it in the newspapers; even then, he did not anticipate that his predecessor and sponsor, Roosevelt, would resent the charge. Or look at the Elkins Act (1903). Supposedly the law aimed to stop rebates and other discriminations by common carriers. Allegedly the rebates had been of great benefit to Standard Oil (Document 20-1), but Rockefeller denied it (Document 21-2). The new law decreed that any departure by a railroad from its published rates was self-evident proof of discrimination; moreover, the man who accepted a rebate was just as guilty as the company that paid it. But notice—one draftsman of the statute was an attorney for the Pennsylvania Railroad. Would it not be logical for a carrier to try to use federal power to avoid being victimized by giant shippers such as steel and petroleum producers? It often happened in this period that an economic interest would try to fight off a competing group by recourse to public favors.

Another feature of the Roosevelt administration was the importance, previously substantial and now growing, of ethnic politics. This theme can be illustrated by reference to two minority groups, blacks and Jews. To consider blacks first, their political power had waned markedly since Reconstruction. The ordinary white at best was indifferent to their plight in the polity; odds were that he was hostile to their participation in civic affairs. Ninety per cent of all Negroes were still south of the Mason-Dixon Line, where they were systematically disfranchised between Reconstruction and 1910. Techniques and results varied from state to state, but a couple of examples can be cited. Louisiana achieved the following reduction in voter registration:

	White	*Black*	*Total*
Registered 1 Jan. 1897	164,088	130,344	294,432
Registered 17 March 1900, new constitution	123,437	5,320	130,757

(Parenthetically note that many of the novel requirements hit at poor whites as well as blacks. One cute device was to make the suffrage dependent upon payment of a poll tax. This trick might be carried further by making the tax payable in the spring when cash is notoriously scarce among farmers. It could be extended further yet by requiring the farmer to produce the receipt for his poll tax at the autumn election, in a country where people were not addicted to elaborate filing systems.)

But a migration of blacks to Northern cities had begun, although it was far short of the dimensions it would attain later, and in some key districts the black vote might be important. So Roosevelt made gestures to win it. Since the death of Frederick Douglass in 1895, the most prominent Negro leader in the country had been Booker T. Washington, president of Tuskegee Institute in Alabama. The president shared a meal with him at the White House. It would be wrong to label this action as flamboyant and hollow; it infuriated the racist extremists, so to them Roosevelt's courtesy was not without meaning. But this positive motion should be seen in context—of the Brownsville outrage for instance. This Texas town was not receptive to three companies of black infantrymen who were transferred to its environs in 1906. The first two weeks saw several outbreaks between civilians and soldiers. At last some men shot up Brownsville and killed a white resident. They were never identified. However, an Army investigator concluded that their Army buddies must know who the culprits were. When nobody came forward to identify them, the president ordered every man in the three companies discharged without honor. Among these (approximately) 450 men were six winners of the Congressional Medal of Honor. A fortnight later Roosevelt informed a friend that because the case was "of vital concern to the whole country, I will not for one moment consider the political effect." Self-deception was becoming the mood of public life.

Another index is Roosevelt's manipulation of the Jewish vote as the waves of immigrants from Russia and Poland rolled into the Eastern cities. In 1903 Congress had established the Department of Commerce and Labor. Three years later the president needed a dramatic move to draw Jewish votes in a New York election, so he named a Jew (significantly, chief executive of the giant department store of R. H. Macy) to head the newly formed department and thus gave him control over immigration. Soon after, a large dinner was held at which the president explained how he had made his choice. The story has it that Roosevelt contended that he had sought only to find the best man for the job, without regard to any other consideration. Certainly he had not thought about the candidate's race or religion or political party. This high-mindedness, he said, could be confirmed by the master of ceremonies. The gentleman in question, himself Jewish, was the top man at the banking firm of Kuhn, Loeb; unfortunately for Roosevelt, he was also deaf. He replied, "Dot's right, Mr. President, you came to me and said 'Chake, who is der best Jew I can appoint Secretary of Commerce?'"

Another segment of the population that deserves notice is the industrial labor force. As already noted, this category is too broad for effective analysis. Some occupations, particularly locomotive engineers, building trades, and the printing trades, were doing quite well. But semiskilled and unskilled workers, whether digging ditches or employed in large factories, had a rough time. The branches of government causing the most trouble for strikers were the police and the courts. In many jurisdictions the favorite indictment for use in labor disputes was the charge of conspiracy; by this sleight of hand, an act that was legal if committed by one man became illegal if committed by several. We cannot examine here the deeds of courts in all the major cities, but representative decisions can be cited. Although exceptions can be found, it is broadly true that the Supreme Court after 1900 seemed to reverse the line of doctrine that it had endorsed earlier in regard to legislative power over working conditions. In 1898 it had upheld a Utah statute fixing a maximum work-day of eight hours in mines. But in *Lochner* v. *New York* (1905) by some elaborate sophistries the Court disallowed a law that banned bakers from working more than ten hours; since the public interest, read the decision, was in no way affected by this topic, the regulation was unconstitutional. The reactionary trend did not stop there. New York also passed a statute pertaining only to women and minors which decreed that they could not work at night nor could they work more than ten hours a day. The Court's judgment said:

> So I think, in this case, that we should say, as an adult female is in no sense a ward of the state, that she is not to be made the special object of the exercise of the paternal power of the state and that the restriction, here imposed upon her privilege to labor, violates the constitutional guarantees.

Does equality for women necessarily imply identical treatment? And what of the children?

In two fields of legislation the Roosevelt terms brought advances: protection of the consumer by inspection of foodstuffs and drugs, and protection of posterity by reducing the exploitation of natural resources. An approach toward the first objective was made by the Meat Inspection Act and the Pure Food and Drug Act of 1906. The federal inspector of meat might be notoriously lax or even corrupt in performing his duty, and the legal sale of patent medicines is greater now than in 1905. But no president should be condemned on the ground that he did not find an instant solution to a complicated problem. The same caution should be used in evaluating the efforts made early in this century to preserve natural resources. The alertness of a Boston bookseller to his environment in 1851 (Document 14-2) should not suggest that many Americans had even begun to grasp the concept of ecology. For this reason the accomplishments of the early twentieth century seem meritorious. There had always been powerful Americans who were devoted to nature; one might think of Presidents Jefferson and John Quincy Adams. But to the typical citizen the landscape conveyed little beyond the hope for a quick fortune. Greed was not quashed by the Roosevelt administrations; it was impeded. Under one law, three million acres in the West were irrigated in four years. More than 2,500 water-power sites were reserved from private development (on the spurious ground that they were to be federal ranger stations). Roosevelt's term of office saw the creation of five national parks, which doubled the number that had existed when he became president.

It remains to say some words about foreign relations. Diplomacy in Europe can best be left for the following chapter on American involvement in

World War I, so the present discussion can be limited to policy toward Latin America, especially the Caribbean, and toward the Far East. Some common fallacies should be rejected at the start. (1) Some circles have relied on the terms "interventionist" and "isolationist." To most historians using these words, the former has applied to the good guys, the latter to the bad. But neither term has much meaning, if any. What kind of intervention, where, when? What kind of isolation, from whom, how? (2) Until the late nineteenth century the United States did avoid committing itself militarily—and to a great extent diplomatically—in the quarrels of Europe (Washington's "Great Rule" steadily adhered to). But American attachments to the European economies were continuous and every effort was made to increase them. (3) In the Pacific and in Latin America, United States involvement was recurrent, and it was political as well as commercial. "Isolationism" was always quite selective.

United States commitments in the Caribbean ensued from the practice of some Latin American nations of forfeiting on their bonds held in Europe. When Venezuela did so, Britain, Germany, and Italy tried to force her to honor her obligations by attempting to impose a blockade on all her ports. The contestants were willing in principle to arbitrate. With Roosevelt taking an active part in the negotiations, this decision was reached. He said later that a refusal by Germany would have led him to intervene with armed force. Historians for years believed that his claim was typical braggadocio, but a recent study proves that he not only made the threat but backed it up by sending a naval squadron toward the area. So far, so good; the Monroe Doctrine has been upheld. But the president's next foray to enforce those tenets was less fortunate. It must be understood in the light of British policy: England had posed to the United States an alternative. Either you must let us curb those Latino countries that commit offenses against our citizens, or you must curb them. Roosevelt chose the latter course. In his 1904 message to Congress he proclaimed:

> Chronic wrongdoing, or an impotence which results in a general loosening of the ties of civilized society, may in America, as elsewhere, ultimately require intervention by some civilized nation, and in the Western Hemisphere the adherence of the United States to the Monroe Doctrine may force the United States, however reluctantly, in flagrant cases of such wrongdoing or impotence, to the exercise of an international police power.

James Monroe and John Quincy Adams had sought to prevent European meddling in the Americas; now the Roosevelt Corollary virtually reversed the policy to justify American meddling.

British goals in the Far East lured the United States into that area also. Not that this nation needed much tempting; its businessmen and to a lesser extent its public officials had been hungry in the Pacific for more than a century. But with the Open Door Notes of 1899 and 1900, the federal policy toward China carried hints of retaliation. The industrial countries of Europe along with Japan were, like buzzards, plucking flesh from China. These formal Open Door Notes responded by stating two American aims: to preserve the territorial integrity of the nation, and to secure there equal commercial treatment for citizens of all foreign governments. A test came in 1905. For three years Great Britain had been publicly allied with Japan. When that country made a surprise attack on Manchuria in 1904, the British hoped to see Russia thrust back into Asia. Then Russia could be used as a counterweight to the German push westward. Confronted by these complicated moves and counter-moves, Roosevelt's initial hope was that hostilities in the Far East would continue until both combatants collapsed; then his country would not face "either a yellow peril or a Slav peril." Later he realized that he might be able to use both of the belligerents to preserve the Open Door in China, so he began maneuvers pointed toward a negotiated peace. Russia was on the verge of popular revolution; Japan was financially threadbare. The two nations met at Portsmouth, New Hampshire in 1905. Due partly to Roosevelt's pressure on Russia, Japan came out ahead. One of her gains was a protectorate over Korea, which would have considerable consequences for the future.

In the interval between the two Open Door Notes, the Boxer Rebellion against all foreigners broke out in northern China. The United States joined with other major powers in sending troops to suppress the outbreak; some of the invaders did not exhibit the finest behavior. Several features of American policy toward China deserve mention. One premise was that production of goods in the United States was so efficient that no European company could compete in the Far East; as *The Times* (London) commented irritably: "Even protectionist organs are for free trade in China, where freedom is for the benefit of American manufacturers." Further, basic flaws in Roosevelt's approach to foreign relations erupted. He had parcelled out the entire earth into "barbarous" distinguished from "civilized" countries. Within this dichotomy, he regarded Australia as more important than India. China he thought had no potential whatever, so he organized a conference where Japan and Russia agreed to a peace for China without any Chinese voice at all. To block Russian expansion in Asia, he agreed to the Japanese holding the dominant influence in Manchuria while the British and Americans were granted prime rights in the Yangtze valley. Going beyond the concession of a Japanese protectorate over Korea, he agreed to let Japan have "suzerainty over" that nation. The other chief provision of the Taft-Katsura Agreement (29 July, 1905; never submitted to the Senate because it was not a treaty) bound the United States for the time being to accept the goals of the Anglo-Japanese alliance. But what sort of aims were behind American policy?

The new American commitments in the Far East led to arguments that the United States needed a greatly enlarged navy. Chief agitators for this program were the president, Admiral Mahan, and such senators as Beveridge and Lodge. Having secured from a reluctant Congress the battleships that he wanted, Roosevelt sent the fleet in 1907 on an around-the-world cruise. This move has been praised as a brilliant stroke for overawing the Japanese, but it still seems like a strange tactic. However one regards it, it proceeded from a false postulate. Having started from the exaggeration that the United States could dominate the western Pacific, Roosevelt had moved to the exaggeration that Japan was a present menace in the eastern Pacific. If so, then why put his fleet in her waters where it could be attacked treacherously? The answer probably lies in a bluster that he had made in 1903: "America's geographical position in the Pacific is such as to insure our peaceful dominion of its waters."

In spite of the costly lessons of World War II, this illusion would persist for decades.

The prolonged depression from 1865 to 1896 had convinced capitalists that they must eliminate competition in order to maintain the prices of their products at a profitable level. In many industries this thrust toward monopoly—together with friendly governments plus advancing technology that lowered costs of production and distribution—did indeed bring profits. It also gave millions of Americans the highest standard of living that the world had ever known. Further, it brought businessmen into numerous and often shifting alliances with the politicians who maneuvered at the summits of governments. These developments had diverse results for different groups of ordinary people. The fortunes of many skilled workers and petty entrepreneurs shot forward dramatically. Politically, some groups of New Immigrants, especially Jews and Italians, gained influence far more quickly than the Irish had done two generations earlier. Other groups, notably blacks and poor Southern whites, actually lost political power that they had previously held. The decade from the Spanish-American War to the financial panic of 1907 can now be seen as a false prosperity. It did little to improve the status of the common man, and its aimless rhetoric befogged the reasons for his misery. Meanwhile the federal authorities energetically pursued the goal of overseas expansion.

SOME NOTABLE EVENTS

1897–

1914 Exports of capital from U.S. exceed imports in every year.

1898 Union Pacific Railroad falls under domination of Edward H. Harriman.

1899 International Paper formed.

1901 U.S. Steel formed; first billion dollar corporation.

Hay-Pauncefote Treaty with Britain for isthmian canal in Central America.

1902 DuPont Corporation acquired by new (du Pont) management.

Newlands Act for land reclamation, 17 June.

1903 Ford Motor Company opens its first plant.

Hay-Herrán Treaty with Colombia is signed for canal rights, but they refuse to ratify.

Panama rebels against Colombia, enabling U.S. to secure canal rights.

Department of Commerce and Labor established.

Elkins Act, mainly against railroad rebates.

1904 Supreme Court orders dissolution of Northern Securities Company.

1905 *Lochner* v. *New York*; Supreme Court rules against state labor regulations.

1906 Harvey Firestone begins to make pneumatic tires.

Hepburn Act gives Interstate Commerce Commission the power to set reasonable rates.

Pure Food and Drug Act.

Brownsville, Texas race riot, 13 August.

1907 Financial panic begins, 13 March.

Moyer-Haywood-Pettibone case in Idaho.

1908 Eugene Debs leads Red Special campaign of Socialist party.

Henry Ford begins to sell the Model T.

1910 Speaker Joseph G. Cannon loses his dictatorial powers in the House.

Ways to Study History XXI

Join a team? This maxim should be ignored, or reversed. Since World War II, research grants have become available from foundations, often awarded in a lump sum to a university on condition that a group of the faculty will dream up some "trail-blazing project." They seldom do. The late Justice Oliver Wendell Holmes, Jr. once wrote that being a judge meant to sail by yourself through the Arctic ice. The same metaphor can be applied to the study of the past. A historian walks into his office or the library, closes a door, and tries to learn what really happened. If lucky, he comes close to success. If he feels depressed when alone, he should not try.

Two eminent men can be seen as illustration. Allan Nevins published about as many important works as any American historian of his generation. For quality of output as well as quantity, he inspires awe. But on some ventures he was thwarted by his research assistants. Thus, he published a multi-volume study of Henry Ford and his motor company. But be wary. The text carries a photographic copy of a contract with the caption: "Tires, at four for $26." The contract was really for wheels; surely Nevins knew a wheel from a tire, but did he check his collaborators' work?

A study of a specific company has commonly been called a work in business history. Probably no practitioner in this specialty has done better work than George Sweet Gibb: first a book about a silverware manufacturer (1946), then an analysis of a textile-machinery builder (1950). Next, judged by the superlative standards of his earlier publications, he came a cropper. He was co-author of one volume (1956) in the mammoth history of the Standard Oil Company (New Jersey). These particular pages of print might give you the impression that the corners of several rugs had never been lifted. Some important issues seem to have been left to slip away between the responsibilities of the team members.

Collaborations can work, but they are treacherous.

Document 21-1

The author of these remarks, Carl Schurz, had been a United States senator and a secretary of the interior. Perhaps more important are two other facts: he was himself an immigrant from Germany, and his warnings were a convocation address at the University of Chicago.

. . . It is an incontestable and very significant fact that the British, the best colonizers in history, have, indeed, established in tropical regions governments, and rather absolute ones, but they have never succeeded in establishing there democratic commonwealths of the Anglo-Saxon type, like those in America or Australia.

The scheme of Americanizing our "new possessions" in that sense is therefore absolutely hopeless. The immutable forces of nature are against it. Whatever we may do for their improvement, the people of the Spanish Antilles will remain in overwhelming numerical predominance, Spanish creoles and negroes, and the people of the Philippines, Filipinos, Malays, Tagals, and so on,—some of them quite clever in their way, but the vast majority utterly alien to us, not only in origin and language, but in habits, traditions, ways of thinking, principles, ambitions,—in short, in most things that are of the greatest importance in human intercourse and especially in political cooperation. And under the influences of their tropical climate they will prove incapable of becoming assimilated to the Anglo-Saxon. They would, therefore, remain in the population of this republic a hopelessly heterogeneous element,—in some respects more hopeless even than the colored people now living among us. . . .

No, we cannot expect that the Porto Ricans, the Cubans, and the Filipinos will maintain orderly governments in Anglo-Saxon fashion. . . .

Document 21-2

Having retired from active participation in Standard Oil in 1897, John D. Rockefeller nonetheless was a witness before a federal commission investigating the problem of trusts. He denied that they had secured unfair rebates from railroads. Rather, so he said, their growth ensued from advantages over other firms which were to the benefit of society.

It is too late to argue about advantages of industrial combinations. They are a necessity. And if Americans are to have the privilege of extending their business in all the States of the Union, and into foreign countries as well, they are a necessity on a large scale, and require the agency of more than one corporation. Their chief advantages are:

(1) Command of necessary capital.

(2) Extension of limitations of business.

(3) Increase of number of persons interested in the business.

(4) Economy in the business.

(5) Improvements and economies which are derived from knowledge of many interested persons of wide experience.

(6) Power to give the public improved products at less prices and still make a profit for stockholders.

(7) Permanent work and good wages for laborers.

I speak from my experience in business with which I have been intimately connected for about 40 years. Our first combination was a partnership and afterwards a corporation in Ohio. That was sufficient for a local refining business. But dependent solely upon local business we should have failed years ago. We were forced to extend our markets and to seek for export trade. This latter made the seaboard cities a necessary place of business, and we soon discovered that manufacturing for export could be more economically carried on at the seaboard, hence refineries at Brooklyn, at Bayonne, at Philadelphia, and necessary corporations in New York, New Jersey, and Pennsylvania. . . .

Document 21-3

It is ironic that Carnegie, who was about to spread his largesse around the world, was heedless of the welfare of his city when he made his fortune. Beatrice Webb, an outstanding English social scientist, visited his factory in Pittsburgh in 1898, and recorded these observations in her diary after a young executive had shown her about.

We were told both by our young man and afterwards by Frick, that they never hesitated to tear up and demolish any of the plant if they thought a new plant would pay handsomely on the new capital to be expended. The value of the old plant was simply written off. It is said that Carnegie's Works replace all their plant every three years. It is, I think, to this lavish generosity towards their brainworkers and stimulus to their co-operative energies combined with this extravagant expenditure on improvements, that the Carnegie business owes its rapid and phenomenal success. . . .

Towards Labour they have acted for the last six years in a niggardly and oppressive fashion. They have abolished Trade Unionism throughout all their works—steel, coke, and mines and railways. . . . These 30 or 40 eager young men, who run the concern, have their whole energies absorbed in money making; they have as the ideal before them the lives of Mr. Carnegie and Mr. Frick—men who directly they have made their pile, leave Pittsburg and, to use the words of our young guide, "entertain finely in Paris and London." Not a member of the firm has any connection with the Federal, State or Municipal Government. It is only another aspect of this kind of Capitalism, that the State of Pennsylvania and the city of Pittsburg are so abjectly corrupt that State and City have become bye-words, even among American politicians. . . .

Document 21-4

When George Washington Plunkett, age 82, died in 1924 he was rich and renowned. He had run a business as a harbor contractor in New York, but his real trade was politics; he was leader of an assembly district for Tammany Hall. His revelations in a set of interviews published in 1905 are an instructive and amusing account of how the system worked.

There's an honest graft, and I'm an example of how it works. I might sum up the whole thing by sayin': "I seen my opportunities and I took 'em."

Just let me explain by examples. My party's in power in the city, and it's goin' to undertake a lot of public improvements. Well, I'm tipped off, say, that they're going to lay out a new park at a certain place.

I see my opportunity and I take it. I go to that place and I buy up all the land I can in the neighborhood. Then the board of this or that makes its plan public, and there is a rush to get my land, which nobody cared particular for before. . . .

What tells in holding your grip on your district is to go right down among the poor families and help them in the different ways they need help. I've got a regular system for this. If there's a fire in Ninth, Tenth, or Eleventh Avenue, for example, any hour of the day or night, I'm usually there with some of my election district captains as soon as the fire engines. If a family is burned out I don't ask whether they are Republicans or Democrats, and I don't refer them to the Charity Organization Society, which would investigate their case in a month or two and decide they were worthy of help about the time they were dead of starvation. I just get quarters for them, buy clothes for them if their clothes were burned up, and fix them up till they get things runnin' again. . . .

How to Get into a War

World War I had been in train for more than two and a half years before the United States was a belligerent. Its origins must be sought abroad. The outbreak of hostilities arose from a wide range of pressures, and some of them should be appraised. Apparent in the issue were changes in military technology, struggles for colonies and markets, rising clamors of nationalism, shifts in the balance of power in Europe. To begin with the last category, all of the major governments except Russia were roughly equal in the efficiency of their administration in mobilizing the resources of the nation. Nor were their rates of population growth widely disparate. What did change dramatically was their relative capacities to produce certain vital industrial goods. Drastically increased possibilities for destruction accompanied this explosive productivity in all the industrial nations.

The weight of this development toward destructiveness shifted enormously because of alterations in the techniques of warfare. Modern weaponry

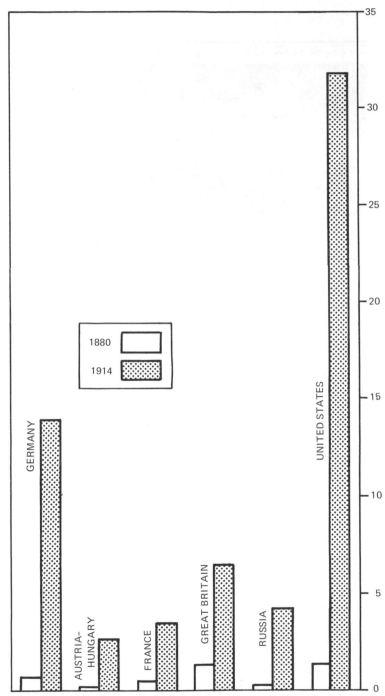

FIGURE 22-1. *International Steel Production, 1800–1914 (millions of tons)*

could consume metal at a pace that was beyond the imagination at the time of the Civil War. Relative strength on the oceans had also shifted. Until about the Crimean War (1854–1856) ships of the line were wooden. They took a long time to build, and they lasted some sixty years. England's accumulation of such vessels was so great that nobody felt like competing for control of the seas. But then came the steel hull, coupled with great strides in naval artillery. One British battleship completed in 1888 could have destroyed the entire fleet of ironclads launched in Britain prior to that decade. Fear of a drastic imbalance in sea power versus Germany prompted a British "naval scare" and a construction program that initiated eight battleships. But their guns still used gunpowder—an explosive so shattering that the weapons had very short lives. This meant that target practice had to be severely restricted. Even prior to the completion of these vessels, another design for big guns using cordite instead of gunpowder was originated. This in turn brought a new type of battleship, and so on. Now that Great Britain no longer had the "stock" of wooden warships, its advantages were reduced to two: (a) a stock of trained naval personnel, and (b) freedom from conscription into the army thus leaving more manpower available for industrial production. But as soon as another country could spare power from its land forces, it could bid for control of the seas. Beginning in 1898, Germany did just that.

One element in the indispensability of naval power was the fact that no nation was self-sufficient in military matériel. Consider nitrate. It supplied the nitrogen essential to all explosives, and nearly all nitrates came from Chile. While Britain dominated the Atlantic, she could cut off the German supply. But in 1910 a scientist at the Kaiser Wilhelm Institute in Berlin (one of the few governmental research establishments in the world at that time) devised a method to capture free nitrogen from the atmosphere. Goodby Chile, goodby English navy. As suggested, cordite had already been invented as an "improvement." Gunpowder consists of sulphur and charcoal (the fuels) plus nitropotassium (the charge, oxidizing element, explosive component). Cordite is the single molecule of nitrocellulose that holds both fuel and oxidizing agent. The latter is far more powerful; the direction of its blast can also be better controlled. By this time a good deal of brain power was at work on implements of aggression. One destructive weapon led to another. Submarines were horribly vulnerable (partly because their hulls were as thin as eggshells) to the better gunnery at longer range of surface vessels. So torpedoes were fabricated that would go farther. Nations were making other types of preparations for conflict. Great Britain's Chancellor of the Exchequer in 1909 created domestic turbulence by asking an increase in the budget of £15 million. Five years later, Germany imposed a military levy of a billion marks, a ghastly burden on a country with the resources that she had then. She cashed in nearly all of her foreign assets. She finished widening the Kiel Canal from that city to Wilhelmshaven, so that her large warships could move from the North Sea to the Baltic without becoming too vulnerable to attack. In the midst of this hurly-burly of preparedness, the French had exhausted most of their possible responses. They had no more able-bodied men who had previously been exempt from the army draft and thus could not expand their forces by the device of eliminating exempt categories. The best expedient they could find was to extend the term of each conscript from two years to three.

The precipitant in this seething pot was the Russo-German rivalry in the Balkans and the Middle East. Germany, as her power grew, had become increasingly resentful that she had been blocked out of the colonization of non-industrial countries, by the United States in Latin America, by other European powers in Africa and Asia. Next she tried to push eastward; a memorable symbol was the Berlin to Baghdad Railroad. This thrust collided with Russian ambitions to expand southward toward the Black Sea and the Bosporus. A violent clash (the Balkan War) began in October 1912; the victors were Serbia, Greece, Albania, and Bulgaria, who triumphed over Austria-Hungary. The latter was the one firm European ally of Germany—which had now miscalculated Habsburg power. In the prelude to World War I (as later in the antecedents of World War II), Germany's ambitions waxed greater than her energies. The moves eastward might well have succeeded if she had limited herself to this expansion on land; instead she had wasted much of her force by trying simultaneously to challenge British suzerainty of the oceans.

Roosevelt was also thinking about naval power, and he showed that he would go to any lengths to get it. The acquisition of the Panama Canal proved that the United States could bully a tiny country in Central America, but everyone knew that anyway. It also showed that we could bully Great Britain, which, facing the German threat, desperately needed to find a friend somewhere. For the present, the background must be stripped down severely. Policy-makers could not agree on the best route for a transisthmian ditch: Nicaragua or the Panama isthmus in Colombia. The situation was further complicated because a treaty of 1850 (Chapter 17) pledged that neither America nor Britain would seek "exclusive control" over a Caribbean ditch. To some minds the matter became urgent during the Spanish-American War; a new battleship at San Francisco took 68 days to go the 13,000 miles to Key West through the Straits of Magellan. Now a peculiar sort of circular logic seeped into minds in Washington: the nation required a Central American canal so that it could move ships more quickly, and it required a two-ocean navy to protect the canal. So the United States procured from England a new agreement that wiped out the 1850 treaty.

The remaining task was to secure a right-of-way. Long since, a French firm had started a canal across the Isthmus of Panama (part of Colombia) but had scrapped the project. It was willing to sell out to the United States; unfortunately, however, its rights were due to expire soon. Thereafter Colombia would be free to seize the physical property and lease it to the highest bidder. In America, Congress pressed the president to get the required real estate, in either of the two desired countries. Roosevelt's emissaries negotiated a treaty with the Colombian government for the Panama route, but the Colombian senate rejected it. Fulminating against the "contemptuous little creatures" trying to thwart his aim, Roosevelt sent a warship to Colombia. It arrived on 2 November, 1903. Two days later, a thousand Panamanians rebelled against Colombia. American forces would not let Colombian troops attack the rebels. In another two days, the American president had recognized the independent republic of Panama. So the canal was built, completed in 1914 a few days after the war began in Europe. Roosevelt offered interpretations of his behavior that look incompatible. He declared that "every action" of his administrations had been "in accordance with the highest, finest, and nicest standards of public governmental ethics." But he also said publicly, "I took the canal zone and let Congress debate, and while the debate goes on the canal does also." Take your choice.

Meanwhile the United States was having its domestic-foreign irritations. That Roosevelt had taken a generally pro-Japan stance at the Portsmouth Conference (late in Chapter 21) does not imply that he took a similar position at home. He had been mainly interested in expanding American business interests in the Orient (as we shall see below), not in favoring Orientals. Meanwhile, Asian immigrants to the United States had aroused hatred for decades. Early in this century the bias manifested itself in discrimination against Japanese children in schools, especially by California. The demand was strong: Keep them out of the country altogether. In 1908 the two nations reached an agreement. The United States conceded that Japanese formerly resident in this country plus close relatives of Japanese currently resident here, should receive entry permits. In return, Japan agreed to discourage emigration of unskilled laborers. This so-called Gentlemen's Agreement would later be an influence on the events of World War II and on the climate of opinion in which that conflict took place.

From the financial panic of 1907 until the outbreak of European war in 1914, American policy in fiscal, foreign, and political affairs was made in a consciousness that the economy was very shaky. Depression was sometimes relieved; ebbs and flows did occur. But depression was endemic along with the basic maldistribution of income. The responses of the federal government, whether under Roosevelt or Taft or Wilson, were anemic. Details need not be explored, but some matters should be mentioned. Whereas Roosevelt had refused to touch the problem of tariff rates, his hand-picked successor plunged in with a call for reduction of import duties. Already Taft was breaking the rules of American politics. The prudent president sends his advance agents to Capitol Hill before he makes any public commitments. They count heads, make deals, swap votes on this for votes on that. Instead, Taft called a special session of Congress for the sole purpose of revising the tariff. When the Payne bill was submitted to the House, the chief executive admitted that its rates were not as low as he had wished, but claimed that they were "substantial reductions." At this stage he should have been wary. The worst was yet to come. Guided by Nelson Aldrich of Rhode Island (son-in-law of the elder Rockefeller), the Senate voted more than 800 amendments. Duties were sharply raised on several iron and steel products, lumber, textiles. The Payne bill had included an inheritance-tax clause; it disappeared.

Now Taft's afflictions multiplied quickly. The final version of the Payne-Aldrich Act brought only a small reduction over-all, and it was regarded as prejudicial to the Midwest. Strong sectional antagonism to the administration emerged. It was aggravated when he bungled the questions of conservation and finally fired a popular administrator from Pennsylvania. These missteps killed any pretense of unity in the Republican Party. The president's fulcrum in the House of Representatives had long been the Speaker, whose power over legislation a decade earlier had been overwhelming. In a sense, his voice had been more decisive than the president's when a bill was being considered. The chief executive could veto a measure, but his veto could be overturned by a two-thirds vote. When the Speaker obstructed a bill, appeal was nearly impossible. Each proposal was required to have a special rule to reach the floor of the House. The Rules Committee had five members. The Speaker was a member, and he appointed two others from his own party and two from the opposition. If he turned thumbs down on a proposal, it was dead. But in 1910 the outraged Midwestern insurgents upset the whole system. They joined with delighted Democrats to decree that in future the Rules Committee should be elected by the whole House. The Speaker has continued to be highly influential, but not the autocrat that he was at the end of the nineteenth century; his power now comes from seniority, from his effect on patronage, from, occasionally, respect.

These formal enactments both reflected and exacerbated the convulsions in the American party system. Wilson's election as president in 1912 and his re-election in 1916 should not be seen as an index of the growing strength of the Democrats. On the contrary, they had lost ground. To a noticeable degree, the Socialists gained where the Democrats lost. Over the years only two avowedly Socialist members of Congress were elected: one a German from Milwaukee, the other a Jew from the lower east side of New York City. But no sweeping interpretation should be based on these scraps of evidence. Much of the Socialist support came from the prairies and the plains: the most popular Party periodicals were published in Kansas and Missouri, while the highest percentage of a state vote that the Socialists ever captured occurred in Oklahoma. These radical encroachments served to shake up the other parties. Already in 1897 Judge Holmes, then on the Supreme Judicial Court of Massachusetts, was writing: "When socialism first began to be talked about, the comfortable classes of the community were a good deal frightened." By 1905 President Roosevelt was alarmed; he thought the growth of socialist beliefs and votes were "far more ominous that any populist or similar movements in the past." These ejaculations were not a formula to either

Democrats or Republicans telling them what adjustments they should make to hold the electorate. A goodly amount of political skirmishing—which had little effect on the economy—can merely be summarized. Roosevelt had a falling out with Taft, partly because of ideology, but mainly because he felt personally affronted. When Taft dismissed Gifford Pinchot from the federal conservation program, Roosevelt felt that his ideas as well as his appointee were being abused.

Meanwhile, the difficulties of trying to expand American business interests in the Far East caused further friction between Roosevelt and Taft on the diplomatic scene. Attempts to draw American capital into land ventures in Asia had been building up over a number of years, and during his presidency, Roosevelt had himself especially tried to promote railroad building. When J. P. Morgan was considering pulling out of a syndicate that had been formed for this purpose, Roosevelt wrote to him: "I cannot expect you or any of our big business men to go into what they think will be to their disadvantage." However, he went on, if the reason for Morgan's projected withdrawal was his fear that the government of the United States might not support him, he should be assured that the administration will "do all that in its power lies to see that you suffer no wrong whatsoever from the Chinese or any other power in this matter." Speaking personally, "My interest of course is simply the interest of seeing American commercial interests prosper in the Orient." Taft worked from this latter assumption too, and tried to use government pressures to further the cause of American private capital in China. Obstructed by a secret agreement between Japan and Russia, the United States failed in Manchuria. By the time in 1910 that American defeat was apparent to most sensible people, Roosevelt was telling Taft that the drive had been doomed from the start. The United States could not have much economic strength in the Far East unless it had military power there. But American voters would never consent to stationing large-scale land forces in Asia. The Open Door, he warned, was empty words if a military power such as Japan chose to ignore it.*

Even after it became obvious that prominent financiers had lost interest, the president and his highest advisers persisted. A shift of stance came with Taft's successor, Wilson. As early as 1902 when he was president of Princeton, Wilson had stated that the United States should "command the economic fortunes of the world." Five years later he said: "Concessions obtained by financiers must be safeguarded by ministers of state, even if the sovereignty of unwilling nations be outraged in the process. Colonies must be obtained or planted, in order that no useful corner of the world may be overlooked or left unused." His subsequent demand at the conference at Versailles for "self-

---

*As late as 1945, no responsible person that I knew in Military Intelligence in Washington would have challenged this postulate: This nation must not commit large armies on the land mass of Asia. The disasters that have followed from the abandonment of this policy, first in Korea and later in Viet Nam, are obvious to anybody who can see. But then, some can't: *Miro, miro, y no ve.*

determination of nations" should be interpreted in the shadow of this attitude. When he entered the White House in 1913, he was expecting "many sharp struggles for foreign trade." He declared then that nothing concerned him more "than the fullest development of the trade of this country and its righteous conquest of foreign markets." Some commentators have written that President Wilson repudiated dollar diplomacy, that his foreign policies were not swayed by the requests of gluttonous lobbyists. The evidence against this view is stubborn. When nationals of the major powers joined together in 1913 to propose the Six Power Loan to China, Wilson refused to accede to a request that he as president should ask American bankers to join the group. But Secretary of State Bryan was forthright about the reasons for the refusal: the Americans would "not have a controlling voice" in the syndicate. The same worthy made a revealing remark on the first day of the National Council of Foreign Trade in Washington in May, 1914, just before World War I began in Europe. The president, he said, had stressed the intention of his administration to "open the doors of all the weaker countries to an invasion of American capital and enterprise." He said too: "My Department is your department; the ambassadors, the ministers, and the consuls are all yours. It is their business to look after your interests and to guard your rights."

These declarations of federal policy make no sense unless they are seen in the context of domestic problems. Let us attempt a quick summation of the dilemma at home. Chiefly because of a hopelessly lopsided distribution of personal incomes, purchasing power was not adequate to buy the goods and services that the economy could produce.* A large part of the maldistribution of income could be attributed, in turn, to the agglutinated formation in the preceding fifty years of a small number of near-monopolies that could usually dictate their own terms at the bargaining table. In the presidential campaign of 1912, the four prominent candidates stood for four different approaches to this situation. President Taft initiated several prosecutions against unpopular trusts, but his total career suggests that he had no desire to alter the fundamental contours of American society. Roosevelt, running for the Progressive Party, repeatedly declared that giant business was here to stay, that the sole course for the federal government to provide justice to the common man was to regulate Standard Oil and similar firms; however, during his nearly eight years in the White House he did not accomplish, or even attempt, significant regulation. Wilson too was emphatic: he wanted to bust them up, to dissolve them into smaller units that would truly compete with each other. Debs, in urging that the only solution was confiscation and public operation,

---

*At the end of World War II, some economists were quite agitated over the relative merits of "underconsumption" and "overproduction" theories of the Great Depression. The dispute seems pointless. What seems central to me is two propositions: An indispensable element in causing the economic collapse was the faulty distribution of incomes. The major cure for the collapse was to give purchasing power to people who would spend it.

was caustic: "Competition was natural enough at one time, but do you think you are competing today? Many of you think you are competing. Against whom? Against Rockefeller? About as I would if I had a wheelbarrow and competed with the Santa Fe from here to Kansas City."

Faced with these alternatives, a plurality (not an impressive one) chose Wilson. Now he had not to talk but to act. He didn't; he went on talking. Much space has been wasted in pseudo-learned tomes on the Federal Trade Commission Act and the Clayton Act, both passed late in 1914. A retrospective view can be cruelly unfair, but now it seems clear that these two laws have changed little in the ways that businessmen behave. The former claimed that it would outlaw "unfair trade practices." A clause in the latter announced that the capacities of employees should not be "an article of commerce." What happened? Although historically the courts have played the leading role in emasculating the Federal Trade Commission, it should be recorded that Wilson started the process by packing it with wealthy conservatives. Perhaps it was never meant to do much; at any rate it never has. The Clayton Act has meant less. When it was acclaimed at its passage as "the Magna Carta of labor" by the president of the American Federation of Labor, he was being an ass, as he frequently was. Promptly upon enactment of this folderol, President Wilson announced that his campaign platform had now been duly passed because the administration had effected the reorganization of the economy.

To be fair to Wilson, two earlier laws must be considered. They did have conseqences. The Underwood-Simmons Tariff Act of 1913 was the first significant reduction in import duties since 1857. Two possible benefits may be suggested here, and they both stem from the same postulate: A sound mechanism for keeping the peace is to treat people more equitably. The new import duties were more kindly to rural areas in the United States at a time when that was probably desirable. And they were more conducive to fair exchanges in international trade at a time when that was probably desirable. The other law, the Federal Reserve Act, is still the law of the land (although, as will be seen in Document 26-1, its operations have been considerably changed). Propellants toward this innovation were many. Defects in the National Banking Act have been, if not scrutinized, at least noted, as have institutional changes in the economy. But when the bias of American politicians was for "whoa" rather than for motion, a new statute could be carried only by urgent needs. The financial panic of 1907 and the unending depression that followed it provided considerable acceleration. Simultaneously, the bankers of New York City seemed to be losing ground to competitors in outlying parts of the country. So the lobbyists came to Washington.

Except for temporary perversions in a few states, Americans have always believed that banks—even the central bank—should be privately owned and privately run (although today several other federal agencies swing considerable weight at the Reserve). (On the basic functions of central

FOR PRESIDENT

EUGENE V. DEBS

FIGURE 22-2. *Campaign Poster for Eugene V. Debs*

The following judgment is sure to be challenged by most American historians, but I will make the assertion nonetheless: Eugene Debs was the most significant politician in the United States in this century. Obviously my statement also requires some definition of a "significant politician": (1) He banking, see Document 26-1.) Thus when the Federal Reserve System was founded in 1913, its charter provided that it should be owned and managed by the private banks that belonged to it, called the "member banks." Twelve Federal Reserve Banks were established, and their location shows vividly where the financial centers of the nation were situated at the time, as shown in Figure 22-3. A map of this kind, if read with an awareness of other developments, can be worth volumes. Note for instance that San Francisco was regarded as the linchpin of a huge area that runs from the eastern border of Utah to the coast; Los Angeles didn't count for shucks. Most of the vast area presided over by Dallas had few people, but production of crude oil had already become vital to the national economy. The Southeast, notoriously outside the national economy at the time, got two Federal Reserve Banks because of its place in the international setting. Why did little old Pennsylvania and New York each get a Bank of its own? Any decent explanation of the sites for these Banks must be tortuous. The reasons of course involved business, but they also involved politics. For instance, five Banks were placed west of the Mississippi, which was quite disproportionate to population and to economic significance, but each state west of the Mississippi had two Senators.

So the trans-Mississippi sections and the Southeast got their Federal Reserve Banks, and they were better off in regard to credit facilities than they had been under the National Banking Act, but they still did not get equitable treatment from the monetary system. When the number of banks failing outright or suspending gold payments rose steeply after 1920, most of these in default were in rural areas of the South and Midwest, not in the East. The

---

must have a clear impact on ordinary voters' expectations from the government. (2) He must help to alter the fundamental structure of the political system.

Debs was born in 1855 in Terre Haute, Indiana, and regarded that town as his home all his life. But he did not really live there. After the American Railway Union was crushed during the Pullman strike (see Chapter 20), he made his living as a travelling lecturer for various radical periodicals almost until he died in 1926. His speeches do not now read well. To modern ears his rhetoric often seems purple, and he seems to repeat the same old exhortations. But his contemporaries did not find him trivial or irrelevant. There is no intention here to load the argument by stating that he was five times the Socialist candidate for President or by pointing out that in 1912 he received one vote for every four received by a Republican incumbent; after all, Bryan was nominated three times and got more votes than Debs ever did. What is vital is that Bryan did not force his opponents into altering their sales pitches, while Debs did.

In one sense this campaign poster is phony: in 1920 Debs was not wearing a bow tie because he was in the Federal prison at Atlanta, Georgia, having been convicted for anti-war agitation under the Sedition Act of 1918. Perhaps the flavor of his thought and the impression he made on others will be conveyed by two brief quotations, both from his internment at Atlanta. To one reporter, Debs commented on the Russian Revolution: "All along the track of the ages, wherever a government has been overthrown by force and violence, that government had been maintained by force and violence." After a visit to Debs, Lincoln Steffens wrote to his sister: "He's a Man—"

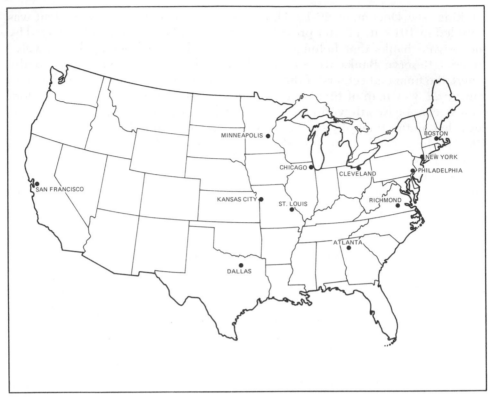

FIGURE 22-3. *Location of the Federal Reserve Banks, 1913*

causes for the concentration of these banking calamities in certain districts cannot be blamed entirely on the new monetary arrangements, but they surely played a big part. The mechanics of the Federal Reserve System need not be dissected in detail. (But see Document 26-1.) The Act created three different categories of member banks depending on size, and stipulated a certain ratio of "reserves" to assets for each. Later amendments altered the arithmetic ratio, but it was the definition of "reserves" that caused endless trouble. For the law allowed cities in smaller places to count as a portion of their reserves the deposits that they carried in banks in larger cities. The latter banks could then count the same money as part of their reserves. As will be seen below, many agricultural regions were in chronic financial difficulties after 1919. When farmers were unable to meet their notes on time, their banks would draw home their deposits from New York or Boston. This unwise set of regulations governing "reserves" thus spread instability through the whole monetary mechanism of the country. The disruption was serious from 1920 forward; it would become disastrous after 1929 (Chapter 26).

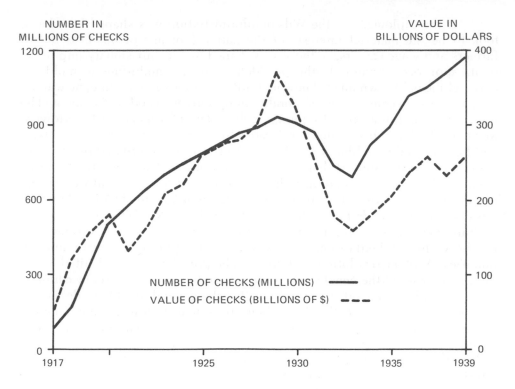

NUMBER IN
MILLIONS OF CHECKS

VALUE IN
BILLIONS OF DOLLARS

NUMBER OF CHECKS (MILLIONS) ———
VALUE OF CHECKS (BILLIONS OF $) ----

FIGURE 22-4. *The Federal Reserve System and the American Economy*

This graph should make immediately visible a few major changes in the condition of the United States from 1917 to 1939. It shows the great increase in the volume of commercial bank deposits and the concomitant use of checks as money; in modern America about 90 per cent of all purchases are being made with checks.

But breaks in the trend should be noted, some chronological, others regional. The chart shows a temporal interruption, in sharp declines from 1929. After 1935 the number of checks being cleared was greater than ever before, while their accumulated value was greatly depressed; more checks were being written for smaller sums. At the depths of the depression, Americans in several areas devised again, as in colonial times, devices for doing business without money—or checks, because they did not have bank accounts. They resorted to "due bills," which might today be called I.O.U.'s. A friend who was then a young man in Montana reports that these pledges of faith would sometimes be endorsed a dozen times from one holder to another, although they did not have as security even a commerical deposit in a bank.

535

If the diplomacy of the Wilson administration was shaped by what it took to be the material interests of the nation (not just of business but of farmers and wage earners, so too was it shaped by the "missionary impulses" of its sponsors, particularly the president. Wilson's ambitions to mold the entire globe in his own image knew no limits of either space or time; he wanted to enact his own conceptions of morality into a universal code of behavior. The implications of this attitude for foreign policy glared forth in his actions toward Mexico, which had been ruled for decades by a corrupt tyrant. But the dictator had been ousted by a liberal in 1911, who in turn was murdered by his chief general two years later. At this point Wilson broke an American tradition that stretched back to the founding fathers. The United States had always recognized as the *de jure* government of a foreign land any faction, however unsavory, that held *de facto* control of the territory. Not Wilson: he was too high-minded. Denouncing the ruling group in Mexico as "a government of butchers," he withheld recognition. Next he started plots that were founded in fantasies. Another revolution took place. The president of the United States did not approve of the new leader in Mexico, so he schemed to replace him by an unscrupulous general. It turned out that the general, unable to defeat the constitutional forces of the incumbent president unless he got tangible American support, began making raids across the Rio Grande to provoke American intervention in Mexico. He got his wish. Earlier, in April 1914, Wilson had sent American naval forces to occupy Vera Cruz to retaliate for the arrest there of American sailors. Now he sent more than 6,000 soldiers into Mexico as a punitive expedition. When an armed clash came with Mexican troops, Wilson drew up a message to Congress. Fortunately, before he delivered it to capitol hill he learned that he had his facts wrong.

However, the president did haul Great Britain, a very reluctant Britain, into supporting his opposition to the Mexican dictator of 1913–1914. Wilson assured the English that he would "teach the South American republics to elect good men." The lesson did not stick.

But Great Britain could not afford to let the Americans down in the Western Hemisphere, because she desperately needed the United States as a counterweight to Germany. World War I began in a few frantic days at the beginning of August, 1914. A jab by one government brought an immediate parry by another, and the fracas was on. It was not a flurry of fists or even the popping of rifles or thrusts of boyonets; it was the drifting of poison gas and the boom of artillery launching thousand-pound shells and the spreading of the miasma of hate. Contemporaries could vaguely predict how horrible their future would be. On the day that Great Britain declared war, the Foreign Minister, Sir Edward Grey, stood in his office in the evening looking out the window. He was addicted to a stable, gentle world. Lover of wild birds and of fishing, he revered the civilized amenities of a country gentleman. His reaction to these dread circumstances was a lament: "The lamps are going out all over Europe; we shall not see them lit again in our lifetime."

What course should the United States follow in such troubled seas? Events refined this general problem into more specific ones. The administration's early response to the European declarations of war showed a level-headed attitude. A significant statement to the press came from Secretary Bryan on 15 August. France had approached Morgan's banking house to ask it to float a war loan in the United States. The firm wanted to know if American authorities would approve the venture. Bryan, having first expounded his arguments to Wilson (Document 22-1) stated: ". . . in the judgment of this Government loans by American bankers to any foreign nation which is at war is inconsistent with the true spirit of neutrality." The president in addressing the Senate on 19 August sketched the reasons for avoiding partiality: "The people of the United States are drawn from many nations, and chiefly from the nations now at war. It is natural and inevitable that there should be the utmost variety of sympathy and desire among them with regard to the issues and circumstances of the conflict. Some will wish one nation, others another, to succeed in the momentous struggle. It will be easy to excite passion and difficult to allay it. . . . The United States must be neutral in fact as well as in name during these days that are to try men's souls. . . ."

Had the administration held to these precepts, the United States might never have become a combatant at all. The reasons for its failure to do so should be inspected. Some historians have argued that the president did not realize the policies that were being advanced because, at the very time the war was starting in Europe, his wife was dying in Washington. If tenable, this argument seems tangential. His speech to the Senate quoted above is not incoherent. Besides, presidents are paid not to be distracted: lesser men do their jobs while they are being sued for divorce, their children are entering mental hospitals, the boss is threatening to fire them. Three other forces that prompted Wilson to alter his policies quickly seem to deserve more extended examination: (1) the condition of the American economy, (2) his own Anglophilism which was shared (or exceeded) by many of his close advisers, (3) extreme legalism, which had been a dominant characteristic in the English colonies from the beginning. (See mid-Chapter 1.)

An obvious extension of Bryan's announced discouragement of war loans would be to place a complete or partial embargo on foreign trade, to ban shipments either to the entire world or just to Europe. But such a move might be disastrous in domestic politics. Wilon had come to the White House as a minority president, and his prospects did not look bright. Worse, the economy had been bobbing down but never far up since 1907; the recession deepened at the turn of 1913–1914.* Most efforts that have been made to justify Wilson's hostility to an embargo seem fragile—that German submarines menaced American lives as well as property (prohibit persons as well as goods), that

---

*Tidiness would require that this sentence be substantiated by quantitative data. None have been compiled. The reliable statisticians do not make even annual estimates of Gross National Product before World War I. But the qualitative evidence is quite strong.

German submarines were a worse danger than British blockades (an embargo would halt both threats), and so on. The imposition of an embargo was not pursued for cold politico-economic reasons. The president's chief adviser, Colonel Edward M. House, wrote to him on 22 July, 1915: "If it came to the last analysis, and we placed an embargo upon munitions of war and foodstuffs to please the cotton men, our whole industrial and agricultural machinery would cry out against it."

So the stand toward war loans that Bryan had announced was quickly reversed. It is questionable whether the president understood finance sufficiently to recognize that policy was taking an about-face. Events proceeded thus: A vice-president of a New York bank wrote to the counsellor of the State Department saying that if temporary credits were not granted to the Allies, the "buying power of these foreign purchasers will go to Australia, Canada, Argentina, and elsewhere. . . . If we allow these purchases to go elsewhere we will have neglected our foreign trade at the time of our greatest need and greatest opportunity." In sending these arguments forward to Wilson, the bureaucrat found ways to imply that they were original with him. The president's reply was a superlative piece of gibberish, in a conversation on 23 August, 1914:

> There is a decided difference between an issue of government bonds, which are sold in open market to investors, and an arrangement for easy exchange in meeting debts incurred in trade between a government and American merchants. The sale of bonds draws gold from the American people. The purchasers of bonds are loaning their savings to the belligerent government, and are, in fact, financing the war. The acceptance of Treasury notes or other evidences of debt in payment for articles purchased in this country is merely a means of facilitating trade by a system of credits which will avoid the clumsy and inpracticable method of cash payments.

What was that "difference" again?

Within a few months the Morgan firm (the elder J. P. had died; the house was now headed by J. P., Jr.) became the procurement agents in the United States for both British military branches, to receive a commission of 2 per cent on all purchases. Soon after the company got a similar contract from the French government. Under these agreements, it seems that the younger Morgan made greater profits during World War I than his father had made in a lifetime. After the war, a partner in the bank observed: "Our firm had never for one moment been neutral; we didn't know how to be. From the very start we did everything we could to contribute to the cause of the Allies." From the mouth of J. P., Jr., in 1936: "In spite of President Wilson's urging impartiality 'even in thought' we found it quite impossible to be impartial as between right and wrong. . . . We agreed that we should do all that was lawfully in our power to help the Allies win the war as soon as possible."

It must be admitted that the interpretation set forth here would be disputed by many students, and some of them have written volumes whereas this account is only a couple of pages. But the observations of informed contemporaries cannot be blinked off, and although one is entitled to ask whether the contemporaries being cited here were either representative or perceptive, I think they were. A joint Anglo-French loan was floated in the autumn of 1915 for a half billion dollars. James J. Hill had a comment: "One who looks only at the plain facts will see that the grant of this credit for the purpose stated is far less an accommodation to the countries that ask it than an act of necessity for the United States." Letters back to the Foreign Office from the British ambassador in Washington point in the same direction. On 21 November, 1915: "The brutal facts are that this country has been saved by the war and by our war demand from a great economical crisis; that in normal times Great Britain and her colonies take forty per cent of the total export trade of the United States. We have therefore the claims of their best customer and at the present moment our orders here are absolutely essential to their commercial prosperity." Again, on 13 August, 1916, "The reason why there has been no embargo on arms and ammunition is not sympathy with us, but the sense that the prosperity of the country on which the administration depends for its existence would be imperilled by such a measure."

Admittedly, in Wilson's mind the issue of an embargo was garbled with the other two determinants of policy: his pro-English bias, and his legalisms. The Anglophilia of the president and his coteries can be seen from both sides. Its negative aspect was a hostility to traits not English. A popular (derogatory) term among them was "hyphenated Americans"; that is, Italian-Americans, Irish-Americans, and so forth. Our ambassador to England, Walter Hines Page, lashed out, "We Americans have got to . . . hang our Irish agitators and shoot our hyphenates and bring up our children with revererence for English history and in the awe of English literature." President Wilson, indicting the critics of the Versailles Treaty after the war, proclaimed, "Hyphens are the knives that are being stuck into this document." On the positive side, most major actors in American foreign policy nearly all thought that England was beautiful.

While there is always a risk of being tedious by racking up a series of quotations, it still seems proper to attempt to capture the tone in which our diplomats communicated with each other. Right after the European War started, the British ambassador called on Wilson, and then reported to Sir Edward Grey: "The President said in the most solemn way that if that [the German] cause succeeds in the present struggle the United States would have to give up its present ideals and devote all its energies to defence, which would mean the end of its present system of Government. . . . I said, 'You and Grey are fed on the same food and I think you understand.' There were tears in his eyes, and I am sure we can, at the right moment, depend on an understanding heart here." Wilson's pro-British sentiments were not new, nor could they be called clandestine. The parliamentary system, so he had written, might well be superior to "congressional government." He had made it clear that in his opinion immigrants from the British Isles were distinctly superior to the riffraff pouring in from eastern and southern Europe. Part of the tragedy is that he had no confidantes who dissented from these opinions. Probably the most prejudiced of his informants was his ambassador in London. The English navy followed its ancient practice of detaining and seizing American exports. The United States followed its ancient practice of insisting: "Free ships make free goods," and drafted some strong protests to Whitehall. On one occasion when the American ambassador had delivered such a protest to Grey at the Foreign Office, he added: "I have now read the despatch, but I do not agree with it; let us conside how it should be answered!" More heartrending yet was his reaction when the State Department instructed him to present at the Foreign Office a comprehensive list of complaints against British violation of the carrying trade of neutrals. His own protest was not against English outrages but against the American note; he wrote home to the State Department (21 October, 1915) that it contained "not a courteous word, not a friendly phrase, nor a kindly turn in it, not an allusion even to old acquaintance, to say nothing of an old friendship . . . there is nothing in its tone to show that it came from an American to an Englishman." Colonel House, while not so hopelessly lopsided, was far from impartial. While in London in January 1916 he said to the American envoy there, "The United States would like Great Britain to do those things which would enable the United States to help Great Britain win the war." A prelude to the next phase of this analysis seems advisable.

Sir Edward Grey does not enjoy a high standing in the ranks of foreign ministers. But the reasons to deprecate him are obscure: he got what he wanted. In his own retrospective sentences:

> Blockade of Germany was essential to the victory of the Allies, but the ill-will of the United States meant their certain defeat. After Paris had been saved by the Battle of the Marne, the Allies could do no more than hold their own against Germany; sometimes they did not even do that. Germany and Austria were self-supporting in the huge supply of munitions. The Allies soon became dependent for an adequate supply on the United States. . . . The object of diplomacy, therefore, was to secure the maximum of blockade that could be enforced without a rupture with the United States.

Grey's diagnosis was right, and he used it to the advantage of his country. The two themes illustrated above may not have caused the United States to enter the war had it not been for a third consideration: the compulsive legalism of the president and most of his aides. It is questionable that "international law" ever means much in a crisis. But what is worse, in the instance at hand, is that Wilson and his corrupted little courtiers in Washington did not act in a judicious fashion. This conclusion can be approached by looking at their handling of three crucial issues:

1. the British treatment of American commerce on the Atlantic
2. the American treatment of armed British merchant ships
3. Germany's use of submarines

Before starting a slightly more detailed discussion of these three issues, another matter can be disposed of quickly. Germany never protested the American sale of armaments to the Allies, although such sales definitely angered the people of Germany. It was common practice then, and still is, for a neutral to sell contraband to a combatant.

From the beginning of the war, the royal navy was pitiless in its encroachments on neutral rights on the Atlantic. It might halt an American ship, search it, seize goods, sometimes escape into a British port under guard. The State Department made repeated protests. It also made indiscreet concessions, as when Secretary Bryan in December, 1914, admitted that a belligerent could legitimately justify its behavior not only by "rules of international law" but by "self-preservation." Given that argument, a nation can validate anything. But at times the Allied high-handedness went so far as to disturb the tranquillity in Washington, where the worst rankling came in the summer of 1916. The Allies began to open and search U.S. mails on the high seas. As the State Department notified the English and French: "To submit to a lawless practice of this character would open the door to repeated violations of international law by the belligerent powers." Even more provocative to the president was publication by the British of a blacklist of hundreds of American persons and companies who, because they had allegedly been trading with the enemy, were declared off-limits to all Commonwealth subjects. After this, Wilson informed Colonel House: "I am seriously considering asking Congress to authorize me to prohibit loans and restrict exportations to the Allies." Would to Providence he had, but he did not.

The disposition of the administration toward the combatants also appeared in its policy toward armed British merchant vessels. The Allied arming of merchant men was made even more questionable because some of the ships found it advantageous to fly the United States flag in order to sink German U-boats. Here was a field (or a sea) on which international law collapsed. A common earlier belief held that a merchantman could be armed for "defensive" purposes although not for offensive ones. However, the hull of a submarine was so fragile that any weapon could be offensive—including depth charges. Germany held that all precedents were irrelevant. A major problem for Washington was whether these armed Allied merchant vessels should be allowed to enter American ports. They had been classified early in the war by the State Department as peaceful ships. But were they? No doubt can exist that the weaponry was a benefit to Allied merchantmen.

	Total Attacked	Sunk by Torpedo	Sunk by Gunfire	Escaped
Defensively armed	310	62	12	236
Unarmed	302	30	205	67

A single incident will expose a further part of the picture. On 19 August, 1915, the German submarine U-27 had stopped a British freighter and given the crew ample time to debark. Then U-27 began bombarding the English vessel to sink it. Another merchantman approached flying an American flag. Permitted to draw near by an unsuspecting submarine, she sank U-27. Wilson posed the problem clearly: "The matter of armed merchantmen is not so simple. . . . It is hardly fair to ask Submarine commanders to give warning by summons if, when they approach as near as they must for that purpose they are to be fired upon." However, this view was expressed privately; publicly the government did not do anything that restrained Allied abuses. Occasionally an armed vessel was allowed into an American port only on condition that its guns be removed, but, as with the blockade and other infractions of neutral rights, the general problem was never solved.

To my mind, the preceding two issues have been badly neglected by many analysts of the period, who seem to have an *idée fixe* about Germany's submarine warfare. The Kaiser managed to have the worst of two worlds. He was so faltering, due in large part to his fear of alienating the United States, that he did not use submarines for a quick knock-out. On the other hand he used them enough that he did alienate the United States. He was first on one foot, then on the other. At the beginning of the war he did not have enough U-boats to do serious damage to his enemies. He built more. Sometimes he authorized their use; the episodes that had the deepest impact on American attitudes are listed in Some Notable Events at the end of this chapter. But for us today, perhaps three generalizations should be proffered. Human beings try to cope with the innovations of the present in terms of old precedents, which often do not apply. Second, as shown in Figure 22-5, by the time the United States entered the war in the spring of 1917, Germany had built its submarine fleet to the point where it could hack out a great toll. Had it not been for American production of Victory ships, the Allied tonnage would have fallen drastically, perhaps fatally. Third, Wilson's personal opinions were crucial. On 20 May, 1915 after the *Lusitania* sinking, he stated: "Each Government should understand that the rights which we claim from it have no connection which we can recognize with what we claim from the other, but that we must insist on our rights from each without regard to what the other does or does not do." A mountainous difficulty was that he was disposed to insist much more strongly to the one side than to the other.

The president sacrificed almost his last inch of side-step when the *Sussex* was sunk in March, 1916. Americans were on board, but not one was killed. Nonetheless, Wilson dispatched an ultimatum saying that if Germany did not abandon its methods of submarine warfare, he would sever diplomatic relations. Germany, for the moment, said it would not sink merchant vessels without warning, but reserved its right to resume unrestricted submarine warfare if the British continued their blockade. When this crisis had been passed, for the moment, the president complained to his secretary of the navy: "I can't keep the country out of war. They talk of me as though I were a god. Any little German lieutenant can put us into the war at any time by some calculated outrage." A chief executive who turns over the foreign policy of his

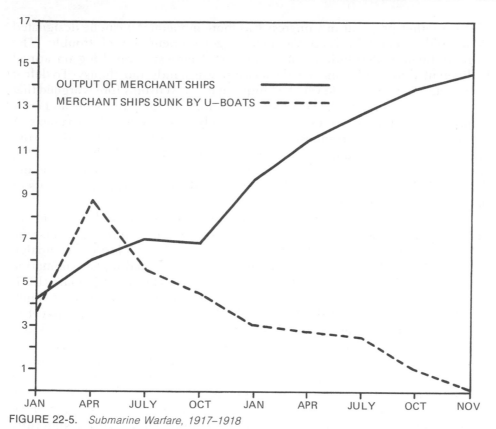

FIGURE 22-5. *Submarine Warfare, 1917–1918*

country to any little lieutenant serving another government has gone too far.

Determined efforts were made in Congress to impede the course of the administration. Consider now only two proposals. Each of them was blocked by the Wilson team using a combination of patronage, disingenuousness, and outright deception. As early as January, 1915, a bill was introduced to ban shipments of munitions from the United States. Insiders, including the president and the British ambassador, thought a stiff fight might be needed to stop its passage since Americans were so upset by violations of neutral commerce. Just at the climax of a struggle in Congress, a U-boat sank Britain's liner *Lusitania*, killing Americans and thus reversing the object of domestic hatred. England had lucked out, due to German ineptitude. By late summer the State Department evolved its final bit of double-think on this question. The new secretary of state (Bryan had resigned in a disagreement with the president during the *Lusitania* crisis) proceeded from the true assertion that the United States had never maintained in peacetime a large military force. He went on with balderdash: "The United States has always depended upon the right and power to purchase arms and ammunition from neutral nations in case of foreign attack. This right, which it claims for itself, it can not deny to others."

543

Another proposal in Congress was more moderate: it can be designated as a mild attempt to keep the federal government out of trouble. The Gore-McLemore Resolution warned against Americans travelling on armed belligerent ships. Unfortunately the measure was windy and clumsy. To defeat it the administration used every technique at hand. Wilson's forces argued that a submarine could not take adequate precautions for the passengers and crew of prizes; therefore they must cease completely to attack merchant vessels. A famous memorandum composed by the State Department at this time conveniently omitted a paragraph from Chief Justice Marshall's decision in the *Nereide* case on the status of the armed merchantman: "She is an open and declared belligerent; claiming all the rights, and subject to all the dangers of the belligerent character."

American relations with Germany remained more or less static for nearly a year; in fact, at times the president seemed to be turning against the Allies. (See early Chapter 24 for Wilson's "peace and social justice" campaign of 1916.) Meanwhile, however, Germany had been expanding her submarine fleet. She decided to try to smash her opponents quickly. On 31 January, 1917, she announced that any vessel, even if unarmed and neutral, that ventured into a forbidden zone around the British Isles and France, would be subject to attack without warning. Wilson had forced his own hand by his previous ultimatum at the time of the *Sussex* episode, and he referred to that sad event when he went before Congress on 3 February to explain his termination of diplomatic relations. His story held two false statements: the *Sussex* did not sink but was towed into Boulogne, and no Americans were killed. Within the month the president had asked for authority to arm United States merchant vessels. When a small group of senators opposed him, Wilson spitefully referred to them as a "little group of willful men, representing no opinion but their own. . . ." He won; the country lost. On that day the issue was decided; with armed American merchant ships venturing into the prohibited zone, an explosive incident was bound to happen. The declaration of war by Congress on 6 April was an anti-climax.

Since no gain could accrue from using these pages to scrutinize the battles and campaigns of American engagements in Europe, the tale can be finished quickly. A few generalizations may be hazarded. First, American entry was essential to Allied victory. Without it the Allies would have gotten nothing better than a draw, and they might well have lost—and we know that German terms of peace were still harsh. Second, a part of the results is recorded in the statistics of fatalities (in millions of men): Germany 1.8, Russia 1.7, France 1.385, Austria-Hungary 1.2, Great Britain .947, United States .106. But these figures hardly begin to show the damage that was done. Distrust became endemic, not only distrust of others but lack of confidence in one's own powers to influence destiny, the revival of an almost seventeenth-century belief that life is preordained. Winston Churchill phrased it thus in 1929:

Events passed very largely outside the scope of conscious choice. Governments and individuals conformed to the rhythm of the tragedy, and swayed and staggered forward in helpless violence, slaughtering and squandering on ever-increasing scales, till injuries were wrought to the structure of human society which a century will not efface, and which may conceivably prove fatal to the present civilization.

But beyond all this was the experience of a new kind of emptiness for the individuals surviving. Boys who were growing up in the years around 1930 can tell you that the damage and the grief did not all go instantly, mercifully, to the grave. They can speak, if only with the intuition of children's hearts, of one-legged men careening about on crutches. They can remember ex-soldiers who were as lethargic as some tuberculars—but with a difference. The *vieux soldat,* as he sat in an arm chair on his lawn, wrapped in blankets even on a warm day, had vague and indifferent eyes. He had been subjected to poison gas. Although he got a small pension, was life on these terms worth much?

Looking first at the European combatants in World War I, we can see that the origins of the conflict were many. They varied from one nation to another. Desire for national glory was a mighty force, as was the desire for colonies that would be subservient economically. A major role was played by improvements in military, particularly naval, technology: substitution of cordite for gunpowder, new methods for securing nitrates, the submarine, heavier artillery, poison gas, to a lesser extent the airplane. But the entry of the United States can be seen in less complex terms. Immediately before and during the early years of the war, the federal government was preoccupied with domestic worries—an economy that continued to be soft, reform of the tariff and of banking laws. When Europe went to war in August 1914, the Wilson administration for a brief time struggled to keep the country neutral. But as Americans became increasingly aware that the prosperity of their economy was dependent on war orders from the Allies, their neutrality steadily melted away. This trend could draw on two persistent pools of energy. Numerous Americans with power in their hands felt that they were partners in the British heritage; they and the English had shared a cultural communion, breaking the same loaf and drinking the same wine. Second, from the time of the first English planters in the New World, Americans had been demented by legalisms. So the United States furnished aid that was indispensable to Allied victory. As we contemplate the ghastly price paid for triumph, it seems that the game was not worth the candle.

SOME NOTABLE EVENTS

1908 Germany lays down four all-big-gun battleships. When Britain responds by starting eight *Dreadnoghts* in 1909, the naval war is on.
Root-Takahira Agreement, 30 Nov.

1909 Payne-Aldrich Tariff.

1910 Germany learns how to fix free nitrogen from the air.

1911 Canadian Parliament refuses to ratify a reciprocity agreement with U.S. about import duties.
Standard Oil and *American Tobacco* decisions by Supreme Court.

1912 Roosevelt gives his "New Nationalism" speech, 21 Feb.
Titanic wrecked on maiden voyage and sinks; 1517 lost, 14–15 April.
Progressive Party issues its platform, 5 Aug.
The Balkan War begins, Oct.

1913 Taft vetoes literacy test for immigrants, 14 Feb.
Wilson is first president since John Adams to make personal appearance before Congress; he asks for tariff reduction.
Underwood-Simmons Tariff also contains income-tax clause.
Pujo Committee issues report on money and banking.
Federal Trade Commission Act, 10 Sept.
Clayton Act.
Federal Reserve Act, 23 Dec.

1914 Wilson orders Marines to occupy Vera Cruz, Mexico.
Austrian archduke is assassinated in Serbia.
World War I begins, 30 July–4 Aug.
Wilson appeals for American neutrality, 19 Aug.

1915 U.S. approves "commercial credits" to Allies, March.
Submarine sinks the *Falaba*; one American drowned, 28 March.
Another U-boat sinks *Lusitania*, 128 Americans killed, 7 May.
U-boat sinks *Arabic*, 19 Aug.
British vessel flying American flag sinks U-27, 19 Aug.
Lansing's *modus vivendi*, Dec.

1916 Jones bill promises independence to Philippines in five years, 4 Feb.
Gore-McLemore Resolution, March.
U-boat sinks the *Sussex*, 24 March; Wilson's ultimatum to Germany.
Rural credits law, 17 July.
Keating-Owen child labor act, 8 Aug.
Federal workmen's compensation law, 19 Aug.
Adamson Act decrees eight-hour day on railroads, 3 Sept.

1917 Wilson's "peace without victory" speech, 22 Jan.
Wilson appeals to Congress for a declaration of war, 2 April.
Congress declares war, 6 April.

1918 Wilson presents Fourteen Points to Congress, 8 Jan.
By May, U.S. has a half million soldiers in France.
Espionage Act, 16 May.
Wilson announces Four Points in speech at Mount Vernon, 4 July.
By November, U.S. had nearly 5 million men under arms, of whom 1,390,000 saw combat service (for fatalities, see Figure 30-1).
Democrats lose both houses of Congress, 5 Nov.
Armistice ends hostilities, 11 Nov.

1919 Versailles Treaty between Allies and Germany, which signs on June 28.
Wilson has a stroke, 2 Oct.

1919–
1920 Versailles Treaty fails of ratification by the Senate.

Ways to Study History XXII

Ransack the archives. Often a scholar is too hasty in concluding that because he holds in his hands a primary source, therefore he has evidence appropriate to his purposes. Repeatedly, in working in the papers of William Jennings Bryan when he was secretary of state, I would find a draft of a memorandum to the president. Fortunately the Wilson Papers were in the same repository, the Library of Congress, and they contained the message that the president had received from Bryan. When the draft was compared to the actual message, the two sometimes diverged widely. The former shows the way that Bryan's mind worked; the latter shows a part of the information, true or false, on which Wilson based a particular decision.

W. Stull Holt has succinctly indicated an additional difficulty that might arise in dealing with documents from either governmental or business files. Both types of institution have developed cryptography to a high state. In the process of either encoding or decoding, a meaning may be altered. As anybody who has dealt with Western Union will know, a message can also be scrambled while it is on the wires.

Holt's article is entitled: "What Wilson Sent and What House Received: Or Scholars Need to Check Carefully," *American Historical Review* (1959–1960). On 29 October, 1918, Colonel Edward M. House was in London as the president's personal envoy. The war was nearing an end. A text written on Wilson's typewriter states: ". . . too much success or security on the part of the Allies will make a genuine peace settlement exceedingly difficult, if not impossible." The cable received by House from the president reads: ". . . too much severity on the part of the Allies will make a genuine peace settlement exceedingly difficult if not impossible." Not only are the nuances shifted, but the two versions look in different directions. Which one is relevant depends on what question the historian is asking.

Document 22-1

The only phase of his career when William Jennings Bryan showed signs of distinction came while he was secretary of state. The reasoning behind his opposition to any loans to belligerents can hardly be faulted. In this memorandum to the president, dated 10 August, 1914, he explained it (see above Chapter 22 on American response to outbreak of war).

First: Money is the worst of all contrabands because it commands everything else. The question of making loans contraband by international agreement has been discussed, but no action has been taken. I know of nothing that would do more to prevent war than an international agreement that neutral nations would not grant loans to belligerents. While such an agreement would be of great advantage, could we not by our example hasten the reaching of such an agreement? We are the one great nation which is not involved and our refusal to loan to any belligerent would naturally tend to hasten a conclusion of the war. We are responsible for the use of our influence through example and as we cannot tell what we can do until we try, the only way of testing our influence is to set the example and test its effect. This is the fundamental reason in support of the suggestion submitted.

Second: There is a special and local reason, it seems to me, why this course would be advisable. . . . If we approved of a loan to France we could not, of course, object to a loan to Great Britain, Germany, Russia, Austria or to any other country, and if loans were made to these countries our citizens would be divided into groups, each group loaning money to the country which it favors and this money could not be furnished without expressions of sympathy. These expressions of sympathy are disturbing enough when they do not rest upon pecuniary interests—they would be still more disturbing if each group was pecuniarily interested in the success of the nation to whom its members had loaned money. . . .

Electricity, Autos, and Chemicals

In much writing about the United States from the day of the Armistice until the Black Tuesday in October, 1929, when the stock market entered upon its long descent—in those unfortunate depictions, the decade was The Golden Twenties, an age of "Fords, flappers, and fanatics." By these accounts, the rich young Americans went to Paris to have fun, and rich old Americans went to their broker in Pasadena to study the word from Wall Street on the ticker. Both of these groups existed, but the average American had no experience of either way of life. Men of my father's generation, whether executives or factory hands, did not even take a week's vacation in the summer. The typical standard of living was rising, but in 1929 it was still far below what most of us have known in our lifetimes. Obviously gross differentials exist in the United States today; they existed also fifty years ago. Thus one task in this chapter is to identify the segments of American society who were eating chicken and those who gnawed the bones.

Breaking down the whole into its parts is much easier for the years after World War I than for any earlier period because we have more accurate measurements. Having said so much, we must admit that formidable difficulties remain. The best to be hoped for is fairly reliable estimates. Informed guesses for Gross National Product (GNP) on an annual basis (not to mention monthly) can be made for the period since 1919. However, zealous and honorable economists will doubtless continue to argue about many questions pertaining to our past. One question is familiar to all: How much did the cost of living change? This query, fundamental as it is to many collective-bargaining contracts and social-welfare schemes, subsumes a host of lesser questions. Thus it cannot be answered with precision and will always be subject to some dispute. However, to shift focus again, we must insist that some estimates are better than others. The effort here is to offer the best we have.

Let us sample the juice we can squeeze from the pulp available. Adjusting all figures to the 1929 level of prices, Gross National Product climbed from $74.2 billion in 1919 to $104.4 in 1929. Further adjusting for the growth in population, GNP per capita went from $710 to $857 over the same span. So in the latter regard the rate of development is not exactly booming—say, a bit less than 2 per cent a year. What is startling is the stability of the price level. Estimates vary, but existing indices peg wholesale prices at the end of the decade with only a difference of 1 or 2 points from where they had been at its beginning, with minor fluctuations in the interim. Probably this outcome resulted from identifiable forces. Over-all growth tended to push prices upward, but two major groups of influences worked as offsets. More details on each will be offered below, but generalizations might be given now. Three clusters of industries must be regarded as sick: farming, (particularly of such staples as cotton and wheat), coal mining, and textile manufacturing. None of these industries was dying in a nationwide sense. Man must have food, but the traditional base of American agriculture was withering. Man must have heat, but coal was being displaced by hydroelectric power, natural gas, fuel oil. He must have clothing, but New England mills were overpowered by Southern producers and by foreign suppliers. Prices were also thrust downward by gigantic increases in output per man-hour in several boom industries, of which the three most important form the title of this chapter. Failing of an imaginative and constructive solution to these downward pressures on prices—hence on profits—Americans turned to the same old solution. They looked for markets abroad. But they wanted to keep the home markets for themselves, so they tried to block out imports. Therefore foreigners had no U.S. dollars to buy American goods. The wily Yankee had a solution to that conundrum. He loaned to foreigners the U.S. funds with which to buy American products. A fine way indeed to manage an economy.

Repeatedly in this chapter it will be necessary to look back at developments on the home front during the war. For instance, in spite of the absence

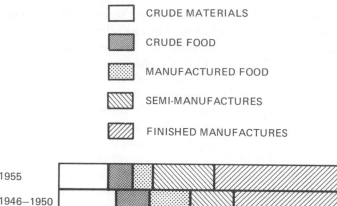

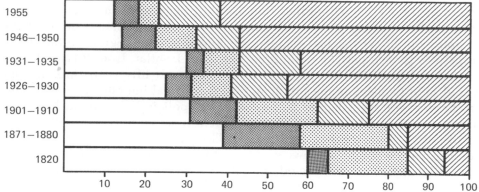

FIGURE 23-1 *Changing Exports from the U.S., 1820-1955*

in the armed forces of about 5 million men in 1917–1918, GNP increased about 15 per cent. Here an index of physical output becomes helpful. For agriculture it barely changed, but for mining and manufacturing the increase came close to 40 per cent, and for transportation it slightly exceeded that mark. Due to the stable production from farms while demand for their output soared, prices paid to them had risen rapidly during the war. But for the husbandman the depression started in 1919, not a decade later. The total value of farm products was $21.4 billion in 1919, down to $11.8 billion by the time of the financial panic. This decline did not result in any shortage of foodstuffs or textile fibers for the American or foreign consumer; on the contrary, surpluses were increased. When a farmer gets less per unit for his crop, his instinct is to produce more units. The decline was in prices:

	Cotton, lb.	Corn, bushel	Wheat, bushel
1919	35.3¢	$1.51	$2.16
1929	16.7¢	.79	1.03
1932	6.5¢	.31	.38

These figures cast immediate doubt on some scholarly interpretations. One author has asked what happened after World War I to LaFollette's Progressive movement in its attempt to sell its reform program in the rural heartland (mid-Chapter 24). His answer is: Nothing. This should not surprise anybody who glances at the above table. When a South Carolina redneck sees the price of cotton fall by half, when a corn-and-hog farmer in Illinois sees the price of corn fall by half,* he gets discouraged about optimistic reform programs.

An individual farmer could do nothing to bolster the sagging prices. The fundamental dilemma of the producers of staples was that they had to sell on a world market, so that the price at which they could export their surplus also determined the price within the United States. Reductions in freight charges, not only by railroads within each country but by improvements in merchant shipping on the oceans, had enabled previously isolated regions to hurl their crops into foreign markets—from the American frontier, from Russia, India, Australia, Argentina, Canada, Mexico. Over the next fifty years three factors would help to alleviate the problem. One was brutal but effective: eliminate the farmer (see mid-Chapter 26 on New Deal policies). The trend has been strong and accelerating to reduce employment in agriculture, particularly the small units—sharecroppers, hired hands. This has made it easier for the large holders and corporate landowners to combine and win political favors; the Farm Bloc in Congress appeared as a cohesive unit after World War I. As will be seen (mid-Chapter 26), one of its chief efforts was to free prices within the United States from their dependence on world prices. Third, mechanization has virtually supplanted manpower in turning out produce from the land (Figure 29-3).**

Before we analyze the problems of the mines, let us pause for a short story about a miner who found some options to exploitation—an English immigrant of extraordinary ingenuity. In the first two decades of the century he worked in Bitumen, Pennsylvania (lovely name that: "coal tar")—one mine, one store. The employee, with five children, could never get out of debt at the store. For fourteen years of steady labor he drew no cash whatever. Each month he got a "statement" showing the residue of his debt. He kept every statement. At length, knowing of a treaty in force between his native country and the United States requiring that any immigrant from the one nation to the other had to be paid in "coin of the realm," he contacted the British embassy in Washington. The upshot was that the coal company was forced to pay the

---

*As a sidelight, consider the   11-to-1 ratio. A good farmer would sell pork on the hoof when a hundredweight brought 11 times as much as he could get for a bushel of corn; when values altered beyond that crucial point, he sold corn.

**The possibilities of modern technology can carry this process to extremes that boggle the mind. It can even cancel out weather, for those willing to invest in one firm's product—a portable trailer about 20' × 6' × 6' which contains horizontal trays at 1' intervals. On Monday you plant oats in the bottom tray; on Tuesday in the next up, and so on. By Sunday you can harvest the bottom tray. This vehicle can grow enough fodder for about three dozen cows.

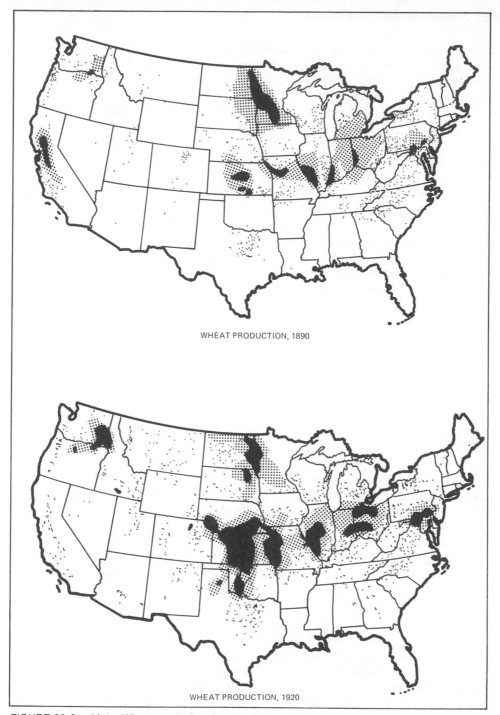

WHEAT PRODUCTION, 1890

WHEAT PRODUCTION, 1920

FIGURE 23-2. *Major Wheat-producing Areas, 1890 and 1920*

miner his fourteen years in back earnings. To retaliate, the company store brought suit against him to pay his overdue bills. He had gone home to England. Moral: The working class could find a multiplicity of ways to hit back at their employers.

The problem of the coal mining industry can be stated quickly; the production of all mineral fuels declined some 30 per cent from 1920 to 1929, due in considerable measure to improvements in the efficiency of industrial processes that had used coal by the thousands of carloads.

Before the decline and prior to World War I coal miners as a group had two shields against exploitation. One was their combination into a union which had influence in many but not all coal fields; at the end of this chapter we will see how it was almost destroyed by 1933. The other form of self-protection was personal mobility. One study for a portion of the industry—anthracite—concludes with a model. Of 200 mine workers (aged 20 years) in 1865, half had died of natural causes by 1902. Another fifteen had died from occupational injuries. Three had become foremen in mines; a few had risen higher in the industry. A handful had become lawyers or politicians or started small businesses. Some had left the region in northeastern Pennsylvania to work in steel or construction or on the railroads. But these types of fluidity were notably reduced after the return of peace in 1918. As coal output slumped, both vertical and horizontal mobility fell with it.

The case of cotton manufacturing was different: The industry migrated. In the basement of Baker Library at the Harvard Business School, any investigator can find large wooden crates holding the office records of defunct textile firms. The bulk of these archives were donated by New England companies some fifty years ago as they went bankrupt; for several segments of the economy the depression began before 1929. To watch the textile industry move southward is to witness a balance of advantages that shifted slowly, then like an avalanche. New England had the benefits of priority. It had established plant, abundant capital, a skilled labor force. Before the Civil War these assets were enhanced because the South had an impervious obstacle to manufacturing: current studies make clear that a plantation was a better investment than a factory. But after the Civil War the balance had begun to tilt. Northern factories were elderly and inefficient. Now it was Northern capital that could find more profitable outlets. Changes in machinery reduced the significance of skilled labor. A Southern industrialist—once beyond the risky and uncertain point where he could get his plant into operation—would have several advantages. He could save transportation costs from being located near his source of raw materials. An almost unlimited supply of cheap labor was available. His worst obstacle would be raising liquid capital in an area that had been eroded by war. So the clamor for "the New South" became a crusade; towns pawned their futures to buy the machines for a new mill. Ironically, the machine-builders of the North sought to save themselves by selling out their customers at home; in payment for their products they accepted stock in

Southern companies. By World War I the migration to the Southern uplands, the Appalachian towns from Virginia to Georgia, was firmly established. Massachusetts cities such as Lowell and Lawrence and Fall River were doomed before 1929. The next year the national president of the Textile Workers could say, "There is, perhaps, more destitution and misery and degradation in the mill towns of New England today . . . than anywhere else in the United States." By this time the North was competing against the South on the worst possible terms. It too could offer cheap labor, and did.

Before this chapter proceeds to the boom industries of the era, it should make clear that not everything was black or white. Two clusters of the economy that were teetering back and forth were steel and railroads. These industries can be made analogous in other ways, both historical and analytical. Each was old in that it was operating in large part with equipment that had been in use for decades. In this respect, each resembled the textile mills of New England; they used ancient equipment because they had stodgy and ignorant executives. Carnegie never made a similar mistake. Bankers had moved into these two fields of finance exactly because they were already established; railroad bonds or stock in U.S. Steel could be sold to the ordinary investor. It was a defect that J. P. Morgan did not know much about the production of steel; the irremediable fault was that he did not place the direction of the company into the hands of men who did understand how to plan future operations, how to coordinate activities, how to check on results. A clear index might be seen in salaries of tycoons in these two industries, which have for a long time been much lower than the earnings of leaders in the boom industries to be examined in a moment. Perhaps it's true that you get what you pay for.

Another similarity with the moribund textile trade was the fact that neither rails nor steel could come to settled terms with its labor force. Two examples from each industry must suffice here. During the war, all railroads had been brought by federal law under the jurisdiction of the United States Railroad Administration, which was to provide an integrated network. After the Armistice, the Brotherhoods countered with a proposal for nationalizing the railroads called the Plumb Plan. It had three basic objectives: (a) the road must give adequate service to users, (b) previous owners of the combined lines should get adequate compensation, (c) charges must not exceed the amount needed to meet the first two aims. This plan was affirmed by members of the Brotherhoods, although many of their leaders opposed it. The A.F.L. also supported it, although president Samuel Gompers did not like it.

To get a clear focus we must look backwards and forwards. In retrospect, we can say that American railroads should have been a unified venture from their beginning in 1830, financed and controlled by the federal government. Apart from a little detachment of promoter-speculators, everyone involved would have benefited from this scheme: investors, workers, maybe even managers. Government-operated national railways were common in Europe. Many American railroads before World War I were sustained by the involuntary donations of bondholders, as arranged through reorganization of capital structures. Since that time they have offered constantly declining services at the continued expense of various levels of government by means of tax levies and public subsidies. In 1919, however, the Plumb Plan did not stand a chance of a fair hearing. National politics would stamp it out in 1920 and 1924, but it was still an influence on the course of those presidential elections. By the latter bout at the polls, the dramatic strike of 1922 had been staged by railroad shopmen. (A "shopman" was anybody not part of the operating crew that rode on the train; he was not unionized; see Chapter 20.) The walkout was provoked by a reduction in wages. The successful effort to stifle the upheaval was greatly aided by a federal judge's injunction, which was almost a duplicate of the one issued against the Pullman boycott. Some railways felt that they had to make concessions, at least on paper. The best-known agreement was the union-management plan on the Baltimore & Ohio, by which the employees agreed to improve efficiency if management would share with them the gains from this. No scholar yet has proven whether management kept its part of the bargain, but every traveller knows whether or not efficiency on the railroads has been improved.

I am not the sort to count lines of space on the front pages of 187 influential newspapers in order to reach a conclusion, and nobody has done the job for me, but it seems likely that the Great Steel Strike of 1919 attracted more attention than any labor conflict since the Pullman boycott. After the Homestead strike of 1892, trade unions had been in tatters in the steel industry. For most occupations, wages during the war had barely kept pace with the cost of living. Steelworkers had a grievance that was not shared by employees in most other industries: they worked twelve hours a day every day—84 hours a week, at a time when the typical work week was 8 hours a day only 6 days a week. Toward the end of the war the A.F.L. began a movement to organize the industry. This attempt was obstructed because fully twenty-five of its member unions claimed jurisdiction over some craft or other in the mills. A decision was made to use a joint organizing committee; after the workers had joined up, they could be parcelled out among the constituent groups. The true director of the organizing committee turned out to be an anarcho-syndicalist from Chicago, who had been preaching industrial unionism for more than a decade. The employers and the press did not really need this excuse for their raucous clamor against the Great Steel Strike as "bolshevist"; they used the same epithet against the Plumb Plan. Beginning on 22 September, 1919, the strike at its peak involved an estimated 376,000 men. They did not have the resources to win. Within four months the walkout was over, and many of its leaders were blacklisted. But the movement was not a complete failure because it rallied opinion, especially in the Protestant churches, against the working conditions in steel mills. Before the decade ended, the companies had felt constrained to institute the eight-hour day.

The Great Steel Strike provides the scenery for a fine short story by Thomas Bell. The union shutdown, which was never strong in the Pittsburgh area, centered in South Chicago and the adjacent Indiana cities that rim Lake Michigan. The narrative centers on a Hungarian immigrant in Gary, Indiana. He speaks only a few words of English, and he neither knows nor cares about trade unions. When other workers shut down the plant, he stays home. One night he wanders down to the picket lines just to see if anything is going on. A riot occurs; a policeman is hit in the head with a club, and he dies. The inoffensive Hungarian is seized, tried, convicted of manslaughter, and spends fifteen years in an Indiana prison. Then another inmate makes a death-bed confession to the pertinent act of violence. Our Hungarian friend is compensated $1,000 for each year he had served unjustly. He takes his "savings," returns to his native district in Hungary, and instantaneously becomes the biggest landowner in the whole region. The title of Bell's story: "The Man Who Made Good in America."

Vast numbers of Americans were having an easier time making good. Four groups of industries can be singled out as the paths to spectacular success after World War I: construction, electric power and its spin-offs, automobiles, industrial chemicals. The next several pages will scrutinize each of these in turn and point out some links among them. Historically, by any of the customary categories the building of homes, warehouses, factories, churches, and other stationary structures had always been the most productive segment of the economy in terms of value of product. This continued to be true. As would happen again after World War II, huge demand for housing had built up during the hostilities that ended in 1918. The portion of national income that is attributable directly to construction doubled between 1919 and 1926, and began to sag slowly from this peak. As will be seen shortly, other boom industries also had topped out before 1929 and started to decline. This construction upsurge was tied to the prosperity of the other new industries that required factories and office buildings and warehouses. It was linked equally to the growth of urban sprawl. To choose four suburbs scattered across the country: growth in population in Queens County (New York) was 100 per cent in the decade; in Grosse Point (Detroit) 700 per cent; in Shaker Heights (Cleveland) 1,000 per cent; in Beverly Hills (Los Angeles) 2,500 per cent.

This outthrust from compacted cities was obviously spurred by growing use of cars. But of the three new conglomerations of growth industries, the first to have a heavy impact was electric power. Again, advance warnings seem timely as we search for terms by which to classify this kind of growth. We may doubt that the word "generator" is appropriate; can it really be applied to any

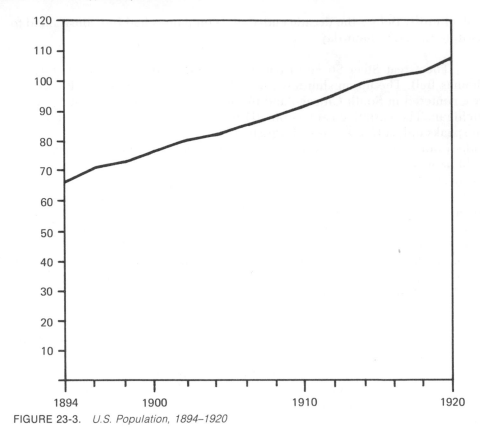

FIGURE 23-3. *U.S. Population, 1894–1920*

source of energy? Second, the phrase "natural resources" can likewise be misleading, since its meaning depends on the ability of human beings at a given time and place to harness and control nature. As understanding of electricity improved, it became possible to transform other types of potential power, especially coal and water, into kinetic current and to transmit it over unprecedented distances. Also the power could be divided into tiny units and sent around to individual motors; the vertical factory with power distributed by means of leather belting could be replaced by the one-story horizontal plant stretching over acres of land. The import of these possibilities for population densities is apparent. Relevant to the same topic is the first giant application of electricity apart from fabrication and lighting—the electric streetcar. From about 1890 to 1910 the construction of trolley lines took the place that had been held by railroads; it spearheaded the expansion of the nation's economy, reaching a peak of $2.5 billion from 1900 to 1909. Without this source of cheap rapid transportation, the spread of cities could not have happened as it did. Another stimulant to the same result was the growth of telephones; the purchase of equipment for expansion of systems doubled from 1900 to 1910, and doubled again in the next decade.

Novel uses spawned markets, so that production of electric energy by central stations rose about twenty times from 1902, the year of our first reliable statistics, to 1929, while many factories were not resorting to central stations at all but had their own generators.* As late as 1907 only 7 per cent of the nation's dwellings had electric current, and that figure soared beyond two thirds by 1930. But long before radio was carrying canned diversions into homes, the motion picture had passed beyond spectator sports as a form of public entertainment. By one reliable account, movies in the decade after 1920 were the fourth largest industry in the nation; attendance at the flicks may have passed attendance at church, and the vice cost about the same as the virtue. Before 1900 Thomas Alva Edison had produced a workable movie camera, and the first commercial show had been exhibited in Manhattan. As early as 1908 at least 8,000 movie houses existed, a number which would nearly double by 1929, and which would begin shrinking rapidly after the advent of television.

Radio was the only electric device to capture the middle-class household before the Great Crash. Refrigerators, washers, dryers, dish washers, toasters, blenders, shavers, hair curlers, knives, stereos—that panoply of appliances that now clutter every proper domicile—were not seen until the depression, and most of them only after World War II. This reflection highlights the rapid expansion of radio. We first have figures for annual sales for 1922. Covering the span from that year to 1929, sales rose 14 times, to reach nearly $1 billion. As a technical innovation broadcasting had been possible as early as 1907. But its exploitation posed several organizational problems: to manufacture sets, build a marketing network, produce programs, establish stations to magnify them in many localities. A serious attack on these obstacles began with the foundation of Radio Corporation of America (1919) which set up the National Broadcasting Co. in 1926. The next year the Columbia Broadcasting System was formed. Understandably the stations were dominated in the early years by reports of real events: the uproarious Democratic national convention of 1924 was heard by multitudes, and the voice of sportscaster Graham McNamee may have been the best-known in the land. But with the networks, patrons were blessed by studio programming featuring Barney Google and Rudy Vallee.

Until 1926, when Henry Ford was persuaded to scrap the Model T for the Model A, his plants achieved wonders of output and profitability. The history of Ford is to a great extent the history of the Model T (as Volkswagen

---

*Each of the developments discussed here was of course crucial to others. We could write a formula: electricity + streets + construction + streetcars + autos + radios = suburbs. Understanding would benefit by juggling the elements in this formula, and several other influences could be inserted.

The Four Stroke Engine

The gasoline engine converts thermal power, created by burning gasoline within the cylinder (thus *internal* combustion engine) to mechanical power, transmitted by the turning crankshaft. To do this requires four distinct operations.

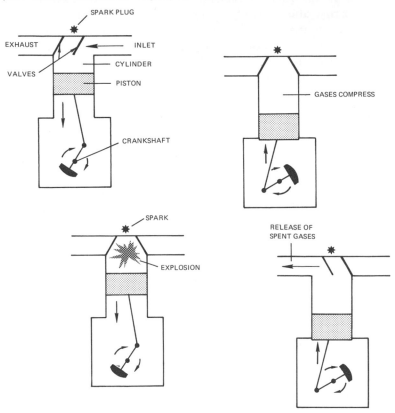

(1) The piston (which must be tightly sealed within the cylinder) is pulled down, drawing a mixture of vaporized gasoline and air through the intake valve into the combustion chamber. The gasoline has been previously changed from a liquid to a vaporous state, thereby mixing it with air, in the carburetor.

(2) The piston is pushed up, compressing the gasoline-and-air mixture to seven or eight times its previous density. It is now almost ready to be exploded by the spark plug.

(3) The intake and outlet valves are closed, the spark plug ignited and the pressure of the exploding gases then forces the piston down, thus turning the crankshaft and providing power as well as momentum for phase four and repeated phases one and two.

(4) The outlet or exhaust valve opens, and the piston rises to expel the spent gases. It is now ready to repeat phase one.

Several other points must be made. First, an inefficient piston (one that does not fit snugly in the cylinder, for example) delivers less power per cycle than a properly operating one. Second, since a piston delivers power during only one of its four strokes, a one-cylinder engine tends to run unevenly: the crankshaft is constantly accelerating and decelerating. This problem is overcome by using several pistons, timed to perform different strokes at any given moment. Third, while gasoline is by far the most common fuel used in the internal combustion engine, almost any substance which will vaporize and ignite at a spark will do—even hair tonic.

for many years was the Beetle). Ford was employed as an engineer at Detroit Edison while he was developing his car. When he started the Ford Motor Company in 1903, he had not yet arrived at his great insight. But three years later he had it, and he persuaded his few associates: he would build an automobile that was sturdy, hence needed few repairs, simple, hence easy to repair, durable, hence depreciation to the buyer would be low, cheap, hence the number of consumers could be broadened, standardized, hence he could, for instance, paint every car black, and unchanging, hence he did not need to re-tool his factories every year. The formula was brilliant. In 1908, when the first Model T was marketed, he sold 10,000. By 1914 the sales reached a quarter of a million; perhaps equally important with his production procedures was Ford's achievement of an efficient set of agencies for merchandising his product. In 1923 the company hit a peak by moving well over two million new vehicles.

The consequences of this expansion should be seen from more than one angle. Original cash investment was $28,500, all from Detroit investors. A lawyer put up $5,000, a coal dealer $2,500. Within a decade both men were millionaires. Or we can look at the situation from the standpoint of employees. In 1914 Ford announced a minimum wage of $5 a day for all production workers. This spectacular change has been derided by many radicals in the last fifty years who have claimed that it brought to the company better workers and that the assembly lines offset the increase in hourly rates by hastening the speed-up (Chapter 26). It was not regarded as a fraud by laborers at the time; they clustered at the Ford employment gates. Most important of all, we must see it in the terms of the typical American. For a portion of the labor force—employees in factories, coal mining, and transportation—these are the number of months that they had to work to earn enough to buy a basic Model T touring car at the factory:

1909	22.2 months
1914	10.8
1919	6.0
1923	3.0

This ratio is about the same now as it was fifty years ago; improvements in the real earnings of workingmen cannot be sought in the realm of automobile prices. The question of whether cars are better now than they were then depends on many dubious elements in the definition of quality. But the impact on society is much easier to elucidate. Railroads and later subways, in their effect on urban growth, were centripetal forces; everybody wanted to live near the station. Trolley lines acted as threads, in that families wanted to live along the line but trolley stops were frequent. The automobile was the true centrifugal influence, hurling suburbs out in many directions. Cars also altered such cultural patterns as courtship practices. Gone forever were the days when

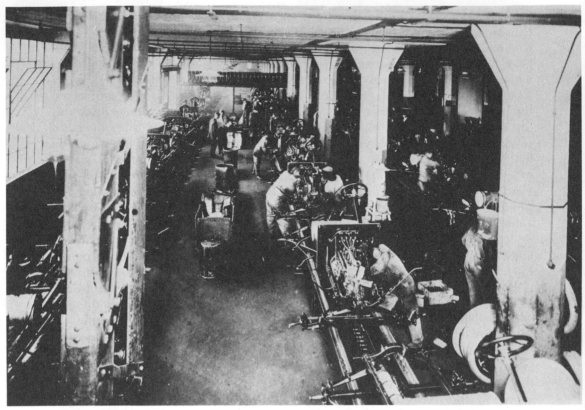

FIGURE 23-4. *Ford Motor Company Assembly Line*   Courtesy of the Ford Motor Company

When the Ford Motor Company started marketing its Model T in 1908, the head of the operation had already determined on the formula that would serve him well for twenty years (see the adjoining pages on Ford's career). Boiled down into theoretical terms, Henry Ford's package depended on the aphorism from Adam Smith that specialization of labor is a function of the size of the market (see the opening of Chapter 3). But Ford's shrewdness reversed the equation: The size of the market depends on the specialization of labor. In retrospect his idea seems simple—Don't bring the man to the job, bring the job to the man. Many revolutionary ideas seem simple after somebody else has had them; compare James Watts' improvements on the steam engine ("How Did It Work?" 2).

It is generally acknowledged that Ford's first assembly line was opened in August, 1913, in his new factory in the Detroit suburb of Highland Park. At that time the assemblage of a Model T chassis took twelve and a half hours of labor. Then the maxim was applied of delivering the work to the worker. In half a year, a chassis was being assembled in one hour and thirty-three minutes. When Ford announced in 1914 that his company would pay a basic wage of $5 a day, he was counting on a reduction of this magnitude in his labor costs. It must be noted that, for every 12 employees who were fabricating automobiles, the company had one man devising tools that would help to make cars cheaper and better.

How did the innovator get the idea for the assembly line? If Ford read Adam Smith, he didn't let on. A common anecdote, of doubtful authenticity, has him watching the carcasses move through a packing plant in Chicago, watching the throats get slashed at one station, the giblets removed at another, the skin peeled off. Packing houses were analysts, breaking their material into components; by contrast, auto assembly factories were synthesizers.

a fellow could only take his girlfriend to the church social or go with her to the kitchen, under her mother's suspicious eyes, to make taffy. The new modes are impossible to quantify, but the qualitative evidence is memorable. A juvenile-court judge in Indiana called the car a "house of prostitution on wheels." Another in Denver told of girls who carried contraceptives around in their compacts.

The third new sheaf of growth industries that began to flare out before 1929 can be cast under the general rubric of industrial chemicals. Again we can indicate the trends by talking about one company, DuPont. As with the big car makers, the interaction of technology with organization must be grasped. Giant corporations in this century have followed one of three strategies for growth. (1) Railroads, steel, and tobacco (processors of metals and of farm products) have shown little or no imagination. They have merely ridden a rising market, selling the same products to a growing number of customers. (2) Some companies have reached out overseas for additional raw materials (oil companies) or customers (auto manufacturers). (3) A few firms diversified into new types of goods made by novel methods to reach new types of customer. Most innovations have come here. The outstanding example has been chemicals. Before outlining the story of how DuPont was coerced by its own problems into instituting a "decentralized" table of organization, it should be observed that almost at the same time three other giants were being forced into similar conclusions: General Motors by its desire for foreign markets, beginning in 1920, Jersey Standard by its quest for foreign supplies, starting 1925, Sears by its decision to establish retail stores, starting 1929.

DuPont had been founded in 1802 to make gunpowder. In 1913 explosives still constituted 97 per cent of its sales. Many other species of chemicals could find markets. Synthetic plastics (in the form of bakelite) had been known since 1869; potash was needed for fertilizers; German dyes were excluded from the American market during World War I, and so on. Technical possibilities did exist. By war's end DuPont had a huge staff: its payrolls went from 5,300 in the autumn of 1914 to more than 85,000 four years later. Obviously the market for its only product was due to fall drastically. It decided to diversify into five other lines—dyestuffs and allied organic chemicals, vegetable oils, paints and varnishes (including lacquers for car bodies), water-soluble chemicals, cellulose-derived synthetics. The immediate result was disaster. For the new products, increased sales meant greater losses. Men who knew only explosives were making decisions about pyroxylin. Men accustomed to reaching a handful of large buyers were incompetent to reach millions of customers for pocket combs. As early as 1919 a committee recommended ways to drastically re-structure the company, but the chief executive resisted. As the postwar recession became more severe, DuPont losses kited. The profits still being made on explosives were not enough to cover deficits on the other products; the firm showed a net loss for the first six months of 1921. At last the company adopted the decentralized or multi-divisional structure. Here are the two chief recommendations made by the subcommittee on reorganization: It made no sense to put all engineers in one category, all salesmen in another, etc., since it is related effort which should be coordinated, and not "like things." Thus those concerned with lacquers should be in one division, with dyes in another. Second, each division should be under the command of one man with full say, subject only to the proviso that if he failed he would be fired. These semi-autonomous divisions would be coordinated by the Executive Committee of the entire firm, which would allocate resources for expansion on the basis of recent performance plus anticipations of future prospects. It would also order the firings of division managers.

Before we look at the great stock market crash of 1929—certainly a significant subject—we must be sure it does not blind us to other basic influences. Plunging security prices may trigger a depression, but they cannot by themselves cause one. Behind them lie several kinds of inequities in the distribution of income, which we have already examined and will again. But first it seems worth while to say a bit about how far federal policies helped to further injustice and to bring about the shortage of consumer purchasing power. The actions of Congress and the federal executive branch can be left until Chapter 24, but the rulings of federal courts and officials that subverted most attempts at trade unionism should not lurk in the shadows unseen. World War I saw the mushrooming of so-called "employee representation plans," which might more properly be termed company unions. This development was spurred by a requirement that employers doing war production should bargain collectively with their workers. Although the company union was a fake, large companies found it a neat piece of flummery. Some 100,000 people were smothered in the device in 1919, nearly 1.5 million by 1926. The extent to which federal officials meant to be impartial about the labor market was shown by their administration of the adjunct rule that exempted workers in "essential industries" from military conscription. When munitions employees at Bridgeport, Connecticut went on strike, President Wilson ordered them restored to the draft rolls unless they returned to work.

Here it must suffice to look at three Supreme Court decisions. *Hitchman Coal & Coke Co.* v. *Mitchell* (1917) began a decade earlier. The coal fields unionized by the Mine Workers were gravely threatened by the competition in consumer markets from non-union companies in Kentucky and West Virginia. Therefore the union sent organizers to the Hitchman mine. No employee was signed to membership, but they did sign pledges to join up as soon as a majority of the workers had similarly decided to do so. The firm then extorted from its employees a yellow-dog contract, promising not to join any union. A federal district judge issued a temporary restraining order against the UMW. Four and a half years later, in December, 1912, he had issued a "perpetual" injunction against any efforts to organize the Hitchman mine. His grounds were three: The UMW was a common-law conspiracy. It violated the Sherman Anti-Trust Act. It was inducing breach of contract. On appeal, a federal circuit court threw out the first two grounds and reversed the third, holding that a worker was free to join the union (although at the risk of losing his job). Thus the breach-of-contract issue came plunk before the Supreme Court. There the decision of the circuit court was reversed. The ruling held that efforts by the UMW to induce "concerted breaches of the contracts" were "unlawful and malicious." In a dissent written by Brandeis, three justices held that since the purpose sought—collective bargaining—was legal, the union's actions could only be illegal if its methods were outside the law, and they were not. (Brandeis had a reverse corollary that was far from friendly to unionism. In *Dorchy* v. *Kansas*, 1926, he held that "a strike may be illegal because of its purpose." Only in California was a strike legal without regard to purpose.)

Within the confines of judicial thinking fifty years ago, only one rejoinder to this line of argument could possibly be effective. It was the reply "judicial restraint," which Justice Holmes elegantly restated in *Truax* v. *Corrigan* (1921). An Arizona law of 1913 had sought to restrict issuance of injunctions against peaceful picketing. Chief Justice Taft wrote the decision that struck down the statute as violating both the due-process and the equal-protection clauses of the 14th Amendment. Even Holmes, for all his eloquence, for all the veneration of judicial restraint, for all the mouthy worship of state rights, could not win his colleagues. He might win us:

> There is nothing I more deprecate than the use of the Fourteenth Amendment beyond the absolute compulsion of its words to prevent the making of social experiments that an important part of the community desires in the insulated chambers afforded by the several States.

This view seemed to him imperative even though "the experiment may seem futile or even noxious to me." His opinion, be it recalled, was in dissent.

Let us sum up backgrounds to the Great Crash: major portions of America were not able to bargain in ways that might have bolstered their purchasing power: farmers were strafed by competition from other countries, coal miners by other sources of energy, New England textile companies by the South, industrial workers by federal and state governments. These groups were the bottom of the pyramid. At the apex were the owners of America, whose flamboyancy was most gaudy on the New York Stock Exchange.

A lopsided impression must be avoided here. One reads many references to chauffeurs or bootblacks who were speculators on Wall Street. Good estimates are that about 7 per cent of the population were buying shares. This is not a negligible proportion, being perhaps 30 per cent of the heads of families. But most of them had slender assets and were mere dabblers. Further, a large portion of their purchases (and of all purchases) were bought on margin; that is, on credit. Further, the margin could go as high as 90 per cent of the selling price of the stocks. Further, a large part of these margin allowances came from call loans—grants of credit by stock brokers that could be cancelled on notice. One huge corporation had accumulated such a reserve of undistributed profits (General Motors) that it had a billion dollars in call loans in New York. Right here is a window into the financial turmoil. Employees of big corporations did not have the bargaining leverage that could have given them the incomes needed to buy the commodities that flowed from the big corporations. Neither did stockholders, for the board of directors would not pay out the profits that investors should have gotten. The company would not spend the money to build new factories or new machinery, because it could not use profitably the physical capital that it already owned.

Obviously there was no real dilemma here: More than one handle could be seen that would set the wheels turning smoothly. But the tycoons were too stupid or too greedy to seize any of them. So the available funds that were not being spent for useful purposes spilled into speculation. Real estate in Florida was reputed to be a hot item; one Miami newspaper in 1924 printed more inches of advertising than any paper had ever printed in a year, and the next summer another Miami sheet ran 504 pages, the largest single issue anywhere up to that time. But that land boom smashed, and the popular destination for money became Wall Street. Many Americans simply were not intelligent enough to use their surplus funds in productive ways. Speculation is easy, since the price of any limited commodity will rise as long as long as increasing numbers of fools want to buy it. Here are some figures at opening time on the New York Stock Exchange on 3 March, 1928, with the price given first and the annual dividend stated last, both in dollars:

American Can	77	2
General Electric	128¾	5
General Motors	139¾	5
R.C.A.	94½	0
Woolworth	180¾	5

Unless special factors intervene (for instance, a high growth rate, as in uranium mining at one time or in photocopy equipment recently), you are wise to unload a common stock when its selling price goes beyond ten times dividends. For all its charming Ivy League graduates and for all its numerous confidence men, the market had gone far out of line. So it crashed.

Thursday, 24 October, 1929 came to be known as Black Thursday. Nearly 13 million shares were sold that day on the New York Stock Exchange, which suffered the widest drop in its history. General Electric, going above 400 a few weeks earlier, opened at 315 and closed at 283. R.C.A. went down during the day from 68¾ to 44½. These numbers only afford a tardy index to what had been happening for a long time. The economy had been vulnerable for the entire decade. A postwar slump had been overcome by booms in construction and auto sales. A slump in 1924 was offset by construction and electrical appliances. A rather severe sag in 1927, due in appreciable measure to the drop in car sales as Ford made his change-over from the Model T, was survived. Perhaps the main element that kept the American economy at least in convalescence before 1929 was its insane symbiosis with the outside world, to be discussed in Chapter 24.

As has been emphasized above, perhaps to a fault, the Great Depression was largely a result of the lopsided distribution of incomes. Persons with savings, unable to perceive a commodity that they could reasonably hope to sell to consumers at a profit, turned instead to the stock exchanges and to other types of speculative ventures. Their blunders were compounded by large corporations who, unwilling to invest their undistributed earnings in their own lines of product, went so far as to deposit them in Wall Street banks which then used their cash surpluses for call loans. Prices of common stocks especially rose to absurd heights, and when the Great Crash came in 1929 its repercussions were both widespread and deep. Although few predicted the disaster, it was predictable. Since the end of World War I, three gigantic segments of the economy—agriculture, coal mining, and textile manufacturing—had been depressed. In addition, major industries had been sustained only by lending to foreigners the American dollars that could then be used to buy American goods; this "subsidize the foreigner" policy applied particularly in Germany and Latin America. However, while some economic sectors were clearly obsolescent, others were having a lusty adolescence. To the Census Bureau, construction continued to be the leading industrial group. But the new energy-source of electricity was more vital. Generators, transformers, high-tension wires, the telephone, the radio, these formed a whole complex of tangible investments. The internal-combustion engine gave us the automobile. Ford dominated the manufacture of cars just as DuPont seized the lead in producing industrial chemicals, from consumer goods such as rayon to producers' goods such as lacquers and solvents. So the decade after 1919 saw millions of Americans live in misery while others thrived beyond their dreams. Conversely, during the Great Depression many almost starved, but others benefited from hard times.

SOME NOTABLE EVENTS

1895 Giant hydroelectric generator installed at Niagara Falls, N.Y.

1896 Telephones in U.S. number one for 175 people; by 1914, one for 10.

1903 Ford Motor Company founded.

1906 Harvey Firestone's factory in Akron takes order for 2,000 sets of pneumatic tires.

1908 Ford markets the first Model T.

1909 Ford builds his first branch assembly plant in Kansas City.

1910 U.S. census: 92,407,000 (47% urban).

1913 U.S. steel production is 31 million tons.

1914 Electric trolleys are running over 40,000 miles of track.

1914–
  1931 Rayon output rose 69 times.

1914 Sales of Model T reach a quarter of a million.

1917 DuPont buys 27.6% of available stock in General Motors.

   Hitchman Coal & Coke Co. v. *Mitchell*

1919 Great Steel Strike begins, 22 Sept.; called off 8 Jan., 1920.

   Plumb Plan for nationalization of railroads is advanced.

   6.7 million passenger cars in use.

   Daily air-mail service from New York to Chicago starts.

   Radio Corporation of America organized.

1920 U.S. census: 106,466,000 (50% urban).

   Transportation Act of 1920 (Esch-Cummins Act) approved, 28 Feb.

   KDKA in Pittsburgh is first radio station to broadcast regularly.

   GM, incorporated in 1908, moves toward decentralized structure.

1921 *Truax* v. *Corrigan*

1922 Annual sales of radios are $60 million; hit $843 million in 1929.

   Baltimore & Ohio Plan ends shopmen's strike on railroads, 15 Sept.

1923 Lacquers introduced to U.S. markets.

   Chrysler begins to produce cars.

1925 Standard Oil (N.J.) begins to change to decentralized structure.

   Florida land boom tops out; collapses in 1926.

1926 National Broadcasting Corporation organized as first major network.

1928 First full-length all-sound movie is released.

   Real earnings of employed wage earners are 32% higher than in 1914.

1929 Sears, Roebuck begins to change to decentralized structure.

   23.1 million passenger cars in use.

Ways to Study History XXIII

Generalize, and then qualify. A promising project can be virtually destroyed if it works with categories that are too broad (see "Ways to Study History X"). It can also be made unbearable for readers if it refuses to conceptualize at all. The latter defect is glaring in *A History of American Life,* edited by Arthur M. Schlesinger, Sr. and Dixon Ryan Fox (1927–1948). Several scholars think that this series set the study of social history back by a full generation. Most of the books came as close to crude empiricism as the historian can get; they were sequences of unrelated facts. They can still be used as reference volumes to learn specific details, but they attempt few interpretations. Anybody who tries to read one from beginning to end is likely to find it tedious.

Scholarly work since World War II has tended to be much more analytical than its ancestors. Moreover, often the analytic framework is stated explicitly. Thomas C. Cochran's *Railroad Leaders, 1845–1890: The Business Mind in Action* (1953) proceeded from the sociological concept of social role. That is, he assumed that the job made the man, not vice versa. What obligations did a railroad executive have? Who defined his duties? What sanctions were applied to ensure compliance? But Cochran's exposition, including 300 pages of extracts from 100,000 letters written by 61 men, makes clear the limits of deviation from the standardized formula.

Alfred D. Chandler's *Strategy and Structure* (1962) expounds the reorganization of four giant corporations—General Motors, DuPont, Standard Oil (New Jersey), and Sears, Roebuck. Each firm adopted a "decentralized" form and thus they were similar. But each came to this innovation for its own reasons, in response to a different set of pressures, with a different group of personnel, dividing their powers in various ways.

Document 23-1

The problem of second-hand, or fifth-hand, goods confronts many industries. Some used products are handled by a scorned fringe of the retailers; to buy discarded jewelry or guitars you must go to a pawnshop. But most residences that are sold by respectable real-estate agencies (they scorn pawnshops) have already been occupied. Similarly the emergence of a used-car market early came to plague the automobile manufacturers. Soon after World War I the Ford Motor Company decided that this end of the dealership should yield to the agency a gross profit of 20 per cent over the cost of purchase of the old vehicle. But when the general sales committee of GM discussed the issue in 1925, they reached a different verdict.

1. Is it definitely established that the used car is the "dealer's own problem" and that it will be an increasingly important part of automobile retailing?

After considerable discussion, the following points were generally agreed upon:

The sale of new cars depends largely upon the used-car situation. This is especially true in the high-priced classes, where 80 per cent of the new-car sales involve trade-ins—in some instances it being necessary to sell two used cars in order to move one new car.

It was unanimously agreed that the future volume of sales on new cars would depend largely upon the efficient selling and servicing of used cars. It is, therefore, necessary for the manufacturer to take an interest in the sale of used cars. . . .

3. Should the dealer who is fortunately situated so that the volume of new-car business is naturally larger than the average, in proportion to capital employed and necessary operating expense and who therefore may enjoy abnormally high profit, be encouraged to allow more liberal prices for used cars taken in trade? . . . It was generally agreed that the Ford policy, whereby the dealer is required to make money on the used-car end, is unsound, at least as applied to our business. . . .

Domestic and Foreign Politics of Self-Deceit, 1916–1928

If a historian means to reject highly popular interpretations, honesty suggests that he should do so at once and bluntly. If it were permissible to determine truth by taking public-opinion polls, a large number of recent commentators would tell you that the great presidents of the twentieth century have been Theodore Roosevelt, Wilson, Franklin Roosevelt, and Kennedy. But while public opinion might grant public office, it does not always look at facts. Staring at the record, it might seem that the three most suitable presidents have been Harding, Coolidge, and Eisenhower. Not that these Republican worthies deserve any high praise. Corruption in high office was perhaps as bad in the Harding administration as it has ever been (but why are folks in such a hurry to forget Major General Harry H. Vaughan of the Truman years, or Eisenhower's crony Sherman Adams?). Coolidge was noted for his genius at sleeping. Eisenhower won note for his ability to garble a sentence. It will be hard to find positive gains that we can credit to any incumbent of the White House in this century. But if almost any action by the chief executive is almost certain to be mistaken, it is best if they do nothing. The man who sits on his hands and does nothing will not help us much, but neither will he provoke much trouble. The three presidents from the GOP who seem to merit a dab of praise accomplished little, but they did not fall into temptations that might have destroyed massive segments of mankind. Two other caveats might be recorded here, one having to do with political party, the other with sectionalism. The word has been bandied about that the Democrats were the "liberals," whatever that may mean. The party did hold prominent members who fought hard for social legislation, such as Alfred E. Smith and Robert Wagner in New York. But the thundering voice in its council came from two groups of reactionaries—the white South and the urban bosses. Republicanism had its own troglodytes; it also had George W. Norris in Nebraska, Robert M. LaFollette (and later his son) in Wisconsin, Fiorello LaGuardia in New York. The struggles of these three men will be discussed below; for the moment let us note that their constituencies also have bearing on the question of regionalism. Two, besides being Republican, were also Midwestern. It is easy to put together a long list of politicians in the heartland who succeeded in their pursuits by fighting in identifiable ways for some form of social justice.

Backtracking again, Wilson's campaign for re-election in 1916 is an illuminating sequence. A cynic would see it, with some reason, as an opportunistic sell-out to reform. The president was running scared. Put in the coarsest sense, he was trying to buy votes. But being a Southern gentleman who had also been president of an Ivy League university, he could not send his bagman down to the polling place as Mark Hanna had done for the Republicans twenty years earlier. He bought, not a vote, but a bloc of voters. His handicaps were great. Personally, he inclined to be frosty. The war was a dilemma to him. Should he be for "preparedness" or against it? Whichaway did the votes lie? What ethnic groups would swing the decision in key areas? For that matter, who could point to the key areas? He backed and filled, hitched and hauled.

Mileage posts can be mapped. The appointment of Louis D. Brandeis to the Supreme Court is worth analysis, coming at the beginning of the campaign on 28 January, 1916. It was fiercely resisted by anti-Semites. Portions, only portions, of big business opposed it because Brandeis had bad-mouthed the "monopolies" and stood as the Louis if not the David of the little man. But men on State Street in Boston had long been hiring him as a shrewd attorney in a railroad reorganization. They could not see a millionaire committing tyrannicide. Jews favored the nomination; so did most voters who held to the standard of fair play. The nomination was confirmed by the Senate. But for us the crucial consideration is this: What motivates a presidential aspirant? For Wilson, later acts serve as a floodlight, with the president backstaging all others. In 1914 and 1915 he had blocked a bill for loans to farmers. Suddenly he became a fervent advocate. We can ask why—but the bill passed.

Next came a splurge on statutes for the kiddies in the cities, for workers on ships and trains. As the election drew closer, the tempo of administration-sponsored legislation was stepped up. A child-labor bill, having languished for six months in the Senate, became law on 1 September after strong pressure from the White House (only to be invalidated by the Supreme Court in *Hammer* v. *Dagenhart*). Two days later the president signed the Adamson Act that decreed an eight-hour day on the railroads; for months the country had been threatened by a nationwide strike, until at last Wilson prevailed over determined opposition by rail executives. Three days after that the Senate agreed to the Revenue Act of 1916. Under the 16th Amendment (1913), Congress had levied a 2 per cent tax on personal incomes above $4,000. The House had doubled this basic levy in 1916; now the Senate added a further surcharge of 13 per cent on incomes over $20,000. The final measure also imposed new taxes on corporations and raised the imposition on inheritances. These steps toward social equity, coming right before a presidential election, show how crude political maneuvers can work for humanitarianism.

But probably the main ingredient in the campaign of 1916 was Wilson's shuffling on international affairs. Early in the year he was gallant for "preparedness." Alleging that constitutional provisions made it impossible to bring the National Guard in the several states under full federal control, the administration asked for a new reserve force to be called the Continental Army. The president also asserted that the United States needed "incomparably the greatest navy in the world." He went on a great tour of the Midwest to muster support for this line. However, he kept his ribs covered. When the Continental Army failed to win congressional favor, Wilson withdrew the proposal and permitted the secretary of war to resign. Years later the victim wrote: "I once heard a description which as nearly fits the case of President Wilson as any other I know. In describing someone it was said, 'He was a man of high ideals but no principles.'"

During the summer Wilson stopped being strong for preparedness and became strong for peace. The catalyst was the Democratic national convention in June. The governor of New York was the keynote speaker. He mentioned that in a number of instances his country had refused to be provoked into war. His audience demanded specifics. He gave some. Unexpectedly, the gathering started to betray strong feelings. It began to chant when informed of each crisis: "What did we do? What did we do?" The keynoter would roar back, "We didn't go to war, we didn't go to war!" On the following day the permanent chairman of the convention gave all the credit, falsely, to the president: "Without orphaning a single American child, without widowing a single American mother, without firing a single gun or shedding a drop of blood, he wrung from the most militant spirit that ever brooded over a battlefield the concession of American demands and American rights." Woodrow Wilson heard the message.

He put together peace with social justice. That was his campaign. By the end of September he was proclaiming that the Republicans meant to involve the nation in war both in Europe and in Mexico. Democratic campaigners were waving the slogan, "He kept us out of war." They were greatly aided by the loudmouth bellicosity of such prominent opponents as Theodore Roosevelt and by the shilly-shallies of the Republican nominee, Charles Evans Hughes, former Republican governor of New York and soon to be Chief Justice of the United States. Again, we have good reason to abandon a common, almost traditional, interpretation of this campaign. With high melodrama it has Hughes going to sleep thinking he had won, but waking up to learn that he lost due to an unexpected reverse in California. This depiction goes way too far. After all, people in a lot of other states voted against the Republicans. The answer may lie in such Democratic plugs as this one on the eve of the election:

The Lesson is Plain:
If You Want WAR, vote for HUGHES!
If You Want Peace with Honor
VOTE FOR WILSON

"Iffy history" is nearly always treacherous, but this conjecture may be offered: If a plebescite had been taken on American entry into World War I, the declaration of war would have been rejected decidedly in the vast realm between the mountains, from the Appalachians to the Rockies, from Pittsburgh to Denver. Wilson's policy would probably have been rejected in the Far West as well. It might have won on the Atlantic coast, but I am not convinced even of that. Wilson was re-elected. So—he helped take us, not out of war, but into it.

While Wilson's tactics in 1916 may seem canny, he followed a course in 1918 that must be called puerile. With the war still on but apparently nearing its close, the president decided to issue his October Appeal. His new wife (m. December, 1915) advised against: "I would not send it out. It is not a dignified thing to do." Right she was. He asked flat-out for a Democratic majority in Congress; the implication was that a denial would be a lack of confidence in him personally. Contrary to his long-standing hallucination, American politics is not a parliamentary system. He got a bloody nose.* In the House the Republicans ended with a 47 vote majority, having gained 25 seats. Their margin in the Senate was only two; they had won five seats.

The president chose to ignore these warnings. Within less than three weeks after Armistice Day the personnel of the commission to the Paris Peace Conference was announced. Chief delegate was the chief executive. The other four were obviously his patsies; not one carried any political clout at all. Sailing for France on 4 December, the president reached Brest nine days later. He then spent nearly a month touring Europe. Often he was acclaimed by adoring throngs. His earlier call in the Fourteen Points for self-determination

---

*Americans apparently do not like to have the president tell them how to vote in Congressional elections. FDR tried the same tactic in the Democratic primaries of 1938; he too got bashed.

was highly popular with many sectors of nationalism in Europe. But what did the slogan mean? How could it be implemented? What was a "nation"? Other members of the American contingent were bothered by Wilson's high-blown cant; one of them commented privately: "I am disquieted to see how hazy and vague our ideas are. We are going to be up against the wiliest politicians in Europe. There will be nothing hazy or vague about their ideas." The most biting comments about Wilson came from the premier of France, Georges Clemenceau. For openers: "God gave us the Ten Commandments and we broke them. Wilson gives us the Fourteen Points. We shall see." And, to Colonel House: "I can get on with you. You are practical. I understand you, but talking to Wilson is something like talking to Jesus Christ!" In 1925: "Wilson was a noble figure, but he did not appreciate the facts or the significance of European history." Clemenceau, on that point, was correct. And, if nobody knew concretely what the United States wanted, Clemenceau knew precisely what France needed: The old-style balance of power, but with a much elevated position for his country. Particularly, France must sap the strength of Germany.

Most details of the Treaty of Versailles need not detain us. Some, however, were to play giant in coming decades. As a summary judgment, the document was abhorrent. It stripped away territories from Germany. It divided up the Austro-Hungarian Empire, meanwhile bestowing the garland of nationhood on such non-nations as Czechoslovakia. In addition, it imposed massive indemnities on the defeated powers. Good economists were quick to see the defects in this program. Apart from exports of gold—neither Germany nor Austria had any in 1919—or the granting of credit by foreigners, international debts must be paid by the transfer of goods. But none of the intended beneficiaries of these indemnities was willing to accept increased imports; on the contrary, they wanted to increase their exports.* Nor should Article 10, Section 1 be overlooked:

> The Members of the League undertake to respect and preserve as against external aggression the territorial integrity and existing political independence of all Members of the League. In case of any such aggression or in case of any threat or danger of such aggression the Council shall advise upon the means by which this obligation shall be fulfilled.

The president saw this provision as the keystone of the peace settlement; Eugene Debs would refer to the League of Nations as "the new capitalist international." Two considerations seem clear. Wilson became obsessed with the menace posed by the Bolshevik revolution in Russia in November, 1917;

---

*This contradiction was eased for a few years by some idiotic processes: Americans make loans to Germans; Germany pays indemnities to Britain and France, which then repay war loans from the U.S. (See Chapter 22 for the role of the Morgan banking interests as beneficiaries of this chain of lending.)

some consequences of his mania will be examined shortly. Also, with considerable encouragement from Mrs. Wilson, he took special note of the "yellow
peril," meaning Japan.

As usual, foreign policy was linked with domestic difficulties. On the
very eve of the declaration of war, the president is said to have spoken to a
reporter as follows:

> Once lead this people into war, and they'll forget there ever was such a thing as
> tolerance. To fight you must be ruthless and brutal, and the spirit of ruthless
> brutality will enter into the very fiber of our national life, infecting Congress, the
> courts, the policeman on the beat, the man in the street.

One scholar has questioned that the president uttered such a paragraph;
another has rebutted that it seems in character for Wilson. If you take the latter
view (I do), it must be said that the chief executive hedged by making it a
self-fulfilling prediction. He was under heavy pressure from that renowned
war-monger Theodore Roosevelt: "He who is not with us, absolutely and
without reserve of any kind, is against us, and should be treated as an alien
enemy." Wilson contributed to the hysteria. During the war he declaimed,
"Woe be to the man that seeks to stand in our way in this day of high resolution
when every principle we hold dearest is to be vindicated and made secure."
(See the statements by our ambassador to England against "hyphenated
Americans," mid-Chapter 22.)

Worked to a frenzy by the invective from high office, masses of
Americans found release in an orgy of bigotry and violence. It reached its peak
in the four years 1916–1920. It had many sources and took many forms, all
ugly. Immigrants were beaten up by mobs. German-language instruction was
abolished in many school districts. Socialists and pacifists ran the risk of being
tarred and feathered. Radical publications were denied the use of the mails.
Leaders of the Socialist party were sent to the county workhouse for advocating resistance to conscription; Eugene Debs later went to the federal prison at
Atlanta on a similar charge. The federal government tried to get better
organization into the repression: on 7 September, 1917, it made simultaneous
raids on radical headquarters across the nation.

One might hope that peace would mean a return to sanity, but events did
not move that way. A manic does not swiftly recover his balance, and mania
was rife. Other reasons can be detected for the persistence of hysteria. The
Democratic party continued to need it. Having suffered a humiliating defeat in
1918, they had no wish to walk the plank again. Their plight declined further
as servicemen returned home to find no jobs. The federal government itself
compounded this difficulty by an abrupt reversal of fiscal policy. In the last
half of 1918, its expenditures were $9 billion in excess of its receipts. For the
next six months, the treasury showed a surplus of $831 million. Inevitably this

retraction caused a drastic reversal of wholesale prices, which fell by 33 per cent from 1920 to 1921. By the latter year an estimated 5 million workers were unemployed.

The Democrats had badly lost the election of 1920. Their last-ditch fight was composed of two main appeals. The administration tried to rally the people to the Treaty of Versailles, especially to the League of Nations. Wilson took the position, understandably, that a mass of amendments and reservations to the treaty would nullify it totally. A majority of the Senate believed, yet more understandably, that the president had abandoned altogether too many traditional American precepts.* Knowing that he would lose in the Foreign Relations Committee, Wilson took the issue to the voters. On 4 September, 1919, he began his famous "swing around the circle" in the West, making 37 speeches in 29 cities. Before the month ended, his gamble was lost when he collapsed in Colorado. He was hurried back to the White House. On 2 October he had a stroke. For several months his activities were at best limited; the vice president was a nobody, and rumors circulated that Mrs. Wilson was making important decisions.

With the president incapacitated, with his retirement certain, with the economic situation shaky, the Democrats had their backs to the wall. Some of their leaders turned vicious. The wolf whose name might endure in infamy was the attorney general, A. Mitchell Palmer. He set in motion the ignoble procession known as the "Palmer raids" against radicals, which he hoped would launch his career toward the White House. Although Palmer wanted the publicity he got, perhaps he ended up with more ignominy than he deserves. He had, if not justification, at least a plausible excuse. Since April numerous efforts had been made to send bombs through the mails to public officials. The front of Palmer's own house was smashed by a bomb (the bombardier was killed). Confronted by such lethal anarchy, few can remain calm. Observers of Canadian affairs may well recall that, after a sequence of bombings, two kidnappings, and a murder in October, 1970, the provincial and federal governments were provoked into policies that the same men would not have undertaken in quieter moments.

Depending on how one chooses to define a "raid," dating of the Palmer raids will differ. It suffices to say that they ran from the autumn of 1919 to the spring of 1920. An early momentous event came just before Christmas when 249 immigrants, alleged radicals, were deported to Russia. The brutalities had scarcely begun. On New Year's Day simultaneous raids were conducted in 33 cities. The number of persons arrested was large; estimates vary from 2,700 to 6,000. They were treated most viciously. In Hartford, any visitor to a supposed revolutionary in jail was himself arrested. Detroit packed them in like sardines:

---

*Particularly such as our time-tested reluctance to make prior commitments to foreign disputes and our belief that the Monroe Doctrine was a divine precept. Wilson, often hailed as an upholder of the American way, had a pronounced tendency to depart from it, especially in foreign affairs.

577

for a week more than a hundred men were kept in a bull-pen that measured 30 feet by 24. These actions, like others before and since, should make us wonder at the chauvinistic paeans to "the American sense of fair play," or the cheerleading that says Americans are devoted to law as well as to order, or the flabby assertion that we have lived by a "politics of consensus." In moments of strain we have the Stamp Act Riots, race riots, anti-draft riots, the Palmer Raids, the Watts Riot of 1965.

The national elections of 1920 must be seen in this context—the sagging economy, the mood of resentment mounting to hysteria. When the presidential polls had been tallied, they revealed that the total votes had shot upward by about 30 per cent. The increase was due in large measure to the enfranchisement of women by the 19th Amendment in August 1920. To a Democrat, the results were horrible. Support for his party remained at the level of 1916, whereas the Republican vote almost doubled. The GOP not only recaptured the marginal elector who had gone Progressive in 1912 and Democratic in 1916, it also won normally Democratic districts. Its candidate Warren G. Harding got more than 60 per cent of the votes; the Democrats a mere 34 per cent, as their tally actually decreased in all sections except the seaboard East and the South. They had brought the drubbing on themselves in considerable measure. For president they had put forward an unknown. The vice presidential nominee was a brash youngish man who had been assistant secretary of the navy. His name was Franklin Delano Roosevelt. Whether his purpose was to win the approval of Woodrow Wilson or not, he sought during the campaign to champion the League of Nations, and in the process fell into some indiscretions. The proposed federation, he said, could be controlled by the United States: Consider the banana republics of Latin America—weren't at least a half dozen of those votes in his side pocket?

Other generalizations can be advanced about national politics during this decade. Seemingly the business cycle did not have much effect on how people voted. Recessions of some magnitude occurred in 1924 and 1927. The number of unemployed in the first of these years rose to 2 million, and it nearly reached that figure in 1927 (due in large part to Ford's shutdown for six months to make the changeover from Model T to Model A). The Republicans continued to prove that they had a semi-permanent presidential majority; as long as they could hold their own ranks together, they could win the White House. Tactically they were shrewd, knowing how to capitalize on such events as a general strike in Seattle and a policeman's strike in Boston—the latter event gave Governor Calvin Coolidge of Massachusetts a chance to break the strike, appear as the champion of law and order, get his name on the front pages, and thus become the Republican nominee for the vice presidency in 1920. His boss, President Harding, was a likable cuss. It is hackneyed to refer to him as the worst chief executive in American history, but recent scholarship makes this verdict debatable. I confess to some prejudice because it was the conservative Harding, not the liberal Wilson, who pardoned Debs. But

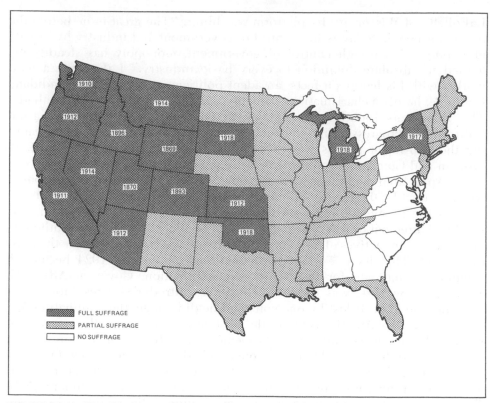

FIGURE 24-1. *The Adoption of Women's Suffrage as of 1919*

Harding was not a bad sort. He was addicted to his friends, whiskey, poker, and having a mistress. He installed as secretary of state Charles Evans Hughes, who in spite of his august demeanor maneuvered the achievements of the Washington Naval Conference of 1921–1922 (late in Chapter 24). Every republic gets the president it deserves, and Harding suited the national mood. Mercifully for him he died before the corrupt leasing of oil reserves at Teapot Dome, Wyoming, and at Elk Hills, California, became public knowledge. Although one result of these scandals was to send a member of the cabinet to prison, the faith of most Americans in the Republican party was not shaken.*

Its ascendancy was challenged in 1924. With support from the dwindling corps of Socialists, the railroad unions, and modest help from other branches of trade unionism, a rejuvenated Progressive party put forward

---

*One of my deep desires is to see a nation admit its vices as well as commemorating its virtues. A series of stamps should be done along this order: Polluted Meat, 1777; Crédit Mobilier; Teapot Dome; deep-freeze scandals during Truman administration, and so on into an obvious series of candidates in the seventies.

LaFollette of Wisconsin. Its platform was blunt: "The great issue before the American people today is the control of government and industry by private monopoly. . . . Through control of government, monopoly has steadily extended its absolute dominion to every basic industry." LaFollette, a hard worker with his hands on facts, an adept politician, was a strong candidate. Coolidge, hardly a charismatic personality, ran for re-election, with a nobody. The Democrats found two nobodies to put forward. One senator from California, a Progressive Republican, wrote to his sons that the issue separating the two major parties was "whether the entrance to the office of J. P. Morgan and Company should be on Wall or Broad Street."

Apart from the independent Progressive move, the zest of the campaign was provided by the Ku Klux Klan. This nativist movement, like its forebears such as the Know-Nothings and the American Progressive Association, was sired by hatred out of fear. The enemy might be blacks, or Jews, or adulterers, or Catholics; for natives of the southern Midwest, the last named were the most dangerous. This issue exploded into national politics in 1924 because a prominent candidate for the Democratic nomination, Governor Alfred E. Smith of New York, was Catholic. His forces introduced a resolution condemning the Klan. It lost by one vote, and he did not get the nomination. We can fairly say that Americans in this decade tended to vote from the viscera, not from the brain. The xenophobia in the Democratic national convention seems a close index to the national temper; Congress had just enacted a new immigration law that clearly discriminated on ethnic grounds. In 1926 the Imperial Wizard and Emperor of the Klan made the viewpoint clear (Document 25-3). These resentments were not confined to any region of the country; they were not rural or small town or big city; they were not defined by social class. William Allen White, great editor of a small-town newspaper in Kansas, ran for governor while opposing the Klan: ". . . the way the Catholics and Jews and colored people were persecuted in Kansas was a dirty shame, and I couldn't rest under it." After his defeat he had this to say about attitudes among trade-unionists, many of them coal miners:

> Here was a funny thing: labor in the Middle West is shot through with the Ku-Klux Klan. It voted for Coolidge . . . because he was right on the Pope. I didn't get much of it because I was wrong on the Pope. . . . Certainly nothing has hit labor such a smash in my memory in politics as the Ku-Klux Klan. . . . It will be a decade before labor recovers what it has lost by flirting with the Ku-Klux Klan.

The Democratic showing in the election of 1924 was more dismal than in 1920: its presidential candidate won only 30 per cent of the popular votes. But Coolidge did not do as well as Harding had done in the preceding election, getting only 54 per cent of the electorate. The wide swing went to LaFollette, who had nearly 5 million votes. He drew more heavily from Democratic than from Republican supporters. His appeal was mainly to the Midwest and the Pacific coast; in California the Democrats were obliterated. Lastly, note that this campaign (not FDR, who in some tomes is made to appear like God at the Creation) brought into prominence a phrase that has passed into the language. The pro tem Committee of One Hundred headed by the editor of the *Nation* announced that it would support the Progressives with this sentence: "We believe that the time has come for a new deal."

In 1928 no third party of substance came forward. Coolidge, although he had been elected only once, chose to doze through the coming contest without having his name in the headlines: his laconic phrase was "I do not choose to run." The Republican candidate was Herbert Hoover, resident in California but a native of the Midwest, a mining engineer who had made a fortune in developments that girdled the globe. His venture into public affairs came as director of American relief efforts in Europe after World War I. Then he became chief of the Department of Commerce, where his aim was to encourage cooperation among companies. This sally had its good side and its bad. Any tinkerer will know the importance of standardizing such commodities as nuts and bolts or lavatory washers by reducing the number of sizes. On the other side, any consumer will know the perils of making it easy for erstwhile competitors to standardize prices. At last Al Smith got the Democratic nomination. He got stomped; Hoover did better than Coolidge had done four years earlier, almost as well as Harding had done in 1920. His 58 per cent of the vote eclipsed Smith's 41 per cent. The anti-Catholic South went strongly against Smith, who lost the normally Democratic Atlanta, Birmingham, Oklahoma City, Dallas, and Houston. But the story must not be allowed to end there. In the North, Smith swung 112 counties away from the GOP; 77 of them had a Catholic preponderance. (See Figure 24-2.)

If we seek to understand how the Republican dominance in presidential elections gave way to a semi-permanent Democratic majority after 1932, these forces become prominent: the movement to cities, where Democratic machines had long been influential and now became dominant; the altered religious and ethnic mix of the population, increasingly felt as immigrant groups moved onto the political stage; the stigma that the GOP was "responsible" for the Great Depression; the Republican persistence in nominating men who were safe but dull, which became fatal when the Democrats found a candidate who was safe but colorful.

The Harding-Coolidge administrations did record achievements, and some follies, in foreign affairs. It has been fashionable to deprecate the Washington Naval Conference of 1921–1922. The humorist Will Rogers gibed that in days of rhetoric "not a rowboat was sunk." Many historians have taken the opposing tack and argued that the agreements went too far in leaving the United States defenseless before its enemies. These judgments are unfair. To defer an arms race is perhaps not the ultimate in human endeavor, but it is

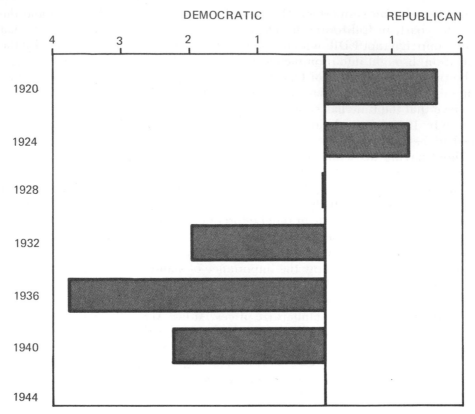

FIGURE 24-2.   *Net Pluralities in Twelve Largest Cities (millions of votes)*

certainly an improvement over our experience in recent decades. The sessions at Washington began on 12 November, 1921. When Secretary of State Hughes got up to speak, nothing much was expected. His proposal of a ten-year "holiday" on the construction of capital ships rocked both press and public as well as delegates and ministries. He wanted not only to suspend the laying down of new battleships but he also offered to destroy thirty American battleships that were partially completed or already afloat; in exchange, he told other naval powers what they would have to do. The final intent was to leave his own country, Britain, and Japan with capital ships in the ratio of 5: 5: 3. In this category, France and Italy would be allowed a third the quota of Great Britain and the United States. He had needed only a few minutes to annihilate (verbally) sixty-six battleships totalling nearly 2 million tons. Let those snort who will, the treaty served at least to postpone a breakneck scramble for military advantage. A companion document, called the Nine-Power Treaty, secured the formal consent of other powers to two long-standing American objectives in China: citizens of all foreign nations could participate on the same terms in the economic development of that country, and China would be allowed to develop an independent suzerainty.

The brutalities of the American diplomacy of the time are well-known. By 1924 United States agents were directly managing the finances of ten Latin-American nations. Nicaragua is an example. The United States in 1912, acting under the jurisdiction of its self-proclaimed Roosevelt Corollary to the Monroe Doctrine (1904), had sent a detachment of marines there, with the explanation that the act was required to insure proper fiscal arrangements (especially collection of import duties plus payments on schedule to European bondholders). American troops remained in Nicaragua as an army of occupation until 1933,* when they were finally withdrawn by President Hoover. Earlier Hoover had told the Hondurans: "We have a desire to maintain not only the cordial relations of governments with each other but also the relations of good neighbors." Thus two phrases conventionally tied to FDR—the New Deal and the Good Neighbor Policy—did not originate in his administration at all.

To recapitulate, agreements made at the Washington Conference had obvious defects when they were made; the concurrence on naval limitations did not touch such significant weapons as destroyers and submarines. Weaknesses in the Nine-Power Treaty became obvious with time; a lack of will to enforce by other signatories made it easy for Japan to brush it away. But the agreements signed in 1922 did ease the situation for a few years, and both the Compromise of 1850 and Crittenden's proposals in 1861 should remind us that deferring a showdown can be a good idea. So, retrospectively, American policies in the Pacific and in Latin America may seem badly flawed, but they were not silly. American actions toward Europe were silly.

Further discussion here can be limited to three sets of actions: the Dawes Plan, the World Court, and the Kellogg-Briand Pact. The first arose from the provision in the Treaty of Versailles requiring Germany to pay massive reparations to Britain and France. Dawes' proposal of 1924 began from a recognition that Germany could not meet the payments, so the annual stipend was reduced. So far, so good. But then the Plan restricted the Reich to payment of this obligation only from funds arising from the transfer of Deutschemarks within Germany. This was lunacy. How were the foreign creditors to redeem their credits if their governments imposed rules that prevented imports from Germany? American fumbling with the World Court was equally inane. Elements in the United States had been arguing that although the Senate would not vote to join the League of Nations, it could at

---

*Smedley Butler, major general (retired) of the Marine Corps, spoke about 1940 at the War Memorial in Indianapolis, Indiana: "I spent much of my adult life wandering around in Latin America, grabbing a government by the neck and shouting, 'Be a democracy, damn you, be a democracy.'"

least adhere to a judicial body with authority to rule on some international disputes. In 1926 the Senate voted several qualifications to its acceptance. These included a stipulation that the United States could withdraw at any time; that Congress would determine the American share of expenses of the World Court; that the body could not consider any dispute involving the United States without American consent; "nor shall adherence to the said protocol and statute be construed to imply a relinquishment by the United States of its traditional attitude toward purely American questions." Having adopted these reservations, the Senate did not take action on the total issue until 1935. Then, for want of the necessary two-thirds vote, the proposal lost.

The colossal folly has been saved for last. The Peace Pact of 1928 should not be likened to the naval pacts of 1922. One helped to stave off an arms race; the other in different circumstances was a stimulant to an already maddened illusion. A commitment to outlaw war will do no good unless governments want to live at peace. Evolution of the Kellogg-Briand Pact can be dated from the arrival in the United States of the French foreign minister in early 1927, but the idea goes earlier. Two Americans in particular, a Chicago lawyer and a professor at Columbia University, had been agitating for a world agreement to outlaw war. They won approbation from the chairman of the Senate Foreign Relations Committee, William J. Borah. Here we encounter, to be trite, a comedy of errors. A top French emissary arrives on these shores, and he has two aims. First, quite reasonably, he wants protection against another invasion by Germany, to which end he seeks to involve the United States in advance. Also the two nations have disagreed about the payment of war debts (Chapter 22 on war loans; early Chapter 28), and he is looking for a way to mend matters. He chooses an inept way. In a public speech to the people of the United States, he states: "France would be ready publicly to subscribe, with the United States, to any mutual engagement tending, as between those two countries, to outlaw war." Policy-makers in Washington were, to say the least annoyed. President Coolidge felt that some barn-stormer from Europe had tried to go over his head to the electorate. Secretary of State Kellogg, who had succeeded at the department when Hughes left in 1925, was irked. Bilateral agreement? Absolutely not.

Then, on May 20–21, a miraculous event helped crystallize (among other things) Franco-American popular ideals about peace and friendship. The young Charles A. Lindbergh flew nonstop and solo from Long Island to Le Bourget Aerodrome outside Paris in 33 hours, 30 minutes, and was hailed as an international hero. No term of negotiations could have done so much for Franco-American negotiations; instantaneously many citizens felt that nothing was too good for their French brothers. Kellogg wrote that, instead of a bilateral treaty, the United States would prefer "an effort to obtain the adherence of all the principal powers of the world to a declaration renouncing war as an instrument of national policy." Now France cooled. She and Britain finally signed, but with a mass of qualifications. Of the fifteen initial signatories, three agreed at once: Japan, Germany, and Italy. The treaty allowed for additional names. USSR was the first to be added.

Out of this convoluted mess another question emerges. What did Lindbergh symbolize for the American people? Did he represent the "rugged individualism" to which some Americans still pledged alliance (Document 24-3)? Or did his achievement foreshadow the future dominance of the machine in a world where the individual would hardly figure at all, as we shall see in later chapters?

With strict moral instruction from those schoolmarms in the White House, Roosevelt and Wilson, many citizens had gotten their feet a good way off the ground and up the success ladder before World War I. The ascent of many financial astronauts was accelerated after an exceptionally hysterical war fever was concluded in the Armistice. Millions went into orbit; the most real of all realities for them was the vicarious (and sometimes vicious) world of make-believe. (This frame of mind, the dominance of fantasy, was splendidly depicted by James Thurber in his short story "The Secret Life of Walter Mitty.") I have placed much responsibility on the pre-war presidents for their contributions to this descent into self-deception. It is rather hard to make a similar charge of personal accountability against Harding or Coolidge. For two generations, Harding's reputation was probably lower than that of any other president. It was rather hard to see why, since his call for a return to "normalcy" exactly caught the mood of a nation tired of political tempests and national heroics. Personally, I side with the columnist who applauded Coolidge for saying nothing, content to sleep through his six years in the White House. The voters did not want him to do anything, so he did very little. When he did act, his behavior was insipid or destructive—as witness the Kellogg-Briand Pact.

SOME NOTABLE EVENTS

1917   Lever Act, 10 August, imposes food rationing.

1918   *Hammer* v. *Dagenhart* invalidates child labor laws.

1919   Paris Peace Conference, 12 January–28 June.
Bomb plots against public officials, April.
Communist parties (several) founded in U.S.
Schenck v. *U.S.*; Holmes on the "clear and present danger" of seditious speech.
Volstead Act, 28 October, outlaws alcoholic beverages.
Palmer raids against alleged radicals begin in earnest, 21 December; last about two months.
Ads begin to appear showing a woman holding a cigarette.

1920   Congressional resolution ratifies peace with Germany.
Transportation Act (also called Esch-Cummins Act), 28 February.
Nineteenth Amendment provides for woman suffrage.
Studebaker stops making horse-drawn vehicles.

1921   Treaty of peace with Germany, 25 August.
Immigration restriction act passes as emergency measure.

1922   Fordney-McCumber tariff compromises business and farm interests.
Treaty of Washington (also called Naval Limitation Treaty, also Five Power Treaty), 21 August.

1924   Congressional resolution for cancellation of oil leases at Teapot Dome and Elk Hill, 8 February.
Immigration Act (National Origins Act), 26 May, establishes immigrant quotas.

1926   Senate votes reservations on U.S. adherence to World Court, 27 January.

1927   Coolidge explains U.S. intervention in Nicaragua, 10 January.
McNary-Haugen grain surplus bill vetoed by Coolidge, 25 February.
Lindbergh flies the Atlantic, 20–21 May.
Sacco and Vanzetti executed, 23 August; many call it political scapegoating.
"Good Neighbor Policy" toward Latin America begins.

1928   Kellogg-Briand Peace Pact, signed by 15 nations on 27 August.

Ways to Study History XXIV

Cling to doubt. Thorstein Veblen, in an essay published more than fifty years ago, declared that skepticism was the beginning of wisdom (Chapter 25). Charles Sanders Peirce argued that the crucial breakthrough of scientists in the nineteenth century was the development of truly detached intellects (Document 25-2). Nature, so Theodore Dreiser asserted, has ways of taking revenge on the cocksure (Chapter 25).

Veblen further argued that skepticism is especially common among persons who have imbibed deeply of two cultures, since they cannot fully accept the values of either. I know not whether Robert H. Ferrell can be termed a "marginal man" in this sense, but certainly he has exhibited the common sense of the proverbial man from Missouri: You got to show me. His study *Peace in Their Time* (1952) shows how the Kellogg-Briand Pact of 1927 came to be drafted and ratified. It begins with the assumption that many phenomena are not what their surface says they are. If the Pact had not helped to confirm and advance the tendency of Americans toward self-delusion, Ferrell's book might be one of the funniest of all works about our history.

The conclusions can only be summarized here. To shore up its defenses against Germany, France wanted a nonaggression pact with the United States. American diplomats were too shrewd for that trap. Then the French foreign minister appealed over their heads to the American people. Although piqued, the executives in Washington were swayed by Charles Lindbergh's nonstop flight across the Atlantic. Feeling unable to say No to the French, the United States counterproposed that all major nations should sign a treaty forswearing warfare. So war would be illegal; but in signing, one nation after another made reservations and qualifications. In Ferrell's words, "The result was that the secretary of state, when he finally 'delivered the goods,' delivered a great amount of wrapping paper."

Document 24-1

Woodrow Wilson never achieved a precise and realistic statement of what he hoped to gain by American entry into World War I. But his oft-cited Fourteen Points seem less adequate in that respect than the Four Points he announced at Mount Vernon, Fourth of July, 1918.

The destruction of every arbitrary power anywhere that can separately, secretly, and of its single choice disturb the peace of the world; or, if it cannot be presently destroyed, at the least its reduction to virtual impotence.

The settlement of every question, whether of territory, of sovereignty, of economic arrangement, or of political relationship, upon the basis of the free acceptance of that settlement by the people immediately concerned. . . .

The consent of all nations to be governed in their conduct towards each other by the same principles of honor and of respect for the common law of civilized society that govern the individual citizens of all modern states in their relations with one another; to the end that all promises and covenants may be sacredly observed, no private plots or conspiracies hatched, no selfish injuries wrought with impunity, and a mutual trust established upon the handsome foundation of a mutual respect for right.

The establishment of an organization of peace which shall make it certain that the combined power of the free nations will check every invasion of right and serve to make peace and justice the more secure by affording a definite tribunal of opinion to which all must submit and by which every international readjustment that cannot be amicably agreed upon by the peoples directly concerned shall be sanctioned.

Document 24-2

The legislative process can be as tortuous as a snake. Some aspects of the procedures that resulted in rejection of the Treaty of Versailles have just been discussed. But glimpses of the precise terms in which the Senate of the United States stated its "reservations" about the League of Nations may also be useful. These are extracts from the resolution that came to vote on 19 March, 1920; the tally was 49 for and 35 against ratification; the motion to adhere to the treaty therefore failed of the necessary two-thirds majority.

1. The United States so understands and construes article 1 that in case of notice of withdrawal from the League of Nations, as provided in said article, the United States shall be the sole judge as to whether all its international obligations and all its obligations under the said covenant have been fulfilled, and notice of withdrawal by the United States may be given by a concurrent resolution of the Congress of the United States.

2. The United States assumes no obligation to preserve the territorial integrity or political independence of any other country by the employment of its military or naval forces, its resources, or any form of economic discrimination. . . .

4. The United States reserves to itself exclusively the right to decide what questions are within its domestic jurisdiction and declares that all domestic and political questions relating wholly or in part to its internal affairs, . . . are solely within the jurisdiction of the United States. . . .

5. The United States will not submit to arbitration or to inquiry by the assembly or by the council of the League of Nations, provided for in said treaty of peace, any questions which in the judgment of the United States depend upon or relate to its long-established policy, commonly known as the Monroe doctrine; said doctrine is to be interpreted by the United States alone and is hereby declared to be wholly outside the jurisdiction of said League of Nations. . . .

Document 24-3

Herbert Hoover was the first president since John Quincy Adams to have spent a major portion of his adulthood abroad. He might also be labelled the first career businessman to occupy the White House. Although he had served in government for a decade by 1928, he had never held elective office. His lack of intimacy with the domestic scene, especially with American politics, contributed to his downfall: no true politician would have shown his dedication to rigid principles. Compare Hoover's campaign speech in 1928 with President Cleveland's philosophy in 1889 (Document 18-1).

When the war closed the most vital of all issues both in our own country and throughout the world was whether governments should continue their war-time ownership and operation of many instrumentalities of production and distribution. We were challenged with a peace-time choice between the American system of rugged individualism and a European philosophy of diametrically opposed doctrines—doctrines of paternalism and state socialism. The acceptance of these ideas would have meant the destruction of self-government through centralization of government. It would have meant the undermining of the individual initiative and enterprise through which our people have grown to unparalleled greatness. . . . Even if governmental conduct of business could give us more efficiency instead of less efficiency, the fundamental objection to it would remain unaltered and unabated. It would destroy political equality. It would increase rather than decrease abuse and corruption. It would stifle initiative and invention. It would undermine the development of leadership. It would cramp and cripple the mental and spiritual energies of our people. . . . For a hundred and fifty years liberalism has found its true spirit in the American system, not in the European systems. . . .

The Life of the Mind, 1898–1929

In *The Theory of the Leisure Class,* Thorstein Veblen explained some aspects of the boom-times mentality of the twenties, some years before they occurred. Every person has an instinct of workmanship, which leads him to be productive and to strive for skillfulness. But he also wants to display the fruits of his labors after he has created them. As long as his product does not greatly exceed his actual needs, these two desires do not conflict. But eventually certain people acquire more goods than they can display, and they need the services of others to consume the excess. Wives are the most immediately available vicarious consumers, causing in part the fist-thumping repugnance at "permitting my wife to work." A producer is not available to consume for another. Servants who perform no useful work, and hangers-on who are supported in luxury, also consume in the service of their benefactor.

The possession of a mob of vicarious consumers might be gratifying to their master, but these functionaries have no opportunity to satisfy their own instincts of workmanship. Often they try to fill this gap by devising a complicated ritual about the trivialities of their lives, and spending time and energy in conforming to it, and watching out for the deviations of others. The cut of a coat, the pronunciation of a word, or the breed of a lap-dog acquire great importance in such a society, though they never quite manage to alleviate its boredom. However, it is worthwhile examining the workings of these and other cultural preoccupations, for it is here that we can begin to see important ingredients of the "roaring" twenties mentality.

By the beginning of the twentieth century the profits of the industrial system had permitted a number of consumers to live ever more luxuriously. Even the original producer need no longer be useful, as he had acquired so very much wealth that further labor on his part had become superfluous. Edith Wharton, the novelist who best portrayed this segment of society, came out of it herself; her family and friends were both astounded and disdainful when she chose to cease being merely decorative and begin a career as a writer. She deplored the pettiness, the ostentation, and the worship of money which flourished around her, but she apparently didn't recognize that these attributes are inevitable in a world of drones. Although usually ironic and precise, Wharton's vision seems clouded by one of the most pervasive features of American life before 1929—nostalgic yearning for an unreal ideal.

In *The House of Mirth* (1905) Wharton's picture of futility among the very rich is most finely drawn. It focuses on a heroine, Lily Bart: although her deceased father lost all his money, Lily continues to be acceptable to society; she is so beautiful and "accomplished" that everyone assumes she will soon make a rich marriage, and then the hostesses of the house parties which she interminably attends will find her a powerful friend and a fearsome opponent. But, because of a delicacy of feeling which those around her do not share, she muffs her opportunity to marry a rich clod. Later, after the husband of her best friend makes some money for her in the stock market, the friend drops Lily from her list. Although tolerant of her husband's infidelities, this woman will not permit any alienation of cash. Later, another friend saves her own reputation at the expense of Lily Bart's. Since a reputation for chastity is the only female attribute which rivals wealth in the marriage market, her fortunes plummet. The hostesses of her circle realize that they need never fear her, and drop her; she winds up a seamstress at a hat shop. There her lower-class co-workers pay her little heed, for "she had 'gone under,' and true to the ideal of their race, they were awed only by success—by the gross tangible image of material achievement." Emulating the rich, the poor worship prosperity.

Another novel published five years earlier, *Sister Carrie,* is Theodore Dreiser's classic portrait of another archetypal American woman with an instinct for the main chance. Carrie Meeker comes to Chicago from the farm to better her condition, but soon, to escape from the grinding monotony of her job at a shoe factory and from the pinch-penny soul of her brother-in-law, she becomes the mistress of a traveling salesman. He introduces her to physical comforts which she had never experienced before, and, more importantly, to acquaintances who outdistance him in wealth and social position. One of these, George Hurstwood, the manager of one of Chicago's most fashionable saloons, lives with an open-handed ease which enchants Carrie, while her beauty and freshness attract him equally. Unhappy with his wife and feeling unneeded by his children, he elopes with Carrie to New York, where they live as man and wife. He buys an interest in another saloon, and they seem to mark time for several years, but inwardly he is dying. In Chicago he was a hail-fellow to many men; in New York he barely manages to remain a cog. Soon enough he loses his business and is no longer even solvent. He sinks into the routine of the unemployed who quickly becomes unemployable, and then to the Bowery bum who depends on soup kitchens even to live.

In the meantime Carrie prospers. The possibilities of New York, which had made Hurstwood feel insignificant, enchant her; she turns to the stage, and before very long has become a famous comic actress, a star. Yet despite the vitality which charmed so many and led to her success, she is a vapid woman. Incapable of genuine emotion, she only occasionally wonders whether life might contain more lasting pleasures than pretty clothes and admiration. The novel dooms Hurstwood to the living death which society imposes on failures and Carrie to the frivolous life which it offers as a prize.

The possibility that any prize might be forthcoming for a woman who had been the mistress of two men shocked *Sister Carrie*'s readers; not for another 20 years could chastity safely be flouted in literature. Yet sexual laxity, although necessary to the book's structure, is but a trivial part of its message. The larger themes, of heartlessness, of hollowness, were perceived by many others of the pre-depression era. T. S. Eliot was one. Though he was an expatriate, his poetry should best be understood within its American context. Nostalgia permeates his work, nostalgia for an implied heroic past which did not whimper. To him everything in the modern era seems stale and tired, with people responding with mechanical formalities to a mechanical world.

> For I have known them all already, known them all:—
> Have known the evenings, mornings, afternoons,
> I have measured out my life with coffee spoons;

In this vision man is a wind-up toy programmed to trudge in circles; he is no longer able to control his destiny or regulate his purposes. His eyes are the only part of him that still lives, and eyes can only view the surfaces of his constantly repeated surroundings, which he can neither change nor understand. If the American Dream of progress and faith in the future was both mythical and unattainable, so much worse would be the fate of those who awakened from it without finding a palpable substitute. The officially authorized Dream required that present pleasures must be subordinated to future perfection, but unfortunately, a realization that such perfection would not be forthcoming in the future was not necessarily, or even probably, an adequate release to allow a modern man to relax and savor the moment. Instead, he would become an Ahab who outlived the whale, a man with no obsession, with nothing at all (See Chapter 14 on Melville.) In such a vision of life as T. S. Eliot's, the most profoundly held emotion is boredom.

The philosopher John Dewey believed that many of America's problems stemmed from the fracturing of work and learning, and that this situation could be eased by a new kind of school. In former days, children learned most of their major lessons by watching and helping their parents or other working adults. Thus the need to learn certain things was immediately apparent, and doing them well produced tangible rewards. But in a society where work went on outside the home, and most people were coming to believe it desirable to separate working and living areas still further, this was no longer possible. To be useful in this changed society, the schools could no longer teach "academic" subjects in a vacuum. In the Laboratory School in Chicago, Dewey devised a system in which all subjects related to a common theme, the themes being different forms of useful labor. Thus a group might be learning about the production of bread. They would raise different kinds of grain, and read and talk about the ways various societies in the past had managed these tasks. Then they would have to thresh and mill grain, and figure out the most efficient ways to measure it. Finally they had to learn processes of baking. While the children were learning about history, mechanics, sociology, and mathematics, all of these lessons were but means to ends, as they would be to actual producers.

This system worked. Children learned faster, remembered longer, and realized that a purpose lay behind their schooling. Unfortunately, the system never became widespread. It would have been extremely expensive. The costs of the extra equipment it required could have been met, but Americans would never entertain the expense of revamping the whole teacher-training establishment. To use the Laboratory School's methods, a teacher needed a wide and generous education, and a mind flexible enough to permit doubt and error. Most teachers were simply drilled in a few irrefutable "facts" to which they clung desperately in the sea of their own ignorance. Their only possible goal was to pound these "facts" into the minds of their charges. To provide a different kind of education would mean luring the very best minds into becoming teachers, and paying them accordingly. At a time when hyped up production of goods was America's pride, and "If you're so smart, why ain't you rich?" one of its common jibes, this could not possibly happen.

Despite its inadequacies, schooling was still regarded as something holy. Children in the black rural South didn't even have the advantage of a semi-regular school run by a graduate of a teacher training academy; if they were lucky, a student at one of the black colleges might wander into the district in the summer time, hawking a little reading and writing for a pittance. W. E. B. DuBois, later to be a noted historian and militant leader, was one of those teachers, and in *The Souls of Black Folk* he recorded his impressions. He saw endurance, and, amazingly, hope. The people he encountered were poor and ignorant, but they had learned to mitigate poverty with laughter, and they hoped that his poor "school" could expand their knowledge of the world. Being black, they were despised, but faith helped to keep them from despising themselves. Although the sturdy white yeoman farmer (already fast disappearing) would have disdained the comparison, they represented most of the virtues which he had been taught to think resided exclusively in himself.

It was becoming increasingly difficult to write of those virtues, and of the optimism which accompanied them, without resorting to the past tense. Willa Cather, who wrote movingly and generously of the farm and small town, always set her stories on these themes in times when the frontier cast its hopeful glow upon them. Although too honest a novelist to give way wholly to nostalgic sugarcoating, Cather's frontier tales have a vitality which would not ring true in the early twentieth century. She recognised that rural life, especially on the frontier, could destroy everything gentle or subtle, but she stressed the ways in which it nurtured strength and hope.

Cather's optimism was always in the form of a memoir. Her novels of her contemporary times present a much sadder picture. In *The Professor's House* the protagonist finally realizes that his life, seemingly so rewarding, has been trickled away in paths he would not have chosen. *A Lost Lady* disintegrates precisely when the dreams of the frontier, represented by her pioneering husband, are no longer possible.

These attitudes—boredom, nostalgia, a sense of futility, a loss of faith—form a personality which we have come to describe as modern. Although they became widespread only after World War I, Herman Melville shared them in the middle of the nineteenth century (Chapter 14). Nonetheless, the year 1920 serves as a useful dividing line in the American mind. Sinclair Lewis published his acid account of American small town life, *Main Street,* in that year. After the 1920 census a majority of the nation's inhabitants resided in urban areas. The Volstead Act established a creaky mechanism to enforce national prohibition. Women across the country were enfranchised in time to help elect Warren Harding. Radio Station KDKA, Pittsburgh, began regular broadcasts. In *This Side of Paradise* F. Scott Fitzgerald trumpeted the start of what was to be called the Jazz Age. Each of these events was something of an exclamation point. The changes which they punctuated had been occurring for some time, but after 1920 it was difficult for even the ostrich to ignore them.

Sinclair Lewis' *Main Street* lampooned the gods of middle America. The small town, where solid goodness was supposed to live, he saw as narrow and fearful. If you would be different, escape or die. Yet its inhabitants were not evil, in Lewis' view; they had been molded by an environment which twisted generosity into gossip and hunger for beauty into cheap sentimental prints. Small-towners lacked the security to afford luxuries, especially the luxury of diversity and change. Lewis showed how the robust optimism of the frontier

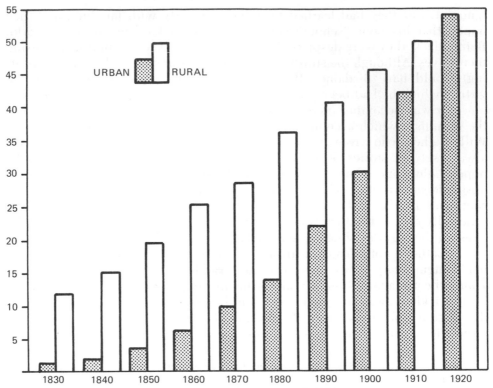

FIGURE 25-1. *Urban and Rural Population in Millions, 1830–1920*

had stagnated, and fear of the future made time-honored respectabilities a haven.

One of the small town's oldest terrors was the city, by now so visibly swamping the country. National prohibition was one of the last thrusts the country could make against the urban menace. By the time of the passage of the 18th Amendment, most rural states were already dry, and dry counties dotted the wet states. Enforcement here did not pose much of a problem, because local opinion supported abstention from alcohol. But enforcing the national law was to be impossible. Gangsters flourished, and respect for all law weakened. Drinking bad liquor acquired the special tingle reserved for the forbidden, and many drinkers learned to be both guilty and coy about its use. The supply of liquor continued undiminished, but only a scattering of aristocrats could use it in a civilized manner.

The prohibitionists did not foresee the results of their noble experiment. One which shocked them the most was the increasing number of women using alcohol. Prohibitionists had always been allied with women suffragists, and the Prohibition Party had endorsed women's suffrage as early as the 1870's, believing all women to be natural prohibitionists. Their disappointment could not have been greater than that of the dedicated women who labored for decades for the right to vote. Suffragists had hoped that it would result in a massive change in American life, that women's votes would be cast for peace and reform. They did not realize that but few women felt their interests to differ from those of their husbands. The only appreciable result of the suffrage was the destruction of feminism for two generations. For some time feminists had decided to ignore other issues and concentrate their energies on getting a Constitutional Amendment passed which would guarantee women the right to vote. That accomplished, they had few immediate goals. When they discovered that postwar American women were more interested in assuming heretofore masculine privileges (alcohol, tobacco, comfortable clothing, gaiety) than in forcing men to live according to the ideals of Victorian womanhood, most ruefully retired from activism. One who did not retire was birth control advocate Margaret Sanger, who worked within this changed context. Some Victorian feminists had favored birth control in the form of continence, not for the sake of limiting reproduction so much as to free women from the imposition of sex. They got nowhere. Mrs. Sanger realized that while few modern women any longer regarded sex as a burden, large families had become economically and socially undesirable in many households. Her efforts to eliminate the laws which made dissemination of birth control information and devices a crime were not very successful, but she performed a real service, both in letting people know that limitation of conception was possible, and in lifting the smokescreen of prudery which had surrounded the subject.

The uninhibited playfulness, the relaxation of moral norms, which popularly characterize the "roaring" twenties accompanied modern man's sense of futility. In part this resulted from the new media (see mid-Chapter 23) which burgeoned at this time, but some of the liveliest participants in the Jazz Age ascribed it to the war. American reaction to World War I was a combination of fervent self-righteousness and optimistic exuberance: a mixture typical in the past and not to be repeated again. There is still something of Tom Sawyer in a people who try to make the world safe for democracy by calling sauerkraut "liberty cabbage." But the real war—the war of mud and disease and mounds of corpses blotted out by the anonymity of artillery and gas rather than by a cavalier's shining sword—blighted innocence. The old simple convictions could not survive such gangrene. The pain of loss and disillusion touched closest to those who had borne the physical brunt of collapse—the veterans—but it was also severe for anyone with high hopes and wide eyes—alert young people, many adventurous children of the wealthy, and especially the ambitious and well educated. So there were many who felt driven to abandon naive high hopes and golden ideals, and they tried to forget their dismay at the loss by devoting themselves to a desperate pursuit of sensation.

But all was not so easy: the merrymakers had been reared to honor purpose and accomplishment. Even if idealism seemed ludicrous and achievement unattainable, they felt guilty at living without either. Two responses were common. The first was to escape to Europe, where hedonism was more respectable. American bustle, the outward sign of American optimism, had always seemed faintly ridiculous on the Continent anyway, and there were plenty of other exiles to cavort with. More importantly, the other Americans in Europe were presumably escaping from the same guilts, and their presence could therefore not reinforce anybody's self-hatred. Everyone was playing hooky together. But most of the revellers eventually went back to school, and often found that they had missed too many lessons. Europe was gay, but finally arid. To the expatriates, too many of the instinctively known features which make a society rich and rounded seemed remote or missing. Even the novels which came out of the exiled experience were about, not Europe, but the group of expatriates which shuttled between the Ritz Bar and the Riviera. Only Hemingway was able to write meaningfully about an actually foreign culture, but to do so he had to live in Spain long enough to make its symbols his own, and that meant not playing quite the same glamorous game. The returned exile had a double problem: the guilts that drove him away in the first place, and a new sense of isolation from a land once familiar that had changed in his absence. It is not surprising that alcoholism was rampant, and suicide and madness common. The only solution lay in a relearning process. America had to be rediscovered, and guilt recognized and put aside.

The second common response of guilty consciences was to lampoon abandoned gods. This produced useful social comment and delightful wit, and it was probably much more healthy than running away. It is no accident that the *New Yorker,* which for decades was to be America's finest comic magazine, started in the twenties. We laugh at things that don't scare us; if unreasonable fear persists, laughter might help exorcise it.

The majority of Americans weren't invited to the party of the intellectuals. H. L. Mencken called them the booboisie, and they provided plenty of opportunities for mirth. While attempting to cling to the old and the known, they acquired new and sensational devices for doing so. Aimee Semple MacPherson, the Scopes trial, and the Ku Klux Klan were much better targets for wit than sober churches or staid WCTU meetings. But these phenomena were manifestations of serious problems. Doubt and a sense of futility were not the exclusive property of the intellectuals; the death of old dreams was apparent to anyone who dared look at corpses. Most people dared not, for no alternative foundation to sanity presented itself. Their only hope was to turn back the clock.

The amazing success of Aimee Semple MacPherson, evangelist and faith healer, is symptomatic. First, she worked in Los Angeles, the symbolic and actual end of the line. California is as far as you can go; in the twenties many went. If the pot of gold isn't under a palm tree, you have nowhere else to look. Second, she achieved an enormous following by means of the radio. Depersonalization was stripping religion of much of its meaning, while sensation became more varied and less pungent. Third, her preaching in the flesh has been described as a wholly sensuous experience. Theologic content was nil, completing the descent from Edwards through Finney and Moody. (Perhaps Billy Graham represents still a further decline, but I doubt it.) The rich decor of Angelus Temple, and the flamboyant presence of the preacher counted for everything. As long as she mouthed soothing syrup which could be taken for old time religion she was satisfying both nostalgic hunger and the thirst for thrills.

The attitudes of the people of Tennessee which led them to prosecute John Thomas Scopes for teaching evolution were more consciously a clinging to old ways. When all the other established patterns of belief seemed to be crumbling, the dicta of religion must be held to the more rigidly. Furthermore, the heresy which most people associated with Darwin—that man was descended from the apes—was especially terrifying, as it erased a sense of superiority precious to people who doubt their own adequacy in a changing world. Actually, of course, neither Darwin nor Scopes (who believed that "evolution is easily reconciled with the Bible") mentioned the question of the origin of the human species at all. Most of the people of Tennessee—and of the rest of the South, and of the rural Midwest—were fundamentalists. They believed that the Bible was literally true. Most of them who had heard of evolution disbelieved it. But enacting and enforcing a law to prevent its teaching made them a laughing stock. The American Civil Liberties Union believed the law an outrage; they volunteered to finance the defense in a test case. Scopes, a biology teacher in Dayton, Tennessee, agreed to be prosecuted; the local merchants foresaw a great opportunity for civic boosterism. When Clarence Darrow, the agnostic antichrist to rural America, agreed to speak for the defense, and William Jennings Bryan, the defender of the faith, came into the case for the prosecution, the stage was set for Armageddon. Newspapers throughout the nation gave the Scopes trial front page coverage, usually only to reinforce the image of the South as a region populated by superstitious yokels. The trial climaxed when Bryan took the stand as an expert on the Bible, and Darrow hopelessly tangled him into a web of his own illogic. Scopes was convicted, (his conviction was later overturned on a technicality) the town of Dayton had its week of hoopla, fundamentalists felt vindicated by Bryan's oratory, and the rest of the country laughed.

The fears which lead people to barricade themselves against knowledge are more pitiable than amusing. During this period the same trepidations led to a more dangerous manifestation than anti-evolutionary efforts. The Ku Klux Klan, which for several years was the real power in several cities and states, arose out of terror and resentment (Document 25-3). We think of the Klan as an anti-black organization, but during the period of its greatest power anti-Catholicism was its most important tenet, with hatred of immigrants a strong subcurrent. Klansmen also attempted to enforce chastity and sobriety, and vocally supported certain Protestant churches. The nature of prejudice is worth some analysis in an attempt to explain the attractiveness of these beliefs: We hate and fear that which we find significantly different; if our own lives are frustrated and unsatisfactory for reasons which we cannot fathom, and our destiny seems to be out of our own control, then hatred of some other group provides a scapegoat. If we can then band together with others who feel the same way, and discharge our anxiety and hatred in a group, our sense of inadequacy will be lessened. Of course this behavior has no effect on the causes of our dissatisfaction, and is inevitably cruel to the persecuted group, but it may make us feel better if it temporarily releases significant frustrations.

The Klan had other attractions. Torchlight parades, burning crosses, masks, and secret rituals were all very exciting. For most of its members, that was excitement enough; they were never involved in actual violence. But for a few they were just an appetizer. Klansmen unquestionably perpetrated lynchings, burnings, and beatings. This violence, more than its unsavory racist and xenophobic beliefs (shared by a great many non-members), brought the Klan into disrepute. But the real outcry came when the Invisible Empire attempted to control politics. In several states and cities they succeeded. Those officials who were not themselves Klan members had to toe the Klan line to keep their posts. This brought the wrath of a batch of ejected politicians down upon the organization, and also exposed its flimsiness. For, possessing power, the Klan had no idea how to use it. Klan leaders soon began wrangling. Combined with financial tangles and scandals about the private morality of many of its luminaries, this infighting was enough to finish the Klan off. Its members drifted away, and by 1928 the organization no longer had any power.

The trial and execution of Nicola Sacco and Bartolomeo Vanzetti crystallized both the prejudices which spawned the Ku Klux Klan and the increasingly vocal opposition to them. The defendants were Italians, Catholics, and above all anarchists. They were convicted of murder in 1921, on faulty procedures. The defendants were convinced that they were being persecuted because they were Italian and radical. Vanzetti wrote to the governor of Massachusetts in 1927, "People don't seem to understand that Italians are unpopular anyway, especially if they are poor and laboring people. Their habits are not the habits of ordinary Americans, and they are suspected. They don't get the same chance before an American jury that an American would get. The jury cannot help being prejudiced against them, and then if on top of that the Italians turn out to be radicals, they have no show at all." By the time of the execution a great many Americans, and practically all the vocal intellectuals, agreed with Vanzetti, and exerted themselves to prevent the death of innocent men (Figure 26-3). They circulated petitions, marched in protest, took out newspaper ads. But the very publicity further circulated the defendants' radical tenets and solidified hatred of them as anarchists while it steadily eroded belief in their guilt in the crime of murder. Thus one group said that Sacco and Vanzetti must be freed, because they had been unjustly convicted of crimes they did not commit, and the rest of the people felt that they must be executed, since to release them would be to condone sins which were unfortunately not illegal.

In the year that Sacco and Vanzetti were executed, Marcus Garvey, leader of the first black movement with widespread lower class support, was deported. Unlike the Urban League and the NAACP, which strived for justice and equality within the American context, and catered almost exclusively to the middle classes of both races, Garvey's Universal Negro Improvement Association stressed racial pride, total segregation, and encouraged a return to Africa. At its peak its membership lay between 100,000 and 200,000, but as Garvey said, "No one will ever know accurately the membership of the Universal Negro Improvement Association, because every second Negro you meet, if not an actual member, is one in spirit." By the twenties American blacks had tried several roads toward the American dream. In the Deep South the subjugation of their working class members was complete. Lynchings declined drastically, but perhaps only because the population they were designed to impress had become sufficiently cowed. W. J. Cash suggests that the entry of the factory system into the South helped to discourage lynchings. Factory owners needed an orderly labor force according to Cash: "For that reason above all, therefore, the masters everywhere are against all excitements and disorders—against whatever operates to fix the attention and emotions of the workman powerfully enough to hinder him from falling swiftly into his robot groove when the whistle blows." In exchange, the factory workers got a "white only" guarantee for their jobs. Many blacks migrated north. There they found less legal segregation of public facilities, and frequently higher paying jobs. But they were crowded into stinking ghettos which made segregation a stronger reality, if not a legality, than in the South, and where their larger pay envelopes were offset by higher costs. Attempts to move out of their inadequate quarters or to use "unsegregated" facilities such as public swimming pools frequently brought on race riots. During World War I some 400,000 black men had joined the army, and some of them had gone overseas, but their patriotism (in this war as in all others before or since) brought no changes in their degraded position in the United States.

Clearly the white man's homilies didn't work for blacks. (They often didn't work for whites either, but this was not quite so obvious.) Moreover, as Garvey was the first leader to realize, it was humiliating for blacks to attempt to shape themselves upon white models, even if their efforts had met with success. They must find pride in being what they were—black. This entailed despising and avoiding everything white. As later groups have discovered

The Cleveland Museum of Art, Hinman B. Hurlbut Collection

FIGURE 25-2. *George Bellows,* Stag at Sharkey's

Stag at Sharkey's is an oil painting by George Bellows, vintage 1907. Bellows was twenty-seven years old, a migrant from Ohio to New York, where he studied with a well-known artist. Sharkey's gym was located across the street, and the young painter went there frequently, but he did not just quiescently loiter. The diagonal slashes across this canvas suggest that his imagination had been touched to the quick.

Nothing is gained by categorizing this type of painting as "realistic." A boxer who tried to fight from either of the stances portrayed here might get pasted hard and often. What is conveyed is in the first place an abstract design. It might be fun to trace (with a ruler if necessary) a straight line to show the directional thrust of each element in the picture. Such an exercise might help analyze the architectonics of the painting, but it omits a good deal. Thomas Eakins ("Ways to Study History XIX") was the palpable American ancestor of Bellows, and Eakins said that nature has no lines, only forms and colors.

which have adopted this attitude, such as the Black Muslims and the Black Panthers, it can lead to a greatly increased sense of dignity and honor. It also creates terror and insecurity among white people. Middle-class integrationist associations can be tolerated, even encouraged, but the economic and psychic well-being of many whites (especially those most anxious about their status) is bolstered by the presence of the black man as cheap labor and as a figure of scorn, and any group which says black people need be neither must be squashed. So Garvey was convicted of fraudulent use of the mails, deported (he was a West Indian), and the UNIA crumbled. It left small apparent effect, except perhaps the remnants of a changed consciousness which were to burst forth again in the 1960's.

Sacco and Vanzetti fired up American intellectuals; Garveyism they ignored. By the end of the decade all had abandoned the Jazz Age ebullience which had flourished in the post-war era. Disillusionment with the plasticity of sensationalism accompanied disillusion with idealism. Scott Fitzgerald's *The Great Gatsby* provides an example. His hero, Gatsby, has made a lot of money, and is leading a fabulous life in one of the flossy towns on Long Island, an abode of the very rich who have nothing to do and want to do it with éclat. Their life is paradise under the money-god, the acme of the American dream. Gatsby comes in search of Daisy, a girl whom he had loved when penniless and who married a stupid (but rich) young sportsman instead. She remembers Gatsby with affection, and his present exotic life as a party-giver to the famous titillates her, so his prospects look ripe. But in a stupid, careless automobile accident, she kills her husband's married mistress, and the shiny surface of all their lives cracks to expose the unsavory truth. Daisy and her husband have always been protected by money, and always will be. Neither good nor evil will ever touch them; they are impervious to responsibility or honest feeling. For them life is a party in a house with lots of servants to sweep up the champagne glasses you drop. Gatsby is more human, but he is a fraud. To be a success he had to invent his glamorous past, and even his name. Fitzgerald's novel ends on a note of deep disillusion: Perhaps the mechanistic technology that America has created necessitated mechanistic emotions which kill the soul; perhaps nature is better than people. The narrator surveys Gatsby's house, now deserted, and sees the land as it once had been, before civilization

---

A connection between these two artists is their mutual fascination with spectator sports. For their times and places, this range of subjects was up-to-date for an artist; by venturing into it, he faced the challenge of depicting experiences that were new in the United States with the growth of cities. Men had been brawling in the streets since the beginning of the nation, but sizeable audiences had not paid to watch them do it.

The two generations that span Eakins and Bellows establish another typical stance in American art. On this side of the Atlantic, the human figure had traditionally been fixed in repose, as it were; now an effort was made to combine the static design of the composition with the dynamics of the actors. No chauvinism is intended here; obviously Michelangelo and Rubens had coped with this problem; but now a new and more determined effort to tackle it was being made in America.

FIGURE 25-3. *Grant Wood*, American Gothic   Courtesy of the Art Institute of Chicago

erupted upon it, and visualizes an unspoiled beauty, a "fresh, green breast of the new world" which inspires his awe. The theme of nostalgia for something hopeful but irretrievably broken is restated here, as well as a hint that nature and human warmth will always be more important than artificial contrivances

Fear of technology as a stultifier is also present in the poetry of Hart Crane. His work shows how people are only able to have "experiences" while perceiving pieces of reality and interrelating them. The human mind takes in different kinds of perceptions—sight, smell, taste, sound, touch—at the same time; only by blending these disparate bits of fact does reality emerge, and reality is constantly changing. Mechanical instruments, such as the camera and the phonograph, not only categorize sensations but tend to freeze them in time. This can provide a useful record of events, and can be the medium of great art when a captured instant in time tells a truth which might be lost in motion, but it can also deaden the mind. After becoming habituated to receiving sensations neatly broken down and marshalled in rank, it can be difficult (as much of Crane's poetry suggests) to experience the natural rhythms of life behind a reality which has not been regimented. Moreover, technological aids make it easy to amplify visual and aural images to the point where they become so much noise. Then to experience anything you have to tune out most of the signals being beamed at you, and to repose in silence becomes almost impossible. Rest and peace, ever more desirable, become ever more unattainable. Crane wrote about the power of technology in New York city; he ended his career in suicide.

For many writers nature offered an escape from pointless urban bustle; rebirth seemed possible there. *Barren Ground,* Ellen Glasgow's account of life on a worn-out farm in Virginia, tells of death and of life. Dorinda Oakley's

---

American Gothic (1930) by Grant Wood is as widely known as any American painting of this century. Each word in the title deserves attention. The Gothic contour of the upper window suggests the Middle Ages, and Wood consciously had chosen as his guides the Flemish primitives of the fifteenth century; he wanted to be the Memling (d. 1495) of the Middle West. The curve of the window is accentuated by the man's eyebrows, the woman's hairline. These two people are blatantly American. The pitchfork symbolizes their rural orientation. Worn but scrupulously clean coveralls, meticulous braid on a jumper, a solid unsmiling stoicism—they all typified the Americans who conquered the prairies. Objects in this painting have a chiselled quality, as they do when you escape from urban smog and see the world etched by sunlight.

Wood was born to a poor farming family in Iowa in 1892. He sank so low that he lived for two years with his mother and sister in a 10′ × 16′ shanty in Cedar Rapids. He climbed back to a position of teaching art at the University of Iowa. He insisted that an artist should stick to the realities that he knew best, in this attitude resembling his predecessors Bingham and Homer (Figures 13-6 and 19-4). But shortly before he died of cancer in 1942, he told Thomas Hart Benton (Figure 27-2) "that when he got well he was going to change his name, go where nobody knew him, and start all over again with a new style of painting."

American Gothic with its pitchfork, prim, upright house, its aura of rectitude, might haunt some viewers now with the trilogy that the Third Reich prescribed for German women: *kinder, küche, kirche* ("kids, kitchen, church," or "family, home, and church").

family had inherited a thousand isolated worthless acres, but their ceaseless labor there cannot lift them out of poverty. Work and religion are the only alternatives to insanity. Dorinda herself is young and blooming, eager for life, but soon the betrayal of the characterless young man she loves destroys her capacity for emotional life, and she becomes, inwardly, as barren as the tired tobacco fields. Yet upon the death of her father she realizes that she need not go on in the traditional way, cultivating a bit of stunted tobacco, letting the piney woods take over a few more acres every year; the land is still good for dairying. She succeeds; for her the barren ground of the novel's title brings forth life in a new way. Her own rebirth is more hesitant and less complete. Although her capacity for passion is, like healthy tobacco, no longer possible, she regains affection and tenderness. Something is irretrievably lost, but the person, like the land, will recover what it can.

This view of nature as the refuge and the healer is superficially reminiscent of the Transcendentalists (Chapter 14), but it avoided most of their excesses. Nature was not necessarily lovely: often it was harsh and ugly. Its quiet and its logic were its important features. Nature provided an escape from hurry and from noise, where it was possible to sort out and discard trivialities. It reaffirmed life, and reduced man to a healthy humility in the face of his own weakness when unprotected by his contrivances.

During World War I, many American soldiers formed the vanguard for a wave of disillusionment that veered sharply away from the values held by hometown civilians in the United States. After the Armistice this rift, you might almost call it a chasm in society, deepened and broadened further. Only the trauma of the Great Depression could serve to institute new bridges between American dreams and disillusionment, and between the common man and the intellectual (Chapter 27). The modern intellectual now saw himself as alienated from his society because the culture itself was fragmented and contradictory. Revolt took many shapes. Veblen wrote ironically about the illusions that spurred his countrymen, about conspicuous consumption and emulation in conflict with the instinct of workmanship. John Dewey singled out the separation of schools from work. A dozen fine writers depicted the shallowness and flummery of their neighbors' ambitions. Encroachments by foreigners and Catholics and Jews and blacks stimulated the idiocies of the Ku Klux Klan. Xenophobia was symbolized by the Sacco-Vanzetti trial. Vast areas of religious commitment were contaminated and vulgarized, from the enthusiastical circuses of Aimee Semple MacPherson and Billy Sunday to the succotash of law and theology that constituted the Scopes trial. Occasionally the victims would try to strike back. Perhaps the most momentous of these counter-cultures would seem, in retrospect, to be the Universal Negro Improvement Association, but it had little impact in its brief life.

SOME NOTABLE EVENTS

1899   Thorstein Veblen, *The Theory of the Leisure Class.*

1900   Theodore Dreiser, *Sister Carrie.*

1905   Edith Wharton, *The House of Mirth.*

1914   Robert Frost, *North of Boston.*

1917   T. S. Eliot, "The Love-song of J. Alfred Prufrock."

1918   Willa Cather, *My Ántonia.*

1920   Volstead Act makes prohibition a reality.

Station KDKA, Pittsburgh, begins regular radio broadcasts.

Sinclair Lewis, *Main Street.*

Majority of Americans are urban dwellers.

1921   Sacco-Vanzetti trial.

1922   T. S. Eliot, *The Wasteland.*

Sinclair Lewis, *Babbitt.*

1923   Aimee Semple MacPherson founds Angelus Temple in Los Angeles.

1925   Scott Fitzgerald, *The Great Gatsby.*

Ellen Glasgow, *Barren Ground.*

Tennessee v. *John Thomas Scopes.*

1927   Deportation of Marcus Garvey.

Sacco and Vanzetti executed.

1929   Hart Crane, *The Bridge.*

Ways to Study History XXV

Be yourself. Obviously this suggestion follows from "Ways to Study History XX" and others. But of all the maxims that lead into these essays on methodology, this one is probably the most difficult to follow. To be human is to have experiences and reactions that—thank the Lord—you do not want to wear on your sleeve. However, the great books reveal an astounding amount about their authors. One of the greatest recent writers explained the matter thus: ". . . the quality that is necessary for the production of the art of literature is simply that of a personality of wide appeal. . . . The quality of literature, in short, is the quality of humanity. It is the quality that communicates, between man and man, the secret of human hearts and the story of our vicissitudes."

In this spirit, a book that ennobles the study of American history is W. E. B. DuBois, *The Souls of Black Folk* (1903). This brief exposition conveys more insight into the hidden life of the United States in the late nineteenth century than a library filled with monographs. Within its few pages are statistics, and autobiography, and biography, and poetry, many songs, sociology, psychology. Yet it adheres; it is a whole. It is a book that no human being could possibly have written, but one did.

DuBois lived for nearly a century. Born black in a small town in western Massachusetts soon after abolition (1868), he survived to die in an independent black state (Ghana) in 1963. In spite of the handicaps imposed because of his color, he did graduate work in Germany and at Harvard; the first volume in the Harvard Historical Monographs is his *The Suppression of the African Slave Trade* (1896). In addition to writing numerous other books, he taught in universities, worked as a magazine editor, helped to organize several groups aimed at overturning the racist system both in the United States and abroad. Nothing patronizing is meant in asserting that he was one of the dozen or so greatest Americans of this century.

Document 25-1

A balanced view of Andrew Carnegie is hard to achieve: his scope was enormous, and both his virtues and his vices bedazzle. Our concern here is limited to his efforts to help the common man to educate himself. In 1889 he was alarmed by demands for social reform, so he published a magazine article entitled "Wealth." In sum it might be labelled as paternalistic feudalism. But he did act upon the precepts published below; in the twenty years preceding his death in 1919, he gave $350 million to promote libraries, formal education, science, and world peace. Many boys remember the local Carnegie Library as a clean, well-lighted place, with books—and warm during cold winters for those too poor to buy fuel.

There remains, then, only one mode of using great fortunes; but in this we have the true antidote for the temporary unequal distribution of wealth, the reconciliation of the rich and the poor—a reign of harmony—another ideal, differing, indeed, from that of the Communist in requiring only the further evolution of existing conditions, not the total overthrow of our civilization. It is founded upon the present most intense individualism, and the race is prepared to put it in practice by degrees whenever it pleases. Under its sway we shall have an ideal state, in which the surplus wealth of the few will become, in the best sense, the property of the many, because administered for the common good, and this wealth, passing through the hands of the few, can be a much more potent force for the elevation of our race than if it had been distributed in small sums to the people themselves. Even the poorest can be made to see this, and to agree that great sums gathered by some of their fellow-citizens and spent for public purposes, from which the masses reap the principal benefit, are more valuable to them than if scattered among them through the course of many years in trifling amounts. . . .

Document 25-2

Charles Sanders Peirce in 1900 published this essay, "The Century's Great Men of Science." Beginning with the question, "How shall we determine that men are great?", he proceeded to distinguish the scientific attitude of his times from that of the preceding century.

The glory of the nineteenth century has been its science, and its scientific great men are those whom I mean to consider here. Their distinctive characteristic throughout the century, and more and more so in each succeeding generation, has been devotion to the pursuit of truth for truth's sake. In this century we have not heard a Franklin asking, "What signifies a philosophy which does not apply itself to some use?"—a remark that could be paralleled by utterances of Laplace, of Rumford, of Buffon, and of many other well-qualified spokesman of eighteenth-century science. It was in the early dawn of the nineteenth that Gauss (or was it Dirichlet?) gave as the reason of his passion for the Theory of Numbers that "it is a pure virgin that never has been and never can be prostituted to any practical application whatsoever." It was my inestimable privilege to have felt as a boy the warmth of the steadily burning enthusiasm of the scientific generation of Darwin, most of the leaders of which at home I knew intimately, and some very well in almost every country of Europe. . . .

To this self-effacement before the grandeur of reason and truth is traceable the greatness of nineteenth-century science, most obviously in mathematics. . . . I must not be led away from my point, to expatiate upon the reposefulness of the new mathematics, upon how it relieves us of that tiresome imp, man, and from the most importunate and unsatisfactory of the race, one's self. Suffice it to say that it is so reasonable, so simple, so easy to read, when the right view has once been attained, that the student may easily forget what arduous labors were expended in constructing the first convenient pathway to that lofty summit, that mastery over intricacies, far beyond that of the eighteenth-century master. . . .

Document 25-3

This brief account of the Ku Klux Klan's purposes, written by Hiram Wesley Evans, the Imperial Wizard, in 1926, relates some of the doubts and fears which led to its foundation. Nostalgia for a heroic past is expressed here, along with the hope that the past could somehow be revitalized. Bigotry arises out of feelings of inferiority, and in this case is strengthened by worship of the pioneering, "old-stock" ancestor. Rigid morality must be clung to, since the shifting ground of ethical ambiguity can only be comfortable to those who find security within themselves.

There is no need to recount the virtues of the American pioneers; but it is too often forgotten that in the pioneer period a selective process of intense rigor went on. From the first only hardy, adventurous and strong men and women dared the pioneer dangers; from among these all but the best died swiftly, so that the new Nordic blend which became the American race was bred up to a point probably the highest in history. This remarkable race character, along with the new-won continent and the new-created nation, made the inheritance of the old-stock Americans the richest ever given to a generation of men.

In spite of it, however, these Nordic Americans for the last generation have found themselves increasingly uncomfortable, and finally deeply distressed. There appeared first confusion in thought and opinion, a groping and hesitancy about national affairs and private life alike, in sharp contrast to the clear, straightforward purposes of our earlier years. There was futility in religion, too, which was in many ways even more distressing. Presently we began to find that we were dealing with strange ideas; policies that always sounded well, but somehow always made us still more uncomfortable.

Finally came the moral breakdown that has been going on for two decades. One by one all our traditional moral standards went by the boards, or were so disregarded that they ceased to be binding. The sacredness of our Sabbath, of our homes, of chastity, and finally even of our right to teach our own children in our own schools fundamental facts and truths were torn away from us. Those who maintained the old standards did so only in the face of constant ridicule.

Document 25-4

Robert Frost (1874–1963) was unquestionably one of the half-dozen greatest American poets of this century. Although he lived the first ten years of his life in San Francisco, his image is inseparable from New England, for reasons that this poem should demonstrate. "After Apple-Picking" was contained in Frost's second book, *North of Boston* (1914) when the author was already 40 years old. He never earned a college degree, and, while he taught for decades in universities, he will always seem remote from academia. He was also apart from modern poetry in that his works do not need the abundance of literary allusions that T. S. Eliot and Wallace Stevens used. Frost won the Pulitzer Prize for American Poetry four times—never without deserving it.

My long two-pointed ladder's sticking through a tree
Toward heaven still,
And there's a barrel that I didn't fill
Beside it, and there may be two or three
Apples I didn't pick upon some bough.
But I am done with apple-picking now.
Essence of winter sleep is on the night,
The scent of apples: I am drowsing off.
I cannot rub the strangeness from my sight
I got from looking through a pane of glass
I skimmed this morning from the drinking trough
And held against the world of hoary grass.
It melted, and I let it fall and break.
But I was well
Upon my way to sleep before it fell,
And I could tell
What form my dreaming was about to take.
Magnified apples appear and disappear,
Stem end and blossom end,
And every fleck of russet showing clear,
My instep arch not only keeps the ache,
It keeps the pressure of a ladder-round.
I feel the ladder sway as the boughs bend.
And I keep hearing from the cellar bin
The rumbling sound
Of load on load of apples coming in.
For I have had too much
Of apple-picking: I am overtired
Of the great harvest I myself desired.
There were ten thousand thousand fruit to touch,
Cherish in hand, lift down, and not let fall.

For all
That struck the earth,
No matter if not bruised or spiked with stubble,
Went surely to the cider-apple heap
As of no worth.
One can see what will trouble
This sleep of mine, whatever sleep it is.
Were he not gone,
The woodchuck could say whether it's like his
Long sleep, as I describe its coming on,
Or just some human sleep.

PART VI

Living with the
Permanent Revolution: *1929–*

The Great Depression and Its Politics

President Hoover, like Martin Van Buren a century earlier, can be regarded as a victim of circumstances. Each man had barely entered the White House when a depression hit the economy, and each bore the blade of resentment. But both deserved it, for in their earlier offices they had sanctioned federal policies that helped to bring on and aggravate the financial crises. Van Buren did not argue against the abolition of the Second Bank of the United States, or the application of the Specie Circular. Nor did Hoover as secretary of commerce oppose the Fordney-McCumber protectionist tariff measure or the fiscal program of Secretary of the Treasury Andrew W. Mellon. One of the half dozen or so wealthiest men in the nation, Mellon's fortune stemmed from one of the true "monopolies"; the Aluminum Corporation of America (Alcoa) was the sole seller of its product. He was also a pioneer owner of the Spindletop well and other Southwestern oil properties.* At the treasury, his policy was to

---

*One year soon somebody will publish a brilliant book about the Mellon family. Of all the large cities in the United States since World War II, none other was dominated by one man as Richard Mellon held sway in Pittsburgh. Wilmington, Delaware was DuPont, but it was family, not individual.

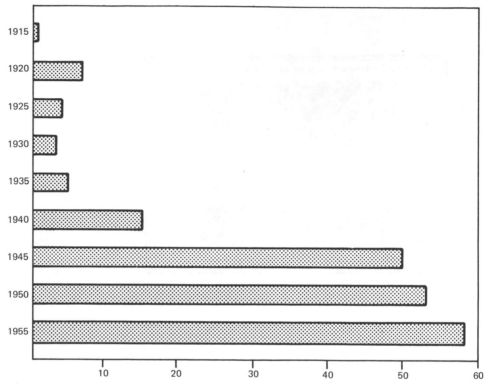

FIGURE 26-1. *Millions of Federal Income Tax Returns Filed, 1915–1955*

run a steady budgetary surplus and pay off the federal debt. At the same time he wanted to cut taxes, especially on fat cats like himself. Due to the rising national income he was able to combine these aims. Forced to compromise in 1924, Mellon came back to win with the Revenue Act of 1926, which cut the maximum surtax on high incomes from 40 to 20 per cent, wiped out the gift tax, cut the estate tax in half. If the major cause of the depression was a maldistribution of income (I think it was), this tax policy that had Hoover's tacit consent must bear a lot of blame.

Hoover's interpretation of the depression did not agree with mine. He had three theses. For months he contended that it did not exist; merely a flurry on the stock market. In his speech accepting the nomination Hoover had said, "We in America today are nearer to the final triumph over poverty than ever before in the history of any land." A campaign slogan had proclaimed, "A chicken in every pot and two cars in every garage." If Hoover was blind, probably he was not deaf; he might have been hearing the pundits of the country. From a Harvard worthy:

The great war produced a number of political revolutions in Europe. It has not yet produced an economic revolution. The only economic revolution now under way is going on in the United States. It is a revolution that is to wipe out the distinction between laborers and capitalists by making laborers their own capitalists and by compelling most capitalists to become laborers of one kind or another, because not many of them will be able to live on the returns from capital. This is something new in the history of the world.

Words of wisdom indeed. Financial analyst Roger Babson (one of the few who sobered up before the crash came) argued for Hoover's election on the grounds that it would assure the prolongation of prosperity. The president of a renowned research organization, the National Industrial Conference Board, proclaimed: "There is no reason why there should be any more panics." Then came the panic.

When it was no longer possible to blink away the hard times, Hoover took two new gambits. He began to admit that the times were troubled, but announced that they would soon cease to be so: "Prosperity is just around the corner." Somehow the corner kept getting farther away. Another Hoover device, baldly chauvinistic, was to proclaim that the American economy had no difficulties of its own. No domestic problem existed; the collapse was strictly an import from the corrupt and decadent foreigners, particularly in Europe. Admittedly, the nationalistic programs of alien nations did not make the American situation easier. However, for the United States as for its president, most dislocations were self-made. The generalization will have to come up in regard to the New Deal, but it is so crucial that it will bear stating more than once. Although Americans can find many episodes in their history to inspire pride, quite a few others should awaken shame. One of the worst episodes is the twelve years from 1929 to 1941. When a majority of the population was confronted with a variety of crises, the national intelligence disappeared in a miasma of rhetoric. An honorable handful spoke for rational and humane actions, but men in power chose not to hear them.

A proper preliminary to further consideration of the economic policies of the Hoover administration is a glance at the international and domestic context. Many nations that relied chiefly on exports of agricultural products or minerals to maintain their foreign balance of payments were confronted now by falling prices on the world market and began to depreciate their currencies. This expedient made the import duties of other countries inadequate, so they in turn resorted to quotas on imports, which by 1933 were systematized by most of the important trading nations plus the British Commonwealth. Next came systematic exchange control—a process whereby the movement of the government's currency into or especially out of the country is impeded or blocked. In the first years of the Great Depression, Great Britain used these devices more than any other nation. She had been subsidizing exports of certain commodities since World War I and now these arrangements were

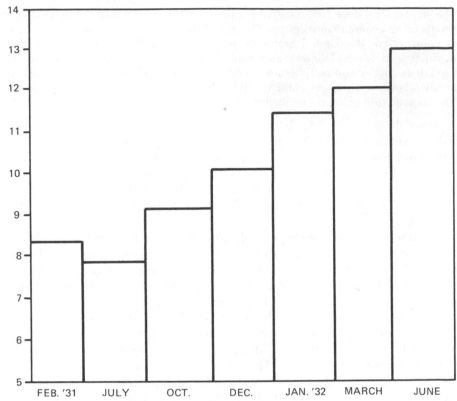

FIGURE 26-2. *Unemployment, 1931–1932 (in millions of workers)*

extended. In addition, a conference at Ottawa, Canada, in 1932 imposed Imperial Preference, which discriminated against goods from without the British sphere. True, these tidal waves from overseas were bad. Maybe the lack of pressure at home was worse. The executive committee of the American Federation of Labor announced in 1931: "Realization of the pernicious effects of wage reductions has prevented a widespread liquidation of wages as we had in the depression of 1921. Growing adherence to the high-wage principle, strengthened by the President's stand against wage cuts, has brought effective support from the leading industrialists of the country." More guff. By the autumn of 1931, when these pronunciamentoes came from the chief labor body, the joke had ended.

Even the president, somewhat to the left of the labor leaders, had recognized a year earlier that the depression was rather serious. He had therefore in October, 1930, appointed the President's Emergency Committee for Employment. One of the three members of this board, a renowned executive of an advertising agency, had expressly warned against use of the word "*un*employment." Two prior attempts had been made to get the Red

Cross to take action, especially in the Appalachian coal fields that had been stricken by drought as well as recession, but this charitable institution refused because depression was "not an Act of God" and thus outside its boundaries. (Who ever put God under their jurisdiction?) Then national action seemed essential, but Hoover hated the idea of laying the problem before Congress. The ultimate funding of the federal relief agency was $157,000, to last for nearly a year. Within that time the farce was ended, the committee disbanded. In the words of a Philadelphia social worker, "As a result of the policy of drift . . . our government will be compelled, by the logic of inescapably cruel events ahead of us, to step into the situation and bring relief on a large scale. . . . Private philanthropy . . . is virtually bankrupt in the face of great disaster." The end of an era seemed in sight.

Until the fall of 1931, it was widely believed that the bad times were similar to periods in the past; no need to get in a flap about the situation. That view became preposterous. Estimates of unemployment varied among contemporaries, and they will therefore continue to vary among historians. The graph in Figure 26-2 shows some that seem reliable, but to most readers these figures will seem ludicrously abstract. An effort should be made to break them down and put them into context. In January, 1932—the height of the season— President Sidney Hillman of the Amalgamated Clothing Workers said that only 10 per cent of his members in New York City had jobs. For the Ford Motor Company, employment went from 128,142 in March, 1929, to 37,000 in August, 1931.

The level of abstraction can be brought to a more concrete level. One of the great athletes of my lifetime has been Stan Musial, who came from a steel town, Donora, in Pennsylvania. With a population in March, 1932, of 13,900, it had 277 persons with jobs. His need to escape was severe. But there were worse spots. In Williamson County, Illinois, in the town of Coello, two people had remunerative employment in a population of 1,350. Now we can bring the level of abstraction down to an even sharper focus. At school in the coal fields, a teacher asked a little girl if she was ill. The pupil replied that she was just hungry. The teacher suggested that she go home and eat. The girl said, "It won't do any good . . . because this is sister's day to eat." Do not permit yourself to believe that incidents like this one are chosen at random; millions of people could tell comparable stories.

The point might be reinforced by anecdotes that are doubtless apocryphal and that admittedly are chosen at random. Here are two. Hoover asks Mellon: "Will you lend me a nickel? I want to phone a friend." Mellon answers: "Here are two nickels. Phone all your friends." The other concerns a man who was considered the greatest baseball player of them all, Babe Ruth, who was engaged in his annual holdout for a better contract. In 1932, he wanted $80,000. After training season had been in action for weeks, it became apparent that none of the lesser executives on the New York Yankees could bring Ruth to terms. Negotiations relapsed onto the desk of the brewery head

Ben Shahn. *Scotts Run, West Virginia.*
Tempera on cardboard. 22¹/₄ × 27⁷/₈.
Collection Whitney Museum of American
Art

FIGURE 26-3.   *Ben Shahn,* Scotts Run, West Virginia
     Ben Shahn had not turned 35 when he burst into the consciousness of the art world in 1932 by exhibiting more than twenty paintings about the Sacco-Vanzetti case (see mid-Chapter 25 on the scapegoat impulse). The series certainly showed indignation. It pointed to stony-eyed judges, to self-righteous review boards. But the content was far from being one-dimensional; Shahn's outrage was toned down by irony and even by touches of humor. Simplicity was present not in the mood but in the technique of the artist. His surfaces tended to be flat; his forms reminiscent of some Picassos in the broad areas of a solid color. His pigment was gouache, a type of water color. In his addiction to this medium, Shahn was the chief exponent since Winslow Homer (Figure 19-4).
     Shahn also resembles Homer in that both men served an early term of apprenticeship to a lithographer. But these similarities came in spite of a vast difference in backgrounds. Homer was

who also owned the Yankees. When their conference began, Ruth kept repeating that he wanted $80,000. Finally the owner shouted, "Babe, that's more than the president gets." Ruth thought it over: "So what? I had a better season than Hoover."

Most poor folks had gags to jolly each other along; when your limbs are shriveled because you cannot get food, when they shake because you cannot buy fuel, laughter becomes the only essential that can be had. Men of power did not laugh; they began at last to admit that much of the furiously invented propaganda was mere ruse. For eighteen months they had frequently used a line that said—well, while employment has fallen a bit, hourly pay has held up. Then the president of U.S. Steel said: "We are living in a fool's paradise if we think that every steel manufacturer in the U.S. has maintained . . . the current rates of wages; it has not been done." His own company in September, 1931, cut wage rates by 10 per cent. General Electric, U.S. Rubber, major textile and coal firms fell into line. Ford put through a 25 per cent reduction. The railroads got the Brotherhoods to agree to a 10 per cent decrease. In New York and Chicago the building trades accepted 25 per cent less. Every stopper had gone down the drain. Nearly every strike was in protest against these pay cuts. Nearly every strike failed. But resentments made manifest can force adaptations. The United Mine Workers, long one of the routine members of the AFL, declared for "unemployment reserves" in January, 1932. The tradition of voluntarism—trade unions should have nothing to do with government— was caving in. The Federation of Labor in New York state came out for jobless insurance.

The governor, Franklin D. Roosevelt, was already on the scene; in August, 1931, he called it a "social duty" for the state to step in when "widespread economic conditions render large numbers of men and women incapable of supporting either themselves or their families because of circumstances beyond their control which make it impossible for them to find remunerative labor." That was good sense, but its impact did not compare to

---

old-stock Yankee, Shahn an immigrant from Lithuania. Homer painted the seas and the woods, Shahn focused on city playgrounds and the bombed-out debris of war. It had to be the latter man, not the former, who tried to depict the jetsam of the depression in this painting of *Scotts Run, West Virginia* (1937). In his last years Shahn turned from industrial landscape to subjects that must be called religious, whether Moses Maimonides or a wheat field.

The variety of Shahn's work is impressive, from jacket designs for paperbound books to monumental murals. But his ambition was steady: "I have always believed that the character of a society is largely shaped and unified by its great creative works, that a society is molded upon its epics, and that it imagines in terms of its created things—its cathedrals, its works of art, its musical treasures, its literary and philosophical works. One might say that a public may be so unified because the highly personal experience is held in common by the many individual members of the public."

his "forgotten man" speech the next spring (8 April, 1932) when he set forth several planks: (a) protect the purchasing power of farmers; (b) save home-owners from losing their houses by foreclosure of mortgages; (c) negotiate tariff reciprocity to win more foreign markets. Thus early FDR emerged as what he was. These three planks must be supplemented by many others at later points in the story. They do reveal, however, his orientation. It aimed at the solid citizen in danger of being treated badly. Folks should be able to keep what they toiled to earn: farmers their farms, homeowners their homes.

Roosevelt's flexibility appealed to "the boys"; meaning the city bosses, "the pols," the small gang in the smoke-filled room at the nominating convention. FDR's attachment to this crew may seem transparent—they had votes—but that is not enough to say. He liked them; they talked the language he knew best. Following a stunt that Lincoln's managers had used as a device to win the presidency, the Democratic boss of the Bronx had employed it to make Roosevelt governor. He held back every single return from his borough until all the rest of the state had reported. When everybody knew what FDR's deficit was, the Bronx made it up.

Roosevelt knew how to use such tactics—and how to beat them. As delegates arrived at the Democratic national convention in Chicago, June, 1932, local boss Edward J. Kelly thought he had everything set. Passes to enter the galleries of the hall were reserved for supporters of Alfred Smith. They rooted and hooted for their champeeeeeen. A brilliant diversion was begun by Senator Huey Long of Louisiana. Clearly a majority of the members were more or less committed to Roosevelt. But for a century, since its first convention in 1832, the party had required a two-thirds majority to make a nomination. Smith and others had substantial support. So why not try to abolish the two-thirds rule? The rule would remain for another four years, but the controversy stirred so much dust that Roosevelt sneaked through. Astute observers were not enchanted. The hallelujahs for FDR that came later were to come—later. One jaundiced commentator wrote: "I have seen many conventions, but this is one of the worst. It is both the stupidest and the most dishonest." An incisive columnist wrote that Roosevelt's main qualification was that he was a young man who wanted very much to be president.

The pundits got scotched. Radio was used as never before (Chapter 27). The Democratic candidate put together a staff of academics who were at best shrewd and at worst pompous; the mouthpiece turned out to have a flowing mellifluous voice. Even more important in beating the Republicans were the faults they could not conquer: their candidate, and their record. Hoover had too many principles to be a strong contender. In the race for the White House a man has to hang loose and easy. With his starched collars and his immobile jowls, Hoover couldn't swing it. The image he projected from a crystal-set radio was stern and demanding, but personality can be emphasized too much. His record killed his chances.

We can only sample the conditions and actions by which the Hoover administration earned apoplectic aversion. An advertisement for a market in Los Angeles in September, 1932, listed these bargains:

Tomatoes, 8 lbs.	5¢
Potatoes, 18 lbs.	25¢
Oranges, 3 dozen	10¢
Lettuce, per head	1¢
Spring lamb chops, lb.	12¹/₂¢
Hamburger, lb.	5¢

Any shopper today might be thrown into paroxysms of glee by sight of such a list, but imagine what it was doing to potato growers or ranchers in 1932. Another bloc of voters that merits attention is the veterans of World War I. Soon after the Armistice they began agitating for a "bonus." In 1924 they got the bill through Congress—with a hitch; payment was to be deferred for twenty years. With the depression, the vets in many localities started agitating for payment *now*. About mid-May, 1932, they started the spontaneous Veterans Bonus March on Washington. Uncoordinated when they left home, they quickly got organized after they reached the capital and set up several shanty colonies or moved into vacant federal office buildings. A showdown came on 28 July. After some relatively minor skirmishes involving the evacuation of government property, the president ordered the army to come over from Fort Myers, Virginia. The contingent was headed by General Douglas MacArthur, Major Dwight D. Eisenhower, and young George S. Patton. It included four troops of cavalry, four companies of infantry, a squadron of mounted machine guns, six tanks. Before they finished, they had evicted the Bonus Expeditionary Force from its encampments. They had killed two men and sprayed a lot of gas around; total casualties could not possibly be determined. The incident probably offended more voters than any other of Hoover's term in office.

The forcibly retired president would rather sourly comment twenty years later in his *Memoirs*: "As we expected, we were defeated in the election." Surely one of the understatements of the decade. The results in November, 1932, stood thus:

	Popular Votes	Per cent of Popular Vote	Electoral Vote
Democrats	22,809,638	57.41	472
Republicans	15,758,901	39.66	59
Others	1,163,181		

This time, as a wag had said of the Democratic nominee in 1924, Hoover lost by acclamation. He won only six states, all in New England or the Middle

States, all except Pennsylvania on the small side. Roosevelt carried more counties than any preceding presidential candidate: 2,721. Hoover had less than 15 per cent as many. But in regard to popular votes, FDR did not set other records in 1932: Harding had shown better in 1920, and Roosevelt, Lyndon Johnson, and Nixon would set superior marks later. Two addenda to these statistics should be noted. The Socialists again neared the million mark. The Prohibitionists still had a dwindling following. The Communists, who would play a strategic role in the next years, could gather barely 100,000 votes. Second, Roosevelt came to the White House with huge majorities in both houses of Congress: nearly 3 to 1 in the Representatives, nearly 2 to 1 in the Senate.

When Roosevelt became president in March, 1933, his massive party support in Congress would have followed him nearly anywhere he wanted to go. Some of his measures would soon meet strong roadblocks by the federal courts, and it would take time to tear down those barricades. But initially his problem was not that he was obstructed by the legislature; he even got a helping hand from several Republicans. His quandary was that he had no ideas and few commitments. Therefore he seldom knew which direction to take. Much has been made of the Brain Trust that he had gathered around him during the campaign and interregnum. In fact, they had little power (academics usually tend to overestimate the influence they can have as wheelers and dealers in Washington.) Roosevelt very much wanted to be re-elected in 1936. As he saw matters, the route to that goal did not lie with a few professors; it lay with the old machines in the South and in urban centers. He could and did ditch Raymond Moley of Columbia. He would not dream of junking Frank Hague of Jersey City or Ed Flynn of the Bronx or Senator Bankhead of Alabama or Little Joe Robinson of Arkansas or Ed Crump in Memphis. It was Roosevelt who picked John Nance Garner of Texas to be vice president. When the head of the CIO, John L. Lewis, memorialized Garner as "a whiskey-drinking, cigar-smoking, poker-playing, evil old man," he was not wrong. But to FDR, Garner could help to sweep the South, and he was not wrong either.

The celebrated Hundred Days that launched the Roosevelt regime were at best a mixed bag. Look at the first three pieces of "emergency" legislation. A major contention of this book is that breakdown of the banking system is indeed an emergency in a modern society (Document 26-1). The most powerful member of the House of Representatives on monetary matters had reached the point of being deliberately insulting on the floor of that body; in his state, he related, a banker tried to marry a white woman and got lynched.* Every bank in the nation was shut down. Stockholders in member banks of the Federal Reserve had a special reason to want to unload their holdings; the law

---

*This flippant anecdote has racist connotations that are contemptible. But it tells a great deal about attitudes toward bankers at the time.

provided that if a bank was not able to pay off its depositors, each share of stock could be assessed at twice its value. Under these circumstances, it might have been possible to establish public control over the volume of the circulating media. (See Document 26-1.) The president had no inclination to do that. The Emergency Banking Act of 1933 did little beyond setting conditions under which a bank could reopen. Since only one copy of the bill had been prepared, it was read aloud to the House. Forty minutes were allowed for debate. From the convening of Congress until adoption by the Senate took less than eight hours. One commentator approvingly notes: "Not for years had Congress acted with such speed and decision." (When Huey Long used similar tactics in Louisiana, he was either demagogue or dictator.)

The other bills in this lamentable trio should provoke laughter. In sequence, the next was the Economy in Government Act, meant to cut federal salaries pretty much across the board. The president was concerned that the national government, with a debt of $5 billion, would go bankrupt, just as a private household will go on the reefs if it spends beyond its means. An average citizen today might reason that a reduction of incomes is not the right method to combat a depression, but the message did not reach Roosevelt. The third of these vital measures legalized the manufacture of beer with an alcoholic content of no more than 3.2 per cent; a revival of the breweries would doubtless help to add jobs.

In all fairness, the administration's proposals did improve. The remainder of the Hundred Days—in fact, the first two years of the New Deal—can be seen from a perspective suggested at that time by the columnist Walter Lippmann. His thesis was that the more important revolution in American society had happened in 1929, not four years later. Lippmann's preoccupation was with federal policy toward the economy of the nation. He concluded that the crucial question was whether the national government should take responsibility for mitigating or even curing a depression. If it once decided that question in the affirmative, its involvement in the economy would be continuous because a required corollary was that it would intervene in prosperous times as well. For some decades, a few city or state governments had advanced programs of public works to relieve unemployment, but even such a humanitarian governor as Altgeld would not accept this notion during the hard times after 1893. Hoover did accept it, so Lippmann argues, and Roosevelt extended his practices, as Hoover himself would probably have done had he won re-election. By this argument a widely used pamphlet with the title *The New Deal—Revolution or Evolution?* is made absurd. The dichotomy dissolves.

The relation of continuity to change is one of the central questions in historical study. Here is a chance to tackle it. What similarities and dissimilarities exist between the Hoover and Roosevelt administrations? The angle of approach soon will be to ask what policies were instituted at various times to aid special segments of the society. First a couple of matters that seem to me relatively marginal should be at least acknowledged. One is the contrast of personality. Hoover may have seemed dignified and reliable to the wealthy businessmen with whom he had associated for so many years, but to ordinary voters he seemed frigid; he never came across. Even in 1928 he did not run a campaign, he stood for office. It was Republican prosperity and the standing GOP vote that put him in the White House. One might have said about him (as Theodore Roosevelt's daughter did say about Coolidge) that he had been weaned on a pickle. FDR was the opposite, all smiles, his honeyed voice over the radio, homey stories about his dog Fala, the appeal of his wife Eleanor. His affection for striking phrases may often have lured him into nonsense, but it helped to capture the electors. Another implement that has done heavy duty for Roosevelt is the contention that he was a master politician. If the analyst limits his gaze to questions of tactics, this is true. Besides his gift for phrasemaking, FDR knew when to time his moves. Hoover in contrast was often pompous, and he could not sense when the rules of the game had altered. Roosevelt was expert at gaining office, surely the elementary requirement for a politician. By 1932 he had worked at the game full-time for more than twenty years, whereas Hoover was in the novitiate. But when the discussion shifts to a deeper level of meaning and speaks of strategy, the gap between the two becomes less clear. Neither can be put beside Jefferson or Van Buren or Lincoln or Mark Hanna as an architect of a major innovation in the structure of American politics. Neither wanted such a change. Considerable metamorphosis was forced on FDR by protests in streets and shops; he did not promote it and damped its fires on frequent occasions.

On to federal policy. The entire subject of foreign relations and World War II must remain until Chapter 28; moreover, the presentation here of domestic affairs will omit social and intellectual history (Chapter 27); further, it halts at 1940. The main suggestion to be made here is that a modification of the direction of thrust from Washington occurred in the spring of 1935. Here we can only dissect the policy organs actually created to deal with important problems, in this order: (a) farmers, (b) the unemployed, (c) industrialists, (d) bankers and investors, (e) homeowners, (f) hydroelectric power and related public works.

Nowhere do the intellectual deficiencies of the New Deal show worse then in its agricultural program. A common gibe has been that the men in Washington had not worked the land; however, this is a defect that can be overcome. But ignorance becomes lethal when it has a young urbanite in a policy meeting pounding on the table to contend that more must be done for the macaroni growers. Coupled with ignorance was infatuation with an obsolescent myth: the American yeoman, the garden of the world, and the family farm all became an intertwined into a bemusing jumble. Because they embodied such a horde of mistakes, the agricultural policies may be taken as a prototype of the analytical failures of the New Deal. The benefits paid under various schemes in the past forty years have gone overwhelmingly to corporations or to banks or to big ranchers or to the wealthy who own plantations along the delta, and not to operators of the family farm. A later vice president (Richard M. Nixon) was indiscreet when he said that the solution to the farm problem was to eliminate the farmer, but he spoke the historical truth. As the *Canadian Magazine* stated the situation in a feature article in 1971: "Good-bye to the Family Farm." (See also Figure 29-3.)

The idea for "farm parity" stemmed from the head of a manufacturer of farm implements, who declared: "You can't sell a plow to a busted customer." Various schemes were put forward for raising the income of farmers to the point where they could buy the same comparative quantity of industrial goods as on the eve of World War I; that is, farm prices and manufacturing prices should rise or fall together. A technique often proposed was to establish a two-price system, by which alleged surpluses of staple crops would be dumped in foreign markets for whatever sums they would bring, to the end of maintaining a floor under prices in the United States. The McNary-Haugen bill, with other elaborate provisions but resting on this mode of reasoning, had been twice passed by Congress and twice vetoed by Coolidge (1927, 1928). The Hoover administration even before the Great Crash had felt compelled to set up a revolving fund of $500 million to make loans to farm cooperatives. Hoover objected quite rightly that the scheme of foreign dumping would further stimulate overproduction of the staples; he might have said also that it would provoke retaliation.

But this scheme became one leg in the New Deal stool. With it they combined three others: federal price fixing, limitation of acreage planted to certain crops, and marketing agreements. By the Agricultural Adjustment Act (AAA) of 1933, the president was permitted to choose among these alternatives. Emphasis was put on the limitation of acreages for selected staples. Hitches developed. The law did not clear Congress until 12 May, when crops had been planted, shoats and calves had been dropped. So it was deemed necessary to plow wheat and cotton under, to burn fields of corn, to convert animals into fertilizer. Folly ran riot. Often, the more fertilizer, the higher the yield per acre. For corn and wheat, the price more than doubled from 1932 to 1934; the price of cotton did double. But the output per acre of cotton rose slightly. The year 1934 was the beginning of a severe drought and the dust storms that would remain for years; the weather probably had more influence on crop reductions than did the federal actions. Further, the deliberate destruction of foodstuffs while millions of Americans went hungry was hard for folks to understand. Secretary of Agriculture Henry A. Wallace said that he could tolerate his own behavior only "as a cleaning up of the wreckage from the old days of unbalanced production. . . . The plowing under of 10 million acres of growing cotton in August, 1933, and the slaughter of 6 million little pigs in September . . . were not acts of idealism in any sane society. They were emergency acts made necessary by the almost insane lack of world statesmanship during the period from 1920 to 1932." A Republican congressman offered sharp rebuttal:

> I think of all the damnable heresies that have ever been suggested in connection with the Constitution, the doctrine of emergency is the worst. It means that when Congress declares an emergency there is no Constitution. This means its death. It is the very doctrine that the German chancellor is invoking today in the dying hours of the parliamentary body of the German republic, namely, that because of an emergency it should grant to the German chancellor absolute power to pass any law, even though that law contradicts the constitution of the German republic. Chancellor Hitler is at least frank about it.

Only a fool would try to equate FDR with Hitler. But even in the United States, events would run beyond the proclamation of an emergency by Congress, so that presidents took to issuing extraordinary decrees. The case of the "relocation" of Japanese-Americans in World War II will be examined in Chapter 28.

It must be conceded that coercion was not the original intent of AAA. But implementation quickly meant a departure from voluntarism. Power lay with landowners and processing corporations. When young lawyers in the administration tried to maintain some rights for tenants and small farmers, they were angrily purged by their superiors (The victims included Alger Hiss, see Chapter 29). A graduate of an Ivy League law school could be quickly placed in another job; those who were smashed to earth were sharecroppers and other poor folks. Croppers were to get half of federal benefit payments on their portion of the tillage, whereas hired hands were to get nothing. A ruthless landowner had little trouble in reducing a cropper to a hired hand. For years many mortgages, especially in the cotton South, had been in arrears. Banks had not foreclosed because no market existed for the land; their wisest course was to forebear in the hope of eventually being repaid. AAA opened a new opportunity. Banks foreclosed, then withdrew the land from production and collected federal benefits. These were used to displace additional men by buying new machinery. Added efficiency helped to undersell private operators and reduce them to tenancy (see Figure 26-4).

Even earlier, the New Deal had moved to help the jobless. In trying to cope with this tragic difficulty, men in office did come up with creative approaches. The failure was that the administration as a whole did not take these innovations, test them, throw out the bad ones and then expand the useful ones. For instance, the first major statute on unemployment was the Civilian Conservation Corps, which can be used to mark the creation of the multi-purpose program. It aimed to achieve not one goal but many. It benefited society for generations to come by taking idle males off the streets; by the spring of 1934 a quarter of a million families had watched a son or two go off to CCC camp. In addition to the pleasure that wages added to his own life, each youth sent dollars back home. Work in the outdoors helped to maintain

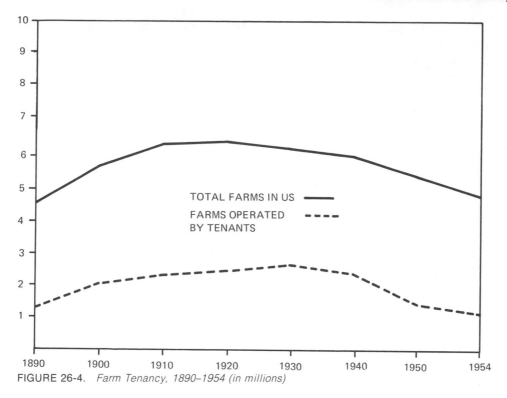

FIGURE 26-4. *Farm Tenancy, 1890–1954 (in millions)*

the health of these young men. The work found for them was creative; the only just criticism might be that it had been too long deferred. Systematic reforestation of the Great Plains and the West was begun by the CCC—but not soon enough to prevent the dust storms of the thirties. (The terror of these storms cannot be exaggerated. An example that sticks in my vision comes from a letter written to *The Nation* in 1937 by a farmwife in Oklahoma. She reported that jackrabbits squatted around her house waiting for food. They could no longer find their own, because they had been blinded by the slashing dust and sand.) A later critic has protested that CCC purposes did not go as far as they should have, with particular reference to schooling of the enrollees. The figures show that he has a point: 5,000 eighth-grade certificates were issued, over 1,000 high-school diplomas. Compared to the number involved, these achievements seem minor. Eight thousand men learned to read and write, but when World War II came, it remained true that millions of conscripts were illiterate.

CCC applied solely to young men. The vast majority of the indigent were sustained at a dismal level by a succession of other bureaus: Federal Emergency Relief Administration (FERA, May, 1933), Public Works Administration (PWA, June, 1933), Civil Works Administration (CWA, November,

1933), Works Progress Administration (WPA, May, 1935). This bewildering succession of agencies, many created by executive orders, has understandably prompted critics to call the New Deal "alphabet soup." Such witticisms may charm; they may also confuse. At their worst, they may divert us from one of FDR's guidelines for administration: namely, to give the same job to several different men and then leave them to cut each other's throats. Thus he ensured that he would be the one person with authority to make a final decision on politically sensitive questions.

Before pushing forward in time, it is advisable to look backward, since our over-all purpose is to compare the Hoover and Roosevelt administrations. The governor of Pennsylvania, one of the states worst beleaguered by distress, wrote to his brother in November, 1931: "I am completely satisfied that the moving impulse behind Hoover's whole handling of the unemployment situation has been his desire to protect the big fellows from additional taxation, as you said." The figures do not dispute this view. In 1930 the federal government actually showed a surplus, and reduced its debt by more than $700 million. A federal surplus might of course suggest heavy taxation, but in this instance it shows that outlays were being trimmed to the bone. Praise the Lord, in 1931, a federal deficit was allowed to the extent of nearly half a billion dollars. A disgruntled Andrew Mellon left Washington. Nor was Hoover pleased; he urged tax increases to bring in another billion dollars a year, together with appropriation cuts to save $350 million. He got no new taxes, and less than half of the cuts he proposed in expenditures. His message to Congress was plaintive: "We cannot squander ourselves into prosperity." Once more, a president was 100 per cent wrong. The childish foibles of these years are hard to understand. Hoover named a former president of the Plumbers' Union to head the United States Employment Service. This official went to address an American Legion conference on unemployment in March, 1931. He exulted in their presence: "I found two of your men jobs this morning in one hour, just using the telephone!" A Legion leader replied, "Fine, I'll give you a list of 750,000 names to place." Hoover's comprehension of the economics of the nation was deplorable; however, as this chapter will try to demonstrate, the leading Democrats did not score much better.

FDR was one of the early advocates of an interstate arrangement for unemployment compensation. The idea was surely a good one, but it lost. He was merely governor of New York. Of more importance on the national scene was Speaker of the House Garner. Bills for federal grants for relief to the needy were knocked down in Congress. I will not pretend to know what went on in Garner's head; perhaps he saw a run for the White House; even though he was 63 years old, he had the asset of 28 years in Congress. In February, 1932, he made an impassioned plea for a balanced federal budget. He left the Speaker's chair to go on the floor and appeal for passage of a federal sales tax. His climax was to ask all members who favored a balanced budget to rise in their seats. But Fiorello LaGuardia succeeded in knocking out the sales tax. A few weeks later Garner had a different proposal: to appropriate some $2.5 billion for public-works projects. About that time Senator Robinson, soon to become the Democratic majority leader, came out with a relief program to total $2.3 billion. The president countered with a proposal of about 15 per cent of that amount, including an onslaught against the Speaker's proposal: "This is not unemployment relief. It is the most gigantic pork barrel ever proposed to the American Congress. It is an unexampled raid on the public treasury. . . ." Such hyperbole should be approached with caution. In Cook County, Illinois, the relief appropriation was running out, and 750,000 job-seekers were seeking in vain. An appeal to the president from Chicago 2 June, 1932, was signed by the head of Marshall Field, three giant meat packers, railroads, International Harvester, the First National Bank, daily newspapers, and mineral processors. Three weeks later the city's mayor appeared in Washington to pose a bleak choice to federal authorities: grant relief to the distressed, or send in the army to put down riots.

The record of both administrations under review in regard to industrialists should make the most gullible wonder. An economist at the Harvard Business School declared bluntly in December, 1930: "We have the dole in America. But the real recipients . . . are not the men who stand for hours before the Salvation Army soup stations." They were, he said, "the great industries of America." Previously noted (late Chapter 24 on the 1928 campaign) was Hoover's fondness for the trade association as a device for reducing competition in an industry. As president he revealed another aspect of his partisanship to big business by sponsoring the Reconstruction Finance Corporation (RFC, January, 1932). This federal agency was designed to make loans to banks, railroads, and other giant corporations in order to save them from disaster. Its president for the first six months was Charles G. Dawes, former vice president of the nation, ambassador to England, re-designer of reparations payments by Germany. He resigned in June and went back to Chicago to tend the affairs of a bank he had organized. His bank got at one swoop an RFC loan of $90 million. Hoover justified such practices by saying that the prosperity of big business would "trickle down" to everybody. One comment on this argument was acidic: To say that the right mechanism for sustaining the poor was to feed the rich was akin to saying that the best way to feed birds was to feed horses.

With the National Recovery Administration (NRA, another product of the Hundred Days), Roosevelt followed this road even farther than Hoover had done. The new president was basically friendly to the agglutinative approach. His experience in Washington during World War I had been with the regulation and coordination of industry, not with forcing it to compete.* He also had served as president of a national trade association, the Construction Council, from 1922 to 1928; this experience, wrote an aide, "taught him that

---

*It also had been focused on the damping of inflation rather than the stoking of deflation; given the circumstances in which FDR now had to operate, he suffered a severe case of "trained incapacity."

purely voluntary self-regulation did not work." Powerful leaders from the Wall Street firm of Lehman Brothers, Jersey Standard, the U.S. Chamber of Commerce, and GE were pushing in the same direction. Textile executives could become metaphoric in their pleas for a shield against deflation: "We are confronted with a condition of rubber money and iron debts. . . ." Spurred by the White House, Congress set up the NRA. The law provided for the producers in each industry to meet in Washington to draw up a code of fair competition. The codes could be enforced by federal sanctions. Predictably, the conferences and the enforcement were dominated by the largest firms. How this collusion worked out can be shown with one illustration, although hundreds of examples could be equally well given. A small lumber yard sold for cash to farmers who carried their purchases away. Its proprietor bought a large shipment of lumber at $24 a thousand feet, planning to sell at $32. Under the Sawmill Code he was required to add 20 per cent for overhead or $6.40, plus $5.20 for handling and delivery, making a total price of $43.60. His farmer-customers could not meet the price; building in the area stopped; the lumber dealer was almost put out of business. After two years these obscenities and NRA powers were cut off by the Supreme Court in the *Schecter* decision, which involved a poultry dealer in Brooklyn. The identity of the plaintiff gave the disillusioned public another barbed jest of the Depression. Taking their cue from the NRA's grotesque poster with its "Blue Eagle" thunderbird symbol, which participants in the detested program were expected to display, writers soon dubbed *Schecter* "the sick chicken case."

While he was trying to coerce the nation with NRA, FDR was also diddling around with monetary policy. We have no reason to think that he ever understood the subject. He was an easy mark for one quack after another. He did not buy every patent medicine, only several. His floundering on the question of the circulating medium was ludicrous. At the beginning of the New Deal, a Cornell professor sold the president on a very old nostrum—"Gresham's law," which can be stated in several ways (see Figure 26-5). One can say that a rise in the price of gold will raise the value of all commodities proportionately, or that an increase in the quantity of money will bring a like rise in the goods. So FDR raised the price of gold. Result: the effect on the general level of prices was very small. In technical language, the velocity of circulation fell. Folks simply took the increased supply of money and tucked it under their mattresses, or put it in banks and let it stagnate there. The fact that some people have more money does not insure that they will want to spend it; the hungry probably will, but the wealthy will spend it only if they see a chance for profit. Simultaneously Roosevelt was considering banking reform. A warehouse full of facts about abuses had been collected. Financiers cheating on their income taxes: one sold $3 million worth of stock in his bank to his wife and later bought back the shares from her. Another banker was caught selling short the stock in his own bank. (To sell short any commodity, including stock in a corporation, is to sell something that you do not own, in the expectation

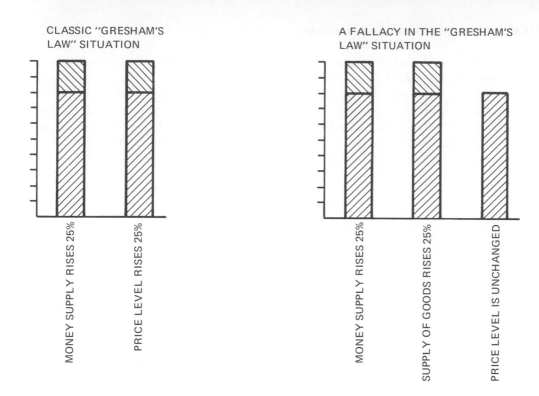

CLASSIC "GRESHAM'S LAW" SITUATION

MONEY SUPPLY RISES 25%
PRICE LEVEL RISES 25%

A FALLACY IN THE "GRESHAM'S LAW" SITUATION

MONEY SUPPLY RISES 25%
SUPPLY OF GOODS RISES 25%
PRICE LEVEL IS UNCHANGED

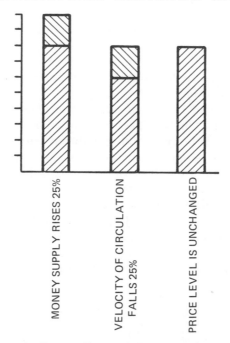

ANOTHER FALLACY IN THE "GRESHAM'S LAW" SITUATION

MONEY SUPPLY RISES 25%
VELOCITY OF CIRCULATION FALLS 25%
PRICE LEVEL IS UNCHANGED

FIGURE 26-5. *Variations on the Quantity Theory of Money and "Greshom's Law"*

that the price in 60 or 90 days will be less than it is today; you sell at today's proffer but deliver at whatever the future price may be. A bank president could find it easy to lower the price of stock in his bank.). Margin buying on the Stock Exchange was financed by the largest industrial firms; Jersey Standard at one time had $100 million loaned (through banks) on call, and its total loans of this type had totalled more than $17.5 billion. So the final day of the Hundred Days saw what was meant to be a lasting statute, and none can gainsay that some of its remedies proved to be useful. The Federal Deposit Insurance Corporation (FDIC) was founded to insure all deposits up to $10,000. No commercial bank which accepted deposits could be connected with a firm selling securities, such as an investment bank or a stockbroker. Interest could not be paid on demand deposits (as in a checking account).

The time has come for a partial assessment. FDR's credit with historians has been exceedingly high. Why? A major reason can be simply stated: They (and most of their students and readers) belonged to precisely the segment of society on whom his administration rained benefits. We might call it the middle 60 per cent of the social strata. The New Deal always had its wealthy supporters, but Roosevelt's name was not popular around the Union League Club, and newspaper publishers did not adore him (count 10 per cent lost). The remaining 30 per cent were the truly disadvantaged, and the president never thought about them much. Their power was negligible, so why bother? But many of them had votes, so they got some benefits too. These tidbits should not be decried. The degree to which folks who have almost nothing can be thankful for a few more crumbs was dramatically expressed two decades later by a black woman in Baltimore. She sang paeans to Roosevelt while assaulting the ingratitude of the contemporary youth. They, she said, don't know what it is to go freeze your butt in an outhouse, and they might be doing it today if it wasn't for That Man.*

Another element in Roosevelt's appeal to many academics can lead to conflicting conclusions. One perspective is offered by a biography (1882) by the English novelist Anthony Trollope about a British prime minister: "He was a statesman for the moment. Whatever was not wanted now, whatever was not practicable now, he drove quite out of his mind." This evaluation would not apply with any richness to Washington, or Hamilton, or Lincoln, but it does seem pertinent to FDR. A harsher analogy can be drawn from a comment by another Englishman, economist John Maynard Keynes: "We are at one of those uncommon junctures of human affairs when we can be saved by the solution of intellectual problems and in no other way." The man who really cut to the quick was the nation's foremost living philosopher, John Dewey (see

---

*The law that seems best to typify the Hundred Days was the Home Owners Loan Act. It contended that men who have worked hard to accumulate property should not be made to give it up under abnormal conditions. The law of 1933, as amended the next year, in effect prohibited foreclosure on a mortgage.

Chapters 25 and 27); under the title "Imperative Need: A New Radical Party," he wrote:

> Events have proved that while those in private control of industry and wealth rule they do not and cannot govern. For government implies order and security at the very least. And what we have is tragic insecurity and essential anarchy. . . . At the time when public officials are calling upon police and militia to keep dairy farmers from emptying milk, the federal government is paying a premium to other farmers for plowing under millions of acres of corn and cotton. If that is not anarchy, no one knows what anarchy is.
>
> This situation continues only because the mass of the people refuse to look facts in the face and prefer to feed on illusions, produced and circulated by those in power with a profusion that contrasts with their withholding of the necessities of life. The day that the mass of the American people awake to the realities of the situation, that day the restoration of democracy will commence, for power and rule will revert to the people.

In 1935 Dewey returned to the attack: "Experimental method is not just messing around nor doing a little of this and a little of that in the hope that things will improve. Just as in the physical sciences, it implies a coherent body of ideas, a theory, that gives direction to effort." A quarter of a century later, a rover boy from the academic-governmental Establishment, acting as an apologist historian of the New Deal, professed to be puzzled by Dewey's protests: "Paradoxically, the New Deal, preferring experiment to abstraction, became repugnant to this theoretical experimentalist."

During the first two years of the Roosevelt administration, the most forward-looking law, the Tennessee Valley Act, put the government into the power and flood control business. This landmark legislation did not get much encouragement from the White House; its chief author was Republican George W. Norris, senator from Nebraska (Chapter 22). Antecedents for such government involvement were several: the Hetch Hetchy struggle in the West for public power; the Muscle Shoals dam in Alabama to produce nitrates during World War I. When war ended, Norris wanted federal operation of the latter development to continue. A bill to that end passed Congress in 1928, vetoed by Coolidge. Another passed in 1931, vetoed by Hoover. These gentlemen would not allow government to compete with free enterprise. Sensing that FDR would not block it, Norris' group made the plan much bolder. Now it would embrace a multi-river system. Further, reverting to the most creative concept of CCC, it would be a multi-purpose enterprise. The easiest part to sell politically was a combination of dams and reforestation as a means to flood control. Tacked on were provisions for recreation areas. The stiffest opposition came to the provisions for hydroelectric power, especially because it was announced that TVA rates could serve as a yardstick for private rates. Leading the objectors was the president of gargantuan Commonwealth and Southern, Wendell Willkie (mid-Chapter 28 on the 1940 campaign). Ironically, after the

FIGURE 26-6. *Norris Dam, Tennessee Valley Authority*

Norris Dam presides over the Clinch River in eastern Tennessee. Although this river is only about 200 miles long from its origins in southwestern Virginia until its juncture with the Tennessee River, the dam is vital to the complex operated by the Tennessee Valley Authority. This agency, as stated by two authorities, "realized from its beginning in 1933 that its progressive conception of regional development would find appropriate expression only in modern architecture."

A strong tendency has existed to denigrate American achievements in the visual arts. But this verdict comes from jurors who have defined the subject in too narrow a way. Consider architecture (surely one of the important arts); Frank Lloyd Wright, expressing the expansive view of many American artists, said that two objects that he had wanted to design, without doing so, were a silo and a steamship. Much American genius has expressed itself in novel forms, as exemplified by the statute was enacted, the private companies were among the chief benefactors. As the cost of electricity fell, more families came into the market. When farm homes got current, they bought radios, refrigerators, washing machines. Private profits rose. Two further comments about TVA seem in order. Its outstanding executive subtitled a book: *Democracy on the March.* This ideal was partly realized; it was a semi-autonomous agency of the federal government. But it soon became another swollen bureaucracy, and the notion that it manifested "grass-roots democracy" has been discredited. Even after allowance for this, the TVA can be seen as an advance in several respects. However, it was not replicated. Proposals for similar projects have been repeatedly made, notably for the Missouri valley; repeatedly they have been turned back by Congress. Perhaps the spreading concern for control of the environment will revive them with added zest.

In the spring of 1935 FDR abruptly shifted his course, not quite a total reverse. What ensued is commonly, and justly, called the Second New Deal—if there had been a First. This switch is always referred to, never explained. An effort to that end should be made. Of the two main causes, one must be deferred until Chapter 27: the rise of democracy in the streets, culminating with the formation of the mass CIO unions. The other can be found in Washington, especially in the White House. A task force in the Treasury Department headed by Mordecai Ezekiel had submitted to the secretary and through him to the president a report proposing an increased program of public works to be financed by federal deficits. For some weeks it seemed that Roosevelt was going to advocate this policy. Then he decided it would not be wise politically. Unfortunately perhaps, the report made explicit the alternative to its proposal: prolonged large-scale unemployment. FDR foresaw rough waters for the New Deal. If he could not help to restore full employment, he would have to capture blocs of voters by the advocacy of specialized programs, particularly designed for the working class.*

*This analysis and the documents underlying it (Roosevelt Library at Hyde Park) were offered in a Senior Honors Thesis by William S. Friedman (1965) at Brandeis University. Other interpretations in this chapter rely on facts contained in other Senior Honors Theses done at the same institution by these students: Miriam A. Epstein (1964), Donald Florman (1965), David A. Levine (1963), Daniel Marcus (1962), and J. Victor Samuels (1963).

---

civil engineers who created Norris Dam. The many rivers of eastern America needed bridges, and they offered additional chances to manipulate beauty. Are we to deny an artistic achievement to the Roeblings, father and son, who built Brooklyn Bridge? And what of David B. Steinman, who refashioned it?

Such questions may necessitate some difficult distinctions. Who is an American? The poet T. S. Eliot was born in St. Louis and educated in the United States but lived most of his adult life in England; an analog is W. H. Auden, bred and reared in England, who lived for decades in the United States. Veering back to the subject of unusual genres in the arts, we might consider Donald McKay, the author of the greatest clipper ships in the mid-nineteenth century. A standard source calls him a "Boston shipbuilder." But he came from Nova Scotia, and those formative years provided him with his visions and with many of his techniques.

The Refrigerator

The operation of the mechanical refrigerator depends upon two laws of physics. First, when a liquid evaporates to a gas, it absorbs heat, and when a gas condenses to a liquid, it loses heat. Second, when pressure is increased the "evaporation point" is raised, and the point at which any material will evaporate to a gas or condense to a liquid is higher. Increased pressure at a given temperature will thus condense a gas to liquid, and lower pressure will evaporate a liquid to a gas. Using these principles for refrigeration requires the selection of a refrigerant material which will evaporate to a gas under normal atmospheric pressure inside a freezer (absorbing heat in the process), and which under pressure (hence a higher "evaporation point") will condense to a liquid at room temperature in a coil outside the freezer, giving off the heat it had absorbed inside. A refrigeration plant operates in these phases:

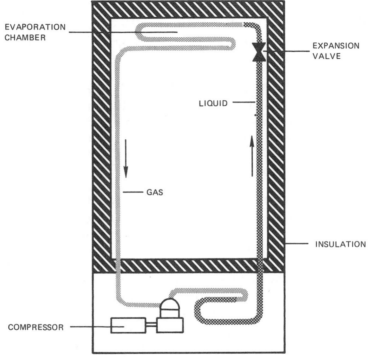

(1) A pump puts the refrigerant under pressure and keeps it in liquid form in a coil outside the freezer; an expansion valve holds it under pressure so that it cannot evaporate prematurely, and the liquid is propelled toward the evaporation chamber.

(2) In the evaporation chamber inside the freezer pressure is relieved; under the lower normal atmospheric pressure the liquid evaporates and absorbs heat.

(3) The refrigerant, now in gas form under normal pressure, is propelled out of the evaporation chamber and toward the compressor.

(4) The refrigerant is compressed by a pump, and under pressure condenses to a liquid and gives off the heat absorbed from inside; it is propelled through the coil outside the freezer, as in phase (1) in the cycle. The refrigerant material is continuously pumped in a steady stream through all phases simultaneously.

Although few American households would today tolerate the inconvenience of the ice box, the importance of mechanical refrigeration does not lie in the domestic sphere. The refrigerated train and truck transport has permitted twentieth century Americans to enjoy a much wider variety of food, especially fruit and vegetables, at all seasons of the year, than was conceivable before their invention.

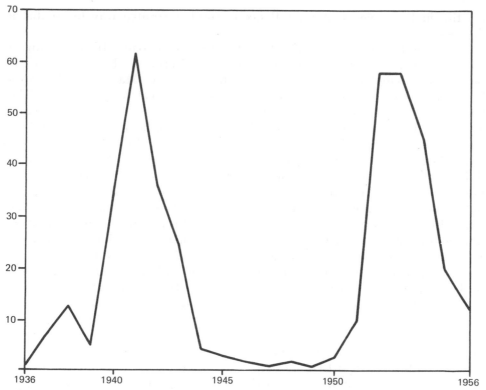

FIGURE 26-7. *Units of Low-rent Federal Housing Completed (in thousands)*

That spring saw three striking new plans. By executive order, no less, the president created the Works Progress Administration (WPA). Disdaining the handout, the agency tried to create jobs on public works. Since the central objective was to put men back to work, they often worked inefficiently in terms of modern technology. Epithets resounded: "Huh, raking leaves!" or "Leaning on a shovel!" These taunts were not only unfair but stupid. In countless towns in the country today you can see a city hall, a library, a bridge, that was built by WPA. Its cultural achievements can be left for the next chapter, as can the groundswell set off by the National Labor Relations Act (NLRA or Wagner Act). The third innovation, and one that Roosevelt had been angling toward for years, was the Social Security Act. In 1931 as a governor he had suggested an interstate meeting to agree on a scheme for compensating the unemployed. That became part of the new law; so did a device for old-age benefits. Undoubtedly over the long run this statute has served to relieve destitution among several segments of society. However, in contrast to WPA with its initial appropriation of nearly $5 billion, Social Security began, not by paying benefits, but by taxing both worker and employer, and thus was deflationary for the first few years. A payroll tax is another strange way to combat a depression.

Then the president decided to rest on his reform oars. His re-election in 1936 was overwhelming: he lost only Maine and Vermont. (The former had its presidential ballot early, giving rise to the jest: "As Maine goes, so goes Vermont.") Then his lack of understanding began to catch up with him. The Supreme Court had certainly behaved outrageously in striking down many New Deal laws for captious reasons; if any court can be accused of "judicial legislation," this one can. On the other hand, many New Deal bills were drafted carelessly or were offensive to the Constitution; the NRA for instance did delegate a monstrous share of power to the chief executive. Details of the famous Court Fight cannot be given here, partly because many of them are only gradually being uncovered, but some points seem established. As he began his move to get more of the bench behind his program by increasing the number of justices on the Court, FDR did not bother to consult his own leaders in Congress. Second, he fabricated an announced reason for his move, claiming that so many of the sitting members were elderly that the Court could not keep up with its calendar. When Chief Justice Hughes was able to produce figures to show that his tribunal was in fact abreast of its work, the rug was jerked from under the president's feet. His proposal lost. In this struggle he erred from beginning to end, and I suspect he need not have lost. Many Americans and many Congressmen were incensed against the conservative majority on the Court. If FDR had explained frankly what he wanted to do and why he wanted to do it, if he had made advance preparations on Capitol Hill, he might have won. Instead he alienated several of his staunchest supporters.

So the president reverted to one of his favorite kicks—balance the budget. The federal debt was actually reduced a little from 1937 to 1938, but unemployment soared from 13.8 per cent to 18.7 per cent of the civilian labor force. What next?—another reverse. The Wagner-Steagall Act (September, 1937) was intended to provide public housing for low-income groups; its results will be examined in Chapter 29. Doing a clear about-face from NRA, Roosevelt appointed a trust-buster to head the anti-trust division of the Justice Department, and a sweeping investigation of the squelching of competition in the economy was launched by the Temporary National Economic Committee. Most important of all, the Fair Labor Standards Act set for workers engaged in interstate commerce both a minimum wage per hour and maximum hours per week. By court decisions plus Congressional action, this law has been frequently upgraded and extended to many additional groups of workers. It must stand as one of the major accomplishments of the New Deal. Elated by the achievement of these reforms, Roosevelt tried to use the Democratic primaries to purge congressmen in his party who had opposed his program. He got scotched. In only one district did he succeed. Our generalization of Chapter 24 (first footnote) still holds.

Our final topic here is Senator Huey Long, for whom my respect is great. Rich kids from the North may well parrot the labels they have heard, calling him power-hungry, a ruthless dictator, or a demagogue. Poor boys from the South are not likely to feel that way about it. The best break that Roosevelt got in the 1936 election was the assassination of Huey Long, because he would have raised cain—all from the left. He had mastered invective: NRA meant "Nuts Running America," or "National Ruin Administration," or "Never Roosevelt Again." Perhaps his larger greatness lay in his years as governor of Louisiana. In a state that had only bogs as roads, he helped pave them. In a state of many bayous, he helped build bridges. In a state of countless diseases, he helped build hospitals. In a state of illiterate adults, he helped to start night schools—for black and white equally.

Critics of his programs need also to be educated on another problem: Many have faulted Long for the rise in the public debt of Louisiana (making it sound like the worst accounts of Reconstruction), but almost any economist today would agree that deficit financing was the right way to fight the depression. Let us end with an anecdote. As governor in 1932, he heard that a bank in Lafayette might fold. With a friend he drove through the night to be right there when banking hours began. Up came a patron to present a check for $18,000 to withdraw his deposits. Huey then waved a state check in the man's face and told him that the state check would more than exhaust the bank's cash. Further, said Long, I got here first. "You agree to leave yours in, and I'll agree to leave the state's in, and nobody'll be hurt." If that was Hitlerism—it was not—the United States needed more of it, in 1932.

Looking back on the Great Depression, it seems clear that neither Hoover nor Roosevelt understood what had provoked it or what to do to cure it. Some of FDR's advisers had the needed insights, but they could never persuade him to implement them in a systematic fashion. He floundered along, shuffling from an advocacy of massive deficits in the federal budget to meet the pressures from blocs of voters, then shifting to a contrary policy of striving to make outgoes match receipts in order to satisfy the dogmas of nineteenth-century economic theory. Meanwhile, citizens suffered. From 1931 to 1940, always at least eight million Americans were unemployed. Social welfare payments and direct relief were far less generous than they would be in 1972. Many employed workers suffered persistent dread that they would lose their jobs. Employers watched the savings of decades disappear like smoke. Farmers saw their land dispersed by dust storms or by floods. By the spring of 1935, Roosevelt despaired of getting the idle segment of the labor force back to work. To save his political neck, he turned to programs that aimed at assuaging large groups in the community. The major reforms of the New Deal stem from this strategic reversal: the Social Security Act, the National Labor Relations Act, the Fair Labor Standards Act. As subsequently broadened in scope, these laws have substantially altered the contours of American society. Considering, however, the strains to which the national life was subjected, it is remarkable that such modest and fairly quiet revisions were sufficient to satisfy the bulk of the electorate.

SOME NOTABLE EVENTS

1929 Black Thursday on New York Stock Exchange, 24 October.

1931 Muscle Shoals bill vetoed by President Hoover, 3 March.

International financial crisis, spring; Great Depression in U.S., autumn.

Japan attacks Mukden, 18 September.

1932 Reconstruction Finance Corporation, 22 January.

Norris-LaGuardia Act, 20 March.

Unemployment in June, 13 million.

Payrolls of Ford fall to 37,000, June; they were 128,142 in March, 1929.

Veterans' Bonus March on Washington, May–July.

Japan recognizes Manchukuo, 15 September.

1933 Emergency Banking Act, 9 March.

Economy in Government Act, 20 March.

Beer (3.2 per cent alcohol) legalized, 22 March.

Federal Emergency Relief Act, 12 May.

Agricultural Adjustment Administration, 12 May.

Tennessee Valley Authority, 18 May.

Truth in Securities Act, 27 May.

London Economic Conference, 12 June–27 July.

Home Owners' Loan Act, 13 June.

Farm Credit Act, 16 June.

Banking Act of 1933 (Glass-Steagall Act), 16 June.

National Recovery Administration, 16 June.

U.S.S.R. recognized by U.S., 16 November.

1934 Gold Reserve Act, 30 January.

Johnson Act, 13 April.

1935 Resettlement Administration, April.

Soldiers' Bonus Bill vetoed by Roosevelt, 22 May.

Schecter Poultry Corporation v. *U.S.*, 27 May.

National Labor Relations Act (Wagner Act), 5 July.

Social Security Acts, 5 August.

Neutrality Act of 1935; Italy invades Ethiopia, 2 October.

1936 Canadian Reciprocal Trade Agreement, 14 May.

Hitler seizes the Rhineland, March.

Spanish Civil War begins, summer.

1937 FDR loses struggle to "pack" the Supreme Court, 5 February–22 July.

Farm Security Administration established, 22 July.

Recession begins, August.

Panay incident, 12 December.

1938 Ludlow resolution for referendum on war beaten in House, 10 January.

Agricultural Adjustment Act of 1938, April 14.

House Committee on Un-American Activities set up, 26 May.

Emergency Relief Appropriation Act, 21 June.

Fair Labor Standards Act, 25 June.

FDR tries to purge his Democratic opponents in Congress; fails.

1939 Administrative Reorganization Act, 3 April.

Hatch Act forbids political activity by federal employees, 2 August.

1940 Alien Registration Act (also called Smith Act), 28 June.

Office of Production Management, 20 December.

FDR says U.S. should become "the great arsenal of democracy."

U.S. unemployment: 7,476,000.

Ways to Study History XXVI

Consult eye-witnesses. Diligent historians for generations have been scouring the countryside to find persons who actually participated in memorable events. In the last twenty years this practice has become far more systematic than ever before. Ways to Study History III briefly examined the use of computers in recent research; the use of tape recorders is another example of how modern tools can be helpful. A taped interview permits more accurate replication of what was said, and preserves it indefinitely. Visitors to the Oral History Project at Columbia University or to the Labor History Archives at Wayne State University can hear what was remembered ten years ago by actors in the crises of fifty years ago.

Incredible gains from this technique are visible in the biography of Huey Long by T. Harry Williams (1970). Long was governor of and then United States senator from Louisiana. Restrained writers had customarily called him a demagogue; the headstrong had used phrases about the Hitler of America. Williams gives a far different portrait of a conventional indigenous type whose distinction was that he had much more than normal style and zeal, and who was, it seems to me, the most creative Southern politician of this century. To reach this picture the author used the traditional sources: manuscripts, public records, periodicals. But also, even though Long was assassinated (an old American habit) in 1935, Williams was able to interview 295 eye-witnesses.

The results refute the old canards. Interviews can bring the past to life.

Document 26-1

Bray Hammond was probably one of the three most acute analysts of the history of American money and banking. He also belongs to the squadron of non-academics, persons not affiliated with any university, who in the last generation contributed so much to our knowledge of our past; his career was spent as a civil servant with the Federal Reserve System, and his research and writing were a pursuit to be indulged on vacations, evenings, weekends. His first-hand knowledge, clear mind, and lucid prose work together in this passage to explain the nature of central banking. Although an explanation of this phenomenon has been made in Chapter 12, the repetition of it here should provide a focus on the Great Depression.

When the System was established and for many years later, the Reserve Banks were usually regarded as a means of "pooling" or "mobilizing" the reserve funds of member banks. To a certain extent this view was correct. But it fell far short of recognizing the full and unique nature of Reserve Bank lending power and Reserve Bank credit. The Reserve Banks are most significant as sources of funds than as reservoirs of funds. In extending credit, either by lending or by purchasing securities, they do not use funds already deposited with them. Their lending power is independent of the funds deposited with them. When they extend credit, they increase both their assets and their liabilities; they originate the funds they lend and the funds they pay for securities.

Anybody who has grasped this interpretation, including the meaning of every word in it, is well on the way to understanding other episodes discussed in this chapter and Chapter 22, as well as in Chapters 28 and 29: in creation of the Open Market Committee in 1933; "monetization of the federal debt" during World War II; why the manipulation of the rediscount rate affected only certain spheres of the economy in recent years.

Document 26-2

The public media have long been harping on the economic theories of an Englishman, John Maynard Keynes. But he did not create all the theories involving government intervention in a national economy, nor did he understand them as well as some Americans who preceded him. Even before Franklin Delano Roosevelt became president, this testimony was offered to the Senate Finance Committee in February, 1933, by Marriner S. Eccles, head of twenty-six banks in Utah and president of several other companies. Besides the analysis reprinted here, he advocated on this occasion federal laws on child labor, minimum wages, unemployment insurance, old-age pensions, plus higher income and inheritance taxes on the wealthy.

Before effective action can be taken to stop the devastating effects of the depression, it must be recognized that the breakdown of our present economic system is due to the failure of our political and financial leadership to intelligently deal with the money problem. In the real world there is no cause nor reason for the unemployment with its resultant destitution and suffering of fully one-third of our entire population. We have all and more of the material wealth which we had at the peak of our prosperity in the year of 1929. Our people need and want everything which our abundant facilities and resources are able to provide for them. The problem of production has been solved, and we need no further capital accumulation for the present, which could only be utilized in further increasing our productive facilities or extending further foreign credits. We have a complete economic plant able to supply a superabundance of not only all of the necessities of our people, but the comforts and luxuries as well. Our problem, then, becomes purely one of distribution. This can only be brought about by providing purchasing power sufficiently adequate to enable the people to obtain the consumption goods which we, as a nation, are able to produce. The economic system can serve no other purpose and expect to survive. . . .

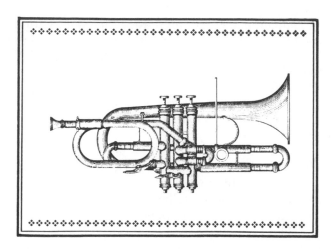

Two Cultures:
Common Men and Intellectuals

In 1959 a renowned English novelist-scientist published a small volume with the title *The Two Cultures and the Scientific Revolution.* His central thesis can be viewed as an ego trip: he implied that he was notable for being conversant with both the humanities and the natural sciences. His self-congratulations were justified in that double-vision is far from common, but he was not unique. To cite only the most famous exemplar, Albert Einstein was a physicist who played the violin and wrote philosophy of quality. Before departing from this theme, an intriguing oddity might be observed. A physicist or chemist is more likely to know something about music and art than is a humanist to know a smidgen about modern science. Between the two, of course, lies mathematics, and therein is the key to the enigma. A person without knowledge of mathematics is barred from contemporary science. This knowledge must be acquired at an early age, whereas a person of any age (perhaps, the older the better) can read a novel or respond to a painting. But his knowledge of any art can be increased if he has pondered the manipulation of numbers. It is not by accident that the highest praise bestowed on a mathematical proof is to call it "elegant."

While the above contentions are limited to a division within the academic community, it appears typical of the much more meaningful polarities in view when we scan a broader horizon, seeking to analyze how the differences between intellectuals and ordinary people enter the panorama. First, an illustration from culture at its lowest. Then, two examples from thought at its highest reaches. Finally, we will look at the democratizing influences: cultural innovations after 1929 that appealed to a wide range of the strata in American society.

Some genre may be more debased than broadcast soap opera, but it is not easy to think of any. This benumbing viper began in Chicago about 1932. Its creators came from various pseudo-intellectual backgrounds; schoolteacher, advertising man, magazine writer, newspaper reporter. Its success was phenomenal. One series, "The Goldbergs," was sponsored continuously by Proctor & Gamble from 1937 until 1945; it had begun as a nighttime show several years earlier but daytime for the housewives seemed to work out better. "Vic and Sade" began in June, 1932, and lasted for thirteen years. One female writer of this pablum made an income estimated at $4,500 a week. Another woman did even better; by the middle of the decade she was earning some $250,000 a year. Later she sold the rights to three of her serials for $175,000. One male writer turned out 100,000 words a week for years.*

The construction of stories was absurd. Any listeners were stultified. Locale was unlikely (usually in small towns). Characters had weird diseases such as temporary blindness or amnesia (did you ever know a person with amnesia?). Children were constantly being killed by automobiles. Men were repeatedly arrested for murder. No woman ever became committed to her lover until he had been crippled. In Thurber's words, the portrait of the American male in soap operas was "Man in a Wheelchair." Such tearjerkers gained audiences running to, in total, some 20 million. A survey reported that 46 per cent of the nation's women were never part of this audience, but think of the other percentage. And how many of the abstainers had daytime jobs? In trying to understand the appeal of the daytime serial, we can begin with its limited demands on audiences. Intellectually it required nothing; anyone could comprehend what it had to say. The pace of action verged toward a dead stop; if a man went to the barber shop for a haircut, the narration of that one haircut could take at least two weeks at the rate of five programs a week. Programs issued no call to a person's physiology; a listener could iron her washing

---

*Facts here gathered in my mother's household have been illuminated by a brilliant series in *The New Yorker* by James Thurber. Journalists have done at least as well as professional historians in interpreting recent America. Many *New Yorker* profiles are superb, and they are exploited often in the pages that follow. Picking almost at random, I think of pieces by S. N. Behrman, Richard O. Boyer, John Hersey, Geoffrey Hellman.

without missing a stroke. Emotionally it was flaccid. In one show a man stopped by to see a lady friend on a hot afternoon. She asked if he wanted anything to drink. He replied that a glass of ice water would be fine. She said: "One cube or two?"

It is probably invalid to say that these programs provided millions of people with vicarious lives. True, many Americans had been made miserable by the depression, and they wanted to flee from reality, but it was not the unemployed and the sharecroppers who owned radios. The common denominator of the soap operas was that they offered so little stimulation to the audience and seemed to offer the average listener some kind of comforting reassurance. But the ability of housewives to get caught up in the juvenilities passes belief. Audiences developed a personal identification with these media "personalities." On one show a man and his beloved got married; the headquarters of the network in New York received moving vans filled with wedding presents. On another, a featured couple was accustomed to talk to each other while in bed—twin beds of course. When the male lead left the show, his replacement continued to talk with his wife while in their beds. An avalanche of letters protested this immorality.

Let us jump from low culture to the highest with what may be the greatest nonfiction work written by an American in the decade after 1929, John Dewey's *Art as Experience.* The operative word is "experience." The fascination of the book is its efforts to define that noun so that it can then define the other noun in the title, with most of its examples being taken from the visual arts. In Dewey's language, we must deny that soap operas promoted any experience whatever (they promoted soap). This topic can be approached by using a coinage that two psychologists devised—a "perfink"—a monstrous term formed by joining sounds from three functions of humans: perception, feeling, thinking. Dewey did not employ this vulgarism, but the concept hints at what he meant by experience; any experience is a "perfink." He went further in saying that it must also involve a muscular response.

Within this framework he tried to resolve a vast range of seeming paradoxes. For instance, he argued that nobody can possibly experience the same painting twice. After the first time, he will be somewhat altered; so also, for him, will be the painting. Here we encounter again the proposition that has been stated above, that all art, all experience, is an interaction of objective with subjective. Obviously this idea was not new with Dewey. The difficulties of distinguishing the *me* from the *not me* are manifold. Dewey stated his conclusion thus: "The moments when the creature is both most alive and most composed and concentrated are those of fullest intercourse with the environment." To be alive, then, is not to be "relaxed" or to "take it easy." Quite the contrary, when speaking about moments of excitement, we use such phrases as "beside myself," "jumped out of my skin," "was transported." A usable analogy to art is religion. An experience in either zone achieves two results: First, it is a temporary loss of Self in that you fuse into external realities.

Second, it is a re-creation and hopefully an extension of Self in that you incorporate more external reality into yourself.

From Dewey's premises some corollaries follow. For one, the outside world assumes a vitalizing role in experience. For instance, you may live in a landscape, or more likely in a culture, that lacks diversity; the barrenness will not stimulate you, and you as a person will wither (see the Dewey discussion in Chapter 25). One environment may offer too little stimulation to the sense organs; another may offer too much; another may offer a chaos of sounds and sights and smells. Any of these imbalances can disrupt a human personality; we all have threshholds beyond which we cannot hold ourselves together. A contribution of art is that it gives us a coordinated sequence of sensations, a process. Because it is not helter-skelter, we can make *human* sense of it. Viewed from this angle, great art has an essential similarity to great theology. To phrase the same insight differently, much of the great art has been religious art—for good reason. Another thrust of Dewey's position might be stated thus (he does not so state it): Art may be for itself, but it can never be of itself or from itself. An essential continuity runs from the events of everyday life to the highest realms of esthetics, and this chain cannot be severed.

Thus the comprehension of an artistic work must be an act, not passive; it must be a "perfink." The English writer A. E. Housman said that conceiving a poem was like cutting yourself shaving. Dewey would have pushed this comment further; he would have said that experiencing a poem was like cutting yourself shaving, except that the reader is not cutting himself as deeply as the poet did. Moreover, these cuts can only come from forces that exist in the external world. Without re-creation of sound waves, light waves, palpable objects, flavors, odors, art could not exist. The quality of an artistic work is a function of its success in grasping the greatest variety and tension of these stimuli in order to harmonize them, impart rhythms to them. Here we come to Dewey's definition of a third of those abstract nouns that are so slippery: Art, Experience, and now Imagination:

> Esthetic experience is imaginative. This fact, in connection with a false idea of the nature of imagination, has obscured the larger fact that all *conscious* experience has of necessity some degree of imaginative quality. For while the roots of every experience are found in the interaction of a live creature with its environment, that experience becomes conscious, a matter of perception, only when meanings enter into it that are derived from prior experiences. . . .

The relevance of this argument to the study of history can be highlighted. Imagination can be the distillation from the past of tinctures (occasionally spirits) relevant to the present. It can also be an injection back into the past of perceptions that we have only gained today. The triad of "past-present-future" can be as functional as "thing-thought-word" or the duo "subjective-objective." But the cutting edge of these propositions must be constantly honed anew.

Finally, for present purposes, Dewey's treatise may be taken as a masterly assertion of what all adults know but can seldom express: That each of us develops a Self by forgetting about Self, by reaching beyond Self, by catching hold of a problem that is so engrossing that we become fused with the problem.

Thus far we have seen a sharp contrast between an illustration out of the depths of American culture, versus one from its heights. But the culture also provided some adhesives. Some of them will be examined in the remainder of this chapter. Several musical genre for instance united listeners of many faiths, colors, classes. New technologies made them accessible to a vastly enlarged audience, and audiences were responsive to a vastly expanded repertoire. Chronologically, first phonograph, then radio. For analytic reasons we might distinguish between innovations in the method of communication, and changes in the nature of the music being heard, but it must never be forgotten that both processes happened simultaneously. Persons who are now nearing the age of 50 will not forget the entranced moments of their childhoods when they sat on the floor in the living room winding up with a hand crank the portable RCA Victor phonograph with the foghorn speaker protruding over the top. Depending on the taste of their parents, they might have listened to racist trash as expressed by the Three Black Crows ("Wheah wuz you when the brains wuz handed out?"). But perhaps they listened to Lawrence Tibbett singing arias. The ambivalence of mechanization cannot be denied. More deceits can be imposed on more people in less time. Conversely, more divinity—using the term in a humanistic rather than a theological sense—can be pumped into the human scene.

Radio was the real jump. Statistics on the matter vary greatly, but probably the best ones are those of the National Association of Broadcasters. They report more than 14 million sets in 1930, twice as many a decade later. Put in other terms, one can guess that 75 per cent of all households in the nation had a radio by 1940. Then, as now, most of what the auditors heard was at best diverting. But not all. NBC had begun broadcasting the New York Symphony Orchestra in 1926, added the Boston Symphony a year later, the Philadelphia Symphony in 1929. The latter had a sponsor—Philco. In 1930 CBS began a series on Sunday afternoons with the New York Philharmonic. NBC countered the next year with a Saturday afternoon series by the Metropolitan Opera.* With the aid of radio, the musical firecracker became a

---

*Again, the momentum of change can be exaggerated easily. The quality of performance that could be heard on the radio thirty-five years ago was better than what can be heard now from a live orchestra except on a few stations.

FIGURE 27-1. *Charles Sheeler,* Upper Deck

skyrocket. Before World War I, the country held about 17 symphony orchestras. By 1939 there were more than 270. Equally important, they were no longer locked into the major cities along the Atlantic seaboard; one of the leading orchestras in the country was in Minneapolis under the direction of Dmitri Mitropoulous. Another was about to emerge in Cleveland under George Szell.

Thus the avenues for offering music proliferated, both by electrical devices and by live performances; the latter particularly were closely connected with the growth of cities that multiplied the existence of many types of spectator sports. As audiences grew, the variety of musical forms was greatly expanded. Hymns in church, a fiddle at the square dance, a player piano in the parlor—these had been the tradition. Now millions of Americans began to hear symphonies, chamber music, oratorios. By 1938–1939 some 10 million families every week were listening to one or another of these programs: Metropolitan Opera, NBC Symphony, New York Philharmonic, Ford's Sunday evening hour. The last in 1937 gained an audience more than double what it had drawn in 1935. Perhaps most telling in the long run, in 1938 more than 70,000 schools were piping the NBC Music Appreciation Hour to more than 7 million children, and nothing prevented adults from listening at home.

The presentation of fine music is one thing; creation of it is something else. It is not really a slander against the United States to say that it did not begin to create original music until the late nineteenth century in Louisiana. The new creation was called "Dixieland." Outstanding scholarship has illuminated some aspects of its origins. (1) Its authors were all black. (2) Although persons who have been around the academic world are likely to hate the term, it, like so many innovations, was a product of cross fertilization; it was born in the mating of African conventions with European instruments. Ashanti migrants in particular brought with them certain styles in rhythm that stressed the "snap" or "sprung beat." Their specific notions about the

---

Charles Sheeler was born in Pennsylvania in 1882. Like Ben Shahn (Figure 26-3), he derived a substantial part of his income from photography. By 1921 Sheeler could collaborate with the great photographer Paul Strand to offer a movie, *Manahatta*. With predictable captions from Walt Whitman (whose poem provided the title), this presentation of New York was memorable for its soaring towers and the tempos of the waterfront.

"Tempo" is still there in his mature paintings, but the viewer must search for it. The forms at first glance seem objective and static, as if fashioned from steel with a turret lathe. In *Upper Deck* (1929) Sheeler found the rhythms that are sought by men who work with camera rather than brush. He also resembles them in choosing to use a subdued palette, a preference perhaps derived from reliance on black and white film.

He could never be content with a head-on depiction of a scene as it was. He affirmed that "a picture could have incorporated in it the structural design implied in abstraction, and be presented in a wholly realistic manner." His respect for photography as a realistic medium was in tension with the abstract cubism of modern France and with the geometric rigors of the Italian Renaissance, though many of his aims would be parallel to theirs.

instrumental composition of a band were preserved in the rural South by their descendants, who drifted after the Civil War into New Orleans, the second biggest port in the nation and a highly cosmopolitan place. For their improvised folk music-makers—drums, loosened teeth in jawbones, hunks of cane made into pipes—they substituted clarinets and cornets and pianos. On these strange mechanisms they tried to achieve the tonal effects that they had gotten in the old ways, including their voices. The offspring of this blend was jazz, which came by Africa, out of Europe, into the United States. A magical creature it has been.

But it has had to cope with the folkways of its adopted land, and here it has met with much trouble. The most likely outlet for a black musician in New Orleans was in its seamy underside: saloons and whorehouses. (Why do the people who go to concerts overlook the fact that Johannes Brahms earned his living playing the piano in a brothel?) But the Establishment was squeamish; during World War I, the Navy closed down the red light district in New Orleans. Was there no way for a Negro trombonist to make it playing his horn? Some had already been working on Mississippi riverboats, had been to Memphis and St. Louis and Kansas City and Chicago. They drifted north, a part of the mass migration of blacks that has been unbroken for a half century; the number of Negroes in both the Northeast and the North Central states doubled from 1920 to 1940. We can almost say that as their customers moved, they moved along. Around 1920, few whites enjoyed their thing. Recording companies listed their products in quite distinct "race" catalogs. Back in Red Eye Joe's "down-home" they may have been hot stuff; now they were just another stupid Sam. One of Louis Armstrong's great sessions (reassembled a few years ago on an LP reissue) was cut in five days in 1926 in a garage in Terre Haute, Indiana, Gene Debs' home town.

This ambience was debilitating (anybody who questions that statement should listen to Armstrong's early records compared to his later ones). Jazz, while it had few white customers, was in danger of losing its black customers; blues and its derivatives were tainted by a degraded past in slavery. Specialized markets in music were being swamped as new channels of distribution favored the big mass-market products; now recording firms wanted a large sale to recoup a high investment. Oligopoly and consolidation of companies developed rapidly until a mere three agencies, the Music Corporation of America, William Morris, and the General Amusement Corporation, were by 1940 the bulk of the band business of the country. It almost seems that in this mass-market "packaging," recording companies were systematically bad-mouthing black musicians. Names of performers were omitted from labels; a famous pianist named Ferdinand "Jelly Roll" Morton on one label became "Fred Morton," on another "Marton"; after he became a star they spelled his name right. But the psychological toll was huge. The clarinet man with Louis Armstrong and His Hot Five in 1926 could improvise with the best in the world, but he called his music "hokum" because he could not play what was written in the score. A trombonist declared that Sidney Bechet was "no musician" because he could not read music.* Such slights abound in the literature of the times—black musicians hating each other, and themselves.

Logically, as entertainers on the make, black musicians applauded the worst white music. They tried, fortunately without perfect execution, to copy it. Armstrong kept proclaiming his adoration of Guy Lombardo. Hack band leaders were applauded as "very modern, almost futuristic"; they could read the score. So could Armstrong, and in another sense as well. He became, not a musician, but a "personality." The star system was being improvised. His early bands were small groups; five performers (not five men, he had a woman too) or seven; the standard Dixieland group was six. The key idea was balance; all other members could nearly match Armstrong in ability. Also crucial was a symmetry in the volume of the instruments. Drums or piano or bass could drown out the others, but didn't. They played subdued rhythm. Trumpet usually carried the melody, trombone below it, clarinet above it doing variations. It was gorgeous. But Armstrong subverted such beauty by surrounding himself with hacks and setting out to be spectacular. Then, sometime around 1930, jazz was cross-bred with pop to invent swing. At its best, as in Benny Goodman's finest cuts, it could be great fun. But it couldn't compare with oldtime Louis playing "Potato Head Blues." Sadder still, young people white and black around 1940 had to learn about Dixieland from white groups because blacks had stopped playing it.

As with music, so with the visual arts. They became available to many more people. Even in fairly large cities, the visitor to an art museum might find nothing beyond reproductions. This was as true in the John Herron Art Institute in Indianapolis as in the Brooklyn Museum. But someone who had never seen anything except plaster casts of discus throwers from ancient Greece could blow his skull when he entered a gallery in the Art Institute of Chicago and confronted Seurat's "Sunday on Grand Jatte Island." Museums had always been created in eccentric ways. The one on Michigan Avenue, which serves the added benefit of blocking the blasts off the Lake in the Windy City, was founded by two self-made millionaires. Besides money, they had taste. They seized upon works by a Spaniard unheard of in the United States, El Greco. They bought early works by Renoir, and the collection now holds a breathtaking assortment of French impressionism. Similarly, the overpowering collection of prints in the Fogg Museum at Harvard was assembled by the wealth and the judgment of one man.

Individualism in the arts (which had first gained momentum in the

---

*Consider (simultaneously) how much America has gained in the glory of spontaneous music and also how, more than they will ever know, Americans have impoverished themselves by putting down the black. I once heard Benny Goodman and the man who had started him on the clarinet, a Negro named Jimmie Noone, take off from "Sweet Georgia Brown." For forty minutes, until both were soaking wet, they swapped choruses, all made up. At the time, 1942, Noone was working as a groundskeeper at Wrigley Field in Chicago. The musical world in the United States could not use him, so it thought—if it thought.

New Britain Museum of American Art, New
Britain, Conn. (Harriet Russell Stanley
Fund). E. Irving Blomstrann, photographer.

FIGURE 27-2. *Thomas Hart Benton,* Arts of the West

Thomas Hart Benton never knew the meaning of the word "serenity." In his paintings there is no repose; you see violent sinuosities of line, screeching oppositions of color, a tumult of action. Trying to depict the enormous variety of life in the United States, he achieved what may be taken as one man's vision of Americans as people on the move. Much of his work, as in this *Arts of the West,* (1932) hovers in the shadowy realm between realism and satire. In cocktail conversations he is often derided (if he is mentioned at all) as the equivalent of Hollywood in the visual arts, but this evaluation is far too glib.

Benton's life (1889–   ) shows the origin of his work. Hailing from the small town of Neosho in southwestern Missouri, he was a son of the (almost) frontier. When he was eighty years old he joined a handful of others to shoot the frothy rapids of an Arkansas river. Besides painting hard, he drank hard and argued hard. In his words, "no American art can come to those who do not live an American life, who do not have an American psychology, and who cannot find in America justification of their lives." (Chapters 24 and 29.)

He was always a tendentious man. He derided the modern city as a "coffin for living and thinking." He himself studied in Paris as a young man, but a quarter century later when he saw Picasso's *Guernica* he scoffed that no decent painting had "come out of France since 1890" (ironically, one of Benton's students about that time was the abstract painter Jackson Pollock). Probably the chief esthetic influence on Benton was the great mural painting of Mexico, but he often tried to adapt its powers to a sheet of canvas on an easel. *Arts of the West,* with its interlocking depiction of a half-dozen scenes, clearly would be suitable for a large wall. Indeed, the recent resurgance of mural painting in the United States might be traced from an effort by Benton in 1930 to portray American activities on a wall at the New School for Social Research in New York City.

1870's) continued after 1929. In that year seven rich collectors founded the Museum of Modern Art in New York. Here also the Whitney Museum of American Art opened in 1930, the first institution to limit itself to esthetic objects created in this country. (Was it possible that the United States could produce beauty?) Colleges and universities busily built up their collections, although unfortunately this activity was concentrated along the East Coast, especially in wealthy Ivy League schools. Notable museums were built in smaller cities; the ones in Buffalo and Dallas and Helena and Youngstown spring to mind. In spite of the continued private or municipal support, the novel element on the scene was federal patronage. This did not take the form of building ponderous new mausoleums in the Corinthian style; even the National Gallery in Washington is the product of philanthropy (the Mellon family, Samuel H. Kress). Rather, federal moneys went to pay room and board for artists. Some of the best painters in the United States today will tell you that the happiest days of their lives were during the Great Depression; they were supported, not handsomely, but well enough to enjoy the sensation of putting pigments on canvas. No time clock; no controls on their messages; for most of them, no students to teach. But WPA workers also ran classes, and started many a pupil on that long climb to a freezing attic studio.

The Art Project of the WPA should remind us that those dreadful years after 1929 were in fact benign for quite a few people (junk dealers and retired servicemen were happy too). It is also a reminder that in the arts, as probably in any human endeavor, personal freedom counts. On the other major projects in the arts—Literature, Music, Theater—more control was imposed. When administration approaches, creativity leaves. These were "group efforts." In every state the writers were required to work on a guidebook to their commonwealth (but see Document 16-3). Some of these tower above others, and any might provide a few useful random facts but none offers much sustenance. The Federal Music Project hit upon a desperate situation. By 1933 some 50,000 professional musicians were out of work, a result not only of the depression but also of movie soundtracks which had knocked countless bands out of the pits. The crude statistics about this project are these. It supported some 15,000 performers. They gave 150,000 programs. They taught a half million youngsters. They collected, on records, about 2,000 folk songs.

What the WPA art projects demonstrated is a truism that every civilized nation in the world knows: that many indispensable forms of culture cannot survive without public subsidy. But now, in the wealthiest country ever, it is difficult in some of the wealthiest cities (Tucson) to get funds for the most basic public culture, the primary schools. If this condition prevails today in regard to the basis of all culture, try to imagine the stresses during the Great Depression. The most striking calamity was the fate of the Federal Theater Project. Started in 1935, it ran until June, 1939. Its budget averaged $7 million a year, and it made only $1 million at the box office. It hired 12,500 performers at an average monthly wage of $83. When it did Sinclair Lewis's "It Can't

Happen Here," the anti-fascist play, opened simultaneously in 21 theaters in 17 states. Eugene O'Neill and G. B. Shaw (notoriously greedy man, he) let the groups do their works for nominal royalties. The Detroit wing did one of the first plays by Arthur Miller. A critic for the New York *Times* called it "the best friend the theater as an institution has ever had in this country."

So what happened? In the spring of 1938 the House Committee on Un-American Activities was set up. In August it began hearings on the Federal Theater Project, which lasted for months. A portion of the hearings went like this, involving the director of the Project and a congressman on the Committee. The director has said that enthusiasm for the Project showed "a certain Marlowesque madness."

> Congressman: "You are quoting from this Marlowe. Is he a
>   Communist?" (Laughter.)
> Director: "I was quoting from Christopher Marlowe . . ."
> [colleague of Shakespeare].

This farce knew no boundaries. After Congress, prodded by HUAC, had wiped out the Theater Project, its former director was packing up her office in Washington. She got a phone call from a congressman. She expected sympathy, but no. He was all business, because he wanted to know about future plans for the theater project in his state. She told him that the establishment was defunct. "You voted it out of existence." She told the date: June 30. After a heavy silence, his shocked voice asked, "Was *that* the Federal Theatre?"

No purpose could be served by writing a sentence or so each about a couple of dozen writers; only a few can be mentioned and then two will be discussed more fully. First, another generalization. In spite of, sometimes because of, the misery surrounding them, American authors produced as many inventive works as in any other decade of our history, including 1850–1860 and 1880–1890. Critics have diminished their homeland by deriding or just ignoring some fine authors. Before expanding that contention, a big exception should be noted. Namely, no new major poet emerged in the United States during the thirties and forties. Comparisons here can be made both over time and in space; in France, England, Germany, a few men were proving that poetry could be vitalized. But during this time the United States did not spawn a new figure of the stature of Robert Frost, E. E. Cummings, Wallace Stevens.

Our sense of respect can really go to work if we poke through the prose of the thirties and forties. At the beginning of the decade Dashiell Hammett, in an outburst that lasted through five novels and a sheaf of short stories, proved that the genre of "mysteries" could recount some lasting truths about the human condition. William Faulkner, sitting way off down there in Oxford, Mississippi near the piney woods, made us believe that he could get inside the stream of consciousness of a mute and simple-minded boy, inside the murderous impulses that build up inside a young black man. To my taste at least, Lillian Hellman virtually invented the American stage with "The Little Foxes" (I personally cannot endorse the numerous accolades for Eugene O'Neill, although he obviously had great influence on the American theater). In *U.S.A.,* John Dos Passos published a tedious novel, but the "profiles" in it are often masterly. If you want to learn fast about Morgan, or Ford, or Debs, or Veblen, here is the best place to go. And we have with us still F. Scott Fitzgerald. When he died in 1940, not even nearing his personal mid-century mark, he was writing a novel that featured a movie producer in Hollywood. Published posthumously and unfinished, the book seems to me to be the most credible love story that has been written by an American in this century.

To mention Fitzgerald is call up memories of Hemingway. The two men, in addition to their other abilities with the English language, had the gift of insulting each other. Both living in Paris during the decade of the expatriate, they were in a bar with friends. Fitzgerald, out of his boyish adulation, blurted, "The rich really *are* different." Hemingway, even younger, found a put-down: "Yeah, they have more money." Fitzgerald subsequently concocted one of his most cutting remarks ever: "Ernest always was willing to lend a helping hand to the man on the ledge a little higher up." Nobody else needs to caricature Hemingway; he did it to himself—his show of virility; his assertive habit of sneaking a snort behind pillars in the galleries of art museums; the rotten novels that he issued in the last half of his life. This included melodramatic claptrap about the Spanish Civil War with a hero who might as well be a Boy Scout master in Traverse City, Michigan, and another book (also about a soldier, officer of course) called *Across the River and Into the Trees* which soon brought the rejoinder *Across the Street and Into the Phone Booth.* Particularly after he killed himself, it became easy to make fun of Hemingway. But a dozen or so of his short stories make us know that as a practitioner of that art almost nobody is fit to play in the same league, that on some days he could make angels and devils dance across the page, that he ranks with Joyce and Kafka and Frank O'Connor.

If his short stories are so ultimately satisfying, why do his novels, including the early ones which are the best ones, seem so dull? One aspect of a tenable explanation might be this: A short story can be compelling even though it deals with only a limited range, confined by number of characters, by space, by time. If it reveals two or three personalities as they existed at a given moment, the reader goes home satisfied. It can be static. But a longer work must present temperaments that are changing, or it becomes trying; if it remains static it reminds you of a record that has cracked, and you begin to fidget at hearing chords repeated. Perhaps Hemingway somewhat reflected the worst weaknesses of Freudianism, in that he seemingly did not believe that a person could change. In a novel of 300 pages, the reader simply ceases to care about what happens to his characters; nothing will happen.

If we conclude that Hemingway's defects were flaws in his character, not in his craft, we might venture the same remark about the outstanding new novelist to appear in the decade, John Steinbeck. But the application would be different. Steinbeck's worst problem was that he could seldom get outside the syndrome that was exposed by Twain so accurately in *Huck Finn* (Chapter 19): the cruelty-sentimentality complex. On one end, we have rather heavy handed cruelty and violence: When a woman gripped by spite goes out with garden shears to cut the heads off chrysanthemums, the symbolic meaning approaches the butchery of another woman (in a novel of the same era) who cuts off her nipples with garden shears. Conversely, we have sentimentality: Steinbeck was prone to slobber over the cute Mexicanos, always happy no matter how dire their malnutrition. But, again as with Hemingway, a man's personal foibles, even his literary faults, should not wall us off from his works. Hemingway—in his use of monosyllables, and even more in his telling of tales strictly by means of dialogue (or interior monologue), did a lot to purify the American language, to scrap the used-up razor blades of "picturesque" verbiage that had no cutting edge. Although Hemingway had revived Mark Twain's technique of using a first-person narrator, he did use many descriptive passages. Steinbeck almost abolished these when he became mature. Although he had written five earlier novels, his first success came with *Of Mice and Men* (1937). His own explanation was that he was trying to write simultaneously the short novel and the play; the book seems to read like a movie script. It has dialogue, plus stage directions, plus nothing else. He stripped it almost bare.

Already in January, 1937, Steinbeck was working on his best work, *The Grapes of Wrath*. Eighteen months later, exhausted, he staggered toward the finish line, and the bound volume came out in 1939. Soon it became a movie that was a big success at the box-offices. It deserved to be, still does, still is. Of all the wide range of books that I have asked students to read for courses about the United States in the twentieth century, the two with the sharpest impact on the most students have been this one and *The Autobiography of Lincoln Steffens* (1931). Two qualities made *The Grapes of Wrath* distinctive. The least noticed has been its innovation in technique. A few pages earlier we looked at Dewey's scheme of art as representing a fusion of subjective with objective. Steinbeck, with astounding audacity, proved that the formula does not always apply; he split the two in the most glaring fashion that one can imagine. He alternated a subjective chapter, then an objective one, a subjective, and so on. His "plot" is about one family, the Joads, and their friend Preacher Casey, who migrate from Oklahoma to become itinerant farmers in California. His larger story tells what happened to millions of poor people in the Southwest during the dust storms and the depression. He convinces readers that he knew what he was writing. If art is disciplined passion, this novel has both elements. Steinbeck stated them while he was doing his research:

> I must go over into the interior valleys. There are five thousand families starving to death over there, not hungry but just actually starving. The government is

trying to feed them and get medical attention to them, with the Fascist group of utilities and banks and huge growers sabotaging the thing all along the line, and yelling for a balanced budget. . . .

Do you know what they're afraid of? They think that if these people are allowed to live in camps with proper sanitary facilities they will organize, and that is the bugbear of the large landowner and the corporation farmer. . . .

Although the Resettlement Administration did found more decent camps for migratory pickers, more than three decades would pass before any sizable number of these workers could establish joint action against growers. (See Chapter 29 on Cesar Chavez).

The central point here is that the Great Depression brought a united front among representatives of various social groups who normally never thought about each other. Steinbeck was far from unique. Steelworkers met lawyers; some sociologists began to suspect that poverty cannot be solved by jargon; writers went to lumbering camps and coal towns to see how common folks lived; photographers and artists dipped into segments of the nation that they had ignored earlier (Figure 26-3). Disaffection from the power sector was extreme and ubiquitous among intellectuals. The young novelist Thomas Wolfe wrote to his mother about the hard times in autumn, 1931: "No one seems to be doing anything about it, everyone is standing around with his mouth open as if he expected the gates of heaven to open the next moment and rain milk and honey all over him. People talk about 'the pendulum swinging backward' and 'conditions are bound to change'—This is foolish talk: conditions are not *bound* to change unless something is done to change them, and at present it seems that any change will be for the worse. . . . I think we are at the end of a period." A few months later, Edmund Wilson, one of the naton's most distinguished younger critics, let fly: "The attitude of the Menckenian gentleman, ironic, beer-loving and 'civilized,' . . . attitude of old-American-stock smugness, . . . the liberal attitude that American capitalism was going to show a new wonder to the world by gradually and comfortably socializing itself and that we should just have to respect it in the meantime . . . the attitude of trying to get a kick out of the sheer size and energy of American enterprises, irrespective of what they were aiming at . . . they are no use in our present predicament, and we can see how superficial they were."

This alienation from the Establishment of many intellectuals came to play a signal role in one of the most astonishing innovations of the decade— formation of unions, organized by industry rather than by craft, in the heartlands of mass production. When labor organizers moved surreptitiously among rubber workers in Akron, auto workers in Flint, shoe workers in St. Louis, they carried with them a small battalion of trained publicity men to turn out pamphlets and plant press releases in the local papers. A trade union might even hope for a square shake on the front pages of some metropolitan dailies. Always before in the United States the onset of depression had meant the decimation of labor organization. Ten unemployed men on every corner had meant an abundance of strikebreakers; companies had not feared strikes because they could not sell their products anyway; the rise in unemployment rates had meant a drop in monthly dues to local and national unions. With the going so rough, many organizations had disappeared. But in the Great Depression, union membership grew by as much as 4 million.* Familiarity with the cause of the working class by so many artists, writers, and movie people helped to acclimate other portions of the public to some of labor's bizarre strategies and tactics, which might otherwise have caused panic or streams of blood instead of the few trickles that developed. Black liberationists after World War II would call this style "democracy in the streets" (mid-Chapter 29). Oldtime buddies in the Industrial Workers of the World would talk about "direct action"; Jimmie Higgins in the hiring hall might counsel "hitting the bricks." Call it how you will, it bore little resemblance to the standard middle-class fantasy about the republic as being orderly lines of voters waiting placidly for their turn at the polls on election day.

If hundreds, thousands, of intellectuals took part in a rising pro-labor movement that furthered the humanization of American factories, their role should not be exaggerated. Some politicians also acted with honor and compassion, and a few have been immortalized in such labels as "the Wagner Act." But recognition that other groups in the society had power and used it should never divert us from the central truth: The glory days of labor progress during the Great Depression would not have happened if democracy had not taken to the streets. For decades the public demonstration in the United States had been a formalized ritual trumped up by the Establishment—flagwaving parades during Wilson's days in the White House, stuffy claptrap on the Fourth of July. When a worker charged at a militiaman, carrying a fistful of bolts and throwing them, the norms of polite society had little bearing.

Marches and meetings began, for understandable reasons, among the unemployed. A wave of public protests was often coordinated by Communists, who formed the National Unemployment Council immediately after the financial crash. Crowds stormed the city hall in Cleveland, Philadelphia, Los Angeles. By 6 March, 1930, the organization felt strong enough to call International Unemployment Day. New York witnessed a parade of 110,000, Detroit of 100,000. By February, 1932, a nationwide demonstration brought forth an estimated half million. Three separate petitions, each with more than a million names, were presented to Congress. Demands did not vary much: improved relief programs, unemployment compensation. Other organizations

---

*The drama of this transition was enormous, but the change was far from universal. As late as 1940 the owner of a half dozen mines around Glen Ferris, West Virginia, was quoted publicly on a strike against his operations: "Put a million dollars on a shelf for a year and you still have a million dollars. Put our employees on a shelf for a year and all you have is a pile of bones."

began to suspect that history was passing them by. The stodgy AFL with its history of "voluntarism" finally declared for unemployment benefits. The Socialists in 1932 set up their own organization for the jobless, and in 1936 it merged with the other national outfit to form the Workers' Alliance. Reliable information about these developments is very hard to find. Guesses at the original membership of the Workers' Alliance range from 93,000 to 500,000. By 1938 it could claim 1,500 locals in 45 states. Although the figures given here can be challenged, the impact of this militancy is beyond question. Recalling the prominence of strikebreakers in earlier mutinies, their obscurity after 1929 seems amazing.

Another breakthrough during the Great Depression was the relatively friendly governmental climate offered to trade unions. Reforms in the 48 states cannot be reported in this space; anyway, three federal laws seem preponderant. The change of tone became manifest before the New Deal. The two Congressional sponsors of the Norris-LaGuardia Act had advocated it long before its enactment in 1932. Key provisions were these: Yellow-dog contracts forbidding unions could not be enforced by federal courts (see late Chapter 23 on unions and the courts). Damage suits against unions were restricted. The statute also contained a policy statement. Since under present conditions, the individual employee could not affect the terms on which he worked, it was mandatory that "he should have full freedom of association, self-organization and designation of representatives of his own choosing, to negotiate the terms and conditions." These terms were virtually used verbatim in the two New Deal provisions that proved vital to the growth of collective bargaining: Section 7 (a) of the law establishing the NRA in 1933, and the National Labor Relations Act of 1935.

At this juncture, we encounter the phenomenon of a snowball rolling down a hill—cumulative effects. Section 7 (a) was meant by most of the officials who administered it to be a fake. In most industries it was a fake. But not in all. Of the three unions that benefited from the law in the two years of its existence, two were in the garment trades. They were led by Sidney Hillman (Amalgamated Clothing Workers, ACW) and by David Dubinsky (International Ladies' Garment Workers Union, ILGWU). The third was John L. Lewis's United Mine Workers (UMW). Even before 1929, these three unions, all in sick industries, had been stricken. The UMW had been almost wiped out. More blows fell after 1929. These three organizations (note that all were organized by industry rather than by craft) wobbled and reeled. Then came Section 7 (a). The leaders saw a chance to recoup. Their organizers swarmed into textile towns and coal camps. Lewis's henchmen had a simple slogan: "FDR wants you to join the union." Membership skyrocketed.

Per capita dues flowed into the coffers of ACW, ILG, UMW. A remarkable decision was made. Old-style time-servers might have simply voted themselves higher salaries and built larger mansions at Miami. But eight national unions, now affluent compared to former times, chose to put some of their unaccustomed wealth into breaking the open shop in mass-production industries. Heading the pack strode the massive bulk of Lewis. Himself corrupt through his career in the labor movement and a hopeless autocrat, he apparently overnight caught the altered tempo of the shops. The man should not be idealized (nor should the working class, for that matter). Countless times his thugs had beaten up dissidents at local meetings; no challenge to the regime was permitted; one socialist who wanted to democratize the UMW was expelled from it four times. But about 1933 Lewis sensed that a tidal wave of rebelliousness was sweeping through factories as well as mines. He would have agreed with Lenin, who after the Russian Revolution was asked: How do you make a revolution? His reply: You get in front of it and run like crazy to stay there. This anecdote belittles both Lenin and Lewis, but it does give a sense of the dynamics of a social explosion. At best the talk about "all that Mr. Roosevelt did for the poor" should be taken with a grain of salt; most of it is hokum. What the poor got, they took; nobody gave it.

An uproar surging in from the shops was the last thing in the world desired by the bureaucrats accustomed to running the AFL. They, together with the members of most AFL affiliates, wanted peace and quiet and steady work. They had no plan to cope with a mass upsurge, but they could not altogether ignore it. Plant after plant throughout the nation was being spontaneously organized by the men and women who worked in it. Sometimes literally wringing their hands, the AFL grannies figured out a format—the federal local. This device was merely a corral to hold the roundup until it could be divvied among ranch owners. That is, the skilled workers would be apportioned among craft unions; then the others in the factory could shift for themselves. Typical was a rubber plant in Akron, where some 4,500 workers set up an independent industrial union. They foolishly applied to the AFL for a charter. Within a few weeks they had been sorted out among 19 craft locals. In bargaining against a giant corporation, such divisions might be advantageous to a few dozen skilled employees; for most of the workers they can only be disastrous. Eugene Debs had understood that back in 1893 (mid-Chapter 20). Beginning about 1934, laborers in giant mills—often with little or no guidance or help from on top, sometimes with resistance from on top—had arrived at an organizational form suited to their needs.

Some academics who rail against "oversimplification" by the common man (whoever he is) have been guilty of oversimplifying the processes being considered here. They seize hotly upon the glib phrase by Samuel Gompers: More, Here, Now. But even that phrase, rightly understood, implied better wages and shorter hours. No general discussion of grievances over working conditions is possible because variations from industry to industry, from district to district, from one establishment within an industry to another, were the crux of the problem. Again, some examples must suffice. Coal miners suffered from silicosis, and many became paraplegics for life when underground timbering gave way. Glass and chemical and rubber factories exuded noxious fumes. An advance taste of hell was imparted to workers by the heat in the open-hearth department. In these jobs, men died young. I have seen young auto workers lie on the floor and retch from exhaustion. With the assembly line, man was adapted to the machine, not the machine to the man. The author of the finest study of the sit-down strike in Flint that crumpled the resistance of General Motors wrote: "It was the speed-up that organized Flint, as it was the one element in the life of all the workers that found a common basis of resentment. Wives who feared the intervention of the union vented their execration on the speed-up which left their husbands trembling and exhausted after their work and narrowed the life of the family to the mere acts of physical continuance." The same tale was told over and over. To these stories of physiological hardship must be added the deprivation of the spirit. Persons who have never been exposed to a world outside that of the whitecollar white apparently find it hard to realize that industrial and manual workers of every ethnic background need dignity just like the rest of the world. Let us consider an item from the file of the CIO Packinghouse Workers in Chicago; an exact copy of a grievance submitted at the Armour plant reads thus:

the string department carries an offensive odor to the extent that it is very hard to find a formular that will take it out of the skin. We have tried everything within our Power, to prevent this awful odor. When a worker takes a street car Every Body tries to get away from this awful smell. So we of the string department are asking the Company to place in our Department a wash room with three showers.

The CIO was built, partly by anger at the lofty policies decreed by top management, partly by gripes against commonplace slurs by petty foremen.

Historians like me are tempted by the dramatic episode, especially when it can be linked to a famous name. So this account cannot omit the clash of giants on the floor of the national AFL convention, during a debate on organizational policy in November, 1935, when Lewis struck the also gargantuan president of the Carpenters in the face. Such a public display of aggression was indeed remarkable since these two despots ordinarily let others do their fighting for them. What provoked them to turn to violence? The Carpenters' boss is perhaps easy to explain; it would not be nasty to label him a hooligan who was desperate to protect both his union's jurisdictional lines and the outlook from which it was derived. For Lewis, with his penchant for histrionics, the turmoil was a way to dramatize the cause of industrial unionism. To an ability at fisticuffs he added a genius for invective. At this 1935 convention eight AFL unions decided to found the Committee for Industrial Organization (CIO), but they would not go the ultimate of full separation from the AFL. Subsequently when CIO chiefs were discussing the situation, it was suggested that they should delay action to explore further into the mind of AFL president William Green. Lewis was jocular: "Explore the mind of Bill Green? Why, Bill and I had offices next door to each other for ten

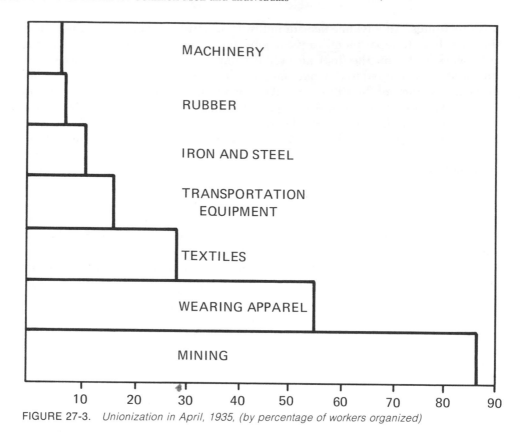

FIGURE 27-3. *Unionization in April, 1935, (by percentage of workers organized)*

years. . . . I have done a lot of exploring in Bill's mind and I give you my word there is nothing there." Maybe another warning is needed against romanticizing Lewis. Several of his associates have pointed to a self-serving motive for his role in the CIO: to keep his control in the UMW. By this account, hundreds of young rebels were challenging for power throughout the mine districts. Lewis siphoned them off by giving them paid jobs on the staff of the Steelworkers Organizing Committee.

The historian who speculates about the motives of any individual (including himself) is risking his life and his sacred honor; it is not a smart thing to do. Whatever the motives were, the results were the wonder of the world. In autos, organization was next to nothing before 1933, and due in considerable part to Roosevelt's devious behavior, progress under the Blue Eagle was slight. The Big Three had hardly been breached. Scattered locals existed in minor companies: White Motors in Cleveland, Auto-Lite in Toledo, some tool-and-die firms in Detroit. But by 1937 both GM and Chrysler had signed exclusive bargaining agreements. Ford did not topple until 1941. As of April, 1935, the percentage of employees in other industries covered by trade-union agreements is shown in Figure 27-3. Within ten years, by 1945, 80 per cent of the workers in all of these industries except textiles were protected by collective agreements.

The giant corporations never did fold up and surrender, but they were forced to make concessions. In retrospect, two episodes seem crucial. The first began on December 26, 1936, in Flint, Michigan, when the workers simply locked themselves in the plant at Fisher Body. No general ever devised better strategy. The company had only two sets of dies to stamp out bodies. Flint handled Buick, Oldsmobile, Pontiac. Fisher of Cleveland did all Chevrolets. As the strike went on, sometimes violently, for six weeks, it was the steadfastness of the ordinary worker that finally won a settlement, although the union produced several leaders of outstanding ability. But one man deserves special mention, Governor Frank Murphy. He was Catholic in a non-Catholic state. He was a Democrat in a Republican state. Now pressure was put on him to send in the National Guard to drive the strikers out of the plants. He must have been strongly tempted, but he let events run their course. Finally on 11 February the bastion of the open shop signed an agreement with the United Auto Workers (UAW). In less than three weeks a major subsidiary of U.S. Steel had signed with the Steelworkers Organizing Committee (SWOC).

These occurrences do not mean that smaller—still huge—firms would at all times follow the lead of the biggest manufacturer in the industry. So-called "Little Steel" fought back bitterly, highlighted by the attacks of South Chicago police outside the Republic plant in South Chicago that caused the death of ten strikers and injury to untold numbers. Ford remained unorganized for years, during which time its Service Department committed thousands of indecencies not to say crimes. Partly because of these strongholds of anti-unionism, the insurgency of industrial workers ran out of steam by about 1938. It revived briefly during World War II, and then was jettisoned by union chieftains.

A final word. The president of the United States was indifferent if not hostile to these efforts to improve the status of the industrial worker. He did champion the Social Security Act. FDR signed but clearly did nothing to promote the National Labor Relations Act. On the Fair Labor Standards Act of 1938 he was neutral. What has been more important in the long run was his unwillingness to use the new power structure of organized labor to alter the regularities of the American party system. In spite of his alleged affinities to Sidney Hillman, Roosevelt was always more comfortable with Ed Flynn and Ed Kelly and Jimmy Byrnes and Sam Rayburn. The mother of a former student of mine once asked, when confronted with some evidence about FDR: "Why did such a marvelous man allow so many terrible things?" It does make a chap wonder.

The persisting ditch between Mr. Citizen and Mr. Egghead had become a moat by 1929. Happily, the next decade framed new bridges between these

Courtesy of the Pennsylvania Academy of
Fine Arts

FIGURE 27-4. *Horace Pippin,* John Brown Going to His Hanging

John Brown Going to His Hanging can be viewed in several ways. Done by Horace Pippin, a black, finished in 1942, it can be seen as a manifestation of yet another upsurge in the campaign for black equality. During World War II quite a few Americans of all derivations and beliefs were horror-stricken by the brutalities that the fascist nations were inflicting on alien minorities. This awareness helped to make them aware of injustice in the United States. It also prompted them to comb the nation's past for heroes who had tried to smash the oppressions.

John Brown was not a happy choice for this role. He was, however, a master of self-righteousness. At his trial in 1859 he had declared: "I never did intend murder, or treason, or the destruction of property, or to excite or incite slaves to rebellion, or to make an insurrection." The unvarnished truth is that he had committed every one of these crimes: murder, treason, destruction of differing segments of society. The germs of a new community can be seen in several areas of culture during the Great Depression. In music a new form appeared as Dixieland jazz, which had appeal to both highbrow and lowbrow. The technology of radio and phonograph made popular music as well as more conventional types available to millions of listeners. The visual arts were offered to wider audiences by a proliferation of museums. Book publishing also had its revolutions. Monthly book clubs infiltrated the middle classes in particular. Novels were converted into films, and original screen plays added to the steady flow of movies. Nearly all Americans knew the Marx Brothers, Chaplin, Jean Harlow, Clark Gable, Gary Cooper. Perhaps most telling of all as an adhesive between formerly divorced groups was the broader base of public support behind the effort to organize the mass-production industries. Civic-minded academics and journalists found little to like about the craft unions of the American Federation of Labor, but they had less difficulty in identifying with the industrial unions of the Congress of Industrial Organizations. As employees in the dominant sectors of the economy were struggling to become unionized, the policies of the federal government usually amounted to benevolent neutrality (which was in itself an advance over the hostility of earlier times). Similarly, the indifference of federal authorities toward attempts to invigorate a higher culture can be seen in their acquiescence while the Federal Arts Projects atrophied away.

---

property, incitation to revolt. Nonetheless, this painting contains historical truth, not about John Brown perhaps, but about the rising militancy of many blacks during the war. Pippin said of his own art, "Pictures just come to my mind, and then I tell my heart to go ahead."

Pippin's three paintings that memorialized John Brown were also a landmark in the revival of the artistic primitives (see Figure 14-1). In this sense they were a bridge over the chasm between the intellectuals and the common man. While saluting Pippin's superb work, we might be puzzled to understand how he conquered his craft. Born in 1888 he went to a one-room country school in Pennsylvania. By his account he was already in trouble with the teacher by the time he was seven because he illustrated his spelling papers with sketches. In consequence he would be kept after school to prepare a respectable paper. When he got home he would be whipped for being late. But he persisted, until at last about 1937 he won some recognition. Within nine years he was dead.

Ways to Study History XXVII

Cross-examine the eye-witnesses for bias. This maxim can be explored by a reverse route through an anecdote. A few years back, no history of Tanganyika had ever been written. The region had just gained its freedom from the British Commonwealth; it would be an independent sovereignty in Africa. The British Colonial Office decided to throw open for scholarly use its records relating to Tanganyika (full independence in December 1961; united with Zanzibar and smaller islands in 1964 to form Tanzania).

An experienced anthropologist had spent several years doing field work in Tanganyika. He now saw an opening to do a firmly based history of that country. His earlier field work had been financed to a large degree by the Social Science Research Council. Chancing to encounter at a conference a grants officer from the SSRC, he asked if they would allow him a modest sum to go to England for a summer to explore the available Colonial Office records. In this fashion he could gain a better estimate of whether his long-term undertaking was feasible. In the language of the natural scientists, he proposed a pilot project; on a firing range the sergeant might call it a trial run. The grants officer, knowing the previous accomplishments of the applicant, was highly encouraging. A formal application was submitted. The anthropologist rented a house in England, made airplane reservations for his entire family—and then he got jolted. A word about procedures in foundations. Any request is normally submitted to outside "referees"; that is, other persons of standing who submit opinions about its worth. This rejection contained an opinion from a referee who leaned heavily against the applicant's reliance on Colonial Office papers because they were "prejudiced sources."

My colleagues chatted for a year trying to recall whether any of them had ever seen an unbiased source. We may doubt that one exists. Historical truth is approached by getting the available primary sources, weighing them against each other, and trying to correct for distortions. No eye-witness is fully trustworthy.

How to Get into a War: Installment II

From 1929 to 1939, the United States faced two major problems. The first: To cure the crushing unemployment—of manpower, of machinery, of money. Whether we think of muscle, of mind, of machines, of bank deposits, the amount of idleness was still appalling as late as 1940. On this score, in spite of raucous (but unsupported) assertions to the contrary, the New Deal failed. Some New Dealers had workable ideas, but their ideas were not usually the ones that were used. The second problem: To stop the spread of fascism without fighting a world war. On this score also, the New Deal failed. Need it have done so badly? Failure to cure unemployment is clearly quite distinct from failure to prevent war. The first could certainly have been alleviated by domestic policies dependent on no outside nations. The second required some cooperation from at least three foreign powers: the U.S.S.R., Great Britain, France. In regard to the latter two countries, that cooperation was never proffered. But Americans have little cause to boast of their record in those terrible years. And Main Street, not the White House, must bear the blame, or most of it.

Ironically, a World Disarmament Conference was scheduled for Geneva on 2 February, 1932. The fascist dictator of Italy, Benito Mussolini, had just named his son-in-law as the new foreign minister. That diplomat called on President Hoover in 1931. Henry Stimson, secretary of state, left a memo of the meeting:

> The President . . . gave us a summary of the attitude of the American man on the street. For a hundred and fifty years we had kept out of Europe; then in 1917 we had been dragged into a great war. We had spent forty billions of dollars in the war, and we had added ten billions more in the shape of loans after the war. We were spending a billion dollars a year on our disabled men. And yet Europe was in a worse condition than she was before the war. This, he said, led to despair as to Europe and European affairs on the part of the ordinary American citizen, and now he just wanted to keep out of the whole business. This was the general attitude of the American public, and he did not see how the United States could take the leadership in any direction.

Hoover was right in his assessment. American foreign policy for the next decade must be read in the light of this statement. But two addenda are needed. That catch-all word "isolationism" will conceal more than it reveals. Second, he was wrong about where the initial crisis would occur; his warnings like Washington's were against political commitments in Europe, whereas the United States was more concerned with economic involvements in Asia.

In the autumn of 1931, a conjunction of circumstances combined to give Japan a relatively free hand. England had just abandoned the gold standard and was trying madly to juggle its finances. The U.S.S.R. was absorbed in its Five-Year Plan and the consequent popular resistance. Civil strife in China was multiplied by a Yangtze flood. Naval construction in the United States and Britain had lagged, while Japan steadily built to its limits under the Washington Treaty of 1922. So in September the Japanese army staged an incident at Mukden and followed with an invasion of Manchuria. For three months the United States, hoping it could strengthen the moderates in Japan, sent only private protests. At last the secretary of state, Henry L. Stimson, declared that the nation would not recognize any government that infringed American rights, the Open Door (end of Chapter 21), or the Kellogg-Briand Pact (end of Chapter 24). Neither Britain nor France would support these doctrines—a division among the antifascist governments that would be re-enacted many times before World War II. Stimson made a strong plea for international cooperation, but one wonders. Already he had told China: "We have not attempted to go into the question of right and wrong. . . . we are not taking sides." For such a moralizing nation, the matter of right and wrong would seem to be critical. By 3 March, 1932, the British ambassador in Washington was writing to the foreign minister: "I know that the Americans are dreadful people to deal with. They cannot make firm promises, but they jolly you along with fair prospects and when you are committed they let you down."

Another generalization may be ventured. It is usually malarkey to speak of "the" foreign policy of the United States. Nearly always there are several in operation, often unknown to the practitioners of a contradictory policy. Manchuria offers an illustration. By April, 1932, Stimson was telling the cabinet that it was "almost impossible" to avoid thinking of war against Japan. He warned that the American navy was not equal to the task of "meeting Japan." President Hoover rejoined that reasons existed for not having an "offensive Navy." When Stimson went off (unofficially of course) for talks with other powers at the League of Nations in Geneva, Hoover cut the ground from under him. At the president's instructions, the undersecretary of state announced that in regard to Manchuria our "government's policy excluded sanctions of economic pressure or military force." Japan set up a puppet government in Manchuria, named it Manchukuo, recognized its legality. The League of Nations issued an innocuous report. On one point Stimson had his way with Hoover, but his victory can hardly be regarded with unqualified enthusiasm. Congress enacted a law for Philippine independence. The president vetoed it because the secretary urged that it would unleash further Japanese expansion. As to that, he was undoubtedly right. During the interregnum between administrations, President-elect Roosevelt seemed to be friendly to Stimson's stiff attitude. Further support for a tough line came from messages sent by the American ambassador in Japan: "There is no bluff in her attitude."

The first diplomatic problem to confront the new president was an International Economic Conference slated to convene in London in June. This episode exemplifies three aspects of the years beginning with 1933: one personal, one intragovernmental, one intergovernmental. (1) FDR had a penchant for secrecy. He sometimes tried sneaky tactics when a candid statement of the truth would probably have worked better (end Chapter 26). Perhaps more frequently, he would assign the same job to two or three men, and leave them free to carve each other's backs. By this mechanism, the only man who could make the final decision was the president. Thus the secretary of state was the formal head of the American delegation to the London Conference. But soon FDR also dispatched an assistant secretary of state as his personal representative. Who had power to speak for the United States? The president. (2) The government in Washington was severely divided on monetary policy. Congress had opened the door for devaluation of the dollar. Although this step was not taken until the Gold Reserve Act of January, 1934, the clauses in both public and private contracts that provided for payment in a fixed quantity of gold had been declared null and void. One faction was pressing for immediate devaluation, arguing that if the price of gold went up, the prices of all other commodities would rise also, and thus domestic production would be encouraged. Opponents screamed that the determining element was the quantity of foreign trade, which could best be expanded by a stabilization of international exchange rates. The latter was the goal of the

London meetings. The former was Roosevelt's decision. While several commentators have complained that he "scuttled" the Economic Conference, he was probably justified. To quote his grounds at the time, "The sound internal economic system of a nation is a greater factor in its well-being than the price of its currency in changing terms of the currencies of other nations." So far, so good, but, the domestic monetary policies of the New Deal for the next two years were at best mediocre. (3) While the impact of Roosevelt's actions on the home economy might be graded LP—low pass—its political impact on the world arena was ghastly—pronounced F. The backbiting within the American delegation was supplemented by squabbles in public among the United States, Britain, and France. Meanwhile the blatantly militarist nations could sit by as delighted spectators. A quick summation might be in place. The countries soon to be the Allies were demonstrating daily that they could not manage their own economies. They had admitted privately to fascist diplomats that their electorates were so polarized that the government was paralyzed. Now they added a public exhibition of how embittered the intergovernmental fracas had become.

My intention is not to saddle FDR, or the State Department, or the American people with sole blame for the next eight years. But when the international order fell in ruins, the United States had wrought its share of the damage.

In November, 1933, the administration did take a promising step. Twenty-six years after the Bolshevik Revolution in Russia, our government acknowledged that it had occurred. The initial opposition in Washington to recognition of the U.S.S.R. had been ideological; President Wilson at the time of the Versailles Conference was obsessed by this new menace to a world made safe for democracy. A rationale had to be found, and it was: The Reds would not pay their debts; they had confiscated American property without compensation. Even after the United States had withdrawn its tiny invading army from Siberia, Secretary of State Hughes continued to harp on these themes.* It took FDR and his advisers to cut through the verbiage. They were urged by some forceful proponents: executives of GE hoped to sell dozens of generators to a new customer, while International Harvester foresaw a giant market for its farm machinery. (Similar influences, especially from wheat farmers, operated on the Canadian recognition of Red China in 1970.) Fittingly, one of the loudest opponents of recognition was the AFL, on the grounds that the U.S.S.R. did not have "free" trade unions; advocates of recognition replied

---

*The hypocrisy was distinct. When the United States enacted prohibition, it rendered worthless hundreds of millions of dollars in private property. When it abrogated the gold clause in all contracts, it greatly reduced the value of many forms of property. But when private American rights were disturbed by Mexico (oil fields) or the U.S.S.R. (railroads), our policy-makers became frenetic with moral outrage.

with sharp questions about the degree of freedom in Lewis' Mine Workers or Hutcheson's Carpenters. The extent to which the governments of the U.S. and the U.S.S.R. lived up to their respective commitments in the exchange of ambassadors will remain in dispute, but it is worth while to know what they agreed to. As stated by President Roosevelt to Peoples Commissar for Foreign Affairs Maxim Litvinov, the Russians would undertake the following:

1. To respect scrupulously the indisputable right of the United States to order its own life within its own jurisdiction in its own way and to refrain from interfering in any manner in the internal affairs of the United States, its territories or possessions.
2. To refrain, and to restrain all persons in Government service and all organizations of the Government or under its direct or indirect control, including organizations in receipt of any financial assistance from it, from any act overt or covert liable in any way whatsoever to injure the tranquillity, prosperity, order, or security of the whole or any part of the United States. . . .

FDR made a reciprocal pledge to Litvinov. This opening might hopefully have led to an antifascist alliance before the situation degenerated into all-out war.

But almost immediately Congress began to move against the other potential partners in such a coalition, in particular Great Britain and France. The Johnson Act of 13 April, 1934, forbade all dealings within the U.S. in the securities of any government that had gone in default to this country on the payment of its war debts from World War I. Inside two months, Finland was the only nation that owed the United States from World War I which had not defaulted. The next harmful move was the Neutrality Act of 1935. This measure was opposed by both FDR and Secretary of State Cordell Hull. They both favored an embargo on arms shipments to belligerents, but they wanted the president to have discretion to ban shipments only to the aggressor but not necessarily to the victim. What they got was a mandatory decree, which passed each house by a virtually unanimous vote. The statute was to run for only six months; when it came up for renewal in February, 1936, Roosevelt sought amendments that would meet his original desires. He failed.

Events were rolling downhill fast. Hitler in March, 1935, repudiated unilaterally the Treaty of Versailles by instituting compulsory military service; long before, Germany had left the League of Nations. Probably noting the American embargo on arms exports, Mussolini launched his armies into Ethiopia on 3 October. In December the foreign ministers of Britain and France came up with the Hoare-Laval Pact that proposed to give more than half of Ethiopia to Italy.* The agreement cost Samuel Hoare his post, but

---

*One of the many disgusting features of this era is the willingness of Britain and France to give away property that did not belong to them; witness also the agreements at Munich, September, 1938.

British foreign policy did not alter appreciably, and Mussolini got the "living space" or *lebensraum* that he and Hitler constantly demanded. Two verbal challenges to these aggressive moves need to be noted. FDR spoke to Congress of the expansionist nations:

> They have therefore impatiently reverted to the old belief in the law of the sword, or to the fantastic conception that they, and they alone, are chosen to fulfill a mission and that all the others among the billion and a half human beings in the world must and shall learn from them and be subject to them.

Litvinov spoke on the sacrifice of Ethiopia in July, 1936:

> I say we do not want a League that is safe for aggressors. We do not want that kind of League, even if it is universal, because it would become the very opposite of an instrument of peace.

When Litvinov spoke, Hitler's intentions were clear. On 7 March, 1936, his troops had moved into the Rhineland. German documents captured later make it clear that if France had resisted the occupation, Hitler's generals had orders to withdraw. France might well have resisted if she had believed she would be supported by England and the United States. By herself, she did not. Thus we arrive at a question that may not be answerable but that must be asked: What was the last possibly day that fascist encroachments could have been stopped without a world war? Some historians put it here. I think they are too early by about thirty months; my date would be Munich. Again, Litvinov had his say about the fall of the Rhineland: "One cannot fight for the collective organization of security without taking collective measures against the violation of international obligations. We, however, do not count among such measures collective capitulation to the aggressor." The Soviet slogan for the next three years would be "collective security."

Japan had struck. Italy had struck. Germany had struck. The pace accelerated. Next the fascists in Spain would strike. In a country long ruled by monarchy, the Catholic church, and nobility, a new republic had been formed. The former rulers found this situation intolerable, so armed insurrection was hurled against the regime. The rebels, headed by Francisco Franco, were supplied with war-planes and other modern munitions by Germany and Italy. The Republic got some material aid from the U.S.S.R., but the supply bases for the opposition were much closer. American policy in this crisis, if can be called by so dignified a term, was predetermined. Congress had made its position clear by its refusal to modify the Neutrality Act; on 6 January, 1937, it forbade exporting munitions "for the use of either of the opposing forces in Spain." The administration had no choice but to impose an embargo on all shipments of armaments to Spain, either to the Republicans or the insurrectionists. Inaction by the federal government was vociferously approved by many elements in American society, not least by the ordinary citizen who wanted chiefly to stay clear of troublesome situations. Of the many elements in the power structure whose voices spoke with affection of the Franco rebellion, probably none were heard more widely than several prelates of the Roman Church. Their view was represented at high levels in the Roosevelt administration; one adherent was Joseph P. Kennedy, American ambassador to Great Britain and father of a future president. To many Americans their government, once proud of its republicanism, was permitting, perhaps encouraging, the lynching by fascist Italian and German arms of a fellow republic. The intellectuals found their greatest moral issue since the Civil War in the United States. Never again after the Spanish civil war would the forces of good seem so clearly arrayed against the forces of evil. But Washington left no doubt as to its contrary attitude. A movement had started in many European countries to recruit International Brigades, volunteers from abroad to fight Franco in Spain. The contingent from the United States was called the Abraham Lincoln Battalion. The few hundred Americans who sneaked abroad to join it were mainly intellectuals; those of working-class or middle-class background were inconsequential. The survivors returning to their homeland were subjected to endless persecutions—revocation of passports, discriminations in their search for work. In spite of the sacrifices made in Spain by thousands of Spaniards and their foreign allies, the Republic would fall in 1939.

Japan struck again in July, 1937, ramming into China determined on conquest. Having already given notice that she would not continue to adhere to the Naval Limitation Treaty of 1922, she threw her strengthened martial might across the Sea of Japan. The onslaught included the bombing of Nanking and other cities. This action was sharply protested by the United States: "any general bombing of an extensive area wherein resides a large populace engaged in peaceful pursuits is unwarranted and contrary to principles of law and humanity." Three comments might be made. (1) Italy had earlier bombed civilians in Ethiopia, and Franco had done so in Spain. (2) These atrocities were regarded with horror even in the allegedly "isolationist" Midwest of the United States. (3) Within a few years (starting in World War II), the American air force would be bombing civilians in several countries, and the typical citizen would view it as normal behavior.

The transition from 1937 to the present seems to me great, but it should not be exaggerated. In 1937, most Americans wanted only to be left alone to worry out their private affairs, as three episodes will reveal. They were simultaneous, almost. The first can use a brief preface. One student of FDR has written: "As a foreign policy maker, Roosevelt during his first term was more pussyfooting politician than political leader." With qualification, this judgment will hold for most of his second term. But in fairness it must be said that he did send up trial balloons several times; he did make some gestures at diplomatic leadership. To illustrate, on 5 October, 1937, the president was in

Chicago to make a speech, where he said: "The peace, the freedom and the security of ninety per cent of the population of the world is being jeopardized by the remaining ten per cent who are threatening a breakdown of all international order and law." And: "We are adopting such measures as will minimize our risk of involvement, but we cannot have complete protection in a world of disorder in which confidence and security have broken down." He suggested that the "peace-loving nations" should "quarantine the aggressor." These pronouncements, if we can judge by the press, were greeted by fire and ice. So Roosevelt pulled his hand from the flames, his foot from the water.

Meanwhile the aggressors, far from being quarantined, were pushing forward on several fronts. The Japanese, advancing rapidly in China, flaunted their contempt for the United States on 12 December, 1937. The USS *Panay,* a gunboat, was at anchor in the Yangtze. Although she flew the American flag, she was attacked by bombers and sunk. American merchant ships nearby were also attacked. Officials in Washington were furious. Secretary of the Navy Claude Swanson wanted war. Harold Ickes, secretary of the interior, pondered the matter: "I confess that Swanson's point of view cannot be lightly dismissed. Certainly war with Japan is inevitable sooner or later, and if we have to fight her, isn't this the best time?" The American mood decreed otherwise. Within days, nearly everybody had lost interest. The hysteria of 1898 was not present in 1937; folks wanted just to go about their personal affairs. When Japan on Christmas Eve offered to pay the full indemnity asked by the United States and to take action against the responsible naval officer, the controversy closed.

But it did force action that indicated for a third time just how the country felt. The Ludlow Amendment to the Constitution had been in the congressional hopper for some time. It provided that, except in case of invasion, war could not be declared without prior approval by a referendum of the nation's voters. The audacity of this move to strip the president and Congress of their traditional powers was astounding. A House committee had been keeping the amendment bottled up. After the *Panay* incident, a petition to bring the measure out onto the floor picked up the required names. Strong pressure from the president brought about fifty Democrats back into line, but even so, the Amendment lost only by a vote of 209 to 188. Within two months, German armies moved into Austria. The *Wehrmacht* was rolling onward. Small wonder that Prime Minister Neville Chamberlain would say, "It is always best and safest to count on nothing from the Americans but words." In April he entered an agreement with Italy that recognized Italian interests in the Mediterranean and Africa; he went so far as to promise to persuade other governments to recognize her sovereignty in Ethiopia.

In the United States, appeasement of fascism had prestigious spokesmen. Lindbergh urged that an accommodation with Hitler "could maintain peace and civilization throughout the world as far into the future as we can see." Henry Ford, pursuant to his longstanding anti-Semitism, accepted from

Hitler the highest medal that the Third Reich could grant, the Award of the Grand Cross of the German Eagle. The Midwestern origins of the latter two men might lead to a false inference, so it should be said that, contrary to the divisions of sentiment from 1914 to 1917, the clash of opinion before World War II seems not to have followed any clear sectional lines. Some of the firmest advocates of a vigorous American stand came from the same region as Ford and Lindbergh. The most celebrated small-town editor in the country, William Allen White of Kansas, headed the Committee to Defend America by Aiding the Allies. Senator Norris of Nebraska, with his long record of gallant opposition—to the powers of Speaker Cannon, to private control of Hetch Hetchy, to the sale of the Muscle Shoals power project to Ford, to the Ku Klux Klan—became an outspoken adversary of the fascist nations. While Sinclair Lewis of Minnesota warned of the dangers of fascism in America, his wife Dorothy Thompson was sending home from Europe an impassioned set of daily newspaper despatches about the emergent menace there. To finish off this selective catalog, which proves nothing but which might raise some doubts, the Republican candidate for president in 1940, Wendell Willkie, had his roots in Indiana. His strong antifascist stand certainly did not delight his fellow partisans who wanted to "stay out of it."

Came the point of no return—Munich. At the time the administration was badly off balance. From his smashing re-election in 1936, FDR's popularity had fallen precipitously, due in the large part to the economic recession (late Chapter 26). By the summer of 1938 barely half of the electorate would report in a poll that they would vote for Roosevelt again.

The significance of Czechoslovakia can hardly be exaggerated. With a population of 15 million and the Skoda munitions works, it had an efficient army of 1.5 million men and an air force of 2,000 planes. Its stragetic location is clear. It was the keystone in France's system of alliances. Further, in 1935 it had signed a treaty of mutual assistance with the U.S.S.R. which was to be implemented only *after* the Franco-Czech agreement had been enforced. Chamberlain pulled the whole rug out. If Germany invades Czechoslovakia, he was asked in Commons, and France goes to her defence, will Britain support France? He gave no guarantees. With strong support among persons of German extraction in the Sudetenland, Hitler hoped to pluck off Czechoslovakia in the spring of 1938. The crisis was fended off. By autumn, the *Wehrmacht* obviously was ready to strike. Hurried meetings were held. Britain and France invited Hitler and Mussolini; nobody from Czechoslovakia took part. Hitler got the Sudetenland, undermining the defenses of the smaller nation. The premier of France was horrified at the triumphal greeting given him on his return to Paris; he thought the concessions to Hitler were a disaster. Chamberlain had no doubts. Stepping from the plane in England he waved a document over his head and shouted: "This means peace in our time." He wrote of Hitler: "In spite of the hardness and ruthlessness I thought I saw in his face, I got the impression that here was a man who could be relied upon when he had given his word." The preceding pledge by the chancellor of the Third Reich had been simple: "This is the last territorial claim I shall make in Europe."

The president seemed almost immobilized. During the Munich crisis his chief public actions were appeals to Hitler to act in the interests of peace. After the Munich agreements, Harold Ickes appealed to him to explain to the American people how grave the international situation had become. Roosevelt refused, saying that nobody would believe him. Then in rapid-fire order came calamities that knocked FDR, and millions of other Americans, off the fence. In March, 1939, German troops moved into Prague and controlled all of Czechoslovakia. In August the Nazi-Soviet non-aggression pact was made public.* Thus further unleashed, *blitzkrieg* gashed into Poland, which fell almost overnight. At first the official reaction in Washington to these catastrophes was to withdraw the nation farther into a shell. The Neutrality Act of 1939 (4 November) forbade all American merchant vessels to enter into certain declared war zones. When the Allies entered the war at the invasion of Poland, they could not count on getting supplies from us.**

Then the president began to act with a firmer hand. The arms embargo was lifted, with the proviso that Allied ships still had to carry the goods away from U.S. ports. German submarines in the next year had a field day on the Atlantic—World War I all over again. The British desperately needed warships that could convoy the freighters. With a heretofore atypical audacity, Roosevelt made the destroyer-bases deal in September, 1940, (at the height of a tough campaign for re-election). The British leased to the United States for 99 years a string of naval and air bases from Newfoundland to British Guiana. They were paid with 50 destroyers of the 1200-ton type, designated "over-age" (were they?). Fortunately for FDR, his opponent for the presidency approved of the destroyer-bases swap. Wendell Willkie hailed from Elwood, Indiana, but since 1933 he had been president of one of the largest electric-power companies in the country (Ickes jested that he was "a simple barefoot Wall Street lawyer.").

---

*For many years, this agreement was hardly debated in scholarly circles; everybody denounced it. Such condemnation seems far too narrow. The Soviet Union had been waving the wand of joint security for years, to see it rejected by Britain and France. It knew that Hitler had ambitions to drive eastward; he had said so in *Mein Kampf* (1925). It saw his armies take Czechoslovakia, and knew they were about to take Poland. The temptation to buy time was strong. What the U.S.S.R. bought was about two years.

**Here mention must be made of hearings before the Nye Committee of the Senate, which beginning in 1934 had taken testimony about the relation to World War I of American business, especially munitions manufacturers and investment bankers (see Chapter 22). Strictures against the Nye hearings by several historians arise from a failure to make the following simple distinction: While these Congressional sessions provide incontrovertible testimony that many American companies from 1914 to 1918 had an unwholesome effect on diplomacy and made exorbitant profits, that disclosure did not really show that the situations prior to American entry into the two wars were analogous. Of course this fear or possible inference of the time might have inhibited earlier American involvement prior to World War II.

However, his views on foreign relations were quite similar at this time to those of FDR. Given slight alternatives as to policy, voters plunked for experience. Roosevelt had a 5 million majority in the popular vote; the electoral vote was 449 to 82. The campaign was as dishonest as most. Self-proclaimed radicals chanted:

> *I hate war, so does Eleanor*
> *But we won't be safe til everybody's dead.*

The president solemnly intoned, "I have said this before, but I shall say it again and again: Your boys are not going to be sent into any foreign wars."

Did everybody suspect that almost everybody was lying? By November, 1940, no outlet was open for the United States to avoid entering World War II except total retreat into the Western Hemisphere, and probably even that strategem would have failed. Events might well have resembled the course of American entry into the earlier Great War—conflict on the oceans followed by an open pronouncement of hostilities. Already by 1941 the United States was involved in an undeclared naval war. But crucial facts about that war were concealed from the American people. One instance, (notorious later) was an attack on a German submarine by an American destroyer, the USS *Greer*. Roosevelt publicly denied that American forces had precipitated any armed clashes. In fact U.S. vessels had been "homing" on Nazi U-boats and radioing their position to British and French warships.

Options had existed. Now they were gone. No alternatives were left. Congress reluctantly and belatedly accepted this truth. FDR had a brilliant idea after the election; befitting him, it was shifty. To avoid aggravating the lingering resentments about unpaid war debts, the United States would lend goods instead of money to the Allies. One senator denounced the resultant bill as "the New Deal's Triple-A foreign policy; it will plow under every fourth American boy." Roosevelt called the charge "the most untruthful, as well as the most dastardly, unpatriotic thing that has ever been said." The bill passed, with an appropriation of $7 billion. However, Congress was nowhere close to voting a declaration of war or to committing American armed forces. Without the attack on Pearl Harbor at the end of 1941, the tenuous threads of American neutrality might have held for at least a year longer. Doubtless eventually they would have been severed by damage to American interests on the oceans—but when?

The Republicans charged that the president connived at the Japanese attack on December 7. This accusation needs to be evaluated, if only because it would serve as the basis for Congressional hearings after the war that would win Republican control of both Houses in 1946. Many people believed it—one sign of the growing distrust within the country—and evidence pointing in that direction is easy to find. These things seem reasonably certain: Roosevelt by the autumn of 1941 was clearly committed to thwarting the expansionist powers; nobody can know whether he was so committed to the degree that he might have asked for a declaration of war without violent provocation by the enemy. In highest circles the opinion was general that war against Japan had to come, a view that we have heard stated in Washington since the invasion of Manchuria (early Chapter 28). Also many officials realized the advantages to this country if Japan did attack. In October, 1941, the United States imposed a special alert on its forces in the Far East. Stimson, now secretary of war, wrote in his diary: ". . . so we face the delicate question of the diplomatic fencing to be done so as to be sure that Japan was put in the wrong and made the first bad move—overt move!" The head of Navy Plans thus described the alert: "It was an attempt to retain the peace as long as possible and to make sure that when war came that it would be initiated by Japan and not by the U.S." Certainly many aspects of American behavior encouraged the Japanese to be the aggressor: the lagging economy, the surging rifts in the body politic, the decision to leave the Philippines by 1946, the reduction in force of America's Pacific fleet during 1941 to build up power in the Atlantic. But none of this constitutes a plot with Japan; nothing here constitutes treason. The most positive verdict that can be rendered on the Republican indictment is the old Scottish judgment—Not proven. Personally I think it is despicably false, and that the men who returned the indictment knew it to be false.

However, other charges are true: carelessness in high places, and a grossly inefficient bureaucracy including civilian and military branches. The lack of system was incredible. Intelligence staffs overseas were picked by the local commanding officer; their contact with G-2 in Washington was at best sporadic. A top Japanese diplomatic code called Magic had been broken. But almost nobody in Washington was allowed to see the decoded messages, and the favored few had the paper taken from their hands almost the moment they got it. Nobody knew who saw it, so they made false assumptions about who had what information. The Navy had the key to Magic, and it did not share its secret with the Army. Another possible source of information in Hawaii was radar, but there were only mobile sets that could not detect low-flying planes, could not detect beyond 130 miles, could not detect within 30 miles. Then, for defense, planes could have flown patrols around Hawaii. To be effective, such patrols would have had to go as far out as 800 miles. The planes were not available. Military authorities had asked for another 180 B-17's; unfortunately, that number of B-17's did not exist in the entire United States. A scream has been heard repeatedly: "Roosevelt was warned." So he was, notably by the American ambassador in Tokyo. The warnings, however, were general, and were hardly needed: everybody knew Japan's aggressive intentions. But when and where would she strike?

Serious errors were made. Japan's striking capacity was falsely estimated because it was thought she would have to use land bombers based on Formosa, and she did not have planes that could make the round trip. So she used aircraft carriers. The consequences for the United States were disastrous. Eight battleships were damaged or destroyed at Pearl Harbor, plus three light cruisers and other invaluable matériel. At least nine hours elapsed before the Japanese assaulted the Philippines. They found the American planes lined up conveniently, wingtip to wingtip, so they wiped out half of the bombers and two thirds of the fighters. The explanation of this folly seems to be that orders had been given to transfer the B-17's to a new and safer air strip. But the facility was not yet fully prepared for large bombers, and B-17's were a precious item in December, 1941.

Looking back at 7 December, 1941, we might ponder a few generalizations. Decision-makers were not getting the information they needed to act intelligibly, or to act at all.* Zany though it was, Naval Intelligence was getting most of its information about the foreign policy of the United States by decoding Japanese messages sent in Magic. A crucial part of the matter was the tendency of a bureaucracy to smother its messages in noise, to generate memoranda that convey no information at all but that are intended to create the illusion that "*I* at least am busy." (Persons familiar with large universities will know the pattern: the only scholars who get any books read, much less written, are those who drop nearly all of their incoming communiqués into the waste basket unopened.) In the words of the most thoughtful student of this disaster, Roberta Wohlstetter: "In short, we failed to anticipate Pearl Harbor not for want of the relevant materials, but because of a plethora of irrelevant ones."

The position of the United States was desperate, but not hopeless. Negatively, in the Pacific both its navy and its air force had been for practical purposes wiped out. Military hardware within this country was in short supply, partly because such intensive efforts had been made to ship equipment to Great Britain; American troops in training were using telephone poles as simulated artillery. Although the size of the armed forces had increased four times, still it counted only some 2 million. Positively the country had three assets that were tangible. Its people nearly equalled in numbers the populations of Germany and Japan combined, and were relatively healthy in spite of depression ravages. Second, its productive potential from already existing plant was huge. Ironically, because of idle capacity of both manpower and machinery—such a scandal for years—size of the armed forces and output of military goods could expand greatly without undue disruption to civilian output. The Liaison Conference that ruled Japan had estimated that the American potential for waging war was seven or eight times that of their own country, but stupidly they paid only "lip service" to this ratio. A canny prognosis was made by the commander of the Japanese navy:

---

*Japan had similar frictions. Her foreign minister complained on the eve of war against the United States that the "high command refused to divulge figures on the numbers of our forces, or any facts relating to operations."

> If you tell me that it is necessary that we fight, then in the first six months to a year of war against the U.S. and England I will run wild, and I will show you an uninterrupted succession of victories; I must also tell you that should the war be prolonged for two or three years, I have no confidence in our ultimate victory.

Third, even though France had been knocked out, the United States had two allies who were still functioning: Great Britain and the U.S.S.R. Without them America's maneuvering room would have disappeared. She would have had no choice but to withdraw into the Western Hemisphere while the Axis ran wild elsewhere.

It remained to convert these three assets into kinetic energy as quickly as may be. As in our consideration of earlier wars, the analysis here will focus on policy and strategy, with little attention to battles and tactics. (The memory of those beastly frays will never be lost to the participants: Midway, the Coral Sea, Guadalcanal, Taiwan, Okinawa, Anzio, Cassino, Omaha Beach, the Bulge.).

American policy was sound—to destroy the military power of the Axis. Nothing less would suffice. But as this policy was spelled out, it became less satisfactory. Conferring at Casablanca on 14 January, 1943, FDR and Churchill announced their aim as "unconditional surrender." In Roosevelt's words: "It does not mean the destruction of the population of Germany, Italy, or Japan, but it does mean the destruction of the philosophies in those countries which are based on conquest and the subjugation of other people." No other approach could have been taken to the Nazis. Theirs was a despotic regime from top to bottom. The removal of a few men at the top would not do the job; the entire political machine had to be smashed. Japan was different. Members of its ruling strata, both industrialists and civil servants, were not thoroughly committed to militarism. A conditional surrender might well have been considered. Crucial to the conditions would be the absolute disbandment of all armed forces and the destruction of all implements of war. Another limitation on Allied policy was its lasting flirtation with the shoring up of pre-war colonialism—the chief obstructionist being Britain and the chief areas in contention being the Far East, the Middle East, and the Balkans.

Strategy also was generally sound. The struggle against Germany was to take first place over the Pacific war. Weird reasons have been given to explain this choice. According to a 1965 study: "This priority was maintained on the sound assumption that Germany without Japan would be as strong as ever, whereas Japan without Germany could not stand long." Neither half of this alleged assumption will hold water. Japan for "six months to a year" did mighty well without German aid. The chief reason for concentration against Germany is that she was an immediate threat to the homelands of two of the Allies, Japan to none. In retrospect, invasion of the British Isles was turned back by the air battles of the autumn of 1940. Clearly it was vital to Britain and the United States that the Soviet Union should not fall, which would release

German might for piratical adventures elsewhere. Thoughtful men have never spent a more tense winter than 1942–1943: if the British had not held at El Alamein, if the Russians had not held at Stalingrad, the Third Reich with Japan might have controlled the Euro-Asian land mass plus Africa.

One error in strategy seems obvious; another is becoming increasingly clear. The first is the Italian campaign. It was a fiasco. Each German soldier tied up ten Allied soldiers. Losses were exorbitant; possible gains could not be decisive. In this instance, FDR allowed himself to be lured by Churchill into buying a white elephant; if the invasion of France had been undertaken sooner, the end of the war would have come earlier. The other questionable strategy was heavy reliance on strategic bombing. Substantial chunks of evidence suggest that bombing of this type has minimal military effect, (Document 28-3; also Chapter 30). The U.S.S.R. did not use strategic bombers. This abstinence was not prompted by humanitarianism; they simply did not believe that strategic bombing was an economical and efficient way to win a war.

Strategy is devised by men. The ranking generals in the army at the outbreak of war were peacetime and stodgy; quickly younger men were jumped over their heads. With remarkably few exceptions, the men commanding armies and fleets during World War II were intelligent and forceful, right up to Chief of Staff George C. Marshall and Chief of Naval Operations Ernest J. King. Of course the generals did load the game in their own favor; the results were fine for them, but lethal for combat soldiers. Of all the Allied armies, ours was the only one that did not rotate units in and out of the front lines. It rotated individual men. Result: If you were in a combat unit early in the war, your chances of survival were slight. Every paratrooper I knew was convinced that the war would last longer than he would. When the second Allied invasion of France pushed northward from Toulon on 15 August, 1944, all three American divisions involved had already made two or more amphibious landings. One sergeant in that landing spoke:

> I came in at Sicily brand-new. I didn't know my tail from third base. I was only 19. I was only a private then, too. Then pretty soon one guy gets knocked off and pretty soon another guy gets knocked off and another guy and another guy and pretty soon I'm the oldest guy in the squad and so they make me the squad leader.
>
> Then Salerno and some of my new guys get knocked off, and I keep getting more and more new guys, and they keep getting knocked off. They pulled us out of Cassino and shipped us to Anzio, and it was the same old story. I guess I must have had about five different squads.
>
> I don't know how I happened to hang around all this time. Maybe I'm just lucky.

An infantryman might still see "the whites of their eyes," but for many combatants, modern warfare was vastly less personal than its antetypes. A former bombardier recalled: "I remember distinctly seeing, from our great height, the bombs explode in the town, flaring like matches struck in fog. I was completely unaware of the human chaos below."

The depersonalization of warfare obviously was made possible by innovations in technology. Equally obviously, the industrial strength of the United States was a main factor in its contribution to Allied victory. The saying was common: "The war is being won on the assembly lines in Detroit." Battlefields played a part, but the common lore at home often tended to slight that element. And in truth it was the miracles of production in factories and on farms that enabled the armed forces to be so lavish in squandering matériel. No purpose could be served here in piling up statistics, but we can look at two critical items: warplanes and shipping. At the time of Pearl Harbor, the annual rate of plane output was 25,000. The president called for 60,000 in 1942. By the war's end, the nation had produced nearly 300,000 planes. The approach to shipping was to take over the designs of an old-fashioned British tramp steamer, to be known as the Liberty ship. Construction of such a vessel in 1941 required 355 days. When 1942 ended, the time had been reduced to 56 days. One shipyard achieved a time of 14 days. At war's end the United States had bottoms on the oceans totalling 36 million tons.

Except for its gaudy, ghastly finale, the conflict was a war of attrition. Victory in Europe meant a steady pounding forward, terminating at Hitler's aerie, Berchtesgaden. Japan was conquered by sweeping sea battles and by a sweaty malignant murderous process of island-hopping, to Okinawa at the threshhold of the final objective. Nobody was sure what would happen next. Would it be necessary to go for the jugular by invading the industrial plains around Tokyo? Universal opinion in Japanese military intelligence in Washington was that Japan would surrender by the autumn (for reasons to be considered below) without an invasion, but nothing was certain. For years, men far from the battle zones had been working toward what would become American policy.

The story of the atomic bomb could reasonably be started at any of several episodes, such as Einstein's papers early in the century that announced his famous relativity formula: $e = mc^2$, (where e stands for the amount of energy released, m for the mass being exploded, and c^2 for the velocity of light squared); matter, accelerated beyond the speed of light, could become pure energy. This account must be foreshortened, so it starts with January, 1939, when two scientists in Berlin split the uranium atom. Those few residents of the United States who understood much about nuclear energy were galvanized by thinking about the new potential for destruction in Hitler's hands. The power released from one atom may be negligible, but what if thousands or millions of atoms could be harnessed into a chain reaction? Significantly, these *cognoscenti* were all recent immigrants, from Germany, Italy, Denmark, a startling number of Jews from Hungary. Ironically, J. Robert Oppenheimer did not attain his later prominence in connection with the atomic bomb

Atomic Power

An axiom of pre-atomic physics stated that matter is neither created nor destroyed: that is, although atoms can combine with each other to form many different kinds of molecules, the atoms themselves remained unchanged. But early in this century it was discovered that certain elements do break down into others, in the process releasing a great deal of energy. The relationship between matter and energy is expressed in Einstein's formula, $E=MC^2$. The amount of energy (E) released by the breakdown of an element is equivalent to the mass (M) of the substance multiplied by the square of the speed of light (C^2).

Thus a very large amount of energy is produced by the disintegration of a small amount of matter. This energy is released from the nucleus of the atom.

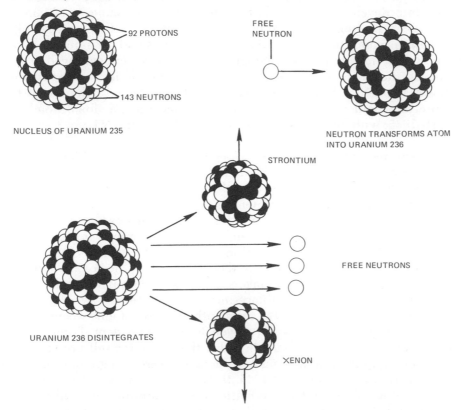

92 PROTONS

143 NEUTRONS

NUCLEUS OF URANIUM 235

FREE NEUTRON

NEUTRON TRANSFORMS ATOM INTO URANIUM 236

STRONTIUM

FREE NEUTRONS

URANIUM 236 DISINTEGRATES

XENON

(1) The nucleus of the Uranium 235 atom contains 92 protons (which carry a positive charge) and 143 neutrons (which have no charge). Since the protons are all straining away from each other (as if they were the positive poles of 92 magnets) a very great amount of energy is needed to hold the nucleus together.

(2) The atom is bombarded with free neutrons. When a neutron becomes attached to the nucleus, it contains 92 protons and 144 neutrons, becoming Uranium 236.

(3) Uranium 236 is a very unstable element and will disintegrate spontaneously into other products, for example strontium and xenon, and release several free neutrons. All of these particles are traveling at enormous speed, and as they hit other parts of the reactor they transmit their energy in the form of heat. The free neutrons go on to break up other Uranium atoms, thus creating the famous "chain reaction" and enormous release of energy.

because of his scientific attainments, which were, so good witnesses say, slight. His distinction came from the fact that in 1930 he was instructor in the only course anywhere in the United States concentrating on nuclear energy (at the California Institute of Technology).

Eminent scientists including Einstein and Leo Szilard immediately tried to emphasize to Roosevelt the devastation that Germany might cause by developing a new weapon. The administration's response was lethargic—a few *thousands* of dollars for research. Not until the summer of 1941 were resources poured into developmental work, for which the code name was Manhattan Project. On 2 December, 1942, a team at the University of Chicago set off the first chain reaction. In the preceding year, resources had been hurled into the effort; at its height, the Manhattan Engineer District employed 539,000 persons at sites in many parts of the nation (The luminaries would turn out to be Los Alamos, New Mexico and Oak Ridge, Tennessee.). By the end of 1944, the director could report that they hoped to have a functional bomb by 1 August, 1945, with an explosive force of 10,000 tons of TNT.

Germany surrendered on 7 May, 1945. Now the problem narrowed down to an overriding question: How could Japan be knocked out of the war? Three alternatives: by (1) direct assault, (2) strangulation coupled with inducements, (3) use of atomic weapons as they became available. Estimates of losses in an invasion varied greatly. Marshall said that casualties should not exceed 30,000 in the first month; Stimson thought the total operation would cost a half million to a million casualties; Douglas MacArthur commanding in the Pacific pointed out that losses could be cut greatly if the Soviets launched a prior attack in Siberia. But why take such risks when possibility (2) seemed well on its way to success; military intelligence estimates were that Japan would surrender by October, 1945, even without use of atomic weapons whose very existence was quite unknown even to Vice President Truman. Naval blockade plus conventional bombing plus the desire for self-preservation of the Emperor and the interlocking bureaucracies were thought to be doing the trick. As early as the autumn of 1944, the Japanese navy was so short of fuel that many of her ships sunk in the Battle of the Philippine Sea could not have made it back home anyway. Shellcases were being made from substitute metals. A shortage of cement had resulted in shoreline fortifications that were nothing but barbed wire, while the only weapons there were machine guns. Mass famine impended. An official government study had predicted that rice supplies for 1945 would fall 14 million tons short of bare subsistence requirements. Stocks of rice for civilians were 40 per cent below the 1941 level, and would yield less than 1,500 calories a day per capita. The movement of Japanese shipping was next to zero. Admiral King and William D. Leahy, the president's personal military adviser, thought the country would surrender to conventional air and naval attacks. But even to invest Japan in this way for a few months would be costly. Although the United States had full sea and air control, she could not prevent the sacrifice of Japanese pilots and planes in suicidal blows in which the enemy filled a plane with dynamite and dived it down the smokestack of an American aircraft carrier. These maniacal youth boasted that they were *kamikaze*—Divine Wind. The wind was lethal.

The further story of the atomic bomb cannot be understood without noting arrival on the stage of the United Nations and Harry S. Truman. Franklin Roosevelt did not live to see the achievement of one of his chief ambitions: the United Nations. FDR died 12 April, 1945; the San Francisco conference that founded the U.N. met from April 25 to June 26. But now Truman was president, and he was not inclined to let foreigners tell him how to use the new American super-weapon. Truman had almost sidled onto the scene. Republicans would never cease taunting that he had tried to run a dinky haberdashery and couldn't make a success of that. As protégé of the corrupt Democratic boss of Kansas City, he had entered the Senate in 1935. Fortune smiled when he became head of a committee to investigate war contracts awarded by the federal government, and he started to get some notice. As the presidential election approached in 1944, Roosevelt feared that Henry A. Wallace had made too many enemies as secretary of agriculture and as vice president. He lopped off a possible drag on the ticket by giving the second spot to Truman, who now succeeded him. As president Truman would win many admirers who bragged that he came out fighting. But often he headed toward the wrong opponent, at the wrong time in the wrong place. He had the compulsion to assert himself often found in men from his background. With notable exceptions, his appointments were dismal, sometimes disastrous. He was too combative for the nation's good.

Truman, Stalin, and Churchill met at Potsdam on 7 July to coordinate strategy for the defeat of Japan. Fourteen days later Truman got the extended report on the successful A-bomb test at Los Alamos on 16 July. Stimson's diary describes a conversation with Churchill on 22 July in which the prime minister said: "Now I know what happened to Truman yesterday. I couldn't understand it. When he got to the meeting after having read this report he was a changed man. He told the Russians just where they got on and off and generally bossed the whole meeting." Atomic diplomacy had begun. Churchill was delighted. Facing a general election at home and a shaky British Empire abroad, he thought that prompt use of the new weapon might not only crush the Japanese but also deter the Soviets. These attitudes rested on an assumption about when another nation, especially the U.S.S.R. could produce an A-bomb. James P. Byrnes, who had become secretary of state on 2 July, said "seven to ten years, at least, to produce a bomb." The general heading the Manhattan Project estimated "no less than five years and probably well over ten." The time actually required was just over four years.

When scientists involved in the Project learned that a bomb had worked, seven of them drew up the Franck Report which called for demonstrating the bomb's power before U.N. representatives on a "barren island." But a contrary decision had already been reached. The president and Stimson had decided that an exclusively civilian group should be formed to advise Truman on use of the bomb. Twelve men were named to the Interim Committee, with Stimson as chairman and Byrnes as the president's agent. They reached three conclusions: (a) Use the bomb as soon as possible. (b) Drop it on a military target surrounded by houses and other highly vulnerable buildings. (c) Give no prior warning. The objective was to effect a holocaust. On these questions, 36 votes were cast. Only one dissent was recorded, on (c).

Not all professional military men are professional militarists. The chief of the air force thought that use of the A-bomb was not needed to win the war because with conventional bombing "we're driving them back to the stone age." Eisenhower, learning at Potsdam of the bomb, said he would hate to see the United States be the first to use such a horrible weapon. After the war, Leahy was bitter: "My own feeling was that in being the first to use it, we had adopted an ethical standard common to the barbarians of the Dark Ages. I was not taught to make war in that fashion and wars cannot be won by destroying women and children." The Strategic Bombing Survey (Document 28-3) concluded: ". . . certainly prior to 31 December, 1945, and in all probability prior to 1 November, 1945, Japan would have surrendered even if the atomic bombs had not been dropped, even if Russia had not entered the war and even if no invasion had been planned or contemplated." From this judgment, says a recent scholar, "there can hardly be a well-grounded dissent."

But each side had its hard-nosed tough guys. In the United States the crucial (in a sense the only important) intransigeant was Truman, who had been rigid on two issues where he should have given ground: He continued to wave the threadbare flag of "unconditional surrender," and he refused to announce the possibility that the Imperial dynasty might be preserved after a surrender. Conversely, several men in Japan's high command seem lunatic. The country was under the sway of the Supreme War Council: the prime minister and foreign minister along with the two ranking officers in the army and navy. Even after the second atomic bomb was dropped, on Nagasaki on 9 November, three of the six members still voted against surrender; they were ready to fight it out on the beaches until the last Japanese was dead (records of the Japanese War Crimes Trials provide an abundance of evidence). Only the intervention of the Emperor broke the tie. When the surrender was announced, some units of the armed forces rebelled at the humiliation. The secretary of war was so mortified he killed himself. Particularly in retrospect, madmen should not be regarded as if they were sane.

Of the many comments made by men who took part in these climactic episodes, two should be quoted. Stimson wrote:

> The face of war is the face of death; death is an inevitable part of every order that a wartime leader gives. The decision to use the atomic bomb was a decision that brought death to over a hundred thousand Japanese. No explanation can change that fact and I do not wish to gloss it over.
>
>   But this deliberate, premeditated destruction was our least abhorrent alternative. . . .

The general commanding the Strategic Air Force was addicted to a West Point maxim: "Seize the high ground" (dating back to a Chinese slogan of 500 B.C.). He cabled a friend in Washington: "Personal. Have looked at good photos of Hiroshima today. The atomic bomb disposes of all high ground."

Failure to use the atomic bomb would have prolonged the war. Thousands of American lives, perhaps millions of Japanese lives, would have been lost. The price of abstinence would have been high. Perhaps no commander-in-chief—least of all in a republic—could abstain from using a new weapon that might save the lives of American boys. Doubtless some men on the Interim Committee were hostile to Japan because the war had been activated by a sneak attack on Pearl Harbor and because American prisoners of war in Japanese hands had been badly mistreated. Doubtless some of the members of this Committee were swayed by racial bias (James Byrnes). It has been said, with considerable evidence, that the bomb was used to forestall any voice by the Soviet Union in the postwar governance of Japan. These assertions do not add up to a justification. The price of using the atomic bomb was high, and most of that price would be paid after the war.

Accompanying their efforts to reverse the flow of unemployment, efforts which never were very successful, the Roosevelt administration had to try to arrest the spread of fascism—hopefully without getting involved in a major war. The League of Nations was patently powerless to prevent the encroachments of the fascist powers—Germany, Italy, and Japan gobbled up chunks of foreign soil while but feeble gestures were made to stop them. In Spain, the reactionary movement led by General Franco and aided by Germany and Italy overthrew a republican government.

Despite the feeling among many Americans that the nation should not involve itself with troubles in Europe, the government realized that close cooperation among non-fascist states was needed to contain this menace, and in 1933 took a step in this direction by recognizing the government of the Soviet Union. Yet attempts to solidify alliances with Great Britain and France were unavailing. By the time of the Munich Agreement in 1938, war was inevitable.

The United States still tried to maintain a posture of public neutrality, while providing supplies for the Allies in Europe. Americans were sure to declare war eventually, but if Japan had not attacked Pearl Harbor on December 7, 1941, entry might have been postponed for as long as a year. Once formally at war, the massive productive capacity of the United States was mobilized for a steady effort, a constant attrition which pushed Germany and Japan under relentless force. New technology was developed as well, climaxing in a weapon which harnessed the power of the atom for destructive purposes.

SOME NOTABLE EVENTS

1931 Hoover proposes moratorium on intergovernmental debts from World War I.

1931–
1932 Japan occupies Manchuria, starting 18 Sept. with Mukden incident.

1932 Stimson's note to Japan and China, 7 Jan.

Stimson's letter to Senator Borah about Manchukuo, 24 Feb.

Japan recognizes Manchukuo, 15 Sept.

1933 Hitler named chancellor of Germany, 30 Jan.

Treaty of Tangku ends Manchurian War, 31 May.

International Economic Conference gathers in London, 12 June.

U.S. recognizes U.S.S.R. 16 Nov.

FDR announces new policy on Latin American relations, 28 Dec.

1934 Platt Amendment on Cuba abrogated, 29 May.

Trade Agreements Act, 12 June.

All governments owing debts to U.S. from World War I except "brave little Finland" have defaulted by June 15.

Tydings-McDuffie Act grants independence to Philippines, but not effective until 4 July, 1946.

Japan denounces Washington Naval Treaty of 1922 on 29 Dec.

1935 Neutrality Act, 31 Aug.

Hoare-Laval Plan for Ethiopia, 10 Dec.

1936 Germany invades Rhineland, 7 March.

1936–
1939 Spanish Civil War, ending with fascist victory.

1937 Neutrality Act, 1 May.

Japan invades China, 7 July.

FDR's "quarantine the aggressor" speech in Chicago, 5 Oct.

Peel Report advocates partition of Palestine.

U.S. gunboat *Panay* sunk by Japanese in China, 12 Dec.

1938 Ludlow Amendment narrowly beaten in House of Representatives, 10 Jan.; vote is 209 to 188.

Germany annexes Austria, 12–13 March.

Mexico expropriates U.S. and British oil properties.

Munich agreements cede about half of Czechoslovakia to Germany, 29–30 Sept.

1939 Germany seizes remainder of Czechoslovakia, March.

Germany invades Poland, 1 Sept.

Neutrality Act of 1939 forbids entry of U.S. merchant vessels into war zones, 4 Nov.

Two scientists at Kaiser Wilhelm Institute in Berlin split the uranium atom.

1939–
1940 Russo-Finnish War, 14 Oct.–12 March.

1940 Germany conquers Norway, 9 April–11 June.

The Netherlands, Belgium, and France fall to Germany, 10 May–10 July.

Battle of Britain is fought in the air. RAF loses nearly a thousand planes, Germany twice as many, 8 Aug.–31 Oct.

U.S. makes "destroyers-bases" deal with Britain, 3 Sept.

Germany, Italy, and Japan sign ten-year military and economic alliance, 27 Sept.

U.S. embargo on shipments of scrap iron and steel to Japan takes effect, 16 Oct.

1941 FDR's "Four Freedoms" speech, 6 Jan.

Lend-Lease Act, 11 March.

Germany invades U.S.S.R. 24 June; FDR promises aid the same day.

Atlantic Charter issued by FDR and Churchill; submitted to Congress on 21 Aug.

Pearl Harbor attacked, 7 Dec.; Congress declares war the next day.

1941–
  1943 Allies retake Africa, 18 Nov.–13 May.
1942 Japanese expansion in Pacific reaches its maximum, early May.

U.S.S.R. assumes counteroffensive, 19 Nov.
1943 Allies take Sicily, 10 July–17 Aug.

Allies begin invasion of Italy, 3 Sept.
1944 D-Day (Operation Overlord); Allies invade western France, 6 June.

Allies invade southern France, 15 Aug. (Operation Dragon).
1945 Germany surrenders, 4 May.

Potsdam Conference, 7 July–2 Aug.

Atomic bomb on Hiroshima, 6 Aug.; called "Little Boy."

Plutonium atomic bomb ("Fat Man") dropped on Nagasaki, 9 Aug.

U.S.S.R. declares war on Japan, 9 Aug.

Japan surrenders, 14 Aug.

Ways to Study History XXVIII

Collaborations can succeed. This assertion has been made rather negatively in Ways to Study History XXI; it should now be re-substantiated. Perhaps the finest of all reference works on the history of the United States is the *Dictionary of American Biography,* edited by Allen Johnson and Dumas Malone (20 volumes plus two Supplements, 1928–1958). Hundreds of contributors have written about thousands of eminent citizens for this series. These volumes have held up amazingly well. Although the final volume in the basic set was issued in 1935, a complete revision today would not require the revision of more than 10 per cent or at most 20 per cent of the information. By such gradual accretions is our knowledge of the past being built up.

The problems confronted by the editors of this compendium can hardly be exaggerated. Its predecessor in the English language had been the *Dictionary of National Biography,* about residents of the British Isles, (22 volumes, 1885–1901). The subjects for many entries had been chosen not for their impact on the country's life but for their family attachments. Likewise authors had been picked for their connections instead of for their scholarship. Many of the careers recounted had not been carefully researched; some entries were either adulatory or condemnatory rather than being detailed narratives.

Who were the significant persons in American history? How much space should each receive? Who is best qualified to write about her (or him)? Because of their skill in meeting these questions, the editors have endowed us with an invaluable guide to our past. More than one instructor has prepared a good lecture while using no other resource than the *D.A.B.* Of course no work of this magnitude can be perfect. There is reason to believe that rascals succeeded in sneaking onto its pages sketches of imagined persons who never existed.

Document 28-1

Some commentators cannot separate Woodrow Wilson from the Fourteen Points. Similarly FDR is often identified with "the Four Freedoms." Acknowledging that the stock in trade of most politicians is words, it nonetheless appears that wars call forth an unusual amount of rhetoric.

Every realist knows that the democratic way of life is at this moment being directly assailed in every part of the world—assailed either by arms or by secret spreading of poisonous propaganda. . . .

As men do not live by bread alone, they do not fight by armaments alone. Those who man our defenses, and those behind them who build our defenses, must have the stamina and courage which come from an unshakable belief in the manner of life which they are defending. . . .

In the future days, which we seek to make secure, we look forward to a world founded upon four essential human freedoms.

The first is freedom of speech and expression everywhere in the world.

The second is freedom of every person to worship God in his own way everywhere in the world.

The third is freedom from want, which, translated into world terms, means economic understandings which will secure to every nation a healthy peacetime life for its inhabitants everywhere in the world.

The fourth is freedom from fear—which, translated into world terms, means a world-wide reduction of armaments to such a point and in such a thorough fashion that no nation will be in a position to commit an act of physical aggression against any neighbor—anywhere in the world.

That is no vision of a distant millenium. It is a definite basis for a kind of world attainable in our own time and generation. That kind of world is the very antithesis of the so-called new order of tyranny which the dictators seek to create with the crash of a bomb.

Document 28-2

In the spring of 1942, the Army removed from the
West Coast 110,000 residents of Japanese ancestry to "relocation centers" in the interior. In
1944, *Korematsu* v. *U.S.*, this military action was
upheld 6-3 by the Supreme Court.

*It is said that we are dealing here with the case of imprisonment of a citizen in a
concentration camp solely because of his ancestry, without evidence or inquiry concerning his
loyalty and good disposition towards the United States. Our task would be simple, our duty clear,
were this a case involving the imprisonment of a loyal citizen in a concentration camp because of
racial prejudice. Regardless of the true nature of the assembly and relocation centers—and we
deem it unjustifiable to call them concentration camps with all the ugly connotations that term
implies—we are dealing with nothing but an exclusion order. To cast this case into outlines of
racial prejudice, without reference to the real military dangers which were presented, merely
confuses the issue. Korematsu was not excluded from the Military Area because of hostility to him
or his race. He was excluded because we are at war with the Japanese Empire, because the
properly constituted military authorities feared an invasion of our West Coast and felt constrained
to take proper security measures, because they decided that the military urgency of the situation
demanded that all citizens of Japanese ancestry be segregated from the West Coast temporarily,
and finally, because Congress, reposing its confidence in this time of war in our military
leaders—as inevitably it must—determined that they should have the power to do just this. There
was evidence of disloyalty on the part of some, the military authorities considered that the need
for action was great, and time was short. We cannot—by availing ourselves of the calm
perspective of hindsight—now say that at that time these actions were unjustified.*

Document 28-3

The United States Strategic Bombing Survey
was a federal team sent to Japan to study the
results of the atomic explosions. The first paragraph here describes some general effects; the
second relates specifically to Hiroshima.

*Penetrating rays such as gamma-rays exposed X-ray films stored in the basement of a
concrete hospital almost a mile from ground zero. Symptoms of their effect on human beings
close to the center of the explosion, who survived other effects thereof, were generally delayed for
two or three days. The bone marrow and as a result the process of blood formation were affected.
The white corpuscle count went down and the human processes of resisting infection were
destroyed. Death generally followed shortly thereafter. . . .*

*Approximately 60,000 to 70,000 people were killed, and 50,000 were injured. Of
approximately 90,000 buildings in the city, 65,000 were rendered unusable and almost all the
remainder received at least light superficial damage. The underground utilities of the city were
undamaged except where they crossed bridges over the rivers cutting through the city. All of the
small factories in the center of the city were destroyed. However, the big plants on the periphery
of the city were almost completely undamaged and 94 percent of their workers unhurt. These
factories accounted for 74 percent of the industrial production of the city. It is estimated that they
could have resumed substantially normal production within 30 days of the bombing, had the war
continued. The railroads running through the city were repaired for the resumption of through
traffic on 8 August, 2 days after the attack. . . .*

The Forbidden Fruits of Affluence

Looking back, it is easy to regard the New Deal as a succession of missed opportunities. More harshly, perhaps more selfishly, stated, many of the problems before the country today have continued because of neglect or indifference by New Dealers. Inflation would be easier to control if a more astute approach to monetary arrangements had been taken in 1933. The mess of the cities could have been relieved somewhat, whereas the Federal Housing Act of 1938 along with freeway construction and other governmental policies have intensified the disease. Racial violence has been endemic to American life, but FDR would not lift a finger, much less wave it, to lance this abscess. Instead of action to elevate the status of women, the nation got a symbol; Eleanor Roosevelt was permitted to serve as ritualistic testimony to the sanctity of motherhood. Perhaps our current politics will serve the country just as badly, but the Roosevelt administration should not be credited with any genius at thinking a problem through, and then building its conclusions into a workable set of institutions.

True, the Great Depression finally ended, but it took the massive spending of the war years to do the job. The soft spots in the economy were merely camouflaged, not eliminated, and they reappeared as soon as war production was curtailed and wartime restrictions were lifted. During the war, two goals were met: employment stayed high, and prices and wages were controlled to prevent galloping inflation. Had this not been done, the costs of scarce consumer goods would have jumped drastically. But soon after VJ Day, the restrictions were lifted, and prices were set free to find their "natural level." Since few factories had yet converted to peacetime production, and since demand had been greatly increased by four years of deprivation, the immediate postwar years saw massive inflation, which a laissez-faire government felt privileged to impede only when it could perceive a "national emergency." World War II had the same influence as other American wars in sending the price level soaring. But after 1933 the federal authorities had even more powerful tools that they could swing in more than one direction. In that year the Federal Reserve Board had started a so-called Open Market Committee that could buy and sell securities on the public exchanges. Using this mechanism, the second great war was financed to a considerable extent by "monetizing the federal debt." This phrase may imply an arcane operation, but what happened was child's play. The Federal Reserve Board printed paper money; the Treasury printed bonds, and they swapped pieces of paper. With such tactics, anybody can be a financier.

Even taking account of the rising price level since 1940, the growth of American prosperity has been impressive. Figures in current prices, billions of dollars, climbed thus:

	1950	1955	1960	1965	1970
Gross National Product	285	398	504	685	924
Personal Incomes	228	311	401	539	804
Federal Expenditures	42	65	77	97	195

The absolute growth of the economy was not accompanied by an equitable distribution of income. As in the past, by far the largest share of the increase went to those who were well-off already. In 1967, the Internal Revenue Service gleaned $1.5 billion dollars in taxes from people earning less than $3,000—exactly the amount which had been allocated to the various poverty programs. And the poverty programs cannot be regarded as mechanisms for returning tax money to those who needed it most, since almost all of their expenditures went to pay for physical plant or the salaries of middle-class administrators. The farm subsidy program provides another example of an attempt to aid the poor which became twisted into a handout for the rich. Half of the $3.5 billion distributed in 1969 went to the richest 15 per cent of the farmers; 20 of the wealthiest got as much as 350,000 of the poorest.

Accompanying the stagnation of poverty was the decay of one of the sacred cows of the American Way, the small businessman. Starting a business has never been easy; most go broke within a year of their hopeful beginnings. But in the decades after World War II the giants of commerce and manufacturing coelesced their power to a degree that had never been possible before. About 200 corporations (out of 200,000) controlled 60 per cent of manufacturing. Three made 95 per cent of the cars, and the largest garnered two billion dollars in after tax profits in one year. Price fixing, wage fixing, and a bland disregard for the consumer's desire for quality and service naturally proceeded from this agglutination of power. Large companies did not restrict themselves to expansion in their original line. The conglomerate, in which many separate companies in unrelated fields are united only by common ownership, is becoming increasingly common. International Telephone and Telegraph, for example, owns among other things Sheraton (hotels), and Bobbs-Merrill (publishing). Aside from the advantages of future profits presumably to be derived from the good management of the executives of the parent company, conglomeration offers two advantages. First, shrewd accounting often allows enormous tax savings. Second, the diverse nature of the various businesses prevents awkward investigation under anti-trust laws, which might become troublesome if a large company tried to gobble up its direct competitors.

Unemployment accompanied inflation. Factories which engaged in war production had been operating under the "cost plus" system, whereby the government paid their expenses, plus 6 per cent. Naturally they had no incentive to keep expenses down, and often hired more men than efficiency demanded. When the sugar plums of government contracts were no longer forthcoming, employers were quick to trim away their surplus manpower. The re-entrance of ex-GIs into the labor market aggravated the problem.

Clearly, careful governmental management was necessary to smooth out economic turbulence. But the actions the government took were both haphazard and repressive. Wages did not escalate as fast as prices (in the four years following the war the cost of living rose an astounding 70 per cent) and the inevitable strikes occurred. Truman tried to stop them by throwing the weight of the federal government on the side of the employer. During the coal strike of 1946, the railroad workers walked out. The president forced them to return to the job by threatening to use the military to run the trains, and broke a coal strike by actually operating the mines with government personel for two months. The numerous strikes, 5,000 in 1946 alone, produced some real gains for workers of many industries, in fringe benefits and improved working conditions as well as in fatter pay envelopes. But inflation more than kept pace, and the constant round of labor disputes provoked much anti-labor feeling which worked to the advantage of the Republican party.

By 1946 the Republicans had won control of both houses of Congress, and used their mandate to pass the Taft-Hartley law. Many union activities were proscribed, and union officials had to sign an affadavit affirming that they were not Communists. Most importantly, the law permitted the president to obtain an injunction postponing any strike for sixty days, which could be extended another twenty. If the dispute continued, he could recommend to Congress any action which he believed to be "appropriate." Most Americans approved the measure. The reforming impulses which had arisen during the depression were clearly yielding to prosperity and the desire for quiet, and the status quo.

On 22 June, 1944, the president signed a major law intended to promote social mobility—the "GI Bill of Rights." In a significant provision, it established a system of federal payments to veterans who wished to continue their education. The resulting flood of new students drastically changed the character of American universities. First, they mushroomed in both size and number. Second, they changed from enclaves catering to the children of the rich into institutions which the middle classes and part of the working classes entered as a matter of course. Given parallel changes which had been occurring in the business world, this broadened educational base was essential. In former years the restriction of higher education to the few didn't matter much. A degree might be the entrée into a few professions, but to little else. In business practical experience counted for much more. But organizations were steadily growing larger, and bureaucratic systems were dominating patterns of advancement. It was more difficult to work your way up through the ranks. The bureaucracy demanded a standard ticket of admission to the executive class, and found it in the form of a university degree. Thus the GI Bill provided a very important service to the many veterans who got not only an education but an all-important diploma.

Most soldiers, like most other Americans, wished to settle into a life where satisfactions were formed chiefly on the personal level. Family, home, enough money to live comfortably—these were the things that mattered. Americans rejected the disruptions inherent in social reform, and were content to forego the satisfactions of public achievement. Thus Truman's re-election in 1948 seems almost as remarkable in retrospect as it did at the time. Both the right and the left wings of the Democratic party had split away, and were expected to take votes from the president. As it happened, the traditional American reluctance to support splinter parties kept the vote for each independent candidate down to about a million apiece. Truman fired his sharpest oratorical barbs not at Thomas E. Dewey, the Republican candidate, but at the Republican 80th Congress, which he excoriated as "do-nothing." But nothing was precisely what the American people wanted done. Probably Truman's appeal was simply himself. He presented an image that retained a nostalgic attractiveness—the little man from down home who zested in battling giants. The people who voted for him could pretend that they were in favor of change and social progress, while they actually prevented those dangers by returning the same hidebound congressmen.

While Truman's election remains somewhat anomalous, that of Dwight

D. Eisenhower in 1952 meshes perfectly with the mood of the times. He retained the enormous popularity which his war record had given him, and his political antecedents were so hazy that he had no bloc of enemies. (A group of liberal Democrats had tried to persuade him to run for the Democratic nomination in 1948; he had never belonged to any political party, and no one was quite sure which one he supported. The perfect candidate.) Eisenhower was soothing, a benign father figure. Nothing drastic was going to happen as long as he was in charge, and the country could go about its business without being shaken up by a lot of turmoil in Washington. His meandering speeches, his passion for golf, his air of stolid rectitude, all inspired love and trust. He probably could have defeated any possible Democratic candidate, and Adlai Stevenson was a piece of cake. The voters thought of Stevenson as an intellectual, a fatal political image. Moreover, his personal platform combined a demand for far-reaching domestic reforms, which most Americans did not want, along with a belligerent attitude in foreign affairs, which most Americans rightly thought was likely to get the country involved in dangerous and unprofitable disputes. Eisenhower, on the other hand, fulfilled his campaign promise to end the Korean War, and although the State Department and the CIA were constantly meddling in the affairs of other countries throughout his two terms, the people didn't know about it, and so didn't have to fret about it (Chapter 30).

The United States fretted about very little during the fifties. Prosperity continued steadily, and few of the prosperous many wanted their consciences pricked by reminders about those for whom respectable middle-class goals were unattainable. Those who persisted in agitating for social change were effectively silenced by the bugbear of Communism. Joseph McCarthy, junior senator from Wisconsin, has been depicted as the center of the witch hunt for Communists, but others all across the country participated. A posture of hostility toward the Soviet Union had been maintained ever since the end of World War II, and American Communists were believed to be all potential spies under orders from Moscow. The age of McCarthy might better be called the age of suppression by Harry S. Truman and such federal agencies as the FBI and the Bureau of Immigration and Naturalization. In the most tyrannical act since the relocation of Japanese-Americans, Truman—not McCarthy—infringed upon his authority as president to decree at his sole discretion on 25 November, 1946, that all federal employees must be "of complete and unswerving loyalty to the United States. . . ." The most detestable phase of the witch hunt began on that day, and held its momentum until John and Robert Kennedy decided to limit its excesses. For a decade, Americans who had nonconforming ideas were faced with a dilemma: keep your mouth shut, or lose your job and occasionally get your head bloodied.

The McCarthy hearings were just the most visible aspect of this repression of dissent. While they were proceeding, the assumption seemed to

FIGURE 29-1   *Centers of U.S. Population, 1870-1970*

be that anyone whose opinions were even slightly left of center was a putative Communist. McCarthy put on a show for a credulous audience by claiming that the government was riddled with subversives, by hauling hundreds of private citizens before a committee where he could examine their political associations. He found a certain number of actual ex-Communists who were willing to accuse their associates of dark deeds, and describe sinister cabals which they had allegedly taken part in. Americans were ready to believe that there was a Communist under every bush, and many governmental and private organizations took steps to uproot the bushes.

Although McCarthy himself did not participate in it, the trial of Alger Hiss for perjury in 1950 typifies the techniques and attitudes of the scare crusaders. Hiss was a former New Dealer (mid-Chapter 26 on AAA) who had worked at the San Francisco Conference which had founded the United Nations. He was convicted of perjury because he denied before a Congressional Committee that he had passed government secrets to the Russians in the thirties. The evidence against him depended on the testimony of one self-declared former Communist who at this point was engaged in hauling former associates before the House Un-American Activities Committee (HUAC). Hiss said that he had once known the man (then going under another name) but was unaware of his Communist affiliation and knew nothing about any espionage. Although a number of dignitaries testified to Hiss' good character, he was convicted. When accused of Communism, a man was guilty until proven innocent, and even then his reputation was smudged.

For the next four years HUAC summoned hundreds of suspected Communists to appear. A few, like Chambers, had pre-arranged to present a list of their former associates and acquaintances, but most preserved a stolid silence, giving the Fifth Amendment's safeguards against self-incrimination as grounds for refusing to answer any questions. Most Americans thought that "taking the Fifth" was self-incrimination enough, but at least witnesses could be protected from a charge of either perjury or contempt of Congress.*

The hearings were a disgraceful spectacle, and subjected both the witnesses and others who feared that they might be called up to unjustifiable badgering, and in some cases to outright persecution. But the activities of other self-appointed Communist hunters around the country were probably more damaging still. In Hollywood, people with known liberal sympathies were driven out of the entertainment industry. For years the only way blacklisted writers could make a living was by having a friend pass off their scripts as his own work—sometimes receiving a fair price, sometimes a pittance. Since the banished writers were among the best in the business, the quality of films plummeted. Not until the sixties was there a significant break in the diet of swill which Hollywood spewed forth. In industry, but particularily in colleges and schools, compulsory loyalty oaths proliferated. Disgraceful enough in themselves, they caused direct hardship to those who refused to sign them and lost their jobs, but their real evil lay in the climate of fear which they engendered. Few dared question the government, or the institutions of the nation, or the established order of things. Teachers in particular didn't dare encourage a doubting spirit among their students.

The students themselves did not seem to mind. Since the placid world of the white middle-class 1950's could satisfy all their ambitions, drastic change could only be for the worse. Few people any longer hoped for personal satisfaction from their jobs, which were "good" when they provided a large enough salary and no worries away from the office. One worked, not to eat, but to get a suburban house, television, a new wardrobe twice a year, a car every three, refrigerator, freezer, transistors, record players, speedboats, and electric toothbrushes. Nothing was expected to last long, and when it broke down no one could be found to fix it. But for the prosperous discarding old things

---

*Use of the Fifth Amendment was not universal. A few witnesses tried to refuse to answer on the grounds that the First Amendment's guarantee of freedom of speech and assembly protected their political beliefs and affiliations from Congressional probing. A few made the Committee look as foolish as it was. Pete Seeger, for example, was asked whether he was a Communist. He replied, "I'm just an old banjo plucker."

FIGURE 29-2. *Henry Hill, G. H. Knoles House*

The home of Dr. and Mrs. George H. Knoles was designed by Henry Hill of the San Francisco firm of Hill and Kruse. Knoles and his wife were looking ahead toward his retirement from the History Department at Stanford University, so they bought several acres on the Pacific Ocean about ten miles south of Carmel, California. The house was placed some 150 feet downward from the highway, on a saddle with a small hillock forming a windbreak between the cottage (for its size would not warrant a more haughty name) and the prevailing westerlies. To the southwest one sees white water along the coast as the breakers explode; to the northwest, coves and hills sweeping to the sea. Seen from California Route 1 above, the triangular shape of the dwelling is striking. The three angles were almost dictated by the forementioned windbreak in tandem with the nature of the views. Materials were stone, redwood, and glass—all rugged to suit the nature of the site. They also conform to what architects call "the interpenetration of space" between indoors and outdoors.

Design of this quality would merit attention anywhere. But new wealth has made California the postwar seedbed for domestic architecture, as Massachusetts was in 1800 or Illinois in 1900. For centuries, Americans had lurched heedlessly across the continent, plundering it as they went. California was clearly the end of the line. A goodly number of its residents seem to have awakened to the reality that they can no longer flee westward, so perhaps they should beautify their home grounds.

provided an opportunity for the gratification of consuming new ones, the only gratification which futile well-paid jobs could offer.

Two important myths prospered with post-war society. One was simply an updated version of the Myth of the Self-Made Man. Everyone could move ahead; everyone could have all the tempting things that television and the magazines presented so enticingly. But now wealth was earned, not by virtue and application, but by personal appearance and a mysterious new entity known as "personality."* If only you used the right toothpaste, kept clean and neat, and smiled brightly you would, if male, get a good job and its accoutrements, and, if female, acquire husband-with-job. Then, if female, you continued by keeping that extention of yourself, your house, properly burnished with all the "right" products—meaning the most recently advertised. Naturally, the cosmetics industry became a giant during these years, and has continued to grow by constantly discovering new ways in which people are unwittingly offending others in their personal habits. Of course the myth did not come true for all, or even most, Americans, but even the defeated continued to believe in it.

The other myth was almost completely new. Americans, like everyone else, had always found satisfactions in family life, but now the Family rose to a high spot in the American pantheon. It consisted of parents and young or adolescent children; the aged had no place in it. This group lived in a private suburban home, supported financially solely by the labors of the father in some other place. The mother cared for the house and children. The Family spent their free time enjoying a variety of activities together; everyone was happy. This new myth, fostered unremittingly by both advertising and entertainment, was partially a response to changing American demography. The age of both men and women at marriage had fallen drastically after the war, and the birth rate had risen. These new families needed housing, and residential suburbs mushroomed in response. There was no room in these subdivisions for either grandparents or productive labor, and no escape from the house for women. As more and more people began living under these conditions the myth developed that they were ideal.

And for many people, suburban private life did offer real satisfactions. The most famous of the post-war subdivisions were the Levittowns on Long Island and in Pennsylvania. They provided cheap, small houses with identical floor plans, taking advantage of every possible economy of scale. The Pennsylvania Levittown housed 70,000 on eight square miles. William Levitt stated the firm's founding premise: "People like people." Suburbs much on the Levittown model, most more expensive, some much more esthetically pleasing, have become ubiquitous. Americans are so accustomed to them that they find it difficult to recognise how great a change they represent. Older residential neighborhoods often display just as much drab sameness, but the

---

**The term "personality" is a perfectly valid one in the study of psychology. But starting in the late forties it became one of the cult words of the popular culture, in the sense of the phrase, "He has a nice personality." Although quite undefinable, "personality" accounted for everything from a child's experiences in kindergarten to the selection of presidents.

similar houses were not erected by one builder at one time. Each individual chose to construct a house quite like his neighbors, because he was familiar with it, because he could afford it. Since a tract was not developed all at once, there was no need to bulldoze out every natural wrinkle on the surface of the land. Moreover, earlier builders had not yet been inoculated by city planning. They didn't realize that residential, commercial, and manufacturing regions must be in as strict quarantine as if they had been infectious diseases. Thus in an earlier era many people could walk to work; everyone could do at least their routine shopping within a block or two of where they lived. As a neighborhood aged, the first floors of some houses would become stores, and certain streets developed into shopping promenades where the residents shopped, strolled, chatted.

In a modern suburb all is changed. The builder has economically uprooted every tree, flattened every hill. Manufacturing is banned, as is all commercial activity except the goods and services the residents need. Thus a mass exodus of wage earners from the neighborhood during the day. The shopping center supposedly fills the functions of the commercial street without its inconveniences—traffic, noise, jostling, parking problems. But the shopping center is merely what its name suggests, a place to buy things. The addition of restaurants, movie theaters, and entertainment cannot disguise its character. Many of the people present on a shopping street are merely out for a walk; others incorporate minor errands. But I can't imagine going to a modern shopping center for such a purpose. Moreover, nearly everyone there has driven in a private car. The planners cluster stores and services because they are supposedly incompatible with houses; they have succeeded in placing them too far from most homes to be conveniently accessible to pedestrians. Even people who live close enough to walk usually prefer to drive: the walk, through treeless, cookie cutter residential streets, is so boring. Despite these disadvantages, almost all Americans want to live in a dormitory suburb; ownership of a private, detached house is a powerful symbol of status and stability. Fewer and fewer can now afford it. Increasingly, poorer families are turning to mobile homes, which allow them to achieve the pride of ownership at a reasonable cost. Assembly line techniques allow trailers, mobile homes, and modular houses to be constructed much more cheaply than a traditional house, without the restrictions imposed by suburban housing codes. Since a mobile home can be placed on a very small site, their owners in some towns can largely sidestep the rocketing land costs which have afflicted all American metropolitan areas in recent years. In 1972, over 80 per cent of all new houses costing less than $20,000 were mobile homes.

The proliferation of the Levittowns and their successors represented a malaise more profound than anything mentioned above. True, they satisfied the hunger for "a home of my own." But they provided no real privacy, and no opportunities to express individuality in more than superficial ways. Few Levittowners really wanted privacy—they needed a community which would hide its lack of intimacy behind a mask of geniality. For intimacy was impossible in a society so fluid; suburban houses are designed with an eye for the inevitable resale.

Some Americans were excluded even from the minimal rewards of docility—prosperity and privacy. The largest single group was shut out because they were black. In the fifties it was still easy for white sympathizers with the black cause to continue in the myopic posture which they had maintained for generations: the problem was Southern. Liberal Northerners shook their heads sadly over segregation, and were outraged at tales of lynching and night riding. Occasionally a specific case might arouse their wrath, as with the Scottsboro case of 1932. Briefly, nine young blacks had been accused of raping two white vagrant girls in a freight car. The girls might be vagrants and probably prostitutes, but they were White Women, the Flower of the South; their testimony assured the defendants' conviction. The NAACP and other groups stepped in for the defense, and the case received much outraged publicity in the North, where its obvious inequities allowed many people to smirk self-righteously about the barbarities of the South. Since most lynchings occurred with the connivance of local authorities, perpetrators were seldom caught and even more rarely punished. It seemed logical to permit federal power to fill this void in justice with a proposed anti-lynching bill, but some Southern senators resisted; they filibustered (on the grounds not of supporting lynching, but of protecting states rights) and defeated the bill. Again, the North pointed an accusing finger. In 1948, in a direct bid for the black vote, Truman eliminated segregation where he could: in the armed forces. These had contained separate black units, often commanded by white officers, since the Civil War. This order had few important practical effects (except the one it was designed to bring about, black votes for Truman), but it indicated the attitude of the federal government.

In the early fifties white Americans still believed that the racial problems of the United States were Southern problems; John Doe was simply blind to the presence of all black people. In *Invisible Man* Ralph Ellison tried to open their eyes to the violent maelstrom beneath a black man's attempts to move up in the South, and to the equally grim picture of his life in the North. Higher education in the black South resembled the old plantation, except that Uncle Tom had been promoted to overseer; the white man remained preeminent. In the North, Ellison saw black solidarity as a mask concealing a perpetual snarl, resulting from a life both physically and emotionally precarious. And white society, which had created these conditions, had simultaneously blinded itself to them. Wishing to reject the black man, white people refused to look at him. But the Southern black was to be constantly in front of their eyes. In 1954 the Supreme Court decided that the Southern system of racial segregation in the public schools was unconstitutional. Racial segregation had been challenged before, and the court had declared it acceptable as long as the facilities provided were "equal." At that time Justice John Marshall Harlan dissented, on grounds which should have been used in 1954; he stated simply that the Constitution is color-blind, segregation is wrong, and it must be stopped. The court was less direct in 1954. The justices based their decision on psychological reasoning which stated that it made black children feel inferior to attend segregated schools, and that such schools were inherently unequal and must be integrated. This left them wide open to the plea of some white parent that it made his child feel inferior to attend integrated schools. But the decision can be criticized on more significant grounds. It decreed integration, but only eventually. The process was to take place "with all deliberate speed," which meant that only token black children were admitted to specific white schools.

Thus Southern schools had plenty of room within which to maneuver. At first some reacted with an outraged refusal to give an inch; they would not permit any integration. Prince Edward County, Virginia, took the desperate step of closing its schools entirely for some years. A number of localities set up "private" schools for whites only, but this expedient was largely thwarted when the courts prevented the states from diverting any public funds to such institutions. Most schools neither integrated nor refused to do so, but simply sat back and waited for a court order directed at them specifically. Then the reaction varied. It might be political suicide to approve or assist integration, but some officeholders indicated their willingness to comply with federal orders, as long as their constituents knew they were being forced. Then the processes of change usually occurred quietly enough.

But often a state governor would attempt to resist federal power; this first occurred in Little Rock, Arkansas, in 1957. At that time virtually all of the Deep South remained segregated. The Little Rock Board of Education set up a plan for gradual integration, which was to begin with the admission of nine black students to Central High School. The federal district court approved. But a group of white mothers petitioned a state court to stop the proceedings, on the grounds that integration would result in violence, and Governor Orval Faubus supported them. He sent the National Guard to the high school, ostensibly to maintain order, but actually to keep the black students out. They were smuggled in after a federal judge ordered him to remove the troops. But then a white mob stormed the school, and the children had to be removed for their own safety. President Eisenhower was outraged, and his reaction showed the rest of the South that it could not resist federal authority indefinitely. He sent a thousand paratroopers to Little Rock to secure orderly desegregation, and for several months the nine black students attended classes under the protection of the army.

This pattern of confrontation over segregated schools was repeated elsewhere, and Southern blacks continued to be external to it. The dispute was between Northern and Southern whites, with Northern middle-class blacks, represented by the NAACP, occasionally participating. But an indigenous Southern black rebellion was proceeding at the same time, led by a minister from Georgia, Martin Luther King. This movement can be dated from

December of 1955, in Montgomery, Alabama, and was precipitated when a tired Negro woman refused to go to her alloted place in the back of a public bus. She was ejected. The black residents of Montgomery responded by boycotting the bus company, which suffered a 65 per cent decrease in revenue, and was forced to capitulate and desegregate the buses on December 21. This episode featured many elements of the black liberation movement in the South that were to be used for the next decade. First, it raised non-violence to a creed. Second, both its leaders and its participants were black, and Southern. Northern whites generally approved, but their aid was superfluous. Third, whites were made conscious of the economic power that blacks had but which they had not exercised in a concerted fashion. Black people acted directly to change a specific wrong, and did not rely on legalistic maneuvering.

The character of Martin Luther King was an important influence in Montgomery, and throughout the Southern struggle. His religious beliefs, devoutly Christian but strongly influenced by Mahatma Ghandi, inspired his followers in a way that a purely secular struggle for civil rights could not have done. King believed that violence was un-Christian, and that gains achieved by violence were ephemeral. On the other hand, an oppressed people need not passively accept the wrongs dealt out to them, or confuse Christian humility with grovelling before white people. He called on black Southerners to pray, to march in unity for their rights, and to resist steadfastly attempts to keep those rights from them. This exhortation was extremely appealing, especially after experience showed that it worked. Often the demonstrators' non-violence was met by a mob, and by clubs and dogs, but King himself was there to take the blows along with his followers. Direct action worked.

Other groups, notably the Student Non-Violent Co-ordinating Committee (SNCC) and the Congress of Racial Equality (CORE) imitated King's techniques. By the early sixties most Northerners had seen the Southern strife on television; the contrast between the orderly, often singing demonstrators and the rock- and bottle-throwing mobs who met them evoked much sympathy. A few expressed their feelings by going south and working in the movement. Their presence enraged even liberal-minded white Southerners. Many Southerners had thought all along that racial troubles were caused by "outside agitators"; the presence of white Northerners seemed to confirm this mistaken notion. And those who sympathized with the black cause rightfully resented the patronizing Northern assumption that prejudice and injustice were restricted to the South. Yankee do-gooders had been anathema since abolitionist times. Eventually this well-meant aid was rejected by the black organizations. They had first welcomed white participation, then accepted it when restrained to subservient positions, then realized that it was often harmful and never necessary. Black people themselves had the power to change the conditions under which they lived; they needed only to organize and be determined to use their power.

Their strength lay in numbers; an efficient, orderly way to express numerical strength is at the polls. By the mid-sixties legal segregation had been crushed through most of the South, but blacks were still disfranchised. Voter registration drives became the crux of the Civil Rights Movement. Early in 1965 Martin Luther King began a campaign to register black voters in Selma, Alabama, a town with an almost even racial split. Ninety-nine per cent of the whites were registered; one per cent of the blacks. Each day several hundred black residents paraded to the county courthouse, ostensibly planning to register. Each day the sheriff turned them back, either by force or by arresting the marchers on a host of charges. Soon 2,000 people were in jail. On February 18 the state police broke up a sympathy demonstration in a nearby town, and one of the participants was killed. King called for a protest march to Montgomery, which was halted by state police a few miles outside Selma. The troopers used whips, clubs, and tear gas to disperse the marchers. The whole deplorable scene was broadcast on national television. It provoked outrage and a number of spontaneous sympathy demonstrations. Four hundred white clergymen flew into Selma to participate in the march. When one of them was murdered by a group of local toughs the tension and protest intensified. Even segregationist Southern newspapers deplored the violence, and realized that such senseless brutality only ensured the passage of tougher federal civil rights measures. On March 17 King won out, and the march to Montgomery took place; four months later the voter registration bill which the South had been opposing became law.

Except for the assassination of Martin Luther King in 1968, the events in Selma were the last ones in the Southern struggle for liberation which won widespread publicity and sympathy in the North. In August of 1965 Northern liberals were joggled out of their complacency by a five-day riot in Watts, a black ghetto in Los Angeles. Throughout the century black laborers had been streaming north, bringing few skills and less money. They qualified for only the most menial jobs, and since most employers followed a policy of "last hired, first fired" with regard to black labor, many were unable to obtain any work at all when times were hard. White bigotry confined blacks in squalid ghettos, where they were charged high rents for poor housing, where recreation facilities were nonexistent, where schools were ramshackle and overcrowded. School segregation was almost as rigid in the North as in the South, but its maintenance did not require legal support. Rigid residential segregation did the job.* When attempts were made to halt *de facto* school segregation by busing children to different schools, white mothers reacted with as much fury as had their counterparts in Little Rock. They rarely dared oppose desegregation as such, but usually based their protest on the need to preserve "neighborhood schools"—which amounted to the same thing.

---

*Residential segregation was not necessarily the rule in the South. One civil rights worker told of conducting a voter registration drive in a small town where residential integration was so absolute that door-to-door canvassing was useless—it was impossible to tell whether a black or white family lived in any given house. They finally solved the problem by consulting the city directory, where white heads of households were designated "Mr." or "Mrs." and blacks received no title.

Superficially, the Watts ghetto was a much more livable place than its counterparts in the East. Its housing was newer, and consisted mostly of detached houses rather than tenements. But since poor blacks could live in no other area, rents were extremely high. Three and four families often had to crowd into a house built for one. Bus service was almost nonexistent, even sparser than for the rest of southern California. Indeed, inferior city services have been a distinguishing mark of black ghettos across the nation. There were very few employers in Watts, as it was built as a residential suburb. It contained no hospitals, no movie houses, almost no opportunities for recreation. Moreover, a high proportion of its residents were unemployed. Accumulated anger at these conditions broke forth in a frenzy of destruction. The same pattern repeated itself in other large Northern cities over the next few years, with the expression of stored fury triggered by some small event, usually a petty act of repression on the part of the police.

But the woeful state of the ghettos had existed for generations. Why were the late sixties the time when they suddenly caught fire? The answer lies in changing expectations. Southern blacks were winning gains, and white liberals were vocally promoting programs to end poverty and discrimination. Yet paper changes were making no visible dent in the asphalt reality, and it was clear that most Northerners bitterly resented any changes which might affect them personally. The white working class were especially afraid, understandably. They enjoyed greater job security than black workers; any moves toward equality or status seemed to threaten what they felt to be a hard-earned relative security or privilege (often at the expense of blacks). Living in neighborhoods adjacent to the ghetto, lower-class whites felt that the brunt of any residential or school desegregation upheaval would fall upon them, while distance and expense protected the middle classes from any unsettling changes involved with a black influx. Often the children of immigrants who had themselves known ghetto conditions, the white working class cherished the notion that hard work and upright behavior had allowed them to advance, but they rejected the notion that poor blacks should want to do likewise.

Yet the fury of the ghetto riots was not turned outward, to white neighborhoods whose residents sat trembling in the midst of a growing arsenal of handguns, but inward, upon the ghetto itself. The destruction was not mindless. First, poor people have been as much conditioned by advertising as rich; they want the good things they see in the commercials. They took them. Moreover, inner city stores are notorious gougers of the credit-dependent poor, who regarded looting as a justifiable reprisal. Second, much property, both business and residential, was destroyed by fire. It appears that these fires were not set at random, but were a deliberate attempt to demolish the records of loan companies and other credit-granting institutions. Third, of the people who died, almost all of them were black and many of them women and children. The evidence indicates that the overwhelming majority of those shot were killed not by snipers, but by police and national guard. Of the people who died in the Detroit riot in 1967, there is no reason to ascribe even one death to a sniper.

The riots were a reaction of the black community to conditions which oppressed them as a group. Throughout the fifties and sixties a few avenues of escape persisted for individuals, the most visible of which was athletics. Professional spectator sports are an urban phenomenon; they require a large, concentrated population to support them. Their participants are highly visible models for the young, and throughout the century boys have looked to sports as an escape from an intolerable and otherwise locked-in environment. A black child knows he can never be president, but he might hope to be Willy Mays. Mays entered major league baseball in 1951, only four years after Jackie Robinson had officially broken the color bar. For the next twenty years Mays remained one of its most thrilling players, standing close to Babe Ruth on the all-time home run list, and remaining a culture hero even after age had blunted his skills. Henry Aaron has been a less colorful superstar. A few years younger than Mays, he has already passed Mays and broken Babe Ruth's home run record. Yet until that feat his exploits never received much publicity, and his name was probably unknown to those who are unfamiliar with baseball. Although it has provided an entrée into the middle class for many blacks, athletics too knows discrimination. White players who are less than great have an edge over their black counterparts; thus the percentage of black all-stars in the major team sports is greater than the overall percentage of black major leaguers. In football, certain positions, especially quarterback, are reserved for whites. White coaches and owners are no less bigoted than whites in general, and they run sports.

But black athletes are not supposed to speak of these things, or of any "controversial" subject. They should be suitably grateful for the opportunities which athletics has given them, and keep their mouths shut about politics. Muhammad Ali broke this rule and paid a heavy price. A very vocal and vivid man, Ali became heavy-weight champion of boxing in February, 1964, and shortly thereafter announced that he had converted to the Black Muslim faith. This provoked both anger and ridicule, and for years sports writers engaged in a put-down of both Ali and black people in general by persisting in calling him by his abandoned "white" name, Cassius Clay. But he continued as both a great fighter and a consummate entertainer, leaving his enemies no loophole through which to do him serious harm. That was provided them in 1967, when he refused induction into the army, stating that his religious convictions made it impossible for him to fight in a war. The World Boxing Association promptly declared his title vacant, in a gross violation of due process, and a Houston jury sentenced him to five years in jail. His appeal dragged on for five years, until finally the Supreme Court issued an injunction forcing the WBA to permit him to compete, and recognized his status as a conscientious objector.

The contrast between the older type of athlete, such as Mays, and a man like Ali parallels the contrast between the old and new black organizations.

The Black Muslims are a strictly segregationist organization which believes that the white man is a sort of Frankenstein's monster created by a black scientist in Africa. He isn't even real. This attitude provides an ironic counterpoint to the persistent white tendency to ignore "invisible" black neighbors. The Muslims' strength has arisen out of the Northern ghettos, particularily in prisons. They tell people who have always considered themselves worthless, "Be proud, be a man, it's good to be black," and alleviate loneliness by group support. Unfortunately, their credo is based on hate, and therefore will never win the support of the whites who hold the power of the nation. Malcolm X, ex-ghetto delinquent, ex-convict, brilliant orator, attempted to establish a breakaway organization which would incorporate both black pride and tolerance for whites, but he was assassinated before he could begin. The Black Panthers are a much smaller, newer group, whose ranks have been greatly thinned by the police and courts. Begun in the San Francisco Bay Area, the organization consists of young men, most of them ex-convicts, many of them ex-drug addicts, who feel that blacks have the right to defend themselves against unprovoked violence. They distrust the operations of the law, which they feel to be rigged against minorities and the poor, and the intentions of whites who attempt to be philanthropic, especially social workers. They have organized free breakfasts for school children and similar projects, which have received very little publicity, but have also been known to march into the legislative buildings in Sacramento armed to the hilt, which has gotten them a great deal of trouble.

Both the Muslims and the Panthers rest their strength in group identity and purpose. But both organizations seem to strike a majority of white Americans with hate and fear. This reaction apparently arises partially out of guilt; fear provokes hate. Whites have oppressed blacks throughout the nation's history, and naturally are apprehensive about the treatment to be meted out if the blacks ever get on top. The sight of a Panther with a gun in his hand brings terror to the surface, and has often provoked a bloody reprisal.

In 1960 the prediction of the upheavals to come would have sounded like an impossible nightmare. John Kennedy was elected president amid feelings of buoyant hope. He presented an image of youth and tinselled glamour, and offered a "New Frontier" to explore. The placid Eisenhower years had conditioned the American people in complacency, but they were growing a little bored. Eisenhower's vice president and chosen candidate for succession, Richard Nixon, lacked the general's personal popularity and grandfatherly aura. Nonetheless, the election was the closest ever, and Kennedy's victory must be regarded as something of a fluke, caused more by Nixon's tactical errors than by anything else. It was certainly not a mandate for change. The Kennedy style blinded his audience to reality, and voters were becoming increasingly willing to act as an audience. Television was becoming their only outlet on the world. Since this medium is perfectly adapted to transmit style and can easily be made to distort content, it was the ideal disseminator of the Kennedy myth. The election itself was probably decided by television, when Kennedy and Nixon met for a series of debates and the former came across as the much more attractive personality. For all JFK's fine words and grandiose programs, his administration accomplished little, which in itself helped to preserve his popularity. Despite their relish of the new air of bustle in Washington, few Americans really wanted change. If there is any harsh reality that lies concealed under the JFK myth, his assassination in November, 1963, assured that it will remain hidden forever, for the image has become far larger than the man.

Lyndon Johnson's image was very different, and did him no good. A consummate politician, he pushed many of Kennedy's social welfare measures through Congress, and at the time of his election in 1964 it seemed that he might become one of the greatest presidents the country had ever had. But even then, while posing as a "peace" candidate, he was planning to increase the involvement of the United States in southeast Asia (Chapter 30). Even before the festering war destroyed his reputation and his career, the American people thought of him as a crafty man, perhaps even a crooked man. His lies caused a credibility gap, but his aura strengthened it. His Texas folksiness, intended to radiate friendly camaraderie, struck middle America as uncouth.

While the war and the demands of minorities for justice were tearing the country apart, the economy boomed throughout the Kennedy and Johnson years. In large part this was caused by the war and defense spending, and by the space program. Electronics, aircraft, rocketry—these industries were buoyed up by a fat cushion of federal money. And the salaries of their well-paid employees helped support a host of other concerns. The gross national product (GNP) went from $214 billion in 1945 to more than a thousand billions of dollars after 1971. But this heart-pounding jump is deceptive in more ways than one. About half of it was only what might be called paper profits, due to the scandalous rate of inflation (Chapter 30 opening). The remainder did indeed represent a rise in the output of goods and services. But, as before, the increase was not disbursed with the well-being of the ordinary citizen in mind. The federal government grabbed off a huge share without any consumer ever seeing the paper money—and most of this portion went for nonproductive or even destructive uses. Much of this newly produced money did not go either for taxes or for consumer expenditures. It went to a handful of huge corporations, who were free to decide whether they wanted to distribute it to their stockholders or to re-invest it in further expansion of their plants (and their power). If put to the latter use, it supplemented governmental deficits as a recurrent boost to the growth of GNP. If passed out as dividends, it might be re-invested by stockholders or it could be spent on consumer goods and services. The amounts involved became mind-boggling. General Motors in 1972 showed net earnings of more than $2 billion. Few states in the union, and fewer national régimes abroad, could approach that figure in total receipts for the year.

The interstate freeway program also pumped dollars into the economy,

FIGURE 29-3. *Combines on a Wheat Ranch*

The Calgary Herald, Calgary, Alberta

This photograph by P. M. Burn of the Calgary *Herald* shows combines sweeping across the wheat fields of the Red Maples Farms in Alberta. Although this picture was not taken in the United States at all, it belongs here for three reasons. It typifies the mechanization of today's agriculture; these combines are threshing while they reap. The scene calls to mind the *Wehrmacht* tanks grinding across the plains of Poland. Second, nature does not respect the international boundary. The bonanza farms of southern Alberta do not differ much from those of Montana or western North Dakota. Perhaps the chief difference is the presence in the Canadian province of chinooks, warm westerly winds that come over the Rockies and cause the temperature to skyrocket; this photograph was taken under such conditions at the beginning of December, 1969. To recoup wheat that had been thought lost to the snows, Red Maples Farms mobilized the three combines it owned plus five borrowed from neighbors.

Third, the proprietors of this spread live in Texas. Although Canadian anxiety about the intrusion of American capital has focussed on a few areas—oil and natural gas, minerals, manufacture of consumer durables—in fact American money is found in many other spheres of the economy. Of foreign investment in Canada, in 1900 Britain furnished 85 per cent and the U.S. 14 per cent. By 1922 the British share had dwindled to 47 per cent, while the U.S. held the majority. By 1946–47 the American portion had swollen to 72 per cent. By 1963 the U.S. controlled 97 per cent of all capital used to make autos in Canada, 90 per cent in rubber manufacture, 66 per cent in electrical goods, 54 per cent in chemicals.

709

and if Johnson's various poverty programs did little for the poor, they were clearly a boon to the thousands of social workers, researchers, and teachers whom they employed. But tangible factors cannot serve as a full explanation of the economic boom, for the psychology of prosperity was its strongest support. In prosperous times people spend money and invest money optimistically. They are more than willing to believe that good times will go on forever, and that attitude helps create a self-fulfilling prophecy. Inflation occurs, but means little to the fully employed, who can expect their salaries to keep pace. For the poor, especially the aging, times worsen as the value of the dollar shrinks, but their influence has always been small. For the majority, growth has become an intoxicant, not subject to question by human values. This benign economic climate nurtured a strange new crop—political and social radicalism.

Radical opinion had been silent; in the mid-sixties it began to speak loudly, in a growing number of voices which often shouted for different things. This was not a regrowth of dormant Communism, although capitalism was a frequent target. The Old Left had deplored the uses to which the system had been put, but felt that in proper hands it was a necessary tool. The New Left distrusted government and had a distaste for organized power, even their own. Its members believed that the system, the structure, of society had to be dismantled, for it forced even the well-meaning to become manipulators of others and destroyers of freedom. Arthur Miller is not a partisan of the New Left, but in his play "Death of a Salesman" he presented a classic portrait of the manipulated man. Willy Loman has tried all his life to cooperate with a system which traps him, drains him, and discards him. As soon as he makes the last payment on his refrigerator the door handle falls off. He finishes paying for his house, and dies. The only pride that a futile life has allowed him is the belief that he was "not only liked, but *well* liked"; the salesman has succeeded in selling himself. None of his "friends" attend his funeral. Loman's pathos is dual: circumstances have made his failure inevitable, and in the end he is not even allowed the delusion of success.

The new radicals rejected the world which created Willy Loman. Most of them were young, and middle class, the children of respectable citizens who had followed the rules and reaped the tangible rewards during the preceding two decades. While the immediate object of youthful anger was the war in Vietnam, a rejection of their parents' values underlay the rebellion. An early rumbling of this movement was heard at the University of California at Berkeley, in 1964. Sparked by resistance to an administrative closing of the campus to outside political activitists, the Free Speech Movement was really a rejection of the modern university. The protesting students at Berkeley felt that the institution had become a factory stamping out graduates without regard to their needs. Education, they insisted, was only valuable when it was interpersonal and flexible. It could not be twisted into a rigid mechanism which poured information into presumably empty heads, and it could not occur in a classroom containing four hundred people. Since sheer size had forced the

University into a rigid bureaucratic mold, many of its students found that it had become valuable to them only as a meeting place where their ideas about the outside world could be formulated; to bar political activity would make it a useless place. The public reacted to the FSM with disbelief and anger. Protesting that students were in school to "learn," and should be grateful for the opportunity, many irate citizens revealed their conception of education as a passive process, with the student as recipient. Since a college diploma had proven itself as the entrance ticket to the middle class, they were bewildered by the uproar.

To understand protesting students, it is necessary to examine the world in which they had grown up. Most came from the regimented world of the middle-class suburb. Their parents, having lived through, if not necessarily experienced, depression and war, still relished security; the next generation took material things for granted, and sought less tangible satisfactions. Love, loyalty, a sense of worth through accomplishment—America provided few opportunities to attain these goals. Instead it offered material wealth and "togetherness." Many young people rejected these trophies, for they were not merely tarnished, they were hollow within. But what should they strive for instead? The university might have offered an answer to some, but had grown too rigid to even hear the question. To others, only immediate sensual gratification, through drugs, through sex, through dancing, seemed worth having. Naturally these activities horrified their elders. As early as the late 1950's, when Elvis Presley wriggled his way into the national consciousness, respectable people prophesied doom. But Dionysian activities such as these do not spark profound change; instead, they absorb the energies of anger. A more serious threat to the norms of American life would come from those who, rejecting society as it was, also turned away from immediate gratification while recognizing that deep changes come slowly. No flare of angry energy could make a better America, and a lifetime of patient effort might do no more than help hold the line. Conditioned by television more than by anything else to live comfortably with sudden change and instant answers, few young Americans had developed the patience to persist in political activities in the face of persistent failure. If the medium is in fact the message, most youthful radicals had been cancelled after a short season.

By 1967 youthful dissent had moved off campus and onto the streets. Having rejected the values of middle-class America, a growing number of young people searched for a different life style, one incorporating more humanity and less money, more love and less war. Although these aims are certainly commendable, they were sought with a naive idealism that doomed itself. Thousands of members of the "love generation" came to San Francisco in the summer of 1967—most of them teenagers, many of them penniless. They slept on the streets, in the parks, jammed together in tiny apartments. Wearing a common uniform of blue jeans and long hair, they were picked up by the police on drug and vagrancy charges, and assaulted, raped, and robbed by assorted hoodlums who found them easy prey. Although the flower children of

711

Haight-Ashbury were a short-lived breed, youthful disillusion with America could not be squelched so quickly as they were.

The continuing war in Vietnam led more and more people into radicalism, as the government refused to heed the wishes of the majority who wanted it stopped. By the late sixties it had become meaningless to speak of "hawks" and "doves"—every sane person wanted out. Most were not radicals, or advocates of social change, or even especially interested in politics, but governmental arrogance and repressive police measures were moving more and more quiet liberals to the left every day. The Democratic National Convention in Chicago provides an example. Although Hubert Humphrey, the vice president, represented the rejected policies of the Johnson administration, control of party machinery sent him into the convention with enough votes to ensure nomination. A group of New Left youth (wearing the familiar badges of hair and clothing which by this time provoked a reflex reaction of violence on the part of many policemen) came into the city to demonstrate their disavowal of the war. A few intended to instigate trouble; most had peaceful plans. When the police were set loose on the demonstrations, a series of riots ensued which tended to radicalize not only their participants, but millions who saw it on television. Watching young people being attacked with clubs and tear gas seemed to confirm the contention that America was a repressive and brutal place; some parents who had deplored their children's appearance and activities began to sympathize, and then to agree that the nation needed some drastic changes.

A similar process occurred in May of 1970. In that month President Nixon, who had promised to wind down the war, sent troops into Cambodia. Students demonstrated on hundreds of college campuses. At Kent State University in Ohio the National Guard was called in to preserve order; guardsmen killed four students. Several inferences can be drawn from the events which followed. First, radicalism was growing; among the young, few any longer trusted the government; many no longer wanted the prosperous middle-class life that their parents had thought so desirable. Kent State was not a Berkeley with a history of activism: it has always been a quiet school in a conservative area. If violence could happen there, it could happen anywhere. Second, the nation's polarities were hardening. Everyone was angry after Kent State: the left was infuriated at a society which gave terrified boys guns to shoot students, and the right hated the students for "provoking" the guard. Dialogue across this gap was becoming almost impossible.

From the mid-sixties on, a movement for equality was gaining momentum among America's numerical majority—its women. Superficially, the demands of women's liberation could be easily met. Equal pay, equal job opportunities, provision for mothers to escape the deadening nest of suburbia—all sound like simple justice. But women's inferior position had been so long engraved into society and into both male and female psychologies that it will probably take generations for even rough parity to be achieved. Little girls were given dolls when boys received footballs. But the real problem lay in the attitudes they were presented with at the same time. Boys were encouraged to look outward, to explore, to contend with nature and with others. Girls were warned to watch out for dangers, to be fearful, to experience triumphs vicariously. Even before they started school, boys learned to feel humiliated when defeated by a girl, and girls to assume their own inadequacy when competing with boys. With these attitudes engraved so early, it was not surprising that many men refused to promote women, talk seriously with women, or respect women. And women frequently confirmed their low opinion by being unreliable and unambitious at work and petty-minded housewives everywhere else. Having been convinced of their own inferiority, they commenced to demonstrate it.

Two reactions to the liberation movement confirm this complementary state of mind. First, male reaction to female demands has been not anger but ridicule. This has been true throughout the history of feminism, and indicates the depth of male contempt. Second, there are a very large number of women who hasten to dissociate themselves from any sympathy with the movement whenever the subject comes up. In a way this is reminiscent of the slaves who hastened to assure visitors that they loved massa and didn't want to be free. But anti-liberationist women hold their position especially vituperatively when in the presence of someone who disagrees with them; they are sincere about it, as the slave was not. I can only believe that such people have become so convinced of their personal inadequacy that they don't want to see any woman lead a full life which would deprive them of built-in sexual excuses for being maimed.

One tangible change in the lives of many women came about in the early sixties with the development of a more reliable means of birth control. Planned conception had been a goal for decades (mid-Chapter 25 on Feminism), but the means for achieving it were awkward to use and often didn't work. Birth control pills, which operate by preventing ovulation, are more safe and sure; their popularity burgeoned. One result has been the desire for sexual freedom which has accompanied youthful dissent, but a more significant product of the "pill" has been economic. In some regions of the South all black families have about the same income. The ones who manage to subsist on it decently, perhaps provide opportunities for their offspring, are those with few children. As use of birth control pills has spread, more and more women have been able to control their own fertility, to make a conscious decision with an enormous impact on themselves and the future of their progeny. This device has probably had a greater impact on more women than any other event in the century.

It has been claimed that women have an enormous amount of power, which they don't use. This is true, and liberationists try to bring it to bear. One instance in which consumer power, which is mostly female (if unorganized) did make some changes, occurred in the late sixties when the grape pickers of California went on strike. Large-scale fruit and vegetable production in the

United States is dependent on migrant labor to do the harvesting; in California the pickers are almost all Mexican-Americans. They are, like their counterparts elsewhere, desperately poor, uneducated, and helpless before the rich, well-organized growers. Although migrant workers have been considered impossible to unionize, César Chavez attempted it when he organized the United Farm Workers. By the force of personality and faith he persuaded numbers of his fellow Chicanos to band together and resist the coercion of the employers despite great hardship. At first, growers would not even recognize the union as a bargaining agent, much less grant an increase in wages or an improvement in working conditions. Chavez called a strike against what he felt was a vulnerable group, the growers of table grapes. A strong agricultural union would normally be in a very powerful position, as the crops must be picked within a short period of time or the grower will face total loss; no lockout is possible. But for the duration of the strike the grapes were picked: the growers simply brought in a fresh supply of workers who had not heard of the strike. When the union persuaded them to go out as well, the process was repeated. But the union won. Chavez achieved this feat by publicizing the plight of the UFW members to audiences throughout the country, and telling them that all grapes were being picked by duped strikebreakers. He asked them therefore not to buy any. The resulting boycott, probably the most hated weapon the many can employ against the few, cut drastically into grape sales, and forced the growers to capitulate. Strengthened by victory, the UFW then struck the lettuce growers.

Another group, less politically radical than the New Left, more numerous than women's liberationists, began clamoring in the late sixties for a halt to the reckless destruction of the environment. Lakes and rivers were dying, ocean fish were becoming too contaminated to eat, city air was often unbreathable, and there were more people every day. Concern over these conditions snowballed, and protest became widespread. Several factors need be distinguished. First, urban air is probably no dirtier than it was a hundred years ago. One need only read a description of Pittsburgh, or Chicago, or Birmingham, to realize that our ancestors did not live in a healthful environment. Water pollution is certainly much worse now. Second, environmental decay is caused in large part by population pressure. If the population continues to grow, probably not even the severest controls will prevent an environmental disaster. Third, the worst threat to the ecology, aside from overpopulation, is technology (Document 30-2). Laboratories are developing, factories producing, and people using (and discarding) vast numbers of substances, in vast quantities, including many that do not occur in nature. These substances are almost all complicated hydrocarbons, known as organic chemicals. Naturally occurring organic matter can be a normal part of the ecological system; if it is introduced in moderate quantities, bacteria will feed on it and it will decay, thus breaking up into its component parts. But no bacteria have developed to feed on the new artificial substances, which means that they persist unchanged to pervade the waters and animal food chains, and affect them disruptively and unpredictably.

If the nation's mood in 1950 was complacent, and in 1960 ebullient, in 1970 it was despairing. Decreased government expenditures in defense and the space program sent the economy reeling. Unemployment rose, among the highly skilled as well as the disadvantaged. During the prosperous years arcane electronics firms ringed Boston, growing fat on NASA money; in the seventies one after another fell. During the summer of 1971 one Bostonian commented wryly, "If you take a taxi around here the odds are even that the driver will be an unemployed Ph.D in Physics." Simultaneously, inflation galloped on. In classical economics, unemployment and inflation are supposed to balance each other; you can't have both at the same time. The United States (and many other industrial nations) proved that indeed you could. Thus the times were insecure for almost everyone. The employed worried about losing their jobs; the educated saw their ticket to prosperity disintegrate to waste paper; those on fixed incomes felt inflation drag them into poverty.

Poverty, which a host of social welfare programs was designed to eliminate, persisted. Predictable groups were poor. First, black families, usually urban, often fatherless. Second, farm workers, usually migrant. Third, the aged, usually living alone. This was the hard core of poverty, but its edges were swelled by the growing numbers of unemployed and chronically under-employed. Only a drastic redistribution of income could aid them; social patchwork could not do the job. But redistribution the government would not undertake, believing that higher taxes taken from the middle class would throw them out of office.

In the early seventies the Asian war dragged on, despite the obvious will of the people that American military involvement in it should have ended long before it finally did, by slow degrees, during 1973. But governmental un-responsiveness had become accepted, if hated. The institution seemed too big to control, a monolithic machine with locked controls. Even if it were controllable, many Americans had come to fear that its masters would never operate it for the public advantage. Getting elected and preserving the inertia of power were the functions of Washington; the people could be endlessly manipulated and spied upon for those ends, but could not themselves affect the future.

One index of a healthy society is a reasonable balance between past-mindedness and future-mindedness: the past neither idolized nor ignored, the future neither defied nor dreaded. Through most of the American past a balance had been maintained. The very mobility of American society has helped to preserve it, for while physical and social migration has forced many changes, it also made the migrants ardent conservators when they could resist change. The War for Independence itself, although in some ways a genuine "revolution," was sparked in large part by a desire to preserve the ancient

715

FIGURE 29-4. *Harrison & Abramovitz, Phoenix Mutual Life Building*

rights of Englishmen from encroachment. By the early seventies this equilibrium became precarious. Most Americans distrusted the future; some were gripped by nostalgia for a more satisfactory past, while others discarded it as irrelevant. It is no accident that the hit television series of the time, *All in the Family,* opened with the song "Those Were the Days," while a substantial part of its audience watched to jeer at a man duped into such sentiments.

A combination of nostalgia and insecurity is understandable enough. American society, still unable to solve the pervasive problem of maldistribution of incomes, masked injustice by an apparent prosperity. Abundance of goods was not accompanied by abundance of services or the pleasures which come from doing useful work, and for a large minority even material things were unobtainable. Since a grossly disproportionate number of the dispossessed were also black, they were sometimes able to focus their anger in ways that the rest of the country could understand. But most of the time white people, prosperous people, relished their self-imposed blindness. Young people also threatened to topple established society, but were sidetracked when their efforts produced few visible results. Having become conditioned to the instantaneous—in news, in food, in answers—they found it hard to deal with slow changes. By the 1970's another question had been raised. Had the American economy and government so hardened itself, in the name of efficiency and speed, that slow changes could not take place? Would drastic means be needed to return more control to a greater number of people?

Americans disturbed by the condition of the environment also worried about the deterioration of the inner cities. This building, the Phoenix Mutual Life Insurance Company's headquarters, is part of Constitution Plaza, a complex designed to expunge blight in the core of Hartford, Connecticut. The beauty of the structure is apparent in the photograph; it is also displayed to travellers between New York and Boston. But its significance goes beyond architectural virtuosity. An overhead walkway ties it to the rest of the Plaza. Underground parking eliminates an eyesore which plagues most American cities. Also the complex offers a goodly amount of greenery and open space—a value often overlooked by those who draft urban building codes. Plans for the building emerged from the New York offices of Harrison & Abramovitz, which also had general responsibility for the United Nations Building in New York.

Apart from its contemporary esthetic and social significance, this building suggests several avenues of contemplation. Hartford has long been a center for insurance; its prosperity depends almost wholly on that industry. Its emergence in this connection begins with Hamilton's plan for funding the federal debt (Chapter 9). Another line of speculation might hit upon the importance of the patron in promoting art: Phoenix Mutual is the twenty-fifth largest life insurance company in the nation in terms of assets. Some firms with even more money are erecting monstrosities.

The company's history is reminiscent of the story of the nation. When formed in 1851, it was called the American Temperance Life Insurance Company, and only served clients who abstained from alcohol. Within a decade its directors felt compelled to widen its appeal, took on the present name, and became less particular as to their clients.

SOME NOTABLE EVENTS

1944 Pocket Books begins to capture mass market; starts paperback revolution.

1946 Truman seizes railroads to avert strike, 24 May.
Republicans win both Houses of Congress, 5 Nov.

1947 Veterans enrolled in U.S. colleges reach peak; of 2.5 million students, 1 million are veterans.
Taft-Hartley Act, 23 June.
Ralph Ellison, *Invisible Man.*

1948 General Motors is first giant employer to grant an "escalator clause" (cost-of living adjustment) in collective-bargaining contract.
Henry A. Wallace nominated by left-wing splinter Progressive party for president, 25 July; increases Truman's chance of defeat for re-election in Nov.
Truman executive order for integration of blacks in armed forces, 26 July.
Alger Hiss called a Communist by Whittaker Chambers, 17 Aug.; on 6 Dec. the charge becomes espionage.

1949 Nobel Prize for Literature to William Faulkner.
Arthur Miller play, "Death of a Salesman."

1950 Hiss convicted of perjury, 21 Jan.
Klaus Fuchs confesses in Great Britain as atomic spy, 3 Feb.
Segregation in colleges and railroad cars banned by Supreme Court, 5 June.
Democrats keep control of both Houses of Congress, 7 Nov.
U.S. Census: 150,697,361 (64 per cent urban).

1951 Color telecast, first in U.S., by C.B.S.
Presidents in future limited to two terms by 22nd Amendment, 26 Feb.
McCarthy asserts that General Marshall was part of "Communist conspiracy," 14 June.

1952 Truman seizes steel mills to avert strike, 8 April; action ruled illegal by Supreme Court, 2 June.
Republicans take both Houses of Congress, 4 Nov.

1953 Mark Harris, *The Southpaw.*
Department of Health, Education, and Welfare created.

1954 Nobel Prize in Literature to Ernest Hemingway.
Army-McCarthy hearings, 22 April–17 June.
Democrats win both Houses of Congress, 2 Nov.
Senate censures McCarthy, 2 Dec.; by 67-22.
Newport Jazz Festival founded.

1955 Salk polio vaccine proven effective, 12 April.
AFL-CIO formed by merger, 5 Dec.
Montgomery, Alabama bus boycott led by Martin Luther King, 1–21 Dec.

1956 First transatlantic telephone cable.
$33.5 billion highway act.

1957 First civil rights bill in eighty years; passed 29 Aug.
First nuclear power station in United States opens in Pennsylvania.

1959 Alaska and Hawaii become states.
St. Lawrence Seaway opens, 26 June.

1960 Black students begin sit-ins.
Federal civil rights voting act.
U.S. Census: 179,324,175 (69.9 per cent urban).
Population of world estimated at 3 billion.

1961 "Freedom rides" begin in March.
Roger Maris hits 61 home runs this season; breaks Babe Ruth's 1927 season record (60).

1962 First television transmission by satellite.

1963 Civil rights march on Washington, 28 Aug.

1964 Free Speech Movement at U. of California, Berkeley, starts in Nov.
Poll tax outlawed by 24th Amendment.
Economic Opportunity Act.

1965   Department of Housing and Urban Development created.

Watts riots in Los Angeles, Aug.

Claude Brown, *Manchild in the Promised Land.*

Autobiography of Malcolm X.

General Motors' profits exceed $2 billion.

1966   Minimum wage set by Congress at $1.40 an hour; covers 38 million workers.

Department of Transportation created.

1967   Gross National Product reaches $750 billion.

First effective organizing drive launched among Mexican-American farm workers in California.

1968   Martin Luther King and Robert F. Kennedy assassinated.

Eldridge Cleaver, *Soul on Ice.*

Ways to Study History XXIX

Check dictionaries. A prize-winning work about Jacksonian America was based in part on a calamitous error about the meaning of the term "working class" to Yankees during the Jackson administration. The book imparted to the phrase its modern meaning, taking it to signify industrial laborers toiling for an hourly wage. But in fact the nineteenth-century use of the term had a far broader import. If we consider the Knights of Labor at their numerical peak in 1886, for instance, they still took the word "labor" as inclusive of the entire labor force except for bankers, saloonkeepers, and lawyers. By this definition Andrew Carnegie was a member of "the working class."

Historians of the modern period work mainly with words. The more precision we can impart to the meaning of those words, the better. Certainly the monumental achievement in historical lexicography so far as English is concerned is the thirteen volumes of *The New English Dictionary on Historical Principles,* begun in 1888 and finished at last forty years later. These volumes are on "historical principles" in that they trace in meticulous detail the changing meanings of a word over centuries of time; some single entries run for several pages. With its supplement of 1933 the set is nearly always called *The Oxford English Dictionary* or merely *O.E.D.* (now available in various forms). But it has two detriments: few of us can afford to spend hundreds of dollars for the dictionary in its regular large-type edition, and a reference library is not always accessible. Second, it records primarily British historical usages. For contemporary (but not historical) American variants, packaged in one handy volume, my own favorite is *Webster's New World Dictionary of the American Language* (1953). Definitions are brief and straightforward; etymologies, so valuable in understanding a word, are fairly full; many idioms are given. Also the items are presented in one alphabetical series, instead of having what some consider a cumbersome appendix for biographies and so on. This last feature (with all the others) is shared by *The American Heritage Dictionary* (1969), and also by the *The Random House Dictionary of the English Language: The Unabridged Edition* (1967), which has additional virtues but which is more costly and bulkier.

Document 29-1

Doubtless many readers have thought that it was unjust to print the parody, "Eisenhower's Gettysburg Address" (Ways to Study History VI), so they might want to read a portion of an actual address that he delivered to graduation exercises at the national academy for local police officers that is conducted by the Federal Bureau of Investigation. The president was presented with an FBI badge. A fellow speaker was the Rev. Norman Vincent Peale, author of *The Power of Positive Thinking.*

Mr. Hoover and my friends:

To say that I am honored by this presentation is indeed an understatement. To say that I am astonished and even astounded is perfectly true, particularly when you realize that on the way over here I was telling Mr. Hoover I couldn't think of a single secret we had in Government that hadn't already appeared in the papers. And this one, he just reminded me, has been a well-kept secret.

I want to say one other thing; that is, that I am moved by the tenor of Dr. Peale's remarks—and just by the way they appealed to me very deeply. He said that there must be an underlying deeply felt religious faith if we are each to bear the burdens that are brought to our particular spot in our lives today, and in view of the tensions and ill-feeling and vituperation and bad words that we read in our papers about each other, sometimes internationally, sometimes closer to home. . . .

And so I couldn't more emphatically endorse what he says today. As we go about our work and each of us in his own capacity does his best, then I believe if we are to be the great civilization that we are destined to be, we must remember there is a God Whom we all trust. . . .

Document 29-2

The deprived groups in American society loomed somewhat bigger in practical politics when President Johnson admonished in his State of the Union message on 8 January, 1964: "this administration here and now declares unconditional war" against poverty. Some dimensions of the problem were summarized in a report to a senate committee later that year.

When Americans look at themselves today, they cannot help seeing a reflection of growing affluence and optimism. The image is thrown back from every side. . . .

But in spite of this, there remains an unseen America, a land of limited opportunity and restricted choice. In it live nearly 10 million families who try to find shelter, feed and clothe their children, stave off disease and malnutrition, and somehow build a better life on less than $60 a week. Almost two-thirds of these families struggle to get along on less than $40 a week.

These are the people behind the American looking glass. There are nearly 35 million of them. Being poor is not a choice for these millions; it is a rigid way of life. It is handed down from generation to generation in a cycle of inadequate education, inadequate homes, inadequate jobs, and stunted ambitions. It is a peculiar axiom of poverty that the poor are poor because they earn little, and they also earn little because they are poor. For the rebel who seeks a way out of this closed circle, there is little help. The communities of the poor generally have the poorest schools, the scarcest opportunities for training. The poor citizen lacks organization, endures sometimes arbitrary impingement on his rights by courts and law enforcement agencies; cannot make his protest heard or has stopped protesting. A spirit of defeatism often pervades his life and remains the only legacy for his children. . . .

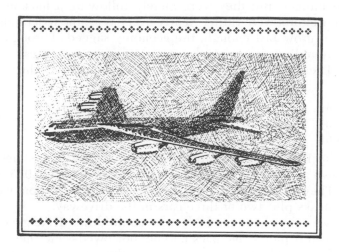

The Decline (and Fall?) of the American Empire

The military-industrial complex, as President Eisenhower would call it later, did not end with V-J Day, nor did it begin then. Such major companies as DuPont had counted the government as a major customer for a century and a half. They had learned the discretion of hiring retired Army officers to handle their negotiations with federal purchasing agencies. But after 1945 the interlocking became tighter and more extensive. Generals such as MacArthur and Somervell were now common on corporate boards of directors. Conversely, business executives (Wilson of GE, Wilson of GM, McNamara of Ford, countless others) became luminaries in Washington. In this two-way traffic, each man was likely to carry with him the attitudes and values to which he had been conditioned by his earlier environment. Most military men were doubtful that war was good, but nearly all knew that defense appropriations were good. Most tycoons from the corporate sector thought that government was bad, but they all knew that federal purchases from private enterprise were splendid.

During the Eisenhower administration at least two members of the cabinet, both from the upper berths of business, tried to check federal expenditures in order to balance the budget. But they were merely following a hackneyed catch-phrase, and their efforts were futile. Nearly every year, the federal debt grew. When it did not grow fast enough, the economy sagged. Through an epoch that shows astounding prosperity by some time-series, we can find pronounced slumps. The nadirs for unemployment as a percentage of the labor force were in

1949	5.5 per cent
1961	6.7 per cent
1971	5.9 per cent

By the yardstick of the 1930's, these figures seem modest, but they shocked millions who had grown accustomed to figures such as 1.9 per cent in 1945 and 2.5 per cent in 1953. They also shocked the unemployed, many of whom were accustomed to thick steaks plus two or three cars in the driveway.

One palliative was obvious to anybody who could think: Hike government expenditures. Even if public agencies had not borrowed—and they did, in amounts worthy of pharaohs—their capacity to pay their bills was growing dramatically. Receipts by the U.S. Treasury were $44.5 billion at the end of World War II. Then they eased downward to $36.5 billion in 1950. That year saw the beginning of the Korean War, and intensification of the Cold War. By 1960 they were closing in on $100 billion, nearly thrice the figure of a decade earlier. By 1970 they had nearly doubled again. Where did these vast resources come from, and where did they go? They came obviously from taxes, which continued, although perhaps to a lesser degree than earlier, to spare the rich and soak the middle incomes. As to where they went, a large portion was never there at all. The inflated figures of 1960 or 1970 merely reflects the general rise in prices, as can be illustrated by the consumer price index (1967 equals 100):

1950	72.1
1955	80.2
1960	88.7
1965	94.5
1970	116.3

After 1970, as the value of the dollar plummeted (memories of the Continental bills of credit and of the Weimar Republic), the cost to the federal government of each nut and bolt rose. The means of payment came from the many unlucky citizens who could not find a way to evade their taxes, and who were simultaneously suffering from the rising cost-of-living. The rest of the increase in federal receipts tended to find its way into the pockets of millions of civil servants—plus a couple of hundred giant companies.

With so much money at stake, and with such a tightly knit community of military-industrial interests, corruption was inevitable. Taxpayers even paid the bills for the corruption. One giant corporation put out a glossy monthly to boast of its achievements in defense and outer-space products; for these goods, there was only one buyer. The same firm was not damaged by the revelation that one of its vice presidents had been procuring prostitutes for potential customers at a sales convention. A company that became big at home before it became a part of outer space was General Dynamics, which repeatedly bought the expensive back cover of *Scientific American* for its "institutional advertising." Successive administrations in Washington, to justify the taxes that made possible these massive expenditures, needed programs that they could sell to millions of Americans. Hence came the overpowering freeways; any prosperous citizen can drive for hours on a six-lane divided highway in Nevada and see very few other cars. Hence came the more modest anti-poverty programs. But the two largest rat-holes down which to pour the wealth of the middle classes were provided by the Cold War. The outer-space program was not designed for scienic ends but for public-relations: Beat the Russians. Direct military appropriations were bigger yet. Although their efficacy in buoying up the domestic economy can hardly be denied, they might be regarded even in that connection as an evasion of the need to think. Abroad, the results were disastrous, as we shall see.

"A man's pride shall bring him low; but honor shall uphold the humble in spirit." (Proverbs xxix:23) The twenty-five years after Hiroshima heard the American orchestra play paeans until they reached a crescendo. A large part of the audience did not listen. The catastrophic approach to foreign relations that had begun with McKinley was pushed to awesome distances in the years from Truman to Johnson, and it is far from certain that Nixon's gestures towards détente will settle Americans back to earth.

For eighteen vital months from July, 1945, to January, 1947, James F. Byrnes headed the State Department. In that period the Allies of World War II—restive with each other at best, united only on the grand policy of smashing the armed might of the Axis, and even within that policy each of them striving to fry its own kettle of fish—these Allies turned into a pack of wolves slashing at each other's throats. Nobody struck a jugular, but body wounds were frequent. Blood and corruption flowed from bodies, gold from treasuries, hardware exploded from factories. Byrnes had neither the understanding nor the character to cope with this melee. Viewing the origins of the Cold War, he could not grasp what was happening; much less could he offer remedies. To his death he remained a small-town politician in South Carolina, elevated to eminence by FDR in 1941 by an appointment as Justice of the United States, resigning from that body in 1942 to become almost an assistant president. He felt no sympathy for the poor, nothing but antagonism to organized labor, and hatred for blacks. His appointment to be secretary of state was as obnoxious as any imaginable.

Already at Potsdam, the U.S.-U.S.S.R. clash was becoming manifest. Truman and Churchill agreed to keep atomic information to themselves, leaving the Soviet Union out. The first major dispute to become public had to do with central Europe and the Balkans. This vast region, as far west as Berlin, had been conquered by Russian armies. Stalin, knowing too well the pro-Nazi governments that had flanked Russia prior to the war, was determined to establish the *cordon sanitaire* which eventually formed the "iron curtain." But at Potsdam, Truman and Churchill had argued that, as Byrnes would say a month later, "Our objective is a government both friendly to the Soviet Union and representative of all the democratic elements of the country." Byrnes was talking about Poland in September. In December he was in Moscow discussing the matter again with Foreign Minister Molotov, surely (from his record during the war and Cold War) one of the most repugnant diplomats of this century. The upshot was that Byrnes and his advisers accepted (they had little choice) the existing pro-Soviet governments in Bulgaria and Rumania. The Russians, at whatever cost in terms of public relations with the outside world, were determined to maintain friendly regimes in all adjacent nations. To that end they had engulfed Latvia, Lithuania, and Estonia in 1940, and they had invaded Finland and sliced off a chunk of its flesh. Having gained effective control of a half-dozen nations to its west, the U.S.S.R. was not about to let any of them lapse into antagonistic or neutral hands.

In this very early postwar period, the lack of international cooperation on atomic energy proved to be critical. Two countries had decided to keep their secret. But it was not theirs, and there was no secret. The theories that had produced the atomic bomb were known to scientists all over the world; the only job that remained for any government was largely engineering: how to manufacture them. We might make a loose analogy by talking about bomb production in the same way as about building machine tools and the assembly line. This task would be immensely expensive, but it was not intellectually taxing. The arms race was on. The U.S.S.R. had an A-bomb by 1949; Red China by 1964. (Soon enough would follow France, India—Argentina?) Who could tell when every puny impoverished country in the world would have one? Would they still be puny? What if some military boss of a government wanted to play with his new toy? The entire world would continue to live with this menace, growing steadily worse as more nations gained the capacity to build atomic weapons. No reliable evidence has become public as to when or in what terms the Soviet Union protested the American-British secrecy on the topic; perhaps her counterthrust was limited to espionage plus developmental work within her own scientific community. In the Western camp, we know what the leaders thought. Truman's alienation from Byrnes reportedly began in December, 1945, when he thought the secretary was too soft at Moscow. The phrase "iron curtain" had been invented by Hitler's minister of propaganda, but its popularity began with a speech by ex-Prime Minister Churchill near Truman's home town in a suburb of Kansas City:

> From Stettin in the Baltic to Triest in the Adriatic, an iron curtain has descended across the Continent. Behind that line lie all the capitals of the ancient states of central and eastern Europe. Warsaw, Berlin, Prague, Vienna, Budapest,

Belgrade, Bucharest and Sofia, all these famous cities and the populations around them lie in the Soviet sphere and all are subject in one form or another, not only to Soviet influence but to a very high and increasing measure of control from Moscow. Athens alone, with its immortal glories, is free to decide its future at an election under British, American and French observation.

Two twists at the end of this passage deserve special note. One is the singling out of Athens. The other is the positioning of Britain ahead of its Allies in talking about interests in Greece. If the Italian invasion of 1943 had any rational purpose, it was not to defeat the Axis; it was to fence the Russians away from the Mediterranean. When civil war erupted in Greece the next year, it was apparent that one side was pro-Soviet while the other had British support. By 1948 this struggle for the Middle East spanned thousands of miles from Greece to Pakistan. Several elements fed into American policy, and they all pushed in the same direction. One was the devotion to loose abstractions that usually sufficed to conceal from most an underlying paranoia; the operative terms were "national security" and "defense of the Free World." There was also the attachment to free enterprise as embodying "the American way of of life"; *ergo,* remorseless opposition to expansion of the socialist bloc. Third, the genocide against Jews in wartime Europe had determined millions of Americans to see Israel established as an independent state—an aim achieved in 1948. Here was a massive voting faction that was both concentrated in key districts and also nearly 100 per cent united in pursuit of a single goal. In terms of domestic politics, the consequence was to warp American policy throughout the Middle East.

Year by year, disruptions multiplied: within the United States, within other nations, between nations. A few mileposts must suffice, in the hope they will reveal some patterns. In the area of nuclear power, the Atomic Energy Commission (AEC) was set up in August, 1946. Clearly, it has helped to develop some peacetime applications of this magnificent force; equally clearly most of its expenditures have been in the proliferation of military hardware. This federal stance aroused opposition at high levels (although not enough to change it); already in September, 1946, Truman fired from the cabinet his predecessor as vice president, Henry Wallace, who had spoken against American policy toward the U.S.S.R. Within three years, so Truman would announce, the Russians had built their own atomic bomb. His response was to order the AEC to construct the more powerful hydrogen bomb.

While American and Soviet power seemed to be growing, the might of Britain and France was patently crumbling. Before his government was felled by Labor in 1945, Churchill had boasted that he had not become PM to reign over the collapse of the Empire: "What we have, we hold." But England could not hold it. In 1947 a populous subcontinent was partitioned into the states of India and Pakistan, which promptly set to slaughtering each other. Within twenty years, the United Kingdom would hardly have a foreign possession left. Neither would France. In Asia and Africa, the Victorian world fell in ruins. The Soviet Union had troubles even maintaining or enforcing its preponderance in contiguous countries. When they supported separatist groups in Iran on their southern borders, they were frustrated by actions in the United Nations. They turned to consolidating their western borders. Pro-Soviet politicians took full power in Czechoslovakia, either with or without popular approval (the point seems uncertain). The U.S. countered with the Marshall Plan (Document 30-1). Since the Russian zone in occupied Germany encircled Berlin (which had been partitioned among the Allies), they were able to seal off all highway access to the city in June, 1948. The United States countered with the Berlin airlift, by which all supplies for almost a year for the three "Western" zones were flown in.

At this stage, many persons were saying that tensions could hardly become worse. They did become worse—war. They did not become apocalyptic—atomic war. The confrontation of the two great powers had now become global because each of them could threaten the other in many zones. Thus the Korean fray that began in 1950 had as its immediate background American gains in Europe. The recovery of several economies of the western Continent, to which the Marshall Plan made a substantial contribution, was startling in its speed. Then the United States persuaded eleven other countries to join in forming the North Atlantic Treaty Organization (NATO), which from its origins in 1949 was almost entirely a military coalition. For that year, American foreign aid of more than $6 billion was exclusively military. Although the federal government adopted the Technical Co-operation or "Point Four" program to help underdeveloped countries, the first appropriation was a mere $35 million. From Europe the center of conflict in 1950 shifted to the Far East. The question of who was the aggressor in Korea is perhaps as pointless as who fired the first shot at the Boston Massacre: neither the U.S.S.R. nor North Korea nor the United States nor South Korea can be held blameless, and some evidence has become public that the U.S.S.R. may have been distressed at the actions of North Korea. The consequences of the Korean War are more clear than its origins. Specifically, it prompted the United States to transplant its Cold War military ambitions to Asia by making pledges to the Koumintang exiles on Taiwan and by enlarging its aid to the French overlords in Vietnam.

The Korean War cannot be understood without noting the elements of continuity and change in the strategies of three nations—none of them Korean. Lenin made explicit what had always been Soviet policy, that Communism would win ascendance by controlling the contiguous countries of the U.S.S.R., China, and India. The dramatic change had come in China, when Communist armies in 1949 had driven the Chiang Kai-shek regime off the mainland to Formosa (Taiwan). This change in sovereignty was altogether predictable, in spite of George Marshall's brilliant efforts to prevent it by a diplomatic mission in 1945–1946. Red armies had made a steadfast fight against the Japanese invaders for a decade, while Kuomintang bureaucrats had occupied themselves in selling American medical supplies on the black market. In comparison to Russia and China, the American role is more difficult to assess. Was it continuous or did it change? Forty years earlier Theodore Roosevelt had insisted that the United States could not be a major power in the Far East; but was this evaluation more true or less true by 1949?

The American move in 1950 was megalomaniac, but it was not solely that. Improvements in transportation and communications appeared to facilitate effective action at distances that had not been thinkable at the beginning of the century. When Korea was stripped away from Japan at the end of World War II, it was split into two warring sovereignties, pro-Soviet and pro-Western. When hostilities of uncertain origin broke out, Red armies swept quickly southward. The U.N. ordered them to withdraw. They did not, and President Truman sent in American troops. Why? To stake out another theme, the Korean War must be seen as a series of power plays in domestic politics. Several of these have been examined in Chapter 29: a Republican sweep in 1946, the trial of Alger Hiss, the repression of radicals. Perhaps most important, the deaf ears that the public turned to the China White Paper. Issued August, 1949, this policy statement on American "abandonment" of China to the Communists was summarized by Truman's new secretary of state in a sentence: "Nothing that this country did or could have done within the reasonable limits of its capabilities would have changed the result, nothing that was left undone by this country has contributed to it." But still the pressure increased for a scapegoat for the loss of China to "Communism." The Republicans had been out of office too long; nobody can measure their resentment at the finesse with which their man had snatched defeat from the mouth of victory in the presidential race of 1948; they were egged on by a China Lobby eager to reconstitute a China where they could act as they pleased. The secretary's sane argument made few converts. Six months later he tried to expound realities again: "The Communists did not create this condition. They did not create this revolutionary spirit. They did not create a great force which moved out from under Chiang Kai-shek. But they were shrewd and cunning to mount it, and to ride this thing into victory and into power."

He still had no audience. This awareness shoved him into backsliding. For three months after American intervention in June, the forces of the North drove southward. Then the United States, using its naval and air superiority, leaped around them and made a beachhead landing far above the North Korean troops. Question: Should they push on north to destroy the enemy? The Chinese issued a clear warning that they would not allow "imperialists" to approach the Yalu River which formed their boundary. President Truman flew to the Far East to confer personally with the American commander, Douglas MacArthur. When asked, "What are the chances for Chinese or Soviet interference?," the general replied, "Very little. Had they interfered in the first or second months it would have been decisive. We are no longer fearful of their intervention." Sixty days later at the brink of the Chinese border he was met by swarms of Chinese infantry, and so he had provoked Chinese intervention despite Truman's warning. First he appealed publicly for more soldiers to fend off the new adversary and fight on to victory (which seemed to include further provocation of China). Impatient, he presented his position in a letter to the minority leader in the House. It was released to the media. MacArthur was sacked for going over the head of the president. Deservedly so, for if any American tradition deserves to be revered, it is the one that places civil, elective authority above the military. If ever a prominent American behaved like an arrogant fool, it was Douglas MacArthur in 1951 (plus his congressional advocates). After 33,000 American deaths, the war ended by treaty. This result could only be achieved by turning out the Democrats, who had become so confined that they could not negotiate with the enemy.

For the next few years the conflict was literally worldwide, and it cannot be neatly segmented into regional clashes. After the United States exploded its first H-bomb in 1952, it was countered the next year by the Soviet Union. Six months later the American secretary of state began to talk about "massive retaliation" if any Communist power launched a nuclear attack against us. Tongues waggled freely, seldom wisely. The first atomic submarine was launched by the U.S. at the beginning of 1954. That same year saw the temporary—very temporary—settlement of an armed confrontation that had raged in the Far East for fifteen years. Resistance in Vietnam to the Japanese occupation had been strong throughout World War II. When France, longtime overlord in the country (known then as French Indochina), tried to reassert their sovereignty at war's end, they met their masters. The outcome was a conference that climaxed on 21 July with a decision to divide the country. The northern half was conceded to the Vietminh (widely known to be Communist as well as nationalist); the southern half was to be ruled by a government which will be discussed in a moment. It was expected that French influence would remain strong in South Vietnam, but this assumption proved false. The United States did not sign this agreement, but it did agree to do nothing to undermine it. The Geneva Convention prescribed that the United States would not go beyond a quota in placing military men in Vietnam. We will see later when and how this agreement was violated. A counterpunch was made by the United States by the inauguration of the Southeast Asia Treaty Organization (SEATO). The Soviet Union instituted the Warsaw Pact as an anti-NATO combine. It seemed that nothing could impede the oscillation of military might.

Then a Third Force started to emerge. This development had more than one facet. It can be summarized as a revolt against colonialism, but the alleged colonizers included powers in both of the major blocs. When delegates from twenty-nine Asian and African nations met in Indonesia for the Bandung Conference, they seemed to cite France and Britain as the chief oppressors,

Red China as the strongest friend. The British government must have been astonished when its occupation of the Suez Canal in 1956 met with virtually unanimous resentment, including that of the United States, so that it was forced to withdraw. But neither of the major powers could go around whistling cheerfully. Their closest neighbors had to be coerced into compliance. The first test for the United States in Central America came in Guatemala. No known Communists were in the cabinet, but it did lean toward the left and it propagated a program of redistribution of the land. The United States through the medium of the Central Intelligence Agency (CIA) is reputed to have played a strong hand in toppling it by a military *putsch*. For non-Communism, we substituted *caudillismo*. In defense, of course, of the Free World. The Soviet Union also intervened in adjacent countries—crudely, by the use of its own brass knuckles. Insurgents in Poland were crushed in June, 1956. An uprising in Hungary was smashed by early November. Egypt, which can be regarded as part of the Third Force but which might have been susceptible to Russian seduction, was invaded by Israel in October, and beaten. In view of the persistent situation in the Mideast, it becomes impossible to talk about an "aggressor nation." We do know that Israel emerged from this conflict, as from the Six Day War in 1967, with accretions to its territory. American policy had been consistently pro-Israeli rather than neutralist.

Then comes a phase of the Russo-American strife that left the earth altogether. Indeed, it left reality altogether. A distinction must be made clearly here. Sane people can applaud the objective of learning more about different kinds of reality, including those of the external solar system. But this goal could have been accomplished at much lower risks in human life and at much lower costs in productive outlays than have been manifest in the space program. Manned satellites have never been needed to explore the moon; they were a good public-relations gambit for the administration, whatever it happened to be. They bred a new breed of culture heroes; they were a circus. They worked great things for the economies of Waltham, Massachusetts, of Houston, Texas, and of Langston Field, Virginia. Nor should we forget Cape Canaveral/Kennedy. Bread and circuses. The competition with the U.S.S.R. was no longer limited to the arms race; it was also a struggle for prestige. Within four months after the Russian *sputnik* the United States had its first earth satellite in orbit.

The razzmatazz did nothing to solve down-to-earth problems. On May Day, 1960, shortly before the leaders of the Big Four (ignoring of course Red China) were slated to meet in Paris, a U.S. "reconnaisance plane" was shot down when it was clearly violating Soviet air space.* The conference never met. Then along came John F. Kennedy with his own style of hoopla. "And so,

---

*The corruption of language by bureaucrats was one of the worst results of the Cold War. The phenomenon was far from new, but seemingly it became more extreme. The U-2 in question was there to spy.

my fellow Americans: Ask not what your country can do for you—ask what you can do for your country." Dedicating himself to the New Frontier (did it ever exist?), he sparred at extending it overseas by announcing the formation of the Peace Corps. The effect of this flamboyant program on underdeveloped areas was about zero. Its major impact was on young Americans, and it can be dissected into three elements. It extended further the magical aura that Kennedy created among students and other young adults (mid-Chapter 29). It provided junkets abroad for thousands of people who could not have afforded to pay their own way. Most important, it taught quite a few participants that poverty existed in the world, so that when they came home they had a deeper commitment to change their native country.

While the administration was taking this initiative that was on balance positive, it continued a policy that was destructive in the extreme. It went on barging around in Latin America like some piratical state. Admittedly the intentions of many Americans to the countries toward the south had been wanton since the filibustering raids of the antebellum era, but only in this century did lust and greed come to dominate policy in the United States. Thereafter the government had sent occupying forces in Nicaragua, into Santo Domingo, wherever it chose; it had tried to bully Mexico over the confiscation of oil rights. Perpetuation of this attitude, which had relaxed under the New Deal, became obvious in three southern neighbors after World War II: Guatemala, Cuba, the Dominican Republic. The first, by scholarly report, was a screaming scandal; the Boston-controlled United Fruit Company, that mammoth importer of bananas, did not want land reform.

Freight cars of paper have been exhausted in writing about Cuba since the insurrectionists took control in 1959. These pages cannot hope to contribute solid conclusions to the heated debate, but they can lay out some guidelines to a discussion. First, the preceding government had been one of the most wretched tyrannies to be found on the globe. The mass base of the revolt was to be found on sugar plantations, while the organized guerrillas came down from the hills. The leaders of the latter included some avowed Marxists. It is contended, however, that the new government was willing to deal with any foreign power that would negotiate freely with them about economic aid, guaranteed markets for raw sugar, and perhaps munitions. Chiefly for ideological reasons, the Eisenhower administration spurned all Cuban advances. Refugees—some of them decent folk who did not want to live under a Marxist regime, some of them hated as men who had prospered under the earlier regime—swarmed into the United States, particularly Florida (only ninety miles from Cuba). They began to organize, on American soil, a plan to reconquer their homeland. Evidence makes clear that the CIA provided them with training and certain types of equipment. Preparations for the invasion were far advanced when the Kennedy administration took office.

What to do? The White House decided, in a clear breach of neutrality, to allow the invaders to push off. Two distinct types of reasoning are reported as having joined in this conclusion. By one account from an adviser, Kennedy reasoned thusly: We have Cubans here who are illegally armed. It is better to get rid of them in Cuba than in the United States. The true fantasists thought the invasion would succeed because the inhabitants of the island would rise up to sustain it, with the wonderful result that Marxist tyranny would vanish from the Caribbean. This wish fulfillment did not last for twenty-four hours after the invaders hit the beach at the Bay of Pigs. For several years after the fiasco of April, 1961, all parties acted from desperation. Rebuffed by the United States and therefore hopelessly dependent on the U.S.S.R. market for its sugar, Cuba foolishly allowed the Russians to install missile bases within its jurisdiction. At this juncture, in a week that involved the cleanest thinking about foreign policy that an American president had done in the century, Kennedy did not prattle about making the Free World safe. He sounded like Thomas Jefferson talking about New Orleans when he said to the Soviet Union: Get them out. The chief executive who thinks cleanly is the one who wins; Kennedy won. But the United States had not learned its full lesson. Having the preponderance of force in Cuba does not prove that you have it everywhere; in parts of Latin America you may not be able to bring it quickly to bear. When a Marxist party came to power in Chile and began to nationalize American companies, the bleats showed dismay. American industrial and governmental disapproval had no quick effect, but the changes the new government was putting through appalled the power elite in Chile. A group of reactionary army officers, in a brief but bloody coup, ousted the Marxist regime and established a dictatorship. Those Americans who may have been relieved to see a Communist government fall had been given quite a scare.

The worst example of the American big-head was manifest in the Far East. It was punctured in a way so startling as to prompt a quite new question: Are there any Great Powers left? The Soviet Union could not hold control in Poland, Czechoslovakia, or Hungary except by armed intervention. Yugoslavia escaped its aegis altogether. Great Britain was humiliated in India and at Suez, France in Indochina and Algeria. These rebukes to major nations had no precedents in the many years from Napoleon to World War II; any country could lose a war, but to lose to a tiny colony was beyond belief. Perhaps the worst putdown of all was inflicted on the United States in Asia.

Given American precepts combined with the logistics involved, the final dilemma of the United States was quite predictable. But it was not inevitable, inasmuch as federal authorities could have changed their assumptions. Indeed, as these pages will show, they were repeatedly warned what would happen if they were content to move forward when they were already "over their heads in the Big Muddy." They could not learn, and each error led to a worse one. It would be idle to talk here about the tactics of specific engagements. It is not even very sensible to talk much about strategy. The rent that could not be mended was in policy, and this error was irremediable. When the United States set out to put down a nationalist rebellion, being carried on by irregular militia, which had the support of all three mammoth countries in the continent, in a strange terrain halfway around the world, it could not win. This assessment, we now know, was made repeatedly by military intelligence and sometimes by the Joint Chiefs of Staff (JCS). The JCS on occasion argued that the importance of Vietnam to American security was being badly exaggerated. But civilians in high office, captive to their own hollow phrases and spurred by spasms of pique, drove a bad policy to its ultimate ruin.

Although American troubles in the Far East can be traced back to the origins of U.S. engagement there, they certainly became worse after World War II. As late as 1947, many officials in Washington were calm and judicious about the fracas in China. When he was recalled from China in January to be head of the State Department, Marshall reported:

> Between this dominant reactionary group in the Government and the irreconcilable Communists who, I must state, did not so appear last February, lies the problem of how peace and well-being are to be brought to the long-suffering and presently inarticulate mass of the people of China. . . .

He explained that Red propaganda against his own nation was more vicious than that issued by the Kuomintang; he also stated that the "reactionaries in the Government have evidently counted on substantial American support regardless of their actions."

The United States would have both of these last problems replicated in Vietnam, and again we will commence in 1945. Japanese occupation of French Indochina had been resisted by guerrillas during the war. When the French tried to re-assert their control, native resistance continued and movements for independence developed. By the winter of 1949–1950 the French were hard pressed. At this point Washington decided to intervene in support of a backward and corrupt native emperor. When France asked for military aid, the head at the State Department wrote in recommending approval: "The choice confronting the U.S. is to support the legal governments in Indochina or to face the extension of Communism over the remainder of the continental area of Southeast Asia and possibly westward." The domino theory was first advanced by the National Security Council* in February, 1950: If one falls, all will fall. So aid is needed. At this stage the policy objective of the United States had been set, and it was never seriously debated at the top levels of government for seventeen years. When a line of action is obviously failing, you would think it would be questioned. But the policymaking hotshots sent around endless

---

*Membership varied, but at least the president, heads of the State Department, Defense Department, and CIA, plus one or more Presidential Assistants for National Security.

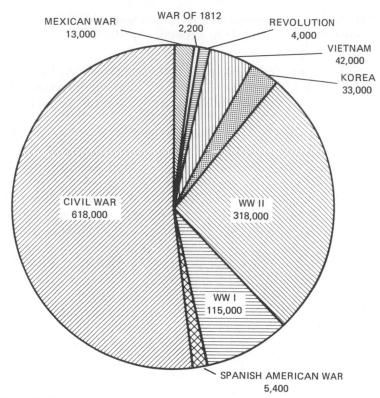

MEXICAN WAR
13,000

WAR OF 1812
2,200

REVOLUTION
4,000

VIETNAM
42,000

KOREA
33,000

CIVIL WAR
618,000

WW II
318,000

WW I
115,000

SPANISH AMERICAN WAR
5,400

FIGURE 30-1   *Deaths of American Soldiers in Major Wars*

memos about the quantity of manpower required, how much hardware was needed, how to conceal their actions from Congress.

If the Truman team defined a goal, the Eisenhower administration took noticeable steps to implement it. Under the two succeeding Democratic regimes the strides got longer; under Nixon they were shortened. Before we look at decisions that revised American commitments of military forces to the Vietnam conflict, we might look at the scale on which manpower was being used:

1954   Geneva Accord permits U.S. to have 342 men in Vietnam.
1961   948 in Nov.
1962   2,646 on 9 Jan.
        5,576 on 30 June.
1963   16,732 by Oct.
1965   184,314 by 31 Dec.
1966   Army command is asking for 542,588 *ground troops* in Aug.
        469,000 troops authorized in Nov. to be delivered in Vietnam by June.

1968	206,756 *more* men requested by U.S. commander.
1969	543,000 troops is peak U.S. strength, April.
1971	196,000 in Nov.

Except for the last entry, from newspapers, these figures have been taken from the most reliable sources that have emerged from the government such as secret reports to the commander-in-chief. They quantify certain trends that cannot be mistaken.

Although an objective had been specified by the Truman administration, it was visibly implemented under Eisenhower. Waning French power in Indochina was shoved beyond the horizon at Dienbienphu in the spring of 1954. The Joint Chiefs of Staff were not greatly concerned: ". . . with reference to the Far East as a whole, *Indochina is devoid of decisive military objectives and the allocation of more than token* U.S. armed forces *in Indochina would be a serious diversion* of limited U.S. capabilities."—date: 26 May, 1954. Even at this time, the Chiefs said that if the American decision was to intervene in what became Vietnam, atomic weapons should be used even if Red China did not take part. By December, the United States had coerced the French into yielding to us all rights to train South Vietnamese troops and to begin a withdrawal that had not been foreseen a few months earlier. As Vietcong infiltration from the North began in 1955, the U.S. was sending increasing numbers of military advisers into the South. Not until 1959 did the CIA pick up evidence of large-scale infiltration of Vietcong southward. In August, 1960, a national intelligence estimate in Washington stated of South Vietnam: "In the absence of more effective Government measures to protect the peasants and to win their positive cooperation, the prospect is for expansion of the areas of Vietcong control in the countryside. . . ."

Eisenhower out, Kennedy in. The imbroglio worsened. In less than three years, American troops in Vietnam were multiplied sixteen times. That was not enough. The folly of sending them there at all was exaggerated by the folly of using "only limited means to achieve excessive ends." The president resisted the pressures to send in ground forces, but in many other respects he exploited the resources—great but not inexhaustible—of his country. As stated in *The Pentagon Papers* (1971): ". . . the limited-risk gamble undertaken by Eisenhower had been transformed into an unlimited commitment under Kennedy." The tactics employed in the expanding involvement will hardly be credited by armchair Americans. Before the Vietcong took over Hanoi in 1954, American-controlled agents contaminated the oil supply for the municipal transit system so that buses would break down. They were training teams to commit sabotage and assassinations, which they prettied up by vague references to "unconventional warfare." They hid their behavior even from themselves behind a barrage of these fancy phrases. When the Mekong Delta suffered a severe flood in 1961, Kennedy's personal military adviser recommended despatching a "relief task force" of 6,000–8,000 men, while specifying that they be "combat troops" who could be diverted into "other activities."

They inflicted upon each other the most unreal dichotomies. When Kennedy sent Vice President Johnson off to Southeast Asia on a fact-finding mission, the latter reported back on 23 May, 1961: "We must decide whether to help these countries to the best of our ability or throw in the towel in the area and pull back our defenses to San Francisco and a Fortress America concept." They exchanged the most grandiose hopes. The JCS estimated that 40,000 Americans could "clean up the Vietcong threat." A general sent on another mission by the president reported that North Vietnam was "extremely vulnerable to conventional bombing." The Kennedy administration made plans for a military "phase-out" in the belief that the Vietcong would be defeated in the field by 1965.

These high-level maneuvers were taken in strict secrecy, but enough facts leaked out that informed guesses could be made about the direction that American policy was taking. Early in the Kennedy administration full-page advertisements against the Vietnam War began to appear in the New York *Times* (paid for by the signatories, in case anybody cares). Originally these ads seemed to come from 200 to 300 academics in the Boston area, but similar protests were appearing in other newspapers near large universities around the nation. The grounds cited by the protestants can be parceled into three categories: (a) Old Far Eastern hands thought that the war was impossible militarily. We had studied other colonial fights against invaders such as the War for Independence, and we had studied the Asian mainland. Air attacks would do little damage because of the absence of vital targets; ground warfare would be a bottomless well for American troops against opponents who could merge at will into their own turf. (b) Broader in their outlook were the natural scientists, who provided the most numbers for these early petitions. They knew facts about nuclear weapons; many of them had been prominent in the development of the atomic bomb. The fallout from a bomb cannot be barricaded within a wall, and they feared that some "limited little war" would become unlimited war. (c) Broadest of all were those who took a moral or a religious stance. Some affirmed that all men are equal in the eyes of God; others were content to say that it was absurd for the United States to go 7,500 miles to fight a little nation that was not bothering us. Obviously these three groups of petitioners overlap, but there were differences in emphasis. Each from his own point of view, all united on one conclusion: the United States was acting in a shameful fashion that violated its own highest traditions. Probably few citizens listened; in a society that is lost in peacetime concerns, that has been depersonalized to a degree where sympathy for your neighbor does not cross your mind, it took the mounting casualty lists to bring mass protests against the war.

Lyndon Johnson saw to that. In the autumn of 1963, the Kennedy team watched warily while a military coup against the premier of South Vietnam took shape. A watchword was: "Sink or swim with Ngo Dinh Diem." Diem sank. A few days later (22 November) Kennedy was assassinated and Johnson became president. Amazing as it may seem in retrospect, many voters who were devoutly opposed to the Vietnam War nonetheless supported his campaign for reelection. This partisanship did not seem incredible at the time. On domestic matters, Johnson's achievements within a year seemed impressive. While Democrats denounced the Republican nominee as a wild man who might (as stated by a cocktail waitress in a Washington hotel) "land us in a depression and a war at the same time," the president posed as the man of reason and restraint in foreign relations. Also feeding the support for Johnson were his own pronouncements. On 29 August, 1964, a tardy celebration of his fifty-sixth birthday was held at Stonewall, Texas, a few miles from his own ranch. After the guests had eaten two tons of beef, the president spoke: "I have had advice to load our planes with bombs and to drop them on certain areas that I think would enlarge the war and escalate the war, and result in our committing a good many American boys to fighting a war that I think ought to be fought by the boys of Asia to help protect their own land." As he spoke thus, Johnson's team was working out an eventual three-phase plan to expand areas for bombing: to go beyond the supply routes across Laos into South Vietnam until attacks were being made on North Vietnam.*

The administration should not bear sole responsibility for later events; Congress must share the blame by virtue of its passage of the Tonkin Gulf resolution on 7 August, 1964: "That the Congress approve and support the determination of the President, as Commander in Chief, to take all necessary measures to repel any armed attack against the forces of the United States and to prevent further aggression." Johnson took this to be almost the equivalent of a declaration of war, so the context should be examined closely. On 30 July, South Vietnamese commandoes had raided North Vietnamese islands in the Gulf. The raids were controlled by the U.S. commander in Vietnam. When the heads of the State and Defense Departments appeared before the senate committee considering the Tonkin Gulf resolve, they lied in their teeth by saying that they had no prior knowledge of the raids of 30 July. Not until 3 August did North Vietnamese PT boats attack a U.S. destroyer. Congress was so complacent that the motion passed the House by 416-0, the Senate by 88-2. Johnson felt unleashed to do as he pleased—after he won re-election.

Conflicts for power between president and Congress can be traced from the origins of the Republic, when George Washington sought the "advice" of the Senate about a treaty (early Chapter 9). Lincoln had his troubles with Congress; Andrew Johnson's difficulties brought about his impeachment.

---

*A further reason for Johnson's colossal victory at the polls in 1964 was his retention of so many advisers from the Kennedy regime; he appealed to young voters by basking in a reflected glow. But the glow had always been a false dawn. When I heard the names of the Boy Scout troop leaders from Cambridge, Massachusetts, whom Kennedy was calling to the capital as advisers, my personal reaction was, "Can the Republic survive?" The question remains.

These struggles ebbed and waned. They hardly appeared for eight years when Harding and Coolidge occupied the White House. During the first six years of FDR's residence at 1700 Pennsylvania, his bitter clashes were almost wholly with the judicial, not with the legislative, branch. While Roosevelt bought Congress, cajoled it, and lied to it, he seldom came to an open break with any strong segment of it. After he died, presidents asserted their supremacy in blatant ways. Their most popular device was the Executive Proclamation. FDR had used it: the "bases for destroyers" swap with the United Kingdom had never been submitted as a treaty. The approach to Fair Employment Practices in 1941 had taken the same legal form. Truman had used it in announcing the loyalty oath for all employees of the executive branch. He used it again in sending American troops into Korea in 1950. Kennedy employed it in dealing with the Cuban missiles crisis. Without doubt, the president is commander-in-chief of the armed forces. Without doubt, Congress is the only agency that can declare war. Without doubt, the boundaries of authority in a tripartite division of authority must meet, and clash, on hazy borders. But where? Johnson pushed the issue far with the Tonkin Gulf Resolution. Richard Nixon pushed it ever farther, beyond matters of security and defense, after congressional committees and grand juries began to investigate the break-in of the Democratic National Headquarters in the Watergate Hotel in Washington in 1972. Asked by a senate committee in the so-called Watergate Affair to produce records that might be relevant to their inquiry, he refused. Was the president "copping out on the Fifth," or was he legitimately and courageously defending the hallowed separation of powers? Congress thought his behavior had passed the limits of presidential privilege, and intended to topple him from the pedestal he had assumed—a post above the law—by the hoary process of impeachment. But before impeachment and trial could proceed, the Supreme Court entered the picture and forced the president to deliver subpoenaed tapes which finally provided irrefutable evidence of Nixon's personal involvement in obstructing justice, and forced his resignation—much to the relief of the Congress and the people. A severe burden was thus thrown on his successor, Gerald Ford, to reburnish the tarnished imagery of the presidency and to seek a more stable balance of power for his office.

From the end of 1964 forward, America's global power delusions fed on themselves. American authorities in Saigon were warning that the situation was desperate; the South Vietnam government was quivering, quaking, frequently toppling. It seemed likely that the Vietcong would conquer the south and win all the marbles. The U.S. aim for sixteen years would be thwarted. It was decided to use Yankee might to enforce the Yankee will. The prognosticators decreed that bombing "must" force the North to negotiate on American terms. The Joint Chiefs of Staff warned that limited bombing would not do the job. A panel including men from all three major intelligence agencies (CIA, Defense, and State Departments) "did not concede very strong chances for breaking the will of Hanoi." The bombing program went forward. It accomplished little. It was amplified. Still little or nothing. Out of frustration, because they did not have any other approaches to try, the United States entered the ground war in April, 1965. By year's end, American forces approached 200,000; they would not drop back to the same level for six years.

American manpower in South Vietnam did indeed escalate (as we saw from the list a few pages back). But the Vietcong seemed to match us man for man; infiltration from the North also escalated. American fatalities escalated. In the United States, demonstrations against the use of napalm, against the Reserve Officer Training Corps, against conscription, began to take violent forms. Dejection about the war escalated to higher floors; in January, 1966, the head of the Defense Department lamented, "We are in an escalating military stalemate." The president's response was to spread the air attacks to oil storage tanks. The Vietcong responded by decentralizing their petroleum depots, which became almost impossible to bomb. The CIA had estimated in advance, in May, 1966, that air strikes against the oil depots would not halt "infiltration of men and supplies." They were right. A study in August said that infiltration was "undiminished." As American soldiers bled and died, resistance at home to the war mounted. Within the administration, disillusionment spread. The undersecretary of state suggested that we "cut our losses." The U.S. commander in Vietnam was asking for more than 500,000 men. As to conditions in South Vietnam, the head of Defense advised the president in October, 1966, that "pacification has if anything gone backward," that more American troops would probably not change the situation, and that U.S. bombing of the North was having "no significant impact" on the war. While the JCS called for more and more men, the secretary of defense decided to resign; perhaps the impressive Tet offensive in January, 1968, had made up his mind. Lyndon B. Johnson, who had yearned for 100 per cent consensus, saw before him a nation more deeply riven than it had been since the Civil War. On 31 March he revealed that he would not stand for re-election.

His successor, Richard Nixon; was virtually handed the election when the Democrats put forward the weakest candidate they could find. If it were not for the uncovering of Nixon's illegal reelection tactics (including burglary, perjury, and obstruction of justice)—which made him famous as the first American president to be forced from office—the Nixon administration might well have been noted for events abroad, and especially for two typical sequences. One was his shifty handling of the court martial of an army lieutenant convicted of complicity in a massacre of civilians at My Lai, Vietnam. To Americans, three segments of this episode were prominent. First, generals who had defied their orders so they could conceal the outrage were quietly released from charges. Second, former soldiers knew that in time of war many outrages are committed, and it seemed unjust that a subordinate officer was being mistreated for symbolic reasons. Third, why did it have to be an infantryman who took the rap, while pilots flying at 20,000 feet could massacre civilians with impunity?

Another fascinating sequence—and probably a constructive one—in Nixon's career was a major asset in his successful campaign for re-election in 1972. As a congressman his public image had been chiefly projected as a staunch foe of Communism. But as vice president he had acted as an important emissary in the negotiations with North Korea. As president he had instituted sweeping cutbacks in American strength in Vietnam (see the list a few pages back). In 1972 he was equipped to say: The Democrats got you into two wars, and I have helped to get you out of both. By the time of the November election, Nixon had not ended the Vietnam War (a year earlier, after he had been chief executive for nearly three years, American forces in Southeast Asia were still ten times what they had been when Kennedy was assassinated) but it did seem that progress was being made.

Not enough progress to suit George McGovern or millions of others. When the Senator for South Dakota began a sustained drive for the Democratic nomination in January, 1971, few thought he could possibly succeed. But in a convention that was drastically different from those of the past—more women, more blacks, more young people—he became the candidate. After eighteen months of brilliant efforts, his campaign came to pieces. Partly the failure was his fault. In a furor over the man he had picked to run for vice president, McGovern seemed to be weak and shifty, whereas his appeal had been to voters who thought him a forthright and principled politician. When he brought forward a plan for a guaranteed annual income, it came out that his staff had done shoddy homework in elaborating a basically sound idea. But in the end, he had a single-plank platform: Stop the Vietnam War. The president pulled that plank right from under the challenger's feet. He came to dramatic reconciliations with the Soviet Union and the People's Republic of China. He seemed to be striving for a settlement in Southeast Asia. Most telling of all, he reduced the casualty lists from Vietnam. Even as his successes abroad seemed to assure his victory, Nixon felt compelled to make his reelection doubly sure by resorting to the illegal campaign tactics whose exposure eventually cost him his power, but none of this bothered many Americans in 1972.

When Nixon substituted massive bombing raids for ground warfare that had cost thousands of American lives, domestic resistance to his program collapsed. The Nixon ticket in 1972 won one of the greatest victories in presidential history; McGovern won electoral votes only in the Dictrict of Columbia plus one state, Massachusetts. The result showed that most Americans were not concerned about the moral issues involved in Southeast Asia. It demonstrated other persisting truths. The sociology of politics was still changing drastically. Movement of the electorate from rural residence to urban, from cities to suburbs, swelling of ghettoes both black and white, both metropolitan and small-town, the explosive participation of black voters—these were trends for vote-seekers to ponder. The election of 1972 also proved further that the party system in politics had died. Most Americans were independent voters. The president, in spite of his startling triumph, could not carry into office a Republican majority in either branch of Congress. But some truths endure. The strategy of the middle 60 per cent, from FDR to Ike to Nixon, has won elections—even though, as Nixon's experiences have shown, a ruthless pursuit of elections might not suffice to hold on to power.

A negotiated cease-fire in Vietnam took effect at the end of January, 1973. What did it mean? From the announced terms, nobody could be sure. One prognosis was that the North Vietnam-Viet Cong coalition would soon seize control of South Vietnam. A gloomier prediction held that if they tried to do so, the president of the United States would again fill the skies with heavy bombers. The most hopeful outlook could be expressed in the directions of a well-known children's game: Return to Square 1. After more than ten years of American effort, the Vietnam War seemed to have achieved no legitimate purpose. It had been the longest war ever fought by the United States. The nation had lost 56,000 servicemen. It had spent $137 billion. How many of his countrymen, even his supporters, believed Richard Nixon when he said that the truce meant "Peace with Honor?" Or was the widespread evaluation the one stated in a song that called him "the genuine plastic man"?

In twenty years, the American sphere of influence had shrunk immeasurably. She had been staved off in Korea. Humbled in Vietnam. Castro still held power in Cuba. Most bitter of all, not only had Red China been given a permanent seat on the Security Council of the United Nations, but the Taiwan regime had been expelled. The vaunted American empire was drooling away into the sands.

For twenty-five years after the close of World War II, the foreign policy of the United States was dictated by the supposed requirements of the Cold War. By this formula, all Communists in every country were subservient to the Soviet Union. Every encroachment by this insidious ideology had to be repelled. If one portion of the Free World fell victim, its neighbors would fall, then their neighbors, and so on, until the entire globe was writhing under tyrannical regimes. Out of this cant came the disposition in governmental circles to bolster every foreign state, no matter how loathesome, so long as it affirmed its hostility to Communism. The previous American tendency to self-deceit was propelled to new depths. When Russia demonstrated that she had fabricated a nuclear bomb, the arms race began in deadly earnest. Weapon gave way to better weapon, each more murderous than the last, while policy-makers embraced the illusion that the road to peace is to prepare for war. Perhaps equally serious was the fantasy that denied that a new Communist government had effective control of mainland China. True, it had taken fifteen years after the Bolshevik revolution for the United States to establish diplomatic relations with the U.S.S.R. but it took twenty-five years for a sober acceptance of truth to occur in regard to the People's Republic of China. In retrospect, it seems that the first major stand-off of the Cold War was the negotiated settlement of the Korean War in 1953. But neither that culmination, nor the French expulsion from Vietnam, taught the American government to tend its own knitting. The miserable outcome was the longest war in our history, with the most humiliating consequences that the United States has ever sustained in a foreign conflict.

SOME NOTABLE EVENTS

1945 Truman, Attlee, and King agree not to share atomic secrets until U.N. agrees on control plan, 15 Nov.
Second conference of foreign ministers on control treaties, Dec.; major split becomes apparent.
Lend-Lease ends; total $50.6 billion.

1945–
1946 Nuremberg trials of Nazi "war criminals."

1945–
1947 U.S. sends Europe $11 billion in aid under UNRRA programs.

1946 Churchill's "iron curtain" address at Fulton, Mo., accelerates cold war, 5 March.
Atomic Energy Commission established, 1 Aug.
Wallace dismissed from cabinet, 20 Sept., after speech attacking U.S. policy toward U.S.S.R., 12 Sept.

1947 Iran charges U.S.S.R. is intervening in her internal affairs, 19 Jan.
India and Pakistan gain independence.
Communists take control of Hungary, 30 April.
Truman Doctrine toward Greece and Turkey, 12 May.
Marshall Plan announced at Harvard, 5 June.
Department of Defense created to unify armed forces.

1948 Communists take control of Czechoslovakia, 25 Feb.
Congress adopts Marshall Plan, 2 April.
Israel becomes a state.

1948–
1949 Berlin airlift, 21 June-12 May.
1949 U.S. takes lead in negotiating treaty with eleven other countries founding NATO, signed 4 April.
NATO ratified by Senate, 21 July.
"Point Four" program of foreign aid.
Truman announces that U.S.S.R. has atomic bomb, 23 Sept.

1950 Truman orders AEC to develop hydrogen bomb, 31 Jan.
South Korea and North Korea go to war, 24 June.
U.N. orders North Korea to cease its invasion of South Korea, 24 June.
Truman commits U.S. forces to repel North Korea, 26–30 June.
U.N. resolution to unify Korea, 7 Oct.

1951–
1953 Korean peace talks.
1951 Marshall Plan ends; total $12.5 billion, 31 Dec.
1952 Allies sign peace contract with West Germany, 26 May.
H-bomb test succeeds at Eniwetok, 10 Nov.
1953 Stalin dies, 5 March.
H-bomb fabrication announced by U.S.S.R., 20 Aug.

1954   Dulles talks of "massive retaliation," 12 Jan.

 Nautilus, first atomic-powered submarine, launched, 21 Jan.

 Geneva Pact divides Vietnam; awards northern sector to Vietminh, 21 July.

 SEATO formed, 8 Sept.

 West Germany awarded sovereignty by Allies, plus right to re-arm and to join NATO, 23 Oct.

1955   President at his request given authority to defend Taiwan, 28 Jan.

 Warsaw Pact, 14 May.

 Bandung Conference brings together 29 Asian and African nations to denounce colonialism, April.

1956   Cominform dissolved.

 British occupation of Suez ends, 13 June.

 Soviets crush Hungarian uprising, 24 Oct.–4 Nov.

 Israel invades Egypt, 29 Oct.

1957   Soviets launch first *Sputnik*, 4 Oct.

1958   DeGaulle wins power in France.

 European Common Market.

 U.S. puts its first earth satellite in orbit, 31 Jan.

1959   Castro forces win control in Cuba, 1 Jan.

1960   Big Four summit meetings in Paris collapse, 16 May.

1961   Kennedy announces Peace Corps, 1 March.

 Bay of Pigs invasion of Cuba shattered, 17 April.

 Berlin Wall starts going up.

1962   U.S. puts its first manned satellite in orbit, 20 Feb.

 Cuban missile crisis between U.S. and U.S.S.R. 22–28 Oct.

1963   Supreme Court rules that compulsory prayer in public schools is unconstitutional, 17 June.

1964   Gulf of Tonkin incident off Vietnam, Aug.

 China explodes its first atomic bomb, 16 Oct.

1965   U.S. armed forces sent to Dominican Republic, 28 April.

1966   France withdraws from NATO, 1 July.

1967   Arab-Israeli War (the Six Day War), 5–10 June.

 Vietnam War protest in Washington by 35,000; more than 600 arrests.

1968   *USS Pueblo* seized by North Koreans in Sea of Japan, 23 Jan.

 Vietcong launches Tet offensive against South Vietnam, 30 Jan.

 U.S.S.R. and other Warsaw Pact nations invade Czechoslovakia, 20–21 Aug.

1969   U.S. begins to reduce its armed forces in Vietnam, 8 July.

 Vietnam War protests across nation draw hundreds of thousands, 15 Oct.

 Vietnam War protest in Washington enlists 250,000, Nov. 15.

 First draft lottery since 1942 is held, 1 Dec.

1970   Nixon sends U.S. troops into Cambodia, 30 April.

 Marxist elected as president of Chile; sworn in 3 Nov.; recognizes Castro regime in Cuba.

1971   South Vietnam-U.S. forces invade Laos, 8 Feb.–24 March.

 Vietnam War protests in Washington, 24 April–5 May.

 Supreme Court affirms right of newspapers to publish *The Pentagon Papers*, 30 June.

1972   Nixon beats McGovern by wide margin, Nov.

1973   Vietnam cease-fire in effect, Jan.

 Watergate investigations intensify, Feb.–Mar.

1974   Clashes and Supreme Court rulings on Executive Privilege.

 Nixon resigns the presidency, Aug. 8; Ford asumes office.

Ways to Study History XXX

Learn foreign languages. Even for those of us who try to remain sensitive to the nuances of words, a meaning can become not only altered but warped or even reversed. Sometimes a slight revision in spelling can help to sharpen perceptions. To write *re-creation* can remind us of what the word *recreation* first implied. A *profess-or* was a person who advocated a set of values rather than an objective automaton who simply "told the facts"; the resemblance of the word to *confessor* should remind us of times when all professors were ordained clerics. In saying *dis-concert-ing* we imply a destruction of harmonies, the production of static, of noise. Although he did not use this exact term, the concept was central to John Dewey's *Art as Experience* (early Chapter 27).

Procedures for taking a fresh look at a word become more productive if the analyst employs more than one language. Often a knowledge of Latin will startle us for what it shows about English; one brilliant essay is built around Shakespeare's mixture of words from Latin roots with a basic vocabulary from Anglo-Saxon. Or consider an example from Spanish. *Cuchilla* is a mountain ridge, while *cuchillo* is the blade of a knife. Anybody who has done rock climbing in Puerto Rico or the Rockies or the High Sierras will grasp the point, although climbers in the White Mountains or the Smokies may be less alert to the analogy.

A disheartening phenomenon of recent years is the laxity of graduate schools in requiring foreign languages coupled with the resistance of students to learning them. With an introductory grammar and a decent dictionary, anybody can learn to read historical works in a foreign language by concentrating two hours a day for three months. Don't waste money on cheap dictionaries. In the modern languages that are most useful to students of American history, for French, *Larousse Dictionaire Moderne* (1960) fills the bill; for Spanish, *Appleton's New Cuyas Dictionary* (1966); for Italian, I have Nicola Spinelli's *Dizionario Scolastico* (1964). *The New Cassell's German Dictionary* (1965) is standard.

Document 30-1

As secretary of state in 1947, George C. Marshall chose his address at the commencement exercises of Harvard on June 5 to make this proposal for the economic reconstruction of Europe.

In considering the requirements for the rehabilitation of Europe, the physical loss of life, the visible destruction of cities, factories, mines, and railroads was correctly estimated, but it has become obvious during recent months that this visible destruction was probably less serious than the dislocation of the entire fabric of European economy. . . . The modern system of the division of labor upon which the exchange of products is based is in danger of breaking down. . . .

It is already evident that, before the United States Government can proceed much further in its efforts to alleviate the situation and help start the European world on its way to recovery, there must be some agreement among the countries of Europe as to the requirements of the situation and the part those countries themselves will take in order to give proper effect to whatever action might be undertaken by this Government. It would be neither fitting nor efficacious for this Government to undertake to draw up unilaterally a program designed to place Europe on its feet economically. This is the business of the Europeans. The initiative, I think, must come from Europe. The role of this country should consist of friendly aid in the drafting of a European program and of later support of such a program so far as it may be practical for us to do so. The program should be a joint one, agreed to by a number of, if not all, European nations.

An essential part of any successful action on the part of the United States is an understanding on the part of the American people of the character of the problem and the remedies to be applied. . . .

Document 30-2

A treaty restricting the testing of all nuclear weapons was signed on 5 August, 1963, by the United States, the United Kingdom, and the U.S.S.R. Soon the document was acceded to by 99 other governments including all powerful countries except France and China. The sponsors professed as follows:

Proclaiming as their principal aim the speediest possible achievement of an agreement on general and complete disarmament under strict international control in accordance with the objectives of the United Nations which would put an end to the armaments race and eliminate the incentive to the production and testing of all kinds of weapons, including nuclear weapons,

Seeking to achieve the discontinuance of all test explosions of nuclear weapons for all time, determined to continue negotiations to this end, and desiring to put an end to the contamination of man's environment by radioactive substances,

Have agreed as follows:

Article I - 1. Each of the Parties to this Treaty undertakes to prohibit, to prevent, and not to carry out any nuclear weapon test explosion, or any other nuclear explosion, at any place under its jurisdiction or control:

(a) in the atmosphere; beyond its limits, including outer space; or underwater, including territorial waters or high seas; or

(b) in any other environment if such explosion causes radioactive debris to be present outside the territorial limits of the State under whose jurisdiction or control such explosion is conducted. . . .

Article II - . . . 2. Any amendment to this Treaty must be approved by a majority of the votes of all the Parties to this Treaty, including the votes of all of the Original Parties. . . .

Article III - 1. This Treaty shall be open to all States for signature. . . .

Article IV - This Treaty shall be of unlimited duration. . . .

Bibliography

PART I

ANDREWS, CHARLES M. *The Colonial Background of the American Revolution.* New Haven, 1924.
——. *The Colonial Period of American History,* 4 vols. New Haven, 1934–38.
BAILYN, BERNARD. *Education in the Forming of American Society.* Chapel Hill, N.C., 1960.
—— and LOTTE BAILYN. *Massachusetts Shipping, 1697–1714: A Statistical Study.* Cambridge, Mass., 1959.
——. *The New England Merchants in the Seventeenth Century.* Cambridge, Mass., 1955.
BAXTER, W. T. *The House of Hancock: Business in Boston, 1724–1775.* Cambridge, Mass., 1945.
BOORSTIN, DANIEL J. *The Americans: The Colonial Experience.* New York, 1958.
BREBNER, JOHN BARTLET. *The Explorers of North America, 1492–1806.* London, 1933.
BRIDENBAUGH, CARL. *Cities in the Wilderness.* New York, 1938.
——. *The Colonial Craftsman.* New York, 1950.
——. *Myths and Realities: Societies of the Colonial South.* Baton Rouge, 1952.
COLBOURN, H. TREVOR, ed. *The Colonial Experience.* Boston, 1965.
CRAVEN, WESLEY FRANK. *The Southern Colonies in the Seventeenth Century.* Baton Rouge, 1949.
DEMOS, JOHN. *Little Commonwealth: Family Life in Plymouth Colony.* New York, 1970.
FOSTER, STEPHEN. *Their Solitary Way: The Puritan Social Ethic in the First Century of Settlement in New England.* New Haven, 1971.
GARVAN, ANTHONY N. *Architecture and Town Planning in Colonial Connecticut.* New Haven, 1951.
GRANT, CHARLES S. *Democracy in the Connecticut Frontier Town of Kent.* New York 1961.
GREENE, JACK P. *Quest for Power: The Lower Houses of Assembly in the Southern Royal Colonies, 1689–1776.* Chapel Hill, N.C., 1963.
GREVEN, PHILIP J. *Four Generations: Population, Land and Family in Colonial Andover, Massachusetts.* Ithaca, N.Y., 1970.
HASKINS, CHARLES LEE. *Law and Authority in Early Massachusetts.* New York, 1962.
HEIMERT, ALAN, and PERRY MILLER, eds. *The Great Awakening.* Indianapolis, 1967.
HINDLE, BROOKE. *The Pursuit of Science in Revolutionary America, 1735–1789.* Chapel Hill, N.C., 1956.
KATZ, STANLEY N., ed. *Colonial America: Essays in Political and Social Development.* Boston, 1971.
LABAREE, LEONARD WOODS. *Conservatism in Early American History.* Ithaca, N.Y., 1948.
LAND, AUBREY C. *The Dulanys of Maryland.* Baltimore, 1955.
LEDER, LAWRENCE H. *Robert Livingston 1654–1728 and the Politics of Colonial New York.* Chapel Hill, N.C., 1961.

LOCKRIDGE, KENNETH A. *A New England Town: . . . Dedham, Massachusetts, 1636–1736.* New York, 1970.

MCLAUGHLIN, ANDREW C. *Foundations of American Constitutionalism.* New York, 1932.

MILLER, PERRY. *Errand into the Wilderness.* Cambridge, Mass., 1956.

——. *Orthodoxy in Massachusetts, 1630–1650.* Cambridge, Mass., 1933.

MORGAN, EDMUND S. *The Puritan Dilemma: The Story of John Winthrop.* Boston, 1958.

——. *The Puritan Family.* Boston, 1956.

——. *Virginians at Home: Family Life in the Eighteenth Century.* Williamsburg, Va., 1952.

MORISON, SAMUEL ELIOT. *The Intellectual Life of Colonial New England.* New York, 1936.

OSGOOD, H. L. *The American Colonies in the Seventeenth Century,* 3 vols. New York, 1904–07.

——. *The American Colonies in the Eighteenth Century,* 4 vols. New York, 1924–25.

PECKHAM, HOWARD H. *The Colonial Wars 1689–1762.* Chicago, 1964.

POWELL, SUMNER CHILTON. *Puritan Village.* Middletown, Conn., 1963.

ROBBINS, CAROLINE. *The Eighteenth Century Commonwealthman.* Cambridge, Mass., 1959.

ROSSITER, CLINTON. *Seedtime of the Republic.* New York, 1953.

RUTMAN, DARRETT B. *Winthrop's Boston.* Chapel Hill, N.C., 1965.

SIMPSON, ALAN. *Puritanism in Old and New England.* Chicago, 1955.

SMITH, JAMES MORTON, ed. *Seventeenth-Century America.* Chapel Hill, N.C., 1959.

TEPASKE, JOHN J., ed. *Three American Empires.* New York, 1967.

TOLLES, FREDERICK B. *James Logan and the Culture of Provincial America.* Boston, 1957.

——. *Meeting House and Counting House: The Quaker Merchants of Colonial Philadelphia 1682–1783.* Chapel Hill, N.C., 1948.

TYLER, MOSES COIT. *A History of American Literature, 1607–1765,* 2 vols. New York, 1878.

UBBELOHDE, CARL. *The American Colonies and the British Empire, 1607–1763.* New York, 1968.

VAUGHAN, ALDEN T. *New England Frontier: Puritans and Indians, 1620–1675.* Boston, 1965.

VER STEEG, CLARENCE L. *The Formative Years, 1607–1763.* New York, 1964.

WILLIAMSON, JAMES A. *The Age of Drake.* London, 1965.

WINSLOW, OLA ELIZABETH. *Samuel Sewall of Boston.* New York, 1964.

ZUCKERMAN, MICHAEL. *Peaceable Kingdom: New England in the Eighteenth Century.* New York, 1970.

Primary Sources

BRADFORD, WILLIAM. *Of Plymouth Plantation,* ed. Samuel Eliot Morison. New York, 1952.

BRUCHEY, STUART, ed. *The Colonial Merchant: Sources and Readings.* New York, 1966.

EDWARDS, JONATHAN. *Representative Selections,* ed. Clarence H. Faust and Thomas H. Johnson. New York, 1935.

ILLICK, JOSEPH E., ed. *America & England, 1558–1776.* New York, 1970.

JACOBSON, DAVID L., ed. *The English Libertarian Heritage.* Indianapolis, 1965.

JENSEN, MERRILL, ed. *English Historical Documents, vol. IX, American Colonial Documents to 1776.* New York, 1964.

MILLER, PERRY, and THOMAS H. JOHNSON, eds. *The Puritans.* New York, 1938.

The New-England Primer, ed. Paul Leicester Ford. New York, 1897. (First published 1687 or thereabouts.)

NYE, RUSSEL B., and NORMAN S. GRABO, eds. *American Thought and Writing,* vol. I. Boston, 1965.

TAYLOR, EDWARD. *Poems.* Earliest edition, Princeton, N.J., 1940.

PART II

BAILYN, BERNARD. *The Ideological Origins of the American Revolution.* Cambridge, Mass., 1967.

BECKER, CARL. *The Declaration of Independence.* Reissued New York, 1942.

BORDEN, MORTON. *Parties and Politics in the Early Republic, 1789–1815.* New York, 1967.

BROWN, RICHARD MAXWELL. *The South Carolina Regulators.* Cambridge, Mass., 1963.

CUNLIFFE, MARCUS. *George Washington: Man and Monument.* Boston, 1958.

——. *The Nation Takes Shape, 1789–1837.* Chicago, 1959.

DICKERSON, OLIVER M. *The Navigation Acts and the American Revolution.* Philadelphia, 1951.

ECHEVERRIA, DURAND. *Mirage in the West: A History of the French Image of American Society.* Princeton, N.J., 1957.

FARRAND, MAX. *The Framing of the Constitution of the United States.* New Haven, Conn., 1913.

FERGUSON, E. JAMES. *The Power of the Purse: A History of American Public Finance, 1776–1790.* Chapel Hill, N.C., 1961.

FISCHER, DAVID HACKETT. *The Revolution of American Conservatism: The Federalist Party in the Era of Jeffersonian Democracy.* New York, 1965.

GILBERT, FELIX. *To the Farewell Address: Ideas of Early American Foreign Policy.* Princeton, N.J., 1961.

GRAHAM, GERALD S. *Sea Power and British North America, 1783–1820.* Cambridge, Mass., 1941.

GREEN, CONSTANCE McL. *Eli Whitney and the Birth of American Technology.* Boston, 1956.

JENSEN, MERRILL. *The New Nation: A History of the United States during the Confederation, 1781–1789.* New York, 1950.

KNOLLENBERG, BERNARD. *Origin of the American Revolution.* New York, 1960.

KURTZ, STEPHEN G. *The Presidency of John Adams.* Philadelphia, 1957.

LABAREE, BENJAMIN WOODS. *The Boston Tea Party.* New York, 1964.

LEVY, LEONARD W. *Legacy of Suppression: Freedom of Speech and Press in Early American History.* Cambridge, Mass., 1960.

McDONALD, FORREST. *E Pluribus Unum: The Formation of the American Republic, 1776–1790.* Boston, 1965.

——. *We the People: The Economic Origins of the Constitution.* Chicago, 1958.

MITCHELL, BROADUS. *Alexander Hamilton,* 2 vols. New York, 1957–62.

MOHL, RAYMOND A. *Poverty in New York, 1783–1825.* New York, 1971.

MORGAN, EDMUND S. *The British of the Republic, 1763–1789.* Chicago, 1956.

—— and Helen M. Morgan. *The Stamp Act Crisis: Prologue to Revolution.* Chapel Hill, N.C., 1953.

MORISON, SAMUEL ELIOT. *The Maritime History of Massachusetts, 1783–1860.* Boston, 1921.

——. *John Paul Jones.* Boston, 1959.

MORRIS, RICHARD B. *The Peacemakers: The Great Powers and American Independence.* New York, 1965.

NETTELS, CURTIS. *Emergence of a National Economy, 1775–1815*. New York, 1962.

PERKINS, BRADFORD. *The First Rapprochement: England and the United States, 1795–1805*. Berkeley, Calif., 1955.

——. *Prologue to War: England and the United States, 1805–1812*. Berkeley, Calif., 1961.

ROBSON, ERIC. *The American Revolution in its Political and Military Aspects, 1763–1783*. London, 1955.

SYDNOR, CHARLES S. *Gentleman Freeholders*. Chapel Hill, N.C., 1952

TREVELYAN, GEORGE OTTO. *The American Revolution*, ed. Richard B. Morris. New York, 1964.

VAN DOREN, CARL. *Benjamin Franklin*. New York, 1938.

WHITE, LEONARD D. *The Federalists: A Study in Administrative History, 1789–1801*. New York, 1948.

——. *The Jeffersonians*. New York, 1951.

WICKWIRE, FRANKLIN B. *British Subministers and Colonial America, 1763–1783*. Princeton, N.J., 1966.

WRIGHT, ESMOND, ed. *Causes and Consequences of the American Revolution*. Chicago, 1966.

Primary Sources

BURNETT, EDMUND CODY, ed. *Letters of Members of the Continental Congress*, 8 vols. Washington, D.C., 1921–38.

CLINTON, SIR HENRY. *The American Rebellion*, ed. William B. Wilcox. New Haven, Conn., 1954.

CRÈVECOEUR, J. HECTOR ST. JOHN. *Letters from an American Farmer*. Several editions, first published 1782.

DEVOTO, BERNARD, ed. *The Journals of Lewis and Clark*. Boston, 1953.

FRANKLIN, BENJAMIN. *Representative Selections*, ed. Chester E. Jorgenson. New York, 1936.

KENYON, CECELIA M., ed. *The Antifederalists*. Indianapolis, 1966.

MORGAN, EDMUND S., ed. *Prologue to Revolution: Sources and Documents on the Stamp Act Crisis, 1764–1766*. Chapel Hill, N.C., 1959.

MORISON, SAMUEL ELIOT, ed. *Sources and Documents Illustrating the American Revolution 1764–1788 and the Formation of the Federal Constitution*. 2nd ed. Boston, 1929.

NYE, RUSSEL B., and NORMAN S. GRABO, eds. *American Thought and Writing*, vol. II. Boston, 1965.

PAINE, THOMAS. *Common Sense*. Many editions, first published 1776.

POLE, J. R., ed. *The Revolution in America, 1754–1788*. Toronto, 1970.

SPECIAL NOTE: The greatest scholarly achievement in American history since World War II has been the establishment of comprehensive and impeccable editions of the works of many of the Founding Fathers: Adams, Franklin, Hamilton, Jefferson, Madison. Any good library will have these sets.

PART III

ARRINGTON, LEONARD J. *Great Basin Kingdom: An Economic History of the Latter-Day Saints, 1830–1900*. Cambridge, Mass., 1958.

BEMIS, SAMUEL FLAGG. *John Quincy Adams and the Foundations of American Foreign Policy.* New York, 1949.

——. *John Quincy Adams and the Union.* New York, 1956.

BILLINGTON, RAY ALLEN. *The Far Western Frontier, 1830–1860.* New York, 1956.

——. *The Protestant Crusade, 1800–1860.* New York, 1938.

BOORSTIN, DANIEL J. *The Americans: The National Experience.* New York, 1965.

CURRENT, RICHARD N. *Daniel Webster and the Rise of National Conservatism.* Boston, 1955.

DANGERFIELD, GEORGE. *The Era of Good Feelings.* London, 1953.

De Tocqueville, Alexis. *Democracy in America,* ed. Phillips Bradley, 2 vols. New York, 1945.

EATON, CLEMENT. *The Growth of Southern Civilization, 1790–1860.* New York, 1961.

——. *Henry Clay and the Art of American Politics.* Boston, 1957.

FURNISS, NORMAN F. *The Mormon Conflict, 1850–1859.* New Haven, Conn., 1960.

GATES, PAUL W. *The Farmer's Age: Agriculture 1815–1860.* New York, 1960.

GENOVESE, EUGENE D. *The Political Economy of Slavery: Studies in the Economy and Society of the Slave South.* New York, 1967.

GOVAN, THOMAS P. *Nicholas Biddle: Nationalist and Public Banker, 1786–1844.* Chicago, 1959.

GRAEBNER, NORMAN A. *Empire on the Pacific: A Study in American Continental Expansion.* New York, 1955.

GREEN, FLETCHER M. *Constitutional Development in the South Atlantic States, 1776–1860.* Chapel Hill, N.C., 1930.

HAMILTON, HOLMAN. *Prologue to Conflict: The Crisis and Compromise of 1850.* Lexington, Ky., 1964.

HAMMOND, BRAY. *Banks and Politics in America from the Revolution to the Civil War.* Princeton, N.J., 1957.

HANDLIN, OSCAR. *Boston's Immigrants, 1790–1800.* Cambridge, Mass., 1941.

HARTZ, LOUIS. *Economic Policy and Democratic Thought: Pennsylvania, 1776–1860.* Cambridge, Mass., 1948.

JAMES, MARQUIS. *Andrew Jackson.* Indianapolis, 1937.

KATZ, MICHAEL B. *The Irony of Early School Reform: Educational Innovation in Mid-nineteenth Century Massachusetts.* Cambridge, Mass., 1968.

LEVIN, HARRY. *The Power of Blackness: Hawthorne, Poe, Melville.* New York, 1958.

LEWIS, R. W. B. *The American Adam: Innocence, Tragedy, and Tradition in the Nineteenth Century.* Chicago, 1955.

LITWACK, LEON F. *North of Slavery: The Negro in the Free States, 1790–1860.* Chicago, 1961.

MATTHIESSEN, F. O. *American Renaissance: Art and Expression in the Age of Emerson and Whitman.* New York, 1941.

MEYERS, MARVIN. *The Jacksonian Persuasion.* Palo Alto, Calif., 1957.

NICHOLS, ROY FRANKLIN. *The Disruption of American Democracy.* New York, 1948.

NYE, RUSSEL B. *Fettered Freedom: Civil Liberties and the Slavery Controversy.* East Lansing, Mich., 1949.

OWSLEY, FRANK LAWRENCE. *Plain Folk of the Old South.* Baton Rouge, 1949.

PERKINS, BRADFORD. *Castlereagh and Adams: England and the United States, 1812–1823.* Berkeley, Calif., 1964.

PHILLIPS, ULRICH B. *Life & Labor in the Old South.* Boston, 1929.

POTTER, DAVID M. *The South and the Sectional Conflict.* Baton Rouge, 1968.

REMINI, ROBERT V. *Andrew Jackson and the Bank War.* New York, 1967.

ROTHMAN, DAVID J. *The Discovery of the Asylum: Social Order and Disorder in the New Republic.* Boston, 1971.

SELLERS, CHARLES G., JR. *James K. Polk: Continentalist, 1843–1846*. Princeton, N.J., 1966.

——. *James K. Polk: Jacksonian*. Princeton, N.J., 1957.

SMITH, TIMOTHY L. *Revivalism and Social Reform: American Protestantism on the Eve of the Civil War*. Knoxville, Tenn., 1957.

STAMPP, KENNETH M. *The Peculiar Institution: Slavery in the Ante-Bellum South*. New York, 1956.

STAROBIN, ROBERT S. *Industrial Slavery in the Old South*. New York, 1970.

STRUIK, DIRK J. *Yankee Science in the Making*. Boston, 1948.

TAYLOR, WILLIAM R. *Cavalier & Yankee: The Old South and the American National Character*. New York, 1961.

THISTLETHWAITE, FRANK. *America and the Atlantic Community: Anglo-American Aspects, 1790–1850*. Philadelphia, 1959.

TURNER, FREDERICK JACKSON. *Rise of the New West, 1819–1829*. New York, 1906.

TYLER, ALICE FELT. *Freedom's Ferment: Phases of American Social History from the Colonial Period to the Outbreak of the Civil War*. Minneapolis, 1944.

WADE, RICHARD C. *Slavery in the Cities: The South 1820–1860*. New York, 1964.

——. *The Urban Frontier: The Rise of Western Cities 1790–1830*. Cambridge, Mass., 1955.

WARD, JOHN WILLIAM. *Andrew Jackson: Symbol for an Age*. Princeton, N.J., 1955.

WHITE, LEONARD D. *The Jacksonians: A Study in Administrative History, 1829–1861*. New York, 1954.

Primary Sources

EMERSON, RALPH WALDO. *Essays: First Series*. Boston, 1841.

FINNEY, CHARLES GRANDISON. *Lectures on Revivals of Religion*, ed. William G. McLoughlin. Cambridge, Mass., 1960.

GRAEBNER, NORMAN A., ed. *Manifest Destiny*. Indianapolis, 1968.

HAWTHORNE, NATHANIEL. *The Scarlet Letter*. Many editions, first published 1850.

LaFEBER, WALTER, ed. *John Quincy Adams and American Continental Empire*. Chicago, 1965.

The Lincoln-Douglas Debates, ed. Robert W. Johannsen. New York, 1965.

MELVILLE, HERMAN. *Moby-Dick*. Many editions, first published 1851.

MULDER, WILLIAM, and A. RUSSELL MORTENSEN, eds. *Among the Mormons: Historic Accounts by Contemporary Observers*. New York, 1958.

OLMSTED, FREDERICK LAW. *The Cotton Kingdom*, ed. Arthur M. Schlesinger. Reissued New York, 1953.

PEASE, WILLIAM H., and JANE H. PEASE, eds. *The Antislavery Argument*. Indianapolis, 1965.

POLE, J. R., ed. *The Advance of Democracy*. New York, 1967.

PROBST, GEORGE E., ed. *The Happy Republic: A Reader in Tocqueville's America*. New York, 1962.

RAWICK, GEORGE P., ed. *The American Slave: A Composite Autobiography*. Westport, Conn., 1972.

THOREAU, HENRY DAVID. *Walden*. Many editions, first published 1854.

WHITMAN, WALT. *Leaves of Grass*. Many editions, first published 1855.

WOODMAN, HAROLD D., ed. *Slavery and the Southern Economy: Sources and Readings*. New York, 1966.

ANDREANO, RALPH, ed. *The Economic Impact of the American Civil War.* Cambridge, Mass., 1962.

ATHERTON, LEWIS. *Main Street on the Middle Border.* Bloomington, Ind., 1964.

BARKER, CHARLES ALBRO. *Henry George.* New York, 1955.

BEER, THOMAS. *The Mauve Decade: American Life at the End of the 19th Century.* New York, 1926.

BOGUE, ALLAN G. *From Prairie to Cornbelt: Farming on the Illinois and Iowa Prairies in the Nineteenth Century.* Chicago, 1963.

BROWN, DEE. *Bury My Heart at Wounded Knee.* New York, 1971.

BUCK, PAUL H. *The Road to Reunion, 1865–1900.* Boston, 1937.

CHARNWOOD, LORD. *Abraham Lincoln.* New York, 1927.

CLARK, VICTOR S. *History of Manufactures in the United States, 1860–1914.* Washington, D.C., 1928.

DESTLER, CHESTER MCARTHUR. *American Radicalism 1865–1901.* New London, Conn., 1946.

FRIEDMAN, MILTON, and ANNA JACOBSON SCHWARTZ. *A Monetary History of the United States, 1867–1960.* Princeton, N.J., 1963.

GATES, PAUL WALLACE. *Fifty Million Acres: Conflicts over Kansas Land Policy, 1854–1890.* Ithaca, N.Y., 1954.

GINGER, RAY. *Age of Excess: The United States from 1877 to 1914.* Second Edition. New York, 1975.

——. *Altgeld's America.* New York, 1958.

HAYS, SAMUEL P. *The Response to Industrialism 1885–1914.* Chicago, 1957.

HICKS, JOHN D. *The Populist Revolt.* Minneapolis, 1931.

HUTCHINS, JOHN G. B. *The American Maritime Industries and Public Policy, 1789–1914.* Cambridge, Mass., 1941.

JOSEPHSON, MATTHEW. *The Politicos, 1865–1896.* New York, 1938.

KIRKLAND, EDWARD CHASE. *Men, Cities and Transportation: A Study in New England History, 1820–1900,* 2 vols. Cambridge, Mass., 1948.

LAFEBER, WALTER. *The New Empire: An Interpretation of American Expansion, 1860–1898.* Ithaca, N.Y., 1963.

LURIE, EDWARD. *Louis Agassiz: A Life in Science.* Chicago, 1960.

MCKITRICK, ERIC L., ed. *Andrew Johnson and Reconstruction.* Chicago, 1960.

SHARKEY, ROBERT P. *Money, Class, and Party: An Economic Study of Civil War and Reconstruction.* Baltimore, 1959.

STAMPP, KENNETH M. *The Era of Reconstruction 1865–1877.* New York, 1965.

STEINMAN, D. B. *The Builders of the Bridge: The Story of John Roebling and His Son.* New York, 1945.

TAYLOR, GEORGE ROGERS. *The Transportation Revolution, 1815–1860.* New York, 1951.

THERNSTROM, STEPHAN. *Poverty and Progress: Social Mobility in a Nineteenth Century City.* Cambridge, Mass., 1964.

THOMAS, BENJAMIN P. *Abraham Lincoln.* New York, 1952.

UNGER, IRWIN. *The Greenback Era: A Social and Political History of American Finance, 1865–1879.* Princeton, N.J., 1964.

WALL, JOSEPH FRAZIER. *Andrew Carnegie.* New York, 1970.

WEBB, WALTER PRESCOTT. *The Great Plains.* Boston, 1931.

WHARTON, VERNON LANE. *The Negro in Mississippi, 1865–1890.* New York, 1947.

WIEBE, ROBERT H. *The Search for Order, 1877–1920.* New York, 1967.

WILEY, BELL IRVIN. *The Plain People of the Confederacy.* Baton Rouge, 1943.

WOODWARD, C. VANN. *Origins of the New South 1877–1913.* Baton Rouge, 1951.

——. *Reunion and Reaction: The Compromise of 1877 and the End of Reconstruction.* Boston, 1951.

WOODWARD, C. VANN. *The Strange Career of Jim Crow*. New York, 1955.
——. *Tom Watson: Agrarian Rebel*. New York, 1938.

Primary Sources

ADAMS, HENRY. *The Education of Henry Adams*. Boston, 1918.

BRYCE, JAMES. *The American Commonwealth*, 2 vols. Many editions, first published 1898.

CURRENT, RICHARD N., ed. *Reconstruction, 1865–1877*. Englewood Cliffs, N.J., 1965.

DENNETT, JOHN RICHARD. *The South as It Is, 1865–1866*, ed. Henry M. Christman. New York, 1967.

DIAMOND, SIGMUND, ed. *The Nation Transformed: The Creation of an Industrial Society*. New York, 1963.

FRANKLIN, JOHN HOPE. *Reconstruction after the Civil War*. Chicago, 1961.

GINGER, RAY, ed. *The Nationalizing of American Life 1877–1900*. New York, 1965.

HAMILTON, ALICE. *Following the Dangerous Trades*. Boston, 1943.

HOWELLS, WILLIAM DEAN. *The Rise of Silas Lapham*. Many editions, first published 1885.

HYMAN, HAROLD M., ed. *The Radical Republicans and Reconstruction, 1861–1870*. Indianapolis, 1967.

LYND, STAUGHTON, ed. *Reconstruction*. New York, 1967.

MAHAN, ALFRED THAYER. *The Influence of Sea Power upon History, 1660–1783*. Boston, 1890.

SULLIVAN, LOUIS. *The Autobiography of an Idea*. New York, 1922.

TROLLOPE, ANTHONY. *North America*, ed. Donald Smalley and Bradford Allen Booth. New York, 1951.

TWAIN, MARK. *The Adventures of Huckleberry Finn*. Many editions, first published 1885.

PART V

ALLEN, FREDERICK LEWIS. *Only Yesterday: An Informal History of the Nineteen-Twenties*. New York, 1931.

BAILEY, THOMAS A. *Woodrow Wilson and the Betrayal*. New York, 1945.

——. *Woodrow Wilson and the Lost Peace*. New York, 1944.

BEALE, HOWARD K. *Theodore Roosevelt and the Rise of America to World Power*. Baltimore, 1956.

BLUM, JOHN MORTON. *The Republican Roosevelt*. Cambridge, Mass., 1954.

——. *Woodrow Wilson and the Politics of Morality*. Boston, 1956.

BRODY, DAVID. *Labor in Crisis: The Steel Strike of 1919*. Philadelphia, 1965.

CHALMERS, DAVID M. *Hooded Americanism: The History of the Ku Klux Klan*. New York, 1965.

CHANDLER, ALFRED D., JR. *Strategy and Structure: Chapters in the History of the Industrial Enterprise*. Cambridge, Mass., 1962.

CREMIN, LAWRENCE A. *The Transformation of the School: Progressivism in American Education, 1876–1957*. New York, 1961.

DAVIS, ALLEN FREEMAN. *Spearheads for Reform: the Social Settlements and the Progressive Movements*. New York, 1967.

GALBRAITH, JOHN KENNETH. *The Great Crash 1929*. Boston, 1965.

GELFAND, LAWRENCE E. *The Inquiry: American Preparations for Peace, 1917–1919*. New Haven, 1963.

GINGER, RAY. *The Bending Cross: A Biography of Eugene Victor Debs.* New Brunswick, N.J., 1949.
——. *Six Days or Forever?: Tennessee v. John Thomas Scopes.* Boston, 1958.
GRAEBNER, NORMAN A., ed. *An Uncertain Tradition: American Secretaries of State in the Twentieth Century.* New York, 1961.
HIGHAM, JOHN. *Strangers in the Land: Patterns of American Nativism, 1860–1925.* New Brunswick, N.J., 1955.
HOFSTADTER, RICHARD. *The Age of Reform: From Bryan to F.D.R.* New York, 1955.
KIRWAN, ALBERT D. *Revolt of the Rednecks.* Lexington, Ky., 1951.
LEVIN, N. GORDON. *Woodrow Wilson and World Politics.* New York, 1968.
LEUCHTENBURG, WILLIAM E. *The Perils of Prosperity, 1914–32.* Chicago, 1958.
LINK, ARTHUR S. *Woodrow Wilson and the Progressive Era, 1910–1917.* New York, 1954.
LOWITT, RICHARD. *George W. Norris: The Making of a Progressive, 1861–1912.* Syracuse, N.Y., 1963.
——. *George W. Norris: The Persistence of a Progressive, 1913–1933.* Urbana, 1971.
MAYER, ARNO J. *Political Origins of the New Diplomacy.* New Haven, 1959.
——. *Politics and Diplomacy of Peacemaking.* New York, 1967.
MURRAY, ROBERT K. *Red Scare: A Study in National Hysteria, 1919–1920.* Minneapolis, 1955.
NEVINS, ALLAN, and FRANK ERNEST HILL. *Ford,* 3 vols. New York, 1954–1963.
PRESTON, WILLIAM, JR. *Aliens and Dissenters: Federal Suppression of Radicals, 1903–1933.* Cambridge, Mass., 1963.
PRINGLE, HENRY F. *Theodore Roosevelt.* New York, 1931.
PROTHRO, JAMES WARREN. *The Dollar Decade: Business Ideas in the 1920's.* Baton Rouge, 1954.
SINCLAIR, ANDREW. *Prohibition: The Era of Excess.* Boston, 1962.
SWARD, KEITH. *The Legend of Henry Ford.* New York, 1948.
WILLIAMS, WILLIAM APPLEMAN. *The Tragedy of American Diplomacy.* Cleveland, 1959.

Primary Sources

ANDERSON, SHERWOOD. *Winesburg, Ohio.* New York, 1919.
CATHER, WILLA. *A Lost Lady.* New York, 1923.
——. *The Professor's House.* New York, 1925.
CROLY, HERBERT. *The Promise of American Life.* New York, 1909.
DREISER, THEODORE. *An American Tragedy.* New York, 1925.
——. *Sister Carrie.* New York, 1900.
DU BOIS, W. E. BURGHARDT. *The Souls of Black Folk.* Chicago, 1903.
FITZGERALD, F. SCOTT. *The Great Gatsby.* New York, 1925.
FRANKFURTER, MARION DENMAN, and GARDNER JACKSON, eds. *The Letters of Sacco and Vanzetti.* New York, 1928.
GINGER, RAY, ed. *American Social Thought.* New York, 1961.
GLASGOW, ELLEN. *Barren Ground.* New York, 1925.
JAMES, HENRY. *The Ambassadors.* Many editions, first published 1903.
——. *The Wings of the Dove.* Many editions, first published 1902.
LEVEN, MAURICE, and others. *America's Capacity to Consume.* Washington, D.C., 1934.
LEWIS, SINCLAIR. *Babbitt.* New York, 1922.
——. *Main Street.* New York, 1920.
LIPPMANN, WALTER. *Drift and Mastery.* New York, 1914.

LONDON, JACK. *The Iron Heel.* Many editions, first published 1907.

——. *Martin Eden.* Many editions, first published 1908.

LYND, ROBERT S., and HELEN MERRILL LYND. *Middletown: A Study in Modern American Culture.* New York, 1929.

MOWRY, GEORGE E., ed. *The Twenties: Fords, Flappers & Fanatics.* Englewood Cliffs, N.J., 1963.

STEFFENS, LINCOLN. *Autobiography.* New York, 1931.

WHARTON, EDITH. *The House of Mirth.* New York, 1905.

PART VI

AGEE, JAMES, and WALKER EVANS. *Let Us Now Praise Famous Men.* Boston, 1941.

ALINSKY, SAUL D. *John L. Lewis: An Unauthorized Biography.* New York, 1949.

ALLEN, FREDERICK LEWIS. *Since Yesterday: The Nineteen-Thirties in America.* New York, 1940.

ARNOLD, THURMAN. *The Bottlenecks of Business.* New York, 1940.

——. *The Folklore of Capitalism.* New Haven, 1937.

AUERBACH, JEROLD S. *Labor and Liberty: The La Follette Committee and the New Deal.* Indianapolis, 1966.

BERLE, ADOLF A., JR., and GARDNER C. MEANS. *The Modern Corporation and Private Property.* New York, 1932.

BERNSTEIN, IRVING. *The Lean Years: A History of the American Worker 1920–1933.* Boston, 1960.

BLUM, JOHN MORTON. *From the Morgenthau Diaries: Years of Crisis, 1928–1938.* Boston, 1959.

BURNS, JAMES M. *Roosevelt,* 2 vols. New York, 1956–1970.

BUTOW, ROBERT J. C. *Tojo and the Coming of the War.* Princeton, N.J., 1961.

CLARK, THOMAS D. *The Emerging South.* New York, 1961.

FEIS, HERBERT. *The Road to Pearl Harbor.* Princeton, N.J., 1950.

FINE, SIDNEY. *The Automobile Under the Blue Eagle.* Ann Arbor, Mich., 1963.

GARDNER, LLOYD C. *Economic Aspects of New Deal Diplomacy.* Madison, Wis., 1964.

HAMMOND, PAUL Y. *The Cold War Years: American Foreign Policy Since 1945.* New York, 1969.

HERSEY, JOHN. *Hiroshima.* New York, 1946.

JACOBS, JANE. *The Death and Life of Great American Cities.* New York, 1961.

JOSEPHSON, MATTHEW. *Sidney Hillman.* Garden City, N.J., 1952.

KNEBEL, FLETCHER, and CHARLES W. BAILEY II. *No High Ground.* New York, 1960.

LEUCHTENBURG, WILLIAM E. *Franklin D. Roosevelt and the New Deal 1932–1940.* New York, 1963.

LUBELL, SAMUEL. *The Future of American Politics.* New York, 1952.

LYND, ROBERT S., and HELEN MERRELL LYND. *Middletown in Transition.* New York, 1937.

McKENNA, MARIAN C. *Borah.* Ann Arbor, Mich., 1961.

MILLS, C. WRIGHT. *The Power Elite.* New York, 1956.

——. *White Collar: The American Middle Classes.* New York, 1951.

MORISON, ELTING E. *Turmoil and Tradition: A Study of the Life and Times of Henry L. Stimson.* Boston, 1960.

MORISON, SAMUEL ELIOT. *The Two-Ocean War: A Short History of the United States Navy in the Second World War.* Boston, 1963.

NEVINS, ALLEN. *Herbert Lehman and His Era.* New York, 1963.

PAIGE, GLENN D. *The Korean Decision (June 24–30, 1950).* New York, 1968.

SCHLESINGER, ARTHUR M., JR. *A Thousand Days: John F. Kennedy in the White House.* Boston, 1965.

SHERWOOD, ROBERT E. *Roosevelt and Hopkins.* New York, 1948.
SILBERMAN, CHARLES E. *Crisis in Black and White.* New York, 1964.
SORENSON, THEODORE C. *Kennedy.* New York, 1965.
TINDALL, GEORGE B. *The Emergence of the New South, 1913–1945.* Baton Rouge, 1967.
WOHLSTETTER, ROBERTA. *Pearl Harbor: Warning and Decision.* Palo Alto, Calif., 1962.
ZINN, HOWARD. *SNCC: The New Abolitionists.* Boston, 1964.

Primary Sources

BERNSTEIN, BARTON J., and ALLEN J. MATUSOW, eds. *The Truman Administration.* New York, 1966.
CLARK, WALTER VAN TILBURG. *The Ox-Bow Incident.* New York, 1940.
CRAIG, GORDON A., and FELIX GILBERT, eds. *The Diplomats, 1919–1939.* Princeton, N.J., 1953.
EISENHOWER, DWIGHT D. *Crusade in Europe.* Garden City, N.J., 1948.
ELLISON, RALPH. *Invisible Man.* New York, 1952.
FAULKNER, WILLIAM. *Selected Short Stories.* New York, 1962.
GINGER, RAY, ed. *Modern American Cities.* Chicago, 1969.
HAMMETT, DASHIELL. *The Glass Key.* New York, 1931.
HEMINGWAY, ERNEST. *Short Stories.* New York, 1938.
HULL, CORDELL. *Memoirs,* 2 vols. New York, 1948.
ICKES, HAROLD L. *Secret Diary,* 3 vols. New York, 1953–1954.
MALCOLM X. *Autobiography.* New York, 1964.
MARTIN, RALPH G., and RICHARD HARRITY, eds. *World War II: A Photographic Record of the War in Europe from D-Day to V-E Day.* Greenwich, Conn., 1962.
McGOVERN, GEORGE, ed. *Agricultural Thought in the Twentieth Century.* Indianapolis, 1967.
MILLER, ARTHUR. *Collected Plays.* New York, 1957.
Report of the National Advisory Commission on Civil Disorders. New York, 1968.
SHEEHAN, NEIL, and others. *The Pentagon Papers.* Chicago, 1971.
SWADOS, HARVEY, ed. *The American Writer and the Great Depression.* Indianapolis, 1966.
WEST, NATHANAEL. *Miss Lonelyhearts.* New York, 1933.

GENERAL BIBLIOGRAPHY

BAILEY, THOMAS A. *A Diplomatic History of the American People.* Many editions, first published New York, 1940.
BALTZELL, E. DIGBY. *Philadelphia Gentlemen: The Making of a National Upper Class.* Glencoe, Ill., 1958.
BERTHOFF, ROWLAND. *An Unsettled People: Social Order and Disorder in American History.* New York, 1971.
BILLINGTON, RAY ALLEN. *America's Frontier Heritage.* New York, 1966.
——. *Westward Expansion.* New York, 1949.
BRANDON, WILLIAM. *American Heritage Book of the Indians.* New York, 1961.
BRUCHEY, STUART. *The Roots of American Economic Growth, 1607–1861.* New York, 1968.
CASH, W. J. *The Mind of the South.* New York, 1941.
CHANNING, EDWARD. *A History of the United States,* 6 vols. New York, 1905–25.
CLARK, THOMAS D. *Frontier America.* New York, 1959.

COHEN, HENNIG, ed. *The American Culture* and *The American Experience*, 2 vols. Boston, 1968.

DIAMOND, SIGMUND. *The Reputation of the American Businessman.* Cambridge, Mass., 1955.

ELIOT, ALEXANDER. *Three Hundred Years of American Painting.* New York, 1957.

FISCHER, DAVID HACKETT. *Historians' Fallacies: Toward a Logic of Historical Thought.* New York, 1970.

FRIEDMAN, JEAN E., and WILLIAM G. SHADE, eds. *Our American Sisters.* Boston, 1973.

GLAAB, CHARLES N., and A. THEODORE BROWN. *A History of Urban America.* New York, 1967.

HANDLIN, OSCAR, and others. *Harvard Guide to American History.* Cambridge, Mass., 1954.

HOFSTADTER, RICHARD. *The American Political Tradition and the Men Who Made It.* New York, 1948.

IMLAH, ALBERT H. *Economic Elements in the Pax Britannica.* Cambridge, Mass., 1958.

JOHNSON, GERALD W. *The Lines Are Drawn: American Life since the First World War as Reflected in the Pulitzer Prize Cartoons.* Philadelphia, 1958.

JOHNSON, THOMAS H. *The Oxford Companion to American History.* New York, 1966.

KELLY, ALFRED H., and WINFRED A. HARBISON. *The American Constitution.* New York, 1948.

KEY, V. O., JR. *Southern Politics in State and Nation.* New York, 1949.

KOUWENHOVEN, JOHN A. *Made in America: The Arts in Modern Civilization.* New York, 1948.

LARKIN, OLIVER W. *Art and Life in America.* New York, 1949.

LASKI, HAROLD J. *The American Democracy.* New York, 1948.

LORD, CLIFFORD L., and ELIZABETH H. LORD. *Historical Atlas of the United States.* New York, 1944.

MENDELOWITZ, DANIEL M. *A History of American Art.* New York, 1960.

MERK, FREDERICK. *Manifest Destiny and Mission in American History.* New York, 1962.

MORRIS, RICHARD B., ed. *Encyclopedia of American History.* New York, 1953.

NORTH, DOUGLASS. *Economic Growth of the United States.* Englewood Cliffs, N.J., 1961.

NYE, RUSSEL B. *The Almost Chosen People: Essays in the History of American Ideas.* East Lansing, Mich., 1966.

PERSONS, STOW. *American Minds: A History of Ideas.* New York, 1958.

PIERSON, WILLIAM H., JR., and MARTHA DAVIDSON, eds. *Arts of the United States.* New York, 1960.

POSTAN, M. M. *Fact and Relevance: Essays on Historical Method.* Cambridge, England, 1971.

POTTER, DAVID M. *People of Plenty: Economic Abundance and the American Character.* Chicago, 1954.

RATNER, SIDNEY. *American Taxation: Its History as a Social Force in Democracy.* New York, 1942.

SALE, RANDALL D., and EDWIN D. KARN. *American Expansion: A Book of Maps.* Homewood, Ill., 1962.

SHANNON, FRED A. *The Farmer's Last Frontier.* New York, 1945.

SHORTER, EDWARD. *The Historian and the Computer: A Practical Guide.* Englewood Cliffs, N.J., 1971.

SMITH, HENRY NASH. *Virgin Land.* Cambridge, Mass., 1950.

TURNER, FREDERICK JACKSON. *The Frontier in American History.* New York, 1920.

U.S. BUREAU OF THE CENSUS. *Historical Statistics of the United States.* Washington, D.C., 1960.

WARNER, SAM BASS JR. *The Private City: Philadelphia in Three Periods of Its Growth.* Philadelphia, 1968.

WEINBERG, ALBERT K. *Manifest Destiny.* Baltimore, 1935.

WILLIAMS, T. HARRY. *Americans at War: The Development of the American Military System.* Baton Rouge, 1960.

WILLIAMS, WILLIAM APPLEMAN. *American Russian Relations, 1781–1947.* New York, 1952.

WOODWARD, C. VANN. *The Burden of Southern History.* Baton Rouge, 1960.

WYLLIE, IRVIN G. *The Self-made Man in America.* New Brunswick, N.J., 1954.

Primary Sources

APTHEKER, HERBERT, ed. *A Documentary History of the Negro People in the United States.* New York, 1951.

BLAIR, WALTER, ed. *Native American Humor (1800–1900).* New York, 1937.

COMMAGER, HENRY STEELE, ed. *Documents of American History.* Many editions, first published, New York, 1934.

KRADITOR, AILEEN S., ed. *Up From the Pedestal: Selected Writings in the History of American Feminism.* Chicago, 1968.

JENSEN, OLIVER, and others. *American Album.* New York, 1968.

WASHBURN, WILCOMB E., ed. *The Indian and the White Man.* Garden City, N.Y., 1964.

WILLIAMS, WILLIAM APPLEMAN, ed. *The Shaping of American Diplomacy.* Chicago, 1956.

THORP, WILLARD, ed. *A Southern Reader.* New York, 1956.

Index of Defined Terms

Subject Index

Poverty, 615, 617, 654–655, 715, 721
see also standards of living, wealth
attitudes toward, 338, 408, 453, 612, 732
in the South, 391, 393, 431
Precious metals, 12–13, 61–63, 115–116, 403–404, 435, 477, 482, 486, 487, 628–629, 667
see also money, paper money
Prejudice, see xenophobia, racism
Present-mindedness, 630
Presidents of the United States, decline in quality of, 435–436
"great", 571–572
Price fixing, 438, 581
Prices, 204, 258, 260, 278, 295, 311, 410, 550–552, 623, 667–668, 692, 724
see also freight rates, inflation, deflation
fall in, 435, 557, 619, 551–552, 561, 566–567
of precious metals, 477
of securities, 566–567
Prisons, 339
see also convict lease system
Privateering, 108, 110, 181–182, 209–210, 217, 244
see also warfare
Profits, 77, 80, 82, 85, 181–183, 185, 234, 235, 258–261, 260, 280, 305, 362, 408, 502, 693, 708
see also economic growth, prosperity
automobile industry, 561, 566
banking, 407, 538
of Southern planters, 401–402, 358–359
oil industry, 401–402
steel industry, 402
Progress, attitudes toward, 285, 351–352, 402, 458
see also optimism, pessimism, nostalgia
Prohibition of alcohol, 430, 594–595, 621
see also temperance movements
Prosperity, 186, 199, 217, 234, 235, 258–261, 314, 498–499, 501–502, 504–506, 692, 697, 698, 708, 710
see also economic growth, profits
among farmers, 410
Protestantism, 18–22, 24
see also religion, Puritanism, Calvinism
Prudery, 346–347, 451, 465, 591, 595
see also sex, hypocrisy

Psychology, 71–72, 699
Public health, 356
see also sanitation, disease
Public housing, 635
Public opinion, 630
Puritanism, 20–22, 23, 40–47, 52, 142
see also religion, Arminianism, Calvinism, Antinomianism
Quantity theory of money, 277
Race riots, 363, 392, 599, 702, 704
see also blacks, riots, violence
Racism, 6, 8, 91, 121, 264–266, 316, 343–345, 347, 362–364, 369, 373, 389–390, 432–433, 434–435, 447, 453, 478, 483, 493, 497–498, 513–514, 517, 520, 527, 580, 597, 599, 601, 607–608, 648–649, 689, 701–707
see also nativism, xenophobia, blacks
exceptions to, 390
Radio, 559, 618, 642–643, 645, 647
Railroads, 311–314, 402, 410–413, 474–475, 479–481, 512, 555–556
see also transportation, freight rates
and government, 313, 395, 474, 480–481, 556
as symbols, 351–352
construction, 312–313, 314, 367, 395, 412
financing of, 415, 426, 555–556
in the South, 386
management, 417, 504
rates, 311
regulation of, 430–431, 512, 513
routes, 370
trunklines, 314
Reconstruction, Congressional plan, 392
Johnson's ideas about, 389
Lincoln's plan for, 387
radical, 390–391
Reform, 331, 338–339, 341–343, 508
see also optimism, progress, social work
Religion, 3–5, 6, 9, 18–24, 31–33, 39, 40–47, 52, 65–75, 78, 83, 85, 92, 133–135, 142, 149, 153–154, 193, 265, 322, 329, 331–335, 338, 348–349, 352, 450–451, 596–597, 703, 706–707
among Indians, 455
and abolitionism, 342–343
and politics, 331
bigotry, 5, 19, 39, 42, 70, 113, 115, 121, 131, 132, 135, 364–365, 378
conversion, 71–72, 332–333

fundamentalism, 597
millenarianism, 341
revivalism, 58–71, 332–333
sectarianism, 333
toleration, 24, 39, 40, 135, 143, 166, 179
Reparations, 583
Retailing, 427, 569
see also advertising, distribution of goods
Revolution, American, results of, 177, 181–184
Revolutions, 48–49, 141–143, 151–171, 210–211, 216, 232, 275, 316–317, 364, 489–490, 527, 536, 732–733
fear of, 474, 480–481, 482, 528
Riots, 160–161, 164, 168, 177, 363, 378, 384, 392, 420, 599, 702, 704
see also violence, disorder
Roman Revival, 286
Sailors, 160–161, 164–165
Sanitation, 356, 453, 515
see also disease, public health
Schecter Poultry Corporation v. U.S., 628
see also jurisprudence, Supreme Court
Science, 66, 74, 78, 597, 607, 641, 680–681, 714–715, 731
Sculpture, 286–287
see also graphic arts
Secession, 381–382, 384
Sectionalism, 231, 243, 244–245, 251–252, 263, 266, 279, 290, 292–293, 366–368, 373–376, 437, 487, 528, 533, 544–555, 572, 574, 581, 701, 703
see also nationalism
Segregation, 483, 599, 701–735
see also blacks, racism
ante-bellum, 345, 363
see also blacks, racism, slavery
Self-deceit, 511, 514, 518, 574–576, 584–585, 587, 612–613, 668, 736–737
Self-made men, 337–338, 417–418, 606
see also myths
Self-righteousness, 214, 407, 485, 494–495, 509, 511, 536, 574–575, 593, 595, 666, 668, 701, 703
Sensationalism, 595, 596–597, 601
Sensuality, 242, 346
Sentimentality, 461, 463, 654
see also hypocrisy, cruelty
Separatism, 292–293, 366, 371–372

Name Index

Great Lakes, 244–245, 268, 438, 506
Great Northern Railroad, 415, 478, 482
Greece, 276, 507, 526, 649, 727
Greeley, Horace, 341, 400
Green, William, 659–660
Grenville, George, 162–163
Grey, Sir Edward, 536, 539–540
Guatamala, 731–732
Guggenheim Art Museum, 503
Gulf of Mexico, 315
Gutman, Herbert, 421
Hague, Frank, 620
Haiti, 6
Hakluyt, Richard, 14–15
Halifax (N.S.), 119
Hamburg, 415
Hamilton, Alexander, 94, 139, 169, 184, 187, 189, 195, 197, 198, 201, 205–212, 214–217, 219, 226–227, 230, 233, 237, 268, 276, 630, 717
Hammett, Dashiell, 652
Hammond, Bray, 639
Hammond, James H., 360, 373
Hancock, John, 57, 63, 164, 192, 227, 238
Hancock, Thomas, 57, 60–61, 63, 116, 189, 396
Hanna, Mark, 486, 572, 622
Hanoi, 736, 740
Harding, Warren G., (Pres. 1921–1923), 482, 571, 578–580, 585, 593, 620, 739
Harlan, John Marshall, 432, 701
Harper, Robert Goodloe, 229
Harper's Ferry (Va.), 390
Harper's Magazine, 462
Harriman, Averell H., 95
Harriman, Edward H., 502, 504, 512
Harrison, William Henry, (Pres. 1841), 241, 253, 323, 326
Hartford, Connecticut, 511, 716–717
Hartford Convention, 244
Harvard University, 41, 43, 62, 94, 97, 255, 347, 394, 554, 606, 649, 745
Havana, 489
Hawaii, 236, 442, 484, 490–491, 676
Hawthorne, Nathaniel, 46, 235, 347, 352
Hay, John, 491
Hearst, William Randolph, 406
Hellman, Geoffrey, 642
Hellman, Lillian, 652
Hemingway, Ernest, 596, 653–654

Henry, Patrick, 173, 193, 214, 226, 247
Henry the Navigator, Prince of Portugal, 3–4
Henry VIII of England, 15, 18, 102, 104
Herblock (Herbert Block), 434
Hersey, John, 642
Hetch Hetchy Dam, 631, 673
Heyward, Nathaniel, 358
Hicks, Edward, 340
Higginson, Thomas Wentworth, 390
Hill, Henry, 698
Hill, James J., 415, 486, 504, 512, 539
Hillman, Sidney, 615, 657, 661
Hiroshima, 685, 689, 725
Hispaniola, 6, 8–9
Hiss, Alger, 624, 696–697, 729
Hitler, Adolph, 624, 669–670, 672–674, 680, 726
Hoare-Laval Pact, 669
Hoare, Samuel, 669
Hobbes, Thomas, 23, 132, 136, 138, 145
Hodes, Suzanne, 344–345
Hollywood, 147, 697
Holmes, Oliver Wendell, Jr., 291, 520, 528, 565
Holt, W. Stull, 547
Homer, Winslow, 464–465, 603, 616–617
Homestead Act, 393, 403, 410, 458
Hooker, Joseph D., 385
Hooker, Thomas, 46, 52
Hoover, Herbert, (Pres. 1929–1933), 581, 583, 588, 611–613, 615, 617–623, 626–627, 631, 637, 666–667
Hoover, J. Edgar, 720
House, Edward M., 538, 540–541, 547, 575
House of Hancock, The, 77
House of Mirth, The, 590
House Un-American Activities Committee, 652, 697
Housman, A.E., 644
Houston, Sam, 317, 381
Howe, Samuel Gridley, 331
Howe, William, 163, 170
Howells, William Dean, 462–463, 472
Hubbard, William, 43, 86
Hudson, Henry, 39
Hudson River, 268, 311
Hudson's Bay Company, 325
Hughes, Charles Evans, 574, 579, 582, 584, 636, 668
Hull, Cordell, 669
Hull-House, 454–455, 507

Human Nature and Conduct, 73
Hume, David, 134–135
Humphrey, Hubert, 712
Hungary, 557, 680, 731, 733
Hutchinson, Anne, 42, 44
Hutchinson, Thomas, 151, 153, 159–160, 165, 180
Ickes, Harold, 672, 674–675
Illinois, 265, 313–314, 334, 337, 363, 370–371, 374, 393, 407, 410, 476, 552, 615, 627, 698
India, 234, 324, 517, 552, 726–728, 733
Indian Territory, 456
Indiana, 265, 335, 390, 393, 451, 533, 557, 563, 648, 673–674
Indianapolis (Ind.), 649
Indiana Territory, 241
Indochina, 733–734, 736
Industrial Revolution, 273, 280, 299
Industrial Workers of the World, 656
Influence of Sea Power Upon History, The, 484
International Harvester Company, 511, 627, 668
International Mercantile Marine, 501, 511
Interstate Commerce Commission, 475
Intolerable Acts, 166
Invisible Man, 701
Iowa, 366, 410, 433, 439, 458, 603
Ireland, 180, 324
Iroquois Indians, 88, 106, 108, 121, 126
Irving, Washington, 347
Isabelle I of Spain, 5, 9
Islam, 3
Israel, 727, 731
Italy, 504, 516, 582, 585, 666, 669–672, 678, 680, 685
Jackson, Andrew, (Pres. 1829–1837), 227, 244–245, 269, 282–285, 287, 289–290, 293–294, 299, 302, 326, 361, 389, 404, 720
Jackson, "Stonewall", 385
Jacksonian Persuasion, The, 389
James, Alice, 347
James Family, The, 425
James, Henry, 285, 462, 472
James I of England, 18, 22, 23, 31
James II of England, 17, 23–24, 49
James, Williams, 71, 347
Jamestown (Va.), 30–31, 32–33, 34, 47, 92, 105
Japan, 442–443, 447, 517–518, 527, 529, 582, 585, 666–667,